American Public School Law

THIRD EDITION

American Public School Law

THIRD EDITION

Kern Alexander
UNIVERSITY DISTINGUISHED PROFESSOR
VIRGINIA TECH UNIVERSITY

M. David Alexander
PROFESSOR
VIRGINIA TECH UNIVERSITY

West Publishing Company
St. Paul   New York   Los Angeles   San Francisco

WEST'S COMMITMENT TO THE ENVIRONMENT
In 1906, West Publishing Company began recycling materials left over from the production of books. This began a tradition of efficient and responsible use of resources. Today, up to 95 percent of our legal books and 70 percent of our college texts are printed on recycled, acid-free stock. West also recycles nearly 22 million pounds of scrap paper annually—the equivalent of 181,717 trees. Since the 1960s, West has devised ways to capture and recycle waste inks, solvents, oils, and vapors created in the printing process. We also recycle plastics of all kinds, wood, glass, corrugated cardboard, and batteries, and have eliminated the use of styrofoam book packaging. We at West are proud of the longevity and the scope of our commitment to the environment.

Copyeditor: Chris Thillen
Compositor: Graphic World, Inc.
Indexing: Sandi Schroeder
Production, Prepress, Printing, and Binding by West Publishing Company

LIBRARY OF CONGRESS CATALOGING-IN-PUBLICATION DATA

Alexander, Kern.
    American public school law / Kern Alexander, M. David Alexander. -
- 3rd ed.
    p. cm.

    Includes index.
    ISBN 0-314-92952-5 (hard)
    1. Educational law and legislation—United States.   I. Alexander,
    M. David.   II. Title.
KF4118.A39   1992
344.73 071—dc20
[347.30471]
                                    91-33177
                                        CIP

Dedicated to our mother and father,
Emma M. Alexander (1910-1989) and
Samuel M. K. Alexander (1908-1990)

CONTENTS IN BRIEF

CONTENTS

CHAPTER 7 The Instructional Program 229

CHAPTER 8 Student Rights 279

CHAPTER 9   Rights of Handicapped Children   359

CHAPTER 10   Desegregation   409

CHAPTER 13   Governmental Immunity from Liability   531

CHAPTER 14   Certification, Contracts, and Tenure   557

CHAPTER 15   Teacher Rights and Freedoms   603

CHAPTER 16   Due Process Rights of Teachers   641

CHAPTER 17   Discrimination in Employment   673

CHAPTER 18   Collective Bargaining   729

CHAPTER 19 Finance 767

TABLE OF CASES

C

I

J

PREFACE

Since its origin in the first half of the nineteenth century, the American public school has been in a state of legal redefinition and change. At different times, in varying political climates, the speed and direction of the evolution has been altered, but the movement has been both inevitable and persistent. The law governing public schools as interpreted and conveyed by this text reflects the past, reports the current status, and frames the issues that may anticipate the future.

This book is designed for graduate students in education or law school students who desire a comprehensive view of the law that governs the state school systems of America. The legal precedents discussed and presented deal with many of the multitude of issues that occur in a country that has developed an extraordinary reliance on the public schools as a mechanism for social and economic improvement. The desire to educate the masses to a high degree of competency resulted in the emergence of the public schools as the common ground of learning for persons of all backgrounds and persuasions. An undertaking of the magnitude of public schools, involving such an amalgam of people, is naturally fertile ground for human differences and perceptions that cause conflict. This book is about those conflicts which were not resolvable through the normal political processes and ultimately necessitated court resolution. What the courts have said in enunciating precedents and the rules of law is valuable information for all those involved with the public schools.

Education in America is large and diverse and, unlike most European systems of education, is federalistic in nature with each of the fifty states having a uniqueness of origin which adds strength and vitality to the whole. Because of the decentralized nature of our educational structure, it is sometimes difficult to identify any single rule of law which prevails in all states. Even with the great sweep of constitutional precedents which the Supreme Court of the United States, from time to time delivers, the law governing our schools can often be difficult to accurately assess and summarize. Beyond constitutional law, which is more focused because the Supreme Court can give the final word, we have a large mass of law pertaining to contracts, property, torts, general administrative law, et cetera which all bear on the administration of the schools. Too, substantial variation may be found from state to state, not merely because of the differing statutory bases, but also because of widely varying perspectives and philosophies of education which the judges, themselves, may have in viewing particular school litigation. And, of course, the social context from which the cases emanate may have strong influence on the outcome of particular disputes.

The reader of this book should, therefore, keep in mind that the authors, of necessity, have had to select cases from among the hundreds of jurisdictions in this country which appear to best exemplify the prevailing view of the courts in the various areas of law. The precedents identified by the authors may not neatly fit the numerous situations and conditions which can exist in all the local school districts across the nation. For this reason, the reader will be well advised to carefully compare the precedents of the book with the rule of law in his or her own locality before drawing hard and fast conclusions. Also, as explained in the first chapter of the text, the reader should, at all times, realize that the facts of the case are of utmost importance and small variations in facts may result in very large differences in rule of law.

This book employs the "case" or "discussion" method of teaching the law. Over the years, this approach to instruction has been utilized largely in business schools and law schools and has been found to be a very effective instructional device for immersing the student in the learning process. Case or discussion teaching enables the instructor to depart from merely lecturing or "telling" about the law to becoming a facilitator of classroom discussion. Using this approach the instructor can circumscribe the issue for the students and then by questioning, probing, and challenging bring out the rules of law. This technique allows each student to relate one rule of law to a particular set of facts which will clarify or distinguish the educational dispute in question. By relating concrete factual situations to the law the student will be better able to recognize similar experiences when they encounter them as practicing teachers or school administrators. For the flegling educator the study of actual cases may well prevent costly repetition. In most instances a better knowledge of both education and the law may have prevented resorting to the courts for redress of an issue. Employment of the case approach gives the student the opportunity to study the law in a setting where the consequences of misjudgment are not so great. Learning by discussing and examining the experiences of others is of course not new; Roger Ascham in 1570 in his dissertation entitled *The Schoolmaster* observed that "Learning teacheth more in one year than experience in twenty; and learning teacheth safely, when experience maketh more miserable than wise. He hasardeth sore that waxeth wise by experience. . . . It is costly wisdom that is brought by experience." The case method in conveying not only the rule of law but the litigious factual experiences of earlier educators provides an inexpensive method of learning valuable lessons.

An effort is made, herein, to present an encompassing book, ranging across civil, criminal, and constitutional law as they touch the student, teacher, and administrator. Several chapters in the book may be of primary interest to teachers who are concerned with such matters as control over the curriculum, teacher tenure, contracts, student rights, and collective bargaining. These aspects of the law which are relevant to the teacher are also essential information for the school administrator. In addition, though, the administrator may, also, have a vital interest in the law of finance, property, desegregation and intergovernmental relations. It is with cognizance of the needs of all educators that additional and separate chapters are included on various topics. Because of the profusion of litigation that has emanated in recent years from federal statutes, separate chapters are provided for issues concerning the education of the handicapped and employment discrimination. In totality, the book represents an attempt to convey to the educator a fully comprehensive treatment of the law, whether emanating from common law, statute or constitutional law.

This third edition is significantly more comprehensive than the previous editions. The evolution of the law of education, while experiencing a gradual ebb and flow of teacher and student rights and freedoms, has, nevertheless, produced a continuous volume of legal precedents. It would be redundant to discuss here all the text modifications from the earlier editions, yet, a few are particularly noteworthy. This new edition greatly expands the discussion of student rights, including a new section on common law reasonableness that enables the reader to more accurately assess the differences between the legal status of students under common law and the more recent concepts of constitutional law. From this discussion one can view the redefinition of the student's constitutional rights and what appears to be a tendency of the federal courts in the 1980s to merge the earlier common law concepts with constitutional law standards. For example, the freedom of the press provisions applicable to student newspapers have now evolved and contracted back to a point of substantial equivalence to earlier common law precedents. Additional precedents regarding student's security against illegal search and seizure and drug testing as well as the various applications of substantive and procedural due process are discussed. Extensive discussion is devoted to the considerations of rights of handicapped children as required by Congress through the new Individuals With Disabilities Act (IDEA). What constitutes a least restrictive environment in the context of separate school placement, the definition of extended school year and the restraints on discipline of handicapped children are all subjects of new and expanded treatment of the text. Of particular concern, too, is, of course, the modern plague, Acquired Immunodeficiency Syndrome (AIDS), and the application of the law to those children affected.

The constancy of legal change as it touches teachers directly is also expanded in the new edition. In this regard, the book deals with the changing nature of the teacher/school board employment relationship as modified by the U.S. Supreme Court's decision in *Connick*. The court's dissection of freedom of speech into its public and private contexts in this case will undoubtedly lead to a plethora of new litigation with the possibly predictable results of reducing teachers' latitude in the exercise of their rights of speech.

Too, the new edition elucidates on the emerging perspective of the U.S. Supreme Court on church-state relations. Recent precedents apparently suggest a movement toward diminishing the height of the "wall of separation." The new doctrine as enunciated by Justice Rehnquist in earlier dissents will probably allow for expanded use of public tax dollars for parochial schools and may, as well, lead to a relaxation of the prohibitions on religious functions in public schools. The emergent theory maintains that the founding fathers actually believed in the nonpreferential approach to separation, meaning essentially that the state can aid, support, or assist, all religions so long as it does not prefer one religion over another. The turn of the Supreme Court in this arena and its retreat from separation is fully explained in this new edition.

Further, this new text reveals that the courts are tending to be more restrained in their view of curricular and instructional matters, allowing school boards more discretion. The removal of Chaucer, Aristophanes or other classics from the school curriculum is not definitively prohibited by the courts today as it may have been a few years ago. This increase of judicial deference in favor of school boards, concerning curricular matters, will undoubtedly raise new legal conflicts and controversies. Other new instructional areas requiring major revision in this edition have to do with the rights and interests of students to question school policies for grading, testing, and promotion.

Finally, changes in many other areas of the law have stimulated additions of new sections of the book, including extension of defamation rulings to public school teachers and administrators, refinement of the legal definition of free public schools, and the questions surrounding the equality of allocation of financial resources among local school districts. Extensive new treatment is provided in a new chapter concerning federal civil rights statutes that prohibit racial, sexual, religious and age discrimination in public school employment. Expanded treatment is given to sexual harassment and Title IX as indicated by prevailing precedents applicable to public schools.

We are in great debt to several persons who contributed to this effort in many different ways. Because this is the third edition, all those persons who were so intimately involved in the original editions are to a large extent responsible for this book as well. This edition, however, would not have come to fruition without the dedicated and timely assistance of Dr. Teressa Caldwell, Dr. Mary Jane Connelly, Paulette Gardner, Linda Pantili, Mary Jane Guy, Dee Bodkins, Fred Keller, John O'Neil, Jeanette McLingberg, and Gloria Whitehurst, all alumni, students or staff at Virginia Tech. In addition we would like to express our appreciation for the constructive suggestions provided by the following reviewers: Gene Gallegos, Western Kentucky University; John McLaughlin, St. Cloud State University; Earl Ogletree, Chicago State University; William T. Rebore, St. Louis University; and William Sharp, University of Akron. We also wish to acknowledge our indebtedness to West Publishing Company and its very able staff, including Elizabeth Hannan, Editor, Sandra J. Engen, Administrative Assistant, and Caroline Nielsen, Promotion Manager. Ms. Hannan very ably organized and coordinated the entire project; Sandra J. Engen devoted months to rapid and accurate copy editing, shaping and molding the project; and Caroline Nielsen to its marketing. We are most appreciative to each for their efficiency, competence and cordiality in making a difficult task a pleasurable and memorable experience.

Blacksburg, Virginia   Kern Alexander
December, 1991   M. David Alexander

CHAPTER 1

The Legal System

■■■■ INTRODUCTION

The law of the school includes all those areas of jurisprudence that bear on the operation of public elementary and secondary schools in the United States. School law as a field of study is a generic term covering a wide range of legal subject matter including the basic fields of contracts, property, torts, constitutional law, and other areas of law that directly affect the educational and administrative processes of the educational system. Because of the breadth of the subject matter involved it is necessary for the school law student to be versed in certain fundamental concepts of the American legal system and to be able to apply this knowledge to situations that daily affect school operation.

Because a public school is a governmental agency, its conduct is circumscribed by precedents of public administrative law supplemented by those legal and historical traditions surrounding an educational organization that is state established, yet locally administered. In this setting legal and educational structural issues must be considered that define the powers to operate, control, and manage the schools. In analyzing the American educational system and comparing it to central state systems of education in foreign countries, one is struck by the diversity of authority under which the American public schools are governed. As a federal and not a national system, the government of the United States comprises a union of states united under one central government. The particular form of American federalism creates a unique educational system, which is governed by laws of

fifty states with component parts amounting to several thousand local school district operating units. Through all of this organizational multiformity, and indeed complexity, runs the legal basis on which the entire system is founded.

The fundamental principles of legal control are those generally prescribed by our constitutional system, from which the basic organic law of the land emanates: the written constitutions of the fifty states and the federal government. Constitutions at both levels of government are basic because the positive power to create public education systems is assumed by state constitutions, and provisions of both the state and federal constitutions serve as restraints to protect the people from unwarranted denial of basic constitutional rights and freedoms.

The power of operation of the public educational system, therefore, originates with a constitutional delegation to the legislature to provide for a system of education. With legislative enactments providing the basis for public school law, it then becomes the role of the courts, through litigation, to interpret the will of the legislature. The combination of constitutions, statutes, and court or case law forms the primary legal foundation on which the public schools are based.

Constitutions

A constitution is a body of precepts that provides a framework of law within which orderly governmental processes can operate.

1

The constitutions of this country are characterized by their provisions for securing fundamental liberty, property, and political rights. One of the basic principles embodied in a constitution is the provision for authorized modification of the document. Experience in human and governmental relations teaches that to be effective a constitution must be flexible and provide for systematic change processes. The Constitution of the United States expressly provides in Article V a process for proposing amendments by a two-thirds vote of each house of Congress or by a convention that shall be called by Congress upon application by two-thirds of the state legislatures. Amendments must be ratified by the legislatures of three-fourths of the states or by conventions in three-fourths of the states.

Another precept reflected in the state and federal constitutions of this country is the importance of a government of separated powers. While all state constitutions do not expressly provide for a separation of all legislative, executive, and judicial departments, in actual practice, all states have governments of separated powers. There is no requirement in the federal constitution that the states have constitutions that require a separation of powers. Theoretically, if a state so desired, it could clothe an officer or an agency with not only executive but plenary judicial and legislative powers. However, as indicated previously, this is not the case and all states have governments with separate branches, each of which exercises checks and balances on the powers of other branches.

All state constitutions make provision for a system of free public schools. Such provisions range from very specific educational provisions to broad mandates that the legislature of the state shall provide funds for the support of a public school system.

Statutes

A statute is an act of government expressing legislative will and constituting a law of the state. Statute is a word derived from the Latin term *statutum*, which means "it is decided." Statutes, in our American form of government, are the most viable and effective means of making new law or changing old law. Statutes enacted at the state or federal level may either follow custom or forge ahead and establish new laws that shape the future.

Statutes in this country are subject to review by the judiciary to determine their constitutionality. This procedure is different from that used in England, where the legislature has ultimate authority and there are no means by which the courts can hold legislation unconstitutional. This is true primarily because in England the constitution, for the most part, is unwritten and the legislature, Parliament, may amend the constitution when it so desires.

The public schools of the United States are governed by statutes enacted by state legislatures. The schools have no inherent powers and the authority to operate them must be found in either express or implied terms of statute. The specificity of statutes in governing the operation of public schools varies from state to state and from subject to subject. As an example, one state may generally require appropriate measures to be followed in budgeting and accounting for public funds, while in another state the legislature may actually specify each line item of the budget for school systems " . . . and prescribe intricate details for fund accounting."

Rules and regulations of both state and local boards of education fall within the category of statutory sources of school law. As a general rule, the legislature cannot delegate its legislative powers to govern the schools to a subordinate agency or official. Boards of education must, in devising rules and regulations for the administration of the schools, do so within the limits defined by the legislature and cannot exercise legislative authority. However, the legislature may through statute expressly or impliedly confer administrative duties upon an agency or official. These administrative powers must be well defined and "canalized" within definitely circumscribed channels.

Court or Case Law

The third source of school law is judge-made or case law, sometimes called common law. The terms "case law" or "common law" are used to distinguish rules of law that are enunciated by the courts from those that have originated in legislative bodies. The term "common law," in its broadest sense, may sometimes be used to contrast the entire system of Anglo-American law with the law of non-English speaking countries sometimes referred to as having systems of civil law. Civil law is a system of statutes in which there is no reliance on precedent. Common Law originated in England, where precedents of various parts of the country became common to the entire country. These customs became crystallized into legal principles that were applied and used as precedent throughout England.

■ POWERS AND FUNCTIONS OF THE COURTS

The question of what powers may be exercised by the judiciary in reviewing decisions or enactments by the other two branches of government is essential to our system of government. The courts have traditionally maintained and enforced the concept of "separation of powers" when confronted with cases involving education. They do not usually question the judgment of either the administrative agencies of the executive branch or the legislative branch. This is true at the federal level as well as the state level.

One court, in describing the hesitancy of the courts to interfere with the other two branches of government, said:

> This reluctance is due, in part, to an awareness of the sometimes awesome responsibility of having to circumscribe the limits of their authority. Even more persuasive is an appreciation of the importance in our system of the concept of separation of powers so that each division of government may function freely within the area of its responsibility. This safeguarding of the separate powers is essential to preserve the balance which has always been regarded as one of the advantages of our system.[1]

In accordance with this reasoning, the courts presume that legislation or administrative actions were enacted conscientiously with due deliberation and are not arbitrary or capricious.[2] When the courts do intervene they perform three types of judicial functions: (a) settle controversies by applying principles of law to a specific set of facts, (b) construe or interpret enactments of the legislature, and (c) determine the constitutionality of legislative or administrative actions.

Applying Principles

In applying principles of law to factual situations, the court may find the disputants to be either school districts, individuals, or both. Although school law cases generally involve the school district itself, they may, in some instances, concern litigation between individuals, for example, a teacher and a student. In many cases, the principles of law governing the situation are vague, and statutory and constitutional guidance are difficult to find. In such instances, the judges must look to judicial precedent for guidance. Cardoza related the process in this manner:

> Where does the judge find the law he embodies in his judgment? There are times when the source is obvious. The rule that fits the case may be supplied by the constitution or by statute. If that is so, the judge looks no further. The correspondence ascertained, his duty is to obey. The constitution overrides a statute, but a statute, if consistent with the constitution, overrides the law of judges. In this sense, judge-made law is secondary and subordinate to the law that is made by legislators . . . . We reach the land of mystery when constitution and statute are silent, and the judge must look to the common law for the rule that fits the case. He is the "living oracle of the law" in Blackstone's vivid phrase.[3]

Interpreting Statutes

The second function of the courts, the task of construing and interpreting statutes, is the most common litigation involving public school operation. Because statutes are merely words, to which many definitions and interpretations may be applied, courts may actually affect the meaning of the legislation. Pound conceives of four ways with which legislation may be dealt by the courts once litigation arises:

1. They might receive it fully into the body of the law as affording not only a rule to be applied but a principle from which to reason, and hold it, as a later and more direct expression of the general will, of superior authority to judge-made rules on the same general subject; and so reason from it by analogy in preference to them.
2. They might receive it fully into the body of the law to be reasoned from by analogy the same as any other rule of law, regarding it, however, as of equal or coordinate authority in this respect with judge-made rules upon the same general subject.
3. They might refuse to receive it fully into the body of the law and give effect to it directly only; refusing to reason from it by analogy but giving it, nevertheless, a liberal interpretation to cover the whole field it was intended to cover.
4. They might not only refuse to reason from it by analogy and apply it directly only, but also give to it a strict and narrow interpretation, holding it down rigidly to those cases which it covers expressly.[4]

The last hypothesis is probably the orthodox, traditional approach; however, the courts today, in interpreting statutes, tend to adhere more and more to the second and third hypotheses.

The philosophy of the courts toward statutory interpretation varies not only among judges and courts but also in the content of the legislation being interpreted. The courts are generally more willing to grant implied authority to perform educational programs where large sums of public monies are not involved. For cases in which taxing authority is in question or in which large capital outlay programs are at issue, the courts tend to require very specific and express statutory authority in order for a school board to perform.[5]

Another, and possibly clearer, explanation of how courts construe statutes may be found in rules of law laid down by several judicial precedents. These rules — the Mischief Rule, the Golden Rule, the Literal Rule, and the Plain Meaning Rule — are useful in delineating the judiciary's options in dealing with statutory construction.[6]

THE MISCHIEF RULE [F]or the sure and true interpretation of all statutes in general (be they penal or beneficial, restrictive or enlarging of the common law) four things are to be discerned and considered:

1. What was the common law before the making of the Act?
2. What was the mischief and defect for which the common law did not provide?
3. What remedy the Parliament hath resolved and appointed to cure the disease of the commonwealth?
4. The true reason of the remedy; and then the office of all the Judges is always to make sure construction as shall suppress the mischief, and advance the remedy, and to suppress subtle inventions and evasions for continuance of the mischief, and *pro privato commodo,* and to add force and life to the cure and remedy, according to the true intent of the makers of the Act, *pro bono publico.*[7]

THE "GOLDEN" RULE But it is to be borne in mind that the office of the judges is not to legislate, but to declare the expressed intention of the Legislature, even if that intention appears to the court injudicious; and I believe that it is not disputed that what Lord Wensleydale used to say is right, namely that we are to take the whole statute together, and construe it all together, giving the words their ordinary signification, unless when so applied they produce an inconsistency, or an absurdity or inconvenience so great as to convince the court that the intention could not have been to use them in their ordinary signification, and to justify the court in putting on them some other signification, which, though less proper, is one which the court thinks the words will bear.[8]

THE LITERAL RULE   If the language of a statute be plain, admitting of only one meaning, the Legislature must be taken to have meant and intended what it has plainly expressed, and whatever it has in clear terms enacted must be enforced though it should lead to absurd or mischievous results. If the language of this subsection be not controlled by some of the other provisions of the statute, it must, since its language is plain and unambiguous, be enforced, and your lordships' House sitting judicially is not concerned with the question whether the policy it embodies is wise or unwise, or whether it leads to consequences just or unjust, beneficial or mischievous.[9]

I should like to have a good definition of what is such an absurdity that you are to disregard the plain words of an Act of Parliament. It is to be remembered that what seems absurd to one man does not seem absurd to another . . . I think it is infinitely better, although an absurdity or an injustice or other objectionable result may be evolved as the consequence of your construction, to adhere to the words of an Act of Parliament and leave the legislature to set it right than to alter those words according to one's notion of an absurdity.[10]

THE PLAIN MEANING RULE   It is elementary that the meaning of a statute must, in the first instance, be sought in the language in which the act is framed, and if that is plain, and if the law is within the constitutional authority of the lawmaking body which passed it, the sole function of the courts is to enforce it according to its terms.   . . .

Where the language is plain and admits of no more than one meaning the duty of interpretation does not arise and the rules which are to aid doubtful meanings need no discussion.   . . .

Statutory words are uniformly presumed, unless the contrary appears to be used in their ordinary and usual sense, and with the meaning commonly attributed to them.[11]

The general rule is perfectly well settled that, where a statute is of doubtful meaning and susceptible upon its face of two construc-

tions, the court may look into prior and contemporaneous acts, the reasons which induced the act in question, the mischiefs intended to be remedied, the extraneous circumstances, and the purpose intended to be accomplished by it to determine its proper construction. But when the act is clear upon its face, and when standing alone it is fairly susceptible of but one construction, that construction must be given to it.   . . .

The whole doctrine applicable to the subject may be summed up in the single observation that prior acts may be resorted to, to *solve,* but not to *create* an ambiguity.[12]

Constitutionality

The functions and responsibility of the judiciary in determining the constitutionality of legislation were set out early in *Marbury v. Madison*[13] in prescribing the power of the United States Supreme Court. This case shaped the American view of the role of the judiciary. Chief Justice Marshall's landmark opinion stated:

It is emphatically the province and duty of the judicial department to say what the law is. Those who apply the rule to particular cases, must of necessity expound and interpret that rule. If two laws conflict with each other, the courts must decide on the operation of each. So, if a law be in opposition to the constitution; if both the law and the constitution apply to a particular case, so that the court must either decide that case, conformably to the law, disregarding the constitution; or conformably to the constitution, disregarding the law; the court must determine which of these conflicting rules governs the case. This is of the very essence of judicial duty. If then the courts are to regard the constitution, and the constitution is superior to any ordinary act of the legislature; the constitution, and not such ordinary act, must govern the case to which they both apply.

In determining the constitutionality of statutes the courts first presume the act to be constitutional and anyone maintaining the contrary must bear the burden of proof. The Florida Supreme Court has related the principle in this manner: "We have held that acts of the legislature carry such a strong presumption of validity that they should be held constitutional if there is any reasonable theory to that end . . . . Moreover, unconstitutionality must appear beyond all reasonable doubt before an Act is condemned . . . ."[14] If a statute can be interpreted in two different ways, one by which it will be constitutional, the courts will adopt the constitutional interpretation.[15]

With specific regard to the United States Supreme Court's review of legislation, either state or federal, the judicial duty in the eyes of Justice Brandeis was that "It must be evident that the power to declare legislative enactment void is one which the judge, conscious of the fallibility of human judgment, will shrink from exercising in any case where he can conscientiously and with due regard to duty and official oath decline the responsibility."[16] Using this basic philosophy, Justice Brandeis, in 1936, set out certain criteria for judicial review that are still generally referred to today in considering the standing of litigants before the Supreme Court.

1. The Court will not pass upon the constitutionality of legislation in a friendly, nonadversary proceeding, declining because to decide such questions is legitimate only in the last resort, and as a necessity in the determination of real, earnest, and vital controversy between individuals.
2. The Court will not anticipate a question of constitutional law in advance of the necessity of deciding it. It is not the habit of the Court to decide questions of a constitutional nature unless absolutely necessary to a decision of the case.
3. The Court will not formulate a rule of constitutional law broader than is required by the precise facts to which it is to be applied.
4. The Court will not pass upon a constitutional question although properly presented by the record, if there is also present some other ground upon which the case may be disposed of. This rule has found most varied application. Thus, if a case can be decided on either of two grounds, one

involving a constitutional question, the other a question of statutory construction or general law, the Court will decide only the latter.
5. The Court will not pass upon the validity of a statute upon complaint of one who fails to show that he or she is injured by its operation. Among the many applications of this rule, none is more striking than the denial of the right of challenge to one who lacks a personal or property right. Thus, the challenge by public officials interested only in the performance of their official duty will not be entertained.
6. The Court will not pass upon the constitutionality of a statute at the instance of one who has availed himself or herself of its benefits.
7. When the validity of an act of Congress is drawn in question, and even if a serious doubt of constitutionality is raised, it is a cardinal principle that this Court will first ascertain whether the construction of the statute is fairly possible by which the question may be avoided.[17]

■ STARE DECISIS

Implicit in the concept of common or case law is the reliance on past court decisions that reflect the historical development of legal controversies. Precedents established in past cases form the groundwork for decisions in the future. In the United States, the doctrine of precedent or the rule of *stare decisis,* "let the decision stand," prevails and past decisions are generally considered to be binding on subsequent cases that have the same or substantially the same factual situations. The rule of *stare decisis* is rigidly adhered to by lower courts when following decisions by higher courts in the same jurisdiction. Courts can limit the impact of the doctrine of precedent by carefully distinguishing the facts of the case from those of the previous case that established the rule of law. Aside from distinguishing factual situations, courts of last resort can reverse their own previous decisions and change a rule of law that they themselves established.

Stare decisis in American law does not constitute the strict adherence to older decisions that are found in English courts. The American rule of today is probably best stated by Justice Brandeis when he said that "stare decisis is usually the wise policy . . . "[18] and by Justice Cardoza, who observed that "I think adherence to precedent should be the rule and not the exception."[19]

THE HISTORICAL DEVELOPMENT OF THE DOCTRINE OF PRECEDENT

(Reprinted with permission, Harold J. Berman and William R. Greiner, *The Nature and Functions of Law*, The Foundation Press, 1966, pp. 491–494.)

—————————

If we go back to the early history of modern English law, we find that by the end of the twelfth century, virtually as soon as records of court proceedings were kept, there developed an interest in judicial decisions as guides to what the law is. Bracton in his treatise on English law, written in the middle of the thirteenth century, referred to about 500 decided cases; he also wrote a Notebook containing digests of 2000 cases. The word "precedent," however, is entirely absent from Bracton's vocabulary; cases for him and for his contemporaries were not binding authorities but merely illustrations of legal principles.

In the fourteenth, fifteenth, and early sixteenth centuries law students kept notes of oral arguments in court cases. These notes, preserved in the so-called Yearbooks, show that not only the students but also the courts were concerned with analogizing and distinguishing cases. Again, however, the decisions were not treated as authorities in any sense, and if a judge did not approve of a decision he would just say it was wrong.

In the sixteenth and seventeenth centuries we get the first systematic reports of cases and the first mention of precedent. Judges then began to say that they are bound by precedents in matters of procedure, and especially in matters of pleading, and the practice of citing previous cases became firmly established. It is interesting to note, however, that in the first known use of the word precedent, in 1557, it is stated that a decision was given "notwithstanding two precedents." Indeed, the doctrine of precedent which developed in those centuries did not provide that a single decision was binding but rather that a line of decisions would not be overturned. Lord Mansfield could still say, in the latter part of the eighteenth century, "The reason and spirit of cases make law; not the letter of particular precedents."

Nevertheless, with the development in the seventeenth century of the distinction between dictum and holding, the way was paved for the modern doctrine. It should be noted that the seventeenth century in England was a time when analogical reasoning also became prevalent in fields other than law.

In the later nineteenth century for the first time there developed the rule that a holding by a court in a previous case is binding on the same court (or on an inferior court) in a similar case. The doctrine was called *stare decisis*—"to stand by the decisions." It was never absolute. The court is only bound "in the absence of weighty reasons." . . .

In the heyday of the doctrine of *stare decisis,* that is, in the last quarter of the nineteenth and the first quarter of the twentieth century, belief was prevalent that certainty in law could be obtained by a scientific use of precedent. The legislature alone was thought to have the function of changing the law; the court's function was "merely" to apply the law, and to apply it in accordance with the holdings of previous decisions. The common law as an organically growing body of experience and doctrine was supposed, in effect, to have been superseded by a body of fixed rules which could be mechanically applied.

The idea that the common law is a body of fixed rules vanished in the second quarter of the twentieth century, and perhaps earlier, in the face of overwhelming changes in social, economic, and political life. The mathematical or mechanical jurisprudence of the late nineteenth century which denied that there is an ethical element in the analogizing and distinguishing of cases can seldom be found today among leaders of legal thought, at least in the United States. This does not mean, however, that the doctrine of precedent has been repudiated. It means, rather, that there has been a return to an older concept of precedent. Precedent is seen as a means of marshalling past experience, of providing a historical context, for making the choice at hand. While condemning the hocus-pocus aspects of the strict nineteenth century doctrine, many American thinkers about law would agree with Lord Mansfield that "the common law works itself pure."

Henry Campbell Black, Nature and Authority of Judicial Precedents

H. Black, The Law of Judicial Precedents 10–11 (1912).

— · — · — · — · — · —

Not as a classification, but as exhibiting the chief aspects or applications of the doctrine of precedents, the subject might be broadly divided into five branches, in each of which there is to be noted one general rule or governing principle, as follows:

First. Inferior courts are absolutely bound to follow the decisions of the courts having appellate or revisory jurisdiction over them. In this aspect, precedents set by the higher courts are imperative in the strictest sense. They are conclusive on the lower courts, and leave to the latter no scope for independent judgment or discretion.

Second. The judgments of the highest court in any judicial system — state or national — are binding on all other courts when they deal with matters committed to the peculiar or exclusive jurisdiction of the court making the precedent. Thus, when the Supreme Court of the United States renders a decision construing the federal constitution or an act of Congress, that decision must be accepted by all state courts, as well as the inferior federal courts, as not merely persuasive, but of absolutely conclusive authority. In the same way, when the supreme court of a state pronounces judgment upon the interpretation of a statute of the state, its decision has imperative force in the courts of the United States, as well as in the courts of another state.

Third. It is the duty of a court of last resort to abide by its own former decisions, and not to depart from or vary them unless entirely satisfied, in the first place, that they were wrongly decided, and, in the second place, that less mischief will result from their overthrow than from their perpetuation. This is the proper application of the maxim, "stare decisis."

Fourth. When a case is presented to any court for which there is no precedent, either in its own former decisions or in the decisions of any court whose rulings, in the particular matter, it is bound to follow, it may consult and be guided by the applicable decisions by any other court, domestic or foreign. In this case, such decisions possess no constraining force, but should be accorded such a measure of weight and influence as they may be intrinsically entitled to receive, the duty of the court being to conform its decision to what is called the "general current of authority" or the "preponderance of authority," if such a standard can be ascertained to exist with reference to the particular question involved.

Fifth. On the principle of judicial comity, a court which is entirely free to exercise its independent judgment upon the matter at issue, and under no legal obligation to follow the decision of another court on the same question, will nevertheless accept and conform to that decision, as a correct statement of the law, when such a course is necessary to secure the harmonious and consistent administration of the law or to avoid unseemly conflicts of judicial authority. But comity does not require any court to do violence to its own settled convictions as to what the law is.

assigned; but it is sufficient that there be nothing in the rule flatly contradictory to reason, and then the law will presume it to be well founded.

BLACKSTONE, COMMENTARIES

1 W. Blackstone, Commentaries *69–70.

— · — · — · — · — ·—

For it is an established rule to abide by former precedents, where the same points come again in litigation: as well to keep the scale of justice even and steady, and not liable to waver with every new judge's opinion; as also because the law in that case being solemnly declared and determined, what before was uncertain, and perhaps indifferent, is now become a permanent rule, which it is not in the breast of any subsequent judge to alter or vary from according to his private sentiments: he being sworn to determine, not according to his own private judgment; but according to the known laws and customs of the land; not delegated to pronounce a new law, but to maintain and expound the old one. Yet this rule admits of exception, where the former determination is most evidently contrary to reason; much more if it be clearly contrary to the divine law. But even in such cases the subsequent judges do not pretend to make a new law, but to vindicate the old one from misrepresentation. For if it be found that the former decision is manifestly absurd or unjust, it is declared, not that such a sentence was *bad law,* but that it was *not law;* that is, that it is not the established custom of the realm, as has been erroneously determined. And hence it is that our lawyers are with justice so copious in their encomiums on the reason of the common law; that they tell us, that the law is the perfection of reason, that it always intends to conform thereto, and that what is not reason is not law. Not that the particular reason of every rule in the law can at this distance of time be always precisely

JOHN HANNA, THE ROLE OF PRECEDENT IN JUDICIAL DECISION

Reprinted with permission from Villanova Law Review Volume 2, No. 3, pp. 367–368. Copyright 1957 by Villanova University.

— · — · — · — · — ·—

Stare decisis or, in its complete form, *stare decisis et non quieta movere* is usually translated "to stand by (or adhere to) decisions and not to disturb what is settled." The classic English version is by Coke: "They said that those things which have been so often adjudged ought to rest in peace." Blackstone says: "The doctrine of the law then is this: that precedents and rules be followed, unless flatly absurd or unjust; for though their reason be not obvious at first view, yet we owe such a deference to former times as not to suppose that they acted wholly without consideration." The general American doctrine as applied to courts of last resort is that a court is not inexorably bound by its own precedents but will follow the rule of law which it has established in earlier cases, unless clearly convinced that the rule was originally erroneous or is no longer sound because of changing conditions and that more good than harm will come by departing from precedent. The alternative to stare decisis as popularly defined would be (1) absolute discretion on the part of a court to decide each case without reference to any precedent; or (2) complete codification of our law, with a requirement that each court look independently to the code for a basis of decision. A more limited reform would be to bar the courts from following precedents of decisions on statutory and constitutional law. None of these alternatives is a matter of much contemporary debate in America. If we define stare decisis in terms of its proper limitations, it should always be applied. We shall stay closer to the points of controversy if we appreciate that our real subject is the theory of judicial precedent.

■ UNDERSTANDING JUDICIAL DECISIONS

In order to determine the rule of a case, it is necessary to find the *ratio decidendi,* or the point on which the judgment balances. This is done primarily by carefully analyzing the facts of the case that are treated by the judge as being material. Only the material facts are relevant to the identification of the *ratio decidendi* of a case. Conclusions of a judge departing from the *ratio* are not binding as precedent and are considered to be *obiter dicta.* Essentially there are two types. First, a statement of law is *obiter* if it is based on facts that were found not to exist, or if the facts are present they are immaterial. Second, it may also be a statement of law that, although based on established facts of the case, does not form the rationale for the decision. A statement of law supporting a dissenting opinion is one example. Another instance of *obiter* may be when a court makes a statement of law leading to one conclusion but then reaches a contrary decision on the facts for a different reason.[20]

Karl N. Llewellyn,[21] late Professor of Law, University of Chicago, in his work *The Bramble Bush* probably offers the best and most concise explanation of what to look for when reading case law. Since the case method is employed in presenting most of the materials in this book, it seems appropriate to quote a portion of Llewellyn's comments on reading and analyzing judicial opinions.

The first thing to do with an opinion, then, is read it. The next thing is to get clear the actual decision, the judgment rendered. Who won, the plaintiff or defendant? And watch your step here. You are after in first instance the plaintiff and defendant below, in the trial court.

In order to follow through what happened you must therefore first know the outcome below; else you do not see what was appealed from, nor by whom. You now follow through in order to see exactly what further judgment has been rendered on appeal. The stage is then cleared of form—although of course you do not yet know all that these forms mean, that they imply. You can turn now to what you peculiarly do know. Given the actual judgments below and above as your indispensable framework—what has the case decided, and what can you derive from it as to what will be decided later?

You will be looking, in the opinion, or in the preliminary matter plus the opinion, for the following: a statement of the facts the court assumes; a statement of the precise way the question has come before the court—which includes what the plaintiff wanted below, and what the defendant did about it, the judgement below, and what the trial court did that is complained of; then the outcome on appeal, the judgment; and finally the reasons this court gives for doing what it did. This does not look so bad. But it is much worse than it looks. For all our cases are decided, all our opinions are written, all our predictions, all our arguments are made, on certain four assumptions. . . . (1) *The court must decide the dispute that is before it.* It cannot refuse because the job is hard, or dubious, or dangerous. (2) *The court can decide only the particular dispute which is before it.* When it speaks to that question it speaks *ex cathedra,* with authority, with finality, with an almost magic power. When it speaks to the question before it, it announces law, and if what it announces is new, it legislates, it makes the law. But when it speaks to any other question at all, it says mere words, which no man needs to follow. Are such words worthless? They are not. We know them as judicial *dicta;* when they are wholly off the point at issue we call them *obiter dicta*—words dropped along the road, wayside remarks. Yet even wayside remarks shed light on the remarker. They may be very useful in the future to him, or to us. But he will not feel bound to them, as to his *ex cathedra* utterance. They came not hallowed by a Delphic frenzy. He may be slow to change them; but not so slow as in the other case. (3) *The court can decide the particular dispute only according to a general rule which covers a whole class of like disputes.* Our legal theory does not admit of single decisions standing on their own. If judges are free, are indeed forced, to decide new cases for which there is no rule, they must at least make a new rule as they decide. So far, good. But how wide or how narrow, is the general rule in this particular case? That is a troublesome matter. The practice of our case-law, however, is I think, fairly stated thus: It pays to be suspicious of general rules which look too wide; it pays to go slow in feeling certain that a wide rule has been laid down at all, or that, if seemingly laid down, it will be followed. For there is a fourth accepted canon: (4) *Everything, everything, everything, big or small, a judge may say in an opinion, is to be read with primary reference to the particular dispute, the particular question before him. You are not to think that the words mean what they might if they stood alone. You are to have your eye on the case in hand, and to learn how to interpret all that has been said merely as a reason for deciding that case that way.* . . .

■■■ CASE OR CONTROVERSY

Article III of the Constitution of the United States limits the power of the judiciary to "decide and pronounce a judgment and carry it into effect between persons and parties who bring a case before it for decision."[22] The judicial branch may settle conflicts that involve only actual "cases" and "controversies."[23] The determination of what constitutes a case and controversy is left to the judgment of the Supreme Court.

The courts of the United States do not sit to decide questions of law presented in a vacuum, but only such questions as arise in a case or controversy.[24] The two terms can be used interchangeably, for, we are authoritatively told, a controversy, if distinguishable at all from a case, is distinguishable only in that it is a less comprehensive term, and includes only suits of a civil nature.[25]

That which is a case or controversy — justiciable in the federal courts — was defined by Chief Justice Hughes in a classic and cryptic statement. He said: "A 'controversy' in this sense must be one that is appropriate for

judicial determination. A justiciable controversy is thus distinguished from a difference or dispute of a hypothetical character; from one that is academic or moot. The controversy must be definite and concrete, touching the legal relations of parties having adverse legal interests. It must be a real and substantial controversy admitting of specific relief through a decree of a conclusive character, as distinguished from an opinion advising what the law would be upon a hypothetical state of facts."[26]

Later, Chief Justice Warren said of the case or controversy requirement that "those two words have an iceberg quality, containing beneath their surface simplicity submerged complexities which go to the very heart of our constitutional form of government. Embodied in the words 'cases' and 'controversies' are two complementary but somewhat different limitations. In part those words limit the business of federal courts to questions presented in an adversary context and in a form historically viewed as capable of resolution through the judicial process. And in part those words define the role assigned to the judiciary in a tripartite allocation of power to assure that the federal courts will not intrude into areas committed to the other branches of government. Justiciability is the term of art employed to give expression to this dual limitation placed upon federal courts by the case and controversy doctrine."[27]

It should also be noted that the limitation to "case or controversy" is intimately related to the doctrine of judicial review. In *Marbury v. Madison*[28] it was central to Marshall's argument that a court has power to declare a statute unconstitutional only as a consequence of the power of the court to decide a case properly before it. Unconstitutional statutes there may be, but unless they are involved in a case properly susceptible of judicial determination, the courts have no power to pronounce that they are unconstitutional. The reluctance of courts to pass on constitutional issues unless absolutely necessary has led to a rigorous set of rules as to what constitutes a justiciable case or controversy.

■ THE AMERICAN COURT SYSTEM

In our federal form of government it is necessary to have a dual judicial system: state and federal. Cases involving public schools may be litigated at either level, and while most actions involve nonfederal questions and are decided by state courts, recent years have brought on a substantial increase in the number of school cases handed down by federal courts.

State Courts

State constitutions generally prescribe the powers and the jurisdiction of the primary or main state courts. The legislature, through power granted in the constitution, provides for the specific operation of the constitutional courts, and it may create new and additional courts if so authorized by the constitution.

State courts can be classified into four categories: courts of last resort, intermediate appellate courts, courts of general jurisdiction, and courts of limited jurisdiction.

Courts of Last Resort

These courts are found at the top of the judicial hierarchy in each state and are established by the state constitution. In 43 states the official name of this highest court is the Supreme Court. The exceptions are Maryland (Court of Appeals), Maine (Supreme Judicial Court sitting as Law Court), Massachusetts (Supreme Judicial Court), New York (Court of Appeals), and West Virginia (Supreme Court of Appeals). Oklahoma and Texas are unique because they have dual-headed systems that have, respectively, a Supreme Court and a Court of Criminal Appeals as the courts of last resort. Except for Texas and Oklahoma, where civil and criminal cases are separated, all of the courts of last resort have mandatory and discretionary jurisdiction for civil, criminal, and adminstrative cases. State statute prescribes where types of cases must be taken and which ones may be heard at the discretion of the highest court. A mandatory case refers to an "appeal of right," which the court must hear and decide on the merits.[29] Mandatory appeals make up about 70 percent of the caseloads of the courts of last resort with discretionary cases constituting the remainder. Discretionary jurisdiction of appellate courts refers to cases in which a party must file a petition to seek redress of the court. The court, then, must exercise its discretion in accepting or rejecting the case.[30]

Intermediate Appellate Courts

These courts have been established in thirty-eight states to hear appeals from trial courts and administrative agencies as specified by state statute.[31] The role of these appellate courts is to review specific trial court proceedings to correct errors in the application of law and procedure[32] and to serve to extend and expand the law for the good of the community. Both of these generic purposes are held in common by both the intermediate appellate courts and the courts of last resort. The intermediate appellate courts hear both mandatory and discretionary cases. In the two-tier appellate state systems, a pattern exists that indicates that the highest court, the court of last resort, tends to control the docket by accepting more discretionary appeals than the intermediate appellate court.[33] Today, as appellate caseloads increase, there is a trend toward creation of new intermediate appellate courts. During the last thirty years, twenty-five states created two-tier systems establishing intermediate appellate courts.[34]

Courts of General Jurisdiction

These courts are major courts of record from which there exists a right of appeal to the intermediate appellate court or, in some cases, to the court of last resort. The jurisdiction of these courts covers all cases except those reserved for limited or special jurisdiction. Courts of general jurisdiction have court filings in broad areas of civil (31 percent), criminal (13 percent), juvenile (4 percent), and traffic (52 percent) cases, and these are heard by nearly 9,000 judges in the state court systems throughout the country.[35] These courts hold a variety of names, including common circuit, chancery, district, superior, and juvenile.

Courts of Limited Jurisdiction

These courts are lower trial courts with specified jurisdiction. These courts are variously named municipal, district justice, justice of the peace, small claims, traffic, and probate. About three-fourths of all the cases in these courts have to do with traffic offenses. Presently, there are over 13,000 courts of limited jurisdiction in the fifty states, handling nearly 100,000 cases each year.

Federal Courts

Article III of the Constitution of the United States provides in part: "The judicial power of the United States, shall be vested in one supreme court, and in such inferior courts as the Congress may from time to time ordain and establish."[36] Pursuant to this provision, Congress has created a network of courts.

Today, the federal court system in the United States includes district courts, courts of appeals, special federal courts, and the Supreme Court.

There is at least one district court in each state and usually more than two; California, Texas, and New York have four each. Cases litigated before federal district courts may largely be classified into two types: (1) cases between citizens of different states and (2) cases involving litigation of federal statutes or the federal constitution. Cases before district courts are usually presided over by one judge. However, in limited situations, involving challenges to apportionment of statewide legislative bodies or apportionment of Congressional districts or otherwise required by Congress, a three-judge court made up of a circuit judge and two district judges may be appointed to hear a case. Decisions of district courts may be appealed to the federal courts of appeals and, in some instances, directly to the Supreme Court of the United States. There are thirteen courts of appeals, one for the District of Columbia, and twelve for numbered circuits. (See Figures 1.1, 1.2, 1.3.)

In addition, federal courts have been established by the Congress to handle special

FIGURE 1.1 ▮▮▮ **The United States Court System**

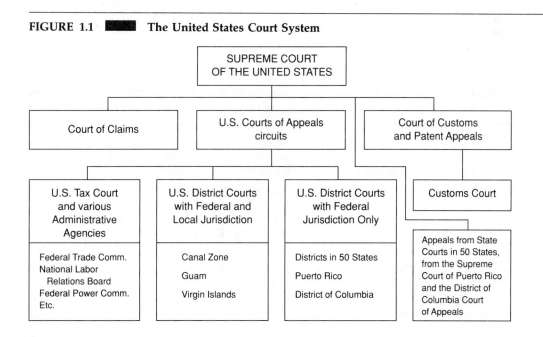

FIGURE 1.2   ███   **General Structure of State Court Systems**

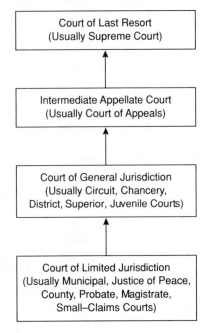

problems or to cover special jurisdictions. These courts are the courts of the District of Columbia, the Court of Claims, the Tax Court, the Customs Courts, the Courts of Customs and Patent Appeals, the Emergency Court of Appeals, and the territorial courts.

The Supreme Court of the United States is the highest court in the land, beyond which there is no redress. Cases may be brought before the Supreme Court by appeal, *writ of certiorari,* or through the original jurisdiction of the Court.

Most school cases that go to the Supreme Court are taken on *writs of certiorari,* certiorari being an original action whereby a case is removed from an inferior to a superior court for trial. Cases may be taken to the Supreme Court from state courts by *writ of certiorari* where a state statute or federal statute is questioned as to its validity under the federal Constitution or where any title, right, privilege, or immunity is claimed under the Constitution. Since most school law cases fall within this category, the *writ of certiorari* is the most common means of getting a case before the Supreme Court.

Archibald Cox, the Role of the Supreme Court in American Society

Reprinted by permission, 50 Marq.L.Rev. 575, 582-84 (1967).

— · — · — · — · — · —

The task of protecting the individual against the aggressions of government, which under our system usually means aggressions willed by representatives of a majority of the people, often conflicts with the Court's special duty of maintaining the frame of government, which includes the separation of legislative and judicial power. Judicial review calls upon the Court to go over the very social, political and economic questions committed to the Congress and State legislatures, yet it can scarcely do so without usurping in some degree the legislative function of weighing and balancing competing interests.   . . .

The conventional escape from this dilemma is to say that the conclusions of Congress will stand unless they are so wrong,

FIGURE 1.3 �\ **The Thirteen Federal Judicial Circuits**

NOTES

1. United States Circuit Court of Appeals, 42 U.S.C.A. § 41. (Number and composition of circuits). The thirteen judicial circuits of the United States are constituted as follows:

Circuits	Composition
District of Columbia	District of Columbia
First	Maine, Massachusetts, New Hampshire, Puerto Rico, Rhode Island
Second	Connecticut, New York, Vermont
Third	Delaware, New Jersey, Pennsylvania, Virgin Islands
Fourth	Maryland, North Carolina, South Carolina, Virginia, West Virginia
Fifth	District of the Canal Zone, Louisiana, Mississippi, Texas
Sixth	Kentucky, Michigan, Ohio, Tennessee
Seventh	Illinois, Indiana, Wisconsin
Eighth	Arkansas, Iowa, Minnesota, Missouri, Nebraska, North Dakota, South Dakota
Ninth	Alaska, Arizona, California, Idaho, Montana, Nevada, Oregon, Washington, Guam, Hawaii
Tenth	Colorado, Kansas, New Mexico, Oklahoma, Utah, Wyoming
Eleventh	Alabama, Florida, Georgia
Federal	All federal judicial districts

upon any state of facts that might rationally be supposed to exist, as to be irrational, arbitrary or capricious, fundamentally unfair or shocking to the conscience of a free people. The formula has substance to command it but the difference between saying that an important law is foolish and saying that it is arbitrary or violates fundamental rights lies chiefly in the strength of the speaker's conviction. Any weighing and balancing of the very same interests appraised by the legislature inescapably evokes personal judgments upon the relative importance of imponderable elements.

Whatever the answer to these questions, the Court's responsibility for the framework of government does less to check the Court's reviewing of laws affecting personal liberty than its scrutiny of statutes regulating business and economic practices. This position has strong roots in constitutional history. The Bill of Rights is the chief express constitutional limitation upon legislative power. It is concerned not with the physical safety of society, jobs or economic activity and security—the bricks and mortar of the community—but with the realm of the spirit. The Framers dreamed that if their hopes for civil liberty were codified, man's energies of mind and spirit, released from fear, would flourish. They also knew that society's respect for the freedom of a man to grow and choose the best he can discern must be founded upon the protection of privacy and just and humane criminal procedure. . . .

■ ENDNOTES

1. Ricker v. Board of Education of Millard County School District, 16 Utah 2d 106, 396 P.2d 416 (1964).

2. Latham v. Board of Education of City of Chicago, 31 Ill.2d 178, 201 N.E.2d 111 (1964).

3. Benjamin N. Cardoza, *The Nature of the Judicial Process* (New Haven and London: Yale University Press, 1962), pp. 18-19.

4. Roscoe Pound, "Common Law and Legislation," 21 *Harvard Law Review*, pp. 383, 385 (1908). Copyright © 1908 by The Harvard Law Review Association.

5. Marion & McPherson Railway Co. v. Alexander, 63 Kan. 72, 64 P. 978 (1901).

6. See H. Hart and A. Sacks, *The Legal Process: Basic Problems in the Making and Application of Law* (Cambridge, 10th ed. 1958), pp. 1144–46. Reprinted by permission of Dean Albert M. Sacks.

7. Heydon's Case, Exchequer, 30 Co. 7a, 76 Eng.Rep. 637 (1584).

8. Lord Blackburn in River Wear Commissioners v. Adamson, 2 App.Cas. 742, 746 (House of Lords, 1877).

9. Lord Atkinson, in Vacher & Sons, Limited v. London Society of Compositers, 107 L.T.Rep. 722 (House of Lords, 1913).

10. Lord Bramwell, in Hill v. East and West India Dock Co., 9 A.C. 448, 464-65 (House of Lords, 1884).

11. Mr. Justice Day, in Caminetti v. United States, 242 U.S. 470, 485–86, 37 S.Ct. 192, 194 (1917).

12. Mr. Justice Brown, in Hamilton v. Rathbone, 175 U.S. 414, 419, 421, 20 S.Ct. 155, 157 (1899).

13. 5 U.S. (1 Cranch) 137 (1803).

14. Bonvento v. Board of Public Instruction of Palm Beach County, 194 So.2d 605 (Fla.1967).

15. Hobbs v. County of Moore, 267 N.C. 665, 149 S.E.2d 1 (1966).

16. Ashwander v. Tennessee Valley Authority, 297 U.S. 288, 56 S.Ct. 466 (1936).

17. Ibid.

18. Burnet v. Coronado Oil & Gas Co., 285 U.S. 393, 52 S.Ct. 443 (1932).

19. Ibid., p. 449.

20. R. J. Walker & M. G. Walker, *The English Legal System* (London: Butterworths, 1972), p. 124.

21. K. N. Llewellyn, *The Bramble Bush, On Our Law and Its Study* (New York: Oceana Publications, 1960), pp. 41-43.

22. Muskrat v. United States, 219 U.S. 346, 31 S.Ct. 250 (1911).

23. Constitution of the United States, Art. III, § 2.

24. Charles Alan Wright, *Law of Federal Courts* (St. Paul, MN: West Publishing Co., 1970).

25. Aetna Life Insurance Co. v. Haworth, 300 U.S. 227, 57 S.Ct. 461, 463, 108 A.L.R. 1000 (1937), quoting from In re Pacific Railway Commission, 32 Fed 241, 255 (C.C.Cal.1887).

26. Ibid.

27. Flast v. Cohen, 392 U.S. 83, 94–95, 88 S.Ct. 1942, 1949-50 (1968).

28. 5 U.S. (1 Cranch) 137, (1803).

29. *State Court Caseload Statistics: Annual Report 1988* (The National Center for State Courts, February 1990), p. 39.

30. Ibid, pp. 38–45.

31. Ibid, p. 18.

32. Ibid.

33. Ibid, pp. 19–20.

34. Ibid.

35. Ibid, p. 5.

36. Constitution of the United States, Art. III, § 1.

CHAPTER 2
Historical Perspective

The law of public education is shaped by the philosophical, political, and social traditions of the United States. In the early years, the colonies naturally assumed the pattern of the class-oriented English educational system in which free and universal education was far beyond the eye of the most progressive leaders. Children of poor and lower-class families received no education at all or were attached as apprentices to learn a trade and develop manual skills.

Even though there was some governmental recognition of the benefits of education, as evidenced by a 1642 statute in Massachusetts in which all parents were charged with seeing to the education of their children and later in 1647 when the legislature required certain towns to appoint a teacher and permitted taxes for education, by and large early colonial legislatures tended to ignore education. The law of 1647 was promulgated to teach all to read the scriptures in order to avoid falling prey to "the old deluder, Satan."

It would not be accurate to say, though, that the Massachusetts legislation of 1642 and 1647 was solely intended for religious purposes. At this time, there was an emerging feeling that education of the youth was essential to the well-being of the state and that a stable social environment could best be facilitated if all persons were literate.

The revolution in England that saw the rise to power of Oliver Cromwell and the Puritans introduced a charitable and humanitarian outlook that was found wanting under the Tudor and Stuart monarchies. There were, during this era, endless debates about the value of education and the necessity for governmental change. Francis Bacon had con-

tributed greatly to this dialogue by urging scientific scholasticism of the Church. In 1641, Jan Amos Comenius, the Moravian exile of Czechoslovakia, internationally known as a preeminent educational thinker, urged that children be taught on realistic lines. Comenius visited England at the invitation of the Puritans to explore the reformation and extension of education. Comenius also advanced the idea of universal books and universal schools to be implemented by the creation of a system of graded schools in all towns and villages. Even the great John Milton contributed to the interchange regarding education with his *Of Education,* wherein he advanced the idea that the "reforming of education . . . be one of the greatest and noblest designs that can be thought on, and for want whereof this nation perishes."[1] Unfortunately, Comenius' idea did not come to fruition as the conflict between Charles I and Parliament escalated and civil war broke out. The influence of the newfound Puritan interest in education nevertheless had a direct effect on America. In 1656, James Harrison argued that the provision of schools was one of the state's primary responsibilities.[2] Unfortunately, with the restoration of Charles II to the throne after the death of Cromwell, the free flow of ideas regarding universal education subsided and lay virtually dormant for another two hundred years.

The emphasis on learning in England and the colonies was, however, feeble compared to the continent, where elementary education was made universal and compulsory for both sexes in the duchy of Wurttemberg in 1565, in the Dutch Republic in 1618, and in the duchy of Weimar in 1619. England itself did not have any provision of governmental education until two centuries later in 1870. England began to *break free* of the control of the privileged who sent their children to the English "public" school (exclusive private schools) that were operated primarily by the Church of England. It was not until 1880 that local attendance bylaws became compulsory. Even Scotland and France were more egalitarian in their perspective toward education, founding systems of universal education in 1696 and 1698 respectively, even though the French system did not provide for secondary education except in Jesuit schools.

The strongest influence of the English on colonial efforts were mostly negative ones, causing pauper school laws to be created. These laws provided that if indigent parents would declare themselves paupers, their children could be sent to specified private or pay schools for a free education.[3] Another vestige of the English system that was used in some colonies was the "rate bill," which required the parent to pay an amount for each child to supplement inadequate school revenues. The amount assessed was collected from the parents through ordinary tax bills. Such rate bills were still in effect in New York State as late as 1867.[4]

It was not until the eighteenth century that a new political philosophy developed that conceived of education as essential to the welfare of the state. Until then, the benefits of education were viewed as largely personal; the external value of education to society had not yet been realized. As the colonies began to struggle for independence from England, the concept of free public education gained momentum. Americans became obsessed with freedom, and schools were viewed as the primary means by which freedom could be obtained and maintained.

During the 1760s and 1770s the idea developed that there should be a free system of education that would provide for a general diffusion of knowledge, cultivate new learning, and nurture the democratic ideals of government. A "system" of education implied at least three attributes. First, there should be some uniformity of access so that the general population would have the opportunity to acquire some appropriate level of learning.

Second, there should be some method by which one could pursue a particular curriculum. Third, there should be some institutional organization whereby a person could progress from primary, to secondary, to college or university.[5] This view was especially well enunciated by Benjamin Rush, who called for the state to be "tied together by one system of education." "The university," he said, "will in time furnish masters for the colleges, and colleges will furnish masters for the free schools, while the free schools, in their turns, will supply the colleges and the universities with scholars, students and pupils. The same systems of grammar, oratory and philosophy, will be taught in every part of the state, and the literary features of Pennsylvania will thus designate one great, and equally enlightened family."[6]

Rush emphasized the need to have a free and uniform system of education that would "render the mass of the people more homogeneous, and thereby fit them more easily for uniform and peaceable government."[7]

As Butts observed, "the really important reason for believing in the value of education is that it can be the foundation of freedom. In the first place, a truly democratic society must rest upon the knowledge, intelligence, and wisdom of all the people."[8] Americans generally embraced the words of Jefferson, that "a people who mean to be their own Governors must arm themselves with the power which knowledge gives." More than any other, Jefferson's words redounded the public or common school philosophy that was to sweep the young nation in generations to come. Typical of Jefferson's position was his letter from Paris in 1786 to his old professor George Wythe written in support of a bill for general education:

I think by far the most important bill in our whole code is that for the diffusion of knowledge among the people. No other sure foundation can be devised for the preservation of freedom and happiness. . . . Preach, my dear sir, a crusade against ignorance; establish and improve the law for educating the common people. Let our countrymen know . . . that the tax which will be paid for this purpose is not more than the thousandth part of what will be paid to kings, priests, and nobles who will rise up among us if we leave the people in ignorance.[9]

In this new era, not only was universal education in greater demand but a discernible shift toward more practical studies was in evidence and the old Latin grammar school began to deteriorate as the major source of learning. After 1750 the enthusiasm for schools based on religious motivations began to die down and the European traditions for both types and methods of education no longer satisfied the American appetite for knowledge.[10] A concept of public education evolved that was uniquely American. During this period general school laws in older states led the progression of public education, requiring maintenance of schools by towns for a definite term each year, imposing taxation, and generally statutorily sanctioning the public school movement that had evolved over a century and a half.[11]

A clearly defined role of the state in education, however, had not emerged by 1796 when George Washington, in his Farewell Address, called for the American people to

[p]romote, then, as an object of primary importance, institutions for the general diffusion of knowledge. In proportion as the structure of a government gives force to public opinion, it is essential that public opinion be enlightened.[12]

To progress from the sporadic and inadequate early general school laws to uniform state systems of free public education was a laborious journey with battles over tax support and sectarianism marking the way. By 1825, it had become commonly recognized that a state system of education would require general and direct taxation of a major source of revenue such as real property. A broad base of taxation became the watchword; "The wealth of the State must educate the children of the State" aptly described the principle of taxation for education that was eventually to emerge.[13]

Established traditions were not easily overcome, and it was difficult to convince many of

the citizens that pauper schools were not the appropriate educational concept since it was believed the poor and poverty-stricken would benefit from free public schools.

A major impetus for education had come from the churches that sought to advance Christianity through knowledge of the Bible. Early states generally recognized and supported these efforts, and several states set aside lands to help church schools. As the new philosophy of public education became entrenched and people started to grasp its benefits, new advocates for state education emerged and conflict with church leaders developed. The inherent discord between sectarian education and free state education was soon manifested in bitter struggles in several states, the story of which is more fully developed in a later chapter of this book.

Into the vortex of these conflicts stepped public education advocates such as Horace Mann of Massachusetts,[14] who preached an educational awakening that was ultimately to form the basis for state systems of public education as we know them today—free secular public schools supported by both local and state general taxation.

The early nineteenth century saw an extraordinary group of dedicated and effective leaders who were "public school men" emerge in several states. They argued against tuition in any shape or form; and most importantly, they maintained that the term "free school" should no longer mean merely a place where the poor were given a free education and all others paid tuition. Class distinctions, they argued, would be reduced if all children could be given a free education financed with revenues from taxes levied on everyone.[15]

This view was reflected in an 1822 report to the Kentucky legislature that advocated free common schools and specifically rejected the pauper school approach:

To be separated from the rest of the community as a distinct and inferior caste, and held out to the world as the objects of public charity, is a degradation too humiliating for the pride of freemen.[16]

In this same state in 1819, the governor, in an eloquent plea to the legislature for creation of a free system of common schools, asserted both the value of education for the welfare of the state and for the equality and livelihood of the people. Although his message fell on deaf legislative ears at that time, his statement is worth repeating because this is the philosophy on which the free common schools of the United States were founded:

Our government depends for its perpetuity upon the virtue and wisdom of the people; virtue is the offspring of wisdom. To be virtuous, the people must be wise. But how shall they be wise, unless the appropriate means are employed? And how shall the appropriate means be extended to the bereaved and destitute, otherwise than by legislative provision? Education is more vitally important in a republican than in any other form of government; for there the right to administer the government is common to all, and when they have the opportunity of administering the government, the means of obtaining the wisdom requisite for its administration should be accessible to all. The wealthy are never without the means of obtaining education; the poor never, or rarely possess them. But the capacity for the acquisition of knowledge, and the display of virtue, is not confined to the wealthy. It is often, and perhaps more frequently found amongst the poor. Instances are not rare in which genius has emerged from poverty, surmounted the difficulties and privations inseparable from that condition, and like the sun burst through a cloud, illumined the social and political horizon by its benignant irradiations. The ornaments and benefactors of society have not unfrequently arisen when but very slight helps were afforded, from the humblest walks of life.[17]

During this period, struggles over public schools were fought with conviction by those on both sides. Cubberley described this era when public, free, nonsectarian, tax-supported schools were first given serious consideration and there was much public debate between church and private school advocates and public school proponents.

The second quarter of the nineteenth century may be said to have witnessed the battle for tax-supported, publicly controlled and directed, and nonsectarian common schools. In 1825 such schools were the distant hope of statesmen and reformers; in 1850 they were becoming an actuality in almost every Northern State. The twenty-five years intervening marked a period of public agitation and educational propaganda; of many hard legislative fights; of a struggle to secure desired legislation, and then to hold what had been secured; of many bitter contests with church and private-school interests, which felt that their "vested rights" were being taken from them; and of occasional referenda in which the people were asked, at the next election, to advise the legislature as to what to do. Excepting the battle for the abolition of slavery, perhaps no question has ever been before the American people for settlement which caused so much feeling or aroused such bitter antagonisms. Old friends and business associates parted company over the question, lodges were forced to taboo the subject to avoid disruption, ministers and their congregations often quarreled over the question of free schools, and politicians avoided the issue. The friends of free schools were at first commonly regarded as fanatics, dangerous to the State, and the opponents of free schools were considered by them as old-time conservatives or as selfish members of society.   . . .

Many thought that tax-supported schools would be dangerous for the State, harmful to individual good, and thoroughly undemocratic. There was danger, too, of making education too common. Schools of any kind were, or should be, for the few, and chiefly for those who could afford private instruction. It was argued that education demands a leisure class and that the poor do not have the necessary leisure, that it was not possible for the government to provide a general educational system, and that all such proposals represented the deliberate confiscation of the property of one class in society for the benefit of another class. These and other arguments were well answered some years later by Horace Mann when he stated, at some length, the political and economic "Ground of the Free School System." Others were afraid that free schools were only a bait, the real purpose being to "religiously traditionalize the children," and then later unite Church and State. Many did not see the need for schools at all, and many more were in the frame of mind of the practical New England farmer who declared that "the Bible and figgers is all I want my boys to know."Strangely enough, the most vigorous opposition often came from the ignorant, improvident, hand-to-mouth laborers, who most needed schools, and free schools at that. Often those in favor of taxation were bitterly assailed, and even at times threatened with personal violence. Henry Barnard, who rendered such useful service in awakening Connecticut and Rhode Island, between 1837 and 1845, to the need for better schools, tells us that a member of the Rhode Island legislature told him that a bill providing a small state tax for schools, which he was then advocating, even if passed by the legislature, could not be enforced in Rhode Island at the point of the bayonet.[18]

Legislatures gradually accepted the idea of free or common schools for all and by statute began to require local school districts to tax themselves to support the public schools. In this early period, it became clear that the states must require rather than permit localities to establish free schools. Local control of education gradually became limited by state constitutions and by actions of state legislatures. Uniformity of education across states, it was decided, would be better brought to fruition by a degree of central state planning rather than through completely decentralized local school control.[19]

By 1852, when Massachusetts enacted the first compulsory attendance law, the responsibility for public education was firmly lodged at the state level. The idea of free common schools was well established, but the implementation of the concept developed slowly. It remained for succeeding generations to deal with the pervasive issues of "uniformity" and "equality," which have grown to be as vital to the public school movement as the word "freedom" was originally.

As a major governmental enterprise the development of the public school system was accompanied by a continuous string of legal controversies in every state in the nation. As a result, court decisions have, to a great extent, given form and substance to the philosophical base on which the public schools are founded. The courts have made it quite clear that "Public education is not merely a function of government; it is of government."[20] In legal

theory, public schools exist not only to confer benefits on the individual but just as importantly they are necessary, indeed essential, to the advancement of civil society.[21] Of such importance is the public education function that the state can, under certain conditions, limit parental control in order to advance the common weal.[22]

The rationale for the creation of a system of free public schools has been reiterated many times by the courts, expounding the importance of an educated citizenry for the general welfare of the people and for the protection of the state.[23]

Recognition of the role and importance of public schools to the well-being of the people and the state was expressed by the Supreme Court of Illinois in 1914. This court declared that public schools were created

> [N]ot out of philanthropic motives, but out of a consideration of the essentials of good government. The conduct and maintenance of schools . . . is no less an "exercise of the functions vested in those charged with the conduct of government," is no less a part of "the science and art of government," and deals no less with the "organization, regulation and administration of a State" in its internal affairs, than the construction and maintenance of roads by the commissioners of highways; the conduct and maintenance of the charitable institutions of the state by the board of administration; the inspection of factories, and the enforcement of the laws for the protection of workers and in regard to the employment of women and children by the factory inspectors; the performance of the industrial board of the duties imposed upon it by law, and the performance of many other duties by public officials that, however beneficial to individuals, are not undertaken from philanthropic or charitable motives, but for the protection, safety, and welfare of the citizens of the state in the interest of good government.[24]

Similarly, it was said by the Supreme Court of New Hampshire:

> The primary purpose of the maintenance of the common school system is the promotion of the general intelligence of the people constituting

the body politic and thereby to increase the usefulness and efficiency of the citizens, upon which the government of society depends. Free schooling furnished by the state is not so much a right granted to pupils as a duty imposed upon them for the public good. If they do not voluntarily attend the schools provided for them, they may be compelled to do so. While most people regard the public schools as the means of great personal advantage to the pupils, the fact is too often overlooked that they are governmental means of protecting the state from the consequences of an ignorant and incompetent citizenship.[25]

This judicial philosophy is stated in various ways by the decisions in other state supreme courts. The high court for Tennessee, for example, saw a need for a uniform system of public schools to promote the general welfare "by educating the people, and thus, by providing and securing a higher state of intelligence and morals, conserve the peace, good order, and well-being of society."[26]

MASSACHUSETTS SCHOOL OF LAW OF 1647

Sec. 1. It being one chief project of the old deluder, Satan, to keep men from the knowledge of the Scriptures, as in former times by keeping them in an unknown tongue, so in these latter times by persuading them from the use of tongues that so at least the true sense and meaning of the original might be clouded by false glosses of saint-seeming deceivers, that learning may not be buried in the grave of our fathers in the church and commonwealth, the Lord assisting our endeavors. . . .

It is therefore ordered by this court and authority thereof, that every township in this jurisdiction, after the Lord hath increased them to the number of fifty householders, shall then forthwith appoint one within their town to teach all such children as shall resort to him to write and read, whose wages shall be paid either by the parents or masters of such children, or by the inhabitants in general, by way of supply, as the major part of those that order the prudentials of the town shall appoint; provided, those that sent their children be not oppressed by paying much more than they can have them taught for in other towns.

Sec. 2. It is further ordered, that where any town shall increase to the number of one hundred families or householders they shall set up a grammar school, the master thereof being able to instruct youth so far as they may be fitted for the university; and if any town neglect the performance hereof above one year, every such town shall pay five pounds per annum to the such school till they shall perform this order. . . .

PREAMBLE TO A BILL FOR THE MORE GENERAL DIFFUSION OF KNOWLEDGE (1779)

From *The Works of Thomas Jefferson,* collected and edited by Paul Leicester Ford, Volume II, Federal Edition (New York: G. P. Putnam's Sons, 1904), pp. 414–426, abridged.

Whereas it appeareth that however certain forms of government are better calculated than others to protect individuals in the free exercise of their natural rights, and are at the same time themselves better guarded against degeneracy, yet experience hath shown, that even under the best forms, those entrusted with power have, in time, and by slow operations, perverted it into tyranny; and it is believed that the most effectual means of preventing this would be, to illuminate, as far as practicable, the minds of the people at large, and more especially to give them knowledge of those facts, which history exhibiteth, that, possessed thereby of the experience of other ages and countries, they may be enabled to know ambition under all its shapes, and prompt to exert their natural powers to defeat its purposes. And whereas, it is generally true that people will be happiest whose laws are best, and are best administered, and that laws will be wisely formed, and honestly administered, in proportion as those who form and administer them are wise and honest; whence it becomes expedient for promoting the publick happiness that those persons, whom nature hath endowed with genius and virtue, should be rendered by liberal education worthy to receive, and able to guard the sacred deposit of the rights and liberties of their fellow citizens, and that they should be called to that charge without regard to wealth, birth or other accidental condition or circumstance; but the indigence of the greater number disabling them from so educating, at their own expense, those of their children whom nature hath fitly formed and disposed to become useful instruments for the public, it is better that such should be sought for and educated at the common expence of all, than that the happiness of all should be confided to the weak or wicked. . . .

which proves the *absolute right* of every human being that comes into the world to an education; and which, of course, proves the correlative duty of every government to see that the means of that education are provided for all.

In regard to the application of this principle of natural law, that is, in regard to the extent of the education to be provided for all, at the public expense, some differences of opinion may fairly exist, under different political organizations; but under a republican government, it seems clear that the minimum of this education can never be less than such as is sufficient to qualify each citizen for the civil and social duties he will be called to discharge; such an education as teaches the individual the great laws of bodily health; as qualifies for the fulfilment of parental duties; as is indispensable for the civil functions of a witness or a juror; as is necessary for the voter in municipal affairs; and finally, for the faithful and conscientious discharge of all those duties which devolve upon the inheritor of a portion of the sovereignty of this great republic.

Horace Mann's Tenth and Twelfth Annual Reports to the Massachusetts Board of Education

From the 10th Annual Report, published in *The Common School Journal*, Vol. IX, No. 9, edited by Horace Mann (Boston: William B. Fowle, 1847); the 12th Annual Report, published separately from the *Journal* by Fowle in 1849.

— – · — · – · — · – · —

From the Tenth Report (1846)

I believe in the existence of a great, immutable principle of natural law, or natural ethics, a principle antecedent to all human institutions and incapable of being abrogated by any ordinances of man, a principle of divine origin, clearly legible in the ways of Providence as those ways are manifested in the order of nature and in the history of the race,

From the Twelfth Report (1848)

The Capacities of Our Present School System to Improve the Pecuniary Condition and to Elevate the Intellectual and Moral Character of the Commonwealth

Under the Providence of God, our means of education are the grand machinery by which the "raw material" of human nature can be worked up into inventors and discoverers, into skilled artisans and scientific farmers, into scholars and jurists, into the founders of benevolent institutions, and the great expounders of ethical and theological science. By means of early education, those embryos of talent may be quickened, which will solve the difficult problems of political and economical law; and by them, too, the genius may be kindled which will blaze forth in the Poets of Humanity. Our schools, far more than they have done, may supply the Presidents and Professors of Colleges, and Superintendents of Public Instruction, all over the land; and send, not only into our sister states, but across the Atlantic, the man of practical science, to superintend the construction of the great works of art. Here, too, may those judicial powers be developed and invigorated, which will make legal principles so clear and convincing as to prevent appeals to force; and, should the clouds of war ever lower over our country, some hero may be found, the nursing of our schools, and ready to become the leader of our armies, the best of all heroes, who will secure the glories of a peace, unstained by the magnificent murders of the battlefield. . . .

Without undervaluing any other human agency, it may be safely affirmed that the Common School, improved and energized, as it can easily be, may become the most effective and benignant of all the forces of civilization. Two reasons sustain this position. In the first place, there is a universality in its operation, which can be affirmed of no other institution whatever. If administered in the spirit of justice and conciliation, all the rising generation may be brought within the circle of its reformatory and elevating influences. And, in the second place, the materials upon which it operates are so pliant and ductile as to be susceptible of assuming a greater variety of forms than any other earthly work of the Creator. . . .

I proceed, then, in endeavoring to show how the true business of the schoolroom connects itself, and becomes identical, with the great interests of society. The former is the infant, immature state of those interests; the latter, their developed, adult state. As "the child is father to the man," so may the training of the schoolroom expand into the institutions and fortunes of the State.

According to the European theory, men are divided into classes—some to toil and earn, others to seize and enjoy. According to the Massachusetts theory, all are to have an equal chance for earning, and equal security in the enjoyment of what they earn. The latter tends to equality of condition; the former to the grossest inequalities. Tried by any Christian standard of morals, or even by any of the better sort of heathen standards, can any one hesitate, for a moment, in declaring which of the two will produce the greater amount of human welfare; and which, therefore, is the more conformable to the Divine will? . . .

I suppose it to be the universal sentiment of all those who mingle any ingredient of benevolence with their notions on Political Economy, that vast and overshadowing private fortunes are among the greatest dangers to which the happiness of the people in a republic can be subjected. Such fortunes would create a feudalism of a new kind; but one more oppressive and unrelenting than that of the Middle Ages. The feudal lords in England, and on the continent, never held their retainers in a more abject condition of servitude, than the great majority of foreign manufacturers and capitalists hold their operatives and laborers at the present day. The means employed are different, but the similarity in results is striking. What force did then, money does now. . . . The baron prescribed his own terms to his retainers; those terms were peremptory, and the serf must submit or perish. . . .

Now, surely, nothing but Universal Education can counter-work this tendency to the domination of capital and the servility of labor. If one class possesses all the wealth and the education, while the residue of society is ignorant and poor, it matters not by what name the relation between them may be called; the latter, in fact and in truth, will be the servile dependents and subjects of the former. But if education be equably diffused, it will draw property after it, by the strongest of all attractions; for such a thing never did happen, and never can happen, as that an intelligent and practical body of men should be permanently poor. . . .

Education, then, beyond all other devices of human origin, is the great equalizer of the conditions of men—the balance-wheel of the social machinery. I do not here mean that it so elevates the moral nature as to make men disdain and abhor the oppression of their fellow-men. This idea pertains to another of its attributes. But I mean that it gives each man the independence and the means, by which he can resist the selfishness of other men. . . .

For the creation of wealth, then—for the existence of a wealthy people and a wealthy nation—intelligence is the grand condition. The number of improvers will increase, as the intellectual constituency, if I may so call it, increases. In former times, and in most parts of the world even at the present day, not one man in a million has ever had such a development of mind, as made it possible for him to become a contributor to art or science. Let this development precede, and contributions, numberless, and of inestimable value, will be sure to follow. That Political Economy, therefore, which busies itself about capital and labor, supply and demand, interest and rents, favorable and unfavorable balances of trade; but leaves out of account the element of a wide-spread mental development, is nought but stupendous folly. The greatest of all the arts in political economy is to change a consumer into a producer; and the next greatest is to increase the producing power—an end to be directly attained, by increasing his intelligence.   . . .

■ EDUCATION PROVISIONS OF STATE CONSTITUTIONS

Some state constitutions have very general provisions for education, requiring that a system of education be established and maintained; while others are more specific, including adjectives such as "thorough and efficient," "uniform," "suitable," or "adequate." Such words are "terms of art" that, when interpreted by the courts, circumscribe the basis to which the legislature must conform in establishing a public school system. While legislatures are given general authority to govern the schools and may go beyond the minimal constitutional mandates, the constitutional prescription must be satisfied. Where legislators fail to fulfill the constitutional requirements, their acts may be invalidated by the courts. The fact that education is specifically set out in state constitutions as a required state function gives education a preferential position relative to other state governmental functions that are not so mentioned.

Provisions for the establishment and maintenance of public schools are enunciated differently in the various state constitutions, yet there exist certain underlying principles that are generally common to all. These may be summarized as follows:

1. *The legislature is required to bear the responsibility for enactment of laws to govern the public or common schools.* This obligation cannot be averted or delegated to other state or local agencies. Legislatures may provide for local discretion, but must ultimately bear the responsibility for the maintenance of a public school system within the context of the wording and meaning of the education provision of the state constitution.
2. *The public schools, by and large, are considered to be a cohesive unit: one organization or organic whole whose particular organizational pattern and subparts are within the prerogative of the legislature.* The word "system," which is used in most constitutions, requires a measure of orderliness and uniformity regardless of the number of local school districts, implies a unitary cohesiveness, and is not intended to create merely a conglomeration of locally independent school agencies.
3. *The schools as public entities are to be of the body politic of the state, controlled by the public and governed by the people.* Early American experiments, ranging from church and private schools to pauper, rate-bill, and academy schools, quasi-private or semipublic in nature, were rejected as constitutional alternatives to public schools. The various devices to foster control by private interests, reducing public participation and preventing full access by the people, run counter to the ideal of a public school.
4. *The nature of the public school is that it be free and common to all with no charges to limit access.* Early attempts to create public schools were hindered by the reluctance of legislatures to tax at a level of sufficiency to operate a completely public system. The idea that education is a family or private concern and should be paid for out of private resources has resulted in imposition of various fees levied on the child's family which can potentially harm access and are

contrary to the philosophical foundation on which public schools are premised. To sustain full participation and access by all the people requires that the schools be financed by all the people through common taxation.

5. *The concept of public common schools as a state governmental enterprise requires that tax resources be allocated throughout the state in a manner that will ensure that the quality of a child's education will not be dependent on private or personal influence or wealth nor on the financial capabilities of the locality or political subdivision of the state.* State constitutions do not envisage a system of schools with widely variant educational opportunity brought about by either political vicissitude or the vagaries of local fiscal fortune.

Each of these principles, to varying degrees, has been emphasized by judicial interpretation of the education provisions in state constitutions. The nomenclature in state constitutions requiring the creation and maintenance of public schools is terminology of art, most of which has a long historical and legal tradition as to usage and intent.

These general principles establishing public schools are implicit in the meaning of words such as to "maintain a general, suitable and efficient system of free schools," as is found in Article XIV of the Arkansas Constitution or "a general uniform and thorough system," as is included in the Montana Constitution, Article XII, § 1. Such wording of education provisions is replete with significant implications for the conduct of education. For example, the Supreme Court of New Jersey held that the words "thorough and efficient" defining system demanded that the state provide equal educational opportunity for all children of the state."[27]

These constitutional provisions can be classified in different ways, but one convenient categorization suggests a minimum of three types.[28] The first of these can be called the adjective or gloss group, wherein the constitution employs words of amplification such as "efficient," "uniform," or "thorough" to specify the qualities of the system required. The second category can simply be called the

system group. Here, the state constitution mandates the establishment and maintenance of a system, but does not prescribe the type of system other than that it be free, public, or common. An example of this type is the California Constitution, which requires that the state provide for a "system of common schools." A third category is what Mize calls the cherish group, or the New England category. A better term may be "virtue," because in this type of provision the virtues of education are lauded and commended, but there is no positive requirement mandating any particular action by the legislature. In this category the New Hampshire Constitution is one of the most descriptive, stating that "It shall be the duty of the legislators and magistrates in all future periods of the government, to cherish the interests of literature and the sciences, and all seminaries and public schools." Including New Hampshire, there are at least four states with virtue provisions: Massachusetts, Rhode Island, and Virginia. Three other states that can be classified as both system and virtue states are California, Vermont, and Connecticut. Virginia rests comfortably in all three categories by reason of some rather unique wording in its bill of rights[29] that is separate from the education provision of its constitution.[30] This provision, Section 15 of the Virginia Bill of Rights, enacted in 1971, taken from Jefferson's Bill For The More General Diffusion of Knowledge, 1779, states:

> That free government rests, as does all progress, upon the broadest possible diffusion of knowledge, and that the Commonwealth should avail itself of those talents which nature has sown so liberally among its people by assuring the opportunity for their fullest development by an effective system of education throughout the Commonwealth.[31]

This admonishment to the Virginia legislature of the value of widespread knowledge in concert with the requirement that the people be given "opportunity for their fullest development" combines the rationale of the virtue provisions with the qualitative standards of the adjectival provisions.

■■■ EDUCATION PROVISION AS LIMITATION ON LEGISLATURE

Historically, state courts have seldom intervened to limit legislative prerogative in interpreting the intent of "education provisions" of state constitutions. Education provisions are typically those that place an affirmative Constitutional obligation on the legislature to create a school system. The courts have most often followed the philosophy expressed by an Illinois court, that refused to substitute its judgment for the legislature's, saying that "The efficiency and fairness of a state system is for the determination of the legislature."[32] Typically, the courts have not viewed the education provisions of state constitutions as limitations on the legislature. The education provisions were not considered to be limitations, but merely elaborations on enabling provisions to be used and defined as the legislature thought necessary. This attitude is expressed by a 1926 Virginia court, which said, "While the Constitution of the state provides, in mandatory terms, that the Legislature shall establish and maintain public free schools, there is neither mandate nor inhibition in the provisions as to the regulation thereof. The Legislature, therefore, has the power to enact any legislation in regard to the conduct, control, and regulation of the public free schools, which does not deny to the citizen the Constitutional right to enjoy life and liberty, to pursue happiness and to acquire property."[33] Thus, words in a state constitution defining the type of education the people required were not to be interpreted by the courts as limitations on legislative prerogative. The power of the legislature would not generally be questioned unless the legislation transgressed on the more important freedom provisions such as the right to life, liberty, happiness, and property.

Lately, however, this view has changed. The courts have become more assertive and have begun to more carefully scrutinize legislation in light of the education provisions. In several instances the courts have held state methods of financing the schools to be unconstitutional as violative of these provisions (see Chapter 19 on School Finance). Such cases are beginning to establish an imposing array of precedents, which give definition to terms such as "thorough," "efficient," "throughout," "uniform," and a host of other adjectives.

A judgment of this type was rendered by the Supreme Court of Kentucky in 1989, invoking the term "efficient" to invalidate the entire system of public schools. The broad sweep of this opinion in enforcing the education provision of a state constitution makes it a particularly significant precedent.

Legislature Fails Constitutional Requirement to Establish an Efficient System of Common Schools

— · — · — · — · — · —

Rose v. The Council for Better Education, Inc.

— · — · — · — · — · —

Supreme Court of Kentucky,
1989. 790 S.W.2d 186

STEPHENS, Chief Justice. The issue we decide on this appeal is whether the Kentucky General Assembly has complied with its constitutional mandate to "provide an efficient system of common schools throughout the state."[1]

In deciding that it has not, we intend no criticism of the substantial efforts made by the present General Assembly and by its predecessors, nor do we intend to substitute our judicial authority for the authority and discretion of the General Assembly. We are, rather, exercising our constitutional duty in declaring that, when we consider the evidence in the record, and when we apply the constitutional requirement of Section 183 to that evidence, it is crystal clear that the General Assembly has fallen short of its duty to enact legislation to provide for an efficient system of common schools throughout the state. In a word, the present system of common schools in Kentucky is not an "efficient" one in our view of the clear mandate of Section 183. The common school system in Kentucky is constitutionally deficient.

In reaching this decision, we are ever mindful of the immeasurable worth of education to our state and its citizens, especially to its young people. The framers of our constitution intended that each and every child in this state should receive a proper and an adequate education, *to be provided for by the General Assembly*. This opinion dutifully applies the constitutional test of Section 183 to the existing system of common schools. We do no more, nor may we do any less.

. . . The overall effect of appellants evidence is a virtual concession that Kentucky's system of common schools is underfunded and inadequate; is fraught with inequalities and inequities throughout the 168 local school districts; is ranked nationally in the lower 20-25% in virtually every category that is used to evaluate educational performance; and is not uniform among the districts in educational opportunities. When one considers the evidence presented by the appellants, there is little or no evidence to even begin to negate that of the appellees. The tidal wave of the appellees' evidence literally engulfs that of the appellants.

In spite of the Minimum Foundation Program and the Power Equalization Program, there are wide variations in financial resources and dispositions thereof which result in unequal educational opportunities throughout Kentucky. The local districts have large variances in taxable property per student. Even a total elimination of all mismanagement and waste in local school districts would not correct the situation as it now exists. A substantial difference in the curricula offered in the poorer districts contrasts with that of the richer districts, particularly in the areas of foreign language, science, mathematics, music and art.

The achievement test scores in the poorer districts are lower than those in the richer districts and expert opinion clearly established that there is a correlation between those scores and the wealth of the district. Student-teacher ratios are higher in the poorer districts. More-

over, although Kentucky's per capital income is low, it makes an even lower per capita effort to support the common schools.

Students in property poor districts receive inadequate and inferior educational opportunities as compared to those offered to those students in the more affluent districts. . . .

In a few simple, but direct words, the framers of our present Constitution, set forth the will of the people with regard to the importance of providing public education in the Commonwealth.

> *General Assembly to provide for school system—* The General Assembly shall, by appropriate legislation, provide for an efficient system of common schools throughout the State. Ky. Const. Sec. 183.

Several conclusions readily appear from a reading of this section. First, it is the obligation, the sole obligation, of the General Assembly to provide for a system of common schools in Kentucky. The obligation to so provide is clear and unequivocal and is, in effect, a constitutional mandate. Next, the school system must be provided throughout the entire state, with no area (or its children) being omitted. The creation, implementation and maintenance of the school system must be achieved by appropriate legislation. Finally, the system must be an efficient one.

It is, of course, the last 'conclusion' that gives us pause and requires study and analysis. What, indeed, is the meaning of the word "efficient" as used in Section 183?

. . . In language which brings together and re-emphasizes earlier decisions, we said,

> The fundamental mandate of the Constitution and Statutes of Kentucky is that there shall be equality and that all public schools shall be nonpartisan and nonsectarian.
>
> Uniformity does not require equal classification but it does demand that there shall be a substantially uniform system and equal school facilities without discrimination as between different sections of a district or a county.

The lack of uniformity and the unequal educational opportunity existing in the county was said to constitute "a violation of both the spirit and intent of Section 183 of our State Constitution." That reasoning therein applies, *a fortiori,* to the entire state system of common schools. Public schools must be efficient, equal and substantially uniform.

As can be seen, this Court, since the adoption of the present Constitution, has, in reflecting on Section 183, drawn several conclusions:

1. The General Assembly is mandated, is duty bound, to create and maintain a system of common schools — throughout the state.
2. The expressed purpose of providing such service is vital and critical to the well being of the state.
3. The system of common schools must be efficient.
4. The system of common schools must be free.
5. The system of common schools must provide equal educational opportunities for all students in the Commonwealth.
6. The state must control and administer the system.
7. The system must be, if not uniform, 'substantially uniform' with respect to the state as a whole.
8. The system must be equal to and for all students.

Opinions of Experts

Numerous well-qualified experts testified in this case. They were all well educated, experienced teachers, educators, or administrators; and all were familiar with the Kentucky system of common schools and with other states' and national school issues.

Dr. Richard Salmon testified that the concept of efficiency was a three part concept. First, the system should impose no financial hardship or advantage on any group of citizens. Further, local school districts must make comparable tax efforts. Second, resources provided by the system must be adequate and uniform throughout the state. Third, the system must not waste resources.

Dr. Kern Alexander opined that an efficient system is one which is unitary. It is one in which there is uniformity throughout the state. It is one in which equality is a hallmark and one in which students must be given equal educational opportunities, regardless of

economic status, or place of residence. He also testified that "efficient" involves pay and training of teachers, school buildings, other teaching staff, materials, and adequacy of all educational resources. Moreover, he, like Dr. Salmon, believed that "efficient" also applies to the quality of management of schools. Summarizing Dr. Alexander's opinion, an efficient system is unitary, uniform, adequate and properly managed.

The definitions of "efficient" were documented and supported by numerous national and local studies, prepared and authorized by many of the giants of the education profession.

The primary expert for the appellees was a local school superintendent who felt that an efficient system is one which is operated as best as can be with the money that was provided. We reject such a definition which could result in a system of common schools, efficient only in the uniformly deplorable conditions it provides throughout the state.

In summary, the experts in this case believed that an "efficient" system of common schools should have several elements:

1. The system is the sole responsibility of the General Assembly.
2. The tax effort should be evenly spread.
3. The system must provide the necessary resources throughout the state — they must be uniform.
4. The system must provide an adequate education.
5. The system must be properly managed.

DEFINITION OF "EFFICIENT." We now hone in on the heart of this litigation. In defining "efficient," we use all the tools that are made available to us. In spite of any protestations to the contrary, we do not engage in judicial legislating. We do not make policy. We do not substitute our judgment for that of the General Assembly. We simply take the plain directive of the Constitution, and, armed with its purpose, we decide what our General Assembly must achieve in complying with its solemn constitutional duty.

Any system of common schools must be created and maintained with the premise that education is absolutely vital to the present and to the future of our Commonwealth. As Herbert Spencer observed, "Education has for its object the formation of character." H. Spencer, *Social Studies* pt. 1, ch. 2, p. 17 (1851). No tax proceeds have a more important position or purpose than those for education in the grand scheme of our government. The importance of common schools and the education they provide Kentucky's children cannot be overemphasized or overstated.

The sole responsibility for providing the system of common schools is that of our General Assembly. It is a duty—it is a constitutional mandate placed by the people on the 138 members of that body who represent those selfsame people.

The General Assembly must not only establish the system, but it must monitor it on a continuing basis so that it will always be maintained in a constitutional manner. The state must carefully supervise it, so that there is no waste, no duplication, no mismanagement, at any level.

The system of common schools must be adequately funded to achieve its goals. The system of common schools must be substantially uniform throughout the state. Each child, *every child,* in this Commonwealth must be provided with an equal opportunity to have an adequate education. Equality is the key word here. The children of the poor and the children of the rich, the children who live in the poor districts and the children who live in the rich districts must be given the same opportunity and access to an adequate education. This obligation cannot be shifted to local counties and local school districts.

This is not to say that local school districts are precluded from enacting these local taxes to supplement the uniform, equal educational effort that the General Assembly must provide. It only means that such local efforts may not be used by the General Assembly as a substitute for providing an adequate, equal and substantially uniform educational system throughout this state.

We do not instruct the General Assembly to enact any specific legislation. We do not direct the General Assembly to raise taxes. It is their decision how best to achieve efficiency.

We only decide the nature of the constitutional mandate. We only determine the intent of the framers. Carrying-out that intent is the duty of the General Assembly.

A child's right to an adequate education is a fundamental one under our Constitution. The General Assembly must protect and advance that right. We concur with the trial court that an efficient system of education must have as its goal to provide each and every child with at least the seven following capacities: (i) sufficient oral and written communication skills to enable students to function in a complex and rapidly changing civilization; (ii) sufficient knowledge of economic, social, and political systems to enable the student to make informed choices; (iii) sufficient understanding of governmental processes to enable the student to understand the issues that affect his or her community, state, and nation; (iv) sufficient self-knowledge and knowledge of his or her mental and physical wellness; (v) sufficient grounding in the arts to enable each student to appreciate his or her cultural and historical heritage; (vi) sufficient training or preparation for advanced training in either academic or vocational fields so as to enable each child to choose and pursue life work intelligently; and (vii) sufficient levels of academic or vocational skills to enable public school students to compete favorably with their counterparts in surrounding states, in academics or in the job market.

The essential, and minimal, characteristics of an "efficient" system of common schools, may be summarized as follows:

1. The establishment, maintenance and funding of common schools in Kentucky is the sole responsibility of the General Assembly.
2. Common schools shall be free to all.
3. Common schools shall be available to all Kentucky children.
4. Common schools shall be substantially uniform throughout the state.
5. Common schools shall provide equal educational opportunities to all Kentucky children, regardless of place of residence or economic circumstances.
6. Common schools shall be monitored by the General Assembly to assure that they are

operated with no waste, no duplication, no mismanagement, and with no political influence.

7. The premise for the existence of common schools is that all children in Kentucky have a constitutional right to an adequate education.

8. The General Assembly shall provide funding which is sufficient to provide each child in Kentucky an adequate education.

9. An adequate education is one which has as its goal the development of the seven capacities recited previously.

We have described, *infra,* in some detail, the present system of common schools. We have noted the overall inadequacy of our system of education, when compared to national standards and to the standards of our adjacent states. We have recognized the great disparity that exists in educational opportunities throughout the state. We have noted the great disparity and inadequacy, of financial effort throughout the state.

In spite of the past and present efforts of the General Assembly, Kentucky's present system of common schools falls short of the mark of the constitutional mandate of "efficient." When one juxtaposes the standards of efficiency as derived from our Constitution, the cases decided thereunder, the persuasive authority from our sister states and the opinion of experts, with the virtually unchallenged evidence in the record, no other decision is possible.

We have decided this case solely on the basis of our Kentucky Constitution, Section 183. We find it unnecessary to inject any issues raised under the United States Constitution or the United States Bill of Rights in this matter. We decline to issue any injunctions, restraining orders, writs of prohibition or writs of mandamus.

We have decided one legal issue—and one legal issue only—viz., that the General Assembly of the Commonwealth has failed to establish an efficient system of common schools throughout the Commonwealth.

Lest there be any doubt, the result of our decision is that Kentucky's *entire system* of common schools is unconstitutional. There is no allegation that only part of the common school system is invalid, and we find no such circumstance. This decision applies to the entire sweep of the system—all its parts and parcels. This decision applies to the statutes creating, implementing and financing the *system* and to all regulations, etc., pertaining thereto. . . .

Since we have, by this decision, declared the system of common schools in Kentucky to be unconstitutional, Section 183 places an absolute duty on the General Assembly to recreate, re-establish a new system of common schools in the Commonwealth. As we have said, the premise of this opinion is that education is a basic, fundamental constitutional right that is available to all children within this Commonwealth. The General Assembly should begin with the same premise as it goes about its duty. The system, as we have said, must be efficient, and the criteria we have set out are binding on the General Assembly as it develops Kentucky's new system of common schools. . . . .

JUDICIAL APPROVAL OF COMMON SCHOOLS

The egalitarian motivation for the common school necessitated the enrollment of all children of all social and economic backgrounds. To enlarge public schools from a system of limited free education for poor children—pauper schools—to common schools at the elementary and high school levels required an ever-increasing commitment of public funds.[34]

The transformation to truly *common* schools required that the public schools be of such quality that they could attract the children of the more affluent in addition to the children of the poor. Ravitch points out that this movement toward common schools was a logical extension of the Jacksonian philosophy of 1828 that heralded the frontier philosophy of equality and the decline of social class based on wealth and position. "Political equality forced the emergence of new political patterns, and the schools, like other social institutions, began to adjust to the demands of the rising middle class."[35]

Opposition to this movement was expressed both politically and in the courts. An early example of such litigation is found in the *Hartman*[36] case in Pennsylvania (decided in 1851), wherein school directors refused to comply with a statute requiring them to create a system of common schools for all children, not just the poor. The school directors defended their position by maintaining that the Pennsylvania Constitution did not permit the legislature to expand the public schools from pauper schools to common schools. The court disagreed.

Legislature Is Not Prohibited from Creating a System of Common Schools by Expanding on the Pauper School Provision in State Constitution

–·–·–·–·–·–

Commonwealth v. Hartman

–·–·–·–·–·–

Supreme Court of Pennsylvania, 1851. 17 Pa. 118.

The appellants, Hartman and five others, had been elected school directors of Lowhill township, Lehigh county. They organized by electing the officers required by the common school law, and made provision for the education of the poor children in that township, but refused to comply with the provisions of the Acts of Assembly of 1848 and 1849, requiring them to provide for the establishment of common schools in that township: and they refused to resign. A petition was presented to the Court of Quarter Sessions, on April 30, 1849, praying the court to declare their offices vacant, and to appoint substitutes. The court granted a rule upon them to appear and answer; and on May 5, 1849, JONES, J., vacated their office and appointed others in their stead to act until the next annual election for directors. The objection made on the part of Hartman and others was that the school

laws of 1848 and 1849 *were unconstitutional,* as being at variance with the provision in the first section of the 7th article of the Constitution of Pennsylvania, which is as follows: Sect. 1. "The legislature shall, as soon as conveniently may be, provide by law for the establishment of schools throughout the state, in such manner that the poor may be taught *gratis.*" It was provided in the Act of Assembly of 11th April, 1848, "That the common school system, from and after the passage of this Act, shall be deemed, held, and taken to be adopted by the several school districts in this Commonwealth," . . . .

In the Act of 7th April 1849, it is provided, "That a system of common school education be and the same is hereby deemed, held, and taken to be adopted, according to the provisions of this Act, in all the counties in this Commonwealth," . . . .

The Act points out the mode of electing directors, and defines their "general powers and duties." It provided that "They shall establish a sufficient number of *common schools* for the education of every individual between the ages of five and twenty-one years, in the districts, who may apply for admission and instruction, either in person, or by parent, guardian, or next friend (italics added)."

The opinion of the court was delivered Dec. 29, 1851, by BLACK, C.J. The only ground on which this court has been urged to reverse the order of the Quarter Sessions, is, that the school law is unconstitutional. We are of opinion that there is nothing in that law, certainly nothing in that part of it to which our attention has been particularly called, which, in the slightest degree, contravenes the constitution. It is to be remembered, that the rule of interpretation for the state constitution differs totally from that which is applicable to the constitution of the United States. The latter instrument must have a strict construction; the former a liberal one. Congress can pass no laws but those which the constitution authorizes either expressly or by clear implication; while the Assembly has jurisdiction of all subjects on which its legislation is not prohibited. The powers, not granted to the government of the Union, are withheld; but the state retains every attribute of sovereignty which is not taken away. In applying this principle to the present case, it is enough to say, that there is no syllable in the constitution which forbids the legislature to provide for a system of general education in any way which they, in their own wisdom, may think best. But it is argued, that for the purpose of promoting education, and carrying out the system of common schools, laws may be passed which will work intolerable wrong, and produce grievous hardship. The answer to this is, that a decent respect for a coordinate branch of the government, compels us to deny that any such danger can ever exist. But if a law, unjust in its operation, and nevertheless not forbidden by the constitution, should be enacted, the remedy lies, not in an appeal to the judiciary, but to the people, who must apply the corrective themselves, since they have not intrusted the power to us.

The constitution, in sect. 1 of article VII, provides that "the legislature shall, as soon as conveniently may be, provide by law for the establishment of schools throughout the state *in such manner that the poor may be taught gratis.*" It seems to be believed that the last clause of this section is a limitation to the power of the legislature, and that no law can be constitutional which looks to any other object than that of teaching the poor gratis. The error consists in supposing this to define the *maximum* of the legislative power, while in truth it only fixes the minimum. It enjoins them to do thus much, but does not forbid them to do more. If they stop short of that point, they fail in their duty; but it does not result from this that they have no authority to go beyond it.

Order affirmed.

EXPANSION OF FREE PUBLIC SCHOOLS

Earlier, education above the elementary school level had to be acquired at private academies for which a tuition fee was charged and few, if any, poor children attended. Common schools were generally looked upon as being for the elementary grades only. Yet, free public high schools soon became a democratic necessity. Cubberley observed that "the rising democracy of the second quarter of the nineteenth century now demanded and obtained the democratic high school."[37] Gradually the high school became an integral part of the free public school system.

The academy had succeeded the old Latin schools with a more practical curriculum designed to more adequately meet the needs of the older youths beyond preparation for college. These academies spread rapidly and were variously known as institutes, seminaries, collegiate institutes, and sometimes colleges. By the early 1800s, Massachusetts had thirty-six academies, New York nineteen, Georgia ten, and some states, including Kentucky and Indiana, by the early 1800s had systems of county academies.[38] The greatest growth of the academies was during the period from 1820 to 1840. Most of these academies were residential schools that charged fees for room and board as well as for tuition. Some were financed by local taxation and a few even had state assistance. The academies, however, were inadequate to meet the burgeoning need for extended educational opportunity. The tuition and fees made accessibility difficult for the poor and, even though their numbers were substantial, they were not numerous enough to be within reasonable walking, wagon, or horseback distance from rural homes to be nonresidential.

The solution was the genesis of the American high school. The American high school had no forerunners and was distinguished from previous European models by its close relationship to the common schools. The high school was an extension of the common elementary school, making it, from the beginning, a higher common school.

The first American high school was established in Boston in 1821, and the increase in the number of high schools was slow, but methodical, for the next thirty years. Skepticism as to the viability of the high school was expressed by many who were imbued with the tradition of the academy. As late as 1874, President Porter of Yale University observed that "the expenditure of money for high schools to prepare boys and girls for college was a doubtful experiment." By 1872, 70 percent of the students entering colleges in the east were graduates of academies, but by 1920, 90 percent of the entering freshmen were graduates of high schools.

Opposition to the high school as an extension of the common school generally came from taxpayers who did not want to bear the increased financial burden, as well as from those advocates of the academies and private sectarian schools who thought that creation of high schools would further diminish the public's reliance on their respective schools.

The court decision generally credited with opening the doors to the public high school as we know it today was the famous *Kalamazoo* case in 1872.[39] No constitutional or legislative provisions in Michigan had previously explicitly established a system of high schools. The legal basis for education was found in legislation in 1817, which contained a provision for public academies, and in the constitution of 1835, which provided for free primary schooling, but neither established a pathway between the primary schooling and the university. Local students aspiring to a university education had entered the preparatory department of the private Kalamazoo College (chartered in 1855). No public accommodation had been made for students' preparation for college until 1858, when the local school superintendent created the union high school at a time when several of these union high schools had been created elsewhere in Michigan. This particular school thrived amid local controversy created by both taxpayers, who objected to paying for the school, and the proprietors of Kalamazoo College, who had lost students to the union high school. Finally, in 1873 a group of prominent citizens filed suit to restrain the school board from expending public funds to support the high school. Ultimately, the case was appealed to the Supreme Court of Michigan, where Judge Thomas M. Cooley rendered a landmark decision.

Even though there was other litigation of this nature during this period, this case was particularly important because of the stature of the court and the judicial rationale by which the high school was justified. Courts are generally reticent, in the absence of express statutory language, to imply authority to perform some public function if the expenditure of funds is involved, but here the court did not hesitate to do so.

This judicial recognition of the importance of public schools provided a philosophical basis for both legislatures and courts to broaden educational opportunity by extending the school system not only upward, but also downward to kindergartens, as well as to expand the scope of education to areas such as vocational education, special education for the handicapped, and compensatory education.

TUITION AND FEES IN PUBLIC SCHOOLS

Courts have generally held that tuition fees, "matriculation" or "registration" fees, and fees for materials, activities, or privileges cannot be levied in public schools.[40] In most cases invalidating fees, the courts have reasoned that the fee was charged as a condition of attendance, which violated the state's constitutional or statutory provisions establishing "free" public schools.

In deciding whether a fee could be charged for school bus transportation, a court in California held that such fees were unconstitutional because transportation is a "fundamental educational activity, which is an integral part of California's system of free public education."[41] In so holding, the court noted that the precedents governing its decision turned on two key points, whether (1) the fee is charged for a necessary school activity, or (2) the fee is charged for an activity that is an essential part of the jurisdiction's system of *free* schools. Underlying the court's rationale was its premise that the "right to a public education must be made available to all equally."[42] Therefore, fees charged for necessary educational activities are unconstitutional because the system is supposed to be free, and second, because an essential service must be provided to all children free and on an equal basis.

Another reason often given by the courts for invalidating fees is the lack of statutory authority to exact the fee. Courts have usually held fees invalid when the fees have been charged for an essential element of a school's activity. When fees have been upheld, the courts have found that there was statutory authorization for the fee, that the purpose for the fee was a reasonable one, or that the term "free schools" did not include the item, such as textbooks, for which the school was charging.[43]

Courts have, on occasion, distinguished tuition fees from incidental fees, and, in at least one jurisdiction, a court has upheld an incidental fee of twenty-five cents per pupil per month to be used for raising funds to pay for fuel to heat the schoolroom, for brooms to sweep the schoolroom, and for water buckets to contain water.[44] In the same jurisdiction, an incidental fee for improvement of grounds, insurance, and other incidental expenses did not violate the state constitution.[45]

However, in other jurisdictions incidental fees have been held invalid. In Georgia,[46] a very early decision held that a state statute requiring each child upon entering municipal public schools to pay the board of education an "incidental fee" was "clearly unconstitutional." However, a court in Illinois ruled that the state constitutional provision requiring the establishment of a thorough and efficient system of free schools did not prevent the state legislature from authorizing school boards to purchase textbooks and rent them to pupils.[47]

In most cases, fees for activities, materials, or privileges have been held invalid.[48] A $25 annual fee required by one school district as a condition to furnishing each high school student a transcript of courses studied and grades achieved was held to be unconstitutional in Idaho.[49] The fee consisted of $12.50 for school activity fees and $12.50 for textbook fees, and had to be paid before a student could receive a transcript. Responding to each of these separately, the court reasoned that the student activity fee was imposed on all students whether they participated in extracurricular activities or not. Therefore the fee was on attendance, not on activity, and as such

contravened the state constitutional mandate that public schools be free. The court did note that since social and extracurricular activities were not necessarily principal elements of a high school career, the state constitution did not prohibit the school district from setting activity fees for students who voluntarily participated. With regard to the textbook fee, the court observed that since textbooks were necessary to the school, they were indistinguishable from other fixed educational expense items such as building maintenance and teachers' salaries, for all of which fees could not be charged.[50]

The requirement that pupils purchase textbooks and school supplies has been held invalid in Michigan.[51] In this case, the school district maintained that the word "free" in the state constitution did not include textbooks and supplies. The Supreme Court of Michigan held that books and supplies were necessary elements of any school's activity and an integral and fundamental part of elementary and secondary education.

---

*Textbook Fee in Elementary Grades
Violates State Constitution*

———·———·———·———

Cardiff v. Bismarck Public School District

———·———·———·———

Supreme Court of North Dakota,
1978. 263 N.W.2d 105.

SAND, Justice. . . . Gary Cardiff and other parents of school children attending elementary schools in the Bismarck Public School District brought an action in Burleigh County district court challenging the authority of the school district to charge rental fees for the use of necessary school textbooks. . . .

The basic issue for our resolution is whether or not § 148 of the North Dakota Constitution provides for free textbooks and prohibits the Legislature from authorizing school districts to charge for textbooks. The parents contend the constitutional provision prohibits charging for textbooks, and the school district contends it merely prohibits charging tuition. . . .

To resolve the first issue we must examine and construe the provisions of § 148 of the North Dakota Constitution, which provides as follows:

> The legislative assembly shall provide at their first session after the adoption of this constitution, for a uniform system of free public schools throughout the state, beginning with the primary and extending through all grades up to and including the normal and collegiate course.

In 1968 this section was amended, as follows:

> The legislative assembly shall provide for a uniform system of free public schools throughout the state, beginning with the primary and extending through all grades up to and including schools of higher education, except that the legislative assembly may authorize tuition, fees and service charges to assist in the financing of public schools of higher education.

In construing a written constitution we must make every effort to determine the intent of the people adopting it. . . .

We must examine the whole instrument in order to determine the true intention of every part so as to give effect to each section and clause. If different portions seem to be in conflict, we must make a true effort to harmonize them if practicable.

In interpreting clauses in a constitution we must presume that words have been employed in their natural and ordinary meaning.

Both parties contended that contemporaneous construction, as an aid in construction and interpretation of the constitution, . . . favored its point of view on the construction of § 148 of the North Dakota Constitution. . . .

From this examination we are left with a firm conviction that the legislative acts referred to do not lend any significant comfort

or aid to the resolution of the basic question under consideration, namely, what does the term "uniform system of free public schools" mean? Contemporaneous construction in this instance is not helpful to either party. The Journal entries of the constitutional convention are not very helpful in determining the meaning of the language, "free public schools."

The first item relating to public schools introduced at the North Dakota Constitutional Convention, as found in the Journal, was File No. 47, § 2, which provided, in part:

> It shall be the duty of the Legislature to establish and maintain a system of free public schools, adequate for education of all children in the state, between the ages of six and eighteen years, inclusive, in the common branches of knowledge, and in virtue and christian morality. . . .

From this brief review it is clear that the framers consistently had in mind a free public school.

A short survey of the constitutional provisions of other states and their case law will shed some light on our question.

ARIZONA:
> The Legislature shall provide for a system of common schools by which a free school shall be established . . . Constitution, Article XI, § 6.

In *Carpio v. Tucson High School District No. 1 of Pima County,* 111 Ariz. 127, 524 P.2d 948 (1974), cert. denied 420 U.S. 982, 95 S.Ct. 1412, 43 L.Ed.2d 664, the court had under consideration Article XI, § 6, of the Arizona Constitution. The court held that textbooks were not required to be furnished to high school students. However, the court referred to an earlier decision, *Shoftstall v. Hollins,* 110 Ariz. 88, 515 P.2d 590 (1973), where the court held that these constitutional provisions had been satisfied when the legislature provided for the means of establishing required courses, qualifications of teachers, textbooks to be used in common schools, etc. Considering this statement and the statement in *Carpio* that "text-

TWO: HISTORICAL PERSPECTIVE   **39**

books have not been provided free in high schools as they have been in the common schools" leaves the impression that under the constitutional provisions of Arizona textbooks in common schools were provided free of charge.

COLORADO:
> The general assembly shall . . . provide for the establishment and maintenance of a thorough and uniform system of free public schools . . . Constitution, Art. IX, § 2.

In *Marshall v. School District RE #3 Morgan County*, 553 P.2d 784 (Colo.1976), the court held that the school district was not required to furnish books free of charge to all students.

INDIANA:
> [I]t shall be the duty of the General Assembly . . . to provide, by law, for a general and uniform system of Common Schools, wherein tuition shall be without charge, and equally open to all. Constitution, Article 8, Section 1.

In *Chandler v. South Bend Community School Corporation*, 160 Ind.App. 592, 312 N.E.2d 915 (1974), the court held that this constitutional provision did not require textbooks to be provided free, but merely to provide a system of common schools where tuition would be without charge.

ILLINOIS:
> Education in public schools through the secondary level shall be free. Constitution, Article X, section 1.

In *Beck v. Board of Education of Harlem Consolidated School District No. 122*, 63 Ill.2d 10, 344 N.E.2d 440 (1976), the court held that workbooks, and other educational material, were not textbooks so as to come within the statutory provision of free textbooks, and as such it did not preclude the school board from charging the parents a fee for supplying the students with such material.

Earlier, in *Hamer v. Board of Education of School District No. 109*, 47 Ill. 2d 480, 265 N.E.2d 616 (1970), the court was specifically concerned with the constitutional provision and

held that under its provisions the school board was not prohibited from purchasing textbooks and renting them to pupils. It further held that the legislature had the power to direct the district school boards to issue textbooks to students free of charge but the constitution did not require it. In a related case entitled *Hamer v. Board of Education of School District No. 109*, County of Lake, 9 Ill.App.3d 663, 292 N.E.2d 569 (1973), the court in effect reaffirmed its earlier decision in the *Hamer* case.

WISCONSIN:
> The legislature shall provide . . . for . . . district schools . . . and such schools shall be free and without charge for tuition . . . Constitution, Article X, section 3.

The court, in *Board of Education v. Sinclair*, 65 Wis.2d 179, 222 N.W.2d 143 (1974), held that the schools may charge a fee for the use of textbooks and items of similar nature authorized by statute and that such did not violate the constitutional provision commanding that schools shall be free without charge for tuition for all children. It basically held that the term "free" referred to school buildings and equipment and what is normally understood by the term "tuition."

IDAHO:
> [I]t shall be the duty of the legislature of Idaho, to establish and maintain a general, uniform and thorough system of public, free common schools. Constitution, Art. 9, sec. 1.

In *Paulson v. Minidoka County School District No. 331*, 93 Idaho 469, 463 P.2d 935 (1970), the court held that school districts could not charge students for textbooks under the state constitutional provision. It also held that public high schools in Idaho are "common schools."

MICHIGAN:
> The legislature shall maintain and support a system of free public elementary and secondary schools . . . Constitution, Article 8, § 2.

In 1908 the Michigan Constitution, Article 11, § 9, in part provided:

The legislature shall continue a system of primary schools, whereby every school district in the state shall provide for the education of its pupils without charge for tuition.

The Michigan court, in *Bond v. Public Schools of Ann Arbor School District,* 383 Mich. 693, 178 N.W.2d 484 (1970), held that the 1963 constitutional provision meant that books and school supplies were an essential part of the system of free public elementary and secondary schools and that the schools should not charge for such items. We note that the 1908 Constitution provided "without charge for tuition," whereas the 1963 Constitution provides for a system of "free public elementary and secondary schools."

MONTANA:
It shall be the duty of the legislative assembly of Montana to establish and maintain a general, uniform and thorough system of public, free, common schools. Constitution, Article XI, Section 1.

In *Granger v. Cascade County School District No. 1,* 159 Mont. 516, 499 P.2d 780 (1972), the school district, as the school district here, contended that the pertinent language simply meant "tuition-free" as far as required courses were concerned and did not prohibit fees and charges for optional extracurricular or elective courses and activities. The Montana parents, however, contended that the schools could not impose fees or charges for anything, whether elective or required, that is encompassed in the constitutional requirement of a "thorough system of public, free, common schools." The fees involved more than just charges for workbooks and textbooks, as in this case. The Montana Supreme Court answered the question in the following manner:

We believe that the controlling principle or test should be stated in this manner: Is a given course or activity reasonably related to a recognized academic and educational goal of a particular school system? If it is, it constitutes part of the free, public school system commanded by Art. XI, Sec. 1 of the Montana Constitution and additional fees or charges cannot be levied, directly or indirectly, against

the student or his parents. If it is not, reasonable fees or charges may be imposed.

The court, however, pointed out that its decision does not apply to supplementary instruction offered by the school district on a private basis during the summer recess or at special times. It should be observed that the school district in the *Granger* case, as well as in the instant case, argued that they had a system of waivers and charges for welfare recipients and other cases of economic hardship. The court rejected this argument.

NEW MEXICO:
A uniform system of free public schools sufficient for the education of, and open to, all children of school age in the state shall be established and maintained. Constitution, Article XII, § 1.

The court, in *Norton v. Board of Education of School District No. 16,* 89 N.M. 470, 553 P.2d 1277 (1976), held that under this constitutional provision courses required of every student shall be without charge to the student. However, reasonable fees may be charged for elective courses. The court also recognized that the board of education shall define what are required or elective courses in the educational system of New Mexico.

SOUTH DAKOTA:
[I]t shall be the duty of the legislature to establish and maintain a general and uniform system of public schools wherein tuition shall be without charge. Constitution adopted 1889, Article VIII, § 1.

We have found no South Dakota case law on the question of tuition or textbooks.

WEST VIRGINIA:
The legislature shall provide by general law, for a thorough and efficient system of free schools. Constitution, Article XII, Section 1.

The court, in *Vandevender v. Cassell,* 208 S.E.2d 436 (W.Va.1974), held that furnishing textbooks free to needy students satisfied the constitutional requirement. But two of the five judges, in a concurring opinion, stated that they did not interpret "free" as pertaining only to indigent pupils. They further stated:

> It is clear to me [us], however, that where state constitutions contain language providing for free schools, such as Article XII, Section 1 of the West Virginia Constitution, that this means free schools for students of all economic classes.

MISSOURI:

> [S]chools and the means of education shall forever be encouraged in this state. [The legislature was required to establish schools] as soon as practicable and necessary, where the poor shall be taught gratis. Constitution of 1820, art. VI, § 1.

> A general diffusion of knowledge and intelligence being essential to the preservation of the rights and liberties of the people, the general assembly shall establish and maintain free public schools for the gratuitous instruction of all persons in this state within ages not in excess of twenty-one years as prescribed by law . . . Constitution, Art. IX, § 1(a), source Constitution of 1875, Art. XI, §§ 1 and 3.

The court held, in *Concerned Parents v. Caruthersville School District No. 18*, 548 S.W.2d 554 (Mo. 1977), that under this constitutional provision school districts were prohibited from charging registration fees or course fees in connection with courses for which academic credit was given.

WASHINGTON:

> The Legislature shall provide for a general and uniform system of public schools. The public school system shall include common schools, and such high schools, normal schools, and technical schools as may hereafter be established. Constitution, art. 9, sec. 2.

The Supreme Court of the State of Washington, in *Litchman v. Shannon*, 90 Wash. 186, 155 P. 783 (1916), said:

> Public schools are usually defined as schools established under the laws of the state, usually regulated in matters of detail by local authorities in the various districts, towns, or counties, and maintained at the public expense by taxation, and open without charge to the children of all the residents of the town or other district.

Earlier, the Supreme Court of Washington, in *School District No. 20, Spokane County v. Bryan*, 51 Wash. 498, 99 P. 28 (1909), defined "common school" as found in its constitution as "one that is common to all children of proper age and capacity, free and subject to, and under the control of, the qualified voters of the school district."

From this study we have concluded that the courts have consistently construed the language "without payment of tuition" or "wherein tuition shall be without charge" or such similar language to mean that a school is prohibited from charging a fee for a pupil attending school. This language has also been construed as not prohibiting the charging of fees for textbooks.

However, as to constitutions containing language such as "free public schools" or "free common schools" or similar language, the courts have generally held, with a few exceptions, that this language contemplates furnishing textbooks free of charge, at least to the elementary schools. The exceptions have generally relied upon extrinsic material such as contemporary construction, history, or practices, as well as the language itself. Although the cases involving language similar to that contained in the North Dakota Constitution are not in themselves conclusive, they nevertheless are helpful, if not persuasive.

A comparison of the key constitutional provisions and existing case law of states which entered the Union at the same time and under similar conditions as North Dakota will be very helpful and valuable in determining the intent of the people of North Dakota in adopting § 148 of the North Dakota Constitution.

At the time North Dakota formulated and adopted its Constitution, three other States — Montana, South Dakota, and Washington — were going through a similar process. All four States were included in the same Enabling Act, Chapter 180, 25 Statutes at Large, 676, and were required to meet the conditions in § 4, which provided

[t]hat provision shall be made for the establishment and maintenance of systems of public schools, which shall be open to all the children of said states, and free from sectarian control.

The key language in the constitutional provisions of the four States is as follows:

Montana: . . . thorough system of public, free common schools.

South Dakota: . . . uniform system of public schools wherein tuition shall be without charge.

North Dakota: . . . uniform system of free public schools throughout the state. . . .

Washington: . . . uniform system of public schools. . . .

We are impressed with the different language employed in the constitutions of the four states, Montana, South Dakota, North Dakota, and Washington, which came into the Union at the same time and under the same Enabling Act. We must assume that each state had available the same information as the other states and was free to choose its constitutional provisions, provided they met the requirements of the Enabling Act. It is significant to note that Montana and North Dakota adopted the "free common schools" and the "free public schools" concept, whereas South Dakota adopted the "public schools wherein tuition shall be without charge" concept, and Washi,gton merely provided for a "uniform system of public schools."

We also note that the Washington Supreme Court, in the *Bryan* case, supra, under the Washington Constitution held that a common school district is free for all children of proper age even though its Constitution merely required a uniform system of public schools. Therefore, if the term "common schools" implies a school for which no tuition may be charged, then the expression "free public schools" should mean something more than merely not permitting the charging of tuition. This position becomes persuasive when we recognize that other states specifically provided that no charge for "tuition" would be allowed.

If the framers of the North Dakota Constitution and the people of North Dakota had in mind only to provide public schools without charging tuition they could have, and probably would have, used the language "without payment of tuition" or "wherein tuition shall be without charge," rather than the language "free public schools." We must assume that the framers of the constitution made a deliberate choice of words which reflected or expressed their thoughts. The term "free public schools" without any other modification must necessarily mean and include those items which are essential to education.

It is difficult to envision a meaningful educational system without textbooks. No education of any value is possible without school books. . . .

We cannot overlook the fact that attendance at school between certain ages was compulsory from the very beginning under penalty of law. This lends support to the contention that textbooks were to be included in the phrase "free public schools." . . .

The word "free" takes on its true and full meaning from the context in which it is used. There can be no doubt that the term means "without charge or cost." In the absence of any other showing we must conclude that the term was commonly understood by the people to mean "without charge or cost." Books and school supplies are a part of the education system. This is true whether we apply the necessary elements of the school's activities test or the integral part of the educational system test.

After a review of the case law and constitutional provisions of other states, and after a careful analysis of the key language of the four states which were admitted under the same Enabling Act, we have come to the conclusion that the term "free public schools" means and includes textbooks, and not merely "free from tuition."

However, our conclusion must necessarily apply only to the elementary schools, as they are the only ones covered in this action. The action in district court was not a class action and factually involved only students enrolled in the elementary schools . . . This opinion therefore is limited to textbooks used in elementary schools in the required subjects, as set out in [statute].   . . .

[T]o the extent that they apply to elementary textbooks [they] are in conflict with § 148 of the North Dakota Constitution and are therefore invalid and unconstitutional as to elementary school textbooks.   . . .

The judgment and order of the district court are both affirmed.

State Constitutional Provision for Free Public Schooling Prohibits Fees for Either Regular or Extracurricular Programs

— · — · — · — · — · —

Hartzell v. Connell

— · — · — · — · — · —

Supreme Court of California, In Bank, 1984. 35 Cal.3d 899, 201 Cal.Rptr. 601, 679 P.2d 35.

BIRD, Chief Justice. May a public high school district charge fees for educational programs simply because they have been denominated "extracurricular"?

The Santa Barbara High School District (District) offers a wide variety of extracurricular activities, ranging from cheerleading to madrigal singing, and from archery to football. Many of these activities are of relatively recent origin. For example, in 1956, Santa Barbara High School fielded six athletic teams while today there are thirty-eight.

Prior to the 1980–1981 school year, any student could participate in these activities free of charge. The programs were financed by a combination of District contributions (mostly state aid and local tax revenues), ticket sales, and fundraising activities conducted by the constituent high schools.

In the spring of 1980, the District school board (Board) decided to cut its budget by $1.1 million. This decision reflected a drop in revenues due to the combined effects of inflation, declining enrollment, and the adoption of Proposition 13. Among the items to be reduced was the District's contribution to the high school extracurricular programs.

The Board considered two plans for adapting the programs to fit its reduced budget. The first plan called for a major cut in interscholastic athletic competition, including the reduction of the high school program from over thirty teams to only eight and the elimination of interscholastic competition at the ninth-grade level. Under this plan, the surviving programs were to remain open to all students free of charge.

The second plan provided for a less extensive cut in athletic competition — elimination of the ninth-grade program only. To make up the difference, it proposed to raise money by charging students fees for participation in dramatic productions, musical performances, and athletic competition.

The Board chose the second option. Under the plan finally adopted, students are required to pay $25 for *each* athletic team in which they wish to participate, and $25 per category for any or all activities in *each* of the following four categories: (1) dramatic productions (e.g., plays, dance performances, and musicals); (2) vocal music groups (e.g., choir and madrigal groups); (3) instrumental groups (e.g., orchestra, marching band, and related groups such as the drill team and flag twirlers); and (4) cheerleading groups.

Thus, a student who desires to play football in the fall and tennis in the spring, in addition to participating in a dramatic production, must pay $75. A more musically inclined student, who plays an instrument, sings in a group, and performs in a musical, also pays $75.

None of the affected activities yield any credit toward graduation.   . . .

The teachers of the credit courses also supervise the noncredit performances.   . . .

In an attempt to ensure that the fees would not prevent any students from participating, the District has implemented a fee-waiver program. Upon a showing of financial need, a student may obtain a "scholarship" to participate without paying the fee. The standard of need is similar to that of the free lunch program. . . .

The District's three high schools granted a total of seventy-seven waivers. . . .

Shortly before the start of the 1980–1981 school year, Barbara Hartzell, a taxpayer with two children in the public schools, and the Coalition Opposing Student Fees, a grouping of community organizations, filed this taxpayers' action against the District, various school officials, and the members of the Board. . . .

The California Constitution requires the Legislature to "provide for a system of common schools by which a *free school* shall be kept up and supported in each district. . . ." (Cal. Const., art. IX, § 5, emphasis added.) This provision entitled "the youth of the State . . . to be educated at the public expense." (*Ward v. Flood* (1874) 48 Cal. 36, 51).

Plaintiffs assert that the imposition of fees for educational extracurricular activities violates the free school guarantee. They are correct.

The first question raised by plaintiffs' challenge is whether extracurricular activities fall within the free education guaranteed by section 5. California courts have not yet addressed this issue. The reported decisions from other jurisdictions reveal two distinct approaches.

One approach restricts the free school guarantee to programs that are "essential to the prescribed curriculum." . . . Under this view, the right to an education does not extend to activities that are "outside of or in addition to the regular academic courses or curriculum of a school." . . . Accordingly, it has been held that students have no right to participate in extracurricular activities. . . .

The second approach holds that the free school guarantee extends to all activities which constitute an "integral fundamental part of the elementary and secondary education" or which amount to "necessary elements of any school's activity." . . . Courts applying this approach have held that "the right to attend school includes the right to participate in extracurricular activities." In particu-

lar, courts have struck down extracurricular activities fees as unconstitutional. . . .

To determine which, if either, of these approaches is consistent with California's free school guarantee, this court must examine the role played by education in the overall constitutional scheme. Because the nature of the free school concept has rarely been addressed by the courts, it will be necessary to explore its underpinnings in some depth.

The free school guarantee was enacted at the Constitutional Convention of 1878–1879. Also adopted was article IX, § 1, which proclaims that "[a] general diffusion of knowledge and intelligence [is] essential *to the preservation of the rights and liberties of the people* . . . ." [Emphasis added.] Joseph W. Winans, chairperson for the convention's Committee on Education, elaborated: "Public education forms the basis of self-government and constitutes the very corner stone of republican institutions." (Debates and Proceedings, Cal. Const. Convention 1878–1879, p. 1087 [hereafter Proceedings].) In support of section 1, delegate John T. Wickes argued that "a liberal education . . . breaks down aristocratic caste; for the man who has a liberal education, if he has no money, if he has no wealth, he can stand in the presence of his fellow-men with the stamp of divinity upon his brow, and shape the laws of the people . . . ." (Proceedings, at p. 1088.)

This theme runs like a unifying thread through the writings of our forefathers. In 1786, Thomas Jefferson wrote from France, then a monarchy: "I think by far the most important bill in our whole code is that for the diffusion of knowledge among the people. No other sure foundation can be devised for the preservation of freedom, and happiness . . . ." (Jefferson, *Letter to George Wythe,* in The Portable Thomas Jefferson (Peterson edit. 1979) pp. 399–400.

John Swett, California's most prominent free school advocate at the time section 5 was adopted, warned: "Our destruction, should it come at all, will be . . . [f]rom the inattention of the people to the concerns of their government. . . . I fear that they may place too implicit confidence in their public servants and fail properly to scrutinize their conduct. . . . Make them intelligent, and they will be vigilant; give them the means of detecting the wrong, and they will apply the remedy." (Quoted in Cloud, The Story of California's Schools (194–), p. 20.) Without education for all, a majority of the people would be—in the words of Horace Mann— "the vassals of as severe a tyranny, in the form of capital, as the lower classes of Europe are bound to in the form of brute force." (Mann, *Twelfth Annual Report,* in Educational Ideas in America: A Documentary History (Rippa edit.1969) p. 199.)

Perhaps the most eloquent expression of the free school idea came not from a political leader or educator, but from the poet, Ralph Waldo Emerson: "We have already taken, at the planting of the Colonies, . . . the initial step, which for its importance, might have been resisted as the most radical of revolutions, thus deciding at the start of the destiny of this country,—this, namely, that the poor man, whom the law does not allow to take an ear of corn when starving, nor a pair of shoes for his freezing feet, is allowed to put his hand into the pocket of the rich, and say, You shall educate me, not as you will, but as I will: not alone in the elements, but, by further provision, in the languages, in sciences, in the useful and in elegant arts." (Emerson, *Education,* in Educational Ideas in America: A Documentary History, supra, at p. 176.)

The contribution of education to democracy has a political, an economic, and a social dimension.

As this court has previously noted, education prepares students for active involvement in political affairs . . . . Education stimulates an interest in the political process and provides the intellectual and practical tools necessary for political action. Indeed, education may well be "the dominant factor in influencing political participation and awareness." . . . . Without high quality education, the populace will lack the knowledge, self-confidence, and critical skills to evaluate independently the pronouncements of pundits and political leaders. . . .

Not only does education provide skills useful in political activity, it also prepares individuals to participate in the institutional structures—such as labor unions and business enterprises—that distribute economic opportunities and exercise economic power. Education holds out a "bright hope" for the "poor and oppressed" to participate fully in the economic life of American society. . . .

Finally, education serves as a "unifying social force" among our varied population, promoting cohesion based upon democratic values. . . . The public schools bring together members of different racial and cultural groups and, hopefully, help them to live together "in harmony and mutual respect." . . .

Viewed in light of these constitutionally recognized purposes, the first of the two tests described above is insufficient to ensure compliance with California's free school guarantee. That approach determines whether a given program falls within the guarantee not by assessing its actual educational value, but by deferring to a school board's decision on whether or not to offer it for formal, academic credit. Under this test, a for-credit program would fall within the guarantee, while a noncredit program with identical content— and equal value in fulfilling the constitutionally recognized purposes of education—could be offered for a fee.

The second approach, on the other hand, does not sever the concept of education from its purposes. It focuses not upon the formalities of credit, but upon the educational character of the activities in question.

It can no longer be denied that extracurricular activities constitute an integral component of public education. Such activities are "generally recognized as a fundamental ingredient of the educational process." . . . They are "[no] less fitted for the ultimate purpose of our public schools, to wit, the making of good citizens physically, mentally, and morally, than the study of algebra and Latin . . . ."

In a variety of legal contexts, courts have emphasized the vital importance of student participation in educational extracurricular programs. . . .

In addition to the particular skills taught, group activities encourage active participation in community affairs, promote the development of leadership qualities, and instill a spirit of collective endeavor. These results are directly linked to the constitutional role of education in preserving democracy, as set forth in article IX, section 1, and elaborated in *Serrano I*, 96 Cal. Rptr. 601, 487 P.2d 1241.

Accordingly, this court holds that all educational activities—curricular or "extracurricular"—offered to students by school districts fall within the free school guarantee of article IX, section 5. Since it is not disputed that the programs involved in this case are "educational" in character, they fall within that guarantee.

Defendants argue, however, that the fee-waiver policy for needy students satisfies the requirements of the free school guarantee. They suggest that the right "to be educated at the public expense" . . . amounts merely to a right *not to be financially prevented* from enjoying educational opportunities. This argument contradicts the plain language of the Constitution.

In guaranteeing "free" public schools, article IX, section 5 fixes the precise extent of the financial burden which may be imposed on the right to an education—none. . . . A school which conditions a student's participation in educational activities upon the payment of a fee clearly is *not* a "free school."

The free school guarantee reflects the people's judgment that a child's public education is too important to be left to the budgetary circumstances and decisions of individual families. It makes no distinction between needy and nonneedy families. Individual families, needy or not, may value education more or less depending upon conflicting budget priorities. As John Swett, the "father of the California public school system," recognized in 1863, "[i]f left to their own unaided efforts, a great majority of the people will fail through want of means to properly educate their children; *another class, with means at command, will fail through want of interest*. The people then, can be educated

only by a system of Free Schools, supported by taxation, and controlled directly by the people." (Swett, *Duties of the State to Public Schools*, reprinted in Swett, History of the Public School System of California (1876) p. 110, emphasis added.)

The free school guarantee lifts budgetary decisions concerning public education out of the individual family setting and requires that such decisions be made by the community as a whole. Once the community has decided that a particular educational program is important enough to be offered by its public schools, a student's participation in that program cannot be made to depend upon his or her family's decision whether to pay a fee or buy a toaster.

Nor may a student's participation be conditioned upon application for a special waiver. The stigma that results from recording some students as needy was recognized early in the struggle for free schools. Thaddeus Stevens once declared, in response to an 1835 proposal that teachers keep a list of "poor scholars": "Sir, hereditary distinctions of rank are sufficiently odious; but that which is founded on poverty is infinitely more so. Such a law should be entitled 'an act for branding and marking the poor, so that they may be known from the rich and proud.'" (Stevens, *A Plea for Free Schools*, in Educational Ideas in America: A Documentary History, supra, at p. 188.) Defendants' extracurricular programs are not truly "free" even to those students who are eligible for waivers. "[T]o a child or his parents financially unable to pay the additional fees and charges imposed by a *free, public school system* any waiver procedure is a degrading experience." . . .

Finally, defendants warn that, if the fees are invalidated, many school districts may be forced to drop some extracurricular activities. They argue that invalidation would—in the name of the free school guarantee—produce the anomalous result of reducing the number of educational opportunities available to students.

This court recognizes that, due to legal limitations on taxation and spending, school districts do indeed operate under difficult financial constraints. However, financial hardship is no defense to a violation of the free school guarantee. . . .

Perhaps, in view of some, public education could be more efficiently financed by peddling it on the open market. Under the California Constitution, however, access to public education is a right enjoyed by all—not a commodity for sale. Educational opportunities must be provided to all students without regard to their families' ability or willingness to pay fees or request special waivers. This fundamental feature of public education is not contingent upon the inevitably fluctuating financial health of local school districts. A solution to those financial difficulties must be found elsewhere—for example, through the political process.

In conclusion, this court holds that the imposition of fees for educational activities offered by public high school districts violates the free school guarantee. The constitutional defect in such fees can neither be corrected by providing waivers to indigent students, nor justified by pleading financial hardship. . . .

In conclusion, the imposition of fees as a precondition for participation in educational-

programs offered by public high schools on a noncredit basis violates the free school guarantee of the California Constitution and the prohibition against school fees contained in title 5, section 350 of the California Administrative Code.

The judgment is reversed.

NOTE

1. Whether a user fee for school bus transportation is constitutionally invalid must rest with state courts in interpreting state constitutional intent. Such fees do not violate the Equal Protection Clause of the Fourteenth Amendment of the U.S. Constitution. In *Kadrmas,* in 1988, the U.S. Supreme Court emphasized that education is not a fundamental right under the Equal Protection Clause, thus, a state's enactment of a law allowing for permissible local user fees for school transportation was not prohibited by the U.S. Constitution. *Kadrmas v. Dickinson Public Schools,* 487 U.S. 450, 108 S.Ct. 2481 (1988).

■■■ ENDNOTES

1. See John Lawson and Harold Silver, *A Social History of Education in England* (London: Methicen & Co., Ltd., 1973), p. 154.

2. Ibid., p. 155.

3. Ellwood P. Cubberley, *A Brief History of Education* (Boston: Houghton Mifflin Company, 1922), p. 374.

4. Ibid., p. 376.

5. Lawrence A. Cremin, *American Education: The National Experience 1783–1876* (New York: Harper & Row Publishers, 1980), p. 125.

6. Benjamin Rush, *Essays, Moral and Philosophical* (2nd ed., Thomas and William Bradford, 1806), pp. 4, 6–7.

7. Ibid., p. 7–8.

8. R. Freeman Butts, "Search for Freedom: The Story of American Education." *NEA Journal* (March 1960): 33–48.

9. Letter from Thomas Jefferson to George Wythe, Paris, August 14, 1786; Bernard Mayo, *Jefferson Himself* (Charlottesville: University Press of Virginia, 1942), p. 89.

10. Cubberley, *A Brief History of Education,* p. 286.

11. Ibid. General school laws were enacted in Connecticut in 1700, 1712, and 1714; Vermont in 1782, in addition to

earlier statutes in Massachusetts (1647); and New Hampshire (1680). Georgia created a state system of academies in 1783. In 1795, New York provided for a state system of elementary education. Delaware established a state school fund in 1796 and Virginia enacted an optional school law in 1796.

12. Ibid., p. 288.

13. Ibid., p. 371.

14. Cremin, *American Education: The National Experience, 1783-1876,* pp. 133-142.

15. Butts, "Search for Freedom: The Story of American Education."

16. *House Journal* 1822, Commonwealth of Kentucky, p. 236.

17. *House Journal* 1818–1819, Commonwealth of Kentucky, p. 13.

18. Ellwood P. Cubberley, *Public Education in the United States,* pp. 164–66. Copyright 1934, renewed 1962 by Ira S. Lillick, adapted by permission of Houghton Mifflin Company.

19. Butts, "Search for Freedom."

20. Newton Edwards, *The Courts and The Public Schools* (The University of Chicago Press, 1955), p. 23.

21. Ibid., p. 24.

22. Meyer v. State of Nebraska, 262 U.S. 390, 43 S.Ct. 625 (1923).

23. Fogg v. Board of Education, 76 N.H. 296, 82 A. 173 (1912).

24. Scown v. Czarnecki, 264 Ill. 305, 106 N.E. 276 (1914).

25. Fogg v. Board of Education, 76 N.H. 296, 82 A. 173, 174–75 (1912).

26. Leeper v. State, 103 Tenn. 500, 53 S.W. 962 (1899).

27. Robinson v. Cahill, 62 N.J. 473, 303 A.2d 273 (1973).

28. This classification is a slight modification of that suggested by James M. Mize, in his article entitled "San Antonio Independent School District v. Rodriguez: A Study of Alternatives Open to State Courts," *University of San Francisco Law Review,* vol. VIII, 1973–74, pp. 105–11.

29. The Constitution of Virginia, 1971, Art. I, § 15.

30. The Constitution of Virginia, 1971, Art. VIII, §§ 1 and 2.

31. Ibid., Art. I, § 15.

32. McLain v. Phelps, 409 Ill. 393, 100 N.E.2d 753 (1951).

33. Flory v. Smith, 145 Va. 164, 134 S.E. 360 (1926).

34. Cubberley, *Public Education in the United States,* p. 260.

35. Diane Ravitch, *The Great School Wars, New York City, 1805–1973* (New York: Basic Books, Inc. Harper, 1974), p. 23.

36. Commonwealth v. Hartman, 17 Pa. 118 (1851).

37. Cubberley, *Public Education,* p. 386.

38. Ibid., p. 247.

39. Stuart v. School District No. 1 of Village of Kalamazoo, 30 Mich. 69 (1874).

40. 41 A.L.R.3rd 755.

41. Salazar v. Honig, 200 Cal.App.3d 1576, 246 Cal. Rptr. 837 (2d Dist. 1988).

42. Ibid.

43. 41 A.L.R. 3rd 755.

44. Kennedy v. County Board of Education, 214 Ala. 349, 107 So. 907 (1926).

45. Vincent v. County Board of Education, 222 Ala. 216, 131 So. 898 (1931).

46. Irvin v. Gregory, 86 Ga. 605, 13 S.E. 120 (1891).

47. Hamer v. Board of Education, 47 Ill. 2d 480, 265 N.E.2d 616 (1970).

48. Mathis v. Gordy, 119 Ga. 817, 47 S.E. 171 (1904).

49. Paulson v. Minidoka County School District, 93 Idaho 469, 463 P.2d 935 (1970).

50. Ibid.

51. Bond v. Public Schools of Ann Arbor School District, 383 Mich. 693, 178 N.W.2d 484 (1970).

CHAPTER 3

Role of the Federal Government

Historically, the federal government has exhibited an active interest in education. Education was much on the minds of the founding fathers, who believed that public virtue and the welfare of the state were dependent on the ability of the people to properly exercise their democratic prerogatives. The founders of the American republic, influenced by John Locke, believed that the citizens were neither innately wise nor foolish, good nor bad, but were products of their learning and exhibited civic responsibilities accordingly. From this assumption it was imminently reasonable to conclude that "mankind could be greatly improved by education."[1] There existed an implicit desire to guarantee the perpetuation of the democratic form of government by educating and "remaking the whole people . . . to conform the principles, morals and manners of our citizens to our republican forms of government."[2] In this light, many statesmen of the new nation believed that education was the best preservative of freedom, and most republicans tied general education and dissemination of knowledge to the success of the new republic.[3]

In the Constitutional Convention of 1787, the matter of education and a national university was advanced by several delegates, including Madison, but to no avail. The problem lay not in the delegates' general belief in the importance of education, but in the pressing concern that the sovereign states and not the federal government should be the proper repository of such power. The hesitancy to vest the power over education in the central government prevailed, and the state orientation of education became the pattern in the United States. Nevertheless, the interest in education at the federal level continued and stimulated educational progress throughout the states.

■ THE LAND ORDINANCES

Even before the adoption of the Constitution, the Continental Congress enacted the Land Ordinances of 1785 and 1787, which provided impetus for creation of educational systems in all the states joining the Union. Initially, the original colonies had claimed almost unlimited territory extending west beyond the Alleghenies. For purposes of mutual accord, the matter was settled in the Continental Congress in 1780 when the existing states ceded their claims to the federal government, creating a national domain. This "common estate" created a common interest and bond among the first states of the new nation, and it was from this National Domain that new states were to be carved for westward expansion.

Although the primary motivation of Congress was to raise revenues for the debt-ridden nation that had just emerged from the War of Independence with England, the provision for education in the ordinances caused the new states to address the issue of education at the very beginning of their statehood. The Land Ordinance of 1785 included a provision reserving the sixteenth section of every township "for the maintenance of public schools within the said township." The purpose of this provision was to make the purchase of land more attractive to men with families who might venture west. Regardless of the profit motive, however, the effect was a very positive force in the expansion of education. The survey plan of 1785 laid out square townships, six miles by six miles, containing a total of thirty-six sections. The sixteenth section, one mile by one mile (640 acres) was dedicated for schools.

Within two years after the enactment of the Ordinance Survey of 1785 in mid-July of 1787, the Continental Congress met and enacted the Ordinance of 1787, known as the Northwest Ordinance. This ordinance is included in Article III, the now-famous provision, which stated that

> [r]eligion, morality, and knowledge being necessary to good government and the happiness of mankind, schools and the means of education shall be forever encouraged.

The Northwest Ordinance set out the requirements necessary for territorial areas to become states. Provisions for education, *habeas corpus,* due process, and religious freedom were all to be provided for in the compact, which was required by the central government as a condition for a territory to become a state.

The legislatures of the new states were thus required, in accordance with the Ordinance of 1785, to oversee the sixteenth-section lands, or to account for the funds if sold; and the Northwest Ordinance of 1787 required that each state have an education provision in its basic law.

Later, when Ohio became a state in 1802, the problem arose as to whether states could tax federal property within their boundaries. A compromise was reached that provided that states would receive "5-percent" of the sale of public lands, if in turn federal property would be exempt from state taxation. These "5-percent" funds, along with income from salt lands and swamp lands, added to the revenues available for the public schools. Later, as a result of Jackson's decentralization efforts, the Surplus Revenue Deposit Act of 1836 distributed $28 million in federal funds back to

state governments, much of which was devoted to school purposes.

These federal initiatives, in combination, provided an important stimulus for the states to assume responsibility for education. When the use and the sale of the land grant and the surplus revenues became inadequate to support state funding of education, the state legislatures began to move slowly toward appropriation of supplemental funds. One can only speculate as to what might have happened had not the federal government given this inertia to the creation of public schools. Perhaps, some states would not have assumed the responsibility at all and would have allowed education to languish as an entirely local function or even, possibly, have allowed education to remain almost entirely in the hands of individuals or charitable and religious groups.

■ INDIRECT FEDERAL ROLE

The early method of federal land grants for education was most notable for two particular aspects. First, the grants were made for the purpose of creating and aiding public schools directly, thus espousing a federal interest in mass general common school education for everyone; and, second, the federal government exercised no control over education as a condition for receiving the grants.[4] From these beginnings, it was established that the federal government was to play an indirect role in the development of public education, to serve a stimulus function without direct control of educational policy and operation.

Over the years, the federal government's role has remained one of indirect support of education; never directly controlling education, but generally in a positive and affirmative manner, the Congress has, from time to time, fashioned educational policy to address certain perceived national interests. The first Morrill Act passed by Congress in 1862, like the early land grants, shaped American education policy by providing a grant of land to each state to be sold with the proceeds to be used for the "endowment, maintenance and support of at least one college where the leading object shall be, without excluding other scientific and classical studies and including military tactics, to teach such branches of learning as are related to agriculture and mechanic arts in such manner as the legislatures of the states may respectively prescribe."[5] In relying on this act, the great land-grant colleges were established and supported. Herein, Congress advanced a role of higher education that transcended the traditional, narrow, European model by expanding and giving credibility to the study of agriculture and engineering, disciplines that a new and developing nation so badly needed. Subsequent legislation, the second Morrill Act of 1890 and the Hatch Act of 1887, the Adams Act of 1906, and other provisions, expanded the activities of the land-grant colleges and introduced grants-in-aid as another type of federal support.

Following these initial steps, the federal government has continued to provide assistance to various phases of education. Categorical grants that were geared toward bringing about a particular educational emphasis became the method of allocation most relied upon. Federal grants of particular importance have been the Smith-Lever Act of 1914, which was quite specific in purpose, prescribing the expenditure of grant funds for, among other things, extension services by county agents for agriculture and homemaking and for training of teachers in these areas; the Smith-Hughes Act of 1917, which provided for funds for vocational education below college level; the National Defense Education Act of 1958, the response to Sputnik I, which instituted several types of programs at the elementary, secondary, and higher education levels to give impetus to scientific training and research; the Higher Education Facilities Act of 1963, creating financial assistance for construction at all levels of higher education; the Vocational Education Act of 1963, substantially increasing federal appropriations for vocational education; and the Elementary and Secondary Education Act of 1965, the most important elementary and secondary program ever enacted by Congress, which provided funding primarily for the education of culturally disadvantaged children.[6]

In each of these acts, the role of the federal government is conveyed by Congress to be one of supplementary assistance to the state systems of education. The Congress has sought to shape educational policy through the indirect means of categorical grants giving direction to certain educational programs once states accept the funds. In each instance, the states have the option of accepting or rejecting the funds, but once they are accepted, the states must abide by the federal guidelines for use of the resources. As states have accepted the conditions of these categorical grants over the years, the role of the federal government in guiding educational choices has become more predominant, and some commentators have maintained that too much control is today vested in the federal government. As a result, even though the federal government's role in education is said to be indirect and secondary, myriad regulations and conditions bear down quite heavily on the public schools and have led some to question the legal scope of federal powers. Unfortunately, legal definition of the role of the federal government in education is as hazy and uncertain as the legal parameters of our federal system of government itself. Courts continue today to ponder the nature of the states' relationship to the central government not only in education, but in all areas of domestic activity.

■ RESERVED STATE POWERS

The powers of the federal government are circumscribed by delegation within the Constitution and are specifically limited by the Tenth Amendment, which provides that "The powers not delegated to the United States by the Constitution, nor prohibited by it to the States, are reserved to the States respectively or to the people." Education is not mentioned in the Constitution and is, therefore, presumably reserved "to the states or to the people." The Tenth Amendment was intended to reconfirm the implicit understanding at the time of the Constitution's adoption that powers not granted to the central government were reserved.[7] James Madison, at the urging of Jefferson, sponsored the Tenth Amendment. In the course of debate that took place while the amendment was still pending, Madison declared: "Interference with the power of the States was no constitutional criterion of the power of Congress. If the power was not given, Congress could not exercise it; if given, they might exercise it, although it should interfere with the laws, or even the Constitutions of the States."[8]

A discrete boundary line between federal and state power was not to evolve, however, in spite of Madison's apparently clear conception of the doctrine. Chief Justice Marshall, in the famous case of *McCulloch v. Maryland*,[9] added ambiguity by noting that the word "expressly" was not included in the Tenth Amendment as it had been in the Articles of Confederation, effectively leaving the issue "whether the particular power which may become the subject of contest has been delegated to the one government, or prohibited to the other" to depend upon a fair construction of the whole instrument.[10] Justice Marshall's view of the Tenth Amendment was merely a restatement of the already presumed and established relationship that is delineated in other parts of the Constitution. In *United States v. Darby*, the Court said:

> The Amendment states but a truism that all is retained which has not been surrendered. There is nothing in the history of its adoption to suggest that it was more than declaratory of the relationship between the national and state governments as it had been established by the Constitution before the amendment or that its purpose was other than to allay fears that the new national government might seek to exercise powers not granted, and that the states might not be able to exercise fully their reserved powers.[11]

Standing alone, the Tenth Amendment does little more than bear witness that our system of government assumes some separation of powers and prevents federal activity without express or implied constitutional authority. As such, there is a presumption of state power, which effectively places the burden on the federal government to justify in court its involvement in affairs that may have been presumed to be left to the states. As Justice Cardoza declared, the Tenth Amendment voices an assumption of "quasi-sovereignty . . . which the state is privileged to redress as a suitor in the courts."[12] This presumption, on behalf of the states, provides a constitutional basis through which a state can seek legal redress in challenging a federal statute. Without the Tenth Amendment, no such action would be possible. In the face of such challenges, the federal government has been forced, on many occasions, to identify other constitutional provisions that justify its activity in regulation of functions that states have assumed to be within their prerogative. In this light, the federal government does not possess general police powers, as such, and in justifying its many activities has invoked implied powers of the general welfare and commerce clauses of the Constitution.

■ FEDERAL CONTROL OF EDUCATION

By virtue of the Tenth Amendment, federal control over education is secondary to the power exercised by the states. While a state can create, organize, and reorganize school districts; employ and dismiss personnel; prescribe curriculum; establish and enforce accreditation standards; and govern all management and operation functions of the public schools directly, the federal government can intervene only in a peripheral and oblique way. Federal controls emanate from three sources: (1) acquiescence by states in accepting federal grants that are provided under the authority given the Congress by the General Welfare Clause; (2) standards or regulations that the Congress has authorized within the Commerce Clause; and (3) constrain actions by courts enforcing federal constitutional provisions protecting individual rights and freedoms.

Education and General Welfare

Two major questions concern education and general welfare: first, does education come under the definition of general welfare; and second, how can Congress provide for education if it does come within the definition? Section 8 of Article I gives Congress the power to tax and spend: "The Congress shall have Power to lay and collect Taxes, Duties, Imports and Excises, to pay the Debts and provide for the common Defense and General Welfare of the United States . . . ."[13]

The interpretation of the general welfare clause has been the subject of much debate and controversy. James Madison contended that the clause "amounted to no more than a reference to other powers enumerated in subsequent clauses of the same section; that, as the United States is a government of limited and enumerated powers, the grant of power to tax and spend for the general welfare must be confined to the enumerated legislative fields committed to the Congress."[14] Madison pointed out that the framers of the Constitution borrowed the phrase from the Articles of Confederation, and it was not looked upon as a phrase to extend the parameters of federal authority. In taking an opposing point of view, Hamilton maintained that this Article conferred upon the Congress a substantive power to tax and spend for purposes that would provide for the general welfare of the United States.

The Supreme Court adopted the Hamiltonian philosophy in a 1936 case that tested the constitutionality of the Agriculture Adjustment Act.[15] The Court stated that Congress was not limited in the expenditure of public monies to the direct or express grants of legislative power found in the Constitution.

In a later case, *Helvering v. Davis*,[16] the Supreme Court upheld the Social Security Act and in so doing ruled conclusively that Congress can tax and spend under the general welfare clause. In this case, the Court said that the general welfare concept is not static but flexible, and Congress may tax and expend public money for general welfare purposes so long as it does not demonstrate a display of arbitrary power. With this elastic definition of general welfare, the Congress is free to define education as general welfare and to tax and appropriate funds for educational purposes.

With the prerogative to broadly define general welfare as inclusive of education, Congress then looks to the taxing power of the clause for the instrumentality to "provide" for education. Jefferson explained the power and purpose of the clause in this manner: "[T]he laying of taxes is the *power* and the general welfare the *purpose* for which the power is to be exercised. They [Congress] are not to lay taxes *ad libitum for any purpose they please,* but only *to pay the debts or provide for the welfare of the Union.* In like manner, they are not *to do anything they please* to provide for the general welfare, but only to *lay taxes* for that purpose (italics added)."[17] This clause therefore expresses not an unlimited power but only a qualified one. Congress has never acted to assert an unlimited power to tax, and the Court has therefore never been compelled to decide the point.[18]

The last sentence in Jefferson's statement raises the point quite clearly that Congress cannot provide for the general welfare in any manner other than through its taxing and appropriation power. With regard to education, this means that Congress can only involve itself in educational matters through the indirect means of appropriation of funds and does not have the power to directly legislate changes in education. It is for this reason that Congress has so consistently used the categorical aid approach to bring about change in education. Constitutionally, regulation of educational functions can be acquired only through conditional grants.

The federal government cannot, therefore, affirmatively and directly require that states alter educational policy; this would be an affront to state autonomy. Constitutionally, the issue is really one of inducement versus compulsion, as one commentator has observed:

> The Constitution counts upon the necessary participation of the states . . . not by direct command but by incentive of not losing the opportunity of participation.[19]

In matters of education, then, the Congress can only effect change through persuasion or by giving the states an option that allows a state to act of its own volition. Welch says:

> The volitional nature of the state's acquiescence to conditional spending programs touches the very core of political autonomy. . . . Undoubtedly, economic necessity often forces states to alter governmental operations to qualify for federal funds; yet, the conditioning of needed funds does not preempt the state's decision-making process. Although the distinction may often be one of form rather than substance, the Court treats it as a critically important question of form. Such observance of form is more than a ritualistic bow to the founders' respect for the states. Apparently, the Court considers the sanctity of a state's decision-making process a necessary component of the Constitution's structure which endows the states with at least a degree of autonomous, volitional control.[20]

A choice of accepting the grant and the conditions attached thereto must be provided the state. Under the General Welfare Clause, then, a state may elect not to participate in a federal program if the conditions are educationally, financially, or legally offensive.[21]

Education and Commerce

Increasingly, Congress has relied on the Commerce Clause to require affirmative action by states. Quite beyond the limitations governing general welfare, the Congress has power under this clause to "regulate Commerce with foreign Nations, and among the several States, and with the Indian Tribes."[22] Education can be affected by congressional action pursuant to this clause in many different ways, but most notably safety, transportation, and labor regulations have touched education. While one would naturally assume that the term "commerce" included commercial activity, to buy, sell, and trade goods to and fro among states, the definition, as applied by the Supreme Court, has been given broader meaning. In *Gibbons* v. *Ogden*,[23] Chief Justice Marshall rejected the narrow "trading" definition and maintained that it was "something more —

intercourse." Commerce, as intercourse, was defined in *Gibbons* as not merely an exchange of goods but as a means for "advancement of society, labor, transportation, *intelligence,* care, and various mediums of exchange [italics added] . . . ."

As a mere limitation on states to prevent interference with interstate commerce, such a definition has little practical effect on education, but when read in its larger context in relation to the "necessary and proper clause,"[24] then Congress may act to improve commerce in an affirmative way rather than merely act to prevent state impediments. This, coupled with the fact that commerce regulation is not limited to interstate but may also, under certain conditions, include intrastate activities, brings public education within the purview of the clause.[25] In this broad context, education could conceivably be brought within the scope of commerce in that the movement of an intelligent citizenry among the states is vital to the growth and prosperity of the nation.

With this definition the courts are presented with a difficult dilemma of weighing the state powers under the Tenth Amendment against the apparent boundless scope of "commerce." Few decisions have been rendered in favor of state prerogative. In expounding the philosophy that the "political process," in which each state has representation in the Congress and this representation will protect state interests, the Supreme Court largely exhibited a hands-off attitude toward the expansion of the federal role through the Commerce Clause.[26]

The expansive view of the Commerce Clause was expounded by the Supreme Court in 1941 in upholding Congress' Fair Labor Standards Act of 1938, which established a national minimum wage and prohibited the shipment in interstate commerce of goods produced by child labor. The Court said:

> The power of Congress over interstate commerce is not confined to the regulation of commerce among the states. It extends to those activities intrastate which so affect interstate commerce or the exercise of the power of Congress as to make regulation of them appropriate

means to the attainment of a legitimate end, the exercise of the granted power of Congress to regulate interstate commerce . . . .[27]

By 1942, Congress' economic regulatory power was viewed by the Supreme Court as being virtually unlimited. In that year, Justice Jackson, Roosevelt's latest appointee, delivered the opinion of the Court:

> Whether the subject of the regulation in question was "production," "consumption," or "marketing" is . . . not material for purposes of deciding the question of federal power before us. That an activity is of a local character may help in a doubtful case to determine whether Congress intended to reach it. The same consideration might help in determining whether in the absence of Congressional action it would be permissible for the state to exert its power on the subject matter, even though in so doing it to some degree affected interstate commerce. But even if appellee's activity be local and though it may not be regarded as commerce, it may still, whatever its nature, be reached by Congress if it exerts a substantial economic effect on interstate commerce, and this irrespective of whether such effect is what might at some earlier time have been defined as "direct" or "indirect."[28]

Later, in 1946, the Court said that the commerce power is "as broad as the economic needs of the nation."[29] At that time the national prerogative, through the Commerce Clause, attained its broadest scope.

This expansive view, though, was apparently changed, if not reversed, in *National League of Cities v. Usery*,[30] handed down by the Supreme Court in 1976. Under litigation was the 1974 Amendments to the Fair Labor Standards Act, which extended wage and hour standards to almost all public employment, including local school districts. In this case, the Court, while admitting that the amendments were within the scope of the Commerce Clause, nevertheless held that the Tenth Amendment was violated. The decision enunciated a more restricted view of the Commerce Clause and interpreted the Tenth Amendment as an affirmative limitation upon the power of Congress to regulate activities of state and local governments.[31] Justice Rehnquist, writing for the majority , maintained that the state's power to determine wages of its own employees is an "undoubted attribute of state sovereignty" and that the functions performed by the affected state employees were "essential to the separate and independent existence" of the state.[32]

Usery, however, was reversed by the Supreme Court on February 19, 1985 in *Garcia v. San Antonio Metropolitan Transit Authority*.[33] In this 5–4 decision, Justice Blackmun, writing for the majority, said that judicial restraint in assuring state sovereignty is unnecessary in our federal system. Blackmun said that the *Usery* test "inevitably invites an unelected federal judiciary to make decisions about state policies it favors and those it dislikes." Blackmun was of the opinion that the balance in the federal system is sufficiently insured by the political processes and constant intervention by the courts is unnecessary. He further stated, "state sovereign interests, then, are more properly protected by procedural safeguards inherent in the structure of the federal system than by judicially created limitations on federal power."

Constitutional Rights and Freedoms of Individuals

Under our system of government, state laws that violate or deny individual rights or freedoms may be invalidated by the courts through application of the United States Constitution. Many of the restraints that educators refer to as "federal control" emanate from the application of federal constitutional provisions to state statutes, regulations, or actions by agents of the public school system. Virtually all the cases that have held state actions unconstitutional have been based on either the First or the Fourteenth Amendments to the Constitution, with a scattering involving the Fourth, Fifth, Sixth, and even the Eighth Amendments. Outside the amendments proper, some early litigation was directed toward the impairment of contracts provision of the Constitution, Article I, Section 10, which prohibits unilateral abrogation of contracts by government. (These cases will be discussed in a later chapter of this text.)

Judicial action through injunctive relief on behalf of a student, teacher, or parent may well serve to limit state options in educational policy issues. Most notable among these has been the pervasive impact of the federal courts in shaping educational policy to effect racial integration in the public schools. Each of these actions is taken by the courts, though, on a case-by-case basis, and judicial control is imposed only where past state action has denied individual constitutional rights.

Suppression of individual freedoms that are given constitutional status in the First Amendment also serves as the basis for frequent litigation and, many times, subsequent judicial control of educational activity. Personal freedoms and civil rights found in the First Amendment pertain to religion, speech, association, press, and assembly. Each of these has been brought into play as a restraint on objectionable activities by state school systems.

Each of these constitutional issues is fully discussed in subsequent chapters of this book, but it is important to note here that it is these legitimate constitutional concerns involving personal freedoms and rights that are primarily responsible for the "federal involvement in education." Such activity by the federal courts in no way violates the sovereign power of the states to operate the public schools.

Beyond these direct judicial controls, whereby the court normally enjoins or mandates, the Congress has evolved certain power from the Fourteenth Amendment to bring about and enforce constitutional purposes. Federal regulation of state employment practices, as justified under the Fourteenth Amendment, has been upheld by the Supreme Court. In *Fitzpatrick v. Bitzer*,[34] Justice Rehnquist appeared to distinguish between Congress' Fourteenth Amendment and Commerce Clause powers by maintaining that the Fourteenth Amendment "clearly contemplates limitations on [the states'] authority." From such precedents, then, it appears that the federal role in education extends to both judicial action to prevent unconstitutional state action and to affirmative Congressional action to effectuate equality through the Fourteenth Amendment.

The Scope of the Commerce Clause Is Defined by Political Process

─ ─ ─ ─ ─ ─ ─ ─

Garcia v. San Antonio Metropolitan Transit Authority

─ ─ ─ ─ ─ ─ ─ ─

Supreme Court of the United States, 1985.
469 U.S. 528, 105 S.Ct. 1005.

Justice BLACKMUN delivered the opinion of the Court. We revisit in these cases an issue raised in the *National League of Cities v. Usery*, 426 U.S. 833 (1976). In that litigation, this Court, by a sharply divided vote, ruled that the Commerce Clause does not empower Congress to enforce the minimum-wage and overtime provisions of the Fair Labor Standards Act (FLSA) against the States "in areas of traditional governmental functions." . . .

The present controversy concerns the extent to which SAMTA (San Antonio Metropolitan Transit Authority) may be subjected to the minimum-wage and overtime requirements of the FLSA. . . .

. . . *National League of Cities, supra,* overruled *Maryland v. Wirtz,* and held that the FLSA could not be applied constitutionally to the "traditional governmental functions" of state and local governments. . . .

Appellees have not argued that SAMTA is immune from regulation under the FLSA on the ground that it is a local transit system engaged in intrastate commercial activity. In a practical sense, SAMTA's operations might well be characterized as "local." Nonetheless, it long has been settled that Congress' authority under the Commerce Clause extends to intrastate economic activities that affect in-terstate commerce. . . . Were

SAMTA a privately owned and operated enterprise, it could not credibly argue that Congress exceeded the bounds of its Commerce Clause powers in prescribing minimum wages and overtime rates for SAMTA's employees. . . .

[F]our conditions must be satisfied before a state activity may be deemed immune from a particular federal regulation under the Commerce Clause. First, it is said that the federal statute at issue must regulate "the 'States as States.'" Second, the statute must "address matters that are indisputably 'attribute[s] of state sovereignty.'" Third, state compliance with the federal obligation must "directly impair [the States'] ability 'to structure integral operations in areas of traditional governmental functions.'" Finally, the relation of state and federal interests must not be such that "the nature of the federal interest . . . justifies state submission." . . .

The controversy in the present cases has focused on the third . . . requirement—that the challenged federal statute trench on "traditional governmental functions." . . .

The central theme of *National League of Cities* was that the States occupy a special position in our constitutional system and that the scope of Congress' authority under the Commerce Clause must reflect that position. Of course, the Commerce Clause by its specific language does not provide any special limitation on Congress' actions with respect to the States. . . . It is equally true, however, that the text of the Constitution provides the beginning rather than the final answer to every inquiry into questions of federalism, for "[b]ehind the words of the constitutional provisions are postulates which limit and control." . . . In order to be faithful to the underlying federal premises of the Constitution, courts must look for the "postulates which limit and control."

What has proved problematic is not the perception that the Constitution's federal structure imposes limitations on the Commerce Clause, but rather the nature and content of those limitations. One approach to defining the limits on Congress' authority to regulate the States under the Commerce Clause is to identify certain underlying elements of political sovereignty that are deemed essential to the States' "separate and independent existence." . . . This approach obviously underlay the Court's use of the "traditional governmental function" concept in *National League of Cities.* It also has led to the separate requirement that the challenged federal statute "address matters that are indisputably 'attribute[s] of state sovereignty.'" . . . In *National League of Cities* itself, for example, the Court concluded that decisions by a State concerning the wages and hours of its employees are an "undoubted attribute of state sovereignty." . . . The opinion did not explain what aspects of such decisions made them such an "undoubted attribute," and the Court since then has remarked on the uncertain scope of the concept. . . . The point of the inquiry, however, has remained to single out particular features of a State's internal governance that are deemed to be intrinsic parts of state sovereignty.

We doubt that courts ultimately can identify principled constitutional limitations on the scope of Congress' Commerce Clause powers over the States merely by relying on *a priori* definitions of state sovereignty. In part, this is because of the elusiveness of objective criteria for "fundamental" elements of state sovereignty, a problem we have witnessed in the search for "traditional governmental functions." There is, however, a more fundamental reason: the sovereignty of the States is limited by the Constitution itself. A variety of sovereign powers, for example, are withdrawn from the States by Article I, § 10. Section 8 of the same Article works an equally sharp contraction of state sovereignty by authorizing Congress to exercise a wide range of legislative powers and (in conjunction with the Supremacy Clause of Article VI) to displace contrary state legislation. . . . By providing for final review of questions of federal law in this Court, Article III curtails the sovereign power of the States' judiciaries to make authoritative determinations of law. . . . Finally, the developed application, through the Fourteenth Amendment, of the greater part of the Bill of Rights to the States limits the sovereign authority that States otherwise would possess to legislate with respect to their citizens and to conduct their own affairs.

The States unquestionably do "retai[n] a significant measure of sovereign authority." . . . They do so, however, only to the extent that the Constitution has not divested them of their original powers and transferred those powers to the Federal Government. . . . If the power was not given, Congress could not exercise it; if given, they might exercise it, although it should interfere with the laws, or even the Constitution of the States. . . .

. . . The power of the Federal Government is a "power to be respected" as well, and the fact that the States remain sovereign as to all powers not vested in Congress or denied them by the Constitution offers no guidance about where the frontier between state and federal power lies. In short, we have no license to employ freestanding conceptions of state sovereignty when measuring congressional authority under the Commerce Clause.

When we look for the States' "residuary and inviolable sovereignty," The Federalist No. 39, p. 285 (B. Wright ed. 1961) (J. Madison), in the shape of the constitutional scheme rather than in predetermined notions of sovereign power, a different measure of state sovereignty emerges. Apart from the limitation on federal authority inherent in the delegated nature of Congress' Article I powers, the principal means chosen by the Framers to ensure the role of the States in the federal system lies in the structure of the Federal Government itself. It is no novelty to observe that the composition of the Federal Government was designed in large part to protect the States from overreaching by Congress. The Framers thus gave the States a role in the selection both of the Executive and the Legislative Branches of the Federal Government. The States were vested with indirect influence over the House of Representatives and the Presidency by their control of electoral qualifications and their role in presidential elections. U.S. Const., Art. I, § 2, and Art. II, § 1. . . .

. . . . In short, the Framers chose to rely on a federal system in which special restraints on federal power over the States inhered principally in the workings of the National Government itself, rather than in discrete limitations on the objects of federal authority. State sovereign interests, then, are more properly protected by procedural safeguards inherent in the structure of the federal system than by judicially created limitations on federal power.

. . . The fact that some federal statutes such as the FLSA extend general obligations to the States cannot obscure the extent to which the political position of the States in the federal system has served to minimize the burdens that the States bear under the Commerce Clause.

We realize that changes in the structure of the Federal Government have taken place since 1789, ... Nonetheless, against this background, we are convinced that the fundamental limitation that the constitutional scheme imposes on the Commerce Clause to protect the "States as States" is one of process rather than one of result. Any substantive restraint on the exercise of Commerce Clause powers must find its justification in the procedural nature of this basic limitation, and it must be tailored to compensate for possible failings in the national political process rather than to dictate a "sacred province of state autonomy." . . .

Insofar as the present cases are concerned, then, we need go no further than to state that we perceive nothing in the overtime and minimum-wage requirements of the FLSA, as applied to SAMTA, that is destructive of state sovereignty or violative of any constitutional provision. . . .

. . . Congress' treatment of public mass transit reinforces our conviction that the national political process systematically protects States from the risk of having their functions in that area handicapped by Commerce Clause regulation.

This analysis makes clear that Congress' action in affording SAMTA employees the protections of the wage and hour provisions of the FLSA contravened no affirmative limit on Congress' power under the Commerce Clause. . . .

Of course, we continue to recognize that the States occupy a special and specific position in our constitutional system and that the scope of Congress' authority under the Commerce Clause must reflect that position. But the principal and basic limit on the federal commerce power is that inherent in all congressional action—the built-in restraints that our system provides through state participation in federal governmental action. The political process ensures that laws that unduly burden the States will not be promulgated. In the factual setting of these cases the internal safeguards of the political process have performed as intended.

These cases do not require us to identify or define what affirmative limits the constitutional structure might impose on federal action affecting the States under the Commerce Clause. . . . We note and accept Justice Frankfurter's observation in *New York v. United States*, 326 U.S. 572, 583, 66 S. Ct. 310, 314, 90 L. Ed. 326 (1946):

> The process of Constitutional adjudication does not thrive on conjuring up horrible possibilities that never happen in the real world and devising doctrines sufficiently comprehensive in detail to cover the remotest contingency. Nor need we go beyond what is required for a reasoned disposition of the kind of controversy now before the Court.

. . . *National League of Cities v. Usery*, 426 U.S. 833, 96 S. Ct. 2465, 49 L. Ed. 2d 245 (1976), is overruled. . . .

NOTES

1. Even though the Supreme Court struck down the Agricultural Adjustment Act in 1936, in *United States v. Butler*, 297 U.S. 1, 56 S.Ct. 312 (1936), the Court interpreted the General Welfare Clause as giving Congress broad powers. In so doing, the Court adopted the Hamilton expansive viewpoint and rejected Madison's more restrictive view. The Court said "Congress is expressly empowered to lay taxes to provide for the general welfare. Funds in the Treasury, as a result of taxation, may be expended only through appropriation, Article 1, § 9, cl. 7. They can never accomplish the objects for which they were collected, unless the

power to appropriate is as broad as the power to tax. The necessary implication is that public funds may be appropriated 'to provide for the general welfare of the United States'."

2. In the case of *Helvering v. Davis*, 301 U.S. 619, 57 S.Ct. 904 (1937), the Supreme Court of the United States was called upon to determine the constitutionality of the Social Security Act of 1935. Although this case does not directly involve education, it provides precedent for interpreting the meaning of the "general welfare clause." In this case, the Court makes two especially important determinations: (a) In drawing the line between what is "general" welfare, and what is "particular," the determination of Congress must be respected by the courts, unless it be plainly arbitrary; (b) The concept of "general welfare" is not static but adapts itself to the crises and necessities of the times. The Court said:

> Congress may spend money in aid of the "general welfare" . . . .There have been great statesmen in our history who have stood for other views. We will not resurrect the contest. It is now settled by decision. . . . The conception of the spending power advocated by Hamilton and strongly reinforced by Story has prevailed over that of Madison, which has not been lacking in adherents. Yet difficulties are left when the power is conceded. The line must still be drawn between one welfare and another, between particular and general. Where this shall be placed cannot be shown through a formula in advance of the event. There is a middle ground or certainly a penumbra in which discretion is at large. The discretion, however, is not confined to the courts. The discretion belongs to Congress, unless the choice is clearly wrong, a display of arbitrary power, not an exercise of judgment. This is now familiar law.
>
> . . .
>
> When such a contention comes here we naturally require a showing that by no reasonable possibility can the challenged legislation fall within the wide range of discretion permitted to the Congress. . . . Nor is the concept of the general welfare static. Needs that were narrow or

parochial a century ago may be interwoven in our day with the well-being of the Nation. What is critical or urgent changes with the times.

3. Powers not expressly or impliedly conferred by the Constitution on the federal government are reserved to the "States respectively or to the people." (Amendment X, Constitution of the United States of America). James Madison, in debate concerning the pending Tenth Amendment, declared that: "Interference with the power of the States was no constitutional criterion of the power of Congress. If the power was not given, Congress could not exercise it; if given, they might exercise it, although it should interfere with the laws, or even the constitutions of the States." (Annals of Congress, 1897, 1791).

4. It is interesting to note that in 1788, before the Tenth Amendment was enacted, Madison described the federal government relationship to the states in the new Constitution thusly:

> The powers delegated by the proposed Constitution to the Federal Government, are few and defined. Those which are to remain in the State Governments are numerous and indefinite. The former will be exercised principally on external objects, as war, peace, negotiation, and foreign commerce; with which the power of taxation will for the most part be connected. The powers reserved to the several States will extend to all the objects, which, in the ordinary course of affairs, concern the lives, liberties and properties of the people; and the internal order, improvement, and prosperity of the State. (The Federalist, No. 45, January 26, 1788)

5. The United States Supreme Court has summarily rejected doctrines of nullification and interposition. The doctrine of interposition being a

> concept based on the proposition that the United States is a compact of States, any one of which may interpose its sovereignty against the enforcement within its borders of any decision of the Supreme Court or act of

Congress, irrespective of the fact that the constitutionality of the act has been established by decision of the Supreme Court . . . .interposition is not a constitutional doctrine . . . [and] if taken seriously, it is illegal defiance of constitutional authority. (*United States v. State of Louisiana*, 364 U.S. 500, 81 S.Ct. 260 (1960).)

The Supreme Court had this to say about interposition as it concerns education. Although "the responsibility of public education is primarily the concern of the States . . . such responsibilities . . . must be exercised consistently with federal constitutional requirements as they apply to state action." *Cooper v. Aaron*, 358 U.S. 1, 78 S.Ct. 1401 (1958).

6. In an early case, the Kentucky Court of Appeals described the relationship of the federal government to the states: "The power of the states to establish and maintain systems of common schools, to raise money for that purpose by taxation, and to govern, control, and regulate such schools when established, is one of 'the powers not delegated to the United States by the Constitution, nor prohibited by it to the states,' and consequently it is reserved to the states respectively or to their people." *Marshall v. Donovan*, 73 Ky. (10 Bush) 681 (1874).

State Statute Impeding Intent of Federal Statute Violates Supremacy Clause

Shepheard v. Godwin

United States District Court of Eastern Virginia, 1968. 280 F.Supp. 869.

ALBERT V. BRYAN, Circuit Judge. . . . "Impacted" school areas are those whose school populations have been substantially enlarged by the attendance of Federal employees' children, but at the same time are losing school tax revenues because of the United States government's immunity from land taxes, both factors arising from increased Federal activities in the area. These conditions prompted Congress to provide financial aid for operation of the local educational facilities, P.L. 874.

In applying a State formula for State assistance to local school districts, Virginia has deducted from the share otherwise allocable to the district a sum equal to a substantial percentage of any Federal "impact" funds receivable by the district.

Residents, real estate owners and taxpayers of the City of Norfolk, later joined by those of the County of Fairfax, Virginia, in behalf of themselves and others similarly situated, here attack this deduction . . . as violative of the purpose and intent of the act of Congress and as transgressing the Fourteenth Amendment. We uphold their contention. . . .

The theory of the deduction in toto was that the Federal moneys were substituting for the taxes lost to the district by reason of the immunity of the Government property, and hence should be charged to the locality, just as the taxes would have been, in fixing the State supplementary aid. . . .

The grievance of the plaintiffs is obvious: any deduction whatsoever of the Federal supplement in apportioning State aid, pro tanto burdens them as taxpayers, for they and the other property owners in Norfolk and Fairfax have to make up the unindemnified portion of the impact costs. They contend that any deduction is prohibited by the purpose and plan of the Federal act.

The rejoinder of the defendant officials is, first, that the impact pupils are counted by the State in computing the minimum program cost in the district, and in accounting with the district for the State's supplementary aid it is not inequitable to insist upon a deduction of a commensurate amount of the impact moneys. At first appealing, this argument ignores the fact that the Federal children are to a large extent paying their own way so far as the *State* is concerned. Quite soundly, the Congressional Committee on Education and Labor in recommending passage of P.L. 874, observed

that the influx of Federal employees, and the withdrawal of real estate from taxes, did not diminish the tax sources of the State or otherwise burden the State. . . .

Our conclusion is that the State formula wrenches from the impacted localities the very benefaction the act was intended to bestow. The State plan must fall as violative of the supremacy clause of the Constitution. Our decision rests entirely on the terms, pattern and policy of the act.

The act makes these propositions clear: (1) the Federal funds are exclusively for supplementation of the local sources of revenues for school purposes; and (2) the act was not intended to lessen the efforts of the State. Those postulates are manifested in the statute by these provisions, especially: that the Federal contribution be paid directly to the local school agency on reports of the local agency, and that the contribution be computed by reference to the expenditures "made from revenues derived from local sources" in comparable school districts.

But the State formula at once sets these precepts at naught. It uses the impact funds to account in part for fulfillment of the State's pledge of supplementary aid to the community; and the State moneys thus saved are available for State retention or such use as Virginia determines. Without the inclusion of the Federal sums the State's annual payments towards supplementary aid would be increased, it is estimated, by more than $10,000,000.

This commandeering of credit for the Federal moneys severely injures both the community and the pupil. First and foremost, it does not relieve the local taxpayers to the extent Congress contemplated. Next, without the exclusive application of the funds to the areas where the need arose and remains, the result may be to lower the standard of education provided in an impacted district. Instead of maintaining the previous standards for the additional pupils, the impact money when thinned by the State would obviously be inadequate to continue that level for the increased school attendance, a result certainly thwarting the aim of the Federal law.

The construction and the implications we put upon the act find confirmation in its legislative history. . . . The exposition underscores the Congressional mandate that the impact payments are for local use and are not to be applied to compensate the State in any respect. Thus, at p. 13, it is stated:

> The effect of the payments provided for in this section is to compensate the local educational agency for loss in its *local* revenues. *There is no compensation for any loss in States revenues* (italics added) . . . .

Since its explanation in 1950 when P.L. 874 was passed that no compensation was intended for the State, Congress has reiterated this intention. In this repetition it definitely disapproves the accounting use Virginia's formula makes of the impact moneys. The House of Representatives Committee Report No. 1814, dated August 5, 1966, in proposing an amendment to P.L. 874 stated:

> Fifteen States offset the amount of Public Law 874 funds received by their school districts by reducing part of their State aid to those districts. *This is in direct contravention to congressional intent.* Impact aid funds are intended to compensate districts for loss of tax revenues due to Federal connection, not to substitute for State funds the districts would otherwise receive.

The committee report and the amendment are cited merely as evidence of Congressional intendment. The amendment provides only an administrative remedy of the Government and does not deprive the plaintiffs of standing to prevent future State infringement of their Constitutional right to the benefits of the aid proposed by Congress. Necessarily, then, the upshot is that the defendants must be enjoined from hereafter in any way denying to the impacted area the exclusive use and enjoyment of the impact funds. . . .

An order implementing this opinion is filed herewith. . . .

State Is Not Obligated to Expend Federal Funds for Purposes That Violate the State Constitution

———————

Wheeler v. Barrera

———————

Supreme Court of the United States, 1974.
417 U.S. 402, 94 S.Ct. 2274, *modified and remanded,*
422 U.S. 1004, 95 S.Ct. 2625 (1975).

Mr. Justice BLACKMUN delivered the opinion of the Court. Title I of the Elementary and Secondary Education Act of 1965, as amended, 20 U.S.C.A. § 241a et seq., provides for federal funding of special programs for educationally deprived children in both public and private schools.

This suit was instituted on behalf of parochial school students who were eligible for Title I benefits and who claimed that the public school authorities in their area, in violation of the Act, failed to provide adequate Title I programs for private school children as compared with those programs provided for public school children. The defendants answered that the extensive aid sought by the plaintiffs exceeded the requirements of Title I and contravened the State's Constitution and state law and public policy. First Amendment rights were also raised by the parties. The District Court, concluding that the State had fulfilled its Title I obligations, denied relief. The United States Court of Appeals for the Eighth Circuit, by a divided vote, reversed. We granted certiorari to examine serious questions that appeared to be present as to the scope and constitutionality of Title I.   . . .

The questions that arise in this case concern the scope of the State's duty to insure that a program submitted by a local agency under Title I provides "comparable" services for eligible private school children.

Plaintiff-respondents are parents of minor children attending elementary and secondary nonpublic schools in the inner city area of Kansas City, Missouri. They instituted this class action in the United States District Court for the Western District of Missouri on behalf of themselves and their children, and others similarly situated, alleging that the defendant-petitioners, the then State Commissioner of Education and the members of the Missouri Board of Education, arbitrarily and illegally were approving Title I programs that deprived eligible nonpublic school children of services comparable to those offered eligible public school children. The complaint sought an injunction restraining continued violations of the Act and an accounting and restoration of some $13,000,000 in Title I funds allegedly misapplied from 1966 to 1969. . . .

In what perhaps may be described as something less than full cooperation by both sides, the possibility of providing "comparable" services was apparently frustrated by the fact that many parochial schools would accept only services in the form of assignment of federally funded Title I teachers to teach in those schools during regular school hours. At the same time, the petitioners refused to approve any program providing for on-the-premises instruction on the grounds that it was forbidden under both Missouri law and the First Amendment and, furthermore, that Title I did not require it. Since the larger portion (over 65%) of Title I funds allocated to Missouri has been used to provide personnel for remedial instruction, the effect of this stalemate is that substantially less money per pupil has been expended for eligible students in private schools, and that the services provided in those schools in no sense can be considered "comparable." . . .

In response to petitioners' argument that Missouri law forbids sending public school teachers into private schools, the court held that the state constitutional provision barring use of "public" school funds in private schools had no application to Title I funds. The court reasoned that although the Act was generally to be accommodated to state law, the question whether Title I funds were "public," within the meaning of the Missouri Constitution, must necessarily be decided by federal law. . . .

In this Court the parties are at odds over two issues: First, whether on this record Title I requires the assignment of publicly employed teachers to provide remedial instruction during regular school hours on the premises of private schools attended by Title I eligible students, and, second, whether that requirement, if it exists, contravenes the First Amendment. We conclude that we cannot reach and decide either issue at this stage of the proceedings.

As the case was presented to the District Court, petitioners clearly had failed to meet their statutory commitment to provide comparable services to children in nonpublic schools. The services provided to the class of children represented by respondents were plainly inferior, both qualitatively and quantitatively, and the Court of Appeals was correct in ruling that the District Court erred in refusing to order relief. But the opinion of the Court of Appeals is not to be read to the effect that petitioners *must* submit and approve plans that employ the use of Title I teachers on private school premises during regular school hours.

The legislative history, the language of the Act, and the regulations clearly reveal the intent of Congress to place plenary responsibility in local and state agencies for the formulation of suitable programs under the Act. There was a pronounced aversion in Congress to "federalization" of local educational decisions. . . . Although this concern was directed primarily at the possibility of HEW's assuming the role of a national school board, it has equal application to the possibility of a federal court's playing an overly active role in supervising the manner of Title I expenditures.

At the outset, we believe that the Court of Appeals erred in holding that federal law governed the question whether on-the-premises private school instruction is permissible under Missouri law. Whatever the case might be if there were no expression of specific congressional intent, Title I evinces a clear intention that state constitutional spending prescriptions not be preempted as a condition of accepting federal funds. The key issue, namely, whether federal aid is money "donated to any state fund for public school purposes," within the meaning of the Missouri Constitution, Art. 9, § 5, is purely a question of state and not federal law. By characterizing the problem as one involving "federal" and not "state" funds, and then concluding that federal law governs, the Court of Appeals, we feel, in effect nullified the Act's policy of accommodating state law. The correct rule is that the "federal law" under Title I is to the effect that state law should not be disturbed. If it is determined, ultimately, that the petitioners' position is a correct exposition of Missouri law, Title I requires, not that the law be preempted, but, rather, that it be accommodated by the use of services not proscribed under state law. The question whether Missouri law prohibits the use of Title I funds for on-the-premises private school instruction is still unresolved.

Furthermore, in the present posture of this case, it was unnecessary for the federal court even to reach the issue whether on-the-premises parochial school instruction is permissible under state law. The state-law question appeared in the case by way of petitioners' defense that it could not provide on-the-premises services because it was prohibited by the State's Constitution. But, as is discussed more fully below, the State is not obligated by Title I to provide on-the-premises instruction. The mandate is to provide "comparable" services. Assuming, *arguendo,* that state law does prohibit on-the-premises instruction, this would not provide a defense to respondents' complaint that comparable services are not being provided. The choice of programs is left to the State with the proviso that comparable (not identical) programs are also made available to eligible private school children. If one form of services to parochial school children is rendered unavailable because of state constitutional proscriptions, the solution is to employ an acceptable alternative form. In short, since the illegality under state law of on-the-premises instruction would not provide a defense to respondents' charge of noncompliance with Title I, there was no reason for the Court of Appeals to reach this issue. By deciding that on-the-premises instruction was not barred by state law, the court in effect issued an advisory opinion. Even

apart from traditional policies of abstention and comity, it was unnecessary to decide this question in the current posture of the case.

The Court of Appeals properly recognized, as we have noted, that petitioners failed to meet their broad obligation and commitment under the Act to provide comparable programs. "Comparable," however, does not mean "identical," and, contrary to the assertions of both sides, we do not read the Court of Appeals' opinion or, for that matter, the Act itself, as ever requiring that identical services be provided in nonpublic schools. Congress recognized that the needs of educationally deprived children attending nonpublic schools might be different from those of similar children in public schools; it was also recognized that in some States certain programs for private and parochial schools would be legally impossible because of state constitutional restrictions, most notably in the church-state area. Title I was not intended to override these individualized state restrictions. Rather, there was a clear intention that the assistance programs be designed on local levels so as to accommodate the restrictions.

Inasmuch as comparable, and not identical, services are required, the mere fact that public school children are provided on-the-premises Title I instruction does not necessarily create an obligation to make identical provision for private school children. Congress expressly recognized that different and unique problems and needs might make it appropriate to utilize different programs in the private schools. A requirement of identity would run directly counter to this recognition. It was anticipated, to be sure, that one of the options open to the local agency in designing a suitable program for private school children was the provision of on-the-premises instruction, and on remand this is an option open to these petitioners and the local agency. If, however, petitioners choose not to pursue this method, or if it turns out that state law prevents its use, three broad options still remain:

First, the State may approve plans that do not utilize on-the-premises private school Title I instruction but, nonetheless, still measure up to the requirement of comparability. . . . In essence, respondents are asking this Court to hold, as a matter of federal law, that one mode of delivering remedial Title I services is superior to others. To place on this Court, or on any federal court, the responsibility of ruling on the relative merits of various possible Title I programs seriously misreads the clear intent of Congress to leave decisions of that kind to the local and state agencies. It is unthinkable, both in terms of the legislative history and the basic structure of the federal judiciary, that the courts be given the function of measuring the comparative desirability of various pedagogical methods contemplated by the Act.

In light of the uncontested statutory proscription in Missouri against dual enrollment, it may well be a significant challenge to these petitioners and the local agencies in their State to devise plans that utilize on-the-premises public school instruction and, at the same time, forgo on-the-premises private school instruction. . . .

Of course, the cooperation and assistance of the officials of the private school are obviously expected and required in order to design a program that is suitable for the private school. It is clear, however, that the Act places ultimate responsibility and control with the public agency, and the overall program is not to be defeated simply because the private school refuses to participate unless the aid is offered in the particular form it requests. The private school may refuse to participate if the local program does not meet with its approval. But the result of this would then be that the private school's eligible children, the direct and intended beneficiaries of the Act, would lose. The Act, however, does not give the private school a veto power over the program selected by the local agency.

In sum, although it may be difficult, it is not impossible under the Act to devise and implement a legal local Title I program with comparable services despite the use of on-the-premises instruction in the public schools but not in the private schools. On the facts of this case, petitioners have been approving plans that do not meet this requirement, and certainly, if public school children continue to receive on-the-premises Title I instruction,

petitioners should not approve plans that fail to make a genuine effort to employ comparable alternative programs that make up for the lack of on-the-premises instruction for the nonpublic school children. A program which provides instruction and equipment to the public school children and the same equipment but no instruction to the private school children cannot, on its face, be comparable. In order to equalize the level and quality of services offered, something must be substituted for the private school children. The alternatives are numerous. Providing nothing to fill the gap, however, is not among the acceptable alternatives.

Second, if the State is unwilling or unable to develop a plan which is comparable, while using Title I teachers in public but not in private schools, it may develop and submit an acceptable plan which eliminates the use of on-the-premises instruction in the public schools and, instead, resorts to other means, such as neutral sites or summer programs that are less likely to give rise to the gross disparity present in this case.

Third, and undoubtedly least attractive for the educationally deprived children, is nonparticipation in the program. Indeed, under the Act, the Commissioner, subject to judicial review, 20 U.S.C.A. § 241k, may refuse to provide funds if the State does not make a bona fide effort to formulate programs with comparable services. 20 U.S.C.A. § 241j.

The second major issue is whether the Establishment Clause of the First Amendment prohibits Missouri from sending public school teachers paid with Title I funds into parochial schools to teach remedial courses. The Court of Appeals declined to pass on this significant issue, noting that since no order had been entered requiring on-the-premises parochial school instruction, the matter was not ripe for review. We agree. As has been pointed out above, it is possible for the petitioners to comply with Title I without utilizing on-the-premises parochial school instruction. Moreover, even if, on remand, the state and local agencies do exercise their discretion in favor of such instruction, the range of possibilities is a broad one and the First Amendment implications may vary according to the precise contours of the plan that is formulated. . . .

It would be wholly inappropriate for us to attempt to render an opinion on the First Amendment issue when no specific plan is before us. A federal court does not sit to render a decision on hypothetical facts, and the Court of Appeals was correct in so concluding.

. . . The comparability mandate is a broad one, and in order to implement the overriding concern with localized control of Title I programs, the District Court should make every effort to defer to the judgment of the petitioners and of the local agency. Under the Act, respondents are entitled to comparable services, and they are, therefore, entitled to relief. As we have stated repeatedly herein, they are not entitled to any particular form of service, and it is the role of the state and local agencies, and not of the federal courts, at least at this stage, to formulate a suitable plan.

On this basis, the judgment of the Court of Appeals is affirmed.

NOTE

Wheeler v. Barrera was later modified and remanded. 422 U.S. 1004, 95 S.Ct. 2625 (1975), but the substance of the original decision was not changed.

Federal Government May Recover Misused Funds from States

— · — · — · — · —

Bell v. New Jersey and Pennsylvania

— · — · — · — · —

Supreme Court of the United States, 1983.
461 U.S. 773, 103 S.Ct. 2187.

JUSTICE O'CONNOR delivered the opinion of the Court. In this case we consider both the rights of the Federal Government when a State misuses funds advanced as part of a federal grant-in-aid program under Title I of the Elementary and Secondary Education Act and the manner in which the Government may assert those rights. We hold that the Federal Government may recover misused funds, that the Department of Education may determine administratively the amount of the debt, and that the State may seek judicial review of the agency's determination.

The respondents, New Jersey and Pennsylvania, received grants from the Federal Government under Title I of the Elementary and Secondary Education Act of 1965 (ESEA), Pub. 89–10, 79 Stat. 27, as amended, 20 U.S.C. § 2701 et seq. (1976 ed. Supp. V). Title I created a program designed to improve the educational opportunities available to disadvantaged children. § 102, 20 U.S.C. § 2701 (1976) ed. Supp. V). Local educational agencies obtain federal grants through state educational agencies, which in turn obtain grants from the Department of Education upon providing assurances to the Secretary that the local educational agencies will spend the funds only on qualifying programs. § 182(a), 20 U.S.C. § 2734 (1976 ed. Supp. V). In auditing New Jersey for the period September 1, 1970, through August 1973, and Pennsylvania for the period July 1, 1967, through June 30, 1973, to ensure compliance with ESEA and the regulations promulgated under ESEA, federal auditors determined that each State had misapplied funds. After review requested by the States, the Education Appeal Board (the Board) modified the findings of the auditors and assessed a deficiency of $1,031,304 against New Jersey and a deficiency of $422,424.29 against Pennsylvania. The Secretary declined to review the orders establishing the deficiencies, and, after a period for comment, the orders became final. Both States filed timely petitions for review in the United States Court of Appeals for the Third Circuit, which consolidated the cases and held that the Department did not have the authority to issue the orders. It therefore did not reach New Jersey's arguments that the State had not in fact misapplied the funds, App. to Pet. for Cert. 3a, or Pennsylvania's arguments challenging the agency's rulemaking procedures and its application of ESEA's limitations provision, ibid. . . .

Turning to the merits, the States first challenge the Secretary's order by asserting that, even if the Board properly determined that they misused the funds, the Federal Government cannot recover the amount misused. Thus, we must decide whether, assuming that a State has misused funds granted to it under Title I of ESEA, it becomes liable to the Federal Government for those funds. The Education Amendments of 1978 (1978 amendments), Pub. 95–561, 92 Stat. 2143, 20 U.S.C. §§ 2701 et seq. (1976 ed. Supp. V), rendered explicit the authority of the Secretary to recover funds misspent by a recipient. § 185, 92 Stat. 2190, 20 U.S.C. § 2835(b) (1976 ed. Supp. V). Although the final determination of the Board in each of these appeals occurred after the enactment of the 1978 amendments, the audits reviewed periods before 1978. Both States take the position that, before the 1978 amendments, the Secretary's sole remedy for noncompliance was prospective: he could withhold funds from a State that did not comply, until the State brought its program into compliance, § 146, 20 U.S.C. § 241j, or he could deny applications for funds for noncomplying programs, § 142, 20 U.S.C. § 241f. Further, they contend that the 1978 amendments operated prospectively only. The Secretary has argued both that the 1978 amendments had retroactive effect and that the right of recovery existed in the pre-1978 version of ESEA. Since we are persuaded that the pre-1978 version contemplated that States misusing federal funds would incur a debt to the Federal Government for the amount misused, we need not address the possible retroactive effect of the 1978 amendments.

Section 207(a)(1) of ESEA, Pub. 89–10, 79 Stat. 27, 32, originally provided:

> The Commissioner shall, subject to the provisions of § 208 [dealing with inadequate appropriations], from time to time pay to each State, in advance or otherwise, the amount which the local educational agencies of that State are eligible to receive under this part. Such payments shall take into account the extent (if any) to which any previous payment to such State educational agency under this title (whether or not in the same fiscal year) was greater or less than the amount which should have been paid to it.

This provision, which remained substantially unchanged as part of Title I until 1970, in our view, gives the Federal Government a right to the amount of any funds overpaid. The plain language of the statute recognizes the right, and the legislative history supports that natural reading. The Senate Report explained, "Since the State is given no authority to retain excess sums paid to it under the title, any excess paid to a State would have to be returned or taken into account in making subsequent payments to the State." S.Rep. No. 146, 89th Cong, 1st Sess., 14 (1965). Indeed, the Committee obtained assurances from the Department that it would recapture these payments, and the debate on the floor termed those assurances "an essential condition for enacting the proposed legislation." 111 Cong. Rec. 7690 (1965). . . . In sum, not only does our conclusion give meaning to the efforts of the 95th Congress, it gives meaning to their understanding of the law that they were amending. Accordingly, we adhere to our view that the pre-1978 version of ESEA requires that recipients be held liable for funds that they misuse.

New Jersey, relying on our decision in *National League of Cities v. Usery*, 426 U.S. 833, 96 S.Ct. 2465, 49 L.Ed.2d 245 (1976), also urges that the imposition of liability for misused funds interferes with state sovereignty, in violation of the Tenth Amendment. It views our construction of the statute as presenting it with "unpalatable" alternatives: making a special appropriation to repay the misused funds, or cutting back its budget for education by the amount owed to the Federal Government. . . . Either alternative, it asserts, infringes its sovereignty.

We cannot agree. Requiring States to honor the obligations voluntarily assumed as a condition of federal funding before recognizing their ownership of funds simply does not intrude on their sovereignty. The State chose to participate in the Title I program and, as a condition of receiving the grant, freely gave its assurances that it would abide by the conditions of Title I. . . . As we must assume at this stage of the litigation, the State failed to fulfill those assurances, and it therefore became liable for the funds misused, as the grant specified. New Jersey has not challenged the program itself as intruding unduly on its sovereignty . . . but challenges only the requirement that it account for funds that it accepted under admittedly valid conditions with which it failed to comply. If the conditions were valid, the State had no sovereign right to retain funds without complying with those conditions. . . .

In these cases, then, we conclude that the Secretary has followed the proper procedures. He has administratively determined the amount of the debt owed by each State to the Federal Government as he is empowered to do. Whether that determination is supported by substantial evidence and by the application of the proper legal standards is a question for

the courts, if the affected parties seek judicial review. Here, New Jersey and Pennsylvania sought that review, and we remand to the Court of Appeals to permit it to undertake to review the challenges raised by each State to the Secretary's determination. Accordingly, the case is reversed and remanded for further proceedings consistent with this opinion.

It is so ordered.

NOTE

1. In *Bennett v. New Jersey*, 470 U.S. 632, 105 S.Ct. 1555 (1985), the Supreme Court ruled on the "retroactive effect," saying that recovery of illegally expended funds is not retroactive because the wording of the law had changed.

◼◼◼ ENDNOTES

1. Forrest McDonald, *Novus Ordo Seclorum* (Lawrence, Kansas: University Press of Kansas, 1985), p. 53.

2. Ibid., pp. 190–91.

3. Ibid., p. 191.

4. Roe L. Johns, Edgar L. Morphet, and Kern Alexander, *The Economics and Financing of Education,* 4th ed. (Englewood Cliffs, N.J.: Prentice-Hall, Inc., 1983), p. 332.

5. U.S.C.A., Title 20, Education 81 to 1686.

6. Ibid.

7. United States v. Sprague, 282 U.S. 716, 51 S.Ct. 220 (1931).

8. Annals of Congress, 1897 (1791). See: Edward S. Corwin (ed.), *The Constitution of the United States of America* (United States Government Printing Office, Wash. D.C., 1964), pp. 1035–36.

9. 17 U.S. (4 Wheat) 316(1819).

10. Ibid., p. 406.

11. United States v. Darby, 312 U.S. 100, 124, 61 S.Ct. 451, 453 (1941).

12. Hopkins Federal Sav. and Loan Ass'n v. Cleary, 296 U.S. 315, 56 S.Ct. 235 (1935).

13. Article I, § 8, cl. 1.

14. United States v. Butler, 297 U.S. 1, 56 S.Ct. 312 (1936).

15. Ibid.

16. 301 U.S. 619, 57 S.Ct. 904 (1937).

17. *3 Writings of Thomas Jefferson,* pp. 147–49 (Library Edition, 1904).

18. Edward S. Corwin, *The Constitution,* rev. by Harold W. Chose and Craig R. Ducet (Princeton University Press, 1978), pp. 139–44.

19. Henry Hart, "The Relations Between State and Federal Law," 54 *Columbia Law Review* 489 (1954).

20. Richard E. Welch III, "At Federalism's Crossroads: National League of Cities v. Usery," *Boston University Law Review* 178 (1977).

21. Wheeler v. Barrera, 417 U.S. 402, 94 S.Ct. 2274 (1974), modified 422 U.S. 1004, 95 S.Ct. 2625 (1975).

22. Article I, § 8, cl. 3.

23. 22 U.S. (9 Wheat) 1 (1824).

24. The power of Congress "To make all Laws which shall be necessary and proper for carrying into Execution the foregoing Powers. . . . " Article I, § 8, cl. 18.

25. Justice Marshall in Gibbons stated: "the power of Congress does not stop at the jurisdictional lines of the several States," but "must be exercised whenever [and wherever] the subject exists. . . . Commerce among the States must, of necessity, be commerce [within] the States." Gibbons v. Ogden, 22 U.S. (9 Wheat) 1 (1824).

26. "[T]he power over commerce . . . is vested in Congress as absolutely as it would be in a single government, having in its constitution the same restrictions on the exercise of the power as are found in the constitution of the United States. The wisdom and the discretion of Congress, their identity with the people, and the influence which their constituents possess at elections, are . . . the sole restraints on which they have relied, to secure them from its abuse. They are the restraints on which the people must often rely solely, in all representative governments." Gibbons v. Ogden, 22 U.S. (9 Wheat) 1 (1824).

27. United States v. Darby, 312 U.S. 100, 61 S.Ct. 451 (1941).

28. Wickard v. Filburn, 317 U.S. 111, 63 S.Ct. 82 (1942).

29. American Power and Light Co. v. Securities and Exchange Commission, 329 U.S. 90, 67 S.Ct. 133 (1946).

30. 426 U.S. 833, 96 S.Ct. 2465 (1976).

31. Welch, "At Federalism's Crossroads: National League of Cities v. Usery," pp. 178–79.

32. National League of Cities v. Usery, 426 U.S. 833, 96 S.Ct. 2465 (1976).

33. Garcia v. San Antonio Metro Transit Auth., 469 U.S. 528, 105 S.Ct. 1005 (1985).

34. 427 U.S. 445, 96 S.Ct. 2666 (1976).

CHAPTER 4

Governance of Public Schools

State government, through statute, regulates and controls education subject only to limitations placed on it by the state and federal constitutions. The courts have consistently held that the power over education is an essential attribute of state sovereignty of the same order as the power to tax, to exercise police power, and to provide for the welfare of the citizenry. In the exercise of this pervasive function, states have established systems of public schools that are operated as administrative arms of the state government.

The broad power of the state extends to provision for education generally within its boundaries and not merely to the public schools alone. Education, in this broader context, encompasses educational purposes and pursuits of the populace and the schools, both public and private. The interest in an educated citizenry is such an important part of state sovereignty that a certain minimal quality of education for all children is required whether their education is acquired in public or private schools.

Court decisions abundantly support the preeminence of the state in control of education. Interestingly, most precedents indicate that the legislature has the prerogative to govern education, when actually education is governed by the democratic legislative process, which requires action by both the legislative and executive branches of government. The legal principles controlling education have been stated many times in different ways by state courts; for example, the legislature has plenary power to set up public schools,[1] the maintenance of common schools is a concern of the state and legislature,[2] or a uniform system of public schools is exclusively within the province of the legislature.[3] The pervasiveness of this power is adequately illustrated by a Michigan decision, which states that "The legislature has entire control over the schools of the state . . . . The division of the territory of the state into districts, the conduct of the schools, the qualifications of teachers, the subjects to be taught therein, are all within its (the state's) control."[4]

An Ohio court has briefly encapsulated this power as follows:

> [T]hat the control of schools, be they public or private, providing elementary and secondary education for the youth of Ohio, reposes in the Legislature of our state. When the General Assembly speaks on matters concerning education it is exercising *plenary* power and its action is subject only to the limitations contained in the Constitution. . . . We can, therefore, indulge in generalities and make a broad statement to the effect that the Legislature of Ohio, in passing laws concerning elementary and secondary schools, is restrained only by its own conscience, [and] fear of the electorate. . . . [5]

The power of the state to control education has sometimes been characterized as emanating from the state's police power.[6] Although police power has not been fully defined by the courts, it is clear that the term encompasses all the elements vested in state sovereignty, including those powers necessary to preserve the peace, morals, good order, and well-being of society.[7] It embraces the broad prerogatives of general welfare. The United States Supreme Court has said: "The police power of a state extends to the protection of the lives, limbs, health, comfort, and quiet of all persons, and to the protection of all property, within the state, and hence to the making of all regulations promotive of domestic order, morals, health, and safety."[8] Within this framework is the power of the state to protect the individual and society through provision for a system of education.

In holding that education is a state function, the courts maintain that the state's authority over education is not a distributive one to be exercised by local government but is a central power residing in the state. The legislature has the prerogative to prescribe the methods of education, and the courts will not intervene unless the legislation is contrary to constitutional provisions.

The state legislature has both the power and the responsibility to enact laws to govern education. In matters of education as in all other functions of state government, the state constitution is fundamental and is determinative of the broad scope within which the legislature can operate. The fact that the legislature is created by the constitution and given law-making authority, in conjunction with the executive branch, is in and of itself a pervasive and general delegation that is not limited to special conditions or situations. By way of explaining this prerogative, the Court of Appeals of New York has said: "The people, in framing the constitution, committed to the legislature the whole law making power of the state, which they did not expressly or impliedly withhold. Plenary power in the legislature of all purposes of civil government is the rule."[9] Unlike the Congress of the United States, which has only those powers delegated to it by the Constitution, state legislatures have plenary power and may pass any act that is not expressly or impliedly forbidden by the state constitution.[10] According to Edwards, "The legislature must do so much; it may do more."[11]

Yet, strictly speaking, the term "plenary," meaning complete, absolute, and unqualified, should be used with proper qualification. Even though the courts have frequently used the term in defining the legislature's prerogative, in actuality, legislative power is subject to definite limits imposed on it by both the federal and state constitutions, as well as by federal statutes—which are supreme and take precedence over state statutes. This limitation must be recognized as of major significance. The term "plenary" can be a particularly poor choice of words in view of recent trends, in which courts have invoked not only the general constitutional restraints of equal protection, liberty, property, and so forth, but have begun to directly circumscribe legislative action within the limits of education clauses of state constitutions. As indicated in Chapter 2 of this book, terms such as "efficient," "thorough," "effective," "uniform," and "system" as used in education clauses have increasingly been invoked by the courts to strike down statutes governing the financing of public schools. Several recent decisions[12] have revitalized the education clauses and their interpretations may, in the future, represent important precedents and, as a consequence, important limitations on legislative power. Thro observes that prior to the 1989 cases, the "education clauses (in state constitutions) were largely useless as tools for school finance reform," but today legislatures are subject to a new duty and responsibility to provide for public schools.[13] The imposition by the courts of this new duty on the state legislatures creates an increased standard to which legislative action must adhere. This standard, emanating from more assertative interpretation of education clauses, is seen by some courts as creating

> a "duty" that is supreme, preeminent and dominant. Flowing from this constitutionally imposed "duty" is its jural correlative, a correspondent "right" permitting control of another's conduct. Therefore, all children residing within the borders of the state possess a "right," arising from a constitutionally imposed "duty" of the State, that the State make ample provision for their education. Further, since the "duty" is characterized as paramount, the correlative "right" has equal stature. . . . Consequently, all children residing within the State's borders have a "right" to be amply provided with an education.[14]

STATE AND LOCAL EDUCATION AGENCIES

All states and the federal government have networks of administrative agencies (usually called boards, commissions, bureaus, or offices) that have been created to implement and administer statutes. State legislatures and the United States Congress have not seen fit historically to actually administer legislative enactments themselves, even though the legislative branch of government could conceivably assume the role of program administration. Traditionally, the view has been that the legislature should not perform the multi-duties of enacting legislation, appropriating funds, and then administering the funds, thereby invading the gray area of executive responsibility. In education, for example, it would be tedious and legislatively cumbersome for a state legislature to attempt to establish by statute rules and regulations governing specific certification requirements for teachers.

In this regard, an Illinois court has said that delegation of public school responsibilities from the General Assembly to subordinate agencies, duly elected school boards, is of practical necessity because the legislature could not itself conveniently or efficiently attend to the details of establishing, maintaining, and operating the public schools.[15]

Jaffe has suggested the reasoning for such delegation of regulatory power by saying:

> Power should be delegated where there is agreement that a task must be performed and it cannot be effectively performed by the legislature without the assistance of a delegate or without an expenditure of time so great as to lead to the neglect of equally important business.[16]

The result has been for the state legislature to create agencies that handle the administrative functions necessary to properly implement legislation. In most states, this delegation by the legislature manifests itself in a state board of education, which may be either elected or appointed and has authority to perform administrative and supervisory func-

tions. An alternative to this approach is to vest officials of the executive branch with regulatory and attendant authority to administer the school system of the state; such officers are generally referred to as chief state school officers. Legislatures may also delegate powers to local school districts.

It is well established that the local school district is a state agency that simply operates at the local level. The Supeme Court of Michigan has said the school district is a legislative creation. "It is true that it was provided for in obedience to a constitutional requirement; and whatever we may think . . . we cannot doubt that such management must be in conformity to the provisions of such laws of a general character as may from time to time be passed, and that the property of the district is in no sense private property, but is public property devoted to the purposes of the state for the general good, just as almshouses and courthouses are, although confided to local management, and applied to uses which are in a sense local, though in another sense general."[17]

Another Michigan decision described the legal relationship between the state and local school districts in this way:

> Fundamentally, provision for and control of our public school system is a state matter, delegated and lodged in the state legislature by the Constitution in a separate article entirely distinct from that relating to local government. The general policy of the state has been to retain control of its school system, to be administered throughout the state under state laws by local state agencies organized with plenary powers independent of the local government with which, by location and geographical boundaries, they are necessarily closely associated and to a greater or lesser extent authorized to co-operate. "Education belongs to the state."[18]

Because local school boards are state bodies, it follows that school board members are state, not local officials.[19] Local school boards are vested with a portion of the sovereignty of the state through delegation, by which they acquire certain administrative functions having attributes of all three branches of government: executive, quasi-judicial, and regulatory or quasi-legislative. As creatures of the legislature or constitution, local school districts abide within their legal prerogatives and cannot give away or redelegate their judgmental powers to other agencies or individuals.

The courts commonly divide the administrative functions of the local school board into two categories, discretionary and ministerial. The meaning of discretionary powers here is those acts that require judgment on the part of the board. Examples of such responsibilities could be the location of a school building site, the employment of a particular teacher, or the purchase of a certain type of school bus. The greatest portion of a board's powers may be classified as discretionary. In exercising these discretionary powers, a board of education is limited only by the requirements and restrictions of the law. As has been pointed out in the case of state education agencies, the courts will not interfere with a board's exercise of discretion even though the judgment is unwise except where the board's action violates the law, abuses authority, or is *ultra vires*.

The operation of school districts is based upon the express or implied authority of statute. The courts in circumscribing the authority of school boards from statutory implication have held that in the absence of statute, travel expenses can be paid for the recruitment of teachers outside the state,[20] a school district can establish a cafeteria,[21] and a school board can establish a school health inspection department made up of doctors, dentists, and nurses.[22] On the other hand, authority has been denied for a school district to pay for surgical and dental operations for pupils,[23] for medical care for pupils injured in athletic contests,[24] and for purchase of basketball uniforms to be used on land not under school control.[25]

Functions of Education Agencies

Functions of public agencies can generally be classified as (1) legislative, (2) executive, and (3) judicial (or quasi-judicial). As agencies of government, both state and local education authorities have these basic powers.

Administration encompasses the rule-making and adjudication processes and incidental powers such as coordinating, supervising, investigating, prosecuting, advising, and declaring.[26] The exercise of administrative functions may be reviewed by the courts to determine if duties have been carried forth within the scope of law and whether proper procedures have been followed.

Delegation of Legislative Powers

Legislative functions of the state agency include the promulgation of rules and regulations made pursuant to and within the scope of statute. The legislative function performed by state agencies has been justified on the grounds that the agency was merely "filling in the details" within the meaning of general statute.[27] In the public interest, it is said the state agency should not have legislative powers since agency officials are not direct representatives of the people with constitutionally sanctioned law-making prerogative. This is a basic tenet of representative government recognized early by John Locke. In his treatises on civil government, he said:

> The legislature cannot transfer the power of making laws to any other hands, for it being but a delegated power from the people, they who have it cannot pass it over to others. . . . [N]obody else can say other men shall make laws for them; nor can they be bound by any laws but such as are enacted by those whom they have chosen and authorized to make laws for them.[28]

Exclusive powers of the legislature should not therefore be delegated to subordinate agencies. In clarification of this theory of government, a Michigan court has said:

> This is not to say, however, that a subordinate body or official may not be clothed with authority to say when the law shall operate, or to whom, or upon what occasion, provided, however, that the standards prescribed for guidance are as reasonably precise as the subject matter requires or permits.[29]

Davis maintains, though, that formulations by state courts that attempt to circumscribe the legislative function of subordinate agencies are largely without substance.[30] While generally it appears that most courts seek to restrain too broad a delegation in order to prevent arbitrary use of uncontrolled power by subordinate officials, the actual legal theory and its implementation by the courts is sometimes difficult to follow. Basically, the theory of delegation appears to have been justified on the grounds of "adequacy of standards." Does the statute provide sufficient delineation of the particular requirement or prohibition so that in light of the surrounding facts and circumstances the agency can ascertain, interpret, and implement the true purpose of the act? The legislature must prescribe a "reasonably adequate standard."[31] Some courts maintain that "definite standards are indispensable, not only to avoid a delegation of the essential legislative power, but to guard against an arbitrary use of the delegated administrative authority."[32] Limitations on legislative delegation to subordinate agencies may have been best described by a Washington court that said:

> The legislature may delegate these legislative controls to an administrative agency of the state; provided, in so doing, it defines what is to be done; the instrumentality which is to accomplish it; and the scope of the instrumentality's authority in so doing, by prescribing reasonable administrative standards.[33]

This statement probably represents the prevailing view of the courts, but the doctrine of delegation is one that must be treated as highly flexible. Courts, for example, tend to restrict agency prerogatives in the area of taxation, property rights, or individual civil rights. On the other hand, state education agencies may have broad latitude in dealing with regulation of purely educational matters such as school district organization. For example, a Wisconsin statute was contested as being unconstitutional because it authorized the state superintendent to merge certain school districts of low assessed valuation with contig-

uous school districts. The Wisconsin Supreme Court said that "the power to exercise discretion in determining whether such districts shall be altered . . . may be delegated without any standard whatsoever to guide in the exercise of the power delegated."[34]

The tendency in recent years has been for the courts to follow a much more lenient policy toward delegation of legislative power.[35] Changes in the nature of modern government and the increasing complexity of society necessitate that public agencies have more general authority to assume broader prerogatives. As it now stands, the delegation principle is still applicable to the state educational process, and it remains in use to prevent unconstitutional usurpation of unauthorized powers; but it is much less pervasive than before. The rule today as expounded by state courts is best exemplified by a New York court[36] that quoted with approval the standard established by the United States Supreme Court, which said that a legislative body

> does not abdicate its functions when it describes what job must be done, who must do it, and what is the scope of his authority. In our complex economy that indeed is frequently the only way in which the legislative process can go forward.[37]

Although the rationale of the courts continues to follow the delegation doctrine, it should be observed that proper delegation and guarantee against arbitrary action by agencies cannot be assured through the specification of standards in legislative declarations. Protection against inappropriate action and injustice in education are to be found more in procedural safeguards and various checks and balances, the most effective of which is, of course, justification of the action to the voters and taxpayers.

Executive Functions

Although functions of education agencies are difficult to compartmentalize, it is possible to identify certain ones that may be more readily described as executive rather than legislative or judicial. In fact, the organizational structures of state education agencies tend to adhere to such definition in that the legislative functions are usually vested in a state board of education, the executive functions in a chief state school officer and his staff, the state department of education, and the quasi-judicial functions may be found within the authority of either or both. A similar situation exists at the local level, where the board makes policy and the superintendent implements it with both sometimes exercising quasi-judicial functions.

The distinction between legislative and executive acts can be expressed as the difference between the general and the particular.

> A legislative act is the creation and promulgation of a general rule of conduct without reference to particular cases; an administrative act cannot be exactly defined, but it includes the adoption of policy, the making and issue of specific direction, and the application of a general rule to a particular case in accordance with the requirements of policy or expediency or administrative practice.[38]

Activities of the education agency that may be classified as purely executive are declaring and enforcing policy as well as advising and supervising implementation of policy. One can easily identify such activities as they are performed daily in state agencies; for example, when a policy is established it must be properly interpreted and conveyed to the local school district administrators, then advice may be given and certain supervisory activities may be followed to assist in implementation. Should problems arise, steps must be taken to assure enforcement of the particular policy.

Executive actions can also be viewed in the more commonly used legislative categories of ministerial and discretionary functions. "Ministerial" refers to those required duties performed by the administrator for which no exercise of judgment is permitted. "Discretionary" functions, as noted above, are judgmental and represent exercise of substantial administrative prerogative. An official can pass on to a subordinate ministerial functions,

but cannot delegate duties that are discretionary in nature. Discretionary functions, of course, represent an area of major overlap with the broader quasi-judicial functions of agencies. The maxim *delegatus non protest delegare* has, on the whole, been more strictly enforced when applied to subdelegation than at the primary or legislative level of delegation. In other words, courts tend to examine more critically the internal delegation of a discretionary function from the state superintendent down to an assistant than from the legislature to the agency itself. For example, where statute vests a specific discretionary power in a state board, the board cannot subdelegate to one board member or to some other officer such as the state superintendent. Similarly, statutory discretion vested in the state superintendent cannot be redelegated to a deputy or assistant. Ministerial functions, on the other hand, can be subdelegated.

As is true at the state level, a local school board cannot delegate discretionary functions, but it may delegate ministerial functions. The exact definition between discretionary powers that cannot be delegated and ministerial powers that can be delegated, is, however, indistinct. A good illustration is provided by a 1987 Colorado case, in which the power to dismiss personnel was delegated. Normally, personnel matters involving hiring and firing of employees are considered to be discretionary or quasi-judicial powers that cannot be delegated; yet the high court of Colorado upheld the dismissal of a school bus driver by the school districts' director of business services, because the court found that such discharges were administrative matters and did not constitute action "significantly related to the policy-making duties" of the school district.[39]

Will has pointed out that there is a discernible trend toward the separation of the legislative function and the executive powers in state educational administration. He describes the pattern in this way:

> Students of state educational administration commonly hold that the central education agency should consist of a state board of education, a chief state school officer, and the

necessary staff. The state board of education is looked upon as the agency's legislative policy-making body, the chief state school officer as the agency's executive officer, and the organized staff as the agency's work force. A virtually complete separation of legislative and executive powers at the administrative level is intended under this pattern.[40]

The powers and duties of the state board of education, the chief state school officer, and the state department of education vary from state to state; however, general rules governing the delegation of legislative powers, the exercises of discretionary authority, and the quasi-judicial role of central state agencies are carefully circumscribed by court decisions.

Quasi-Judicial Functions

In their tripartite capacity, administrative agencies hand down many more decisions affecting individuals than do the formal courts of this country. Decisions by educational tribunals form an important source of law under which education operates. Authority for decisions by educational tribunals may be found at federal, state, and local levels. At the federal level, statute often vests the United States Commissioner of Education with quasi-judicial authority to render decisions in disputes over federal grant processes and procedures that may have direct impact on individuals or states. At the state level, quasi-judicial authority may be given to state boards of education, to state superintendents, or, in some cases, to other legislatively authorized bodies. New Jersey and New York are good examples of such powers being vested in the chief state school officer.

The state commissioner of education in New Jersey has the authority to decide cases involving internal administrative operations of the public schools of that state. A New Jersey court has said that a statute providing that the state commissioner shall decide all controversies under the school laws of the state is evidence of legislative purpose to set up a comprehensive system of internal appeals with broad powers. Such an authority invested in administrative tribunals assures that controversies are justly disposed of in accordance with the law.[41]

In another New Jersey case illustrating the judicial function of the state commissioner of education, the court said that the commissioner must enforce all rules and regulations prescribed by the state board and decide all questions arising under rules and regulations of the state board.[42]

Determinations by these tribunals are binding on the parties involved and serve additionally to establish a type of quasi-judicial *stare decisis* within the agencies' jurisdiction. Agencies, in exercise of their judicial powers, are required generally to merely provide fair treatment to the parties involved. Some states, through administrative procedure acts, may provide specific definition of the requirements of fairness, and, when administrative tribunals are dealing with disputes involving constitutional interests, more elaborate procedures are necessary. In the absence, though, of statutory or constitutional restraints, the courts have been very liberal in allowing educational tribunals to establish their own procedures. In so doing, courts more or less adhere to a requirement similar to the English doctrine of *audi alteram partem* of natural justice that requires tribunals to adjudicate fairly. Fairness is not always easily defined but may be roughly equated to reasonableness and good faith. These two standards are not the same but may be viewed as complementary. It has been said that "some of the most honest people are the most unreasonable; and some excesses may be sincerely believed in but yet be quite beyond the limits of reasonableness."[43] It is true, however, that the actions of one conducting a hearing could be so unreasonable as to be arbitrary and capricious and as such appear to be taken in bad faith.

The objective is for justice to be rendered by tribunals whether they are courts of law or administrative agencies. When persons stand before tribunals, there is an implicit assumption that the tribunal will act "neutrally in a principled way" because there is a natural right of justice for requiring that tribunals not help nor hinder one side more than the other.[44]

Fairness of a hearing may also be explained in terms of equality before the law. It is expected that persons coming before a tribunal will be treated equally and the determination favorable or unfavorable toward one or the other will be described on the merits of the case. Equality, as an aspect of fairness, requires that "rules of law shall be applied according to their terms without regard to the person(s) involved . . . ." This equal application of laws is guaranteed not only by common law, but by constitutional provisions guaranteeing due process.[45]

A particularly perplexing problem is presented when the tribunal is itself a party to the action that comes before it. Because school boards have tripartite jurisdiction—legislative, executive, and quasi-judicial—it is not uncommon for a board to sit in judgment in its own cause. Because of the nature of our governmental system, however, this problem cannot be avoided.

This particular issue, whether a school board can sit in judgment when it is a party in the dispute, has been litigated before the U.S. Supreme Court. The Court held that the mere fact that a public agency is, as a body, a party to a dispute before it is not alone an indication of bias sufficient to violate due process.[46]

In the Absence of Bias, a School Board May Sit in Its Quasi-Judicial Capacity in Judgment of a Case to Which It Is a Party

—·—·—·—·—·—

Hortonville Joint School District No. 1 v. Hortonville Education Association

—·—·—·—·—·—

Supreme Court of the United States, 1976.
426 U.S. 482, 96 S.Ct. 2308.

Mr. Chief Justice BURGER delivered the opinion of the Court. We granted certiorari in this case to determine whether School Board members, vested by state law with the power to employ and dismiss teachers, could, consistent with the Due Process Clause of the Fourteenth Amendment, dismiss teachers engaged in a strike prohibited by state law.

The petitioners are a Wisconsin school district, the seven members of its School Board, and three administrative employees of the district. Respondents are teachers suing on behalf of all teachers in the district and the Hortonville Education Association (HEA), the collective-bargaining agent for the district's teachers.

During the 1972–1973 school year Hortonville teachers worked under a master collective-bargaining agreement; negotiations were conducted for renewal of the contract, but no agreement was reached for the 1973–1974 school year. The teachers continued to work while negotiations proceeded during the year without reaching agreement. On March 18, 1974, the members of the teachers' union went on strike, in direct violation of Wisconsin law. . . .

On April 1, most of the striking teachers appeared before the Board with counsel. Their attorney indicated that the teachers did not want individual hearings, but preferred to be treated as a group. Although counsel agreed that the teachers were on strike, he raised several procedural objections to the hearings. He also argued that the Board was not sufficiently impartial to exercise discipline over the striking teachers and that the Due Process Clause of the Fourteenth Amendment required an independent, unbiased decision-maker. . . .

The sole issue in this case is whether the Due Process Clause of the Fourteenth Amendment prohibits this School Board from making the decision to dismiss teachers admittedly engaged in a strike and persistently refusing to return to their duties.

Respondents' argument rests in part on doctrines that have no application to this case. They seem to argue that the Board members had some personal or official stake in the decision whether the teachers should be dismissed . . . and that the Board has manifested some personal bitterness toward the teachers, aroused by teacher criticism of the Board . . . .

[T]he teachers did not show, and the Wisconsin courts did not find, that the Board members had the kind of personal or financial stake in the decision that might create a conflict of interest, and there is nothing in the record to support charges of personal animosity. . . .

The only other factor suggested to support the claim of bias is that the School Board was involved in the negotiations that preceded and precipitated the striking teachers' discharge. Participation in those negotiations was a statutory duty of the Board. The Wisconsin Supreme Court held that this involvement, without more, disqualified the Board from deciding whether the teachers should be dismissed:

> The board was the collective bargaining agent for the school district and thus was engaged in the collective bargaining process with the teachers' representative, the HEA. It is not difficult to imagine the frustration on the part of the board members when negotiations broke down, agreement could not be reached and the employees resorted to concerted activity. . . . They were . . . not uninvolved in the events which precipitated decisions they were required to make. . . .

Mere familiarity with the facts of a case gained by an agency in the performance of its statutory role does not, however, disqualify a decisionmaker. . . . Nor is a decisionmaker disqualified simply because he has taken a position, even in public, on a policy issue related to the dispute , in the absence of a showing that he is not "capable of judging a particular controversy fairly on the basis of its own circumstances." . . .

Due process, as this Court has repeatedly held, is a term that "negates any concept of inflexible procedures universally applicable to every imaginable situation." . . .

Determining what process is due in a given setting requires the Court to take into account the individual's stake in the decision at issue as well as the State's interest in a particular procedure for making it. . . . Our assessment of the interests of the parties in this case leads to the conclusion that . . . the public interest in maintaining uninterrupted classroom work required that teachers striking in violation of state law be discharged.

The teachers' interest in these proceedings is, of course, self-evident. They wished to avoid termination of their employment, obviously an important interest, but one that must be examined in light of several factors. Since the teachers admitted that they were engaged in a work stoppage, there was no possibility of an erroneous factual determination on this critical threshold issue. . . . The Board's decision whether to dismiss striking teachers involves broad considerations, and does not in the main turn on the Board's view of the "seriousness" of the teachers' conduct or the factors they urge mitigated their violation of state law. It was not an adjudicative decision, for the Board had an obligation to make a decision based on its own answer to an important question of policy: What choice among the alternative responses to the teachers' strike will best serve the interests of the school system, the interests of the parents and children who depend on the system, and the interests of the citizens whose taxes support it? . . .

State law vests the governmental, or policymaking, function exclusively in the School Board and the State has two interests in keeping it there. First, the Board is the body with overall responsibility for the governance of the school district; it must cope with the myriad day-to-day problems of a modern public school system including the severe consequences of a teachers' strike; by virtue of electing them the constituents have declared the Board members qualified to deal with these problems, and they are accountable to the voters for the manner in which they perform. Second, the state legislature has given to the Board the power to employ and dismiss teachers, as a part of the balance it has struck in the area of municipal labor relations; altering those statutory powers as a matter of federal due process clearly changes that balance. Permitting the Board to make the decision at issue here preserves its control over school district affairs, leaves the balance of power in labor relations where the state legislature struck it, and assures that the decision whether to dismiss the teachers will be made by the body responsible for that decision under state law.

Respondents have failed to demonstrate that the decision to terminate their employment was infected by the sort of bias that we have held to disqualify other decisionmakers as a matter of federal due process. A showing that the Board was "involved" in the events preceding this decision, in light of the important interest in leaving with the Board the power given by the state legislature, is not enough to overcome the presumption of honesty and integrity in policymakers with decisionmaking power. . . . Accordingly, we hold that the Due Process Clause of the Fourteenth Amendment did not guarantee respondents that the decision to terminate their employment would be made or reviewed by a body other than the School Board.

The judgment of the Wisconsin Supreme Court is reversed, and the case is remanded for further proceedings not inconsistent with this opinion.

Reversed and remanded.

Delegation of Authority Must Be Accompanied by Specific Standards

— - — - — - — - —

Fremont RE–1 School District v. Jacobs

— - — - — - — - —

Supreme Court of Colorado, 1987.
737 P.2d 816.

ROVIRA, Justice. Respondent Joyce Jacobs, a bus driver for the Fremont RE–1 School District, filed suit in May 1983 after she was fired by Norman Lemons, the school district's director of business services, in February 1983. She alleged that her firing was unlawful because the school board could not delegate to

the director of business services the power to discharge her. . . . We now conclude that the school board could lawfully delegate to its agents the task of firing bus drivers and that the standards set forth by the Fremont School Board in this case were adequate as a matter of law. . . .

Undisputed facts in the record show that prior to the firing of Jacobs the Fremont Board of Education had adopted a policy for the discharge of "classified personnel"—which included bus drivers like Jacobs and also secretaries, office clerks, bookkeepers, and maintenance employees. The policy, which was published in an employee handbook, provided that:

> The Board of Education delegates to the Superintendent of Schools the authority to dismiss classified personnel. Further, the Superintendent of Schools may delegate this authority to the Director of Business Services and/or the Director of Personnel. Classified employees shall be employed for such time as the District is in need of, or desirous of, the services of such employees. The duration of employment is unspecified and solely rests at the discretion of the District. . . .
>
> [D]ismissal of classified employees shall be unaffected by the employee's religious beliefs, marital status, racial or ethnic background, sex, or participation in community affairs.

In February 1983, following a disagreement between Jacobs and her superiors stemming from a disciplinary action Jacobs had taken on her bus, she was discharged by Lemons. Later, after Jacobs filed suit, the school board ratified her discharge.

The sole question presented for review here is whether the board of education could lawfully delegate to the superintendent of schools and, through him, to Lemons the authority to dismiss Jacobs. An examination of the relevant statutes discloses that the legislature has imposed upon school boards certain "duties," . . . , and has granted them certain "powers," . . . . The Fremont school board points out that the legislature has granted school boards the "power" to discharge personnel . . . , but has not made employee discharge a "duty" of school boards . . . . It argues, therefore, that the school board was authorized to delegate the responsibility for discharging employees.

We disagree with this line of argument. As we read the statutes, section 22–32–109 sets forth mandatory "duties" of school boards and section 22–32–110 sets forth discretionary "powers." The listing of employee discharge as a "power" under section 22–32–110 indicates only that a school board may, but need not, exercise its authority to fire employees. The statutes, as we read them, do not specify the scope of a school board's authority to delegate its duties and powers — they merely indicate which powers a school board *may* exercise and which duties it *must* perform. . . .

We turn, therefore, to the rule of construction we adopted in *Big Sandy School District No. 100–J v. Carroll,* 164 Colo. 173, 433 P.2d 325 (1967), a case which presented us with a similar issue. In that case, members of a school board informally authorized the superintendent to hire a principal-teacher and provided him with a signed, blank contract. Thereafter, the superintendent apparently hired one Barney Carroll for the post, but discharged him ten days later. Carroll sued for breach of contract. The issue, as a result, was whether the superintendent had authority to hire a principal-teacher without the school board's explicit approval of the job applicant and his rate of pay. In examining the Colorado statute then in effect, we initially noted that it was the school board's "duty" to employ teachers. We then discussed and applied the established rule of construction applicable to quasi-municipal corporations like the school district:

> [T]he general rule is that . . . a quasi-municipal corporation . . . may delegate to subordinate officers and boards powers and functions which are ministerial or administrative in nature, where there is a fixed and certain standard or rule which leaves little or nothing to the judgment or discretion of the subordinate. However, legislative or judicial powers, involving judgment and discretion on the part of the municipal body, which have been vested by statute in a municipal corporation may *not* be delegated unless such has been expressly authorized by the legislature.

. . . Analyzing the facts under this standard, we concluded that the power to employ teachers and fix their wages is a nondelegable statutory power which the legislature has conferred solely on the school board. It was thus not subject to delegation without explicit legislative authorization.

The principle announced in *Big Sandy* serves several salutary purposes. By placing limits on the delegation of power by school boards, it assures the public that school board members — who are subject to public election — must take responsibility for significant policy decisions associated with management of the school district. . . . Further, the rule protects school districts from incurring significant liabilities based on actions taken by school administrators without the full considered approval of the school board. Lastly, by limiting delegation as a rule of statutory construction, questions concerning the constitutionality of delegation of legislative powers are avoided. . . .

However, we are convinced that the *Big Sandy* rule should not be extended beyond the limited purposes it serves. As a practical matter, school districts require a significant degree of administrative flexibility in order to function smoothly on a day-to-day basis between meetings of their school boards. As school organizations have grown in size and their functions have become more diverse and complex, the need for administrative delegation has become all the more imperative. If the law were to insist on strict limitations on delegation of authority, school board members might tend to become mired in the details of routine operations, and the effectiveness and usefulness of school administrators might be hampered. As a result, the trend in this area of the law has been to allow greater flexibility and away from the insistence on detailed and definite standards. . . . In this vein, we have said:

> The modern tendency of the courts is toward greater liberality in permitting grants of discretion to administrative officials in order to facilitate the administration of the laws as the complexity of governmental and economic conditions increases.

. . . In a somewhat different context, we have held that

> [t]he [School] Board can select reasonable means to carry out its duties and responsibilities incidental to the sound development of employer-employee relations, as long as the means selected are not prohibited by law or against public policy.

. . . Analyzing the question before us with these principles in mind, we conclude that the discharge of a bus driver is an administrative function subject to delegation by the school board. In our view, this action was not significantly related to the policy-making duties of the Fremont school board. . . . In reaching this conclusion, we note that the character of this action—the discharge of a bus driver—is collateral to the school board's educational mission and the significance of this action is not so great that the law should demand the formal accountability of school board members before recognizing the validity of the action. . . .

We recognize that in the past we have held that the power to hire teachers and fix their wages and the power to dismiss them are nondelegable powers. . . . However, the hiring and firing of teachers directly affect the educational mission of the school district, and a central purpose for the election of school board members is to obtain their judgment on such matters. Actions that do not have a significant impact on institutional policy, on the other hand, are properly characterized as administrative in character and therefore are delegable. . . . We do not believe the discharge of a bus driver significantly affects the Fremont school board's institutional policy; therefore, we agree with the court of appeals that the power to discharge Jacobs was properly delegable.

However, we disagree with the holding of the court of appeals that further investigation of the adequacy of the standards limiting the discretion of the school administrators is required in this case. In our view, the standards set forth by the Fremont school board were adequate as a matter of law. Under the school board's employee handbook, "classified employees" served at the will of the district except that they could not be dismissed on account of their religious beliefs, marital status, racial or ethnic background, sex or participation in community affairs.

Ordinarily, a delegation of discretion this broad might run afoul of even the liberalized rules that have been applied to administrative delegation in recent cases. The requirement of standards to limit administrative discretion is designed to assure that administrative action will be rational and consistent and that subsequent judicial review will be available and effective. . . . However, the law has traditionally accorded employers—including government agencies—broad discretion in the discharge of employees who are terminable at will. The general rule is that, absent a violation of constitutional rights, judicial review is not available to review the firing of an employee who is terminable at will. . . . Such an employee may be dismissed without any justifying cause whatever. . . .

Further, the traditional rule with respect to local government employees has been that

> local government employees hold their posts at the pleasure of the proper local government authorities and can be dismissed without cause, in the absence of restrictions or limitations provided by law.

. . . Here, no additional restrictions or limitations relevant to this case have been provided by law. To the contrary, the Colorado legislature has explicitly provided tenure for specified teachers but has adopted no comparable protections for "classified employees" like Jacobs. . . . Furthermore, the Fremont school board has explicitly categorized classified employees as terminable at will with a few limitations not pertinent here. As a result, we are not convinced the rule of construction applied in *Big Sandy* should operate to override the considered policy choices of the legislature and the school board.

The court of appeals' insistence on specific standards for dismissal, however, might indirectly convert Fremont's terminable at will employees to employees terminable only for cause — unless the school board were willing to decide itself every case involving the discharge of a "classified employee." Further, the adoption of more specific standards for dismissal could well create "property" rights for classified employees that would entitle them to a panoply of procedural due process protections. . . . Additionally, the adoption of specific dismissal standards might convert what is now an administrative function into a judicial function, which is not subject to delegation under the *Big Sandy* rule absent explicit legislative authorization. . . . Consequently, it may be meaningless to hold that the discharge power may be delegated if more specific standards are adopted; if more specific standards are adopted, the power may no longer be delegable. We decline to overrule the policy decisions of the Colorado legislature and the Fremont school board in such a roundabout fashion. In our view, the standards adopted by the school board are sufficient as a matter of law.

Accordingly, the judgment of the court of appeals is affirmed in part and reversed in part, and we remand to the court with instructions that it reinstate summary judgment on behalf of the petitioners [school board].

NOTES

1. The decision of the Commissioner of Education of New York in interpreting a statute is to be given great weight by the courts and unless irrational or unreasonable it will be upheld. *Board of Education of Roslyn Union Free School District v. Nyquist,* 90 Misc.2d 955, 396 N.Y.S.2d 567 (1977).
2. Administrative agencies in quasi-judicial hearings have traditionally not been held to the intricate procedural requirement of the courts. However, there are fundamental requirements of fairness which must be observed. A West Virginia court had this to say concerning the conduct of hearings by administrative agencies.

> An administrative body, clothed by law with quasi-judicial powers, must never de-

part from those elemental principles of discreetness and circumspection which our system of law requires in all tribunals which purport to conduct trials. . . . There was a time in the history of English jurisprudence when a felon was not entitled to have the assistance of an attorney at law, but in America, the very word "hearing," both in common and legal parlance, implies some kind of trial, formal or informal, and presupposes permission to have legal aid if desired. *State ex rel. Rogers v. Board of Education of Lewis County,* 125 W.Va. 579, 25 S.E.2d 537 (1943).

3. Legislation in Texas has been interpreted to mean that all administrative steps should be taken to resolve a dispute before appeal can be taken to the courts. Exception to this rule is only found where an action involves a question of taxation, *City of Dallas v. Mosely,* 286 S.W. 497 (Tex. Civ. App. 1926), if the facts are undisputed and the issue is one purely of law and not of education; in such instances, direct access to the courts is available. *Alvin Independent School District v. Cooper,* 404 S.W.2d 76 (Tex. Civ. App. 1966).
4. A Maryland court has held that the State Board of Education has the last word on any matter concerning educational policy or administration of the system of public instruction; however, it cannot finally decide pure questions of law nor exercise its visitatorial power fraudulently, in bad faith or in breach of trust. Where the State Board of Education of Maryland set a rule of a county board of education requiring fingerprint cards of all employees to be submitted to local police, the court upheld the action of the State Board as being a valid exercise of its authority. *Wilson v. Board of Education of Montgomery County,* 234 Md. 561, 200 A.2d 67 (1964).
5. A Missouri court has held that, where four local school districts were unable to reorganize because of refusal of one to discuss the matter, the state board of education was vested with exclusive jurisdiction to make the decision for the board and once this decision by the state board was approved

by the voters, the school district became officially and legally organized. State ex inf. Eagleton ex rel. *Reorganized School District R–I of Miller County v. Van Landuyt,* 359 S.W.2d 773 (Mo.1962).

_____

Judicial Review of Education Agency Actions

Whether the administrative actions be legislative, executive, or judicial, the courts agree that school boards or officials may exercise those powers expressly granted by statute, and those fairly and necessarily implied.

> The rule respecting such powers is that, in addition to the powers expressly given by statute to an officer or board of officers, he or it has by implication such additional powers as are necessary for the due and efficient exercise of the powers expressly granted or which may be fairly implied from the statute granting the express powers.[47]

While some flexibility in discretion is necessary, indeed indispensable for the schools to operate efficiently, the courts cannot usurp the legislative function by too broad an interpretation of administrative powers.[48]

In challenging the exercise of administrative powers by an educational agency, be they express or implied, the aggrieved parties are required by the courts to exhaust their administrative remedies before they are allowed to bring an action before the courts. Such a rule assures the courts that issues have been properly treated at lower levels, within the realm of administrative authority, thus preventing continuous involvement of the courts in educational disputes where legitimate legal controversy is not present. Examples of the hesitancy of courts to intervene until administrative remedies are exhausted may be found in many instances.[49]

In New York, the state administrative decisions are considered to have substantial weight owing largely to a statute that provides that decisions of the commissioner of education "shall be final and conclusive, and not subject to question or review in any place or court whatsoever." While this provision on its face would appear to preclude any judicial intervention, the true "intent" has been interpreted to mean that the decisions of the commissioner would stand so long as they were not arbitrary.[50]

The general rule of law is probably best expounded by an Illinois court, which stated:

> A court of review cannot substitute its judgment for the judgment of the administrative tribunal. The question is not simply whether the court of review agrees or disagrees with the finding below. It has been said that courts should not disturb administrative findings unless such findings are arbitrary, or constitute an abuse of discretion, or are without substantial foundation in evidence, or are obviously and clearly wrong, or unless an opposite conclusion is clearly evident.[51]

While this rule governing judicial review of administrative actions is generally followed by courts across the country, the individual interpretations of the rule are widely variant, ranging from rather strict adherence to what some would consider to be relative disregard. As a matter of fact, courts may exercise their prerogatives to intervene and alter administrative action with several different legal bases. Ministerial actions of government agencies have been successfully challenged under the ancient legal doctrines of nonfeasance, misfeasance, or malfeasance. Failure to perform properly may be remedied by the courts by use of the common law remedy, *writ of mandamus.* If the aggrieved party is seeking to prevent an inappropriate action, then an *injunction* may be the appropriate legal remedy.

On the other hand, if discretionary actions are in question, then the person challenging the action may proceed from a broader legal basis. As mentioned above, fairness and reasonableness of action are requisite to appropriate use of the quasi-judicial authority of an agency. More directly, discretionary powers may be viewed quite broadly, and if an agency acts beyond the scope of its powers it may well be *ultra vires*. A discretionary power may be abused in either good faith or in bad faith, but in both instances the action may be voided by the courts.[52] Beyond inquiry into *vires*, judicial intervention may be justifiable if:

1. A power granted to an agency is not properly applied. Here the courts will seek to determine whether the agency had either express or implied statutory power to perform as it did, and if the statute was broad enough with possibly a plurality of purposes sufficient to support the action. The court will generally apply certain tests including seeking to ascertain

   a. the true purpose for the action
   b. the dominant purpose
   c. if there was an unauthorized or illicit purpose,[53] or if the action was taken in bad faith.

2. Exercise of discretionary power may also be challenged if the agency, official, or tribunal was influenced by considerations that could not have been lawfully taken into account or if it ignored obviously relevant considerations. Plaintiff, though, must show that irrelevant considerations were actually relied upon in the decision. Certainly if extraneous or irrelevant matters are set out as reasons in support of the decision, then courts may consider the result to be invalid.

3. Prescription of law is not followed in effecting administrative actions. While most instances that come to mind here involve ministerial functions (e.g., following election procedures or budgetary submission processes), the educational agency's action may also be challenged if it fails to recognize or appreciate the amplitude of its discretion.[54] For example, a state authority may have the statutory power to grant salary increases or increase fringe benefits but misconstrues and through misunderstanding fails to recognize the discretion. Here it is not the reasonableness of the decision made by the agency but the failure of the agency to recognize its power that is judicially questionable.

4. A public education board binds itself through its own regulation in such a way as to constrict or disable itself from fulfilling the primary purposes for which it was created. Where a public body is entrusted by the legislature with certain powers and duties either express or implied for public purposes, the body cannot divest itself of such powers and duties. Regulations or bylaws that effectively thwart statutory intent, for example, by contracting away a power or requiring the exercise of a broad power in a restrictive way, may be unreasonable and incompatible with public purpose.

Courts do not penalize a state agency for possible error in the exercise of discretion where judgment or opinion of the public officials is in contest. If there are reasonable grounds, the judge has no further duty to inquire. The criterion of reasonableness is not subjective, but objective in the sense that it must be weighed in light of surrounding facts and circumstances.

This rule applies to actions of local school agencies as well as to state education agencies. The Supreme Court of Virginia has refused to intervene and question a school division action even if the court would quite probably not have agreed with the result of the decision. The Court said:

> [W]here there is rational legal and factual basis for a school board's administrative determination, the Court will not overturn such decision and substitute its own judgment even if it would have reached a contrary conclusion.[55]

The Court is concerned with whether the judgment rendered by the board is founded on "rational, legal and factual" information, not whether the Court, viewing the same situation and evidence, would have reached a contrary decision. The party who assails a school board's decision must prove that the board acted arbitrarily and without regard for the evidence, and thus illegally, before a court will upset a board's decision.[56]

*Regulation of Common Schools Is within
the Power of the Legislature*

— · — · — · — · — · —

State Ex Rel. Clark v. Haworth

— · — · — · — · — · —

Supreme Court of Indiana, 1890.
122 Ind. 462, 23 N.E. 946.

ELLIOTT, J. . . . It is sufficient, to bring the question clearly enough before the mind for investigation and consideration, to say that the relator petitioned for a writ of mandate to compel the appellee, as school trustee of Monroe township, in the county of Howard, to certify to the county superintendent of schools the number of text-books required by the children of the township for use in the public schools, and to procure and furnish such books as the law requires . . . Elliott's Supp. § 1289 (Acts 1889, p. 74.)

The act assailed does not impinge in the slightest degree upon the right of local self-government. The right of local self-government is an inherent, and not a derivative, one. Individualized, it is the right which a man possesses in virtue of his character as a free man. It is not bestowed by legislatures, nor derived from statutes. But the courts which have carried to its utmost extent the doctrine of local self-government have never so much as intimated that it exists as to a matter over which the constitution has given the law-making power supreme control; nor have they gone beyond the line which separates matters of purely local concern from those of state control. Essentially and intrinsically, the schools in which are educated and trained the children who are to become the rulers of the commonwealth are matters of state, and not of local, jurisdiction. In such matters the state is a unit, and the legislature the source of power. The authority over schools and school affairs is not necessarily a distributive one, to be exercised by local instrumentalities; but, on the contrary, it is a central power, residing in the legislature of the state. It is for the law-making power to determine whether the authority shall be exercised by a state board of education, or distributed to county, township, or city organizations throughout the state. With that determination the judiciary can no more rightfully interfere than can the legislature with a decree or judgment pronounced by a judicial tribunal. The decision is as conclusive and inviolable in the one case as in the other; and an interference with the legislative judgment would be a breach of the constitution which no principle would justify, nor any precedent excuse.

. . . Judge Cooley has examined the question with care, and discussed it with ability; and he declares that the legislature has plenary power over the subject of the public schools. He says, in the course of his discussion, that "to what degree the legislature shall provide for the education of the people at the cost of the state, or of its municipalities, is a question which, except as regulated by the constitution, addresses itself to the legislative judgment exclusively." Again, he says, "The governing school boards derive all their authority from the statute, and can exercise no powers except those expressly granted, and those which result by necessary implication from the grant." Const.Lim. (5th Ed.) p. 225, note 1. No case has been cited by counsel, and none has been discovered by us,—although we have searched the reports with care,—which denies the doctrine that the regulation of the public schools is a state matter, exclusively within the dominion of the legislature. . . .

As the power over schools is a legislative one, it is not exhausted by exercise. The legislature, having tried one plan, is not precluded from trying another. It has a choice of methods, and may change its plans as often as it deems necessary or expedient; and for mistakes or abuses it is answerable to the people, but not to the courts. It is clear, therefore, that, even if it were true that the legislature had uniformly intrusted the management of school affairs to local organizations, it would not authorize the conclusion that it might not change the system. To deny the power to change, is to affirm that progress is impossible, and that we must move forever "in the dim footsteps of antiquity." But the legislative power moves in a constant stream, and is not exhausted by its exercise in any number of instances, however great. It is not true, however, that the authority over schools was originally regarded as a local one. On the contrary, the earlier cases asserted that the legislature could not delegate the power to levy taxes for school purposes to local organizations, but must itself directly exercise the power; thus denying, in the strongest possible form, the theory of local control. . . . All the public schools have been established under legislative enactments, and all rules and regulations have been made pursuant to statutory authority. Every school that has been established owes its existence to legislation, and every school officer owes his authority to the statute.

It is impossible to conceive of the existence of a uniform system of common schools without power lodged somewhere to make it uniform; and, even in the absence of express constitutional provisions, that power must necessarily reside in the legislature. If it does reside there, then that body must have, as an incident of the principal power, the authority to prescribe the course of study, and the system of instruction, that shall be pursued and adopted, as well as the books which shall be used. This general doctrine is well entrenched by authority. *Hovey v. State,* 119 Ind. 395, 21 N.E.Rep. 21; *Hovey v. Riley,* 119 Ind. 386, 21 N.E.Rep. 890; *State v. Hawkins,* 44 Ohio St. 98, 5 N.E.Rep. 228; *State v. Harmon,* 31 Ohio St. 250. Having this authority, the legislature may not only prescribe regulations for using such books, but it may also declare how the books shall be obtained and distributed. If it may do this, then it may provide that they shall be obtained through the medium of a contract awarded to the best or lowest bidder, since, if it be true, as it unquestionably is, that the power is legislative, it must also be true that the legislature has an unrestricted discretion, and an unfettered choice of methods. It cannot be possible that the courts can interfere with this legislative power, and adjudge that the legislature shall not adopt this method or that

method; for, if the question is at all legislative, it is so in its whole length and breadth. . . .

Either the state has power to regulate and control the schools it owns, or it has not. That it does not have the power, we venture to say, no one will affirm. If it does have the power, it must reside in the law-making department, for it is impossible for it to exist elsewhere. If the power does reside in the law-making department, then that department must exercise its discretion, and adopt such measures as it deems best; and, if the measures adopted lead to the exclusion of some book-owners, it is an incident that no ingenuity can escape, nor any system avoid. The denial of the right to select the books is the denial of the right of regulation and control, and we cannot conceive it possible to deny this right. If the right of regulation and control exists, then the fact that the exercise of the right does not exclude some publisher is an inseparable and unavoidable condition of the exercise of the right. Without it, the right is annihilated. If a clear and manifest legislative right cannot be exercised without conferring privileges in the nature of a monopoly, then, as the authorities all agree, a monopoly may be created; for a denial of the right will not be suffered. This doctrine is discussed by Judge Cooley in his work on Torts, and by Mr. Tiedeman in his work on the Police Power, to which we refer without comment. Cooley, Torts, 277; Tied.Lim. 315 *et seq.* But we need not enter the field traveled by those authors, for here there is no denial of a right to sell books to a community. All that is here done is to provide that the person who receives, after fair and open competition, the contract for supplying books to the school children, shall enjoy an exclusive privilege for the period prescribed by the statute. Judge Cooley says that "it is held competent for the state to contract with a publisher to supply all the schools of the state with textbooks of a uniform character and price." Const.Lim. (5th Ed.) p. 225, note 1. . . .

Judgment reversed, with instructions to proceed in accordance with this opinion. . . .

NOTES

1. The Supreme Court of New York has held that the requirement of the New York State Constitution stating that "the legislature shall provide for the maintenance and support of a system of free common schools, wherein all the children of this state may be educated" gave the legislature power to govern the educational system of the state. *Cohen v. State,* 52 Misc.2d 324, 275 N.Y.S.2d 719 (1966). Such power allows the legislature to create school districts and to establish different types and structures of school boards to govern and regulate the local school districts.

2. The Supreme Court of Tennessee early explained the role of the legislature in exercising police power over public education:

> We are of the opinion that the legislature, under the constitutional provision, may as well establish a uniform system of schools and a uniform administration of them, as it may establish a uniform system of criminal laws and of courts to execute them. The object of the criminal laws is, by punishment, to deter others from the commission of crimes, and thus preserve the peace, morals, good order and well-being of society; and the object of the public-school system is to prevent crime, by educating the people, and thus, by providing and securing a higher state of intelligence and morals, conserve the peace, good order, and well-being of society. The prevention of crime, and preservation of good order and peace, is the highest exercise of the police power of the state, whether done by punishing offenders or educating the children. What is the scope and meaning of the term "police power" has never been defined. The supreme court of the United States has expressly declined to define its limits. Stone v. Mississippi, 101 U.S. 814, 25 L.Ed. 1079 (1879). In *Mayor, etc., v. Miln,* [36 U.S. 102,] 11 Pet. 139, 9 L.Ed. 648 (1835), it is said: "It embraces every law which concerns the welfare of the whole people, of the state or any individual within it, whether it relates to their rights or duties, whether it respects them as men or citizens of the state, whether in their public or private relations, whether it relates to the rights of persons or property of the whole people of the state or of any individual within it." In *Railroad Co. v. Husen,* 95 U.S. 465, 24 L.Ed. 527 (1877), it is said: "The police power of a state extends to the protection of the lives, limbs, health, comfort, and quiet of all persons, and to the protection of all property, within the state, and hence to the making of all regulations promotive of domestic order, morals, health, and safety." In *Smith v. State,* 100 Tenn. 494, 46 S.W. 566, it is said, in substance, that it extends to all questions of health, morals, safety, order, comfort, and well-being of the public, and that this enumeration does not make the list complete. Similar language has but recently been used in the case of *Harbison v. Iron Co.,* [103 Tenn. 421] 53 S.W. 955, and this is no new doctrine, either in this state or in the United States. *Leeper v. State,* 103 Tenn. 500, 53 S.W. 962 (1899).

School Districts Can Exercise Only Those Powers Fairly Implied or Expressly Granted By Statute

McGilvra v. Seattle School District No. 1

Supreme Court of Washington, 1921.
113 Wash. 619, 194 P.2d 817.

PARKER, J. The plaintiffs, McGilvra and others, residents and taxpayers of Seattle school district No. 1, of King county, suing for themselves and in behalf of all others similarly situated, commenced this action in the superior court for that county seeking an injunction to restrain the school district and its officers from maintaining in one of its school buildings and expending funds of the school district for the maintenance therein of a so-called clinic, which, as we proceed we think it will appear would be more properly designated as a "hospital," for the medical, surgical, and dental treatment of the physical ailments of pupils of the schools of the district, whose parents or guardians are financially unable to furnish such treatment. Trial in the superior court upon the merits resulted in findings and judgment denying the relief prayed for, from which the plaintiffs have appealed to this court.   . . .

The question to be here answered is: Have the school district and its officers legal authority for so furnishing the use of, and equipping rooms in its buildings and the maintenance therein of such clinic, by the expenditure of the taxpayers' funds collected and placed at their disposal, for the sole purpose of maintaining the public schools of the district? At the outset let us be reminded in the language of Judge Dillon, in his work on Municipal Corporations, quoted with approval by this court in *State ex rel. Winsor v. Mayor and Council,* 10 Wash. 4, 37 Pac. 761, that

> [i]t is a general and undisputed proposition of law that a municipal corporation possesses and can exercise the following powers, and no others: First, those granted in express words; second, those necessarily or fairly implied in or incident to the powers expressly granted; third, those essential to the declared objects and purposes of the corporation—not simply convenient but indispensable. Any fair or reasonable doubt concerning the existence of power is resolved by the courts against the corporation, and the power is denied.

This view of the law is of added weight when applied to school districts, because they are municipal corporations with powers of a much more limited character than are cities, or towns, or even than counties.   . . .

We are quite unable to find in . . . statutory provisions any power given to the school district officers, other than the power to cause inspection of the buildings and premises of the district to be made with a view

to making them sanitary and healthful, and to cause inspection of persons with a view to the exclusion from the school premises of all persons afflicted with contagious diseases, to the end that such diseases shall not obtain a foothold among the pupils and other persons whose duties require them to be upon the school premises.

Counsel for the school district officers call our attention to, and rely upon, our decision in *State ex rel. School District No. 56 v. Superior Court,* 69 Wash. 189, 124 Pac. 484, and *Sorenson v. Perkins & Co.,* 72 Wash. 16, 129 Pac. 577, commonly known as the "playground" and "gymnasium" cases, wherein it was held that a school district has the power to acquire, by expenditure of the funds of the district, additional land for playgrounds for the pupils, and also at the expense of the district to construct and equip gymnasiums. We do not think these cases are of any controlling force touching the present inquiry. Playgrounds in connection with public schools have for generations been so common that it must be presumed that the Legislature by giving the general power to maintain public schools incidentally intended to also give the authority to provide such playgrounds in connection therewith; and, while gymnasiums in connection with public schools have not been so common, the work and exercise of the students carried on therein is manifestly so intimately connected with the education of the pupil as to warrant the assumption that the Legislature intended the school districts and their officers to possess the power of providing the same as a proper public school equipment. The rendering of medical, surgical, and dental services to the pupils, however, is, and always has been, we think, so foreign to the powers to be exercised by a school district or its officers, that such power cannot be held to exist in the absence of express legislative language so providing.   . . .

The specific legislative enumeration of these powers which it seems could with much sounder reason be considered as implied powers in the absence of express language in the statute than the claimed powers here in question, argues, in the light of well-settled rules of statutory construction, that the Legislature has not intended that there should be an exercise of such claimed powers. We see no argument lending any substantial support, in a legal way, to the view that a school district and its officers possess the powers they are seeking to exercise and threatening to continue to exercise. There is much in the argument of counsel for the school officers which might be considered as lending support to the view that such powers ought to be possessed by the school district and its officers, and it is probable that counsel has many well meaning people upon his side of that question. The Legislature may give heed to such arguments, but the courts cannot do so.

The judgment of the trial court is reversed, and the case remanded to that court, with directions to render a judgment enjoining the school district and its officers from furnishing or equipping upon the school premises, or elsewhere, appliances for the medical, surgical, or dental treatment of the physical ailments of the pupils of the schools at the expense of the district, and from employing physicians, dentists, or nurses for the rendering of such medical, surgical, or dental treatment; it being understood, however, that such injunction shall not restrain the school district or its officers from the doing of these things at the expense of the district in connection with, and as may be necessary in, the maintenance of the parental schools of the district and the proper care of the pupils committed to such schools.

NOTE

1. Boards of education are creatures of statute and, as such, have only those powers that are expressly granted by statute or are necessarily implied therefrom. *Schwing v. McClure*, 120 Ohio St. 335, 166 N.E. 230 (1929); See also: *Tax Deferred Annuities Corp. v. Cleveland Board of Education*, 24 Ohio App. 3d 105, 493 N.E. 2d 305 (1985).

County Board of Education Has Implied Authority to Establish Day Care Centers

Clark v. Jefferson County Board of Education

Supreme Court of Alabama, 1982.
410 So.2d 23.

MADDOX, Justice. Does a county board of education have legal authority to operate a child care center? That is the sole question presented by this appeal.

The Jefferson County Board of Education offers child care services as an adjunct to its regular academic program.   .   .   .

Participation in these programs is voluntary and on a fee basis. The community education program of the Board and the child care program, in particular, are "self-sufficient" in that all expenses are met by fees generated from the programs. All programs are conducted within existing school facilities.

Appellant Clara Clark owns two day care centers in Jefferson County and one in Shelby County under the name of Happy House Day Care Center, Inc. The Jefferson County facilities owned and operated by Clark are in Irondale and Hoover. Clark identified several facilities which she contends are in competition with her Irondale facility, including at least one child care program operated by the Jefferson County Board of Education.

.   .   .

The trial judge held that the operation of a child care center was an activity within the broad powers granted to county boards of education.   .   .   .

We first state, in summary form, Clark's argument that the Board has no authority to operate a child care program. She says that county boards of education, creatures of statute, can exercise only those powers which are expressly conferred upon them, that the powers granted to county boards by Code 1975, §§

16–8–8, and 16–8–9, to administer and supervise is limited to *public schools,* and that a day care program is not a part of a *public school* because "public schools" are those established and maintained for persons between the ages of 7 and 21. . . . Clark's position is aptly stated by this quote from her brief: "No statute authorizes the education of children between one day and 5 years old."

The County Board contends that "the curricular and extracurricular offerings of the public school systems within this state, as in all states, are established by local boards of education in the exercise of their broad discretionary authority conferred by statute" and that in Alabama, this grant of authority is manifested throughout Chapter 8 of Title 16 of the Alabama Code. . . .

The Board, therefore, says that where there is a broad grant of statutory authority, no specific grant of authority to operate a child care program is required. . . .

The Board also calls our attention to evidence introduced during the trial which shows that the State Board of Education has actively and officially supported the implementation and development of Community Education in local school systems. Illustrative of this evidence is a position statement adopted by the Alabama State Board of Education on March 23, 1977, which reads as follows:

> The State Board of Education in its efforts to provide the highest quality education for the citizens of Alabama recognizes the components of community education as a most positive influence on the lifelong learning process and the democratic way of life. . . .

Other exhibits included a publication which showed that the Alabama State Department of Education defines "community education" as follows:

WHAT IS COMMUNITY EDUCATION?

Community education is a concept that stresses an expanded role for public education and provides a dynamic approach to individual and community improvement. . . .

The publication includes a page which shows that "day care" is one of the activities under the umbrella of "people of all ages together using a community school and community resources."

The concept of community education is probably best expressed in a publication entitled "Community Education: A Position Statement," which was adopted by the Alabama State Board of Education in March, 1977, and which is included in the record. . . . The publication states that "the State Board of Education, recognizing the importance of and supporting the concepts involved in Community Education, adopted a resolution in March, 1975, urging all local school systems 'to actively pursue the community education concept.'" . . .

Based on the foregoing facts, and applying the law to those facts, we conclude that the judgment of the trial court is due to be affirmed.

The legislature has made broad grants of authority to the Alabama State Board of Education, the Alabama State Department of Education and to the individual county boards of education to administer and supervise the public schools. It is apparent that the Alabama State Board of Education, pursuant to authority granted it by law, has encouraged the development of "community education," of which "day care" is a part, and has determined that community education is in the best interest of the public schools in Alabama. . . .

We have carefully considered Clark's argument that a public body, without statutory authority, is encroaching upon an area of private enterprise.

Upon consideration of the facts and the law, we hold that while there is no specific statutory grant of authority to local boards of education to operate day care centers, there is authority for such activity under the broad grants of power which we have evaluated and discussed in this opinion. We, therefore, affirm the judgment of the trial court.

Affirmed.

––·––·––·––·––

Hennessey v. Independent School District No. 4, Lincoln County

––·––·––·––·––

Supreme Court of Oklahoma, 1976.
552 P.2d 1141.

DOOLIN, Justice. This is an action filed in the district court by the Wellston Parent Teacher Association (PTA) seeking a writ of mandamus to require Independent School District No. 4, Lincoln County School Board (Board) to allow PTA use of school facilities for its meetings.   . . .

Board has uniformly permitted outside organizations such as Lions Club, Young Homemakers' Organization, Booster Club, 4H Club, Boy Scouts, Bible Lovers' League and Vocational Agriculture Teachers to use the building as authorized by 70 O.S.1971 § 5–130.   . . .

At some time after PTA's first request was denied, Board adopted rules for use of school property by outside organizations. These rules, in addition to general platitudes, contained the following provisions:

> The Wellston School Board will not tolerate nor continue affiliation with any organization that it determines to be disruptive to or *unsupportive* of the school board or any part of the school system.   . . .

Board's refusal to allow PTA to use its building fails for the following reasons:

First, there is no evidence any of Board's stated rules, constitutional or otherwise, have been violated. The record is absolutely void of any testimony as to any legitimate reason why PTA should be forbidden use of the building, or that PTA is not supportive of the school system. The Superintendent of Schools testified he had no personal knowledge of any past action of PTA that would be considered a violation of Board's regulations.

The general statement in the minutes of the Board that use by PTA of school facilities would not be in best interests of community is unsupported by *any* evidence. To the contrary, it was shown that in the past PTA has sponsored many admittedly worthwhile activities for the community children. The superintendent admitted the guidelines and objectives of PTA are all worthwhile. He indicated PTA's request was refused because a vote of the teachers showed a majority of them were not interested in becoming members of PTA. PTA is chartered and supported by both the state and national Parent-Teacher Association. There is nothing in either organization's rules or guidelines requiring teachers to be members in order to be recognized.

Board's reasoning is *circulus in probanda;* PTA is not comparable to other organizations, because the Board does not officially recognize it, since it is not comparable to other organizations. 70 O.S.1971 § 5–130 was certainly not intended to omit PTA objectives from its list of permitted purposes and it cannot be successfully argued PTA is not comparable to the acceptable organizations.

The other grounds for reversal are constitutional. Board's rules and regulations as set forth above and their implementation violate the first and fourteenth amendments to the Constitution of the United States as an abridgment of freedom of speech, and a denial of equal protection and further are a violation of the Constitution of Oklahoma Art. 2, § 22. A regulation by a governmental body such as a school board which permits a public official or body to determine what expressions or views will be permitted or allows the board to engage in invidious discrimination among groups by use of a statute granting discretionary powers and by a system of selective enforcement cannot stand.   . . .

There is no doubt 70 O.S.1971 § 5–130 gives Board absolute discretionary authority as to whether or not to open a school building to activities and meetings of outside organizations. The only absolute discretion exercised however is whether to open the building to outside organizations or not to open it. Once this discretion has been exercised and the decision has been made to permit use of property for any of the enumerated purposes, then it must not adopt a discriminatory and unconstitutional policy as to who will be allowed access to its facilities. Its classifications must be reasonable. Discretion of an administrative body must not be used in a discriminatory matter. Administrative action must have a reasonable or rational basis if it is to avoid the stigma of arbitrariness. All governmental bodies must remain within bounds of the Constitution.

A school board may withhold school facilities altogether from use by nonscholastic groups or may make *reasonable* classifications in determining availability. The state may control the use made of its premises but not without regard to the Constitution. The equal protection clause precludes a school from censoring expressions because it does not like its content or message, and it requires a state authority to deal with similarly situated organizations in an even-handed manner. The privilege of using a school should be available on a reasonable basis.

A state is under no duty to make school buildings available for public gatherings and a school board is not prevented from barring its use for unlawful purposes. But where a school district allows a number of organizations to use its facilities for non-academic purposes, a board must not unconstitutionally discriminate against any comparable applicant in deciding who will and who will not be permitted its use.

Reversed.

NOTES

1. Where the legislature empowers local school boards to perform certain functions, the courts will not interfere with the exercise of those powers unless the school board's actions are found to be "palpably arbitrary, unreasonable or capricious." *Tyska By Tyska v. Board of Education of Township High School District 214*, Cook County, 117, Ill. App. 3d 917, 73 Ill. Dec. 209, 453 N.E. 2d 1344 (1983).

2. The Supreme Court of Nebraska has defined the Legislature's power to delegate authority as follows:

The law appears to be well settled that the Legislature may properly delegate authority to an executive or administrative agency to formulate rules and regulations to carry out the expressed legislative purpose, or to implement such expressed purpose in order to provide for the complete operation and enforcement of the statute. The purpose of the delegation of authority ordinarily must be limited by express standards which have the effect of restricting the actions of the agency to the expressed legislative intent. In *State ex rel. Martin v. Howard*, 96 Neb. 278, 147 N.W. 689, this court approved the following: "In order to justify the courts in declaring invalid as a delegation of legislative power a statute conferring particular duties or authority upon administrative officers, it must clearly appear beyond a reasonable doubt that the duty or authority so conferred is a power that appertains exclusively to the legislative department, and the conferring of it is not warranted by the provisions of the Constitution. . . . Authority to make rules and regulations to carry out an expressed legislative purpose, or for the complete operation and enforcement of a law within designated limitations, is not an exclusively legislative power. Such authority is administrative in its nature and its use by administrative officers is essential to the complete exercise of the powers of all the departments." . . .

The difference between a delegation of legislative power and the delegation of authority to an administrative agency to carry out the expressed intent of the Legislature and the details involved has long been a difficult and important question. Increased complexity of our social order, and the multitude of details that necessarily follow, has led to a relaxation of the specific standards in the delegating statute in favor of more general ones where a specialized state agency is concerned. It is almost impossible for a legislature to prescribe all the rules and regulations necessary for a specialized agency to accomplish the legislative purpose. The delegation of authority to a specialized department under more generalized standards has been the natural trend as the need for regulation has become more evident and complex. . . . *School District No. 8 of Sherman County v. State Board of*

Education, 176 Neb. 722, 127 N.W.2d 458 (1964).

3. The courts have held that discretionary administrative powers may be delegated while legislative powers cannot. In this regard, the Supreme Court of Nebraska has said:

> The legislature cannot delegate legislative authority to an individual. It can prescribe the terms and conditions which may bring into operation a dissolution or consolidation of school districts. This is the legislative act. It then can authorize the county superintendent to determine if the facts exist which call the law into operation. *Bierman v. Campbell,* 175 Neb. 877, 124 N.W.2d 918 (1963).

An Illinois court has said that the legislature may not delegate legislative authority but it may "give an administrative body discretionary powers to decide an issue if it establishes standards under which that discretion may be exercised." *People ex rel. Community Unit School District No. 1 v. Decatur School District No. 61,* 45 Ill.App.2d 33, 194 N.E.2d 659 (1963).

4. The courts have held that the Superintendent of Public Instruction of Illinois is the head of the public school system of that state and has been vested by the General Assembly with the duty of establishing standards in education, along the lines delineated by statute. *Games v. County Board of School Trustees of McDonough County,* 13 Ill.2d 78, 147 N.E.2d 306 (1958).

5. A Massachusetts court has held that the state Commissioner of Education has the power to compel local school officials to produce information by racial census. The court said that the Commissioner had the implied authority to do in an ordinary and reasonable manner those things required for the efficient exercise of powers and satisfactory performance of duties. *School Committee of New Bedford v. Commissioner of Education,* 349 Mass. 410, 208 N.E.2d 814 (1965).

6. In a Kentucky case concerning the constitutionality of delegation of legislative power to agencies in general and county boards of education in particular, the court said:

> It has been suggested that the statute in this respect . . . is unconstitutional as being a delegation of legislative power to the several county boards of education. Such bodies may and do have conferred upon them legislative authority in a degree, for rules and regulations partake of that function. But delegation of legislative power in relation to constitutional limitations means delegation of discretion as to what the law shall be, and does not mean that the legislature may not confer discretion in the administration of the law itself . . . . Many are the instances where powers more nearly approaching the legislative prerogative than this have been vested in executive or administrative agencies and sustained as valid. This authority given the school boards is administrative and not legislative, and the act does not offend the Constitution in this regard. *Board of Education of Bath County v. Goodpaster,* 260 Ky. 198, 84 S.W.2d 55 (1935).

7. A decision by the Commissioner of Education of New York requiring school boards to furnish transportation to nonpublic school children was held not to be arbitrary even though the decision was rendered under two "somewhat inconsistent rules". *Board of Education of Cornwall Central School Dist. v. Nyquist,* 61 A.D.2d 132, 401 N.Y.S.2d 589 (1978).

■ SCHOOL OFFICERS

A school officer, as distinguished from an employee, is one who possesses a delegation of sovereign power of the state. An Indiana court[57] has defined a public office as "a position to which a portion of the sovereignty of the state attaches for the time being, and which is exercised for the benefit of the public." The most important characteristic that may be said to distinguish an office from an employment is that the duties of an office must involve an exercise of some part of the sovereignty; there are powers and duties conferred by the legislature or the constitution. The duties must be performed independently, without the control of a superior power, unless statute provides for a subordinate office. Other characteristics that typically identify the office are a permanency or continuity of office, a required oath of office, and a procedure for removal that is usually fixed by statute. In addition, employees may exercise only ministerial powers and have no authority to exercise discretionary powers.

A superintendent of a local school district is, in most states, considered an employee. A case in point is that of a local superintendent in California who was discharged by the board of education and claimed he could be discharged only by the grand jury since he was a school officer. The school code provided that the school board shall "elect" a superintendent for a four-year term. Other provisions of the code said the school board may "employ" a superintendent. The superintendent in this case asserted that the term "elect" was indicative of public office. The court, however, held that the terms "elect" and "employ" in this case meant the same thing. The court further pointed out that the position of superintendent did not exercise a sovereign power, was not created by the constitution or statute, and statutes did not impose independent police power duties upon the individual.[58]

Public officers are not allowed to hold two offices that are in conflict. Offices may be incompatible when one exercises control over the other, one office is subordinate to another, or the offices are held in more than one branch of the government at the same time. For example, a judge cannot also be a prosecuting attorney, a legislator cannot also be a school board member, and a governor cannot also be a legislator. Extending this principle further, it has been held that teachers, even though they are only employees, cannot also serve as board members in the same school district.[59]

Some state constitutions may say that a person cannot hold two lucrative offices regardless of whether one is subordinate to the other. The Indiana Constitution provides, "No person holding a lucrative office or appointment under the United States or under this State, shall be eligible to a seat in the General Assembly; nor shall any person hold more than one lucrative office at the same time, except as in this Constitution expressly prohibited . . . ."[60] Such "lucrative offices" have been held to prevent a person from serving both as a justice of the peace and a school board member, or to be sheriff while serving as a school board member.

Nearly all states have statutes that prevent public officers from having an interest in contracts made with the agencies they administer. A case illustrating a conflict of interest occurred when a board member with an interest in an insurance company wrote a policy for his own school district. The court held that this board member could be removed because he had wrongfully gained advantage through his public position.[61]

A conflict of interest may be in the form of nepotism. Nepotism can be prohibited by common law, statute, or state constitutional provision. Nepotism is defined by the courts as the "bestowal of patronage by public officers in appointing others to positions by reason of blood or marital relationship to the authority."[62] Thus, violation may occur where a school board appoints the blood kin or spouse of a board member to a position with the schools.

A public office, theoretically, is a public duty; and an officer must have the consent of the governing power before he can resign. In other words, a public office is held at the will of both parties, and the public has a right to the services of its citizens. Therefore, to be valid a resignation must be accepted. Without acceptance, the resignation is of no effect and the officer remains in office.[63] Although this is one theory of vacation of a public office, some states provide for an "absolute" right to resign.[64] In states in which the officer has an "absolute" right to resign, if he tenders a resignation, he cannot withdraw it. There is immediate unconditional acceptance. In states that follow the "public duty" theory, a resignation probably can be withdrawn prior to acceptance or prior to an effective date if resignation specifies such a date. An Illinois court has held that resignations in advance are not legal. In a case in which a mayor required board members to put resignations in writing at the time of appointment, and the mayor later accepted, the court said that such resignations were invalid as they were not contemplated by the law.[65]

Statutes provide the procedure to be used for the removal of public officers. In the absence of statute, removal is an incidental power of the appointing agency. For removal for cause, only a notice and a hearing are generally required. Cause may be malfeasance; improper or illegal performance of duties; or breach of good faith, inefficiency, and incapacity. A public officer cannot be removed during a term of office, when the term is fixed by statute, unless for cause. In a case in which school board members took "kickbacks" from a contractor for violation of competitive bid law, the court removed the board. The court held that even in the absence of statute, the board members could be punished under common law for wilful misconduct in office.[66]

Constitutional Prohibition of Nepotism Is Violated Where School Board Enters into Teaching Contract with Spouse of Board Member

— · — · — · — · —

Smith v. Dorsey

— · — · — · — · —

Supreme Court of Mississippi, 1988.
530 So. 2d 5.

EN BANC. On Petition for Rehearing
Griffin, Justice, for the Court.

In this appeal this Court is asked to construe Section 109 as applied to contracts of teachers whose spouses are school board members. Stated differently, may a local school board contract with spouses of its members?

Proceedings in the lower court were held on October 9, 1986. Testimony at trial and stipulated exhibits include documents issued to defendants by the Secretary of State certifying them as Claiborne County School Board members; contracts for employment for their spouses—Jo Anne Collins Smith, Mary Jennings, Ernestine Williams and Catherine Knox—as teachers in the Claiborne County School District, at the time defendants served as board members; the teachers' payroll records from 1980–1986; and minutes of the Claiborne County School Board from 1980–1986.

On October 10, 1986, the chancellor entered an order finding all defendants to be in violation of Section 109. He further adjudicated the defendants' spouses' contracts to be null and void, and that each defendant had an indirect interest in these contracts as he had been a Trustee of the Claiborne County Board of Education when said Board approved one or more contracts for the employment of the defendants' spouses.

Finally, the chancellor ordered claims of restitution be made against the spouses of the defendants because of the Section 109 violations. The Court found that these violations as to all defendants and their spouses had existed for several years up to and including the present date.

This appeal followed.

Article 4, Section 109 of the Mississippi Constitution of 1890 provides:

> No public officer or member of the legislature shall be interested, directly or indirectly, in any contract with the state, or any district, county, city or town thereof, authorized by any law passed or order made by any board of which he may be or may have been a member, during the term for which he shall have been chosen, or within one year after the expiration of such term.

In *Frazier, supra* [504 So.2d 675 (Miss. 1987)] at 693, we said that this section prohibits any officer from:
(a) having any direct or indirect interest in any contract
(b) with the state or any political subdivision
(c) executed during his term of office or one year thereafter, and

(d) authorized by any law, or order of any board of which he was a member.

The chancellor found that each defendant had an indirect interest in his spouse's contract as prohibited by Section 109. We would agree. . . .

However, without hesitation we find that logic dictates some manifest interest by appellants herein in the public school employment contracts of their wives. Appellants are directly responsible for the hiring and firing of their spouses. Additionally, the record indicates that these school board members share fully in the process behind which the salaries are awarded to public school teachers in their district. This is not to say that we question the integrity or fairness of these board members in any way; we simply recognize that each has an indirect interest in his wife's contract which violates the constitutional provision.

Next, we address the question of restitution ordered by the lower court and brought up on appeal.

In the trial below plaintiffs and appellees herein neither plead nor raised the question of any bad faith committed by appellants for their role in the employment of their spouses. Nor did the chancellor make any finding of such.

In our review of the record, we can see no allegation by these Claiborne County taxpayers that they did not receive value for services performed by the teachers, whose time of employment ranged from two (2) to thirty-three (33) years. Further, in at least one instance the record shows that a spouse of one board member had been teaching long before his election to that body.

We have no doubt that such circumstances involving husband and wife teams in which one teaches and the other serves as a member of the school board are commonplace across this state, with no thought to any wrongdoing by the parties involved.

The record reflects that the conduct of the defendants here had been the general practice in Claiborne County for many years, and we would concede that a similar case could be made in many other counties of the state. The claim for restitution, however, should be denied on other grounds. There is no way the parties can be put back in their original position before the teaching contracts were entered. For restitution to be equitable, there would have to be some way of restoring to the teachers the value of the services they have rendered to the schools. Obviously, this cannot be done. To require restitution under the facts of this case would place these school teachers in a position where they would have served as public school teachers without pay, and in several instances for a number of years. The equitable remedy of restitution should not be enforced in such an inequitable way.

We hold that the above premise, coupled with the fact that there is no allegation or finding of bad faith on the part of the appellants, would make it grossly inequitable to require restitution on the peculiar facts presented here. . . .

We, therefore, uphold the chancellor's order finding appellants herein have been and are in violation of Sec. 109; declaring the contracts of appellants's spouses to be null and void; and enjoining any further payment of salaries, etc. to said spouses while appellants remain as members of the Board of the Claiborne County School District and for a period of one year after the defendants shall leave their official capacities . . . .

NOTES

1. No conflict of interest exists where the husband of a public school teacher serves in the state legislature. The fact that the spouse serving in the legislature votes on general public school laws and educational appropriations does not create a constitutional conflict. *Frazier v. State By and Through Pittman*, 504 So.2d 675 (Miss. 1987).

2. A state criminal statute prohibiting "self-dealing and nepotism" is violated by a county school superintendent who nominates his wife for a central administration position. *West Virginia Education Association v. Preston County Board of Education*, ____W.Va. ____, 297 S.E. 2d 444 (1982).

SCHOOL ELECTIONS

Legal issues relating to school elections are nearly as diverse as the general election laws of a state. No attempt is made here to fully encompass this wide body of law, but it is necessary to generally examine election law with regard to reapportionment precedents and to those legal requirements pertaining to compliance with election statutes.

Until 1962, the view of the courts prevailed that legislative representation and how it was apportioned throughout a state was a matter for only the legislature to determine. Malapportionment and rotten boroughs were of grave concern to many, and the problems became more acute as population mobility left some voters with very little legislative power while others reaped disproportionately great political muscle. Judicial precedent, which permitted this to transpire, was found in *Colegrove v. Green*,[67] in which case Justice Frankfurter, writing for the Supreme Court, opted to keep the courts out of the "political thicket." Frankfurter said:

> To maintain this action would cut very deep into the very being of Congress. Courts ought not to enter this political thicket. The remedy for unfairness in distributing is to secure state legislatures that will apportion properly, or to invoke the ample powers of Congress . . . . The Constitution has left the performance of many duties in our governmental scheme to depend on the fidelity of the executive and legislative action and, ultimately, in the vigilance of the people in exercising their political rights.[68]

After this decision, it soon became clear that the problems of apportionment would not be corrected by the legislators themselves, and the people were powerless to fully exercise their political rights. In reevaluation of its position, the Supreme Court handed down a new precedent in *Baker v. Carr*[69] in 1962. In so doing, the court found that the Equal Protection Clause was violated by the resulting discrimination against some voters, which was not reasonable or rational but instead was arbitrary and capricious.

This case has had bearing on school district elections in the same manner as it has influenced statewide elections; if officials are elected by popular vote, then the Constitution assures "that each person's vote counts as much, insofar as it is practicable, as any other person's."[70]

---

*Equality of Voting Power Is Required
in Local District Elections*

––––––––––––

Hadley v. Junior College District of Metropolitan Kansas City, Mo.

––––––––––––

Supreme Court of the United States, 1970.
397 U.S. 50, 90 S.Ct. 791.

Mr. Justice BLACK delivered the opinion of the Court. This case involves the extent to which the Fourteenth Amendment and the "one man, one vote" principle apply in the election of local governmental officials. Appellants are residents and taxpayers of the Kansas City School District, one of eight separate school districts that have combined to form the Junior College District of Metropolitan Kansas City. Under Missouri law separate school districts may vote by referendum to establish a consolidated junior college district and elect six trustees to conduct and manage the necessary affairs of that district. The state law also provides that these trustees shall be apportioned among the separate school districts on the basis of "school enumeration," defined as the number of persons between the ages of six and twenty years, who reside in each district. In the case of the Kansas City School District this apportionment plan results in the election of three trustees, or 50 percent of the total number from that district. Since that district contains approximately 60 percent of the total school enumeration in the junior college district, appellants brought suit claiming that their right to vote for trustees was being unconstitutionally diluted in violation of the Equal Protection Clause of the Fourteenth Amendment. The Missouri Supreme Court upheld the trial court's dismissal of the suit, stating that the "one man, one vote" principle was not applicable in this case. . . . [F]or the reasons set forth below we reverse and hold that the Fourteenth Amendment requires that the trustees of this junior college district be apportioned in a manner that does not deprive any voter of his right to have his own vote given as much weight, as far as is practicable, as that of any other voter in the junior college district. . . .

This Court has consistently held in a long series of cases that in situations involving elections, the States are required to insure that each person's vote counts as much, insofar as it is practicable, as any other person's. We have applied this principle in congressional elections, state legislative elections, and local elections. The consistent theme of those decisions is that the right to vote in an election is protected by the United States Constitution against dilution or debasement. While the particular offices involved in these cases have varied, in each case a constant factor is the decision of the government to have citizens participate individually by ballot in the selection of certain people who carry out governmental functions. Thus in the case now before us, while the office of junior college trustee differs in certain respects from those offices considered in prior cases, it is exactly the same in the one crucial factor — these officials are elected by popular vote. . . . While there are differences in the powers of different officials, the crucial consideration is the right of each qualified voter to participate on an equal footing in the election process. It should be remembered that in cases like this one we are asked by voters to insure that they are given equal treatment, and from their perspective the harm from unequal treatment is the same in any election, regardless of the officials selected. . . .

It has also been urged that we distinguish for apportionment purposes between elections for "legislative" officials and those for "administrative" officers. Such a suggestion would leave courts with an . . . unmanageable principle since governmental activities "cannot easily be classified in the neat categories favored by civics texts," . . . and it must also be rejected. We therefore hold today that as a general rule, whenever a state or local government decides to select persons by popular election to perform governmental functions, the Equal Protection Clause of the Fourteenth Amendment requires that each qualified voter must be given an equal opportunity to participate in that election, and when members of an elected body are chosen from separate districts, each district must be established on a basis that will insure, as far as is practicable, that equal numbers of voters can vote for proportionally equal numbers of officials. . . .

Although the statutory scheme reflects to some extent a principle of equal voting power, it does so in a way that does not comport with constitutional requirements. This is so because the Act necessarily results in a systematic discrimination against voters in the more populous school districts. This discrimination occurs because whenever a large district's percentage of the total enumeration falls within a certain percentage range it is always allocated the number of trustees corresponding to the bottom of that range. Unless a particularly large district has exactly $33\frac{1}{3}$ percent, 50 percent or $66\frac{2}{3}$ percent of the total enumeration it will always have proportionally fewer trustees than the small districts. As has been pointed out, in the case of the Kansas City School District, approximately 60 percent of the total enumeration entitles that district to only 50 percent of the trustees. Thus while voters in large school districts may frequently have less effective voting power than residents of small districts, they can never have more. Such built-in discrimination against voters in large districts cannot be sustained as a sufficient compliance with the constitutional mandate that each person's vote count as much as another's, as far as practicable. . . . We have said before that mathematical exactitude is not required . . . but a plan that does not automatically discriminate in favor of certain districts is.

In holding that the guarantee of equal voting strength for each voter applies in all elections of governmental officials, we do not feel that the States will be inhibited in finding ways to insure that legitimate political goals of representation are achieved. We have previously upheld against constitutional challenge an election scheme that required that candidates be residents of certain districts that did not contain equal numbers of people. . . . Since all the officials in that case were elected at large, the right of each voter was given equal treatment. We have also held that where a State chooses to select members of an official body by appointment rather than election, and that choice does not itself offend the Constitution, the fact that each official does not "represent" the same number of people does not deny those people equal protection of the laws. . . . And a State may, in certain cases, limit the right to vote to a particular group or class of people. . . . But once a State has decided to use the process of popular election and "once the class of voters is chosen and their qualifications specified, we see no constitutional way by which equality of voting power may be evaded." . . .

NOTES

1. A statute limiting the franchise in school elections to parents of children enrolled in the public schools and owners and leasees of taxable real property denies equal protection. *Kramer v. Union Free School District No. 15*, 395 U.S. 621, 89 S.Ct. 1886 (1969).

   Similarly, the Supreme Court has held unconstitutional a statute that limited electors in a public utility bond election to only "property taxpayers." *Cipriano v. City of Houma*, 395 U.S. 701, 89 S.Ct. 1897 (1969).

2. The Civil Rights Acts of 1957 and 1960 protect voters in federal elections from intimidation and interference and requires State election officials to preserve federal election records. 42 U.S.C.A. §§ 1971(b), 1974–1974 (b). Also, state laws requiring literacy to vote cannot be ambiguous and vague violating the Fifteenth Amendment. *Smith v.*

Allwright, 321 U.S. 649, 64 S.Ct. 757 (1944).

3. The one-person, one-vote standard is not applicable to appointive boards. *Sailors v. Board of Education of Kent County*, 387 U.S. 105, 87 S. Ct. 1549 (1967).

4. Where there is no fraud, bad faith, or misleading of the voters, it is a well-settled rule that statutory provisions that are treated as mandatory before an election will be construed as directory after the election. *Lindahl v. Independent School District No. 306*, 270 Minn. 164, 133 N.W.2d 23 (1965).

5. A Minnesota court, in *Bakken v. Schroeder*, 269 Minn. 381, 130 N.W.2d 579 (1964), stated that challenges to consolidation proceedings will not serve to invalidate the election unless there is proof of prejudice and that statutory requirements are treated as directory rather than mandatory when election proceedings are contested following the election. In a case involving a challenge, the court quoted an earlier decision, *Erickson v. Sammons*, 242 Minn. 345, 65 N.W.2d 198 (1954), and said:

   It is the general rule that, before an election is held, statutory provisions regulating the conduct of the election will usually be treated as mandatory and their observance may be insisted upon and enforced. After an election has been held, the statutory regulations are generally construed as directory and such rule of construction is in accord with the policy of this state, which from its beginning has been that, in the absence of fraud or bad faith or constitutional violation, an election which has resulted in a fair and free expression of the will of the legal voters upon the merits will not be invalidated because of a departure from the statutory regulations governing the conduct of the election except in those cases where the legislature has clearly and unequivocally expressed an intent that a specific statutory provision is an essential jurisdictional prerequisite and that a departure therefrom shall have the drastic consequence of invalidity. . . .

6. Where a statute requires a resolution by the board of education for the initiation of a bond election the courts have held that the

resolution need not be formal, "Be it resolved," nor need it even be in writing. The statute is fulfilled by any official action by the board. *Lindahl v. Independent School District No. 306,* 270 Minn. 164, 133 N.W.2d 23 (1965).

7. The Supreme Court of Texas, in *McKinney v. O'Conner,* 26 Tex. 5 (1861), has stated the rule for elections as

> rules prescribing the manner in which the qualified electors shall hold the election, at the time and place designated, and those prescribing the manner in which their act, when done, shall be authenticated, so as to import verity on its face, are directory. Irregularities in their observance will not vitiate an election, unless they be such that the true result of the ballot cannot be arrived at with reasonable certainty. The ultimate test of the validity of an election is involved in the questions: *Did the qualified electors, at the time and place designated, acting in concert, either actively or by acquiescence, hold an election and cast their votes in the ballot box; and has it been done in a manner sufficiently conformable to the directions of the law, as that the true* result can be arrived at with reasonable certainty? (Emphasis supplied.)

8. Judicial reluctance to overthrow an election was illustrated in *Stafford v. Stegle,* 271 S.W.2d 833 (Tex.Civ.App.1954), wherein the court said:

> While those charged with conducting elections would use every precaution possible to see that elections are conducted strictly in accordance with the provisions of the Election Code, nevertheless, after an election has been held and it appears that it has been fairly conducted and the result correctly declared and there [are] no charges of fraud, misconduct or illegality, the entire election will not be set aside for irregularities in the manner of conducting the election, unless the statutes governing such matters state that the election must be vitiated.

9. In a case contending a lack of sufficiency of notice for a special election, a Missouri court said that: "Generally, statutory provisions as to notice of special elections are mandatory, must be strictly followed, the failure to properly call a special election will invalidate it. . . . A special election, however, will not be vitiated by failure to comply strictly with the statutory requirements with respect to the giving of notice where the electors were in fact informed of the time, place, and purpose of the election and generally voted on the question submitted; where it is not shown that the electors did not participate in the election because of lack of notice or knowledge or that a different result would have obtained if the full statutory notice had been given. *State v. Whittle,* 401 S.W.2d 401 (Mo.1966).

■ SCHOOL BOARD MEETINGS

A fundamental rule of school board meetings is that the meeting must be held within the geographic boundaries of the school district. A Missouri court has explained the reasons for this requirement in this manner:

> [I]t is obvious that considerations of public policy demand that the official meetings of public bodies be held within the limits of their territorial jurisdictions; otherwise, public servants might do in secret that which they would not attempt to do under public scrutiny, and thereby much injury might be done the public welfare . . . . . It would be just as proper for the state legislature to hold its sessions outside the state or for a county court to transact business in another county . . . . .

The courts have traditionally been rather lenient concerning the procedure used by boards of education in meetings. Unless the rules of procedure are prescribed by statute, a board of education may establish its own rules of procedure. Where neither statutes nor adopted board procedures are used, the generally accepted rules of parliamentary procedure will control. As indicated, the courts are indulgent concerning procedure and will not insist on a specific set of rules. The court is primarily concerned that every board member has been given a right to be heard and to vote.

The actual board meeting is an important prerequisite to an action by a board of education. Action taken separately or individually, by board members outside a board meeting, has no validity. Likewise, promises made by individual board members outside official meetings have no legal validity. However, a board of education, if it chooses, may ratify a previous individual commitment made by a board member. Official action at a later meeting is necessary for ratification.

Allegation that Board Had Made Decision Prior to Official Meeting Not Sustained by Facts

— — — — — — — —

Aldridge v. School District of North Platte

— — — — — — — —

Supreme Court of Nebraska, 1987.
225 Neb. 580, 407 N.W. 2d 495.

WHITE, Justice. Gary R. Aldridge appeals from an order of the district court for Lincoln County, Nebraska, granting summary judgment in favor of the appellees, the school district of North Platte and six members of its board of education.   . . .

The petition in this case attacked decisions made by the board in regard to the employment status of the superintendent of schools. On August 31, 1984, the superintendent was found guilty of third degree sexual assault. The board called a meeting on September 5, 1984, a week before the next scheduled meeting. The meeting was largely attended, and when the matter concerning the superintendent's conviction arose, board member Linda L. Gale requested that there be no discussion on the subject. Dallas F. Darland, a board member, announced that he had been tendered a resignation by the superintendent and read aloud the letter, which stated that the superintendent would resign voluntarily in December. Darland moved to accept the offer

to resign; the motion was seconded and passed. Board member Myra Satterfield then made a motion to suspend the superintendent from his duties with pay until his resignation was effective. The motion also was seconded and passed. There was no discussion of these motions except for the reading of the letter and the making of the motions.

Aldridge's petition alleges two causes of action: first, that a quorum of the board met with the attorney for the school district and discussed and made policy in violation of the public meetings law; and second, that the motion by Satterfield to suspend the superintendent with pay passed without public discussion based on the prior nonpublic briefing and meeting alleged in the first count.

In his deposition Aldridge stated he based his allegations that the public meetings law was violated on two facts: that a major motion passed without discussion and that a witness saw a quorum (four of six) of the board members at the school board attorney's office earlier in the day of the September 5 meeting. The witness, Kathy Seacrest, testified on deposition that she saw four board members in the "entryway" of the attorney's office and that two of them were leaving as she left. She heard no discussion or comments made by the members.

A reading of the depositions of the board members exposes no discrepancies in their stories. The four members met with the attorney to discuss the legal ramifications of various options to remove the superintendent from office. Each feared a long legal battle and was informed that the superintendent had due process and contractual rights in his employment. Each was aware that certain of the benefits would vest in December and that the superintendent knew this. They specifically denied that a quorum ever met to decide policy and testified that they left the office having made no decision in the matter.   . . .

At oral argument counsel for Aldridge argued that Gale's statement limiting discussion on the issue was a violation of the public meetings law. The petition shows two causes of action: that an illegal meeting of a quorum of the board took place prior to the public meeting and that, without public discussion, the board passed a motion based on the previous illegal deliberations. The petition does not maintain that public discussion may not be limited or prohibited by the board at its meetings. See Neb.Rev.Stat. § 84–1412(2) (Cum.Supp. 1984). . . .

Appellant's counsel conceded at argument that the attorney for the board could advise members two at a time without violating the public meetings law. However, he still argues that the lack of discussion at the meeting implies that the real decision was made illegally prior to the meeting.

The appellant based his case on Seacrest's statements that she saw four board members in the attorney's office. She corroborated their statements that two were leaving as two were waiting. Obviously, no meeting of the board members in which a quorum was present occurred. . . .

The appellees' testimony establishes that no improper meeting occurred. The appellant then had the burden to introduce evidence in opposition to the motion for summary judgment that would tend to prove that a meeting did occur. . . . He could not produce such evidence. Since no issue of fact existed, the motion for summary judgment was properly granted in favor of the appellees.

Affirmed.

NOTES

1. A teacher's association can videotape proceedings of a school board meeting. A court in New Jersey, in upholding videotaping of a board meeting, reasoned that video cameras and recorders are so commonplace today that one would have great difficulty showing that their use would in some manner impede the deliberations or harm the public interest. On the school board's behalf, the court did say that the videotaping equipment could not be used in such a manner as to disrupt the meeting. The court, though, was not sympathetic with school board members who wanted to ban the cameras merely because the cameras' presence made the members feel uncomfortable or inhibited. *Maurice River Board of*

Education v. Maurice River Tp. Teachers Ass'n, 193 N.J.Super. 488, 475 A.2d 59 (App.Div. 1984). See also: *Sony Corp. of America v. Universal City Studios, Inc.,* 464 U.S. 417, 104 S.Ct. 774 (1984).

2. *Procedure.* As pointed out earlier, courts are rather flexible as to the procedure used by local school boards.

   In 1960, a New Hampshire court upheld action by a school board when there was considerable irregularity in parliamentary procedure. The court said that a board's action could not be voided so long as no statutes were violated. If the machinery of government were not allowed a little play in its joints it would not work. *Lamb v. Danville School Board,* 102 N.H. 569, 162 A.2d 614 (1960).

   However, the courts will not go too far in upholding flimsy procedure. In a Missouri case, two board members, without notifying a third, got together informally at home and decided to call a special school election. No minutes were kept. The court said that school elections called as a result of the meeting were invalid. The board meeting was not a legal one: "While there is no question but that the motives of the (board members) . . . were of the highest, we think their manner of getting together had no more dignity than any ordinary fence-row conference."

3. *Executive Sessions.* Executive sessions, where the board retires to privacy, may be used for discussion, but not for action. Where a board met in open session, adjourned for an hour or so, reconvened in executive session, and then met again in open session, and teachers' contracts were terminated in the open session after discussion in the executive session, the teachers sued, questioning the validity of the action. The court said the meeting was a legal one, despite the fact that the contracts were discussed in the executive session. The requirements of the law were met when the official action of the board was taken in open session. *Alva v. Sequoia Union High School District,* 98 Cal.App.2d 656, 220 P.2d 788 (1950); *Dryden v. Marcellus Community Schools,* 401 Mich. 76, 257 N.W.2d 79 (1977).

In a later case, in Illinois, the board of education voted in an executive session to condemn land. The action was challenged and the court held that the action in the executive session was "not an effective exercise of the power of the board to commence condemnation." However, since the board had later ratified the action in an official meeting, the condemnation proceedings were legal. *Goldman v. Moore,* 35 Ill.2d 450, 220 N.E.2d 466 (1966).*State ex rel. Stewart v. Consolidated School District,* 281 S.W.2d 511 (Mo.App. 1955).

Boards of education should adopt rules of procedure. However, when they do, they are bound by their own rules. In an early Kentucky case, illustrating the binding force of a board rule, a board made a rule that purchases of supplies and materials of $500 or less could be made without bid. Pianos were purchased in an amount of $2,500 without bids. The membership of the board changed and the new board refused to pay for the pianos. The vendor sued. The action of the vendor was unsuccessful. The court held that the school board rules had the force of law upon the board itself, which the board could not disregard. *Montenegro-Riehm Music Co. v. Board of Education of Louisville,* 147 Ky. 720, 145 S.W. 740 (1912).

An Ohio school board passed a rule that provided that bus drivers involved in five accidents causing police investigation shall be dismissed. A bus driver arrived home from a vacation trip at three in the morning, arose four hours later to drive a school bus. The bus left the road and struck an embankment seventeen feet from the highway. No one was injured. The board dismissed the driver and the driver sued. The court held for the driver saying that the rule of five accidents of the board was "unfortunate." Since there was evidence of only one accident and even though the discharge of the driver was desirable, the board could not discharge him because of its own regulation. *State ex rel. Edmundson v. Board of Education,* 2 Ohio Misc. 137, 201 N.E.2d 729 (Com.Pl.1964).

4. *Quorum.* A quorum under common law is a simple majority of the total membership. In the absence of statute, the common law rule will be applied. *Gunnip v. Lautenklos,* 33 Del. 415, 94 A.2d 712 (1953). See also: *Matawan Regional Teachers Association v. Matawan-Aberdeen Regional Board of Education,* 223 N.J. Super. 504, 538 A.2d 1331 (1988).

A Kentucky court has held that where there was one vacancy on a five-member board the four remaining members represented a quorum. *Trustees v. Brooks,* 163 Ky. 200, 173 S.W. 305 (1915). The number required for a quorum is not reduced by a reduction in the membership due to vacancies. This means that in the case of a five-member board, which has three vacancies, the two remaining board members cannot take action.

5. *Voting.* Boards, in the absence of statute, may establish voting procedures (voice vote, show of hands, secret ballot). There is no authority for a board member to allow someone else to vote for him.

When a board member refuses to vote, the general rule is that this vote is considered as an assent to the will of the majority. *Mullins v. Eveland,* 234 S.W.2d 639 (Mo.App.1950). In a Tennessee case, in which a board of seven members considered a motion to execute a contract, three voted in favor, two opposed, and two did not vote. The court said the motion carried by a vote of five to two. Those not voting were considered as assenting to the majority. *Collins v. Janey,* 147 Tenn. 477, 249 S.W. 801 (1923).

Common law does not require that individual votes be recorded in the board minutes so long as the totals are made a part of the record. *Diefenderfer v. Budd,* 563 P.2d 1355 (Wyo.1977).

6. *Minutes and Records.* Courts hold that the school boards can act only through their minutes. The minutes of a board member are the only legal evidence of what has transpired during the meeting. An Illinois court has said that: "Proper minutes and records should be kept by a board of education to the end that the persons who are carrying the tax load may make refer-

ence thereto and the future boards may be advised of the manner of disposition of questions that have arisen." *Hankenson v. Board of Education,* 10 Ill.App.2d 79, 134 N.E.2d 356 (1956). *Reversed* on different issue, 10 Ill. 2d 560, 141 N.E. 2d 5, (1957).

A board secretary may record minutes after the meeting has adjourned. *Kent v. School District,* 106 Okl. 30, 233 P. 431 (1925).

Memoranda kept by the board secretary cannot be examined by the public prior to transcribing the minutes. In a 1954 case, on the day after a board meeting, citizens requested permission to examine the minutes. The school board secretary had not as yet transcribed his notes and refused permission to the group. The court upheld the board and said "the clerk's untranscribed notes reasonably are not classifiable as a public writing . . . whereas the transcribed minutes, in final form, but awaiting only approval and placement in the journal, are a public writing . . . ." *Conover v. Board of Education,* 1 Utah 2d 375, 267 P.2d 768 (1954).

The form and wordage used in school board minutes are looked upon with indulgence by the court. "Although they may be unskillfully drawn, if by fair and reasonable interpretation their meaning can be ascertained, they will be sufficient to answer the requirements of law." *Noxubee County v. Long,* 141 Miss. 72, 106 So. 83 (1925).

A public records law may require that names of applicants screened for a superintendent's position be released to the press. *Attorney General v. School Committee of Northampton,* 375 Mass. 127, 375 N.E.2d 1188 (1978).

7. *Notice of Meetings.* In order for a board meeting to be legal, proper notice must be given and all members must be notified in time to be given an opportunity to participate. A reasonable time in advance of a meeting for notice to be given is "sufficient time to the party notified for preparation and attendance at the time and place of such meeting." *Green v. Jones,* 144 W.Va. 276, 108 S.E.2d 1 (1959).

When a board meeting was called with a few minutes' notice, the chairman was unable to attend, and the board employed a teacher, the court held the employment invalid. "(The chairman) was hardly bound to quit the work he had started to do and rush over to attend a suddenly called meeting of the board. The notice should have given him reasonable opportunity to attend. It did not." *Wood v. School District,* 137 Minn. 138, 162 N.W. 1081 (1917).

Notice should include the time and the place of the meeting. Members should be notified of any changes.

When a meeting is held without notice, and all members are present and consent to act, the requirement of notice is waived.

Notice is not required for regular board meetings because members have constructive notice. For example, boards usually establish a regular meeting date each month for which special notice is not required. Notice is only required for special board meetings.

8. *Bylaws.* In the absence of statute to the contrary, a board's bylaws are binding on the board. School boards cannot set aside or render nugatory a bylaw by suspension of a mere rule of order for the convenience of transacting business.

A bylaw must be changed using appropriate procedures, with notice, and following proper regulatory processes. See: *Matawan Regional Teachers Association v. Matawan-Aberdeen Regional School District Board of Education,* 223 N.J. Super. 504, 538 A. 2d 1331 (App.Div.1988).

■ OPEN MEETINGS AND PUBLIC RECORDS LAWS

In recent years, state legislatures have sought to make public board meetings more open and public records more accessible to the public. Even though there has always been a general common-law right of the citizenry to be informed through openness of public meetings and public records, actual implementation of the ideal often fell short of the mark. Technicalities regarding when meetings were open, the justification for executive sessions, notice, and the logistics of access to public records have presented problems that legislatures have attempted to resolve by enactment of statutes specifically governing meetings and records. As a result of this legislation, much new litigation has transpired that endeavors to interpret the meaning of the statutes.

The most important difference between the traditional common law covering public meetings and the new statutes is that public school boards could adjourn to executive session to discuss virtually any matter bearing on operation of the schools, while the new laws narrowly define the purposes and procedures for the conduct of closed or executive sessions. Most sunshine laws require both deliberations and actions to be taken in public; the exception being only for a limited number of sensitive matters that would, if aired in public, be personally detrimental to some party or would harm the public interest. The underlying purpose of both open meeting and public records laws is to display to the public marketplace and subject to public appraisal the truth about official acts of public servants.[71]

School Committee's Closed-Session Discussion and Approval of Drug Search Was Exempt from Open-Meetings Law

—·—·—·—·—·—

Rhode Island Affiliate, American Civil Liberties Union, Inc. v. Bernasconi

—·—·—·—·—·—

Supreme Court of Rhode Island, 1989.
557 A. 2d 1232.

FAY, Chief Justice. This case comes before us on appeal from a Superior Court order granting the defendants' motion to dismiss pursuant to Rule 12(b)(6) of the Superior Court Rules of Civil Procedure. The plaintiffs, Rhode Island Affiliate, American Civil Liberties Union (ACLU) and Steven Brown, Executive Director, contend that the trial justice erred in granting that motion. . . .

On January 26 and February 12, 1987, the Chariho school committee (school committee), held regularly scheduled public meetings. During the meetings, the school committee voted unanimously to enter into closed executive session pursuant to G.L. 1956 (1984 Reenactment) § 42–46–5(a)(1) and (2). These provisions allow a public body to hold a closed meeting, in limited circumstances, following an affirmative vote of the majority of its members.

On April 8, 1987, plaintiffs filed an action to impose civil fines against defendants, in their individual capacities and in their capacities as members of the school committee, for violations of the Rhode Island Open Meetings Law. Chapter 46 of title 42. The plaintiffs alleged, on information and belief, that the school committee discussed and approved a plan to search student lockers at the Chariho Regional Junior–Senior High School. Thereafter, state and local police conducted a search of approximately 800 lockers at the school. The plaintiffs maintained that these closed sessions of the school committee violated multiple provisions of the open-meetings law. . . .

. . . [P]laintiffs aver that the school committee's closed-session discussion and approval of a drug search is not a matter exempted from the requirement that meetings of a public body remain open to the public. Assuming, as required, that all allegations in the complaint are true, we find that the topic of a drug search falls within the statutory guidelines enunciated in §§ 42–46–4 and 42–46–5. This topic clearly implicates security matters as contemplated by § 42–46–5(a)(3). Additionally, these closed sessions may involve or lead to investigative proceedings concerning allegations of civil or criminal misconduct. *See* § 42–46–5(a)(4). We believe that the sale and use of drugs in a school system represents a serious threat to the security, health, and welfare of a student body. It would be inconceivable for this court to find that the topic is not a legitimate concern for a closed session. Therefore, we hold that the discussion and approval of a drug search is exempted by §§ 42–46–4 and 42–46–5. . . .

The plaintiffs further argue that the school committee violated § 42–46–6(b), as amended by P.L.1984, ch. 372, § 1, which requires notice of agenda topics. In the present case, defendants did not include the matter of the drug search on the agenda for the January and/or February meetings. We may infer, however, that defendants provided adequate notice of the meetings pursuant to § 42–46–6(a) and (c). We note that any announcement of this subject matter would be self-defeating and hold that defendants' action does not operate to their detriment. . . .

For the reasons stated, the plaintiffs' appeal is denied and dismissed. The judgment appealed from is affirmed, and the case is remanded to the Superior Court for further proceedings consistent with this opinion.

NOTES

1. *Open Meetings.* The gathering of school board members on occasion at various restaurants, sometimes before and sometimes after official board meetings, did not violate the Oregon Open Meetings Law even though, at times, a quorum was present. The court held that there was not a "convening of the body" of the board for the purpose of making "a decision or to deliberate toward a decision." *Harris v. Nordquist,* 96 Or. App. 19, 771 P. 2d 637 (1989).

Where a quorum of school board members attended a meeting of another school board in an adjacent town where the topic discussed was possible merger, the court ruled that the open meetings law was not violated because the board members were not "meeting for the purpose of exercising the school board's responsibilities, power or duties." *Paulton v. Volkmann,* 141 Wis. 2d 370, 415 N.W. 2d 528 (App. 1987).

A Wisconsin court has held that failure to announce with specificity the reason for going into closed session did not violate the state's open-meetings law. *State v. Van Lare,* 125 Wis. 2d 40, 370 N.W. 2d 271 (App. 1985).

The Open Meetings Act of Illinois has been held not to require notice in the school board agenda of topics to be considered in closed session. In so holding, the court expanded on the rationale for openness of public boards as that which provides the greatest "public advantage."

> While we keep in mind that the purpose of the Act is to promote the openness of public business, we must not overlook the larger, overriding purpose of the Act within which the promotion of openness is subsumed and made a constituent part—aiding the conduct of the people's business, or, in other words, securing public advantage. (*People ex rel. Hopf v. Barger* (1975), 30 Ill.App.3d 525, 332 N.E.2d 649.) In promoting the ultimate goal of requiring public bodies to carry out their business in the manner most beneficial to the public they represent, there are occasions on which it is not to the public's advantage that a public body carry on its business in a meeting open to the public. Therefore, it is not always possible for both of the above stated purposes of the Act to be promoted in harmony. It is our belief that where the purposes of the Act cannot be promoted in harmony, priority should be given to the more dominant or overriding purpose.
>
> This is particularly true in the instant case where the purpose of promoting openness is not separate and distinct from the overriding purpose of promoting the ultimate goal of public advantage. Openness is in most circumstances an element fundamental in furthering public advantage; however, in some instances openness simply prevents or defeats public advantage.
>
> For example, consideration of topics concerning matters such as personal information, bargaining position and negotiating strategy makes it necessary that a public body meet in private, lest it run the risk that the business undertakings will be rendered, for all practical purposes, ineffective and meaningless. Public knowledge of their officials' intentions and actions resulting from compulsory public deliberative sessions when considering matters such as the purchase of real estate would destroy any advantage to be gained from negotiation and work a severe detriment upon the

officers and the public they represent. (*Collinsville Community Unit School District Number 10 v. Witte* (1972), 5 Ill.App. 3d 600, 603, 283 N.E.2d 718, 720–21.) Likewise, forcing public officers to discuss sensitive issues in meetings open to the public may result in these topics being intentionally overlooked, at the public's expense. Premised by a familiarity with the common use of discretion which results in many sensitive issues being better left alone, especially when the audience is large and confidence is wanting, consider the negative effects resulting from open discussion of personal problems that might impede upon the work place of a public office, such as alcohol abuse, tardiness, poor hygiene or cigarette smoking. While these problems might be resolved if the appropriate public body were able to discuss the matter freely, it is unlikely that this will occur when such matters cannot be discussed in confidence. As a result, work quality continues to wane, at the public's expense.

Gosnell v. Hogan, 179 Ill.App.3d 161, 128 Ill. Dec. 252, 534 N.E. 2d 434 (5 Dist. 1989).

Citizen May Review Teacher's Personnel File under Authority of State Public Record Law

— · — · — · — · —

Hovet v. Hebron Public School District

— · — · — · — · —

Supreme Court of North Dakota, 1988. 419 N.W.2d 189.

VANDE WALLE, Justice. Meredith Hovet appealed from a judgment of dismissal declaring his personnel file to be a public record open for inspection by the public under the provisions of Sections 44–04–18 and 15–29–10, N.D.C.C., and Article XI, Section 6, of the North Dakota Constitution. We affirm.

Hovet was employed by the Hebron Public School District (School District) as a teacher of business education and physical education during the 1986–1987 school year and had been so employed for the previous three school years. During the course of this employment a personnel file was maintained by the School District.

By a letter dated May 21, 1987, Madonna Tibor requested that the School District allow her to review Hovet's personnel file. Subsequently the superintendent for the School District agreed to provide a review of Hovet's personnel file on June 2, 1987.

Hovet then filed a complaint seeking a permanent injunction enjoining the School District from allowing the review of his personnel file by anyone other than a legal representative of the School District. At this time Hovet also sought a temporary restraining order prohibiting the review. A hearing was held and a temporary restraining order was granted. . . .

Hovet and the School District each argued that the personnel file was confidential. Tibor argued that the personnel file was a public record open to inspection. Thereafter the trial court determined that Hovet's personnel file was a public record open for inspection under Section 44–04–18 and 15–29–10, N.D.C.C., and Article XI, Section 6, of the North Dakota Constitution. The trial court issued a judgment of dismissal. It is from this judgment that Hovet appealed. We note that the School District has aligned itself with Hovet and against Tibor on appeal.

Hovet and the School District concede that the personnel file is a governmental record, but argue that it is a record not open to public inspection because certain statutes protect a teacher's personnel file from inspection under the open-records law. The concession that the personnel file is a governmental record is based upon this court's decisions . . . .

Open governmental records in North Dakota are required by our Constitution and our statutes. Article XI, Section 6, of the North Dakota Constitution provides:

> Unless otherwise provided by law, all records of public or governmental bodies, boards, bureaus, commissions, or agencies of the state or any political subdivision of the state,

or organizations or agencies supported in whole or in part by public funds, or expending public funds, shall be public records, open and accessible for inspection during reasonable office hours."

Section 44–04–18, N.D.C.C., tracks and implements Article XI, Section 6. It provides:

1. Except as otherwise specifically provided by law, all records of public or governmental bodies, boards, bureaus, commissions or agencies of the state or any political subdivision of the state, or organizations or agencies supported in whole or in part by public funds, or expending public funds, shall be public records, open and accessible for inspection during reasonable office hours.
2. Violations of this section shall be punishable as an infraction.

The first argument of Hovet and the School District is that Section 15–47–38, N.D.C.C., provides an implied exception to the open-records law. Section 15–47–38 specifies the procedures to be utilized when a school board discharges a teacher or decides to not renew a teacher's contract. Among these procedures are the following: For a nonrenewal decision the reasons for nonrenewal must be drawn from specific and documented findings arising from formal reviews conducted by the board with respect to the teacher's overall performance; that such proceedings must be held in an executive session unless both parties agree to open them to the public; that no action for libel or slander shall lie for statements expressed orally or in writing at the executive sessions. Hovet and the School District argue that these procedures are designed to facilitate openness in the proceedings and to protect the teacher's reputation. They reason that opening to the public a teacher's personnel file—which would be reviewed at these proceedings—harms the above-stated goals. Thus, they conclude, an exception for teachers' personnel files from the open-records law must be implied.

This argument, however, ignores the language of the open-records law. Section 44–04–18(1), N.D.C.C., provides that all gov-

ernmental records are open to the public "Except as otherwise *specifically* provided by law, ..." [Emphasis added.] Our Code provides that "Words used in any statute are to be understood in their ordinary sense, unless a contrary intention plainly appears, ..." The word "specific" usually is defined to mean "Explicitly set forth; particular, definite." . . . This definition is opposite to the meaning of "implied," which is defined to mean "suggested, involved, or understood although not clearly or openly expressed." . . . Thus, because the open-records law provides that governmental records are to be open to the public "Except as otherwise specifically provided by law," an exception to the open-records law may not be implied. In order that a record may be excepted from the open-records law the Legislature must specifically address the status of that type of record—e.g., statements that a certain type of record is confidential or that it is not open to the public. . . .

Thus, for an exception to the open-records law to exist under our constitutional and statutory provisions, it must be specific, i.e., the Legislature must directly address the status of the record in question, for a specific exception, by the plain terms of those provisions, may not be implied. Therefore, the contention that an exception to the open-records law for teacher personnel files should be implied from Section 15–47–38, N.D.C.C., must fail.

Hovet next alleges that he has a right to privacy guaranteed to him by the United States Constitution and the North Dakota Constitution, which will be violated if the public is allowed to inspect his personnel file. Teachers, like students, do not "shed their constitutional rights . . . at the schoolhouse gate." *Tinker v. Des Moines Community School Dist.*, ... But we rejected the claim that a governmental employee's personnel file is protected by a constitutional right to privacy in *City of Grand Forks v. Grand Forks Herald*, ... Our position has not changed.

In *Grand Forks Herald* we decided that personnel records are not protected by the right to privacy arising under the Federal Constitution because personnel records do not concern a subject to which the Federal right to privacy has been recognized as applying. As we noted, the Federal right to privacy is limited to "cases involving governmental intrusions into matters relating to marriage, procreation, contraception, family relationships, child rearing, and education." . . .

In *Grand Forks Herald* we also refused to find that a governmental employee's personnel record was protected by a right to privacy arising from the North Dakota Constitution. We noted that there is no explicit right to privacy under our Constitution, and we declined to consider whether such a right to privacy could be inferred under our Constitution. Even if a right to privacy existed under our Constitution, there would be no right of privacy "in a personnel record of a person employed by a public agency, ..." 307 N.W.2d at 580. [VandeWalle, J., concurring specially.] A teacher's personnel file has not been shown to be different from the personnel files of other governmental employees. Therefore, we reject Hovet's argument.

In arguing that a teacher's personnel file is protected by a right to privacy Hovet has referred us to the case of *Trahan v. Larivee*, 365 So.2d 294 (La.App.1978). In *Trahan* the court refused to allow public inspection of the evaluation reports of city directors even though it concluded that those reports were public records under the Louisiana public records law because to do so would be an impermissible invasion of privacy under the Louisiana Constitution. However, *Trahan* is readily distinguishable in that the Louisiana Constitution has an express guarantee of the right to privacy at Article I, Section 5, Louisiana Constitution. Therefore, we decline to follow *Trahan*.

Hovet next contends that school students have a right to privacy which will be violated if a teacher's personnel file is open to public inspection. In making this argument Hovet notes that names of students may be placed in a teacher's personnel file in notations concerning the teacher.

Considering what we stated in the previous section about the right to privacy under the Federal and State Constitutions, we decline to consider this issue. Even if a student

had a privacy interest in this case, to consider this issue would violate the general rule that "A litigant may assert only his own constitutional rights, unless he can present 'weighty countervailing policies.' " . . . Hovet has not raised sufficiently "weighty countervailing policies" for us to depart from the general rule.

We recognize that Hovet and the School District have raised some strong public-policy arguments for the exception of teacher personnel records from the open-records law. However, as the trial court noted, "such policy considerations are for the legislature and the courts must apply the law as it exists."
. . .

The judgment is affirmed. . . .

NOTES

1. *Public Records.* Florida statute defines public records as

> all documents, papers, letters, maps, books, tapes, photographs, films, sound recordings or other material, regardless of physical form or characteristics, made or received pursuant to law or ordinance or in connection with the transaction of official business by any agency. Section 119.011 (1), West's Florida Statutes Annotated.

In holding that the transcript of a dismissal proceeding, held by a school board to determine the fitness of a school administrator, must be released on request of a newspaper, the Supreme Court of Iowa said that, as a method of public policy; "Disclosure is favored over non-disclosure, and exemptions from disclosure are to be strictly construed and granted sparingly." *Board of Directors of Davenport Community School District v. Quad City Times*, 382 N.W. 2d 80 (Iowa 1986).

2. Where a public records statute provided that "records of any executive session may remain secret as long as publication may defeat purposes of the executive session, but no longer," the court held that closed-session minutes of a hearing charging sexual harrassment of an employee must be

released on request to the newspaper after the employee had resigned. The court said:

> The lawful purposes of the executive sessions called by the school committee were to discuss the litigation that the school committees was engaged with the director. By the time this case was filed, the director had resigned, and the litigation was terminated. Thus, the lawful purposes, . . . for which the executive sessions were held were no longer extant.

One is likely to be perplexed with this result because the minutes may have continuing harmful effects on the employee. In this case, however, the trial judge concluded that the purpose of the executive session was not to discuss or preserve the employee's reputation, but rather to consider complaints or charges brought against the employee. *Foudy v. Amherst-Pelham Regional School Committee,* 402 Mass. 179, 521 N.E. 2d 391 (1988).

3. A request was made to review a teacher's personnel file, in particular the college transcript of the teacher. The court ruled that the Family Educational Rights and Privacy Act did not protect the transcript. Also the teacher's right to privacy under the federal Constitution was rejected, and the Texas open-records law required disclosure of the transcript. *Klein Independent School District v. Mattox,* 830 F.2d 576 (5th Cir. 1987).

ENDNOTES

1. State Tax Commission v. Board of Education of Jefferson County, 235 Ala. 388, 179 So. 197 (1938).

2. Board of Education v. Stoddard, 294 N.Y. 667, 60 N.E.2d 757 (1945).

3. Moore v. Board of Education, 212 N.C. 499, 193 S.E. 732 (1937).

4. Child Welfare Society of Flint v. Kennedy School District, 220 Mich. 290, 189 N.W. 1002 (1922).

5. Board of Education of Aberdeen-Huntington Local School District v. State Board of Education, 116 Ohio App. 515, 189 N.E.2d 81 (1962).

6. Campbell v. Aldrich, 159 Or. 208, 79 P.2d 257 (1938), appeal dismissed 305 U.S. 559, 59 S.Ct. 87 (1938).

7. Leeper v. State, 103 Tenn. 500, 53 S.W. 962 (1899).

8. Hannibal and St. J. Railroad Co. v. Husen, 95 U.S. (5 Otto) 465 (1877).

9. People v. Draper, 15 N.Y. 532 (1857).

10. See Newton Edwards, *The Courts and the Public Schools* (University of Chicago Press, 1955), p. 27; also, Commonwealth v. Hartman, 17 Pa. 118 (1851); Moseley v. Welch, 209 S.C. 19, 39 S.E.2d 133 (1946); Board of Education of Chicago v. Upham, 357 Ill. 263, 191 N.E. 876 (1934); Board of Education v. State Board of Education, 116 Ohio App. 515, 189 N.E.2d 81 (1962); Associated Schools of Independent District No. 63 v. School District No. 83 of Renville County, 122 Minn. 254, 142 N.W. 325 (1913).

11. Edwards, *The Courts and the Public Schools,* p. 28.

12. See Helena Elementary School District No. 1. v. State, 236 Mont. 44, 769 P. 2d 684 (1989); Rose v. Council for Better Education, Inc., 790 S.W. 2d 186 (Ky. 1989); Edgewood Independent School District v. Kirby, 777 S.W. 2d 391 (Tex. 1989). These school finance cases are discussed in more detail in Chapter 19 in this book.

13. William E. Thro, "The Third Wave: The Impact of the Montana, Kentucky and Texas Decisions on the Future of Public School Finance Reform Litigation," *Journal of Law and Education* 19, no. 2, (Spring 1990): 240.

14. Seattle School Dist. No. 1 v. State, 90 Wn. 2d 476, 511-513, 514, 585 P. 2d 71 91–92 (1978).

15. Tyska by Tyska v. Board of Education, 117 Ill. App. 3d 917, 73 Ill. Dec. 209, 453 N.E. 2d 1344 (1983).

16. Louis L. Jaffe, Essay on Delegation of Legislative Power 47 *Col.L.Rev.* 359, 361 (1947).

17. Attorney General v. Lowrey, 131 Mich. 639, 92 N.W. 289 (1902).

18. MacQueen v. City Com'n. of City of Port Huron, 194 Mich. 328, 160 N.W. 627 (1916).

19. Board of Educ. Louisville v. Society of Alumni of Louisville Male High School, 239 S.W.2d 931 (Ky.1951).

20. School District No. 1, Multnomah County v. Bruck, 225 Or. 496, 358 P.2d 283 (1960).

21. Goodman v. School District No. 1, 32 F.2d 586 (8th Cir. 1929).

22. Hallett v. Post Printing & Publishing Co., 68 Colo. 573, 192 P. 658 (1920).

23. McGilvra v. Seattle School District No. 1, 113 Wash. 619, 194 P. 817 (1921).

24. Jarrett v. Goodall, 113 W.Va. 478, 168 S.E. 763 (1933).

25. Brine v. City of Cambridge, 265 Mass. 452, 164 N.E. 619 (1929).

26. Kenneth Culp Davis, *Administrative Law Treatise,* vol. 1 (St. Paul, Minn.: West Publishing Company, 1958), p. 5.

27. Ibid., p. 102.

28. John Locke, *Two Treatises of Civil Government,* Book II, Ch. XI, Sec. 141.

29. Osius v. City of St. Clair Shores, 344 Mich. 693, 75 N.W.2d 25 (1956).

30. Davis, *Administrative Law Treatise,* p. 103.

31. Ward v. Scott, 11 N.J. 117, 93 A.2d 385 (1952).

32. Ibid.

33. State v. Kinnear, 70 Wn.2d 482, 423 P.2d 937 (1967).

34. School District No. 3 of Town of Adams v. Callahan, 237 Wis. 560, 297 N.W. 407 (1941).

35. Schinck v. Board of Education of Westwood Consolidated School Dist., 60 N.J.Super 448, 159 A.2d 396 (1960).

36. Jokinen v. Allen, 15 Misc.2d 124, 182 N.Y.S.2d 166 (1958).

37. Bowles v. Willingham, 321 U.S. 503, 64 S.Ct. 641 (1944).

38. S. A. de Smith, *Judicial Review of Administrative Action* (London: Stevens & Sons, 1973), p. 60.

39. Fremont RE–1 School District v. Jacobs, 737 P. 2d 816 (Colo. 1987).

40. Robert F. Will, *State Education, Structure and Organization* (United States Department of Health, Education and Welfare, United States Office of Education, 1964), pp. 8–10.

41. Laba v. Board of Education of Newark, 23 N.J. 364, 129 A.2d 273 (1957).

42. In re Masiello, 25 N.J. 590, 138 A.2d 393 (1958).

43. R. v. Roberts, 2 K.B. 695 (1924). See also Kern Alexander, "Administrative Prerogative: Restraints of Natural Justice on Student Discipline," *Journal of Law and Education* 7, no. 3 (July 1978): 331–58.

44. Joseph Raz, *The Morality of Freedom* (Oxford: Clarendon Press, 1986), p. 113.

45. Lloyd L., Weinreb, *Natural Law and Justice* (Cambridge, Mass.: Harvard University Press, 1987), p. 166.

46. Hortonville Joint School District No. 1 v. Hortonville Education Association, 426 U.S. 482, 96 S. Ct. 2308 (1976).

47. A. H. Andrews Co. v. Delight Special School District, 95 Ark. 26, 128 S.W. 361 (1910).

48. Edwards, *The Courts and the Public Schools,* p. 147.

49. Knox County Board of Education v. Fultz, 241 Ky. 265, 43 S.W.2d 707 (1931); Lyerley v. Manila School District 15, 214 Ark. 245, 215 S.W.2d 733 (1948); Board of Education v. County Board of School Trustees, 25 Ill.App.2d 390, 166 N.E.2d 472 (1960); Detroit Edison Co. v. East China Township School District No. 3, 366 Mich. 638, 115 N.W.2d 298 (1962); School District No. 12, Phillips County v. Hughes, 170 Mont. 267, 552 P.2d 328 (1976).

50. Board of Education of City of New York v. Allen, 6 N.Y.2d 127, 188 N.Y.S.2d 515, 160 N.E.2d 60 (1959).

51. Board of Education v. County Board of School Trustees, 32 Ill.App.2d 1, 176 N.E.2d 633 (1961).

52. de Smith, *Judicial Review of Administrative Action,* p. 283.

53. Ibid., pp. 288, 289.

54. Ibid., p. 279.

55. Bristol Virginia School Board v. Quarles, 235 Va. 108, 119–120, 366 S.E. 2d 82, 89 (1988).

56. Wood v. Board of Supervisors of Halifax County, 236 Va. 104, 372 S.E. 2d 611 (1988).

57. Shelmadine v. City of Elkhart, 75 Ind.App. 493, 129 N.E. 878 (1921).

58. Main v. Claremont Unified School District, 161 Cal.App.2d 189, 326 P.2d 573 (1958).

59. Maddox v. State, 220 Ark. 762, 249 S.W.2d 972 (1952).

60. Constitution of Indiana, Art. 2, § 9.

61. People v. Becker, 112 Cal.App.2d 324, 246 P.2d 103 (1952).

62. State ex rel. Robinson v. Keefe, 111 Fla. 701, 149 So. 638 (1933).

63. Green v. Jones, 144 W.Va. 276, 108 S.E.2d 1 (1959).

64. Leech v. State, 78 Ind. 570 (1881).

65. People v. Reinberg, 263 Ill. 536, 105 N.E. 715 (1914).

66. Commonwealth v. Fahey, 156 Pa.Super. 254, 40 A.2d 167 (1944).

67. 328 U.S. 549, 66 S.Ct. 1198 (1946).

68. Ibid.

69. 369 U.S. 186, 82 S.Ct. 691 (1962).

70. Hadley v. Junior College District of Metropolitan Kansas City, Mo., 397 U.S. 50, 90 S.Ct. 791 (1970).

71. Conover v. Board of Education, 1 Utah 2d 375, 267 P. 2d 768 (1954).

CHAPTER 5

Church and State

The conflicts caused by religious interaction with public policy decisions multiplied and intensified during the decade of the eighties. Much rancor and ill will have been manifested among various churches and sects as abortion, school prayer, Bible reading, and tax benefits for parochial schools have been widely debated. Even more broadly, the news is replete with stories of religious strife worldwide. The problems created by the intermingling of religious and political issues have appeared to intensify rather than abate as America's founding fathers would have hopefully anticipated.[1]

■ WALL OF SEPARATION

In 1879 the Supreme Court in *Reynolds v. United States*[2] first invoked the famous *dictum* of Jefferson, calling for the erection of a "wall of separation between church and state." Over a century of judicial struggle has resulted in precious little resolution of the church and state conflict. In fact, it appears that the plethora of litigation over the years has merely tended to obscure the boundaries of separation envisaged by Jefferson. Indeed, lately, it seems that the vision of separation, the foundational premise[3] of religious freedom, may be becoming so obscure as to have undiscernable contours and boundaries. Indeed, the new membership of the Supreme Court will most likely reflect the position of Chief Justice Rehnquist, who in dissent in *Wallace v. Jaffree* roundly condemned the idea and desirability of a "wall of separation," saying that it is "a metaphor based on bad

history, a metaphor which has proved useless as a guide to judging" and that it "should be frankly and explicitly abandoned."[4]

Thus, the issue of separation and the interrelationship between religion and government retains its characteristic preeminence as a devisive issue in American society. To better understand the problem requires a brief look backward to the antecedents of the church-state issues touching the schools of this country. Centuries of religious strife in Europe left an indelible mark on the minds of the fathers of the American Constitution. Controversy over religion has not abated and today causes as much international and domestic discord as it did a thousand years ago. Diversity of religious background among the American colonies was so great, and religious sentiments so deep, that representatives at the Constitutional Convention in Philadelphia in 1787 were loath to address the issue lest the convention founder on the shoals of religious dissension. Avoidance was implicitly agreed upon by all, and everyone more or less adopted the position of John Adams, who assumed that if the issue was not mentioned both the state and religion would be best served. Adams expressed the hope that "Congress will never meddle with religion further than to say their own prayers, and to fast and to give thanks once a year."[5] Some believed that simple omission was not the appropriate solution to the religious dilemma and although it was not acted upon by the convention, Pinckney of South Carolina sought to make the absence of congressional power in religion explicit by proposing that the new Constitution provide that "the Legislature of the United States shall pass no law on the subject of religion."[6] Even though no general religious provision was acted upon, there is little doubt that the failure resulted from the delegates' firm belief that such a provision was not necessary to preserve religious liberty. While no general religious separation provision was thought to be needed, the convention did decide to specifically prohibit states from imposing religious tests for federal office. Madison explained that it might be implied that "without [an] exception, a power would have been given to impose an oath involving religious test as a qualification for office."[7] Obviously, it was in the interest of the central government to prevent states with different religious ties to require religious tests for federal office. With cognizance of this, the convention adopted Pinckney's motion that "no religious test shall ever be required as a qualification to any office or public trust under the United States"; this became the last clause of Article VI in the Constitution.

Thus, when the Constitution was ratified by the states only the "religious test" of office provision was included and no other reference was made regarding religious toleration. This omission was not taken lightly when the states were called upon to ratify the document. Six states ratified but proposed amendments guaranteeing religious liberty and two other states, North Carolina and Rhode Island, refused to ratify until a bill of rights including religious freedom was promulgated.[8] Although Madison defended the omission, saying, "the government has no jurisdiction over it [religion],"[9] it was argued by others that there was no security for the rights of conscience. Jefferson ultimately convinced Madison that a religious provision in a bill of rights was necessary. Commenting on the proposed constitution in a letter to Madison from Paris, where Jefferson was serving as ambassador, he said:

> I will now add what I do not like. First, the omission of a bill of rights providing clearly and without the aid of sophisms for freedom of religion, freedom of the press, protection against monopolies, the eternal and unremitting force of the habeas corpus laws, and trials by juries.   .   .   . [A] bill of rights is what the

people are entitled to against every government on earth, general or particular, and what no just government should refuse or rest on inference.[10]

The very uncertainty itself of whether such rights were implied in the Constitution was evidence enough that a bill of rights protecting religious freedom and assuring disestablishment was necessary. Madison, with Jefferson's urging and his own experience in persuading the states to ratify only after promising amendments as specific affirmation of individual rights and freedoms, stated that he now favored amendments to provide for "all essential rights, particularly the rights of Conscience in the fullest latitude, the freedom of the press, trial by jury, etc."[11] In accordance with this position, Madison introduced to the House of Representatives, in 1789, a compilation of proposals for amendments that he maintained would prevent encroachments by the sovereign power into individual rights and liberties. Madison's proposals before the House were to finally become the Bill of Rights, which were approved by the requisite number of states in 1791. Prominent among these rights was the separation of church and state provision, which guaranteed religious freedom and prohibited establishment of religion by government. The First Amendment states:

> Congress shall make no law respecting an establishment of religion, or prohibiting the free exercise thereof; or abridging the freedom of speech, or of the press; or the right of the people peaceably to assembly and to petition the Government for a redress of grievances.

■■■ RELIGIOUS INTOLERANCE

Much of the history of western civilization has had its basis in religious controversy. Disputes between tribal chiefs and priests were fertile ground for discord that materially affected both church and state. In more primitive eras, the state did not attempt to delineate religious from secular activities, with some polytheistic societies merely cataloguing and assigning gods to a particular divine hierarchy, as in the Code of Hammurabi.[12] In most instances, the state and religion were entwined in the interests and affairs of the day, but it was very clear that of the two forces, the state was supreme. In ancient Greece, the head of state was also chief priest and served as the supreme guardian of religion. As the Athenian republic became well established, the unity of religion with state continued.[13]

Rome, too, was originally a state of many gods, with the innovation that great heads of state, upon death, were placed among the ranks of the gods.[14] So long as there were many gods to worship and everyone recognized the state was supreme, little conflict developed; however, with the advent of Christianity, full-fledged discord became apparent. Christians ascribed to a dogmatic exclusiveness that was not tolerated by the Romans. Religious persecution of Christians began with Nero, with the justification that they were "enemies of mankind" and "arsonists," conveniently serving as scapegoats for the burning of Rome.[15] Persecution continued until Constantine issued the Edict of Milan in 312 or 313 A.D., a document of great importance in religious history, providing "that liberty of worship shall not be denied to any, but that the mind and will of every individual shall be free to manage divine affairs according to his own choice."[16] From this point on, the Christian religion became dominant as Constantine adopted it as a primary means of consolidating his empire.[17]

In the centuries that followed, the Christian church gained power and authority, to the point that it became quite clear that the church was supreme over any head of state. Strength of the Church was demonstrated by Pope Gelasius I in 496, when he proclaimed to the emperor:

> There are two things, most august emperor, by which this world is chiefly ruled: the sacred authority of the priesthood and the royal power. Of these two the priests carry the greater weight, because they will have to render account in the divine judgment even for the kings of men.[18]

Although Christianity had, under the Romans, been the oppressed, when it gained dominion it became the oppressor and little tolerance was exhibited. St. Augustine strongly advanced the conviction that the civil power of the state should be used to suppress dissidents of the Church. Compulsion was the watchword and St. Augustine espoused the belief that "freedom to err" was the worst killer of the soul. In keeping with that philosophy, "the Medieval Church was intolerant, was the source and author of persecution, justified and defended the most violent measures which could be taken against those who differed from it."[19]

From this basis, the development of medieval Europe was almost solely that of continual struggle between church and state, with kings rebelling against the church, and the sword of the state being readily put to use to stamp out heretics and nonconformists.

While most people are aware of the centuries of intolerance on the European continent, the most extreme example of which is probably the Spanish Inquisition, our more direct church-state antecedents derive from English origins. With the Reformation, problems of church and state were compounded as new religious doctrines were advanced and various ideologies began to emerge as separate and viable religions. Intolerance prevailed, whether Catholics or Protestants were in power. Henry VIII's conflict with Rome blossomed into bloody internal strife as Edward VI, Mary, and Elizabeth took the throne and in succession persecuted religious opponents. For her deeds, Mary was remembered in history as "Bloody Mary." During Elizabeth's long reign, the Church of England was firmly established as the state religion, and the supremacy of the state over the church was complete. Ecclesiastical offices were regulated by her proclamations and opposing religious viewpoints were not tolerated. From this point in England, there existed a church that was Protestant in nature and entirely subject to state authority and control. Intra-Protestant struggles developed, and internal Protestant religious peace was not actually achieved in England until 1689 with the act of Toleration.

Even though the great religious wars of Europe were not of the same era with the lifespan of the constitutional forefathers of the United States, the strife of the Old World was still much in their minds. The Supreme Court of the United States has best expressed the situation:

> The centuries immediately before and contemporaneous with the colonization of America had been filled with turmoil, civil strife, and persecution, generated in large part by established sects determined to maintain their absolute political and religious supremacy. With the power of government to support them, at various times and places, Catholics had persecuted Protestants, Protestants had persecuted Catholics, Protestant sects had persecuted other Protestant sects, Catholics of one shade of belief had persecuted Catholics of another shade of belief, and all of these had from time to time persecuted Jews.[20]

When the matter of religion was to be considered in 1787, there were essentially three rationalizations for church-state relationships that had arisen out of the Reformation: the Erastian (named after the German philosopher Erastus), the theocratic, and the separatist. Dominant among these was the Erastian view, which assumed state superiority over ecclesiastical affairs and religion was used to further the interests of the state. It was during the Elizabethan era in England that the Erastian philosophy was fully implemented. The second, the theocratic, was founded in the idea that the church is supreme and the state should be used to further ecclesiastical policy. Third, complete separation, was advanced as the proper course by minority dissident groups in Europe, but did not find full expression until 1791 in America.[21] It was, however, John Locke on whom both Madison and Jefferson relied for their basic philosophical ideas concerning separation. In his *Letter Concerning Toleration,* Locke maintained that "The care of souls cannot belong to the civil magistrate because his power consists only in outward force, but true and saving religion consists in the inward persuasion of the mind . . . ."[22]

Locke's ideas were developed and expanded under fire in the great dispute in Virginia over established religion that had been carefully protected by statutes promulgated by the Anglican church until the Revolution. These laws provided for religious services according to the laws and orders of the Church of England: compulsory attendance at religious services, regulation of nonconformists, glebe lands for support of the clergy, and a system of governmentally sanctioned vestries empowered to levy tithes for upkeep of the church and ministers' salaries.

■ COLONIAL ESTABLISHMENTS

The colonies during the seventeenth and eighteenth centuries reflected the precedent of single church establishments of Europe. While the intensity of the force of the preferred church varied among the colonies, there nevertheless existed strong and unquestioned establishments of the Congregational church in New England—Massachusetts, Connecticut, and New Hampshire; and of the Anglican church in the South—Virginia, North Carolina, and South Carolina. Another group of colonies—New York, New Jersey, Maryland, and Georgia—evolved through periods of preference of different churches, and tax support for Protestant churches as the population changed. In New York, for example, the Dutch Reformed church was initially established, but as the colony grew, a heterogeneous group of other believers entered, including Calvinists, Lutherans, Mennonites, Quakers, Catholics, and Jews. When the English took over New Netherland and it became New York, the inclinations of the Stuarts toward Catholicism forced more toleration for all religious groups. The ultimate effect was that by 1693, New York, while Anglican, was reasonably tolerant toward Catholics, and generally provided tax support for all Protestant ministries.[23] Because the religious preference of New York was largely unclear, a battle raged for years between the royal governors and the Anglican clergy, who demanded the clear and uncertain establishment of the Church of England. The policy ultimately became one of multiple establishment whereby a variety of churches were provided funding by the state.

A third group of colonies—Rhode Island, Pennsylvania, and Delaware—had a large measure of religious freedom, which generally prevailed from their origins. Pennsylvania advanced toleration that generally followed William Penn's philosophy as expounded in his *Frame of Government,* promoting freedom of religion.[24] Delaware broke off from Pennsylvania in 1702 and continued this policy of religious freedom and the prohibition of use of public funds for church purposes.

But Rhode Island, under Roger Williams, was the prototype of religious tolerance that came ultimately to prevail. From the time that Williams landed in Massachusetts in 1631, conflict developed with the Puritan establishment. Because of his insistence on separation of civil and ecclesiastical aspects of society, Williams was banished in 1635. In 1636, he formed a plantation in Rhode Island territory and in 1643, a patent was obtained from Charles I to form a new colony. Williams' ideas regarding the separation of church and state were predominant in Rhode Island, evolving from four basic theses: (1) attempts by the state to enforce religious orthodoxy, produce persecution and religious wars and pervert God's plan for the regeneration of souls; (2) God has not blessed a particular form of government, and governments will vary with the nature of the people governed; (3) political and religious diversity could not be avoided; (4) the human conscience must be totally free, through religious freedom and the separation of church and state.[25] These ideas were elaborated in Williams' *Bloudy Tenet of Persecution* in 1644.

Williams' ideas undoubtedly influenced the American attitude toward disestablishment that became prevalent after the war for independence, but Williams' legacy apparently had little carry-over influence on those who formed the new federal Constitution in 1787 and the subsequent First Amendment.[26]

■ RELIGIOUS ASSESSMENTS

Jefferson, more than any other individual, led in enunciating and implementing the separation principle. In 1776, while he was in Philadelphia writing the *Declaration of Independence,* he drafted a proposed constitution for Virginia that stated: "All persons shall have full and free liberty of religious opinion; nor shall any be compelled to frequent or maintain any religious institution."[27] Although this particular measure was not passed, it nevertheless set the tone for religious freedom for Virginia in the era to come. In spite of Jefferson's position, however, in 1779, a bill was introduced in the Virginia legislature declaring that "the Christian Religion shall in all times coming be deemed and held to be the established Religion of the Commonwealth."[28] It required every person to enroll his name with the county clerk and designate the society that he intended to support, whereupon the clerk would present the roll for the appropriate religious group to determine assessment rates; these were then collected by the sheriff and the proceeds were turned over to the church. Taxes obtained from persons failing to enroll in a religious society had their payments spread across all religious groups.[29]

In 1784, the bill was called up for a vote; entitled a "Bill Establishing a Provision for Teachers of the Christian Religion," it was sponsored by Patrick Henry. Although the bill was defeated, from the preceding and ensuing debate, two of the most important documents in religious freedom were written, Jefferson's *Bill for Establishing Religious Freedom* and Madison's *Memorial and Remonstrance against Religious Assessments.* Jefferson's bill was written and introduced in the Virginia General Assembly in 1779, but was not enacted into law until January, 1786.

Madison's *Memorial,* in opposition to Henry's bill for religious assessments, was of great historical significance. The philosophy stated therein has often been referred to by the United States Supreme Court in support of its opinions. The *Memorial* presents several arguments against the religious assessment bill, but more importantly it conveys a philosophy of separation that, along with Jefferson's, provided the logic and rationale for the "wall of separation" provisions of the First Amendment in 1791.

AN ACT FOR ESTABLISHING RELIGIOUS FREEDOM

by Thomas Jefferson (written and introduced in 1779, enacted in 1786).

— — — ·— ·— ·— ·—

Well aware that Almighty God hath created the mind free; that all attempts to influence it by temporal punishments or burdens, or by civil incapacitations, tend only to beget habits of hypocrisy and meanness, and are a departure from the plan of the Holy Author of our religion, who being Lord both of body and mind, yet chose not to propagate it by coercions on either, as was in his Almighty power to do;

That the impious presumption of legislators and rulers, civil as well as ecclesiastical, who, being themselves but fallible and uninspired men, have assumed dominion over the faith of others, setting up their own opinions and modes of thinking as the only true and infallible, and as such endeavoring to impose them on others, hath established and maintained false religions over the greatest part of the world, and through all time;

That to compel a man to furnish contributions of money for the propagation of opinions which he disbelieves, is sinful and tyrannical; that even the forcing him to support this or that teacher of his own religious persuasion, is depriving him of the comfortable liberty of giving his contributions to the particular pastor whose morals he would make his pattern, and whose power he feels most persuasive to righteousness, and is withdrawing from the ministry those temporal rewards, which proceeding from an approbation of their personal conduct, are an

additional incitement to earnest and unremitting labors for the instruction of mankind;

That our civil rights have no dependence on our religious opinions, any more than our opinions in physics or geometry; that, therefore, the proscribing any citizen as unworthy the public confidence by laying upon him an incapacity of being called to the offices of trust and emolument, unless he profess or renounce this or that religious opinion, is depriving him injuriously of those privileges and advantages to which in common with his fellow citizens he has a natural right;

That it tends also to corrupt the principles of that very religion it is meant to encourage, by bribing, with a monopoly of worldly honors and emoluments, those who will externally profess and conform to it; that though indeed these are criminal who do not withstand such temptation, yet neither are those innocent who lay the bait in their way;

That to suffer the civil magistrate to intrude his powers into the field of opinion and to restrain the profession or propagation of principles, on the supposition of their ill tendency, is a dangerous fallacy, which at once destroys all religious liberty, because he being of course judge of that tendency, will make his opinions the rule of judgment, and approve or condemn the sentiments of others only as they shall square with or differ from his own;

That it is time enough for the rightful purposes of civil government, for its officers to interfere when principles break out into overt acts against peace and good order;

And finally, that truth is great and will prevail if left to herself, that she is the proper and sufficient antagonist to error, and has nothing to fear from the conflict, unless by human interposition disarmed of her natural weapons, free argument and debate, errors ceasing to be dangerous when it is permitted freely to contradict them.

Be it therefore enacted by the General Assembly, That no man shall be compelled to frequent or support any religious worship, place or ministry whatsoever, nor shall be enforced, restrained, molested, or burthened in his body or goods, nor shall otherwise suffer on account of his religious opinions or belief; but that all men shall be free to profess, and by argument to maintain, their opinions in matters of religion, and that the same shall in nowise diminish, enlarge, or affect their civil capacities.

And though we well know this Assembly, elected by the people for the ordinary purposes of legislation only, have no power to restrain the acts of succeeding assemblies, constituted with the powers equal to our own, and that therefore to declare this act irrevocable, would be of no effect in law, yet we are free to declare, and do declare, that the rights hereby asserted are of the natural rights of mankind, and that if any act shall be hereafter passed to repeal the present or to narrow its operation, such act will be an infringement of natural right.

MEMORIAL AND REMONSTRANCE AGAINST RELIGIOUS ASSESSMENTS

by James Madison (1785).

— · — · — · — · — · —

To the Honorable General Assembly of the Commonwealth of Virginia. A Memorial and Remonstrance.

We, the subscribers, citizens of the said Commonwealth, having taken into serious consideration, a Bill printed by order of the last Session of General Assembly, entitled "A Bill establishing a provision for teachers of the Christian Religion," and conceiving that the same, if finally armed with the sanctions of a law, will be a dangerous abuse of power, are bound as faithful members of a free State, to remonstrate against it, and to declare the reasons by which we are determined. We remonstrate against the said Bill,

Because we hold it for a fundamental and undeniable truth, "that religion, or the duty which we owe to our Creator, and the manner of discharging it, can be directed only by reason and conviction, not by force or violence."[30] The Religion then of every man must

be left to the conviction and conscience of every man; and it is the right of every man to exercise it as these may dictate. This right is in its nature an unalienable right. . . .

Because, it is proper to take alarm at the first experiment on our liberties. We hold this prudent jealousy to be the first duty of citizens, and one of [the] noblest characteristics of the late Revolution. The freemen of America did not wait till usurped power had strengthened itself by exercise, and entangled the question in precedents. They saw all the consequences in the principle, and they avoided the consequences by denying the principle. We reverse this lesson too much, soon to forget it. Who does not see that the same authority which can establish Christianity, in exclusion of all other Religions, may establish with the same ease any particular sect of Christians, in exclusion of all other Sects? That the same authority which can force a citizen to contribute three pence only of his property for the support of any one establishment, may force him to conform to any other establishment in all cases whatsoever?

Because, the bill violates that equality which ought to be the basis of every law, and which is more indispensable, in proportion as the validity or expediency of any law is more liable to be impeached. If "all men are by nature equally free and independent,"[31] all men are to be considered as entering into Society on equal conditions; as relinquishing no more, and therefore retaining no less, one than another, of their natural rights. Above all are they to be considered as retaining an "equal title to the free exercise of Religion according to the dictates of conscience."[32] Whilst we assert for ourselves a freedom to embrace, to profess and to observe the Religion which we believe to be of divine origin, we cannot deny an equal freedom to those whose minds have not yet yielded to the evidence which has convinced us. If this freedom be abused, it is an offense against God, not against man: To God, therefore, not to men, must an account of it be rendered. As the Bill violates equality by subjecting some to peculiar burdens; so it violates the same principle, by granting to others peculiar exemptions. Are the Quakers and Menonists the only sects who think a compulsive support of their religions unnecessary and unwarrantable? Can their piety alone be entrusted with the care of public worship? Ought their Religions to be endowed above all others, with extraordinary privileges, by which proselytes may be enticed from all others? We think too favorably of the justice and good sense of these denominations, to believe that they either covet preeminencies over their fellow citizens, or that they will be seduced by them, from the common opposition to the measure. . . .

What influence in fact have ecclesiastical establishments had on Civil Society? In some instances they have been seen to erect a spiritual tyranny on the ruins of Civil authority; in many instances they have been seen upholding the thrones of political tyranny; in no instance have they been seen the guardians of the liberties of the people. Rulers who wished to subvert the public liberties, may have found an established clergy convenient auxiliaries. A just government, instituted to secure and perpetuate it, needs them not. Such a government will be best supported by protecting every citizen in the enjoyment of his Religion with the same equal hand which protects his person and his property; by neither invading the equal rights by any Sect, nor suffering any Sect to invade those of another.

Because the proposed establishment is a departure from that generous policy, which offering an asylum to the persecuted and oppressed of every Nation and Religion, promised a lustre to our country, an accession to the number of its citizens. What a melancholy mark is the Bill of sudden degeneracy? Instead of holding forth an asylum to the persecuted, it is itself a signal of persecution. It degrades from the equal rank of citizens all those whose opinions in Religion do not bend to those of the Legislative authority. Distant as it may be, in its present form, from the Inquisition it differs from it only in degree. The one is the first step, the other the last in the career of intolerance. . . .

Because, it will destroy that moderation and harmony which the forbearance of our laws to intermeddle with Religion, has produced amongst its several sects. Torrents of blood have been spilt in the old World, by vain attempts of the secular arm to extinguish Religious discord, by proscribing all difference in Religious opinions. Time has at length revealed the true remedy. Every relaxation of narrow and rigorous policy, wherever it has been tried, has been found to assuage the disease. The American Theatre has exhibited proofs, that equal and complete liberty, if it does not wholly eradicate it, sufficiently destroys its malignant influence on the health and prosperity of the State. If with the salutary effects of this system under our own eyes, we begin to contract the bonds of Religious freedom, we know no name that will too severely reproach our folly. At least let warning be taken at the first fruit of the threatened innovation. The very appearance of the Bill has transformed that "Christian forbearance,[33] love and charity," which of late mutually prevailed, into animosities and jealousies, which may not soon be appeased. What mischiefs may not be dreaded should this enemy to the public quiet be armed with the force of a law? . . .

Because, finally, "the equal right of every citizen to the free exercise of his Religion according to the dictates of conscience" is held by the same tenure with all our other rights. If we recur to its origin, it is equally the gift of nature; if we weigh its importance, it cannot be less dear to us; if we consult the Declaration of those rights which pertain to the good people of Virginia, as the "basis and foundation of Government,"[34] it is enumerated with equal solemnity, or rather studied emphasis. Either then, we must say, that the will of the Legislature is the only measure of their authority; and that in the plentitude of this authority, they may sweep away all our fundamental rights; or, that they are bound to leave this particular right untouched and sacred: Either we must say, that they may control the freedom of the press, may abolish the trial by jury, may swallow up the Executive and Judiciary powers of the State; nay that they may despoil us of our very right of suffrage, and erect themselves into an independent and hereditary assembly: or we must say, that they have no authority to enact into law the Bill under consideration. We, the subscribers, say, that the General Assembly of this Commonwealth have no such authority: And that no effort may be omitted on our part against so dangerous an usurpation, we oppose to it, this remonstrance; earnestly praying, as we are in duty bound, that the Supreme Lawgiver of the Universe, by illuminating those to whom it is addressed, may on the one hand turn their councils from every act which would affront his holy prerogative, or violate the trust committed to them: and on the other, guide them into every measure which may be worthy of his [blessing, may re] dound to their own praise, and may establish more firmly the liberties, the prosperity, and the Happiness of the Commonwealth.

■ THE PUBLIC SCHOOL AND RELIGION

Public education is founded on three fundamental assumptions that relate either directly or indirectly to the issue of church and state. First, education is a benefit to the entire society and the legislature has the power to tax all for support. Essential to this concept is that general taxation is used for support and that taxation is not levied merely on those who use the public schools—the childless and those who sent their children to private schools must all pay their fair share. Thaddeus Stevens in 1835, in dramatically defeating a legislative proposal to repeal general taxation for education, enunciated the principle of universal responsibility for universal education in Pennsylvania. It was claimed that it was unjust to tax people to educate children of others; Stevens responded thusly:

It is for their own benefit, inasmuch as it perpetrates the government and ensures the due administration of the laws under which they live, and by which their lives and property are protected. Why do they not urge the same objection against all other taxes? The industri-

ous, thrifty, rich farmer pays a heavy county tax to support criminal courts, build jails, and pay sheriffs and jail keepers, and yet probably he never has had and probably never will have any direct personal use for them. . . . He cheerfully pays burdensome taxes which are necessarily levied to support and punish convicts, but loudly complains of that which goes to prevent his fellowbeing from becoming a criminal and to obviate the necessity of those humiliating institutions.[35]

To Stevens, education was a public obligation that must be nurtured to develop the entire civic intelligence to better govern through an elective republic. Those who do not directly benefit from public education certainly gain indirectly through association with an enlightened citizenry.

Second, education provided by the state must be secular and individual religious beliefs should not be inhibited. An important element of the secular state envisioned by Jefferson was a system of public schools that could convey all necessary temporal knowledge and yet not impede religious freedom. The power of the state could not be used to inculcate religious beliefs, nor could the authority of the state to tax be used to assist religious training.

The First Amendment has two religious clauses that protect the individual's religious liberty, "the establishment" clause and the "free exercise" clause. These two combined prevent the use of public schools to proselytize and, correspondingly, forbid the expenditure of public tax funds to support religion. An extract from an opinion by the Supreme Court of Iowa forcefully illuminates this:

If there is any one thing which is well settled in the policies and purposes of the American people as a whole, it is the fixed and unalterable determination that there shall be an absolute and unequivocal separation of church and state, and that our public school system, supported by the taxation of the property of all alike—Catholic, Protestant, Jew, Gentile, believer and infidel—shall not be used directly or indirectly for religious instruction, and above all that it shall not be made an instrumentality of proselyting influence, in favor of any religious organization, sect, creed, or belief.[36]

The third assumption, that the state can compel all parents to provide their children with a minimum secular education, is essential to the concept of general mass education. Every government has as a goal its own continuation and preservation, and in a republic an educated electorate is fundamental. As such, the state must be conceived as *parens patriae* in enforcing minimum educational and welfare requirements. The validity of the state's interest was established several years ago in *Prince v. Massachusetts*.[37]

The primary issue emanates from placing the force and power of the state, whether it be through taxation or other public policy decision, in a position to either enhance or inhibit religion. This was one of the most obstinate problems that Horace Mann was forced to overcome in his great crusade to found free common schools in Massachusetts. Mann vigorously maintained that the only purpose of religious education in the schools was to convey to each child the idea and respect of religious liberty. According to him, the child should be able

> to judge for himself according to the dictates of his own reason and conscience, what his religious obligations are and whither they lead. But if a man is taxed to support a school where religious doctrines are inculcated which he believes to be false, and which he believes that God condemns, then he is excluded from the school by the divine law, at the same time that he is compelled to support it by the human law. This is a double wrong.[38]

Today the public schools of America are secular and not merely nonsectarian; this is necessary if separation of church and state is to be complete. The important position of education in the governmental process is the key to maintaining religious liberty. Pfeffer observes that to be secular does not mean to be "Godless"; it is merely a guarantee that the state will not dictate or encroach on religious beliefs of the individual. He says:

> A secular state requires a secular state school; but the secularization of the state does not mean the secularization of society. Only by accepting a totalitarian philosophy, either in religion or politics or both, can the state be equated with society. We are a religious people even though our government is secular. Our democratic state must be secular, for it does not purport or seek to pre-empt all of societal life. Similarly the public school need not and should not be the totality of the education process.[39]

In this regard, our Constitution precludes religious indoctrination in the public schools and prohibits use of public funds in supporting religion in parochial schools and it also proscribes the state from preempting all the child's time, thereby allowing substantial opportunity for religious training outside the school by parents and churches.[40]

■ TEXTBOOKS AND TRANSPORTATION FOR PAROCHIAL SCHOOL PUPILS

The United States Supreme Court, in the case of *Cochran v. Louisiana,* ruled that a state plan to provide textbooks to parochial school students does not violate the Fourteenth Amendment.[41] The Court in this decision was not asked to determine whether the First Amendment was violated. The decision in the *Cochran* case was rendered in 1930, ten years before the Court decided in the *Cantwell* case that the religious liberties of the First Amendment not only provided protection against actions by the Congress but, when applied through the Fourteenth Amendment, protected the individual from arbitrary acts of the states.[42] However, the Court in this case did identify and adopt the "child benefit" concept that has subsequently been used in many instances to defend the appropriation of public funds for private and parochial school use.

The Supreme Court in the *Everson v. Board of Education* case, a 1947 decision, held that the use of public funds for transportation of parochial school children does not violate the First Amendment. However, many state constitutions impose stricter regulations concerning separation of church and state than does the United States Constitution and, as a result, the highest courts in several states have ruled that their state constitutions would be violated if public funds were used to provide transportation for parochial school pupils.

In the *Everson* case, the legislature of New Jersey enacted a law that allowed boards of education to provide transportation for parochial school children at public expense. A school board, acting under this statute, authorized reimbursement of parents for bus fares spent in sending their children to parochial schools. The plaintiff attacked the statute on the grounds that it violated the First and Fourteenth Amendments of the federal Constitution. The Court, in a 5–4 decision, ruled that the statute did not violate the Constitution. The Court adopted the "child benefit" doctrine and reasoned that the funds were expended for the benefit of the individual child and not for religious purposes. The transportation law was a general program that provided assistance in getting children safely to and from school regardless of their religion.

In 1968, the Supreme Court in *Board of Education v. Allen* applied the reasoning of the *Cochran* and *Everson* cases in upholding as constitutional a New York statute that provided textbooks distributed free of charge to students attending parochial schools. The court stated that there was no indication that the books were being used to teach religion and that since private schools serve a public purpose and perform a secular as well as a sectarian function, such an expenditure of public funds is not unconstitutional.[43]

Establishment Clause Does Not Prohibit Spending Tax Funds to Pay Bus Fares for Parochial School Students

— — — — — — — —

Everson v. Board of Education

— — — — — — — —

Supreme Court of the United States, 1947.
330 U.S. 1, 67 S.Ct. 504.

Mr. Justice BLACK delivered the opinion of the Court. A New Jersey statute authorizes its local school districts to make rules and contracts for the transportation of children to and from schools. The appellee, a township board of education, acting pursuant to this statute authorized reimbursement to parents of money expended by them for the bus transportation of their children on regular buses operated by the public transportation system. Part of this money was for the payment of transportation of some children in the community to Catholic parochial schools. These church schools give their students, in addition to secular education, regular religious instruction conforming to the religious tenets and modes of worship of the Catholic Faith. The superintendent of these schools is a Catholic priest.

The appellant, in his capacity as a district taxpayer, filed suit in a State court challenging the right of the Board to reimburse parents of parochial school students. He contended that the statute and the resolution passed pursuant to it violated both the State and the Federal Constitutions. That court held that the legislature was without power to authorize such payment under the State constitution. 132 N.J.L. 98, 39 A.2d 75. The New Jersey Court of Errors and Appeals reversed, holding that neither the statute nor the resolution passed pursuant to it was in conflict with the State constitution or the provisions of the Federal Constitution in issue. 133 N.J.L. 350, 44 A.2d 333. The case is here on appeal under 28 U.S.C. § 344(a), 28 U.S.C.A. § 344(a). . . .

The only contention here is that the State statute and the resolution, in so far as they authorized reimbursement to parents of children attending parochial schools, violate the Federal Constitution in these two respects, which to some extent, overlap. First. They authorize the State to take by taxation the private property of some and bestow it upon others, to be used for their own private purposes. This, it is alleged, violates the due process clause of the Fourteenth Amendment. Second. The statute and the resolution forced inhabitants to pay taxes to help support and maintain schools which are dedicated to, and which regularly teach, the Catholic Faith. This is alleged to be a use of State power to support church schools contrary to the prohibition of the First Amendment which the Fourteenth Amendment made applicable to the states.

First. The due process argument that the State law taxes some people to help others carry out their private purposes is framed in two phases. The first phase is that a state cannot tax A to reimburse B for the cost of transporting his children to church schools. This is said to violate the due process clause because the children are sent to these church schools to satisfy the personal desires of their parents, rather than the public's interest in the general education of all children. This argument, if valid, would apply equally to prohibit state payment for the transportation of children to any nonpublic school, whether operated by a church, or any other nongovernment individual or group. But, the New Jersey legislature has decided that a public purpose will be served by using tax-raised funds to pay the bus fares of all school children, including those who attend parochial schools. The New Jersey Court of Errors and Appeals has reached the same conclusion. The fact that a state law, passed to satisfy a public need, coincides with the personal desires of the individuals most directly affected is certainly an inadequate reason for us to say that a legislature has erroneously appraised the public need. . . .

It is much too late to argue that legislation intended to facilitate the opportunity of children to get a secular education serves no public purpose. *Cochran v. Louisiana State Board of Education,* 281 U.S. 370, 50 S.Ct. 335, 74 L.Ed. 913 . . . .The same thing is no less true of legislation to reimburse needy parents, or all parents, for payment of the fares of their children so that they can ride in public buses to and from schools rather than run the risk of traffic and other hazards incident to walking or "hitchhiking." See *Barbier v. Connolly,* 113 U.S. at page 31, 5 S.Ct. at page 359. . . . Nor does it follow that a law has a private rather than a public purpose because it provides that tax-raised funds will be paid to reimburse individuals on account of money spent by them in a way which furthers a

public program. See *Carmichael v. Southern Coal & Coke Co.,* 301 U.S. 495, 518, 57 S.Ct. 868, 876, 81 L.Ed. 1245 . . . . Subsidies and loans to individuals such as farmers and home owners, and to privately owned transportation systems, as well as many other kinds of businesses, have been commonplace practices in our state and national history.

Insofar as the second phase of the due process argument may differ from the first, it is by suggesting that taxation for transportation of children to church schools constitutes support of a religion by the State. But if the law is invalid for this reason, it is because it violates the First Amendment's prohibition against the establishment of religion by law. This is the exact question raised by appellant's second contention, to consideration of which we now turn.

Second. The New Jersey statute is challenged as a "law respecting an establishment of religion." The First Amendment, as made applicable to the states by the Fourteenth, *Murdock v. Commonwealth of Pennsylvania,* 319 U.S. 105, 63 S.Ct. 870, 872, 87 L.Ed. 1292 . . . . commands that a state "shall make no law respecting an establishment of religion, or prohibiting the free exercise thereof." These words of the First Amendment reflected in the minds of early Americans a vivid mental picture of conditions and practices which they fervently wished to stamp out in order to preserve liberty for themselves and for their posterity. Doubtless their goal has not been entirely reached; but so far has the Nation moved toward it that the expression "law respecting an establishment of religion," probably does not so vividly remind present-day Americans of the evils, fears, and political problems that caused that expression to be written into our Bill of Rights. . . .

The "establishment of religion" clause of the First Amendment means at least this: Neither a state nor the Federal Government can set up a church. Neither can pass laws which aid one religion, aid all religions, or prefer one religion over another. Neither can force nor influence a person to go to or to remain away from church against his will or force him to profess a belief or disbelief in any religion. No person can be punished for entertaining or professing religious beliefs or disbeliefs, for church attendance or nonattendance. No tax in any amount, large or small, can be levied to support any religious activities or institutions, whatever they may be called, or whatever form they may adopt to teach or practice religion. Neither a state nor the Federal Government can, openly or secretly, participate in the affairs of any religious organizations or groups and vice versa. In the words of Jefferson, the clause against establishment of religion by law was intended to erect "a wall of separation between Church and State." *Reynolds v. United States,* 98 U.S. at page 164, 25 L.Ed. 244.

We must consider the New Jersey statute in accordance with the foregoing limitations imposed by the First Amendment. But we must not strike that state statute down if it is within the state's constitutional power even though it approaches the verge of that power. . . . New Jersey cannot consistently with the "establishment of religion" clause of the First Amendment contribute tax-raised funds to the support of an institution which teaches the tenets and faith of any church. On the other hand, other language of the amendment commands that New Jersey cannot hamper its citizens in the free exercise of their own religion. Consequently, it cannot exclude individual Catholics, Lutherans, Mohammedans, Baptists, Jews, Methodists, Non-believers, Presbyterians, or the members of any other faith, *because of their faith, or lack of it,* from receiving the benefits of public welfare legislation. While we do not mean to intimate that a state could not provide transportation only to children attending public schools, we must be careful, in protecting the citizens of New Jersey against state-established churches, to be sure that we do not inadvertently prohibit New Jersey from extending its general State law benefits to all its citizens without regard to their religious belief.

Measured by these standards, we cannot say that the First Amendment prohibits New Jersey from spending tax-raised funds to pay the bus fares of parochial school pupils as a part of a general program under which it pays the fares of pupils attending public and other schools. It is undoubtedly true that children are helped to get to church schools. There is even a possibility that some of the children might not be sent to the church schools if the parents were compelled to pay their children's bus fares out of their own pockets when transportation to a public school would have been paid for by the State. The same possibility exists where the state requires a local transit company to provide reduced fares to school children including those attending parochial schools, or where a municipally owned transportation system undertakes to carry all school children free of charge. Moreover, state-paid policemen, detailed to protect children going to and from church schools from the very real hazards of traffic, would serve much the same purpose and accomplish much the same result as state provisions intended to guarantee free transportation of a kind which the state deems to be best for the school children's welfare. And parents might refuse to risk their children to the serious danger of traffic accidents going to and from parochial schools, the approaches to which were not protected by policemen. Similarly, parents might be reluctant to permit their children to attend schools which the state had cut off from such general government services as ordinary police and fire protection, connections for sewage disposal, public highways and sidewalks. Of course, cutting off church schools from these services, so separate and so indisputably marked off from the religious function, would make it far more difficult for the schools to operate. But such is obviously not the purpose of the First Amendment. That Amendment requires the state to be neutral in its relations with groups of religious believers and non-believers; it does not require the state to be their adversary. State power is no more to be used so as to handicap religions, than it is to favor them. . . .

The First Amendment has erected a wall between church and state. That wall must be kept high and impregnable. We could not approve the slightest breach. New Jersey has not breached it here.

Affirmed.

NOTES

1. In a case where a public school district assigned a male with less seniority than a female to drive a school bus for male Hasidic Jews who attended a private church school, the Jewish students refused to ride the bus with the female driver because it violated their religious beliefs. A federal court ruled that the school district's assigning of a male bus driver instead of a female, violated the Constitution because it advanced religion. Moreover, the court found that the assigning of the male in place of the female constituted sex discrimination in violation of the Civil Rights Act of 1964, Title VII. *Bollenbach v. Board of Education of Monroe-Woodbury Central School District,* 659 F.Supp. 1450 (S.D.N.Y. 1987).

2. A Pennsylvania statute that allowed the transportation of private school children beyond school district boundary lines was ruled constitutional. *School District of Pittsburgh v. Commonwealth Department of Education,* 33 Pa.Cmwlth. 535, 382 A.2d 772 (1978), appeal dismissed 443 U.S. 901, 99 S.Ct. 3091 (1979). See also *Springfield School District v. Department of Education,* 483 Pa. 539, 397 A.2d 1154 (1979), appeal dismissed 443 U.S. 901, 99 S.Ct. 3091 (1979).

3. Relate the historical background and rationale of Jefferson's *Bill for Establishing Religious Freedom* and Madison's *Memorial and Remonstrance Against Religious Assessments* to *Everson.*

4. In the *Everson* case, is the state's contribution under the New Jersey law in defraying the cost of conveying pupils to a place where they will receive primarily religious instruction in fact a substitution of resources for parents and an encouragement to aid religion?

5. Statutes that authorize public transportation for parochial school children to travel to and from the private schools do not constitute mandatory authority for the public schools to also transport such children for educational field trips. *Cook v. Griffin,* 47 A.D.2d 23, 364 N.Y.S.2d 632

(1975). See also: *Wolman v. Walter,* 433 U.S. 229, 97 S.Ct. 2593 (1977).

Loan of Textbooks to Parochial School Students Does Not Violate Establishment Clause

———————————

Board of Education of Central School District No. 1 v. Allen

———————————

Supreme Court of the United States, 1968.
392 U.S. 236, 88 S.Ct. 1923.

Mr. Justice WHITE delivered the opinion of the Court. A law of the State of New York requires local public school authorities to lend textbooks free of charge to all students in grades seven through twelve; students attending private schools are included. This case presents the question whether this statute is a "law respecting an establishment of religion, or prohibiting the free exercise thereof," and so in conflict with the First and Fourteenth Amendments to the Constitution, because it authorizes the loan of textbooks to students attending parochial schools. We hold that the law is not in violation of the Constitution.

. . .

Beginning with the 1966–1967 school year, local school boards were required to purchase textbooks and lend them without charge "to all children residing in such district who are enrolled in grades seven to twelve of a public or private school which complies with the compulsory education law."[44] The books now loaned are "text-books which are designated for use in any public, elementary or secondary schools of the state or are approved by any boards of education," and which—according to a 1966 amendment—"a pupil is required to use as a text for a semester or more in a particular class in the school he legally attends."

Appellant Board of Education of Central School District No. 1 in Rensselaer and Columbia Counties brought suit in the New York courts against appellee James Allen. The complaint alleged that § 701 violated both the State and Federal Constitutions; that if appellants, in reliance on their interpretation of the Constitution, failed to lend books to parochial school students within their counties appellee Allen would remove appellants from office; and that to prevent this, appellants were complying with the law and submitting to their constituents a school budget including funds for books to be lent to parochial school pupils. Appellants therefore sought a declaration that § 701 was invalid, an order barring appellee Allen from removing appellants from office for failing to comply with it, and another order restraining him from apportioning state funds to school districts for the purchase of textbooks to be lent to parochial students. . . .

Everson and later cases have shown that the line between state neutrality to religion and state support of religion is not easy to locate. "The constitutional standard is the separation of Church and State. The problem, like many problems in constitutional law, is one of degree." *Zorach v. Clauson,* 343 U.S. 306, 314, 72 S.Ct. 679, 684, 96 L.Ed. 954 (1952). . . . Based on *Everson, Zorach, McGowan,* and other cases, *Abington Tp. School District v. Schempp,* 374 U.S. 203, 83 S.Ct. 1560, 10 L.Ed.2d 844 (1963), fashioned a test subscribed to by eight Justices for distinguishing between forbidden involvements of the State with religion and those contacts which the Establishment Clause permits:

> The test may be stated as follows: what are the purpose and the primary effect of the enactment? If either is the advancement or inhibition of religion then the enactment exceeds the scope of legislative power as circumscribed by the Constitution. That is to say that to withstand the strictures of the Establishment Clause there must be a secular legislative purpose and a primary effect that neither advances nor inhibits religion. *Everson v. Board* of Education . . . . 374 U.S. at 222, 83 S.Ct., at 1571.

This test is not easy to apply, but the citation of *Everson* by the *Schempp* Court to support its general standard made clear how the *Schempp* rule would be applied to the facts of *Everson.* The statute upheld in *Everson* would be considered a law having "a secular legislative purpose and a primary effect that neither advances nor inhibits religion." We reach the same result with respect to the New York law requiring school books to be loaned free of charge to all students in specified grades. The express purpose of § 701 was stated by the New York Legislature to be furtherance of the educational opportunities available to the young. Appellants have shown us nothing about the necessary effects of the statute that is contrary to its stated purpose. The law merely makes available to all children the benefits of a general program to lend school books free of charge. Books are furnished at the request of the pupil and ownership remains, at least technically, in the State. Thus no funds or books are furnished to parochial schools, and the financial benefit is to parents and children, not to schools. Perhaps free books make it more likely that some children choose to attend a sectarian school, but that was true of the state-paid bus fares in *Everson* and does not alone demonstrate an unconstitutional degree of support for a religious institution. . . .

The major reason offered by appellants for distinguishing free textbooks from free bus fares is that books, but not buses, are critical to the teaching process, and in a sectarian school that process is employed to teach religion. However this Court has long recognized that religious schools pursue two goals, religious instruction and secular education. In the leading case of *Pierce v. Society of Sisters,* 268 U.S. 510, 45 S.Ct. 571, 69 L.Ed. 1070 (1925), the Court held that although it would not question Oregon's power to compel school attendance or require that the attendance be at an institution meeting State-imposed requirements as to quality and nature of curriculum, Oregon had not shown that its interest in secular education required that all children attend publicly operated schools. A premise of this holding was the view that the State's interest in education would be served sufficiently by reliance on the secular teaching that accompanied religious training in the schools maintained by the Society of Sisters. Since *Pierce*, a substantial body of case law has confirmed the power of the States to insist that attendance at private schools, if it is to satisfy state compulsory-attendance laws, be at institutions which provide minimum hours of instruction, employ teachers of specified training, and cover prescribed subjects of instruction. Indeed, the State's interest in assuring that these standards are being met has been considered a sufficient reason for refusing to accept instruction at home as compliance with compulsory education statutes. These cases were a sensible corollary of *Pierce v. Society of Sisters:* if the State must satisfy its interest in secular education through the instrument of private schools, it has a proper interest in the manner in which those schools perform their secular educational function. Another corollary was *Cochran v. Louisiana State Board of Education*, 281 U.S. 370, 50 S.Ct. 335, 74 L.Ed. 913 (1930), where appellants said that a statute requiring school books to be furnished without charge to all students, whether they attended public or private schools, did not serve a "public purpose," and so offended the Fourteenth Amendment. Speaking through Chief Justice Hughes, the Court summarized as follows its conclusion that Louisiana's interest in the secular education being provided by private schools made provision of textbooks to students in those schools a properly public concern: "[The State's] interest is education, broadly; its method, comprehensive. Individual interests are aided only as the common interest is safeguarded." 281 U.S., at 375, 50 S.Ct., at 336.

Underlying these cases, and underlying also the legislative judgments that have preceded the court decisions, has been a recognition that private education has played and is playing a significant and valuable role in raising national levels of knowledge, competence, and experience. Americans care about the quality of the secular education available to their children. They have considered high quality education to be an indispensable ingredient for achieving the kind of nation,

and the kind of citizenry, that they have desired to create. Considering this attitude, the continued willingness to rely on private school systems, including parochial systems, strongly suggests that a wide segment of informed opinion, legislative and otherwise, has found that those schools do an acceptable job of providing secular education to their students. This judgment is further evidence that parochial schools are performing, in addition to their sectarian function, the task of secular education.

Against this background of judgment and experience, unchallenged in the meager record before us in this case, we cannot agree with appellants either that all teaching in a sectarian school is religious or that the processes of secular and religious training are so intertwined that secular textbooks furnished to students by the public are in fact instrumental in the teaching of religion. This case comes to us after summary judgment entered on the pleadings. Nothing in this record supports the proposition that all textbooks, whether they deal with mathematics, physics, foreign languages, history, or literature, are used by the parochial schools to teach religion. No evidence has been offered about particular schools, particular courses, particular teachers, or particular books. We are unable to hold, based solely on judicial notice, that this statute results in unconstitutional involvement of the State with religious instruction or that § 701, for this or the other reasons urged, is a law respecting the establishment of religion within the meaning of the First Amendment. . . .

Mr. Justice BLACK, dissenting. . . . I believe the New York law held valid is a flat, flagrant, open violation of the First and Fourteenth Amendments which together forbid Congress or state legislatures to enact any law "respecting an establishment of religion." For that reason I would reverse the New York Court of Appeals' judgment. . . .

The *Everson* and *McCollum* cases plainly interpret the First and Fourteenth Amendments as protecting the taxpayers of a State from being compelled to pay taxes to their government to support the agencies of private religious organizations the taxpayers oppose.

To authorize a State to tax its residents for such church purposes is to put the State squarely in the religious activities of certain religious groups that happen to be strong enough politically to write their own religious preferences and prejudices into the laws. This links state and churches together in controlling the lives and destinies of our citizenship — a citizenship composed of people of myriad religious faiths, some of them bitterly hostile to and completely intolerant of the others. It was to escape laws precisely like this that a large part of the Nation's early immigrants fled to this country. It was also to escape such laws and such consequences that the First Amendment was written in language strong and clear barring passage of any law "respecting an establishment of religion."

It is true, of course, that the New York law does not as yet formally adopt or establish a state religion. But it takes a great stride in that direction and coming events cast their shadows before them. The same powerful sectarian religious propagandists who have succeeded in securing passage of the present law to help religious schools carry on their sectarian religious purposes can and doubtless will continue their propaganda, looking toward complete domination and supremacy of their particular brand of religion.[45] And it nearly always is by insidious approaches that the citadels of liberty are most successfully attacked.[46]

I know of no prior opinion of this Court upon which the majority here can rightfully rely to support its holding this New York law constitutional. In saying this, I am not unmindful of the fact that the New York Court of Appeals purported to follow *Everson v. Board of Education,* in which this Court, in an opinion written by me, upheld a New Jersey law authorizing reimbursement to parents for the transportation of children attending sectarian schools. That law did not attempt to deny the benefit of its general terms to children of any faith going to any legally authorized school. Thus, it was treated in the same way as a general law paying the streetcar fare *of all school children,* or a law providing midday lunches for all children, or a law to provide police protection for children going to and from school, or general laws to provide police and fire protection for buildings, including, of course, churches and church school buildings as well as others.

As my Brother DOUGLAS so forcefully shows, in an argument with which I fully agree, upholding a State's power to pay bus or streetcar fares for school children cannot provide support for the validity of a state law using tax-raised funds to buy school books for a religious school. The First Amendment's bar to establishment of religion must preclude a State from using funds levied from all of its citizens to purchase books for use by sectarian schools, which, although "secular," realistically will in some way inevitably tend to propagate the religious views of the favored sect. Books are the most essential tool of education since they contain the resources of knowledge which the educational process is designed to exploit. In this sense it is not difficult to distinguish books, which are the heart of any school, from bus fares, which provide a convenient and helpful general public transportation service. With respect to the former, state financial support actively and directly assists the teaching and propagation of sectarian religious viewpoints in clear conflict with the First Amendment's establishment bar; with respect to the latter, the State merely provides a general and nondiscriminatory transportation service in no way related to substantive religious views and beliefs.

This New York law, it may be said by some, makes but a small inroad and does not amount to complete state establishment of religion. But that is no excuse for upholding it. It requires no prophet to foresee that on the argument used to support this law others could be upheld providing for state or federal government funds to buy property on which to erect religious school buildings or to erect the buildings themselves, to pay the salaries of the religious school teachers, and finally to have the sectarian religious groups cease to rely on voluntary contributions of members of their sects while waiting for the Government to pick up all the bills for the religious schools. Arguments made in favor of this New York law point squarely in this direction, namely, that the fact that government has not heretofore aided religious schools with tax-raised funds amounts to a discrimination against those schools and against religion. And that there are already efforts to have government supply the money to erect buildings for sectarian religious schools is shown by a recent Act of Congress which apparently allows for precisely that. See Higher Education Facilities Act of 1963, 77 Stat. 363, 20 U.S.C.A. § 701 et seq.

I still subscribe to the belief that tax-raised funds cannot constitutionally be used to support religious schools, buy their school books, erect their buildings, pay their teachers, or pay any other of their maintenance expenses, even to the extent of one penny. The First Amendment's prohibition against governmental establishment of religion was written on the assumption that state aid to religion and religious schools generates discord, disharmony, hatred, and strife among our people, and that any government that supplies such aids is to that extent a tyranny. And I still believe that the only way to protect minority religious groups from majority groups in this country is to keep the wall of separation between church and state high and impregnable as the First and Fourteenth Amendments provide. The Court's affirmance here bodes nothing but evil to religious peace in this country. . . .

NOTES

1. Observe that Justice Black wrote the majority opinion in *Everson* and dissented in *Allen*. This is particularly interesting since the majority opinion by Justice White relied heavily on the interpretation and meaning of the majority in *Everson*.
2. The *Cochran* case in Louisiana was preceded by *Borden v. Louisiana State Board of Education,* 168 La. 1005, 123 So. 655 (1929), which held that the Acts of 1928, Nos. 100 and 143, the same acts contested in *Cochran,* were not violative of religious constitutional prohibitions, nor did the acts violate constitutional provisions prohibiting public funds for private or benevolent purposes and were not adverse to due process requirements.

3. Appellants in *Allen* argue that transportation of parochial pupils may be constitutional whereas providing textbooks is not. How does the Court react to this argument? Compare the Court's opinion to the dissenting opinion of Justice Jackson in the *Everson* case.
4. What is the implication of Justice White's statement that "parochial schools are performing, in addition to their sectarian function, the task of secular education?"
5. How does Justice Black, in dissent in *Allen,* distinguish textbooks from transportation in *Everson* in which he wrote the majority opinion?

■ PUBLIC FUNDS FOR PAROCHIAL SCHOOLS

The decision by the Supreme Court in the *Allen* case[47] created many questions on the part of both public and parochial school leaders throughout the country. The language of Justice White, speaking for the majority, was unclear, failing to delineate First Amendment restrictions in providing state aid to parochial schools. White applied the public purpose theory and reasoned that the state could give assistance to religious schools so long as the aid was provided for only secular services in the operation of parochial schools. He said that

> a wide segment of informed opinion, legislative and otherwise, has found that those schools [parochial] do an acceptable job of providing secular education to their students. *This judgment is further evidence that parochial schools are performing, in addition to their sectarian function, the task of secular education.*

This statement was taken by many parochial school educators to mean that a state could permissibly provide funds to parochial schools for such things as teachers' salaries, operation, building, and so on, so long as the funds were used by the parochial school only for "public secular purposes." State legislatures were suddenly flooded with hundreds of bills to provide state support to parochial schools; some were passed and others, for various reasons, failed.

It was into this fertile area of conjecture that the Supreme Court of the United States walked in 1971 when it was asked to rule on the constitutionality of two such state acts from Pennsylvania and Rhode Island. Both states, relying on the vagueness of *Allen,* were attempting to aid parochial schools. The Supreme Court struck down the statutes of both states. The court found the "secular purpose" standard alone to be inadequate and added its own standard of "excessive entanglement." This new standard seeks to prevent the state from infringing on the separate rights of religion by becoming too intermingled with the process of religion. The Supreme Court summarized three tests for determining constitutionality of a state statute and applied and discussed each of these in *Lemon v. Kurtzman.* The tests are (1) the statute must have a secular legislative purpose, (2) its principal or primary effect must be one that neither advances nor inhibits religion, and (3) it must not foster excessive government entanglement with religion. Subsequent Supreme Court cases have explained the law as prescribed by these tests.[48]

The Supreme Court, on 25 June 1973, delivered three opinions regarding financial aid to private schools. The first case was *Levitt v. Committee,* where the New York legislature in 1970 appropriated funds for reimbursing nonpublic school expenses for various services performed by the nonpublic schools. These services included

> administration, grading and the compiling and reporting of the results of tests and examinations, maintenance of records of pupils enrollment and reporting hereon, maintenance of pupil health records, recording of personnel qualifications and characteristics and the preparation and submission to the state of various other reports as provided for or required by law or regulation.[49]

The most expensive of these services was the administration, grading, compiling, and reporting of tests, which included both state-prepared examinations and teacher-prepared tests. The New York statute made no provision for auditing[50] the expenditures to determine the private schools expenditures. The Supreme Court ruled that the funds impermissibly aided religion, violating the Establishment Clause.

Almost immediately after the *Levitt* case was rendered, the New York legislature sought to remedy the defects by enacting a revised statute unencumbered by the unconstitutional aspects. The new statute was to pay the actual cost incurred by the nonpublic schools in complying with state reporting mandates that included a pupil evaluation program, basic educational data system, regent examinations, and other state-prepared examinations, as well as several reporting requirements designed to confirm school performance of the other functions. Payments were to be audited by the state, a requirement that had not been included in the earlier law. With these changes, the statute was litigated before the Supreme Court, in the case of the *Committee for Public Education and Religious Liberty v. Regan,*[51] 1980. The law, this time, passed constitutional muster. The legislature had been successful in skillfully paring and shaping the law to skirt the edges of unconstitutionality to permit aid to parochial schools.

In a second case, *Committee for Public Education and Religious Liberty v. Nyquist,*[52] the challenge was based on a New York statute designed to aid nonpublic schools. The New York legislature had amended the education and tax laws to provide financial aid to nonpublic elementary and secondary schools by way of (1) grants to nonpublic schools for "maintenance and repair" of facilities and equipment,[53] (2) tuition reimbursement plan for nonpublic school parents whose children were enrolled in elementary and secondary schools,[54] and (3) tax relief for parents who did not qualify for the tuition reimbursement plan. In evaluating each provision, the U.S. Supreme Court ruled that all three provisions violated the Establishment Clause because they subsidized and, thereby, advanced religion.

The third case, rendered in 1973, brought down a Pennsylvania law entitled "Parent

Reimbursement Act for Nonpublic Education" that compensated parochial school parents for a portion of their private school tuition expenses.[55] The Court found that there was no constitutionally significant difference between the Pennsylvania and the New York statutes, both being in violation of the Establishment Clause.

By mid-decade of the 1970s, the Supreme Court was again faced with an even more complex and circuitous Pennsylvania effort to aid nonpublic schools.[56] One part of the law, Act 194, provided auxiliary services to children enrolled in nonpublic schools, including counseling, testing, psychological services, speech and hearing therapy, and services for disadvantaged and exceptional children. The court ruled that because the services were provided in predominantly church-related schools, excessive entanglement existed. The second part, Act 195, extended a direct loan of textbooks and instructional materials and equipment to parochial schools. The law defined instructional materials and equipment as photographs, maps, charts, globes, films, projection equipment, recording equipment, and so forth. The Court ruled that because the textbooks were secular and were the same as those used in the public schools, their benefits accrued only to the parents or students and not the parochial school. The Court refused to bring instructional materials under the constitutional umbrella that had been fashioned by *Cochran* and *Allen*. Even though the instructional materials and equipment were merely loaned to the parochial school, the Court ruled that the primary effect of the law was to advance religion.

Still more litigation ensued in 1977 from Ohio, a state aggressively persistent in its efforts to provide public funds to aid private schools. In this case, Justice Blackmun commented, "This is still another case presenting the recurrent issue of the limitations imposed by the Establishment Clause of the First Amendment . . . on state aid to pupils in church-related elementary and secondary schools."[57] Here, the Ohio law provided funds to nonpublic schools for (1) textbooks, (2) testing and scoring of standard-

ized tests, (3) diagnostic services, (4) therapeutic services, (5) instructional materials and equipment, and (6) field trips by nonpublic school children. The law required that the textbooks purchased by private schools with state funds be the same as those used in the public schools. The books were to be loaned to the pupils in nonpublic schools. The Supreme Court disected the issues and concluded that based on its decisions in *Allen* and *Meek* the textbook provision was constitutional, as were the state payments for testing and scoring. Similarly, the Court upheld the payment for diagnostic services as distinguishable from teaching or counseling, reasoning that such services encompassed no educational content and were not closely associated with the educational mission of the nonpublic school.[58] Concerning the therapeutic, guidance, and remedial services to be provided in public schools, public centers, or in mobile units located off the nonpublic school premises, the Supreme Court held that because the locus of the service was not on parochial school property, there was no excessive entanglement. Lastly, the Court ruled that the loan of instructional materials and equipment to parochial schools was unconstitutional because there was no way of ensuring their secular use.[59] The field trip scheme met the same fate of unconstitutionality.

These cases, when combined, bear witness to the political pressure that is today exerted on state legislatures to aid parochial schools and suggest intensified efforts to use public tax funds to support private and parochial schools.

Tax Credits and Deductions

The issue of aid to nonpublic schools in the form of tax credits or tax deductions is not a new idea. In 1972, a lower federal district court invalidated Ohio's Parental Reimbursement Grant, which provided a tax credit[60] to nonpublic school parents, a decision that was summarily affirmed by the U.S. Supreme Court in 1973.[61] As described earlier, the Supreme Court addressed the tax benefit in *Nyquist* and found a New York statute for nonpublic school parents was unconstitutional.[62] Again, in 1979, the Supreme Court confronted the tax benefit issue, at which time it summarily affirmed the Third Circuit Court of Appeals decision[63] invalidating a tax benefit program for nonpublic school parents in New Jersey. This program allowed nonpublic school parents a $100 tax deduction for each dependent child's attendance at a tuition-charging nonpublic school. In yet another case, the U.S. Court of Appeals, First Circuit, ruled in 1980 in *Norberg*, a Rhode Island case, that a statute allowing nonpublic school parents a state income tax deduction for tuition, textbooks, and transportation expenses was unconstitutional as violative of the Establishment Clause.[64]

Perhaps the leading case on the subject of tax credits resulted from a Minnesota statute that allowed all parent taxpayers to deduct from their income taxes a legislatively specified amount. In approving this scheme of aid to private schools, the U.S. Supreme Court[65] appeared to chart a new direction of even greater leniency in provision of public monies for parochial schools. In validating the Minnesota plan, the Court distinguished its rejection of the earlier tax deduction or credit plans by noting that each of those limited tax benefits were available only to parents of private school children, while the Minnesota deduction was available to parents of *all* children in both private and public schools. The Court did not seem to be concerned that tax deduction benefits to public school parents would be minimal, because public schools do not charge tuition or transportation fees and textbooks are, by and large, free. The primary benefits would then, of course, accrue largely to the advantage of parochial school parents. Justice Rehnquist, in applying the three-part test for the 5–4 majority, found that the statute had a secular purpose, that it did not advance or promote religion, and that governmental entanglement with the church was minimal and unimportant.

Importantly, Rehnquist, in justifying the decision, expressed a view of the Court (which is apparently in its ascendency) to the effect that parochial schools are a viable and important alternative to public schools fostering "wholesome competition" and that states are

justified in giving them tax support.[66] This same view is a slightly different version of that expressed by Justice White in 1968 in *Board of Education v. Allen*.[67] There the Court justified the loan of textbooks on the grounds that parochial schools were performing an important secular function that was of sufficient public importance to merit public financial assistance.

Buchanan has said that the present situation of condoning aid to private schools supports a "total subsidy" position.[68] He maintains that any aid will be constitutional if the aid has a secular purpose, and if the aid is offered to religious and nonreligious entities, as in Minnesota, where the tax deduction or credit is available to *all* parents.[69]

In a *Grand Rapids* case[70] in 1985, the Supreme Court, under the hand of Justice Brennan, momentarily returned to a more strict adherence to separation. In this case, a Grand Rapids plan offered benefits to parochial schools through shared time and community education programs financed by the public school system. Justice Brennan, writing for the majority, found that the plan had the primary effect of advancing religion.

Justice Brennan again prevailed in the 1985 *Aguilar* decision,[71] in which he formed a majority coalition of justices enabling the Court to strike down a New York City plan that provided federal Title I, Elementary and Secondary Education Act of 1965 funds to pay for the education of eligible parochial school students on parochial school premises. The Supreme Court found that such a benefit to the parochial schools offended the Establishment Clause. Justice Brennan went to great length to explain why this particular plan, which involved the use of public school teachers in parochial schools as well as an elaborate monitoring system, violated the excessive entanglement test.

In reviewing the education cases interpreting the Establishment Clause, one is struck by the failure of the Court to delineate a workable definition prescribing the boundaries of constitutionality. Levy has observed that the "Supreme Court has been inexcusably inconsistent in its interpretation of the Establishment Clause."[72] By and large, the court has kept religion out of public schools, and has generally prevented public tax funds from flowing to parochial schools. Today, however, there is an obvious trend toward a judicially sanctioned permissiveness in giving public dollars to religious schools. Levy has noted that "the court has reaped the scorn of a confused and aroused public because it has been erratic and unprincipled in its decisions. It sometimes heeds history; other times it ignores history and distorts it."[73] This is not entirely the fault of the Supreme Court, because the Court itself has been forced to respond to a consistent and seemingly endless array of attempts by legislatures, in states with large percentages of parochial school students, to circumvent separation barriers in efforts to allow tax funds to flow to religious schools. The repeated attempts to override or change the precedents established by the Court, making them more favorable to private schools, have produced a series of technical exceptions that make infeasible, if not impossible, the creation of generally applicable rules of constitutional law. The persistence of these legislative blows at an already crumbling wall of separation has given credence to the arguments of those who have traditionally asserted that the creation of a wall of separation of church and state is an inappropriate and impractical pursuit.

The future of the Establishment Clause appears to entail a continuing erosion of the wall as far as aid to parochial schools is concerned. The new majority on the Supreme Court, including Justices Souter, Kennedy, Scalia, O'Conner, White, Rehnquist, and Thomas, have indicated by deed or background that they will favor public aid to parochial schools. The philosophical rationale for this position was enunciated by Chief Justice Rehnquist in his dissent in *Wallace v. Jaffree* in 1985,[74] where he maintained that the true intent of the Establishment Clause was merely to prohibit a "national religion" or the "official designation of any church as a national one" as well as to discourage the preference of any particular religious sect over another. It did not intend, according to Rehnquist, to create "government neutrality between religion and irreligion, nor did it

prohibit the federal government from providing nondiscriminating aid to religion."[75] This nonpreferential philosophy would, therefore, allow state and federal tax funds to go to religious schools so long as one or a few religious sects were not preferred over others. The fact that one religious group may control over 80 percent of America's private schools would apparently make no difference in the application of this nonpreferential philosophy.[76] This position is, of course, diametrically opposed to the intent enunciated in Madison's *Memorial and Remonstrance,* which declared that government should not aid one religion or *all* religions. The Rehnquist's nonpreferential stance, however, probably represents the wave of the future.

State Aid to Parochial Schools through Salary Supplements and Purchase of Services Constitutes Impermissible Entanglement between Church and State

—-—-—-—-—

Lemon v. Kurtzman

—-—-—-—-—

Supreme Court of the United States, 1971.
403 U.S. 602, 91 S.Ct. 2105.

Mr. Chief Justice BURGER delivered the opinion of the Court. These two appeals raise questions as to Pennsylvania and Rhode Island statutes providing state aid to church-related elementary and secondary schools. Both statutes are challenged as violative of the Establishment and Free Exercise Clauses of the First Amendment and the Due Process Clause of the Fourteenth Amendment.

Pennsylvania has adopted a statutory program that provides financial support to nonpublic elementary and secondary schools by way of reimbursement for the cost of teachers' salaries, textbooks, and instructional materials in specified secular subjects. Rhode Island has adopted a statute under which the State pays directly to teachers in nonpublic elementary schools a supplement of 15 percent of their annual salary. Under each statute state aid has been given to church-related educational institutions. We hold that both statutes are unconstitutional.

The Rhode Island Salary Supplement Act[77] was enacted in 1969. It rests on the legislative finding that the quality of education available in nonpublic elementary schools has been jeopardized by the rapidly rising salaries needed to attract competent and dedicated teachers. The Act authorizes state officials to supplement the salaries of teachers of secular subjects in nonpublic elementary schools by paying directly to a teacher an amount not in excess of 15 percent of his current annual salary. As supplemented, however, a nonpublic school teacher's salary cannot exceed the maximum paid to teachers in the State's public schools, and the recipient must be certified by the state board of education in substantially the same manner as public school teachers.

In order to be eligible for the Rhode Island salary supplement, the recipient must teach in a nonpublic school at which the average per-pupil expenditure on secular education is less than the average in the State's public schools during a specified period. Appellant State Commissioner of Education also requires eligible schools to submit financial data. If this information indicates a per-pupil expenditure in excess of the statutory limitation, the records of the school in question must be examined in order to assess how much of the expenditure is attributable to secular education and how much to religious activity.

The Act also requires that teachers eligible for salary supplements must teach only those subjects that are offered in the State's public schools. They must use "only teaching materials which are used in the public schools." Finally, any teacher applying for a salary supplement must first agree in writing "not to teach a course in religion for so long as or during such time as he or she receives any salary supplements" under the Act.

Appellees are citizens and taxpayers of Rhode Island. . . . Appellants are state officials charged with administration of the Act, teachers eligible for salary supplements under the Act, and parents of children in

church-related elementary schools whose teachers would receive state salary assistance.

A three-judge federal court was convened pursuant to 28 U.S.C.A. §§ 2281, 2284. It found that Rhode Island's non-public elementary schools accommodated approximately 25 percent of the State's pupils. About 95 percent of these pupils attended schools affiliated with the Roman Catholic church. To date some 250 teachers have applied for benefits under the Act. All of them are employed by Roman Catholic schools. •

The court held a hearing at which extensive evidence was introduced concerning the nature of the secular instruction offered in the Roman Catholic schools whose teachers would be eligible for salary assistance under the Act. Although the court found that concern for religious values does not necessarily affect the content of secular subjects, it also found that the parochial school system was "an integral part of the religious mission of the Catholic Church."

The District Court concluded that the Act violated the Establishment Clause, holding that it fostered "excessive entanglement" between government and religion. In addition two judges thought that the Act had the impermissible effect of giving "significant aid to a religious enterprise." 316 F.Supp. 112. We affirm.

Pennsylvania has adopted a program that has some but not all of the features of the Rhode Island program. The Pennsylvania Nonpublic Elementary and Secondary Education Act[78] was passed in 1968 in response to a crisis that the Pennsylvania Legislature found existed in the State's nonpublic schools due to rapidly rising costs. The statute affirmatively reflects the legislative conclusion that the State's educational goals could appropriately be fulfilled by government support of "those purely secular educational objectives achieved through nonpublic education . . . ."

The statute authorizes appellee state Superintendent of Public Instruction to "purchase" specified "secular educational services" from nonpublic schools. Under the "contracts" authorized by the statute, the State directly reimburses nonpublic schools solely for their actual expenditures for teachers' salaries, textbooks, and instructional materials. A school seeking reimbursement must maintain prescribed accounting procedures that identify the "separate" cost of the "secular educational service." These accounts are subject to state audit. The funds for this program were originally derived from a new tax on horse and harness racing, but the Act is now financed by a portion of the state tax on cigarettes.

There are several significant statutory restrictions on state aid. Reimbursement is limited to courses "presented in the curricula of the public schools." It is further limited "solely" to courses in the following "secular" subjects: mathematics, modern foreign languages,[79] physical science, and physical education. Textbooks and instructional materials included in the program must be approved by the state Superintendent of Public Instruction. Finally, the statute prohibits reimbursement for any course that contains "any subject matter expressing religious teaching, or the morals or forms of worship of any sect."

The Act went into effect on July 1, 1968, and the first reimbursement payments to schools were made on September 2, 1969. It appears that some $5 million has been expended annually under the Act. The State has now entered into contracts with some 1,181 nonpublic elementary and secondary schools with a student population of some 535,215 pupils—more than 20 percent of the total number of students in the State. More than 96 percent of these pupils attend church-related schools, and most of these schools are affiliated with the Roman Catholic church.

Appellants brought this action in the District Court to challenge the constitutionality of the Pennsylvania statute. The organizational plaintiffs-appellants are associations of persons resident in Pennsylvania declaring belief in the separation of church and state; individual plaintiffs-appellants are citizens and taxpayers of Pennsylvania. Appellant Lemon, in addition to being a citizen and a taxpayer, is a parent of a child attending public school in Pennsylvania. Lemon also alleges that he purchased a ticket at a race track and thus had paid the specific tax that supports the expenditures under the Act. . . . The District Court held that the individual plaintiffs-appellants had standing to challenge the Act, 310 F.Supp. 42. . . .

The court granted appellees' motion to dismiss the complaint for failure to state a claim for relief. 310 F.Supp. 35. It held that the Act violated neither the Establishment nor the Free Exercise Clause, Chief Judge Hastie dissenting. We reverse.

In *Everson v. Board of Education,* 330 U.S. 1, 67 S.Ct. 504, 91 L.Ed. 711 (1947), this Court upheld a state statute that reimbursed the parents of parochial school children for bus transportation expenses. There Mr. Justice Black, writing for the majority, suggested that the decision carried to "the verge" of forbidden territory under the Religion Clauses. Id., at 16, 67 S.Ct., at 511. Candor compels acknowledgment, moreover, that we can only dimly perceive the lines of demarcation in this extraordinarily sensitive area of constitutional law.

The language of the Religion Clauses of the First Amendment is at best opaque, particularly when compared with other portions of the Amendment. Its authors did not simply prohibit the establishment of a state church or a state religion, an area history shows they regarded as very important and fraught with great dangers. Instead they commanded that there should be "no law *respecting* an establishment of religion." A law may be one "respecting" the forbidden objective while falling short of its total realization. A law "respecting" the proscribed result, that is, the establishment of religion, is not always easily identifiable as one violative of the Clause. A given law might not *establish* a state religion but nevertheless be one "respecting" that end in the sense of being a step that could lead to such establishment and hence offend the First Amendment.

In the absence of precisely stated constitutional prohibitions, we must draw lines with reference to the three main evils against which the Establishment Clause was intended to afford protection: "sponsorship, financial support, and active involvement of the sovereign in religious activity." *Walz v. Tax Commission,* 397 U.S. 664, 668, 90 S.Ct. 1409, 1411, 25 L.Ed.2d 697 (1970).

Every analysis in this area must begin with consideration of the cumulative criteria developed by the Court over many years. Three such tests may be gleaned from our cases. First, the statute must have a secular legislative purpose; second, its principal or primary effect must be one that neither advances nor inhibits religion, *Board of Education v. Allen,* 392 U.S. 236, 243, 88 S.Ct. 1923, 1926, 20 L.Ed.2d 1060 (1968); finally, the statute must not foster "an excessive government entanglement with religion." *Walz,* supra, at 674, 90 S.Ct. at 1414.

Inquiry into the legislative purposes of the Pennsylvania and Rhode Island statutes affords no basis for a conclusion that the legislative intent was to advance religion. On the contrary, the statutes themselves clearly state that they are intended to enhance the quality of the secular education in all schools covered by the compulsory attendance laws. There is no reason to believe the legislatures meant anything else. A State always has a legitimate concern for maintaining minimum standards in all schools it allows to operate. As in *Allen,* we find nothing here that undermines the stated legislative intent; it must therefore be accorded appropriate deference.

In *Allen* the Court acknowledged that secular and religious teachings were not necessarily so intertwined that secular textbooks furnished to students by the State were in fact instrumental in the teaching of religion. 392 U.S., at 248, 88 S.Ct., at 1929. The legislatures of Rhode Island and Pennsylvania have concluded that secular and religious education are identifiable and separable. In the abstract we have no quarrel with this conclusion.

The two legislatures, however, have also recognized that church-related elementary and secondary schools have a significant religious mission and that a substantial portion of their activities is religiously oriented. They have therefore sought to create statutory restrictions designed to guarantee the separation between secular and religious educational functions and to ensure that State financial aid supports only the former. All these

provisions are precautions taken in candid recognition that these programs approached, even if they did not intrude upon, the forbidden areas under the Religion Clauses. We need not decide whether these legislative precautions restrict the principal or primary effect of the programs to the point where they do not offend the Religion Clauses, for we conclude that the cumulative impact of the entire relationship arising under the statutes in each State involves excessive entanglement between government and religion. . . .

(a)   Rhode Island Program

The District Court made extensive findings on the grave potential for excessive entanglement that inheres in the religious character and purpose of the Roman Catholic elementary schools of Rhode Island, to date the sole beneficiaries of the Rhode Island Salary Supplement Act.

The church schools involved in the program are located close to parish churches. This understandably permits convenient access for religious exercises since instruction in faith and morals is part of the total educational process. The school buildings contain identifying religious symbols such as crosses on the exterior and crucifixes, and religious paintings and statues either in the classrooms or hallways. Although only approximately thirty minutes a day are devoted to direct religious instruction, there are religiously oriented extracurricular activities. Approximately two-thirds of the teachers in these schools are nuns of various religious orders. Their dedicated efforts provide an atmosphere in which religious instruction and religious vocations are natural and proper parts of life in such schools. Indeed, as the District Court found, the role of teaching nuns in enhancing the religious atmosphere has led the parochial school authorities to attempt to maintain a one-to-one ratio between nuns and lay teachers in all schools rather than to permit some to be staffed almost entirely by lay teachers.

On the basis of these findings the District Court concluded that the parochial schools constituted "an integral part of the religious mission of the Catholic Church." The various characteristics of the schools make them "a powerful vehicle for transmitting the Catholic faith to the next generation." This process of inculcating religious doctrine is, of course, enhanced by the impressionable age of the pupils, in primary schools particularly. In short, parochial schools involve substantial religious activity and purpose.

The substantial religious character of these church-related schools gives rise to entangling church-state relationships of the kind the Religion Clauses sought to avoid. Although the District Court found that concern for religious values did not inevitably or necessarily intrude into the content of secular subjects, the considerable religious activities of these schools led the legislature to provide for careful governmental controls and surveillance by state authorities in order to ensure that state aid supports only secular education. . . .

The Rhode Island Legislature has not, and could not, provide state aid on the basis of a mere assumption that secular teachers under religious discipline can avoid conflicts. The State must be certain, given the Religion Clauses, that subsidized teachers do not inculcate religion — indeed the State here has undertaken to do so. To ensure that no trespass occurs, the State has therefore carefully conditioned its aid with pervasive restrictions. An eligible recipient must teach only those courses that are offered in the public schools and use only those texts and materials that are found in the public schools. In addition the teacher must not engage in teaching any course in religion.

A comprehensive, discriminating, and continuing state surveillance will inevitably be required to ensure that these restrictions are obeyed and the First Amendment otherwise respected. Unlike a book, a teacher cannot be inspected once so as to determine the extent and intent of his or her personal beliefs and subjective acceptance of the limitations imposed by the First Amendment. These prophylactic contacts will involve excessive and enduring entanglement between state and church.

There is another area of entanglement in the Rhode Island program that gives concern. The statute excludes teachers employed by nonpublic schools whose average per-pupil expenditures on secular education equal or exceed the comparable figures for public schools. In the event that the total expenditures of an otherwise eligible school exceed this norm, the program requires the government to examine the school's records in order to determine how much of the total expenditures is attributable to secular education and how much to religious activity. This kind of state inspection and evaluation of the religious content of a religious organization is fraught with the sort of entanglement that the Constitution forbids. It is a relationship pregnant with dangers of excessive government direction of church schools and hence of churches. The Court noted "the hazards of government supporting churches" in *Walz v. Tax Commission,* supra, 397 U.S., at 675, 90 S.Ct., at 1414, and we cannot ignore here the danger that pervasive modern governmental power will ultimately intrude on religion and thus conflict with the Religion Clauses.

(b) Pennsylvania Program

The Pennsylvania statute also provides state aid to church-related schools for teachers' salaries. The complaint describes an educational system that is very similar to the one existing in Rhode Island. According to the allegations, the church-related elementary and secondary schools are controlled by religious organizations, have the purpose of propagating and promoting a particular religious faith, and conduct their operations to fulfill that purpose. Since this complaint was dismissed for failure to state a claim for relief, we must accept these allegations as true for purposes of our review.

As we noted earlier, the very restrictions and surveillance necessary to ensure that teachers play a strictly nonideological role give rise to entanglements between church and state. The Pennsylvania statute, like that of Rhode Island, fosters this kind of relationship. Reimbursement is not only limited to courses offered in the public schools and materials approved by state officials, but the statute excludes "any subject matter expressing religious teaching, or the morals or forms of worship of any sect." In addition, schools seeking reimbursement must maintain accounting procedures that require the State to establish the cost of the secular as distinguished from the religious instruction.

The Pennsylvania statute, moreover, has the further defect of providing state financial aid directly to the church-related schools. This factor distinguishes both *Everson* and *Allen,* for in both those cases the Court was careful to point out that state aid was provided to the student and his parents—not to the church-related school. . . . In *Walz v. Tax Commission,* supra, 397 U.S., at 675, 90 S.Ct., at 1414, the Court warned of the dangers of direct payments to religious organizations:

> Obviously a direct money subsidy would be a relationship pregnant with involvement and, as with most governmental grant programs, could encompass sustained and detailed administrative relationships for enforcement of statutory or administrative standards . . . .

The history of government grants of a continuing cash subsidy indicates that such programs have almost always been accompanied by varying measures of control and surveillance. The government cash grants before us now provide no basis for predicting that comprehensive measures of surveillance and controls will not follow. In particular the government's post-audit power to inspect and evaluate a church-related school's financial records and to determine which expenditures are religious and which are secular creates an intimate and continuing relationship between church and state.

A broader base of entanglement of yet a different character is presented by the divisive political potential of these state programs. In a community where such a large number of pupils are served by church-related schools, it can be assumed that state assistance will entail considerable political activity. Partisans of parochial schools, understandably concerned with rising costs and sincerely dedicated to both the religious and secular educational missions of their schools, will inevitably champion this cause and promote political action to achieve their goals. Those who oppose state aid, whether for constitutional, religious, or fiscal reasons, will inevitably respond and employ all of the usual political campaign techniques to prevail. Candidates will be forced to declare and voters to choose. It would be unrealistic to ignore the fact that many people confronted with issues of this kind will find their votes aligned with their faith.

Ordinarily political debate and division, however vigorous or even partisan, are normal and healthy manifestations of our democratic system of government, but political division along religious lines was one of the principal evils against which the First Amendment was intended to protect. . . . The potential divisiveness of such conflict is a threat to the normal political process.
. . .

The potential for political divisiveness related to religious belief and practice is aggravated in these two statutory programs by the need for continuing annual appropriations and the likelihood of larger and larger demands as costs and populations grow.
. . .

In *Walz* it was argued that a tax exemption for places of religious worship would prove to be the first step in an inevitable progression leading to the establishment of state churches and state religion. That claim could not stand up against more than 200 years of virtually universal practice imbedded in our colonial experience and continuing into the present.

The progression argument, however, is more persuasive here. We have no long history of state aid to church-related educational institutions comparable to 200 years of tax exemption for churches. Indeed, the state programs before us today represent something of an innovation. We have already noted that modern governmental programs have self-perpetuating and self-expanding propensities. These internal pressures are only enhanced when the schemes involve institutions whose legitimate needs are growing and whose interests have substantial political support. Nor can we fail to see that in constitutional adjudication some steps, which when taken were thought to approach "the verge," have become the platform for yet further steps. A certain momentum develops in constitutional theory and it can be a "downhill thrust" easily set in motion but difficult to retard or stop. Development by momentum is not invariably bad; indeed, it is the way the common law has grown, but it is a force to be recognized and reckoned with. The dangers are increased by the difficulty of perceiving in advance exactly where the "verge" of the precipice lies. As well as constituting an independent evil against which the Religion Clauses were intended to protect, involvement or entanglement between government and religion serves as a warning signal.

Finally, nothing we have said can be construed to disparage the role of church-related elementary and secondary schools in our national life. Their contribution has been and is enormous. Nor do we ignore their economic plight in a period of rising costs and expanding need. Taxpayers generally have been spared vast sums by the maintenance of these educational institutions by religious organizations, largely by the gifts of faithful adherents.

The merit and benefits of these schools, however, are not the issue before us in these cases. The sole question is whether state aid to these schools can be squared with the dictates of the Religion Clauses. Under our system the choice has been made that government is to be entirely excluded from the area of religious instruction and churches excluded from the affairs of government. The Constitution decrees that religion must be a private matter for the individual, the family, and the institutions of private choice, and that while some involvement and entanglement are inevitable, lines must be drawn.

The judgment of the Rhode Island District Court in No. 569 and No. 570 is affirmed. The judgment of the Pennsylvania District Court in No. 89 is reversed, and the case is remanded for further proceedings consistent with this opinion. . . .

Tuition Reimbursement to Parents of Parochial School Children Is Unconstitutional

– – · – – · – – · – –

Sloan v. Lemon

– – · – – · – – · – –

Supreme Court of the United States, 1973.
413 U.S. 825, 93 S.Ct. 2982.

Mr. Justice POWELL delivered the opinion of the Court. . . . Pennsylvania's "Parent Reimbursement Act for Nonpublic Education" provides for reimbursement to parents who pay tuition for their children to attend the State's nonpublic elementary and secondary schools. Qualifying parents are entitled to receive $75 for each dependent enrolled in an elementary school, and $150 for each dependent in a secondary school, unless that amount exceeds the amount of tuition actually paid. The money to fund this program is to be derived from a portion of the revenues from the State's tax on cigarette sales, and is to be administered by a five-member committee appointed by the Governor, known as the "Pennsylvania Parent Assistance Authority." In an effort to avoid the "entanglement" problem that flawed its prior aid statute, *Lemon v. Kurtzman, supra,* the new legislation specifically precludes the administering authority from having any "direction, supervision or control over the policy determinations, personnel, curriculum, program of instruction or any other aspect of the administration or operation of any nonpublic school or schools." Similarly, the statute imposes no restrictions or limitations on the uses to which the reimbursement allotments can be put by the qualifying parents.

Like the New York tuition program, the Pennsylvania law is prefaced by "legislative findings," which emphasize its underlying secular purposes: parents who send their children to nonpublic schools reduce the total cost of public education; "inflation, plus sharply rising costs of education, now combine to place in jeopardy the ability of such parents fully to carry this burden"; if the State's 500,000 nonpublic school children were to transfer to the public schools, the annual operating costs to the State would be $400 million, and the added capital costs would exceed $1 billion; therefore, "parents who maintain students in nonpublic schools provide a vital service" and deserve at least partial reimbursement for alleviating an otherwise "intolerable public burden." We certainly do not question now, any more than we did two Terms ago in *Lemon v. Kurtzman,* the reality and legitimacy of Pennsylvania's secular purposes.   . . .

For purposes of determining whether the Pennsylvania tuition reimbursement program has the impermissible effect of advancing religion, we find no constitutionally significant distinctions between this law and the one declared invalid today in *Nyquist.* Each authorizes the States to use tax-raised funds for tuition reimbursements payable to parents who send their children to nonpublic schools. Neither tells parents how they must spend the amount received. While the Pennsylvania grants are more generous ($75 to $150 as opposed to $50 to $100), and while Pennsylvania imposes no ceiling on the number of children for whom parents may claim tuition reimbursement or on the percentage of the tuition bill for which parents may be reimbursed, these considerations are irrelevant to the First Amendment question.   . . .

Intervenors suggest that New York's law might be differentiated on the ground that because tuition grants there were available only to parents in an extremely low income bracket (less than $5,000 of taxable income), it would be reasonable to predict that the grant would, in fact, be used to pay tuition, rendering the parent a mere "conduit" for public aid to religious schools. Since Pennsylvania authorizes grants to all parents of children in nonpublic schools—regardless of income level—it is argued that no such assumption can be made as to how individual parents will spend their reimbursed amounts.

Our decision, however, is not dependent upon any such speculation. Instead we look to the substance of the program, and no matter how it is characterized its effect remains the same. The State has singled out a class of its citizens for a special economic benefit. Whether that benefit be viewed as a simple tuition subsidy, as an incentive to parents to send their children to sectarian schools, or as a reward for having done so, at bottom its intended consequences is to preserve and support religion-oriented institutions. We think it plain that this is quite unlike the sort of "indirect" and "incidental" benefits that flowed to sectarian schools from programs aiding *all* parents by supplying bus transportation and secular textbooks for their children. Such benefits were carefully restricted to the purely secular side of church-affiliated institutions and provided no special aid for those who had chosen to support religious schools. Yet such aid approached the "verge" of the constitutionally impermissible. *Everson v. Board of Education,* 330 U.S. 1, 16, 67 S.Ct. 504, 511, 91 L.Ed. 711 (1947). In *Lemon v. Kurtzman,* we declined to allow *Everson* to be used as the "platform for yet further steps" in granting assistance to "institutions whose legitimate needs are growing and whose interests have substantial political support." Again today we decline to approach or overstep the "precipice" against which the Establishment Clause protects. We hold that Pennsylvania's tuition grant scheme violates the constitutional mandate against the "sponsorship" or "financial support" of religion or religious institutions. . . .

In holding today that Pennsylvania's post-*Lemon v. Kurtzman* attempt to avoid the Establishment Clause's prohibition against government entanglements with religion has failed to satisfy the parallel bar against laws having a primary effect that advances religion, we are not unaware that appellants and those who have endeavored to formulate systems of state aid to nonpublic education may feel that the decisions of this Court have, indeed, presented them with the "insoluble paradox" to which Mr. Justice White referred in his separate opinion in *Lemon v. Kurtzman.* But if novel forms of aid have not readily been sustained by this Court, the "fault" lies not with the doctrines which are said to create a paradox but rather with the Establishment Clause itself: "Congress" and the States by virtue of the Fourteenth Amendment "shall make no law respecting an establishment of religion." With that judgment we are not free to tamper, and while there is "room for play in the joints," . . . the Amendment's proscription clearly forecloses Pennsylvania's tuition reimbursement program.

Affirmed.

Shared Time and Community Education Programs for Nonpublic School Students Have Primary Effect of Advancing Religion

—·—·—·—·—·—

School District of the City of Grand Rapids v. Ball

—·—·—·—·—·—

United State Supreme Court, 1985.
473 U.S. 373, 105 S.Ct. 3216.

Justice BRENNAN delivered the opinion of the Court. The School District of Grand Rapids, Michigan, adopted two programs in which classes for nonpublic school students are financed by the public school system, taught by teachers hired by the public school system, and conducted in "leased" classrooms in the nonpublic schools. Most of the nonpublic schools involved in the programs are sectarian religious schools. This case raises the question whether these programs impermissibly involve the government in the support of sectarian religious activities and thus violate the Establishment Clause of the First Amendment.

At issue in this case are the Community Education and Shared Time programs offered in the nonpublic schools of Grand Rapids, Michigan. These programs, first instituted in the 1976–1977 school year, provide classes to nonpublic school students at public expense in classrooms located in and leased from the local nonpublic schools.

The Shared Time program offers classes during the regular school day that are intended to be supplementary to the "core curriculum" courses that the State of Michigan requires as a part of an accredited school program. Among the subjects offered are "remedial" and "enrichment" mathematics, "remedial" and "enrichment" reading, art, music, and physical education. A typical nonpublic school student attends these classes for one or two class periods per week; approximately "ten percent of any given nonpublic school student's time during the academic year would consist of Shared Time instruction." . . . Although Shared Time itself is a program offered only in the nonpublic schools, there was testimony that the courses included in that program are offered, albeit perhaps in a somewhat different form, in the public schools as well. All of the classes that are the subject of this case are taught in elementary schools, with the exception of Math Topics, a remedial math course taught in the secondary schools.

The Shared Time teachers are full-time employees of the public schools, who often move from classroom to classroom during the course of the school day. A "significant portion" of the teachers (approximately 10%) "previously taught in nonpublic schools, and many of those had been assigned to the same nonpublic school where they were previously employed." The School District of Grand Rapids hires Shared Time teachers in accordance with its ordinary hiring procedures. The public school system apparently provides all of the supplies, materials, and equipment used in connection with Shared Time instruction.

The Community Education Program is offered throughout the Grand Rapids community in schools and on other sites, for children as well as adults. The classes at issue here are taught in the nonpublic elementary schools and commence at the conclusion of the regular school day. Among the courses offered are Arts and Crafts, Home Economics, Spanish, Gymnastics, Yearbook Production, Christmas Arts and Crafts, Drama, Newspaper, Humanities, Chess, Model Building, and Nature Appreciation. . . .

Both programs are administered similarly. The Director of the program, a public school employee, sends packets of course listings to the participating nonpublic schools before the school year begins. The nonpublic school administrators then decide which courses they want to offer. The Director works out an academic schedule for each school, taking into account, *inter alia,* the varying religious holidays celebrated by the schools of different denominations.

Nonpublic school administrators decide which classrooms will be used for the programs, and the Director then inspects the facilities and consults with Shared Time teachers to make sure the facilities are satisfactory. The public school system pays the nonpublic schools for the use of the necessary classroom space by entering into "leases" at the rate of $6 per classroom per week. The "leases," however, contain no mention of the particular room, space, or facility leased and teachers' rooms, libraries, lavatories, and similar facilities are made available at no additional charge. . . . Each room used in the programs has to be free of any crucifix, religious symbol, or artifact, although such religious symbols can be present in the adjoining hallways, corridors, and other facilities used in connection with the program. During the time that a given classroom is being used in the programs, the teacher is required to post a sign stating that it is a "public school classroom." However, there are no signs posted outside the school buildings indicating that public school courses are conducted inside or that the facilities are being used as a public school annex.

Although petitioners label the Shared Time and Community Education students as "part-time public school students," the students attending Shared Time and Community Education courses in facilities leased from a nonpublic school are the same students who attend that particular school otherwise. . . . There is no evidence that any public school student has ever attended a Shared Time or Community Education class in a nonpublic school. . . .

Forty of the forty-one schools at which the programs operate are sectarian in character. The schools of course vary from one another, but substantial evidence suggests that they share deep religious purposes. . . . The District Court found that the schools are "pervasively sectarian," . . . and concluded "without hesitation that the purposes of these schools is to advance their particular religions," . . . and that "a substantial portion of their functions are subsumed in the religious mission." . . .

The First Amendment's guarantee that "Congress shall make no law respecting an establishment of religion," as our cases demonstrate, is more than a pledge that no single religion will be designated as a state religion. . . . It is also more than a mere injunction that governmental programs discriminating among religions are unconstitutional. . . . The Establishment Clause instead primarily proscribes "sponsorship, financial support, and active involvement of the sovereign in religious activity." . . .

Since *Everson* made clear that the guarantees of the Establishment Clause apply to the States, we have often grappled with the problem of state aid to nonpublic, religious schools. In all of these cases, our goal has been to give meaning to the sparse language and broad purposes of the Clause, while not unduly infringing on the ability of the States to provide for the welfare of their people in accordance with their own particular circumstances. Providing for the education of school-children is surely a praiseworthy purpose. But our cases have consistently recognized that even such a praiseworthy, secular purpose cannot validate government aid to parochial schools when the aid has the effect of promoting a single religion or religion generally or when the aid unduly entangles the government in matters religious. For just as religion throughout history has provided spiritual comfort, guidance, and inspiration to many, it can also serve powerfully to divide societies and to exclude those whose beliefs are not in accord with particular religions or sects that

have from time to time achieved dominance.
The solution to this problem adopted by the
Framers and consistently recognized by this
Court is jealously to guard the right of every
individual to worship according to the dictates of conscience while requiring the government to maintain a course of neutrality
among religions, and between religion and
nonreligion. Only in this way can we "make
room for as wide a variety of beliefs and creeds
as the spiritual needs of man deem necessary"
and "sponsor an attitude on the part of
government that shows no partiality to any
one group and lets each flourish according to
the zeal of its adherents and the appeal of its
dogma." . . .

We have noted that the three-part test first
articulated in *Lemon v. Kurtzman,* . . .
guides "[t]he general nature of our inquiry in
this area," . . . .

> Every analysis in this area must begin with
> consideration of the cumulative criteria devel-
> oped by the Court over many years. Three such
> tests may be gleaned from our cases. First, the
> statute must have a secular legislative purpose;
> second, its principal or primary effect must be
> one that neither advances nor inhibits reli-
> gion, . . . finally, the statute must not fos-
> ter "an excessive government entanglement
> with religion." . . .

These tests "must not be viewed as setting the
precise limits to the necessary constitutional
inquiry, but serve only as guidelines with
which to identify instances in which the
objectives of the Establishment Clause have
been impaired." . . . We have particularly relied on *Lemon* in every case involving
the sensitive relationship between government and religion in the education of our
children. The government's activities in this
area can have a magnified impact on impressionable young minds, and the occasional
rivalry of parallel public and private school
systems offers an all-too-ready opportunity
for divisive rifts along religious lines in the
body politic. . . . The *Lemon* test concen-
trates attention on the issues—purposes, effect, entanglement—that determine whether

a particular state action is an improper
"law respecting an establishment of religion." We therefore reaffirm that state action alleged to violate the Establishment
Clause should be measured against the *Lemon*
criteria.

As has often been true in school aid cases,
there is no dispute as to the first test. Both the
District Court and the Court of Appeals found
that the purpose of the Community Education
and Shared Time programs was "manifestly
secular." . . . We find no reason to disagree with this holding, and therefore go on to
consider whether the primary or principal
effect of the challenged programs is to advance or inhibit religion.

Our inquiry must begin with a consideration of the nature of the institutions in which
the programs operate. Of the 41 private
schools where these "part-time public
schools" have operated, 40 are identifiably
religious schools. . . . The District Court
found, however, that "[b]ased upon the massive testimony and exhibits, the conclusion is
inescapable that the religious institutions receiving instructional services from the public
schools are sectarian in the sense that a
substantial portion of their functions are subsumed in the religious mission." . . .

Given that 40 of the 41 schools in this case
are thus "pervasively sectarian," the challenged public-school programs operating in
the religious schools may impermissibly advance religion in three different ways. First,
the teachers participating in the programs
may become involved in intentionally or
inadvertently inculcating particular religious
tenets or beliefs. Second, the programs may
provide a crucial symbolic link between government and religion, thereby enlisting—at
least in the eyes of impressionable youngsters—the powers of government to the
support of the religious denomination operating the school. Third, the programs may
have the effect of directly promoting religion
by impermissibly providing a subsidy to the
primary religious mission of the institutions
affected. . . .

The programs before us today share the
defect that we identified in *Meek [v. Pittenger]*.

With respect to the Community Education Program, the District Court found that "virtually every Community Education course conducted on facilities leased from nonpublic schools has an instructor otherwise employed full time by the same nonpublic school." . . . These instructors, many of whom no doubt teach in the religious schools precisely because they are adherents of the controlling denomination and want to serve their religious community zealously, are expected during the regular school day to inculcate their students with the tenets and beliefs of their particular religious faiths. Yet the premise of the program is that those instructors can put aside their religious convictions and engage in entirely secular Community Education instruction as soon as the school day is over. Moreover, they are expected to do so before the same religious-school students and in the same religious-school classrooms that they employed to advance religious purposes during the "official" school day. Nonetheless, as petitioners themselves asserted, Community Education classes are not specifically monitored for religious content. . . .

We do not question that the dedicated and professional religious school teachers employed by the Community Education program will attempt in good faith to perform their secular mission conscientiously. . . . Nonetheless, there is a substantial risk that, overtly or subtly, the religious message they are expected to convey during the regular school day will infuse the supposedly secular classes they teach after school. . . .

The Shared Time program, though structured somewhat differently, nonetheless also poses a substantial risk of state-sponsored indoctrination. The most important difference between the programs is that most of the instructors in the Shared Time program are full-time teachers hired by the public schools. Moreover, although "virtually every" Community Education instructor is a full-time religious school teacher, . . . only "[a] significant portion" of the Shared Time instructors previously worked in the religious schools. . . . Nonetheless, as with the Community Education program, no attempt is made to monitor the Shared Time courses for religious content. . . .

Thus, despite these differences between the two programs, our holding in *Meek* controls the inquiry with respect to Shared Time, as well as Community Education. Shared Time instructors are teaching academic subjects in religious schools in courses virtually indistinguishable from the other courses offered during the regular religious-school day. The teachers in this program, even more than their Community Education colleagues, are "performing important educational services in schools in which education is an integral part of the dominant sectarian mission and in which an atmosphere dedicated to the advancement of religious belief is constantly maintained." . . . Teachers in such an atmosphere may well subtly (or overtly) conform their instruction to the environment in which they teach, while students will perceive the instruction provided in the context of the dominantly religious message of the institution, thus reinforcing the indoctrinating effect. As we stated in *Meek*, "[w]hether the subject is 'remedial reading,' 'advanced reading,' or simply 'reading,' a teacher remains a teacher, and the danger that religious doctrine will become intertwined with secular instruction persists." . . . Unlike types of aid that the Court has upheld, such as state-created standardized tests, . . . there is a "substantial risk" that programs operating in this environment would "be used for religious educational purposes." . . .

The Court of Appeals of course recognized that respondents adduced no evidence of specific incidents of religious indoctrination in this case. . . . But the absence of proof of specific incidents is not dispositive. When conducting a supposedly secular class in the pervasively sectarian environment of a religious school, a teacher may knowingly or unwillingly tailor the content of the course to fit the school's announced goals. If so, there is no reason to believe that this kind of ideological influence would be detected or reported by students, by their parents, or by the school system itself. The students are presumably attending religious schools precisely in order to receive religious instruction. After spending the balance of their school day in classes heavily influenced by a religious perspective, they would have little motivation or ability to discern improper ideological content that may creep into a Shared Time or Community Education course. Neither their parents nor the parochial schools would have cause to complain if the effect of the publicly-supported instruction were to advance the schools' sectarian mission. And the public school system itself has no incentive to detect or report any specific incidents of improper state-sponsored indoctrination. Thus, the lack of evidence of specific incidents of indoctrination is of little significance.

Our cases have recognized that the Establishment Clause guards against more than direct, state-funded efforts to indoctrinate youngsters in specific religious beliefs. Government promotes religion as effectively when it fosters a close identification of its powers and responsibilities with those of any—or all—religious denominations as when it attempts to inculcate specific religious doctrines. If this identification conveys a message of government endorsement or disapproval of religion, a core purpose of the Establishment Clause is violated. . . .

It follows that an important concern of the effects test is whether the symbolic union of church and state effected by the challenged governmental action is sufficiently likely to be perceived by adherents of the controlling denominations as an endorsement, and by the nonadherents as a disapproval, of their individual religious choices. The inquiry into this kind of effect must be conducted with particular care when many of the citizens perceiving the governmental message are children in their formative years. . . . The symbolism of a union between church and state is most likely to influence children of tender years, whose experience is limited and whose beliefs consequently are the function of environment as much as of free and voluntary choice.

Our school-aid cases have recognized a sensitivity to the symbolic impact of the union of church and state. Grappling with problems in many ways parallel to those we face today . . . .

In the programs challenged in this case, the religious school students spend their typical school day moving between religious-school and "public-school" classes. Both types of classes take place in the same religious-school building and both are largely composed of students who are adherents of the same denomination. In this environment, the students would be unlikely to discern the crucial difference between the religious-school classes and the "public-school" classes, even if the latter were successfully kept free of religious indoctrination. . . . Consequently, even the student who notices the "public school" sign temporarily posted would have before him a powerful symbol of state endorsement and encouragement of the religious beliefs taught in the same class at some other time during the day. . . .

This effect—the symbolic union of government and religion in one sectarian enterprise—is an impermissible effect under the Establishment Clause. . . .

Aside from cash payments, the Court has distinguished between two categories of programs in which public funds are used to finance secular activities that religious schools would otherwise fund from their own resources. In the first category, the Court has noted that it is "well established . . . that not every law that confers an 'indirect,' 'remote,' or 'incidental' benefit upon religious institutions is, for that reason alone, constitutionally invalid." . . . In such "indirect" aid cases, the government has used primarily secular means to accomplish a primarily secular end, and no "primary effect" of advancing religion has thus been found. . . .

In the second category of cases, the Court has relied on the Establishment Clause prohibition of forms of aid that provide "direct and substantial advancement of the sectarian enterprise." . . . In such "direct aid" cases, the government, although acting for a secular purpose, has done so by directly supporting a religious institution. . . .

Thus, the Court has never accepted the mere possibility of subsidization, . . . as sufficient to invalidate an aid program. On the other hand, this effect is not wholly unimportant for Establishment Clause purposes. If it were, the public schools could gradually take on themselves the entire responsibility for teaching secular subjects on religious school premises. The question in each case must be whether the effect of the proffered aid is "direct and substantial," . . . or indirect and incidental. "The problem, like many problems in constitutional law, is one of degree." . . .

We have noted in the past that the religious school has dual functions, providing its students with a secular education while it promotes a particular religious perspective. . . . The programs challenged here, which provide teachers in addition to the instructional equipment and materials, have a similar — and forbidden — effect of advancing religion. This kind of direct aid to the educational function of the religious school is indistinguishable from the provision of a direct cash subsidy to the religious school that is most clearly prohibited under the Establishment Clause. . . .

We conclude that the challenged programs have the effect of promoting religion in three ways. The state-paid instructors, influenced by the pervasively sectarian nature of the religious schools in which they work, may subtly or overtly indoctrinate the students in particular religious tenets at public expense. The symbolic union of church and state inherent in the provision of secular, state-provided instruction in the religious school buildings threatens to convey a message of state support for religion to students and to the general public. Finally, the programs in effect subsidize the religious functions of the parochial schools by taking over a substantial portion of their responsibility for teaching secular subjects. For these reasons, the con-

clusion is inescapable that the Community Education and Shared Time programs have the "primary or principal" effect of advancing religion, and therefore violate the dictates of the Establishment Clause of the First Amendment. . . .

It is so ordered. . . .

Federal Funds to Pay Salaries of Public School Teachers Teaching in Parochial Schools Violates the Establishment Clause

— — — — — — — —

Aguilar v. Felton

— — — — — — — —

Supreme Court of the United States, 1985.
473 U.S. 402, 105 S.Ct. 3232.

Justice BRENNAN delivered the opinion of the Court. The City of New York uses federal funds to pay the salaries of public employees who teach in parochial schools. In this companion case to *School District of Grand Rapids v. Ball*, 473 U.S. 373 105 S.Ct. 3216, we determine whether this practice violates the Establishment Clause of the First Amendment.

The program at issue in this case, originally enacted as Title I of the Elementary and Secondary Education Act of 1965, authorizes the Secretary of Education to distribute financial assistance to local educational institutions to meet the needs of educationally deprived children from low-income families. The funds are to be appropriated in accordance with programs proposed by local educational agencies and approved by state educational agencies. . . .

Since 1966, the City of New York has provided instructional services funded by Title I to parochial school students on the premises of parochial schools. Of those students eligible to receive funds in 1981–1982, 13.2% were enrolled in private schools. Of that group, 84% were enrolled in schools affiliated with the Roman Catholic Archdiocese of New York and the Diocese of Brooklyn and 8% were enrolled in Hebrew day schools. . . .

The programs conducted at these schools include remedial reading, reading skills, remedial mathematics, English as a second language, and guidance services. These programs are carried out by regular employees of the public schools (teachers, guidance counselors, psychologists, psychiatrists and social workers) who have volunteered to teach in the parochial schools. The amount of time that each professional spends in the parochial school is determined by the number of students in the particular program and the needs of these students.

The City's Bureau of Nonpublic School Reimbursement makes teacher assignments, and the instructors are supervised by field personnel, who attempt to pay at least one unannounced visit per month. The field supervisors, in turn, report to program coordinators, who also pay occasional unannounced supervisory visits to monitor Title I classes in the parochial schools. The professionals involved in the program are directed to avoid involvement with religious activities that are conducted within the private schools and to bar religious materials in their classrooms. All material and equipment used in the programs funded under Title I are supplied by the Government and are used only in those programs. The professional personnel are solely responsible for the selection of the students. Additionally, the professionals are informed that contact with private school personnel should be kept to a minimum. Finally, the administrators of the parochial schools are required to clear the classrooms used by the public school personnel of all religious symbols. . . .

In *School Districts of the City of Grand Rapids v. Ball*, . . . the Court has today held unconstitutional under the Establishment Clause two remedial and enhancement programs operated by the *Grand Rapids Public School District*, in which classes were provided to private school children at public expense in classrooms located in and leased from the local private schools. The New York programs challenged in this case are very similar to the programs we examined in *Ball*. In both cases, publicly funded instructors teach classes composed exclusively of private school students in private school buildings. In both cases, an overwhelming number of the participating private schools are religiously affiliated. In both cases, the publicly funded programs provide not only professional personnel, but also all materials and supplies necessary for the operation of the programs. Finally, the instructors in both cases are told that they are public school employees under the sole control of the public school system.

The appellants attempt to distinguish this case on the ground that the City of New York, unlike the Grand Rapids Public School District, has adopted a system for monitoring the religious content of publicly funded Title I classes in the religious schools. At best, the supervision in this case would assist in preventing the Title I program from being used, intentionally or unwittingly, to inculcate the religious beliefs of the surrounding parochial school. But appellants' argument fails in any event, because the supervisory system established by the City of New York inevitably results in the excessive entanglement of church and state, an Establishment Clause concern distinct from that addressed by the effects doctrine. Even where state aid to parochial institutions does not have the primary effect of advancing religion, the provision of such aid may nonetheless violate the Establishment Clause owing to the nature of the interaction of church and state in the administration of that aid.

The principle that the state should not become too closely entangled with the church in the administration of assistance is rooted in two concerns. When the state becomes enmeshed with a given denomination in matters of religious significance, the freedom of religious belief of those who are not adherents of that denomination suffers, even when the governmental purpose underlying the involvement is largely secular. In addition, the freedom of even the adherents of the denom-

ination is limited by the governmental intrusion into sacred matters. "[T]he First Amendment rests upon the premise that both religion and government can best work to achieve their lofty aims if each is left free from the other within its respective sphere." . . .

The critical elements of the entanglement proscribed in *Lemon* and *Meek* are thus present in this case. First, as noted above, the aid is provided in a pervasively sectarian environment. Second, because assistance is provided in the form of teachers, ongoing inspection is required to ensure the absence of a religious message. . . . In short, the scope and duration of New York's Title I program would require a permanent and pervasive State presence in the sectarian schools receiving aid.

This pervasive monitoring by public authorities in the sectarian schools infringes precisely those Establishment Clause values at the root of the prohibition of excessive entanglement. Agents of the State must visit and inspect the religious school regularly, alert for the subtle or overt presence of religious matter in Title I classes. . . . In addition, the religious school must obey these same agents when they make determinations as to what is and what is not a "religious symbol" and thus off limits in a Title I classroom. In short, the religious school, which has as a primary purpose the advancement and preservation of a particular religion must endure the ongoing presence of state personnel whose primary purpose is to monitor teachers and students in an attempt to guard against the infiltration of religious thought.

The administrative cooperation that is required to maintain the educational program at issue here entangles Church and State in still another way that infringes interests at the heart of the Establishment Clause. Administrative personnel of the public and parochial school systems must work together in resolving matters related to schedules, classroom assignments, problems that arise in the implementation of the program, requests for additional services, and the dissemination of information regarding the program. Furthermore, the program necessitates "frequent contacts between the regular and the remedial teachers (or other professionals), in which each side reports on individual student needs, problems encountered, and results achieved." . . .

We have long recognized that underlying the Establishment Clause is "the objective . . . to prevent, as far as possible, the intrusion of either [Church or State] into the precincts of the other." . . . Although "[s]eparation in this context cannot mean absence of all contact," . . . the detailed monitoring and close administrative contact required to maintain New York's Title I program can only produce "a kind of continuing day-to-day relationship which the policy of neutrality seeks to minimize." . . . The numerous judgments that must be made by agents of the state concern matters that may be subtle and controversial, yet may be of deep religious significance to the controlling denominations. As government agents must make these judgments, the dangers of political divisiveness along religious lines increase. At the same time, "[t]he picture of state inspectors prowling the halls of parochial schools and auditing classroom instruction surely raises more than an imagined specter of governmental 'secularization of a creed.'" . . .

Despite the well-intentioned efforts taken by the City of New York, the program remains constitutionally flawed owing to the nature of the aid, to the institution receiving the aid, and to the constitutional principles that they implicate—that neither the State nor Federal Government shall promote or hinder a particular faith or faith generally through the advancement of benefits or through the excessive entanglement of church and state in the administration of those benefits.

Affirmed.

NOTES

1. Justice Rehnquist and Reagan appointees to the Supreme Court have, in recent years, criticized the tripartite test established in *Lemon.* In two nonschool church-state cases in the mid-eighties, the Supreme Court did not use the *Lemon* test. (*Marsh v.*

Chambers, 463 U.S. 783, 103 S.Ct. 3330 (1983); *Larson v. Valente,* 456 U.S. 228, 102 S.Ct. 1673 (1982). In these cases, the court appears to downgrade the importance of the *Lemon* test. Moreover, the test was described as a "guideline" in *Committee v. Nyquist,* then as "no more than [a] useful signpost" in *Mueller v. Allen,* 463 U.S. 388, 103 S.Ct. 3062, (1983). Later, the court stated that the *Lemon* test has never been binding on the court (*Lynch v. Donnelly,* 465 U.S. 668, ____, 104 S.Ct. 1355, 1984).

2. *Free Exercise.* It should be remembered that the Supreme Court has distinguished between the freedom of individual beliefs, which is absolute and the freedom of individual conduct, which is not absolute. The Free Exercise Clause protects an individual "from certain forms of governmental compulsion; it does not afford an individual a right to dictate the conduct of the Government's internal procedures." Maintaining an ordered or organized society that guarantees religious freedom to such a vast variety of religious beliefs, as held in this country, requires some religious practices to yield to the common good. Religious beliefs can be accommodated, but there is a point at which accommodation would restrict the operation of government and the prerogative of the representative body of the people of the legislature. See *Mozert v. Hawkins County Board of Education,* 827 F.2d 1058 (6th Cir. 1987); *Bowen v. Roy,* 476 U.S. 693, 106 S.Ct. 2147 (1986).

3. Lease of classroom space from a parochial school by the public school system was held to be constitutional where the public schools actually faced a severe classroom shortage and the classrooms were in a separable part of the parochial school where no religious manifestations were present. A significant effort had been made by the public schools, it was found, to prevent intermingling of the two school programs. *Thomas v. Schmidt,* 397 F.Supp. 203 (D.R.I.1975).

4. Lease of public school facilities for religious activities was held unconstitutional where the rental charge covered only the cost of janitorial services and the lease extended for an indefinite period of time. The court found that such nominal rent is functionally a subsidy to the church. *Resnick v. East Brunswick Township Board of Education,* 135 N.J.Super. 257, 343 A.2d 127 (Ch.1975).

5. Following the precedent established by the United States Supreme Court in *Nyquist,* the United States Court of Appeals for the Third Circuit struck down a $4.4 million tax deduction plan that would have assisted parents with children in parochial schools. The statute enacted in 1976 provided for a personal income tax deduction of $1000 for each child attending a nonpublic elementary and secondary school on a full-time basis. The federal court found that the statute had a secular purpose, but failed to meet the primary effect test and thus was constitutionally deficient because it advanced religion. Since the act violated the primary effect standard the court saw no need to evaluate it under the excessive entanglement criterion. The United States Supreme Court in a vote of 6 to 3 upheld without a hearing the lower court's decision. *Public Funds for Public Schools of New Jersey v. Byrne,* 590 F.2d 514 (3d Cir. 1979).

State Financing of Auxiliary Services and Direct Loans for Instructional Materials and Equipment for Parochial Schools Is Unconstitutional

— · — · — · — · —

Meek v. Pittenger

— · — · — · — · —

Supreme Court of the United States, 1975.
421 U.S. 349, 95 S.Ct. 1753.

Mr. Justice STEWART announced the judgment of the Court and delivered the opinion of the Court (Parts I, II, IV, and V), together with an opinion (Part III), in which Mr. Justice BLACKMUN and Mr. Justice POWELL joined. This case requires us to determine once again whether a state law providing assistance to nonpublic, church-related, elementary and secondary schools is constitutional under the Establishment Clause of the First Amendment, made applicable to the States by the Fourteenth Amendment. . . .

With the stated purpose of assuring that every schoolchild in the Commonwealth will equitably share in the benefits of auxiliary services, textbooks, and instructional material provided free of charge to children attending public schools, the Pennsylvania General Assembly in 1972 added Acts 194 and 195, July 12, 1972, Pa.Stat.Ann., Tit. 24, § 9–972, to the Pennsylvania Public School Code of 1949, Pa.Stat.Ann., Tit. 24, §§ 1–101 to 27–2702.

Act 194 authorizes the Commonwealth to provide "auxiliary services" to all children enrolled in nonpublic elementary and secondary schools meeting Pennsylvania's compulsory-attendance requirements. "Auxiliary services" include counseling, testing, and psychological services, speech and hearing therapy, teaching and related services for exceptional children, for remedial students, and for the educationally disadvantaged, "and such other secular, neutral, nonideological services as are of benefit to nonpublic school children and are presently or hereafter provided for public school children of the Commonwealth." Act 194 specifies that the teaching and services are to be provided in the nonpublic schools themselves by personnel drawn from the appropriate "intermediate unit," part of the public school system of the Commonwealth established to provide special services to local school districts.

Act 195 authorizes the State Secretary of Education, either directly or through the intermediate units, to lend textbooks without charge to children attending nonpublic elementary and secondary schools that meet the Commonwealth's compulsory-attendance requirements. The books that may be lent are limited to those "which are acceptable for use in any public, elementary, or secondary school of the Commonwealth."

Act 195 also authorizes the Secretary of Education, pursuant to requests from the appropriate nonpublic school officials, to lend directly to the nonpublic schools "instruc-

tional materials and equipment, useful to the education" of nonpublic school children. "Instructional materials" are defined to include periodicals, photographs, maps, charts, sound recordings, films, "or any other printed and published materials of a similar nature." "Instructional equipment," as defined by the Act, includes projection equipment, recording equipment, and laboratory equipment. . . .

In judging the constitutionality of the various forms of assistance authorized by Acts 194 and 195, the District Court applied the three-part test that has been clearly stated, if not easily applied, by this Court in recent Establishment Clause cases. . . . First, the statute must have a secular legislative purpose. . . . Second, it must have a "primary effect" that neither advances nor inhibits religion. . . . Third, the statute and its administration must avoid excessive government entanglement with religion. . . .

These tests constitute a convenient, accurate distillation of this Court's efforts over the past decades to evaluate a wide range of governmental action challenged as violative of the constitutional prohibition against laws "respecting an establishment of religion," and thus provide the proper framework of analysis for the issues presented in the case before us. It is well to emphasize, however, that the tests must not be viewed as setting the precise limits to the necessary constitutional inquiry, but serve only as guidelines with which to identify instances in which the objectives of the Establishment Clause have been impaired.

. . .

The District Court held that the textbook loan provisions of Act 195 are constitutionally indistinguishable from the New York textbook loan program upheld in *Board of Education v. Allen,* 392 U.S. 236, 88 S.Ct. 1923, 20 L.Ed.2d 1060. We agree. . . .

Like the New York program, the textbook provisions of Act 195 extend to all schoolchildren the benefits of Pennsylvania's well-established policy of lending textbooks free of charge to elementary and secondary school students. As in *Allen,* Act 195 provides that the textbooks are to be lent directly to the student, not to the nonpublic school itself, although, again as in *Allen,* the administrative practice is to have student requests for the books filed initially with the nonpublic school and to have the school authorities prepare collective summaries of these requests which they forward to the appropriate public officials. Thus, the financial benefit of Pennsylvania's textbook program, like New York's, is to parents and children, not to the nonpublic schools. . . . Moreover, the record in the case before us, like the record in *Allen* . . . contains no suggestion that religious textbooks will be lent or that the books provided will be used for anything other than purely secular purposes.

In sum, the textbook loan provisions of Act 195 are in every material respect identical to the loan program approved in *Allen.* Pennsylvania, like New York, "merely makes available to all children the benefits of a general program to lend school books free of charge." As such, those provisions of Act 195 do not offend the constitutional prohibition against laws "respecting an establishment of religion."

Although textbooks are lent only to students, Act 195 authorizes the loan of instructional material and equipment directly to qualifying nonpublic elementary and secondary schools in the Commonwealth. The appellants assert that such direct aid to Pennsylvania's nonpublic schools, including church-related institutions, constitutes an impermissible establishment of religion. . . .

The only requirement imposed on nonpublic schools to qualify for loans of instructional material and equipment is that they satisfy the Commonwealth's compulsory-attendance law by providing, in the English language, the subjects and activities prescribed by the standards of the State Board of Education. Commonwealth officials, as a matter of state policy, do not inquire into the religious characteristics, if any, of the nonpublic schools requesting aid pursuant to Act 195. The Coordinator of Nonpublic School Services, the chief administrator of Acts 194 and 195, testified that a school would not be barred from receiving loans of instructional material and equipment even though its dominant

purpose was the inculcation of religious values, even if it imposed religious restrictions on admissions or on faculty appointments, and even if it required attendance at classes in theology or at religious services. In fact, of the 1,320 nonpublic schools in Pennsylvania that comply with the requirements of the compulsory-attendance law and thus qualify for aid under Act 195, more than 75% are church-related or religiously affiliated educational institutions. Thus, the primary beneficiaries of Act 195's instructional material and equipment loan provisions, like the beneficiaries of the "secular educational services" reimbursement program considered in *Lemon v. Kurtzman,* and the parent tuition-reimbursement plan considered in *Sloan v. Lemon,* are nonpublic schools with a predominant sectarian character. . . .

The church-related elementary and secondary schools that are the primary beneficiaries of Act 195's instructional material and equipment loans typify such religion-pervasive institutions. The very purpose of many of those schools is to provide an integrated secular and religious education; the teaching process is, to a large extent, devoted to the inculcation of religious values and belief . . . . Substantial aid to the educational function of such schools, accordingly, necessarily results in aid to the sectarian school enterprise as a whole. "[T]he secular education those schools provide goes hand in hand with the religious mission that is the only reason for the schools' existence. Within the institution, the two are inextricably intertwined." . . . For this reason, Act 195's direct aid to Pennsylvania's predominantly church-related, nonpublic elementary and secondary schools, even though ostensibly limited to wholly neutral, secular instructional material and equipment, inescapably results in the direct and substantial advancement of religious activity . . . and thus constitutes an impermissible establishment of religion.

Unlike Act 195, which provides only for the loan of teaching material and equipment, Act 194 authorizes the Secretary of Education, through the intermediate units, to supply professional staff, as well as supportive materials, equipment, and personnel, to the nonpublic schools of the Commonwealth. The "auxiliary services" authorized by Act 194 remedial and accelerated instruction, guidance counseling and testing, speech and hearing services — are provided directly to nonpublic school children with the appropriate special need. But the services are provided only on the nonpublic school premises, and only when "requested by nonpublic school representatives." . . . The appellants concede the validity of this secular legislative purpose. Nonetheless, they argue that Act 194 constitutes an impermissible establishment of religion because the auxiliary services are provided on the premises of predominantly church-related schools. . . .

We need not decide whether substantial state expenditures to enrich the curricula of church-related elementary and secondary schools, like the expenditure of state funds to support the basic educational program of those schools, necessarily result in the direct and substantial advancement of religious activity. For decisions of this Court make clear that the District Court erred in relying entirely on the good faith and professionalism of the secular teachers and counselors functioning in church-related schools to ensure that a strictly nonideological posture is maintained.

In *Earley v. DiCenso*, a companion case to *Lemon v. Kurtzman*, the Court invalidated a Rhode Island statute authorizing salary supplements for teachers of secular subjects in nonpublic schools. The Court expressly rejected the proposition, relied upon by the District Court in the case before us, that it was sufficient for the State to assume that teachers in church-related schools would succeed in segregating their religious beliefs from their secular educational duties. . . .

The prophylactic contacts required to ensure that teachers play a strictly nonideological role, the Court held, necessarily give rise to a constitutionally intolerable degree of entanglement between church and state. . . . The same excessive entanglement would be required for Pennsylvania to be "certain," as it must be, that Act 194 personnel do not advance the religious mission of the church-related schools in which they serve. . . .

That Act 194 authorizes state funding of teachers only for remedial and exceptional students, and not for normal students participating in the core curriculum, does not distinguish this case from *Earley v. DiCenso* and *Lemon v. Kurtzman*. Whether the subject is "remedial reading," "advanced reading," or simply "reading," a teacher remains a teacher, and the danger that religious doctrine will become intertwined with secular instruction persists. The likelihood of inadvertent fostering of religion may be less in a remedial arithmetic class than in a medieval history seminar, but a diminished probability of impermissible conduct is not sufficient: "The State must be certain, given the Religion Clauses, that subsidized teachers do not inculcate religion." . . . And a state-subsidized guidance counselor is surely as likely as a state-subsidized chemistry teacher to fail on occasion to separate religious instruction and the advancement of religious beliefs from his secular educational responsibilities.

The fact that the teachers and counselors providing auxiliary services are employees of the public intermediate unit, rather than of the church-related schools in which they work, does not substantially eliminate the need for continuing surveillance. To be sure, auxiliary-services personnel, because not employed by the nonpublic schools, are not directly subject to the discipline of a religious authority. . . . But they are performing important educational services in schools in which education is an integral part of the dominant sectarian mission and in which an atmosphere dedicated to the advancement of religious belief is constantly maintained. . . . The potential for impermissible fostering of religion under these circumstances, although somewhat reduced, is nonetheless present. To be certain that auxiliary teachers remain religiously neutral, as the Constitution demands, the State would have to impose limitations on the activities of auxiliary personnel and then engage in some form of continuing surveillance to ensure that those restrictions were being followed.

In addition, Act 194, like the statutes considered in *Lemon v. Kurtzman* and *Committee for Public Education & Religious Liberty v. Nyquist*, creates a serious potential for divisive conflict over the issue of aid to religion—"entanglement in the broader sense of continuing political strife." . . . The recurrent nature of the appropriation process guarantees annual reconsideration of Act 194 and the prospect of repeated confrontation between proponents and opponents of the auxiliary services program. The Act thus provides successive opportunities for political fragmentation and division along religious lines, one of the principal evils against which the Establishment Clause was intended to protect. . . . This potential for political entanglement, together with the administrative entanglement which would be necessary to ensure that auxiliary-services personnel remain strictly neutral and nonideological when functioning in church-related schools, compels the conclusion that Act 194 violates the constitutional prohibition against laws "respecting an establishment of religion."

The judgment of the District Court as to Act 194 is reversed; its judgment as to the textbook provisions of Act 195 is affirmed, but as to that Act's other provisions now before us its judgment is reversed.

It is so ordered.

Judgment reversed in part and affirmed in part.

NOTE

1. In a Vermont suit by a taxpayer against a town school district the question was presented: does the payment of tuition for attendance of students at a religious school by a public entity create a fusion of secular and sectarian education? The court held the payment of students' tuition to the religious denominational high school violates the Federal Constitution. The court quoted the United States Supreme Court in *Zorach v. Clauson*, 343 U.S. 306, 72 S.Ct. 679 (1952) stating: "Government may not finance religious groups nor undertake religious instruction nor blend secular and sectarian education nor use secular institu-

tions to force one or some religion on any person." *Swart v. South Burlington Town School District*, 122 Vt. 177, 167 A.2d 514 (1961).

Tax Deductions Benefiting Parents of Parochial School Children Do Not Violate the Establishment Clause

–·–·–·–·–·–

Mueller v. Allen

–·–·–·–·–·–

Supreme Court of the United States, 1983.
463 U.S. 388, 103 S.Ct. 3062.

Justice REHNQUIST delivered the opinion of the Court. Minnesota allows taxpayers, in computing their state income tax, to deduct certain expenses incurred in providing for education of their children. . . .

Minnesota, like every other state, provides its citizens with free elementary and secondary schooling. It seems to be agreed that about 820,000 students attended this school system in the most recent school year. During the same year, approximately 91,000 elementary and secondary students attended some 500 privately supported schools located in Minnesota, and about 95% of these students attended schools considering themselves to be sectarian.

Minnesota, by a law originally enacted in 1955 and revised in 1976 and again in 1978, permits state taxpayers to claim a deduction from gross income for certain expenses incurred in educating their children. The deduction is limited to actual expenses incurred for the "tuition, textbooks and transportation" of dependents attending elementary or secondary schools. A deduction may not exceed $500 per dependent in grades K through six and $700 per dependent in grades seven through twelve. . . .

Today's case is no exception to our oft-repeated statement that the Establishment Clause presents especially difficult questions of iznterpretation and application. It is easy enough to quote the few words comprising that clause—"Congress shall make no law respecting an establishment of religion." It is not at all easy, however, to apply this Court's various decisions construing the Clause to governmental programs of financial assistance to sectarian schools and the parents of children attending those schools. Indeed, in many of these decisions "we have expressly or implicitly acknowledged that 'we can only dimly perceive the lines of demarcation in this extraordinarily sensitive area of constitutional law.'." *Lemon v. Kurtzman,* 403 U.S. 602, 609, 612, 91 S.Ct. 2105, 2109, 2111, 29 L.Ed.2d 745 (1971), quoted with approval in *Nyquist,* 413 U.S., at 761, 93 S.Ct. at 2959.

One fixed principle in this field is our consistent rejection of the argument that "any program which in some manner aids an institution with a religious affiliation" violates the Establishment Clause. . . .

Petitioners place particular reliance on our decision in *Committee for Public Education v. Nyquist,* supra, where we held invalid a New York statute providing public funds for the maintenance and repair of the physical facilities of private schools and granting thinly disguised "tax benefits," actually amounting to tuition grants, to the parents of children attending private schools. As explained below, we conclude that § 290.09(22) bears less resemblance to the arrangement struck down in *Nyquist* than it does to assistance programs upheld in our prior decisions and those discussed with approval in *Nyquist.*

The general nature of our inquiry in this area has been guided, since the decision in *Lemon v. Kurtzman,* 403 U.S. 602, 91 S.Ct. 2105, 29 L.Ed.2d 745 (1971), by the "three-part" test laid down in that case:

> First, the statute must have a secular legislative purpose; second, its principal or primary effect must be one that neither advances nor inhibits religion . . . ; finally, the statute must not foster "an excessive government entanglement with religion." Ibid., at 612–613, 91 S.Ct., at 2111.

While this principle is well settled, our cases have also emphasized that it provides "no more than [a] helpful signpost" in dealing with Establishment Clause challenges. *Hunt v. McNair,* 413 U.S., at 741, 93 S.Ct., at 2873. With this caveat in mind, we turn to the specific challenges raised against § 290.09(22) under the *Lemon* framework.

Little time need be spent on the question of whether the Minnesota tax deduction has a secular purpose. Under our prior decisions, governmental assistance programs have consistently survived this inquiry even when they have run afoul of other aspects of the *Lemon* framework. See, e.g., *Lemon v. Kurtzman,* supra; *Meek v. Pittenger,* 421 U.S., at 363, 95 S.Ct., at 1762; *Wolman v. Walter,* 433 U.S., at 236, 97 S.Ct., at 2599. This reflects, at least in part, our reluctance to attribute unconstitutional motives to the states, particularly when a plausible secular purpose for the state's program may be discerned from the face of the statute.

A state's decision to defray the cost of educational expenses incurred by parents—regardless of the type of schools their children attend—evidences a purpose that is both secular and understandable. . . .

We turn therefore to the more difficult but related question whether the Minnesota statute has "the primary effect of advancing the sectarian aims of the nonpublic schools." In concluding that it does not, we find several features of the Minnesota tax deduction particularly significant. First, an essential feature of Minnesota's arrangement is the fact that § 290.09(22) is only one among many deductions—such as those for medical expenses, Minn.Stat. § 290.09(10) and charitable contributions, Minn.Stat. § 290.21—available under the Minnesota tax laws. . . . Under our prior decisions, the Minnesota legislature's judgment that a deduction for educational expenses fairly equalizes the tax burden of its citizens and encourages desirable expenditures for educational purposes is entitled to substantial deference.

Other characteristics of § 290.09(22) argue equally strongly for the provision's constitutionality. Most importantly, the deduction is available for educational expenses incurred by *all* parents, including those whose children attend public schools and those whose children attend nonsectarian private schools or sectarian private schools. . . .

In this respect, as well as others, this case is vitally different from the scheme struck down in *Nyquist*. There, public assistance amounting to tuition grants, was provided only to parents of children in *nonpublic* schools. This fact had considerable bearing on our decision striking down the New York statute at issue; we explicitly distinguished both *Allen* and *Everson* on the grounds that "In both cases the class of beneficiaries included *all* schoolchildren, those in public as well as those in private schools." Moreover, we intimated that "public assistance (e.g., scholarships) made available generally without regard to the sectarian-nonsectarian or public-nonpublic nature of the institution benefited," might not offend the Establishment Clause. We think the tax deduction adopted by Minnesota is more similar to this latter type of program than it is to the arrangement struck down in *Nyquist*. . . .

We also agree with the Court of Appeals that, by channeling whatever assistance it may provide to parochial schools through individual parents, Minnesota has reduced the Establishment Clause objections to which its action is subject. It is true, of course, that financial assistance provided to parents ultimately has an economic effect comparable to that of aid given directly to the schools attended by their children. It is also true, however, that under Minnesota's arrangement public funds become available only as a result of numerous, private choices of individual parents of school-age children. For these reasons, we recognized in *Nyquist* that the means by which state assistance flows to private schools is of some importance: we said that "the fact that aid is disbursed to parents rather than to . . . schools" is a material consideration in Establishment Clause analysis, albeit "only one among many to be considered." . . .

We find it useful, in the light of the foregoing characteristics of § 290.09(22), to compare the attenuated financial benefits flowing to parochial schools from the section to the evils against which the Establishment Clause was designed to protect. These dangers are well-described by our statement that

"what is at stake as a matter of policy [in Establishment Clause cases] is preventing that kind and degree of government involvement in religious life that, as history teaches us, is apt to lead to strife and frequently strain a political system to the breaking point." It is important, however, to "keep these issues in perspective."

> At this point in the 20th century we are quite far removed from the dangers that prompted the Framers to include the Establishment Clause in the Bill of Rights. The risk of significant religious or denominational control over our democratic processes—or even of deep political division along religious lines—is remote, and when viewed against the positive contributions of sectarian schools and such risk seems entirely tolerable in light of the continuing oversight of this Court. *Wolman*, 433 U.S., at 263, 97 S.Ct., at 2613.

The Establishment Clause of course extends beyond prohibition of a state church or payment of state funds to one or more churches. We do not think, however, that its prohibition extends to the type of tax deduction established by Minnesota. The historic purposes of the clause simply do not encompass the sort of attenuated financial benefit, ultimately controlled by the private choices of individual parents, that eventually flows to parochial schools from the neutrally available tax benefit at issue in this case.

Petitioners argue that, notwithstanding the facial neutrality of § 290.09(22), in application the statute primarily benefits religious institutions. Petitioners rely, as they did below, on a statistical analysis of the type of persons claiming the tax deduction. They contend that most parents of public school children incur no tuition expenses, and that other expenses deductible under § 290.09(22) are negligible in value; moreover, they claim that 96% of the children in private schools in 1978–1979 attended religiously affiliated institutions. Because of all this, they reason, the bulk of deductions taken under § 290.09(22) will be claimed by parents of children in sectarian schools. Respondents reply that petitioners have failed to consider the impact of deductions for items such as transportation, summer school tuition, tuition paid by parents whose children attended schools outside the school districts in which they resided, rental or purchase costs for a variety of equipment, and tuition for certain types of instruction not ordinarily provided in public schools.

We need not consider these contentions in detail. We would be loath to adopt a rule grounding the constitutionality of a facially neutral law on annual reports reciting the extent to which various classes of private citizens claimed benefits under the law. Such an approach would scarcely provide the certainty that this field stands in need of, nor can we perceive principled standards by which such statistical evidence might be evaluated. Moreover, the fact that private persons fail in a particular year to claim the tax relief to which they are entitled — under a facially neutral statute — should be of little importance in determining the constitutionality of the statute permitting such relief.

Finally, private educational institutions, and parents paying for their children to attend these schools, make special contributions to the areas in which they operate. "Parochial schools, quite apart from their sectarian purpose, have provided an educational alternative for millions of young Americans; they often afford wholesome competition with our public schools; and in some States they relieve substantially the tax burden incident to the operation of public schools." *Wolman*, at 262, 97 S.Ct., at 2613 (POWELL, J., concurring and dissenting). If parents of children in private schools choose to take especial advantage of the relief provided by § 290.09(22), it is no doubt due to the fact that they bear a particularly great financial burden in educating their children. More fundamentally, whatever unequal effect may be attributed to the statutory classification can fairly be regarded as a rough return for the benefits, discussed above, provided to the state and all taxpayers by parents sending their children to parochial schools. In the light of all this, we believe it wiser to decline to engage in the type of empirical inquiry into those persons benefited by state law which petitioners urge.

Thus, we hold that the Minnesota tax deduction for educational expenses satisfies the primary effect inquiry of our Establishment Clause cases.

Turning to the third part of the *Lemon* inquiry, we have no difficulty in concluding that the Minnesota statute does not "excessively entangle" the state in religion. The only plausible source of the "comprehensive, discriminating, and continuing state surveillance" necessary to run afoul of this standard would lie in the fact that state officials must determine whether particular textbooks qualify for a deduction. In making this decision, state officials must disallow deductions taken from "instructional books and materials used in the teaching of religious tenets, doctrines or worship, the purpose of which is to inculcate such tenets, doctrines or worship." Making decisions such as this does not differ substantially from making the types of decisions approved in earlier opinions of this Court. In *Board of Education v. Allen*, 392 U.S. 236, 88 S.Ct. 1923, 20 L.Ed.2d 1060 (1968), for example, the Court upheld the loan of secular textbooks to parents or children attending nonpublic schools; though state officials were required to determine whether particular books were or were not secular, the system was held not to violate the Establishment Clause. See also *Wolman v. Walter; Meek v. Pittenger*. The same result follows in this case.

For the foregoing reasons, the judgment of the Court of Appeals is Affirmed.

■ ANTIESTABLISHMENT PROVISIONS IN STATE CONSTITUTIONS

The ideals of toleration and freedom of conscience are reflected in the state constitutions, as well as in the First Amendment of the U.S. Constitution. A state law that is constitutional under the First Amendment of the United States Constitution may not be constitutional under the state constitution. Some of the state provisions establish strong and effective barriers preventing the mixing of affairs of state with those of religion. The history, tradition, and religious influence of both Protestant and Catholic churches in the various states, though, have led to judicial interpretations that have, in many instances, weakened the separation of church and state. As political pressure for use of tax funds for support of religious schools has intensified, primarily in states with greater numbers of parochial schools, the establishment principles of those state constitutions have been interpreted by state courts to be less restrictive. For example, even though the states of Rhode Island, New York, Pennsylvania, Ohio, and Illinois have strongly worded constitutional prohibitions against establishment of religion, lenient judicial interpretations have given the legislatures substantial latitude in aiding parochial schools. In these states, the courts have generally ruled that the state constitutional restraints are no more, and probably less, restrictive than the First Amendment of the U.S. Constitution.

As an example, the various pressures for aid to parochial schools in Rhode Island, ironically the state of Roger Williams, have caused the courts to negate the meaning of the strong disestablishment language of the Rhode Island Constitution, which says, "we, therefore, declare that no man shall be compelled to frequent or to *support* any religious worship, place, or ministry whatever" (italics added).[80] The Supreme Court of Rhode Island, in considering the constitutionality of textbook aid to parochial schools, noted that the allegedly offending statute was less vulnerable to attack under the Rhode Island Constitution than under the First Amendment. This court held that the Rhode Island Constitution erected a lower wall of separation than the First Amendment, said:

> Nor can we agree with appellees that the language of the constitution of this state prohibiting establishment of religion or the interference with the free exercise thereof is more restrictive than the language of the federal constitution as interpreted in *Allen*. . . . [81]

Similarly, an apparently strong and definitive prohibition in the Illinois Constitution forbidding state aid to church schools, stating that neither the state, school district, nor public corporation "shall ever make any appropriation or pay from any public fund whatever, anything in aid of any church or sectarian purpose, or to help support or sustain any school . . . controlled by any church or sectarian denomination whatever,"[82] has been substantially weakened by state court interpretation. The Supreme Court of Illinois has held that the Illinois Constitution is no more restrictive than the First Amendment.[83]

This view of the Illinois court appears to reflect a prevailing pattern of precedents of state courts in interpreting their own constitutions closely adhering to the constitutional tests that the U.S. Supreme Court applied to the First Amendment case in *Lemon v. Kurtzman*.[84]

In Connecticut that state's supreme court followed the *Everson* precedent, and upheld a state statute that provided public funds for transportation of parochial school students.[85] The "public purpose" theory used by the U.S. Supreme Court in *Everson* was cited as controlling rationale for the Connecticut Constitution. The Connecticut Court said:

> It cannot be said that their transportation does not serve the purpose of education, and [e]ducation in itself serves a public purpose. . . . [86]

Similarly, the Indiana Constitution has been held to be no more forceful in the separation of church and state than is the First Amendment.[87] Moreover, most states, such as Iowa,[88] Kansas,[89] Maine,[90] Michigan,[91] Minnesota,[92] New Jersey,[93] and Wisconsin,[94] have applied the U.S. Supreme Court's First Amendment rationale to the church-state provisions of their own constitutions. The judicial precedents of many of these states explicitly follow the establishment of religion tests used by the U.S. Supreme Court.

It remains to be seen whether a lessening of the strictures by the U.S. Supreme Court in interpreting the Establishment Clause of the First Amendment—a distinct possibility as indicated by the decision in *Mueller v. Allen*[95] and the new makeup of the membership of the Court, — will in turn elicit a corresponding lowering of the establishment standards of state constitutions as decided by the respective state supreme courts. It is possible, of course, that state supreme courts will choose instead to maintain a higher standard in the protection of religious liberties. There is precedent for greater assertiveness on the part of state courts in the protection of individual rights and freedoms.[96]

The history and legal precedents of some states do indicate that there may be substantial resistance to reinterpretation of state constitutions, which would diminish present religious liberty protections. Several states, including Colorado, Hawaii, Idaho, Kentucky, Missouri, Montana, and Wyoming, have constitutional provisions that would suggest strong and definite opposition to legislative action to use public moneys to aid parochial schools. For example, Article V, § 34 of the Colorado Constitution forbids the state appropriation for educational purposes to any person or corporation not under absolute control of the state or to any denominational or sectarian institution.[97] Moreover, Article IX, § 7 of the Colorado Constitution provides that:

> Neither the general assembly, nor any county, city, town, township, school district or other public corporation, shall ever make any appropriation, or pay from any public fund or moneys whatever, anything in aid of any church or sectarian society, or for any sectarian purpose, or to help support or sustain any school, academy, seminary, college, university or other literary or scientific institution, controlled by any church or sectarian denomination whatsoever . . . .[98]

Similarly, the Hawaii Constitution is quite specific in banning the use of public money for aid to parochial schools. In *Spears v. Honda*,[99] a 1968 case, the Supreme Court of Hawaii refused the permissive interpretation advanced by the U.S. Supreme Court in *Everson*, saying that:

> We find that the framers did not open the door one bit. The language of the Constitution itself is unequivocal. It explicitly states "Nor shall

public funds be appropriated for the support or benefit of any sectarian or private educational institution."[100]

In the same vein, the Idaho Supreme Court has said:

> The Idaho Constitution places much greater restriction upon the power of state government to aid activities undertaken by religious sects than does the First Amendment to the Constitution of the United States.[101]

The Supreme Court of Missouri has made it quite clear that the Missouri constitutional restraint is more restrictive than the federal First Amendment.[102] The Missouri Supreme Court has said that "The constitutional policy of our state has decreed the absolute separation of church and state, not only in governmental matters, but in educational ones as well."[103] This court has further stated that

> it is the unqualified policy of the State of Missouri that no public funds or properties, either directly or indirectly, be used to support or sustain any school affected by religious influences or teachings or by any sectarian or religious beliefs . . . . .[104]

In comparing the Missouri establishment standard to the Establishment Clause of the First Amendment, the Missouri Court said:

> [I]t becomes readily apparent that the provisions of the Missouri Constitution declaring that there shall be a separation of church and state are not only more explicit but [also] more *restrictive than the Establishment Clause of the United States Constitution*" (italics added).[105]

There is little doubt that the Missouri Constitution is a definitive obstacle to legislation designed to provide public funds for parochial schools.

Both Montana and Wyoming have religious liberty protections that are stronger than those of the First Amendment. The Montana Supreme Court in 1971,[106] in barring the employment of public schools teachers in parochial schools, noted that the practice would probably have violated the First

Amendment as interpreted by the *Lemon v. Kurtzman*[107] tripartite test, but the Montana court made it clear that the Montana Constitution was actually more pervasive than the federal Constitution. The Montana Constitution of 1972 maintained the strict separation language of the old 1889 constitution, which prohibited appropriations "for religious, charitable, industrial, educational or benevolent purposes to any private corporation not under the control of the state."[108] It is unlikely that such strong language could be watered down to the point that it would permit the use of state funds for parochial schools, whether the aid was extended through direct or indirect funding devices. In support of this supposition, Howard has noted that "Montana's Constitution appears to establish stricter barriers to denominational schools and colleges than does the First Amendment to the United States Constitution."[109]

There are several other examples of such strong constitutional restraints. A notable provision is in the Wyoming Constitution, Article 1, § 19, which simply states that "No money of the state shall ever be given or appropriated to any sectarian or religious society or institution." The conclusiveness of this provision is to impose "strong bars to any state funding for private or sectarian schools."[110]

The Oregon Constitution, like Missouri, has an antiestablishment provision that has been held to constitute a more restrictive barrier than the First Amendment in preventing the flow of public funds to church schools. Article I, § 5 of Oregon's Constitution states in part: No money shall be drawn from the Treasury for the benefit of any religious [sic], or theological institution . . . .

The Supreme Court of Oregon has interpreted this provision as precluding the use of public funds to provide textbooks to students in parochial schools.[111] In so holding, the court rejected the "child benefit" theory and found that textbooks, being essential to the educational process and not an incidental, were an asset to the religious institution. In 1991 proponents of parochiaid in Oregon placed on the ballot a proposed amendment to Article I, § 5 that would have allowed tax credits for parents sending their children to parochial schools. The plan called for tax credits of up to $2,500 per child for tuition and costs incurred for private schools or for home school education. This effort was roundly defeated by the Oregon voters in the spring of 1991.

Therefore, the antiestablishment provisions of state constitutions may be strong or weak, effectual or ineffectual, depending on their wording and the interpretations of the state supreme courts. Some state supreme courts, such as Illinois, have emasculated relatively strong constitutional provisions, while other state courts have given weaker statements even stronger meaning.

Whether the state supreme courts, though, will follow new U.S. Supreme Court precedents such as *Mueller v. Allen* in a diminution of religious liberty and an erosion of the wall of separation remains to be seen.

Oregon Law Providing Textbooks to Parochial Schools Cannot Be Justified on "Child Benefit Theory"

–––·––·––·––

Dickman v. School District No. 62 C

–––·––·––·––

Supreme Court of Oregon, 1961.
232 Or. 238, 366 P.2d 533, *cert. denied* 371 U.S. 823, 83 S.Ct. 41 (1962).

O'Connell, J.   This is a suit in equity brought by plaintiff taxpayers against School District No. 62C, its board and clerk, to enjoin defendants from supplying textbooks without charge for the use of pupils enrolled in St. John's The Apostle School, a parochial school maintained and operated by the Catholic church. Plaintiffs also seek a judicial declaration that the so-called free textbook statute (ORS 337.150), under which distribution was made to the St. John's school and other parochial schools, does not authorize defendants to supply textbooks free of charge to church or parochial schools, or if the statute is so construed that it be declared unconstitutional. . . .

For a period of several years the defendant district has furnished free textbooks for the use of the pupils of St. John's school. In a period of three school years these books have cost the district approximately $4,000. The books were purchased by the district from money in its General Fund, a part of which was derived from taxes levied upon real property in the district, including real property owned by plaintiffs. . . . The district retains title to the books, a matter of little practical significance however, because the books are not ordinarily retrieved by the district. Textbooks furnished for the use of parochial school students do not differ from those delivered to public schools. A school is not entitled to receive free textbooks unless it complies with standards established by the Oregon statutes as implemented by administrative regulation. The St. John's school met these standards.

The evidence establishes, and the trial judge found, that the purpose of the Catholic church in operating in the St. John's school and other similar schools under its supervision is to permeate the entire educational process with the precepts of the Catholic religion. . . .

. . . The principal issue presented to us is whether the expenditure of public funds by the defendant school district for the purpose of furnishing textbooks free of charge to pupils of a parochial school is within these constitutional prohibitions.

We have concluded that the expenditure authorized by ORS 337.150 is within the proscription of Article I, § 5 of the Oregon Constitution. . . . [T]he statute violates also the First or Fourteenth Amendments to the United States Constitution. Nor is it necessary to consider whether Article VIII, § 2 of the Oregon Constitution has been violated.

Article I, § 5 prohibiting the use of public moneys "for the benefit of any religious (sic) or theological institution," was designed to keep separate the functions of state and church and to prevent the influence of one upon the other. In this respect our constitution follows the general pattern of other state constitutions and may be regarded as expressing, in more specific terms, the policy of the First Amendment as it has been explained in the Everson case.

The historical setting in which constitutional provisions such as Article I, § 5 were written and the factors which prompted their adoption have been thoroughly explained elsewhere; it is not necessary, therefore, to restate those observations here. We need only say that we regard the separation of church and state no less important today than it was at the time Article I, § 5 and its counterpart in other constitutions were adopted.

The general policy is clear. Our problem is to determine whether that policy is violated by the distribution of free textbooks to parochial schools under ORS 337.150. . . .

Defendants' principal argument in support of the statute is that the expenditure of public funds for the purpose of furnishing books to pupils of parochial and public schools benefits the pupils who receive these books and not the schools themselves. . . .

This so-called "child benefit theory" has been applied in other cases in which the expenditure of public funds is made for the purpose of meeting the educational needs of pupils, including those attending parochial schools. The difficulty with this theory is, however, that unless it is qualified in some way it can be used to justify the expenditure of public funds for every educational purpose, because all educational aids are of benefit to the pupil. This criticism is made in *Gurney v. Ferguson*, 190 Okla 254, 255, 122 P2d 1002, 1003–1004 (1942). In passing upon expenditures for the transportation of children attending parochial schools the court said:

It is true this use of public money and property aids the child, but it is no less true that practically every proper expenditure for school purposes aids the child. We are convinced that this expenditure, in its broad and true sense, and as commonly understood, is an expenditure in furtherance of the constitutional duty or function of maintaining schools as organizations or institutions. The state has no authority to maintain a sectarian school. Surely the expenditure of public funds for the erection of school buildings, the purchasing and equipping and the upkeep of same; the payment of teachers, and for other proper related purposes is expenditure made for schools as such. Yet the same argument is equally applicable to those expenditures as to the present one.

And, as observed by the same court, if the expenditure is not in aid of schools the use of school funds would be unauthorized and illegal. . . .

The furnishing of textbooks even more clearly constitutes an educational aid. In the Everson case the expenditure for the transportation of parochial school pupils was upheld on the theory that the state could provide for the protection of all school children from traffic hazards irrespective of the religious or public character of schools which they attended. Assuming that the court's reasoning in Everson is sound, it is not applicable to the case at bar. The expenditure of public funds for textbooks supplied to pupils of parochial schools is clearly identified with the educational process, and does not warrant the assumption made in the Everson case that the expenditure is for the general welfare thus justifying the use of the state's police power. . . .

It is argued that the aid to school children is for a public purpose because the compulsory school law compels all children to attend school and that the state may, therefore, make expenditures to further compliance. But this begs the basic question—the state may not compel compliance through the device of furnishing aid to religious schools if that aid is in violation of the constitution. Moreover, the state does not compel pupils to attend *parochial* schools . . . .

The theory has been advanced in some cases that since the parochial schools are performing a task which the state itself must perform through the use of the public schools, the expenditures made are not "aid" but "remuneration" for services rendered and, therefore, not prohibited by the constitutional principle of separation of church and state. The distinction is specious and its application could be urged in the justification of the expenditure of public moneys for all educational needs of parochial schools.

In the instant case the evidence establishes that the defendant school district expended approximately $4,000 for textbooks used in the St. John's school. This constitutes a substantial benefit. The benefit is of such a character as to bring it within the proscription of Article I, § 5. . . .

We recognize that whether an expenditure is an aid to a religious institution in its religious function or in some other capacity is a question of degree. But it seems clear that the line must be drawn to include within the constitutional proscription the furnishing of textbooks to pupils of parochial schools. This conclusion is compelled because such books are an integral part of the educational process. As we have already pointed out, the teaching of the precepts of Catholicism is an inseparable part of the educational process in the St. John's school. Considering the purpose of Article I, § 5, we are unable to see any substantial distinction between the furnishing of textbooks and the furnishing of blackboards, desks, laboratory instruments, or other equipment clearly necessary to the operation of the school. In comparing these various essential tools we agree with the dissenting opinion in *Everson v. Board of Education of Ewing Twp.,* 133 NJL 350, 359, 44 A2d 333 (1945) that there is no way of "satisfactorily distinguishing one item of expense from another in the long process of child education."

It is argued that the strict notions of separation in vogue at the time of the adoption of our constitutional provisions no longer exist and that these provisions should be interpreted to reflect this change in attitude. Conceding that such change has occurred, there are still important considerations warranting the resolve that the wall of separation between church and state "must be kept high and impregnable." *Everson v. Board of Education,* supra, 330 US at p. 18, 67 S Ct at p. 513, 91 L ed at 725, 168 ALR at 1406. . . . These considerations convince us that the wall of separation in this state must also be kept "high and impregnable" to meet the demands of Article I, § 5.

We are not unmindful of the fact that parents who send their children to Catholic schools must bear the double burden of supporting not only their own parochial schools but the public schools as well. But the additional burden is self-imposed; instruction in the public schools is available to all. Catholic schools operate only because Catholic parents feel that the precepts of their faith should be integrated into the teaching of secular subjects. Those who do not share in this faith need not share in the cost of nurturing it. Article I, § 5 so ordains. . . .

The trial judge was of the opinion that the expenditures in question constituted a violation of the constitutional principle of separation of church and state, but he concluded that he was bound by *Everson v. Board of Education,* 330 US 1, 67 S Ct 504, 91 L ed 711, 168 ALR 1392 (1946). A decision of the Supreme Court of the United States holding that certain legislation is not in violation of the federal constitution is not an adjudication of the constitutionality of the legislation under a state constitution. In such a case it is not only within the power of the state courts, it is their duty to decide whether the state constitution has been violated. Our views on the policy or interpretation of a particular constitutional provision do not always coincide with those of the Supreme Court of the United States. As we have indicated, *Everson v. Board of Education,* supra, is distinguishable from the case at bar. Even if it were not, our conclusion would be the same.

The judgment is reversed. The trial court is directed to enter a decree in accordance with the prayer in plaintiffs' complaint.

NOTE

1. The Supreme Court of Oklahoma has held that Article II, § 5 of that state's constitution prevents use of public funds to transport parochial school students to school. *Gurney v. Ferguson,* 190 Okl. 254, 122 P.2d 1002 (1941); *Board of Education v. Antone,* 384 P.2d 911 (Okl. 1963).

   In *Antone* the court wrote:

   The law leaves to every man the right to entertain such religious views as appeal to his individual conscience, and to provide for the religious instruction and training of his own children to the extent and in the manner he deems essential or desirable. When he chooses to seek for them educational facilities which combine secular and religious instruction, he is faced with the necessity of assuming the financial burden which that choice entails.

   In specifically rejecting the *Everson* precedent as applicable to Oklahoma, the Oklahoma Supreme Court pointed out that *Everson* was merely an interpretation of federal law and did not negate the more restrictive provisions of the Oklahoma constitution.

   The Oklahoma Supreme Court said further:

   As we pointed out in *Gurney v. Ferguson* . . . if the cost of school buses and the operation and maintenance thereof is in aid of the public schools, then it would seem to necessarily follow that when pupils of parochial schools are transported by them, such service is in aid of that school. Any such aid or benefit, either directly or indirectly, is expressly prohibited by the above quoted provision of the constitutoin of Oklahoma. *Antone,* supra, 384 P.2d 911 (1963); the constitutional provision referred to is Article II, § 5 of the Constitution of Oklahoma.

▪▪▪ RELEASED TIME FOR RELIGIOUS INSTRUCTION

The practice of releasing public school children during regular school hours for religious instruction first began in the United States in Gary, Indiana, in 1914. Since then, the Supreme Court has had before it two cases involving release time. The first was the *McCollum* case in 1948,[112] in which pupils were released to attend religious instruction in the classrooms of the public school building. Students who did not want to participate were not released, but were required to leave their classrooms and go to another part of the building to pursue their secular studies. The Supreme Court held that this "release time" program violated the First Amendment of the Constitution.

In 1952, the Supreme Court was once again called upon to test the constitutionality of "release time." In this case a New York statute permitted pupils to leave the school building and grounds to attend religious centers for religious instruction.[113] Students who did not wish to participate in such services stayed in their classrooms, and no supervision or approval of their activities was required. The Supreme Court found that this statute did not violate the doctrine of separation of church and state. The Court pointed out that while the Constitution forbids the government financing of religious groups and the promotion of religious instruction, the First Amendment does not require governmental hostility toward religion. From this decision it is clear that the Supreme Court does not prohibit some cooperation between schools and churches, but the nature and degree of the cooperation is important; and, if it exceeds certain reasonable limitations, the relationship will violate the Constitution.

Released Time for Religious Instruction on Public School Premises Is Unconstitutional

— · — · — · — · —

People of State of Illinois Ex Rel. McCollum v. Board of Education of School District No. 71, Champaign County, Illinois

— · — · — · — · —

Supreme Court of the United States, 1948. 333 U.S. 203, 68 S.Ct. 461.

Mr. Justice BLACK delivered the opinion of the Court. This case related to the power of a state to utilize its tax-supported public school system in aid of religious instruction insofar as that power may be restricted by the First and Fourteenth Amendments to the Federal Constitution. . . .

Appellant's petition for mandamus alleged that religious teachers, employed by private religious groups, were permitted to come weekly into the school buildings during the regular hours set apart for secular teaching, and then and there for a period of thirty minutes substitute their religious teaching for the secular education provided under the compulsory education law. The petitioner charged that this joint public-school religious-group program violated the First and Fourteenth Amendments to the United States Constitution. The prayer of her petition was that the Board of Education be ordered to "adopt and enforce rules and regulations prohibiting all instruction in and teaching of all religious education in all public schools in Champaign District Number 71 . . . and in all public school houses and buildings in said district when occupied by public schools." . . .

Although there are disputes between the parties as to various inferences that may or may not properly be drawn from the evidence concerning the religious program, the following facts are shown by the record without dispute. In 1940 interested members of the Jewish, Roman Catholic, and a few of the Protestant faiths formed a voluntary association called the Champaign Council on Religious Education. They obtained permission from the Board of Education to offer classes in religious instruction to public school pupils in grades four to nine inclusive. Classes were made up of pupils whose parents signed printed cards requesting that their children be permitted to attend; they were held weekly, thirty minutes for the lower grades, forty-five minutes for the higher. The council employed the religious teachers at no expense to the school authorities, but the instructors were subject to the approval and supervision of the superintendent of schools. The classes were taught in three separate religious groups by Protestant teachers, Catholic priests, and a Jewish rabbi, although for the past several years there have apparently been no classes instructed in the Jewish religion. Classes were conducted in the regular classroom of the school building. Students who did not choose to take the religious instruction were not released from public school duties; they were required to leave their classrooms and go to some other place in the school building for pursuit of their secular studies. On the other hand, students who were released from secular study for the religious instructions were required to be present at the religious classes. Reports of their presence or absence were to be made their secular teachers.

The foregoing facts, without reference to others that appear in the record, show the use of tax-supported property for religious instruction and the close cooperation between the school authorities and the religious council in promoting religious education. The operation of the state's compulsory education system thus assists and is integrated with the program of religious instruction carried on by separate religious sects. Pupils compelled by law to go to school for secular education are released in part from their legal duty upon the condition that they attend the religious classes. This is beyond all question a utilization of the tax-established and tax-supported public school system to aid religious groups to spread their faith. And it falls squarely under the ban of the First Amendment (made applicable to the States by the Fourteenth) as we interpreted it in *Everson v. Board of Education*, 330 U.S. 1, 67 S.Ct. 504. . . .

To hold that a state cannot consistently with the First and Fourteenth Amendments utilize its public school system to aid any or all religious faiths or sects in the dissemination of their doctrines and ideals does not, as counsel urge, manifest a governmental hostility to religion or religious teachings. A manifestation of such hostility would be at war with our national tradition as embodied in the First Amendment's guaranty of the free exercise of religion. For the First Amendment rests upon the premise that both religion and government can best work to achieve their lofty aims if each is left free from the other within its respective sphere. Or, as we said in the *Everson* case, the First Amendment has erected a wall between Church and State which must be kept high and impregnable.

Here not only are the state's tax supported public school buildings used for the dissemination of religious doctrines. The State also affords sectarian groups an invaluable aid in that it helps to provide pupils for their religious classes through the use of the state's compulsory public school machinery. This is not separation of Church and State.

The cause is reversed and remanded to the State Supreme Court for proceedings not inconsistent with this opinion.

Reversed and remanded.

NOTE

1. *Released Time.* Courts upholding discretionary power of boards of education to provide released time programs: *People ex rel. Lewis v. Graves*, 245 N.Y. 195, 156 N.E. 663 (1927); *People ex rel. Latimer v. Board of Education of City of Chicago*, 394 Ill. 228, 68 N.E.2d 305 (1946); *Dilger v. School District 24 CJ*, 222 Or. 108, 352 P.2d 564 (1960). Some decisions indicated parents had the right to have children excused or released from school for religious purposes: *Lewis v. Spaulding*, 193 Misc. 66, 85 N.Y.S.2d 682 (1948), appeal dismissed 299 N.Y. 564, 85 N.E.2d 791 (1949); *Gordon v. Board of Education of City of Los Angeles*, 78 Cal.App.2d 464, 178 P.2d 488 (1947); *Perry v. School District No. 81*, Spokane, 54 Wn.2d 886, 344 P.2d 1036 (1959)

Released Time for Public School Students to Attend Religious Classes Off Public School Grounds Is Constitutional

– – – – – – – – – – –

Zorach v. Clauson

– – – – – – – – – – –

Supreme Court of the United States, 1952. 343 U.S. 306, 72 S.Ct. 679.

Mr. Justice DOUGLAS delivered the opinion of the Court. New York City has a program which permits its public schools to release students during the school day so that they may leave the school buildings and school grounds and go to religious centers for religious instruction or devotional exercises. A student is released on written request of his parents. Those not released stay in the classrooms. The churches make weekly reports to the schools, sending a list of children who have been released from public school but who have not reported for religious instruction.

This "released time" program involves neither religious instruction in public school classrooms nor the expenditure of public funds. All costs, including the application blanks, are paid by the religious organizations. The case is therefore unlike *McCollum v. Board of Education,* 333 U.S. 203, 68 S.Ct. 461, 92 L.Ed. 249, which involved a "released time" program from Illinois. In that case the classrooms were turned over to religious instructors. We accordingly held that the program violated the First Amendment which (by reason of the Fourteenth Amendment) prohibits the states from establishing religion or prohibiting its free exercise.

Appellants, who are taxpayers and residents of New York City and whose children attend its public schools, challange the present law, contending it is in essence not different from the one involved in the *McCollum* case. Their argument, stated elaborately in various ways, reduces itself to this: the weight and influence of the school is put behind a program for religious instruction; public school teachers police it, keeping tab on students who are released; the classroom activities come to a halt while the students who are released for religious instruction are on leave; the school is a crutch on which the churches are leaning for support in their religious training; without the cooperation of the schools this "released time" program, like the one in the *McCollum* case, would be futile and ineffective. The New York Court of Appeals sustained the law against this claim of unconstitutionality. . . .

It takes obtuse reasoning to inject any issue of the "free exercise" of religion into the present case. No one is forced to go to the religious classroom and no religious exercise or instruction is brought to the classrooms of the public schools. A student need not take religious instruction. He is left to his own desires as to the manner or time of his religious devotions, if any.

There is a suggestion that the system involves the use of coercion to get public school students into religious classrooms. There is no evidence in the record before us that supports that conclusion. The present record indeed tells us that the school authorities are neutral in this regard and do no more than release students whose parents so request. If in fact coercion were used, if it were established that any one or more teachers were using their office to persuade or force students to take the religious instruction a wholly different case would be presented. Hence we put aside that claim of coercion both as respects the "free exercise" of religion and "an establishment of religion" within the meaning of the First Amendment. . . .

We would have to press the concept of separation of Church and State to these extremes to condemn the present law on constitutional grounds. . . .

We are a religious people whose institutions presuppose a Supreme Being. We guarantee the freedom to worship as one chooses. We make room for as wide a variety of beliefs and creeds as the spiritual needs of man deem necessary. We sponsor an attitude on the part of government that shows no partiality to any one group and that lets each flourish according to the zeal of its adherents and the appeal of its dogma. When the state encourages religious instruction or cooperates with religious authorities by adjusting the schedule of public events to sectarian needs, it follows the best of our traditions. For it then respects the religious nature of our people and accommodates the public service to their spiritual needs. To hold that it may not would be to find in the Constitution a requirement that the government show a callous indifference to religious groups. That would be preferring those who believe in no religion over those who do believe. Government may not finance religious groups nor undertake religious instruction nor blend secular and sectarian education nor use secular institutions to force one or some religion on any person. But we find no constitutional requirement which makes it necessary for government to be hostile to religion and to throw its weight against efforts to widen the effective scope of religious influence. The government must be neutral when it comes to competition between sects. It may not thrust any sect on any person. It may not make a religious observance compulsory. It may not coerce anyone to attend church, to observe a religious holiday, or to take religious instruction. But it can close its doors or suspend its operations as to those who want to repair to their religious sanctuary for worship or instruction. No more than that is undertaken here. . . .

In the *McCollum* case the classrooms were used for religious instruction and the force of the public school was used to promote that instruction. Here, as we have said, the public schools do no more than accommodate their schedules to a program of outside religious instruction. We follow the *McCollum* case. But we cannot expand it to cover the present released time program unless separation of Church and State means that public institutions can make no adjustments of their schedules to accommodate the religious needs of the people. We cannot read into the Bill of Rights such a philosophy of hostility to religion.

Affirmed.

NOTES

1. *Shared Time.* "Dual Enrollment" or "shared time" is an arrangement between a public school and a private school by which the shared use of the public school facilities is provided for public school teachers or students. A pupil may be a part-time student in a public school while concurrently attending a nonpublic school part-time.

2. The United States Court of Appeals, Tenth Circuit, has held that provisions in a released time program, in which students attended church-related seminaries and received public school credit for classes that were "mainly denominational" in content,

was unconstitutional. Also, unconstitutional was a procedure whereby the public school bore the burden of gathering the seminary's attendance slips. *Lanner v. Wimmer*, 662 F.2d 1349 (10th Cir.1981).

3. In a case involving "shared time" the Supreme Court of Missouri held that use of public moneys to send speech teachers of a school district into parochial schools for speech therapy was not for the purpose of maintaining free public schools and was, therefore, unconstitutional (Section 5 of Article IX, Missouri Constitution). Also, when the school district provided speech therapy for parochial school children in buildings maintained by the school district and parochial children who desired such therapy were released from school for part of their regular six-hour day, such practice violated compulsory attendance laws that required each school child to attend school regularly for six hours a school day. *Special District for the Education and Training of Handicapped Children of St. Louis County v. Wheeler*, 408 S.W.2d 60 (Mo.1966).

4. An Illinois court reached a conclusion different from that of the Missouri court concerning shared time. Plaintiffs in this case sought to enjoin the Board of Education from maintaining a dual enrollment program where children were enrolled part-time in a public school and part-time in a nonpublic school, on the grounds that the program violated statutory and constitutional provisions. The court held that the dual enrollment program did not violate either statutory or constitutional provisions.

> The object of compulsory attendance law is that all children be educated and not that they be educated in any particular manner or place, and part-time enrollment in a public school and part-time enrollment in a nonpublic school under a dual enrollment program permitted so long as the child receives a complete education. *Morton v. Board of Education of City of Chicago*, 69 Ill. App.2d 38, 216 N.E.2d 305 (1966).

5. How does the released time program of the *Zorach* case differ from the program in the *McCollum* case?

6. What does the court say about the relationship between church and state? What is the role of the state in dealing with religion?

7. Relate the reasoning in the decisions by the Supreme Court in *McCollum* and *Zorach* to the concept of dual enrollment. What legal principles of the cases may be applied in a case involving dual enrollment?

8. In regard to a shared time program where the school district leased parochial school facilities and public school teachers taught classes therein, the court held that neither the state nor federal constitutions were violated. This was true even in light of the fact that classes were conducted in the same building. *Citizens to Advance Public Education v. Porter*, 65 Mich.App. 168, 237 N.W.2d 232 (1975).

9. In a case where parents of a nonschool student filed suit to compel a public school district to enroll their child in a band class, the Supreme Court of Michigan held that (1) nonessential elective courses offered to public school students must be offered to resident nonpublic school students on a shared time basis, and (2) provision of nonessential elective courses to resident nonpublic school students on a shared time basis does not violate the Establishment Clause where shared time instruction is conducted on public school premises. *Snyder v. Charlotte Public School District, Eaton County*, 421 Mich. 517, 365 N.W.2d 151 (1984).

■ PRAYER AND BIBLE READING IN THE PUBLIC SCHOOLS

Prayer and Bible reading in the public schools have been the source of much judicial controversy. Over half the states have, at some point, permitted or required prayer and Bible reading in public schools. Prior to 1962, at least twelve states and the District of Columbia required Bible reading. The typical attitude of the courts was that the Bible and general prayer were not sectarian in nature, and their use did not violate constitutional religious guarantees.[114] That the Bible was not sectarian was even reflected in statute, the North Dakota legislature had observed that:

> [t]he Bible shall not be deemed a sectarian book. It shall not be excluded from any public school. It may be the option of the teacher to read in school without sectarian comment, not to exceed ten minutes daily. No pupil shall be required to read it nor be present in the schoolroom during the reading thereof contrary to the wishes of his parents or guardian or other person having him in charge.[115]

Volitional

Voluntariness of the exercise, whether it was Bible reading or prayer, was thought to be an important factor as evidenced by this type of legislation. Proponents of religious exercise generally relied upon voluntariness, tradition, and nonsectarianism of the Bible as the primary defense of the practice.[116] In 1962, however, the United States Supreme Court, in *Engel v. Vitale*,[116] found a New York Regents prayer unconstitutional, and a year later held both prayer and Bible reading offensive to the First Amendment even though the defendants claimed that the exercises were voluntary and the Bible was nondenominational. This result could probably have been anticipated since the position established by the Court in *McCollum* in 1948 indicated that neither the nature of the religious instruction nor the voluntariness of the exercise were valid defenses. In *McCollum*, Justice Frankfurter stated:

> That a child is offered an alternative may reduce the constraint; it does not eliminate the operation of influence by the school in matters sacred to conscience and outside the school's domain. The law of imitation operates, and nonconformity is not an outstanding characteristic of children. The result is an obvious pressure upon children to attend.   . . .   [117]

Likewise, the nondenominational nature of a prayer was found to be no defense when the issue was raised in *Engel*. The Court explained that neither the fact that a prayer is denominationally neutral nor that it is voluntary can serve to free it from the limitations of the Establishment Clause of the First Amendment. According to the Court:

> The Establishment Clause, unlike the Free Exercise Clause, does not depend upon any showing of direct governmental compulsion and is violated by the enactment of laws which establish an official religion whether those laws operate directly to coerce non-observing individuals or not. . . . [118]

Secular Purpose

The result of *Engel, Schempp,* and their companion case, *Murray*,[119] in 1963, was that religious exercises in the public schools are clearly unconstitutional. Neither state, nor school, nor teacher can hold religious services of any type in the public schools. The Court did point out, however, that the study of the Bible as part of a secular program of education for its literary and historic values would not be unconstitutional.

In 1980, the Supreme Court, in *Stone v. Graham*,[120] followed the precedents of *Schlempp* and *Murray* in holding a Kentucky statute unconstitutional that required the posting of the Ten Commandments on the walls of each public school classroom. In spite of an avowal by the state that the posting was premised on a secular legislative purpose, the High Court said that no legislative recitation of a supposed secular purpose could deny that the Ten Commandments are a sacred text of the Jewish and Christian faiths.

Silent Meditation

During the past few years, a plethora of school prayer cases have been rendered by the courts. Legislatures have passed statutes permitting voluntary prayer in public schools,[121] state constitutions have been changed,[122] challenges have been made to prayers at football games[123] and graduation exercises, and there have been cases in which teachers have maintained that the Free Exercise Clause of the First Amendment permitted them to conduct prayers in the classroom.[125]

The United States Supreme Court in 1985 held, in *Wallace v. Jaffree*,[126] that a period of silence for meditation or voluntary prayer in the public school is unconstitutional. The Court ruled that the purpose of the legislative enactment was not secular and, therefore, violated the Establishment Clause.

In 1984 the people of West Virginia voted to amend the state constitution permitting public schools to designate time at the beginning of the day for student contemplation, meditation, or prayer. A federal court ruled that the "prayer amendment" failed all three aspects of the *Lemon* test and therefore violated the Establishment Clause of the First Amendment. The court, in referring to the "Prayer Amendment," said it was "a hoax conceived in political expediency . . . perpetrated upon those sincere citizens of West Virginia who voted for this amendment to the West Virginia Constitution in belief that even if it violated the United States Constitution, 'majority rule' would prevail."[127]

Ceremonial Invocations

The Courts have been virtually unanimous in holding that prayer, whether at a football game or a graduation exercise, violates the Establishment Clause.[128] Yet, some have allowed prayer by rationalizing that prayer is a secular and not a religious activity. In *Marsh v. Chambers*,[129] the Supreme Court found that some invocations are civil or secular. Using this rationale, one U.S. Circuit Court of Appeals ruled that invocations at graduation have a dual purpose. They may be ceremonial and also religious. If they are ceremonial, then the secular prayer is constitutional. Thus, ceremonial invocation, may be delivered at commencement exercises.[130] Another U.S. Circuit, however, has rejected this reasoning, holding that prayers at public events are, in fact, public endorsements of Christianity.[131]

––·––·––·––·––

School District of Abington Township v. Schempp and Murray v. Curlett

––·––·––·––·––

Supreme Court of the United States, 1963.
374 U.S. 203, 83 S.Ct. 1560.

Mr. Justice CLARK delivered the opinion of the Court. Once again we are called upon to consider the scope of the provision of the First Amendment to the United States Constitution which declares that "Congress shall make no law respecting an establishment of religion, or prohibiting the free exercise thereof . . . ." These companion cases present the issues in the context of state action requiring that schools begin each day with readings from the Bible. While raising the basic questions under slightly different factual situations, the cases permit of joint treatment. In light of the history of the First Amendment and of our cases interpreting and applying its requirements, we hold that the practices at issue and the laws requiring them are unconstitutional under the Establishment Clause, as applied to the States through the Fourteenth Amendment.

The Facts in Each Case: No. 142. The Commonwealth of Pennsylvania by law, 24 Pa.Stat. § 15–1516, as amended, Pub.Law 1928 (Supp.1960) Dec. 17, 1959, requires that "At least ten verses from the Holy Bible shall be read, without comment, at the opening of each public school on each school day. Any child shall be excused from such Bible reading, or attending such Bible reading, upon the written request of his parent or guardian." The Schempp family, husband and wife and two of their three children, brought suit to enjoin enforcement of the statute, contending that their rights under the Fourteenth Amendment to the Constitution of the United States are, have been, and will continue to be violated unless this statute be declared unconstitutional as violative of these provisions of the First Amendment. They sought to enjoin the appellant school district, wherein the Schempp children attend school, and its officers and the Superintendent of Public Instruction of the Commonwealth from continuing to conduct such readings and recitation of the Lord's Prayer in the public schools of the district pursuant to the statute. . . .

No. 119. In 1905 the Board of School Commissioners of Baltimore City adopted a rule pursuant to Art. 77, § 202 of the Annotated Code of Maryland. The rule provided for the holding of opening exercises in the schools of the city, consisting primarily of the "reading, without comment, of a chapter in the Holy Bible and/or the use of the Lord's Prayer." The petitioners, Mrs. Madalyn Murray and her son, William J. Murray III, are both professed atheists. Following unsuccessful attempts to have the respondent school board rescind the rule, this suit was filed for mandamus to compel its rescission and cancellation. It was alleged that William was a student in a public school of the city and Mrs. Murray, his mother, was a taxpayer therein; that it was the practice under the rule to have a reading on each school morning from the King James version of the Bible; that at petitioners' insistence the rule was amended[132] to permit children to be excused from the exercise on request of the parent and that William had been excused pursuant thereto; that nevertheless the rule as amended was in violation of the petitioners' rights "to freedom of religion under the First and Fourteenth Amendments" and in violation of "the principle of separation between church and state, contained therein."

Applying the Establishment Clause principles to the cases at bar we find that the States are requiring the selection and reading at the opening of the school day of verses from the Holy Bible and the recitation of the Lord's Prayer by the students in unison. These exercises are prescribed as part of the curricular activities of students who are required by law to attend school. They are held in the school buildings under the supervision and with the participation of teachers employed in those schools. None of these factors, other than compulsory school attendance, was present in the program upheld in *Zorach v. Clauson*. The trial court in No. 142 has found that such an opening exercise is a religious ceremony and was intended by the State to be so. We agree with the trial court's finding as to the religious character of the exercises. Given that finding, the exercises and the law requiring them are in violation of the Establishment Clause.

There is no such specific finding as to the religious character of the exercises in No. 119, and the State contends (as does the State in No. 142) that the program is an effort to extend its benefits to all public school children without regard to their religious belief. Included within its secular purposes, it says, are the promotion of moral values, the contradiction to the materialistic trends of our times, the perpetuation of our institutions and the teaching of literature. The case came up on demurrer, of course, to a petition which alleged that the uniform practice under the rule had been to read from the King James version of the Bible and that the exercise was sectarian. The short answer, therefore, is that the religious character of the exercise was admitted by the State. But even if its purpose is not strictly religious, it is sought to be accomplished through readings, without comment, from the Bible. Surely the place of the Bible as an instrument of religion cannot be gainsaid, and the State's recognition of the pervading religious character of the ceremony is evident from the rule's specific permission of the alternative use of the Catholic Douay version as well as the recent amendment permitting nonattendance at the exercises. None of these factors is consistent with the contention that the Bible is here used either as an instrument for nonreligious moral inspiration or as a reference for the teaching of secular subjects.

The conclusion follows that in both cases the laws require religious exercises and such exercises are being conducted in direct violation of the rights of the appellees and petitioners. Nor are these required exercises mitigated by the fact that individual students may absent themselves upon parental request, for that fact furnishes no defense to a claim of unconstitutionality under the Establishment Clause. . . . Further, it is no defense to urge that the religious practices here may be relatively minor encroachments on the First Amendment. The breach of neutrality that is today a trickling stream may all too soon become a raging torrent and, in the words of Madison, "it is proper to take alarm at the first experiment on our liberties." *Memorial and Remonstrance Against Religious Assessments.* . . .

It is insisted that unless these religious exercises are permitted a "religion of secularism" is established in the schools. We agree of course that the State may not establish a "religion of secularism" in the sense of affirmatively opposing or showing hostility to religion, thus "preferring those who believe in no religion over those who do believe." *Zorach v. Clauson*, 343 U.S., at 314, 72 S.Ct., at 684, 96 L.Ed. 954. We do not agree, however, that this decision in any sense has that effect. In addition, it might well be said that one's education is not complete without a study of comparative religion or the history of religion and its relationship to the advancement of civilization. It certainly may be said that the Bible is worthy of study for its literary and historic qualities. Nothing we have said here indicates that such study of the Bible or of religion, when presented objectively, as part of a secular program of education, may not be effected consistently with the First Amendment. But the exercises here do not fall into those categories. They are religious exercises, required by the States in violation of the command of the First Amendment that the Government maintain strict neutrality, neither aiding nor opposing religion.

Finally, we cannot accept that the concept of neutrality, which does not permit a State to require a religious exercise even with the consent of the majority of those affected, collides with the majority's right to free exercise of religion. While the Free Exercise Clause clearly prohibits the use of state action to deny the rights of free exercise to *anyone*, it has never meant that a majority could use the machinery of the State to practice its beliefs. Such a contention was effectively answered by Mr. Justice Jackson for the Court in *West Virginia Board of Education v. Barnette*, 319 U.S.

624, 638, 63 S.Ct. 1178, 1185, 87 L.Ed. 1628 (1943):

> The very purpose of a Bill of Rights was to withdraw certain subjects from the vicissitudes of political controversy, to place them beyond the reach of majorities and officials and to establish them as legal principles to be applied by the courts. One's right to . . . freedom of worship . . . and other fundamental rights may not be submitted to vote; they depend on the outcome of no elections.

The place of religion in our society is an exalted one, achieved through a long tradition of reliance on the home, the church and the inviolable citadel of the individual heart and mind. We have come to recognize through bitter experience that it is not within the power of government to invade that citadel, whether its purpose or effect be to aid or oppose, to advance or retard. In the relationship between man and religion, the State is firmly committed to a position of neutrality. Though the application of that rule requires interpretation of a delicate sort, the rule itself is clearly and concisely stated in the words of the First Amendment. Applying that rule to the facts of these cases, we affirm the judgment in No. 142. In No. 119, the judgment is reversed and the cause remanded to the Maryland Court of Appeals for further proceedings consistent with this opinion.

It is so ordered.

Judgment in No. 142 affirmed; judgment in No. 119 reversed and cause remanded with directions.

State Statute Authorizing a Period for Meditation or Voluntary Prayer Violates the Establishment Clause

Wallace v. Jaffree

Supreme Court of the United States, 1985.
472 U.S. 38, 105 S.Ct 2479.

Justice STEVENS delivered the opinion of the Court. At an early stage of this litigation, the constitutionality of three Alabama statutes was questioned: (1) § 16–1–20, enacted in 1978, which authorized a one-minute period of silence in all public schools "for meditation"; (2) § 16–1–20.1, enacted in 1981, which authorized a period of silence "for meditation or voluntary prayer"; and (3) § 16–1–20.2, enacted in 1982, which authorized teachers to lead "willing students" in a prescribed prayer to "Almighty God . . . the Creator and Supreme Judge of the world."

At the preliminary-injunction stage of this case, the District Court distinguished § 16–1–20 from the other two statutes. It then held that there was "nothing wrong" with § 16–1–20, but that § 16–1–20.1 and 16–1–20.2 were both invalid because the sole purpose of both was "an effort on the part of the State of Alabama to encourage a religious activity." After the trial on the merits, the District Court did not change its interpretation of these two statutes, but held that they were constitutional because, in its opinion, Alabama has the power to establish a state religion if it chooses to do so.

The Court of Appeals agreed with the District Court's initial interpretation of the purpose of both §§ 16–1–20.1 and 16–1–20.2, and held them both unconstitutional. We have already affirmed the Court of Appeals' holding with respect to § 16–1–20.2. Moreover, appellees have not questioned the holding that § 16–1–20 is valid. Thus, the narrow question for decision is whether § 16–1–20.1, which authorizes a period of silence for "meditation or voluntary prayer," is a law respecting the establishment of religion within the meaning of the First Amendment. . . .

On August 2, 1982, the District Court held an evidentiary hearing on appellees' motion for a preliminary injunction. At that hearing, State Senator Donald G. Holmes testified that he was the "prime sponsor" of the bill that was enacted in 1981 as § 16–1–20.1. He explained that the bill was an "effort to return voluntary prayer to our public schools . . . it is a beginning and a step in the right direction." Apart from the purpose to return voluntary prayer to public school, Senator Holmes unequivocally testified that he had "no other purpose in mind." A week after the hearing, the District Court entered a preliminary injunction. The court held that appellees were likely to prevail on the merits because the enactment of §§ 16–1–20.1 and 16–1–20.2 did not reflect a clearly secular purpose.

In November 1982, the District Court held a four-day trial on the merits. The evidence related primarily to the 1981–1982 academic year—the year after the enactment of § 16–1–20.1 and prior to the enactment of § 16–1–20.2. The District Court found that during that academic year each of the minor plaintiffs' teachers had led classes in prayer activities, even after being informed of appellees' objections to these activities.

In its lengthy conclusions of law, the District Court reviewed a number of opinions of this Court interpreting the Establishment Clause of the First Amendment, and then embarked on a fresh examination of the question whether the First Amendment imposes any barrier to the establishment of an official religion by the State of Alabama. After reviewing at length what it perceived to be newly discovered historical evidence, the District Court concluded that "the establishment clause of the first amendment to the United States Constitution does not prohibit the state from establishing a religion." In a separate opinion, the District Court dismissed appellees' challenge to the three Alabama statutes because of a failure to state any claim for which relief could be granted. The court's dismissal of this challenge was also based on its conclusion that the Establishment Clause did not bar the States from establishing a religion.

The Court of Appeals consolidated the two cases; not surprisingly, it reversed. The Court of Appeals noted that this Court had considered and had rejected the historical arguments that the District Court found persuasive, and that the District Court had misapplied the doctrine of *stare decisis*. The Court of Appeals then held that the teachers' religious activities violated the Establishment Clause of the First Amendment. With respect to § 16–1–20.1 and

§ 16–1–20.2, the Court of Appeals stated that "both statutes advance and encourage religious activities." The Court of Appeals then quoted with approval the District Court's finding that § 16–1–20.1, and § 16–1–20.2, were efforts "'to encourage a religious activity. Even though these statutes are permissive in form, it is nevertheless state involvement respecting an establishment of religion.'" Thus, the Court of Appeals concluded that both statutes were "specifically the type which the Supreme Court addressed in *Engel* . . . .

Our unanimous affirmance of the Court of Appeals' judgment concerning § 16–1–20.2 makes it unnecessary to comment at length on the District Court's remarkable conclusion that the Federal Constitution imposes no obstacle to Alabama's establishment of a state religion. Before analyzing the precise issue that is presented to us, it is nevertheless appropriate to recall how firmly embedded in our constitutional jurisprudence is the proposition that the several States have no greater power to restrain the individual freedoms protected by the First Amendment than does the Congress of the United States.

As is plain from its text, the First Amendment was adopted to curtail the power of Congress to interfere with the individual's freedom to believe, to worship, and to express himself in accordance with the dictates of his own conscience. Until the Fourteenth Amendment was added to the Constitution, the First Amendment's restraints on the exercise of federal power simply did not apply to the States. But when the Constitution was amended to prohibit any State from depriving any person of liberty without due process of law, that Amendment imposed the same substantive limitations on the States' power to legislate that the First Amendment had always imposed on the Congress' power. This Court has confirmed and endorsed this elementary proposition of law time and time again. . . .

Just as the right to speak and the right to refrain from speaking are complementary components of a broader concept of individual freedom of mind, so also the individual's freedom to choose his own creed is the counterpart of his right to refrain from accepting the creed established by the majority. At one time it was thought that this right merely proscribed the preference of one Christian sect over another, but would not require equal respect for the conscience of the infidel, the atheist, or the adherent of a non-Christian faith such as Mohammedism or Judaism. But when the underlying principle has been examined in the crucible of litigation, the Court has unambiguously concluded that the individual freedom of conscience protected by the First Amendment embraces the right to select any religious faith or none at all. This conclusion derives support not only from the interest in respecting the individual's freedom of conscience, but also from the conviction that religious beliefs worthy of respect are the product of free and voluntary choice by the faithful, and from recognition of the fact that the political interest in forestalling intolerance extends beyond intolerance among Christian sects — or even intolerance among "religions" — to encompass intolerance of the disbeliever and the uncertain. As Justice Jackson eloquently stated in *Board of Education v. Barnette,* 319 U.S. 624, 642, 63 S.Ct. 1178, 1187, 87 L.Ed. 1628 (1943):

> If there is any fixed star in our constitutional constellation, it is that no official, high or petty, can prescribe what shall be orthodox in politics, nationalism, religion, or other matters of opinion or force citizens to confess by word or act their faith therein.

The State of Alabama, no less than the Congress of the United States, must respect that basic truth.

When the Court has been called upon to construe the breadth of the Establishment Clause, it has examined the criteria developed over a period of many years. Thus, in *Lemon v. Kurtzman,* . . . we wrote:

> Every analysis in this area must begin with consideration of the cumulative criteria devel-

oped by the Court over many years. Three such tests may be gleaned from our cases. First, the statute must have a secular legislative purpose; second, its principal or primary effect must be one that neither advances nor inhibits religion, *Board of Education v. Allen,* . . . finally, the statute must not foster 'an excessive government entanglement with religion'. . . .

It is the first of these three criteria that is most plainly implicated by this case. As the District Court correctly recognized, no consideration of the second or third criteria is necessary if a statute does not have a clearly secular purpose. For even though a statute that is motivated in part by a religious purpose may satisfy the first criterion, . . . the First Amendment requires that a statute must be invalidated if it is entirely motivated by a purpose to advance religion.

In applying the purpose test, it is appropriate to ask "whether government's actual purpose is to endorse or disapprove of religion." In this case, the answer to that question is dispositive. For the record not only provides us with an unambiguous affirmative answer, but it also reveals that the enactment of § 16–1–20.1 was not motivated by any clearly secular purpose — indeed, the statute had *no* secular purpose.

The sponsor of the bill that became § 16–1–20.1, Senator Donald Holmes, inserted into the legislative record — apparently without dissent — a statement indicating that the legislation was an "effort to return voluntary prayer" to the public schools. Later Senator Holmes confirmed this purpose before the District Court. In response to the question whether he had any purpose for the legislation other than returning voluntary prayer to public schools, he stated, "No, I did not have no other purpose in mind." The State did not present evidence of *any* secular purpose.
. . .

The legislative intent to return prayer to the public schools is, of course, quite different from merely protecting every student's right to engage in voluntary prayer during an appropriate moment of silence during the school day. The 1978 statute already protected that right, containing nothing that prevented any student from engaging in voluntary prayer during a silent minute of meditation. Appellants have not identified any secular purpose that was not fully served by § 16–1–20 before the enactment of § 16–1–20.1. Thus, only two conclusions are consistent with the text of § 16–1–20.1: (1) the statute was enacted to convey a message of State endorsement and promotion of prayer; or (2) the statute was enacted for no purpose. No one suggests that the statute was nothing but a meaningless or irrational act.   . . .

The Legislature enacted § 16–1–20.1 despite the existence of § 16–1–20 for the sole purpose of expressing the State's endorsement of prayer activities for one minute at the beginning of each school day. The addition of "or voluntary prayer" indicates that the State intended to characterize prayer as a favored practice. Such an endorsement is not consistent with the established principle that the Government must pursue a course of complete neutrality toward religion.

The importance of that principle does not permit us to treat this as an inconsequential case involving nothing more than a few words of symbolic speech on behalf of the political majority. For whenever the State itself speaks on a religious subject, one of the questions that we must ask is "whether the Government intends to convey a message of endorsement or disapproval of religion." The well-supported concurrent findings of the District Court and the Court of Appeals — that § 16–1–20.1 was intended to convey a message of State-approval of prayer activities in the public schools — make it unnecessary, and indeed inappropriate, to evaluate the practical significance of the addition of the words "or voluntary prayer" to the statute. Keeping in mind, as we must, "both the fundamental place held by the Establishment Clause in our constitutional scheme and the myriad, subtle ways in which Establishment Clause values can be eroded," we conclude that § 16–1–20.1 violates the First Amendment.

The judgment of the Court of Appeals is affirmed.

It is so ordered.

NOTES

1. *Prayers.* The U.S. Supreme Court, in *Marsh v. Chambers,* 463 U.S. 783, 103 S.Ct. 3330 (1983), upheld the validity of opening prayers at legislative sessions. The Eleventh Circuit, though, refused to apply *Marsh* to schools and held that *Lemon* controlled. *Jager v. Douglas County School District,* 862 F.2d 824 (11th Cir. 1989).

2. *Graduation Ceremonies.* A student of the Orthodox Jewish faith objected to graduation ceremonies being held on Saturday, the Jewish Sabbath. Students received their diplomas whether they attended graduation ceremonies or not. Attendance at graduation was *not* a prerequisite for receiving a diploma; therefore, the court held that having Saturday graduation did not violate the Free Exercise Clause. The court noted that if graduation was compulsory in order to receive a diploma, then the state would need to establish a compelling governmental interest for such action. *Smith v. Board of Educ., North Babylon Union Free School District,* 844 F.2d 90 (2d Cir. 1988).

3. *Invocations.* The Supreme Court of California has held that religious invocation and benedictions at a public high school graduation ceremony violate the First Amendment. *Sands v. Morongo Unified School District,* 53 Cal. 3d 863, 281 Cal. Rptr. 34, 809 P.2d 809(1991); see also *Lundberg v. West Monona Community School District,* 731 F.Supp. 331 (N.D. Iowa 1989).

4. *Benedictions.* The First Circuit Court of Appeals has ruled that a benediction invoking the deity delivered by a member of the clergy at a public high school graduation violates the Establishment Clause. *Weisman v. Lee,* 908 F.2d 1090, 1990 (1st Cir. 1990). *Certiorari* granted, *Lee v. Weisman,* 111 S.Ct. 1305 (March 18, 1991). The United States Supreme Court having recently accepted this Rhode Island case on appeal will probably rule on it in 1992. The "Lemon test," a twenty-year-old doctrine, will be revisited. Will the Supreme Court develop a new method to review

cases involving the Establishment Clause of the First Amendment? In a nineteen-page brief, the Solicitor General of the United States requested that the Supreme Court not follow twenty years of precedence and abandon the Lemon test. This brief, representing the position of the Bush government, argues that the Supreme Court should search for a "contemporaneous" or modern understanding.

5. *Graduation Prayers.* The Sixth Circuit Court has distinguished between classroom and graduation prayer, saying that the latter provides less opportunity for religious indoctrination or peer pressure. The court noted that the type of prayers recited placed the seal of approval on Christian views and also invoked the name of Jesus as the Savior. The court said that in order for prayers to be allowed, they must be "civil" in nature. *Stein v. Plainwell Community Schools,* 822 F.2d 1406 (6th Cir. 1987).

The United States Court of Appeals, Fifth Circuit, has held that the Establishment Clause is not violated by prayer at graduation ceremonies. The prayer, though, must be given by student volunteers, in a nonsectarian, nonproselytizing manner. *Jones v. Clear Creek Independent School District,* 930 F.2d 416 (5th Cir 1991).

6. *Prayer in Band Class.* Where students and parents brought suit challenging a public school band teacher's prayers before concerts and practices, a parent complained, and the superintendent and school board did nothing to stop the prayers and gave tacit approval to the band director's action. The court found the school board had violated the First Amendment and awarded attorney's fees and costs to the parents. *Steele v. Van Buren Public School District,* 845 F.2d 1492 (8th Cir. 1988).

7. *Dancing.* Whether dancing is a religious activity has been ruled upon by the courts. In a case where a local school board policy prohibited dancing on school property, the students and parents filed suit, claiming the policy violated the Establishment Clause. Religious groups of the small rural community opposed dancing and spoke out in support of the school policy. The court ruled that dancing was not religious, but that it was not unconstitutional for a school board to have a rule that is compatible with belief of a large, vocal segment of the community. The court, in holding for the board, stated that the plaintiff's remedy is to be found at the ballot box and not in the Constitution. *Clayton by Clayton v. Place,* 884 F.2d 376 (8th Cir. 1989).

8. Many decisions were rendered by state courts before the *Engel* and *Schempp* cases, which found that morning religious activities did not violate constitutional or statutory provisions. Some of these were *Hackett v. Brooksville Graded School District,* 120 Ky. 608, 87 S.W. 792 (1905); *Donahoe v. Richards,* 38 Me. 379, 61 Am.Dec. 256 (1854); *Moore v. Monroe,* 64 Iowa 367, 20 N.W. 475 (1884); *Billard v. Board of Education of City of Topeka,* 69 Kan. 53, 76 P. 422 (1904); *Knowlton v. Baumhover,* 182 Iowa 691, 166 N.W. 202 (1918); *McCormick v. Burt,* 95 Ill. 263 (1880).

Other state courts listed below held that religious exercises offended their constitutions: *State ex rel. Weiss v. District Board,* 76 Wis. 177, 44 N.W. 967 (1890); *State ex rel. Freeman v. Scheve,* 65 Neb. 853, 91 N.W. 846 (1902); *People ex rel. Ring v. Board of Education of District 24,* 245 Ill. 334, 92 N.E. 251 (1910); *Herold v. Parish Board of School Directors,* 136 La. 1034, 68 So. 116 (1915); *State ex rel. Finger v. Weedman,* 55 S.D. 343, 226 N.W. 348 (1929).

9. *Religious Garb in Public Schools.* Whether public school teachers can wear religious garb of any particular religious order or society has been litigated on several occasions. While there is no precise definition of what constitutes religious garments, some states have sought prohibition of any apparel showing the person belongs to a particular sect, denomination, or order. See Donald E. Boles, *The Two Swords* (Ames, Ia.: Iowa State University Press, 1967), p. 222.

In 1894, the Supreme Court of Pennsylvania held that the wearing by nuns of garb and insignia of the Sisterhood of St.

Joseph while teaching in the public schools did not constitute sectarian teaching. *Hysong v. School District of Gallitzin Borough,* 164 Pa. 629, 30 A. 482 (1894). The court reasoned that to deny wearing of such apparel would violate the teachers' religious liberty. Later, the Legislature of Pennsylvania prohibited the wearing of garb by public school teachers while in performance of their duties. This statute was subsequently upheld by the Pennsylvania Supreme Court. This time the court maintained that the Act was a reasonable exercise of state power in regulating the educational system to prevent sectarian control. The court found that the legislation "is directed against acts, not beliefs, and only against acts of the teacher while engaged in the performance of his or her duties as such teacher." *Commonwealth v. Herr,* 229 Pa. 132, 78 A. 68 (1910).

10. Bibles can be distributed on the sidewalk in front of a public school. In a case where an individual was barred from distributing Gideon Bibles on the sidewalk in front of a high school, the plaintiff claimed that the sidewalk was used for teachers to picket, pass out leaflets, and other activities and was, therefore, a "public forum." The court held that the school district's policy violated the individual's First Amendment and Equal Protection rights. *Bacon v. Bradley-Bourbonnais High School Dist. No. 307,* 707 F.Supp. 1005 (C.D. Ill. 1989).

■ EQUAL ACCESS ACT

The Equal Access Act, passed by the U.S. Congress in 1984, was based on the free speech determination of *Widmar v. Vincent.*[133] In *Widmar,* the University of Missouri had refused to allow a religious group the use of university facilities because of possible violation of the Establishment Clause. The Court ruled that to refuse religious groups access to facilities while allowing other groups to use the same facilities violated the student rights of free speech. The Reagan administration,

using this case as rationale, applied the equal access concept to noncurricular high school activities in order to allow religious functions in public schools. The Equal Access Act provides that if a school district receives federal money and allows noncurricular activities and club meetings, then it is unlawful to deny students the right to meet for religious activities. Therefore, if a high school has noncurricular meetings, such as a photography club, and this activity is not directly related to a specific class or a class requirement, then the school has created a *limited open forum.* If a limited open forum exists, then all groups, regardless of their religious, political, or philosophical beliefs, are allowed to form and hold meetings and activities in the public high school. Such groups must be student initiated and not sponsored by the school.

The Supreme Court, on 4 June 1990, upheld the constitutionality of the Equal Access Act. In *Board of Education v. Mergens,*[134] the court ruled that if a school allows any noncurricular groups to meet, then a limited open forum is created and any student-initiated group would have a right to assemble. These groups would be allowed to convene during noninstructional time when other groups, such as the class club, meet.

Students Have a Right to Organize Their Own Groups in Public Schools Whether They Be Religious, Political, or Philosophical

---

Board of Education of the Westside Community Schools v. Mergens

---

Supreme Court of the United States, 1990.
____ U.S. ____, 110 S.Ct. 2356.

Justice O'Connor delivered the opinion of the Court except as to Part III. This case requires us to decide whether the Equal Access Act, 98

Stat. 1302, 20 U.S.C. §§ 4071–4074, prohibits Westside High School from denying a student religious group permission to meet on school premises during noninstructional time, and if so, whether the Act, so construed, violates the Establishment Clause of the First Amendment.

Respondents are current and former students at Westside High School, a public secondary school in Omaha, Nebraska. At the time this suit was filed, the school enrolled about 1,450 students and included grades 10 to 12; in the 1987–1988 school year, ninth graders were added. Westside High School is part of the Westside Community School system, an independent public school district. . . .

Students at Westside High School are permitted to join various student groups and clubs, all of which meet after school hours on school premises. The students may choose from approximately 30 recognized groups on a voluntary basis. . . .

School Board Policy 5610 concerning "Student Clubs and Organizations" recognizes these student clubs as a "vital part of the total education program as a means of developing citizenship, wholesome attitudes, good human relations, knowledge and skills." . . . Board Policy 5610 also provides that each club shall have faculty sponsorship and that "clubs and organizations shall not be sponsored by any political or religious organization, or by any organization which denies membership on the basis of race, color, creed, sex or political belief." Board Policy 6180 on "Recognition of Religious Beliefs and Customs" requires that "[s]tudents adhering to a specific set of religious beliefs or holding to little or no belief shall be alike respected." In addition, Board Policy 5450 recognizes its students' "Freedom of Expression," consistent with the authority of the Board.

There is no written school board policy concerning the formation of student clubs. Rather, students wishing to form a club present their request to a school official who determines whether the proposed club's goals and objectives are consistent with school board policies and with the school district's "Mission and Goals"—a broadly worded "blueprint" that expresses the district's commitment to teaching academic, physical, civic, and personal skills and values.

In January 1985, respondent Bridget Mergens met with Westside's principal, Dr. Findley, and requested permission to form a Christian club at the school. The proposed club would have the same privileges and meet on the same terms and conditions as other Westside student groups, except that the proposed club would not have a faculty sponsor. According to the students' testimony at trial, the club's purpose would have been, among other things, to permit the students to read and discuss the Bible, to have fellowship, and to pray together. Membership would have been voluntary and open to all students regardless of religious affiliation.

Findley denied the request, as did associate superintendent Tangdell. In February 1985, Findley and Tangdell informed Mergens that they had discussed the matter with superintendent Hanson and that he had agreed that her request should be denied. The school officials explained that school policy required all student clubs to have a faculty sponsor, which the proposed religious club would not or could not have, and that a religious club at the school would violate the Establishment Clause. In March 1985, Mergens appealed the denial of her request to the Board of Education, but the Board voted to uphold the denial. . . .

Respondents, . . . then brought this suit in the United States District Court for the District of Nebraska seeking declaratory and injunctive relief. They alleged that petitioners' refusal to permit the proposed club to meet at Westside violated the Equal Access Act, 20 U.S.C. §§ 4071–4074, which prohibits public secondary schools that receive federal financial assistance and that maintain a "limited open forum" from denying "equal access" to students who wish to meet within the forum on the basis of the content of the speech at such meetings, ... Respondents further alleged that petitioners' actions denied them their First and Fourteenth Amendment rights to freedom of speech, association, and the free exercise of religion. Petitioners responded that the Equal Access Act did not apply to Westside and that, if the Act did apply, it violated the Establishment Clause of the First Amendment and was therefore unconstitutional. . . .

In *Widmar v. Vincent,* 454 U.S. 263 (1981), we invalidated, on free speech grounds, a state university regulation that prohibited student use of school facilities "for purposes of religious worship or religious teaching." In doing so, we held that an "equal access" policy would not violate the Establishment Clause under our decision in *Lemon v. Kurtzman,* . . . . In particular, we held that such a policy would have a secular purpose, would not have the primary effect of advancing religion, and would not result in excessive entanglement between government and religion. . . . We noted, however, that "[u]niversity students are, of course, young adults. They are less impressionable than younger students and should be able to appreciate that the University's policy is one of neutrality toward religion."

In 1984, Congress extended the reasoning of *Widmar* to public secondary schools. Under the Equal Access Act, a public secondary school with a "limited open forum" is prohibited from discriminating against students who wish to conduct a meeting within that forum on the basis of the "religious, political, philosophical, or other content of the speech at such meetings." . . . Specifically, the Act provides:

> It shall be unlawful for any public second-ary school which receives Federal financial assistance and which has a limited open forum to deny equal access or a fair opportunity to, or discriminate against, any students who wish to conduct a meeting within that limited open forum on the basis of the religious, political, philosophical, or other content of the speech at such meetings. 20 U.S.C. § 4071(a).

A "limited open forum" exists whenever a public secondary school "grants an offering to or opportunity for one or more noncurriculum related student groups to meet on school premises during noninstructional time." "Meeting" is defined to include "those activ-ities of student groups which are permitted under a school's limited open forum and are not directly related to the school curriculum." "Noninstructional time" is defined to mean "time set aside by the school before actual classroom instruction begins or after actual classroom instruction ends." Thus, even if a public secondary school allows only one "noncurriculum related student group" to meet, the Act's obligations are triggered and the school may not deny other clubs, on the basis of the content of their speech, equal access to meet on school premises during noninstructional time.

The Act further specifies that "[s]chools shall be deemed to offer a fair opportunity to students who wish to conduct a meeting within its limited open forum" if the school uniformly provides that the meetings are voluntary and student-initiated; are not spon-sored by the school, the government, or its agents or employees; do not materially and substantially interfere with the orderly con-duct of educational activities within the school; and are not directed, controlled, con-ducted, or regularly attended by "nonschool persons." . . . "Sponsorship" is defined to mean "the act of promoting, leading, or participating in a meeting. The assignment of a teacher, administrator, or other school em-ployee to a meeting for custodial purposes does not constitute sponsorship of the meet-ing." If the meetings are religious, employees or agents of the school or government may attend only in a "nonparticipatory capacity." Moreover, a State may not influence the form of any religious activity, require any person to participate in such activity, or compel any school agent or employee to attend a meeting if the content of the speech at the meeting is contrary to that person's beliefs. . . .

Finally, the Act does not "authorize the United States to deny or withhold Federal financial assistance to any school," . . . or "limit the authority of the school, its agents or employees, to maintain order and discipline on school premises, to protect the well-being of students and faculty, and to assure that attendance of students at the meetings is voluntary," . . . .

The parties agree that Westside High School receives federal financial assistance and is a public secondary school within the meaning of the Act. . . . The Act's obligation to grant equal access to student groups is therefore triggered if Westside maintains a "limited open forum"—*i.e.,* if it permits one or more "noncurriculum related student groups" to meet on campus before or after classes.

Unfortunately, the Act does not define the crucial phrase "noncurriculum related student group." Our immediate task is therefore one of statutory interpretation. We begin, of course, with the language of the statute. . . . The common meaning of the term "curriculum" is "the whole body of courses offered by an educational institution or one of its branches." Webster's Third New International Dictionary 557 (1976); see also Black's Law Dictionary 345 (5th ed. 1979) ("The set of studies or courses for a particular period, designated by a school or branch of a school"). Cf. *Hazelwood School Dist. v. Kuhlmeier,* 484 U.S., at 271 (high school newspaper produced as part of the school's journalism class was part of the curriculum). Any sensible interpretation of "noncurriculum related student group" must therefore be anchored in the notion that such student groups are those that are not related to the body of courses offered by the school. The difficult question is the degree of "unrelatedness to the curriculum" required for a group to be considered "noncurriculum related."

The Act's definition of the sort of "meeting[s]" that must be accommodated under the statute, . . . sheds some light on this question. "[T]he term 'meeting' includes those activities of student groups which are . . . not *directly related* to the school curriculum." . . . Congress' use of the phrase "directly related" implies that student groups directly related to the subject matter of courses offered by the school do not fall within the "noncurriculum related" category and would therefore be considered "curriculum related."

The logic of the Act also supports this view, namely, that a curriculum-related student group is one that has more than just a tangential or attenuated relationship to courses offered by the school. Because the purpose of granting equal access is to prohibit discrimination between religious or political clubs on the one hand and other noncurriculum-related student groups on the other, the Act is premised on the notion that a religious or political club is itself likely to be a noncurriculum-related student group. It follows, then, that a student group that is "curriculum related" must at least have a more direct relationship to the curriculum than a religious or political club would have.

Although the phrase "noncurriculum related student group" nevertheless remains sufficiently ambiguous that we might normally resort to legislative history, . . . we find the legislative history on this issue less than helpful. Because the bill that led to the Act was extensively rewritten in a series of multilateral negotiations after it was passed by the House and reported out of committee by the Senate, the committee reports shed no light on the language actually adopted. During congressional debate on the subject, legislators referred to a number of different definitions, and thus both petitioners and respondents can cite to legislative history favoring their interpretation of the phrase. . . .

We think it significant, however, that the Act, which was passed by wide, bipartisan majorities in both the House and the Senate, reflects at least some consensus on a broad legislative purpose. The committee reports indicate that the Act was intended to address perceived widespread discrimination against religious speech in public schools, ... The committee reports also show that the Act was enacted in part in response to two federal appellate court decisions holding that student religious groups could not, consistent with the Establishment Clause, meet on school premises during noninstructional time. . . . A broad reading of the Act would be consistent with the views of those who sought to end discrimination by allowing students to meet and discuss religion before and after classes.

In light of this legislative purpose, we think that the term "noncurriculum related student group" is best interpreted broadly to mean any student group that does not *directly* relate to the body of courses offered by the school. In our view, a student group directly relates to a school's curriculum if the subject matter of the group is actually taught, or will soon be taught, in a regularly offered course; if the subject matter of the group concerns the body of courses as a whole; if participation in the group is required for a particular course; or if participation in the group results in academic credit. We think this limited definition of groups that directly relate to the curriculum is a commonsense interpretation of the Act that is consistent with Congress' intent to provide a low threshold for triggering the Act's requirements.

For example, a French club would directly relate to the curriculum if a school taught French in a regularly offered course or planned to teach the subject in the near future. A school's student government would generally relate directly to the curriculum to the extent that it addresses concerns, solicits opinions, and formulates proposals pertaining to the body of courses offered by the school. If participation in a school's band or orchestra were required for the band or orchestra classes, or resulted in academic credit, then those groups would also directly relate to the curriculum. The existence of such groups at a school would not trigger the Act's obligations.

On the other hand, unless a school could show that groups such as a chess club, a stamp-collecting club, or a community service club fell within our description of groups that directly relate to the curriculum, such groups would be "noncurriculum related student groups" for purposes of the Act. The existence of such groups would create a "limited open forum" under the Act and would prohibit the school from denying equal access to any other student group on the basis of the content of that group's speech. Whether a specific student group is a "noncurriculum related student group" will therefore depend on a particular school's curriculum, but such determinations would be subject to factual findings well within the competence of trial courts to make.

Petitioners contend that our reading of the Act unduly hinders local control over schools and school activities, but we think that schools and school districts nevertheless retain a significant measure of authority over the type of officially recognized activities in which their students participate. . . . First, schools and school districts maintain their traditional latitude to determine appropriate subjects of instruction. To the extent that a school chooses to structure its course offerings and existing student groups to avoid the Act's obligations, that result is not prohibited by the Act. . . . Second, the Act expressly does not limit a school's authority to prohibit meetings that would "materially and substantially interfere with the orderly conduct of educational activities within the school." . . . The Act also preserves "the authority of the school, its agents or employees, to maintain order and discipline on school premises, to protect the well-being of students and faculty, and to assure that attendance of students at meetings is voluntary." . . . Finally, because the Act applies only to public secondary schools that receive federal financial assistance, . . . a school district seeking to escape the statute's obligations could simply forgo federal funding. Although we do not doubt that in some cases this may be an unrealistic option, Congress clearly sought to prohibit schools from discriminating on the basis of the content of a student group's speech, and that obligation is the price a federally funded school must pay if it opens its facilities to noncurriculum-related student groups. . . .

The parties in this case focus their dispute on 10 of Westside's approximately 30 voluntary student clubs: Interact (a service club related to Rotary International); Chess; Subsurfers (a club for students interested in scuba diving); National Honor Society; Photography; Welcome to Westside (a club to introduce new students to the school); Future Business Leaders of America; Zonta (the female counterpart to Interact); Student Advisory Board (student government); and Student Forum (student government). . . . Petitioners contend that all of these student activities are curriculum-related because they further the goals of particular aspects of the school's curriculum. Welcome to Westside, for example, helps "further the School's overall goal of developing effective citizens by requiring student members to contribute to their fellow students." . . . The student government clubs "advance the goals of the School's political science classes by providing an understanding and appreciation of government processes." Subsurfers furthers "one of the essential goals of the Physical Education Department—enabling students to develop lifelong recreational interests." Chess "supplement[s] math and science courses because it enhances students' ability to engage in critical thought processes." Participation in Interact and Zonta "promotes effective citizenship, a critical goal of the WHS curriculum, specifically the Social Studies Department."

To the extent that petitioners contend that "curriculum related" means anything remotely related to abstract educational goals, however, we reject that argument. To define "curriculum related" in a way that results in almost no schools having limited open fora, or in a way that permits schools to evade the Act by strategically describing existing student groups, would render the Act merely hortatory. . . . ("[A] limited open forum should be triggered by what a school does, not by what it says"). As the court below explained:

> Allowing such a broad interpretation of 'curriculum-related' would make the [Act] meaningless. A school's administration could simply declare that it maintains a closed forum and choose which student clubs it wanted to allow by tying the purposes of those clubs to some broadly defined educational goal. At the same time the administration could arbitrarily deny access to school facilities to any unfavored student club on the basis of its speech content. This is exactly the result that Congress sought to prohibit by enacting the [Act]. A public secondary school cannot simply declare that it maintains a closed forum and then discriminate against a particular student group on the basis of the content of the speech of that group. . . .

Rather, we think it clear that Westside's existing student groups include one or more "noncurriculum related student groups." Although Westside's physical education classes apparently include swimming, . . . counsel stated at oral argument that scuba diving is not taught in any regularly offered course at the school, ... Based on Westside's own description of the group, Subsurfers does not directly relate to the curriculum as a whole in the same way that a student government or similar group might. . . . Moreover, participation in Subsurfers is not required by any course at the school and does not result in extra academic credit. Thus, Subsurfers is a "noncurriculum related student group" for purposes of the Act. Similarly, although math teachers at Westside have encouraged their students to play chess, chess is not taught in any regularly offered course at the school, . . . and participation in the chess club is not required for any class and does not result in extra credit for any class, ... The chess club is therefore another "noncurriculum related student group" at Westside. Moreover, Westside's principal acknowledged at trial that the Peer Advocates program—a service group that works with special education classes—does not directly relate to any courses offered by the school. . . . Peer Advocates would therefore also fit within our description of a "noncurriculum related student group." The record therefore supports a finding that Westside has maintained a limited open forum under the Act.

Although our definition of "noncurriculum related student activities" looks to a school's actual practice rather than its stated policy, we note that our conclusion is also supported by the school's own description of its student activities. . . . [T]he school states that Band "is included in our regular curriculum"; Choir "is a course offered as part of the curriculum"; Distributive Education "is an extension of the Distributive Education class"; International Club is "developed through our foreign language classes"; Latin Club is "designed for those students who are taking Latin as a foreign language"; Student Publications "includes classes offered in preparation of the yearbook (Shield) and the student newspaper (Lance)"; Dramatics "is an extension of a regular academic class"; and Orchestra "is an extension of our regular curriculum." These descriptions constitute persuasive evidence that these student clubs directly relate to the curriculum. By inference, however, the fact that the descriptions of student activities such as Subsurfers and chess do not include such references strongly suggests that those clubs do not, by the school's own admission, directly relate to the curriculum. We therefore conclude that Westside permits "one or more noncurriculum related student groups to meet on school premises during noninstructional time," . . . . Because Westside maintains a "limited open forum" under the Act, it is prohibited from discriminating, based on the content of the students' speech, against students who wish to meet on school premises during noninstructional time.

The remaining statutory question is whether petitioners' denial of respondents' request to form a religious group constitutes a denial of "equal access" to the school's limited open forum. Although the school apparently permits respondents to meet informally after school, . . . respondents seek equal access in the form of official recognition by the school. Official recognition allows student clubs to be part of the student activities program and carries with it access to the school newspaper, bulletin boards, the public address system, and the annual Club Fair. Given that the Act explicitly prohibits denial of "equal access . . . to . . . any students who wish to conduct a meeting within [the school's] limited open forum" on the basis of the religious content of the speech at such meetings, . . . we hold that Westside's denial of respondents' request to form a Christian club denies them "equal access" under the Act.

Because we rest our conclusion on statutory grounds, we need not decide—and therefore express no opinion on—whether the First Amendment requires the same result.

Petitioners contend that even if Westside has created a limited open forum within the meaning of the Act, its denial of official recognition to the proposed Christian club must nevertheless stand because the Act violates the Establishment Clause of the First Amendment, as applied to the States through the Fourteenth Amendment. Specifically, petitioners maintain that because the school's

recognized student activities are an integral part of its educational mission, official recognition of respondents' proposed club would effectively incorporate religious activities into the school's official program, endorse participation in the religious club, and provide the club with an official platform to proselytize other students.

We disagree. In *Widmar,* we applied the three-part *Lemon* test to hold that an "equal access" policy, at the university level, does not violate the Establishment Clause. . . . We concluded that "an open-forum policy, including nondiscrimination against religious speech, would have a secular purpose," . . . and would in fact *avoid* entanglement with religion. . . . We also found that although incidental benefits accrued to religious groups who used university facilities, this result did not amount to an establishment of religion. First, we stated that a university's forum does not "confer any imprimatur of state approval on religious sects or practices." Indeed, the message is one of neutrality rather than endorsement; if a State refused to let religious groups use facilities open to others, then it would demonstrate not neutrality but hostility toward religion. "The Establishment Clause does not license government to treat religion and those who teach or practice it, simply by virtue of their status as such, as subversive of American ideals and therefore subject to unique disabilities." . . . Second, we noted that "[t]he [University's] provision of benefits to [a] broad . . . spectrum of groups"—both nonreligious and religious speakers—was "an important index of secular effect." . . .

We think the logic of *Widmar* applies with equal force to the Equal Access Act. As an initial matter, the Act's prohibition of discrimination on the basis of "political, philosophical, or other" speech as well as religious speech is a sufficient basis for meeting the secular purpose prong of the *Lemon* test. . . . Congress' avowed purpose—to prevent discrimination against religious and other types of speech—is undeniably secular. Even if some legislators were motivated by a conviction that religious speech in particular was valuable and worthy of protection, that alone would not invalidate the Act, because what is relevant is the legislative *purpose* of the statute, not the possibly religious *motives* of the legislators who enacted the law. Because the Act on its face grants equal access to both secular and religious speech, we think it clear that the Act's purpose was not to "'endorse or disapprove of religion,'" . . . .

Petitioners' principal contention is that the Act has the primary effect of advancing religion. Specifically, petitioners urge that, because the student religious meetings are held under school aegis, and because the state's compulsory attendance laws bring the students together (and thereby provide a ready-made audience for student evangelists), an objective observer in the position of a secondary school student will perceive official school support for such religious meetings. . . .

We disagree. First, although we have invalidated the use of public funds to pay for teaching state-required subjects at parochial schools, in part because of the risk of creating "a crucial symbolic link between government and religion, thereby enlisting—at least in the eyes of impressionable youngsters—the powers of government to the support of the religious denomination operating the school," . . . there is a crucial difference between *government* speech endorsing religion, which the Establishment Clause forbids, and *private* speech endorsing religion, which the Free Speech and Free Exercise Clauses protect. We think that secondary school students are mature enough and are likely to understand that a school does not endorse or support student speech that it merely permits on a nondiscriminatory basis. . . . The proposition that schools do not endorse everything they fail to censor is not complicated. "[P]articularly in this age of massive media information . . . the few years difference in age between high school and college students [does not] justif[y] departing from *Widmar*." . . .

Indeed, we note that Congress specifically rejected the argument that high school students are likely to confuse an equal access policy with state sponsorship of religion.

. . . Given the deference due "the duly enacted and carefully considered decision of a coequal and representative branch of our Government," . . . we do not lightly second-guess such legislative judgments, particularly where the judgments are based in part on empirical determinations.

Second, we note that the Act expressly limits participation by school officials at meetings of student religious groups, §§ 4071(c)(2) and (3), and that any such meetings must be held during "noninstructional time," . . . . The Act therefore avoids the problems of "the students' emulation of teachers as role models" and "mandatory attendance requirements," . . . . To be sure, the possibility of *student* peer pressure remains, but there is little if any risk of official state endorsement or coercion where no formal classroom activities are involved and no school officials actively participate. Moreover, petitioners' fear of a mistaken inference of endorsement is largely self-imposed, because the school itself has control over any impressions it gives its students. To the extent a school makes clear that its recognition of respondents' proposed club is not an endorsement of the views of the club's participants, . . . students will reasonably understand that the school's official recognition of the club evinces neutrality toward, rather than endorsement of, religious speech.

Third, the broad spectrum of officially recognized student clubs at Westside, and the fact that Westside students are free to initiate and organize additional student clubs, . . . Although a school may not itself lead or direct a religious club, a school that permits a student-initiated and student-led religious club to meet after school, just as it permits any other student group to do, does not convey a message of state approval or endorsement of the particular religion. Under the Act, a school with a limited open forum may not lawfully deny access to a Jewish students' club, a Young Democrats club, or a philosophy club devoted to the study of Nietzsche. To the extent that a religious club is merely one of many different student-initiated voluntary clubs, students should perceive no message of government endorsement of religion. Thus, we conclude that the Act does not, at least on its face and as applied to Westside, have the primary effect of advancing religion. . . .

Petitioners' final argument is that by complying with the Act's requirement, the school risks excessive entanglement between government and religion. The proposed club, petitioners urge, would be required to have a faculty sponsor who would be charged with actively directing the activities of the group, guiding its leaders, and ensuring balance in the presentation of controversial ideas. Petitioners claim that this influence over the club's religious program would entangle the government in day-to-day surveillance of religion of the type forbidden by the Establishment Clause.

Under the Act, however, faculty monitors may not participate in any religious meetings, and nonschool persons may not direct, control, or regularly attend activities of student groups. . . . Moreover, the Act prohibits school "sponsorship" of any religious meetings, . . . which means that school officials may not promote, lead, or participate in any such meeting, ... Although the Act permits "[t]he assignment of a teacher, administrator, or other school employee to the meeting for custodial purposes," *ibid.*, such custodial oversight of the student-initiated religious group, merely to ensure order and good behavior, does not impermissibly entangle government in the day-to-day surveillance or administration of religious activities. . . . Indeed, as the Court noted in *Widmar*, a denial of equal access to religious speech might well create greater entanglement problems in the form of invasive monitoring to prevent religious speech at meetings at which such speech might occur. . . .

Accordingly, we hold that the Equal Access Act does not on its face contravene the Establishment Clause. Because we hold that petitioners have violated the Act, we do not decide respondents' claims under the Free Speech and Free Exercise Clauses. For the foregoing reasons, the judgment of the Court of Appeals is affirmed.

It is so ordered.

▉ FLAG SALUTE

The flag-salute ceremony in the United States originated in 1892 after a substantial rise in national sentiment to stimulate patriotism in the schools. In 1898, New York passed the first flag-salute statute only one day after the United States declared war on Spain.[135] By 1940, eighteen states had statutes making provision for "some sort of teaching regarding the flag."[136] Even though the statutes did not specifically require individual recitation, the reality of the classroom regimentation tended to make such statutory pronouncement unnecessary.[137] Opposition sprang up on sporadic bases from certain religious groups, the most persistent of which was Jehovah's Witnesses. In early litigation, the Georgia Supreme Court held that the Witnesses' religious freedom was not violated since the flag salute was merely an exercise in patriotism and not a religious rite.[138] Other rulings were unfavorable to the plaintiffs, the most intolerant of which stated that "Those who do not desire to conform with the demands of the statute can seek their school elsewhere."[139] In California, that state's high court upheld the expulsion of pupils for refusing to salute the flag.[140] Similarly, a New York court in 1939 held that "The flag has nothing to do with religion"; therefore, religious freedoms could not be offended.[141]

Nationalistic fervor just before World War II brought on more heated controversy, and the Supreme Court, in 1940, rendered a decision. In this case, Justice Frankfurter, speaking for an eight-to-one majority, held that freedom of religion guaranteed by the First Amendment was not violated by a Pennsylvania statute that required a flag salute and pledge of allegiance. Significantly, the opinion concluded that:

> Conscientious scruples have not, in the course of the long struggle for religious toleration, relieved the individual from obedience to a general law not aimed at the promotion or restriction of religious beliefs. The mere possession of religious convictions which contradict the relevant concerns of a political society does

not relieve the citizen from the discharge of political responsibilities.[142]

This decision engendered substantial controversy, and the legal and academic community generally disapproved of the decision as an infringement on individual constitutional rights.[143] Some state courts tended to ignore the federal constitutional implications and held that flag-salute requirements violated their own state constitutions.[144] Other state courts followed the decision.[145] Disenchantment with the *Gobitis* decision was so great and the constitutional foundation so weak that the case was officially overruled in *West Virginia State Board of Education v. Barnette* in *1943.*[146] In reconsideration of the issues, Justice Jackson, writing for a six-man majority, held that a state may require pupils to attend educational exercises based on American history and civics to teach patriotism, but that ceremonies involving compulsory rituals, such as flag salute, were unconstitutional. Justices Black, Douglas, and Murphy had changed their minds, and even though Frankfurter remained steadfast, the precedent of *Gobitis* was overturned. The swing vote of the three justices was predictable by the announcement a year earlier, in 1942, in *Jones v. Opelika,*[147] that: "Since we joined in the opinion in the *Gobitis* case, we think this is an appropriate occasion to state that we now believe that it was . . . wrongly decided."

---

*Required Participation in Flag Salute Is
Unconstitutional*

––– ––– ––– ––– –––

West Virginia State Board of Education v. Barnette

––– ––– ––– ––– –––

Supreme Court of the United States, 1943.
319 U.S. 624, 63 S.Ct. 1178.

Mr. Justice JACKSON delivered the opinion of the Court. Following the decision by this Court on June 3, 1940, in *Minersville School*

District v. Gobitis, 310 U.S. 586, 60 S.Ct. 1010, 84 L.Ed. 1375, 127 A.L.R. 1493, the West Virginia legislature amended its statutes to require all schools therein to conduct courses of instruction in history, civics, and in the Constitutions of the United States and of the State "for the purpose of teaching, fostering and perpetuating the ideals, principles and spirit of Americanism, and increasing the knowledge of the organization and machinery of the government." Appellant Board of Education was directed, with advice of the State Superintendent of Schools, to "prescribe the courses of study covering these subjects" for public schools. The Act made it the duty of private, parochial and denominational schools to prescribe courses of study "similar to those required for the public schools."

The Board of Education on January 9, 1942, adopted a resolution containing recitals taken largely from the Court's *Gobitis* opinion and ordering that the salute to the flag become "a regular part of the program of activities in the public schools," that all teachers and pupils "shall be required to participate in the salute honoring the Nation represented by the Flag; provided, however, that refusal to salute the Flag be regarded as an Act of insubordination, and shall be dealt with accordingly." . . .

Appellees, citizens of the United States and of West Virginia, brought suit in the United States District Court for themselves and others similarly situated asking its injunction to restrain enforcement of these laws and regulations against Jehovah's Witnesses. The Witnesses are an unincorporated body teaching that the obligation imposed by law of God is superior to that of laws enacted by temporal government. Their religious beliefs include a literal version of Exodus, Chapter 20, verses 4 and 5, which says: "Thou shalt not make unto thee any graven image, or any likeness of anything that is in heaven above, or that is in the earth beneath, or that is in the water under the earth; thou shalt not bow down thyself to them nor serve them." They consider that the flag is an "image" within this command. For this reason they refuse to salute it. . . .

This case calls upon us to reconsider a precedent decision, as the Court throughout its history often has been required to do.

Before turning to the *Gobitis* case, however, it is desirable to notice certain characteristics by which this controversy is distinguished.

The freedom asserted by these appellees does not bring them into collision with rights asserted by any other individual. It is such conflicts which most frequently require intervention of the State to determine where the rights of one end and those of another begin. But the refusal of these persons to participate in the ceremony does not interfere with or deny rights of others to do so. Nor is there any question in this case that their behavior is peaceable and orderly. The sole conflict is between authority and rights of the individual. The State asserts power to condition access to public education on making a prescribed sign and profession and at the same time to coerce attendance by punishing both parent and child. The latter stand on a right of self-determination in matters that touch individual opinion and personal attitude. . . .

Nor does the issue as we see it turn on one's possession of particular religious views or the sincerity with which they are held. While religion supplies appellees' motive for enduring the discomforts of making the issue in this case, many citizens who do not share these religious views hold such a compulsory rite to infringe constitutional liberty of the individual. It is not necessary to inquire whether non-conformist beliefs will exempt from the duty to salute unless we first find power to make the salute a legal duty.

The *Gobitis* decision, however, *assumed,* as did the argument in that case and in this, that power exists in the State to impose the flag salute discipline upon school children in general. The Court only examined and rejected a claim based on religious beliefs of immunity from an unquestioned general rule. The question which underlies the flag salute controversy is whether such a ceremony so touching matters of opinion and political attitude may be imposed upon the individual by official authority under powers committed to any political organization under our Constitution. . . .

The Fourteenth Amendment, as now applied to the States, protects the citizen against the State itself and all of its creatures — Boards of Education not excepted. These have, of course, important, delicate, and highly discretionary functions, but none that they may not perform within the limits of the Bill of Rights. That they are educating the young for citizenship is reason for scrupulous protection of Constitutional freedoms of the individual, if we are not to strangle the free mind at its source and teach youth to discount important principles of our government as mere platitudes. . . .

The very purpose of a Bill of Rights was to withdraw certain subjects from the vicissitudes of political controversy, to place them beyond the reach of majorities and officials and to establish them as legal principles to be applied by the courts. One's right to life, liberty, and property, to free speech, a free press, freedom of worship and assembly, and other fundamental rights may not be submitted to vote; they depend on the outcome of no elections. . . .

National unity as an end which officials may foster by persuasion and example is not in question. The problem is whether under our Constitution compulsion as here employed is a permissible means for its achievement. . . .

If there is any fixed star in our constitutional constellation, it is that no official, high or petty, can prescribe what shall be orthodox in politics, nationalism, religion, or other matters of opinion or force citizens to confess by word or act their faith therein. If there are any circumstances which permit an exception, they do not now occur to us.

We think the action of the local authorities in compelling the flag salute and pledge transcends constitutional limitations on their power and invades the sphere of intellect and spirit which it is the purpose of the First Amendment to our Constitution to reserve from all official control.

The decision of this Court in *Minersville School District v. Gobitis* and the holding of those few per curiam decisions which preceded and foreshadowed it are overruled, and the judgment enjoining enforcement of the West Virginia Regulation is affirmed. . . .

NOTE

1. When a student was offered the option of either leaving the classroom or standing silently during the Pledge of Allegiance, the court held that to leave the classroom is a benign type of punishment for nonparticipation, while to compel the student to stand in silence was to compel an act of acceptance to the Pledge over the student's deeply held contrary convictions. The requirement of the school was therefore unconstitutional regardless of option. *Goetz v. Ansell*, 477 F.2d 636 (2d Cir.1973).

◼︎ ENDNOTES

1. Wallace v. Jaffree, 472 U.S. 38, 107, 105 S.Ct. 2479, 2516 (1985).

2. 98 U.S. (8 Otto) 145 (1879).

3. Everson v. Board of Education, 330 U.S. 1, 67 S.Ct. 504 (1947).

4. Wallace, op. cit., at 2517.

5. Evarts B. Green, *Religion and the State in America* (New York: New York University Press 1941), p. 83.

6. Jonathan Elliot, *The Debates in the Several State Conventions on the Adoption of the Federal Constitution*, 2d ed. (Philadelphia: J.B. Lippincott & Co., 1988), p. 131.

7. Leo Pfeffer, *Church, State and Freedom* (Boston: Beacon Press, 1967), p. 123.

8. R. Freeman Butts, *The American Tradition in Religion and Education* (Boston: Beacon Press, 1950), p. 72.

9. Pfeffer, *Church, State and Freedom*, p. 125.

10. Ibid.

11. Ibid., p. 126.

12. Pfeffer, *Church, State and Freedom*, p. 4.

13. Ibid.

14. Ibid.

15. Williston Walker, *A History of the Christian Church* (New York: Charles Scribner's Sons, 1929), p. 464.

16. *History of Christianity in the Light of Modern Knowledge* (London: Blackie and Son, 1929), p. 464.

17. Pfeffer, *Church, State and Freedom*, p. 14.

18. M. Searle Bates, *Religious Liberty: An Inquiry* (New York and London: International Missionary Council, 1945), p. 134.

19. Alexander J. Carlyle, *The Christian Church and Liberty* (London: J. Clark, 1924), p. 96.

20. Everson v. Board of Education, 330 U.S. 1, 67 S.Ct. 504 (1947).

21. Pfeffer, *Church, State and Freedom*, p. 26.

22. John Locke, *A Letter Concerning Toleration* (Liberal Arts Press, 1955), pp. 17–18.

23. R. Freeman Butts and Lawrence A. Cremin, *A History of Education in American Culture* (New York: Henry Holt and Company, 1753), p. 15.

24. Ibid., p. 22.

25. Ibid., p. 21.

26. Ibid.

27. Saul K. Padover, *The Complete Jefferson* (New York: Duell, Sloan & Pearce, 1943).

28. Ibid.

29. Pfeffer, *Church, State and Freedom*, p. 109.

30. Decl. Rights, Art. 16. [Note in the original.]

31. Decl. Rights, Art. 1 [Note in the original.]

32. Art. 16 [Note in the original.]

33. Art. 16 [Note in the original.]

34. Decl. Rights-title [Note in the original.]

35. V.T. Thayer, *The Attack Upon the American Secular School* (Boston: Beacon Press, 1951), pp. 26–27.

36. Knowlton v. Baumhover, 182 Iowa 691, 166 N.W. 202 (1918).

37. 321 U.S. 158, 64 S.Ct. 438 (1944).

38. Joseph L. Blow, *Cornerstones of Religious Freedom in America* (Boston: Beacon Press, 1949), pp. 179–82.

39. Pfeffer, *Church, State and Freedom*, p. 338.

40. Wisconsin v. Yoder, 406 U.S. 205, 92 S.Ct. 1526 (1972).

41. Cochran v. Louisiana State Board of Education, 281 U.S. 270, 50 S.Ct. 335 (1930).

42. Cantwell v. Connecticut, 310 U.S. 296, 60 S.Ct. 900 (1940).

43. Board of Education of Central School District v. Allen, 392 U.S. 236, 88 S.Ct. 1923 (1968).

44. New York Education law, § 701 (1967 suppl.)

45. See dissenting opinion of Mr. Justice Douglas.

46. See Boyd v. United States, 116 U.S. 616, 6 S.Ct. 524 (1886).

47. Board of Education of Central School District No. 1 v. Allen, 392 U.S. 236, 88 S.Ct. 1923 (1968).

48. Sloan v. Lemon, 413 U.S. 825, 93 S.Ct. 2982 (1973), rehearing denied 414 U.S. 881, 94 S.Ct. 30 (1973); Committee for Public Education and Religious Liberty v. Nyquist, 413 U.S. 756, 93 S.Ct. 2955 (1973).

49. Levitt v. Committee for Public Education and Religious Liberty, 413 U.S. 472, 474, 93 S.Ct. 2814, 2816 (1973).

50. Payments were $27 for each pupil in average daily attendance (ADA) in grades 1 to 6 and $45 for each pupil in ADA in grades 7 to 12, in two installments during the year.

51. Committee for Public Education and Religious Liberty v. Regan, 444 U.S. 646, 650, 100 S.Ct. 840, 845 (1980).

52. Committee for Public Education and Religious Liberty v. Nyquist, 413 U.S. 756, 93 S.Ct. 2955 (1973).

53. The school had to qualify by having a high concentration of low-income families; and the amount of the

grant was $30 per pupil, or $40 per pupil if the facility was more than 25 years old. The grant could not exceed 50 percent of the average per-pupil cost for equivalent services in the public schools. Nyquist, 413 U.S. at 761, 93 S. Ct. at 2959.

54. A parent must have a taxable income of less than $5,000 and would be reimbursed $50 per grade school child and $100 per high school child so long as these amounts did not exceed 50 percent of the tuition.

55. Sloan v. Lemon, 413 U.S. 825, 93 S.Ct. 2982 (1973).

56. Meek v. Pittenger, 421 U.S. 349, 363, 95 S.Ct. 1753, 1762 (1975).

57. Wolman v. Walter, 433 U.S. 229, 232, 97 S.Ct. 2593, 2597 (1977).

58. Ibid., p. 2603.

59. Ibid., p. 2606.

60. Kosydar v. Wolman, 353 F.Supp. 744 (S.D. Ohio 1972).

61. Kosydar affirmed by 413 U.S. 901, 93 S.Ct. 3062 (1973) as Grit v. Wolman.

62. Committee v. Nyquist, op. cit.

63. Byrne v. Public Funds for Public Schools, 442 U.S. 907, 99 S.Ct. 2818, (1979), affirming 590 F.2d 514 (3d Cir. 1979).

64. Rhode Island Federation of Teachers, AFL-CIO et al. v. Norberg, 630 F.2d 855 (1st Cir. 1980).

65. Mueller v. Allen, 463 U.S. 388, 103 S.Ct. 3062 (1983).

66. Ibid.

67. 392 U.S. 236, 88 S.Ct. 1923 (1968).

68. G. Sidney Buchanan, "Governmental Aid to Religious Entities: The Total Subsidy Position Prevails," *58 Fordham L. Rev.* 53 (October 1989).

69. Ibid.

70. School District of City of Grand Rapids v. Ball, 473 U.S. 373, 105 S.Ct. 3216 (1985).

71. Aguilar v. Felton, 473 U.S. 402, 105 S.Ct. 3232 (1985).

72. Leonard Levy, *The Establishment Clause, Religion and the First Amendment* (New York: MacMillan Publishing Company, 1986), p. 162.

73. Ibid., p. 163.

74. 472 U.S. 38, 107, 114, 105 S.Ct. 2479, 2516, 2519, (1985).

75. Ibid.

76. Levy, *The Establishment Clause*, p. 92.

77. R.I.Gen.Laws § 16-51-1 et seq.

78. 24 Pa.Stat. §§ 5601–5609.

79. Latin, Hebrew, and classical Greek are excluded.

80. Rhode Island Constitution, Article I, § 3.

81. Bowerman v. O'Connor, 104 R.I. 519, 247 A.2d 82 (1968).

82. Constitution of Illinois, Article I, § 3.

83. Board of Education v. Bakalis, 54 Ill. 2d 448, 299 N.E.2d 737 (1973). See A.E Dick Howard, *State Aid to Private Higher Education* (Charlottesville, Va.: The Michie Company, 1977), p. 254.

84. 403 U.S. 602, 91 S.Ct. 2105 (1971).

85. Snyder v. Town of Newton, 147 Conn. 374, 161 A.2d 770 (1960), *appeal dismissed*, 81S.Ct. 692 365 U.S. 299 (1961).

86. Ibid., 161 A. 2d at 774–775.

87. State ex rel. Johnson v. Boyd, 217 Ind. 348, 28 N.E. 2d 256 (1940); Buford v. Southeast Dubois County School Corp., 472 F.2d 890 (7th Cir.), *cert denied*, 411 U.S. 967, 93 S.Ct. 2151 (1973); *Opinion of Attorney General*, 241, 1967.

88. Article I, § 3; Knowlton v. Baumhover, 166 N.W. 202 (1918). Howard, *State Aid to Private Higher Education*, p. 303. Howard states that "Article I, Section 3 of the Iowa Supreme Court will adopt the same interpretation of this section as the United States Supreme Court has adopted for the First Amendment."

89. Howard, *State Aid to Private Higher Education*, p. 314; see Wright v. School District, 151 Kan. 485, 99 P. 2d 737 (1940).

90. Squires v. City of Augusta, 155 Me. 151, 153 A.2d 80 (1959); Opinion of the Justices, 261 A. 2d 58 (Me. 1970).

91. In re Opinion on the Constitutionality of Amendatory Act. No. 100 in the Public Acts of 1970, 384 Mich. 82, 180 N.W. 2d 265 (1970).

92. Americans United Inc. v. Independent School District No. 622, 288 Minn. 196, 179 N.W. 2d 146 (1970).

93. Everson v. Board of Education, 330 U.S. 1, 67 S.Ct. 504 (1947).

94. State ex rel. Warren v. Nusbaum (III), 219 N.W. 2d 577 (1974).

95. 463 U.S. 388, 103 S.Ct. 3062 (1983).

96. San Antonio Independent School Dist. v. Rodriguez, 411 U.S. 1, 93 S.Ct. 1278 (1973) *rehearing denied* 411 U.S. 959, 93 S.Ct. 1919 (1973). See Chapter 19 of this book.

97. People ex rel. Vollmar v. Stanley, 81 Colo. 276, 255 P. 610 (1927); Howard, *State Aid*, pp. 154–57.

98. West's Colorado R.S.A. Constitution, Article IX, § 7.

99. 51 Hawaii 1, 449 P. 2d 130 (1968).

100. Ibid.

101. Board of County Commissioners v. Idaho Health Facilities Authority, 96 Idaho 498, 531 P.2d 588 (1974).

102. Paster v. Tussey, 512 S.W. 2d 97 (Mo. 1974), *cert. denied* 419 U.S. 1111, 95 S.Ct. 785 (1975).

103. Harfst v. Hoegen, 349 Mo. 808, 163 S.W. 2d 609, 614 (1941).

104. Berghorn v. Reorganized School Dist. No. 8, 364 Mo. 121, 260 S.W. 2d 573, 582–583 (1953).

105. Paster v. Tussey, *op cit.*, pp. 101–2.

106. State ex rel. Chambers v. School District No. 10, 155 Mont. 422, 472 P. 2d 1013 (1970).

107. 403 U.S. 602, 91 S.Ct. 2105 (1971).

108. Article V, § II(5).

109. Howard, *State Aid*, p. 250.

110. Ibid., p. 987.

111. Dickman v. School District, 232 Or. 238, 366 P.2d 533 (1961), *cert. denied* 371 U.S. 823, 83 S.Ct.41 (1962): See also Fisher v. Clackamas County School, 13 Or. App. 56, 507 P.2d 839 (1973).

112. People of State of Illinois ex rel. McCollum v. Board of Education of School District No. 71, 333 U.S. 203, 68 S.Ct. 461 (1948).

113. Zorach v. Clauson, 343 U.S. 306, 72 S.Ct. 679 (1952).

114. Hackett v. Brooksville Graded School District, 120 Ky. 608, 87 S.W. 792 (1905).

115. North Dakota Compiled Laws, Sec. 1388 (1913).

116. Engel v. Vitale, 370 U.S. 421, 82 S.Ct. 1261 (1962).

117. People of State of Illinois ex rel. McCollum v. Board of Education, 333 U.S. 203, 68 S.Ct. 461 (1948).

118. Engel v. Vitale, op cit.

119. School District of Abington Township v. Schempp and Murray v. Curlett, 374 U.S. 203, 83 S.Ct. 1560 (1963).

120. 449 U.S. 39, 101 S.Ct. 192 (1980).

121. 472 U.S. 38, 105 S.Ct. 2479 (1985); Duffy v. Las Cruces Public Schools, 557 F.Supp. 1013 (D.N.M. 1983).

122. Walter v. West Virginia Bd. of Educ., 610 F.Supp. 1169 (S.D.W.Va. 1985).

123. Jager v. Douglas County School Dist., 862 F.2d 824 (11th Cir. 1989).

124. Smith by Smith v. North Babylon Union Free School District, 844 F.2d 90 (2d Cir. 1988); Graham v. Central Community School Dist. of Decatur County, 608 F.Supp. 531 (S.D. Iowa 1985); Weisman v. Lee, 908 F.2d 1090 (1st Cir. 1990); Lundberg v. West Monona Community School Dist., 731 F.Supp. 331 (N.D. Iowa 1989); Stein v. Plainwell Community Schools, 822 F.2d 1406 (6th Cir. 1987).

125. Breen v. Runkel, 614 F.Supp. 355 (W.D. Mich. 1985); May v. Evansville-Vanderburgh School Corp., 787 F.2d 1105 (7th Cir. 1986).

126. Wallace, op cit.

127. Walter, op cit.

128. Jager, op cit.

129. Marsh v. Chambers, 463 U.S. 783, 103 S.Ct. 3330 (1983).

130. Stein v. Plainwell Community Schools, 822 F.2d 1406 (6th Cir. 1987).

131. Jager v. Douglas County School District, op cit.

132. The rules as amended provide as follows:

> Opening Exercises. Each school, either collectively or in classes, shall be opened by the reading, without comment, of a chapter in the Holy Bible and/or the use of the Lord's Prayer. The Douay version may be used by those pupils who prefer it. Appropriate patriotic exercises should be held as a part of the general opening exercise of the school or class. Any child shall be excused from participating in the opening exercises or from attending the opening exercises upon the written request of his parent or guardian.

133. Widmar v. Vincent, 454 U.S. 263, 102 S.Ct. 269 (1981).

134. Board of Education of Westside Community Schools v. Mergens, _____ U.S. _____, 110 S.Ct. 2356 (1990).

135. Donald E. Boles, *The Two Swords* (Ames, Ia.: The Iowa State University Press, 1967), p. 139.

136. D. R. Manwaring, *Render Unto Caesar: The Flag-Salute Controversy* (Chicago: University of Chicago Press, 1962).

137. Ibid.

138. Leoles v. Landers, 184 Ga. 580, 192 S.E. 218 (1937), *appeal dismissed* 302 U.S. 656, 58 S.Ct. 364 (1937).

139. Hering v. State Board of Education, 117 N.J.L. 455, 189 A. 629 (1937).

140. Gabrielli v. Knickerbocker, 12 Cal.2d 85, 82 P.2d 391 (1938).

141. People ex rel. Fish v. Sandstrom, 279 N.Y. 523, 18 N.E.2d 840 (1939).

142. Minersville School District v. Gobitis, 310 U.S. 586, 60 S.Ct. 1010 (1940).

143. Boles, op cit., p. 148.

144. State v. Smith, 155 Kan. 588, 127 P.2d 518 (1942); Bolling v. Superior Court, 16 Wn.2d 373, 133 P.2d 803 (1943).

145. In re Latrecchia, 128 N.J.L. 472, 26 A.2d 881 (1942); State v. Davis, 58 Ariz. 444, 120 P.2d 808 (1942).

146. 319 U.S. 624, 63 S.Ct. 1178 (1943).

147. 316 U.S. 584, 62 S.Ct. 1231 (1942); see Bates, op cit., pp. 151–52.

CHAPTER 6

School Attendance

Operating within constitutional provisions, legislatures have prescribed the admission and residence requirements for attendance in the public schools. Where state constitutions have established the age span within which all have a right to attend public schools, legislatures must provide at least the specified minimum education, but are not restricted from creating additional educational opportunities. For example, the constitutional requirement that a state provide schools for all children between the ages of five and twenty years does not prevent the legislature from establishing a nursery school for four-year-olds. Neither does such a provision prohibit the establishment of institutions for higher education.

When a state establishes a system of public education, it cannot arbitrarily withhold services from a particular class of persons. While a state is not required by the federal constitution to provide public education at all, when it does so provide, it must be open and available to all.[1] In this regard, children whose parents are illegal aliens are entitled to attend public schools so long as they reside in the United States. The United States Supreme Court has said that if a state is to deny the child of illegal alien parents a free public education, then the state must demonstrate the denial advances a substantial state interest. It is insufficient for the state to claim the denial of a free education is justified on the grounds that the presence of undocumented children requires the state to spread scarce fiscal resources among greater numbers of children.[2]

States, though, can impose restrictions on school attendance provided they are reasonably related to a valid state purpose. Reasonableness may relate to the health, safety, and welfare of other children or may have to do with the orderly organization and administration of school systems. Residence requirements based on geographical boundaries drawn within and between school districts have been upheld provided there is no intent to invidiously discriminate against a certain class of student. Indeed, the drawing of attendance zones has been upheld as a valid exercise of state prerogative where boundaries were drawn to effectuate integration.

Most state laws require that children be residents of the school district in which they attend school. A school district has the legal authority to challenge the residence of a student. A student who changes guardianship solely for the purposes of attending a particular school may be denied attendance.[3] The United States Supreme Court has held that an appropriately defined and uniformly applied residence law is constitutionally valid. The state's interest in assuring appropriate educational services to be enjoyed by the residents is rationale enough to support such a requirement.[4]

To establish residence, one must be physically present and intend to remain at that location. The Supreme Court of Maine, in an early decision, held that residence was established "when a person takes up his abode in a given place, without any present intention to remove therefrom . . . ."[5]

191

*Undocumented Children of Alien Parents
Cannot Be Denied a Public Education*

–––·––·––·–––

Plyler v. Doe

–––·––·––·–––

Supreme Court of the United States, 1982.
457 U.S. 202, 102 S.Ct. 2382.

Mr. Justice BRENNAN delivered the opinion of the Court. The question presented by these cases is whether, consistent with the Equal Protection Clause of the Fourteenth Amendment, Texas may deny to undocumented school-age children the free public education that it provides to children who are citizens of the United States or legally admitted aliens.

Since the late nineteenth century, the United States has restricted immigration into this country. Unsanctioned entry into the United States is a crime, 8 U.S.C. § 1325, and those who have entered unlawfully are subject to deportation, 8 U.S.C. §§ 1251–1252. But despite the existence of these legal restrictions, a substantial number of persons have succeeded in unlawfully entering the United States, and now live within various States, including the State of Texas.

In May 1975, the Texas legislature revised its education laws to withhold from local school districts any state funds for the education of children who were not "legally admitted" into the United States. The 1975 revision also authorized local school districts to deny enrollment in their public schools to children not "legally admitted" to the country. Tex.E-duc.Code Ann. § 21.031 (Vernon Cum-.Supp.1981). These cases involve constitutional challenges to those provisions. . . .

The Fourteenth Amendment provides that "No State shall . . . deprive any person of life, liberty, or property, without due process of law; nor deny to *any person within its jurisdiction* the equal protection of the laws." Appellants argue at the outset that undocumented aliens, because of their immigration status, are not "persons within the jurisdiction" of the State of Texas, and that they

therefore have no right to the equal protection of Texas law. We reject this argument. Whatever his status under the immigration laws, an alien is surely a "person" in any ordinary sense of that term. Aliens, even aliens whose presence in this country is unlawful, have long been recognized as "persons" guaranteed due process of law by the Fifth and Fourteenth Amendments. Indeed, we have clearly held that the Fifth Amendment protects aliens whose presence in this country is unlawful from invidious discrimination by the Federal Government.

Appellants seek to distinguish our prior cases, emphasizing that the Equal Protection Clause directs a State to afford its protection to persons *within its jurisdiction* while the Due Process Clauses of the Fifth and Fourteenth Amendments contain no such assertedly limiting phrase. In appellants' view, persons who have entered the United States illegally are not "within the jurisdiction" of a State even if they are present within a State's boundaries and subject to its laws. Neither our cases nor the logic of the Fourteenth Amendment supports that constricting construction of the phrase "within its jurisdiction." We have never suggested that the class of persons who might avail themselves of the equal protection guarantee is less than coextensive with that entitled to due process. To the contrary, we have recognized that both provisions were fashioned to protect an identical class of persons, and to reach every exercise of State authority.

> The Fourteenth Amendment to the Constitution is not confined to the protection of citizens. It says: "Nor shall any state deprive any person of life, liberty or property without due process of law; nor deny to any person within its jurisdiction the equal protection of the laws." *These provisions are universal in their application, to all persons within the territorial jurisdiction*, without regard to any differences of race, color, or of nationality; and the protection of the laws is a pledge of the protection of equal laws. (Emphasis added.)

In concluding that "all persons within the territory of the United States," including aliens unlawfully present, may invoke the

Fifth and Sixth Amendment to challenge actions of the Federal Government, we reasoned from the understanding that the Fourteenth Amendment was designed to afford its protection to all within the boundaries of a State. . . .

There is simply no support for appellants' suggestion that "due process" is somehow of greater stature than "equal protection" and therefore available to a larger class of persons. To the contrary, each aspect of the Fourteenth Amendment reflects an elementary limitation on state power. To permit a State to employ the phrase "within its jurisdiction" in order to identify subclasses of persons whom it would define as beyond its jurisdiction, thereby relieving itself of the obligation to assure that its laws are designed and applied equally to those persons, would undermine the principal purpose for which the Equal Protection Clause was incorporated in the Fourteenth Amendment. The Equal Protection Clause was intended to work nothing less than the abolition of all caste and invidious class-based legislation. That objective is fundamentally at odds with the power the State asserts here to classify persons subject to its laws as nonetheless excepted from its protection. . . .

Use of the phrase "within its jurisdiction" thus does not detract from, but rather confirms, the understanding that the protection of the Fourteenth Amendment extends to anyone, citizen or stranger, who *is* subject to the laws of a State, and reaches into every corner of a State's territory. That a person's initial entry into a State, or into the United States, was unlawful, and that he may for that reason be expelled, cannot negate the simple fact of his presence within the State's territorial perimeter. Given such presence, he is subject to the full range of obligations imposed by the State's civil and criminal laws. And until he leaves the jurisdiction—either voluntarily, or involuntarily in accordance with the Constitution and laws of the United States—he is entitled to the equal protection of the laws that a State may choose to establish.

Our conclusion that the illegal aliens who are plaintiffs in these cases may claim the benefit of the Fourteenth Amendment's guarantee of equal protection only begins the inquiry. The more difficult question is whether the Equal Protection Clause has been violated by the refusal of the State of Texas to reimburse local school boards for the education of children who cannot demonstrate that their presence within the United States is lawful, or by the imposition by those school boards of the burden of tuition on those children. . . .

The Equal Protection Clause directs that "all persons similarly circumstanced shall be treated alike." But so too, "The Constitution does not require things which are different in fact or opinion to be treated in law as though they were the same." The initial discretion to determine what is "different" and what is "the same" resides in the legislatures of the States. A legislature must have substantial latitude to establish classifications that roughly approximate the nature of the problem perceived, that accommodate competing concerns both public and private, and that account for limitations on the practical ability of the State to remedy every ill. In applying the Equal Protection Clause to most forms of state action, we thus seek only the assurance that the classification at issue bears some fair relationship to a legitimate public purpose.

But we would not be faithful to our obligations under the Fourteenth Amendment if we applied so deferential a standard to every classification. The Equal Protection Clause was intended as a restriction on state legislative action inconsistent with elemental constitutional premises. Thus we have treated as presumptively invidious those classifications that disadvantage a "suspect class," or that impinge upon the exercise of a "fundamental right." With respect to such classifications, it is appropriate to enforce the mandate of equal protection by requiring the State to demonstrate that its classification has been precisely tailored to serve a compelling governmental interest. In addition, we have recognized that certain forms of legislative classification, while not facially invidious, nonetheless give rise to recurring constitutional difficulties; in these limited circumstances we have sought the assurance that the classification reflects a reasoned judgment consistent with the ideal of equal protection by inquiring whether it may fairly be viewed as furthering a substantial interest of the State. We turn to a consideration of the standard appropriate for the evaluation of § 21.031.

Sheer incapability or lax enforcement of the laws barring entry into this country, coupled with the failure to establish an effective bar to the employment of undocumented aliens, has resulted in the creation of a substantial "shadow population" of illegal migrants — numbering in the millions — within our borders. This situation raises the specter of a permanent caste of undocumented resident aliens, encouraged by some to remain here as a source of cheap labor, but nevertheless denied the benefits that our society makes available to citizens and lawful residents. The existence of such an underclass presents most difficult problems for a Nation that prides itself on adherence to principles of equality under law.

The children who are plaintiffs in these cases are special members of this underclass. Persuasive arguments support the view that a State may withhold its beneficence from those whose very presence within the United States is the product of their own unlawful conduct. These arguments do not apply with the same force to classifications imposing disabilities on the minor *children* of such illegal entrants. At the least, those who elect to enter our territory by stealth and in violation of our law should be prepared to bear the consequences, including, but not limited to, deportation. But the children of those illegal entrants are not comparably situated. Their "parents have the ability to conform their conduct to societal norms," and presumably the ability to remove themselves from the State's jurisdiction; but the children who are plaintiffs in these cases "can affect neither their parents' conduct nor their own status." Even if the State found it expedient to control the conduct of adults by acting against their children, legislation directing the onus of a parent's misconduct against his children does not comport with fundamental conceptions of justice. . . .

Of course, undocumented status is not irrelevant to any proper legislative goal. Nor is

undocumented status an absolutely immutable characteristic since it is the product of conscious, indeed unlawful, action. But § 21.031 is directed against children, and imposes its discriminatory burden on the basis of a legal characteristic over which children can have little control. It is thus difficult to conceive of a rational justification for penalizing these children for their presence within the United States. Yet that appears to be precisely the effect of § 21.031.

Public education is not a "right" granted to individuals by the Constitution. But neither is it merely some governmental "benefit" indistinguishable from other forms of social welfare legislation. Both the importance of education in maintaining our basic institutions, and the lasting impact of its deprivation on the life of the child, mark the distinction. . . .

In sum, education has a fundamental role in maintaining the fabric of our society. We cannot ignore the significant social costs borne by our Nation when select groups are denied the means to absorb the values and skills upon which our social order rests. . . .

Paradoxically, by depriving the children of any disfavored group of an education, we foreclose the means by which that group might raise the level of esteem in which it is held by the majority. But more directly, "education prepares individuals to be self-reliant and self-sufficient participants in society." Illiteracy is an enduring disability. The inability to read and write will handicap the individual deprived of a basic education each and every day of his life. The inestimable toll of that deprivation on the social, economic, intellectual and psychological well-being of the individual, and the obstacle it poses to individual achievement, makes it most difficult to reconcile the cost or the principle of a status-based denial of basic education with the framework of equality embodied in the Equal Protection Clause. . . .

These well-settled principles allow us to determine the proper level of deference to be afforded § 21.031. Undocumented aliens cannot be treated as a suspect class because their presence in this country in violation of federal law is not a "constitutional irrelevancy." Nor is education a fundamental right; a State need not justify by compelling necessity every variation in the manner in which education is provided to its population. But more is involved in this case than the abstract question whether § 21.031 discriminates against a suspect class, or whether education is a fundamental right. Section 21.031 imposes a lifetime hardship on a discrete class of children not accountable for their disabling status. The stigma of illiteracy will mark them for the rest of their lives. By denying these children a basic education, we deny them the ability to live within the structure of our civic institutions, and foreclose any realistic possibility that they will contribute in even the smallest way to the progress of our Nation. In determining the rationality of § 21.031, we may appropriately take into account its costs to the Nation and to the innocent children who are its victims. In light of these countervailing costs, the discrimination contained in § 21.031 can hardly be considered rational unless it furthers some substantial goal of the State. . . .

To be sure, like all persons who have entered the United States unlawfully, these children are subject to deportation. 8 U.S.C. §§ 1251–1252. But there is no assurance that a child subject to deportation will ever be deported. An illegal entrant might be granted federal permission to continue to reside in this country, or even to become a citizen. See, e.g., 8 U.S.C. §§ 1252, 1253(h), 1254. In light of the discretionary federal power to grant relief from deportation, a State cannot realistically determine that any particular undocumented child will in fact be deported until after deportation proceedings have been completed. It would of course be most difficult for the State to justify a denial of education to a child enjoying an inchoate federal permission to remain. . . .

Appellants argue that the classification at issue furthers an interest in the "preservation of the state's limited resources for the education of its lawful residents." . . . Apart from the asserted state prerogative to act against undocumented children solely on the basis of their undocumented status—an asserted prerogative that carries only minimal force in the circumstances of this case—we

discern three colorable state interests that might support § 21.031.

First, appellants appear to suggest that the State may seek to protect the State from an influx of illegal immigrants. While a State might have an interest in mitigating the potentially harsh economic effects of sudden shifts in population, § 21.031 hardly offers an effective method of dealing with an urgent demographic or economic problem. There is no evidence in the record suggesting that illegal entrants impose any significant burden on the State's economy. . . .

Second, while it is apparent that a state may "not . . . reduce expenditures for education by barring [some arbitrarily chosen class of] children from its schools," appellants suggest that undocumented children are appropriately singled out for exclusion because of the special burdens they impose on the State's ability to provide high quality public education. But the record in no way supports the claim that exclusion of undocumented children is likely to improve the overall quality of education in the State. . . . In terms of educational cost and need, however, undocumented children are "basically indistinguishable" from legally resident alien children.

Finally, appellants suggest that undocumented children are appropriately singled out because their unlawful presence within the United States renders them less likely than other children to remain within the boundaries of the State, and to put their education to productive social or political use within the State. Even assuming that such an interest is legitimate, it is an interest that is most difficult to quantify. The State has no assurance that any child, citizen or not, will employ the education provided by the State within the confines of the State's borders. In any event, the record is clear that many of the undocumented children disabled by this classification will remain in this country indefinitely, and that some will become lawful residents or citizens of the United States. It is difficult to understand precisely what the State hopes to achieve by promoting the creation and perpetuation of a subclass of illiterates within our boundaries, surely adding to the problems and costs of unemployment, welfare, and crime. It is thus clear that whatever savings might be achieved by denying these children an education, they are wholly insubstantial in light of the costs involved to these children, the State, and the Nation.

If the State is to deny a discrete group of innocent children the free public education that it offers to other children residing within its borders, that denial must be justified by a showing that it furthers some substantial state interest. No such showing was made here. Accordingly, the judgment of the Court of Appeals in each of these cases is Affirmed.

NOTES

1. Physical presence and intent to remain in the school district is sufficient to establish residency in a school district even though parents or legal guardians lived elsewhere. *Byrd v. Livingston Independent School District*, 674 F.Supp. 225 (E.D. Tex. 1987). See also *Orozco by Arroyo v. Sobol*, 674 F.Supp. 125 (S.D. N.Y. 1987).

2. *Homeless Children.* A lower New York state court has ruled that children who live in a shelter for the homeless in a school district were entitled to be educated in the schools of that district regardless of whether their residency would be short or long, temporary or permanent, and regardless of whether their mother expressed a desire to have the children registered in the district where they previously attended school. *Delgado v. Freeport Public School District*, 131 Misc. 2d 102, 499 N.Y. S. 2d 606 (1986)

   A federal district court in New York held that New York school authorities had denied due process of law to "homeless" children when they were excluded from school on grounds of nonresidency without proper notice. The homeless mother and her children were entitled to nominal damages of $1 for violation of their procedural due process rights. *Harrison v. Sobol*, 705 F.Supp. 870 (S.D. N.Y. 1988).

Bona Fide Residence Requirement That Furthers State Interest Is Constitutional

Martinez v. Bynum

Supreme Court of the United States, 1983. 461 U.S. 321, 103 S.Ct. 1838.

Justice POWELL delivered the opinion of the Court. This case involves a facial challenge to the constitutionality of the Texas residency requirement governing minors who wish to attend public free schools while living apart from their parents or guardians.

Roberto Morales was born in 1969 in McAllen, Texas, and is thus a United States citizen by birth. His parents are Mexican citizens who reside in Reynosa, Mexico. He left Reynosa in 1977 and returned to McAllen to live with his sister, petitioner Oralia Martinez, for the primary purpose of attending school in the McAllen Independent School District. Although Martinez is now Morales's custodian, she is not—and does not desire to become—his guardian. As a result, Morales is not entitled to tuition-free admission to the McAllen schools. Section 21.031(b) and (c) of the Texas Education Code would require the local school authorities to admit him if he or "his parent, guardian, or the person having lawful control of him" resided in the school district, Tex.Educ.Code Ann. § 21.031(b) and (c) (Supp.1982), but §21.031(d) denies tuition-free admission for a minor who lives apart from a "parent, guardian, or other person having lawful control of him under an order of a court" if his presence in the school district is "for the primary purpose of attending the public free schools." Respondent McAllen Independent School District therefore denied Morales's application for admission in the fall of 1977. . . .

This Court frequently has considered constitutional challenges to residence requirements. On several occasions the Court has invalidated requirements that condition receipt of a benefit on a minimum period of residence within a jurisdiction, but it always has been careful to distinguish such durational residence requirements from bona fide residence requirements. . . .

We specifically have approved bona fide residence requirements in the field of public education. The Connecticut statute before us in *Vlandis v. Kline,* 412 U.S. 441, 93 S.Ct. 2230, 37 L.Ed.2d 63 (1973), for example, was unconstitutional because it created an irrebuttable presumption of nonresidency for state university students whose legal addresses were outside of the State before they applied for admission. The statute violated the Due Process Clause because it in effect classified some bona fide state residents as nonresidents for tuition purposes. But we "fully recognize[d] that a State has a legitimate interest in protecting and preserving . . . the right of its own bona fide residents to attend [its colleges and universities] on a preferential tuition basis." This "legitimate interest" permits a "State [to] establish such reasonable criteria for in-state status as to make virtually certain that students who are not, in fact, bona fide residents of the State, but who have come there solely for educational purposes, cannot take advantage of the in-state rates." Last Term, in *Plyler v. Doe,* 457 U.S. 202, 102 S.Ct. 2382, 72 L.Ed.2d 786 (1982), we reviewed an aspect of Tex.Educ.Code Ann. § 21.031 — the statute at issue in this case. Although we invalidated the portion of the statute that excluded undocumented alien children from the public free schools, we recognized the school districts' right "to apply . . . established criteria for determining residence."
. . .

A bona fide residence requirement, appropriately defined and uniformly applied, furthers the substantial state interest in assuring that services provided for its residents are enjoyed only by residents. Such a requirement with respect to attendance in public free schools does not violate the Equal Protection Clause of the Fourteenth Amendment. It does not burden or penalize the constitutional right of interstate travel, for any person is free to move to a State and to establish residence there. A bona fide residence requirement simply requires that the person *does* establish

residence before demanding the services that are restricted to residents. . . .

The provision of primary and secondary education, of course, is one of the most important functions of local government. Absent residence requirements, there can be little doubt that the proper planning and operation of the schools would suffer significantly. The State thus has a substantial interest in imposing bona fide residence requirements to maintain the quality of local public schools.

The central question we must decide here is whether § 21.031(d) is a bona fide residence requirement. Although the meaning may vary according to context, "residence" generally requires both physical presence and an intention to remain. As the Supreme Court of Maine explained over a century ago,

> when . . . a person voluntarily takes up his abode in a given place, with intention to remain permanently, or for an indefinite period of time; or, to speak more accurately, when a person takes up his abode in a given place, without any present intention to remove therefrom, such place of abode becomes his residence . . . . *Inhabitants of Warren v. Inhabitants of Thomaston,* 43 Me. 406, 418 (1857).

This classic two-part definition of residence has been recognized as a minimum standard in a wide range of contexts time and time again. . . . But at the very least, a school district generally would be justified in requiring school-age children or their parents to satisfy the traditional, basic residence criteria — i.e., to live in the district with a bona fide intention of remaining there — before it treated them as residents.

Section 21.031 is far more generous than this traditional standard. It compels a school district to permit a child such as Morales to attend school without paying tuition if he has a bona fide intention to remain in the school district indefinitely, for he then would have a reason for being there other than his desire to attend school: his intention to make his home in the district. Thus § 21.031 grants the benefits of residency to all who satisfy the traditional requirements. The statute goes further and extends these benefits to many children even if they (or their families) do not intend to remain in the district indefinitely. As long as the child is not living in the district for the sole purpose of attending school, he satisfies the statutory test. . . .

The Constitution permits a State to restrict eligibility for tuition-free education to its bona fide residents. We hold that § 21.031 is a bona fide residence requirement that satisfies constitutional standards. The judgment of the Court of Appeals accordingly is

Affirmed.

_____

NOTES

1. School districts may inquire as to the reason for the change in the custody of a child and can deny admission if the parent's purpose is to circumvent the school district's zoning requirements. *Matter of Curry,* 113 Mich.App. 821, 318 N.W.2d 567 (1982).

2. A change in student residence simply to participate in an athletic program may be denied by athletic association rules without violating a student's property rights. *Pennsylvania Interscholastic Athletic Association, Inc. v. Greater Johnstown School District,* 76 Pa.Cmwlth. 65, 463 A.2d 1198 (1983).

3. The Supreme Court of Arkansas has held that children residing in one school district could pay tuition and attend school in another school district, but only if both school districts agree to the arrangement. *Delta Special School District No. 5 v. McGehee Special School District No. 17,* 280 Ark. 489, 659 S.W.2d 508 (1983).

4. The word "domicile" is derived from the Latin "domus" meaning home or dwelling house. The word may be defined, by law, as the true place of habitation. A Washington statute was upheld as constitutional by the United States Supreme Court when it defined "domicile" as "a person's true, fixed and permanent home and place of habitation. It is the place where he intends to remain, and to which he expects to return when he leaves without intending to establish a new domicile elsewhere." *Sturgis v. Washington,* 414 U.S. 1057, 94 S.Ct. 563 (1973). A bona fide residence requirement may have the same legal connotation

as domicile. Domicile and residence are usually in the same place, but the terms are not identical. A person may have two residences, but can have only one domicile. Whether the term "residence" or "domicile" is used, the key is the "intention to remain."

_____

◼ COMPULSORY SCHOOL ATTENDANCE

While the benefits of universal education were recognized at an early stage of our national development, the idea that all youth should be compelled to attend school came later. Even though the first compulsory attendance law was enacted in Massachusetts in 1853 and in New York one year later, the idea was not firmly established until the turn of the century, by which time 32 states had enacted such laws.

That the state's interests should take precedence over parental rights to govern the activities of the child is the basis for both compulsory attendance and child labor laws. The employment records of the nineteenth century and early twentieth century indicate that it took both types of legislation to take children out of the work force and put them in school.

In large cities children were virtually enslaved—in factories and shops, from daylight until dark—working for abysmally low wages. In the south, public school advocates and the labor unions crusaded against the abuse of child labor. In 1900 three out of ten workers in mills of the South were children under sixteen years of age, and 57.5 percent of those children were between ten and thirteen. Those under ten were not enumerated for statistical purposes. It was estimated that 75 percent of the spinners in the cotton mills of North Carolina were fourteen or younger. The number of children under sixteen working in the mills increased sixfold between 1880 and 1900. In 1894, the only child labor law that was on the books of a leading textile state was in Alabama. The law was enacted in 1887 and repealed in 1895, on demand of a large Massachusetts company that opened a mill in Alabama in 1895.[6]

The *Manufacturers Record*[7] attacked child labor laws as "radical," "unreasonable," and "inflammatory"; and others charged that taking away child labor would cripple the economy of the South. Fortunately, by 1912 all southern states had adopted an age-and-hour limit and some prohibition against night work of children, yet in most states the age limit for employment was only twelve and the work week was sixty hours.

Thus, a combination of industrial exploitation and the inability of parents to make decisions in the best interest of their own children greatly retarded educational progress for many years. It was not until compulsory attendance laws and child labor laws were enforced, in concert, that the public schools became a viable social phenomenon.

Even today, there are some who maintain that compulsory attendance should be abolished and all children should be given the option and opportunity to attend school, but not be compelled to do so. Milton Friedman, the Nobel Laureate in Economics, argues that compulsory attendance laws are unnecessary and should be abolished. In his national bestseller of 1980, *Free to Choose,* he observed:

> But it is far from clear that there is any justification for the compulsory attendance laws themselves. . . . Like most laws, compulsory attendance laws have costs as well as benefits. We no longer believe the benefits justify the costs.[8]

Friedman's primary objection to compulsory attendance laws seems to be that such laws are merely an unwarranted justification for government control over parents. This argument is, of course, not a new one. It is of nineteenth-century vintage, during which era great acrimony was raised by opponents of public schools who saw compulsory attendance as an unnecessary governmental device that would deny parental authority and weaken private schools. Though the logical connection is relatively difficult to rationalize, it was basically argued that society had no right to force anyone to be educated, and if they were educated, they should do so of their own volition using their own resources.

It was argued that the child and parent should be given freedom to choose or not choose education. "What right," it was exclaimed, "has society to force me to learn reading, if I do not want to? or writing, if I can get along without it? or numbering, if I will know enough of it by the practical schooling of hard life? or geography, if I can make my way through life without maps?"[9] It was further argued that those who advocated compulsory attendance implicitly assumed that "a man cannot be honest and industrious without having passed through a primary school . . . ."[10] Finally, it was maintained that the general welfare of the people did not justify the government's requirement that all attend school.[11]

The argument against compulsory attendance also played a role in the struggle to desegregate the public schools of the South during the 1950s and 1960s. The desegregation movement both prior to and subsequent to *Brown v. Board of Education*[12] led several southern states to abolish their compulsory attendance laws, apparently on the theory that equal protection of the laws would not apply if one were not required to attend school; or possibly on the more perverse notion that if black children were truant from school, there was no legal obligation on the part of the state to see that they were educated. The legislature of Virginia, for example, repealed its compulsory attendance laws in 1959 and adopted the general policy of massive resistance to desegregation.[13] Without compulsory attendance the "freedom of choice" program, coupled with the tuition vouchers for whites to attend private schools, combined to create formidable desegregation problems.[14] Alabama went a step further, amending its constitution in 1956 to prevent any challenge to legislative discretion in the matter of control of public education attendance policy or rights pertaining thereto.

In short, the issue of compulsory school attendance has been and continues to be a volatile area of dispute between those who argue for broader and universal education versus those who seek a more limited use of education for particularized purposes and interests. The argument is an historical one, with the basic motivations changing little over the years. The courts have generally resolved the dilemma by maintaining that education is vital to the welfare of the state, and that the requirement that all persons be exposed to schooling is not an unreasonable or arbitrary exercise of state power. On the other hand, the courts do not compel the state legislatures to require attendance in a school; so those states that have little interest in universal education or for some reason seek to limit educational opportunity by either rescinding attendance laws or by greatly expanding the reasons for exemptions are free to do so at their own volition.

Parens Patriae

Legal authority for the state to require school attendance is found in the common-law doctrine of *parens patriae*, which maintains, essentially, that as a father to all persons, the state has the inherent prerogative to provide for the commonwealth and individual welfare. It can through the exercise of the police power of the legislature establish reasonable laws, not repugnant to the constitution, as it may judge for the good of the state. As guardian over everyone, the state has the authority to protect those who are not legally competent to act in their own behalf, *non sui juris* (literally, "not his own master"). This protection was quite naturally interpreted to apply to minor children who, because of their age, were unable to take care of themselves. Unavoidably, the state's interest in the child was to collide with parental interest and this, today, still forms the framework on which most compulsory education and curriculum controversies are litigated. It is well established, going back into English law, that the state's or the King's prerogative is superior to that of the parent when the parent's natural right is improperly exercised. Authority for the power of the state was clearly stated in English precedent and *parens patriae* was adopted throughout the United States "to the

end that the health, patriotism, morality, efficiency, industry, and integrity of its citizenship may be preserved and protected, looking to the preservation and stability of the state."[15] In this country, the desirability of the doctrine as a rudiment of governmental responsibility was well expressed in an 1882 Illinois case, wherein the court said:

> It is the unquestioned right and imperative duty of every enlightened government, in its character of *parens patriae*, to protect and provide for the comfort and well-being of such of its citizens as by reason of infancy . . . were unable to take care of themselves. The performance of these duties is justly regarded as one of the most important of governmental functions, and all constitutional limitations must be so understood and construed as not to interfere with its proper and legitimate exercise.[16]

A child has a right to be protected not only from the patent abuses of his parents but also against the ignorance of his parents. The state has recognized more truth than fiction in the adage, "There are no delinquent children, only delinquent parents." In support of this view, juvenile courts and welfare agencies of the state have traditionally intervened between parent and child in cases of parental abuse. Public education may thus serve as a mechanism to free the child from the shackles of unfit parents.

To protect the child from the parent requires affirmative state action. A child has no constitutional protection from the parent; such protection must come in the form of statutory action by the state to protect the child, examples of which are compulsory attendance laws and requirements that children be exposed to certain kinds of educational curricula. On the other hand, the state's action must be supported by a compelling or, at least, a rational state interest before either the child's or the parent's rights can be restricted or infringed upon.

In the United States today, a dual set of precedents has emerged. One tends to limit *parens patriae*, as is evidenced by court-imposed limitations on state handling of juvenile cases.[17] This precedent was illustrated by the exception from state compulsory attendance laws in *Yoder*.[18] The second precedent is judicial authorization for legislatures to protect the infant from parental abuse, as was reflected by the United States Supreme Court in *Ford v. Ford* in 1962:

> Unfortunately, experience has shown that the question of custody, so vital to a child's happiness and well-being, frequently cannot be left to the discretion of the parents. This is particularly true where, as here, the estrangement of husband and wife beclouds parental judgment with emotion and prejudices.[19]

The language of the Supreme Court in *Pierce v. Society of Sisters*[20] indicated that only limited tolerance would be given the state in interfering with the parent's control of the child:

> In this day and under our civilization, the child of man is his parent's child and not the state's. . . . It is not seriously debatable that the parental right to guide one's child intellectually and religiously is a most substantial part of the liberty and freedom of the parent.

This does not mean that parental rights fully preempt those of the state. On the contrary, it would appear that a parent may forfeit his right to control his child by either omission or commission. In such case, the parent has no immunity from state intervention.

Nearly twenty years after *Pierce*, in 1943, the Supreme Court more clearly defined its position toward state intervention in *Prince v. Massachusetts*.[21] Here, a legal guardian was found guilty of contributing to the delinquence of a minor by permitting her nine-year-old ward to sell Jehovah's Witnesses publications on a public street. The act was found to be in violation of Massachusetts' child labor laws. The Supreme Court addressed the conflicting claims of parent and state, saying:

> [T]he family itself is not beyond regulation in the public interest . . . acting to guard the general interest in youth's well being, the state as *parens patriae* may restrict the parent's con-

trol by requiring school attendance, regulating or prohibiting the child's labor and in many other ways.

In *Yoder*, the court said that the power of the parent, even when linked to free exercise of religion, may be subject to limitation if it appears that parental decisions will jeopardize the health or safety of the children or have "potential for significant social burdens."

A common thread running through these precedents is a renewed judicial concern for the child, with the parental interest and the state interest secondary. However, the general welfare is always a concern of the state and the maxim *salus populi suprema lex esto*, "let the welfare of the people be the supreme law," is sufficient justification for the exercise of the *parens patriae* doctrine.

State intervention to compel attendance includes distinguishable premises: the state may provide education for all who cannot appropriately educate themselves, protect infants from those who would deny them education, and compel all citizens to act in ways most beneficial to the child and society.[22] Reflecting state concern in these areas, compulsory attendance laws require schooling and provide enforcement to protect the child from undesirable parental conduct.[23]

Cases involving challenges to compulsory attendance laws generally emanate from disputes between parents and officials. This may be due, in part, to the old notion that "the basic right of a juvenile is not to liberty but to custody."[24] It may also result directly from enforcement provisions in compulsory attendance laws that penalize the parent, rather than the child.

Confrontation between state and parent instead of between state and child is probably the result of two subtle theories suggested by Kleinfeld.[25] One is that parents have a duty to a child to educate him, and the state may compel fulfillment of this duty. The other is that parents have a duty to the state to educate their children, which the state may compel them to perform.

Whether the judgment of the parent should prevail over the collective judgment of the state in educational matters is a much broader question, however, than may be evidenced by simple challenges to compulsory attendance laws. In a dispute between parent and state regarding an educational matter, parents may be pictured as intelligent, well-meaning, and motivated for the betterment of the child. This is not always the case. The invocation of the doctrine of *parens patriae* in matters of education may result from broken homes where parents will not assist or support the child in obtaining an education. Where children have sought financial assistance from parents toward a common school education, the courts have uniformly termed such education as "necessary" and granted the support. Common school education is a "necessary," as are food, lodging, clothing, and medicine.[26]

In the courts' view, education has traditionally been of such importance that even items assisting school attendance have been considered necessary for child support purposes. For example, one early Texas court held that a buggy may be a "necessary" if it is needed to convey a child to and from school.[27] In some states, the courts have given alimony in divorce decrees that considers education to be a "necessary" over and beyond the normal public school education.[28]

Exercise of *parens patriae* by the state may result in more severe action than that of requiring a child to attend school or mandating that a parent furnish resources for attendance in school or college. The child-parent relationship can be partly or totally severed by judicial enforcement of divorce, neglect,[29] or child abuse statutes.[30] The concept of *parens patriae* extends to compulsory medical care over the objection of parents. Some states have explicit statutory language declaring a parent neglectful if he fails to provide medical care for his child. Under a finding of neglect, the court is empowered to provide the necessary medical care.[31] Courts, acting as *parens patriae*, have made children wards of the state and required medical care in the absence of statute, under common law.[32]

It should be noted that the invocation of *parens patriae* by the state does not restrict parental authority in all cases. In some instances, such action may even strengthen it. In cases in which parents are unable to control their own children, the child's action produces not only disharmony within the family but sometimes becomes a nuisance to the public, generally. For such situations, some states have enacted "stubborn child laws"[33] that protect the public from children who are "runaways, night walkers, common railers and brawlers."

Instruction in Private Schools

When compulsory attendance laws are mentioned, one usually thinks of children being compelled to attend only public schools. However, many alternatives and exceptions exist. A child may attend a private, profit, nonprofit, sectarian, or secular school, or with state statutory permission be permitted to have home instruction. A child may also be exempt from required attendance because of religion, marriage, physical or mental incapacity, distance of travel, and so on. Courts have established many precedents that even today are in a state of transition.

Few cases have defined "private school" as used in compulsory attendance laws.[34] Precise definition is lacking, because in several jurisdictions children are not required to attend either public or private schools but must obtain "equivalent instruction."[35]

The state cannot, however, impose too many regulations on private schools. In holding Ohio's regulation of private schools overly restrictive, tending to make private schools the images of public schools, the court said that the overregulation of the private schools emanated from state education agency regulations. These regulations governed "the content of the curriculum that [was] taught, the manner in which it [was] taught, the person or persons who [taught] it, the physical layout of the building in which the students [were] taught, the hours of instruction, and the educational policies intended to be achieved through the instruction offered."[36]

Most courts have held that to be "recognized," a private school must provide instruction equivalent to the free instruction furnished in public schools. To have equivalent instruction, it is also necessary for the private school to comply with the statutory period of attendance.[37]

Equivalent Instruction

The state has the prerogative to define what constitutes equivalent instruction, and the private school must accommodate the state. Although vaguely defining the term "equivalent" as meaning "equal," the courts generally refer to the qualifications of the instructor and the available teaching materials as the primary criteria for determining equivalency of instruction. Should the state require that students be tested, it makes no difference that the private school would rather opt for some other measure of equivalency.[38] The court will uphold the state standards so long as they are reasonable and are not too vague for proper implementation. State equivalency regulations may require that children (a) be taught by a certified teacher; (b) be taught a minimum specified, listed curriculum; (c) fulfill specified minimum attendance standards that are appropriate and will be upheld by the courts; (d) or pass tests as specified by the state.[39]

However, in Missouri, where the state compulsory attendance law provided that home instruction be permitted as an alternative to compulsory attendance if the instructional program is "substantially equivalent" to that of a public or private school, a U.S. District Court ruled that the provision was unconstitutionally vague because nowhere in the statute were the terms defined. No guidelines were issued to interpret, and both parents and school officials could only guess at its meaning.[40]

Thus, as with all laws touching on individual freedoms, appropriate governmental restraints must be specifically and properly defined or they will be invalidated by the courts as too vague to be enforceable.[41]

Courts may thus continue to find that tests, certification of teachers, and other measures constitute a reasonable exercise of state power.[42]

Although the state can require instruction equivalent to that of a public school, it cannot deny the parent the right to send his or her child to a private school. In a 1925 case, *Pierce v. Society of Sisters,* a private school itself, as a corporation, claimed denial of due process of law because an Oregon compulsory attendance statute required all children ages eight to sixteen to attend public schools.[43] The appellees in the case were the Roman Catholic order of the Society of Sisters and Hill Military Academy, both private, profit-making corporations. The schools claimed that enforcement of the compulsory attendance law would deprive them of students, destroy the profitable features of their businesses, and diminish the value of their property.

The compulsory education controversy had been raised by those who were concerned that private schools created religious hostility and prejudice, and that American government and loyalty to democratic ideals could best be taught in public schools. Further, the law was enacted at the time when there was a great worldwide fear of the spread of Bolshevists, syndicalists, and communists; and there was concern that private schools could be started and fostered by such groups. In 1922, the Oregon voters adopted an initiative—by a margin of 115,000 to 103,000—requiring that all children between the ages of eight and sixteen years attend a public school or be exempted by permission of the county school superintendent.

In ruling in the plaintiffs' favor, in *Pierce,* the United States Supreme Court decided the case on the grounds that the state cannot, through improper regulation, deprive a business corporation of its patrons or customers. The law deprived the corporations of a liberty protected by the Fourteenth Amendment. In this regard, the Court commented on the rights of both parent and child:

> The fundamental theory of liberty upon which all governments in this union repose excludes any general power of the state to standardize its children by forcing them to accept instruction from public teachers only. The child is not the mere creature of the state; those who nurture him and direct his destiny have the right, coupled with the high duty, to recognize and prepare him for additional obligations.[44]

Religious interests may be used as rationale by private school operators to maintain that their schools should remain open regardless of adherence to state curriculum regulations. Courts will weigh religious interests against state interests and the result may hang in balance on the facts involved. For example, even a church itself may be closed if worship services are held in a residential area of a city and the religious chanting during worship services disturbs the neighborhood.[45] With private religious schools, though, the facts and the interests involved may concern more esoteric questions, such as whether accommodation of minimal state educational requirements is, in and of itself, an encroachment on religious interests. In Nebraska, a lengthy and highly publicized conflict developed when the state closed a private religious school because it did not adhere to state requirements for private schools. The Supreme Court of Nebraska held that the state interests prevailed over the religious interests of the private school proprietors and parents.[46] Religious convictions do not exempt operators of private schools from compliance with reasonable state school laws.[47] In this regard an appeals court in Michigan has held that parochial schools can be required to submit to the state records of enrollment of pupils attending the schools and the qualifications of teachers. Similarly, the state can enforce curriculum and teacher certification requirements.[48]

Compulsory Education Law Requiring All Children to Attend Public Schools Violates Due Process Clause

— — — — — — —

Pierce v. Society of the Sisters of the Holy Names of Jesus and Mary

— — — — — — —

Supreme Court of the United States, 1925.
268 U.S. 510, 45 S.Ct. 571.

Mr. Justice McREYNOLDS delivered the opinion of the Court. These appeals are from decrees, based upon undenied allegations, which granted preliminary orders restraining appellants from threatening or attempting to enforce the Compulsory Education Act adopted November 7, 1922 (Laws Or.1923, p. 9), under the initiative provision of her Constitution by the voters of Oregon. Judicial Code, § 266 (Comp.St. § 1243). . . .

The challenged act, effective September 1, 1926, requires every parent, guardian, or other person having control or charge or custody of a child between eight and sixteen years to send him "to a public school for the period of time a public school shall be held during the current year" in the district where the child resides; and failure so to do is declared a misdemeanor. There are exemptions—not specially important here—for children who are not normal, or who have completed the eighth grade, or whose parents or private teachers reside at considerable distances from any public school, or who hold special permits from the county superintendent. The manifest purpose is to compel general attendance at public schools by normal children, between eight and sixteen, who have not completed the eighth grade. And without doubt enforcement of the statute would seriously impair, perhaps destroy, the profitable features of appellees' business and greatly diminish the value of their property.

Appellee the Society of Sisters is an Oregon corporation, organized in 1880, with power to care for orphans, educate and instruct the youth, establish and maintain academies or schools, and acquire necessary real and personal property. It has long devoted its property and effort to the secular and religious education and care of children, and has acquired the valuable good will of many parents and guardians. . . . It owns valuable buildings, especially constructed and equipped for school purposes. The business is remunerative—the annual income from primary schools exceeds $30,000—and the successful conduct of this requires long time contracts with teachers and parents. The Compulsory Education Act of 1922 has already caused the withdrawal from its schools of children who would otherwise continue, and their income has steadily declined. The appellants, public officers, have proclaimed their purpose strictly to enforce the statute.

After setting out the above facts, the Society's bill alleges that the enactment conflicts with the right of parents to choose schools where their children will receive appropriate mental and religious training, the right of the child to influence the parents' choice of a school, the right of schools and teachers therein to engage in a useful business or profession, and is accordingly repugnant to the Constitution and void. And, further, that unless enforcement of the measure is enjoined the corporation's business and property will suffer irreparable injury.

Appellee Hill Military Academy is a private corporation organized in 1908 under the laws of Oregon, engaged in owning, operating, and conducting for profit an elementary, college preparatory, and military training school for boys between the ages of five and twenty-one years. . . . It owns considerable real and personal property, some useful only for school purposes. The business and incident good will are very valuable. . . .

The Academy's bill states the foregoing facts and then alleges that the challenged act contravenes the corporation's rights guaranteed by the Fourteenth Amendment and that unless appellants are restrained from proclaiming its validity and threatening to enforce it irreparable injury will result. The prayer is for an appropriate injunction. . . .

The court ruled that the Fourteenth Amendment guaranteed appellees against the deprivation of their property without due process of law consequent upon the unlawful interference by appellants with the free choice of patrons, present and prospective. It declared the right to conduct schools was property and that parents and guardians, as a part of their liberty, might direct the education of children by selecting reputable teachers and places. . . .

No question is raised concerning the power of the state reasonably to regulate all schools, to inspect, supervise and examine them, their teachers and pupils; to require that all children of proper age attend some school, that teachers shall be of good moral character and patriotic disposition, that certain studies plainly essential to good citizenship must be taught, and that nothing be taught which is manifestly inimical to the public welfare.

The inevitable practical result of enforcing the act under consideration would be destruction of appellees' primary schools, and perhaps all other private primary schools for normal children within the state of Oregon. Appellees are engaged in a kind of undertaking not inherently harmful, but long regarded as useful and meritorious. Certainly there is nothing in the present records to indicate that they have failed to discharge their obligations to patrons, students or the state. And there are no peculiar circumstances or present emergencies which demand extraordinary measures relative to primary education.

Under the doctrine of *Meyer v. Nebraska*, we think it entirely plain that the Act of 1922 unreasonably interferes with the liberty of parents and guardians to direct the upbringing and education of children under their control. As often heretofore pointed out, rights guaranteed by the Constitution may not be abridged by legislation which has no reasonable relation to some purpose within the competency of the state. The fundamental theory of liberty upon which all governments in this Union repose excludes any general power of the state to standardize its children by forcing them to accept instruction from public teachers only. The child is not the mere creature of the state; those who nurture him and direct his destiny have the right, coupled with the high duty, to recognize and prepare him for additional obligations.

Appellees are corporations, and therefore, it is said, they cannot claim for themselves the liberty which the Fourteenth Amendment guarantees. Accepted in the proper sense, this is true. . . . But they have business and property for which they claim protection. These are threatened with destruction through the unwarranted compulsion which appellants are exercising over present and prospective patrons of their schools. And this court has gone very far to protect against loss threatened by such action. . . .

Generally, it is entirely true, as urged by counsel, that no person in any business has such an interest in possible customers as to enable him to restrain exercise of proper power of the state upon the ground that he will be deprived of patronage. But the injunctions here sought are not against the exercise of any proper power. Appellees asked protection against arbitrary, unreasonable, and unlawful interference with their patrons and the consequent destruction of their business and property. Their interest is clear and immediate . . . .

The decrees below are affirmed.

■ RELIGION: THE AMISH EXCEPTION

After *Pierce v. Society of Sisters*,[49] it was rather uniformly assumed that children could be compelled to attend a public, private, or parochial school, but that no child had a right *not* to attend school at all.

Early cases established that the child's and the parents' rights of religious freedom, as protected by the First Amendment of the United States Constitution, were not sufficient to diminish the state's power to compel compulsory attendance. Justice Cardozo, in a concurring opinion in *Hamilton v. Regents*[50] (a case dealing with the rights of a conscientious objector), maintained that undesirable results may evolve where religious scruples predominate over reasonable state laws. In delivering the opinion Cardozo said:

> Manifestly a different doctrine would carry us to lengths that have never yet been dreamed of. The conscientious objector, if his liberties were to be thus extended, might refuse to contribute taxes in furtherance of any other end condemned by his conscience as irreligious or immoral. The right of private judgment has never yet been so exalted above the powers and the compulsion of the agencies of government. One who is a martyr to a principle — which may

turn out in the end to be a delusion or an error — does not prove by his martyrdom that he has kept within the law.[51]

Following this rationale, other courts have concluded that the individual cannot be permitted, on religious grounds, to be the judge of his duty to obey reasonable civil requirements enacted in the interest of public welfare.

In a 1945 Virginia case, the parents of three families sought to prevent the enforcement of compulsory attendance laws on religious grounds. These parents interpreted the Bible as commanding parents to teach and train their own children. They believed that sending their children to public schools was incompatible with the primary religious obligation they felt they owed their Maker. Their willful intent to violate the law was solely because of sincere religious convictions. Yet the court decided against the parents, and declared:

> No amount of religious fervor he [parent] may entertain in opposition to adequate instruction should be allowed to work a lifelong injury to his child. Nor should he, for this religious reason, be suffered to inflict another illiterate citizen on his community or his state.[52]

Although the religious issue was the *ratio decidendi* in this case, the court ruled that the parents were not capable of adequately educating the children themselves.

Religious grounds have been ruled insufficient to limit the number of days a child attends school. A Moslem parent claimed that his religion prevented him from sending his children to school on Fridays. Regardless of the validity of his religious motives, the court said the state allowed parental choice among public, private, and parochial schools. The parent and child did not, however, have the option of nonattendance on Fridays.[53]

Thus, the prevailing view of the courts was that religious beliefs cannot impair achievement of the state's objective — universal compulsory education. The precedent-setting case that has altered this view is *Wisconsin v.*

Yoder.[54] This case contested the power of the state to require the school attendance of Amish children after the eighth grade. Although the issue in this case is limited to the compulsory attendance of Amish children between the time they complete the eighth grade and the time they reach sixteen years of age, it nevertheless has profound implications for all future cases involving compulsory attendance.

The decision of the Court in this case can be summarized in three points. First, although the state has power to impose reasonable regulation, this power must be balanced against fundamental rights and interests of individuals. Second, beliefs that are philosophical rather than personal are not sufficient to invoke free exercise of religion. Third, where parents show that enforcement of compulsory education will endanger their religious beliefs, the *parens patriae* power of the state must give way to the free exercise clause of the First Amendment.

Two dramatic limitations on the general applicability of *Yoder* are the objection of the Amish only to post-eighth-grade compulsory attendance of fourteen- and fifteen-year-olds and the well-established Amish customs of living near the soil and shunning modern society generally. These features of the case tend to diminish the compelling interest of the state; they eliminate the possibility of illiteracy by providing at least eight years of schooling and negate the chance of these children becoming unproductive members of society.

The ultimate question of who will determine the child's destiny is not answered by *Yoder*. The court is content, instead, to speak rather vaguely of balancing the fundamental religious freedom of the parents against the interest of the state.

Litigation following *Yoder* indicates that the courts will tend to circumscribe the "Amish exception" very narrowly, and that in most instances requests to have other churches, religions, or religious views added to the list of valid exemptions from compulsory attendance are not likely to be granted. Actions by Fundamentalist Baptists seeking to convince the courts that the Amish exemption should extend to their religion have been to

no avail.[55] Where the Amish exception is applied to one religious group and not to another,[56] the courts have held that equal protection is not violated.

State Cannot Compel Amish Children to Attend Public High School

—·—·—·—·—·—

State of Wisconsin v. Yoder

—·—·—·—·—·—

Supreme Court of the United States, 1972.
406 U.S. 205, 92 S.Ct. 1526.

. . . . Respondents Jonas Yoder and Wallace Miller are members of the Old Order Amish religion, and respondent Adin Yutzy is a member of the Conservative Amish Mennonite Church. They and their families are residents of Green County, Wisconsin. Wisconsin's compulsory school-attendance law required them to cause their children to attend public or private school until reaching age sixteen but the respondents declined to send their children, ages fourteen and fifteen, to public school after they completed the eighth grade. The children were not enrolled in any private school, or within any recognized exception to the compulsory-attendance law, and they are conceded to be subject to the Wisconsin statute.

On complaint of the school district administrator for the public schools, respondents were charged, tried, and convicted of violating the compulsory-attendance law in Green County Court and were fined the sum of $5 each. Respondents defended on the ground that the application of the compulsory-attendance law violated their rights under the First and Fourteenth Amendments. . . .

The history of the Amish sect was given in some detail, beginning with the Swiss Anabaptists of the sixteenth century who rejected institutionalized churches and sought to return to the early, simple, Christian life deemphasizing material success, rejecting the competitive spirit, and seeking to insulate themselves from the modern world. As a result of their common heritage, Old Order Amish communities today are characterized by a fundamental belief that salvation requires life in a church community separate and apart from the world and worldly influence. This concept of life aloof from the world and its values is central to their faith. . . .

Formal high school education beyond the eighth grade is contrary to Amish beliefs, not only because it places Amish children in an environment hostile to Amish beliefs with increasing emphasis on competition in class work and sports and with pressure to conform to the styles, manners, and ways of the peer group, but also because it takes them away from their community, physically and emotionally, during the crucial and formative adolescent period of life. . . .

The Amish do not object to elementary education through the first eight grades as a general proposition because they agree that their children must have basic skills in the "three R's" in order to read the Bible, to be good farmers and citizens, and to be able to deal with non-Amish people when necessary in the course of daily affairs. They view such a basic education as acceptable because it does not significantly expose their children to wordly values or interfere with their development in the Amish community during the crucial adolescent period. While Amish accept compulsory elementary education generally, wherever possible they have established their own elementary schools in many respects like the small local schools of the past. In the Amish belief higher learning tends to develop values they reject as influences that alienate man from God. . . .

There is no doubt as to the power of a State, having a high responsibility for education of its citizens, to impose reasonable regulations for the control and duration of basic education. See, e.g., *Pierce v. Society of Sisters*, 268 U.S. 510, 534, 45 S.Ct. 571, 573, 69 L.Ed. 1070 (1925). Providing public schools ranks at the very apex of the function of a State. Yet even this paramount responsibility was, in *Pierce*, made to yield to the right of parents to provide an equivalent education in a privately operated system. There the Court held that Oregon's statute compelling attendance in a public school from age eight to age sixteen unreasonably interfered with the interest of parents in directing the rearing of their offspring, including their education in church-operated schools. As that case suggests, the values of parental direction of the religious upbringing and education of their children in their early and formative years have a high place in our society. . . . Thus, a State's interest in universal education, however highly we rank it, is not totally free from a balancing process when it impinges on fundamental rights and interests, such as those specifically protected by the Free Exercise Clause of the First Amendment, and the traditional interest of parents with respect to the religious upbringing of their children so long as they, in the words of *Pierce*, "prepare [them] for additional obligations." 268 U.S., at 535, 45 S.Ct., at 573.

It follows that in order for Wisconsin to compel school attendance beyond the eighth grade against a claim that such attendance interferes with the practice of a legitimate religious belief, it must appear either that the State does not deny the free exercise of religious belief by its requirement, or that there is a state interest of sufficient magnitude to override the interest claiming protection under the Free Exercise Clause. . . .

The essence of all that has been said and written on the subject is that only those interests of the highest order and those not otherwise served can overbalance legitimate claims to the free exercise of religion. We can accept it as settled, therefore, that, however strong the State's interest in universal compulsory education, it is by no means absolute to the exclusion or subordination of all other interests. . . .

We come then to the quality of the claims of the respondents concerning the alleged encroachment of Wisconsin's compulsory school-attendance statute on their rights and the rights of their children to the free exercise of the religious beliefs they and their forbears have adhered to for almost three centuries. In evaluating those claims we must be careful to determine whether the Amish religious faith and their mode of life are, as they claim, inseparable and interdependent. A way of life, however virtuous and admirable, may not be interposed as a barrier to reasonable state regulation of education if it is based on purely secular considerations; to have the protection of the Religion Clauses, the claims must be rooted in religious belief. Although a determination of what is a "religious" belief or practice entitled to constitutional protection may present a most delicate question, the very concept of ordered liberty precludes allowing every person to make his own standards on matters of conduct in which society as a whole has important interests. Thus, if the Amish asserted their claims because of their subjective evaluation and rejection of the contemporary secular values accepted by the majority, much as Thoreau rejected the social values of his time and isolated himself at Walden Pond, their claims would not rest on a religious basis. Thoreau's choice was philosophical and personal rather than religious, and such belief does not rise to the demands of the Religion Clauses.

Giving no weight to such secular considerations, however, we see that the record in this case abundantly supports the claim that the traditional way of life of the Amish is not merely a matter of personal preference, but one of deep religious conviction, shared by an organized group, and intimately related to daily living.   .   .   .

As the society around the Amish has become more populous, urban, industrialized, and complex, particularly in this century, government regulation of human affairs has correspondingly become more detailed and pervasive. The Amish mode of life has thus come into conflict increasingly with requirements of contemporary society exerting a hydraulic insistence on conformity to majoritarian standards. So long as compulsory education laws were confined to eight grades of elementary basic education imparted in a nearby rural schoolhouse, with a large proportion of students of the Amish faith, the Old Order Amish had little basis to fear that school attendance would expose their children to the worldly influence they reject. But modern compulsory secondary education in rural areas is now largely carried on in a consolidated school, often remote from the student's home and alien to his daily home life. As the record so strongly shows, the values and programs of the modern secondary school are in sharp conflict with the fundamental mode of life mandated by the Amish religion; modern laws requiring compulsory secondary education have accordingly engendered great concern and conflict. The conclusion is inescapable that secondary schooling, by exposing Amish children to worldly influences in terms of attitudes, goals, and values contrary to beliefs, and by substantially interfering with the religious development of the Amish child and his integration into the way of life of the Amish faith community at the crucial adolescent stage of development, contravenes the basic religious tenets and practice of the Amish faith, both as to the parent and the child.

The impact of the compulsory-attendance law on respondents' practice of the Amish religion is not only severe, but inescapable, for the Wisconsin law affirmatively compels them, under threat of criminal sanction, to perform acts undeniably at odds with fundamental tenets of their religious beliefs. .   .   .

In sum, the unchallenged testimony of acknowledged experts in education and religious history, almost 300 years of consistent practice, and strong evidence of a sustained faith pervading and regulating respondents' entire mode of life support the claim that enforcement of the State's requirement of compulsory formal education after the eighth grade would gravely endanger if not destroy the free exercise of respondents' religious beliefs.   .   .   .

The State advances two primary arguments in support of its system of compulsory education. It notes, as Thomas Jefferson pointed out early in our history, that some degree of education is necessary to prepare citizens to participate effectively and intelligently in our open political system if we are to preserve freedom and independence. Further, education prepares individuals to be self-reliant and self-sufficient participants in society. We accept these propositions.

However, the evidence adduced by the Amish in this case is persuasively to the effect that an additional one or two years of formal high school for Amish children in place of their long-established program of informal vocational education would do little to serve those interests. Respondents' experts testified at trial, without challenge, that the value of all education must be assessed in terms of its capacity to prepare the child for life. It is one thing to say that compulsory education for a year or two beyond the eighth grade may be necessary when its goal is the preparation of the child for life in modern society as the majority live, but it is quite another if the goal of education be viewed as the preparation of the child for life in the separated agrarian community that is the keystone of the Amish faith. . . .

The State attacks respondents' position as one fostering "ignorance" from which the child must be protected by the State. No one can question the State's duty to protect children from ignorance but this argument does not square with the facts disclosed in the record. Whatever their idiosyncrasies as seen by the majority, this record strongly shows that the Amish community has been a highly successful social unit within our society, even if apart from the conventional "mainstream." Its members are productive and very law-abiding members of society; they reject public welfare in any of its usual modern forms. The Congress itself recognized their self-sufficiency by authorizing exemption of such groups as the Amish from the obligation to pay social security taxes. . . .

Insofar as the State's claim rests on the view that a brief additional period of formal education is imperative to enable the Amish to participate effectively and intelligently in our democratic process it must fall. The Amish alternative to formal secondary school education has enabled them to function effectively in their day-to-day life under self-imposed limitations on relations with the world, and to survive and prosper in contemporary society as a separate, sharply identifiable and highly self-sufficient community for more than 200 years in this country. In itself this is strong evidence that they are capable of fulfilling the social and political responsibilities of citizenship without compelled attendance beyond the eighth grade at the price of jeopardizing their free exercise of religious belief. When Thomas Jefferson emphasized the need for education as a bulwark of a free people against tyranny, there is nothing to indicate he had in mind compulsory education through any fixed age beyond a basic education. Indeed, the Amish communities singularly parallel and reflect many of the virtues of Jefferson's ideal of the "sturdy yeoman" who would form the basis of what he considered as the ideal of a democratic society. Even their idiosyncratic separateness exemplifies the diversity we profess to admire and encourage.

The requirement for compulsory education beyond the eighth grade is a relatively recent development in our history. Less than sixty years ago, the educational requirements of almost all of the States were satisfied by completion of the elementary grades, at least where the child was regularly and lawfully employed. The independence and successful social functioning of the Amish community for a period approaching almost three centuries and more than 200 years in this country are strong evidence that there is at best a speculative gain, in terms of meeting the duties of citizenship, from an additional one or two years of compulsory formal education. Against this background it would require a more particularized showing from the State on this point to justify the severe interference with religious freedom such additional compulsory attendance would entail. . . . There is no intimation that the Amish employment of their children on family farms is in any way deleterious to their health or that Amish parents exploit children at tender years. Any such inference would be contrary to the record before us. Moreover, employment of Amish children on the family farm does not present the undesirable economic aspects of eliminating jobs that might otherwise be held by adults.

Finally, the State, on authority of *Prince v. Massachusetts,* argues that a decision exempting Amish children from the State's requirement fails to recognize the substantive right of the Amish child to a secondary education, and fails to give due regard to the power of the State as *parens patriae* to extend the benefit of secondary education to children regardless of the wishes of their parents. Taken at its broadest sweep, the Court's language in *Prince* might be read to give support to the State's position. However, the Court was not confronted in *Prince* with a situation comparable to that of the Amish as revealed in this record; this is shown by the Court's severe characterization of the evils that it thought the legislature could legitimately associate with child labor, even when performed in the company of an adult. 321 U.S., at 169–170, 64 S.Ct., at 443–444. The Court later took great care to confine *Prince* to a narrow scope in *Sherbert v. Verner,* when it stated:

> On the other hand, the Court has rejected challenges under the Free Exercise Clause to governmental regulation of certain overt acts prompted by religious beliefs or principles, for "even when the action is in accord with one's religious convictions, [it] is not totally free from legislative restrictions." Braunfeld v. Brown, 366 U.S. 599, 603, 81 S.Ct. 1144, 1146, 6 L.Ed.2d 563. The conduct or actions so regulated have invariably posed some substantial threat to public safety, peace or order. See, e.g., *Reynolds v. United States,* 98 U.S. 145, 25 L.Ed. 244; *Jacobson v. Massachusetts,* 197 U.S. 11, 25 S.Ct. 358, 49 L.Ed. 643; *Prince v. Massachusetts,* 321 U.S. 158, 64 S.Ct. 438, 88 L.Ed. 645. . . . 374 U.S., at 402–403, 83 S.Ct., at 1793.

This case, of course, is not one in which any harm to the physical or mental health of the child or to the public safety, peace, order, or

welfare has been demonstrated or may be properly inferred. The record is to the contrary, and any reliance on that theory would find no support in the evidence.   . . .

Our holding in no way determines the proper resolution of possible competing interests of parents, children, and the State in an appropriate state court proceeding in which the power of the State is asserted on the theory that Amish parents are preventing their minor children from attending high school despite their expressed desires to the contrary. Recognition of the claim of the State in such a proceeding would, of course, call into question traditional concepts of parental control over the religious upbringing and education of their minor children recognized in this Court's past decisions. It is clear that such an intrusion by a State into family decisions in the area of religious training would give rise to grave questions of religious freedom comparable to those raised here and those presented in *Pierce v. Society of Sisters,* 268 U.S. 510, 45 S.Ct. 571, 69 L.Ed. 1070 (1925). On this record we neither reach nor decide those issues.

The State's argument proceeds without reliance on any actual conflict between the wishes of parents and children. It appears to rest on the potential that exemption of Amish parents from the requirements of the compulsory-education law might allow some parents to act contrary to the best interests of their children by foreclosing their opportunity to make an intelligent choice between the Amish way of life and that of the outside world. The same argument could, of course, be made with respect to all church schools short of college. There is nothing in the record or in the ordinary course of human experience to suggest that non-Amish parents generally consult with children of ages fourteen to sixteen if they are placed in a church school of the parents' faith.

Indeed it seems clear that if the State is empowered, as *parens patriae,* to "save" a child from himself or his Amish parents by requiring an additional two years of compulsory formal high school education, the State will in large measure influence, if not determine, the religious future of the child. Even more markedly than in *Prince,* therefore, this case involves the fundamental interest of parents, as contrasted with that of the State, to guide the religious future and education of their children. The history and culture of Western civilization reflect a strong tradition of parental concern for the nurture and upbringing of their children. This primary role of the parents in the upbringing of their children is now established beyond debate as an enduring American tradition. . . . The record strongly indicates that accommodating the religious objections of the Amish by forgoing one, or at most two, additional years of compulsory education will not impair the physical or mental health of the child, or result in an inability to be self-supporting or to discharge the duties and responsibilities of citizenship, or in any other way materially detract from the welfare of society.

In the fact of our consistent emphasis on the central values underlying the Religion Clauses in our constitutional scheme of government, we cannot accept a *parens patriae* claim of such all-encompassing scope and with such sweeping potential for broad and unforeseeable application as that urged by the State.

For the reasons stated we hold, with the Supreme Court of Wisconsin, that the First and Fourteenth Amendments prevent the State from compelling respondents to cause their children to attend formal high school to age sixteen. Our disposition of this case, however, in no way alters our recognition of the obvious fact that courts are not school boards or legislatures, and are ill-equipped to determine the "necessity" of discrete aspects of a State's program of compulsory education. This should suggest that courts must move with great circumspection in performing the sensitive and delicate task of weighing a State's legitimate social concern when faced with religious claims for exemption from generally applicable educational requirements. It cannot be overemphasized that we are not dealing with a way of life and mode of education by a group claiming to have recently discovered some "progressive" or more enlightened process for rearing children for modern life.

Aided by a history of three centuries as an identifiable religious sect and a long history as a successful and self-sufficient segment of American society, the Amish in this case have convincingly demonstrated the sincerity of their religious beliefs, the interrelationship of belief with their mode of life, the vital role that belief and daily conduct play in the continued survival of Old Order Amish communities and their religious organization, and the hazards presented by the State's enforcement of a statute generally valid as to others. Beyond this, they have carried the even more difficult burden of demonstrating the adequacy of their alternative mode of continuing informal vocational education in terms of precisely those overall interests that the State advances in support of its program of compulsory high school education. In light of this convincing showing, one that probably few other religious groups or sects could make, and weighing the minimal difference between what the State would require and what the Amish already accept, it was incumbent on the State to show with more particularity how its admittedly strong interest in compulsory education would be adversely affected by granting an exemption to the Amish. . . .

Nothing we hold is intended to undermine the general applicability of the State's compulsory school-attendance statutes or to limit the power of the State to promulgate reasonable standards that, while not impairing the free exercise of religion, provide for continuing agricultural vocational education under parental and church guidance by the Old Order Amish or others similarly situated. The States have had a long history of amicable and effective relationships with church-sponsored schools, and there is no basis for assuming that, in this related context, reasonable standards cannot be established concerning the content of the continuing vocational education of Amish children under parental guidance, provided always that state regulations are not inconsistent with what we have said in this opinion.

Affirmed.

*State Justified in Denial of "Amish Exception"
to Baptist School*

———·—·———·—·———·—·———

Johnson v. Charles City
Community Schools Board
of Education

———·—·———·—·———·—·———

Supreme Court of Iowa, 1985. 368 N.W.2d 74.

Considered en banc.

HARRIS, Justice. Plaintiffs are the pastor and certain members of a fundamentalist Baptist church in Charles City. The controversy arose following their organization of a parochial school. The parents were charged with violating Iowa's compulsory attendance law, Iowa Code section 299.1 (1983). The section is quite typical in that it places the sanction for failure to attend on the parent rather than the child. The parents here responded by bringing two separate proceedings. One was a declaratory judgment action which challenged our statutory education requirements, not only the compulsory attendance statute but also certain reporting requirements in chapter 299. The second response was to apply to the state board of public instruction for relief under section 299.24, popularly called the Amish exception.

· · ·

The district court denied declaratory relief and affirmed on the administrative appeal. We agree with plaintiffs' contention that the religious freedoms guaranteed them under the first amendment entitle them to educate their children at the private religious school they have established. The same guarantees accord them the right to operate the school with minimal necessary supervision by the state. · · ·

Both challenges are rooted in the plaintiffs' deeply held religious beliefs. They perceive their school, which they describe as their "week day educational ministry," to be an integral part of the exercise of their religion. It is named Calvary Baptist Christian Academy.

When it was set up in the fall of 1980 the school was not incorporated separately from the church. The curriculum chosen, the Accelerated Christian Education Program, has not as yet been challenged as inadequate by any state authorities. At the bottom of this litigation is the fact that plaintiffs are unwilling to submit to any state inquiry on the matter. In their view, the educational content and process of their school, because it is so central to their religion, is not properly subject to state oversight. · · ·

According to the trial court's findings, beginning in the 19th century, there has been growing concern among Christian "fundamentalist" churches with what they consider to be the calamitous threat of secular humanism. The trial court pointed out in its findings:

· · ·

Iowa law does not require that all children attend public schools, reflecting a long tradition of friendly coexistence between private and public schools. · · · This accommodation, dating from the first years of our statehood, was reached at least three quarters of a century before the United States Supreme Court ruled that a state cannot compel all students to be educated in public schools. *Pierce v. Society of Sisters,* 268 U.S. 510, 45 S.Ct. 571, 69 L.Ed. 1070 (1925).

The *Pierce* opinion, however, carefully and expressly excluded from its sweep any limitation or curtailment of

> the power of the state reasonably to regulate all schools, to inspect, supervise, and examine them, their teachers and pupils; to require that all children of proper age attend some school, that teachers shall be of good moral character and patriotic disposition, that certain studies plainly essential to good citizenship must be taught, and that nothing be taught which is manifestly inimical to the public welfare.

268 U.S. at 534, 45 S.Ct. at 573, 69 L.Ed. at 1077.

The power thus acknowledged in the states to provide out of social necessity for minimum educational standards has enjoyed continuing endorsement in later opinions. · · · ("There is no doubt as to the power of a State, having a high responsibility for education of its citizens, to impose reasonable regulations for the control and duration of basic education."); *Lemon v. Kurtzman,* 403 U.S. 602, 614, 91 S.Ct. 2105, 2112, 29 L.Ed.2d 745, 756 (1971) ("[S]tate requirements under school-attendance laws are examples of necessary and permissible contact" between government and religious organizations, illustrating the impossibility of "total separation of [church and state] in an absolute sense."); *Sherbert v. Verner,* 374 U.S. 398, 403, 83 S.Ct. 1790, 1793, 10 L.Ed.2d 965, 970 (1963) (free exercise of religion may be subordinate to overriding, compelling state interest in regulation of proper subject). . . .

While the state authority to intrude into private religious schools is, as we shall point out, confined to a necessary minimum, a clear authority, even a duty, does exist.

The foregoing authorities also make it clear that first amendment considerations *limit* the extent to which a state can intrude into the educational affairs of a private religious school. Under *Pierce,* parents are free, notwithstanding compulsory education statutes, to provide for a private education in a religious forum of their own choosing. This fundamental right would be hollow to the point of nonexistence if the state were to so closely superintend the school as to compromise its religious independence. . . .

In their appellate brief and upon oral submission of their appeal the plaintiffs, as mentioned, suggest that their position of absolute and total rejection of any public regulation can and should be accommodated by Iowa's educational scheme. Yet they concede the general right of the public to demand education for all its children. Plaintiffs suggest that the public could satisfy its rightful role while at the same time protecting plaintiffs' first amendment rights by merely testing the children.

We reject the suggestion because it does not do enough for the children. To merely test the children, as we shall explain in a later division, does not satisfy the state's rightful role. Whatever limitations are imposed on the state's general right and duty to see to the education of its youth, the right extends beyond occasional testing. It plainly extends

to such matters as basic parameters for curriculum and teacher qualifications. . . .

A principal difficulty in plaintiffs' assertion is that anyone can make it, not only high-minded and sincere people, but also a host of others whose childrens' educations also are at stake.

The state has a clear right to set minimum educational standards for all its children and a corresponding responsibility to see to it that those standards are honored. When such standards are set in place, compliance with them falls within the ambit of the fundamental contract between the citizen and society. It need scarcely be said that each of us, in order to enjoy membership in an organized social order, is pledged to adhere to a number of minimum norms. Of these, one of the most central is society's duty to educate its children.

The nature and extent of education remain largely a matter of personal choice. But there are basic minimums and, this being true, it is up to the people as a whole to set them. One way they have done this is to enact compulsory education statutes. A citizen must submit to them, persuade society to change them, or join a society without them. . . .

It is enough here to reject the challenge plaintiffs do raise. We reject it because the state can reasonably regulate the basic educational requirements of all children within its borders. The state can inquire into private educational institutions in order to see this is done. . . .

It remains for us to consider plaintiffs' appeal from the district court decision on judicial review. . . .

This was the proceeding in which plaintiffs sought a determination that their school should escape state control under section 299.24, the Amish exception.

This provision was noted in *Wisconsin v. Yoder,* 406 U.S. at 208, 92 S.Ct. at 1529, 32 L.Ed.2d at 21 n. 3, as Iowa's resolution of the conflict between compulsory education and the uniquely isolated Amish culture in our midst. Under section 299.24 certain religious societies can apply to the state superintendent for an exemption from the compulsory attendance laws. Upon being satisfied the requirements of the statute are met the superintendent, subject to the approval of the state board of public instruction, may, but is not required to, grant the exemption.

The district court quoted the material parts of section 299.24 as follows:

> When members or representatives of a local congregation of a reorganized church . . . established for ten years or more within the State of Iowa prior to July 1, 1967, which professes principles or tenets that differ substantially from the objectives, goals, and philosophy of education embodied in the standards set forth in section 257.25, and rules adopted in implementation thereof. . . .

The board of education denied the application in the belief there was no essential conflict between plaintiffs' legitimate educational goals and those specified in section 257.25. Section 257.25 specifies in considerable detail the educational standards for public schools in Iowa. The district court held there was nothing unreasonable, arbitrary, or capricious in the denial. It also held the denial did not render section 299.24 unconstitutional as applied to the plaintiffs.

Plaintiffs' administrative appeal challenges both of these determinations. Plaintiffs contend they fall within the ambit of the statute's language and hence qualify for the exemption. They also contend it is unconstitutional to deny them the exemption. Our scope of review differs for the two contentions. . . .

In view of the historical background for section 299.24 (the plaintiffs themselves call it the "Amish exception") we do not think the legislature intended the exemption to be available to any and all church groups who seek to provide for a religiously oriented education. If this had been the legislative goal a much broader statute would have been required. . . . plainly, all parochial schools in the state are not intended for the exemption. The statute calls, not for a religious evaluation by the superintendent, but for an analysis of the educational goals of the group applying for exemptions and a comparison of those goals with those set up for public school children. Because of the con-

viction that religion is the basis for education, held by these plaintiffs and by all who support parochial education, the superintendent faces a mixed and somewhat complex question.

To obtain an exemption under section 299.24, plaintiffs had to prove their church "professes principles or tenets that differ substantially from the objectives, goals, and philosophy of education embodied in standards set forth in section 257.25, and rules adopted in implementation thereof . . . ." As this provision has been interpreted and applied in this case, the "standards" in section 257.25 consist entirely of the listing in subsections 257.25(3) and (4) of subjects that must be taught in grades one through eight. No relevant implementing rules are involved. Therefore plaintiffs could establish their right to an exemption only if their church professes principles or tenets that differ substantially from the "objectives, goals, and philosophy of education" embodied in the areas of study listed in subsections (3) and (4) of section 257.25.

Plaintiffs offered no evidence that any principle or tenet of their church is in conflict with teaching the subjects listed in the statute. Rather, they insisted only that their church be able to teach those subjects in its own way with books and teachers of its own exclusive choice. Nothing in section 257.25, as interpreted and applied here, would deny them that opportunity. Thus the state board cannot be said to have acted unreasonably, arbitrarily or capriciously in rejecting their exemption request.

What prevents plaintiffs from having their way is not any objective, goal or philosophy of education embodied in section 257.25, but the requirement in section 299.1 that their church employ only certified teachers. Their church's opposition to that requirement, however, is not made a basis for obtaining an exemption under section 299.24. They must look to section 257.25, not section 299.1, to establish their right to exemption.

We conclude, giving due and required deference to the administrative findings of the superintendent, that the plaintiffs have not established any substantial dissimilarity between their educational goals and those specified for public schools, certainly none which sets them apart from all the many other parochial schools in the state. . . .

We next consider the first of two constitutional facets of plaintiffs' challenge to the administrative denial of their application for an Amish exemption. They first argue it was a violation of their first amendment rights to deny them the exemption.

Section 299.24 was our legislature's response to precisely the same concerns later involved in *Wisconsin v. Yoder*. The statute, its subject, purpose, meaning, and application are fully explained in the *Yoder* opinion.

The United States Supreme Court employed a balancing test to weigh the acknowledged and valid public interest in imposing reasonable regulations and minimum educational standards against the fundamental right of the Amish to direct the religious upbringing of their children. A number of factors were considered in the weighing:

1. The sincerity of their commitment to a long established religion;
2. An intricate and crucial interrelationship between those beliefs and their mode of life;
3. The vital role their beliefs and life mode play in the survival of Amish culture;
4. The hazards of enforcing compulsory education laws against them; and
5. The adequacy, in terms of their peculiar needs, of the informal vocational education provided to their youth past the eighth grade.

The court found that the state failed to show how, on balance, its legitimate interest in assuring educated and self-reliant citizens justified a requirement that Amish children attend school for two additional years (past eighth grade) in contravention of their religious beliefs. The state moreover failed to prove that exempting the Amish from two additional years of education would seriously curtail the efficient operation of their school laws.

When the same factors are placed in balance on this record the opposite conclusion asserts itself. Sincerity of belief is the only

factor wholly common to both the Amish and these plaintiffs. The beliefs of the plaintiffs are greatly less interwoven with their daily mode of life. The Amish culture is greatly more isolated from mainstream American life. Plaintiffs' children, for all the distinctive religious convictions they will be given, will live, compete for jobs, work, and move about in a diverse and complex society. Their educational needs are plainly not as circumscribed as those of Amish children. Neither does exposure to the more general American culture pose such an immediate threat to plaintiffs' mode of living as is the case with the Amish.

Whatever they may feel about their children's religious needs, the plaintiffs have not established that their children's educational needs are significantly different from those of other children. The superintendent's determination not to grant plaintiffs an Amish exception did not infringe upon their religious rights under the first amendment.

Plaintiffs also ground their appeal from the decision on judicial review upon an equal protection claim. . . .

On an equal protection challenge the first question is whether some fundamental right is involved. The answer determines the burden to be borne by the challenger. . . . Without doubt, and plaintiffs agree, the state has a compelling interest in educating its youth.
. . .

For reasons we have already explained we think this vital state interest is served by the classification. Education is of transcendent importance to all children. . . .

The educational needs of the children involved here are, as we have said, much different and much greater than the needs of Amish children. Even at school age there is much greater mixing by these children in general society. Some church members send their children to other schools, a matter which would ostracize children from Amish culture.
. . .

The principal difference is to consider the world for which the children here will have to be prepared. They will have to compete with well-educated children, will associate with them in a society very different from the simple, rural, and largely isolated one that lies ahead for Amish children. The state was fully justified in the classification. The equal protection challenge is rejected.   . . .

Affirmed.

NOTE

1. *Religious Exemption.* The Virginia compulsory attendance statute provides that "[a] school board . . . [s]hall excuse from attendance at school any pupil who, together with his parents, by reason of *bona fide* religious training or belief, is conscientiously opposed to attendance at school." This statutory provision also states, "The term *bona fide* religious training or belief does not include essentially political, sociological, or philosophical views or merely a personal moral code." The Virginia Supreme Court ruled a school board did not need to state the reasons for denying a religious exemption. *Johnson v. Prince William County School Board,* 404 S. E. 2d 209 (Va. 1991).

Home Instruction

The state may compel all children to attend a school, public or private, and home instruction will not suffice as an exemption from compulsory attendance requirements unless state statute so specifies. The rationale for subordinating a parent's desire to keep his or her child at home to the state's interest in compelling the child to attend a school is best summarized by Butts and Cremin:

> Clearly, the child has a right to education. If governments are instituted among men to secure to all enjoyment of their rights, then what objection could be raised to the government compelling parents and guardians to send their children to school?[57]

To allow parents, at will, to nullify the effects of compulsory attendance laws would have not only a detrimental effect on society as a whole, but, importantly, would allow the parent to limit and restrict the ultimate development and future prospects of the child. In this regard parents find themselves in the difficult position of arguing that less opportunity is preferable to more opportunity.

Assuming that parents could provide as thoroughly comprehensive and varied a curriculum at home as at school, courts still may hold that having the child physically in school with other children is a valuable socialization process, the fostering of which is in the state's interest and for which home instruction cannot be an adequate substitute.

Several states refuse to allow home instruction because it is believed that the sequestration of children in the home, insulated from society and other children, will inhibit social consciousness and prevent the child from living a normal and productive life. A New Jersey court has said that "Cloister and shelter have their place, but not in the everyday give and take of life."[58]

Moreover, a legislature's denial of home instruction does not violate equal protection of the Fourteenth Amendment. A New Mexico court has held that the state need only to show that such denial is rationally related to a legitimate state purpose. The state's desire to have children attend school with other children of their age is an appropriate and defensible state interest. This court said, "By bringing children into contact with some person, other than those in the excluded group, those children are exposed to at least one other set of attitudes, values, morals, lifestyles and intellectual abilities."[59]

An Oregon appellate court has held that the state does not violate equal protection when it distinguishes between children taught by parents or a private teacher in home instruction, and those taught in a private school. The state may clearly have a rational basis for such distinctions.[60]

In states that permit home instruction, the key elements in determining the validity of home instruction are generally the educational level of the parents and the regularity and time of instruction. Obviously, states permitting home instruction must prescribe certain minimal standards for such instruction or their compulsory attendance laws would be nullified.

Courts will uphold reasonable state criteria to qualify for exemption from compulsory attendance. Where a statute provided that parents show a "manifest educational hardship," it was not sufficient that parents show merely the one criterion of manifest educational hardship to validly qualify for exemption from compulsory attendance. A state board of education may require adherence to one or more of the criteria, such as the competency of parents to teach, the scope of the subject matter, the child's potential for interaction with peers and adults, and the teaching methods to be employed, before the exemption is considered valid.[61]

An early Washington case rejected the home as a private school. In that case, the parent claimed his home instruction was authorized by a statute providing that children must attend "the public school of the district in which the child resides, for the full time such school may be in session, or . . . attend a private school for the same time." The parent further claimed that he was a qualified and competent teacher giving home instruction within the definition to the statute. This claim was rejected by the court, which explained:

> We do not think that the giving of instruction by a parent to a child, conceding the competency of the parent to fully instruct the child in all that is taught in the public schools, is within the meaning of the law "to attend a private school." Such a requirement means more than home instruction; it means that the same character of school as the public school, a regular, organized and existing institution making a business of instructing children of school age in the required studies and for the full time required by the laws of this state. . . . There may be a difference in institution and government, but the purpose and end of both public and private schools must be the same—the education of children of school age. The parent who teaches his children at home, whatever be his reason for desiring to do so, does not maintain such a school.[62]

Home instruction has been rejected because of difficulty of supervision. The state bears the responsibility of reasonable supervision to guarantee that students obtain an adequate education. If home instruction imposes an unreasonable burden on the state's performance of its duties, the instruction is not allowed. For example, a situation may exist where parents use education units so small or facilities of such doubtful quality that supervision creates an unusual expense for the state. The state requires that proper educational facilities be provided for the child and supplied in a way that the state can ascertain facts about the instructional program and maintain proper direction without undue cost.[63]

Critics have charged that home instruction does not comply with statutory requirements that a child attend a public, private, denominational, or parochial school and be taught by a competent instructor. In Kansas, the legislature reenacted a compulsory attendance law, leaving out a former provision for home instruction as a valid exemption from compulsory attendance. The court said that exclusion of home instruction, while including private, denominational, and parochial school instruction as valid, indicated legislative intent to disallow home instruction as an excuse for nonattendance.[64]

Another Kansas case distinguished between a "private school" and "scheduled home instruction." Here parents operated a "school," serving as tutors themselves, with only their own children in attendance. The only grades taught were those in which their own children were enrolled. The court interpreted this as falling short of the definition of a private school, and ruled that the instruction given did not meet statutory requirements. In the view of the court, the program was nothing more than "home instruction."[65]

Where reference to home instruction was excluded from the statute, a California court refused to officially regard home instruction programs as qualified "private schools."[66]

Other cases, however, have established that home instruction may constitute "private school" instruction in contemplation of the law. For example, a parent who employs a competent, noncertified school teacher to instruct his child in the same curriculum and for the same period of time as the public schools is complying with the law which requires instruction in a public, private, or parochial school.[67] In commenting on this situation, the court said:

> The law was made for the parent who does not educate his child, and not for the parent who employs a teacher and pays him out of his private purse, and so places within the reach of the child the opportunity and means of acquiring an education equal to that obtainable in the public schools of the State.

In summary, if a state statute allows for home instruction as an alternative to compulsory attendance, the burden falls on the state to show that the parent is not, in fact, providing such instruction. If the state has set out few standards governing home instruction, the inadequacy of such instruction may be difficult to prove. The state must produce evidence documenting the parent's failure to furnish adequate home instruction, and the parent must respond to such evidence.[68] However, the final burden of proof rests on the state to show that the instruction failed to meet state requirements.[69]

State's Use of Achievement Tests to Monitor Home Instruction Is Constitutionally Valid

– – · – · – – · – –

Murphy v. State of Arkansas

– – · – · – – · – –

United States Court of Appeals, Eighth Circuit, 1988. 852 F.2d 1039.

HEANEY, Circuit Judge. Appellants challenge the decision of the district court upholding the constitutionality of the Arkansas Home School Act, Ark. Code Ann. §§ 6-15-501 – 6-15-507. We affirm the decision of the district court.

Doty and Phyllis Murphy are evangelical Christians who believe that "Christian Scriptures require parents to take personal responsibility for every aspect of their children's training and education." They have six children, ages four through eighteen. The Murphys educate their children at home, providing an "education that is pervasively religious in nature and which does not conflict with the religious beliefs they hold, based upon their understanding of the scriptures."

Under Arkansas law, a parent must educate her children through the age of sixteen. This requirement may be satisfied by sending the child to public, private, or parochial school or by educating the child at home. The Arkansas Home School Act, Ark.Code Ann. §§ 6-15-501 – 6-15-507, requires parents intending to school their children at home to notify in writing the superintendent of their local school district prior to the commencement of each school year. The notice must provide information concerning the name, age, and grade of each student, the core curriculum to be offered, the schedule of instruction and the qualifications of the person teaching. The parent must also agree to submit the children to standardized achievement tests each year and, when the children reach the age of fourteen, to a minimum performance test. All of these tests are administered, interpreted, and acted upon by the Arkansas Department of Education. Finally, the parent must provide any information to the superintendent which might indicate the need for special educational services for the children.

The achievement test administered to a student schooled at home is chosen by the parent from a list of nationally recognized tests provided by the director of the State Department of Education or the director's designee. The parent may be present when the standardized test is administered, but both parent and student are under the supervision of a test administrator. The results of the standardized tests are used for several purposes. Most significantly, if a home school student does not achieve a composite score within eight months of grade level in designated subjects, the student must be placed in a public, private, or parochial school. No such annual testing is required for students in public, private, or parochial schools. If children not schooled at home are, for some reason, tested, no remedial placement is required for those who do not achieve certain scores.

The Murphys allege that the Arkansas statutory scheme deprives them of the right to free exercise of religion, the right of due process of law, the right of equal protection of the laws, and the right of privacy and parental liberty in violation of the United States Constitution. The Murphys brought an action for a declaratory judgment in federal district court. That court awarded judgment to the state.

The Free Exercise Clause

The Murphys assert that Ark.Code Ann. § 6-15-504, requiring that a standardized test be given to their children under the supervision of a test administrator deprives them of the right to free exercise of religion as guaranteed by the first amendment. They argue that the irreligious beliefs require they must be *completely* responsible for *every* aspect of their children's education. In contrast, the Arkansas Home School Act places responsibility for testing and interpreting test results with the State of Arkansas, rather than with the parents.

To determine whether governmental conduct infringes upon an individual's first amendment free exercise rights, a court must first inquire whether the challenged governmental action interferes with the claimant's "sincerely held religious beliefs." Second, if such a belief is interfered with, the court must determine whether the governmental action is the least restrictive means of achieving some compelling governmental interest. . . .

In the case before us, the parties have stipulated that the testing requirements of the Arkansas law interfere with the Murphys' sincerely held religious beliefs. Thus, we will go no further in examining the subtleties of the Murphys' beliefs. Consequently, the resolution of the free exercise claim involves answering two related questions: First, does the state have a compelling interest in the education of all children? Second, if so, is the Arkansas statutory scheme the least restrictive means of achieving that objective? We believe that the answer to both of these questions is yes.

The government has a compelling interest in educating all of its citizens. Education of the citizenry is and always has been a preeminent goal of American society. Reaching back through the collective memory of the Republic, the fundamental importance of education in the design of our system of government rapidly becomes clear. Article III of the Northwest Ordinance states in part: "Religion, morality, and knowledge being necessary to good government and the happiness of mankind, schools and the means of education shall forever be encouraged." In *Yoder*, the Supreme Court adopted Thomas Jefferson's often expressed belief that education was a "bulwark" against tyranny. . . .

> Thomas Jefferson pointed out early in our history, that some degree of education is necessary to prepare citizens to participate effectively and intelligently in our open political system if we are to preserve freedom and independence. Further, education prepares individuals to be self-reliant and self-sufficient participants in society.

406 U.S. at 221, 92 S.Ct. at 1536.

The fundamental importance of education in terms of access and achievement in American society was further underscored by the Court in *Brown v. Board of Education* . . . .

It is the very foundation of good citizenship. Today it is a principal instrument in awakening the child to cultural values, in preparing him for later professional training, and in helping him to adjust normally to his environment. In these days, it is doubtful that any child may reasonably be expected to succeed in life if he is denied the opportunity of an education. . . .

Thus, as the district court correctly noted, it is "settled beyond dispute, as a legal matter, that the state has a compelling interest in ensuring that all its citizens are being adequately educated."

Given the existence of a compelling governmental interest, we must next inquire whether Arkansas' home testing system is the least restrictive means to achieve that purpose. In doing so, we recognize that the state must have a mechanism by which it can confidently and objectively be assured that its citizens are being adequately educated.

Upon examination, it would appear that Arkansas has created the least restrictive system possible to assure its goal. By providing the option of home schooling, Arkansas allows parents vast responsibility and accountability in terms of their children's education — control far in excess of limitations on religious rights that have been previously upheld. . . . Arkansas requires neither that the parent instructing the home-schooled child be a certified teacher nor that the parent follow a mandated curriculum. The state's only safeguard to ensure adequate training of the home-schooled student is the standardized achievement test. Even regarding this test, the state allows wide latitude to the parents. The parent may choose a test administered from a list of nationally recognized standard achievement tests and may be present while the test is administered.

Finally, the Murphys make no showing, as made by the Amish in *Yoder,* that the state can be assured its interest will be attained if appellants' religious beliefs are accommodated. We reject the Murphys' argument that parental "testing" of children provides a sufficient safeguard to assure the state's interest in education is protected. Likewise, parental affidavits concerning the children's progress would also be insufficient. In the end, we believe that the state has no means less restrictive than its administration of achievement tests to ensure that its citizens are being properly educated.

Equal Protection

The Murphys argue that the Arkansas Home School Act violates the equal protection clause of the fourteenth amendment. Specifically, they claim that those who school their children at home for religious reasons are a suspect class or that parental control over a child's education involves a fundamental right. . . . Thus, the Murphys contend that the state appears irrationally to allow parents to educate their children in religious private schools without any state regulatory

supervision but subjects children schooled at home to the various requirements of the Home School Act.

While home school families impelled by deep-seated religious convictions might be the type of "discrete and insular minorit[y]" . . . , the broad secular category of individuals who prefer to school their children at home is not. Clearly, the statute is aimed at this second category of individuals.

It could be argued that the statute, while superficially neutral, has a discriminatory impact on the category of deeply religious individuals impelled by their convictions to school their children at home. Yet, even if such discriminatory impact were shown — which it has not been — this would not be sufficient to invoke strict scrutiny. The Murphys would still bear the burden of proving discriminatory purpose or intent. . . . Because no such showing of either discriminatory impact or discriminatory intent has been made, strict scrutiny analysis is inappropriate here.

Second, we find no persuasive arguments advanced that there is a fundamental right of parents to supervise their children's education to the extent that the Murphys contend. The recognition of such a right would fly directly in the face of those cases in which the Supreme Court has recognized the broad power of the state to compel school attendance and regulate curriculum and teacher certification. . . . Thus, again, strict scrutiny cannot be invoked in this case.

Given that strict scrutiny analysis does not apply, we move to the question of whether Arkansas has a rational reason to subject home schooling to regulatory requirements, while at the same time freeing private schools from virtually any regulation. This step by the legislature in Arkansas may at first glance offend common sense, and, sitting as a legislature, we might not have made this same decision. However, our job is *not* to sit as a legislature and the constitutional standard of rationality under the equal protection clause is a relaxed one. In this area of the law, the Supreme Court has declared its willingness to uphold any classification based "upon [any] state of facts that reasonably can be conceived to constitute a distinction, or difference in state policy . . . ."

We believe that such a state of facts exists here. First, it could be argued that the notion of an actual independent school, away from home, implies more formality and structure than a home school. This could lead the state to believe that more serious instruction would be occurring there than in the relaxed atmosphere of a child and parents in their own home. Second, the notion that more than one family is likely to be sending their children to the private school may provide an additional objective indication of the private school's quality that is not present in the context of individual home schools. Finally, unlike a home-school, parents sending a child to a private school have to pay money for education, and, hence, would be more likely to demand their money's worth of instructional quality from the private school. All these possibilities together could provide Arkansas with a passable reason for the challenged distinction under the minimum rationality standards of the equal protection clause.

Right of Privacy

The Murphys argue that the right of privacy should be extended to protect parental decisions concerning the direction of a child's education from state interference. . . .

> The Court has repeatedly stressed that while parents have a constitutional right to send their children to private schools and a constitutional right to select private schools that offer specialized instruction, they have no constitutional right to provide their children with private school education unfettered by reasonable government regulation. . . . Indeed, the Court in *Pierce* expressly acknowledged "the power of the State reasonably to regulate all schools, to inspect, supervise and examine them, their teachers and pupils."

427 U.S. at 178, 96 S.Ct. at 2598 (citations omitted).

The Supreme Court has spoken clearly on this issue, and we are bound by its decision. Moreover, we agree with the Court's reasoning and its conclusion. We thus decline to extend the right of privacy to this situation.

For the foregoing reasons, the decision of the district court is affirmed.

NOTES

1. The state statutory requirement that a child being educated at home be taught by a person who is legally certified does not offend a parent's religious beliefs. The court held that the state had a compelling interest in the education of children and the requirement of teacher certification was among the least personally intrusive methods available to satisfy that interest. *State v. Melin,* 428 N.W.2d 227 (N.D. 1988).

   This same court had earlier held the requirement of teacher certification did constitute a burden on the parents' religious freedom, but in balancing the parents' religious interests against the compelling interest of the state, certification was among the least intrusive means of satisfying that interest in education. *State v. Patzer,* 382 N.W.2d 631 (N.D. 1986).

2. Parents of children enrolled in home instruction program in Indiana showed unusual vehemence against public school authority when filing an action for monetary damages against a school superintendent for his attempts to gain information from the parents to verify compliance with a home instruction law. The court held in denying the damages that the parents had frustrated attempts to verify their compliance and that the superintendent exhibited no hostility toward the parents in seeking to obtain adherence to the law. *Mazanec v. North Judson–San Pierre School Corporation,* 798 F.2d 230 (7th Cir. 1986).

Other Reasons for Nonattendance

Litigation regarding exceptions from school attendance are usually of two types. The first involves the aforementioned cases in which parents seek exemption for their children from school attendance in favor of private school or home instruction, or perhaps, of no formal education at all. The second common source of litigation emanates from simple truancy wherein children merely fail to attend school without offering or claiming alternative forms of education.

Excessive Absences

Excused absences from school must be authorized by statute or regulation and usually allow for a reasonable number of days of nonattendance for illness, family emergency, educational travel, medical appointments, or approved school activities. To violate such rules may result in an action against parents for failure to see that the child is attending school. A situation illustrative of such a case emanated from an action in a Maryland case where two women, each with two children, allowed the children to miss a total of seventy school days. The state sought conviction of the women for violation of the compulsory attendance laws. The women defended, claiming their constitutional rights of due process were violated because the law imposed "strict liability" by prosecuting parents for actions of their children. The court held that the law, on the contrary, did not prosecute parents for the failure of their children; but prosecuted them for their own failure to see that their children attended school. Performance of such an affirmative duty as imposed by the law is offended by "passive acquiescence (by the parent) in the child's nonattendance of school."[70]

Travel

Parental insistency on taking their children from school for no authorized purpose may be grounds for conviction under attendance laws. In one such case, school board policy limited excused absences for educational trips to one trip per year not to exceed five days. The parents of four children had already expended leave time on a trip to Washington, D.C., and later requested additional time to travel to Europe. The school refused permission; the parents took the children and departed for Europe anyway. Upon the family's return, the school filed a truancy action

against the parents that led to conviction. The appellate court upheld the lower court, concluding that the discretionary authority over such matters rested with the local school board.[71]

Students themselves cannot be punished for truancy if the state law only imposes penalties against parents. In a Washington case, the court reversed a truancy fine against students because the state statute provided that "parents, guardians, and the persons in this state having custody . . . shall cause such child to attend . . . school." Under such a law, which is typical of most states, failure of the students to attend school may result in orders, fines, and contempt citations against the parents of truants, but not against the truants themselves.[72]

Illness

Parents who claim that their child is ill and cannot attend school must show valid medical proof of illness. An Illinois case illustrates how a claim of illness may well result in a charge of truancy. Under Illinois law, a child is considered to be truant if absent without "valid cause," which is defined as illness, death in the immediate family, a family emergency, or other circumstances that cause concern to the parent for the child's health or safety. In this case, the student was absent from school for 339½ days during a two-year period. Testimony from the student's doctor indicated that he had conducted tests and found that the child had certain allergies, but these were not of such magnitude to warrant absences from school. Having no other proof of illness to justify the noncompliance with the law, the parents' conviction was upheld.[73]

Marriage

Exemption from compulsory attendance is a dubious benefit of marriage, yet courts have agreed that when a minor of less than sixteen years (otherwise required to attend school) is married, he or she is usually exempt from further compulsory attendance.

One of the precedents in this area was rendered by the Supreme Court of Louisiana. A fifteen-year-old girl and her husband sought to set aside a judgment of a lower court committing her to the State Industrial School for Girls as a result of her truancy and alleged juvenile delinquency.[74] The girl did not deny truancy but claimed that her legal marriage exempted her from attendance. Although marriage of a female under sixteen years of age was prohibited by law, the court ruled that once a girl is married, she enjoys the status of wife and has a right to live as such, emancipated from both school and parents. The court stated:

> The marriage relationship, regardless of the age of the persons involved, creates conditions and imposes obligations upon the parties that are obviously inconsistent with compulsory school attendance or with either the husband or wife remaining under the legal control of parents or other persons.

In another Louisiana case, a truant, neglected girl of fourteen was married only a few days after the truant officer had taken her into custody.[75] The lower court committed the girl to a state girls' school for an indefinite period of time. The judge, exercising *parens patriae,* was of the opinion that the girl needed the care and protection of the state. The Supreme Court of Louisiana, while sympathetically viewing the judge's concern for the girl's welfare, held that the lower juvenile court could not commit her to the girls' school or prevent her from assuming the responsibilities of a married woman. The court stated that the power of such public policy determinations rested with the legislature and not the court.

A New York court followed the rationale of these two cases. In one of the cases a girl resisted attempts to force her to attend school because she was married and wanted to be a housewife and homemaker.[76] The court, while recognizing the state's sovereignty concerning compulsory attendance, decided for the girl, observing that times and mores had changed since the compulsory attendance law was passed. The court expressed doubt that the legislature had anticipated the question of such youthful marriage in passing the law.

In the eyes of the law, then, youthful marriage is a valid exemption from compulsory attendance laws. Effectively, marriage removes both state and parental control over minors. Consequently, married minors have the choice and the right to decide on their own further education.

VACCINATION

To protect the health and welfare of citizens, states have required school children to be vaccinated. Courts have generally held that, if a parent violates a statute requiring vaccination, the parent is subject to arrest or fine, even if he or she claims religious, conscientious, or scientific objections.

In 1905, the United States Supreme Court held that a board of health requirement that all persons in Cambridge, Massachusetts, be vaccinated did not violate personal liberties found under the Fourteenth Amendment. In this case, the Court noted that "the liberty secured by the Constitution of the United States to every person within its jurisdiction does not impart an absolute right on each person to be, at all times and in all circumstances, wholly freed from restraint. There are manifold restraints to which every person is necessarily subject for the common good."[77]

Although this particular decision directly challenged the vaccination regulation rather than compulsory attendance, the Supreme Court,[78] nevertheless, cited several state court decisions approving state statutes and making vaccination of children a condition of the right to attend public schools.[79]

In *Viemeister v. White,*[80] a turn-of-the-century New York decision, the appellant argued that vaccination not only did not prevent smallpox but tended instead to bring on other harmful diseases. The court, while not ruling that vaccination was a smallpox preventive, nevertheless maintained that laymen and physicians alike commonly believed that it did prevent smallpox. The court concluded that, even if it could not be conclusively proved that the vaccination was a preventive, in our republican form of government the legislature has the right to pass laws based on common belief and the will of the people to promote health and welfare.

Is a parent guilty of violating the compulsory attendance law, then, if he sends his child to school without vaccination and the child is sent home by school authorities? Answering this question in the affirmative, a New York court said that attendance at a public school imposes certain conditions on a child. These requirements must be met in order for the child to attend. However, the court went on to say that under the public health law, vaccination was required only for children attending public schools not private schools. The parent could offer private equivalent education to the child and avoid vaccination. Here, however, the parent had not provided equivalent education and was, therefore, subject to penalty under the compulsory attendance law.[81]

In an earlier New York case, little tolerance was evidenced for parents who used vaccination as an excuse to prevent their children's attendance in public schools.

It is obvious that a parent should not be allowed to escape his duty to send his children to school as provided by law on any excuse which is not an ample justification for such course. Our public school system has been developed with great pains and solicitude, and its maintenance and support have been recognized as so important for the welfare of the state that they have been provided for and safeguarded in the Constitution itself. As a part of this system a statute has been passed requiring attendance at school of children within certain limits. If indifferent or selfish parents, for ulterior purposes, such as the desire to place young children at labor, instead of school, or from capricious or recalcitrant motives, may be allowed to manufacture easy excuses for not sending their children to school, a ready method will have been developed for evading the statute compelling such attendance, and, if the statute requires parents to see to it that their children attend and take advantage of this school system may be lightly and easily evaded, the purposes of the state in providing and insisting on education will be frustrated and impaired. Failure to comply with the statute ought not to be excused, except for some good reason.[82]

The earlier cases concerning school vaccinations were not generally related to First Amendment religious protections. As observed above, the Supreme Court did not clarify the application of the "no state" provision of the Fourteenth Amendment until 1940, in *Cantwell v. Connecticut*.[83] The precedent of religious exemption from compulsory attendance, established in *Yoder*,[84] holds implications for cases involving religious freedom from vaccination. At this time, though, the precedents indicate that statutes requiring vaccination do not violate the free exercise of religion.

Parents in *State v. Drew* refused to have their child vaccinated, giving reasons as "partly religious and partly because they did not want that poison injected into their child." The Supreme Court of New Hampshire upheld the parents' conviction for violating the compulsory attendance law and said:

The defendant's individual ideas, whether "conscientious," "religious," or "scientific" do not appear to be more than opinions. . . . The defendant's views cannot affect the validity of the statute or entitle him to be excepted from its provisions. . . . It is for the Legislature, not for him or for us, to determine the question of policy involved in public health regulations.[85]

Where an epidemic is imminent, there is no question concerning the state's power to protect the citizenry by requiring vaccination. However, when there is no evidence of the imminence of an epidemic, how do the courts view the issue? Can the state's requirement of vaccination be a reasonable and permissible restraint on constitutional rights in the absence of epidemic?

In *Maas*,[86] the defendant argued that compulsory vaccination and immunization were not needed because there had been no smallpox or diphtheria for almost a decade. The court disagreed and ruled that the absence of an emergency does not warrant a denial of the exercise of preventive means. The court said, "A local board of education need not await an epidemic, or even a single sickness or death, before it decides to protect the public. To hold otherwise would be to destroy prevention as a means of combating the spread of disease."

Likewise, in *Stull v. Reber*,[87] the fact that there had been no smallpox in the borough for forty years did not prevent enforcement of the compulsory vaccination regulation. Health authorities were not required to wait for an epidemic before acting. [88] Neither does the fact that an epidemic has already started to prevent compulsory vaccination.[89]

If the state board of health enacts a compulsory vaccination regulation made pursuant to statute, the general statutory requirements requiring all pupils to comply with law are sufficient grounds for the board of education to enforce the statute.[90]

All the aforementioned cases contested duly promulgated board rules that were enacted pursuant to state statutes. However, where no statute exists to empower school or health boards to pass compulsory vaccination regulations, the issues shift quite drastically. A board cannot enact regulations unless they are based on existing statutes. Where the board acts regardless of statute, the act is *ultra vires* (in excess of legal authority). Further, a board

rule restricting school attendance cannot prevail over a legislative act granting free unlimited admittance to public schools.

Accordingly, two Illinois courts have decided that in the absence of a compulsory vaccination statute, an unvaccinated child cannot be denied a public education.[91] In both of these cases, however, it appeared that the school boards made little effort to draw enabling implications from health or education statutes.

In summary, one can reasonably draw several conclusions regarding compulsory attendance and vaccination: (1) The legislature has power to enact a statute providing for vaccination and including a penalty for noncompliance. (2) Neither the parent nor the child has a constitutional right to schooling without complying with the statutory requirement of vaccination. (3) A parent cannot escape conviction for failing to have his child vaccinated by demanding that the child be admitted to school unvaccinated. (4) Religious objection has not generally prevented enforcement of compulsory vaccination and attendance requirements.

◼◼◼◼ ENDNOTES

1. Griffin v. County School Board of Prince Edward County, 377 U.S. 218, 84 S.Ct. 1226 (1964).

2. Plyler v. Doe, 457 U.S. 202, 102 S.Ct. 2382 (1982).

3. In the Matter of Proios, 111 Misc.2d 252, 443 N.Y.S.2d 828 (Sur.1981).

4. Martinez v. Bynum, 461 U.S. 321, 103 S.Ct. 1838 (1983).

5. Inhabitants of Warren v. Inhabitants of Thomaston, 43 Me. 406 (1857).

6. C. Vann Woodward, *Origins of the New South, 1877–1913* (Baton Rouge, La.: Louisiana State University Press, 1971), pp. 416–17.

7. *Manufacturer's Record*, XLII (August 28, 1902), pp. 93–95.

8. Milton and Rose Friedman, *Free to Choose* (New York: Harcourt Brace Jovanovich, 1980), pp. 162–63.

9. S. G. Messmer, "Compulsory Education," *American Ecclesiastical Review* 6 (1892): 279–98.

10. Ibid.

11. R. Freeman Butts and Lawrence A. Cremin, *A History of Education in American Culture* (New York: Henry Holt and Company, 1953), pp. 357–58.

12. 347 U.S. 483, 74 S.Ct. 686 (1954).

13. Acts of Assembly, Chapter 2, p. 4, (1959), repealing Virginia Code 1950 § 22.251 to 22–275.

14. See Chapter 10, "Desegregation," of this book for more detail on desegregation; see also A. E. Dick Howard, *Commentaries on the Constitution of Virginia* (Charlottesville, Va.: University Press of Virginia, 1974), Vol. II, p. 893.

15. Strangway v. Allen, 194 Ky. 681, 240 S.W. 384 (1922).

16. County of McLean v. Humphrey, 104 Ill. 378 (1882).

17. In re Gault, 387 U.S. 1, 87 S.Ct. 1428 (1967).

18. Wisconsin v. Yoder, 406 U.S. 205, 92 S.Ct. 1526 (1972).

19. 371 U.S. 187, 83 S.Ct. 273 (1962).

20. 268 U.S. 510, 45 S.Ct. 571 (1925).

21. 321 U.S. 158, 166, 64 S.Ct. 438, 442 (1944).

22. Andrew Jay Kleinfeld, "The Balance of Power Among Infants, Their Parents and the State," *ABA Family Law Quarterly* 5 (1971): 107.

23. Salem Community School Corp. v. Easterly, 150 Ind.App. 11, 275 N.E.2d 317 (1971).

24. Ibid., p. 92.*Kleinfeld, op.cit., p. 92.*

25. Ibid., p. 93.

26. Morris v. Morris, 92 Ind.App. 65, 171 N.E. 386 (1930); Sisson v. Schultz, 251 Mich. 553, 232 N.W. 253 (1930).

27. Heffington v. Jackson and Norton, 43 Tex.Civ.App. 560, 96 S.W. 108 (1906).

28. Luques v. Luques, 127 Me. 356, 143 A. 263 (1928).

29. Hiram D. Gordon, "Terminal Placements of Children and Permanent Termination of Parental Rights: The New York Permanent Neglect Statute," *St. Johns Law Review* 46 (1971): 215.

30. Harvey J. Eger and Anthony J. Popeck, "The Abused Child: Problems and Proposals," *Duquesne Law Review* 8 (1969–70): 136.

31. State v. Perricone, 37 N.J. 463, 181 A.2d 751 (1962); People v. Pierson, 176 N.Y. 201, 68 N.E. 243 (1903).

32. Morrison v. State, 252 S.W.2d 97 (Mo.App.1952).

33. Massachusetts Gen.Laws Ann., ch. 272, § 53 (1958).

34. See Alexander v. Bartlett, 14 Mich.App. 177, 165 N.W.2d 445 (1968).

35. 14 A.L.R.2d 1369; Knox v. O'Brien, 7 N.J.Super. 608, 72 A.2d 389 (1950).

36. State v. Whisner, 47 Ohio St.2d 181, 351 N.E.2d 750 (1976).

37. State v. Garber, 197 Kan. 567, 419 P.2d 896 (1966).

38. Murphy v. State of Arkansas, 852 F.2d 1039 (1988).

39. Ibid.

40. Ellis v. O'Hara, 612 F.Supp. 379 (E.D. Mo. 1985).

41. Murphy v. State of Arkansas, 852 F.2d 1039 (1988).

42. *Ibid.*

43. Pierce v. Society of the Sisters of the Holy Names of Jesus and Mary, 268 U.S. 510, 45 S.Ct. 571 (1925).

44. Morris, op. cit.

45. Grosz v. City of Miami Beach, Florida, 721 F.2d 729 (11th Cir.1983).

46. State ex rel. Douglas v. Faith Baptist Church, 207 Neb. 802, 301 N.W.2d 571 (1981), *appeal dismissed* 454 U.S. 803, 102 S.Ct. 75 (1981).

47. State ex rel. Douglas v. Calvary Academy, 217 Neb. 450, 348 N.W.2d 898 (1984). See also: McCurry v. Tesch, 738 F.2d 271 (8th Cir.1984).

48. Sheridan Road Baptist Church v. Department of Education, 132 Mich.App.1, 348 N.W.2d 263 (1984).

49. Pierce, op. cit.

50. 293 U.S. 245, 55 S.Ct. 197 (1934).

51. Rice v. Commonwealth, 188 Va. 224, 49 S.E.2d 342, 3 A.L.R.2d 1392 (1948).

52. Commonwealth v. Bey, 57 York Leg.Rec. (Pa.) 200, 92 Pitts.Leg.J. 84 (1944).

53. See also in re Currence, 42 Misc.2d 418, 248 N.Y.S.2d 251 (1963). Here religious observance was no defense for withdrawing a boy from school weekly on Wednesday afternoons and Thursday mornings.

54. 406 U.S. 205, 92 S.Ct. 1526 (1972).

55. Fellowship Baptist Church v. Benton, 815 F.2d 485 (8th Cir., 1987).

56. Ibid.

57. Butts and Cremin, *A History of Education in American Culture,* p. 357.

58. Knox v. O'Brien, 7 N.J.Super. 608, 72 A.2d 389 (1950).

59. State v. Edgington, 99 N.M. 715, 663 P.2d 374 (1983).

60. State v. Bowman, 60 Or.App. 184, 653 P.2d 254 (1982).

61. Appeal of Pierce, 122 N.H. 762, 451 A.2d 363 (1982).

62. State v. Counort, 69 Wash. 361, 124 P. 910 (1912).

63. State v. Hoyt, 84 N.H. 38, 146 A. 170 (1929).

64. State v. Well, 99 Kan. 167, 160 P. 1025 (1916).

65. State v. Lowry, 191 Kan. 701, 383 P.2d 962 (1963).

66. People v. Turner, 121 Cal.App.Supp.2d 861, 263 P.2d 685 (1953).

67. State v. Peterman, 32 Ind.App. 665, 70 N.E. 550 (1904).

68. Sheppard v. State, 306 P.2d 346 (Okl.Crim.App.1957).

69. State v. Massa, 95 N.J.Super. 382, 231 A.2d 252 (1967).

70. In re Jeanette L., 71 Md. App. 70, 523 A.2d 1048 (1987).

71. Commonwealth v. Hall, 309 Pa.Super. 407, 455 A.2d 674 (1983).

72. State v. Turner, 9 Wn.2d 731, 658 P.2d 658 (1983).

73. People v. Berger, 109 Ill.App.3d 1054, 65 Ill.Dec. 600, 441 N.E.2d 915 (1982).

74. State v. Priest, 210 La. 389, 27 So.2d 173 (1946).

75. In re State, 214 La. 1062, 39 So.2d 731 (1949).

76. In re Rogers, 36 Misc.2d 680, 234 N.Y.S.2d 172 (1962).

77. Jacobson v. Commonwealth of Massachusetts, 197 U.S. 11, 25 S.Ct. 358 (1905).

78. Ibid., p. 364.

79. Blue v. Beach, 155 Ind. 121, 56 N.E. 89 (1900); Morris v. Columbus, 102 Ga. 792, 30 S.E. 850 (1898); State v. Hay, 126 N.C. 999, 35 S.E. 459 (1900); Abeel v. Clark, 84 Cal. 226, 24 P. 383 (1890); Bissell v. Davison, 65 Conn. 183, 32 A. 348 (1894); Hazen v. Strong, 2 Bt. 427 (1830); Duffield v. School Dist. of Williamsport, 162 Pa. 476, 29 A. 742 (1894).

80. 179 N.Y. 235, 72 N.E. 97 (1904).

81. People v. McIlwain, 151 N.Y.S. 366 (1915).

82. People v. Ekerold, 211 N.Y. 386, 105 N.E. 670 (1914).

83. 310 U.S. 296, 60 S.Ct. 900, 128 ALR 1352 (1940).

84. *Yoder,* op. cit.

85. State v. Drew, 89 N.H. 54, 192 A. 629 (1937).

86. Board of Education of Mountain Lakes v. Maas, 56 N.J.Super. 245, 152 A.2d 394 (App. Div. 1959).

87. 215 Pa. 156, 64 A. 419 (1906).

88. Hill v. Bickers, 171 Ky. 703, 188 S.W. 766 (1916).

89. Board of Trustees v. McMurtry, 169 Ky. 457, 184 S.W. 390 (1916).

90. Mosier v. Barren County Board of Health, 308 Ky. 829, 215 S.W.2d 967 (1948).

91. Potts v. Breen, 167 Ill. 67, 47 N.E. 81 (1897); People ex rel. LaBaugh v. Board of Education of District No. 2, 177 Ill. 572, 52 N.E. 850 (1899).

CHAPTER 7

The Instructional Program

Upon entering a public school a child becomes subject to state and local administrative regulations, as well as to state laws governing public education. These regulations are an exercise of state police power, which is the inherent sovereign power allowing the state to provide for the health, safety, and well-being of its citizens. Such provisions establish the framework within which each child is afforded a free public education.

Education may be viewed differently by educators, parents, students, or various special interest groups, but few would argue that a public educational program should not be expansive and broadening of one's perspective and knowledge. The public school has been quite accurately defined as a "marketplace of ideas."

The critical position of education in a democratic society is self-evident. Over the years the courts have come to conclude that society is best served by an educational system that teaches "through wide exposure to that robust exchange of ideas which discovers truth 'out of a multitude of tongues [rather] than through any kind of authoritative selection.'"[1] Thus, because of the importance of the schools and because this "robust exchange of ideas" is so vital to the educational process, the perpetuation of that exchange is, at all levels of the educational system, "a special concern of the First Amendment."[2] No school can function as a marketplace of ideas unless both students and faculty enjoy an atmosphere conducive to debate and scholarly inquiry.[3] The First Amendment not only creates a marketplace of intellectual ideas for the students but also benefits the teacher in the presentation of ideas.

Courts have generally given wide latitude to the state in matters involving the educational program. In one notable case, parents sought a *writ of mandamus* to prevent using the novel *Slaughterhouse Five* as a part of the instructional program. The parents alleged that the material was obscene, profane, and repugnant to the religious provisions of the First Amendment.

The court, in an exposition on the law, first observed that, although there may have been religious references in the work, the book itself did not violate the students' and parents' religious freedom. To declare otherwise, the court concluded, would censor and prevent the public schools from making use of many great works of the past.

If plaintiffs' contention was correct, then public school students could no longer marvel at Sir Galahad's saintly quest for the Holy Grail, nor be introduced to the dangers of Hitler's *Mein Kampf* nor read the mellifluous poetry of John Milton and John Donne. Unhappily, Robin Hood would be forced to forage without Friar Tuck and Shakespeare would have to delete Shylock from *The Merchant of Venice*. Is this to be the state of our law? Our Constitution does not command ignorance; on the contrary, it assures the people that the state may not relegate them to such a status and guarantees to all the precious and unfettered freedom of pursuing one's own intellectual pleasures in one's own personal way.[4]

Even more to the point, the court observed that the judges are not to be the experts in what educational programs are offered in the schools. Citing Justice Brennan's admonition in *Schempp*,[5] the court contended that curriculum determination should be entrusted to the experienced school officials of the nation's public schools and not to the judges. The appellate court reprimanded the lower trial court for imposing its judgment of "right" and "morality" over that of the school authorities. Such action by a court was forbidden by the state constitution and a matter for the lawfully elected school board to determine. The appellate court concluded that the judicial censor was *persona non grata* in the formation of public education curriculum policies.

Because the public school is a creature of the legislature[6] and the local school board is the recipient of governance powers delegated by the legislature, the school board occupies a critical juncture in the free flow of ideas and information.[7]

The educational program of the public school has both academic and disciplinary aspects. Courts have been very hesitant to enter into the academic arena. The position of the courts is stated by the United States Supreme Court in a higher education case that has applicability for elementary and secondary school operation. In *Horowitz*, the Court said:

> Academic evaluations of a student, in contrast to disciplinary determinations, bear little resemblance to the judicial and administrative fact-finding proceedings to which we have traditionally attached a full learning requirement. . . . Like the decision of an individual professor as to the proper grade for a student in his course, the determination whether to dismiss a student for academic reasons requires expert evaluation of cumulative information and is not readily adapted to the procedural tools of judicial or administrative decisionmaking. . . . Courts are particularly ill-equipped to evaluate academic performance.[8]

The courts have generally supported the school boards when they have expanded the school program or introduced innovative curricula. Thus far, the courts have agreed that the school has the power to regulate and develop curricula for the well-being of the students. These cases also remind us that not all parental discontent is aimed at broadening student knowledge and choice. In many instances, parents seek to restrict or "contract the spectrum of knowledge." As a result, the courts will tend to weigh parental grievances very carefully, even when a parent feels that a constitutional right is being offended.

This judicial position has been demonstrated when a school board sought to reduce the length of the school day, thereby restricting the educational program. For lack of funds, the school board decided to hold one-half sessions and to teach certain subjects on a compressed schedule.[9] The Supreme Court of Michigan decided that in the absence of state board regulations limiting local school board authority in this area, the reduction in the school program was valid.

Although the content of the school program itself is an area of concern to parents, an even more direct concern is the placement of their children. Aside from the recent statutory emphasis and litigation dealing with handicapped children, much of the controversy between parent and school has arisen during the child's first few years of schooling. It is at this level that the parent and the child are experiencing the removal of the child from the home and placing him or her in the hands of strangers at school.

In one such New York State case, a mother petitioned the court for an order directing the board of education to admit her son to the first grade.[10] Previously, the boy had established an unenviable reputation as a "disciplinary problem." The school had demoted the boy from the first grade back to kindergarten, an action the parent maintained was arbitrary, capricious, unreasonable, and in violation of the Fourteenth Amendment and the New York Constitution. The board defended itself by maintaining the school principal had made an "educational decision" based on the boy's inability to perform first-grade work, his test results, and his lack of self-control. The petitioner was unable to rebut the test results. The court held that the placement of the child was within the school's authority to provide rules and regulations for promotion from grade to grade, based not on age but on training, knowledge, and ability.[11]

In a similar New York State decision, the parents of a five-year-old child sought to compel the school board to accept the child into the first grade.[12] According to New York law, a five-year-old is entitled to attend public schools, and the boy's parents claimed that kindergarten was not the public schools. The court disagreed with the parent, holding that when a kindergarten is established it becomes a part of the public school system. Since the boy was already in public school, the court maintained, the parents had no right to insist that the boy be admitted to a particular grade or class in the public school.

Most precedents indicated that the courts, though sympathetic with the intentions of the parent, generally defer to authorized and trained educational experts in matters of school policy. In recent years, however, there has been a greater tendency by the courts to delve deeper into the justification and rationale supporting educational policy. School authorities, therefore, are well advised to document placement and curriculum decisions with a solid educational rationale.

However, the collective judgment of the school does hold substantial influence with the courts. Courts hesitate to substitute their knowledge of children for that of educators. Yet, although the school has generally prevailed in curriculum and placement disputes with parents, the school's power is by no means absolute. Where legitimate constitutional concerns are present, the courts stand ready to invalidate the offending regulations, particularly if the action of the school tends to contract rather than expand knowledge. Such judicial intervention is not uncommon and has been demonstrated in several notable United States Supreme Court cases.[13]

Board Has the Power to Enforce Reasonable Rules Prescribing Specific Curriculum

State Ex Rel. Andrews v. Webber

Supreme Court of Indiana, 1886.
108 Ind. 31, 8 N.E. 708.

HOWK, C.J. . . . The relator . . . said that he was the father and natural guardian of one Abram Andrew, who was a white male child, between the ages of six and twenty-one years, to-wit, of the age of twelve years . . . .The said Abram Andrew being sufficiently advanced in his studies, in accordance with the relator's desire and consent, and in compliance with his legal rights in the premises, was admitted as a pupil in such high school, to receive instruction therein, and thereafter, until his suspension, as hereinafter stated, was regular in his attendence and deportment, and was obedient and respectful to his teachers, and properly subordinate to the rules and regulations of such school; that among the exercises prescribed by such superintendent, with the sanction of such board of trustees, for the pupils of the high school, was a requirement that each of the pupils should, at stated intervals, employ a certain period of time in the study and practice of music, and that they should provide themselves with prescribed books for that purpose; that the relator, believing it was not for the best interest of said Abram Andrew, and not in accordance with the relator's wishes regarding the instruction of his said son, in a respectful manner asked of such superintendent that Abram Andrew might be excused from the study and practice of music at such exercises, and directed Abram Andrew not to participate therein, all in good faith, and in a respectful manner, and with no intention of in any manner interfering with the government, rules, and regulations of such schools, except in so far as he might legally control and direct the education of his said son, which purpose and desire were fully communicated by him to such superintendent.

But the relator said that, notwithstanding his said desire and request so communicated to such superintendent as aforesaid, the superintendent, on or about the fourteenth day of October, 1885, in disregard of the relator's wishes and request, required said Abram Andrew to participate in the practice and study of music, and upon the refusal of said Abram Andrew to participate in such exercises and study, which he did without disrespect to such superintendent, and entirely because of the relator's direction, which was so communicated to such superintendent as aforesaid, the superintendent suspended said Abram Andrew from such school, without assigning any cause therefor. . . .

This action is brought by the father and natural guardian of the suspended pupil, to compel, by mandate, the governing authorities of the school corporation to revoke such suspension, and to readmit such pupil to the high school.

The question for our decision in this case, as it seems to us, may be thus stated: Is the rule or regulation for the government of the pupils of the high school of the school city of La Porte, in relation to the study and practice of music, a valid and reasonable exercise of the discretionary power conferred by law upon the governing authorities of such school corporation? In section 4497, Rev.St.1881, in force since August 16, 1869, it is provided as follows: "The common schools of the state shall be taught in the English language; and the trustee shall provide to have taught in them orthography, reading, writing, arithmetic, geography, English grammer, physiology, history of the United States, and good behavior, and such other branches of learning, and other languages, as the advancement of pupils may require, and the trustees from time to time direct." Under this statutory provision and others of similar purport and effect, to be found in our school laws, it was competent, we think, for the trustees of the school city of

La Porte to enact necessary and reasonable rules for the government of the pupils of its high school, directing what branches of learning such pupils should pursue, and regulating the time to be given to any particular study, and prescribing what book or books should be used therein. Such trustees were and are required, by the express provisions of section 4444, Rev.St.1881, in force since March 8, 1873, to "take charge of the educational affairs" of such city of La Porte; "they may also establish graded schools, or such modifications of them as may be practicable, and provide for admitting into the higher departments of the graded school, from the primary schools of their townships, such pupils as are sufficiently advanced for such admission."

The power to establish graded schools carries with it, of course, the power to establish and enforce such reasonable rules as may seem necessary to the trustees, in their discretion, for the government and discipline of such schools, and prescribing the course of instruction therein. Confining our opinion strictly to the case in hand, we will consider and decide these two questions, in the order of their statement, namely: (1) Has the appellant's relator shown, by the averments of his verified complaint, that the rule or regulation for the government of the pupils of the high school, in the school city of La Porte, of which he complains, was or is an unreasonable exercise of the discretionary power conferred by law upon the trustees of such school corporation and the superintendent of its schools? (2) Conceding or assuming such rule or regulation to be reasonable and valid, has the relator shown, in his complaint herein, any sufficient or satisfactory excuse for the noncompliance therewith, and the disobedience thereof, of his son, Abram Andrew, a pupil of such high school, or any sufficient or legal ground for the revocation of the suspension of his son, or for his son's readmission, as a pupil in such high school?

As to the first of these questions . . . we think that the legislature has given the trustees of the public school corporations the discretionary power to direct, from time to time, what branches of learning, in addition to those specified in the statute, shall be taught in the public schools of their respective corporations. Where such trustees may have established a system of graded schools, or such modifications of them as may be practicable, within their respective corporations, they are clothed by law with the discretionary power to prescribe the course of instruction in the different grades of their public schools. We are of opinion that the rule or regulation of which the relator complains in the case under consideration was within the discretionary power conferred by law upon the governing authorities of the school city of La Porte; that it was not an unreasonable rule; but that it was such a one as each pupil of the high school, in the absence of sufficient excuse, might lawfully be required to obey and comply with. . . .

. . . The only cause or reason assigned by the relator for requiring his son to disobey such rule or regulation was that he did not believe it was for the best interest of his son to participate in the musical studies and exercises of the high school, and did not wish him to do so. The relator has assigned no cause or reason, and it may be fairly assumed that he had none, in support either of his belief or his wish. The important question arises, which should govern the public high school of the city of La Porte, as to the branches of learning to be taught and the course of instruction therein, — the school trustees of such city, to whom the law has confided the direction of these matters, or the mere arbitrary will of the relator, without cause or reason in its support? We are of opinion that only one answer can or ought to be given to this question. The arbitrary wishes of the relator in the premises must yield and be subordinated to the governing authorities of the school city of La Porte, and their reasonable rules and regulations for the government of the pupils of its high school. . . .

For the reasons given, our conclusion is that no error was committed by the court below in sustaining appellees' demurrer to the relator's complaint.

The judgment is affirmed, with costs.

Denial of Promotion for Failure to Complete Requisite Reading Level Does Not Violate Constitutional Rights

—··—··—··—··—

Sandlin v. Johnson

—··—··—··—··—

United States Court of Appeals,
Fourth Circuit, 1981.
643 F.2d 1027.

MURNAGHAN, Circuit Judge. Four second-grade students filed the case as a class action on behalf of themselves and eighteen other similarly situated second graders against the principal of their school, and the superintendent of schools and school board of Pittsylvania County, Virginia. Plaintiffs attended the Whitmell Elementary School. Only one member of their class was promoted to the third grade at the end of the 1977-1978 school year. The stated and undisputed ground for denial of promotion was the students' failure to complete the requisite level of the Ginn Reading Series. While plaintiffs do not deny that they failed to demonstrate the required reading level, they argue that they are nevertheless capable of reading at the third-grade level. They sued pursuant to 42 U.S.C. § 1983 claiming a denial of equal protection of the law because, as their Complaint had it:

> By either the defendants' negligent and careless supervision of the instruction of plaintiffs or by their arbitrary and negligent grading and classification of these plaintiffs, plaintiffs have been effectively denied third-grade educational opportunities commensurate with their abilities and in accord with educational opportunities provided other students similarly situated in the Pittsylvania County School System.

Plaintiffs contended that defendants' actions damaged them by delaying the completion of their education and their obtaining employment, by foreclosing "certain lucrative employment . . . because of a lack of education provided them commensurate with their abilities," and by burdening them with the stigma of failure. . . .

Defendants responded that they had provided equal opportunities to plaintiffs, that while plaintiffs' intelligence was such that they were capable of reading at the third-grade level, they had failed to progress to that level of mastery, and that promoting plaintiffs before they had mastered the requisite reading skills would be counterproductive and would increase plaintiffs' reading deficiencies. . . .

There is no allegation in the case that plaintiffs were classified on the basis of race or any other basis calling for heightened scrutiny, i.e., religious affiliation, alienage, illegitimacy, gender or wealth. Nor is public education a fundamental right which would trigger strict scrutiny of claims of denial of equal protection. Thus, in reviewing the equal protection claim, the only question, as recognized by all parties, is whether the classification by the governmental entity which is at issue here is rationally related to a permissible governmental end.

Defendants here classified plaintiffs according to their attained reading level. The stated purpose for the classification was to enable the school to provide students with the level of instruction most appropriate to their abilities and needs. The objective was to further the education, the preparation for life of the plaintiffs. The governmental end is a permissible one, and defendants' classification scheme is clearly rationally related to achieving it. Defendants, therefore, have not implicated any constitutional right of plaintiffs by classifying them according to their reading level.

Plaintiffs also claim that defendants or the teachers under their supervision negligently and carelessly failed to ensure that plaintiffs were properly and appropriately taught. What appellants denominate a denial of equal educational opportunity sounds rather in tort as a breach of some duty owed by teachers or school boards to their pupils to give them an education. If there is any such cause of action, it does not rise to the level of a constitutional

claim and, therefore, is not cognizable in an action pursuant to 42 U.S.C. § 1983. . . .

Decisions by educational authorities which turn on evaluation of the academic performance of a student as it relates to promotion are peculiarly within the expertise of educators and are particularly inappropriate for review in a judicial context. ("We decline to further enlarge the judicial presence in the academic community and thereby risk deterioration of many beneficial aspects of the faculty-student relationship.") We, therefore, affirm the district court's dismissal.

Affirmed. (Held for the school board.)

Statute Prohibiting Teaching of Foreign Language Violates Substantive Due Process

—————————

Meyer v. Nebraska

—————————

Supreme Court of the United States, 1923.
262 U.S. 390, 43 S.Ct. 625.

Mr. Justice McREYNOLDS delivered the opinion of the Court. Plaintiff in error was tried and convicted in the district court for Hamilton county, Nebraska, under an information which charged that on May 25, 1920, while an instructor in Zion Parochial School he unlawfully taught the subject of reading in the German language to Raymond Parpart, a child of ten years, who had not attained and successfully passed the eighth grade. The information is based upon "An act relating to the teaching of foreign languages in the state of Nebraska," approved April 9, 1919 (Laws 1919, c. 249), which follows:

Section 1. No person, individually or as a teacher, shall, in any private, denominational, parochial or public school, teach any subject to any person in any language than the English language.

Sec. 2. Languages, other than the English language, may be taught as languages only after a pupil shall have attained and successfully passed the eighth grade as evidenced by a certificate of graduation issued by the county superintendent of the county in which the child resides.

. . . The Supreme Court of the state affirmed the judgment of conviction. It declared the offense charged and established was "the direct and intentional teaching of the German language as a distinct subject to a child who had not passed the eighth grade," in the parochial school maintained by Zion Evangelical Lutheran Congregation, a collection of Biblical stories being used therefor. And it held that the statute forbidding this did not conflict with the Fourteenth Amendment, but was a valid exercise of the police power. The following excerpts from the opinion sufficiently indicate the reasons advanced to support the conclusion.

> The salutary purpose of the statute is clear. The Legislature had seen the baneful effects of permitting foreigners, who had taken residence in this country, to rear and educate their children in the language of their native land. The result of that condition was found to be inimical to our own safety. To allow the children of foreigners, who had emigrated here, to be taught from early childhood the language of the country of their parents was to rear them with that language as their mother tongue. It was to educate them so that they must always think in that language, and, as a consequence, naturally inculcate in them the ideas and sentiments foreign to the best interests of this country. The statute, therefore, was intended not only to require that the education of all children be conducted in the English language, but that, until they had grown into that language and until it had become a part of them, they should not in the schools be taught any other language. The obvious purpose of this statute was that the English language should be and become the mother tongue of all children reared in this state. The enactment of such a statute comes reasonably within the police power of the state. . . .

. . . The problem for our determination is whether the statute as construed and applied unreasonably infringes the liberty guaranteed to the plaintiff in error by the Four-

teenth Amendment. "No state . . . shall deprive any person of life, liberty or property without due process of law."

While this court has not attempted to define with exactness the liberty thus guaranteed, the term has received much consideration and some of the included things have been definitely stated. Without doubt, it denotes not merely freedom from bodily restraint but also the right of the individual to contract, to engage in any of the common occupations of life, to acquire useful knowledge, to marry, establish a home and bring up children, to worship God according to the dictates of his own conscience, and generally to enjoy those privileges long recognized at common law as essential to the orderly pursuit of happiness by free men. . . . The established doctrine is that this liberty may not be interfered with, under the guise of protecting the public interest, by legislative action which is arbitrary or without reasonable relation to some purpose within the competency of the state to effect. Determination by the Legislature of what constitutes proper exercise of police power is not final or conclusive but is subject to supervision by the courts. . . .

The American people have always regarded education and acquisition of knowledge as matters of supreme importance which should be diligently promoted. The Ordinance of 1787 declares: "Religion, morality and knowledge being necessary to good government and the happiness of mankind, schools and the means of education shall forever be encouraged." Corresponding to the right of control, it is the natural duty of the parent to give his children education suitable to their station in life; and nearly all the states, including Nebraska, enforce this obligation by compulsory laws.

Practically, education of the young is only possible in schools conducted by especially qualified persons who devote themselves thereto. The calling always has been regarded as useful and honorable, essential, indeed, to the public welfare. Mere knowledge of the German language cannot reasonably be regarded as harmful. Heretofore it has been commonly looked upon as helpful and desirable. Plaintiff in error taught this language in school as part of his occupation. His right thus to teach and the right of parents to engage him so to instruct their children, we think, are within the liberty of the amendment.   . . .

That the state may do much, go very far, indeed, in order to improve the quality of its citizens, physically, mentally and morally, is clear; but the individual has certain fundamental rights which must be respected. The protection of the Constitution extends to all, to those who speak other languages as well as to those born with English on the tongue. Perhaps it would be highly advantageous if all had ready understanding of our ordinary speech, but this cannot be coerced by methods which conflict with the Constitution—a desirable end cannot be promoted by prohibited means.   . . .

The power of the State to compel attendance at some school and to make reasonable regulations for all schools, including a requirement that they shall give instructions in English, is not questioned. Nor has challenge been made of the state's power to prescribe a curriculum for institutions which it supports. Those matters are not within the present controversy. Our concern is with the prohibition approved by the Supreme Court. *Adams v. Tanner*, 244 U.S. 594, 37 S.Ct. 662, 61 L Ed. 1336, pointed out that mere abuse incident to an occupation ordinarily useful is not enough to justify its abolition, although regulation may be entirely proper. No emergency has arisen which renders knowledge by a child of some language other than English so clearly harmful as to justify its inhibition with the consequent infringement of rights long freely enjoyed. We are constrained to conclude that the statute as applied is arbitrary and without reasonable relation to any end within the competency of the State.

As the statute undertakes to interfere only with teaching which involves a modern language, leaving complete freedom as to other matters, there seems no adequate foundation for the suggestion that the purpose was to protect the child's health by limiting his mental activities. It is well known that proficiency in a foreign language seldom comes to one not instructed at an early age, and experience shows that this is not injurious to the health, morals or understanding of the ordinary child.

The judgment of the court below must be reversed and the cause remanded for further proceedings not inconsistent with this opinion.

Reversed.

State Can Validly Require a Course in Sex Education for All Students

Cornwell v. State Board of Education

United States District Court, Maryland, 1969. 314 F.Supp. 340 (D.Md.1969), affirmed 428 F.2d 471 (4th Cir.1970), cert. denied 400 U.S. 942, 91 S.Ct. 240 (1970).

HARVEY, District Judge. In this civil action, Baltimore County taxpayers are suing the Maryland State Board of Education seeking to prevent the implementation in the Baltimore County Schools of a program of sex education. In particular, the plaintiffs, who are school children and their parents, seek to have this Court declare unconstitutional a bylaw duly adopted by the State Board. The provision in question is By-Law 720, Section 3, Subsection 4, which provides as follows:

It is the responsibility of the local school system to provide a comprehensive program of family life and sex education in every elementary and secondary school for all students as an integral part of the curriculum including a planned and sequential program of health education.

. . . In determining whether there is here a substantial question of constitutionality, this Court concludes initially that no question whatsoever arises under the Fourteenth Amendment. There is first no denial of substantive due process to the plaintiffs. Under Section 6 of Article 77 of the Maryland Code (as amended and re-codified by Chapter 405 of the Acts of 1969), the State Board is directed to determine the educational policies of the state and to enact bylaws for the administration of the public school system, which when enacted and published shall have the force of law. Assuredly it cannot be said that the bylaw here is an arbitrary or unreasonable exercise of the authority vested in the State Board to determine a teaching curriculum, nor that there is no basis in fact for the legislative policy expressed in the bylaw. Furthermore, it does not appear that the bylaw denies equal protection of the laws, as on its face it applies to all pupils equally.

Plaintiffs allege that the enactment of this bylaw was based on a study made in reference to pregnant pupils. But whatever the genesis of the bylaw, it is not the study that is being attacked here but the bylaw itself, and it is being attacked on its face. It is the provisions of the bylaw then that must be examined in the light of the United States Constitution. The plaintiffs' argument that the bylaw is defective because it applies to nonpregnant as well as to pregnant pupils is difficult to follow. There would appear to be just as much reason for the State Board to provide sex education for the non-pregnant (and, incidentally, for the non-impregnating) as for those students who, because of a lack of information on the subject (or for other reasons), have become pregnant or who have caused pregnancy.

The plaintiffs further assert that they have the exclusive constitutional right to teach their children about sexual matters in their own homes, and that such exclusive right would prohibit the teaching of sex in the schools. No authority is cited in support of this novel proposition, and this Court knows of no such constitutional right. This Court, then, is satisfied that the claims asserted in this complaint under the Fourteenth Amendment are so insubstantial that they do not confer jurisdiction here.

In support of their First Amendment claim, the plaintiffs assert that they have been denied the free exercise of their religious concepts and that the teaching of sex in the

Baltimore County Schools will in fact establish religious concepts. . . .

Applying the principles that have been established by the various cases, it is quite clear to this Court that the purpose and primary effect of the bylaw here is not to establish any particular religious dogma or precept, and that the bylaw does not directly or substantially involve the state in religious exercises or in the favoring of religion or any particular religion. The bylaw may be considered quite simply as a public health measure. As the Supreme Court indicated in *Prince v. Massachusetts,* 321 U.S. 158, 64 S.Ct. 438, 88 L. Ed 645 (1944), the State's interest in the health of its children outweighs claims based upon religious freedom and the right of parental control. The Court in that particular case said this (at pages 168-169):

> A democratic society rests . . . upon the healthy, well-rounded growth of young people into full maturity as citizens . . . . It is too late now to doubt that legislation appropriately designed to reach such evils is within the state's police power, whether against the parent's claim to control of the child or one that religious scruples dictate contrary action.

In summary, then, the Court concludes that the federal question here is plainly insubstantial. Construing the allegations in a light most favorable to the plaintiffs, as the Court must do on these motions to dismiss, this Court finds that the constitutional questions relied upon are obviously without merit. The unsoundness and insubstantiality of the plaintiffs' position is clearly indicated by the various decisions of the Supreme Court to which I have alluded.

For these reasons then, the two motions to dismiss are granted.

NOTES

1. Sex education does not invade the privacy of school children or parents. *Medeiros v. Kiyosaki,* 52 Hawaii 436, 478 P.2d 314 (1970).
2. The Supreme Court of New Jersey has upheld a State Board of Education regulation that requires each school district to

develop and implement a family life education program in the public elementary and secondary school curricula. The focus of the program was to be on teaching about human sexuality. The regulation included an "excusal clause" establishing procedures by which a parent could withdraw his or her child if the course conflicted with religious belief or conscience. The court held that the regulation did not violate either the Free Exercise or Establishment Clause of the First Amendment. Concerning free exercise, the court placed emphasis on the fact that the regulation contained an "excusal" provision. In applying the Establishment Clause, the court pointed out that the regulation does not enhance any particular religious viewpoint nor does it favor a "secular" view over a "religious" one. *Smith v. Ricci,* 89 N.J. 514, 446 A.2d 501 (1982).

3. The federal circuit court in *Cornwell* dismissed parents' free exercise argument even though there was no provision for the student to be excused. In *Medeiros* in Note 1 and *Smith* in Note 2, above, however, the courts relied on "excusal" provisions in the regulations to offset the free exercise issue.

Academic Freedom Extends to Protect Teacher in Use of "Dirty" Word If Conveyed for Demonstrated Educational Purpose

— · — · — · — · — · —

Keefe v. Geanakos

— · — · — · — · — · —

United States Court of Appeals,
First Circuit, 1969.
418 F.2d 359.

ALDRICH, Chief Judge. . . . Reduced to fundamentals, the substance of plaintiff's position is that as a matter of law his conduct which forms the basis of the charge did not warrant discipline. Accordingly, he argues,

there is no ground for any hearing. He divides this position into two parts. The principal one is that his conduct was within his competence as a teacher, as a matter of academic freedom, whether the defendants approved of it or not. The second is that he had been given inadequate prior warning by such regulations as were in force, particularly in the light of the totality of the circumstances known to him, that his actions would be considered improper, so that an ex post facto ruling would, itself, unsettle academic freedom. The defendants, essentially, deny plaintiff's contentions. They accept the existence of a principle of academic freedom to teach, but state that it is limited to proper classroom materials as reasonably determined by the school committee in the light of pertinent conditions, of which they cite in particular the age of the students. Asked by the court whether a teacher has a right to say to the school committee that it is wrong if, in fact, its decision was arbitrary, counsel candidly and commendably (and correctly) responded in the affirmative. This we consider to be the present issue. . . .

On the opening day of school in September 1969 the plaintiff gave to each member of his senior English class a copy of the September 1969 *Atlantic Monthly* magazine, a publication of high reputation, and stated that the reading assignment for that night was the first article therein. September was the educational number, so-called, of the *Atlantic,* and some seventy-five copies had been supplied by the school department. Plaintiff discussed the article, and a particular word that was used therein, and explained the word's origin and context, and the reasons the author had included it. The word, admittedly highly offensive, is a vulgar term for an incestuous son. Plaintiff stated that any student who felt the assignment personally distasteful could have an alternative one.

The next evening the plaintiff was called to a meeting of the school committee and asked to defend his use of the offending word. Following his explanation, a majority of the members of the committee asked him informally if he would agree not to use it again in the classroom. Plaintiff replied that he could not, in good conscience, agree. His counsel states, however, without contradiction, that in point of fact plaintiff has not used it again. No formal action was taken at this meeting. Thereafter plaintiff was suspended, as a matter of discipline, and it is now proposed that he should be discharged.

The Lifton article, which we have read in its entirety, has been described as a valuable discussion of "dissent, protest, radicalism, and revolt." It is in no sense pornographic. We need no supporting affidavits to find it scholarly, thoughtful and thought-provoking. The single offending word, although repeated a number of times, is not artificially introduced, but, on the contrary, is important to the development of the thesis and the conclusions of the author. Indeed, we would find it difficult to disagree with plaintiff's assertion that no proper study of the article could avoid consideration of this word. It is not possible to read the article, either in whole or in part, as an incitement to libidinous conduct, or even thoughts. If it raised the concept of incest, it was not to suggest it, but to condemn it; the word was used, by the persons described, as a superlative of opprobrium. We believe not only that the article negatived any other concept, but that an understanding of it would reject, rather than suggest the word's use.

. . .

Hence the question in this case is whether a teacher may, for demonstrated educational purposes, quote a "dirty" word currently used in order to give special offense, or whether the shock is too great for high school seniors to stand. If the answer were that the students must be protected from such exposure, we would fear for their future. We do not question the good faith of the defendants in believing that some parents have been offended. With the greatest of respect to such parents, their sensibilities are not the full measure of what is proper education.

We of course agree with defendants that what is to be said or read to students is not to be determined by obscenity standards for adult consumption. . . . At the same time, the issue must be one of degree. A high school senior is not devoid of all discrimination or resistance. Furthermore, as in all other instances, the offensiveness of language and the

particular propriety or impropriety is dependent on the circumstances of the utterance. . . . We accept the conclusion of the court below that "some measure of public regulation of classroom speech is inherent in every provision of public education." But when we consider the facts at bar as we have elaborated them, we find it difficult not to think that its application to the present case demeans any proper concept of education. The general chilling effect of permitting such rigorous censorship is even more serious.

We believe it equally probable that the plaintiff will prevail on the issue of lack of any notice that a discussion of this article with the senior class was forbidden conduct. The school regulation upon which defendants rely, although unquestionably worthy, is not apposite. It does not follow that a teacher may not be on notice of impropriety from the circumstances of a case without the necessity of a regulation. In the present case, however, the circumstances would have disclosed that no less than five books, by as many authors, containing the word in question were to be found in the school library. It is hard to think that any student could walk into the library and receive a book, but that his teacher could not subject the content to serious discussion in class.

Such inconsistency on the part of the school has been regarded as fatal. . . . We, too, would probably so regard it. At the same time, we prefer not to place our decision on this ground alone, lest our doing so diminish our principal holding, or lead to a bowdlerization of the school library.

Finally, we are not persuaded by the district court's conclusion that no irreparable injury is involved because the plaintiff, if successful, may recover money damages. Academic freedom is not preserved by compulsory retirement, even at full pay.

The immediate question before us is whether we should grant interlocutory relief pending appeal. This question, as defendants point out, raises the ultimate issue of the appeal itself. The matter has been extensively briefed and argued by both sides. We see no purpose in taking two bites, and believe this a case for action under Local Rule 5. The order of the district court denying an interlocutory injunction pending a decision on the merits is reversed and the case is remanded for further proceedings consistent herewith.

NOTES

1. In a case in which a secondary school teacher wrote on the blackboard using a four-letter word to illustrate changes in standards of morality, the court held that the teacher must be able to show that the instructional method used is in keeping with the preponderant opinion of the teaching profession. The court said:

> While secondary schools are not rigid disciplinary institutions, neither are they open forums in which mature adults, already habituated to social restraints, exchange ideas on a level of parity. Moreover, it cannot be accepted as a premise that the student is voluntarily in the classroom and willing to be exposed to a teaching method which, though reasonable, is not approved by the school authorities or by the weight of professional opinion. A secondary school student, unlike most college students, is usually required to attend school classes, and may have no choice as to his teacher.
>
> Bearing in mind these competing considerations, this court rules that when a secondary school teacher uses a teaching method which he does not prove has the support of the preponderant opinion of the teaching profession or of the part of it to which he belongs, but which he merely proves is relevant to his subject and students, is regarded by experts of significant standing as serving a serious educational purpose, and was used by him in good faith the state may suspend or discharge a teacher for using that method but it may not resort to such drastic sanctions unless the state proves he was put on notice either by a regulation or otherwise that he should not use that method. *Mailloux v. Kiley*, 323 F.Supp. 1387 (D.Mass.1971).

On appeal of this case, the higher court cast some doubt on the feasibility of the rule measuring the validity of a teaching method on the preponderant opinion of other edu-

cators and noted that each case must be examined on an independent basis, the court considering that "the propriety of regulations or sanctions must depend on such circumstances as the age and sophistication of the students, the closeness of the relation to the specific [teaching" technique used and some concededly valid educational objective, and the context and manner of presentation." *Mailloux v. Kiley*, 448 F.2d 1242 (1st Cir.1971).

2. In 1973, a group of teachers requested a pilot program, Global Studies, as an alternative to the conventional history course. Students were given a choice between Global Studies and the conventional course, and most chose the conventional one. Two teachers filed a grievance regarding the student registration procedure because of the decline in students in Global Studies and the fact that they had to teach the traditional class. When they lost the grievance at all levels they filed suit claiming, inter alia, that their academic freedom had been violated and asserted the right of a teacher to select teaching methods and materials. The Supreme Court of Washington ruled that

> if Global Studies detracts from the scope of a conventional history course — because it emphasizes small groups, independent reading and writing, and inquiry — discovery techniques — [the teachers] may be compelled to abandon their own preferred techniques and to teach history in a more conventional manner. While teachers should have some measure of freedom in teaching techniques employed, they may not ignore or omit essential course material or disregard the course calendar. *Millikan v. Board* of Directors of Everett School Dist. No. 2, 93 Wn.2d 522, 611 P.2d 414 (1980)

3. The United States Court of Appeals, Sixth Circuit has held that academic freedom

> does not encompass the right of a nontenured teacher to have her teaching style insulated from review by her superiors . . . just because her methods and

philosophy are considered acceptable within the teaching profession. *Hetrick v. Martin,* 480 F.2d 705, 709 (6th Cir.1973), cert. denied 414 U.S. 1075, 94 S.Ct. 592 (1973). See also *Adams v. Campbell County School District, Campbell County, Wyoming,* 511 F.2d 1242 (10th Cir.1975); *Saunders v. Reorganized School District No. 2,* 520 S.W.2d 29 (Mo.1975); *Clark v. Holmes,* 474 F.2d 928 (7th Cir.1972), cert. denied, 411 U.S. 972, 93 S.Ct. 2148 (1973); *Parducci v. Rutland,* 316 F.Supp. 352 (M.D.Ala.1970)

Teacher's Dismissal Upheld for Objectionable Film that under Circumstances was Not Expressive nor Communicative

— - — - — - — - —

Fowler v. Board of Education of Lincoln County, Kentucky

— - — - — - — - —

United States Court of Appeals, Sixth Circuit, 1987. 819 F. 2d 657.

MILBURN, Circuit Judge. . . . Plaintiff Jacqueline Fowler was a tenured teacher employed by the Lincoln County, Kentucky, school system for fourteen years. She was discharged in July, 1984 for insubordination and conduct unbecoming a teacher. The basis for this action was that she had an "R" rated movie, *Pink Floyd — The Wall,* shown to her high school students on the last day of the 1983-84 school year. The students in Fowler's classes were in grades nine through eleven and were of the ages fourteen through seventeen.

The day on which the movie was shown, May 31, 1984, was a noninstructional day used by teachers for completing grade cards. A group of students requested that Fowler allow the movie to be shown while she was completing the grade cards. Fowler was unfamiliar with the movie and asked the students whether it was appropriate for viewing at

school. Charles Bailey, age fifteen, who had seen the movie on prior occasions, indicated that the movie had "one bad place in it."

. . .

When Fowler had the movie shown on the morning of May 31, 1984, she instructed Charles Bailey, the fifteen-year-old student who had seen the movie, to edit out any parts that were unsuitable for viewing at school. He did so by attempting to cover the 25″ screen with an 8½″ by 11″ letter-sized file folder.

. . .

There is conflicting testimony as to whether, or how much, nudity was seen by the students. At the administrative hearing, several students testified that they saw no nudity. . . . One student testified that she saw "glimpses" of nudity, but "nothing really offending." . . .

There is also conflicting testimony regarding the amount of sexual innuendo existing in the "unedited" version of the film. Because some parts of the film are animated, they are susceptible to varying interpretations. One particularly controversial segment of scenes is animated in which flowers appear on the screen, are transformed into the shape of male and female sex organs and then engage in an act of intercourse. . . .

Once again, there is conflicting testimony concerning the effectiveness of the editing attempt. . . .

In addition to the sexual aspects of the movie, there is a great deal of violence. One scene involves a bloody battlefield. . . . Another scene shows children being fed into a giant sausage machine. . . .

On the afternoon of May 31, 1984, Principal Jack Portwood asked Fowler to give him the video tape, and she did so. After the movie was viewed by the superintendent and members of the Lincoln County Board of Education, proceedings were instituted to terminate Fowler's contract.

Plaintiff Fowler received her termination notice on or about June 19, 1984. The notice advised her that a hearing would be held on July 10, 1984, and she subsequently advised the board of her intention to appear at the hearing and contest the charges.

On July 10, 1984, plaintiff Fowler appeared with counsel at the administrative hearing. She testified that, despite the fact that she had never seen the movie before having it shown to her students, and despite the fact that she was posting grades on report cards and left the room several times while the movie was being shown, she believed it had significant value. She believed the movie portrayed the dangers of alienation between people and of repressive educational systems. She testified that she would show an edited version of the movie again if given the opportunity to explain it. She stated that she did not at any time discuss the movie with her students because she did not have enough time.

The board viewed the movie once in its entirety and once as it had been edited in the classroom. The board then retired into executive session. Following this executive session, the board returned to open session and voted unanimously to terminate plaintiff's employment for insubordination and conduct unbecoming a teacher. . . .

The district court concluded that Fowler's conduct was protected by the First Amendment, and that she was discharged for exercising her constitutionally protected rights. . . .

In the present case the district court concluded that Mrs. Fowler was entitled to the protection of the First Amendment *while acting as a teacher*. That a teacher does have First Amendment protection under certain circumstances cannot be denied. . . . Likewise, a motion picture is a form of expression which may be entitled to the protection of the First Amendment. . . .

However, I conclude that Fowler's conduct in having the movie shown under the circumstances present here did not constitute expression protected by the First Amendment. It is undisputed that Fowler was discharged for the showing of the movie, *Pink Floyd — The Wall*. Such conduct, under the circumstances involved, clearly is not "speech" in the traditional sense of the expression of ideas through use of the spoken or written word. . . .

However, not every form of conduct is protected by the First Amendment right of free speech. . . .

In the present case, it is undisputed that Fowler did not see the movie before she had it shown to her class on the morning of May 31, 1984, a noninstructional day. Fowler agreed to allow the movie to be shown, at the students' request, because May 31 was "their treat type of day." . . . It is also undisputed that she left the room on several occasions while the film was being shown. Under circumstances such as these, I cannot conclude that Fowler possessed "[a]n intent to convey a particularized message" to her students. . . . The mere fact that at some point she may have developed an approval of the content of the movie is not, standing alone, a sufficient basis for the conclusion that her conduct in having the movie shown was a form of expression entitled to protection under the First Amendment.

> If any sort of conduct that people wish to engage in is to be considered "speech" simply because those who engage in conduct are, in one sense, necessarily expressing their approval of it, the line between "speech" protected by the First Amendment and conduct not so protected will be destroyed. . . .

Moreover, the surrounding circumstances in the present case indicate that there was little likelihood "that the message would be understood by those who viewed it." . . . As we have noted, the "R" rated movie was shown on a noninstructional day to students in Fowler's classes in grades nine through eleven who were of ages ranging from fourteen through seventeen. Furthermore, Fowler never at any time made an attempt to explain any message that the students might derive from viewing the movie. . . .

[C]onduct is protected by the First Amendment *only* when it is expressive or communicative in nature. In the present case, because plaintiff's conduct in having the movie shown cannot be considered expressive or communicative, under the circumstances presented, the protection of the First Amendment is not implicated. . . .

Plaintiff argues that Ky.Rev.Stat. § 161.-790(1)(b), which proscribes "conduct unbecoming a teacher," is unconstitutionally vague as applied to her because the statute failed to give notice that her conduct would result in discipline. We find this argument to be without merit. . . .

In the present case, plaintiff Fowler had a fifteen-year-old student show a controversial, highly suggestive and somewhat sexually explicit movie to a group of high school students aged fourteen to seventeen. She did not preview the movie, despite the fact that she had been warned that portions were unsuitable for viewing in this context. She made no attempt at any time to explain the meaning of the movie or to use it as an educational tool. Rather, she had it shown for the purpose of keeping her students occupied during a noninstructional day while she was involved in posting grades on report cards. We conclude that the statute proscribing "conduct unbecoming a teacher" gave her adequate notice that such conduct would subject her to discipline. Accordingly, we conclude that the statute is not unconstitutionally vague as applied to Fowler's conduct. . . .

In the present case, we conclude that plaintiff's conduct, although not illegal, constituted serious misconduct. Moreover, there was a direct connection between this misconduct and Fowler's work as a teacher. She introduced a controversial and sexually explicit movie into a classroom of adolescents without preview, preparation or discussion. In the process, she abdicated her function as an educator. Her having the movie shown under the circumstances involved demonstrates a blatant lack of judgment. Having considered the entire record, including the viewing of the movie, which we describe as gross and bizarre and containing material completely unsuitable for viewing by a classroom of students aged fourteen to seventeen, we conclude that such conduct falls within the concept of conduct unbecoming a teacher under Kentucky law.

Accordingly, for the reasons stated, the judgment of the district court is vacated, and this cause is dismissed.

■■■ CURRICULUM AND THE PALL OF ORTHODOXY

The Supreme Court has said that the courts should not intervene in conflicts that arise in the daily operation of the schools, so long as the conflicts do not involve basic constitutional values. However, the courts will not "tolerate laws which cast a pall of orthodoxy over the classroom."[14]

The Supreme Court stated in *Sweezy v. New Hampshire:*[15]

> Scholarship cannot flourish in an atmosphere of suspicion and distrust. Teachers and students must always remain free to inquire, to study and to evaluate. . . . [The state cannot] chill that free play of the spirit which all teachers ought especially to cultivate and practice.[16]

Since the beginnings of the public schools, the nature and content of the curriculum has been subject to continuing and perplexing debate. As observed elsewhere in this book, one of the primary obstacles that faced early public school reformers was the formulation of a commonly accepted curriculum that would not unduly advance any particularized or specialized interest to the exclusion of others. Early experience found that the most difficult of such interests to overcome had to do with religious sectarianism and the hundreds of beliefs that touched on human values, morality, and ethics. A public school system that did not advance the cause of a particular group quickly encountered discord and conflict as a result. Cognizant of this problem, the early public school leaders sought to build a nonsectarian common school curriculum that would not be offensive to any particular religious view or sectarian viewpoint. In this pursuit, the public schools have been condemned by conservative religious groups for being ungodly or irreligious. Such groups, too, have sought to impose their beliefs on the public schools in an attempt to make their particular views the official policy of the state. This has not materially changed over the years, for it was this same issue that led to vigorous opposition to public schools initially. Butts and Cremin noted that what Horace Mann's "attackers were urging was not that religion, ethics and morals be taught in the schools, but that their particular sectarian doctrines be taught."[17]

In his concurring opinion in *McCollum*, Justice Jackson observed that

> authorities list 256 separate and substantial religious bodies to exist in the United States. Each of them . . . has as good a right (as any other) to demand that the courts compel the schools to sift out of their teaching everything that is objectionable to any of these warring sects or inconsistent with any of their doctrine. If we are to eliminate everything that is objectionable to any of these warring sects or inconsistent with any of their doctrines, we will leave public education in shreds.[18]

To identify and avoid all such conflicts was difficult if not impossible. Fortunately, though, the tenacity with which most sects imposed their particular tenets on the public varied considerably, allowing for some considerable flexibility. Butts and Cremin have noted that

> so long as each religious sect held firmly and uncompromisingly to a set of specific religious doctrines in opposition to all other sects, the tendency would be to insist upon religious schools that taught those tenets and only those tenets. . . . It is entirely possible that if some kind of nonsectarian outlook in religion had not appeared, the rise of the public school open to all religious groups alike would not have been possible.[19]

Over the years the intolerance for beliefs of others has, however, subsided very little and the tendency for some sects to continue their objections to public schools is commonplace.

There, too, has been a tendency for religious fundamentalism to ebb and flow in popular appeal over the years, making the imposition of particular sectarian beliefs more politically viable at certain times than at others. The attitudes of legislatures, school boards, and even the courts, have sometimes reflected these popularized views. It is because of the great difficulty in accommodating these divisive forces that the public schools have sought to convey a general attitude of secular impartiality to the views of various sects. The courts have generally enforced the view that the public schools should deal with temporal matters and remain apart and separate from ecclesiastical affairs.

The legal controversies that normally arise in this area generally involve some particular group seeking to impose a particular belief by restricting the school curriculum or demanding that certain textbooks, films, courses, or programs be excluded from the instructional program. In response, the courts have traditionally felt most comfortable in upholding the expansion rather than the contraction of knowledge.

In *Pico*,[20] the Supreme Court reinforced the "pall of orthodoxy" rule by forbidding removal of books by a local school board that was responding to political pressure from a local group of conservative parents. The court observed that the expansion of information and knowledge was the most desirable end to education policy and said that "the right to receive ideas is a necessary predicate to the recipient's meaningful exercise of his own rights of speech, press, and political freedom."[21]

This general precedent, that expansion of information and knowledge is paramount, and that even school boards' actions will be invalidated if they impair the flow of ideas was closely followed in 1982 by U.S. Court of Appeals, Eighth Circuit, in *Pratt*.[22] Here the court ruled that a school board's removal of a film from the school library was constitutionally invalid because the "First Amendment precludes local authorities from imposing a 'pall of orthodoxy' on classroom instruction which implicates the state in propagation of a particular religious or ideological viewpoint."[23]

More recently, though, a new judicial pattern has emerged that may suggest a possible retreat from the "pall of orthodoxy" rule. The present U.S. Supreme Court has indicated that it is willing to allow the final decision regarding the curriculum and the availability of books, films, and materials to reside fully within the prerogative of the local school board, even though there may be a resulting constriction on the flow of information and a possible diminution of knowledge. This position was implied by the Supreme Court in *Hazelwood School District v. Kuhlmeier*,[24] where excision of two pages from a student newspaper was upheld because, as the court said, such regulation is permissible so long as it is "reasonable related to legitimate pedagogical concerns."[25] Such a reasonableness standard is less definitive and gives the local school board greater flexibility in determining whether to restrict or expand the curriculum. In this case, the Supreme Court gave further justification for restriction of curriculum content by observing that "a school must be able to take into account the emotional maturity of the intended audience."[26]

In following this precedent of giving greater latitude to local school boards in controlling (and possibly limiting) curriculum, books, and materials, the U.S. Court of Appeals, Eleventh Circuit, followed *Kuhlmeier* and upheld a school board's action in removing material from the curriculum because the removal was related to "legitimate pedagogical concerns."[27]

The new direction of the courts appears to place less emphasis on a broadly conceived standard that secures the expansion of knowledge preventing the "casting of a pall of orthodoxy" and allows more flexibility in allowing curriculum decisions to be made on the basis of local school board judgment and, possibly, local political pressure.

Local School Board May Not Remove Books from School Libraries Simply Because It Dislikes the Ideas Contained in the Books

—————·—·—·———

Board of Education, Island Trees Union Free School District No. 26 v. Pico

—————·—·—·———

Supreme Court of the United States, 1982.
457 U.S. 853, 102 S.Ct. 2799.

Justice BRENNAN announced the judgment of the Court, and delivered an opinion in which Justice MARSHALL and Justice STEVENS joined, and in which Justice BLACKMUN joined except for Part II-A-(1). The principal question presented is whether the First Amendment imposes limitations upon the exercise by a local school board of its discretion to remove library books from high school and junior high school libraries.

Petitioners are the Board of Education of the Island Trees Union Free School District No. 26, in New York, and Richard Ahrens, Frank Martin, Christina Fasulo, Patrick Hughes, Richard Melchers, Richard Michaels, and Louis Nessim. When this suit was brought, Ahrens was the President of the Board, Martin was the Vice President, and the remaining petitioners were Board members. The Board is a state agency charged with responsibility for the operation and administration of the public schools within the Island Trees School District, including the Island Trees High School and Island Trees Memorial Junior High School. Respondents are Steven Pico, Jacqueline Gold, Glenn Yarris, Russell Rieger, and Paul Sochinski. When this suit was brought, Pico, Gold, Yarris, and Rieger were students at the High School, and Sochinski was a student at the Junior High School.

In September 1975, petitioners Ahrens, Martin, and Hughes attended a conference sponsored by Parents of New York United (PONYU), a politically conservative organization of parents concerned about education legislation in the State of New York. At the conference these petitioners obtained lists of books described by Ahrens as "objectionable," and by Martin as "improper fare for school students." It was later determined that the High School library contained nine of the listed books, and that another listed book was in the Junior High School library. [The nine books in the High School library were: *Slaughterhouse Five*, by Kurt Vonnegut, Jr.; *The Naked Ape*, by Desmond Morris; *Down These Mean Streets*, by Piri Thomas; *Best Short Stories of Negro Writers*, edited by Langston Hughes; *Go Ask Alice*, of anonymous authorship; *Laughing Boy*, by Oliver LaFarge; *Black Boy*, by Richard Wright; *A Hero Ain't Nothin' But A Sandwich*, by Alice Childress; and *Soul On Ice*, by Eldridge Cleaver. The book in the Junior High School library was *A Reader for Writers*, edited by Jerome Archer. Still another listed book, *The Fixer*, by Bernard Malamud, was found to be included in the curriculum of a twelfth grade literature course.] In February 1976, at a meeting with the superintendent of schools and the principals of the High School and Junior High School, the Board gave an "unofficial direction" that the listed books be removed from the library shelves and delivered to the Board's offices, so that Board members could read them. When this directive was carried out, it became publicized, and the Board issued a press release justifying its action. It characterized the removed books as "anti-American , anti-Christian, anti-Semitic, and just plain filthy," and concluded that "It is our duty, our moral obligation, to protect the children in our schools from this moral danger as surely as from physical and medical dangers."

A short time later, the Board appointed a "Book Review Committee," consisting of four Island Trees parents and four members of the Island Trees schools staff, to read the listed books and to recommend to the Board whether the books should be retained, taking into account the books' "educational suitability," "good taste," "relevance," and "appropriateness to age and grade level." In July, the Committee made its final report to the Board,

recommending that five of the listed books be retained [*The Fixer, Laughing Boy, Black Boy, Go Ask Alice*, and *Best Short Stories by Negro Writers*] and that two others be removed from the school libraries [*The Naked Ape* and *Down These Mean Streets*]. As for the remaining four books, the Committee could not agree on two, *Soul on Ice* and *A Hero Ain't Nothin' But A Sandwich*] took no position on one [*A Reader for Writers*] The reason given for this disposition was that all members of the Committee had not been able to read the book], and recommended that the last book be made available to students only with parental approval [*Slaughterhouse Five*]. The Board substantially rejected the Committee's report later that month, deciding that only one book should be returned to the High School library without restriction [*Laughing Boy*], that another should be made available subject to parental approval [*Black Boy*], but that the remaining nine books should "be removed from elementary and secondary libraries and [from] use in the curriculum." [As a result, the nine removed books could not be assigned or suggested to students in connection with school work. However, teachers were not instructed to refrain from discussing the removed books or the ideas and positions expressed in them.] The Board gave no reasons for rejecting the recommendations of the Committee that it had appointed.

Respondents reacted to the Board's decision by bringing the present action. They alleged that petitioners had

> ordered the removal of the books from school libraries and proscribed their use in the curriculum because particular passages in the books offended their social, political and moral tastes and not because the books, taken as a whole, were lacking in educational value.

Respondents claimed that the Board's actions denied them their rights under the First Amendment. They asked the court for a declaration that the Board's actions were unconstitutional. . . .

We emphasize at the outset the limited nature of the substantive question presented by the case before us. Our precedents have long recognized certain constitutional limits upon the power of the State to control even the curriculum and classroom. For example, *Meyer v. Nebraska*, 262 U.S. 390, 43 S.Ct. 625, 67 L.Ed. 1042 (1923), struck down a state law that forbade the teaching of modern foreign languages in public and private schools, and *Epperson v. Arkansas*, 393 U.S. 97, 89 S.Ct. 266, 21 L.Ed.2d 228 (1968), declared unconstitutional a state law that prohibited the teaching of the Darwinian theory of evolution in any state-supported school. But the current action does not require us to re-enter this difficult terrain, which *Meyer* and *Epperson* traversed without apparent misgiving. For as this case is presented to us, it does not involve textbooks, or indeed any books that Island Trees students would be required to read. Respondents do not seek in this Court to impose limitations upon their school board's discretion to prescribe the curricula of the Island Trees schools. On the contrary, the only books at issue in this case are *library* books, books that by their nature are optional rather than required reading. Our adjudication of the present case thus does not intrude into the classroom, or into the compulsory courses taught there. Furthermore, even as to library books, the action before us does not involve the *acquisition* of books. Respondents have not sought to compel their school board to add to the school library shelves any books that students desire to read. Rather, the only action challenged in this case is the *removal* from school libraries of books originally placed there by the school authorities, or without objection from them. . . . [T]he issue before us in this case is a narrow one, both substantively and procedurally. . . . Does the First Amendment impose *any* limitations upon the discretion of petitioners to remove library books from the Island Trees High School and Junior High School? . . .

The Court has long recognized that local school boards have broad discretion in the management of school affairs. . . . [B]y and large, "public education in our Nation is committed to the control of state and local authorities," and . . . federal courts should not ordinarily "intervene in the resolution of conflicts which arise in the daily operation of school systems." *Tinker v. Des Moines School Dist.*, 393 U.S. 503, 507, 89 S.Ct. 733, 736, 21 L.Ed.2d 731 (1969), noted that we have "repeatedly emphasized . . . the comprehensive authority of the States and of school officials . . . to prescribe and control conduct in the schools." We have also acknowledged that public schools are vitally important "in the preparation of individuals for participation as citizens," and as vehicles for "inculcating fundamental values necessary to the maintenance of a democratic political system." We are therefore in full agreement with petitioners that local school boards must be permitted "to establish and apply their curriculum in such a way as to transmit community values," and that "there is a legitimate and substantial community interest in promoting respect for authority and traditional values be they social, moral, or political."

At the same time, however, we have necessarily recognized that the discretion of the States and local school boards in matters of education must be exercised in a manner that comports with the transcendent imperatives of the First Amendment. . . .

In short, "First Amendment rights, applied in light of the special characteristics of the school environment, are available to . . . students."

Of course, courts should not "intervene in the resolution of conflicts which arise in the daily operations of school systems" unless "basic constitutional values" are "directly and sharply implicate[d]" in those conflicts. But we think that the First Amendment rights of students may be directly and sharply implicated by the removal of books from the shelves of a school library. Our precedents have focused "not only on the role of the First Amendment in fostering individual self-expression but also on its role in affording the public access to discussion, debate, and the dissemination of information and ideas." And we have recognized that "The State may not, consistently with the spirit of the First Amendment, contract the spectrum of available knowledge." . . . This [the right to receive information and ideas] is an inherent corollary of the rights of free speech and press that are explicitly guaranteed by the Constitution, in two senses. First, the right to receive ideas follows ineluctably from the *sender's* First Amendment right to send them: "The right of freedom of speech and press . . . embraces the right to distribute literature, . . . and necessarily protects the right to receive it." "The dissemination of ideas can accomplish nothing if otherwise willing addressees are not free to receive and consider them. It would be a barren marketplace of ideas that had only sellers and no buyers."

More importantly, the right to receive ideas is a necessary predicate to the *recipient's* meaningful exercise of his own rights of speech, press, and political freedom. Madison admonished us that

> a popular Government, without popular information, or the means of acquiring it, is but a Prologue to a Farce or a Tragedy; or, perhaps both. Knowledge will forever govern ignorance: And a people who mean to be their own Governors, must arm themselves with the power which knowledge gives.   . . .

In sum, just as access to ideas makes it possible for citizens generally to exercise their rights of free speech and press in a meaningful manner, such access prepares students for active and effective participation in the pluralistic, often contentious society in which they will soon be adult members. Of course all First Amendment rights accorded to students must be construed "in light of the special characteristics of the school environment." But the special characteristics of the school *library* make that environment especially appropriate for the recognition of the First Amendment rights of students.

A school library, no less than any other public library, is "a place dedicated to quiet, to knowledge, and to beauty." . . . The school library is the principal locus of such freedom. . . .

Petitioners emphasize the inculcative function of secondary education, and argue that they must be allowed *unfettered* discretion to "transmit community values" through the Island Trees schools. But that sweeping claim overlooks the unique role of the school library.

It appears from the record that use of the Island Trees school libraries is completely voluntary on the part of students. Their selection of books from these libraries is entirely a matter of free choice; the libraries afford them an opportunity at self-education and individual enrichment that is wholly optional. Petitioners might well defend their claim of absolute discretion in matters of *curriculum* by reliance upon their duty to inculcate community values. But we think that petitioners' reliance upon that duty is misplaced where, as here, they attempt to extend their claim of absolute discretion beyond the compulsory environment of the classroom, into the school library and the regime of voluntary inquiry that there holds sway.

In rejecting petitioners' claim of absolute discretion to remove books from their school libraries, we do not deny that local school boards have a substantial legitimate role to play in the determination of school library content.   . . .

Petitioners rightly possess significant discretion to determine the content of their school libraries. But that discretion may not be exercised in a narrowly partisan or political manner. If a Democratic school board, motivated by party affiliation, ordered the removal of all books written by or in favor of Republicans, few would doubt that the order violated the constitutional rights of the students denied access to those books. The same conclusion would surely apply if an all-white school board, motivated by racial animus, decided to remove all books authored by blacks or advocating racial equality and integration. Our Constitution does not permit the official suppression of *ideas*. Thus whether petitioners' removal of books from their school libraries denied respondents their First Amendment rights depends upon the motivation behind petitioners' actions. If petitioners *intended* by their removal decision to deny respondents access to ideas with which petitioners disagreed, and if this intent was the decisive factor in petitioners' decision, then petitioners have exercised their discretion in violation of the Constitution. To permit such intentions to control official actions would be to encourage the precise sort of officially prescribed orthodoxy unequivocally condemned in *Barnette*. On the other hand, respondents implicitly concede that an unconstitutional motivation would *not* be demonstrated if it were shown that petitioners had decided to remove the books at issue because those books were pervasively vulgar. And again, respondents concede that if it were demonstrated that the removal decision was based solely upon the "educational suitability" of the books in question, then their removal would be "perfectly permissible." In other words, in respondents' view such motivations, if decisive of petitioners' actions, would not carry the danger of an official suppression of ideas, and thus would not violate respondents' First Amendment rights.

As noted earlier, nothing in our decision today affects in any way the discretion of a local school board to choose books to *add* to the libraries of their schools. Because we are concerned in this case with the suppression of ideas, our holding today affects only the discretion to *remove* books. In brief, we hold that local school boards may not remove books from school library shelves simply because they dislike the ideas contained in those books and seek by their removal to "prescribe what shall be orthodox in politics, nationalism, religion, or other matters of opinion." . . .

School Board's Removal of Works by Aristophanes and Chaucer from Curriculum Is Reasonably Related to Legitimate Pedagogical Concerns

–·–·–·–·–·–

Virgil v. School Board of Columbia County, Florida

–·–·–·–·–·–

United States Court of Appeals,
Eleventh Circuit, 1989.
862 F. 2d 1517.

ANDERSON, Circuit Judge. This case presents the question of whether the first amendment prevents a school board from removing a previously approved textbook from an elective high school class because of objections to the material's vulgarity and sexual explicitness. We conclude that a school board may, without contravening constitutional limits, take such action where, as here, its methods are "reasonably related to legitimate pedagogical concerns." Accordingly, we affirm the judgment of the district court.

The essential facts were stipulated by the parties to this dispute. Since about 1975 the educational curriculum at Columbia High School has included a course entitled "Humanities to 1500" offered as part of a two-semester survey of Western thought, art and literature. In 1985 the school designed the course for eleventh- and twelfth-grade students and prescribed as a textbook Volume I of *The Humanities: Cultural Roots and Continuities*. This book contained both required and optional readings for the course.

Among the selections included in Volume I of *Humanities* which were neither required nor assigned are English translations of *Lysistrata*, written by the Greek dramatist Aristophanes in approximately 411 B.C., and *The Miller's Tale*, written by the English poet Geoffrey Chaucer around 1380-1390 A.D. During the fall semester of the 1985-86 school year, a portion of *Lysistrata* was read aloud in class during a session of the Humanities course.

In the spring of 1986, after the first semester had ended, the Reverend and Mrs. Fritz M. Fountain, the parents of a student who had taken the class in the fall of 1985, filed a formal complaint concerning Volume I of *Humanities* with the School Board of Columbia County. The Fountains also submitted a Request for Examination of School Media. Their objections centered upon *Lysistrata* and *The Miller's Tale*.

In response to this parental complaint, the School Board on April 8, 1986 adopted a Policy on Challenged State Adopted Textbooks to address any complaints regarding books in use in the curriculum. Pursuant to the new policy, the School Board appointed an advisory committee to review Volume I of *Humanities*. Upon examination, the committee recommended that the textbook be retained in the curriculum, but that *Lysistrata* and *The*

Miller's Tale not be assigned as required reading.

At its April 22, 1986 meeting the School Board considered the advisory committee's report. Silas Pittman, Superintendent of the Columbia County School System, offered his disagreement with the committee's conclusion, and recommended that the two disputed selections be deleted from Volume I or that use of the book in the curriculum be terminated. Adopting the latter proposal, the School Board voted to discontinue any future use of Volume I in the curriculum.

Pursuant to the Board decision, Volume I of *Humanities* was placed in locked storage and has been kept there ever since. . . .

On November 24, 1986 parents of students at Columbia High School filed an action against the School Board and the Superintendent seeking an injunction against the textbook removal and a declaration that such action violated their first amendment rights. . . .

It has long been clear that public school students do not "shed their constitutional rights to freedom of speech or expression at the schoolhouse gate." . . . At the same time, the Supreme Court has held that the rights of students in public schools are not automatically coextensive with the rights of adults, . . . and has recognized the central role of public schools in transmitting values necessary to the development of an informed citizenry. . . .

In matters pertaining to the curriculum, educators have been accorded greater control over expression than they may enjoy in other spheres of activity. . . .

[C]ourts that have addressed the issue have failed to achieve a consensus on the degree of discretion to be accorded school boards to restrict access to curricular materials. . . .

The most direct guidance from the Supreme Court is found in the recent case of *Hazelwood School District v. Kuhlmeier*, 484 U.S. 260, 108 S.Ct. 562, 98 L.Ed.2d 592 (1988).* In

Hazelwood the Court upheld the authority of a high school principal to excise two pages from a school-sponsored student newspaper on the grounds that articles concerning teenage pregnancy and divorce were inappropriate for the level of maturity of the intended readers, the privacy interests of the articles' subjects were insufficiently protected, and the controversial views contained therein might erroneously be attributed to the school. *Hazelwood* established a relatively lenient test for regulation of expression which "may fairly be characterized as part of the school curriculum." Such regulation is permissible so long as it is "reasonably related to legitimate pedagogical concerns." . . .

In applying that test the Supreme Court identified one such legitimate concern which is relevant to this case: "a school must be able to take into account the emotional maturity of the intended audience in determining whether to disseminate student speech on potentially sensitive topics . . . [e.g.] the particulars of teenage sexual activity." . . .

In applying the *Hazelwood* standard to the instant case, two considerations are particularly significant. First, we conclude that the Board decisions at issue were curricular decisions. The materials removed were part of the textbook used in a regularly scheduled course of study in the school. Plaintiffs argue that this particular course was an elective course, and not a required course. However, common sense indicates that the overall curriculum offered by a school includes not only the core curriculum (i.e., required courses) but also such additional, elective courses of study that school officials design and offer. Each student is expected to select from the several elective courses which school officials deem appropriate in order to fashion a curriculum tailored to his individual needs.

One factor identified in *Hazelwood* as relevant to the determination of whether an activity could fairly be characterized as part of the curriculum is whether "the public might reasonably perceive [the activity] to bear the imprimatur of the school." . . . It is clear that elective courses designed and offered by the school would be so perceived. . . .

---

* See Chapter 8 of this book for details of *Hazelwood School District v. Kuhlmeier.*

Plaintiffs further point out that the materials removed in this case not only were part of an elective course, but were optional, not required readings. For the reasons just mentioned, we conclude that the optional readings removed in this case were part of the school curriculum. Just as elective courses are designed by school officials to supplement required courses, optional readings in a particular class are carefully selected by the teacher as relevant and appropriate to supplement required readings in order to further the educational goals of the course. This is especially true in the instant circumstances, where the optional readings were included within the text itself, and thus had to accompany the student every time the text was taken home. Such materials would obviously carry the imprimatur of school approval.

The second consideration that is significant in applying the *Hazelwood* standard to this case is the fact that the motivation for the Board's removal of the readings has been stipulated to be related to the explicit sexuality and excessively vulgar language in the selections. It is clear from *Hazelwood* and other cases that this is a legitimate concern. School officials can "take into account the emotional maturity of the intended audience in determining . . . [the appropriateness of] potentially sensitive topics" such as sex and vulgarity. . . .

Since the stipulated motivation of the School Board relates to legitimate concerns, we need only determine whether the Board action was *reasonably* related thereto. It is of course true, as plaintiffs so forcefully point out, that *Lysistrata* and *The Miller's Tale* are widely acclaimed masterpieces of Western literature. However, after careful consideration, we cannot conclude that the school board's actions were not reasonably related to its legitimate concerns regarding the appropriateness (for this high school audience) of the sexuality and vulgarity in these works. Notwithstanding their status as literary classics, *Lysistrata* and *The Miller's Tale* contain passages of exceptional sexual explicitness, as numerous commentators have noted. In assessing the reasonableness of the Board's action, we also take into consideration the fact that most of the high school students involved ranged in age from fifteen to just over eighteen, and a substantial number had not yet reached the age of majority. We also note that the disputed materials have not been banned from the school. The *Humanities* textbook and other adaptations of *Lysistrata* and *The Miller's Tale* are available in the school library. No student or teacher is prohibited from assigning or reading these works or discussing the themes contained therein in class or on school property. . . . Under all the circumstances of this case, we cannot conclude that the Board's action was not reasonably related to the stated legitimate concern.

We decide today only that the Board's removal of these works from the curriculum did not violate the Constitution. Of course, we do not endorse the Board's decision. Like the district court, we seriously question how young persons just below the age of majority can be harmed by these masterpieces of Western literature. However, having concluded that there is no constitutional violation, our role is not to second guess the wisdom of the Board's action.

The judgment of the district court is affirmed.

Requirements that Students Study Basic Reader Series Is Not Unconstitutional as Violative of Student's Religious Beliefs

— - — - — - — - —

Mozert v. Hawkins County Board of Education

— - — - — - — - —

United States Court of Appeals,
Sixth Circuit, 1987.
827 F. 2d 1058.

LIVELY, Chief Judge. This case arose under the Free Exercise Clause of the First Amendment, made applicable to the states by the Fourteenth Amendment. The district court held that a public school requirement that all students in grades one through eight use a prescribed set of reading textbooks violated the constitutional rights of objecting parents and students. . . .

Early in 1983 the Hawkins County, Tennessee Board of Education adopted the Holt, Rinehart and Winston basic reading series (the Holt series) for use in grades 1-8 of the public schools of the county. . . .

Like many school systems, Hawkins County schools teach "critical reading" as opposed to reading exercises that teach only word and sound recognition. "Critical reading" requires the development of higher order cognitive skills that enable students to evaluate the material they read, to contrast the ideas presented, and to understand complex characters that appear in reading material. . . .

The plaintiff Vicki Frost is the mother of four children, three of whom were students in Hawkins County public schools in 1983. At the beginning of the 1983-84 school year Mrs. Frost read a story in a daughter's sixth grade reader that involved mental telepathy. Mrs. Frost, who describes herself as a "born again Christian," has a religious objection to any teaching about mental telepathy. Reading further, she found additional themes in the reader to which she had religious objections. After discussing her objections with other parents, Mrs. Frost talked with the principal of Church Hill Middle School and obtained an agreement for an alternative reading program for students whose parents objected to the assigned Holt reader. The students who elected the alternative program left their classrooms during the reading sessions and worked on assignments from an older textbook series in available office or library areas. Other students in two elementary schools were excused from reading the Holt books. In November 1983 the Hawkins County School Board voted unanimously to eliminate all alternative reading programs and require every student in the public schools to attend classes using the Holt series. Thereafter the plaintiff students refused to read the Holt series or attend reading classes where the series was being used. . . .

On December 2, 1983, the plaintiffs, consisting of seven families—14 parents and 17 children—filed this action pursuant to 42 U.S.C. § 1983. In their complaint the plaintiffs asserted that they have sincere religious beliefs which are contrary to the values taught or inculcated by the reading textbooks and that it is a violation of the religious beliefs and convictions of the plaintiff students to be required to read the books and a violation of the religious beliefs of the plaintiff parents to permit their children to read the books. The plaintiffs sought to hold the defendants liable because "forcing the student-plaintiffs to read school books which teach or inculcate values in violation of their religious beliefs and convictions is a clear violation of their rights to the free exercise of religion protected by the First and Fourteenth Amendments to the United States Constitution. . . .

Vicki Frost was the first witness for the plaintiffs and she presented the most complete explanation of the plaintiffs' position. The plaintiffs do not belong to a single church or denomination, but all consider themselves born again Christians. Mrs. Frost testified that the word of God as found in the Christian Bible "is the totality of my beliefs." There was evidence that other members of their churches, and even their pastors, do not agree with their position in this case.

Mrs. Frost testified that she had spent more than 200 hours reviewing the Holt series and had found numerous passages that offended her religious beliefs. She stated that the offending materials fell into seventeen categories which she listed. These ranged from such familiar concerns of fundamentalist Christians as evolution and "secular humanism" to less familiar themes such as "futuristic supernaturalism," pacifism, magic and false views of death.

In her lengthy testimony Mrs. Frost identified passages from stories and poems used in the Holt series that fell into each category. Illustrative is her first category, futuristic supernaturalism, which she defined as teaching "Man As God." Passages that she found offensive described Leonardo da Vinci as the human with a creative mind that "came closest to the divine touch." . . . . Mrs.

Frost testified that it is an "occult practice" for children to use imagination beyond the limitation of scriptural authority. She testified that the story that alerted her to the problem with the reading series fell into the category of futuristic supernaturalism. Entitled "A Visit to Mars," the story portrays thought transfer and telepathy in such a way that "it could be considered a scientific concept," according to this witness. This theme appears in the testimony of several witnesses, *i.e.*, the materials objected to "could" be interpreted in a manner repugnant to their religious beliefs.

Mrs. Frost described objectionable passages from other categories in much the same way. Describing evolution as a teaching that there is no God, she identified 24 passages that she considered to have evolution as a theme. . . .

Another witness for the plaintiffs was Bob Mozert, father of a middle school and an elementary school student in the Hawkins County system. His testimony echoed that of Vicki Frost in large part, though his answers to questions tended to be much less expansive. . . .

The first question to be decided is whether a governmental requirement that a person be exposed to ideas he or she finds objectionable on religious grounds constitutes a burden on the free exercise of that person's religion as forbidden by the First Amendment. . . .

It is also clear that exposure to objectionable material is what the plaintiffs objected to albeit they emphasize the repeated nature of the exposure. The complaint mentioned only the textbooks that the students were required to read. It did not seek relief from any method of teaching the material and did not mention the teachers' editions. The plaintiffs did not produce a single student or teacher to testify that any student was ever required to affirm his or her belief or disbelief in any idea or practice mentioned in the various stories and passages contained in the Holt series. However, the plaintiffs appeared to assume that materials clearly presented as poetry, fiction and even "make-believe" in the Holt series were presented as facts which the students were required to believe. Nothing in the record supports this assumption. . . .

. . . Proof that an objecting student was *required* to participate beyond reading and discussing assigned materials, or was disciplined for disputing assigned materials, might well implicate the Free Exercise Clause because the element of compulsion would then be present. But this was not the case either as pled or proved. The record leaves no doubt that the district court correctly viewed this case as one involving exposure to repugnant ideas and themes as presented by the Holt series.

Vicki Frost testified that an occasional reference to role reversal, pacifism, rebellion against parents, one-world government and other objectionable concepts would be acceptable, but she felt it was the repeated references to such subjects that created the burden. . . .

. . . Mrs. Frost testified that it would be acceptable for the schools to teach her children about other philosophies and religions, but if the practices of other religions were described in detail, or if the philosophy was "profound" in that it expressed a world view that deeply undermined her religious beliefs, then her children "would have to be instructed to [the] error [of the other philosophy]." It is clear that to the plaintiffs there is but one acceptable view — the Biblical view, as they interpret the Bible. Furthermore, the plaintiffs view every human situation and decision, whether related to personal belief and conduct or to public policy and programs, from a theological or religious perspective. . . .

The Supreme Court has recently affirmed that public schools serve the purpose of teaching fundamental values "essential to a democratic society." These values "include tolerance of divergent political and religious views" while taking into account "consideration of the sensibilities of others." . . . The Court has noted with apparent approval the view of some educators who see public schools as an "assimilative force" that brings together "diverse and conflicting elements" in our society "on a broad but common ground." . . . The critical reading approach furthers these goals. Mrs. Frost stated specifically that she objected to stories that develop "a religious tolerance that all religions are merely different roads to God." Stating that the plaintiffs reject this concept, presented as a recipe for an ideal world citizen, Mrs. Frost said, "We cannot be tolerant in that we accept other religious views on an equal basis with ours." While probably not an uncommon view of true believers in any religion, this statement graphically illustrates what is lacking in the plaintiffs' case.

The "tolerance of divergent . . . religious views" referred to by the Supreme Court is a civil tolerance, not a religious one. It does not require a person to accept any other religion as the equal of the one to which that person adheres. It merely requires a recognition that in a pluralistic society we must "live and let live." If the Hawkins County schools had required the plaintiff students either to believe or say they believe that "all religions are merely different roads to God," this would be a different case. No instrument of government can, consistent with the Free Exercise Clause, require such a belief or affirmation. However, there was absolutely no showing that the defendant school board sought to do this; indeed, the school board agreed at oral argument that it could not constitutionally do so. Instead, the record in this case discloses an effort by the school board to offer a reading curriculum designed to acquaint students with a multitude of ideas and concepts, though not in proportions the plaintiffs would like. While many of the passages deal with ethical issues, on the surface at least, they appear to us to contain no religious or anti-religious messages. Because the plaintiffs perceive every teaching that goes beyond the "three Rs" as inculcating religious ideas, they admit that any value-laden reading curriculum that did not affirm the truth of their beliefs would offend their religious convictions.

Although it is not clear that the plaintiffs object to all critical reading, Mrs. Frost did testify that she did not want her children to make critical judgments and exercise choices in areas where the Bible provides the answer. There is no evidence that any child in the Hawkins County schools was required to make such judgments. It was a goal of the school system to encourage this exercise, but

nowhere was it shown that it was required. When asked to comment on a reading assignment, a student would be free to give the Biblical interpretation of the material or to interpret it from a different value base. The only conduct compelled by the defendants was reading and discussing the material in the Holt series, and hearing other students' interpretations of those materials. This is the exposure to which the plaintiffs objected. What is absent from this case is the critical element of compulsion to affirm or deny a religious belief or to engage or refrain from engaging in a practice forbidden or required in the exercise of a plaintiff's religion. . . .

Since we have found none of the prohibited forms of governmental compulsion in this case, we conclude that the plaintiffs failed to establish the existence of an unconstitutional burden. Having determined that no burden was shown, we do not reach the issue of the defendants' compelling interest in requiring a uniform reading series or the question, raised by the defendant, of whether awarding damages violated the Establishment Clause. . . .

. . . . There was no evidence that the conduct required of the students was forbidden by their religion. Rather, the witnesses testified that reading the Holt series "could" or "might" lead the students to come to conclusions that were contrary to teachings of their and their parents' religious beliefs. This is not sufficient to establish an unconstitutional burden. . . .

The judgment of the district court granting injunctive relief and damages is reversed, and the case is remanded with directions to dismiss the complaint. No costs are allowed. The parties will bear their own costs on appeal.

NOTES

1. *Sequel to Mozert.* Following the determination in the Hawkins County case, Vickie Frost, a "born again Christian," was arrested for failure to leave school grounds after being told on several occasions by the principal that her repeated removal of her child from reading class and her conduct-

ing of reading lessons in the school parking lot, in the family car, was in violation of school policy. Frost sued, claiming denial of freedom of expression and due process because she was denied custody of her child during the school day. The court held that the school board had not deprived Frost of her freedom of expression nor had she been deprived of custody of her child without due process. Further, the court held that the city police were not liable for arresting her on school grounds. Her presence on school grounds and repeated refusal to leave was in violation of state statute forbidding trespass on school property. *Frost v. Hawkins County Board of Education*, 851 F.2d 822 (6th Cir. 1988).

2. *Secular Humanism and Textbooks.* Plaintiffs in an Alabama Case, *Smith v. Board of School Commissioners of Mobile County*, 827 F.2d 684 (11th Cir. 1987), claimed that use of certain home economics textbooks required students to accept tenets of humanistic psychology, a term that the lower court found to be a "manifestation of humanism." Humanism or secular humanism, it was maintained, was a religion advanced by the public schools through the use of home economics, history, and social studies textbooks that "implied that a person uses the same process in deciding a moral issue that he uses in choosing one pair of shoes over another." It was contended that these home economics, history, and social studies textbooks inferred that "the student must determine right and wrong based only on his own experience, feelings and [internal] values" and that such "moral choice is only to be decided by the student." The plaintiffs further asserted that the textbooks assumed that "self-actualization is the goal of every human being, and that man has no supernatural attributes . . . , that there are only temporal and physical consequences for man's actions, and that these results, alone, determine the morality of an action." This "belief strikes at the heart of many theistic religious beliefs that certain actions are in and of themselves immoral, whatever the consequences." By not seeking ecclesiastical answers in resolving human deci-

sions, the schools, it was claimed, denied or inhibited religion and advanced secularism. In support of the charge that the schools were purely temporal, the plaintiffs cited a recommended decision process cited by the textbooks which called for resolving problems by (1) defining the problem, (2) establishing your goals, (3) listing your goals in priority order, (4) looking for resources, (5) studying the alternatives, (6) making a decision, (7) carrying out the decision, and (8) evaluating the results. Because this process did not invoke divine guidance or include a step for spiritual involvement, the plaintiffs and the lower court concluded that the textbooks advanced secular humanism as a religion and denied theistic religious views. The appeals court found for the School Board and in so doing, concluded:

> . . . Examination of the contents of these textbooks, including the passages pointed out by Appellees as particularly offensive, in the context of the books as a whole and the undisputedly nonreligious purpose sought to be achieved by their use, reveals that the message conveyed is not one of endorsement of secular humanism or any religion. Rather, the message conveyed is one of a governmental attempt to instill in Alabama public school children such values as independent thought, tolerance of diverse views, self-respect, maturity, self-reliance and logical decision-making. This is an entirely appropriate secular effect. Indeed, one of the major objectives of public education is the "inculcat[ion of] fundamental values necessary to the maintenance of a democratic political system." . . .
>
> Nor do these textbooks evidence an attitude antagonistic to theistic belief. The message conveyed by these textbooks with regard to theistic religion is one of neutrality: the textbooks neither endorse theistic religion as a system of belief, nor discredit it. . . .
>
> There is no doubt that these textbooks were chosen for the secular purpose of education in the areas of history and social studies, and we find that the primary effect of the use of these textbooks is consistent with that stated purpose. We do not believe

that an objective observer could conclude from the mere omission of certain historical facts regarding religion or the absence of a more thorough discussion of its place in modern American society that the State of Alabama was conveying a message of approval of the religion of secular humanism.

. . . .

There simply is nothing in this record to indicate that omission of certain facts regarding religion from these textbooks of itself constituted an advancement of secular humanism or an active hostility towards theistic religion prohibited by the establishment clause.

◼ EVOLUTION VERSUS CREATIONISM

The classic argument over Darwin's theory of evolution and the biblical account of creation has been often debated in legislatures and the courts of the United States. Proponents of teaching "creation science" in the public schools convinced at least two legislatures, those of Arkansas and Louisiana, and the Texas State Board of Education that the account of creation in the Bible was as scientific as Darwin's theory and it was, therefore, a legitimate scientific theory, meriting its inclusion as a part of the public school curriculum. Because creationism was viewed by some as a scientific theory, state authorities mandated it be taught alongside evolution. The tenets of creationism are derived from the first two chapters of Genesis in the Bible and include the following judgments: (1) that the earth and universe are relatively young, perhaps only 6,000 to 10,000 years old; (2) that the present physical form of earth is explained by "catastrophism" including a worldwide flood; and (3) that all living things (including humans) were created miraculously, essentially in their present forms.

The National Academy of Sciences and many scientists, individually, have spoken out against the notion that "creation science" is science at all and have opposed its imposition in public school classrooms. The Academy, in an official release on the subject, said:

[T]he Academy states unequivocally that the tenets of "creation science" are not supported by scientific evidence, that creationism has no place in a *science* curriculum at any level, that its proposed teaching would be impossible in any constructive sense for well-informed and conscientious science teachers, and that its teaching would be contrary to the nation's need for a scientifically literate citizenry and for a large, well-informed pool of scientific and technical personnel.[28]

The Academy further observed that creationism is not a science per se and cannot be characterized as such, and to claim that creationism should be given equal time in the classrooms indicates a misunderstanding of the definition of science. Science, according to the Academy, is a systematic organization of knowledge about the universe and its parts. This knowledge is founded on evidence and verifiable consequences of experimentation and observation. Science is a process of formulation of hypotheses, continuous testing, corrections, and new conclusions and findings—it evolves and changes. Creationism, on the other hand, has no foundation in evidence, experimentation, or observation and is, therefore, not a science. Creationism is based on belief and revelation and cannot change regardless of evidence to the contrary.

The effect of the creationism movement was felt by major textbook publishers nationwide who responded to creationists' demands, especially those in Texas, where the State Board of Education adopted textbook guidelines that encouraged censorship. The Texas rule[29] required that all science textbooks identify evolution as only "one of several explanations of the origins of human kind," and that evolution must be treated as a theory rather than fact. As a result, the publishers decreased coverage of evolution in their science textbooks and one even deleted the word "evolution" completely. Finally, after a decade of acrimony, which had a substantial effect on the content of textbooks, the Texas State Board of Education abrogated the rule in April 1984.

The situation in Texas was merely a modern version of the issues that precipitated the famous "John Scopes monkey trial" in Dayton, Tennessee, which matched the famous lawyer Clarence Darrow against the great politician William Jennings Bryan. A technical victory was won by Bryan for the state, but Darrow won a popular victory in his devastating cross-examination of Bryan. Although the statute that made it a criminal offense to teach evolution in the public school classrooms of Tennessee was not overturned, it was largely ignored and went unenforced after Scopes' conviction.

In 1968, an antievolution statute in Arkansas was challenged as violative of the First Amendment.[30] The United States Supreme Court found in the statute an implicit state sanction of the Christian doctrine of creation from the Book of Genesis, and the Court declared it unconstitutional.

In a later version of the issue, which coincided with the aforementioned episodes in Texas, the Governor of Arkansas signed into law in 1981 a bill that required balanced treatment for creation science and evolution in the public schools. Proponents of the new statute maintained that not only was creationism a science, but that Darwin's theory of evolution actually constituted a kind of obverse religion, secular humanism, and, as such, its use in the classroom was tantamount to teaching an atheistic religion in public schools.

The statute was promptly challenged as violative of the religion provisions of the First Amendment. The State of Arkansas defended, first, by maintaining that a literal interpretation of Genesis did not necessarily mean that creation science was religious; second, the state's reference to creation did not imply that the creation was caused by a supreme being or God; and, third, to teach in public schools about the concept of a creator was not religious per se. The federal court in *McLean v. Arkansas Board of Education*[31] held against the state on all counts. The judge observed that creation science was not a science at all; but, instead, a religious doctrine. For the state to impose such a belief on the youth in public schools violated the First Amendment.

In January 1985, a federal district judge held a Louisiana creation statute, similar to Arkansas', unconstitutional because it "pro-motes the beliefs of some theistic sects to the detriment of others." According to the judge, the so-called balanced treatment statute removed the state from a position of neutrality toward advancing a particular religious belief. This case was appealed to the U.S. Supreme Court, and the Louisiana statute was held to be unconstitutional. The Court observed that the true legislative intent was to impose into the public schools the teaching of creationism as a religious doctrine, and the statute was therefore unconstitutional.[32]

---

*Statute Forbidding the Teaching of Evolution
Is Unconstitutional*

—··—··—··—··—

Epperson v. State of Arkansas

—··—··—··—··—

Supreme Court of the United States, 1968.
393 U.S. 97, 89 S.Ct. 266.

Mr. Justice FORTAS delivered the opinion of the Court. This appeal challenges the constitutionality of the "anti-evolution" statute which the State of Arkansas adopted in 1928 to prohibit the teaching in its public schools and universities of the theory that man evolved from other species of life.
. . .

The Arkansas law makes it unlawful for a teacher in any state-supported school or university "to teach the theory or doctrine that mankind ascended or descended from a lower order of animals," or "to adopt or use in any such institution a textbook that teaches" this theory. Violation is a misdemeanor and subjects the violator to dismissal from his position.

The present case concerns the teaching of biology in a high school in Little Rock. According to the testimony, until the events here in litigation, the official textbook furnished for the high school biology course did not have a section on the Darwinian Theory. Then, for the academic year 1965-1966, the school administration, on recommendation of the teachers of biology in the school system, adopted and prescribed a textbook which contained a chapter setting forth "the theory about the origin . . . of man from a lower form of animal."

Susan Epperson, a young woman who graduated from Arkansas' school system and then obtained her master's degree in zoology at the University of Illinois, was employed by the Little Rock school system in the fall of 1964 to teach tenth grade biology at Central High School. At the start of the next academic year, 1965, she was confronted by the new textbook (which one surmises from the record was not unwelcome to her). She faced at least a literal dilemma because she was supposed to use the new textbook for classroom instruction and presumably to teach the statutorily condemned chapter; but to do so would be a criminal offense and subject her to dismissal. . . . Only Arkansas and Mississippi have such "anti-evolution" or "monkey" laws on their books. There is no record of any prosecutions in Arkansas under its statute. It is possible that the statute is presently more of a curiosity than a vital fact of life in these States. Nevertheless, the present case was brought, the appeal as of right is properly here, and it is our duty to decide the issues presented.

At the outset, it is urged upon us that the challenged statute is vague and uncertain and therefore within the condemnation of the Due Process Clause of the Fourteenth Amendment. The contention that the Act is vague and uncertain is supported by language in the brief opinion of Arkansas' Supreme Court. That court, perhaps reflecting the discomfort which the statute's quixotic prohibition necessarily engenders in the modern mind, stated that it "expresses no opinion" as to whether the Act prohibits "explanation" of the theory of evolution or merely forbids "teaching that the theory is true." Regardless of this uncertainty, the court held that the statute is constitutional.

On the other hand, counsel for the State, in oral argument in this Court, candidly stated that, despite the State Supreme Court's equivocation Arkansas would interpret the statute "to mean that to make a student aware of the theory . . . just to teach that there was

such a theory" would be grounds for dismissal and for prosecution under the statute; and he said "that the Supreme Court of Arkansas' opinion should be interpreted in that manner." He said: "If Mrs. Epperson would tell her students that 'Here is Darwin's theory, that man ascended or descended from a lower form of being,' then I think she would be under this statute liable for prosecution.

In any event, we do not rest our decision upon the asserted vagueness of the statute. On either interpretation of its language, Arkansas' statute cannot stand. It is of no moment whether the law is deemed to prohibit mention of Darwin's theory, or to forbid any or all of the infinite varieties of communication embraced within the term "teaching." Under either interpretation, the law must be stricken because of its conflict with the constitutional prohibition of state laws respecting an establishment of religion or prohibiting the free exercise thereof. The overriding fact is that Arkansas' law selects from the body of knowledge a particular segment which it proscribes for the sole reason that it is deemed to conflict with a particular religious doctrine; that is, with a particular interpretation of the Book of Genesis by a particular religious group. . . .

Judicial interposition in the operation of the public school system of the Nation raises problems requiring care and restraint. Our courts, however, have not failed to apply the First Amendment's mandate in our educational system where essential to safeguard the fundamental values of freedom of speech and inquiry and of belief. By and large, public education in our Nation is committed to the control of state and local authorities. Courts do not and cannot intervene in the resolution of conflicts which arise in the daily operation of school systems and which do not directly and sharply implicate basic constitutional values. On the other hand, "[t]he vigilant protection of constitutional freedoms is nowhere more vital than in the community of American schools," *Shelton v. Tucker,* 364 U.S. 479, 487, 81 S.Ct. 247, 251, 5 L.Ed.2d 231 (1960). As this Court said in *Keyishian v. Board of Regents,* the First Amendment "does not tolerate laws that cast a pall of orthodoxy over the classroom."

385 U.S. 589, 603, 87 S.Ct. 675, 683, 17 L.Ed.2d 629 (1967). . . .

There is and can be no doubt that the First Amendment does not permit the State to require that teaching and learning must be tailored to the principles or prohibitions of any religious sect or dogma. . . .

In the present case, there can be no doubt that Arkansas has sought to prevent its teachers from discussing the theory of evolution because it is contrary to the belief of some that the Book of Genesis must be the exclusive source of doctrine as to the origin of man. No suggestion has been made that Arkansas' law may be justified by considerations of state policy other than the religious views of some of its citizens. It is clear that fundamentalist sectarian conviction was and is the law's reason for existence. Its antecedent, Tennessee's "monkey law," candidly stated its purpose: to make it unlawful "to teach any theory that denies the story of the Divine Creation of man as taught in the Bible, and to teach instead that man has descended from a lower order of animals." Perhaps the sensational publicity attendant upon the *Scopes* trial induced Arkansas to adopt less explicit language. It eliminated Tennessee's reference to "the story of the Divine Creation of man" as taught in the Bible, but there is no doubt that the motivation for the law was the same: to suppress the teaching of a theory which it was thought "denied" the divine creation of man. . . .

The judgment of the Supreme Court of Arkansas is reversed.

Louisiana Statute Requiring Balanced Treatment of Creation Science and Evolution Science Violates First Amendment

— · — · — — · — · —

Edwards v. Aguillard

— · — · — — · — · —

Supreme Court of the United States, 1987.
482 U.S. 578, 107 S. Ct. 2573.

Justice BRENNAN delivered the opinion of the Court. The question for decision is whether Louisiana's "Balanced Treatment for Creation-Science and Evolution-Science in Public School Instruction" Act (Creationism Act), La.Rev.Stat.Ann. §§ 17:286.1-17:286.7 (West 1982), is facially invalid as violative of the Establishment Clause of the First Amendment.

The Creationism Act forbids the teaching of the theory of evolution in public schools unless accompanied by instruction in "creation science." § 17:286.4A. No school is required to teach evolution or creation science. If either is taught, however, the other must also be taught. The theories of evolution and creation science are statutorily defined as "the scientific evidences for [creation or evolution] and inferences from those scientific evidences." . . .

Appellees, who include parents of children attending Louisiana public schools, Louisiana teachers, and religious leaders, challenged the constitutionality of the Act in District Court, seeking an injunction and declaratory relief. . . .

The Establishment Clause forbids the enactment of any law "respecting an establishment of religion." The Court has applied a three-pronged test to determine whether legislation comports with the Establishment Clause. First, the legislature must have adopted the law with a secular purpose. Second, the statute's principal or primary effect must be one that neither advances nor inhibits religion. Third, the statute must not result in an excessive entanglement of government with religion. . . . State action violates the Establishment Clause if it fails to satisfy any of these prongs.

In this case, the Court must determine whether the Establishment Clause was violated in the special context of the public elementary and secondary school system. States and local school boards are generally afforded considerable discretion in operating public schools. . . .

The Court has been particularly vigilant in monitoring compliance with the Establishment Clause in elementary and secondary schools. Families entrust public schools with the education of their children, but condition their trust on the understanding that the classroom will not purposely be used to advance religious views that may conflict with the private beliefs of the student and his or her family. Students in such institutions are impressionable and their attendance is involuntary. . . . The State exerts great authority and coercive power through mandatory attendance requirements, and because of the students' emulation of teachers as role models and the children's susceptibility to peer pressure. . . . Furthermore, "[t]he public school is at once the symbol of our democracy and the most pervasive means for promoting our common destiny. In no activity of the State is it more vital to keep out divisive forces than in its schools . . . ."

Consequently, the Court has been required often to invalidate statutes which advance religion in public elementary and secondary schools. . . .

Therefore, in employing the three-pronged *Lemon* test, we must do so mindful of the particular concerns that arise in the context of public elementary and secondary schools. We now turn to the evaluation of the Act under the *Lemon* test.

Lemon's first prong focuses on the purpose that animated adoption of the Act. "The purpose prong of the *Lemon* test asks whether government's actual purpose is to endorse or disapprove of religion." . . . A governmental intention to promote religion is clear when the State enacts a law to serve a religious purpose. This intention may be evidenced by promotion of religion in general, . . . or by advancement of a particular religious belief, ... If the law was enacted for the purpose of endorsing religion, "no consideration of the second or third criteria is necessary." . . . In this case, the petitioners have identified no clear secular purpose for the Louisiana Act.

True, the Act's stated purpose is to protect academic freedom. La.Rev.Stat.Ann. § 17:286.2 (West 1982). This phrase might, in common parlance, be understood as referring to enhancing the freedom of teachers to teach what they will. The Court of Appeals, however, correctly concluded that the Act was not designed to further that goal. We find no merit in the State's argument that the "legislature may not [have] use[d] the terms 'academic freedom' in the correct legal sense. They might have [had] in mind, instead, a basic concept of fairness; teaching all of the evidence." . . . Even if "academic freedom" is read to mean "teaching all of the evidence" with respect to the origin of human beings, the Act does not further this purpose. The goal of providing a more comprehensive science curriculum is not furthered either by outlawing the teaching of evolution or by requiring the teaching of creation science.

While the Court is normally deferential to a State's articulation of a secular purpose, it is required that the statement of such purpose be sincere and not a sham. . . .

It is clear from the legislative history that the purpose of the legislative sponsor, Senator Bill Keith, was to narrow the science curriculum. During the legislative hearings, Senator Keith stated: "My preference would be that neither [creationism nor evolution] be taught." Such a ban on teaching does not promote—indeed, it undermines—the provision of a comprehensive scientific education.

It is equally clear that requiring schools to teach creation science with evolution does not advance academic freedom. The Act does not grant teachers a flexibility that they did not already possess to supplant the present science curriculum with the presentation of theories, besides evolution, about the origin of life. . . .

Furthermore, the goal of basic "fairness" is hardly furthered by the Act's discriminatory preference for the teaching of creation science and against the teaching of evolution. While requiring that curriculum guides be developed for creation science, the Act says nothing of comparable guides for evolution. . . . Similarly, research services are supplied for creation science but not for evolution. . . . Only "creation scientists" can serve on the panel that supplies the resource services. The Act forbids school boards to discriminate against anyone who "chooses to be a creation-scientist" or to teach "creationism," but fails to protect those who choose to teach evolution or any other non-creation science theory, or who refuse to teach creation science. . . .

If the Louisiana legislature's purpose was solely to maximize the comprehensiveness and effectiveness of science instruction, it would have encouraged the teaching of all scientific theories about the origins of humankind.[8] But under the Act's requirements, teachers who were once free to teach any and all facets of this subject are now unable to do so. Moreover, the Act fails even to ensure that creation science will be taught, but instead requires the teaching of this theory only when the theory of evolution is taught. Thus we agree with the Court of Appeals' conclusion that the Act does not serve to protect academic freedom, but has the distinctly different purpose of discrediting "evolution by counterbalancing its teaching at every turn with the teaching of creation science . . . ."

. . .

. . . There is a historic and contemporaneous link between the teachings of certain religious denominations and the teaching of evolution. It was this link that concerned the Court in *Epperson v. Arkansas*, 393 U.S. 97, 89 S.Ct. 266, 21 L.Ed.2d 228 (1968), which also involved a facial challenge to a statute regulating the teaching of evolution. . . . Although the Arkansas anti-evolution law did not explicitly state its predominant religious purpose, the Court could not ignore that "[t]he statute was a product of the upsurge of 'fundamentalist' religious fervor" that has long viewed this particular scientific theory as contradicting the literal interpretation of the Bible. . . .

These same historic and contemporaneous antagonisms between the teachings of certain religious denominations and the teaching of evolution are present in this case. The preeminent purpose of the Louisiana legislature was clearly to advance the religious viewpoint that a supernatural being created humankind. The term "creation science" was defined as embracing this particular religious doctrine by those responsible for the passage of the Creationism Act. Senator Keith's leading expert on creation science, Edward Boudreaux, testified at the legislative hearings that the theory of creation science included belief in the existence of a supernatural creator. (noting that "creation scientists" point to high probability that life was "created by an intelligent mind").[12] Senator Keith also cited testimony from other experts to support the creation-science view that "a creator [was] responsible for the universe and everything in it." . . .

The legislative history therefore reveals that the term "creation science," as contemplated by the legislature that adopted this Act, embodies the religious belief that a supernatural creator was responsible for the creation of humankind.

Furthermore, it is not happenstance that the legislature required the teaching of a theory that coincided with this religious view. The legislative history documents that the Act's primary purpose was to change the science curriculum of public schools in order to provide persuasive advantage to a particular religious doctrine that rejects the factual basis of evolution in its entirety. . . . The legislation therefore sought to alter the science curriculum to reflect endorsement of a religious view that is antagonistic to the theory of evolution.

In this case, the purpose of the Creationism Act was to restructure the science curriculum to conform with a particular religious viewpoint. Out of many possible science subjects taught in the public schools, the legislature chose to affect the teaching of the one scientific theory that historically has been opposed by certain religious sects. As in *Epperson*, the legislature passed the Act to give preference to those religious groups which have as one of their tenets the creation of humankind by a divine creator. . . . Because the primary purpose of the Creationism Act is to advance a particular religious belief, the Act endorses religion in violation of the First Amendment.

We do not imply that a legislature could never require that scientific critiques of prevailing scientific theories be taught. . . . But because the primary purpose of the Creationism Act is to endorse a particular religious doctrine, the Act furthers religion in violation of the Establishment Clause. . . .

We agree with the lower courts that these affidavits do not raise a genuine issue of material fact. The existence of "uncontroverted affidavits" does not bar summary judgment.

The Louisiana Creationism Act advances a religious doctrine by requiring either the banishment of the theory of evolution from public school classrooms or the presentation of a religious viewpoint that rejects evolution in its entirety. The Act violates the Establishment Clause of the First Amendment because it seeks to employ the symbolic and financial support of government to achieve a religious purpose. The judgment of the Court of Appeals therefore is

Affirmed.

■ STUDENT TESTING AND PROMOTION

The state has the authority to establish standards for promotion and graduation. In recent years, states have begun to rely more and more on the standardized test as a criterion to determine students' competencies. So long as such measures of academic attainment are reasonable and nondiscriminatory, the courts will not intervene. Courts have traditionally given school officials and teachers wide latitude in deciding on appropriate academic requirements. The United States Supreme Court, in *Horowitz*, pointed out that "Courts are particularly ill-equipped to evaluate academic performance."[33] This judicial position of nonintervention was adopted early by the courts. In a 1913 case in Massachusetts, the court said that "So long as the school committee acts in good faith their conduct in formulating and applying standards and making decisions touching this matter is not subject to review by any other tribunal."[34]

Courts, of course, are not equipped to evaluate the academic standards of the myriad areas of subject matter and to review student performance. The courts confine themselves to determining whether due process is given, whether discrimination exists, or if a student suffers ill treatment from arbitrary or capricious action by the school. In *Gaspar v. Bruton*,[35] the United States Court of Appeals for the Tenth Circuit observed that "The courts are not equipped to review academic records based upon academic standards within the particular knowledge, experience and expertise of academicians. . . . Thus, when presented with a challenge . . . . for failure re academic standards, the court may grant relief, as a practical matter, only in those cases where the student presents positive evidence of ill will or bad motives."

Due Process and Testing

In recent years, states have moved to competency tests as minimal criteria for the awarding of high school diplomas. Because of society's great reliance on high school and college diplomas as measures of attainment, the diploma is of special interest to the student. The diploma, therefore, meets the criteria for a property interest under the Due Process Clause of the Fourteenth Amendment as enunciated in *Board of Regents v. Roth* by the United States Supreme Court. There the Court stated that "To have a property interest in a benefit, a person clearly must have more than an abstract need or desire for it. He must have more than a unilateral expectation of it. He must, instead, have a legitimate claim of entitlement to it."[36] Certainly, a diploma is a benefit that everyone needs, and when a student progresses academically for twelve years, one may logically assume that the diploma will be forthcoming. The reasonableness of expectation of receipt of a diploma is, of course, contingent on the school standards and normal academic progress.

In requiring that students pass minimal competency tests in order to graduate, states have established new criteria to which a student must respond in order to have a reasonable expectation of graduation. The criteria for graduation, level of test scores, type of questions, and the difficulty of items are all issues requiring subjective academic judgment. Substantive due process, property, and liberty interests do not apply to such subjective standards. It is the objective standards over which the courts will exercise scrutiny. The United States Supreme Court in *Mathews v. Eldridge*[37] enunciated the rationale for invoking due process, saying that the dictates of due process are (1) the nature of the private interest denied by official action, (2) the risk of erroneous deprivation if appropriate procedures are not followed, and (3) the state's interest in imposing the particular requirements or denying the benefit.

Where tests are concerned, "risk of erroneous deprivation" may be caused by tests that do not measure the content that they are supposed to measure. If the tests do not measure the content then they lack validity. A second test concept is reliability that requires that the measure must yield consistent results.

These issues of validity and reliability became the foci of the court in the case of *Debra P. v. Turlington,* in which the Florida functional literacy examination was challenged. In the original litigation, the plaintiffs prevailed on the due process issues because the state could not show that the school curriculum prepared the students for the items tested.[38] The United States Court of Appeals for the Fifth Circuit, in addressing test validity as a due process issue, remanded the case for further findings of fact to determine whether the literacy test covered "material actually taught in Florida's classrooms." To provide this information, the Florida Department of Education went through an elaborate process of surveying teachers to determine the content of courses they were teaching in order to verify that the questions on the literacy test were addressed in the classroom. On rehearing of the case, the federal district court accepted the evidence submitted by the state indicating validity of the questions and ruled for the state.

Debra P. is an important due process precedent because it expands the judicial view of objective criteria to the extent that test questions come under the scrutiny of the court. This case tends to narrow the state's prerogative in interpreting what has traditionally been a subjective consideration. By more carefully circumscribing objective criteria in terms of statistical measures of validity and reliability, the court effectively extends the realm of judicial scrutiny into student evaluation processes. In so doing, the court shifts the burden of proof and forces the state to demonstrate that the test was a fair assessment of what was taught.

Debra P. has subsequently been used as precedent by other courts. In *Anderson v. Banks,* a federal district court in Georgia required the school district to show that the questions on the California Achievement Test (CAT) had actually been covered in the high school curriculum before the court would allow the test to be used for an exit examination. The school district sustained this burden by conducting a study that matched objectives measured by the CAT with the school curriculum. Second, the study showed that the textbook content closely paralleled the types of items used and the content measured on the CAT. This was sufficient to meet the court's due process requirements. The court, in quoting *Debra P.*, said that "To require school officials to produce testimony that every teacher finished every lesson and assigned every problem in the curriculum would impose a paralyzing burden on school authorities . . . ."[39]

Equal Protection and Testing

Courts are very much aware of the potential for use of tests as a means to justify racial discrimination in violation of equal protection. In 1967, a federal district judge in Washington, D.C., held that the use of tests for tracking students was unconstitutional. The court found that the effect of the tests was to categorize students according to race, and, that little opportunity was afforded to move from one track to another. Similarly, the use of IQ tests to evaluate students for placement in classes for the mentally retarded was invalidated by a federal court in California because the state could not show how the IQ tests were related to the intellectual capabilities of the students.[40] The effect of these tests was to place an inordinate number of black children in the mentally retarded category.[41]

The "effect" standard required that school officials show a compelling interest to administer such tests if the result was to effectively separate the races in the schools. School officials were uniformly unable to sustain this compelling interest burden and were, thus, virtually foreclosed from using standardized tests for placement or promotion.

Then the United States Supreme Court, in *Washington v. Davis*,[42] set down a new precedent that required plaintiffs to show not merely that the "effect" of the tests was to racially discriminate, but that the state in adopting the tests had the "intent" to discriminate. In this case, the Court found that to use tests producing racially disparate results was not a violation of equal protection unless it could be shown that there was official intent to discriminate.

Since the *Davis* decision, lower courts have refined the intent standard with a moderating criterion called "institutional intent." This standard requires that officials show a substantial nonracial objective, not a compelling interest if discriminatory results can be reasonably foreseen. This compromise test has been defined this way: "Where the school board adopts policies that foreseeably further an illegitimate objective, and it cannot justify or adequately explain such policies in terms of legitimate educational objectives, one must presume that the school board would not have adopted such a policy but for an illegitimate purpose. Consistent with this perspective, "institutional segregative intent' may be said to exist where a school board adopts a more, rather than a less, segregative policy and cannot justify its choice in terms of legitimate educational objectives."[43]

The important issue is to determine what is a "compelling" state interest as opposed to what is merely a "reasonable" state interest. There is little doubt that tests can be used as diagnostic instruments even though classifications fall along racial lines. But there may be some legitimate question as to whether such tests can be used as a culling device to weed out those who are not as academically able as others, especially where no opportunity for academic redress is offered the student. Most importantly, though, the "institutional intent" standard shifts the burden of proof to the school district where with the simple "intent" test the plaintiff must show evidence that the state had the purpose and intent to discriminate.

Functional Literacy Test May Be Required as Prerequisite for High School Diploma, but Test Must Be a Valid Measure of Instruction

— — — — — — —

Debra P. v. Turlington

— — — — — — —

United States District Court, Middle District of Florida, 1983.
564 F.Supp. 177, affirmed 730 F.2d 1405
(11th Cir. 1984).

GEORGE C. CARR, District Judge. In 1978, the Florida Legislature approved an amendment to the Educational Accountability Act of 1976, Fla.Stat. § 229.55 et seq., which required public school students in the State of Florida to pass a functional literacy examination in order to receive a state high school diploma. Fla.Stat. § 232.246(1)(b). Shortly after its enactment, Florida high school students filed a class action challenging the constitutionality of the literacy test requirement. This Court found that the test violated both the equal protection and due process clauses of the Constitution and enjoined its use as a diploma sanction until the 1982-83 school year. *Debra P. v. Turlington*, 474 F.Supp. 244 (M.D.Fla.1979). On appeal, the Fifth Circuit Court of Appeals affirmed many of this Court's findings. *Debra P. v. Turlington*, 644 F.2d 397 (5th Cir.1981). However, the appellate court remanded the case for further factual findings on two key issues. Specifically, this Court was directed to make further findings on whether or not the functional literacy test, the Florida Student State Assessment Test, Part II (SSAT-II), covers material actually taught in Florida's classrooms. In addition, the Court of Appeals requested this Court to reexamine the "role and effect of the 'vestiges' of past discrimination" upon twelfth-grade black students.   . . .

The SSAT-II is a test of student's ability to successfully apply basic communications and mathematics skill to everyday life situations. . . . The test covers twenty-four basic skills. Of these, eleven are designated as communications skills and thirteen are designated as mathematics skills. . . .

The Court of Appeals has upheld the denial of a diploma to these students so long as the "test is a fair test of that which was taught." The Court reasoned that "[i]f the test is not fair, it cannot be said to be rationally related to a state interest" and therefore it would be violative of the Equal Protection Clause. In other words, the SSAT-II is only constitutional if it is instructionally valid. . . .

Put simply, the task assigned to this Court by the Court of Appeals was to find out if Florida is teaching what it is testing. Unfortunately, the answer to this apparently easy question is quite complex.

In an effort to carry its burden of proving that the test is instructionally valid, the defendants commissioned . . . a private consultant firm, to develop a study . . . . The survey asked teachers whether they had provided instruction relating to the twenty-four skills tested on the SSAT-II. If they had, the teachers were then asked if they had provided sufficient instruction for a student to master the skills. The teachers were required to answer separately for each individual skill. In addition, although the survey was anonymous, the teachers were asked to identify whether they were an elementary or secondary teacher and, if a secondary teacher, they were to identify their major field of emphasis.

The second part of the study . . . was a survey sent to the sixty-seven school districts and four university laboratory schools in Florida. . . .

The third component of the . . . study consisted of a series of site visits to verify the accuracy of the district reports. . . .

The fourth component of the . . . study was a student survey administered by the site visitors to one or two eleventh-grade social studies and English classes. The survey asked the students to state whether or not they had been taught in school how to answer the types of questions found on the SSAT-II. The sample questions provided to the students included questions on all twenty-four SSAT-II skills.

At trial, the defendant offered three expert witnesses who opined, based on the array of data outlined above, that Florida was teaching what it was testing. . . .

. . . [E]vidence suggests, the resolution of the instructional validity issue depends both on whose experts are believed and on what sort of proof is required. With regard to the former, it is important to understand that the instructional validity issue, and the related concept of minimum competency testing, are relatively new and highly controversial subjects which seem to have polarized the educational community. Thus, in large part, this Court has been called upon to settle not only a legal argument but also a professional dispute. . . .

But, what does the Constitution require in this instance? It may not be fair to expect students with differing interests and abilities to learn the same material at the same rate, but is it unconstitutional? Similarly, it may be inequitable that some students, through random selection, are assigned to mediocre teachers while others are given excellent instructors, but does this inequity rise to the level of a constitutional violation?

These questions lead to other issues concerning the appropriate burden of proof. The plaintiffs argue that the defendants have not carried their burden because they have not attempted to follow students throughout their entire careers. They also assert that there is insufficient evidence of what actually goes on in the classrooms. But, absent viewing a videotape of every student's school career, how can we know what really happened to each child? Even assuming that such videotapes were available, how could this Court decide, in constitutional terms, which students received appropriate instruction and which did not? Suppose that there is one student who never encountered a teacher who taught the SSAT-II skills, or a teacher who taught the skills well, should the entire test be declared invalid? What if the number of students were 3,000 rather than one?

It is necessary to consider these questions in order to appreciate the dilemma confronted by this Court. Instructional validity is an elusive concept. Moreover, unlike some of the other claims made by the plaintiffs at the first trial, the instructional validity issue strikes at the heart of the learning and teaching process. It also lends itself to individualized determinations rather than objective treatment.

Instructional validity is a subpart of content validity which together with curricular validity, insures that a test covers matters actually taught. As the Court of Appeals noted, and as this Court previously found, the SSAT-II is a "good test of what the students *should* know." . . . That is, the subjects tested parallel the curricular goals of the State. To this end, the Department of Education publishes minimum performance standards and also "periodically examine[s] and evaluate[s] procedures, records, and programs in each district to determine compliance with law and rules established by the state board." Thus, although the individual districts are still somewhat autonomous, they no longer have the authority to decide that they will not teach certain minimum skills. In the same vein, the Department of Education, the individual districts, and the separate schools are required to submit annual reports of how well school instructional programs are helping students acquire minimum performance skills. In sum, since at least 1979, school administrators and teachers have been well aware of the minimum performance standards imposed by the State and their duty to teach these skills.
. . .

The districts also receive funding from the State to remediate students who need special educational assistance in order to master the basic skills. . . . Each district school board is also required to establish pupil progression plans to insure that students are not promoted without consideration of each student's mastery of basic skills. The State has also established uniform testing standards for grades three, five, eight and eleven to monitor the acquisition of basic skills by students statewide.

These legislative requirements bolster the conclusion that the SSAT-II is, at least, curricularly valid. They lend support to the opinions of the defendants' experts that the SSAT-II is instructionally valid. It is clear from the survey results that the terms of the Educational Accountability Act are not just hollow words found in a statute book. Rather, the district reports, teacher surveys, and site visit audits, as interpreted by the defendants' experts, all indicate that the directives of the Act are a driving force in all of Florida's public schools.

Nevertheless, it is the plaintiffs' position that the instructional validity of the test cannot be established by showing that the skills tested are included in a recognized curriculum. To the contrary, they believe that the only touchstone of the test's validity is proof of what graduating seniors were *actually*, not theoretically, taught. Without such proof, the plaintiffs posit that no one can tell whether the students had a "fair" opportunity to learn. . . .

As noted above, it is impossible to prove conclusively the degree to which every one of the more than 100,000 graduating seniors were exposed to the SSAT-II skills. What is known, is that the districts have reported that these skills are included in their curriculum and that a substantial number of public school teachers have stated that they adhere to this curriculum by including these skills in their course of instruction. In addition, and of even greater significance in determining the constitutionality of the test, it is known that students are given five chances to pass the SSAT-II between the tenth and twelfth grades of school and that, if they fail, they are offered remedial help. They also have the option of staying in school for an additional year in order to "receive special instruction designed to remedy [their] identified deficiencies." Certainly, some remedial programs and teachers will be more effective than others. However, this disparity cannot be said to be unfair in a constitutional sense. While it might be preferable from an educator's standpoint to insure that students learn the requisite skills during their regular courses rather than in remedial sessions, the Constitution clearly does not mandate such a result. What is required is that the skills be included in the official curriculum and that the majority of the teachers recognize them as being something they should teach. Once these basic facts are proven, as they have been in this case, the only logical inference is that the teachers are doing the job they are paid to do and are teaching these skills. It strains credibility to hypothesize that teachers, especially remedial teachers, are uniformly avoiding their responsibilities at the expense of their pupils.   .   .   .

For the reasons stated above, and based on a review of the evidence presented by both sides, the Court finds that the defendants have carried their burden of proving by a preponderance of the evidence that the SSAT-II is instructionally valid and therefore constitutional. Although the instruction offered in all the classrooms of all the districts might not be ideal, students are nevertheless afforded an adequate opportunity to learn the skills tested on the SSAT-II before it is used as a diploma sanction.

As noted earlier, deciding that the SSAT-II is a fair test of that which is taught in the Florida public schools does not end this Court's inquiry. The Court must still decide whether or not the State should be enjoined from imposing the diploma sanction because the vestiges of past purposeful discrimination have an unconstitutional impact on black high school students.

No one disputes the fact that the SSAT-II failure rate among black students is disproportionately high. Of the three thousand twelfth-grade students who have not passed the test, about 57 percent are black even though blacks only constitute about 20 percent of the entire student body. While these statistics are alarming, they do not, standing alone, answer the constitutional question this Court must confront.

In order for this Court to continue to prohibit the State from using the SSAT-II as a diploma sanction, the disproportionate failure rate among today's high school seniors must be found to have been caused by past purposeful segregation or its lingering effects. If the disparate failure of blacks is not due to the present effects of past intentional segregation or if the test is necessary to remedy those

effects, then the four-year injunction entered in 1979 cannot be extended.   .   .   .

[T]he plaintiffs seem to argue that the SSAT-II will be invalid as long as any vestiges of discrimination exist.

In the 1979 trial, this Court found, "the most significant burden which accompanied black children into the integrated schools was the existence of years of inferior education." This burden is not shouldered by the Class of 1983. Unlike the Class of 1979, black and white members of the Class of 1983 have had the same textbooks, curricula, libraries and attendance requirements throughout their public school years. Thus, while no two students can have an identical academic experience, their educational opportunities have nonetheless been equal in a constitutional sense. Moreover, to the extent that insidious racism is a problem in the schools, it would seem that a test like the SSAT-II, with objective standards and goals, would lead to its eradication.
.   .   .

Twelve years have passed since the Florida public schools became physically unitary. Since that time, the State of Florida has undertaken massive efforts to improve the education of all of its school children. The SSAT-II is an important part of those efforts. Its use can be enjoined only if it perpetuates the effects of past school segregation or if it is not needed to remedy those effects. Applying this standard to the facts presented at both the 1979 and 1983 trials, the Court finds that the injunction should not be extended. The State of Florida may deny diplomas to the members of the Class of 1983 who have not passed the SSAT-II.

NOTES

Achievement or Ability Grouping

1. Where plaintiff black children alleged that a school district's use of achievement test for ability grouping violated their rights under the Equal Protection Clause and the Civil Rights Act of 1964, the court ruled that the former was not violated because the evidence indicated that achievement grouping was a sound educational practice,

and that disadvantaged children, including black students, had made significant academic progress since the inception of the achievement grouping program. Regarding the charge of discrimination under the Civil Rights Act, the court said that "disparate impact" test of the act required that the plaintiffs show by a preponderance of evidence that a racially neutral practice, such as achievement tests, have a racially disproportionate impact. If the plaintiffs are able to sustain such evidence, then the burden of proof shifts to the defendant to prove substantial legitimate justification for its action. In this case the defendants bore the burden and were able to show that the school district achievement grouping practices had a manifest, demonstrable relationship to classroom education and, thus, did not violate Title VI of the Civil Rights Act of 1964. *Georgia State Conference of Branches of NAACP v. State of Georgia*, 775 F.2d 1403 (11th Cir. 1985).

■ GRADING AND ACADEMIC REQUIREMENTS

Educational processes of public schools are generally systematic and incremental in nature. Student progress is normally measured and evaluated accordingly. The school fits the conceptual bases discussed early by Benjamin Rush and Jefferson in their correspondence, wherein they called for a uniform system of education that would provide essential curriculum for the masses and an orderly means of incremental learning—elementary, secondary, higher education, and so on.[44] The organization of the graded class system in which students build on the knowledge gained from previous schooling assumes, implicitly, some evaluation process to determine knowledge gained.

Because such evaluations are so important to the individual's future, it is inevitable that litigation should arise regarding grading, testing, and sanction of a student's educational progress.

The courts have been reluctant to intervene in the internal academic affairs of schools, preferring to defer to the judgment of professional educators where issues of student evaluation are concerned. This reticence was illustrated by the U.S. Supreme Court in a 1978 higher education case, where a fine line was drawn distinguishing academic penalties from disciplinary actions. The Court observed that academic considerations are by their "nature more subjective and evaluative than the typical factual questions presented in the average disciplinary decision" and that such academic judgments should be left to educators.[45] More recently, the Supreme Court upheld faculty judgment in denying a student the opportunity to retake an examination that was a prerequisite to obtaining a degree because the student had a poor overall academic standing and had failed to score at an acceptable level on a particular examination. The Court upheld the school's action, even though some other students had been allowed to retake the examination.[46] The Court said that "when judges are asked to review the substance of a genuinely academic decision . . . , they should show great respect for the faculty's professional judgment."[47]

Withholding Diploma

It is within the sound judgment of school authorities to determine if and when a pupil has completed the prescribed courses entitling him to a diploma. However, there is no direct relationship between participation in a graduation exercise and the issuance of a diploma. Once the pupil has completed successfully all of the required courses, the issuance of a diploma is a ministerial act that the school officials must perform. Refusal of a pupil to perform some act that is not a part of curriculum nor is required by school regulation prior to graduation will not justify withholding of the diploma. Thus, school authorities may deny a student participation in graduation ceremonies as a disciplinary measure, but may not withhold the diploma unless the student is academically deficient.[48]

In a 1921 case in which a student's refusal to wear a cap and gown to graduation resulted in the board's withholding the pupil's diploma, the court mandated that the diploma be granted and stated:

> A diploma, therefore is *prima facie* evidence of educational worth, and is the goal of the matriculate. . . . The issuance of a diploma by the school board to a pupil who satisfactorily completes the prescribed course of study and who is otherwise qualified is mandatory, and, although such duty is not expressly enjoined upon the board by statute, it does arise by necessary and reasonable implication. . . . This Plaintiff . . . having complied with all the rules and regulations precedent to graduation, may not be denied her diploma by the arbitrary action of the school board subsequent to her being made the recipient of the honors of graduation. *Valentine v. Independent School Dist. of Casey*, 191 Iowa 1100, 183 N.W. 434 (1921).[49]

Grade Reduction

Challenges to school grading policies have usually been couched in due process of law. In response to such an allegation, a court in Michigan held that a student has no vested property interest in a particular grade, and that a school board has the implied authority to set grading policies even though state statute does not expressly grant such authority.[50]

Courts have generally held that grades cannot be reduced as a disciplinary measure for violation of school rules. Where a student, while on a school field trip, drank a glass of wine in violation of school rules, the school suspended her for five days, expelled her from the cheerleading squad and the National Honor Society, prohibited her participation in school activities during the days she was expelled from school, and, in addition, imposed a further penalty of grade reduction. The school policy called for the reduction of grades in all classes by two percentage points for each day of suspension. Upon challenge, the court held for the student and ruled that a school board may not impose a grade reduction sanction for infractions that are not related to education. To do so, the court maintained, was to misrepresent the student's

true scholastic achievement for college entrance and other purposes.[51]

Yet, attendance at school and academic performance may be reasonably connected, and failure to attend school may affect the overall educational process. If a school board decides that attendance is essential to fulfill academic requirements and rules are so promulgated, then the courts are not likely to intervene.[52]

Thus, while school authorities have broad authority in the evaluation of students, the exercise of the authority cannot be so broad and indiscriminate as to permit unreasonable or improper exercise of discretion. What constitutes appropriate use of discretion largely depends on how well the school documents its rationale and how closely that rationale relates to the desirable educational end that the rule is designed to achieve.

Extracurricular Grade Standards

Lately, much has been written about the relationship between the regular and the extracurricular activities of the school and the importance of requiring reasonable minimum academic standards as conditions precedent to participation. Minimal participation standards have been imposed in several states, and in some instances litigation has resulted. The Montana Supreme Court has held that a school district requirement that a student maintain a 2.0 or "C" grade average for the preceding nine weeks in order to participate in extracurricular activities was a valid exercise of school board authority.[53] The court reasoned that participation in extracurricular activities is not a fundamental right under either the Montana or federal constitutions, and that therefore, the board need only show that its, rule was reasonable and rational. The reasonableness of the board's action was found in its desire to develop the full educational potential of each person in providing a basic quality education and providing incentive for those students who wish to participate in extracurricular activities. In a similar case, a Louisiana court held that requiring a 1.6 grade average to participate in cheerleading tryouts was rationally related to promotion of academic excellence and was not violative of equal protection.[54]

In such cases the rule will be upheld if its purpose is rationally related to the educational objective of the school. Because courts have generally held that participation in extracurricular activities and interscholastic athletics do not rise to the level of a constitutionally protected right, there is no entitlement of procedural due process protections, and the school board does not need to bear the more severe equal protection burden of showing that it has a compelling reason to invoke such a rule.[55]

School Board Policy Imposing Academic Sanctions for Nonattendance Is Not Ultra Vires, nor Does It Violate Due Process or Equal Protection Guarantees

— · — · — · — · — · —

Campbell v. Board of Education of Town of New Milford

— · — · — · — · — · —

Supreme Court of Connecticut, 1984.
193 Conn. 93, 475 A.2d 289.

PETERS, Associate Justice. This case concerns the validity of the policy of a local school board that imposes academic sanctions for nonattendance upon high school students. . . . The plaintiff claimed that the defendants' policy was ultra vires in light of governing state statutes, and unconstitutional in light of operative provisions of the Connecticut constitution and the United States constitution. The trial court rendered judgment for the defendants and the plaintiff has appealed.

The underlying facts are undisputed. The New Milford attendance policy, set out in an annually distributed student handbook, provides two sets of academic sanctions for students who are absent from school. Course credit is withheld from any student who,

without receiving an administrative waiver, is absent from any year-long course for more than twenty-four class periods. In the calculation of the twenty-four maximum absences, all class absences are included except absences on school-sponsored activities or essential administrative business. In addition to the twenty-four absence limit, the course grade of any student whose absence from school is unapproved is subject to a five-point reduction for each unapproved absence after the first. In any one marking period, the grade may not, however, be reduced to a grade lower than 50, which is a failing grade. The grade reduction for unexcused absences is, like the twenty-four maximum absence policy, subject to administrative waiver. The policy of the school board entails extensive opportunities for counseling after a student's first confirmed unapproved absence from a class and thereafter.

The stated purpose of the attendance policy is educational rather than disciplinary. A student's disciplinary suspension from school, for reasons unrelated to attendance, is considered an approved rather than an unapproved absence. Such an absence cannot result in the diminution of a class grade although it may be counted, unless waived, as part of the twenty-four maximum absences for class credit. A student's absence from school, whether approved or unapproved, is not a ground for suspension or expulsion.

A student's report card lists, for each course, grades for each marking period, a final examination grade, a final grade, the amount of credit awarded, and the number of approved and unapproved absences. The report card conspicuously bears the following legend: "A circled grade indicates that the grade was reduced due to unapproved absences." In the case of the named plaintiff, his report card indicated grade reductions by the circling of grades in each of his academic courses, with the result that in three of the courses his final grade was lowered from passing to failing. In a fourth course, Architectual Drafting II, where the plaintiff's final grade was passing despite an indicated reduction for unapproved absences, the report card assigned him no credit because of a total of thirty-eight absences, thirty-one of which were approved and seven of which were unapproved. Any report card thus discloses, on its face, those grades which are affected by the enforcement of the attendance policy.

The plaintiff's appeal argues that the trial court erred in ruling that the defendants' attendance policy: (1) was not ultra vires or preempted by governing state statutes; (2) did not violate the rights of the plaintiff class to substantive due process under the Connecticut and the United States constitutions; (3) did not deprive the plaintiff class of procedural due process under the Connecticut and the United States constitutions; (4) did not deny the rights of the plaintiff class to equal protection of the law under the Connecticut and the United States constitutions. We find no error.

The plaintiff's first argument on appeal is that the defendant school board's policy is invalid because it conflicts with a number of state statutes. This argument is twofold, that the attendance policy is ultra vires because it exceeds the authority conferred upon local school boards by state law and that the policy is preempted by state statutes with which it is inconsistent. We find neither argument persuasive.

The authority of local boards of education derives from their role as agents of the state. "[T]he furnishing of education for the general public, required by article eighth, § 1, of the Connecticut constitution, is by its very nature a state function and duty." . . . This responsibility has been delegated to local boards which, as "agencies of the state in charge of education in the town . . . possess only such powers as are granted to them by the General Statutes expressly or by necessary implication." . . .

The trial court found authority for the defendant school board's attendance policy in General Statutes §§ 10-220 and 10-221.

The first of these statutes, § 10-220, requires a local school board to "implement the educational interests of the state" and to "provide such other educational activities as in its judgment will best serve the interests of the school district." The second statute, § 10-221, instructs local boards of education to "pre-scribe rules for the management, studies, classification and discipline of the public schools." In addition, the trial court noted that General Statutes §§ 10-184 and 10-199 permit local school boards to investigate and to regulate "the irregular attendance of pupils at school."

The plaintiff contends that these statutes do not furnish support for the defendant school board's policy because its policy is properly to be characterized not as an academic regulation assigning a uniform grading value to classroom presence but rather as unauthorized punishment for nonattendance. . . .

We do not read the school board's authority in so limited a fashion. The authority to adopt uniform rules concerning irregularity of attendance is necessarily implied in the conjunction of statutory provisions authorizing local implementation of the educational mission of the state. Significantly, § 10-220 expressly charges local boards with responsibility for the oversight of the school attendance of children from the ages of seven to sixteen made mandatory by § 10-184. Furthermore, the plaintiff's concession that school teachers, upon the instruction of local school boards, may properly consider class participation in the assignment of grades, logically implies the existence of an educational nexus between classroom presence and grading. If local school boards can delegate to others the authority to impose academic sanctions for nonattendance, the decision to adopt uniform school-wide rules for such sanctions can hardly be deemed ultra vires.

None of the out-of-state cases upon which the plaintiff relies compels the conclusion that school-wide academic sanctions for nonattendance should generally be adjudged to be ultra vires. It may well be improper to reduce a student's grade for nonattendance as an additional punishment for unrelated conduct leading to a suspension from class; . . . but this school board's program does not permit such double punishment. It would indubitably be unlawful to apply a nonattendance program in an unreasonable, capricious, arbitrary or inequitable manner; . . . but no such allegation has been factually demonstrated. It would finally be troublesome to bar a truant student from further class attendance and from taking a final examination; . . . but the defendant board's program neither removes such a student from class nor excuses further compliance with the state's compulsory education law. In short, the plaintiff has cited no authority for his claim that attendance rules promulgated by local school boards, if carefully drafted and fairly applied, are to be deemed per se ultra vires. Our own research has likewise revealed no such case-law. We agree that such regulations fall within the authority granted to local school boards by the statutes of this state. . . .

. . . [T]he plaintiff urges that the state statutes governing academic discipline, which require that a suspended or expelled student be afforded alternate educational opportunities; General Statutes §§ 10-233c and 10-233d; be read as a mandate that any student be given full academic credit for completion of academic work, and as a prohibition of locally-imposed academic sanctions for nonattendance.

The defendant school board's reply to these arguments calls upon us to recognize a distinction between sanctions which are disciplinary in nature and sanctions which relate to academic requirements. The question is not whether we concur in the judgment of the defendant board of education that "[l]earning experiences that occur in the classroom are . . . essential components of the learning process" or that "[t]ime lost from class tends to be irretrievable in terms of opportunity for instructional interaction." The policy decision that academic credentials should reflect more than the product of quizzes, examinations, papers and classroom participation nonetheless constitutes an academic judgment about academic requirements. We agree with the defendants' characterization of their policy. . . .

Even if the defendant school board's attendance policy is authorized by the relevant state statutes, the plaintiff class asserts that the policy cannot pass constitutional muster. The plaintiff relies on provisions of our state and federal constitutions to raise three different constitutional claims: a right to substantive due process, a right to procedural due process, and a right to equal protection of the laws. The trial court, upon consideration of these claims, found no infringement of the plaintiff's constitutional rights. We agree.

The plaintiff's challenge to the New Milford attendance policy as violative of the requirements of substantive due process claims infringement of students' fundamental rights to public education, of students' liberty interests in their academic reputation and of students' property interests in grades reflecting academic achievement. The first of these claims is based on article eighth, § 1, of the Connecticut constitution; the others rely on article first, §§ 8 and 10, of the Connecticut constitution and the fourteenth amendment to the United States constitution.

Of these substantive due process claims, the most serious is the charge of impairment of a fundamental right, because, if such an impairment were properly before us, the validity of the questioned governmental regulation would require strict scrutiny to determine whether the regulation was compellingly justified and narrowly drafted. . . . We must therefore decide the applicability of the fundamental rights guaranteed by article eighth, § 1, to a school board's policy of imposing uniform school-wide academic sanctions for nonattendance. In *Horton v. Meskill*, 172 Conn. 615, 648-49, 376 A.2d 359 (1977), we held, in the context of state-wide disparities in the financing of public school education, that "elementary and secondary education is a fundamental right, [and] that pupils in the public schools are entitled to the equal enjoyment of that right." The plaintiff argues that *Horton v. Meskill* implies that strict scrutiny must be the test for any and all governmental regulations affecting public school education. We disagree. The underlying issue in *Horton v. Meskill* was the provision of "a substantially equal educational opportunity" for Connecticut students in the state's "free public elementary and secondary schools." . . .

This school board policy, which is neither disciplinary; . . . nor an infringement of equal educational opportunity, does not jeopardize any fundamental rights under our state constitution.

The standard by which the plaintiff's remaining substantive due process claims must be measured is therefore the more usual rational basis test. . . . In order to succeed on these claims, the plaintiff bears the heavy burden of proving that the challenged policy has no reasonable relationship to any legitimate state purpose; . . . and that the plaintiff class has suffered a specific injury as a result of the policy's enforcement. . . . The plaintiff has established neither the legal nor the factual predicate for meeting this burden of proof.

The plaintiff argues that it is unconstitutionally arbitrary and capricious for the defendant school board to require student grades to reflect more than academic achievement. With respect to the plaintiff's liberty interest, we can find no factual impairment of whatever rights the plaintiff might possibly assert. Inspection of the report card of the named plaintiff discloses the relationship between his academic performance and the reduction in his grades and class credit that resulted from application of the attendance policy. The plaintiff has failed to show how a student's reputation could be injured by a report card in this form. With respect to the plaintiff's property interest, we find it difficult to understand how a uniform school-wide policy that links class grades with attendance can be on its face more arbitrary, as a constitutional matter, than are similar judgments by individual teachers who may justifiably, according to the plaintiff, adjust classroom grades to reflect classroom participation. . . . On this record, the plaintiff class has not proven infringement of its liberty or property interest in a fair grading system. . . .

The plaintiff's final constitutional claim invokes the equal protection provisions of article first, § 20, of the Connecticut constitution and the fourteenth amendment to the United States constitution. . . . It is irrational, and a violation of equal protection, according to the plaintiff, to waive grade reduction for students who do "outstanding" work and to impose such sanctions on students whose work is, because of academic difficulties unrelated to class absence, only average.

The defendants offer several answers to this argument. Factually, they deny the premise that the waiver provision favors students on account of their ability rather than on account of their effort, since work may be considered "outstanding" in light of a particular student's past performance. Legally, they note that the waiver provision imports a reasonable element of flexibility into the assessment of a student's total classroom performance. Finally, they remind us that a district-wide policy is more likely to assure equality of treatment for all students than is a policy administered on an ad-hoc basis by individual classroom teachers. We find the defendants' arguments persuasive and therefore reject the plaintiff's equal protection claim.

There is no error.

In this opinion the other Judges concurred.

NOTES

1. A member of the National Honor Society cheated on a calculus examination by etching the formulas on his calculator. The court upheld the student's dismissal from the society. *Jacob v. School Board of Lee County*, 519 S.2d 1002 (Fla. App. 1987).
2. Denial of membership in the National Honor Society does not give rise to a property interest. *Price v. Young*, 580 F. Supp. 1 (ED. Ark. 1983) [See also: Karnstein v. Pewaukee School Board, 557 F.Supp. 565 (E.D. Wis. 1983).

▓▓ BILINGUAL EDUCATION PROGRAMS

A school's curriculum must provide special instructional services for limited-English-proficiency students. As to the nature and method of instruction required, the courts have left substantial school board discretion. In 1974 the U.S. Supreme Court held, in *Lau v. Nichols,* that the failure of the San Francisco public school system to provide for the lingual needs of non–English-speaking Chinese students violated section 601 of the Civil Rights Act of 1964.[56] The Court said that

> there is no equality of treatment merely by providing students the same facilities, textbooks, teachers, and curriculum; for students who do not understand English are effectively foreclosed from any meaningful education.

Later, in 1978, the Ninth Circuit Court of Appeals held that neither the federal Constitution nor the civil rights laws required that all courses, instructional materials, instructors, and testing procedures be bicultural or bilingual.[57] The Court indicated that compensatory education programs for non–English-speaking children were sufficient to satisfy the court's mandate in *Lau v. Nichols.*

In 1974, the U.S. Congress had enacted the Equal Educational Opportunities Act (EEOA), which requires that school systems develop appropriate programs for limited-English-proficiency students. The act states in pertinent part that

> no state shall deny educational opportunity to an individual on account of his or her race, color, sex, or national origin, by . . . the failure by an educational agency to take appropriate action to overcome language barriers that impede equal participation by its students in its instructional programs.[58]

In applying this law the Fifth Circuit Court of Appeals, in 1981, in *Castaneda I,* observed that Congress, while requiring appropriate remedial programs, gave local school districts "a substantial amount of latitude" in meeting these obligations.[59] In this case the court found that the challenged bilingual programs were nondiscriminatory. Later, in 1986, in a sequel to *Castaneda I,* the Fifth Circuit *upheld* the school district's ability grouping and classroom assignment system as not being racial-

ly and ethnically discriminatory. The court said:

> We by no means imply, however, that a state must provide a program of bilingual education to all limited English speaking students in order to satisfy § 1703(f) of the EEOA. We hold fast to our conviction, voiced in *Castaneda I,* that in enacting § 1703(f) Congress intended to leave state and local educational authorities a substantial amount of latitude in choosing the programs and techniques they would use. (See *Castaneda I,* 648 F.2d at 1009.)[60]

Of significance in this court's validation of the school district's bilingual program was the fact that a majority of the teachers were native speakers of the Spanish language and the remainder were "proficient in Spanish." Further, the court was satisfied that adequate steps had been taken to ensure that these teachers had appropriate in-service teacher training to "develop and hone the skills necessary to be an adequate bilingual teacher."[61]

Guidelines emerging from the *Castaneda* cases may be summarized from the court's conclusion in *Castaneda I,* that the appropriateness of remediation programs in satisfying the EEOA may be evaluated with three queries: (1) Is the school district's program based upon reorganized, sound educational theory or principles? (2) Is the school district's program or practice designed to implement the adopted theory? (3) Has the program produced satisfactory results?[62]

Concerning the pertinent federal legislation, Congress had passed a Bilingual Education Act in 1968[63] and, as discussed above, revised it in the Bilingual Education Act in 1974.[64] In the former, supplemental funding was provided for school districts to address the educational needs of low-income students with limited-English proficiency. The Bilingual Education Act of 1974 expanded coverage to include children other than those from low-income families. The act also provided a more precise definition of the bilingual education program required in English and the child's native language to the extent needed for the child to make effective progress.

School System's Failure to Provide English Language Instruction to Chinese-Speaking Children Violates the Civil Rights Act of 1964

— ·— ·— ·— ·—

Lau v. Nichols

— ·— ·— ·— ·—

Supreme Court of the United States, 1974.
414 U.S. 563, 94 S.Ct. 786.

Mr. Justice DOUGLAS delivered the opinion of the Court. . . . This class suit brought by non-English-speaking Chinese students against officials responsible for the operation of the San Francisco Unified School District seeks relief against the unequal educational opportunities, which are alleged to violate the Fourteenth Amendment. No specific remedy is urged upon us. Teaching English to the students of Chinese ancestry who do not speak the language is one choice. Giving instructions to this group in Chinese is another. There may be others. Petitioners ask only that the Board of Education be directed to apply its expertise to the problem and rectify the situation. . . .

The Court of Appeals reasoned that "every student brings to the starting line of his educational career different advantages and disadvantages caused in part by social, economic and cultural background, created and continued completely apart from any contribution by the school system." Yet in our view the case may not be so easily decided. This is a public school system of California and § 71 of the California Education Code states that "English shall be the basic language of instruction in all schools." That section permits a school district to determine "when and under what circumstances instruction may be given bilingually." That section also states as "the policy of the state" to insure "the mastery of

English by all pupils in the schools." And bilingual instruction is authorized "to the extent that it does not interfere with the systematic, sequential, and regular instruction of all pupils in the English language."

Moreover, § 8573 of the Education Code provides that no pupil shall receive a diploma of graduation from grade twelve who has not met the standards of proficiency in "English," as well as other prescribed subjects. Moreover, by § 12101 of the Education Code children between the ages of six and sixteen years are (with exceptions not material here) "subject to compulsory full-time education."

Under these state-imposed standards there is no equality of treatment merely by providing students with the same facilities, textbooks, teachers, and curriculum; for students who do not understand English are effectively foreclosed from any meaningful education.

Basic English skills are at the very core of what these public schools teach. Imposition of a requirement that, before a child can effectively participate in the educational program, he must already have acquired those basic skills is to make a mockery of public education. We know that those who do not understand English are certain to find their classroom experiences wholly incomprehensible and in no way meaningful.

We do not reach the Equal Protection Clause argument which has been advanced but rely solely on § 601 of the Civil Rights Act of 1964, 42 U.S.C.A. § 2000d, to reverse the Court of Appeals.

That section bans discrimination based "on the ground of race, color, or national origin," in "any program or activity receiving Federal financial assistance." The school district involved in this litigation receives large amounts of federal financial assistance. HEW, which has authority to promulgate regulations prohibiting discrimination in federally assisted school systems, 42 U.S.C.A. § 2000d-1, in 1968 issued one guideline that "school systems are responsible for assuring that students of a particular race, color, or national origin are not denied the opportunity to obtain the education generally obtained by other students in the system." 33 CFR 4955. In 1970 HEW made the guidelines more specific, requiring school districts that were federally funded "to rectify the language deficiency in order to open" the instruction to students who had "linguistic deficiencies," 35 Fed.Reg. 11595.

By § 602 of the Act HEW is authorized to issue rules, regulations, and orders to make sure that recipients of federal aid under its jurisdiction conduct any federally financed projects consistently with § 601. HEW's regulations, 45 CFR § 80.3(b)(1), specify that the recipients may not

> provide any service, financial aid, or other benefit to an individual which is different, or is provided in a different manner, from that provided to others under the program.   . . .
>
> Restrict an individual in any way in the enjoyment of any advantage or privilege enjoyed by others receiving any service, financial aid, or other benefit under the program.

Discrimination among students on account of race or national origin that is prohibited includes "discrimination . . . in the availability or use of any academic . . . or other facilities of the grantee or other recipient." Id., § 80.5(b).

Discrimination is barred which has that *effect* even though no purposeful design is present: a recipient "may not . . . utilize criteria or methods of administration which have the effect of subjecting individuals to discrimination" or have "the effect of defeating or substantially impairing accomplishment of the objectives of the program as respect individuals of a particular race, color or national origin." Id., § 80.3(b)(2).

It seems obvious that the Chinese-speaking minority receive fewer benefits than the English-speaking majority from respondents' school system which denies them a meaningful opportunity to participate in the educational program—all earmarks of the discrimination banned by the regulations. In 1970 HEW issued clarifying guidelines (35 Fed.Reg. 11595) which include the following:

> Where inability to speak and understand the English language excludes national origin-

minority group children from effective participation in the educational program offered by a school district, the district must take affirmative steps to rectify the language deficiency in order to open its instructional program to these students (Pet.Br.App. 1a).

> Any ability grouping or tracking system employed by the school system to deal with the special language skill needs of national origin-minority group children must be designed to meet such language skill needs as soon as possible and must not operate as an educational deadend or permanent track. (Pet.Br. p. 2a).

Respondent school district contractually agreed to "comply with title VI of the Civil Rights Act of 1964 . . . and all requirements imposed by or pursuant to the Regulation" of HEW (45 CFR pt. 80) which are "issued pursuant to that title . . . " and also immediately to "take any measures necessary to effectuate this agreement." The Federal Government has power to fix the terms on which its money allotments to the States shall be disbursed. . . . Whatever may be the limits of that power . . . they have not been reached here. Senator Humphrey, during the floor debates on the Civil Rights Act of 1964, said:

> Simple justice requires that public funds, to which all taxpayers of all races contribute, not be spent in any fashion which encourages, entrenches, subsidizes, or results in racial discrimination.

We accordingly reverse the judgment of the Court of Appeals and remand the case for the fashioning of appropriate relief.

Reversed.

NOTES

1. A school district may admit students who achieve in the top 15 percent to a preferred, college-preparatory high school without violating the Civil Rights Act or the Fourteenth Amendment, even though the percentage of black and Spanish-American is disproportionately low. The court found that the school district's legitimate interest outweighed any harm imagined or suf-

fered by students whose achievement had not qualified them for admission. *Berkelman v. San Francisco* Unified School District, 501 F.2d 1264 (9th Cir.1974).

2. A federal district court has within its inherent legal prerogative the equitable power to fashion a bilingual-bicultural program that will assure that Spanish-surnamed children receive meaningful education. *Serna v. Portales Municipal Schools,* 499 F.2d 1147 (10th Cir., 1974).

ENDNOTES

1. Keyishian v. Board of Regents, 385 U.S. 589, 603, 87 S.Ct. 675, 683, 684 (1967), quoting United States v. Associated Press, 52 F.Supp. 362, 372 (S.D.N.Y.1943), affirmed 326 U.S. 1, 65 S.Ct. 1416 (1945); see Weiman v. Updegraff, 344 U.S. 183, 197-198, 73 S.Ct. 215, 221-222 (1952) (Frankfurter, J., concurring).

2. Keyishian v. Board of Regents, 385 U.S. 589, 603, 87 S.Ct. 675, 683, 684 (1967).

3. "Academic Freedom in the Public Schools; The Right to Teach," *New York University Law Review,* vol. 48 (Dec. 1973): 1183.

4. Todd v. Rochester Community Schools, 41 Mich.App. 320, 200 N.W.2d 90 (1972).

5. School District of Abington Township v. Schempp, 374 U.S. 203, 300, 83 S.Ct. 1560, 1612 (1963).

6. Sturgis v. County of Allegan, 343 Mich. 209, 72 N.W.2d 56 (1955).

7. Kelly v. Dickson County School District, 64 Lack.Jur. 13 (1962).

8. Board of Curators of University of Missouri v. Horowitz, 435 U.S. 78, 98 S.Ct. 948 (1978).

9. Welling v. Board of Education, 382 Mich. 620, 171 N.W.2d 545 (1969).

10. Pittman v. Board of Education of Glen Cove, 56 Misc.2d 51, 287 N.Y.S.2d 551 (1967).

11. Ibid.

12. Isquith v. Levitt, 285 App.Div. 833, 137 N.Y.S.2d 497 (1955).

13. 262 U.S. 390, 43 S.Ct. 625 (1923).

14. Keyishian v. Board of Regents, 385 U.S. 589, 87 S.Ct. 675 (1967).

15. 354 U.S. 234, 77 S.Ct. 1203 (1957).

16. Ibid., at 250, 77 S.Ct. at 1212.

17. R. Freeman Butts and Lawrence A. Cremin, *A History of Education in American Culture* (New York: Henry Holt and Company, 1953), p. 273.

18. People ex. rel. McCollum v. Board of Education, 333 U.S. 203, 68 S.Ct. 461 (1948).

19. Butts and Cremin, *A History of Education,* p. 165.

20. Board of Education, Island Trees Union Free School District No. 26 v. Pico, 457 U.S. 853, 102 S.Ct. 2799 (1982).

21. Ibid.

22. Pratt v. Independent School District No. 831, Forest Lake, Minnesota, 670 F.2d 771 (8th Cir. 1982).

23. Ibid.

24. 484 U.S. 260, 108 S.Ct. 562 (1988). This case is more fully discussed in Chapter 8 of this book.

25. Ibid.

26. Ibid, at 273, 108 S.Ct. at 571.

27. Virgil v. School Board of Columbia County, Florida, 862 F.2d 1517 (11th Cir. 1989).

28. *Science and Creationism, A View from the National Academy of Sciences,* Committee on Science and Creationism, National Academy of Sciences (Washington, D.C.: National Academy Press, 1984), pp. 7–8.

29. Rule 81.71(a)(5), *Texas Administrative Code.*

30. Epperson v. State of Arkansas, 393 U.S. 97, 89 S.Ct. 266 (1968).

31. 529 F.Supp. 1255 (E.D.Ark., 1982).

32. Edwards v. Aguillard, 482 U.S. 578, 107 S.Ct. 2573 (1987).

33. Board of Curators of University of Missouri v. Horowitz, 435 U.S. 78, 98 S.Ct. 948 (1978).

34. Barnard v. Inhabitants of Shelburne, 216 Mass. 19, 102 N.E. 1095 (1913).

35. 513 F.2d 843, 851 (10th Cir.1975).

36. 408 U.S. 564, 92 S.Ct. 2701 (1972).

37. 424 U.S. 319, 96 S.Ct. 893 (1976).

38. Debra P. v. Turlington, 474 F.Supp. 244 (M.D. Fla.1979), affirmed 644 F.2d 397 (5th Cir.1981).

39. Anderson v. Banks, 540 F.Supp. 761, 765 (S.D.Ga.1982).

40. Hobson v. Hansen, 269 F.Supp. 401 (D.D.C.1967), affirmed *sub nom.* Smuck v. Hobson, 408 F.2d 175 (D.C.Cir.1969).

41. P. v. Riles, 343 F.Supp. 1306 (N.D.Cal.1972), affirmed 502 F.2d 963 (9th Cir.1974).

42. 426 U.S. 229, 96 S.Ct. 2040 (1976).

43. "Reading the Mind of the School Board: Segregative Intent and the De Facto/De Jure Distinction." 86 *Yale L.J.* (1976): 317, 335.

44. Lawrence A. Cremin, *American Education, The National Experience, 1783–1876* (New York: Harper and Row, 1980), p. 117.

45. Board of Curators of the University of Missouri v. Horowitz, 435 U.S. 78, 98 S.Ct. 948 (1978).

46. Regents of the University of Michigan v. Ewing, 474 U.S. 214, 106 S.Ct. 507 (1985).

47. Ibid.

48. Swany v. San Ramon Valley Unified School District, 720 F.Supp. 764 (N.C.Cal. 1989).

49. Valentine v. Independent School District of Casey, 191 Iowa.1100, 183 N.W. 434 (1921).

50. Slocum v. Holton Board of Education, 171 Mich.App. 92, 429 N.W.2d 607 (1988).

51. Katzman v. Cumberland Valley School District, 84 Pa. Cmwlth. 474 479 A.2d 671 (1984).

52. Campbell v. Board of Education of Town of New Milford, 193 Conn. 93, 475 A.2d 289 (1984).

53. State v. Board of Trustees of School Dist. No. 1, 223 Mont. 269, 726 P.2d 801 (1986).

54. Rousselle v. Plaquemines Parish School Board, 527 So.2d 376 (La. App. 1988).

55. Truby v. Broadwater, ____W.Va. ____,332 S.E.2d 284 (1985).

56. 414 U.S. 563, 94 S.Ct. 786 (1974).

57. Guadalupe Organization, Inc. v. Tempe Elementary School District No. 3, 587 F.2d 1022 (9th Cir. 1978).

58. 20 U.S.C.A. § 1703(f).

59. Castaneda v. Pickard, 648 F.2d 989 (5th Cir. 1981).

60. Castaneda v. Pickard, 781 F.2d 456 (5th Cir. 1986).

61. Ibid.

62. Castaneda v. Pickard, 648 F.2d at 1009-1010; see also Martha McCarthy and Nelda H. Cambron-McCabe, *Public School Law*, (2d ed.) (Boston: Allyn and Bacon, Inc., 1987), pp. 186–87.

63. 20 U.S.C.A. § 880b et seq.

64. 20 U.S.C.A. § 880b-1(a) (4) (A).

CHAPTER 8

Student Rights

School authorities are vested with broad powers for the establishment and conduct of the educational program. This prerogative, however, is by no means absolute, and school officials must act within the scope of reasonable regulations. Rules are usually held to be reasonable if they materially contribute to the maintenance and advancement of the educational process. Court decisions in recent years indicate the judiciary is ever diligent in the requirement of reasonableness and fairness in protecting the constitutional rights of students. The courts, though, even under the weight of a great quantum of challenges to school board authority, continue to give school boards wide discretion in promulgating and interpreting regulations governing student conduct. In a 1982 case, the U.S. Supreme Court reversed a U.S. Circuit Court decision in which the court substituted its own interpretation of a school board rule for that of the school board.[1] Too, earlier, in *Wood v. Strickland,* the Supreme Court stated that a lower federal court erred "in substituting its own notions for a school board's definition of its rules."[2] The Supreme Court said, "The Court of Appeals was ill advised to supplant the interpretation of the regulation of those officers who adopted it and are entrusted with its enforcement."[3]

A school board rule, however, cannot be so broad or vague as to allow arbitrary interpretation and application. Such overbreadth can result in a violation of a student's right of due process. In acknowledging such eventuality, the Supreme Court has said in *dictum* that "A case may be hypothesized in which a school board's interpretation of its rules is so extreme as to be in violation of due process."[4] School regulations are generally held to be sufficiently definitive if they provide students with adequate information as to what is expected of them and are so stated that persons of common intelligence are not required to guess at their meaning. Reasonable certainty of interpretation requires only the use of ordinary and commonly used terminology. Reasonableness, however, is not predicated on formal adoption and publication of rules before they can have effect, and the absence of a preexisting rule on the books does not prohibit official action. Absence of such formality may, though, make it much more difficult to convince a court that a rule was necessary and that its enforcement was not capricious.

This chapter discusses the power of school boards in promulgation of rules of student conduct and the reasonableness of the application by school administrators and teachers. Much of the chapter is devoted to limitations that the courts may impose to protect students where governmental actions have been unreasonable, vague, arbitrary, or contrary to constitutional rights or freedoms.

▮▮ COMMON LAW AND THE STUDENT

Court decisions throughout the years have established a common law of the school, under which the teacher and the student have mutual responsibilities and obligations. The mutuality of the relationship is predicated on society's expectations of the school in the advancement of the common good of the community. The teacher's responsibility is diverse and multifaceted, owing both to the community and to the student. The courts have recognized that in order for teachers to address the diversity of expectations placed upon them, they must be given sufficient latitude in the control of the conduct of the school for appropriate decorum and learning atmosphere to prevail. In keeping with this objective, the courts have allowed teachers general control over students in the school setting. Edwards has summarized the view of the courts with regard to the teacher's authority by observing, "There is inherent in his position the authority to govern the school in a reasonable and humane way . . . ."[5]

The reference to "inherent" authority means that the teacher does not derive all of his or her authority from direct enunciations of statute or regulation, but, in addition, holds by virtue of the special teacher/student relationship a built-in obligation to promote the harmony of the school by requiring discipline while protecting and advancing the interest of the child. As such, the teacher has much unprescribed discretion to advance learning and to prohibit those disharmonies inimical to learning. Within this scope is constituted the common law of the school. The Wisconsin Supreme Court has perhaps best explained the common law with regard to the teacher's power and authority.

> While the principal or teacher in charge of a public school is subordinate to the school board or board of education of his district or city, and must enforce rules and regulations adopted by the board for the government of the school, and execute all its lawful orders in that behalf, he does not derive all his power and authority in the school and over his pupils from the affirmative action of the board. He stands for the time being *in loco parentis* to his pupils, and because of that relation, he must necessarily exercise authority over them in many things concerning which the board may have remained silent.[6]

On the other hand, the student has a corresponding and reciprocal obligation to the school not only to partake of its benefits, but by action and deed, to assist in the advancement of its purposes and causes. The student fulfills this obligation by respect for school decorum with conduct and manners appropriate to the situation. This behavior requires a degree of subordination of the student's individual freedom for the general good and lawful purposes of the school. The student's responsibility was clearly defined by the forementioned Wisconsin court.

> In the school, as in the family, there exist on the part of the pupils the obligations of obedience to lawful commands, subordination, civil deportment, respect for the rights of other pupils and fidelity to duty. These obligations are inherent in any proper school system, and constitute, so to speak, the common law, and is subject, whether it has or has not been reenacted by the district board in the form of written rules and regulations. Indeed it would seem impossible to frame rules which would cover all cases of insubordination and all acts of vicious tendency which the teacher is liable to encounter daily and hourly.[7]

The situation of the student in school is not significantly different from that of the citizen in society; some reduction in individual freedom is necessary throughout society. In fact, a commonwealth, or Latin *civitas*, is formed by individuals consenting to submit their wills for unity of the whole or common good. Hobbes, in *Leviathan*, spoke of a covenant in which a *quid pro quo* was given between the protector and the protected, a contract for mutual benefit. He described it this way:

> [I]t is a real unity of them all, in one and the same person, made by covenant of every man, in such a manner, as if every man should say to every man, I authorize and give up my right of governing myself, to this condition, that thou give up the right to him, and authorize all his actions in like manner. This done, the multitude united in one person, is called a commonwealth . . . .[8]

In a less severe conceptualization, Rousseau defined the common interest in forming society and government, to the effect that each individual must "acquire his rights by discharging his duties",[9] and this forms a social compact wherein

> [e]ach of us puts his person and all his power in common under the supreme direction of the general will, and, in our corporate capacity, we receive each member as an indivisible part of the whole.
>
> At once, in place of the individual personality of each contrasting party, this act of association creates a corporate and collective body, . . . , and receiving from this act its unity, its common identity, its life, and its will.[10]

It is this commonality of the social purpose of public schools that creates the obligations and responsibilities on the part of the school, the teacher, and the student. The exchange of autonomy for benefits as defined by philosophers as diverse as Hobbes and Rousseau can easily be translated into the circumstances of the public school. The common good is advanced by the common law of the school, which prescribes acceptable social conditions and standards for the operation of the schools. Again, Rousseau makes the critical connection.

> Public education, therefore, under regulation prescribed by the Sovereign, is one of the fundamental rules of popular or legitimate government. If children are brought up in common in the bosom of equality; if they are imbued with the laws of the State and precepts of general will; if they are surrounded by examples and objects which constantly remind them of the tender mother who nourishes them, . . . we cannot doubt that they will learn to cherish one another mutually as brothers, to will nothing contrary to the will of society . . . , and to become, in time, defenders and fathers of the country of which they will have been so long children.[11]

Thus, the common law of the school, as prescribed by extensive judicial precedent, reflects a synthesis, characterized by the school, wherein the highest interest of the individual and the pre-eminent interest of the community coincide.[12] The individual, the student, "[i]n pursuing his own interest, . . . pursues that of the community, and in promoting the interest of the community, he promotes his own."[13] This "harmony of interests"[14] is defined and furthered by the common law of the public school.

Therefore, it may be understood in the context of both law and philosophy the reasoning of the common law, which conveys to the teacher the authority to maintain an orderly atmosphere of learning, a benefit to both the student and the community. The rule of law as enunciated by an early Missouri court is thus clearly understood:

> The teacher of a school as to the children of his school, while under his care, occupies, for the time being, the position of parent or guardian, and it is his right and duty not only to enforce discipline to preserve order and to teach, but also to look after the morals, the health and the safety of his pupils; to do and require his pupils to do whatever is reasonably necessary to preserve and conserve all these interests . . . .[15]

Reasonableness

Reasonableness of a school rule in the control of students has at least two aspects—the jurisdictional reach of the school's authority beyond the school grounds and the nature and degree of the discipline visited upon the student. Reasonableness is the common-law watchword of the teacher/student relationship. To act reasonably is the primary test of tort law and is a favorite definition of proper and expected conduct in society, generally.

The meaning of reasonableness in the abstract is difficult to determine, but when coupled with facts found in scholastic circumstances, the term usually takes on greater lucidity. In its detached sense, though, it means that which is proper, rational, and fair; and precludes conduct that can be characterized as immoderate, excessive, and unsuitable to the particular conditions or circumstances. Because the authority of the teacher cannot be completely circumscribed by state law or by school regulations, and every eventuality in school cannot be anticipated by applicable rule, considerable judicial flexibility must be allowed in determining reasonable behavior of the teacher. Further, the reciprocal responsibilities of the students must also be viewed in the context of reasonableness.

In Loco Parentis

Though the term *in loco parentis* translated to English means "in the place of a parent," the courts have never intended that school authorities or teachers stand fully in the place of parents in control of their children. School officials' and teachers' prerogatives are circumscribed by and limited to school functions and activities. The concept emanated from English law that governed the private schools of that country, usually giving schoolmasters extraordinary, and sometimes unconscionable, powers over pupil conduct. Even though common law approves of the concept, the boundaries of the teacher's authority is marked by requirements of reasonableness and restraint. Blackstone himself, in his *Commentaries,* observed that the schoolmaster had only that portion of parental powers necessary for the conduct of the school.[16] In *Lander v. Seaver,*[17] the Supreme Court of Vermont makes the very important point that power of the schoolmaster over the child is not coextensive with the parent.[18] Importantly, this court observed that because the teacher does not have the natural affection of the parent for the child, his or her acts of discipline must therefore be viewed circumspectly by the courts. Because the teacher has no innate natural parental concern for the child, "he may not be trusted with all a parent's authority . . . ."[19]

Nevertheless, even with its limitations, the doctrine of *in loco parentis,* as a vestige of common law, is viable and operates to help define the school and student relationship in the public school today. Its justification is found in the necessity for an orderly and well-behaved student in keeping with an agreeable learning environment. The doctrine is probably best defined by a Nebraska court as follows:

[G]eneral education and control of pupils who attend public schools are in the hands of school boards, superintendents, principals, and teachers. This control extends to health, proper surroundings, necessary discipline, promotion of morality and other wholesome influences, while parental authority is temporarily superceded.[20]

Recent trends in constitutional law that have more clearly defined the interests of the student in the context of public school operation have acted to more sharply define the legal concept, but not to replace it.

In *New Jersey v. T.L.O.,* the U.S. Supreme Court held that although the *in loco prentis* doctrine did not exempt school officials from Fourth Amendment search and seizure restrictions, the doctrine, yet, "retains vitality in appropriate circumstances."[21] Other Supreme Court cases have also recognized the continuing viability of the doctrine.[22] Significantly, the Supreme Court in *Bethel,* 1986, reiterated the importance of the *in loco parentis* doctrine in protecting children "especially in a captive audience from exposure to sexually explicit, indecent, or lewd speech."[23]

Thus, not only does *in loco parentis* appear to be an active legal concept, but in recent years it has taken on new and more definitive meaning.

Court Is Not Concerned with Wisdom of Regulation but Whether It Is Reasonable

—·—·—·—·—·—

Flory v. Smith

—·—·—·—·—·—

Supreme Court of Appeals of Virginia, 1926.
145 Va. 164, 134 S.E. 360.

CAMPBELL, J. The object of this suit is to test the legality of a rule promulgated by the school board of Gloucester county. This rule is as follows:

"Student Regulation.—Leaving the campus between the hours of 9 A.M. and 3:35 P.M. is strictly prohibited, unless students are accompanied by a teacher." . . .

It was the desire of the appellees that their children be relieved of the restriction placed upon them by the rule stated, *supra,* and that the children be permitted to eat their midday meal, either in the home, situated about a mile distant from the school, or to eat same with their father at the hotel in the town.

The special privilege was denied by the principal of the school. . . .

The court, on final hearing, overruled the demurrer and entered a decree enjoining and restraining E.D. Flory, principal of the school, from prohibiting and preventing the children of appellees "from eating their midday meals either in the home of their parents or with their father in Botetourt Hotel. . . . "

While the Constitution of the state provides in mandatory terms that the Legislature shall establish and maintain public free schools, there is neither mandate nor inhibition in the provisions as to the regulation thereof. The Legislature, therefore, has the power to enact any legislation in regard to the conduct, control, and regulation of the public free schools, which does not deny to the citizen the constitutional right to enjoy life and liberty, to pursue happiness and to acquire property.

In the conduct of the public schools it is essential that power be vested in some legalized agency in order to maintain discipline and promote efficiency. In considering the exercise of this power, the courts are not concerned with the wisdom or unwisdom of the act done. The only concern of the court is the reasonableness of the regulation promulgated. To hold otherwise would be to substitute judicial opinion for the legislative will. . . .

While appellees allege in their bill "that it is their right to select and provide the best and most suitable food for the nourishment of their children, and to select the mode and manner by which such food shall be received by their children, to the end that their children may be best nourished and their physical development may be best promoted," it is nowhere alleged that the physical condition of the children is such that results detrimental to their physical well-being will follow if the right alleged is denied.

While it may be argued with force that a warm meal at midday is preferable to a cold lunch, it is not conclusive that the latter is destructive of health. It is a matter of common knowledge that in the towns and rural sections the vast majority of school children partake of a cold lunch at midday. In the larger cities, where paternalism is further advanced, children are encouraged to partake of hot food furnished them for a consideration.

Considering the regulation from the viewpoint afforded us by the bill of complaint, demurrer, and answer, we are unable to say that the regulation is an unreasonable one. However, while a rule may be legally reasonable, it should not be without elasticity. In the enforcement of every law there should be brought into play the element of common sense.

We have no serious trouble in disposing of the contention that appellees have a property right in the public schools of the commonwealth. . . .

While it may be a restraint upon liberty and an infringement upon happiness for the Legislature to inhibit a parent from sending his child to any school, it is neither restraint nor infringement for the Legislature to enact laws to debar a child from the mere privilege of acquiring an education at the expense of the state until he is willing to submit himself to all reasonable regulations enacted for the purpose of promoting efficiency and maintaining discipline. There is a marked difference between the inherent right to conduct a private school—that is, to select and pursue a given legitimate vocation—and the right to attend a public school. . . .

The last contention of appellees is that they have been penalized without notice and deprived of their right to seek redress by appeal. . . . Immediately upon the suspension of appellees' child, notice of such suspension was given to the father. We are of the opinion that this was sufficient notice; that upon the receipt thereof he had the absolute right to have the matter reviewed by the county school board within a reasonable time from the date of the receipt of such notice.

For the reasons stated, the decree of the circuit court must be reversed, and this court will enter a decree dismissing the bill of complaint.

Reversed.

NOTE

1. For other related cases on this point, see *Bozeman v. Morrow*, 34 S.W.2d 654 (Tex.Civ. App.1931); *Richardson v. Braham*, 125 Neb. 142, 249 N.W. 557 (1933); and *Haffner v. Braham*, 125 Neb. 147, 249 N.W. 560 (1933).

Teacher Has Authority to Punish Pupil for Offenses Committed after Returning Home from School

— · — · — · — · —

O'Rourke v. Walker

— · — · — · — · —

Supreme Court of Errors of Connecticut, 1925.
102 Conn. 130, 128 A. 25.

KEELER, J. (after stating the facts as above). It is conceded in the brief of the appealing plaintiff that the school board or other proper authority may make reasonable rules concerning the conduct of pupils, and inflict reasonable corporal punishment for the infraction of such rules, and that in the absence of rules so established, the teacher may make all necessary and proper rules for the regulation of the school. We so held in *Sheehan v. Sturges*, 53 Conn. 481, 2 A. 841. The plaintiff further concedes that—

> The conduct of pupils outside of school hours and school property may be regulated by rules established by the school authorities if such conduct directly relates to and affects the management of the school and its efficiency.

This we understand to be the rule abundantly established by authority. 5 C.J. 755. However, plaintiff proceeds to say that this conceded rule of law is qualified in this important particular:

> But no rule can be adopted which attempts to control the conduct of pupils outside of school hours after they have reached their homes.

. . . In Mechem on Public Officers, § 730, the law is summarized in accordance with the decided weight of authority as follows:

> The authority of the teacher is not confined to the school room or grounds, but he may prohibit and punish all acts of his pupils which are detrimental to the good order and best interests of the school, whether such acts are committed in school hours or while the pupil is on his way to or from school or after he has returned home.

Examination of the authorities clearly reveals the true test of the teacher's right and jurisdiction to punish for offenses not committed on the school property or going and returning therefrom, but after the return of the pupil to the parental abode, to be not the time or place of the offense, but its effect upon the morale and efficiency of the school, whether it in fact is detrimental to its good order, and to the welfare and advancement of the pupils therein. If the conduct punished is detrimental to the best interests of the school, it is punishable, and in the instant case, under the rules of the school board, by corporal infliction. The effect of the rule claimed by the plaintiff, if applied, would result in a serious loss of discipline in school, and possible harm to innocent pupils in attendance. Supposing that some strong-armed juvenile bully attending school lived upon the next block and sought for a brief moment the asylum of his home, and thence sallied forth and beat, abused, and terrorized his fellow pupils as they pass by returning home; then by the claim urged by plaintiff he would be immune from punishment by the school authorities, while if he began his assaults before he had passed within the bounds of his own front yard he would be liable to proper punishment for any harm done. Now the harm done to the morale of the school is the same. The injured and frightened pupils are dismayed and discouraged in going to and coming from the school, and demoralized while in attendance. It will not do to say, as plaintiff's counsel argue, that the proper resort to correct such an abuse is the parents of such offenders, or the public prosecutors. Some parents would dismiss the matter by saying that they could give no attention to children's quarrels; many would champion their children as being all right in their conduct. The public authorities would very properly say, unless the offense resulted in quite serious injury, that such affrays were too trifling to deserve their attention. Yet the harm to the school has been done, and its proper conduct and operation seriously harmed, by such acts. Correction will usually be sought in vain at the hands of parents; it can only be successfully applied by the teacher. It is not likely that any milder punishment than corporal infliction would act as a deterrent in cases like the present. The abuse of little girls by young bullies is a base and brutal offense.

In the instant case it will be observed that while the plaintiff had reached his home after school, his victims had not. This is an important fact, even if the rule claimed by plaintiff should be upheld as a general statement. The claim made in argument that the small girls who were abused were trespassers upon the property of plaintiff's mother is of no avail. There is nothing in the record to show that plaintiff was acting under direction of his mother, and even if he were, such conduct as the court has found to exist would not be lawful.

There is no error.

The other Judges concurred.

NOTES

1. As a teacher passed by an automobile in a shopping center on a Sunday evening, a student in the automobile shouted, "There's Stear." Another student in the car then yelled, "He's a prick." On Monday morning the teacher explained the facts to the vice-principal. The vice-principal confronted the student who admitted calling Mr. Stear a prick, whereupon the student was given an in-school suspension, was not allowed to participate in the senior trip, was not permitted to attend any extracurricular activities, and was placed on other restrictions while at school, such as being required to sit at the restricted table in the cafeteria.

   The student challenged the disciplinary action as a violation of his freedom of speech and denial of a property right to an education. The court stated, "It is the opinion of the court that the First Amendment rights of the plaintiff were not violated. His conduct involved an invasion of the right of teacher Stear to be free from being loudly insulted in a public place by 'lewd, lascivious or indecent words or language.'" The court went on to say, "It is our opinion that when a high school student refers to a high school teacher in a public place on a Sunday by a lewd and obscene name in such a loud voice that the teacher and others hear the insult, it may be deemed a matter for discipline in the discretion of the school authorities. To countenance such student conduct even in a public place without imposing sanctions could lead to devastating consequences in the school." Furthermore, since the student continued his education while serving the in-school suspension, he was not deprived of any property right. *Fenton v. Stear*, 423 F.Supp. 767 (W.D.Pa.1976).

2. Two students, one in a jeep and the other in a pickup truck, impeded the progress of a school bus traveling to school loaded with children. The driver of the jeep positioned his vehicle in front of the bus while the pickup truck was behind, and by alternatively slowing and speeding up obstructed the operation of the bus. Upon arriving at school, the students who had been positively identified were cited by the Wyoming highway patrol and suspended by the school. They challenged the disciplinary action by the school authorities. The court stated, "It matters little that the proscribed

conduct occurred on a public highway. It is generally accepted that school authorities may discipline pupils for out-of-school conduct having a direct and immediate effect on the discipline or general welfare of the school. This is particularly true where the discipline is reasonably necessary for the student's physical or emotional safety and well-being of other students." *Clements v. Board of Trustees of Sheridan County School Dist. No. 2,* 585 P.2d 197 (Wyo.1978); see also 53 A.L.R.3d 1124, 68 Am.Jur.2d, Schools, §§ 256 and 266.

3. In the case of *Jones v. Cody,* 132 Mich. 13, 92 N.W. 495, 62 L.R.A. 160 (1902), a principal enforced a requirement that pupils go directly home after school. A local storekeeper refused to allow the principal to enter her store to send some of the loitering pupils home. The principal then required strict adherence to his rule and the storekeeper sued the principal for loss of profits. The court upheld the rule and indicated that it was not only the right, but the duty of the school to see that children went directly home from school. The court reasoned that if the child did not reach home when scheduled, his parents would be put on notice and would go looking for him, thereby affording greater protection for the safety and well-being of the child.

4. Would a rule prohibiting pupils from attending movies or other social functions on school nights be upheld by courts today? In this regard, what limitations may be imposed on school officials today? Does such a rule grant too much authority to school officials?

5. Courts will not tolerate frivolous suits. In a case in which a student was demoted from first trumpet to second trumpet by the band master, and then refused to go on a band trip and was then dismissed from the band the parents filed suit. The court, in a strongly worded opinion, found for the school authorities and required the child's mother to pay legal fees of $2,250 because of the frivolous, unreasonable, and groundlessness of the action. The court stated, "This complaint is another example of a prevalent disposition by parties and lawyers to litigate over every source of unhappiness to which humankind may be subject. While it might be considered unfortunate that a boy be dismissed from the high school band, it is much more unfortunate that his mother saw fit to take the matter to court and that she was able to find a lawyer willing to do her bidding." *Bernstein v. Menard,* 557 F.Supp. 90, 557 F.Supp. 92 (E.D.Va. 1983).

6. In another case involving academic punishment a school district's rules provided that a pupil may miss no more than twelve days, excused or unexcused. A student missed physical science class fourteen times although he only missed four complete days and cut other classes even though he was on school grounds much of the time watching football films. He was expelled from school for excessive absenteeism. The student challenged the expulsion saying he missed only four days, which was not excessive. The Supreme Court of Arkansas upheld the school officials saying, "the decision to dismiss [the student] was one within the power of the board. This court does not have the power to substitute its judgment for that of such a board. We can only determine whether the judgment was arbitrary, capricious, or contrary to law. We cannot so find in this case." *Williams v. Board of Education for Marianna School District* 274 Ark, 530, 626 S.W.2d 361 (1982).

The Schoolmaster Stands in loco parentis *in the Control of Pupil Behavior*

– – · – – · – – · – – ·

Lander v. Seaver

– – · – – · – – · – – ·

Supreme Court of Vermont, 1859.
32 Vt. 114, 76 Am.Dec. 156.

Trespass for assault and battery. Defendant pleaded the general issue, and two special pleas in bar. The first special plea alleged that defendant was a schoolmaster; that plaintiff was one of his pupils, and was guilty of misbehavior as such pupil; that for the purpose of punishing him for it, defendant did, in his school, a little beat and bruise the plaintiff, but that no unnecessary injury was done him. This was alleged to be the trespass complained of by plaintiff. The second special plea justified upon the same ground, except that the pupil's offense was stated to have been the use of saucy and disrespectful language towards defendant after the close of the school, but in the presence of other pupils of defendant; that such language tended to degrade the latter in the opinion of such other pupils. The plaintiff replied *de injuria,* etc. The jury rendered a verdict for defendant, and judgment being entered thereon, the plaintiff appealed. The offense of the pupil, a boy eleven years of age, was committed an hour and a half after the close of school, after he had returned home, and while he was driving his father's cow past the teacher's house. Plaintiff, in the presence of some fellow-pupils, and of the master, called the latter "old Jack Seaver." The next morning after school convened, defendant reprimanded the plaintiff for said language, and whipped him with a small rawhide. . . .

The defendant was a teacher in a public school in Burlington; the plaintiff, his pupil. The first question presented is, Has a schoolmaster the right to punish his pupil for acts of misbehavior committed after the school has been dismissed, and the pupil has returned home and is engaged in his father's service?

I.   It is conceded that his right to punish extends to school hours, and there seems to be no reasonable doubt that the supervision and control of the master over the scholar extend from the time he leaves home to go to school till he returns home from school. Most parents would expect and desire that teachers would take care that their children, in going to and returning from school, should not loiter, or seek evil company, or frequent vicious places of resort. But in this case, as appears from the bill of exceptions, the offense was committed an hour and a half after the school was dismissed, and after the boy had returned home, and while he was engaged in his father's service. When the child has returned home, or to his parents' control, then the parental authority is resumed and the control of the teacher ceases, and then, for all ordinary acts of misbehavior, the parent alone has the power to punish. It is claimed, however, that in this case "the boy, while in the presence of other pupils of the same school, used toward the master and in his hearing contemptuous language, with a design to insult him, and which had a direct and immediate tendency to bring the authority of the master over his pupils into contempt and lessen his hold upon them and his control over the school." This, under the charge of the court, must have been found by the jury.

This misbehavior, it is especially to be observed, has a direct and immediate tendency to injure the school, to subvert the master's authority, and to beget disorder and insubordination. It is not misbehavior generally, or towards other persons, or even towards the master in matters in no way connected with or affecting the school; for as to such misconduct, committed by the child after his return home from school, we think the parents, and they alone, have the power of punishment.

But where the offense has a direct and immediate tendency to injure the school and bring the master's authority into contempt, as in this case, when done in the presence of other scholars and of the master, and with a design to insult him, we think he has the right to punish the scholar for such acts if he comes again to school.

The misbehavior must not have merely a remote and indirect tendency to injure the school. All improper conduct or language may perhaps have, by influence and example, a remote tendency of that kind. But the tendency of the acts so done out of the teacher's supervision for which he may punish must be direct and immediate in their bearing upon the welfare of the school, or the authority of the master and the respect due to him. Cases may readily be supposed which lie very near the line, and it will often be difficult to distinguish between the acts which have such an immediate bearing and those which have such a remote tendency. Hence each case must be determined by its peculiar circumstances. . . . By common consent and by the universal custom in our New England schools, the master has always been deemed to have the right to punish such offenses. Such power is essential to the preservation of order, decency, decorum, and good government in schools. Upon this point the charge of the court was substantially correct.

II. The court charged the jury that although the punishment inflicted on the plaintiff was excessive in severity and disproportioned to the offense, still if the master in administering it acted with proper motives, in good faith, and, in his judgment, for the best interests of the school, he would not be liable; that the school-master acts in a judicial capacity, and that the infliction of excessive punishment, when prompted by good intentions and not by malice or wicked motives, or an evil mind, is merely an honest error of opinion, and does not make him liable to the pupil for damages. The plaintiff claims that this was erroneous. . . .

We think the schoolmaster does not belong to the class of public officers vested with such judicial and discretionary powers. He is included rather in the domestic relation of master and servant, and his powers and duties are usually treated of as belonging to that class. . . .

It is also said that he stands *in loco parentis*, and is invested with all the authority and immunity of the parent. . . .

The parent, unquestionably, is answerable only for malice or wicked motives or an evil heart in punishing his child. This great, and to some extent irresponsible, power of control and correction is invested in the parent by nature and necessity. It springs from the natural relation of parent and child. It is felt rather as a duty than a power. . . . This parental power is little liable to abuse, for it is continually restrained by natural affection, the tenderness which the parent feels for his offspring, an affection ever on the alert, and acting rather by instinct than reasoning.

The schoolmaster has no such natural restraint. Hence he may not safely be trusted with all a parent's authority, for he does not act from the instinct of parental affection. He

should be guided and restrained by judgment and wise discretion, and hence is responsible for their reasonable exercise. The limit upon the parental authority transferred to the master is well expressed by Judge Blackstone. He says: "The master is *in loco parentis,* and has such a portion of the powers of the parent committed to his charge as may be necessary to answer the purposes for which he is employed." An English annotator, in a note to the passage, very properly adds: "This power must be temperately exercised, and no schoolmaster should feel himself at liberty to administer chastisement co-extensive with the parent." . . .

The law, as we deem it to exist, is this: A schoolmaster has the right to inflict reasonable corporal punishment. He must exercise reasonable judgment and discretion in determining when to punish, and to what extent. In determining upon what is a reasonable punishment, various considerations must be regarded, the nature of the offense, the apparent motive and disposition of the offender, the influence of his example and conduct upon others, and the sex, age, size, and strength of the pupil to be punished. Among reasonable persons, much difference prevails as to the circumstances which will justify the infliction of punishment, and the extent to which it may properly be administered. On account of this difference of opinion, and the difficulty which exists in determining what is a reasonable punishment, and the advantage which the master has by being on the spot to know all the circumstances, the manner, look, tone, gestures, and language of the offender (which are not always easily described), and thus to form a correct opinion as to the necessity and extent of the punishment, considerable allowance should be made to the teacher by way of protecting him in the exercise of his discretion. Especially should he have this indulgence when he appears to have acted from good motives, and not from anger or malice. Hence the teacher is not to be held liable on the ground of excess of punishment, unless the punishment is clearly excessive, and would be held so in the general judgment of reasonable men. If the punishment be thus clearly excessive, then the master should be held liable for such excess, though he acted from good motives in inflicting the punishment; and in his own judgment considered it necessary, and not excessive. But if there is any reasonable doubt whether the punishment was excessive, the master should have the benefit of the doubt. . . .

IV. Whether a rawhide was a proper instrument of punishment, was left to the jury with very suitable instructions.

The evidence to show that the rawhide was used in other schools in the vicinity was properly admitted to rebut the charge of malice, by showing that he did not resort to an unusual instrument of punishment.

The testimony to show the plaintiff did not claim an excess of punishment on the first trial was proper, as tending to prove that that claim on the then pending trial was not well founded.

Judgment reversed.

■ CONSTITUTIONAL DUE PROCESS

As pointed out elsewhere in this book, the Fourteenth Amendment to the federal Constitution provides that no state shall deprive a person of his life, liberty, or property without due process of law. Stated positively, a state may deprive a person of his life, liberty, or property so long as the individual is given due process.

There are two types of due process. One is called *procedural due process*. This means that if a person is to be deprived of his life, liberty, or property, a prescribed constitutional procedure must be followed. The Supreme Court of the United States has said that in order to give an individual procedural due process as required by the federal Constitution, three basic factors must be present. The person must have proper notice that he is about to be deprived of his life, liberty, or property; he must be given an opportunity to be heard; and the hearing must be conducted fairly.

A second type of due process is called *substantive due process*. To satisfy this constitu-

tional requirement, if a state is going to deprive a person of his life, liberty, or property, the state must have a valid objective and the means used must be reasonably calculated to achieve the objective. Early interpretations by the United States Supreme Court recognized only the procedural aspects of due process of law.[24] It was not until 1923 that the Supreme Court defined due process of law as possessing "substantive" protections.[25] Substantive due process was defined by one court as follows:

> The phrase "due process of law," when applied to substantive rights, as distinguished from procedural rights, means that the state is without power to deprive a person of life, liberty or property by an act having no reasonable relation to any proper governmental purpose, or which is so far beyond the necessity of case as to be an arbitrary exercise of governmental power.[26]

Substantive Due Process

In *Meyer v. Nebraska*,[27] the Supreme Court related substantive protection of the due process clause of the Fourteenth Amendment to education when it held unconstitutional a Nebraska statute forbidding the teaching in public or private schools of foreign languages to pupils below the eighth grade. Since the United States Constitution provided no express relief for offending the statute, the Court extended the due process clause to protect the teacher. The Court related the teacher's right to teach to an expanded substantive interpretation of "liberty" and said:

> The problem for our determination is whether the statute as construed and applied unreasonably infringes the liberty guaranteed to the Plaintiff in error by the Fourteenth Amendment. "No state shall . . . deprive any person of life, liberty, or property, without due process of law."
>
> While this court has not attempted to define with exactness the liberty thus guaranteed, the term has received much consideration and some of the included things have been definitely stated. Without doubt, it denotes not merely freedom from bodily restraint but also

the right of the individual to contract, to engage in any of the common occupations of life, to acquire useful knowledge, to marry, establish a home and bring up children, to worship God according to the dictates of his own conscience, and generally to enjoy those privileges long recognized at common law as essential to the orderly pursuit of happiness by free men. . . . The established doctrine is that this liberty may not be interfered with, under the guise of protecting the public interest, by legislative action which is arbitrary or without reasonable relation to some purpose within the competency of the State to effect. . . . His [the teacher's] right thus to teach and the right of parents to engage him so to instruct their children, we think, are within the liberty of the Amendment.[28]

With this decision, the Supreme Court not only acknowledged the substantive protections of due process covering life, liberty, and property but clearly extended them to protect a person's right of education,[29] travel,[30] and appearance.[31] Substantive due process rights also generally encompass the First Amendment freedoms of religion, speech, press, and assembly.

Corporal Punishment, The Eighth Amendment, and Substantive Due Process

The courts have upheld the right of school authorities to physically punish children in order to preserve school propriety and discipline. Cases have generally dealt with the degree and reasonableness of the discipline and not with whether corporal punishment could be administered at all.

A teacher's right to discipline students is subject to the reasonableness that is applicable to parents in disciplining their own children. Courts have advanced two standards governing a teacher's corporal punishment of a child: (1) the reasonableness standard, that it "must be exerted within bounds of reason and humanity"; and (2) the good faith standard. With regard to the former, the authority of a teacher over the pupil is considered a delegation by the state to the teacher of at least a portion of parental authority. As such, there is

a presumption in favor of the correctness of the teacher's actions. Concerning the second, the teacher must not have been activated by malice, nor have inflicted the punishment wantonly or excessively. The teacher may not be liable for error in judgment, even though the punishment is too severe, if the punishment is not of a nature to cause injury and he or she acts in good faith.

The legality of corporal punishment in the public schools has been drawn into question in recent years as several state legislatures have statutorily abolished physical punishment as a means of discipline. A recent study indicated that nineteen states have abolished corporal punishment in the public schools, and ten of these laws have been enacted since 1988. Yet, under common law and constitutional law precedents, corporal punishment remains permissible.

Eighth Amendment

In *Ingraham v. Wright*,[32] the U.S. Supreme Court ruled flatly that corporal punishment, as administered in the schools, could not be construed to violate the Eighth Amendment. The Court said the amendment's prohibition against cruel and unusual punishment did not apply to paddling in the schools; rather, it was designed to protect those convicted of crimes from punishment that is inhumane, vicious, or barbarous. The amendment's intent is threefold: to limit the kinds of punishment that can be imposed on those convicted of crimes, to proscribe punishment grossly disproportionate to the severity of the crime, and to impose substantive limits on what can be made criminal and punished as such. In this light, the Court concluded that it is difficult to conceive of corporal punishment as being within the scope of the Eighth Amendment. According to the Court, the amendment was not so intended.

Liberty Interest

At present, the courts are in conflict over whether at some level of severity corporal punishment may be so excessive as to deny a student's substantive liberty interests. The Supreme Court, in *Ingraham*, declared that "corporal punishment in public schools implicates a constitutionally protected liberty interest."[33] The Court noted that "among the liberty interests 'long recognized at common law as essential to the orderly pursuit of happiness of free man' " is the "right to be free from, and obtain judicial relief for, unjustified intrusions on personal security," including "bodily restraint and punishment."[34]

Yet, the Supreme Court noted that ordinary corporal punishment does not violate substantive rights. Further, if the Supreme Court did believe that substantive due process interests come into play at a certain level of severity, it apparently did not feel that the severe beating that the students suffered in *Ingraham* was of sufficient magnitude to invoke such substantive interests. Therefore, the Supreme Court left the issue hanging. The Fifth Circuit Court of Appeals, in dealing with *Ingraham* at the lower court level, had observed that substantive rights could not be reduced to a review of the severity of corporal punishment in each case, an untenable position in which the courts would find themselves counting the weight and number of paddle licks.[35]

The U.S. Courts of Appeals for the Fourth[36] and Tenth[37] Circuits, have, however, sought more definitive standards with regard to punishment. Both have maintained that punishment may be so severe as to constitute denial of a substantive due process interest. The Appeals Court for the Fourth Circuit, in *Hall v. Tawney*,[38] said that the scope and magnitude was of a different level than commonly considered in tort law, whether "ten licks rather than five licks" is excessive; rather, the court observed that "substantive due process is concerned with violation of personal rights of privacy and bodily security of so different an order of magnitude" that an overly simplistic application, such as counting of licks, is not necessarily appropriate.

The U.S. Court of Appeals for the Tenth Circuit, in *Garcia v. Miera*,[39] has followed the rationale of *Hall v. Tawney* and disagreed with the Fifth Circuit's conclusion in *Ingraham*. This court concluded "that grossly excessive corporal punishment may indeed constitute a violation of substantive due process rights."[40]

The views expressed in *Hall* and *Garcia* have been followed and reinforced by precedents from the Third and Eighth Circuits. The Third Circuit has said that

> [a] decision to discipline a student, if accomplished through excessive force and appreciable physical pain, may constitute an invasion of the child's Fifth Amendment liberty interest in his personal security and a violation of substantive due process prohibited by the Fourteenth Amendment.[41]

The Eighth Circuit said we agree that "at some point the administration of corporal punishment may violate a student's liberty interest in his personal security and substantive due process rights."[42]

Even though the nebulous nature of the U.S. Supreme Court's decision in *Ingraham* leaves the question in doubt, and the U.S. Courts of Appeals are not in agreement, it appears that the view enunciated in *Hall* and *Garcia* may portend the prevailing precedent whereby a substantive due process interest is implicated if corporal punishment is excessively immoderate, "inhumane or brutal."[43]

Cruel and Unusual Punishment Clause of Eighth Amendment Does Not Apply to Corporal Punishment in Schools

— · — · — · — · —

Ingraham v. Wright

— · — · — · — · —

Supreme Court of the United States, 1977.
430 U.S. 651, 97 S.Ct. 1401.

Mr. Justice POWELL delivered the opinion of the Court. This case presents questions concerning the use of corporal punishment in public schools: first, whether the paddling of students as a means of maintaining school discipline constitutes cruel and unusual punishment in violation of the Eighth Amendment; and second, to the extent that paddling is constitutionally permissible, whether the Due

Process Clause of the Fourteenth Amendment requires prior notice and an opportunity to be heard. . . .

Petitioners' evidence may be summarized briefly. In the 1970–1971 school year many of the 237 schools in Dade County used corporal punishment as a means of maintaining discipline pursuant to Florida legislation and a local school board regulation. The statute then in effect authorized limited corporal punishment by negative inference, proscribing punishment which was "degrading or unduly severe" or which was inflicted without prior consultation with the principal or the teacher in charge of the school. The regulation. . . contained explicit directions and limitations. . . .

Petitioners focused on Drew Junior High School, the school in which both Ingraham and Andrews were enrolled in the fall of 1970. In an apparent reference to Drew, the District Court found that "[t]he instances of punishment which could be characterized as severe, accepting the students' testimony as credible, took place in one junior high school."
. . .

The District Court made no findings on the credibility of the students' testimony. Rather, assuming their testimony to be credible, the court found no constitutional basis for relief.
. . .

A panel of the Court of Appeals voted to reverse. . . . Upon rehearing, the en banc court rejected these conclusions and affirmed the judgment of the District Court. . . .

In addressing the scope of the Eighth Amendment's prohibition on cruel and unusual punishment this Court has found it useful to refer to "[t]raditional common law concepts" . . . and to the "attitude[s] which our society has traditionally taken."
. . . So, too, in defining the requirements of procedural due process under the Fifth and Fourteenth Amendments, the Court has been attuned to what "has always been the law of the land" . . . and to "traditional ideas of fair procedure." . . . We therefore begin by examining the way in which our traditions and our laws have responded to the use of corporal punishment in public schools.

The use of corporal punishment in this country as a means of disciplining school children dates back to the colonial period. It has survived the transformation of primary and secondary education from the colonials' reliance on optional private arrangements to our present system of compulsory education and dependence on public schools. Despite the general abandonment of corporal punishment as a means of punishing criminal offenders, the practice continues to play a role in the public education of school children in most parts of the country. Professional and public opinion is sharply divided on the practice, and has been for more than a century. Yet we can discern no trend toward its elimination.

At common law a single principle has governed the use of corporal punishment since before the American Revolution: teachers may impose reasonable but not excessive force to discipline a child. . . . The basic doctrine has not changed. The prevalent rule in this country today privileges such force as a teacher or administrator "reasonably believes to be necessary for [the child's] proper control, training, or education." . . . To the extent that the force is excessive or unreasonable, the educator in virtually all States is subject to possible civil and criminal liability.

Although the early cases viewed the authority of the teacher as deriving from the parents, the concept of parental delegation has been replaced by the view—more consonant with compulsory education laws—that the State itself may impose such corporal punishment as is reasonably necessary "for the proper education of the child and for the maintenance of group discipline." . . . All of the circumstances are to be taken into account in determining whether the punishment is reasonable in a particular case. Among the most important considerations are the seriousness of the offense, the attitude and past behavior of the child, the nature and severity of the punishment, the age and strength of the child, and the availability of less severe but equally effective means of discipline. . . .

Of the twenty-three States that have addressed the problem through legislation, twenty-one have authorized the moderate use of corporal punishment in public schools. Of these States only a few have elaborated on the common law test of reasonableness, typically providing for approval or notification of the child's parents, or for infliction of punishment only by the principal or in the presence of an adult witness. Only two States, Massachusetts and New Jersey, have prohibited all corporal punishment in their public schools. Where the legislatures have not acted, the state courts have uniformly preserved the common law rule permitting teachers to use reasonable force in disciplining children in their charge.

Against this background of historical and contemporary approval of reasonable corporal punishment, we turn to the constitutional questions before us.

The Eighth Amendment provides, "Excessive bail shall not be required, nor excessive fines imposed, nor cruel and unusual punishments inflicted." Bail, fines and punishment traditionally have been associated with the criminal process, and by subjecting the three to parallel limitations the text of the Amendment suggests an intention to limit the power of those entrusted with the criminal law function of government. An examination of the history of the Amendment and the decisions of this Court construing the proscription against cruel and unusual punishment confirms that it was designed to protect those convicted of crimes. We adhere to this longstanding limitation and hold that the Eighth Amendment does not apply to the paddling of children as a means of maintaining discipline in public schools.

The history of the Eighth Amendment is well known. The text was taken, almost verbatim, from a provision of the Virginia Declaration of Rights of 1776, which in turn derived from the English Bill of Rights of 1689. The English version, adopted after the accession of William and Mary, was intended to curb the excesses of English judges under the reign of James II. . . .

At the time of its ratification, the original Constitution was criticized in the Massachusetts and Virginia Conventions for its failure to provide any protection for persons convicted of crimes. This criticism provided the impetus for inclusion of the Eighth Amendment in the Bill of Rights. . . .

In light of this history, it is not surprising to find that every decision of this Court considering whether a punishment is "cruel and unusual" within the meaning of the Eighth and Fourteenth Amendments has dealt with a criminal punishment. . . .

In the few cases where the Court has had occasion to confront claims that impositions outside the criminal process constituted cruel and unusual punishment, it has had no difficulty finding the Eighth Amendment inapplicable. . . .

Petitioners acknowledge that the original design of the Cruel and Unusual Punishments Clause was to limit criminal punishments, but urge nonetheless that the prohibition should be extended to ban the paddling of school children. Observing that the Framers of the Eighth Amendment could not have envisioned our present system of public and compulsory education, with its opportunities for noncriminal punishments, petitioners contend that extension of the prohibition against cruel punishments is necessary lest we afford greater protection to criminals than to school children. It would be anomalous, they say, if schoolchildren could be beaten without constitutional redress, while hardened criminals suffering the same beatings at the hands of their jailers might have a valid claim under the Eighth Amendment. . . . Whatever force this logic may have in other settings, we find it an inadequate basis for wrenching the Eighth Amendment from its historical context and extending it to traditional disciplinary practices in the public schools.

The prisoner and the schoolchild stand in wholly different circumstances, separated by the harsh facts of criminal conviction and incarceration. . . .

The schoolchild has little need for the protection of the Eighth Amendment. Though attendance may not always be voluntary, the public school remains an open institution. Except perhaps when very young, the child is not physically restrained from leaving school during school hours; and at the end of the school day, the child is invariably free to return home. Even while at school, the child brings with him the support of family and friends and is rarely apart from teachers and other pupils who may witness and protest any instances of mistreatment.

The openness of the public school and its supervision by the community afford significant safeguards against the kinds of abuses from which the Eighth Amendment protects the prisoner. In virtually every community where corporal punishment is permitted in the schools, these safeguards are reinforced by the legal constraints of the common law. Public school teachers and administrators are privileged at common law to inflict only such corporal punishment as is reasonably necessary for the proper education and discipline of the child; any punishment going beyond the privilege may result in both civil and criminal liability. . . . As long as the schools are open to public scrutiny, there is no reason to believe that the common law constraints will not effectively remedy and deter excesses such as those alleged in this case.

We conclude that when public school teachers or administrators impose disciplinary corporal punishment, the Eighth Amendment is inapplicable. The pertinent constitutional question is whether the imposition is consonant with the requirements of due process.

The Fourteenth Amendment prohibits any State deprivation of life, liberty or property without due process of law. Application of this prohibition requires the familiar two-stage analysis: we must first ask whether the asserted individual interests are encompassed within the Fourteenth Amendment's protection of "life, liberty or property"; if protected interests are implicated, we then must decide what procedures constitute "due process of law." . . . Following that analysis here, we find that corporal punishment in public school implicates a constitutionally protected liberty interest, but we hold that the traditional common law remedies are fully adequate to afford due process.

"[T]he range of interests protected by procedural due process is not infinite." . . . Among the historic liberties so protected was a right to be free from and to obtain judicial relief, for unjustified intrusions on personal security.

While the contours of this historic liberty interest in the context of our federal system of government have not been defined precisely, they always have been thought to encompass freedom from bodily restraint and punishment. . . . It is fundamental that the state cannot hold and physically punish an individual except in accordance with due process of law.

This constitutionally protected liberty interest is at stake in this case. There is, of course a *de minimis* level of imposition with which the Constitution is not concerned. But at least where school authorities, acting under color of state law, deliberately decide to punish a child for misconduct by restraining the child and inflicting appreciable physical pain, we hold that Fourteenth Amendment liberty interests are implicated.

"[T]he question remains what process is due." . . . Were it not for the common law privilege permitting teachers to inflict reasonable corporal punishment on children in their care, and the availability of the traditional remedies for abuse, the case for requiring advance procedural safeguards would be strong indeed. But here we deal with a punishment — paddling — within that tradition, and the question is whether the common law remedies are adequate to afford due process. . . . Whether in this case the common law remedies for excessive corporal punishment constitute due process of law must turn on an analysis of the competing interests at stake, viewed against the background of "history, reason, [and] the past course of decisions." The analysis requires consideration of three distinct factors: "first, the private interest that will be affected . . . ; second, the risk of an erroneous deprivation of such interest . . . and the probable value, if any, of additional or substitute procedural safeguards; and, finally, the [state] interest, including the function involved and the fiscal and administrative burdens that the additional or substitute procedural requirement would entail." . . .

Because it is rooted in history, the child's liberty interest in avoiding corporal punishment while in the care of public school authorities is subject to historical limitations. . . .

The concept that reasonable corporal punishment in school is justifiable continues to be recognized in the laws of most States. . . . It represents "the balance struck by this country" . . . between the child's interest in personal security and the traditional view that some limited corporal punishment may be necessary in the course of a child's education. Under that longstanding accommodation of interests, there can be no deprivation of substantive rights as long as disciplinary corporal punishment is within the limits of the common law privilege.

This is not to say that the child's interest in procedural safeguards is insubstantial. The school disciplinary process is not "a totally accurate, unerring process, never mistaken and never unfair. . . ." . . . In any deliberate infliction of corporal punishment on a child who is restrained for that purpose, there is some risk that the intrusion on the child's liberty will be unjustified and therefore unlawful. In these circumstances the child has a strong interest in procedural safeguards that minimize the risk of wrongful punishment and provide for the resolution of disputed questions of justification.

We turn now to a consideration of the safeguards that are available under applicable Florida law.

Florida has continued to recognize, and indeed has strengthened by statute, the common law right of a child not to be subjected to excessive corporal punishment in school. Under Florida law the teacher and principal of the school decide in the first instance whether corporal punishment is reasonably necessary under the circumstances in order to discipline a child who has misbehaved. But they must exercise prudence and restraint. For Florida has preserved the traditional judicial proceedings for determining whether the punishment was justified. If the punishment inflicted is later found to have been excessive—not reasonably believed at the time to be necessary for the child's discipline or training—the school authorities inflicting it may be held liable in damages to the child and, if malice is

shown, they may be subject to criminal penalties.

Although students have testified in this case to specific instances of abuse, there is every reason to believe that such mistreatment is an aberration. The uncontradicted evidence suggests that corporal punishment in the Dade County schools was, "[w]ith the exception of a few cases . . . unremarkable in physical severity." Moreover, because paddlings are usually inflicted in response to conduct directly observed by teachers in their presence, the risk that a child will be paddled without cause is typically insignificant. In the ordinary case, a disciplinary paddling neither threatens seriously to violate any substantive rights nor condemns the child "to suffer grievous loss of any kind." . . .

In those cases where severe punishment is contemplated, the available civil and criminal sanctions for abuse—considered in light of the openness of the school environment—afford significant protection against unjustified corporal punishment. Teachers and school authorities are unlikely to inflict corporal punishment unnecessarily or excessively when a possible consequence of doing so is the institution of civil or criminal proceedings against them. . . .

But even if the need for advance procedural safeguards were clear, the question would remain whether the incremental benefit could justify the cost. Acceptance of petitioners' claims would work a transformation in the law governing corporal punishment in Florida and most other States. Given the impracticability of formulating a rule or procedural due process that varies with the severity of the particular imposition, the prior hearing petitioners seek would have to precede *any* paddling, however moderate or trivial.

Such a universal constitutional requirement would significantly burden the use of corporal punishment as a disciplinary measure. Hearings—even informal hearings—require time, personnel, and a diversion of attention from normal school pursuits. . . .

Elimination or curtailment of corporal punishment would be welcomed by many as a societal advance. But when such a policy choice may result from this Court's determination of an asserted right to due process, rather than from the normal processes of community debate and legislative action, the societal costs cannot be dismissed as insubstantial.   . . . In view of the low incidence of abuse, the openness of our schools, and the common law safeguards that already exist, the risk of error that may result in violation of a schoolchild's substantive rights can only be regarded as minimal. Imposing additional administrative safeguards as a constitutional requirement might reduce that risk marginally, but would also entail a significant intrusion into an area of primary educational responsibility. We conclude that the Due Process Clause does not require notice and a hearing prior to the imposition of corporal punishment in the public schools as that practice is authorized and limited by the common law.   . . .

NOTES

1. Teachers may paddle students in spite of parental opposition. One federal district court upheld the spanking of a child over the parents' protest and said that even though parents generally have control of their children's discipline, "[T]he state has a countervailing interest in the maintenance of order in the school sufficient to sustain the right of teachers and school officials to administer reasonable corporal punishment" over the parent's objections. *Baker v. Owen*, 395 F.Supp. 294 (M.D. N.C.1975), affirmed without opinion 423 U.S. 907, 96 S.Ct. 210 (1975).

2. In a Texas case, a teacher whipped a pupil with a switch for fighting after school; the court held that the fact that the fighting occurred after school did not deprive the teacher of his legal right to punish the pupil. *Hutton v. State*, 23 Tex.App. 386, 5 S.W. 122 (1887). The court stated:

> The authority of the teacher is not confined to the school room or grounds, but

he may prohibit and punish all acts of his pupils which are detrimental to the good order and best interests of the school, whether such acts are committed in school hours or while the pupil is on his way to or from school or after he has returned home.

3. In a New York case, a teacher was accused of being malicious in the punishment of a boy. The teacher had been assigned to see that the pupils who were not taking part in class-day assembly should leave the school premises. One boy refused to leave; he had a record of bad behavior and he had been drinking. The boy used profane language when the teacher insisted that he leave. The teacher put his hands on the throat of the boy and either pushed or threw him over a hedge. The boy accused the teacher of assault and battery. The court ruled for the teacher and stated that

> people will differ as to what force is reasonable in manner and moderate in degree. Taking into consideration the prior conduct of the complainant, the lack of malice on the part of the defendant, the nature of the offense of the pupil, his motive, the effect of his conduct on other pupils, and his size and strength, I find and decide that the guilt of the defendant has not been proved beyond a reasonable doubt. *People ex rel. Hogan v. Newton*, 185 Misc. 405, 56 N.Y.S.2d 779 (1945).

4. An example of excessive and unreasonable punishment by a teacher is illustrated in an 1872 Kentucky case. In this case, a teacher was taking part in a playground activity with the pupils and one pupil differed with the opinion of the teacher on a trivial matter. The teacher in turn beat the boy. The court said:

> The authority of a teacher to hold his pupil to strict accountability in school for disorderly behavior did not justify him in assaulting and beating the pupil on the playground. *Hardy v. James*, 5 Ky. 36 Opin. (1872).

*Students' Substantive Due Process Rights May Be
Violated If Punishment Is Grossly Excessive as to Be
Shocking to the Conscience*

— · — · — · — · —

Garcia by Garcia v. Miera

— · — · — · — · —

United States Court of Appeals,
Tenth Circuit, 1987.
817 F.2d 650.

LOGAN, Circuit Judge. . . . Teresa Garcia, an elementary school pupil in New Mexico, by her parents and next friends, Max and Sandra Garcia, sued the defendants in their individual capacities for denying her substantive due process in violation of 42 U.S.C. § 1983 because of two beatings suffered at their hands. After considerable discovery, the defendants filed a motion for summary judgment, which the court granted. The district court concluded that the defendants were shielded from liability "by the defense of good faith immunity," R. I, 306, because the "law governing whether excess corporal punishment can give rise to a substantive due process claim is not clearly established." Garcia has appealed the court's order, contending that at the time of the beatings excessive corporal punishment by school officials did violate her clearly established substantive due process rights.

In 1982 Garcia was a nine-year-old student in the third grade at the Penasco Elementary School in Penasco, New Mexico. On February 10, 1982, defendant-appellee Theresa Miera, the school principal, summoned Garcia to her office for hitting a boy who had kicked her. Miera instructed Garcia to go to her chair to be paddled. Garcia refused and told Miera that her father had said that "Mrs. Miera had better shape up."

Miera responded by calling defendant J.D. Sanchez, a teacher at the school, for assistance. Sanchez held Garcia upside down by her ankles while Miera struck Garcia with a wooden paddle. The paddle "was split right down the middle, so it was two pieces, and when it hit, it clapped [and] grabbed." Miera hit Garcia five times on the front of the leg between the knee and the waist. After the beating, Garcia's teacher, Ruth Dominez, "noticed blood coming through [Garcia's] clothes," and, on taking Garcia to the restroom, was shocked to see a "welt" on Garcia's leg. The beating made a two-inch cut on her leg that left a permanent scar. Shortly after this incident, Garcia's mother and father told Miera "not to spank Teresa again unless we were called, to make sure it was justified, and [Miera] said okay, no problems."

The second beating at issue occurred on May 13, 1983. Miera summoned Garcia to her office for saying that defendant Judy Mestas had been seen kissing a student's father, Denny Mersereau, on a school bus during a recent field trip and that Mestas had sent love letters to Mersereau through his son.

Miera proceeded to strike Garcia two times with the paddle on the buttocks. Garcia then refused to be hit again. Miera responded by calling defendant Edward Leyba, an administrative associate at the school. Leyba pushed Garcia toward a chair over which she was to bend and receive three additional blows. Garcia and Leyba struggled and Garcia hit her back on Miera's desk, from which she suffered back pains for several weeks. Garcia then submitted to the last three blows. The beating caused severe bruises on Garcia's buttocks, which did not stop hurting for two to three weeks. The report of the school nurse indicates that as a result of the beating Garcia's "buttocks [were] bright red with [a] crease across both." Dr. Albrecht, a physician who treated Garcia, stated: "I've done hundreds of physicals of children who have had spankings. . . . and I have not seen bruises on the buttocks as Teresita had, from routine spankings . . . [T]hey were more extensive, deeper bruises. . . ." Betsy Martinez, a nurse who examined Garcia, stated that if a child had received this type of injury at home she "would have called [the police department's] Protective Services." The extent and severity of Garcia's bruises is independently supported by photographs of Garcia's buttocks taken on May 13 and May 18. Throughout the May 13 incident, Garcia kept asking Miera to allow her to call her mother. The principal refused, saying that she knew the law.

Some of these allegations were disputed by defendants in their affidavits and testimony. For purposes of reviewing the district court's grant of summary judgment to defendants, however, we must determine whether the allegations and facts recited above, if believed by the trier of fact, would establish a constitutional wrong for which plaintiff could recover.

We first consider whether corporal punishment of a school child, in any degree of excessiveness, can violate substantive rights under the Due Process Clause. Despite the Supreme Court's explicit disclaimer that it was deciding that issue in *Ingraham v. Wright,* 430 U.S. 651, 97 S.Ct. 1401, 51 L.Ed.2d 711 (1977), we believe that *Ingraham* requires us to hold that, at some point, excessive corporal punishment violates the pupil's substantive due process rights. Rejecting the four dissenters' views that corporal punishment could violate the Eighth Amendment, the majority found the Due Process Clause applicable. The Court declared that "corporal punishment in public schools implicates a constitutionally protected liberty interest." It recognized that among the liberty interests " 'long recognized at common law as essential to the orderly pursuit of happiness by free men' " is the "right to be free from, and to obtain judicial relief for, unjustified intrusions on personal security," including "bodily restraint and punishment." . . . "[W]here school authorities, acting under color of state law, deliberately decide to punish a child for misconduct by restraining the child and inflicting appreciable physical pain, we hold that Fourteenth Amendment liberty interests are implicated." This language plainly indicates that the infliction of corporal punishment can affect a fundamental right susceptible to substantive due process protection. . . .

Although the *Ingraham* opinion focuses on procedural due process, it discusses the history of corporal punishment in the law and applies a balancing test between the child's interest in personal security and the traditional view that a school may need to be able to impose "limited" or "reasonable" corporal punishment: "[T]here can be no deprivation of *substantive* rights as long as disciplinary corporal punishment is within the limits of the common-law privilege." . . .

Although *Ingraham* makes clear that ordinary corporal punishment violates no substantive due process rights of school children, by acknowledging that corporal punishment implicates a fundamental liberty interest protected by the Due Process Clause, we believe that opinion clearly signaled that, at some degree of excessiveness or cruelty, the meting out such punishment violates the substantive due process rights of the pupil.

Indeed, such a view is compelling and the general principles underlying it have been recognized at least since *Rochin v. California,* 342 U.S. 165, 72 S.Ct. 205, 96 L.Ed. 183 (1952), when the Supreme Court held that the forcible use of a stomach pump by police officers violated the individual's rights under the Due Process Clause. The Court declared that official conduct that "shocks the conscience," force that is "brutal" or "offensive to human dignity," offends the Due Process Clause. . . .

This circuit applied that notion in the context of a school, albeit one for problem children, in *Milonas v. Williams,* 691 F.2d 931 (10th Cir.1982), *cert. denied,* 460 U.S. 1069, 103 S.Ct. 1524, 75 L.Ed.2d 947 (1983). We there affirmed the issuance of a permanent injunction against the Provo Canyon School for Boys enjoining, *inter alia,* the school's use of a practice nicknamed the "hair dance." The hair dance was a form of disciplinary action whereby a school employee would "grab one of the student's arms and clutch the boy's hair with his other hand." Our decision in *Milonas* expressly endorsed the district court's finding that the "hair dance permitted unreasonably harsh school responses to the conduct of disturbed boys." We rejected the argument that such physical abuse was reasonably related to the legitimate objectives of the Provo Canyon School, and concluded that the defendants' actions violated the plaintiffs' due process rights. . . .

We here reaffirm our view, set out in *Milonas,* that at some point of excessiveness or brutality, a public school child's substantive due process rights are violated by beatings administered by government-paid school officials. . . .

We believe the necessary inference from the Supreme Court's *Ingraham* decision is that excessive corporal punishment less offensive than the definition quoted above does not rise to the level of a constitutional substantive due process violation. Such lesser violations implicate only a pupil's procedural due process rights. Thus, if the state were to provide no adequate remedy to deter this lesser degree of official conduct and compensate the victim of that misconduct, we would find a violation of procedural due process.

We thus envision three categories of corporal punishment. Punishments that do not exceed the traditional common law standard of reasonableness are not actionable; punishments that exceed the common law standard without adequate state remedies violate procedural due process rights; and finally, punishments that are so grossly excessive as to be ·shocking to the conscience violate substantive due process rights, without regard to the adequacy of state remedies. . . .

. . . [W]e believe that the Court's refusal in *Ingraham* to address the substantive due process claim does not, without more, mandate a conclusion that the law was not clearly established. . . . [T]he concept of the substantive due process right is implicit in *Ingraham.* Indeed, before the first beating of Garcia, the author of the *Ingraham* majority, Justice Powell, describing the contours of substantive due process, had cited with approval the proposition that "corporal punishment of students may have violated due process if it 'amounted to a brutal and inhumane abuse of official power literally shocking to the conscience.' " . . .

We agree that a direct conflict exists between the Fourth Circuit in *Hall,* which has rejected, and the Fifth Circuit in *Ingraham,* which has upheld, the constitutionality of grossly excessive corporal punishment. But the decisions of one circuit court of appeals are not binding upon another circuit. . . . To give preclusive effect to a conflict among the circuits would effectively bind this circuit by the decisions of others. Moreover, the binding would always be in denigration of the constitutional right at issue. . . .

Despite the Fifth Circuit's position, we believe the law was clearly established before *Milonas* that some high level of force in a corporal punishment context would violate a child's substantive due process rights. We think a reasonably competent legal advisor to a school district should have realized that egregious invasions of a student's personal security would be unconstitutional. . . .

The threshold for recovery on the constitutional tort for excessive corporal punishment is high. But the allegations with respect to the first beating, that this nine-year-old girl was held up by her ankles and hit several times with a split board of substantial size on the front of her legs until they bled — supported by evidence of a permanent scar — are sufficient. The allegations with respect to the second beating, that the punishment was severe enough to cause pain for three weeks — supported by pictures of the injured buttocks, an affidavit from an examining doctor that in his long experience he had not seen bruises like that from routine spankings, and an affidavit from an examining nurse that if a child had received this type of injury at home she would have reported it as child abuse — are also sufficient. These claims may not survive the crucible of the trial, but they overcome defendants' motion for summary judgment.

Reversed and remanded for further proceedings consistent herewith.

NOTES

1. *Interscholastic Athletics as a Substantive Due Process Interest.* "A clear majority of the courts" has held that students do not have

a legitimate entitlement to participate in interscholastic athletics. *Brands v. Sheldon Community School,* 671 F.Supp. 627 (N.D. Iowa 1987).

See *Colorado Seminary v. NCAA,* 570 F.2d 320 (10th Cir. 1978); *Hamilton v. Tennessee Secondary School Athletic Association,* 552 F.2d 681 (6th Cir. 1976); *Mitchell v. Louisiana High School Athletic Association,* 430 F.2d 1155 (5th Cir. 1970). In a case from the U.S. Court of Appeals, Eighth Circuit, the court stated that "a student's interest in participating in a single year of interscholastic athletics amounts to a mere expectation rather than a constitutionally protected claim of entitlement." *In re United States ex. rel. Missouri State High School Activities Association,* 682 F.2d 147 (8th Cir. 1982) quoting *Walsh v. Louisiana High School Athletic Association,* 616 F.2d 152, (5th Cir. 1980), cert. denied, 449 U.S. 1124, 101 S.Ct. 939 (1981).

In *Brands,* the Court noted that "once awarded, a college scholarship may give rise to a property interest in its continuation," *Hall v. University of Minnesota,* 530 F.Supp. 104 (D. Minn. 1982).

In *Brands* the Court further said that

> [w]hen scholarships are awarded at the discretion of a college coach, and such discretion has not yet been exercised, no property interest in the receipt of a scholarship can exist, and the plaintiff can not invoke his expectation that he would earn a scholarship at the state tournament in order to claim a property interest. *Brand v. Sheldon Community School,* supra.

2. The U.S. Court of Appeals for the Fifth Circuit in *Woodard v. Los Fresnos Independent School Dist.,* 732 F. 2d 1243 (5th Cir. 1984), has pointed out that even though "the infliction of punishment may transgress constitutionally protected liberty interests," that "if the state affords the student adequate post punishment remedies to deter unjustified or excessive punishment and to redress that which may nevertheless occur, the student receives all the process that is constitutionally due."

3. In following its own precedent in *Cunningham v. Beavers,* 858 F.2d 269 (5th Cir. 1988), the Fifth Circuit court ruled in a Texas case that severe spankings, leaving black and blue marks, on two little girls for the offense of snickering, did not implicate substantive due process, and that relief, if any existed, was to be found in Texas common law.

4. *Arbitrary and Capricious Action.* If a school board's actions are arbitrary and capricious, then a substantive due process denial may be shown by the student. *Brands v. Sheldon Community School,* 671 F.Supp. 627 (N.D. Iowa 1987).

5. *Rule of Privileged Force.* A teacher may claim that use of force in controlling or disciplining a student is privileged and as such is a defense against a civil assault charge. Such a privilege emanates from the concept of *in loco parentis,* but is couched in different terminology. This rule has been defined as follows:

> [A]ny force used must be that which the teacher **reasonably** believes necessary (1) to enforce compliance with a **proper** command issued for the purpose of controlling, training or educating the child, or (2) to punish the child for prohibited conduct; and in either case, the force or physical contact must be reasonable and not disproportionate to the activity or the offense. *Hogenson v. Williams,* 542 S.W.2d 456 (Tex. Civ. App.-Texarkana 1976).

6. *Mandatory Punishment.* The Supreme Court of Mississippi has held that a rule with prescribed mandatory punishment is valid. The Court explained:

> As a matter of state substantive due process, a school board's disciplinary rule or scheme is enforceable when fairly viewed it furthers a substantial legitimate interest of the school.
>
> Mandatory school disciplinary rules are not unconstitutional simply because they are mandatory.
>
> The fact that a school rule may be worded in mandatory language does not deprive school boards and their subordinates of the authority to administer the rule with flexibility and leniency.

Clinton Municipal Separate School District v. Byrd, 477 So. 2d 237 (Miss. 1985).

Procedural Due Process

The requirement of procedural due process is neither novel nor new to the law. As discussed elsewhere in this book, Article 39 of the Magna Carta required due process and the common law has long required a fair hearing by an impartial tribunal as a fundamental staple of justice.

Procedural due process or natural justice encompasses two basic or elemental standards of fairness:

1. The rule against bias: No man shall be a judge in his own case, or *nemo judex in causa sua,* and
2. The right to a hearing: No man shall be condemned unheard, or *audi alteram partem.*

The right to a hearing requires that the accused know the case against him or her and have an opportunity to state his or her own case. Each party must have the chance to present his or her version of the facts and to make submissions relevant to the case. Fairness is the hallmark of this process, and though the extent of process required is sometimes in question, the principle that "no one should be condemned unheard" prevails.

The Fifth and Fourteenth Amendments of the U.S. Constitution provide that neither the federal government nor a state shall "deprive any person of life, liberty or property, without due process of law." Originally, these provisions were interpreted to apply to judicial proceedings only and not to quasi-judicial proceedings conducted by educational agencies. Because school officials stood *in loco parentis,* in a privileged relationship to students, particular legal standards of fair play were not required. It was not until the landmark case of *Dixon v. Alabama*[44] in 1961 that this changed. *Dixon* established that procedural due process does manifestly apply to schools and other governmental agencies, and that deviations from minimal fairness in disciplinary action, depending on the magnitude and severity, may well deny the student a constitutional interest.

Later, in *Soglin v. Kauffman,*[45] the court said the point at which disciplinary actions should be subject to constitutional scrutiny is when the action involves suspension "for any period of time substantial enough to prevent one from obtaining credit for a particular term."

The circumstances and the interests of the parties involved are paramount in prescribing the standards of procedural due process.[46] The United States Supreme Court has said:

> Due process unlike some legal rules is not a technical conception with a fixed content, unrelated to time, place and circumstances . . .. It is a delicate process of adjustment inescapably involving the exercise of judgment by those whom the Constitution entrusted the unfolding of its process.[47]

In providing procedural due process, the courts are not uniform in their requirements, but all insist that fundamental fairness must be afforded and "both sides must be given an opportunity to present their sides of the story in detail."[48]

In *Due v. Florida Agr. and Mechanical University,* the court outlined three minimal due process requirements.

> First, the student should be given adequate notice in writing of the specific ground or grounds and the nature of the evidence on which the disciplinary proceedings are based. Second, the student should be given an opportunity for a hearing in which the disciplinary authority provides a fair opportunity for hearing of the student's position, explanations and evidence. The third requirement is that no disciplinary action be taken on grounds which are not supported by any substantial evidence.[49]

Fundamental fairness prescribed in these early cases for long suspension or expulsion of students has been extended to temporary, short-term suspensions by the United States Supreme Court in *Goss v. Lopez.*[50] The formality and intensity, though, of the procedural process is not fixed, the requirement being only that the process be commensurate with the length of suspension or the detriment that may be imposed on the student.

Procedural Due Process Required for Students When Expelled

Dixon v. Alabama State Board of Education

United States Court of Appeals,
Fifth Circuit, 1961.
294 F.2d 150, cert. denied 368 U.S. 930,
82 S.Ct. 368 (1961).

RIVES, Circuit Judge. The question presented by the pleadings and evidence, and decisive of this appeal, is whether due process requires notice and some opportunity for hearing before students at a tax-supported college are expelled for misconduct. We answer that question in the affirmative.

The misconduct for which the students were expelled has never been definitely specified. Defendant Trenholm, the President of the College, testified that he did not know why the plaintiffs and three additional students were expelled and twenty other students were placed on probation. The notice of expulsion which Dr. Trenholm mailed to each of the plaintiffs assigned no specific ground for expulsion, but referred in general terms to "this problem of Alabama State College."
. . .

As shown by the findings of the district court . . . the only demonstration which the evidence showed that *all* of the expelled students took part in was that in the lunch grill located in the basement of the Montgomery County Courthouse. The other demonstrations were found to be attended "by several if not all of the plaintiffs." We have carefully read and studied the record, and agree with the district court that the evidence does not affirmatively show that *all* of the plaintiffs were present at any but the one demonstration.
. . . . The most elaborate grounds for expulsion were assigned in the testimony of Governor Patterson:

Q.   There is an allegation in the complaint, Governor, that—I believe it is paragraph six, the defendants' action of expulsion was taken without regard to any valid rule or regulation concerning student conduct and merely retaliated against, punished, and sought to intimidate plaintiffs for having lawfully sought service in a publicly owned lunch room with service; is that statement true or false?

A.   Well, that is not true; the action taken by the State Board of Education was—was taken to prevent—to prevent incidents happening by students at the College that would bring—bring discredit upon—upon the School and be prejudicial to the School, and the State—as I said before, the State Board of Education took—considered at the time it expelled these students several incidents, one at the Court House at the lunch room demonstration, the one the next day at the trial of this student, the marching on the steps of the State Capitol, and also this rally held at the church, where—where it was reported that—that statements were made against the administration of the School. In addition to that, the—the feeling going around in the community here due to—due to the reports of these incidents of the students, by the students, and due to reports of incidents occurring involving violence in other States, which happened prior to these things starting here in Alabama, all of these things were discussed by the State Board of Education prior to the taking of the action that they did on March 2 and as I was present and acting as Chairman, as a member of the Board, I voted to expel these students and to put these others on probation because I felt that that was what was in the best interest of the College. And the—I felt that the action should be—should be prompt and immediate, because if something—something had not been done, in my opinion, it would have resulted in violence and disorder, and that we wanted to prevent, and we felt that we had a duty to the—to the—to the parents of the students and to the State to require that the students behave themselves while they are attending a State College, and that is [sic] the reasons why we took the action that we did. That is all.

Superintendent of Education Stewart testified that he voted for expulsion because the students had broken rules and regulations

pertaining to all of the State institutions
. . . .

The evidence clearly shows that the question for decision does not concern the sufficiency of the notice or the adequacy of the hearing, but is whether the students had a right to any notice or hearing whatever before being expelled. . . . After careful study and consideration, we find ourselves unable to agree with the conclusion of the district court that no notice or opportunity for any kind of hearing was required before these students were expelled.

It is true, as the district court said, that "there is no statute or rule that requires formal charges and/or a hearing . . . " but the evidence is without dispute that the usual practice at Alabama State College had been to give a hearing and opportunity to offer defenses before expelling a student. . . .

Whenever a governmental body acts so as to injure an individual, the Constitution requires that the act be consonant with due process of law. The minimum procedural requirements necessary to satisfy due process depend upon the circumstances and the interests of the parties involved. . . .

The precise nature of the private interest involved in this case is the right to remain at a public institution of higher learning in which the plaintiffs were students in good standing. It requires no argument to demonstrate that education is vital and, indeed, basic to civilized society. Without sufficient education the plaintiffs would not be able to earn an adequate livelihood, to enjoy life to the fullest, or to fulfill as completely as possible the duties and responsibilities of good citizens.

There was no offer to prove that other colleges are open to the plaintiffs. If so, the plaintiffs would nonetheless be injured by the interruption of their course of studies in mid-term. It is most unlikely that a public college would accept a student expelled from another public college of the same state. Indeed, expulsion may well prejudice the student in completing his education at any other institution. Surely no one can question that the right to remain at the college in which

the plaintiffs were students in good standing is an interest of extremely great value.

Turning then to the nature of the governmental power to expel the plaintiffs, it must be conceded, as was held by the district court, that that power is not unlimited and cannot be arbitrarily exercised. Admittedly, there must be some reasonable and constitutional ground for expulsion or the courts would have a duty to require reinstatement. The possibility of arbitrary action is not excluded by the existence of reasonable regulations. There may be arbitrary application of the rule to the facts of a particular case. Indeed, that result is well nigh inevitable when the Board hears only one side of the issue. In the disciplining of college students there are no considerations of immediate danger to the public, or of peril to the national security, which should prevent the Board from exercising at least the fundamental principles of fairness by giving the accused students notice of the charges and an opportunity to be heard in their own defense. Indeed, the example set by the Board in failing so to do, if not corrected by the courts, can well break the spirits of the expelled students and of others familiar with the injustice, and do inestimable harm to their education. . . .

For the guidance of the parties in the event of further proceedings, we state our views on the nature of the notice and hearing required by due process prior to expulsion from a state college or university. They should, we think, comply with the following standards. The notice should contain a statement of the specific charges and grounds which, if proven, would justify expulsion under the regulations of the Board of Education. The nature of the hearing should vary depending upon the circumstances of the particular case. The case before us requires something more than an informal interview with an administrative authority of the college. By its nature, a charge of misconduct, as opposed to a failure to meet the scholastic standards of the college, depends upon a collection of the facts concerning the charged misconduct, easily colored by the point of view of the witnesses. In such circumstances, a hearing which gives the Board or the administrative authorities of the college an opportunity to hear both sides in considerable detail is best suited to protect the rights of all involved. This is not to imply that a full-dress judicial hearing, with the right to cross-examine witnesses, is required. Such a hearing, with the attending publicity and disturbance of college activities, might be detrimental to the college's educational atmosphere and impractical to carry out. Nevertheless, the rudiments of an adversary proceeding may be preserved without encroaching upon the interests of the college. In the instant case, the student should be given the names of the witnesses against him and an oral or written report on the facts to which each witness testifies. He should also be given the opportunity to present to the Board, or at least to an administrative official of the college, his own defense against the charges and to produce either oral testimony or written affidavits of witnesses in his behalf. If the hearing is not before the Board directly, the results and findings of the hearing should be presented in a report open to the student's inspection. If these rudimentary elements of fair play are followed in a case of misconduct of this particular type, we feel that the requirements of due process of law will have been fulfilled.

The judgment of the district court is reversed and the cause is remanded for further proceedings consistent with this opinion.

Reversed and remanded.

---

*Temporary Suspension Requires
Procedural Due Process*

—··—··—··—··—

Goss v. Lopez

—··—··—··—··—

Supreme Court of the United States, 1975.
419 U.S. 565, 95 S.Ct. 729.

Mr. Justice WHITE delivered the opinion of the Court. This appeal by various administrators of the Columbus, Ohio, Public School System (CPSS) challenges the judgment of a three-judge federal court, declaring that appellees—various high school students in the CPSS—were denied due process of law contrary to the command of the Fourteenth Amendment in that they were temporarily suspended from their high schools without a hearing either prior to suspension or within a reasonable time thereafter, and enjoining the administrators to remove all references to such suspensions from the students' records.

Ohio law, Rev.Code Ann. § 3313.64 (1972), provides for free education to all children between the ages of six and twenty-one. Section 3313.66 of the Code empowers the principal of an Ohio public school to suspend a pupil for misconduct for up to ten days or to expel him. In either case, he must notify the student's parents within twenty-four hours and state the reasons for his action. A pupil who is expelled, or his parents, may appeal the decision to the Board of Education and in connection therewith shall be permitted to be heard at the board meeting. The Board may reinstate the pupil following the hearing. No similar procedure is provided in § 3313.66 or any other provision of state law for a suspended student. Aside from a regulation tracking the statute, at the time of the imposition of the suspensions in this case the CPSS itself had not issued any written procedure applicable to suspensions. Nor, so far as the record reflects, had any of the individual high schools involved in this case. Each, however, had formally or informally described the conduct for which suspension could be imposed.

The nine named appellees, each of whom alleged that he or she had been suspended from public high school in Columbus for up to ten days without a hearing pursuant to § 3313.66, filed an action under 42 U.S.C.A. § 1983 against the Columbus Board of Education and various administrators of the CPSS. The complaint sought a declaration that § 3313.66 was unconstitutional in that it permitted public school administrators to deprive plaintiffs of their rights to an education without a hearing of any kind, in violation of the procedural due process component of the Fourteenth Amendment. It also sought to enjoin the public school officials from issuing future suspensions pursuant to § 3313.66 and to require them to remove references to the past suspensions from the records of the students in question.

The proof below established that the suspensions arose out of a period of widespread student unrest in the CPSS during February and March 1971. Six of the named plaintiffs, Rudolph Sutton, Tyrone Washington, Susan Cooper, Deborah Fox, Clarence Byars, and Bruce Harris, were students at the Marion-Franklin High School and were each suspended for ten days on account of disruptive or disobedient conduct committed in the presence of the school administrator who ordered the suspension. One of these, Tyrone Washington, was among a group of students demonstrating in the school auditorium while a class was being conducted there. He was ordered by the school principal to leave, refused to do so, and was suspended. Rudolph Sutton, in the presence of the principal, physically attacked a police officer who was attempting to remove Tyrone Washington from the auditorium. He was immediately suspended. The other four Marion-Franklin students were suspended for similar conduct. None was given a hearing to determine the operative facts underlying the suspension, but each, together with his or her parents, was offered the opportunity to attend a conference, subsequent to the effective date of the suspension, to discuss the student's future.

Two named plaintiffs, Dwight Lopez and Betty Crome, were students at the Central High School and McGuffey Junior High School, respectively. The former was suspended in connection with a disturbance in the lunchroom which involved some physical damage to school property. Lopez testified that at least seventy-five other students were suspended from his school on the same day. He also testified below that he was not a party to the destructive conduct but was instead an innocent bystander. Because no one from the school testified with regard to this incident, there is no evidence in the record indicating the official basis for concluding otherwise. Lopez never had a hearing.

Betty Crome was present at a demonstration at a high school other than the one she was attending. There she was arrested together with others, taken to the police station, and released without being formally charged. Before she went to school on the following day, she was notified that she had been suspended for a ten-day period. Because no one from the school testified with respect to this incident, the record does not disclose how the McGuffey Junior High School principal went about making the decision to suspend Crome, nor does it disclose on what information the decision was based. It is clear from the record that no hearing was ever held.

There was no testimony with respect to the suspension of the ninth named plaintiff, Carl Smith. The school files were also silent as to his suspension, although as to some, but not all, of the other named plaintiffs the files contained either direct references to their suspensions or copies of letters sent to their parents advising them of the suspension.

On the basis of this evidence, the three-judge court declared that plaintiffs were denied due process of law because they were "suspended without hearing prior to suspension or within a reasonable time thereafter," and that Ohio Rev.Code Ann. § 3313.66 (1972) and regulations issued pursuant thereto were unconstitutional in permitting such suspensions. It was ordered that all references to plaintiffs' suspensions be removed from school files.

Although not imposing upon the Ohio school administrators any particular disciplinary procedures and leaving them "free to adopt regulations providing for fair suspension procedures which are consonant with the educational goals of their schools and reflective of the characteristics of their school and locality," the District Court declared that there were "minimum requirements of notice and a hearing prior to suspension, except in emergency situations." In explication, the court stated that relevant case authority would: (1) permit "[i]mmediate removal of a student whose conduct disrupts the academic atmosphere of the school, endangers fellow students, teachers or school officials, or damages property"; (2) require notice of suspension proceedings to be sent to the students' parents within twenty-four hours of the decision to conduct them; and (3) require a hearing to be held, with the student present, within seventy-two hours of his removal. Finally, the court stated that, with respect to the nature of the hearing, the relevant cases required that statements in support of the charge be produced, that the student and others be permitted to make statements in defense or mitigation, and that the school need not permit attendance by counsel.

The defendant school administrators have appealed the three-judge court's decision. Because the order below granted plaintiffs' request for an injunction—ordering defendants to expunge their records—this Court has jurisdiction of the appeal pursuant to 28 U.S.C.A. § 1253. We affirm.

At the outset, appellants contend that because there is no constitutional right to an education at public expense, the Due Process Clause does not protect against expulsions from the public school system. This position misconceives the nature of the issue and is refuted by prior decisions. The Fourteenth Amendment forbids the State to deprive any person of life, liberty, or property without due process of law. Protected interests in property are normally "not created by the Constitution. Rather, they are created and their dimensions are defined" by an independent source such as state statutes or rules entitling the citizen to certain benefits. *Board of Regents v. Roth,* 408 U.S. 564, 577, 92 S.Ct. 2701, 2709, 33 L.Ed.2d 548 (1972). . . .

The Due Process Clause also forbids arbitrary deprivations of liberty. "Where a person's good name, reputation, honor, or integrity is at stake because of what the government is doing to him," the minimal requirements of the Clause must be satisfied. *Wisconsin v. Constantineau,* 400 U.S. 433, 437, 91 S.Ct. 507, 510, 27 L.Ed.2d 515 (1971); *Board of Regents v. Roth,* supra, 408 U.S. at 573, 92 S.Ct. at 2707. School authorities here suspended appellees from school for periods of up to ten days based on charges of misconduct. If sustained and recorded, those charges could seriously damage the students' standing with their fellow pupils and their teachers as well as interfere with later opportunities for higher education and employment. It is apparent that

the claimed right of the State to determine unilaterally and without process whether that misconduct has occurred immediately collides with the requirements of the Constitution.

Appellants proceed to argue that even if there is a right to a public education protected by the Due Process Clause generally, the Clause comes into play only when the State subjects a student to a "severe detriment or grievous loss." The loss of ten days, it is said, is neither severe nor grievous and the Due Process Clause is therefore of no relevance. Appellants' argument is again refuted by our prior decisions; for in determining "whether due process requirements apply in the first place, we must look not to the 'weight' but to the *nature* of the interest at stake." *Board of Regents v. Roth,* supra, at 570–571, 92 S.Ct. at 2705–2706. Appellees were excluded from school only temporarily, it is true, but the length and consequent severity of a deprivation, while another factor to weigh in determining the appropriate form of hearing, "is not decisive of the basic right" to a hearing of some kind. *Fuentes v. Shevin,* 407 U.S. 67, 86, 92 S.Ct. 1983, 1997, 32 L.Ed. 2d 556 (1972). The Court's view has been that as long as a property deprivation is not *de minimis,* its gravity is irrelevant to the question whether account must be taken of the Due Process Clause. *Sniadach v. Family Finance Corp.,* 395 U.S. 337, 342, 89 S.Ct. 1820, 1823, 23 L.Ed. 2d 349 (1969) (Harlan, J. concurring); *Boddie v. Connecticut,* 401 U.S. 371, 378–379, 91 S.Ct. 780, 786, 28 L.Ed. 2d 113 (1971); *Board of Regents v. Roth,* supra, 408 U.S., at 570 n. 8, 92 S.Ct., at 2705. A ten-day suspension from school is not *de minimis* in our view and may not be imposed in complete disregard of the Due Process Clause.

A short suspension is, of course, a far milder deprivation than expulsion. But, "education is perhaps the most important function of state and local governments," *Brown v. Board of Education,* 347 U.S. 483, 493, 74 S.Ct. 686, 691, 98 L.Ed. 873 (1954), and the total exclusion from the educational process for more than a trivial period, and certainly if the suspension is for ten days, is a serious event in the life of the suspended child. Neither the property interest in educational benefits tem-

porarily denied nor the liberty interest in reputation, which is also implicated, is so insubstantial that suspensions may constitutionally be imposed by any procedure the school chooses, no matter how arbitrary.
. . .

There are certain bench marks to guide us, however. *Mullane v. Central Hanover Trust Co.,* 339 U.S. 306, 70 S.Ct. 652, 94 L.Ed. 865 (1950), a case often invoked by later opinions, said that "[m]any controversies have raged about the cryptic and abstract words of the Due Process Clause but there can be no doubt that at a minimum they require that deprivation of life, liberty or property by adjudication be preceded by notice and opportunity for hearing appropriate to the nature of the case." Id., at 313, 70 S.Ct. at 657. "The fundamental requisite of due process of law is the opportunity to be heard," *Grannis v. Ordean,* 234 U.S. 385, 394, 34 S.Ct. 779, 783, 58 L.Ed. 1363 (1914), a right that "has little reality or worth unless one is informed that the matter is pending and can choose for himself whether to . . . contest." *Mullane v. Central Hanover Trust Co.,* supra, 339 U.S. at 314, 70 S.Ct. at 657. At the very minimum, therefore, students facing suspension and the consequent interference with a protected property interest must be given *some* kind of notice and afforded *some* kind of hearing. "Parties whose rights are to be affected are entitled to be heard; and in order that they may enjoy that right they must first be notified." *Baldwin v. Hale,* 1 Wall. 223, 233, 17 L.Ed. 531 (1864).

It also appears from our cases that the timing and content of the notice and the nature of the hearing will depend on appropriate accommodation of the competing interests involved. *Cafeteria Workers v. McElroy,* supra, 367 U.S. at 895, 81 S.Ct. at 1748; *Morrissey v. Brewer,* supra, 408 U.S. at 481, 92 S.Ct. at 2600. The student's interest is to avoid unfair or mistaken exclusion from the educational process, with all of its unfortunate consequences. The Due Process Clause will not shield him from suspensions properly imposed, but it disserves both his interest and the interest of the State if his suspension is in fact unwarranted. The concern would be mostly academic if the disciplinary process

were a totally accurate, unerring process, never mistaken and never unfair. Unfortunately, that is not the case, and no one suggests that it is. Disciplinarians, although proceeding in utmost good faith, frequently act on the reports and advice of others; and the controlling facts and the nature of the conduct under challenge are often disputed. The risk of error is not at all trivial, and it should be guarded against if that may be done without prohibitive cost or interference with the educational process.

The difficulty is that our schools are vast and complex. Some modicum of discipline and order is essential if the educational function is to be performed. Events calling for discipline are frequent occurrences and sometimes require immediate, effective action. Suspension is considered not only to be a necessary tool to maintain order but a valuable educational device. The prospect of imposing elaborate hearing requirements in every suspension case is viewed with great concern, and many school authorities may well prefer the untrammeled power to act unilaterally, unhampered by rules about notice and hearing. But it would be a strange disciplinary system in an educational institution if no communication was sought by the disciplinarian with the student in an effort to inform him of his dereliction and to let him tell his side of the story in order to make sure that an injustice is not done. "[F]airness can rarely be obtained by secret, one-sided determination of facts decisive of rights. . . ." "Secrecy is not congenial to truth-seeking and self-righteousness gives too slender an assurance of rightness. No better instrument has been devised for arriving at truth than to give a person in jeopardy of serious loss notice of the case against him and opportunity to meet it."
. . .

We do not believe that school authorities must be totally free from notice and hearing requirements if their schools are to operate with acceptable efficiency. Students facing temporary suspension have interests qualifying for protection of the Due Process Clause and due process requires, in connection with a suspension of ten days or less, that the student be given oral or written notice of the charges against him and, if he denies them, an explanation of the evidence the authorities have and an opportunity to present his side of the story. The Clause requires at least these rudimentary precautions against unfair or mistaken findings of misconduct and arbitrary exclusion from school.

There need be no delay between the time "notice" is given and the time of the hearing. In the great majority of cases the disciplinarian may informally discuss the alleged misconduct with the student minutes after it has occurred. We hold only that, in being given an opportunity to explain his version of the facts at this discussion the student first be told what he is accused of doing and what the basis of the accusation is. Lower courts which have addressed the question of the *nature* of the procedures required in short suspension cases have reached the same conclusion. *Tate v. Board of Education*, 453 F.2d 975, 979 (CA8 1972); *Vail v. Board of Education*, 354 F.Supp. 592, 603 (NH 1973). Since the hearing may occur almost immediately following the misconduct, it follows that as a general rule notice and hearing should precede removal of the student from school. We agree with the District Court, however, that there are recurring situations in which prior notice and hearing cannot be insisted upon. Students whose presence poses a continuing danger to persons or property or an ongoing threat of disrupting the academic process may be immediately removed from school. In such cases, the necessary notice and rudimentary hearing should follow as soon as practicable, as the District Court indicated.

In holding as we do, we do not believe that we have imposed procedures on school disciplinarians which are inappropriate in a classroom setting. Instead we have imposed requirements which are, if anything, less than a fair-minded school principal would impose upon himself in order to avoid unfair suspensions. Indeed, according to the testimony of the principal of Marion-Franklin High School, that school had an informal procedure, remarkably similar to that which we now require, applicable to suspensions generally but which was not followed in this case. Similarly, according to the most recent memorandum

applicable to the entire CPSS, school principals in the CPSS are now required by local rule to provide at least as much as the constitutional minimum which we have described.

We stop short of construing the Due Process Clause to require, countrywide, that hearings in connection with short suspensions must afford the student the opportunity to secure counsel, to confront and cross-examine witnesses supporting the charge, or to call his own witnesses to verify his version of the incident. Brief disciplinary suspensions are almost countless. To impose in each such case even truncated trial-type procedures might well overwhelm administrative facilities in many places and, by diverting resources, cost more than it would save in educational effectiveness. Moreover, further formalizing the suspension process and escalating its formality and adversary nature may not only make it too costly as a regular disciplinary tool but also destroy its effectiveness as part of the teaching process.

On the other hand, requiring effective notice and informal hearing permitting the student to give his version of the events will provide a meaningful hedge against erroneous action. At least the disciplinarian will be alerted to the existence of disputes about facts and arguments about cause and effect. He may then determine himself to summon the accuser, permit cross-examination, and allow the student to present his own witnesses. In more difficult cases, he may permit counsel. In any event, his discretion will be more informed and we think the risk of error substantially reduced.

Requiring that there be at least an informal give-and-take between student and disciplinarian, preferably prior to the suspension, will add little to the factfinding function where the disciplinarian himself has witnessed the conduct forming the basis for the charge. But things are not always as they seem to be, and the student will at least have the opportunity to characterize his conduct and put it in what he deems the proper context.

We should also make it clear that we have addressed ourselves solely to the short suspension, not exceeding ten days. Longer suspensions or expulsions for the remainder of the school term, or permanently, may require more formal procedures. Nor do we put aside the possibility that in unusual situations, although involving only a short suspension, something more than the rudimentary procedures will be required.

The District Court found each of the suspensions involved here to have occurred without a hearing, either before or after the suspension, and that each suspension was therefore invalid and the statute unconstitutional insofar as it permits such suspensions without notice or hearing. Accordingly, the judgment is

Affirmed.

Procedural Due Process Is a Flexible Concept

McClain v. Lafayette County Board of Education

United States Court of Appeals,
Fifth Circuit, 1982.
673 F.2d 106, rehearing denied
687 F.2d 121 (1982).

COLEMAN, Circuit Judge. On September 23, 1980, Michael carried a switchblade knife to school. The physical education teacher saw the knife in the student's possession and took him forthwith to the principal's office where . . . Michael admitted that he had the knife. He also admitted that he knew that it was against the rule. His explanation was that he had found the knife, forgot that he had it in his pocket, and unintentionally had brought it to school.

The principal sent Michael back to class and later the same day directed him to appear in his office the following morning with his mother.

On September 24, 1980, Michael and his mother met with Mr. Bigham in his office where they were informed that Michael would be indefinitely suspended for his pos-

session of the knife. At that time the principal gave Mrs. McClain a letter informing her that Michael was "indefinitely suspended" because of his possession and display of a switchblade knife and that she had a right to attend the Lafayette County School Board meeting which was to be held on September 30, 1980 to "request re-admittance" for Michael.

Mrs. McClain arranged an appointment in accordance with the third paragraph of the letter. She, along with Michael, attended the meeting of the Lafayette County School Board on the night of September 30, 1980. The principal and the physical education teacher attended the meeting and related their accounts of the switchblade knife event leading to Michael's suspension. Tape recordings of statements taken from other students during the course of the investigation which followed Michael's September 24 suspension were played. Mrs. McClain and Michael were given the opportunity to question anyone present, and they were also afforded the opportunity to explain any facts or circumstances which might have a bearing on the Board's decision regarding Michael's reinstatement.

Lafayette County High School provides each of its students with a *Student Handbook* at the start of the school year. . . . [T]he *Student Handbook* was read aloud to Michael and other members of his class on the first day of classes. In addition, Mrs. McClain testified that she had read the *Handbook*.

The School Board voted to change Michael's indefinite suspension to a suspension for the remainder of the school year. Mrs. McClain was notified later on the night of the meeting of the Board's actions.

This suit for injunctive relief soon followed and the District Court held an evidentiary hearing, filed findings of fact, and denied injunctive relief.

On appeal, the McClains contend that Michael's procedural due process rights were violated when he was suspended for an indefinite period of time from the high school without first being given a hearing. They argue that this indefinite suspension was in fact a long-range suspension, which should have been preceded by a fair, impartial and meaningful hearing on both the charges and the appropriate punishment. Furthermore, they contend even if the suspension by Mr. Bigham were viewed as a short-range suspension, Michael's procedural due process rights were violated during the School Board meeting because he was not given adequate notice of the type of hearing and the charges, the names of his accusers and a summary of their expected testimonies, the right to retain and to be represented by counsel, nor the right to confront and cross-examine the witnesses.

> [T]he State is constrained to recognize a student's legitimate entitlement to a public education as a property interest which is protected by the Due Process Clause and which may not be taken away for misconduct without adherence to the minimum procedures required by the Clause. *Goss v. Lopez,* 419 U.S. 565, 574 [95 S.Ct. 729, 736, 42 L.Ed.2d 725] (1975).
>
> Once it is determined that due process applies, the question remains what process is due. *Morrissey v. Brewer,* 408 U.S. 471, 481 [92 S.Ct. 2593, 2600, 33 L.Ed.2d 484] (1972).
>
> At the very minimum . . . students facing suspension and the consequent interference with a protected property interest must be given *some* kind of notice and afforded *some* kind of hearing . . . .
>
> [D]ue process requires, in connection with a suspension of ten days or less, that the student be given oral or written notice of the charges against him and, if he denies them, an explanation of the evidence the authorities have and an opportunity to present his side of the story . . . . There need be no delay between the time "notice" is given and the time of the hearing. In the great majority of the cases the disciplinarian may informally discuss the alleged misconduct with the student minutes after it has occurred. We hold only that, in being given an opportunity to explain his version of the facts at this discussion, the student first be told what he is accused of doing and what the basis of the accusation is. 419 U.S. at 579, 581, 582 [95 S.Ct. at 738, 739, 740.]

The Supreme Court has cautioned that "suspensions or expulsions for the remainder of the school term, or permanently, may require more formal procedures." Id. at 584, 95 S.Ct. at 741.

The District Court held that the standards of *Goss v. Lopez,* supra, were met. Michael admitted the possession of the knife when first taken to the principal. Indeed, he could hardly have done otherwise because the physical education teacher saw him in possession of it and took it from him. Never at any time or place, including the hearing in the District Court, did Michael deny it. He did say that he forgot about having this large jackknife, and a switchblade at that, in his pocket. This is not the kind of defense to carrying a deadly weapon that a jury or other factfinder must accept.

Relying upon *Dixon v. Alabama State Board of Education,* 294 F.2d 150, 159 (5th Cir., 1961), plaintiff argues that he should have been given the names of the witnesses against him and an oral or written report of their testimonies. Plaintiff contends that the taped testimony denied him a right of confrontation. Though the *Dixon* Court did find that the students in that case should have been given the list of witnesses against them, the Court noted, "The nature of the hearing should vary depending upon the circumstances of the particular case." Id. at 158.

We can conceive of situations in which the playing of the tapes as done here might be a denial of due process. Not in this instance, however. The issue was whether Michael had carried a switchblade knife to school. There is no representation that the tapes presented any untruths or dealt with any other issue. Therefore, they were merely cumulative on an issue in which Michael had conceded his guilt and has never afterward denied it.

The nub of the matter is that the student was given an opportunity to present his side of the case, including anything by way of denial or mitigation. He and his mother appeared and participated. There has never been any doubt of Michael's guilt in carrying this deadly weapon to school. There was nothing fundamentally unfair or legally prejudicial in the proceedings.

The judgment of the District Court denying injunctive relief is

Affirmed.

NOTES

1. *Procedural Technicality and Hearsay.* When a high school principal read statements made by teachers in an expulsion hearing, the students challenged, claiming that hearsay evidence could not be used in such school hearings. The United States Court of Appeals, Fifth Circuit, stated:

> There is a seductive quality to the argument—advanced here to justify the importation of technical rules of evidence into administrative hearings conducted by laymen—that, since a free public education is a thing of great value, comparable to that of welfare sustenance or the curtailed liberty of a parolee, the safeguards applicable to these should apply to it. . . .
> In this view we stand but a step away from the application of the *strictissimi juris* due process requirements of criminal trials to high school disciplinary processes. And if to high school, why not to elementary school? It will not do. Basic fairness and integrity of the fact-finding process are the guiding stars. Important as they are, the rights at stake in a school disciplinary hearing may be fairly determined upon the "hearsay" evidence of school administrators charged with the duty of investigating the incidents. We decline to place upon a board of laymen the duty of observing and applying the common-law rules of evidence. *Boykins v. Fairfield Board of Education,* 492 F.2d 697 (5th Cir.1974) cert. denied, 420 U.S. 962, 92 S.Ct. 1350 (1975).

Although *Boykins* predates *Goss v. Lopez*, the hearsay principle was reaffirmed by the Fifth Circuit in *Tasby v. Estes*, 643 F.2d 1103 (5th Cir. 1981). Other courts' opinions have been somewhat mixed concerning hearsay evidence. *Tasby v. Estes* (hearsay may be allowed in hearings for serious student offenses); *Linwood v. Board of Education*, 463 F.2d 763 (7th Cir. 1972), *cert. denied* 409 U.S. 1027, 93 S.Ct. 475 (1972) (hearsay may be allowed by implication in expulsion hearing); *Whiteside v. Kay*, 446 F.Supp. 716 (W.D.La.1978) (hearsay may be allowed by implication at expulsion hearing); *Racine Unified School District v. Thompson,* 107 Wis.2d 657, 321 N.W.2d 334 (1982) (hearsay evidence may be allowed from school teachers or staff); *Fielder v. Board of Education,* 346 F.Supp. 722 (D.Neb.1972) (hearsay may not be allowed by implication at expulsion hearing); *DeJesus v. Penberthy*, 344 F.Supp. 70 (D. Conn.1972) (hearsay may not be allowed in hearing for thirty-day suspension).

2. *Double Jeopardy.* When faced with both criminal and school disciplinary punishments, students have claimed that constitutional prohibition against double jeopardy comes into play. In *Paine v. Board of Regents of University of Texas System*, 355 F.Supp. 199 (W.D.Tex.1972), affirmed 474 F.2d 1397 (5th Cir.1973), a group of students faced criminal prosecution for drug use and suspension from the university. The court rejected their double jeopardy claims, stating:

> Through two separate governmental organs, the *legislative branch* and the *Board of Regents*, the State does indeed impose two successive sanctions for the same offense: judicially imposed punishment and automatic suspension from the University of Texas System. However, the state laws defining criminal conduct and authorizing its punishment are intended to vindicate public justice in regard to the individual offender while . . . the Regents' Rule mandating . . . suspension of student drug or narcotic offenders is intended to protect the university community and the educational goals of the institution from such adverse influence as the offender may wield if he is allowed to remain a student. Thus the two sanctions imposed by the state upon plaintiffs have *sufficiently different underlying purposes* to permit characterization of the first as "criminal" or "punitive" and the second as "civil," "remedial" or "administrative." Since the Double Jeopardy Clause operates only upon sanctions of the first type successively imposed for the same offense, plaintiffs may not avail themselves of its protection here. See also *Clements v. Board of Trustees of Sheridan County School Dist. No. 2,* 585 P.2d 197 (Wyo.1978).

3. *Miranda Warning*. A student is not entitled to a *Miranda* warning prior to being questioned by school authorities. *Boynton v. Casey*, 543 F.Supp. 995 (D.Me.1982); see: *Baxter v. Palmigiano*, 425 U.S. 308, 96 S.Ct. 1551 (1976).

4. *Charges and Evidence*. An informal discussion of the student's offense and the circumstances of the incident may be sufficient to inform the student of the evidence against him. *Lamb v. Panhandle Community School District No. 2*, 826 F.2d 526 (7th Cir. 1987).

5. *Cross-Examination*. While acknowledging that "the value of cross-examination to the discovery of truth cannot be overemphasized" (*Davis v. Alaska*, 415 U.S. 308, 94 S.Ct. 1105 (1974)), the U.S. Court of Appeals for the Sixth Circuit held in 1988 that protecting student witnesses in testifying against fellow students was of paramount importance if order and discipline are to be maintained in the school. This Court of Appeals has discussed in some detail the rationale for differing standards of cross-examination between the criminal courts and public schools. The Court states:

> The value of cross-examining student witnesses in school disciplinary cases, however, is somewhat muted by the fact that the veracity of a student account of misconduct by another student is initially assessed by a school administrator—in this case, the school principal—who has, or has available to him, a particularized knowledge of the student's trustworthiness. The school administrator generally knows firsthand (or has access to school records which disclose) the accusing student's disciplinary history, which can serve as a valuable gauge in evaluating the believability of the student's account. Additionally, the school administrator often knows, or can readily discover, whether the student witness and the accused have had an amicable relationship in the past. Consequently, the process of cross-examining the student witness may often be merely duplicative of the evaluation process undertaken by the investigating school administrator.
>
> The value of cross-examining student witnesses in pre-expulsion proceedings

must be set against the burden that such a practice would place upon school administration. Today's public schools face severe challenges in maintaining the order and discipline necessary for the impartation of knowledge. A recent study conducted by the Fullerton, California, Police Department and the California Department of Education, for instance, shows that, while schoolteachers in the 1940's listed talking, chewing gum, and running in the hallways as the primary disciplinary problems they encountered, today's schoolteachers are more concerned with drug abuse, rape, robbery, assault, burglary, arson, and bombings. Bowen, *Getting Tough*, TIME, Feb. 1, 1988, at 54. Indeed, in a recent Supreme Court decision involving the fourth amendment restraints on school administrators, the Court noted that "drug use and violent crime in the schools have become major social problems." . . . (citing 1 NIE, U.S. Dept. of Health, Education and Welfare, Violent Schools—Safe Schools: The Safe School Study Report to the Congress (1978)).

> In this turbulent, sometimes violent, school atmosphere, it is critically important that we protect the anonymity of students who "blow the whistle" on their classmates who engage in drug trafficking and other serious offenses. Without the cloak of anonymity, students who witness criminal activity on school property will be much less likely to notify school authorities, and those who do will be faced with ostracism at best and perhaps physical reprisals. Giving due weight to the important interest a student accused of serious misconduct has in his public education, we conclude that the necessity of protecting student witnesses from ostracism and reprisal outweighs the value to the truth-determining process of allowing the accused student to cross-examine his accusers. *Newsome v. Batavia Local School Dist.*, 842 F.2d 920 (6th Cir. 1988).

6. *Bias*. One of the primary elements of ancient natural justice and modern procedural due process is the requirement that the hearing officers or the tribunal sitting in judgment over an offender must be impartial and not be motivated by bias. The question, therefore, arises as to

whether a school administrator can be both the accuser and an impartial dispenser of justice.

In *Brewer v. Austin Independent School District*, 1985, the U.S. Court of Appeals, Fifth Circuit, said:

> A school administrator involved in the initiation and investigation of charges is not thereby disqualified from conducting a hearing on the charges, although the facts of an occasional case may demonstrate that a school official's involvement in an incident created a bias "such as to preclude his affording the student an impartial hearing."

Where a student claimed that a principal or other administrator was biased and unable to be impartial, the court said that school administrators cannot be disqualified from hearings unless the plaintiff student can show that administrators "possessed either a pre-existing animus towards him, or had developed a bias because of their involvement in the incident, they would not have been able to act as decisionmakers." *Newsome v. Batavia Local School District*, 842 F.2d 920 (6th Cir. 1988).

7. *New Evidence.* New evidence cannot be introduced against a student, before a closed session with a school board, if the student is not aware of the information and it was not originally brought to the student's attention in the notice of the hearing or in the preliminary hearing. Minimal due process requires that students have notice of the charges against them and an explanation of the evidence the authorities intend to use in the disciplinary action. See *Goss v. Lopez*, 419 U.S. 565, 95 S.Ct. 729 (1975); and *Newsome v. Batavia Local School District*, 842 F.2d 920 (6th Cir. 1988).

8. *Admissibility of Evidence.* Procedural due process has been held denied where the accuser sent an affidavit based on a photo of the student and did not personally appear at the hearing. *Smith v. Miller*, 213 Kan.1, 514 P.2d 377 (1973). Similarly, a student's expulsion was invalidated by a court where the accusing teacher was not called and did not come to the hearing. *Dillon v. Pulaski County Special School District*, 594 F.2d 699 (8th Cir. 1979).

9. *In-school Suspension.* Is procedural due process required? Temporary isolation using in school "timeout" has been held to be a *de minimis* punishment not interfering with property or liberty interests. *Dickens by Dickens v. Johnson County Board of Education*, 661 F. Supp. 155 (E.D. Tenn. 1987).

In *Fenton v. Stears*, 423 F. Supp. 767 (W.D. Pa. 1976), schools officials required a student to attend a detention hall instead of joining the class sightseeing trip. While so confined to his small "prison," as he called it, the student was required to do school work. The court held that such punishment was *de minimis* and procedural due process is not required.

An informal "give-and-take" session between school principal and students prior to a ten-day suspension may satisfy procedural due process requirements. *Keough v. Tate County Board of Education*, 748 F.2d 1077 (5th Cir. 1984)

10. *Admission of Offense.* If a student admits the offensive conduct, then there is no issue with regard to procedural errors except those errors which may pertain to the school's determination of appropriateness of punishment. *Brewer v. Austin Independent School District*, 779 F.2d 260 (5th Cir.1985)

▇▇ CHILD ABUSE*

While the phenomena of child abuse and neglect are ageless, only recently have they been given national attention.[51] Commencing

---

* Reprinted with permission, Richard G. Salmon and M. David Alexander, "Child Abuse and Neglect: Implications for Educators," *West's Education Law Reporter*, vol. 28, pp. 9–19 (1986)].

in 1962, state legislatures began enacting legislation designed to deal with problems of child abuse and neglect, and in 1974 a federal statute, the Child Abuse Prevention and Treatment Act, was enacted.[52] The purpose of this legislation was to provide federal financial assistance to the states that had implemented programs for identification, prevention, and treatment of instances of child abuse and neglect.[53] Currently, all fifty states plus the District of Columbia, Puerto Rico, and the Virgin Islands have enacted various forms of child abuse and neglect statutes.[54] A component of the 1974 act was the National Center on Child Abuse and Neglect, which developed the Model Child Protection Act (Model Act).[55] The Model Act has been used extensively throughout the nation for development of individual state child abuse legislation.[56]

Definition

The Model Act included the following succinct definition of child abuse and neglect:

> [C]hild abuse and neglect means the physical or mental injury, sexual abuse, negligent treatment, or maltreatment of a child under the age of eighteen by a person who is responsible for the child's welfare under circumstances which indicate that the child's health or welfare is harmed or threatened thereby, as determined in accordance with regulations prescribed by the Secretary.[57]

Commonly contained within state child abuse and neglect statutes is a purpose statement that outlines the intent of the legislation. Typically, the primary purpose of child abuse and neglect statutes is to identify children who are being abused or neglected so that state protection may be provided.[58] Often, as in the case of Virginia, the state desires to preserve "the family life of the parents and children, where possible, by enhancing parental capacity for adequate child care."[59]

In contrast with the rather general federal definition of child abuse and neglect, state definitions tend to be more specific as typified by the Virginia definition:

Abused or neglected child shall mean any child less than eighteen years of age whose parents or other person responsible for his care:

1. Creates or inflicts, threatens to create or inflict, or allows to be created or inflicted upon such a child a physical or mental injury by other than accidental means, or creates a substantial risk of death, disfigurement, impairment of bodily or mental functions;
2. Neglects or refuses to provide care necessary for his health; provided, however, that no child who in good faith is under treatment solely by spiritual means through prayer in accordance with tenets and practices of a recognized church or religious denomination shall for that reason alone be considered to be an abused or neglected child; or
3. Abandons such child; or
4. Commits or allows to be committed any sexual act upon a child in violation of the law.[60]

Nearly all states have accepted the federal definition of child as a person under the age of eighteen but vary widely in regard to definitions of abuse and neglect.[61] Some states provide separate definitions of what constitutes child abuse and neglect, while other states have not attempted to distinguish between them.[62] In a recent survey of state child abuse statutes, child abuse and neglect were defined as follows:

> Implicit in most definitions of abuse is that the injury is deliberately inflicted. Abuse includes bodily violence (beating, squeezing, poisoning, burning, cutting, and exposing to heat or cold); sexual molestation (ranging from inappropriate fondling to intercourse); and psychological or mental injury (insults and accusations, prevention of sleep, and sensory overload relating to light, sound, pain, itching, stench, and aversive taste).
>
> Neglect is generally an omission—a failure to provide for a child's physical or emotional needs or both. Neglect includes deprivation of physiological necessities such as drink, nourishment, clothing, shelter, and sanitation. In addition, neglect encompasses the failure to fulfill psychological needs for sensory stimulation and social communication. These parental failures do not amount to neglect, however, if they are beyond the parents' control.[63]

Reporting

An integral component of state child abuse and neglect statutes is the mandated reporting of suspected instances of child abuse and neglect by certain professionals. During initial legislation, child abuse and neglect legislation required only physicians to report instances of suspected child abuse and neglect.[64] Currently, in addition to medical personnel such as nurses, surgeons, medical examiners or coroners, dentists, osteopaths, optometrists, chiropractors, and podiatrists, other professionals including school teachers and officials, police, peace or law enforcement officers, social workers, and day-care personnel often are required to report instances of child abuse and neglect.[65] Forty-nine states have mandated that teachers report to certain authorities suspected instances of child abuse and neglect.[66] . . .

If the reports of suspected child abuse and neglect are determined to be unfounded, teachers are said to fear possible liability suits for slander, libel, defamation of character, invasion of privacy, and breach of confidence. However, all states have enacted legislation which grants immunity to reporters of child abuse and neglect from criminal and civil liability if the report *is made in good faith*. For example, the Virginia immunity statute states: "A person making a report . . . shall be immune from any civil or criminal liability in connection therewith unless it is proven that such person acted with malicious intent."[67]

. . .

A 1985 Oregon case, *McDonald v. State, By and Through CSD*[68] serves to illustrate the statutory immunity granted reporters of child abuse and neglect. In this case, a teacher observed scratches on the neck of one of her pupils and had him examined by a child development specialist. When questioned about how he had acquired the scratches, the child told two stories. One version attributed the scratches to his kitten, and the second version suggested that the child's mother had made the scratches by choking him, as the child said she had done on several occasions. The principal was informed, who in turn instructed the child development specialist to report the incident to the state's Children's Services Division. The child was removed from parental custody and placed in a foster home. Subsequently, the parents appeared in court where the allegations of child abuse were ruled groundless and the child reinstated with his parents. The parents brought suit against Children's Services Division, principal, teacher, and others. The court dismissed the parents' complaint and indicated regardless that two versions of the derivation of scratches were told and that the principal relied only upon the opinion of the child development specialist, both the principal and teacher had acted in good faith and had reasonable grounds to report suspected child abuse.

Penalty for Failure to Report

In order to gain compliance from those persons required to report instances of child abuse and neglect, most states permit the assessment of penalties for knowing and willful failure to report.[69] Most states have enacted criminal penalties for those persons guilty of not reporting suspected cases of child abuse and neglect.[70] Some states have legislated both criminal and civil penalties, and a few states provide only for civil remedies.[71]

Those states that have established criminal penalties for persons found guilty of not reporting instances of child abuse and neglect commonly classify such an offense as a misdemeanor.[72] Punishments normally include fines up to $1000, jail sentences up to one year, or both.[73]

. . . [T]he threat of criminal prosecution, possibly due to inaction by persons responsible for initiating criminal proceedings, has not resulted in high level of reporting compliance by teachers. As a result, some interest is being given to initiation of civil suits against teachers for their failure to report instances of child abuse and neglect. . . .

Civil liability may be imposed against teachers who fail to report instances of child abuse and neglect in states that either have not specified penalties for non reporters or have established criminal sanctions. In *Landeros v. Flood*,[74] the court ruled that a physician could be held civilly liable for injuries sustained by a child if he had negligently failed to diagnose and report suspected child abuse. However, teachers failing to report instances of child abuse and neglect are much more vulnerable to civil suits in states that have legislatively established provisions of civil liability for mandatory reporters.[75]

Defenses for Failure to Report

Included within child abuse and neglect statutes for most states that provide criminal penalties for failure of mandatory reporters to report instances of child abuse and neglect are statements such as, "reasonable cause to believe," "cause to believe,"[76] or as in the case of Oklahoma, "reason to believe."[77] Such statements are considered to provide an objective standard on which to determine compliance.[78] Less rigorous statements, such as "knows or suspects" are considered to provide a subjective standard and one that may permit mandatory reporters to shield their own poor judgements.[79] Regardless of whether the standard is objective or subjective, a teacher charged with failure to report suspected child abuse and neglect under the criminal code of a state likely will attempt to show that there was not "reasonable cause to believe" that child abuse and neglect had occurred.[80]

In regard to civil liability for failure to report instances of suspected child abuse and neglect, the teacher will have to defeat allegations of negligence.[81]

■ FREEDOM OF SPEECH AND EXPRESSION

Few areas of the law are more misunderstood by laypeople than those connected with First Amendment rights, especially as they relate to freedom of speech and expression. While it is true that the right to speak one's mind carries with it at least the moral obligation to mind one's speech, this rule of thumb is not the prevailing yardstick or standard used by the courts in resolving issues in this area.

The Supreme Court has relied primarily on two tests to determine whether the state can control freedom of speech or expression: (1) clear and present danger and (2) material and substantial disruption. In 1919, the Court[82] said that the question to be asked is whether the words used are used in such circumstances and are of such a nature as to create a "clear and present danger" that they will bring about the substantial evils . . . which may harm the state. In subsequent decisions[83] the Court further defined the concept. Justice Brandeis said that

> no danger flowing from speech can be deemed clear and present, unless the incidence of the evil apprehended is so imminent that it may befall before there is opportunity for full discussion. If there be time to expose through discussion the falsehood and fallacies, to avert the evil by the processes of education, the remedy to be applied is more speech, not enforced silence.[84]

Government cannot limit speech where the dangers are merely perceived or are not "present" or "imminent." Justice Black observed that "What finally emerges from the 'clear and present danger' cases is a working principle that the substantive evil must be extremely serious and the degree of imminence extremely high before utterances can be punished."[85]

Material and Substantial Disruption

The second rationale, "material and substantial disruption," is the standard applied to public education by the Supreme Court in the famous *Tinker* case. The Court in this case made it clear that school authorities would not be permitted to deny a student his fundamental right of freedom of expression simply because of "a mere desire to avoid discomfort and unpleasantness that always accompany an unpopular viewpoint."[86]

The material and substantial disruption standard is, however, so broad that proper interpretation of specific school incidents is sometimes difficult. It is important to note that the precedent set in *Tinker* was based on facts relating to the intense political controversy surrounding the Vietnam War. Therefore, the curtailment of expression at this level of political concern is of significant constitutional magnitude. The Supreme Court, though, acknowledges that even expression at this level of importance can be limited if the school officials can reasonably forecast material and substantial disruption. As to when and how such restraint can take place, the Court in *Tinker* is rather nebulous. The interpretation and application of the standard is left to later court decisions in applying other factual situations.

One such decision that provides good guidance for school officials is *Guzick v. Drebus*,[87] a federal circuit court decision in which *Tinker* was applied to a situation in Shaw High School in Cleveland. Here the school forbade the wearing of buttons in an antiwar protest because the history of student disturbance and the wearing of insignia of various kinds strongly suggested to school officials that disuption would ensue. This fear was so pronounced that the court agreed that the officials could reasonably forecast substanial disruption. Thus, in a particular setting where disruptive antecedents can be documented and long-standing uniform rules can be applied, even political expression can be restrained.

Tinker Redefined

More recently, the U.S. Supreme Court has provided additional clarification to the *Tinker* standard.[88] Here the court draws a line between the "political message" of the armbands of *Tinker* and other content that is less compellingly subject to First Amendment protection. In this case, *Bethel School District No. 403 v. Fraser*,[89] a student made a lewd speech full of sexual innuendos, and the school responded by suspending him. The Court

observed that *Tinker* could not be interpreted to mean that public schools had to tolerate indecent speech that offended both the teachers and other students of the school. The Court observed that in *Tinker*, the expression did not intrude "upon the work of the schools or the rights of other students." The Court further noted, "Surely it is a highly appropriate function of public school education to prohibit the use of vulgar and offensive terms in public discourse."[90]

Bethel, then, not only provides more definition for student conduct than does *Tinker*, but represents somewhat of a retrenchment of pre-Tinker precedents where school boards were given much greater latitude in controlling student behavior.

Student Appearance

The great weight of judicial authority supports the proposition that a board of education possesses the authority to regulate pupil dress and personal appearance if they become so extreme as to interfere with school's favorable learning atmosphere. An illustration of this judicial position was provided several years ago when the Arkansas Appellate Court[91] upheld a school regulation that forbade the wearing of low-necked dresses, any immodest dress, or the use of face paints or cosmetics. An application of somewhat more recent vintage is the right of a school district to require pupils to participate in physical education programs and to wear clothing suitable for these occasions. The majority rule in these instances is that the pupils must participate in physical education programs, but they may not be required to wear "immodest" attire.[92]

Students and parents have relied on several legal issues in contesting student appearance regulations, including freedom of speech of the First Amendment, the due process and equal protection clauses of the Fourteenth Amendment, the Ninth Amendment, which provides for retention of rights by the people, and even the Civil Rights Acts. The cases convey a lack of agreement by the courts in the application of these rights to students in public schools.

Haircuts

As an indication of this lack of a clear precedent, the courts appear to be about evenly split on the constitutional status of haircuts. The courts have been unable to agree and enunciate any consistent constitutional guideline for schools to follow in dealing with the issue of personal appearance, generally, and haircuts, specifically. While the precedents generally follow *Tinker*, it is difficult to see precisely how untidy hair can rise to the level of a constitutional concern for either the student or the school. From the student's viewpoint, it is difficult to convincingly show that a haircut will in some fashion harm a constitutionally protected interest. That is, of course, providing that the school officials had in mind clipping the hair and not pulling it out. On the other hand, school officials are hard-pressed to show that untidy hair is of much educational significance, and certainly, that unkept or long hair would substantially disrupt the school. In fact, one federal appellate court has rejected further involvement in the haircut disputes, saying that "we refuse to take our judicial clippers to this hairy issue"; and the U.S. Supreme Court has rejected the entire question by pointing out that the issue is *de minimis*.

Nevertheless, much litigation has enveloped this problem. The Federal Circuit Courts of Appeals are divided as to whether and under what conditions schools may regulate student hairstyles. The Third, Fifth, Sixth, Ninth, Tenth, and Eleventh have upheld school regulation of haircuts while the First, Second, Fourth, Seventh, and Eighth have ruled that grooming has attendant constitutional rights. In *King v. Saddleback Jr. College Dist.*,[93] the court ruled that long hair was not protected by the constitutional rights of privacy. The Sixth Circuit ruled that hair that was a distracting influence could be regulated.[94] In the same year, the First Circuit found that

students' hair was protected by the Due Process Clause of the Fourteenth Amendment, (establishing "a sphere of personal liberty.")[95]

In the case of *Ferrell v. Dallas Independent School District*,[96] a suit was brought to enjoin school officials from refusing to enroll male pupils who had failed to comply with a school regulation banning long hair. The United States District Court for the Northern District of Texas denied any injunctive relief, and the pupils appealed. The court of appeals held that the regulation promulgated by the principal was valid.

In another case, the Fifth Circuit ruled against three male pupils who refused to shave in compliance with a good-grooming rule of their school. This court noted, with approval, the sentiment of the district court that "the Court felt somewhat put upon by having to fit a controversy over shaving into an inordinately busy schedule. It was viewed as a problem for school administrators. . . . The entire problem seems minuscule in light of other matters involving the school system.[97]

The Fourth Circuit,[98] in reviewing all the relevant appellate haircut decisions, concluded that the state interest may overcome the student's constitutional interest if the evidence indicates that the health and safety of the student are jeopardized. In so holding, this court, though, did acknowledge that hair style is a constitutionally protected right, "to be secure in one's person" as guaranteed by substantive due process.

Thus, buried in the haircut cases is a full panoply of constitutional provisions including freedom of expression, substantive due process, and equal protection. Whether these constitutional standards apply to restrict the authority of school officials depends more on the jurisdiction than on the constitutional concept invoked by the plaintiff. The impact of *Bethel* on these cases is yet to be determined, but, if current judicial trends continue to vest more discretion in school officials, it is likely that lower courts will increasingly allow for less student latitude.

Denial of Freedom of Expression Must be Justified by a Reasonable Forecast of Substantial Disruption

– · – · – · – · – ·

Tinker v. Des Moines Independent Community School District

– · – · – · – · – ·

Supreme Court of the United States, 1969.
393 U.S. 503, 89 S.Ct. 733.

Mr. Justice FORTAS delivered the opinion of the Court. Petitioner John F. Tinker, fifteen years old, and petitioner Christopher Eckhardt, sixteen years old, attended high schools in Des Moines, Iowa. Petitioner Mary Beth Tinker, John's sister, was a thirteen-year-old student in junior high school.

In December 1965, a group of adults and students in Des Moines held a meeting at the Eckhardt home. The group determined to publicize their objections to the hostilities in Vietnam and their support for a truce by wearing black armbands during the holiday season and by fasting on December 16 and New Year's Eve. Petitioners and their parents had previously engaged in similar activities, and they decided to participate in the program.

The principals of the Des Moines schools became aware of the plan to wear armbands. On December 14, 1965, they met and adopted a policy that any student wearing an armband to school would be asked to remove it, and if he refused he would be suspended until he returned without the armband. Petitioners were aware of the regulation that the school authorities adopted.

On December 16, Mary Beth and Christopher wore black armbands to their schools. John Tinker wore his armband the next day. They were all sent home and suspended from school until they would come back without their armbands. They did not return to school until after the planned period for wearing

armbands had expired—that is, until after New Year's Day.

This complaint was filed in the United States District Court by petitioners, through their fathers, under § 1983 of Title 42 of the United States Code. It prayed for an injunction restraining the respondent school officials and the respondent members of the board of directors of the school district from disciplining the petitioners, and it sought nominal damages. After an evidentiary hearing the District Court dismissed the complaint. It upheld the constitutionality of the school authorities' action on the ground that it was reasonable in order to prevent disturbance of school discipline. 258 F.Supp. 971 (1966). The court referred to but expressly declined to follow the Fifth Circuit's holding in a similar case that the wearing of symbols like the armbands cannot be prohibited unless it "materially and substantially interfere[s] with the requirements of appropriate discipline in the operation of the school." *Burnside v. Byars*, 363 F.2d 744, 749 (1966).

On appeal, the Court of Appeals for the Eighth Circuit considered the case *en banc*. The court was equally divided, and the District Court's decision was accordingly affirmed, without opinion. 383 F.2d 988 (1967). We granted certiorari. 390 U.S. 942, 88 S.Ct. 1050, 19 L.Ed.2d 1130 (1968).

The District Court recognized that the wearing of an armband for the purpose of expressing certain views is the type of symbolic act that is within the Free Speech Clause of the First Amendment.   . . . As we shall discuss, the wearing of armbands in the circumstances of this case was entirely divorced from actually or potentially disruptive conduct by those participating in it. It was closely akin to "pure speech" which, we have repeatedly held, is entitled to comprehensive protection under the First Amendment.

. . .

First Amendment rights, applied in light of the special characteristics of the school environment, are available to teachers and students. It can hardly be argued that either students or teachers shed their constitutional rights to freedom of speech or expression at the schoolhouse gate. This has been the unmistakable holding of this Court for almost fifty years. . . .

The school officials banned and sought to punish petitioners for a silent, passive expression of opinion, unaccompanied by any disorder or disturbance on the part of petitioners. There is here no evidence whatever of petitioners' interference, actual or nascent, with the schools' work or of collision with the rights of other students to be secure and to be let alone. Accordingly, this case does not concern speech or action that intrudes upon the work of the schools or the rights of other students.

Only a few of the 18,000 students in the school system wore the black armbands. Only five students were suspended for wearing them. There is no indication that the work of the schools or any class was disrupted. Outside the classrooms, a few students made hostile remarks to the children wearing armbands, but there were no threats or acts of violence on school premises.

The District Court concluded that the action of the school authorities was reasonable because it was based upon their fear of a disturbance from the wearing of the armbands. But, in our system, undifferentiated fear or apprehension of disturbance is not enough to overcome the right to freedom of expression. Any departure from absolute regimentation may cause trouble. Any variation from the majority's opinion may inspire fear. Any word spoken, in class, in the lunchroom, or on the campus, that deviates from the views of another person may start an argument or cause a disturbance. But our Constitution says we must take this risk, *Terminiello v. Chicago,* 337 U.S. 1, 69 S.Ct. 894, 93 L.Ed.1131 (1949); and our history says that it is this sort of hazardous freedom—this kind of openness—that is the basis of our national strength and of the independence and vigor of Americans who grow up and live in this relatively permissive, often disputatious, society.

In order for the State in the person of school officials to justify prohibition of a particular expression of opinion, it must be able to show that its action was caused by something more than a mere desire to avoid the discomfort and unpleasantness that always accompany an unpopular viewpoint. Certainly where there is no finding and no showing that engaging in the forbidden conduct would "materially and substantially interfere with the requirements of appropriate discipline in the operation of the school," the prohibition cannot be sustained. *Burnside v. Byars,* supra, 363 F.2d at 749.

In the present case, the District Court made no such finding, and our independent examination of the record fails to yield evidence that the school authorities had reason to anticipate that the wearing of the armbands would substantially interfere with the work of the school or impinge upon the rights of other students. Even an official memorandum prepared after the suspension that listed the reasons for the ban on wearing the armbands made no reference to the anticipation of such disruption.

On the contrary, the action of the school authorities appears to have been based upon an urgent wish to avoid the controversy which might result from the expression, even by the silent symbol of armbands, of opposition to this Nation's part in the conflagration in Vietnam. It is revealing, in this respect, that the meeting at which the school principals decided to issue the contested regulation was called in response to a student's statement to the journalism teacher in one of the schools that he wanted to write an article on Vietnam and have it published in the school paper. (The student was dissuaded.)

It is also relevant that the school authorities did not purport to prohibit the wearing of all symbols of political or controversial significance. The record shows that students in some of the schools wore buttons relating to national political campaigns, and some even wore the Iron Cross, traditionally a symbol of Nazism. The order prohibiting the wearing of armbands did not extend to these. Instead, a particular symbol—black armbands worn to exhibit opposition to this Nation's involvement in Vietnam—was singled out for prohibition. Clearly, the prohibition of expression of one particular opinion, at least without evidence that it is necessary to avoid material and substantial interference with schoolwork or discipline, is not constitutionally permissible.

In our system, state-operated schools may not be enclaves of totalitarianism. School officials do not possess absolute authority over their students. Students in school as well as out of school are "persons" under our Constitution. They are possessed of fundamental rights which the State must respect, just as they themselves must respect their obligations to the State. In our system, students may not be regarded as closed-circuit recipients of only that which the State chooses to communicate. They may not be confined to the expression of those sentiments that are officially approved. In the absence of a specific showing of constitutionally valid reasons to regulate their speech, students are entitled to freedom of expression of their views. As Judge Gewin, speaking for the Fifth Circuit, said, school officials cannot suppress "expressions of feelings with which they do not wish to contend." *Burnside v. Byars*, supra, 363 F.2d at 749.

. . .

If a regulation were adopted by school officials forbidding discussion of the Vietnam conflict, or the expression by any student of opposition to it anywhere on school property except as part of a prescribed classroom exercise, it would be obvious that the regulation would violate the constitutional rights of students, at least if it could not be justified by a showing that the students' activities would materially and substantially disrupt the work and discipline of the school. . . . In the circumstances of the present case, the prohibition of the silent, passive "witness of the armbands," as one of the children called it, is no less offensive to the constitution's guarantees.

As we have discussed, the record does not demonstrate any facts which might reasonably have led school authorities to forecast substantial disruption of or material interference with school activities, and no disturbances or disorders on the school premises in fact occurred. These petitioners merely went about their ordained rounds in school. Their deviation consisted only in wearing on their sleeve a band of black cloth, not more than two inches wide. They wore it to exhibit their

disapproval of the Vietnam hostilities and their advocacy of a truce, to make their views known, and, by their example, to influence others to adopt them. They neither interrupted school activities nor sought to intrude in the school affairs or the lives of others. They caused discussion outside of the classrooms, but no interference with work and no disorder. In the circumstances, our Constitution does not permit officials of the State to deny their form of expression.

We express no opinion as to the form of relief which should be granted, this being a matter for the lower courts to determine. We reverse and remand for further proceedings consistent with this opinion.

Reversed and remanded.

---

*Rule Banning Buttons Is Not Unconstitutional
If It Is Reasonably Related to Prevention
of Disruptive Conduct*

— · — · — · — · —

Guzick v. Drebus

— · — · — · — · —

United States Court of Appeals,
Sixth Circuit, 1970.
431 F.2d 594.

Memorandum Opinion and Order

LAMBROS, District Judge. This is an action arising under the provisions of Title 42 U.S.C.A. § 1983. This section provides as follows:

> Every person who, under color of any statute, ordinance, regulation, custom, or usage, of any State or Territory, subjects, or causes to be subjected, any citizen of the United States or other person within the jurisdiction thereof to the deprivation of any rights, privileges, or immunities secured by the Constitution and laws, shall be liable to the party injured in an action at law, suit in equity, or other proper proceeding for redress.

The complaint, in summary, alleges the following: Thomas Guzick, Jr., is seventeen years of age and is a student at Shaw High School in East Cleveland, Ohio. Defendant, Donald L. Drebus, is the principal of Shaw High School. The other defendants are: Nelson F. Leist, Superintendent of the East Cleveland School District; and Robert Henderson, Charles Hamilton, Leslie Reardon, Erwin Schrader, and George Beasley, who are members of the East Cleveland Board of Education. Plaintiff desires to wear a button on his lapel while attending school at Shaw High. The button reads:

April 5 Chicago
G.I.Civilian
Anti-War
Demonstration
Student Mobilization Committee

He wore this button to school on March 11, 1969. The school principal, Mr. Drebus, ordered the plaintiff to remove the button. Upon the plaintiff's refusal to remove the button, Mr. Drebus suspended him from Shaw High School until such time as he returned to school without the button. The complaint alleges that the acts of Mr. Drebus in suspending the plaintiff have been ratified, approved, or encouraged by the other defendants in their official capacities. Plaintiff alleges that his right to wear this button is protected by the First Amendment to the Constitution, and that his suspension deprives him of rights guaranteed by the Constitution; and, further, that his suspension was without just cause, without a hearing, and without due process of law. The complaint alleges that similar buttons are being worn in other high schools in the Cleveland area, and that the acts of the defendants denying the plaintiff his right to wear a similar button deprives him of the equal protection of the law as guaranteed by the Fourteenth Amendment. The complaint seeks a temporary restraining order enjoining the defendants from interfering with the plaintiff's right to wear the button while attending school and from refusing to reinstate the plaintiff. It also seeks a preliminary and permanent injunction directed toward securing the same relief. The complaint further seeks a declaratory judgment that any rule or regulation of the East Cleveland Board of Education proscribing the wearing of such buttons is unconstitutional, and the complaint further seeks damages in the amount of $1000.00 per day for every day the plaintiff is compelled to miss school and for costs and attorneys' fees. . . .

In a case where there are substantial factual disputes raised by the testimony of the various witnesses, their demeanor on the stand and their relative degree of knowledge are particularly important. The court has, therefore, reviewed the evidence and its impressions of the various witnesses and has reached its considered judgment as to the actual facts in this case.

The city of East Cleveland, Ohio, is a suburb located east of Cleveland. At one time, it was an almost exclusively white community. In the last few years, however, many Negroes have moved into the community from Cleveland, which is immediately adjoining; and East Cleveland now is a racially mixed community. . . .

Approximately 70 percent of the students at Shaw High School are black. Approximately 30 percent are white. There has been considerable friction between the students of the two races. There has also been friction among students of the same race. Nonetheless, Shaw High School has not, as yet, had a serious racial disturbance.

At the same time, many other high schools in the area have had such disturbances. At John Hay High, a predominately black school approximately one mile to the west, there have been repeated disturbances; and, in fact, John Hay High School was forced to close for a number of days as a result of these. East High School and Glenville High School have also had serious disturbances. East High was also required to close. Both of these high schools have a high percentage of black students.

Collinwood High School, which is racially mixed, has had serious disturbances. Indeed, these required the closing of the school at one time this year.

So far there have been no crippling disruptions at Shaw High. The situation, however, is not peaceful.

Although there have been no crippling disruptions of school activities, Shaw High has a significant, perhaps serious, discipline problem. Students have been threatened in both the men's rooms and locker rooms, among other places. These threats have often been accompanied by violence. Money has been extorted from students under these circumstances. The problem has been of such significance that the P.T.A. and other groups in the community have become concerned. There have been numerous fights at Shaw, both between blacks and whites and among students of the same race. These fights have occurred both during school hours and in the evening.

Tension at Shaw High is at an incendiary point. The school officials spend a great portion of their time disciplining students in an attempt to control this situation. In January of this year, black students attempted to organize a walkout. Such walkouts have occurred in a number of the other schools in the area. Shaw High officials were forced to call police to the school. The walkout was aborted, and only one student actually left the school.

These are but a few of the incidents described to the Court. It appears that the principal reason why more such incidents have not occurred is the extensive effort by school officials to avert such situations by maintaining discipline and discussing these problems with the students and their parents.

For many years Shaw High has had an informal rule with respect to the wearing of emblems and other insignia. The rule has never been published; nevertheless, it has been applied uniformly and consistently for at least forty years at both Shaw High School and Kirk Junior High. To summarize the rule, it provides that students will not be permitted to wear buttons, emblems, or other insignia on school property during school hours unless these emblems or insignia are related to a school activity.

This informal rule has been applied in a wide variety of situations. School officials have applied it against the high school fraternities and sororities which existed at Shaw in the 1940s. Emblems signifying or indicating membership in any of these fraternities were prohibited. Students wearing them were asked to remove them or leave school.

Subsequently, informal clubs replaced the outlawed high school fraternities. The rule was applied to these clubs. Pins, emblems, lavalieres, lettering on clothing, and other insignia have not been permitted at Shaw High School. . . . The problem again exists as a result of the racial mixture at Shaw. Buttons, pins, and other emblems have been used as identifying "badges." They have portrayed and defined the divisions among students in the school. They have fostered an undesirable form of competition, division and dislike. The presence of these emblems, badges and buttons are taken to represent, define and depict the actual division of the students in various groups. . . .

The rule has acquired a particular importance in recent years. Students have attempted to wear buttons and badges expressing inflammatory messages, which, if permitted, and as the evidence indicates, would lead to substantial racial disorders at Shaw. Students have attempted to wear buttons with the following messages inscribed thereon. "White is right"; "Say it loud, Black and Proud"; "Black Power." Other buttons have depicted a mailed black fist, commonly taken to be the symbol for black power.

There have been occasions when the wearing of such insignia has led to disruptions at Shaw and at Kirk Junior High. A fight resulted in the cafeteria when a white student wore a button which read "Happy Easter, Dr. King." (Dr. Martin Luther King was assassinated in the Easter season.) On another occasion, students at Kirk Junior High entered the corridors wearing a distinctive headdress. They proceeded down the corridors striking and attacking certain other students whom they had expected would join them in wearing the headdress, but who had not done so.

School authorities have attempted to eliminate the wearing of buttons, emblems, other insignia, and distinctive forms of dress characteristic of a particular club or group. The evidence discloses a number of instances in which various individuals and groups attempted to wear such insignia or clothing and

in which the school officials prohibited it.
. . .

On March 11, 1969, the plaintiff, Thomas Guzick, Jr., in the company of Hunter Havens, went to the office of the principal of Shaw High, Mr. Donald Drebus. Both the plaintiff and Mr. Havens wore a button on their clothing inscribed with the message:

April 5 Chicago
G.I. Civilian
Anti-War
Demonstration
Student Mobilization Committee

Plaintiff also carried certain leaflets which he and Mr. Havens desired to distribute at Shaw High School.

The conversation had that morning between the two students and Mr. Drebus is in dispute. It appears, however, that the students requested permission to pass out the leaflets at the school. Mr. Drebus refused permission, stating that Shaw High had a policy against distribution of leaflets. Mr. Drebus demanded that the students remove the buttons which they were wearing. The students asserted that they had a constitutional right to wear such buttons. Hunter Havens removed his. The plaintiff, however, refused to remove his button, even after a warning by Mr. Drebus that he would suspend the plaintiff from school if he refused to remove it. Upon the plaintiff's further refusal to remove the button, he was suspended from school until such time as he returned without the button. Subsequently, the plaintiff filed suit with this Court seeking a legal determination whether he is entitled under the Constitution to wear this button at Shaw High School.

As outlined above, the Court has concluded that Shaw High School has had a long-standing and consistently-applied rule prohibiting the wearing of buttons and other insignia on school grounds during school hours, unless these are related to a school-sponsored activity. The Court finds that this rule has been a significant factor in preserving peace and good order at Shaw High School and in preventing provocations, distractions,

and disruptive conduct. The Court finds that if this policy of excluding buttons and other insignia is not retained, some student will attempt to wear provocative or inciting buttons and other emblems. If these provocative buttons and insignia are permitted to be worn, they will further amplify an already serious discipline problem, they will exacerbate an already tense racial situation, and they will inevitably cause substantial disruptions in the educational process at Shaw High.

The Court further finds that if students are permitted to wear *some* buttons but not others, similar disruptions of the educational process will occur. Many students will not understand the justification for any rule that prohibits the wearing of certain buttons while permitting others. Many will not accept the distinction.
. . .

The Court finds that the prohibition of buttons and other insignia at Shaw High significantly contributes to the preservation of peace and order, and that the blanket prohibition of buttons and other insignia is reasonably related to the prevention of the distractions and disruptive and violent conduct at Shaw High. The Court finds that if all buttons are permitted or if any buttons are permitted, a serious discipline problem will result, racial tensions will be exacerbated, and the educational process will be significantly and substantially disrupted.

On February 24, 1969, the United States Supreme Court decided *Tinker v. Des Moines Independent Community School District*, 393 U.S. 503, 89 S.Ct. 733. This is the landmark case in the area of the student's rights to free speech in the public schools, and it has formed the basis of this litigation. . . .

The Court noted that the wearing of an expressive arm band is "closely akin" to "pure speech." It was, in substance, the silent expression of an idea. . . .

The regulation in the *Tinker* case was not applied in an even-handed manner. Other buttons and symbols of political and controversial significance were permitted to be worn in the school. The Court concluded that the regulation was directed at the principle expressed in this particular demonstration — that is, opposition to the Vietnam War. The school authorities, the Court concluded, wanted not to introduce the Vietnam controversy into the school.

Certain factors present in the *Tinker* case, and upon which the Court rested its decision, are not present here. The rule prohibiting the wearing of emblems at Shaw High School is one of long standing. It has been applied evenhandedly both in politically controversial and noncontroversial areas. . . . They have applied this rule consistently; they have applied it equally. The rule is applied (and it is applied in this case) without regard to the content and the ideas sought to be expressed in the emblem. It is applied without regard to the status of the wearer or to the message, inflammatory or innocuous, sought to be expressed.

Furthermore, there is in the present case much more than an "undifferentiated fear or apprehension" of disturbances likely to result from the wearing of buttons at Shaw High School. The wearing of buttons and other emblems and insignia has occasioned substantial disruptive conduct in the past at Shaw High. It is likely to occasion such conduct if permitted henceforth. The wearing of buttons and other insignia will serve to exacerbate an already tense situation, to promote divisions and disputes, including physical violence among the students, and to disrupt and interfere with the normal operation of the school and with appropriate discipline by the school authorities. . . .

The school authorities have adopted the policy of excluding all insignia and emblems, in view of the explosive situation and the likelihood of substantial disruption if provocative emblems are permitted. This Court is unprepared to say that the rule excluding all buttons is unreasonable, in view of the difficulty in applying a selective rule and in view of the real likelihood that such a rule would itself contribute to disruption. This Court is also unprepared to say that the school authorities were unreasonable in rejecting such a selective rule. . . . This Court concludes

that such a rule is reasonably related to the prevention of disruptive conduct at Shaw High School.

The wearing of buttons or, as in the *Tinker* case, wearing of arm bands is itself and without accompanying conduct "closely akin" to "pure speech." Nevertheless, wearing of such insignia has other characteristics different from pure speech. A button is not merely a statement; it is an identification tag. It identifies the wearer as an adherent or member of one group or class. It identifies him as not being a member of other groups or classes. This identification aspect exists independent of the nature of the message contained in the button. Thus, for example, a button on which appears a mailed black fist certainly identifies the wearer with a particular political persuasion. This is apart from any message sought to be conveyed by the button.

The button also demonstrates that the wearer has a particular and keen interest in the goals and outlook of the group with which the button identifies him. It marks the wearer as a proponent; it also may mark him as someone's opponent. In so doing, buttons have an inherent tendency to divide a body of individuals into separate sub-groups, each identified by its own insignia, each declaring by a particular decoration its position in relation to other individuals. Such an effect may not be significant in the context of many high schools in this country. But because of the "peculiar situation" at Shaw High, this divisive influence is likely and, indeed, almost certain to lead to disruptive conduct. When there is added the fact that many of these expressive buttons are likely to convey that expression in a most inflammatory and, perhaps, insulting manner, it is apparent that a most dangerous situation will result.

Free speech is the single most important element upon which this nation has thrived. Wherever reasonably possible, it must be upheld, cherished, and nurtured. There are, however, situations in which free speech, or manifestations which are "closely akin" to free speech, must be exercised with care and restraint; and there are situations in which the manifestations of speech may even be prohibited altogether. It has been demonstrated that the identifying aspects of buttons and other insignia have led to considerable disruption at Shaw High in the past. It has also been demonstrated that such insignia would be likely and, indeed, more likely to lead to such disruptions if permitted now.

We bear in mind that the buttons and other insignia are not speech themselves. Rather, they are a pictorial manifestation of speech. As such, they acquire other characteristics which would not be possessed by the spoken word itself. Buttons and other insignia have an inherently identifying nature. They are in a sense "badges." It is this aspect of emblems and other insignia that has caused difficulty at Shaw High. It is this aspect, and not the actual speech of any of the students, which has been prohibited and which is at issue here.

. . .

The prohibition of buttons and other insignia at Shaw High is the result of a history of problems which the Shaw High authorities have encountered as a result of this activity. The prohibition against buttons is reasonably related in preventing the occurrence of disruptive conduct. It is also reasonably related to what is administratively possible at Shaw High School. If any buttons are permitted to be worn at Shaw High, it is likely that students will require that all buttons be permitted. In any event, the wearing of any buttons will lead to disruptive, even violent, activities, will materially and substantially affect the normal educational processes at Shaw High, and will diminish significantly the ability of the school officials to maintain proper discipline.

In this case, it is relevant that the school authorities *did* prohibit the wearing of all symbols and applied the rule uniformly and consistently. This was not the case in *Tinker.*

It is also relevant that the wearing of a button by the plaintiff in this case was associated with a distribution of leaflets. This was not the case in *Tinker.*

An evidentiary pattern has developed in this case which specifically shows to this Court that the school authorities had a constitution-ally valid reason to regulate student conduct regarding the wearing of buttons and other emblems and symbols. This was not the case in *Tinker.* . . .

It is also relevant that leaflets of all kinds are being distributed and circulated throughout the public schools, and specifically at Shaw High School, and finding their way on the bulletin boards. Many of these are of a harmless nature, but many of these are downright immoral and sinister, such as, defendants' Exhibit B distributed by SDS, which was posted on the Shaw High School bulletin board. It encouraged a demonstration in Washington opposing our political leaders and, among other things, contained this phrase: "Don't let the bastards grind you down!"

It is also relevant in the instant case that one of the pamphlets which was circulated at Shaw High School by the Student Mobilization Committee advertised a city-wide meeting to consider a possible high school strike.

The regulation prohibiting the wearing of the button is an appropriate standard of behavioral conduct which is reasonably relevant to the mission and function of Shaw High School.

The regulation is not discriminatory nor unreasonable, arbitrary or capricious. The rule does not deny a federally protected constitutional right.

Upholding the Shaw High School rule prohibiting buttons or other symbols does not sound the death knell for student freedom of speech.

The evidence in this case has made it abundantly clear that the school authorities have a factual basis upon which to forecast substantial disruption of, or material interference with, school activities if student behavioral conduct regarding the wearing of buttons is not regulated.

Therefore, the Court finds the issues in this case in favor of the defendants; and the plaintiff's claim for injunctive relief and damages is denied.

It is, therefore, ordered that this cause be and is hereby dismissed and terminated.

Students' Lewd and Indecent Speech Is Not Protected by First Amendment

———————————

Bethel School District No. 403 v. Fraser

———————————

Supreme Court of the United States, 1986.
478 U.S. 675, 106 S.Ct. 3159.

Chief Justice BURGER delivered the opinion of the Court. We granted certiorari to decide whether the First Amendment prevents a school district from disciplining a high school student for giving a lewd speech at a school assembly.

On April 26, 1983, respondent Matthew N. Fraser, a student at Bethel High School in Bethel, Washington, delivered a speech nominating a fellow student for student elective office. Approximately 600 high school students, many of whom were 14-year-olds, attended the assembly. Students were required to attend the assembly or to report to the study hall. The assembly was part of a school-sponsored educational program in self-government. Students who elected not to attend the assembly were required to report to study hall. During the entire speech, Fraser referred to his candidate in terms of an elaborate, graphic, and explicit sexual metaphor.

Two of Fraser's teachers, with whom he discussed the contents of his speech in advance, informed him that the speech was "inappropriate and that he probably should not deliver it," and that his delivery of the speech might have "severe consequences."

During Fraser's delivery of the speech, a school counselor observed the reaction of students to the speech. Some students hooted and yelled; some by gestures graphically simulated the sexual activities pointedly alluded to in respondent's speech. Other students appeared to be bewildered and embarrassed by the speech. One teacher reported that on the day following the speech, she found it necessary to forgo a portion of the scheduled class lesson in order to discuss the speech with the class.

A Bethel High School disciplinary rule prohibiting the use of obscene language in the school provides:

> Conduct which materially and substantially interferes with the educational process is prohibited, including the use of obscene, profane language or gestures.

The morning after the assembly, the Assistant Principal called Fraser into her office and notified him that the school considered his speech to have been a violation of this rule. Fraser was presented with copies of five letters submitted by teachers, describing his conduct at the assembly; he was given a chance to explain his conduct, and he admitted to having given the speech described and that he deliberately used sexual innuendo in the speech. Fraser was then informed that he would be suspended for three days, and that his name would be removed from the list of candidates for graduation speaker at the school's commencement exercises.

Fraser sought review of this disciplinary action through the School District's grievance procedures. . . . The examiner determined that the speech fell within the ordinary meaning of "obscene," as used in the disruptive-conduct rule, and affirmed the discipline in its entirety. Fraser served two days of his suspension, and was allowed to return to school on the third day.

Respondent, by his father as guardian *ad litem*, then brought this action [and] . . . alleged violation of his First Amendment right to freedom of speech and sought both injunctive relief and monetary damages under 42 U.S.C. § 1983. . . .

The Court of Appeals for the Ninth Circuit affirmed the judgment of the District Court, 755 F.2d 1356 (1985), holding that respondent's speech was indistinguishable from the protest armband in *Tinker v. Des Moines Independent Community School Dist.*, 393 U.S.

503, 89 S.Ct. 733, 21 L.Ed.2d 731 (1969). The court explicitly rejected the School District's argument that the speech, unlike the passive conduct of wearing a black armband, had a disruptive effect on the educational process. The Court of Appeals also rejected the School District's argument that it had an interest in protecting an essentially captive audience of minors from lewd and indecent language in a setting sponsored by the school, reasoning that the school board's "unbridled discretion" to determine what discourse is "decent" would "increase the risk of cementing white, middle-class standards for determining what is acceptable and proper speech and behavior in our public schools." . . . Finally, the Court of Appeals rejected the School District's argument that, incident to its responsibility for the school curriculum, it had the power to control the language used to express ideas during a school-sponsored activity.

We granted certiorari, . . . We reverse.

This Court acknowledged in *Tinker v. Des Moines Independent Community School Dist.,* . . . that students do not "shed their constitutional rights to freedom of speech or expression at the schoolhouse gate." . . . The Court of Appeals read that case as precluding any discipline of Fraser for indecent speech and lewd conduct in the school assembly. That court appears to have proceeded on the theory that the use of lewd and obscene speech in order to make what the speaker considered to be a point in a nominating speech for a fellow student was essentially the same as the wearing of an armband in *Tinker* as a form of protest or the expression of a political position.

The marked distinction between the political "message" of the armbands in *Tinker* and the sexual content of respondent's speech in this case seems to have been given little weight by the Court of Appeals. In upholding the students' right to engage in a nondisruptive, passive expression of a political viewpoint in *Tinker*, this Court was careful to note that the case did "not concern speech or action that intrudes upon the work of the schools or the rights of other students."

It is against this background that we turn to consider the level of First Amendment protection accorded to Fraser's utterances and actions before an official high school assembly attended by 600 students.

The role and purpose of the American public school system was well described by two historians, saying "public education must prepare pupils for citizenship in the Republic. . . . It must inculcate the habits and manners of civility as values in themselves conducive to happiness and as indispensable to the practice of self-government in the community and the nation." C. Beard & M. Beard, New Basic History of the United States 228 (1968). . . .

These fundamental values of "habits and manners of civility" essential to a democratic society must, of course, include tolerance of divergent political and religious views, even when the views expressed may be unpopular. But these "fundamental values" must also take into account consideration of the sensibilities of others, and, in the case of a school, the sensibilities of fellow students. The undoubted freedom to advocate unpopular and controversial views in schools and classrooms must be balanced against the society's countervailing interest in teaching students the boundaries of socially appropriate behaviour. Even the most heated political discourse in a democratic society requires consideration for the personal sensibilities of the other participants and audiences.

In our Nation's legislative halls, where some of the most vigorous political debates in our society are carried on, there are rules prohibiting the use of expressions offensive to other participants in the debate. The Manual of Parliamentary Practice, drafted by Thomas Jefferson and adopted by the House of Representatives to govern the proceedings in that body, prohibits the use of "impertinent" speech during debate and likewise provides that "[n]o person is to use indecent language against the proceedings of the House." Jefferson's Manual of Parliamentary Practice, §§ 359, 360, reprinted in Manual and Rules of House of Representatives, H.R. Doc. No. 97–271, pp. 158–159 (1982); see *id.,* at 111, n. *a* (Jefferson's Manual governs the House in all cases to which it applies). The Rules of Debate applicable in the Senate likewise provide that a Senator may be called to order for imputing improper motives to another Senator or for referring offensively to any State. . . . Can it be that what is proscribed in the halls of Congress is beyond the reach of school officials to regulate?

The First Amendment guarantees wide freedom in matters of adult public discourse. A sharply divided Court upheld the right to express an antidraft viewpoint in a public place, albeit in terms highly offensive to most citizens. . . . It does not follow, however, that simply because the use of an offensive form of expression may not be prohibited to adults making what the speaker considers a political point, that the same latitude must be permitted to children in a public school. . . .

Surely it is a highly appropriate function of public school education to prohibit the use of vulgar and offensive terms in public discourse. Indeed, the "fundamental values necessary to the maintenance of a democratic political system" disfavor the use of terms of debate highly offensive or highly threatening to others. Nothing in the Constitution prohibits the states from insisting that certain modes of expression are inappropriate and subject to sanctions. The inculcation of these values is truly the "work of the schools." . . . The determination of what manner of speech in the classroom or in school assembly is inappropriate properly rests with the school board.

The process of educating our youth for citizenship in public schools is not confined to books, the curriculum, and the civics class; schools must teach by example the shared values of a civilized social order. Consciously or otherwise, teachers—and indeed the older students—demonstrate the appropriate form of civil discourse and political expression by their conduct and deportment in and out of class. Inescapably, like parents, they are role models. The schools, as instruments of the state, may determine that the essential lessons of civil, mature conduct cannot be conveyed in a school that tolerates lewd, indecent, or offensive speech and

conduct such as that indulged in by this confused boy.

The pervasive sexual innuendo in Fraser's speech was plainly offensive to both teachers and students—indeed to any mature person. By glorifying male sexuality, and in its verbal content, the speech was acutely insulting to teenage girl students. . . . The speech could well be seriously damaging to its less mature audience, many of whom were only 14 years old and on the threshold of awareness of human sexuality. Some students were reported as bewildered by the speech and the reaction of mimicry it provoked.

This Court's First Amendment jurisprudence has acknowledged limitations on the otherwise absolute interest of the speaker in reaching an unlimited audience where the speech is sexually explicit and the audience may include children. . . . These cases recognize the obvious concern on the part of parents, and school authorities acting *in loco parentis* to protect children—especially in a captive audience—from exposure to sexually explicit, indecent, or lewd speech.

We have also recognized an interest in protecting minors from exposure to vulgar and offensive spoken language. . . .

We hold that petitioner School District acted entirely within its permissible authority in imposing sanctions upon Fraser in response to his offensively lewd and indecent speech. Unlike the sanctions imposed on the students wearing armbands in *Tinker*, the penalties imposed in this case were unrelated to any political viewpoint. The First Amendment does not prevent the school officials from determining that to permit a vulgar and lewd speech such as respondent's would undermine the school's basic educational mission. A high school assembly or classroom is no place for a sexually explicit monologue directed towards an unsuspecting audience of teenage students. Accordingly, it was perfectly appropriate for the school to disassociate itself to make the point to the pupils that vulgar speech and lewd conduct is wholly inconsistent with the "fundamental values" of public school education. Justice Black, dissenting in *Tinker*, made a point that is especially relevant in this case:

I wish therefore, . . . to disclaim any purpose . . . to hold that the federal Constitution compels the teachers, parents and elected school officials to surrender control of the American public school system to public school students. 393 U.S., at 522, 526, 89 S.Ct., at 744, 746.

Respondent contends that the circumstances of his suspension violated due process because he had no way of knowing that the delivery of the speech in question would subject him to disciplinary sanctions. This argument is wholly without merit. We have recognized that "maintaining security and order in the schools requires a certain degree of flexibility in school disciplinary procedures, and we have respected the value of preserving the informality of the student-teacher relationship." *New Jersey v. T.L.O.*, 469 U.S., at ___, 105 S.Ct., at 743. Given the school's need to be able to impose disciplinary sanctions for a wide range of unanticipated conduct disruptive of the educational process, the school disciplinary rules need not be as detailed as a criminal code which imposes criminal sanctions. . . . Two days' suspension from school does not rise to the level of a penal sanction calling for the full panoply of procedural due process protections applicable to a criminal prosecution. . . . The school disciplinary rule proscribing "obscene" language and the pre-speech admonitions of teachers gave adequate warning to Fraser that his lewd speech could subject him to sanctions.

The judgment of the Court of Appeals for the Ninth Circuit is

Reversed.

Justice BLACKMUN concurs in the result.

Justice BRENNAN, concurring in the judgment.

Respondent gave the following speech at a high school assembly in support of a candidate for student government office:

'I know a man who is firm—he's firm in his pants, he's firm in his shirt, his character is firm—but most . . . of all, his belief in you, the students of Bethel, is firm.

'Jeff Kuhlman is a man who takes his point and pounds it in. If necessary, he'll take an issue and nail it to the wall. He doesn't attack things

in spurts—he drives hard, pushing and pushing until finally—he succeeds.'

Jeff is a man who will go to the very end—even the climax, for each and every one of you.

'So vote for Jeff for A.S.B. vice-president—he'll never come between you and the best our high school can be.'

The Court, referring to these remarks as "obscene," "vulgar," "lewd," and "offensively lewd," concludes that school officials properly punished respondent for uttering the speech. Having read the full text of respondent's remarks, I find it difficult to believe that it is the same speech the Court describes. To my mind, the most that can be said about respondent's speech—and all that need be said—is that in light of the discretion school officials have to teach high school students how to conduct civil and effective public discourse, and to prevent disruption of school educational activities, it was not unconstitutional for school officials to conclude, under the circumstances of this case, that respondent's remarks exceeded permissible limits. Thus, while I concur in the Court's judgment, I write separately to express my understanding of the breadth of the Court's holding. . . .

NOTES

1. Lower courts have begun to follow the *Bethel* precedent in giving school officials greater discretion in regulating student conduct. A case in point is *Gano*, an Idaho case, where a federal district court upheld the suspension of a student for drawing and having printed on T-shirts a caricature of the principal, vice-principal, and Dean of Men sitting against a fence, holding alcoholic beverages and acting drunk. The plaintiff wore one of the T-shirts to school. The court in holding against the student said that in Idaho the schools are statutorily charged with teaching the "effects of alcohol." To depict the school administrators in a drunken stupor was to not only falsely accuse them of being drunk, but to do damage to the school's decorum as well. The court said:

The administrators are role models, as stated by the United States Supreme Court, and their position would be severely compromised if this T-shirt was circulated among students.

Further, the court noted that:

This case appears to clearly fall within the *Bethel* precedent.

Gano v. School District No. 411 of Twin Falls County, State of Idaho, 674 F.Supp. 796 (D. Idaho 1987).

2. In a case where students dressed as persons of the opposite sex, and were escorted from the school prom by police at the request of school officials, the court held for the officials, saying that students were not denied First Amendment, Due Process, or Equal Protection rights. [*Harper v. Edgewood Bd. of Educ.,* 655 F.Supp. 1353 (S.D. Ohio 1987)]. In so holding the court cited *Gfell v. Rickelman,* wherein the Sixth Circuit upheld grooming codes regarding hair length as reasonably related to "the maintenance of discipline, promotion of safety . . . and the furtherance of valid educational purposes." 441 F.2d 444 (6th Cir. 1971). In further quoting *Gfell,* the court said that

regulations which deal generally with dress and the like are a part of the disciplinary process which is necessary in maintaining a balance as between the rights of individual students and the rights of the whole in the functioning of schools. *Gfell,* 441 F.2d at 446.

3. In a 1987 case, a federal district court was able to relate the wearing of earrings to the buttons of *Guzick* and the armbands of *Tinker* and to square its ruling with *Bethel* as well. In this case, a student wanted to wear an earring because he believed it expressed his individuality and would, possibly, be attractive to young women at the school. Each time he wore the earring, on several occasions, he was suspended under a school board rule that forbade all gang symbols including jewelry and emblems. The wearing of earrings by males was included in the ban, although girls could wear earrings. The board had earlier, in 1984, passed the rule because of gang problems between 1981 and 1985, when the board discovered that students had been intimidated by gang members, and that the gangs had warring factions in and around the school. The rule did not, however, specifically ban the wearing of earrings. In upholding the board rule and its enforcement the court, citing *Bethel,* said that the board of education

has the responsibility to teach not only English and History, but the role of young men and women in our democratic society. They are taught to have individual rights and that those rights must be balanced with the rights of others. The direction and manner of this instruction rests with the Board, not the federal court.

Concerning protection of political expression, the court noted that the student's "message" was one of "individuality" and not one of "politics," thus it was not within the scope of the First Amendment. *Olesen v. Board of Education of School Dist. No. 228,* 676 F.Supp. 820 (N.D. Ill. 1987).

4. The influence of *Bethel* is further evidenced by a 1989 case from the Fifth Circuit, in which a student was disqualified from a school election because of "rude" and "discourteous" remarks he made about the school principal in a campaign speech in school assembly. The court upheld the school in declaring the student ineligible. In so doing, the court cited *Bethel,* saying that

the determination of what manner of speech in the classroom or in school assembly is inappropriate properly rests with the school board. *Bethel School District No. 403 v. Fraser,* 478 U.S. 675, 683, 106 S.Ct. 3159, 3164 (1986).

The court further referenced, pursuant to *Bethel* logic, "The art of stating one's views without unnecessarily hurting the feelings of others surely has a legitimate place in any high school curriculum, and we are not prepared to say that the lesson Unicoi High tried to teach Dean Poling (the student) and his captive audience was illegitimate." *Poling v. Murphy*, 872 F.2d 757 (6th Cir. 1989).

5. A United States District Court in California upheld the suspension of high school pupils for ten days for use of profanity and/or vulgarity appearing in an off-campus newspaper, "Oink." The more damaging portions of the publication appeared to be a "vulgar retouching of what appears to be a photograph of President Nixon." *Baker v. Downey City Board of Education*, 307 F.Supp. 517 (D.Cal. 1969).

6. A clear case of disruptive school activities by nonstudents arose when twelve youths entered the office of the secretary of the school principal and told her "they were going to interrupt us that day," locked the secretary out of her office, moved furniture about, scattered papers, and dumped some books on the floor, all of which resulted in the dismissal of school. The conviction of the defendants was affirmed in *State v. Midgett*, 8 N.C.App. 230, 174 S.E.2d 124 (1970).

7. Suspension of black students for disrupting a student assembly because the tune "Dixie" was played was upheld by the United States Court of Appeals, Eighth Circuit. The Court said that "On the record we cannot say that the tune 'Dixie' constitutes a badge of slavery or that the playing of the tune under the facts as presented constituted officially sanctioned racial abuse. Such a ruling would lead to the prohibition of the playing of many of our most famous tunes." *Tate v. Board of Education of Jonesboro, Arkansas*, 453 F.2d 975 (8th Cir.1972).

8. Students can be temporarily suspended from school for disrupting school by engaging in a sit-in and not attending classes. *Gebert v. Hoffman*, 336 F.Supp. 694 (E.D. Pa.1972).

9. Symbols and insignia such as the Confederate flag, indicating the desire to maintain a segregated school, must be removed. *Smith v. St. Tammany Parish School Board*, 448 F.2d 414 (5th Cir.1971).

◼ STUDENT PUBLICATIONS

Freedom of the press is a cornerstone of the basic freedoms of the Constitution. In settling the Pentagon papers dispute between the New York Times and the United States Government, the Supreme Court said:

> In the First Amendment the Founding Fathers gave the free press the protection it must have to fulfill its essential role in our democracy. The press was to serve the governed, not the governors. The Government's power to censor the press was abolished so that the press would remain forever free to censure the Government.[99]

That a free press was essential to the proper functioning of a democratic government was well established among the framers of the U.S. Constitution. Blackstone, the great English jurist, reflected these sentiments when he observed that "The liberty of the press is indeed essential to the nature of a free state."[100] By the time the First Amendment was written by Madison, "[f]reedom of the press had become part . . . of government and the protection of civil liberties."[101]

The press, though, does have some limitations that have been debated over the years. It was maintained by Alexander Hamilton in 1804 that freedom of the press "consists of the right to publish, with impunity, truth, with good motives, for justifiable ends, though reflecting on government, magistracy, or individuals."[102] The expectation that the press would endeavor to be truthful, publish with proper motivation, without malice, for appropriate ends is a standard that the press has had difficulty in maintaining. Because what constitutes proper motives, appropriate ends, and truth, rests largely in the eye of the beholder, much litigation has ensued in defining the role that the press will play in society. Truth and proper motives, especially in the discussion of politics, has always been a nebulous and largely unenforceable standard. That the freedom of the press was to be defended on the basis of truth was thus an unsatisfactory condition. Thompson early observed that to maintain truth as a defense was like asking a jury to decide which is "the most palatable food, agreeable drink, or beautiful color."[103] In spite of the problems with proving truth in defense of publication, this standard prevailed in 1964, when the U.S. Supreme Court in the *New York Times v. Sullivan* held that public persons could not succeed in a libel action against the press by compelling the defense to show truth and good motives.[104] Today, the publication of falsehoods with malice can be maintained by private persons against the press, but public persons can not likewise prevail.

The courts have always been particularly suspicious of prior restraint; that is, when a publication is censored before it can reach the street. The historical view has been that the freedom of thought and enquiry should not be subject to previous restraints, but only to subsequent redress through civil or criminal action after publication. McKean, in 1797, observed that "Every free man has an undoubted right to lay what sentiments he pleases before the public . . . but take the consequences."[105]

The issue of prior restraint versus retrospective redress has been largely obviated by the Supreme Court decision in the Pentagon papers case.[106] Today there is no question that government cannot exercise prior restraint, except possibly in the most extreme circumstance, when the governmental interest is so absolutely compelling that there is little doubt that the health and safety of the people will be harmed.

Freedom of press in the public schools, however, is governed by an entirely different constitutional precedent. Regulation of student newspapers is subject to the Supreme Court decision in *Hazelwood School District v. Kuhlmeier*,[107] in which the Court distinguished government censorship outside of schools from that of student newspapers. Here the Court ruled that prior restraint was permissible because the student newspaper was not a "public forum," and the restraint was reasonably related to a valid educational purpose. The Court found that the "material and substantial disruption" standard of *Tinker* did

not apply, because in *Hazelwood* the student newspaper was school sponsored; whereas in *Tinker*, free expression was exhibited by armbands that were not school sponsored, but instead were individual political expression. The Court said, "[W]e conclude that the standard articulated in *Tinker* for determining when a school may punish student expression need not also be the standard for determining when a school may refuse to lend its name and resources to the dissemination of student expression."[108]

The Court thus removed the *Tinker* burden of proof from school officials with regard to regulation of student newspapers.

In spite of *Hazelwood*, however, school officials do not have an entirely free hand in censorship of student newspapers. School officials are not permitted to exercise powers of censorship merely as a matter of taste or fancy.[109] Rather, school determinations should be based on a school rule that advances an educational purpose and is uniformly enforced.[110] Without such rules, coupled with proper enforcement, substantive due process rights may be implicated.[111]

Schools May Regulate the Content of School-Sponsored Newspapers

Hazelwood School District v. Kuhlmeier

United States Supreme Court, 1988.
484 U.S. 260, 108 S.Ct. 562.

Justice WHITE delivered the opinion of the Court. This case concerns the extent to which educators may exercise editorial control over the contents of a high school newspaper produced as part of the school's journalism curriculum.

Petitioners are the Hazelwood School District in St. Louis County, Missouri; various school officials; . . . Respondents are three former Hazelwood East students who were staff members of Spectrum, the school newspaper. They contend that school officials violated their First Amendment rights by deleting two pages of articles from the May 13, 1983, issue of Spectrum.

Spectrum was written and edited by the Journalism II class at Hazelwood East. The newspaper was published every three weeks or so during the 1982–1983 school year. More than 4,500 copies of the newspaper were distributed during that year to students, school personnel, and members of the community.

The Board of Education allocated funds from its annual budget for the printing of Spectrum. These funds were supplemented by proceeds from sales of the newspaper. The printing expenses during the 1982–1983 school year totaled $4,668.50; revenue from sales was $1,166.84. The other costs associated with the newspaper—such as supplies, textbooks, and a portion of the journalism teacher's salary—were borne entirely by the Board.

The Journalism II course was taught by Robert Stergos for most of the 1982–1983 academic year. Stergos left Hazelwood East to take a job in private industry on April 29, 1983, when the May 13 edition of Spectrum was nearing completion, and petitioner Emerson took his place as newspaper adviser for the remaining weeks of the term.

The practice at Hazelwood East during the spring 1983 semester was for the journalism teacher to submit page proofs of each Spectrum issue to Principal Reynolds for his review prior to publication. On May 10, Emerson delivered the proofs of the May 13 edition to Reynolds, who objected to two of the articles scheduled to appear in that edition. One of the stories described three Hazelwood East students' experiences with pregnancy; the other discussed the impact of divorce on students at the school.

Reynolds was concerned that, although the pregnancy story used false names "to keep the identity of these girls a secret," the pregnant students still might be identifiable from the text. He also believed that the article's references to sexual activity and birth control were inappropriate for some of the younger students at the school. In addition, Reynolds was concerned that a student identified by name in the divorce story had complained that her father "wasn't spending enough time with my mom, my sister and I" prior to the divorce, "was always out of town on business or out late playing cards with the guys," and "always argued about everything" with her mother. . . . Reynolds believed that the student's parents should have been given an opportunity to respond to these remarks or to consent to their publication. He was unaware that Emerson had deleted the student's name from the final version of the article.

Reynolds believed that there was no time to make the necessary changes in the stories before the scheduled press run and that the newspaper would not appear before the end of the school year if printing were delayed to any significant extent. He concluded that his only options under the circumstances were to publish a four-page newspaper instead of the planned six-page newspaper, eliminating the two pages on which the offending stories appeared, or to publish no newspaper at all. Accordingly, he directed Emerson to withhold from publication the two pages containing the stories on pregnancy and divorce. He informed his superiors of the decision, and they concurred.

Respondents subsequently commenced this action in the United States District Court.
. . .

The District Court concluded that school officials may impose restraints on students' speech in activities that are " 'an integral part of the school's educational function' "—including the publication of a school-sponsored newspaper by a journalism class—so long as their decision has " 'a substantial and reasonable basis.' " . . .

The Court of Appeals for the Eighth Circuit reversed. . . . The court held at outset that Spectrum was not only "a part of the school adopted curriculum," but also a public forum, because the newspaper was "intended to be and operated as a conduit for student viewpoint." The court then concluded that Spectrum's status as a public forum precluded school officials from censoring its contents except when " 'necessary to avoid material and substantial interference with school work or discipline . . . or the rights of others.' " . . .

We granted certiorari, . . . and we now reverse.

Students in the public schools do not "shed their constitutional rights to freedom of speech or expression at the schoolhouse gate." . . . They cannot be punished merely for expressing their personal views on the school premises—whether "in the cafeteria, or on the playing field, or on the campus during the authorized hours," . . . unless school authorities have reason to believe that such expression will "substantially interfere with the work of the school or impinge upon the rights of other students."

We have nonetheless recognized that the First Amendment rights of students in the public schools "are not automatically coextensive with the rights of adults in other settings," *Bethel School District No. 403 v. Fraser*, 478 U.S. 675, ____, 106 S.Ct. 3159, 3164, 92 L.Ed.2d 549 (1986), and must be "applied in light of the special characteristics of the school environment." . . . A school need not tolerate student speech that is inconsistent with its "basic educational mission," . . . even though the government could not censor similar speech outside the school. Accordingly, we held in *Fraser* that a student could be disciplined for having delivered a speech that was "sexually explicit" but not legally obscene at an official school assembly, because the school was entitled to "disassociate itself" from the speech in a manner that would demonstrate to others that such vulgarity is "wholly inconsistent with the 'fundamental values' of public school education." We thus recognized that "[t]he determination of what manner of speech in the classroom or in school assembly is inappropriate properly rests with the school board," . . . rather than with the federal courts. It is in this context that respondents' First Amendment claims must be considered.

We deal first with the question whether Spectrum may appropriately be characterized as a forum for public expression. The public schools do not possess all of the attributes of streets, parks, and other traditional public forums that "time out of mind, have been used for purposes of assembly, communicating thoughts between citizens, and discussing public questions." . . . Hence, school facilities may be deemed to be public forums only if school authorities have "by policy or by practice" opened those facilities "for indiscriminate use by the general public," . . . or by some segment of the public, such as student organizations. . . . If the facilities have instead been reserved for other intended purposes, "communicative or otherwise," then no public forum has been created, and school officials may impose reasonable restrictions on the speech of students, teachers, and other members of the school community. "The government does not create a public forum by inaction or by permitting limited discourse, but only by intentionally opening a nontraditional forum for public discourse." . . .

The policy of school officials toward Spectrum was reflected in Hazelwood School Board Policy 348.51 and the Hazelwood East Curriculum Guide. Board Policy 348.51 provided that "[s]chool sponsored publications are developed within the adopted curriculum and its educational implications in regular classroom activities." . . . The Hazelwood East Curriculum Guide described the Journalism II course as a "laboratory situation in which the students publish the school newspaper applying skills they have learned in Journalism I." The lessons that were to be learned from the Journalism II course, according to the Curriculum Guide, included development of journalistic skills under deadline pressure, "the legal, moral, and ethical restrictions imposed upon journalists within the school community," and "responsibility and acceptance of criticism for articles of opinion." Journalism II was taught by a faculty member during regular class hours. Students received grades and academic credit for their performance in the course.

School officials did not deviate in practice from their policy that production of Spectrum was to be part of the educational curriculum and a "regular classroom activit[y]." The District Court found that Robert Stergos, the journalism teacher during most of the

1982–1983 school year, "both had the authority to exercise and in fact exercised a great deal of control over *Spectrum.*" . . . For example, Stergos selected the editors of the newspaper, scheduled publication dates, decided the number of pages for each issue, assigned story ideas to class members, advised students on the development of their stories, reviewed the use of quotations, edited stories, selected and edited the letters to the editor, and dealt with the printing company. Many of these decisions were made without consultation with the Journalism II students. The District Court thus found it "clear that Mr. Stergos was the final authority with respect to almost every aspect of the production and publication of *Spectrum,* including its content." Moreover, after each Spectrum issue had been finally approved by Stergos or his successor, the issue still had to be reviewed by Principal Reynolds prior to publication. Respondents' assertion that they had believed that they could publish "practically anything" in Spectrum was therefore dismissed by the District Court as simply "not credible." These factual findings are amply supported by the record, and were not rejected as clearly erroneous by the Court of Appeals. . . .

School officials did not evince either "by policy or by practice," . . . any intent to open the pages of Spectrum to "indiscriminate use," by its student reporters and editors, or by the student body generally. Instead, they "reserve[d] the forum for its intended purpos[e]," . . . as a supervised learning experience for journalism students. Accordingly, school officials were entitled to regulate the contents of Spectrum in any reasonable manner. It is this standard, rather than our decision in *Tinker,* that governs this case.

The question whether the First Amendment requires a school to tolerate particular student speech—the question that we addressed in *Tinker*—is different from the question whether the First Amendment requires a school affirmatively to promote particular student speech. The former question addresses educators' ability to silence a student's personal expression that happens to occur on the school premises. The latter question concerns educators' authority over school-

sponsored publications, theatrical productions, and other expressive activities that students, parents, and members of the public might reasonably perceive to bear the imprimatur of the school. These activities may fairly be characterized as part of the school curriculum, whether or not they occur in a traditional classroom setting, so long as they are supervised by faculty members and designed to impart particular knowledge or skills to student participants and audiences.

Educators are entitled to exercise greater control over this second form of student expression to assure that participants learn whatever lessons the activity is designed to teach, that readers or listeners are not exposed to material that may be inappropriate for their level of maturity, and that the views of the individual speaker are not erroneously attributed to the school. Hence, a school may in its capacity as publisher of a school newspaper or producer of a school play "disassociate itself," . . . not only from speech that would "substantially interfere with [its] work . . . or impinge upon the rights of other students," . . . but also from speech that is, for example, ungrammatical, poorly written, inadequately researched, biased or prejudiced, vulgar or profane, or unsuitable for immature audiences. A school must be able to set high standards for the student speech that is disseminated under its auspices—standards that may be higher than those demanded by some newspaper publishers or theatrical producers in the "real" world—and may refuse to disseminate student speech that does not meet those standards. In addition, a school must be able to take into account the emotional maturity of the intended audience in determining whether to disseminate student speech on potentially sensitive topics, which might range from the existence of Santa Claus in an elementary school setting to the particulars of teenage sexual activity in a high school setting. A school must also retain the authority to refuse to sponsor student speech that might reasonably be perceived to advocate drug or alcohol use, irresponsible sex, or conduct otherwise inconsistent with "the shared values of a civilized social order," . . . or to associate the school with any position other than neutrality on matters of political controversy. Otherwise, the schools would be unduly constrained from fulfilling their role as "a principal instrument in awakening the child to cultural values, in preparing him for later professional training, and in helping him to adjust normally to his environment." . . .

Accordingly, we conclude that the standard articulated in *Tinker* for determining when a school may punish student expression need not also be the standard for determining when a school may refuse to lend its name and resources to the dissemination of student expression. Instead, we hold that educators do not offend the First Amendment by exercising editorial control over the style and content of student speech in school-sponsored expressive activities so long as their actions are reasonably related to legitimate pedagogical concerns.

This standard is consistent with our oft-expressed view that the education of the Nation's youth is primarily the responsibility of parents, teachers, and state and local school officials, and not of federal judges. . . . It is only when the decision to censor a school-sponsored publication, theatrical production, or other vehicle of student expression has no valid educational purpose that the First Amendment is so "directly and sharply implicate[d]," as to require judicial intervention to protect students' constitutional rights.

We also conclude that Principal Reynolds acted reasonably in requiring the deletion from the May 13 issue of Spectrum of the pregnancy article, the divorce article, and the remaining articles that were to appear on the same pages of the newspaper.

The initial paragraph of the pregnancy article declared that "[a]ll names have been changed to keep the identity of these girls a secret." The principal concluded that the students' anonymity was not adequately protected, however, given the other identifying information in the article and the small number of pregnant students at the school. Indeed, a teacher at the school credibly testified that she could positively identify at least one of the girls and possibly all three. It is likely that many students at Hazelwood East would have

been at least as successful in identifying the girls. Reynolds therefore could reasonably have feared that the article violated whatever pledge of anonymity had been given to the pregnant students. In addition, he could reasonably have been concerned that the article was not sufficiently sensitive to the privacy interests of the students' boyfriends and parents, who were discussed in the article but who were given no opportunity to consent to its publication or to offer a response. The article did not contain graphic accounts of sexual activity. The girls did comment in the article, however, concerning their sexual histories and their use or nonuse of birth control. It was not unreasonable for the principal to have concluded that such frank talk was inappropriate in a school-sponsored publication distributed to 14-year-old freshmen and presumably taken home to be read by students' even younger brothers and sisters.

The student who was quoted by name in the version of the divorce article seen by Principal Reynolds made comments sharply critical of her father. The principal could reasonably have concluded that an individual publicly identified as an inattentive parent -- indeed, as one who chose "playing cards with the guys" over home and family — was entitled to an opportunity to defend himself as a matter of journalistic fairness. These concerns were shared by both of Spectrum's faculty advisers for the 1982–1983 school year, who testified that they would not have allowed the article to be printed without deletion of the student's name.

Principal Reynolds testified credibly at trial that, at the time that he reviewed the proofs of the May 13 issue during an extended telephone conversation with Emerson, he believed that there was no time to make any changes in the articles, and that the newspaper had to be printed immediately or not at all. It is true that Reynolds did not verify whether the necessary modifications could still have been made in the articles, and that Emerson did not volunteer the information that printing could be delayed until the changes were made. We nonetheless agree with the District Court that the decision to excise the two pages containing the problematic articles was reasonable given the particular circumstances of this case. These circumstances included the very recent replacement of Stergos by Emerson, who may not have been entirely familiar with Spectrum editorial and production procedures, and the pressure felt by Reynolds to make an immediate decision so that students would not be deprived of the newspaper altogether.

In sum, we cannot reject as unreasonable Principal Reynolds' conclusion that neither the pregnancy article nor the divorce article was suitable for publication in Spectrum. Reynolds could reasonably have concluded that the students who had written and edited these articles had not sufficiently mastered those portions of the Journalism II curriculum that pertained to the treatment of controversial issues and personal attacks, the need to protect the privacy of individuals whose most intimate concerns are to be revealed in the newspaper, and "the legal, moral, and ethical restrictions imposed upon journalists within [a] school community" that includes adolescent subjects and readers. Finally, we conclude that the principal's decision to delete two pages of Spectrum, rather than to delete only the offending articles or to require that they be modified, was reasonable under the circumstances as he understood them. Accordingly, no violation of First Amendment rights occurred.

The judgment of the Court of Appeals for the Eighth Circuit is therefore

Reversed.

NOTES

1. *Underground Newspapers.* A school policy governing unofficial or underground newspapers and giving school officials the power to exercise prior review and restraint may be constitutionally valid. Thus, a school rule that prohibited publication of material that was pervasively indecent or vulgar was held permissible, though the terms were poorly defined and contained large elements of subjectivity to the extent that reasonable people might disagree as to

the meaning. *Bystrom v. Fridley High School Independent School District, No. 14,* 822 F.2d 747 (8th Cir. 1987).

2. The school rule, though, may be too broad and so vague as to give school authorities unbridled discretion in exercising prior restraint. In *Burch v. Barker,* the Ninth Circuit held that a high school prior restraint policy was unconstitutional for lack of specificity for distribution and approval procedures; but, most importantly, the school policy was overly broad concerning the content-based requirements for the exercise of prior restraint. *Burch v. Barker,* 861 F.2d 1149 (9th Cir. 1988).

■ SEARCH AND SEIZURE

The Fourth Amendment of the United States Constitution provides: "The right of people to be secure in their persons, houses, papers, and effects, against unreasonable searches and seizures shall not be violated, and no warrants shall issue, but upon probable cause . . . ."

To search or not to search a pupil's desk, locker, pockets, purses, book-bags, coats, shoes and socks, and automobile is a question frequently confronting school administrators. Oftentimes, the issue must be decided forthwith because of the gravity of the situation—bomb threats, dangerous weapons, illegal drugs—which could result in serious injury to school pupils.[112]

The legality of search and seizure in the public schools balances primarily on whether the court views the school teacher or administrator as a parent or a police officer. To assume that the school administrator or teacher represents the state and seeks to obtain seized goods for purposes of criminal prosecution would require a warrant.

The Fourth Amendment has five important components. First, it enunciates and protects the *right* of people "to be secure in their persons, houses, papers and effects." Second, it protects persons from *unreasonable* searches and seizures. Third, a search cannot be instituted without government showing *probable cause* or giving evidence that a search is necessary. Fourth, the search must be *specific,* describing the place to be searched and the articles to be seized. Last, a *magistrate* or *judge* is interposed between the individual and the government, requiring that the government justify with evidence the necessity of the search.

Application of three of these five components is easily made to student searches in public schools. Students have a right of privacy — to be secure in their persons, papers and effects — and this right protects them against unreasonable searches and seizures. Moreover, any search must be specific as to what is sought in the search and the location where it is secreted. The courts do not, however, require that school officials be able to provide evidence constituting probable cause or that they obtain a warrant from a judge justifying a search.

Reasonable Suspicion

School officials need only have "reasonable suspicion," a standard less rigorous of proof than the requirement of "probable cause, in order to conduct a legal search." Suspicion itself implies a belief or opinion based upon facts or circumstances that do not amount to proof.[113] Until James Madison composed the Fourth Amendment, the terms "reasonable suspicion," "reason to suspect," "sufficient foundation," and "probable cause" had been used more or less interchangeably. Virginia's recommendation for amendments to the proposed constitution, in 1788, used the words "legal and sufficient cause" for issuance of warrants.[114] "Probable cause" as used by Madison in the Fourth Amendment "required more than mere suspicion or even reasonable suspicion."[115]

Although the standard of "reasonable suspicion" is a lower standard than that of the "probable cause," required for police to obtain a warrant, it is not so unrestrictive as to place no restraint on school personnel.[116] A New York court held that school personnel conducting a strip search of fifth-grade students after classroom thefts violated the children's Fourth Amendment rights because there were no acts that allowed school officials to particularize which student might have actually taken the money. The court maintained that there must be some available facts that together provide reasonable grounds to search, and the search must be conducted in order to further a legitimate school purpose such as the maintenance of discipline in the school.

A student's freedom from unreasonable search and seizure must be balanced against the need for school officials to maintain order and discipline and to protect the health and welfare of all the students. Where an assistant principal threatened to call a student's parents, forcing the student to reluctantly, but voluntarily, empty his pockets producing a pipe and marijuana, the court held that such a search was legitimate. Where the scope of intrusion is slight and there is no police involvement, school officials are held only to a "reasonable cause to believe" standard.[117]

The Supreme Court in *New Jersey v. T.L.O.,* 1985, established the prevailing precedent regarding school searches and seizures. The Court in this case held that the Fourth Amendment did apply to schools and that in order for searches to be constitutionally valid reasonableness must prevail. The Court stated that "the legality of a search of a student should depend on the reasonableness, under all circumstances, of the search."[118] According to the Court in *T.L.O.,* the constitutional validity of a search is to be determined at two levels. The first level involves consideration of whether the search is initially justified at its inception. The inception of the search is the point at which reasonable suspicion comes into play. Was the motivation for the search reasonable in light of the information obtained by the school official? The second level concerns the reasonableness of the search itself, and the "measures adopted for the search must be reasonably related to the objectives of the search and not excessively intrusive in light of the age and sex of the student and the nature of the infraction."[119] A search is not reasonable if it lacks specificity, or if it excessively intrudes on the student's privacy.

Inception of Search

The facts leading to the initiation of the search must indicate the suspicion was reasonable. In a case where a student was observed in an office where items had been stolen and was also found to have unauthorized objects concealed in his clothing, the court concluded that reasonable suspicion was established for a search of the student's locker.[120] In another case, reasonable suspicion was established where a school administrator had previously heard reports that a student was involved in drugs. A subsequent search of the student's locker and car revealed drugs and therefore was found reasonable and constitutional.[121]

In another drug case a student's car was searched, revealing cocaine, after the assistant principal observed that the student had glassy eyes, a flushed face, slurred speech, smelled of alcohol, and walked with an unsteady gait. The court found that this was ample evidence to support reasonable suspicion.[122]

Intrusiveness of Search

Whether a search is reasonable is a subjective determination and the courts determine the standard on the individual facts of each case. It is clear, though, that excessively intrusive searches must be supported by a relatively strong degree of suspicion by the school officials. The courts will require a corresponding relationship between the extensiveness of grounds supporting reasonable suspicion and the degree to which a search intrudes on a student's privacy. Where money was missing from a schoolroom and a teacher searched the books of two students and then required them to remove their shoes, the court found that the fact that the two students had been alone in the room where the stolen money disappeared was sufficient to support reasonable suspicion to conduct a limited search.[123]

A more extensive and intrusive search, however, may require more evidence to establish reasonable suspicion. In a case where an assistant principal spied a boy carrying a small calculator case with an odd bulge, the principal searched the case and found marijuana. The court held that merely noticing a bulge was not sufficient to establish reason-

able suspicion and pointed out that reasonable suspicion must be established by a clear articulation of facts, with rational inferences drawn from those facts, in order to warrant the conclusion of reasonable suspicion. This court noted that without having prior knowledge of the student's involvement in drug use, the mere observation of the calculator case was insufficient to establish a reason to suspect something illegal was hidden in the case.[124]

Where a girl was forced to remove her jeans and submit to visual inspection of her brassiere, the court held that the fact that she had ducked behind a car and had given a school security guard a false name was insufficient to establish reasonable suspicion. The court noted that without further specific information, the school had no more reason to believe that the girl was hiding drugs than to believe that she was skipping class, stealing hubcaps, or anything else, legal or illegal.[125]

Context of Search

Further, the courts have held that "what is reasonable depends on the context within which the search takes place."[126] A context indicating loosely articulated factual background that is not necessarily related to a specific violation is too nebulous to support "reasonable suspicion." The lack of specificity in a wide search of large groups of students without specific knowledge of rule violations by any particular students is not reasonable.[127] Some individualized suspicion is essential as a prerequisite to a constitutional search. One court has cautioned that even though general searches are easier and may be more effective in finding illegal contraband, such searches will not survive the reasonableness test without individualized suspicion unless other safeguards are available to assure respect for individual privacy.[128]

Guidelines for Searches

These precedents, therefore, suggest that even though school officials must adhere to the lesser standards of "reasonable suspicion" rather than "probable cause," the courts will nevertheless be vigilant in scrutinizing the conditions attendant to school searches. Certain conclusions can be drawn that provide guidelines governing school searches.

1. Students have a right to privacy of their persons, papers, and effects.
2. In determining whether a search is reasonable, the courts will consider the magnitude of the offense and extent of the intrusiveness on the student's privacy.
3. To establish reasonable suspicion justifying the inception of a search requires that the school official have some evidence regarding the particular situation, including possibly the background of the student, that would lead to the conclusion that something is hidden in violation of school rules.
4. A search must be supported by *specificity* as to the offense and a particularized knowledge as to where the illegal contraband is located as well as to the identity of the offending student. This guideline is taken from the Fourth Amendment, which requires that issuance of a warrant is dependent on particularity: "describing the place to be searched, and the persons or things to be seized."[129]

Canine Searches

In recent years, because of the use of drugs in public schools, officials have used dogs to sniff out contraband. These canine searches have been viewed by the courts with mixed reactions.

The Tenth Circuit Court of Appeals in *Zamora v. Pomeroy*[130] upheld the use of dogs in the exploratory sniffing of lockers. The court noted that since the schools gave notice at the beginning of the year that the lockers might be periodically opened, the lockers were jointly possessed by both student and school. The court further stated that since the school officials had a duty to maintain a proper educational environment it was necessary for them to inspect lockers, and, even though there might be a slight Fourth Amendment infringement, it was not significant.

The Seventh Circuit Court in *Doe v. Renfrow*[131] held that school officials stood *in loco parentis* and had a right to use dogs to seek out drugs, especially because of the diminished

expectations of privacy inherent in the public schools. School officials had a duty to maintain an educational environment that was conducive to learning. This decision may be contrary to *New Jersey v. T.L.O.*, in which the Supreme Court expressly limited the application of *in loco parentis*.

In a federal district court case, *Jones v. Latexo Independent School District*,[132] the decision was different from that in *Doe* and *Zamora*. The school district in *Jones* used dogs to sniff both students and automobiles. The court ruled, in the absence of individual suspicion, that the sniffing of the students was too intrusive and not reasonable. Because the students did not have access to their automobiles during the school day, the school's interest in sniffing the cars was minimal, and therefore also unreasonable.

In *Horton v. Goose Creek Independent School District*[133] the court stated, "The problem presented in this case is convergence of two troubling questions. First, is the sniff of a drug-detecting dog a 'search' within the purview of the Fourth Amendment? Second, to what extent does the Fourth Amendment protect students against searches by school administrators seeking to maintain a safe environment conducive to education?"[134] In response to the first question the court stated, "We accordingly hold that the sniff of the lockers and cars did not constitute a search and, therefore, we need make no inquiry into the reasonableness of the sniffing of the lockers and automobiles."[135] Concerning the second question the court ruled that school officials may search students if they have "reasonable cause" but "the instrusion on dignity and personal security that goes with the type of canine inspection of the student's person involved in this case cannot be justified by the need to prevent abuse of drugs and alcohol when there is no individualized suspicion; and we hold it unconstitutional."[136]

Strip Searches

The courts have allowed school officials to search students if they have reasonable suspicion that the student is in possession of something that is illegal, against school regulation, or may be harmful to the health and safety of other students. But the courts have determined that the reasonable suspicion standard does not always apply when a strip search is conducted. As one court stated, "We are also of the view that as the intrusiveness of the search intensifies, the standard of Fourth Amendment 'reasonableness' approaches probable cause, even in the school context. Thus, when a teacher conducts a highly intrusive invasion such as a strip search in this case, it is reasonable to require that probable cause be present."[137] In *Bellnier v. Lund,*[138] the court ruled that a teacher who strip-searched the class trying to locate a missing three dollars violated the Fourth Amendment. However, in *Bellnier* the court noted that the relative slight danger of the missing money had to be considered and if something more dangerous were present, it might be different. In *Rone,*[139] school officials were specific in knowing the facts surrounding the student's drug activity before searching. In *Renfrow,* school officials used dogs "unsupported by particularized facts, reasonable suspicion, or probable cause"[140] to detect drug odors and then strip-searched a student. Here the court said:

It does not require a constitutional scholar to conclude that a nude search of a thirteen-year-old child is an invasion of constitutional rights of some magnitude. More than that: It is a violation of any known principal of human decency. Apart from any constitutional readings and rulings, simple common sense would indicate that the conduct of the school officials in permitting such a nude search was not only unlawful but outrageous under settled indisputable principles of law.[141]

Exclusionary Rule

School officials should be concerned with removing contraband from the school environment for the betterment of other students and not for use in the criminal prosecution of students. Because materials seized in public schools are frequently illegal and may be turned over to law enforcement officials, the Exclusionary Rule has been often raised. Can

illegal materials seized by school officials be used in criminal prosecutions?

In 1914, in *Weeks v. United States,*[142] the Supreme Court established that evidence (in this instance lottery tickets, private letters, and papers) seized without a warrant could not be used in federal courts for federal prosecution. This doctrine, the *Weeks Doctrine,* thereafter excluded evidence obtained illegally by federal officials from use in federal trials.

In *Wolf v. People of the State of Colorado,* 1949,[143] the question arose concerning the issue of whether materials illegally seized could be used in state courts. The question was:

Does a conviction by a state court for a state offense deny the "due process of law" required by the Fourteenth Amendment, solely because evidence that was admitted at the trial was obtained under circumstances which would have rendered it inadmissible in a prosecution for violation of a federal law in a court of the United States because there deemed to be an infraction of the Fourth Amendment as applied in *Weeks v. United States.*[144]

The court reasoned that the *Weeks Doctrine* did not apply to states because other remedies could be used to negate arbitrary police actions in conducting illegal searches.[145]

In *Mapp v. Ohio* in 1961[146] the Supreme Court reversed the *Wolf Doctrine* and expanded the *Weeks Doctrine* or Exclusionary Rule to ban illegally seized evidence in state courts. This extension of the Exclusionary Rule has been litigated numerous times in public education cases. The courts generally have allowed materials seized by school officials to be used in a criminal prosecution. Therefore the Exclusionary Rule has not been applied.

Drug Testing

The private business sector and state and federal governmental agencies are now resorting to mandatory testing as a means to deter drug use and to ensure job health and safety. The United States Supreme Court in 1989 ruled on two cases, one of which concerned the testing of railway employees and the other the testing of customs service employees. The Court ruled that a drug or alcohol test, whether it be a blood test, urine test, or a breath test, constitutes a search. "The [Supreme] Court has long recognized that . . . intrusion into the body for blood to be tested for alcohol content and the ensuing chemical analysis constitutes searches".[147] Although the testing of rail workers and customs officials constitutes a search, the court upheld the testing programs because of the government's compelling interest in protecting the public safety. With railway workers, the overriding factor was the government's interest in preventing accidents and casualties and the major factor in the customs service case was that workers carry firearms.[148] In these cases, individualized suspicion was not required because of the government's compelling need to preserve the health and safety of the public.

No case involving the drug testing of public school students has been litigated by the U.S. Supreme Court, and the lower-court decisions are split. In two cases testing was held unconstitutional, and one court has held testing to be constitutional. In one case litigated in New Jersey, the state required school children to have a physical examination to ensure physical fitness and, as a part of this examination, the local school board required that students be tested for drugs and alcohol.[149] The school official argued that this was not a search, because it was a part of a medical procedure and the purpose was to remedy any drug or alcohol problem that the child might have. The court ruled that the testing program did not comport with the *T.L.O.* reasonableness standard and if the medical arguments were accepted, the spectrum of items could be limitless. The program, the court said, "violates [the student's] right to be free of unreasonable search and seizure, . . . due process . . . [and] the [student's] legitimate expectation of privacy and personal security."

The Seventh Circuit ruled that the Tippecanoe County Schools, Indiana,[150] could randomly test students who participated in interscholastic programs. Although the court found that the search fell under the penumbra of the Fourth Amendment, the testing conformed to the reasonableness standard established in *T.L.O.* The court viewed as an important qualifying element the procedure established to allow the student due process if the results were positive.

In another case involving drug testing of students who participated in interscholastic programs, the court held that students' constitutional rights were violated[151] by the school district's requirement of urine tests administered to all students participating in interscholastic programs. After the initial tests of all students, random testing was mandated throughout the year. Because most of the students participated in activities such as athletics and band, 176 students out of 296 in the total student body were given urine tests for drugs. The court held that the critical requirement of individualized suspicion was missing and that random testing constituted an impermissible search. Without such specification the reasonableness of a search cannot be defended, except possibly in the extenuating circumstance where the school's interests appear to be so great as to be compelling.

Search of Students by School Officials
Is Constitutionally Permissible if Reasonable
and Not Excessively Intrusive

— - — - — - — - —

New Jersey v. T. L. O.

— - — - — - — - —

Supreme Court of the United States, 1985.
469 U.S. 325, 105 S.Ct. 733.

JUSTICE WHITE delivered the opinion of the Court. We granted certiorari in this case to examine the appropriateness of the exclusionary rule as a remedy for searches carried out in violation of the Fourth Amendment by public school authorities. Our consideration of the proper application of the Fourth Amendment to the public schools, however, has led us to conclude that the search that gave rise to the case now before us did not violate the Fourth

Amendment. Accordingly, we here address only the questions of the proper standard for assessing the legality of searches conducted by public school officials and the application of that standard to the facts of this case.

On March 7, 1980, a teacher at Piscataway High School in Middlesex County, N.J., discovered two girls smoking in a lavatory. One of the two girls was the respondent T. L. O., who at that time was a 14-year-old high school freshman. Because smoking in the lavatory was a violation of a school rule, the teacher took the two girls to the Principal's office, where they met with Assistant Vice Principal Theodore Choplick. In response to questioning by Mr. Choplick, T. L. O.'s companion admitted that she had violated the rule. T. L. O., however, denied that she had been smoking in the lavatory and claimed that she did not smoke at all.

Mr. Choplick asked T. L. O. to come into his private office and demanded to see her purse. Opening the purse, he found a pack of cigarettes, which he removed from the purse and held before T. L. O. as he accused her of having lied to him. As he reached into the purse for the cigarettes, Mr. Choplick also noticed a package of cigarette rolling papers. In his experience, possession of rolling papers by high school students was closely associated with the use of marihuana. Suspecting that a closer examination of the purse might yield further evidence of drug use, Mr. Choplick proceeded to search the purse thoroughly. The search revealed a small amount of marihuana, a pipe, a number of empty plastic bags, a substantial quantity of money in one-dollar bills, an index card that appeared to be a list of students who owed T. L. O. money, and two letters that implicated T. L. O. in marihuana dealing.

Mr. Choplick notified T. L. O.'s mother and the police, and turned the evidence of drug dealing over to the police. At the request of the police, T. L. O.'s mother took her daughter to police headquarters, where T. L. O. confessed that she had been selling marihuana at the high school. On the basis of the confession and the evidence seized by Mr. Choplick, the State brought delinquency charges against T. L. O. in the Juvenile and

Domestic Relations Court of Middlesex County. Contending that Mr. Choplick's search of her purse violated the Fourth Amendment, T. L. O. moved to suppress the evidence found in her purse as well as her confession, which, she argued, was tainted by the allegedly unlawful search. . . .

The New Jersey Supreme Court agreed with the lower courts that the Fourth Amendment applies to searches conducted by school officials. The court also rejected the State of New Jersey's argument that the exclusionary rule should not be employed to prevent the use in juvenile proceedings of evidence unlawfully seized by school officials. Declining to consider whether applying the rule to the fruits of searches by school officials would have any deterrent value, the court held simply that the precedents of this Court establish that "if an official search violates constitutional rights, the evidence is not admissible in criminal proceedings."

With respect to the question of the legality of the search before it, the court agreed with the Juvenile Court that a warrantless search by a school official does not violate the Fourth Amendment so long as the official "has reasonable grounds to believe that a student possesses evidence of illegal activity or activity that would interfere with school discipline and order." However, the court, with two justices dissenting, sharply disagreed with the Juvenile Court's conclusion that the search of the purse was reasonable. According to the majority, the contents of T. L. O.'s purse had no bearing on the accusation against T. L. O., for possession of cigarettes (as opposed to smoking them in the lavatory) did not violate school rules, and a mere desire for evidence that would impeach T. L. O.'s claim that she did not smoke cigarettes could not justify the search. Moreover, even if a reasonable suspicion that T. L. O. had cigarettes in her purse would justify a search, Mr. Choplick had no such suspicion, as no one had furnished him with any specific information that there were cigarettes in the purse. Finally, leaving aside the question whether Mr. Choplick was justified in opening the purse, the court held that the evidence of drug use that he saw inside did not justify the extensive "rummaging" through T. L. O.'s papers and effects that followed.

In determining whether the search at issue in this case violated the Fourth Amendment, we are faced initially with the question whether that Amendment's prohibition on unreasonable searches and seizures applies to searches conducted by public school officials. We hold that it does.

It is now beyond dispute that "the Federal Constitution, by virtue of the Fourteenth Amendment, prohibits unreasonable searches and seizures by state officers." Equally indisputable is the proposition that the Fourteenth Amendment protects the rights of students against encroachment by public school officials:

> The Fourteenth Amendment, as now applied to the States, protects the citizen against the State itself and all of its creatures — Boards of Education not excepted. These have, of course, delicate, and highly discretionary functions, but none that they may not perform within the limits of the Bill of Rights. That they are educating the young for citizenship is reason for scrupulous protection of constitutional freedoms of the individual, if we are not to strangle the free mind at its source and teach youth to discount important principles of our government as mere platitudes. *West Virginia State Bd. of Ed. v. Barnette,* 319 U.S. 624, 637, 63 S.Ct. 1178, 1185, 87 L.Ed. 1628 (1943).

It may well be true that the evil toward which the Fourth Amendment was primarily directed was the resurrection of the pre-Revolutionary practice of using general warrants or "writs of assistance" to authorize searches for contraband by officers of the Crown. But this Court has never limited the Amendment's prohibition on unreasonable searches and seizures to operations conducted by the police. Rather, the Court has long spoken of the Fourth Amendment's strictures as restraints imposed upon "governmental action" — that is, "upon the activities of sovereign authority." . . .

Notwithstanding the general applicability of the Fourth Amendment to the activities of civil authorities, a few courts have concluded that school officials are exempt from the dictates of the Fourth Amendment by virtue of the special nature of their authority over schoolchildren. Teachers and school administrators, it is said, act *in loco parentis* in their dealings with students: their authority is that of the parent, not the State, and is therefore not subject to the limits of the Fourth Amendment.

Such reasoning is in tension with contemporary reality and the teachings of this Court. We have held school officials subject to the commands of the First Amendment, . . . and the Due Process Clause of the Fourteenth Amendment, ... If school authorities are state actors for purposes of the constitutional guarantees of freedom of expression and due process, it is difficult to understand why they should be deemed to be exercising parental rather than public authority when conducting searches of their students. More generally, the Court has recognized that "the concept of parental delegation" as a source of school authority is not entirely "consonant with compulsory education laws." Today's public school officials do not merely exercise authority voluntarily conferred on them by individual parents; rather, they act in furtherance of publicly mandated educational and disciplinary policies. . . . In carrying out searches and other disciplinary functions pursuant to such policies, school officials act as representatives of the State, not merely as surrogates for the parents, and they cannot claim the parents' immunity from the strictures of the Fourth Amendment.

To hold that the Fourth Amendment applies to searches conducted by school authorities is only to begin the inquiry into the standards governing such searches. Although the underlying command of the Fourth Amendment is always that searches and seizures be reasonable, what is reasonable depends on the context within which a search takes place. The determination of the standard of reasonableness governing any specific class of searches requires "balancing the need to search against the invasion which the search entails." On one side of the balance are arrayed the individual's legitimate expectations of privacy and personal security; on the other, the government's need for effective methods to deal with breaches of public order. . . .

The State of New Jersey has argued that because of the pervasive supervision to which children in the schools are necessarily subject, a child has virtually no legitimate expectation of privacy in articles of personal property "unnecessarily" carried into a school. This argument has two factual premises: (1) the fundamental incompatibility of expectations of privacy with the maintenance of a sound educational environment; and (2) the minimal interest of the child in bringing any items of personal property into the school. Both premises are severely flawed.

Although this Court may take notice of the difficulty of maintaining discipline in the public schools today, the situation is not so dire that students in the schools may claim no legitimate expectations of privacy. We have recently recognized that the need to maintain order in a prison is such that prisoners retain no legitimate expectations of privacy in their cells, but it goes almost without saying that "[t]he prisoner and the schoolchild stand in wholly different circumstances, separated by the harsh facts of criminal conviction and incarceration." We are not yet ready to hold that the schools and the prisons need be equated for purposes of the Fourth Amendment.

Nor does the State's suggestion that children have no legitimate need to bring personal property into the schools seem well anchored in reality. Students at a minimum must bring to school not only the supplies needed for their studies, but also keys, money, and the necessaries of personal hygiene and grooming. In addition, students may carry on their persons or in purses or wallets such nondisruptive yet highly personal items as photographs, letters, and diaries. Finally, students may have perfectly legitimate reasons to carry with them articles of property needed in connection with extracurricular or recreational activities. In short, schoolchildren may find it necessary to carry with them a variety of legitimate, noncontraband items, and there is no reason to conclude that they have necessarily waived all rights to privacy in such items merely by bringing them onto school grounds.

Against the child's interest in privacy must be set the substantial interest of teachers and administrators in maintaining discipline in the classroom and on school grounds. Maintaining order in the classroom has never been easy, but in recent years, school disorder has often taken particularly ugly forms: drug use and violent crime in the schools have become major social problems. . . . Accordingly, we have recognized that maintaining security and order in the schools requires a certain degree of flexibility in school disciplinary procedures, and we have respected the value of preserving the informality of the student-teacher relationship.

How, then, should we strike the balance between the schoolchild's legitimate expectations of privacy and the school's equally legitimate need to maintain an environment in which learning can take place? It is evident that the school setting requires some easing of the restrictions to which searches by public authorities are ordinarily subject. The warrant requirement, in particular, is unsuited to the school environment: requiring a teacher to obtain a warrant before searching a child suspected of an infraction of school rules (or of the criminal law) would unduly interfere with the maintenance of the swift and informal disciplinary procedures needed in the schools. Just as we have in other cases dispensed with the warrant requirement when "the burden of obtaining a warrant is likely to frustrate the governmental purpose behind the search," we hold today that school officials need not obtain a warrant before searching a student who is under their authority.

The school setting also requires some modification of the level of suspicion of illicit activity needed to justify a search. Ordinarily, a search—even one that may permissibly be carried out without a warrant—must be based upon "probable cause" to believe that a violation of the law has occurred. However, "probable cause" is not an irreducible requirement of a valid search. The fundamental command of the Fourth Amendment is that searches and seizures be reasonable, and although "both the concept of probable cause and the requirement of a warrant bear on the reasonableness of a search, . . . in certain

limited circumstances neither is required."
. . .

We join the majority of courts that have examined this issue in concluding that the accommodation of the privacy interests of schoolchildren with the substantial need of teachers and administrators for freedom to maintain order in the schools does not require strict adherence to the requirement that searches be based on probable cause to believe that the subject of the search has violated or is violating the law. Rather, the legality of a search of a student should depend simply on the reasonableness, under all the circumstances, of the search. Determining the reasonableness of any search involves a twofold inquiry: first, one must consider "whether the . . . action was justified at its inception," second, one must determine whether the search as actually conducted "was reasonably related in scope to the circumstances which justified the interference in the first place." Under ordinary circumstances, a search of a student by a teacher or other school official will be "justified at its inception" when there are reasonable grounds for suspecting that the search will turn up evidence that the student has violated or is violating either the law or the rules of the school. Such a search will be permissible in its scope when the measures adopted are reasonably related to the objectives of the search and not excessively intrusive in light of the age and sex of the student and the nature of the infraction.

This standard will, we trust, neither unduly burden the efforts of school authorities to maintain order in their schools nor authorize unrestrained intrusions upon the privacy of schoolchildren. By focusing attention on the question of reasonableness, the standard will spare teachers and school administrators the necessity of schooling themselves in the niceties of probable cause and permit them to regulate their conduct according to the dictates of reason and common sense. At the same time, the reasonableness standard should ensure that the interests of students will be invaded no more than is necessary to achieve the legitimate end of preserving order in the schools.

There remains the question of the legality of the search in this case. We recognize that the "reasonable grounds" standard applied by the New Jersey Supreme Court in its consideration of this question is not substantially different from the standard that we have adopted today. Nonetheless, we believe that the New Jersey court's application of that standard to strike down the search of T. L. O.'s purse reflects a somewhat crabbed notion of reasonableness. Our review of the facts surrounding the search leads us to conclude that the search was in no sense unreasonable for Fourth Amendment purposes.

The incident that gave rise to this case actually involved two separate searches, with the first—the search for cigarettes—providing the suspicion that gave rise to the second—the search for marihuana. Although it is the fruits of the second search that are at issue here, the validity of the search for marihuana must depend on the reasonableness of the initial search for cigarettes, as there would have been no reason to suspect that T. L. O. possessed marihuana had the first search not taken place. Accordingly, it is to the search for cigarettes that we first turn our attention.

The New Jersey Supreme Court pointed to two grounds for its holding that the search for cigarettes was unreasonable. First, the court observed that possession of cigarettes was not in itself illegal or a violation of school rules. Because the contents of T. L. O.'s purse would therefore have "no direct bearing on the infraction" of which she was accused (smoking in a lavatory where smoking was prohibited), there was no reason to search her purse. Second, even assuming that a search of T. L. O.'s purse might under some circumstances be reasonable in light of the accusation made against T. L. O., the New Jersey court concluded that Mr. Choplick in this particular case had no reasonable grounds to suspect that T. L. O. had cigarettes in her purse. At best, according to the court, Mr. Choplick had "a good hunch."

Both these conclusions are implausible. T. L. O. had been accused of smoking, and had denied the accusation in the strongest possible terms when she stated that she did not smoke at all. Surely it cannot be said that under these circumstances, T. L. O.'s possession of cigarettes would be irrelevant to the charges against her or to her response to those charges. T. L. O.'s possession of cigarettes, once it was discovered, would both corroborate the report that she had been smoking and undermine the credibility of her defense to the charge of smoking. To be sure, the discovery of the cigarettes would not prove that T. L. O. had been smoking in the lavatory; nor would it, strictly speaking, necessarily be inconsistent with her claim that she did not smoke at all. But it is universally recognized that evidence, to be relevant to an inquiry, need not conclusively prove the ultimate fact in issue, but only have "any tendency to make the existence of any fact that is of consequence to the determination of the action more probable or less probable than it would be without the evidence." The relevance of T. L. O.'s possession of cigarettes to the question whether she had been smoking and to the credibility of her denial that she smoked supplied the necessary "nexus" between the item searched for and the infraction under investigation. Thus, if Mr. Choplick in fact had a reasonable suspicion that T. L. O. had cigarettes in her purse, the search was justified despite the fact that the cigarettes, if found, would constitute "mere evidence" of a violation.

Of course, the New Jersey Supreme Court also held that Mr. Choplick had no reasonable suspicion that the purse would contain cigarettes. This conclusion is puzzling. A teacher had reported that T. L. O. was smoking in the lavatory. Certainly this report gave Mr. Choplick reason to suspect that T. L. O. was carrying cigarettes with her; and if she did have cigarettes, her purse was the obvious place in which to find them. Mr. Choplick's suspicion that there were cigarettes in the purse was not an "inchoate and unparticularized suspicion or 'hunch,' " rather, it was the sort of "common-sense conclusio[n] about human behavior" upon which "practical people"—including government officials—are entitled to rely. Of course, even if the teacher's report were true, T. L. O. *might* not have had a pack of cigarettes with her; she might have borrowed a cigarette from some-

one else or have been sharing a cigarette with another student. But the requirement of reasonable suspicion is not a requirement of absolute certainty: "sufficient probability, not certainty, is the touchstone of reasonableness under the Fourth Amendment.   . . . " Because the hypothesis that T. L. O. was carrying cigarettes in her purse was itself not unreasonable, it is irrelevant that other hypotheses were also consistent with the teacher's accusation. Accordingly, it cannot be said that Mr. Choplick acted unreasonably when he examined T. L. O.'s purse to see if it contained cigarettes.

Our conclusion that Mr. Choplick's decision to open T. L. O.'s purse was reasonable brings us to the question of the further search for marihuana once the pack of cigarettes was located. The suspicion upon which the search for marihuana was founded was provided when Mr. Choplick observed a package of rolling papers in the purse as he removed the pack of cigarettes. Although T. L. O. does not dispute the reasonableness of Mr. Choplick's belief that the rolling papers indicated the presence of marihuana, she does contend that the scope of the search Mr. Choplick conducted exceeded permissible bounds when he seized and read certain letters that implicated T. L. O. in drug dealing. This argument, too, is unpersuasive. The discovery of the rolling papers concededly gave rise to a reasonable suspicion that T. L. O. was carrying marihuana as well as cigarettes in her purse. This suspicion justified further exploration of T. L. O.'s purse, which turned up more evidence of drug-related activities: a pipe, a number of plastic bags of the type commonly used to store marihuana, a small quantity of marihuana, and a fairly substantial amount of money. Under these circumstances, it was not unreasonable to extend the search to a separate zippered compartment of the purse; and when a search of that compartment revealed an index card containing a list of "people who owe me money" as well as to letters, the inference that T. L. O. was involved in marihuana trafficking was substantial enough to justify Mr. Choplick in examining the letters to determine whether they contained any further evidence. In short, we cannot conclude that the search for marihuana was unreasonable in any respect.

Because the search resulting in the discovery of the evidence of marihuana dealing by T. L. O. was reasonable, the New Jersey Supreme Court's decision to exclude that evidence from T. L. O.'s juvenile delinquency proceedings on Fourth Amendment grounds was erroneous. Accordingly, the judgment of the Supreme Court of New Jersey is

Reversed.

---

*School Officials May Be Obligated
to Inspect School Lockers*

—··—·—··—·—··—·

People v. Overton

—··—·—··—·—··—·

Court of Appeals of New York, 1967.
20 N.Y.2d 360, 283 N.Y.S.2d 22, 229 N.E.2d 596,
affirmed on reargument 24 N.Y.2d 522, 301
N.Y.S.2d 479, 249 N.E.2d 366 (1969).

KEATING, Judge. Three detectives of the Mount Vernon Police Department having obtained a search warrant went to the Mount Vernon High School. The warrant directed a search of the persons of two students and, also, of their lockers.

The detectives presented the warrant to the vice-principal, Dr. Panitz, who sent for the two students, one of whom was the defendant, Carlos Overton. The detectives searched them and found nothing. A subsequent search of Overton's locker, however, revealed four marijuana cigarettes.

The defendant moved to invalidate that portion of the search warrant which directed a search of his locker, on the ground that the papers were defective upon which it was based. This motion was granted. The court denied the motion to suppress, however, on the grounds that the vice-principal had consented to the search and that he had a right to

do so. The Appellate Term reversed and dismissed the information, holding that the consent of the vice-principal could not justify an otherwise illegal search. The People have appealed from this order of the Appellate Term.

It is axiomatic that the protection of the Fourth Amendment is not restricted to dwellings. A depository such as a locker or even a desk is safeguarded from unreasonable searches for evidence of a crime (*United States v. Blok*, 88 U.S.App.D.C. 326, 188 F.2d 1019).

There are situations, however, where someone other than the defendant in possession of a depository may consent to what otherwise would have been an illegal search. Such a case was *United States v. Botsch*, 364 F.2d 542 [2d Cir. 1966], cert. den. 386 U.S. 937, 87 S.Ct. 959, 17 L.Ed.2d 810. In that case, the defendant had rented a shed from one Stein. Stein retained a key to the shed and accepted deliveries on behalf of the defendant. When the police approached Stein and informed him of their suspicion that the defendant was receiving goods obtained through fraud, Stein consented to a search of the shed.

In upholding the search, the court noted two significant factors. First, Stein had a key to the shed and, second, more than a mere landlord-tenant relationship existed, since Stein was empowered to take deliveries on behalf of the defendant. The court also noted that Stein had a right to exculpate himself from implication in the defendant's scheme.

Considering all these factors cumulatively, the court concluded that, in this situation, Stein could give consent to the search. Thus, the search was not unreasonable in contravention of the Fourth Amendment.

Dr. Panitz, in this case, gave his consent to the search of Overton's locker. The dissenting opinion suggests, however, that Dr. Panitz' consent was not freely given, because he acted under compulsion of the invalid search warrant. If this were the case, his consent might be rendered somewhat questionable. However, Dr. Panitz testified that: "Being responsible for the order, assignment, and maintenance of the physical facilities, if *any* report were given to me by *anyone* of an article or item of the nature that does not belong there, or of an illegal nature, I would inspect the locker." (Italics supplied.)

This testimony demonstrates beyond doubt that Dr. Panitz would have consented as he did regardless of the presence of the invalid search warrant.

The power of Dr. Panitz to give his consent to this search arises out of the distinct relationship between school authorities and students.

The school authorities have an obligation to maintain discipline over the students. It is recognized that when large numbers of teenagers are gathered together in such an environment, their inexperience and lack of mature judgment can often create hazards to each other. Parents, who surrender their children to this type of environment, in order that they may continue developing both intellectually and socially, have a right to expect certain safeguards.

It is in the high school years particularly that parents are justifiably concerned that their children not become accustomed to antisocial behavior, such as the use of illegal drugs. The susceptibility to suggestion of students of high school age increases the danger. Thus, it is the affirmative obligation of the school authorities to investigate any charge that a student is using or possessing narcotics and to take appropriate steps, if the charge is substantiated.

When Overton was assigned his locker, he, like all the other students at Mount Vernon High School, gave the combination to his home room teacher who, in turn, returned it to an office where it was kept on file. The students at Mount Vernon are well aware that the school authorities possess the combinations of their lockers. It appears understood that the lock and the combination are provided in order that each student may have exclusive possession of the locker vis-à-vis other students, but the student does not have such exclusivity over the locker as against the school authorities. In fact, the school issues regulations regarding what may and may not be kept in the lockers and presumably can spot check to insure compliance. The vice-

principal testified that he had, on occasion, inspected the lockers of students.

Indeed, it is doubtful if a school would be properly discharging its duty of supervision over the students, if it failed to retain control over the lockers. Not only have the school authorities a right to inspect but this right becomes a duty when suspicion arises that something of an illegal nature may be secreted there. When Dr. Panitz learned of the detectives' suspicion, he was obligated to inspect the locker. This interest, together with the nonexclusive nature of the locker, empowered him to consent to the search by the officers.

Accordingly, the order of the Appellate Term should be reversed and the matter remitted to that court for consideration of the other points raised by the defendant which were not decided on the prior appeal.

---

*Search of Student by School Official
Working in Conjunction
with Police Liaison Officer Held Reasonable*

—··—·—··—·—

Cason v. Cook

—··—·—··—·—

United States Court of Appeals
Eighth Circuit, 1987.
810 F.2d. 1988.

. . . Shy [Cason] was a student at North High School in Des Moines, Iowa. At approximately 12:20 p.m. on that date, [May 1, 1983] a student approached the appellee Connie Cook, the vice-principal of North High School, and told her that her locker had been broken into and that she was missing a pair of sweatpants and a duffle bag. She also reported that a friend was missing a pair of sweatpants. At approximately 12:40 p.m., another student approached Ms. Cook and reported that her wallet and coin purse had been taken from her gym locker. The student reported that the wallet contained $65 along with several credit cards. Ms. Cook recorded a detailed description of the missing items.

Standing with Ms. Cook when these reports were made was the appellee Wanda Jones, a police officer who had been assigned to North High School as a liaison officer pursuant to an established police liaison program between the Des Moines Police Department and the school district. The liaison program is funded jointly by the police department and the school district. The officer does not wear a police uniform and drives an unmarked automobile. The liaison officer is instructed to cooperate with the school officials.

After receiving the reports of stolen items, Ms. Cook decided to investigate the alleged thefts and asked Ms. Jones if she would accompany her to the locker room. Ms. Cook interviewed several students in the locker room and was supplied with the names of four students who had been seen in the locker area around the time of the thefts: Shy Cason, Jerrie Harvey, Monica Harvey and Tabatha Prather. These four students did not have permission to be in the locker area at this time nor were they assigned to the gym class of the prior period. Ms. Cook also recalled having seen Shy, Jerrie and Monica together in the lobby just prior to receiving the reports of the thefts.

Ms. Cook and Ms. Jones then proceeded to the office where Ms. Cook checked the schedules of the four students. Ms. Cook again asked Ms. Jones to accompany her as she interviewed each of the students. Jerrie was removed from her classroom by Ms. Cook and was taken into an empty classroom where she was questioned. Ms. Jones did not participate in this questioning and in fact, remained in the hallway during this time period. Shy and Monica were then removed from their classroom and taken into an empty restroom. Shy testified that Monica remained outside and that she was taken into the restroom and that Ms. Cook locked the door. Ms. Jones was also inside the locked restroom but again did not participate in any questioning of Shy.

Ms. Cook informed Shy why she was being questioned and allowed Shy an opportunity to respond. After Shy admitted being in the locker room but denied having any of the missing items, Ms. Cook told Shy that she was going to search her purse. Ms. Cook then took Shy's purse and dumped the contents onto a shelf in the restroom. In Shy's purse was a coin purse that matched exactly the description of the missing coin purse. After this purse was found, Shy testified that Ms. Jones conducted a pat-down search of Shy from her shoulders to her toes while Shy was made to stand against the wall with her hands up and legs spread.

Monica and Shy were then taken to the office area and on the way, Shy was asked by Ms. Cook to open her locker and a search of the locker was conducted by Ms. Cook. At the office, Monica and Shy were placed in separate rooms with Ms. Jones remaining with Monica while Ms. Cook continued to question Shy. Ms. Jones did not participate in the questioning of either Shy or Monica at this point. It was learned that Shy and Jerrie were in fact involved with the thefts and Jerrie was summoned to come to the office. Ms. Jones did participate in a joint interview with Shy and Jerrie and when the two girls could not agree on the events that had transpired in the locker room, Ms. Jones presented each girl with a juvenile appearance card. Juvenile appearance cards are utilized by the police liaison program whenever possible in lieu of an arrest. The card required each of the girls and their parents to report to Ms. Jones' office at the police station on May 19, 1983.

Shy's mother was not made aware of the events of this day until she arrived to pick up Shy after school. No attempt was made to contact Shy's mother prior to any questioning or the search of Shy and her possessions. While at school, Shy was not informed of a right to remain silent or of a right to counsel. Both Shy and her mother signed a waiver and consent form before they visited with Ms. Jones at her office on the 19th. Each of the girls was suspended from school and after meeting with Ms. Jones no further action was taken.

. . . In 1985, the Supreme Court addressed the Fourth Amendment and its application in the school setting. . . . [T]he Court held that the Fourth Amendment right

to be free from unreasonable search and seizure applies to a search by a school official.
. . .

After the Court determined that the Fourth Amendment applied in the school setting, it further discussed the extent of the protection afforded the schoolchildren. Balancing the interests of the children's privacy and the need to maintain discipline in the school setting, the Court held that the warrant requirement was unsuited to the school environment: "requiring a teacher to obtain a warrant before searching a child suspected of an infraction of school rules (or of the criminal law) would unduly interfere with the maintenance of the swift and informal disciplinary procedures needed in the schools." . . . In addition to eliminating the warrant requirement, the Court also reduced the level of suspicion of illicit activity that is needed to justify a search. "[T]he legality of a search of a student should depend simply on the reasonableness, under all the circumstances, of the search." . . .

In determining whether a given search is reasonable, the Court provided further guidance: The inquiry into the reasonableness of a search is twofold: First, the action must be justified at its inception and second, the scope of the search must be reasonably related to the circumstances which justified the interference in the first place. . . . A search satisfies the first inquiry when there are reasonable grounds for suspecting that the search will uncover evidence of a rule or criminal violation. The second inquiry is satisfied when "the measures adopted are reasonably related to the objectives of the search and not excessively intrusive in light of the age and sex of the student and the nature of the infraction." . . .

The Court did note, however, that it was *not* addressing the question of what standard would apply when a search is conducted by school officials *in conjunction with* or *at the behest of* law enforcement agencies and expressed no opinion on that subject. . . . This is the precise question that is presented to this court by the case at bar: Whether the reasonableness standard should apply when a school official acts in conjunction with a police

liaison officer. The district court found that the reasonableness standard was the correct standard and that the appellee Cook had met this standard and thus there was no violation of the appellant's constitutional rights. We agree.

There is no evidence to support the proposition that the activities were at *the behest of* a law enforcement agency. The uncontradicted evidence showed that Ms. Cook, the school official, conducted the investigation of the thefts that had been reported to her. Ms. Jones' involvement was limited to a pat-down search conducted after a coin purse matching the description of the one stolen was found and to briefly interviewing Shy and Jerrie and presenting juvenile appearance cards to the girls. At most, then, this case represents a police officer working *in conjunction with* school officials.

In *Martens v. District No. 220*, 620 F.Supp. 29 (N.D.Ill.1985), the district court addressed a very similar question. The school official had received an anonymous phone call implicating the plaintiff in drug-related activities. The plaintiff was called into the office but refused to consent to a search until his parents were contacted. *Id.* at 30. While waiting in the office, a deputy sheriff came in (the deputy had come to the school on another matter). The deputy told the plaintiff that based on his experience it would be best to cooperate. The deputy then asked the plaintiff to empty his pockets and the plaintiff complied.

The court recognized that the involvement of the police officer distinguished this case from *T.L.O.*; however, the court held that, "[T]he interest that prompted the *T.L.O.* Court to waive the warrant requirement and to adopt a reasonableness standard—preserving swift and informal disciplinary procedures— would not be served by imposing warrant and probable cause requirements here" in light of the limited role of the deputy. The district court noted that the deputy had not helped to develop the facts that prompted the search of the plaintiff nor had he directed that the plaintiff be detained and searched. There was no indication that but for the deputy's involvement, the plaintiff would not have been searched. Finding that the school official's actions were based on reasonable suspicion and reasonable in scope, the court held that there was no constitutional violation. . . .

We find the reasoning of the district court in *Martens* to be persuasive. The imposition of a probable cause warrant requirement based on the limited involvement of Ms. Jones would not serve the interest of preserving swift and informal disciplinary procedures in schools. Ms. Jones did not conduct any of the initial interviews of the students and participated in a pat-down search only after evidence was discovered. Ms. Cook, on the other hand, made the initial determination to investigate the reported thefts and conducted the investigation. This school official procured the names of four students who had been seen in the locker room area at an unscheduled time and without permission. Ms. Cook also recalled having personally observed these same students together in the hall just prior to receiving the reports of the thefts. The students were removed from their classrooms by Ms. Cook and each was provided with an explanation as to the reason for their removal and was provided with an opportunity to respond prior to any search.

It was Ms. Cook who conducted the search of Shy's purse which led to the discovery of the coin purse. It was only after this discovery that Ms. Jones conducted a limited pat-down search of Shy. The only other involvement of the police liaison officer occurred when the students were unable to agree on the events that had transpired in the locker room. This involvement was limited to some questioning and the issuance of juvenile appearance cards.

It is clear that the correct standard to apply under the circumstances presented in this case is the standard enunciated by the Court in *T.L.O.:* Whether the search was reasonable under all of the circumstances. Based on the foregoing discussion of the facts, the initial search of the appellant's purse was based on a reasonable suspicion that Shy Cason had been involved in a violation of school rules and of the criminal law. The subsequent pat-down search was made when this suspicion was increased due to the finding of physical evidence in the appellant's possession. In

addition, the scope of the search was reasonable. The theft victim had reported $65 as missing along with her wallet. Due to the nature of this missing item, patting down the appellant was not "excessively intrusive in light of the age and sex of the student and the nature of the infraction." . . . We do not hold that a search of a student by a school official working in conjunction with law enforcement personnel could never rise to a constitutional violation, but only that under the record as presented to the court, no such violation occurred here. . . .

Since we have found no constitutional violation, the remaining allegations against the Des Moines Police Department, the appellee Anderson and the Des Moines Independent School District need not be addressed. . . .

Accordingly, the order of the district court is affirmed.

---

*Search of Student's Car and
Locked Briefcase Held Constitutional*

— — — — — — — —

State of Washington v. Slattery

— — — — — — — —

Court of Appeals of Washington,
Division 1, 1990.
56 Wn. App.820, 787 P.2d. 932.

COLEMAN, Chief Judge. On February 26, 1987, a student contacted Vice Principal Sterling Thurston in his office at Thomas Jefferson High School. The student told Thurston that Mike Slattery was selling marijuana in the parking lot. Thurston believed the information to be reliable because of his past experience with the informant and because he had received other reports that Slattery was involved with drugs.

Thurston called Slattery into his office and asked him to empty his pockets. Slattery was carrying $230 cash in small bills and a piece of paper with a telephone pager number on it.

Thurston recently had learned that pagers are often used by drug dealers. Thurston then called security. A security officer searched Slattery's locker, but found nothing. When Thurston told Slattery that they would have to search his car, Slattery refused. One of the security officers told Slattery that they would get into his car one way or another. After speaking to his mother on the telephone, Slattery gave the officials his keys.

The officials found a pager and a notebook inside the car. The notebook had names with dollar amounts written next to the names. The officials then opened the locked trunk of the car. Inside they found a locked briefcase. Slattery first said that he did not know who owned the briefcase, then said a friend owned it and that he did not know the combination. The security officers then pried open the briefcase and discovered what turned out to be 80.2 grams of marijuana. The police were called and Slattery was arrested. . . .

The Fourth Amendment to the United States Constitution and the Washington Constitution, article 1, section 7, protects persons from unreasonable searches and seizures.[1] Government agents, therefore, must have a search warrant unless some other condition justifies a warrantless search. . . . When, as here, school officials are acting under the authority of the State, Fourth Amendment and Constitution, article 1, section 7 protections apply. . . . Some of the conditions that have been used to justify exceptions to the warrant requirement are (1) searches incident to arrest, . . . (2) exigent circumstances, . . . (3) searches of students conducted by school authorities, *New Jersey v. T.L.O.*, ... The school search exception applies in this case.

Under the school search exception, school officials may search students if, under all the circumstances, the search is reasonable. . . . Whether a search is reasonable depends upon the satisfaction of two criteria. First, the action must have been justified at its inception. . . . Second, the search conducted must have been reasonably related in scope to the circumstances that justified the interference in the first place. . . . The rationale for the school search exception is

that school teachers and administrators have a substantial interest "in maintaining discipline in the classroom and on school grounds," which weighs against a child's interest in privacy.

Appellant concedes that it may have been reasonable to search him and his locker, but argues that it was unreasonable to extend the search to his car and the locked briefcase in the car. The school search exception is a limited one, appellant argues, and applies only to unintrusive searches, such as of a school locker. . . .

. . . The vice principal was told that appellant, who was nearly 18 years old, was selling marijuana in the parking lot. The vice principal had reason to believe the information, based upon his past experience with the informant and reports the vice principal had received earlier from others that appellant was involved with drugs. Appellant was carrying a large amount of money in small bills and a pager number that reasonably could lead the principal to expect to find drugs in appellant's possession. Drug use was a serious, ongoing problem at the school. School officials were confronted with exigent circumstances that warranted an immediate search because Slattery or a friend could have removed his car from the school grounds.

When the school officials did not find any drugs on Slattery or in his locker, they logically went outside to search his car, which was parked in the school parking lot where the informant had said Slattery had been selling marijuana. The officials found a notebook with names and dollar amounts next to the names and a telephone pager—then the officials found a locked briefcase.

The school officials' initial search of Slattery's person was justified at its inception. They had reasonable grounds for suspecting that the search of Slattery would turn up evidence that he had violated the law. The searches of Slattery's locker, car, and briefcase were reasonably related in scope to the circumstances which justified the interference in the first place. To limit the school search exception to a search of a student's body or his locker would be anomalous in light of the rationales of *T.L.O.*

▆▆ ENDNOTES

1. Board of Education of Rogers, Arkansas v. McCluskey, 458 U.S. 966, 102 S.Ct. 3469 (1982).

2. 420 U.S. 308, 95 S.Ct. 992 (1975).

3. Ibid.

4. Board of Education of Rogers, Arkansas v. McCluskey, op cit., 488 U.S. at 970, 102 S.Ct. at 3471.

5. Newton Edwards, *The Courts and the Public Schools* (Chicago: University of Chicago Press, 1955), p. 604.

6. State *ex rel. Burpee* v. Burton, 45 Wis. 150, 30 Am. Rep. 706, (1878).

7. Ibid.

8. Thomas Hobbes, *Leviathan* (New York: Collier, MacMillan Publishing Company, 1962), p. 132. Hobbes conveyed the newly published *Leviathan* to Mr. Francis Godolphin, Paris, April 15/25, 1651.

9. Jean-Jacques Rousseau, *The Social Contract and Discourses,* translated by G. D. H. Cole, (London: J. M. Dent & Sons Ltd: Everyman's Library); *A Discourse on Political Economy,* first published in 1758, p. 149.

10. Ibid. p. 192.

11. Ibid.

12. Edward Hallett Carr, *The Twenty Years' Crisis, 1919–1939* (New York: Harper Torchbooks, Harper & Row Company, 1964; originally published in 1939), p. 42.

13. Ibid.

14. Ibid.

15. State v. Randall, 79 Mo. App. 226 (1899).

16. See Lander v. Seaver, 32 Vt. 114, 76 Am. Dec. 156 (1859).

17. Ibid.

18. Ibid.

19. Ibid.

20. Richardson v. Braham, 125 Neb. 142, 249 N.W. 557 (1933).

21. 469 U.S. 325, 105 S.Ct. 733 (1985).

22. Ginsberg v. New York, 390 U.S. 629, 88 S.Ct. 1274 (1968); Board of Education of Island Trees v. Pico, 457 U.S. 853 102 S.Ct. 2799 (1982).

23. Bethel School District No. 403 v. Frazer, 478 U.S. 675, 106 S.Ct. 3159 (1986).

24. Hurtado v. California, 110 U.S. 516, 4 S.Ct. 111 (1884).

25. Adkins v. Children's Hospital, 261 U.S. 525, 43 S.Ct. 394 (1923).

26. Valley National Bank of Phoenix v. Glover, 62 Ariz. 538, 159 P.2d 292 (1945).

27. 262 U.S. 390, 43 S.Ct. 625 (1923); see Pierce v. Society of Sisters, 268 U.S. 510, 45 S.Ct. 571 (1925).

28. Ibid.

29. Meyer v. Nebraska, op cit.; Pierce v. Society of Sisters, op cit.

30. Kent v. Dulles, 357 U.S. 116, 78 S.Ct. 1113 (1958); United States v. Guest, 383 U.S. 745, 86 S.Ct. 1170 (1966); Shapiro v. Thompson, 394 U.S. 618, 89 S.Ct. 1322 (1969).

31. Richards v. Thurston, 424 F.2d 1281 (1st Cir.1970); Breen v. Kahl, 296 F.Supp. 702 (W.D.Wis.1969), affirmed 419 F.2d 1034 (7th Cir.1969), cert. denied 398 U.S. 937, 90 S.Ct. 1836 (1970).

32. 430 U.S. 651, 97 S.Ct. 1401, (1977).

33. Ibid.

34. Ingraham v. Wright, 525 F.2d 909 (5th Cir. 1976).

35. Ibid.

36. Hall v. Tawney, 621 F.2d 607 (4th Cir. 1980).

37. Garcia v. Miera, 817 F.2d 650 (10th Cir. 1987).

38. Hall v. Tawney, op cit.

39. Ibid.

40. Ibid.

41. Metzger v. Osbeck, 841 F.2d 518 (3d Cir. 1988).

42. Wise v. Pea Ridge School District, 855 F.2d 560 (8th Cir. 1988).

43. Hall v. Tawney, op cit.

44. 294 F.2d 150 (1961), *cert. denied,* 368 U.S. 930, 82 S.Ct. 368 (1961).

45. 295 F.Supp. 978 (W.D.Wis.1968), affirmed 418 F.2d 163 (7th Cir.1969).

46. Hobson v. Bailey, 309 F.Supp. 1393 (W.D.Tenn.1970); Zanders v. Louisiana State Board of Education, 281 F.Supp. 747 (W.D.La.1968).

47. Joint Anti-Fascist Refugee Committee v. McGrath, 341 U.S. 123, 71 S.Ct. 624 (1951) (concurring opinion of Justice Frankfurter).

48. Dixon v. Alabama State Board of Education, 294 F.2d 150 (5th Cir.1961), cert. denied 368 U.S. 930, 82 S.Ct. 368 (1961). For an excellent discussion of procedural due process, see William G. Buss, "Procedural Due Process for School Discipline: Probing the Constitutional Outline," *University of Pennsylvania Law Review* 119 (1971): 545–641.

49. 233 F.Supp. 396 (N.D.Fla.1963).

50. 419 U.S. 565, 95 S.Ct. 729 (1975).

51. Marjorie R. Freiman, "Unequal and Inadequate Protection Under the Law: State Child Abuse Statutes," *George Washington Law Review* 50, no. 2 (January 1982): 243–44.

52. Ibid., p. 252.

53. Public Law 93–247, 88 Stat. 4 (1974) [codified as amended at 42 U.S.C.A. § 5101–5107.

54. Freiman, "Unequal and Inadequate Protection."

55. 42 U.S.C.A. § 5112.

56. Freiman, "Unequal and Inadequate Protection," pp. 253–54.

57. 42 U.S.C.A. § 5102.

58. Freiman, "Unequal and Inadequate Protection," p. 254.

59. Commonwealth of Virginia, Va. Code 1950, Chapter 12.1, § 63.1–248.1.

60. Ibid., § 63.1–248.2.

61. Freiman, "Unequal and Inadequate Protection," pp. 252–69.

62. Arthur Schwartz and Harold Hirsh, "Child Abuse and Neglect: A Survey of the Law," *Medical Trial Technique Quarterly* 28 (Winter 1982): 298–302.

63. Ibid., p. 247.

64. Jody Aaron, "Civil Liability for Teachers' Negligent Failure to Report Suspected Child Abuse," *Wayne Law Review* 28 (1981): 187.

65. Sanford N. Katz, et al., "Legal Research on Child Abuse and Neglect: Past and Future," *Family Law Quarterly* XI, no. 2 (Summer 1977): 151.

66. Freiman, "Unequal and Inadequate Protection," p. 259 (footnote).

67. Commonwealth of Virginia, Va. Code 1950, at § 63.1–248.5.

68. 71 Or.App. 751, 694 P.2d 569, 22 Ed.Law Rep. 1001 (1985).

69. Freiman, "Unequal and Inadequate Protection," p. 263.

70. Ibid.

71. Ibid.

72. Schwartz, "Child Abuse and Neglect," p. 311.

73. Ibid.

74. 17 Cal.3d 399, 131 Cal.Rptr. 69, 551 P.2d 389 (1976).

75. Aaron, "Civil Liability."

76. Schwartz, "Child Abuse and Neglect," p. 304.

77. State of Oklahoma, *Oklahoma Statutes Annotated*. Title 21, § 846.

78. Frieman, "Unequal and Inadequate Protection," pp. 260–61.

79. Ibid.

80. Schwartz, "Child Abuse and Neglect," pp. 304–5.

81. Aaron, "Civil Liability," p. 191. See also Chapter 11 on tort liability of this book for further discussions of a teacher's potential liability.

82. Schenck v. United States, 249 U.S. 47, 39 S.Ct. 247 (1919).

83. Whitney v. California, 274 U.S. 357, 47 S.Ct. 641 (1927); Bridges v. California, 314 U.S. 252, 62 S.Ct. 190 (1941).

84. Whitney v. California, op cit.

85. Bridges v. California, op cit.

86. Tinker v. Des Moines Independent Community School District, 393 U.S. 503, 89 S.Ct. 733 (1969).

87. 431 F.2d 594, (6th Cir. 1970).

88. Tinker, op cit. at 737.

89. Bethel School District No. 403 v. Fraser, 478 U.S. 675, 106 S.Ct. 3159 (1986).

90. Bethel, op cit.

91. Pugsley v. Sellmeyer, 158 Ark. 247, 250 S.W. 538 (1923).

92. Mitchell v. McCall, 273 Ala. 604, 143 So.2d 629 (1962).

93. 445 F.2d 932 (9th Cir. 1971).

94. Jackson v. Dorrier, 424 F.2d 213 (6th Cir. 1970), cert denied, 400 U.S. 850, 91 S.Ct. 55 (1970).

95. Richards v. Thurston, 424 F.2d 1281, (1st Cir. 1970). See also Breen v. Kahl, 419 F.2d 1034 (7th Cir. 1969) holding regulation unconstitutional.

96. 392 F.2d 697 (5th Cir. 1968).

97. Stevenson v. Board of Education of Wheeler County, Georgia, 426 F.2d 1154 (5th Cir. 1970).

98. Massie v. Henry, 455 F.2d 779 (4th Cir. 1972). See also Humphries v. Lincoln Parish School Board, 467 So.2d 870 (La. App. Cir. 1985); Dominco v. Rapids Parish School Board, 675 F.2d 100 (5th Cir. 1982).

99. New York Times Co. v. United States, 403 U.S. 713, 91 S.Ct. 2140 (1971).

100. William Blackstone, *Commentaries on the Laws of England* book 4, chapter II, (London, 1765–1769), p. 153.

101. Levy, op cit., p. 213.

102. People v. Croswell, 3 Johnson's (N.Y.) Cases 336 (1804).

103. John Thompson, *An Enquiry, Concerning the Liberty, and Licentiousness of the Press* (New York, 1801), 84 pp., reprinted by DeCapo Press, 1970.

104. 376 U.S. 254, 84 S.Ct. 710 (1964).

105. "Trial of William Cobbett," Nov. 1797, in Francis Wharten, ed., *State Trials of the United States During the Administration of Washington and Adams* (Philadelphia, 1849), pp. 323–24. See also Levy, op cit., p. 197.

106. New York Times v. United States, op cit.

107. 484 U.S. 260 108 S.Ct. 562 (1988).

108. Hazelwood, op cit. at 570.

109. 393 U.S. 503, 513, 89 S.Ct. 733, 740 (1969).

110. Leeb v. DeLong, 198 Cal. App. 3d 47, 243 Cal. Rptr. 494 (4 Dist. 1988). See Trachtman v. Anker, 563 F.2d 512 (2d Cir. 1977), cert denied. 435 U.S. 925, 98 S.Ct. 1491 (1978).

111. Baughman v. Freienmuth, 478 F.2d 1345 (4th Cir. 1973).

112. See "Search and Seizure in Education," Mary Jane Connelly, Ph.D. diss., Virginia Tech University, 1982.

113. *Black's Law Dictionary* (St. Paul, Minn.: West Publishing Company), 1968, p. 1616.

114. Levy, op cit., p. 242.

115. Ibid.

116. Bellnier v. Lund, 438 F.Supp. 47 (N.D.N.Y. 1977).

117. State v. Stein, 203 Kan. 638, 456 P.2d 1 (1969), cert. denied 397 U.S. 947, 90 S.Ct. 966 (1970).

118. New Jersey v. T.L.O., 469 U.S. 325, 105 S.Ct. 733 (1985).

119. Ibid.

120. R.D.L. v. State, 499 So.2d 31 (Fla. App. 2 Dist. 1986).

121. State v. Slattery, 56 Wn.App.820, 787 P.2d 932 (1990).

122. Shamberg v. State, 762 P.2d 488 (Alaska App. 1988). See also Coffman v. State 782 S.W.2d 249 (Tex. App. 1989).

123. Wynn v. Board of Education of Vestavia Hills, 508 So.2d 1170 (Ala. 1987).

124. Shamberg v. State, 762 P.2d 488 (Alaska App. 1988).

125. Cales v. Howell Public Schools, 635 F.Supp. 454 (E.D. Mich. 1985).

126. T.L.O., op cit.

127. Kuehn v. Reston School District No. 403, 103 Wn.2d 594, 694 P.2d 1078 (1985).

128. Burnham v. West, 681 F.Supp. 1160 (E.D.Va.1987).

129. Levy, op cit., p.244.

130. 639 F.2d 662 (10th Cir. 1981).

131. 475 F.Supp.1012 (N.D.Ind 1979), opinion adopted on this issue and reversed on another issue 631 F.2d 91 (7th Cir.1980), 635 F.2d 582 (7th Cir. 1980), rehearing denied cert. denied 451 U.S. 1022, 101 S.Ct. 3015 (1981).

132. 499 F.Supp. 223 (E.D.Tex.1980).

133. 690 F.2d 470 (5th Cir.1982).

134. Ibid., p. 475.

135. Ibid., p. 477.

136. Ibid., pp. 481–82.

137. M.M. v. Anker, 607 F.2d 588 (2d Cir.1979).

138. 438 F.Supp. 47 (N.D.N.Y.1977).

139. Rone v. Daviess County Board of Education, 655 S.W.2d 28 (Ky.App.1983).

140. Renfrow, op cit.

141. Doe v. Renfrow 631 F.2d 91 (7th Cir.1980).

142. 232 U.S. 383, 34 S.Ct. 341 (1914).

143. 338 U.S. 25, 69 S.Ct. 1359 (1949).

144. Wolf, 338 U.S. at 25, 69 S.Ct. at 1360.

145. Wolf, 338 U.S. at 26, 69 S.Ct. at 1361.

146. 367 U.S. 643, 81 S.Ct. 1684 (1961).

147. Skinner v. Railway Labor Executives' Association, 489 U.S. 602, 109 S.Ct. 1402 (1989).

148. National Treasury Employees Union v. Von Raab, 489 U.S. 656, 109 S.Ct. 1384 (1989).

149. Odenheim v. Carlstadt-East Rutherford Regional School District, 211 N.J. Super. 54, 510 A.2d 709 (Ch. 1985).

150. Schaill v. Tippecanoe County School Corporation, 864 F.2d 1309 (7th Cir. 1988).

151. Brooks v. East Chambers Consolidated Independent School District, 730 F.Supp. 759 (S.D. Tex. 1989).

CHAPTER 9

Rights of Handicapped Children

Programs for handicapped children developed slowly in public schools. Meager financial resources and public apathy combined to prevent significant efforts to extend an equal educational opportunity to the handicapped until relatively recently.

During the 1940s through 1960s, several states distributed categorical funds to local school districts for handicapped programs. A few states required local school districts to establish programs for the handicapped in order to receive state foundation program allocations; but such efforts were not comprehensive and failed to address the special needs of most handicapped children, particularly those who were severely handicapped.

It was not until the latter part of the 1960s and early 1970s that pervasive concern for the equality of educational opportunity swept the nation. During the Johnson presidency that concern had expanded to touch the handicapped. The watershed in development of handicapped programs in public schools, however, came with a few key court decisions and the federal government's landmark legislation in 1975 entitled the Education for All Handicapped Children Act (EAHCA). From that point, comprehensive educational programs were rapidly developed in all states.[1]

To better understand the recent court cases involving this federal legislation, it is instructive to briefly review the early antecedents of provision of educational opportunity for the handicapped.

◼ A HISTORY OF NEGLECT*

Special education programs in the United States originated during the early nineteenth century, when isolated advocates of handicapped children established educational programs for specific handicaps or pressured state legislatures to pass legislation to achieve this purpose. The earliest known school for handicapped students was established in Hartford, Connecticut, in 1817. Thomas Hopkins Gallaudet founded the American Asylum for the Education of the Deaf and Dumb (now the American School for the Deaf) two years after returning from France, where he was newly trained in the French method of manual communication for the deaf. Gallaudet brought with him a deaf teacher, Laurent Clerc, and together the two men traveled to various American cities soliciting money from private sources to establish their school.[2]

The Connecticut legislature appropriated $5,000 for the school in 1816, and by 15 April 1817, it opened its doors to seven students. In 1819, the school's future was assured when the federal government turned over 23,000 acres of land to the school, which the school in turn sold, accruing over $300,000. During the same year, other states began providing the

* The authors wish to express sincere appreciation to Patricia Anthony, Ph.D., University of Massachusetts, Amherst, for preparation of this portion of the chapter on rights of handicapped children.

tuition moneys necessary to send deaf children to the American School.[3]

A second school, the New York Institution for the Education of the Deaf and Dumb, was opened in New York in 1818. This school was funded by private donations, but in 1821 the State of New York appropriated funds for its support. The New York school was the first day school for deaf students, but soon evolved into a residential school program.

Pennsylvania was the site of the third school founded in this country for deaf students. Initially established in 1820, also as a private school, the state began supporting it in 1821 with funds to provide an education for fifty students. From 1823 to 1844, three new state schools were built for deaf students in Kentucky, Ohio, and Virginia. From 1844 to 1860, seventeen new schools for deaf students were established, and in 1864 the National Deaf Mute College was founded in Washington, D.C. The name later was changed to Gallaudet College in honor of the man who first began deaf education in the United States.

The need for educational services for other handicaps was not ignored. In 1830, due to the tireless efforts of Horace Mann, the Massachusetts State Legislature passed into law a "Resolve for Erecting a Lunatic Hospital,"[4] and the first state hospital for the mentally ill was founded in the city of Worcester, Massachusetts. Mann, of course, was best known for his labors in establishing free compulsory public education for all children.

Elected in 1827 by the town of Dedham, Massachusetts, to the Massachusetts State Legislature, Mann sought legislative support in abolishing the deplorable living conditions of the insane.[5] Forming a committee to study the plight of the insane, Mann toured poorhouses and gaols (jails) throughout Massachusetts, gathering evidence to encourage legislative action. In 1830, Mann's bill was passed by both the Massachusetts House and Senate.

Other states were not idle in efforts to aid handicapped children. In 1832, New York established a school for blind students, and by 1852, New York, Pennsylvania, and Massachusetts all had appropriated money for programs for mentally retarded children.[6] In 1869, day programs for deaf students were started

in Boston and in 1896, programs for mentally retarded students were started in Providence, Rhode Island. Public school classes for physically handicapped and blind students were begun in Chicago in 1900. Consequently, by the early twentieth century, handicapped children had gained entry into the public schools in several states.

Severely handicapped students had a difficult time conforming to the structure and expectations of public school systems. Schools were ill equipped to handle students who exhibited aberrant characteristics. In 1893, a Massachusetts court ruled that student behavior resulting from "imbecility" was grounds for expulsion, thereby barring many mentally retarded students from public schools.[7] A later decision[8] ruled that a handicapped student, although academically capable, could be excluded from regular public school classes because his handicap had "a depressing and nauseating effect on the teachers and school children."[9]

This ruling prevented severely handicapped children suffering from cerebral palsy or poliomyelitis from attending regular public school day classes. Since special classes for these severely handicapped students had not yet been created in many cities, parents of such children had to resort to residential schools, private tutors, or forgo formal education completely.

THE TURNING POINT

Despite these earlier judicial setbacks, social conditions of the twentieth century impacted favorably upon the growth of education services for the handicapped. The return home of disabled World War I veterans focused national attention upon the need for handicapped educational programs.

In 1918, the Soldiers' Rehabilitation Act was passed by Congress, followed in 1920 by the Smith-Bankhead Act.[10] Both pieces of legislation offered vocational rehabilitation services in the form of job training and counseling. By 1944, these acts were amended to include services for mentally ill individuals and the mentally retarded, as well as to provide additional funds for research and training programs.[11]

Another condition significantly affecting handicapped children's quest for equal educational opportunity was the court-ordered desegregation of the public schools.[12] While specifically referring to the rights of black children, the legal mandate of *Brown v. Board of Education* set a precedent for the extension of educational access to all children, including the handicapped.[13]

A significant turning point for handicapped children's rights occurred in 1971, when a federal district court ruled that retarded children in Pennsylvania were entitled to a free public education.[14] The ruling stipulated that whenever possible, retarded children must be educated in regular classrooms rather than be segregated from the normal school population. The court said a

> free, public program of education and training appropriate to the child's capacity, within the context of a presumption that, among the alternative programs of education and training required by statute to be available, placement in a regular public school class is preferable to placement in a special public school class [i.e., a class for "handicapped" children] and placement in a special public school class is preferable to placement in any other type of program of education and training . . . .[15]

Procedural due process and periodic reevaluations of retarded children were also part of the court's consent agreement.

The Mills Case

In 1972, *Mills v. Board of Education of the District of Columbia*[16] expanded the Pennsylvania (PARC) decision to include all handicapped children. Emphasizing the need for appropriate educational services in the District of Columbia, the court pointed out that there are "22,000 retarded, emotionally disturbed, blind, deaf, and speech, or learning disabled children, and perhaps as many as 18,000 of these children are not being furnished with programs of specialized education."[17] In granting summary judgment in favor of the plaintiffs, the court adopted a comprehensive plan that had been formulated by the District of Columbia Board of Education. Included in the plan were provisions for (1) a free appropriate education, (2) an Individualized Educational Plan (IEP), and (3) due process procedures. The groundwork for future federal legislation in the area of handicapped children's rights to an education had been laid.

Procedural Due Process Is Required to Reassign Handicapped Children

—————————————————

Mills v. Board of Education of District of Columbia

—————————————————

United States District Court,
District of Columbia, 1972.
348 F.Supp. 866.

WADDY, District Judge. This is a civil action brought on behalf of seven children of school age by their next friends in which they seek a declaration of rights and to enjoin the defendants from excluding them from the District of Columbia Public Schools and/or denying them publicly supported education and to compel the defendants to provide them with immediate and adequate education and educational facilities in the public schools or alternative placement at public expense. They also seek additional and ancillary relief to effectuate the primary relief. They allege that although they can profit from an education either in regular classrooms with supportive services or in special classes adapted to their needs, they have been labeled as behavioral problems, mentally retarded, emotionally disturbed or hyperactive, and denied admission to the public schools or excluded therefrom after admission, with no provision for alternative educational placement or periodic review. . . .

The genesis of this case is found (1) in the failure of the District of Columbia to provide publicly supported education and training to plaintiffs and other "exceptional" children, members of their class, and (2) the excluding, suspending, expelling, reassigning and transferring of "exceptional" children from regular public school classes without affording them due process of law.

The problem of providing special education for "exceptional" children (mentally retarded, emotionally disturbed, physically handicapped, hyperactive and other children with behavioral problems) is one of major proportions in the District of Columbia. The precise number of such children cannot be stated because the District has continuously failed to comply with Section 31–208 of the District of Columbia Code which requires a census of all children aged three to eighteen in the District to be taken. Plaintiffs estimate that there are "22,000 retarded, emotionally disturbed, blind, deaf, and speech or learning disabled children, and perhaps as many as 18,000 of these children are not being furnished with programs of specialized education." According to data prepared by the Board of Education, Division of Planning, Research and Evaluation, the District of Columbia provides publicly supported special education programs of various descriptions to at least 3,880 school-age children. However, in a 1971 report to the Department of Health, Education and Welfare, the District of Columbia Public Schools admitted that an estimated 12,340 handicapped children were not to be served in the 1971–72 school year.

Each of the minor plaintiffs in this case qualifies as an "exceptional" child. . . .

Although all of the named minor plaintiffs are identified as Negroes the class they represent is not limited by their race. They sue on behalf of and represent all other District of Columbia residents of school age who are eligible for a free public education and who have been, or may be, excluded from such education or otherwise deprived by defendants of access to publicly supported education. . . .

Plaintiffs' entitlement to relief in this case is clear. The applicable statutes and regulations and the Constitution of the United States require it.

Section 31–201 of the District of Columbia Code requires that:

> Every parent, guardian, or other person residing [permanently or temporarily] in the District of Columbia who has custody or control of a child between the ages of seven and sixteen years shall cause said child to be regularly instructed in a public school or in a private or parochial school or instructed privately during the period of each year in which the public schools of the District of Columbia are in session. . . .

Under Section 31–203, a child may be "excused" from attendance only when

> upon examination ordered by . . . [the Board of Education of the District of Columbia, the child] is found to be unable mentally or physically to profit from attendance at school: Provided, however, That if such examination shows that such child may benefit from specialized instruction adapted to his needs, he shall attend upon such instruction.

Failure of a parent to comply with Section 31–201 constitutes a criminal offense. D.C. Code 31–207. The Court need not belabor the fact that requiring parents to see that their children attend school under pain of criminal penalties presupposes that an educational opportunity will be made available to the children. The Board of Education is required to make such opportunity available. . . .

A fortiori, the defendants' conduct here, denying plaintiffs and their class not just an equal publicly supported education but all publicly supported education while providing such education to other children, is violative of the Due Process Clause.

Not only are plaintiffs and their class denied the publicly supported education to which they are entitled, many are suspended or expelled from regular schooling or specialized instruction or reassigned without any prior hearing and are given no periodic review thereafter. Due process of law requires a hearing prior to exclusion, termination of classification into a special program. . . .

The Answer of the defendants to the Complaint contains the following:

> These defendants say that it is impossible to afford plaintiffs the relief they request unless:
>
> 1. The Congress of the United States appropriates millions of dollars to improve special education services in the District of Columbia; or
> 2. These defendants divert millions of dollars from funds already specifically appropriated for other educational services in order to improve special educational services. These defendants suggest that to do so would violate an Act of Congress and would be inequitable to children outside the alleged plaintiff class.

This Court is not persuaded by that contention.

The defendants are required by the Constitution of the United States, the District of Columbia Code, and their own regulations to provide a publicly supported education for these "exceptional" children. Their failure to fulfill this clear duty to include and retain these children in the public school system, or otherwise provide them with publicly-supported education, and their failure to afford them due process hearing and periodic review, cannot be excused by the claim that there are insufficient funds. In *Goldberg v. Kelly,* 397 U.S. 254, 90 S.Ct. 1011, 25 L.Ed.2d 287 (1969) the Supreme Court, in a case that involved the right of a welfare recipient to a hearing before termination of his benefits, held that constitutional rights must be afforded citizens despite the greater expense involved. The Court stated at page 266, 90 S.Ct. at page 1019, that "the State's interest that this [welfare recipient's] payments not be erroneously terminated, clearly outweighs the State's competing concern to prevent any increase in its fiscal and administrative burdens." Similarly the District of Columbia's interest in educating the excluded children clearly must outweigh its interest in preserving its financial resources. If sufficient funds are not available to finance all of the services and programs that are needed and desirable in the system then the available funds must be expended equitably in such a manner that no child is entirely excluded from a publicly supported education consistent with his needs and ability to benefit therefrom. The inadequacies of the District of Columbia Public School System whether occasioned by insufficient funding or administrative inefficiency, certainly cannot be permitted to bear more heavily on the "exceptional" or handicapped child than on the normal child.   . . .

Inasmuch as the Board of Education has presented for adoption by the Court a proposed "Order and Decree" embodying its present plans for the identification of "exceptional" children and providing for their publicly supported education, including a time table, and further requiring the Board to formulate and file with the Court a more comprehensive plan, the Court will not now appoint a special master as was requested by plaintiffs.   . . .

. . . it is hereby ordered, adjudged and decreed that summary judgment in favor of plaintiffs and against defendants be, and hereby is, granted, and judgment is entered in this action as follows:

1. That no child eligible for a publicly supported education in the District of Columbia public schools shall be excluded from a regular public school assignment by a rule, policy, or practice of the Board of Education of the District of Columbia or its agents unless such child is provided (a) adequate alternative educational services suited to the child's needs, which may include special education or tuition grants, and (b) a constitutionally adequate prior hearing and periodic review of the child's status, progress, and the adequacy of any educational alternative.

2. The defendants, their officers, agents, servants, employees, and attorneys and all those in active concert or participation with them are hereby enjoined from maintaining, enforcing or otherwise continuing in effect any and all rules, policies and practices which exclude plaintiffs and the members of the class they represent from a regular public school assignment without providing them at public expense (a)

adequate and immediate alternative education or tuition grants, consistent with their needs, and (b) a constitutionally adequate prior hearing and periodic review of their status, progress and the adequacy of any educational alternatives; and it is further ORDERED that:

3. The District of Columbia shall provide to each child of school age a free and suitable publicly supported education regardless of the degree of the child's mental, physical or emotional disability or impairment. Furthermore, defendants shall not exclude any child resident in the District of Columbia from such publicly supported education on the basis of a claim of insufficient resources.

4. Defendants shall not suspend a child from the public schools for disciplinary reasons for any period in excess of two days without affording him a hearing pursuant to the provisions of Paragraph 13.f., below, and without providing for his education during the period of any such suspension.

5. Defendants shall provide each identified member of plaintiff class with a publicly supported education suited to his needs within thirty (30) days of the entry of this order. . . .

9. Defendants shall utilize public or private agencies to evaluate the educational needs of all identified "exceptional" children and, within twenty (20) days of the entry of this order, shall file with the Clerk of this Court their proposal for each individual placement in a suitable educational program, including the provision of compensatory educational services where required. . . .

10. Within forty-five (45) days of the entry of this order, defendants shall file with the Clerk of the Court, with copy to plaintiffs' counsel, a comprehensive plan which provides for the identification, notification, assessment, and placement of class members. Such plan shall state the nature and extent of efforts which defendants have undertaken or propose to undertake to

a. describe the curriculum, educational objectives, teacher qualifications, and

ancillary services for the publicly supported educational programs to be provided to class members; and,

b. formulate general plans of compensatory education suitable to class members in order to overcome the present effects of prior educational deprivations.

. . .

12. Within forty-five (45) days of the entry of this order, defendants shall file with this Court a report showing the expunction from or correction of all official records of any plaintiff with regard to past expulsions, suspensions, or exclusions effected in violation of the procedural rights . . . .

13. Hearing Procedures.

a. Each member of the plaintiff class is to be provided with a publicly supported educational program suited to his needs, within the context of a presumption that among the alternative programs of education, placement in a regular public school class with appropriate ancillary services is preferable to placement in a special school class.

b. Before placing a member of the class in such a program, defendants shall notify his parent or guardian of the proposed educational placement, the reasons therefore, and the right to a hearing before a Hearing Officer if there is an objection to the placement proposed. . . .

e. Whenever defendants take action regarding a child's placement, denial of placement, or transfer . . . the following procedures shall be followed.

1. Notice required hereinbefore shall be given in writing by registered mail to the parent or guardian of the child.

2. Such notice shall:

a. describe the proposed action in detail;

b. clearly state the specific and complete reasons for the proposed action, including the specification of any tests or reports upon which such action is proposed;

c. describe any alternative educational opportunities available on a permanent or temporary basis;

d. inform the parent or guardian of the right to object to the proposed action at a hearing before the Hearing Officer;

e. inform the parent or guardian that the child is eligible to receive, at no charge, the services of a federally or locally funded diagnostic center for an independent medical, psychological and educational evaluation and shall specify the name, address and telephone number of an appropriate local diagnostic center;

f. inform the parent or guardian of the right to be represented at the hearing by legal counsel; to examine the child's school records before the hearing, including any tests or reports upon which the proposed action may be based; to present evidence, including expert medical, psychological and educational testimony; and to confront and cross-examine any school official, employee, or agent of the school district or public department who may have evidence upon which the proposed action was based.

3. The hearing shall be at a time and place reasonably convenient to such parent or guardian. . . .

5. The hearing shall be a closed hearing unless the parent or guardian requests an open hearing.

6. The child shall have the right to a representative of his own choosing, including legal counsel.

7. The decision of the Hearing Officer shall be based solely upon the evidence presented at the hearing.

8. Defendants shall bear the burden of proof as to all facts and as to the appropriateness of any placement, denial of placement or transfer.

9. A tape recording or other record of the hearing shall be made and transcribed and, upon request, made available to the parent or guardian or his representative.

10. At a reasonable time prior to the hearing, the parent or guardian, or his counsel, shall be given access to all public school system and other public office records pertaining to the child, including any tests or reports upon which the proposed action may be based.

11. The independent Hearing Officer shall be an employee of the District of Columbia, but shall not be an officer, employee or agent of the Public School System.   . . .

13. The parent or guardian, or his representative, shall have the right to present evidence and testimony, including expert medical, psychological or educational testimony.

14. Within thirty (30) days after the hearing, the Hearing Officer shall render a decision in writing.

. . .

■ CONGRESSIONAL ACTION

The reasoned treatment of the handicapped question by the courts in the *PARC* and *Mills* cases initiated an enhanced level of public consciousness to the plight of handicapped children. A near dormant humanitarian impulse of the public was awakened by these legal actions and presently spilled over to the legislative bodies of the country. An important, and indeed momentous, occasion was the concerted efforts by the U.S. Congress to redress the problem. Immediately following the *PARC* and *Mills* decisions, federal legislation was introduced in both chambers of Congress seeking to eliminate discrimination against the handicapped in both the world of work and the public education system of the country. This legislative action eventually culminated in the passage of two laws—the

Vocational Rehabilitation Act of 1973[18] and the EAHCA in 1975.

Vocational Rehabilitation Act of 1973

Section 504 of the Vocational Rehabilitation Act states:

> No otherwise qualified handicapped individual in the United States . . . shall, solely by reason of his handicap, be excluded from the participation in, be denied the benefits of, or be subjected to discrimination under any program or activity receiving Federal financial assistance.[19]

Section 504 applies to all agencies receiving federal funds for any purpose, and such funds may be forfeited if charges of agency discrimination against handicapped persons are sustained.

Although § 504 is concerned with the discrimination of handicapped individuals in work situations, it also addresses the problems encountered by handicapped children in seeking equal educational opportunity. Five mandates are encompassed in § 504 that pertain directly to the educational needs of handicapped children:

> (a) location and notification, (b) free appropriate public education, (c) educational setting, (d) evaluation and placement, and (e) procedural safeguards.[20]

These provisions of § 504 have been used successfully in obtaining desirable school programs and services for individual handicapped students. Specifically, the provisions for a free appropriate public education and educational setting[21] enabled a child with cystic fibrosis to attend regular classes while receiving supportive services for a daily suctioning procedure[22] and recently were instrumental in assisting children with acquired Immunodeficiency Syndrome (AIDS) to remain in school.[23]

The strength of this act was dealt a substantial, if temporary, blow by the U.S. Supreme Court in *Grove City College v. Bell*.[24] The Court held that Title IX,[25] a statute prohibiting

sex discrimination, did not apply comprehensively to all aspects of an educational institution but only to those parts of the educational institution receiving federal assistance. Because the wording of the Title IX provision was similar to that of § 504, the Supreme Court decision severely crippled the latter act's effectiveness. This Supreme Court precedent led to at least one lower court ruling in which the Sixth Circuit Court of Appeals, in 1986, held that because a student had not attempted to be included in a particular program receiving federal funding that he could not obtain redress under § 504.[26]

The Supreme Court itself was not completely definitive as to whether *Grove City* applied to § 504, because in 1987 it allowed relief for a handicapped teacher, in *School Boards of Nassau County v. Arline*,[27] who claimed § 504 relief, ignoring the possible application of the *Grove City* restraint to § 504. The teacher in *Arline* was not required to show that the specific program in which she was endeavoring to participate was a federally funded program.

The questions surrounding this constricted view of § 504 were, however, obviated by Congressional action that corrected the defect by enacting the Civil Rights Restoration Act in 1987.[28] This act amended § 504 of the Rehabilitation Act by clarifying the language to remove all doubt that the law applies to all operations of public educational institutions.

Individuals With Disabilities Education Act (IDEA)

In 1975, federal legislation in the form of the EAHCA, Public Law 94–142, was enacted. Incorporating many provisions of earlier litigation and legislation, Public Law 94–142 (as of October 1990, IDEA) assured the right of all handicapped children to a public school education.

The need for this law was expressed by Congress:

1. there are more than eight million handicapped children in the United States today;
2. the special educational needs of such children are not being fully met;

3. more than half of the handicapped children in the United States do not receive appropriate educational services which would enable them to have full equality of opportunity;

4. one million of the handicapped children in the United States are excluded entirely from the public school system and will not go through the educational process with their peers;

5. there are many handicapped children throughout the United States participating in regular school programs whose handicaps prevent them from having a successful educational experience because their handicaps are undetected.[29]

To ensure handicapped children basic educational rights, Public Law 94–142 incorporated certain tenets: (1) a free appropriate public education, (2) an individualized education program, (3) special education services, (4) related services, (5) due process procedures, and (6) the least restrictive environment (LRE) in which to learn.[30]

Congress authorized immediate implementation of all sections of the EAHCA on a priority basis: first, addressing the needs of handicapped children who were currently receiving no educational services at all; and second, upgrading the inadequately served needs of the most severely handicapped children. The act further required that all handicapped children between the ages of three and eighteen receive appropriate education services by 1 September 1978; by 1 September 1980, all handicapped children from age three to twenty-one were to receive appropriate educational services.[31]

Amendments to EAHCA

Since its enactment in 1975, the EAHCA has been amended numerous[32] times; and each time, Congress has reaffirmed the original intent. A 1978 amendment stressed the importance of applied research and related activities to improve the educational opportunities of the handicapped, and reiterated the state's responsibility to refine and improve existing programs. In 1983, the bill was amended to clarify the term "special education" as services

designated "to meet the unique, 'educational' needs of the handicapped child" and specifically expanded services for deaf-blind children. The committee report supporting the legislation emphasized the need to improve education for the severely handicapped.[33] This legislation further reinforced § 624, which sought to augment research, innovation, training, and dissemination activities in connection with centers and services for the handicapped.[34]

The amendments in 1986 extended the age groups covered, mandating that all preschool handicapped children aged three to five years be entitled to public education, and establishing a new federal education program for handicapped babies from birth through age two. The Senate Committee report supporting the law stated that the provision was now made "for universal access to services for all handicapped children beginning at birth."[35] The 1986 amendments, however, focused in particular on the needs of deaf-blind and multiple-handicapped children, extending provisions for specialized, intensive professional and allied services, methods, and aids that are found to be most effective.[36] In addition the 1986 act, called the Handicapped Children's Protection Act (HCPA), enables handicapped children, parents, or guardians to receive attorney's fees if they are successful in litigation against state or local agencies.[37] Finally in 1990 we have the name change to Individuals with Disabilities Education Act (IDEA).

■■■ JUDICIAL INTERPRETATION OF EAHCA

The federal legislation beginning with P.L. 94–142 (EAHCA) has resulted in many court decisions that interpret the statute's intent. In Chapter 1 of this book, we observed that a primary function of the courts is to interpret statutes to determine their true intent. This has been the primary function of the courts in dealing with handicapped children's issues since the enactment of the federal laws. Since 1975, the pervasive nature of EAHCA (IDEA) tends to obviate the need for constitutional inquiry. The handicapped cases are devoted almost entirely to judicial responses to conflicts between school districts and parents of handicapped children seeking definition of provisions of the federal handicap legislation. These cases can be classified several different ways, but primarily fall into groups wherein the courts define the meanings of the following statutory provisions:

- Free Appropriate Public Education
- Procedural Safeguards
- Individualized Education Program (IEP)
- Least Restrictive Environment
- Separate School Placement
- Related Services
- Discipline and "Stay Put"
- Attorney's Fees
- Tuition Reimbursement

Judicial opinions interpreting these portions of the handicapped legislation are discussed in the following paragraphs.

Free Appropriate Public Education

To qualify for federal funds under the EAHCA, a state must adopt a policy "that assures all handicapped children the right to a free appropriate public education." The act does not define "appropriate education" but does expressly define "free appropriate public education."

> The term 'free appropriate education' means special education and related services which (A) have been provided at public expense, under public supervision and direction, and without charge, (B) meet the standards of the state education agency, (C) include an appropriate preschool, elementary, or secondary education in the state involved, and (D) are provided in conformity with the individualized education program required under Section 1414 (a) (5) of this title.[38]

A free appropriate education must be specifically designed to meet the unique needs of the child. The program is designed for the child "to benefit." The act requires no substantive measures regarding the level of education; therefore, the state does not have to

maximize the potential of the children, only provide a program that benefits the child. The Supreme Court in *Rowley* stated, "We therefore conclude that the 'basic floor of opportunity' provided by the Act consists of access to specialized instruction and related services which are individually designed to provide educational benefit to the handicapped child."[39]

The educational methods to be used are the responsibility of the state, and the courts may review them to determine compliance with the act. The legal concerns are primarily twofold: "First, has the state complied with procedures set forth in the Act. And, second, is the individualized educational program developed pursuant to the Act's procedures reasonably calculated to enable the child to receive educational benefits."[40]

What constitutes a "benefit," though, is not easily discerned or readily agreed upon. In a vigorous dissent in *Rowley*, Justice White took issue with the use of the term "benefit," pointing out that in the case of a deaf student, instruction by "a teacher with a loud voice" could be viewed as an educational placement providing some benefit.[41]

Concerning benefit, itself, and whether it is required at all was treated at length in the *Timothy W. v. Rochester, New Hampshire, School District*.[42] Here the U.S. Court of Appeals for the First Circuit concluded that the EAHCA did not require that a child prove that he or she could benefit from the educational services before participation. The court said that the act was intended for *all* handicapped, and that the most severely handicapped were to be given priority, not excluded. For a child to be compelled to show potential benefit as a condition precedent was neither intended nor contemplated by the Congress in enacting the law.

Extended School Year

Whether a handicapped child is entitled to an extended school year depends on the individual child's IEP, which determines an appropriate education for each child. In *Battle v. Commonwealth of Pennsylvania*,[43] a federal circuit court ruled that a state could be required to provide educational programs beyond the regular school year. The court stated, "At the center of the controversy . . . is the definition of 'free appropriate public education.' "[44] The state of Pennsylvania through administrative policy set a limit of 180 days of instruction per year for all children, handicapped or not. The case was brought by children who were Severely or Profoundly Impaired (SPI) or Severely Emotionally Disturbed (SED), claiming that the administrative policy denied them a free appropriate education as required by the EAHCA. The court found that during the summer break, all children regressed in their learning process. Although all children regressed, handicapped children regressed more and required longer to recoup skills than did nonhandicapped children. The state claimed that the regression was caused by a multitude of factors, such as teacher incompetency, parental failure, and lack of functionality of skills taught. The court agreed that all of the factors attributed to the regression, but that the program break was a major factor. The court said that no clear legislative guidance is provided, and the issues are convoluted.

> 'Where as in this case, the handicap in question profoundly affects the child's learning abilities, this comparison reaches a level of difficulty, which, in the absence of legislative guidance, approaches the perimeter of judicial competence.' [45]

The *Battle* court, though, reasoned that because the federal statute requires special education programs be individualized to "meet the unique needs" of each child, a fixed term of 180 days was contrary to the federal intent. The court said:

> Rather than ascertaining the reasonable educational needs of each child in light of reasonable education goals and establishing a reasonable program to attain those goals, the 180 day rule imposes with rigid certainty a program restriction which may be wholly inappropriate to the child's educational objectives.[46]

The Fifth Circuit in *Crawford v. Pittman*[47] found a similar limited school year policy was in violation of EAHCA; this court concluded

that Mississippi's policy of refusing to consider or provide special education of a duration longer than 180 days is inconsistent with its obligations under the Act. Rigid rules like the 180 day limitation violate not only the Act's procedural command that each child receive individual consideration but also its substantive requirements that each child receive some benefit and that lack of funds not bear more heavily on handicapped than non-handicapped children.

The Eighth Circuit, too, ruled that a Missouri policy limiting the education of handicapped children violated the EAHCA, as did the Eleventh Circuit[48] in invalidating a Georgia policy. After the cases of *Battle*,[49] *Yaris*,[50] *Crawford*,[51] and *Georgia Association of Retarded Citizens*,[52] the issue is no longer in doubt as to whether a handicapped child can legally have available an extended school year as part of a free appropriate education, but rather what standards should be used to determine which child receives the extended school year services. The aforementioned cases all used as a criterion the fact that a child would regress during the summer break and concluded that if the learning regression is substantial enough to preclude rapid recoupment at the beginning of the next school year, then an extended school program is required.

Regression-Recoupment Dilemma

The *regression-recoupment* analysis has been commonly supported by expert testimony, but conflicts are apparent. One court noted:

> The school district's employees and consultants were unanimous in that they observed no significant regression, while doctors, therapists, and former teachers testified on behalf of [the student] that a continuous structural program . . . was required to prevent significant regression.[53]

In *Alamo Heights*[54] a more multifaceted standard emerged that uses regression-recoupment as a factor but also employs other factors. Here, the standard maintains that

> if a child will experience severe or substantial regression during the summer months in the

absence of a summer program, the handicapped child may be entitled to year round services. The issue is whether the benefits accrued to the child during the regular school year will be significantly jeopardized if he is not provided an educational program during the summer months. This is, of course, a general standard, but it must be applied to the individual by the ARD [Admission, Review and Dismissal] Committee in the same way that juries apply other general legal standards such as negligence and reasonableness.[55]

In 1990, in *Johnson v. Independent School District No. 4 of Bixby*,[56] the court agreed with the *Alamo* analysis, saying that the use of the regression-recoupment analysis as the only test violated the right of the child to have his or her program individualized. This argument basically assumes that any fixed standard, such as the 180-day rule, must fall because it is static and negates the individualization that the act requires. The Third Circuit in *Polk*[57] also rejected the regression argument as the sole factor in determining the child's need for extended services. *Johnson* cited *Rowley* as providing a rationale for using many factors, pointing out that the Supreme Court in *Rowley* said that, "We do not attempt today to establish any one test for determining the adequacy of educational benefits conferred upon all children covered by the Act."[58] *Johnson* further concluded:

> In addition to degree of regression and the time necessary for recoupment, courts have considered many factors important in their discussions of what constitutes an "appropriate" educational program under the Act.[59]

In yet another case, *Cordrey*, the Sixth Circuit followed the twofold test from *Rowley* to determine what constituted an appropriate education: (1) whether the state has complied with all procedures set forth in the act, and (2) was the individualized educational program reasonably calculated to enable the child to receive educational benefits.[60] In this case the court found that "hard empirical proof" of regression-recoupment is clearer and simpler, but the regression standard should not be interpreted to require absolutely that a child demonstrate regression in order to prove need for a summer program.[61] The court said that "the ESY [Extended School Year] standard should be open to developments in special education science, but not bound to any particular one."[62]

Thus, according to *Rowley*, a "free appropriate" education is defined in rather "general and somewhat imprecise" language, but if procedural guidelines are followed and a specialized program is developed for the child's needs, then the requirements of the act are met. The specialized program may or may not include extended school year services. This is a question that must be resolved based on the individual needs of each child.

Procedural Safeguards

As indicated in the *Mills* and *Rowley*[63] cases, proper procedures are a vital aspect in assuring that appropriate educational services are extended to handicapped children. The necessary due process specifications delineated in *Mills* were followed and embellished by the EAHCA in 1975. Section 1415 of that act contains procedures that are mandatory. Most importantly, the procedures specify that parents must be given notice and an opportunity to participate in the development of a child's education program. Inclusive is the requirement that parents be informed of all methods and procedures by which conflicts and grievances may be appealed and resolved. Implicit therein is the assurance that hearings regarding the child's placement will be impartial and unbiased. The law, § 1415, emphasizes this standard of fairness by giving the parent a right to have the hearing conducted by a person who is neither an employee of the school district nor of the state department of education.[64]

As stated in *Rowley*, a reviewing court must make sure that procedures are followed by the district. A school district making a placement decision without reference to the IEP violates the requirements of the law and free appropriate education.[65] On the other hand, if an insignificant procedural error is made not resulting in the child's loss of educational opportunity,[66] the court will decline to "exalt form over substance" by enforcing a technical infraction from the act's procedural standards.[67]

If the results of the hearing are not to the satisfaction of the parent or the school district, then appeal can be made to the state department of education.[68] During the time in which appeals are taken, the child must remain or "stay put" in his or her "then current" program.[69] As discussed later in this chapter, indefinite suspension during pendency of appeal violates this section of the law.[70] Appeal to either state or federal courts may be taken after a decision has been rendered by the state department of education.[71]

Individualized Education Program (IEP)

The purpose, of course, of all these procedural safeguards is to ensure to the parent and child that an appropriate individualized educational program (IEP) will be provided. The IEP goes beyond merely providing a place for the child in the public schools, but, more extensively, must design and reduce to writing an educational plan that takes into account the identification of the child's educational needs, the annual instructional goals and objectives, the specific educational programs and services to be provided, and the necessary evaluation procedures to monitor the child's progress. An IEP is "more than a mere exercise in Public Relations,"[72] indeed it is the "centerpiece of the statute's education delivery system for disabled children."

> The term "individualized education program" means a written statement for each child with a disability developed in any meeting by a representative of the local educational agency or an intermediate educational unit who shall be qualified to provide, or supervise the provision of, specially designed instruction to meet the unique needs of children with disabilities . . . .[73]

This statement describing the child's educational goals and specifying required services is developed by a multidisciplinary team. For initial evaluation and placement the IEP team must have as members a school official, the child's teacher(s), parents and other person(s) qualified to interpret evaluation results. Because the IEP must be jointly prepared by school officials and parents and reviewed annually, a condition of possible contention is staged. Contests between parents and school districts over the nature of the IEP have created a plethora of handicapped litigation in recent years, all of which has begun to form a formidable body of case law.

---

*The "Free Appropriate Public Education"
Clause of the Education of the Handicapped Act
Does Not Require a State to Maximize the Potential
of Each Handicapped Child*

———————

Board of Education of Hendrick Hudson Central School District Board of Education v. Rowley

———————

Supreme Court of the United States, 1982.
458 U.S. 176, 102 S.Ct. 3034.

JUSTICE REHNQUIST delivered the opinion of the Court. This case presents a question of statutory interpretation. Petitioners contend that the Court of Appeals and the District Court misconstrued the requirements imposed by Congress upon States which receive federal funds under the Education of the Handicapped Act. We agree and reverse the judgment of the Court of Appeals.

The Education of the Handicapped Act provides federal money to assist state and local agencies in educating handicapped children, and conditions such funding upon a State's compliance with extensive goals and procedures. . . .

This case arose in connection with the education of Amy Rowley, a deaf student at the Furnace Woods School in the Hendrick Hudson Central School District, Peekskill, N.Y. Amy has minimal residual hearing and is an excellent lipreader. During the year before she began attending Furnace Woods, a meeting between her parents and school administrators resulted in a decision to place her in a regular kindergarten class in order to determine what supplemental services would be necessary to her education. Several members of the school administration prepared for Amy's arrival by attending a course in sign-language interpretation, and a teletype machine was installed in the principal's office to facilitate communication with her parents who are also deaf. At the end of the trial period it was determined that Amy should remain in the kindergarten class, but that she should be provided with an FM hearing aid which would amplify words spoken into a wireless receiver by the teacher or fellow students during certain classroom activities. Amy successfully completed her kindergarten year.

As required by the Act, an IEP was prepared for Amy during the fall of her first-grade year. The IEP provided that Amy should be educated in a regular classroom at Furnace Woods, should continue to use the FM hearing aid, and should receive instruction from a tutor for the deaf for one hour each day and from a speech therapist for three hours each week. The Rowleys agreed with parts of the IEP but insisted that Amy also be provided a qualified sign-language interpreter in all her academic classes in lieu of the assistance proposed in other parts of the IEP. Such an interpreter had been placed in Amy's kindergarten class for a two-week experimental period, but the interpreter had reported that Amy did not need his services at that time. The school administrators likewise concluded that Amy did not need such an interpreter in her first-grade classroom. They reached this conclusion after consulting the school district's Committee on the Handicapped, which had received expert evidence from Amy's parents on the importance of a sign-language interpreter, received testimony from Amy's teacher and other persons familiar with her academic and social progress, and visited a class for the deaf.

When their request for an interpreter was denied, the Rowleys demanded and received a hearing before an independent examiner. After receiving evidence from both sides, the examiner agreed with the administrators' determination that an interpreter was not necessary because "Amy was achieving educationally, academically, and socially" without such assistance. The examiner's decision was affirmed on appeal by the New York Commissioner of Education on the basis of substantial evidence in the record. Pursuant to the Act's provision for judicial review, the Rowleys then brought an action in the United States District Court for the Southern District of New York, claiming that the administrators' denial of the sign-language interpreter constituted a denial of the "free appropriate public education" guaranteed by the Act. . . .

We granted certiorari to review . . . . Such review requires us to consider two questions: What is meant by the Act's requirement of a "free appropriate public education"? And what is the role of state and federal courts in exercising the review granted by 20 U.S.C. § 1415? We consider these questions separately.

This is the first case in which this Court has been called upon to interpret any provision of the Act . . . "(t)he Act itself does not define 'appropriate education,'" but leaves "to the courts and the hearing officers" the responsibility of "giv(ing) content to the requirement of an 'appropriate education.'" Petitioners contend that the definition of the phrase "free appropriate public education," used by the courts below overlooks the definition of that phrase actually found in the Act. Respondents agree that the Act defines "free appropriate public education," but contend that the statutory definition is not "functional" and thus "offers judges no guidance in their consideration of controversies involving 'the identification, evaluation, or educational placement of the child or the provision of a free appropriate public education.'" . . .

We are loath to conclude that Congress failed to offer any assistance in defining the meaning of the principal substantive phrase used in the Act. It is beyond dispute that, contrary to the conclusions of the courts below, the Act does expressly define "free appropriate public education":

The term "free appropriate public education" means *special education* and *related services* which (A) have been provided at public expense, under public supervision and direction, and without charge, (B) meet the standards of the State educational agency, (C) include an appropriate preschool, elementary, or secondary school education in the State involved, and (D) are provided in conformity with the individualized education program required under section 1414(a)(5) of this title. § 1401(18) (emphasis added).

"Special education," as referred to in this definition, means "specially designed instruction, at no cost to parents or guardians, to meet the unique needs of a handicapped child, including classroom instruction, instruction in physical education, home instruction, and instruction in hospitals and institutions." § 1401(16). "Related services" are defined as "transportation, and such developmental, corrective, and other supportive services . . . as may be required to assist a handicapped child to benefit from special education." § 1401(17).

Like many statutory definitions, this one tends toward the cryptic rather than the comprehensive, but that is scarcely a reason for abandoning the quest for legislative intent.
. . .

According to the definitions contained in the Act, a "free appropriate public education" consists of educational instruction specially designed to meet the unique needs of the handicapped child, supported by such services as are necessary to permit the child "to benefit" from the instruction. . . .

Noticeably absent from the language of the statute is any substantive standard prescribing the level of education to be accorded handicapped children. Certainly the language of the statute contains no requirement like the one imposed by the lower courts—that States maximize the potential of handicapped children "commensurate with the opportunity provided to other children." That standard was expounded by the District Court without reference to the statutory definitions or even to the legislative history of the Act. Although we find the statutory definition of "free appropriate public education" to be helpful in

our interpretation of the Act, there remains the question of whether the legislative history indicates a congressional intent that such education meet some additional substantive standard. For an answer, we turn to that history.

That the Act imposes no clear obligation upon recipient States beyond the requirement that handicapped children receive some form of specialized education is perhaps best demonstrated by the fact that Congress, in explaining the need for the Act, equated an "appropriate education" to the receipt of some specialized educational services. The Senate Report states: "[T]he most recent statistics provided by the Bureau of Education for the Handicapped estimate that of the more than eight million children . . . with handicapping conditions requiring special education and related services, only 3.9 million such children are receiving an appropriate education." This statement, which reveals Congress' view that 3.9 million handicapped children were "receiving an appropriate education" in 1975, is followed immediately in the Senate Report by a table showing that 3.9 million handicapped children were "served" in 1975 and a slightly larger number were "unserved." A similar statement and table appear in the House Report.

It is evident from the legislative history that the characterization of handicapped children as "served" referred to children who were receiving some form of specialized educational services from the States, and that the characterization of children as "unserved" referred to those who were receiving no specialized educational services. . . .

Respondents contend that "the goal of the Act is to provide each handicapped child with an equal educational opportunity." We think, however, that the requirement that a State provide specialized educational services to handicapped children generates no additional requirement that the services so provided be sufficient to maximize each child's potential "commensurate with the opportunity provided other children." Respondents and the United States correctly note that Congress sought "to provide assistance to the States in carrying out their responsibilities under

. . . the Constitution of the United States to provide equal protection of the laws." But we do not think that such statements imply a congressional intent to achieve strict equality of opportunity or services.

The educational opportunities provided by our public school systems undoubtedly differ from student to student, depending upon a myriad of factors that might affect a particular student's ability to assimilate information presented in the classroom. The requirement that States provide "equal" educational opportunities would thus seem to present an entirely unworkable standard requiring impossible measurements and comparisons. Similarly, furnishing handicapped children with only such services as are available to nonhandicapped children would in all probability fall short of the statutory requirement of "free appropriate public education"; to require, on the other hand, the furnishing of every special service necessary to maximize each handicapped child's potential is, we think, further than Congress intended to go. Thus to speak in terms of "equal" services in one instance gives less than what is required by the Act and in another instance more. The theme of the Act is "free appropriate public education," a phrase which is too complex to be captured by the word "equal" whether one is speaking of opportunities or services.

. . .

In explaining the need for federal legislation, the House Report noted that "no congressional legislation has required a precise guarantee for handicapped children, i.e., a basic floor of opportunity that would bring into compliance all school districts with the constitutional right of equal protection with respect to handicapped children."

Assuming that the Act was designed to fill the need identified in the House Report — that is, to provide a "basic floor of opportunity" consistent with equal protection — neither the Act nor its history persuasively demonstrates that Congress though that equal protection required anything more than equal access. Therefore, Congress' desire to provide specialized educational services, even in furtherance of "equality," cannot be read as imposing any particular substantive educational standard upon the States.

The District Court and the Court of Appeals thus erred when they held that the Act requires New York to maximize the potential of each handicapped child commensurate with the opportunity provided nonhandicapped children. Desirable though that goal might be, it is not the standard that Congress imposed upon States which receive funding under the Act. Rather, Congress sought primarily to identify and evaluate handicapped children, and to provide them with access to a free public education.

Implicit in the congressional purpose of providing access to a "free appropriate public education" is the requirement that the education to which access is provided be sufficient to confer some educational benefit upon the handicapped child. It would do little good for Congress to spend millions of dollars in providing access to a public education only to have the handicapped child receive no benefit from that education. The statutory definition of "free appropriate public education," in addition to requiring that States provide each child with "specially designed instruction," expressly requires the provision of "such . . . supportive services . . . as may be required to assist a handicapped child *to benefit* from special education." (Emphasis added.) We therefore conclude that the "basic floor of opportunity" provided by the Act consists of access to specialized instruction and related services which are individually designed to provide educational benefit to the handicapped child.

The determination of when handicapped children are receiving sufficient educational benefits to satisfy the requirements of the Act presents a more difficult problem. The Act requires participating States to educate a wide spectrum of handicapped children, from the marginally hearing-impaired to the profoundly retarded and palsied. It is clear that the benefits obtainable by children at one end of the spectrum will differ dramatically from those obtainable by children at the other end, with infinite variations in between. One child may have little difficulty competing successfully in an academic setting with nonhandicapped children while another child may encounter great difficulty in acquiring even the most basic of self-maintenance skills. We do not attempt today to establish any one test for determining the adequacy of educational benefits conferred upon all children covered by the Act. Because in this case we are presented with a handicapped child who is receiving substantial specialized instruction and related services, and who is performing above average in the regular classrooms of a public school system, we confine our analysis to that situation.

The Act requires participating States to educate handicapped children with nonhandicapped children whenever possible. When that "mainstreaming" preference of the Act has been met and a child is being educated in the regular classrooms of a public school system, the system itself monitors the educational progress of the child. Regular examinations are administered, grades are awarded, and yearly advancement to higher grade levels is permitted for those children who attain an adequate knowledge of the course material. The grading and advancement system thus constitutes an important factor in determining educational benefit. Children who graduate from our public school systems are considered by our society to have been "educated" at least to the grade level they have completed, and access to an "education" for handicapped children is precisely what Congress sought to provide in the Act.

When the language of the Act and its legislative history are considered together, the requirements imposed by Congress become tolerably clear. Insofar as a State is required to provide a handicapped child with a "free appropriate public education," we hold that it satisfies this requirement by providing personalized instruction with sufficient support services to permit the child to benefit educationally from that instruction. Such instruction and services must be provided at public expense, must meet the State's educational standards, must approximate the grade levels used in the State's regular education, and must comport with the child's IEP. In addition, the IEP, and therefore the personalized instruction, should be formulated in accordance with the requirements of the Act and, if the child is being educated in the regular classrooms of the public education system, should be reasonably calculated to enable the child to achieve passing marks and advance from grade to grade.   . . .

In assuring that the requirements of the Act have been met, courts must be careful to avoid imposing their view of preferable educational methods upon the States. The primary responsibility for formulating the education to be accorded a handicapped child, and for choosing the educational method most suitable to the child's needs, was left by the Act to state and local educational agencies in cooperation with the parents or guardian of the child. The Act expressly charges States with the responsibility of "acquiring and disseminating to teachers and administrators of programs for handicapped children significant information derived from educational research, demonstration, and similar projects, and [of] adopting, where appropriate, promising educational practices and materials." § 1413(a)(3). In the face of such a clear statutory directive, it seems highly unlikely that Congress intended courts to overturn a State's choice of appropriate educational theories in a proceeding conducted pursuant to § 1415(e)(2).

We previously have cautioned that courts lack the "specialized knowledge and experience" necessary to resolve "persistent and difficult questions of educational policy." *San Antonio Independent School Dist. v. Rodriguez,* 411 U.S. 1, 42, 93 S.Ct. 1278, 1301, 36 L.Ed.2d 16 (1973). We think that Congress shared that view when it passed the Act. As already demonstrated, Congress' intention was not that the Act displace the primacy of States in the field of education, but that States receive funds to assist them in extending their educational systems to the handicapped. Therefore, once a court determines that the requirements of the Act have been met, questions of methodology are for resolution by the States.

Entrusting a child's education to state and local agencies does not leave the child without protection. Congress sought to protect individual children by providing for parental involvement in the development of state plans and policies, and in the formulation of the child's individual educational program. As the Senate Report states:

> The Committee recognizes that in many instances the process of providing special education and related services to handicapped children is not guaranteed to produce any particular outcome. By changing the language [of the provision relating to individualized educational programs] to emphasize the process of parent and child involvement and to provide a written record of reasonable expectations, the Committee intends to clarify that such individualized planning conferences are a way to provide parent involvement and protection to assure that appropriate services are provided to a handicapped child.

As this very case demonstrates, parents and guardians will not lack ardor in seeking to ensure that handicapped children receive all of the benefits to which they are entitled by the Act.

Applying these principles to the facts of this case, we conclude that Court of Appeals erred in affirming the decision of the District Court. Neither the District Court nor the Court of Appeals found that petitioners had failed to comply with the procedures of the Act, and the findings of neither court would support a conclusion that Amy's educational program failed to comply with the substantive requirements of the Act. On the contrary, the District Court found that the "evidence firmly establishes that Amy is receiving an 'adequate' education, since she performs better than the average child in her class and is advancing easily from grade to grade." In light of this finding, and of the fact that Amy was receiving personalized instruction and related services calculated by the Furnace Woods school administrators to meet her educational needs, the lower courts should not have concluded that the Act requires the provision of a sign-language interpreter. Accordingly, the decision of the Court of Appeals is reversed, and the case is remanded for further proceedings consistent with this opinion.

So ordered.

The EAHCA Mandates the Education of All Handicapped and Does Not Require a Child to Demonstrate a Benefit as a Condition Precedent to Participation.

—————————

Timothy W. v. Rochester, New Hampshire School District

—————————

United States Court of Appeals,
First Circuit, 1989.
875 F.2d 954.

BOWNES, Circuit Judge. Plaintiff-appellant Timothy W. appeals an order of the district court which held that under the Education for All Handicapped Children Act, a handicapped child is not eligible for special education if he cannot benefit from that education, and that Timothy W., a severely retarded and multiply handicapped child was not eligible under that standard. We reverse.

Timothy W. was born two months prematurely on December 8, 1975, with severe respiratory problems, and shortly thereafter experienced an intracranial hemorrhage, subdural effusions, seizures, hydrocephalus, and meningitis. As a result, Timothy is multiply handicapped and profoundly mentally retarded. He suffers from complex developmental disabilities, spastic quadriplegia, cerebral palsy, seizure disorder and cortical blindness. His mother attempted to obtain appropriate services for him, and while he did receive some services from the Rochester Child Development Center, he did not receive any educational program from the Rochester School District when he became of school age.

On February 19, 1980, the Rochester School District convened a meeting to decide if Timothy was considered educationally handicapped under the state and federal statutes, thereby entitling him to special education and related services. . . . In a meeting on March 7, 1980, the school district decided that Timothy was not educationally handicapped — that since his handicap was so severe he was not "capable of benefitting" from an education, and therefore was not entitled to one. During 1981 and 1982, the school district did not provide Timothy with any educational program. . . .

In response to a letter from Timothy's attorney, on January 17, 1984, the school district's placement team met. . . . The placement team recommended that Timothy be placed at the Child Development Center so that he could be provided with a special education program. The Rochester School Board, however, refused to authorize the placement team's recommendation to provide educational services for Timothy, contending that it still needed more information. The school district's request to have Timothy be given a neurological evaluation, including a CAT Scan, was refused by his mother. . . .

On November 17, 1984, Timothy filed a complaint in the United States District Court, pursuant to 42 U.S.C. § 1983, alleging that his rights under the Education for All Handicapped Children Act (20 U.S.C. § 1400 *et seq.*), the corresponding New Hampshire state law (RSA 186–C), § 504 of the Rehabilitation Act of 1973 (29 U.S.C. § 794), and the equal protection and due process clauses of the United States and New Hampshire Constitutions, had been violated by the Rochester School District. The complaint sought preliminary and permanent injunctions directing the school district to provide him with special education, and $175,000 in damages.

A hearing was held in the district court on December 21, 1984. . . . On January 3, 1985, the district court denied Timothy's motion for a preliminary injunction, and on January 8, stated it would abstain on the damage claim pending exhaustion of the state administrative procedures. . . .

In September, 1986, Timothy again requested a special education program. In October, 1986, the school district continued to refuse to provide him with such a program, claiming it still needed more information. Various evaluations were done at the behest of the school district. On December 30, 1985, Dr. Cecilia Pinto-Lord, a neurologist, had given Timothy a negative prognosis for learning, but did indicate he had some awareness of his environment; on October 10, 1986, Dr. Pinto-Lord stated that acquisition of new skills by Timothy was very unlikely. . . .

On May 20, 1987, the district court found that Timothy had not exhausted his state administrative remedies before the New Hampshire Department of Education, and precluded pretrial discovery until this had been done. On September 15, 1987, the hearing officer in the administrative hearings ruled that Timothy's capacity to benefit was not a legally permissible standard for determining his eligibility to receive a public education, and that the Rochester School District must provide him with an education. The Rochester School District, on November 12, 1987, appealed this decision to the United States District Court by filing a counterclaim, and on March 29, 1988, moved for summary judgment. Timothy filed a cross motion for summary judgment.

Hearings were held on June 16 and 27, 1988, pursuant to Fed.R.Civ.P. 65(a)(2), relating "solely to the issue of whether or not Timothy W. qualifie[d] as an educationally handicapped individual." In addition to the large record containing the reports described above, additional testimony was obtained from various experts. Timothy's experts, Kathy Schwaninger, consultant to United Cerebral Palsy, and Rose Bradder, Program Coordinator at the Child Development Center, testified that Timothy would benefit from a special educational program including physical and occupational therapy, with emphasis on functional skills. The school district presented Carrie Foss, Executive Director of the Child Development Center, who disagreed with her own staff and testified that Timothy had shown no progress. The district court relied heavily on another school district witness, Dr. Patricia Andrews, a developmental pediatrician, who testified that Timothy probably does not have the capacity to learn educational skills and activities. She also testified: that she was not an expert in the education of handicapped children; that her only contact with Timothy was when he was two months old; that he might have the capacity to respond to his environment and change in some ways; that the X-ray bubble test performed on Timothy in 1976, which she was using as a basis for concluding that Timothy had virtually no brain cortex and therefore no capacity to learn, was not the most sophisticated and accurate technology currently available; and that even a CAT scan could not predict Timothy's ability to learn.

On July 15, 1988, the district court rendered its opinion entitled "Order on Motion for Judgment on the Pleadings or in the Alternative, Summary Judgment." . . . The court then reviewed the materials, reports and testimony and found that "Timothy W. is not capable of benefitting from special education. . . . As a result, the defendant [school district] is not obligated to provide special education under either EAHCA [the federal statute] or RSA 186–C [the New Hampshire statute]." Timothy W. has appealed this order. Neither party objected to the procedure followed by the court.

The primary issue is whether the district court erred in its rulings of law. Since we find that it did, we do not review its findings of fact.

A. The Plain Meaning of the Act Mandates a Public Education for All Handicapped Children

. . . The language of the Act could not be more unequivocal. The statute is permeated with the words "*all* handicapped children" whenever it refers to the target population. It never speaks of any exceptions for severely handicapped children. Indeed, as indicated *supra,* the Act gives priority to the most severely handicapped. Nor is there any language whatsoever which requires as a prerequisite to being covered by the Act, that a handicapped child must demonstrate that he

or she will "benefit" from the educational program. Rather, the Act speaks of the *state's* responsibility to design a special education and related services program that will meet the unique "needs" of all handicapped children. The language of the Act in its entirety makes clear that a "zero-reject" policy is at the core of the Act, and that no child, regardless of the severity of his or her handicap, is to ever again be subjected to the deplorable state of affairs which existed at the time of the Act's passage, in which millions of handicapped children received inadequate education or none at all. In summary, the Act mandates an appropriate public education for all handicapped children, regardless of the level of achievement that such children might attain.

B. Timothy W.: A Handicapped Child Entitled to An Appropriate Education

Given that the Act's language mandates that all handicapped children are entitled to a free appropriate education, we must next inquire if Timothy W. is a handicapped child, and if he is, what constitutes an appropriate education to meet his unique needs. . . .

There is no question that Timothy W. fits within the Act's definition of a handicapped child: he is multiply handicapped and profoundly mentally retarded. He has been described as suffering from severe spasticity, cerebral palsy, brain damage, joint contractures, cortical blindness, is not ambulatory, and is quadriplegic.

APPROPRIATE PUBLIC EDUCATION: The Act and the implementing regulations define a "free appropriate public education" to mean "special education and related services which are provided at public expense . . . [and] are provided in conformity with an individualized education program." 34 C.F.R. § 300.4; 20 U.S.C. § 1401(a)(18).

(a) "*Special education*" means "specially designed instruction, at no cost to the parent, to meet the unique needs of a handicapped child, including classroom instruction, instruction in *physical education,* home instruction, and instruction in hospitals and institutions." 34 C.F.R. § 300.14(a)(1); 20 U.S.C. § 1401(a)(16) (emphasis added). It is of significance that the Act explicitly provides for education of children who are so severely handicapped as to require hospitalization or institutionalization. Timothy W.'s handicaps do not require such extreme measures, as he can be educated at home. . . .

The record shows that Timothy W. is a severely handicapped and profoundly retarded child in need of special education and related services. Much of the expert testimony was to the effect that he is aware of his surrounding environment, makes or attempts to make purposeful movements, responds to tactile stimulation, responds to his mother's voice and touch, recognizes familiar voices, responds to noises, and parts his lips when spoon fed. The record contains testimony that Timothy W.'s needs include sensory stimulation, physical therapy, improved head control, socialization, consistency in responding to sound sources, and partial participation in eating. The educational consultants who drafted Timothy's individualized education program recommended that Timothy's special education program should include goals and objectives in the areas of motor control, communication, socialization, daily living skills, and recreation. The special education and related services that have been recommended to meet Timothy W.'s needs fit well within the statutory and regulatory definitions of the Act.

We conclude that the Act's language dictates the holding that Timothy W. is a handicapped child who is in need of special education and related services because of his handicaps. He must, therefore, according to the Act, be provided with such an educational program. There is nothing in the Act's language which even remotely supports the district court's conclusion that "under [the Act], an initial determination as to a child's ability to benefit from special education, must be made in order for a handicapped child to qualify for education under the Act." The language of the Act is directly to the contrary: a school district has a duty to provide an educational program for every handicapped child in the district, regardless of the severity of the handicap.

An examination of the legislative history reveals that Congress intended the Act to provide a public education for all handicapped children, without exception; that the most severely handicapped were in fact to be given priority attention; and that an educational benefit was neither guaranteed nor required as a prerequisite for a child to receive such education. These factors were central, and were repeated over and over again, in the more than three years of congressional hearings and debates, which culminated in passage of the 1975 Act. . . .

A. Education for All Handicapped Children

. . . Moreover, the legislative history is unambiguous that the primary purpose of the Act was to remedy the then current state of affairs, and provide a public education for *all* handicapped children. As the Committee Chairman, Senator Williams stated:

> We must recognize our responsibility to provide education for *all* children which meets their unique needs. The denial of the right to education and to equal opportunity within this Nation for handicapped children—whether it be outright exclusion from school, the failure to provide an education which *meets the needs of a single handicapped child,* or the refusal to recognize the handicapped child's right to grow—is a travesty of justice and a denial of equal protection of the law.

. . .

B. Priority For The Most Severely Handicapped

Not only did Congress intend that all handicapped children be educated, it expressly indicated its intent that the most severely handicapped be given priority. This resolve was reiterated over and over again in the floor debates and congressional reports, as well as in the final legislation.

The principal author, Senator Williams, stated that the bill "assures that handicapped children in the greatest need will be given *priority* by requiring that services be provided first to those children not receiving an education; and second, *to those children with the most severe handicaps* receiving an inadequate education." 121 Cong.Rec.S37413 (1975) (emphasis added). . . .

If the order of the district court denying Timothy W. the benefits of the Act were to be implemented, he would be classified by the Act as in even greater need for receiving educational services than a severely multi-handicapped child receiving inadequate education. He would be in the *highest priority* — as a child who was not receiving any education at all.

C.   Guarantees of Educational Benefit Are Not A Requirement For Child Eligibility

In mandating a public education for all handicapped children, Congress explicitly faced the issue of the possibility of the non-educability of the most severely handicapped. The Senate Report stated, "The Committee recognizes that in many instances the process of providing special education and related services to handicapped children is *not guaranteed to produce any particular outcome.*" Senate Report at 11 (1975), 1975 U.S.Code Cong. & Admin. News, 1435, (emphasis added). . . .

Thus, the district court's major holding, that proof of an educational benefit is a prerequisite before a handicapped child is entitled to a public education, is specifically belied, not only by the statutory language, but by the legislative history as well. We have not found in the Act's voluminous legislative history, nor has the school district directed our attention to, a single affirmative averment to support a benefit/eligibility requirement. But there is explicit evidence of a contrary congressional intent, that *no* guarantee of any particular educational outcome is required for a child to be eligible for public education.

We sum up. In the more than three years of legislative history leading to passage of the 1975 Act, covering House and Senate floor debates, hearings, and Congressional reports, the Congressional intention is unequivocal: Public education is to be provided to all handicapped children, unconditionally and without exception. It encompasses a universal right, and is not predicated upon any type of guarantees that the child will benefit from the special education and services before he or she is considered eligible to receive such educa-

tion. Congress explicitly recognized the particular plight and special needs of the severely handicapped, and rather than excluding them from the Act's coverage, gave them priority status. The district court's holding is directly contradicted by the Act's legislative history, as well as the statutory language.   . . .

The statutory language of the Act, its legislative history, and the case law construing it, mandate that all handicapped children, regardless of the severity of their handicap, are entitled to a public education. The district court erred in requiring a benefit/eligibility test as a prerequisite to implicating the Act. School districts cannot avoid the provisions of the Act by returning to the practices that were widespread prior to the Act's passage, and which indeed were the impetus for the Act's passage, of unilaterally excluding certain handicapped children from a public education on the ground that they are uneducable.

The law explicitly recognizes that education for the severely handicapped is to be broadly defined, to include not only traditional academic skills, but also basic functional life skills, and that educational methodologies in these areas are not static, but are constantly evolving and improving. It is the school district's responsibility to avail itself of these new approaches in providing an education program geared to each child's individual needs. The only question for the school district to determine, in conjunction with the child's parents, is what constitutes an appropriate individualized education program (IEP) for the handicapped child. We emphasize that the phrase "appropriate individualized education program" cannot be interpreted, as the school district has done, to mean "no educational program."

The judgment of the district court is reversed, judgment shall issue for Timothy W. The case is remanded to the district court which shall retain jurisdiction until a suitable individualized education program (IEP) for Timothy W. is effectuated by the school district. Timothy W. is entitled to an interim special educational placement until a final IEP is developed and agreed upon by the parties.

The district court shall also determine the question of damages.

Costs are assessed against the school district.

———

Least Restrictive Environment

The EAHCA advances the general philosophy that handicapped children should be educated with regular children in the normal educational setting whenever possible. The idea is to give the handicapped child opportunity to socialize and interact with other nonhandicapped children, and further, to reduce as much as possible any formal education processes that would tend to stigmatize or differentiate the handicapped child. This objective is clearly set out in the regulation, which provides that

> to the maximum extent appropriate, handicapped children, including children in public or private institutions or other care facilities, [should be] educated with children who are not handicapped, and that separate schooling, or other removal of handicapped children from the regular educational environment [should] occur only when the nature or severity of the handicap is such that education in regular classes with the use of supplementary aids and services cannot be achieved satisfactorily. . . . [74]

This regulation requires that the broadest opportunity should be afforded the student on a "continuum of alternative placements" and that when "selecting the *least restrictive environment*, consideration [must be] given to any potential harmful effect on the child. . . ."[75]

What precisely the "least restrictive environment" requirement means operationally has been fertile ground for speculation, frequently leading to court action. To mainstream a child is generally considered to be the least restrictive environment. Regulations pursuant to the EAHCA provide for a "continuum of alternative placements."[76] At one end of this continuum is the regular classroom, as the least restrictive environment, and at the other, the hospital, as the most restrictive.[77] Though mainstreaming is not specifically referred to by statute, it is generally considered to be the least restrictive environment.

In *Roncker v. Walter*, the Sixth Circuit Court of Appeals[78] observed that

> the Act does not require mainstreaming in every case but its requirement that mainstreaming be provided to the maximum extent appropriate indicated a very strong congressional preference.

A determination by the school that a child should not be mainstreamed but should be placed in a separate class requires a showing that a segregated facility would offer superior educational services. It cannot be assumed *ipso facto* that a segregated education is superior merely because it is more costly or because it is separate. The law establishes a "strong preference in favor of mainstreaming."[79] If a separate facility is considered to be superior to mainstreaming, it must be determined why, and whether it is possible for the same services to be offered in the nonsegregated mainstream setting. If such additional and commensurate services can be offered in the regular classroom, then a separate and segregated placement would be inappropriate.

If, though, the "marginal benefits received from mainstreaming are far outweighed by the benefits gained from services which could not be feasibly provided in the nonsegregated setting," then the courts will hold that mainstreaming is not the appropriate placement.[80]

In one such case, a school district recommended the placement of a student in a self-contained classroom for hearing-impaired students for at least half of the school day with integration into the regular classroom. The parents objected and insisted that the child be placed in a regular classroom all day with the assistance of a full-time speech instructor. The court held that the dispute arose over the appropriate educational methodology, and that the school district had the discretion to make the final decision. The lawsuit was dismissed.[81]

Individualized Education Program Proposed by School Officials Complied with EAHCA

---·---·---·---

Lachman v. Illinois State Board of Education

---·---·---·---

United States Court of Appeals,
Seventh Circuit, 1988.
852 F.2d 290.

ESCHBACH, Senior Circuit Judge. Benjamin Lachman is a profoundly deaf seven-year-old child who resides within the district boundaries of the East Maine, Illinois School District No. 63 ("the school district"). The school district is a member of the Maine Township Special Education Program ("MSTEP") and through MSTEP contracts with Northern Suburban Special Education District to provide services for its hearing-impaired students through a Regional Hearing Impaired Program ("RHIP"). Since the time Benjamin became eligible for participation in the RHIP preschool program, in September, 1984, his parents and the school district have disagreed as to the manner in which his education should be facilitated. . . .

The Lachmans believe that Benjamin can best be educated at a neighborhood school near his home, in a regular classroom with the assistance of a full-time cued speech instructor.[2] In contrast, the school district has consistently proposed that all or at least half of Benjamin's school day be spent in a RHIP self-contained classroom with other hearing-impaired children. . . .

Cued speech is a technique for aiding hearing-impaired persons to understand spoken language. It is used in conjunction with speech (lip) reading and employs eight hand shapes held in four positions close to the mouth to clarify phonetic ambiguities.

In the Spring of 1986, with the approach of Benjamin's enrollment in kindergarten, the controversy between the Lachmans and the school district crystallized. Because the Lachmans did not agree with the Individualized

Education Program ("IEP") that the school district proposed for Benjamin, they initiated the due process review procedure established by § 615 of the Act. . . .

On November 15, 1986, the Lachmans, as Benjamin's guardians, brought suit on his behalf against the school district, MSTEP and the Illinois State Board of Education. At its core, the complaint alleges that the IEP proposed by the RHIP and the school district, and approved by the Illinois State Board of Education, fails to provide Benjamin with a free appropriate public education as required by § 612(1) of the EAHCA. . . .

The district court fashioned its analysis along the lines of the Supreme Court's interpretation, in *Board of Education of the Hendrick Hudson Central School District Board of Education, Westchester County v. Rowley,* 458 U.S. 176, 102 S.Ct. 3034, 73 L.Ed.2d 690 (1982), of the procedural and substantive requirements imposed by the EAHCA. The critical portion of the district court's substantive analysis is set forth below.

> The purpose of the Act was to open the door of public education to handicapped children by means of specialized educational services rather than to guarantee any particular substantive level of education once the child was enrolled. The Act does not require a state to maximize the potential of each child commensurate with the opportunity provided nonhandicapped children. . . .
>
> Courts must avoid imposing their view of preferable educational methods upon the responsible authorities. Once it is shown that the Act's requirements have been met, questions of methodology are for resolution by the responsible authorities.
>
> Clearly, the consultation and procedural requirements of the Act have been met in this case. Careful, impartial consideration has been given to Benjamin's individual educational needs. A full, free appropriate public education has been offered to him. Plaintiffs, because of their and Benjamin's success with cued speech, assert, with support from their experts, that it is the proper methodology by which Benjamin should be educated. But defendants' experts give equal credence to total communication.
>
> Defendants must provide a free appropriate public education for all of the handicapped

children in their particular district. They have done so. Plaintiffs are not entitled to have defendants provide a separate educational opportunity for Benjamin.

Based on the foregoing analysis, the district dismissed the Lachmans' complaint. They appeal from that dismissal.

It is well established that in reviewing the outcomes reached through the § 1415(b) and (c) administrative appeals procedure, a district court is to make an independent decision as to whether the requirements of the Act have been satisfied. . . .

The district court correctly ascertained that *Rowley, supra,* is the definitive Supreme Court pronouncement to date as to the standards a school district must meet in order to satisfy its § 1412(1) obligation to provide all handicapped students with a free appropriate public education. In *Rowley,* the Court directed the lower courts to engage in the following two-part inquiry in suits, like the present one, brought under § 615(e)(2) of the Act.

> First, [the court must inquire whether] the State has complied with the procedures set forth in the Act[.] And second, [the court must ask] is the individualized educational program developed through the Act's procedures reasonably calculated to enable the child to receive educational benefits? If these requirements are met, the State has complied with the obligations imposed by Congress and the courts can require no more.

458 U.S. at 207, 102 S.Ct. at 3051 (footnotes omitted). Appellants do not contend that the appellee education officials failed to comply with the procedures set forth in the Act. Accordingly, we need not address the first part of the *Rowley* test. In determining whether the IEP proposed by the school district secures to Benjamin the right to a free appropriate free public education guaranteed him by § 612(1) of the Act, our analysis will be limited to the second *Rowley* inquiry.

In *Rowley,* the Supreme Court was not directly confronted with a claim that the § 1412(5)(B) mainstreaming goal had not been satisfied. In that opinion, the Court made only a passing reference to the "preference" for mainstreaming handicapped children reflected in § 612(5)(B) of the Act. *Rowley,* 458 U.S. at 202–03, 102 S.Ct. at 3049. Thus, the Lachmans claim that the district court erred because, in applying the *Rowley* test for satisfaction of the Act's general (§ 612(1)) requirement that Benjamin be provided a free appropriate public education, it failed to adequately address the issues raised by the § 1412(5)(B) preference for mainstreaming handicapped children. . . .

Rowley makes clear that "once a court determines that the requirements of the Act have been met, questions of methodology are for resolution by the State." . . . The mainstreaming preference articulated in § 1412(5)(B) is one of the "requirements of the Act" referred to in the above excerpt from *Rowley.* Because the parties' disagreement as to the extent to which Benjamin is to be mainstreamed is inexorably intertwined with their disagreement as to the choice between the cued speech and total communication methodologies, we must first ascertain which of those issues, if any, predominates here.

In order to divine the true crux of the dispute that prompted the present cause of action, we must establish the nature of the mainstreaming obligation created by § 1412(5)(B) and clarify the relationship of that statutory language to the general § 1412(1) requirement that handicapped children be provided with a free appropriate public education. Several post-*Rowley* decisions by the U.S. Courts of Appeals for the Sixth, Eighth and Ninth Circuits, as well as a small number of reported district court opinions, have addressed this topic.

In *Roncker v. Walter,* 700 F.2d 1058 (6th Cir.), *cert. denied,* 464 U.S. 864, 104 S.Ct. 196, 78 L.Ed.2d 171 (1983), the Sixth Circuit observed that:

> The Act does not require mainstreaming in every case but its requirement that mainstreaming be provided to the *maximum* extent appropriate indicates a very strong congressional preference. The proper inquiry is whether a proposed placement is appropriate under the Act. In some cases, a placement which may be considered better for academic reasons may not

be appropriate because of the failure to provide for mainstreaming.

The court in *Roncker* next identified the question of "whether the services which make the segregated placement superior can be feasibly provided in a non-segregated setting" as the key to determining if a proposed segregated placement is inappropriate under the Act. If those services can feasibly be provided in a non-segregated setting, the *Roncker* court stated it would deem the segregated placement inappropriate under the Act. Also relevant to our analysis is the observation in *Roncker* that the Act's "strong preference" for mainstreaming must be balanced against "the possibility that some handicapped children simply must be educated in segregated facilities either because . . . any marginal benefits from mainstreaming are far outweighed by the benefits gained from services which could not feasibly be provided in the non-segregated setting."

The remainder of the relevant reported case law pertaining to § 1412(5)(B) reflects a perception that the mainstreaming preference the statutory provision creates was not meant by Congress to be implemented in an unqualified manner. Instead, it is clear that the courts considering this issue have determined that the Act's mainstreaming preference is to be given effect only when it is clear that the education of the particular handicapped child can be achieved satisfactorily in the type of mainstream environment sought by the challengers to the IEP proposed for that child.

. . . .

We are convinced that appellants' effort to characterize the sole, true issue in this case as whether the proposed IEP satisfies the § 1412(5)(B) mainstreaming preference is misdirected. Undoubtedly, this case does present a valid question of whether the IEP proposed by the school district and affirmed by the Illinois State Board of Education would result in Benjamin being mainstreamed to the "maximum extent appropriate" as contemplated by § 1412(5)(B). However, on careful examination, it becomes apparent that a determination of whether the IEP proposed for Benjamin provides for mainstreaming to the maximum

extent appropriate can be made only within the context of the methodology employed to facilitate his education.

The degree to which a challenged IEP satisfies the mainstreaming goal of the EAHCA simply cannot be evaluated in the abstract. Rather, that laudable policy objective must be weighed in tandem with the Act's principal goal of ensuring that the public schools provide handicapped children with a free appropriate education. . . . A major part of the task of local and state officials in fashioning what they believe to be an effective program for the education of a handicapped child is the selection of the methodology or methodologies that will be employed. "The primary responsibility for formulating the education to be accorded a handicapped child, *and for choosing the educational method most suitable to the child's needs,* was left by the Act to state and local educational agencies in cooperation with the parents or guardians of the child." . . .

The Lachmans' contention that their son can be fully mainstreamed rests squarely on their belief in, and preference for, the cued speech technique. They do not maintain that the fully-mainstreamed placement they seek would be possible without the use of cued speech and the utilization of a cued speech instructor working at Benjamin's side, full-time, in the classroom. Further, appellants do not claim that Benjamin could be mainstreamed to any greater extent than called for in the proposed IEP, if the total communication methodology is utilized. The reasons relied on by the school district for refusing to place Benjamin in a regular classroom full-time focus on its lack of confidence in the cued speech technique as a means for facilitating immediate, full mainstreaming in Benjamin's case. Instead, the school district believes that the total communication concept is the most appropriate way to facilitate Benjamin's early primary education and it has selected that methodology for his IEP.

On the facts of this case, it is clear that the § 1412(5)(B) issue of mainstreaming is subsumed by the parties' disagreement as to methodology. In the absence of the parties' difference of opinion as to that question of educational methodology, there would be no disagreement between them as to the extent of mainstreaming that could presently be achieved for Benjamin. Given the nature of the disagreement between the parties and the concomitant thrust of the Lachmans' cause of action, we can only conclude that the district court did not err when it framed its substantive analysis in a manner closely tracking the *Rowley* opinion, without expressly addressing the § 1412(5)(B) mainstreaming issue.

We have determined that the core, dispositive issue in the controversy that underlies this cause of action is one centering on a disagreement between appellant parents and appellee school district as to the most appropriate method whereby the education of the parents' handicapped child is to be facilitated. Accordingly, in reviewing the decision of the court below, we, like the district court, must take great care to avoid displacing the educational policy judgments made by appellees. That substantial deference to the decisions of those state and local public education officials is warranted here is confirmed by the statements of the Supreme Court in *Rowley* as to the role of the courts under the EAHCA in reviewing the decisions made by state and local public education officials.

> In assuring that the requirements of the Act have been met, courts must be careful to avoid imposing their view of preferable education methods upon the States. The primary responsibility for formulating the education to be accorded a handicapped child, and for choosing the educational method most suitable to the child's needs, was left by the Act to state and local educational agencies in cooperation with the parents and guardians of the child. . . . [I]t seems highly unlikely that that Congress intended courts to overturn a State's choice of appropriate educational theories in a proceeding brought pursuant to § 1415(e)(2).
>
> We previously have cautioned that courts lack the "specialized knowledge and experience" necessary to resolve "persistent and difficult questions of educational policy." We think Congress shared that view when it passed the Act. . . . Therefore, once a court determines that the requirements of the Act have been met, questions of methodology are for resolution by the States.

Rowley, 458 U.S. at 207–08, 102 S.Ct. at 3052–53 (citation omitted). . . .

The district court expressly found that defendant/appellee education officials had complied with the Act. Our review leads us to the same conclusion. *Rowley* and its progeny leave no doubt that parents, no matter how well-motivated, do not have a right under the EAHCA to compel a school district to provide a specific program or employ a specific methodology in providing for the education of their handicapped child. . . . It is clear that the IEP proposed by the school district is based upon an accepted, proven methodology for facilitating the early primary education of profoundly hearing-impaired children. Further, nothing in the record indicates that the proposed IEP does not provide that Benjamin will be educated in a regular classroom environment to the maximum extent appropriate as required by § 612(5)(B) of the Act. Given these findings, we conclude that the proposed IEP will provide Benjamin Lachman with a free appropriate public education as required by § 612(1) of the Act. Accordingly, the judgment of the district court is affirmed.

————

Separate School Placement

The use of private schools for appropriate educational placement has been the subject of bitter dispute between parents of handicapped children and local school administrators.[82] Increasingly, courts have had to decide whether "parents have the right under the law to write a prescription for an ideal education for their child and to have the prescription filled at public expense."[83]

Results of judicial intervention are mixed. However, in most cases, if a public school program is available, and judged to be appropriate for the child's needs, the courts have tended to favor local district administrative decisions.

When no appropriate placement can be provided within the local public schools, "special education and related services . . . including nonmedical care and room and board must be [provided] at no cost to the parents of the child."[84] This holds true even when it has been contended that twenty-four-hour residential care is necessary for noneducational reasons, that is, emotional problems or custodial care.

On the "placement continuum," placement in a separate residential school is toward the extreme end nearest hospitalization. Placement in a separate school, though, is an option that is commonly used. The law explicitly contemplates residential placement as an appropriate alternative, specifying that

> [i]f placement in a public or private residential program is necessary to provide special education and related services to a handicapped child, the program, including nonmedical care and room and board, must be at no cost to the parents of the child.[85]

The necessity and presumption of the appropriateness of placement in a regular classroom has been contested, in favor of a separate school, by parents from differing viewpoints. Some parents strongly inveigh against mainstreaming and insist that their child be placed in a particularized environment of a separate facility or school. On the other hand, some parents strongly resolve to have their child in the company of other children in a regular classroom in a public school. This latter position was taken by parents in a recent Virginia case, in which a parent sought to compel the school board to remove her child from a private special education school and place him in a regular classroom.[86] The Fourth Circuit Court of Appeals found the private school placement to be appropriate and upheld the school board. The court reasoned that mainstreaming was indeed the preferred objective; however, this preference is overcome when the individual needs of a child are such that separate school placement is appropriate. In this particular case, the student was autistic and the private school was one that emphasized vocational education. The court agreed with the school board that mainstreaming would have resulted in the boy merely "monitoring" classes and would have been of little benefit, whereas

the special vocational training gave the student special tutorial instruction more appropriate to his needs. Thus, circumstances may be such that mainstreaming is not the preferred alternative.

A school board cannot refuse private school placement of a handicapped child if the appropriate education cannot be provided within the school district. When a parent unilaterally places a child in a private placement and the court later determines this placement to be proper and the school-developed IEP inappropriate, then relief should be granted. In speaking to this issue, the U.S. Supreme Court in *School Committee of Burlington v. Department of Education* stated that "appropriate relief would include a prospective injunction directing the school officials to develop and implement at public expense an IEP placing the child in a private school."[87]

The act does not impose financial, geographical, or other limitations on the placement so long as it is determined to be appropriate. Appropriateness of placement is not "location-specific."[88] In what is perhaps an extreme case, the placement of a child in a school in Tokyo, Japan, was upheld by the courts.[89] In this instance the child was autistic, and as he had gotten older his behavior had become more aggressive. His parents, as a consequence, withdrew him from the school district's special education program. Upon recommendation of a private center for such children, he was placed in a private residential center in Tokyo. After two years there, he was transferred to a new center in Boston, a branch of the Tokyo school. The school district challenged the appropriateness of both the Tokyo and Boston placements, but the court upheld the placements. The case turned on the fact that the state had not developed assessment standards for autistic students, and therefore, without standards of its own, could not challenge the Tokyo and Boston placements as being inappropriate.[90] The federal district court that ruled in favor of the parents before the appeal to the Eleventh Circuit admitted that it was somewhat "troubled" by sending a child as far away as Tokyo, and because of the potentially prohibitive costs, required careful monitoring of the expenditures. This necessity, though, was obviated by the eventual Boston placement.

The moral of the story, as far as this case is concerned, is that the state should be prepared with formal standards to assess the various needs of handicapped children and to be equipped to offer alternative acceptable placements.

Before Ordering Residential Placement for a Handicapped Child, the Court Will Weigh the Mainstreaming Policy Which Encourages Placement of the Child in the Least Restrictive Environment

— · — · — · — · —

Kruelle v. New Castle County School District

— · — · — · — · —

United States Court of Appeals,
Third Circuit, 1981.
642 F.2d 687.

ADAMS, Circuit Judge. [D]id the district court err in determining that Paul Kruelle is entitled to residential placement under the Education Act?

Appellee is profoundly retarded and is also afflicted with cerebral palsy. At age thirteen he has the social skills of a six-month-old child and his I.Q. is well below thirty. As found by the district court, "he cannot walk, dress himself, or eat unaided. He is not toilet trained. He does not speak, and his receptive communication level is extremely low. In addition to his physical problems, he has had a history of emotional problems which result in choking and self-induced vomiting when experiencing stress."

The chronicle of Paul's educational placements begins in 1973, when he entered the Barber Center Preschool Program in Pennsylvania, where the Kruelle family then resided. Paul next spent three years in the public school system in a mixed class with the trainable mentally retarded. By 1977 Paul's behavior had significantly deteriorated. He was vomiting food in school and having frequent temper tantrums. That summer Paul received in-home instruction to compensate for his rejection of the school environment.

In September 1977, at the behest of the public educational authorities, Paul was placed in the private day program at the Barber Center. Admission was based on the local school agencies' certification that "an appropriate education for this child cannot be met in a special education program operated either by the school district or Intermediate Unit" in Pennsylvania. Despite initial improvement, by early 1978 Paul again manifested the vomiting and choking that apparently is caused by emotional stress. Because of the severity and increased frequency of the vomiting, both the school authorities and Paul's parents concluded that twenty-four-hour residential placement was needed.

After a short period in respite care, Paul was admitted in June 1978 to the Barber Center's New Community Living Arrangement Program for multiply-handicapped children. Although not a "residential" placement in the sense of having the living environment and school facilities on the same premises, this combination school program and group home did provide around-the-clock training by skilled caretakers. The local and state educational agencies, Department of Public Welfare and Social Security Administration provided funding for the program. Most importantly, except for a brief hospital stay for pneumonia, Paul appears to have adjusted well to this joint CLA residence-school program.

The Kruelle family then moved to Delaware. Paul was immediately enrolled in the Meadowood School and placed in respite care at the home of Mrs. Albanese. Mrs. Albanese had extensive experience in the care and training of handicapped children. Although the teachers at Meadowood indicated that Paul made observable progress at the school and Mrs. Albanese noted some improvements from her continuation of Paul's day-time training, after two weeks the Kruelles withdrew Paul from Meadowood. Having objected from the start to the lack of a residential placement in Delaware, as well as to Paul's assignment to a mixed class of trainable mentally retarded, which had previously failed, the Kruelles next began through the administrative process, an unsuccessful quest for a residential program.

Parents or guardians challenging a child's educational placement are offered an impartial hearing under the Education Act. 20 U.S.C. § 1415(b)(2). In states such as Delaware, where the hearing is conducted by a local or an intermediate educational unit, the party may appeal to the state educational agency. 20 U.S.C. § 1415(c). Both the district hearing officer and the state-level review officer determined that the individual educational program (IEP) proposed by the Meadowood staff was "appropriate" within the meaning of the Education Act. The district hearing officer found that residential placement was "too restrictive," while the state review officer asserted that the full-time services sought "were more in the nature of parenting than education." The Kruelle's request for Paul's placement in a residential setting was therefore denied.

In October, 1979, Paul's parents, pro se, sought review of the administrative decision by filing a civil suit in district court. The multiple defendants included the local New Castle County School District (NCCSD), the supervisory State Board of Education, the Superintendent of the Division of Public Instruction, Dr. Kenneth Madden as well as the state authorities with general jurisdiction over programs for handicapped children in Delaware — the Division of Health and Social Services and the Division of Mental Retardation. Both sides requested the opportunity to present additional evidence at the court hearing.

Dr. Angert, who had previously served as a consultant for the NCCSD but who had no firsthand knowledge of Paul's experience at Meadowood, was the principal witness for the Kruelles. Although he generally was inclined against residential placement, he recommended such a program for Paul, because of Paul's need for a consistent environment. Dr. Angert believed, in light of Paul's history, that "inconsistency of approach, environment or caretakers typically led to stress and self-destructive behaviors such as vomiting." Ac-

cordingly, he urged a twenty-four-hour placement "with programming by people who know how to do it" in order to maximize Paul's chances of learning. *Kruelle v. Biggs*, 489 F.Supp. at 173. The defendant school and state authorities continued to maintain that the day program at Meadowood satisfied Paul's educational needs, and any necessity for residential placement arose from social and emotional problems clearly beyond the competency and responsibility of school officials.

Much like Dr. Angert, the district court concluded that Paul required a greater degree of consistency than many other profoundly retarded children. Specifically, it held that the present educational program provided by the NCCSD was not a free appropriate public education within the meaning of the Act. Then, in a supplemental order, the district court directed the State Education Board to provide Paul with a full-time residential program. The local and state school authorities now appeal this decision challenging both the residential placement and the imposition of the order against the state agency as erroneous interpretations of the requirements of the Education Act. We affirm. . . .

The Education Act, however, is not silent on what qualifies as a free appropriate public education (FAPE). In fact, the 1975 statute and regulations promulgated thereunder, for the first time, give definitional content to the term "appropriate education" and its component parts, "special education" and "related services."

Theoretically, the scope and details of an appropriate education which the local educational agencies are obligated to provide as a condition to receiving federal grants under the statute, are left primarily to state definition. But the term "special education" is given specific content:

The term "special education" means specially designed instruction, at no cost to parents or guardians, to meet the unique needs of a handicapped child, including classroom instruction, instruction in physical education, home instruction, and instruction in hospitals and institutions. 20 U.S.C. § 1401(16).

Similarly, "related services" is extensively defined:

> The term "related services" means transportation, and such developmental corrective, and other supportive services (including speech pathology and audiology, psychological services, physical and occupational therapy, recreation, and medical and counseling services, except that such medical services shall be for diagnostic and evaluation purposes only) as may be required to assist a handicapped child to benefit from special education, and includes the early identification and assessment of handicapping conditions in children. 20 U.S.C. § 1401(17).

Moreover, the regulations promulgated under the Act explicitly contemplate residential placement:

> If placement in a public or private residential program is necessary to provide special education and related services to a handicapped child, the program, including nonmedical care and room and board, must be at no cost to the parents of the child.

> Comment. This requirement applies to placements which are made by public agencies for educational purposes, and includes placements in State-operated schools for the handicapped, such as a State school for the deaf or blind. 45 C.F.R. § 121a.302.

In light of these provisions, a court is not without guidance in determining whether a residential setting is consistent with the purpose and directives of the Education Act. And most courts confronted with the question whether residential placement is necessary to meet the goals of an individual education plan have answered in the affirmative.

Another salient feature of the Education Act, for our purposes, is the congressional rejection of court deference to agency determinations. The statute contemplates a *de novo* review role by the district courts, including the hearing of additional evidence and an independent decision by the district courts based on the preponderance of the evidence. 20 U.S.C. § 1415(e)(2). Thus, in evaluating the ruling by the district court here, what is critical is not whether the judge reversed the conclusions of the state agencies, but whether he properly applied the preponderance of the evidence standard prescribed by Congress.

Significantly, all parties concede that Paul needs full-time assistance from the state of Delaware beyond that available in any day school program. It is also uncontroverted that the Education Act specifically provides for residential placement in certain instances. The question, then, is whether the trial judge correctly construed the Education Act as requiring more continuous supervision for Paul than he was receiving under the Meadowood Program in order to meet the standard of a free appropriate education.

Based on our careful review of the record, we cannot find that the district court erred in holding that the six-hour day provided by the Meadowood program was an inappropriate education given the terms of the Act.   . . .

Analysis must focus, then, on whether full-time placement may be considered necessary for educational purposes, or whether the residential placement is a response to medical, social or emotional problems that are segregable from the learning process. . . .

The relevant question in the present case is whether residential placement is part and parcel of a "specially designed instruction . . . to meet to the unique needs of a handicapped child," in conformity with § 1401(16). And we cannot conclude that the district judge misapplied the statutory standard in determining that "because of his combination of physical and mental handicaps, [Paul] requires a greater degree of consistency of programming than many other profoundly retarded children" and that "it would appear that full-time care is necessary in order to allow Paul to learn." Indeed, it would be difficult to conceive of a more apt case than Paul's for which the unique needs of a child required residential placement. . . .

Of course, before ordering residential placement, a court should weigh the mainstreaming policy embodied in the Education Act which encourages placement of the child in the least restrictive environment. The district judge here, however, carefully undertook such a calculation. He noted that in the past attempts to provide in-home care and after-school instruction had been singularly unsuccessful; all had occasioned regression for Paul. . . . once a court concludes that residential placement is the only realistic option for learning improvement, the question of "least restrictive" environment is also resolved. "Only when alternatives exist must the court reach the issue of which is the least restrictive." If day school cannot provide an appropriate education it is, by definition, not a possible alternative.

Admittedly, the unequivocal congressional directive to provide an appropriate education for all children regardless of the severity of the handicap, 20 U.S.C. § 1412(2)(C), places a substantial burden on states in certain instances. The language and the legislative history of the Act simply do not entertain the possibility that some children may be untrainable. . . . Under the Education Act, . . . schools are required to provide a comprehensive range of services to accommodate a handicapped child's educational needs, regardless of financial and administrative burdens, and if necessary, to resort to residential placement. The district court's order, consequently, did not impose a duty beyond the contemplation of the Education Act; rather it carried out the implications of an undeniably broad statutory intent. . . .

NOTE

1. In *Clevenger v. Oak Ridge School Board,* 744 F.2d 514 (1984), the U.S. Court of Appeals, 6th Circuit, stated:

> [C]ost can be a legitimate consideration when devising an appropriate program . . . . Nevertheless, cost considerations are only relevant when choosing between several options, all of which offer an appropriate education.

Related Services

Under Public Law 94–142, supportive services that enable handicapped children to benefit from special education must be made available without cost to the parents. The act defines related services:

> The term "related services" means transportation, and such developmental, corrective, and other supportive services (including speech pathology and audiology, psychological services, physical and occupational therapy, recreation, and medical and counseling services, except that such medical services shall be for diagnostic and evaluative purposes only) as may be required to assist a handicapped child to benefit from special education. . . . [91]

The Federal Regulations promulgated pursuant to the act further define [34 C.F.R. § 300.13(b)(8)] "psychological services" as "planning and managing a program of psychological services, including psychological counseling for children and parents," and "counseling services" [34 C.F.R. § 300.13(b)(2)] are defined as "services provided by qualified social workers, psychologists, guidance counselors, or other qualified personnel."

Confusion has arisen regarding which medical services fall within the domain of Public Law 94–142. In *Irving Independent School District v. Tatro,*[92] clean intermittent catheterization (CIC) was required by the Supreme Court in spite of the fact that the school district had claimed the service was not required under Public Law 94–142 guidelines,[93] which exempt medical services except those for diagnostic and evaluation purposes.[94] The Court in *Tatro* stated, "Only those services necessary to aid a handicapped child to benefit from special education must be provided" under the act.[95]

Further, a federal district court has ruled that psychotherapy is a related service, although not specifically mentioned in either the act or regulations.[96] Here, the court required out-of-district transportation and stated that "unless the transportation request is shown to be unreasonable, the EAHCA requires that such transportation be provided as a related service."[97]

When a child is placed in a facility for medical purposes and not for educational placement, then the child is not within the purview of the Handicapped Act. Where a child was placed in a hospital for psychiatric care, the court stated, "Although 'related services' may include medical services, the Act does not require a school system to provide services by a physician except those necessary for diagnostic and evaluation purposes."[98] Residential placement, however, is a related service in which social and emotional issues are intertwined with educational problems.[99]

Catheterization Falls within Definition of Related Services

— — — — — — — — — —

Irving Independent School District v. Tatro

— — — — — — — — — —

Supreme Court of the United States, 1984.
468 U.S. 883, 104 S.Ct. 3371.

CHIEF JUSTICE BURGER delivered the opinion of the Court. We granted certiorari to determine whether the Education of the Handicapped Act or the Rehabilitation Act of 1973 requires a school district to provide a handicapped child with clean intermittent catheterization during school hours.

Amber Tatro is an eight-year-old girl born with a defect known as spina bifida. As a result, she suffers from orthopedic and speech impairments and a neurogenic bladder, which prevents her from emptying her bladder voluntarily. Consequently, she must be catheterized every three or four hours to avoid injury to her kidneys. In accordance with accepted medical practice, clean intermittent catheterization (CIC), a procedure involving the insertion of a catheter into the urethra to drain the bladder, has been prescribed. The procedure is a simple one that may be performed in a few minutes by a layperson with less than an hour's training. Amber's parents, babysitter, and teenage brother are all quali-

fied to administer CIC, and Amber soon will be able to perform this procedure herself.

In 1979 petitioner Irving Independent School District agreed to provide special education for Amber, who was then three and one-half years old. In consultation with her parents, who are respondents here, petitioner developed an individualized education program for Amber under the requirements of the Education of the Handicapped Act, 84 Stat. 175, as amended significantly by the Education for All Handicapped Children Act of 1975, 89 Stat. 773, 20 U.S.C. §§ 1401(19), 1414(a)(5). The individualized education program provided that Amber would attend early childhood development classes and receive special services such as physical and occupational therapy. That program, however, made no provision for school personnel to administer CIC. . . .

This case poses two separate issues. The first is whether the Education of the Handicapped Act requires petitioner to provide CIC services to Amber. The second is whether § 504 of the Rehabilitation Act creates such an obligation. We first turn to the claim presented under the Education of the Handicapped Act.

States receiving funds under the Act are obliged to satisfy certain conditions. A primary condition is that the state implement a policy "that assures all handicapped children the right to a free appropriate public education." 20 U.S.C. § 1412(1). Each educational agency applying to a state for funding must provide assurances in turn that its program aims to provide "a free appropriate public education to all handicapped children." § 1414(a)(1)(C)(ii).

A "free appropriate public education" is explicitly defined as "special education and related services." § 1401(18). The term "special education" means

> specially designed instruction, at no cost to parents or guardians, to meet the unique needs of a handicapped child, including classroom instruction, instruction in physical education, home instruction, and instruction in hospitals and institutions. § 1401(16).

"Related services" are defined as

> transportation, and such developmental, corrective, and other *supportive services (including* speech pathology and audiology, psychological services, physical and occupational therapy, recreation, and *medical* and counseling *services, except that such medical services shall be for diagnostic and evaluation purposes only) as may be required to assist a handicapped child to benefit from special education,* and includes the early identification and assessment of handicapping conditions in children. § 1401(17) (emphasis added).

The issue in this case is whether CIC is a "related service" that petitioner is obliged to provide to Amber. We must answer two questions: first, whether CIC is a "supportive servic[e] . . . required to assist a handicapped child to benefit from special education"; and second, whether CIC is excluded from this definition as a "medical servic[e]" serving purposes other than diagnosis or evaluation.

The Court of Appeals was clearly correct in holding that CIC is a "supportive servic[e] . . . required to assist a handicapped child to benefit from special education." It is clear on this record that, without having CIC services available during the school day, Amber cannot attend school and thereby "benefit from special education." CIC services therefore fall squarely within the definition of a "supportive service."

As we have stated before, "Congress sought primarily to make public education available to handicapped children" and "to make such access meaningful." *Board of Education of Hendrick Hudson Central School District v. Rowley,* 458 U.S. 176, 192, 102 S.Ct. 3034, 3043, 73 L.Ed.2d 690 (1982). A service that enables a handicapped child to remain at school during the day is an important means of providing the child with the meaningful access to education that Congress envisioned. The Act makes specific provision for services, like transportation, for example, that do no more than enable a child to be physically present in class, see 20 U.S.C. § 1401(17); and the Act specifically authorizes grants for

schools to alter buildings and equipment to make them accessible to the handicapped, § 1406; see S.Rep. No. 94–168, p. 38 (1975); 121 Cong. Rec. 19483–19484 (1975) (remarks of Sen. Stafford). Services like CIC that permit a child to remain at school during the day are no less related to the effort to educate than are services that enable the child to reach, enter, or exit the school.

We hold that CIC services in this case qualify as a "supportive servic[e] . . . required to assist a handicapped child to benefit from special education."

We also agree with the Court of Appeals that provision of CIC is not a "medical servic[e]," which a school is required to provide only for purposes of diagnosis or evaluation. See 20 U.S.C. § 1401(17). We begin with the regulations of the Department of Education, which are entitled to deference. See, e.g., *Blum v. Bacon,* 457 U.S. 132, 141, 102 S.Ct. 2355, 2361, 72 L.Ed. 2d 728 (1982). The regulations define "related services" for handicapped children to include "school health services," 34 CFR § 300.13(a) (1983), which are defined in turn as "services provided by a qualified school nurse or other qualified person," § 300.13(b)(10). "Medical services" are defined as "services provided by a licensed physician." § 300.13(b)(4). Thus, the Secretary has determined that the services of a school nurse otherwise qualifying as a "related service" are not subject to exclusion as a "medical service," but that the services of a physician are excludable as such.

This definition of "medical services" is a reasonable interpretation of congressional intent. Although Congress devoted little discussion to the "medical services" exclusion, the Secretary could reasonably have concluded that it was designed to spare schools from an obligation to provide a service that might well prove unduly expensive and beyond the range of their competence. From this understanding of congressional purpose, the Secretary could reasonably have concluded that Congress intended to impose the obligation to provide school nursing services.

Congress plainly required schools to hire various specially trained personnel to help handicapped children, such as "trained occupational therapists, speech therapists, psychologists, social workers and other appropriately trained personnel." S.Rep. No. 94–168, supra, at 33. School nurses have long been a part of the educational system, and the Secretary could therefore reasonably conclude that school nursing services are not the sort of burden that Congress intended to exclude as a "medical service." By limiting the "medical services" exclusion to the services of a physician or hospital, both far more expensive, the Secretary has given a permissible construction to the provision.

Petitioner's contrary interpretation of the "medical services" exclusion is unconvincing. In petitioner's view , CIC is a "medical service," even though it may be provided by a nurse or trained layperson; that conclusion rests on its reading of Texas law that confines CIC to uses in accordance with a physician's prescription and under a physician's ultimate supervision. Aside from conflicting with the Secretary's reasonable interpretation of congressional intent, however, such a rule would be anomalous. Nurses in petitioner's school district are authorized to dispense oral medications and administer emergency injections in accordance with a physician's prescription. This kind of service for nonhandicapped children is difficult to distinguish from the provision of CIC to the handicapped. It would be strange indeed if Congress, in attempting to extend special services to handicapped children, were unwilling to guarantee them services of a kind that are routinely provided to the nonhandicapped.

To keep in perspective the obligation to provide services that relate to both the health and educational needs of handicapped students, we note several limitations that should minimize the burden petitioner fears. First, to be entitled to related services, a child must be handicapped so as to require special education. See 20 U.S.C. § 1401(1); 34 CFR § 300.5 (1983). In the absence of a handicap that requires special education, the need for what otherwise might qualify as a related service does not create an obligation under the Act. See 34 CFR § 300.14, Comment (1) (1983).

Second, only those services necessary to aid a handicapped child to benefit from special education must be provided, regardless how easily a school nurse or layperson could furnish them. For example, if a particular medication or treatment may appropriately be administered to a handicapped child other than during the school day, a school is not required to provide nursing services to administer it.

Third, the regulations state that school nursing services must be provided only if they can be performed by a nurse or other qualified person, not if they must be performed by a physician. See 34 CFR §§ 300.13(a), (b)(4), (b)(10) (1983). It bears mentioning that here not even the services of a nurse are required; as is conceded, a layperson with minimal training is qualified to provide CIC.   . . .

Finally, we note that respondents are not asking petitioner to provide *equipment* that Amber needs for CIC. Tr. of Oral Arg. 18–19. They seek only the *services* of a qualified person at the school.

We conclude that provision of CIC to Amber is not subject to exclusion as a "medical service," and we affirm the Court of Appeals' holding that CIC is a "related service" under the Education of the Handicapped Act.

Respondents sought relief not only under the Education of the Handicapped Act but under § 504 of the Rehabilitation Act as well. After finding petitioner liable to provide CIC under the former, the District Court proceeded to hold that petitioner was similarly liable under § 504 and that respondents were therefore entitled to attorney's fees under § 505 of the Rehabilitation Act, 29 U.S.C. § 794a. We hold today, in *Smith v. Robinson,* ____U.S. ____, 104 S.Ct. 3457, 80 L.Ed.2d (1984), that § 504 is inapplicable when relief is available under the Education of the Handicapped Act to remedy a denial of educational services. Respondents are therefore not entitled to relief under § 504, and we reverse the Court of Appeals' holding that respondents are entitled to recover attorney's fees. In all other respects, the judgment of the Court of Appeals is affirmed.

It is so ordered.

NOTES

1. *In-school nurse.* Related services do not extend to require the school to provide an in-school nurse needed to attend to a child's daily medical needs. A child in a physical condition so severe as to require constant nursing care is beyond the requirements of "related services" and falls in the realm of "medical services." *Detsel v. Board of Education,* 637 F.Supp. 1022 (N.D.N.Y. 1986); affirmed 820 F.2d 587 (2d Cir. 1987); *cert denied* 108 S.Ct. 495 (1987).

2. *Treatment for Emotional Problems.* The departing line between related services and medical services is most difficult to define when a child has an emotional handicap. In addressing this issue, a federal district court was called upon to apportion expenses used between related and medical services in this nebulous area of mental and psychological treatment. After trial, the district court concluded that counseling, psychological services, and periodic psychiatric evaluations for medication purposes were "related services when provided by a psychologist, social worker, or other professional." Even though this decision was reversed on procedural grounds, this broad view of related services is likely to prevail. *Antkowiak v. Ambach,* 838 F.2d 635 (2d Cir. 1988).

3. *Provision of Extracurricular Activities.* The EAHCA does not require that school districts provide extracurricular activities for handicapped children. *Rettig v. Kent City School District,* 788 F.2d 328 (6th Cir. 1986).

Discipline and Stay-Put

The mainstreaming of handicapped children has underscored the need for guidelines governing the disciplining of handicapped students. Neither § 504 nor Public Law 94–142 addresses this issue, leaving it to the courts to decipher the legal ramifications involved.

Two provisions of the Education for All Handicapped Children Act must be considered when disciplinary action is taken with a handicapped student: appropriate education and least restrictive environment. P.L. 94–142 mandates that a handicapped student must be provided a free appropriate education in the least restrictive environment. Acceptable environments for the placement of a handicapped child range from least restrictive (a regular classroom) to highly restrictive (an institution). However, each environment can be termed "least restrictive" depending upon the seriousness of a particular handicap, and the student's ability to cope within a specific environment.

Courts have consistently ruled that handicapped students must be given special consideration in disciplinary proceedings.[100] Earlier court decisions prohibited expulsion, noting that, under Public Law 94–142, services must be provided through alternative placement in one of the other educational environments offered.[101]

In 1981, expulsion again surfaced as an issue, when nine mentally retarded students in the state of Florida sued local districts and the state, claiming that they had been denied an appropriate education due to expulsion.[102] The court upheld expulsion in *S–1 v. Turlington*[103] as a viable form of discipline to be used with handicapped students. The court, however, pointed out that cessation of all educational programs violated the rights of handicapped students, consequently even after expelling a student, services must be provided.

Suspension, on the other hand, has been viewed favorably by the courts as an appropriate disciplinary action for handicapped students, when it has been determined that misconduct is not related to the student's handicap. If it is related to the handicapping condition, an alternate or more restrictive placement should be considered, rather than suspension or expulsion.[104]

The "Stay-Put" Provision

The Education of the Handicapped Act contains a pendency of review provision that prohibits school authorities from unilaterally excluding a handicapped child from school during review proceedings to determine the placement of the student. Section 1415(e)(3) of the act states that "the child shall remain in the then current educational placement" until proper placement can be determined. This so-called stay-put provision raises the question as to whether a child can be excluded from school for an indefinite period of time for dangerous or disruptive conduct growing out of a disability. *S–1 v. Turlington*[105] and other cases[106] left doubt as to whether there was, in fact, a "dangerousness" exclusion implied by the act. In *Honig v. Doe*, the U.S. Supreme Court resolved the issue by making it clear that the EAHCA (1) confers a substantive right to education on disabled students, (2) prohibits school officials from unilaterally excluding a disabled student from the classroom for dangerous or disruptive conduct for an indeterminate period of time where conduct grows out of a disability, and (3) permits school officials to temporarily suspend a student for up to ten days to protect the safety of others and to provide a "cooling down." During which time an IEP meeting can be initiated to review the child's placement. If the school needs more than ten days to change the placement to a more restrictive environment, they may petition the court for an injunction, since the act does not apply to the courts. Yet, even though the "stay put" provision requires that the child remain in school, it does not forbid the use of reasonable measures to control an offending child who endangers himself or others. The school may employ methods such as study carrels, timeouts, detention or other restriction of privileges in the interest of the safety and decorum of the school. Such measures do not constitute a change of placement.

"Stay-Put" Provision Prohibits
School Authorities from Unilaterally Excluding
Disabled Students from Classroom for Dangerous
Conduct Growing Out of Disability

— · — · — · — · —

Honig v. Doe

— · — · — · — · —

Supreme Court of the United States, 1988.
484 U.S. 305, 108 S.Ct. 592.

Justice BRENNAN delivered the opinion of the Court. As a condition of federal financial assistance, the Education of the Handicapped Act requires States to ensure a "free appropriate public education" for all disabled children within their jurisdictions. In aid of this goal, the Act establishes a comprehensive system of procedural safeguards designed to ensure parental participation in decisions concerning the education of their disabled children and to provide administrative and judicial review of any decisions with which those parents disagree. Among these safeguards is the so-called "stay-put" provision, which directs that a disabled child "shall remain in [his or her] then current educational placement" pending completion of any review proceedings, unless the parents and state or local educational agencies otherwise agree. 20 U.S. C. § 1415(e)(3). Today we must decide whether, in the face of this statutory proscription, state or local school authorities may nevertheless unilaterally exclude disabled children from the classroom for dangerous or disruptive conduct growing out of their disabilities. In addition, we are called upon to decide whether a district court may, in the exercise of its equitable powers, order a State to provide educational services directly to a disabled child when the local agency fails to do so.

. . .

The present dispute grows out of the efforts of certain officials of the San Francisco Unified School District (SFUSD) to expel two emotionally disturbed children from school indefinitely for violent and disruptive conduct related to their disabilities. In November 1980, respondent John Doe assaulted another student at the Louise Lombard School, a developmental center for disabled children. Doe's April 1980 IEP identified him as a socially and physically awkward 17 year old who experienced considerable difficulty controlling his impulses and anger. Among the goals set out in his IEP was "[i]mprovement in [his] ability to relate to [his] peers [and to] cope with frustrating situations without resorting to aggressive acts." Frustrating situations, however, were an unfortunately prominent feature of Doe's school career: physical abnormalities, speech difficulties, and poor grooming habits had made him the target of teasing and ridicule as early as the first grade; his 1980 IEP reflected his continuing difficulties with peers, noting that his social skills had deteriorated and that he could tolerate only minor frustration before exploding.

On November 6, 1980, Doe responded to the taunts of a fellow student in precisely the explosive manner anticipated by his IEP: he choked the student with sufficient force to leave abrasions on the child's neck, and kicked out a school window while being escorted to the principal's office afterwards. Doe admitted his misconduct and the school subsequently suspended him for five days. Thereafter, his principal referred the matter to the SFUSD Student Placement Committee (SPC or Committee) with the recommendation that Doe be expelled. . . .

After unsuccessfully protesting these actions by letter, Doe brought this suit against a host of local school officials and the state superintendent of public education. Alleging that the suspension and proposed expulsion violated the EHA, he sought a temporary restraining order cancelling the SPC hearing and requiring school officials to convene an IEP meeting. The District Judge granted the requested injunctive relief and further ordered defendants to provide home tutoring for Doe on an interim basis; shortly thereafter, she issued a preliminary injunction directing defendants to return Doe to his then current educational placement at Louise Lombard School pending completion of the IEP review process. Doe re-entered school on December 15, 5½ weeks, and 24 school days, after his initial suspension.

Respondent Jack Smith was identified as an emotionally disturbed child by the time he entered the second grade in 1976. School records prepared that year indicated that he was unable "to control verbal or physical outburst[s]" and exhibited a "[s]evere disturbance in relationships with peers and adults." Further evaluations subsequently revealed that he had been physically and emotionally abused as an infant and young child and that, despite above average intelligence, he experienced academic and social difficulties as a

result of extreme hyperactivity and low self-esteem. Of particular concern was Smith's propensity for verbal hostility; one evaluator noted that the child reacted to stress by "attempt[ing] to cover his feelings of low self worth through aggressive behavior[,] . . . primarily verbal provocations."

Based on these evaluations, SFUSD placed Smith in a learning center for emotionally disturbed children. . . .

At the beginning of the next school year, Smith was assigned to a full-day program; almost immediately thereafter he began misbehaving. School officials met twice with his grandparents in October 1980 to discuss returning him to a half-day program; although the grandparents agreed to the reduction, they apparently were never apprised of their right to challenge the decision through EHA procedures. The school officials also warned them that if the child continued his disruptive behavior—which included stealing, extorting money from fellow students, and making sexual comments to female classmates—they would seek to expel him. On November 14, they made good on this threat, suspending Smith for five days after he made further lewd comments. His principal referred the matter to the SPC, which recommended exclusion from SFUSD. . . .

After learning of Doe's action, Smith sought and obtained leave to intervene in the suit. The District Court subsequently entered summary judgment in favor of respondents on their EHA claims and issued a permanent injunction. In a series of decisions, the District Judge found that the proposed expulsions and indefinite suspensions of respondents for conduct attributable to their disabilities deprived them of their congressionally mandated right to a free appropriate public education, as well as their right to have that education provided in accordance with the procedures set out in the EHA. The District Judge therefore permanently enjoined the school district from taking any disciplinary action other than a two- or five-day suspension against any disabled child for disability-related misconduct, or from effecting any other change in the educational placement of any such child without parental consent pending completion of any EHA proceedings. In addition, the judge barred the State from authorizing unilateral placement changes and directed it to establish an EHA compliance-monitoring system or, alternatively, to enact guidelines governing local school responses to disability-related misconduct. Finally, the judge ordered the State to provide services directly to disabled children when, in any individual case, the State determined that the local educational agency was unable or unwilling to do so.

On appeal, the Court of Appeals for the Ninth Circuit affirmed the orders with slight modifications. *Doe v. Maher*, 793 F.2d 1470 (1986). Agreeing with the District Court that an indefinite suspension in aid of expulsion constitutes a prohibited "change in placement" under § 1415(e)(3), the Court of Appeals held that the stay-put provision admitted of no "dangerousness" exception and that the statute therefore rendered invalid those provisions of the California Education Code permitting the indefinite suspension or expulsion of disabled children for misconduct arising out of their disabilities. The court concluded, however, that fixed suspensions of up to 30 school days did not fall within the reach of § 1415(e)(3), and therefore upheld recent amendments to the state education code authorizing such suspensions. Lastly, the court affirmed that portion of the injunction requiring the State to provide services directly to a disabled child when the local educational agency fails to do so.

Petitioner Bill Honig, California Superintendent of Public Instruction, sought review in this Court, claiming that the Court of Appeals' construction of the stay-put provision conflicted with that of several other courts of appeals which had recognized a dangerousness exception, . . . and that the direct services ruling placed an intolerable burden on the State. We granted certiorari to resolve these questions, . . . and now affirm. . . .

The language of § 1415(e)(3) is unequivocal. It states plainly that during the pendency of any proceedings initiated under the Act, unless the state or local educational agency and the parents or guardian of a disabled child otherwise agree, "the child *shall* remain in the then current educational placement." § 1415(e)(3) (emphasis added). Faced with this clear directive, petitioner asks us to read a "dangerousness" exception into the stay-put provision on the basis of either of two essentially inconsistent assumptions: first, that Congress thought the residual authority of school officials to exclude dangerous students from the classroom too obvious for comment; or second, that Congress inadvertently failed to provide such authority and this Court must therefore remedy the oversight. Because we cannot accept either premise, we decline petitioner's invitation to re-write the statute.

Petitioner's arguments proceed, he suggests, from a simple, common-sense proposition: Congress could not have intended the stay-put provision to be read literally, for such a construction leads to the clearly unintended, and untenable, result that school districts must return violent or dangerous students to school while the often lengthy EHA proceedings run their course. We think it clear, however, that Congress very much meant to strip schools of the *unilateral* authority they had traditionally employed to exclude disabled students, particularly emotionally disturbed students, from school. In so doing, Congress did not leave school administrators powerless to deal with dangerous students; it did, however, deny school officials their former right to "self-help," and directed that in the future the removal of disabled students could be accomplished only with the permission of the parents or, as a last resort, the courts.

As noted above, Congress passed the EHA after finding that school systems across the country had excluded one out of every eight disabled children from classes. . . .

Congress attacked such exclusionary practices in a variety of ways. It required participating States to educate *all* disabled children, regardless of the severity of their disabilities, 20 U.S.C. § 1412(2)(C), and included within the definition of "handicapped" those children with serious emotional disturbances. § 1401(1). It further provided for meaningful parental participation in all aspects of a child's educational placement, and barred schools, through the stay-put provision, from changing that placement over the parent's objection until all review proceedings were completed. Recognizing that those proceedings might prove long and tedious, the Act's drafters did not intend § 1415(e)(3) to operate inflexibly, see 121 Cong.Rec. 37412 (1975) (remarks of Sen. Stafford), and they therefore allowed for interim placements where parents and school officials are able to agree on one. Conspicuously absent from § 1415(e)(3), however, is any emergency exception for dangerous students. This absence is all the more telling in light of the injunctive decree issued in *PARC*, which permitted school officials unilaterally to remove students in " 'extraordinary circumstances.' " 343 F.Supp., at 301. Given the lack of any similar exception in *Mills*, and the close attention Congress devoted to these "landmark" decisions, see S.Rep., at 6, U.S.Code Cong. & Admin.News p. 1430, we can only conclude that the omission was intentional; we are therefore not at liberty to engraft onto the statute an exception Congress chose not to create.

Our conclusion that § 1415(e)(3) means what it says does not leave educators hamstrung. The Department of Education has observed that, "[w]hile the [child's] placement may not be changed [during any complaint proceeding], this does not preclude the agency from using its normal procedures for dealing with children who are endangering themselves or others." Comment following 34 CFR § 300.513 (1987). Such procedures may include the use of study carrels, timeouts, detention, or the restriction of privileges. More drastically, where a student poses an immediate threat to the safety of others, officials may temporarily suspend him or her for up to 10 school days. This authority, which respondent in no way disputes, not only ensures that school administrators can protect the safety of others by promptly removing the most dangerous of students, it also provides a "cooling down" period during which officials can initiate IEP review and seek to persuade the child's parents to agree to an interim placement. And in those cases in which the

parents of a truly dangerous child adamantly refuse to permit any change in placement, the 10-day respite gives school officials an opportunity to invoke the aid of the courts under § 1415(e)(2), which empowers courts to grant any appropriate relief. . . . As the EHA's legislative history makes clear, one of the evils Congress sought to remedy was the unilateral exclusion of disabled children by *schools,* not courts, and one of the purposes of § 1415(e)(3), therefore, was "to prevent *school* officials from removing a child from the regular public school classroom over the parents' objection pending completion of the review proceedings." . . . The stay-put provision in no way purports to limit or pre-empt the authority conferred on courts by § 1415(e)(2), . . . indeed, it says nothing whatever about judicial power.

In short, then, we believe that school officials are entitled to seek injunctive relief under § 1415(e)(2) in appropriate cases. In any such action, § 1415(e)(3) effectively creates a presumption in favor of the child's current educational placement which school officials can overcome only by showing that maintaining the child in his or her current placement is substantially likely to result in injury either to himself or herself, or to others. In the present case, we are satisfied that the District Court, in enjoining the state and local defendants from indefinitely suspending respondent or otherwise unilaterally altering his then current placement, properly balanced respondent's interest in receiving a free appropriate public education in accordance with the procedures and requirements of the EHA against the interests of the state and local school officials in maintaining a safe learning environment for all their students.

We believe the courts below properly construed and applied § 1415(e)(3), except insofar as the Court of Appeals held that a suspension in excess of 10 school days does not constitute a "change in placement." We therefore affirm the Court of Appeals' judgment on this issue as modified herein. Because we are equally divided on the question whether a court may order a State to provide services directly to a disabled child where the local agency has failed to do so, we affirm the Court of Appeals' judgment on this issue as well.

Affirmed.

NOTE

1. In *Honig v. Doe*, the Supreme Court stated that a school district may suspend a child who is dangerous to himself or others for up to ten days without violating the stay-put provision. If the school district needs more than ten days to develop a new IEP with a more restrictive environment, or the parents do not agree with the new placement, then the school district may request that the courts issue an injunction to either keep the child out of school or temporarily place the child until an appropriate placement may be formulated.

In post-*Honig* litigation, school districts have requested injunctions because of the dangerous propensities of a child. One school district obtained an injunction to keep a seventeen-year-old autistic and behavior-disordered student out of school pending a new placement. The student became overtly sexually and physically aggressive, posing a danger to himself, fellow students, and the faculty and staff. Before issuing an injunction, the Federal District Court stated that four factors must be considered:

> (1) whether the plaintiff is reasonably likely to succeed on the merits of the action; (2) whether the plaintiff will be irreparably harmed absent the injunction or will have an adequate remedy at law; (3) whether the prospective injury to the plaintiff outweighs the injury the injunction may impose upon the defendant; (4) whether a preliminary injunction will disserve the public interest. *Board of Education of Township High School District Number 211, Cook County, Illinois v. Corral*, 1989 W.L. 57041 (N.D. Ill. 1989).

In another case, the school district recommended limiting the student's participation to a behavioral management class or home care because the child was a danger to himself and other students. The parents

disagreed with this new placement. The child's behaviors included striking other students and staff, tearing off wooden door jambs, tearing up carpet, threatening to jump out a second floor window, and so on. When the parent refused placement in a behavioral class or home instruction, the school sought and received an injunction from the court. The court said the child was "an ongoing major threat to others, as well as to himself." *Texas City Independent School District v. Jorstad*, 752 F.Supp. 231 (S.D. Tex. 1990).

Attorney's Fees

Attorney's fees may be awarded by the courts to parents who win law suits against school districts [§ 1415(e)(4)(B)]. Attorney's fees were permitted by a 1986 amendment entitled the Handicapped Children's Protection Act (HCPA), allowing "reasonable attorney's fees" to parents who prevail in a hearing or a court action. This amendment was considered necessary because Congress observed that the weight of heavy attorney's fees could conceivably make parents reluctant to raise valid complaints challenging school district actions. The amendment was initiated following a Supreme Court decision in 1984, in *Smith v. Robinson*,[107] which found that parents, in bringing EAHCA actions, could not claim attorney's fees under either § 1983 of the Civil Rights Act of 1871 or § 504 of the Rehabilitation Act.

Those who opposed the amendment maintained that an undefined right to attorney's fees was tantamount to giving a blank check for lawyer's fees not only for judicial action but also for due process hearings and preliminary reviews in extrajudicial settings. The Congress finally resolved the issue for purposes of the amendment by including specifications and limitations for courts to follow in awarding attorney's fees. The amendment, Handicapped Children's Protection Act of 1986 (HCPA) (Public Law 99–372), further provided that, in addition to the EAHCA, recovery could be sustained under the Rehabilitation Act and the Civil Rights Act as well. The only restriction to invoking the last two acts is that the handicapped student must have exhausted EAHCA procedures. Even though attorney's fees are now allowed under EAHCA, money damages are still generally unavailable under the EAHCA itself and can be obtained only under the other acts.

Fees for Lay Advocates

Statutory provisions for attorney's fees do not extend to special education lay advocates who are not lawyers. To permit such fees would in the court's opinion encourage a plethora of unlicensed legal practitioners to have access to public resources, which would not be in the public's best interest.[108]

Private or Publicly Funded Attorneys

Section 1988 of the HCPA states that "reasonable fees are to be calculated according to the prevailing market rates in the relevant community, regardless of whether plaintiff is represented by private or non-profit counsel."[109]

Tuition Reimbursement

A state may be liable for reimbursement of parents for tuition and other necessary costs incurred in the education of handicapped children.

The Supreme Court in *Dellmuth*, while acknowledging that Congress has the power under § 5 of the Fourteenth Amendment to specifically abrogate Eleventh Amendment immunity of states, held that such abrogation is valid only in cases where the statute meets a simple, but stringent, test, which states:

> Congress may abrogate the State's constitutionally secured immunity from suit in federal court only by making its intention unmistakably clear in the language of the statute.[111]

The Court in *Dellmuth* found that no such specific abrogation was present in the EAHCA. In so holding, the Court contrasted the language of EAHCA, which is "ambiguous at best," to the Rehabilitation Act, which clearly states that "[a] state shall not be immune under the Eleventh Amendment . . . from suit . . . [for] discrimination by recipients of Federal financial assistance."[112]

Subsequent to *Dellmuth*, the Congress responded with a clear and unmistakable abrogation of state immunity for violation of the EAHCA. The new law, § 1403 of the Education of Individuals with Disabilities Act, 1990 states in part that "[a] state shall not be immune under the Eleventh Amendment" (see the discussion of the Eleventh Amendment in the Chapter 13 entitled "Governmental Immunity from Liability"). Thus, a school district may be financially responsible for reimbursement for tuition and other costs for special educational services beyond the public school.

ACQUIRED IMMUNODEFICIENCY SYNDROME (AIDS)

A major problem facing society and public schools is the dreaded and lethal acquired immunodeficiency syndrome (AIDS). The first known case of this highly contagious disease was reported by the Centers for Disease Control (CDC) in 1981. By December 1986, 28,098 patients had been identified as having AIDS.[113]

AIDS is a disease believed to be caused by a retrovirus that destroys the immune system: "A retrovirus is a class of viruses with special genetic material which allows them to produce copies of themselves inside the cells they infect, killing the host cells in the process."[114] A person may test positive for the virus and transmit the virus to others, but himself be asymptomatic. The person who tests seropositive and displays a number of symptoms characteristic of the disease may not be considered to have AIDS. It is estimated, depending on the source, that 30 to 90 percent of those who are seropositive "healthy carriers"[115] will develop AIDS. When a person exhibits symptoms of a weakened immune system, he or she is no longer a carrier of the virus, but has been attacked by the virus, and has AIDS Related Complex (ARC). At this stage, the individual is susceptible to disease because of the weakened immune system. There are no known cures for AIDS, and the disease is fatal.

Because of the finality of this disease, there has been widespread concern and fear within society. One court stated:

> While we wait for medical science to save us from what many think may be such a raging, indiscriminate inferno, it is the task of this court to deal with the here and now of this lethal, inevitability fatal disease, for which there is currently no inoculation and no cure. The mystery of the virus and its communicability challenges jurists legally to be assured our decisions do not lead us to allow proliferation of this disease by our ignorance.[116]

A number of cases have arisen in the public schools where children who have AIDS or children who have tested positive have been excluded from the regular classroom. The school districts have attempted to continue the child's education with homebound instruction or by other means. Numerous legal questions have arisen relating to AIDS, but the most prominent has been whether a school district can exclude a child who has AIDS or tests positive for the AIDS virus.

AIDS cases involving public school children have been litigated under the Rehabilitation Act of 1973, § 504 (29 U.S.C.A. § 794); the Education of the Handicapped Act (20 U.S.C.A. § 1415(e)(2)); Due Process and Equal Protection of the U.S. Constitution; and various state statutes. The two major areas of contention have been the Rehabilitation Act of 1973 and the Education for All Handicapped Children Act.

Rehabilitation Act of 1973

The Rehabilitation Act of 1973 states:

> No otherwise qualified handicapped individual in the United States, as defined in section 705(7) of this title, shall, solely by reason of his handicap, be excluded from the participation in, be denied the benefits of, or be subjected to discrimination under any program or activity receiving Federal financial assistance. . . .

Therefore, for an AIDS child to successfully litigate under § 504, the student must be a "handicapped individual" and must be "otherwise qualified" to attend a regular classroom under § 504.

The law defines "handicapped individual" as a person who "(i) has a physical . . . impairment which substantially limits one or more of [his or her] major life activities, (ii) has a record of impairment, or (iii) is regarded as having such impairment (29 U.S.C.A. § 706(7)(B)). In *Doe*[117] the court used the third standard of physical impairment as the basis for declaring an AIDS child handicapped under § 504. This rationale was based on the Supreme Court decision in *Arline*, in which the court stated:

> [The] basic purpose of § 504 . . . is to ensure that handicapped individuals are not denied jobs or other benefits because of the prejudiced attitudes or the ignorance of others. By amending the definition of "handicapped individual" to include not only those who are actually physically impaired but also those who are regarded as impaired and who, as a result, are substantially limited in a major life activity, Congress acknowledged that society's accumulated myths and fears about disability and disease are as handicapping as are the physical limitations that flow from actual impairment. Few aspects of a handicap give rise to the same level of public fear and misapprehension as contagiousness. . . . The Act is carefully structured to replace such reflexive reactions to actual or perceived handicaps with actions based on reasoned and medically sound judgments. . . .

Because of the seriousness of the AIDS disease, a student is likely to prevail also on the standard of "impairment of a major life activity." Several courts have ruled that a person is covered under § 504 while he or she is seropositive and has not developed AIDS; simply having the virus has been considered a handicapping condition. In *Thomas* the court said, "[A]ny person infected with AIDS virus, even an asymptomatic carrier, is handicapped due to impairment of the hemic and reproductive systems, which makes procreation and childbirth dangerous to others." The majority of courts have determined that se-ropositive and AIDS students are covered by § 504; therefore, the child is covered by the Rehabilitation Act as handicapped.

The next question arising after determining that a child is handicapped is whether he or she is "otherwise qualified" to attend a regular classroom. A person who presents a significant risk to others in the workplace or classroom will not be otherwise qualified if the risk cannot be eliminated through reasonable accommodation. The courts have used four factors when addressing the issue of otherwise qualified.:

> (a) the nature of the risk (how the disease is transmitted), (b) the duration of the risk (how long is the carrier infectious), (c) the severity of the risk (what is the potential harm to third parties), and (d) the probabilities the disease will be transmitted and will cause varying degrees of harm.[118]

Relying on the majority of medical evidence, the courts have decided that an AIDS child does not present a risk to other children in the classroom. A number of courts have cited the Surgeon General of the United States, who has said:

> There is no known risk of non-sexual infection in most of the situations we encounter in our daily lives. We know that family members living with individuals who have the AIDS virus do not become infected except through sexual contact. There is no evidence of transmission (spread) of the AIDS virus by everyday contact even though these family members shared food, towels, cups, razors, even toothbrushes, and kissed each other.

When speaking specifically to the classroom environment, the surgeon general said:

> None of the identified cases of AIDS in the United States are known or are suspected to have been transmitted from one child to another in school, day care or foster care settings. Transmission would necessitate exposure of open cuts to the blood or other body fluids of the infected child, a highly unlikely occurrence. Even then, routine safety procedures for han-dling blood or other body fluids . . . would be effective in preventing transmission from children with AIDS to other children in school. . . . Casual social contact between children and persons infected with AIDS virus is not dangerous.[119]

The United States Centers for Disease Control (CDC) and the American Medical Association and other organizations have also maintained that a child with AIDS does not constitute a risk in a public school classroom. Therefore, based on § 504, a child is handicapped if he or she has AIDS and is otherwise qualified to attend a public school classroom, and cannot be excluded from school.

EAHCA and AIDS

Another issue with AIDS students is whether they are covered by the Education of the Handicapped Act (EAHCA). The EAHCA defines "handicapped children" as

> mentally retarded, hard of hearing, deaf, speech or language impaired, visually handicapped, seriously emotionally disturbed, ortho-pedically impaired, *or other health impaired children,* or children with specific learning disabilities *who by reason thereof require special education and related services* (italics added).[120]

In the case of AIDS student, the category that would most closely fit is "other health impaired children." This phrase is defined as

> [l]imited strength, vitality or alertness due to chronic or acute health problems such as a heart condition, tuberculosis, rheumatic fever, nephritis, asthma, sickle-cell anemia, *hemophilia,* epilepsy, lead poisoning, leukemia, or diabetes, *which adversely affects a child's educational performance* (italics added).[121]

AIDS is not listed as an example of an acute or chronic health problem by the EAHCA. In October of 1984, the Department of Education addressed the applicability of EAHCA to AIDS victims. The department stated that AIDS is not considered to be "handicapped" as a term defined in EAHCA, unless the child needs special education. The opinion states:

Children with AIDS could be eligible for special education programs under the category of "other health impaired," if they have chronic or acute health problems which adversely affect their educational performance.

The EAHCA would apply to AIDS victims only if the virus adversely affects their educational performance. If a child is seropositive or a "healthy carrier," then he or she is not covered under EAHCA, but if the child becomes an AIDS victim and this diminishes his or her educational performance, then the EAHCA must be enforced to meet the needs of the child.

Is a Child with AIDS a Significant Risk, and If So, Could the Child Be Reasonably Accommodated? Case Remanded to Determine Risk.

Martinez v. School Board of Hillsborough County, Florida

United States Court of Appeals, Eleventh Circuit, 1988. 861 F.2d 1502.

VANCE, Circuit Judge: This case involves the appropriate educational placement of a mentally retarded child infected with the human immunodeficiency virus, the virus that causes Acquired Immunodeficiency Syndrome (AIDS). Appellant, Eliana Martinez, is seven years old and has an I.Q. of 41. This classifies her as a trainably mentally handicapped child. Eliana was born prematurely and received thirty-nine blood transfusions in the first four months of life. In April 1985 Eliana was diagnosed as suffering from AIDS Related Complex. She now is in the late stages of AIDS but her condition has been stabilized for several months. The court below found that Eliana is not toilet trained and suffers from thrush, a disease that can produce blood in the saliva. Eliana sucks her thumb and

forefinger frequently, resulting in saliva on her fingers. In the past Eliana has suffered from skin lesions. When these occurred, Mrs. Rosa Martinez, her adoptive mother, has kept her at home. . . .

Two overlapping federal statutes establish the framework for determining appropriate educational placement for handicapped children—the Education of the Handicapped Act (the "EHA"), and section 504 of the Rehabilitation Act of 1973 ("section 504"). . . .

When the EHA and section 504 are read together, a complementary set of standards emerges to determine the appropriate educational setting for a handicapped child. The EHA requires participating states to provide a "free appropriate public education" to handicapped children. 20 U.S.C. § 1412(2)(B) (1982). Educational authorities must develop an individualized educational program stating the educational program and setting forth specific goals for each handicapped child. . . .

Section 504 of the Rehabilitation Act more broadly provides:

> No otherwise qualified handicapped individual . . . shall, solely by reason of his handicap, be excluded from the participation in, be denied the benefits of, or be subjected to discrimination under any program or activity receiving Federal financial assistance or under any program or activity conducted by any Executive agency or by the United States Postal Service.

29 U.S.C. § 794 (1982). In considering whether an exclusion is prohibited by section 504, a trial judge must first determine whether the individual is "otherwise qualified." When a person is handicapped with a contagious disease this task requires the judge to conduct an individualized inquiry and to make appropriate findings of fact, "based on reasonable medical judgments . . . about (a) the nature of the risk (how the disease is transmitted), (b) the duration of the risk (how long is the carrier infectious), (c) the severity of the risk (what is the potential harm to third parties) and (d) the probabilities the disease will be transmitted and will cause varying degrees of harm." . . . As a second step

the court must evaluate whether reasonable accommodations would make the handicapped individual otherwise qualified.

When a child with an infectious disease seeks relief under both the EHA and section 504 of the Rehabilitation Act, the relationship between these two statutory frameworks is particularly intricate. The trial judge must first determine the most appropriate educational placement for the handicapped child under EHA procedures. Next,the court must determine whether the child is otherwise qualified within the meaning of section 504 to be educated in this setting, despite the communicable disease. . . . If not, the court must consider whether reasonable accommodations could reduce the risk of transmission so as to make the child otherwise qualified to be educated in that setting. In considering accommodations that would make the child "otherwise qualified," the court must bear in mind the requirement that to the maximum extent appropriate, the child is to be educated in the least restrictive environment.

Eliana is entitled to a free appropriate public education under the EHA. She suffers from two handicaps under section 504 of the Rehabilitation Act: she is mentally retarded and has AIDS; each condition results in a "physical or mental impairment which substantially limits one or more major life activities." . . . Applying the standards under these two statutes to the facts of this case, the trial court first had to determine the most appropriate educational placement for Eliana under the EHA. Next, it had to consider whether Eliana was otherwise qualified to be educated in this setting. If the trial court found that Eliana was not otherwise qualified, it then had to consider whether reasonable accommodations would make her so. If, after reasonable accommodations, a significant risk of transmission would still exist, Eliana would not be otherwise qualified. *See Arline,* 107 S.Ct. at 1131 n. 16.

As the parties agreed, the appropriate educational placement for Eliana under the EHA would be the regular TMH classroom if she did not suffer from AIDS. This presented the question whether the exclusion of Eliana from that setting is unlawful under section 504. In conducting this inquiry, the trial court had to determine whether Eliana was otherwise qualified to be educated in the regular TMH classroom. The trial court found a "remote theoretical possibility" of transmission with respect to tears, saliva and urine. This does not rise to the "significant" risk level that is required for Eliana to be excluded from the regular TMH classroom. . . . The court below made no findings with respect to the overall risk of transmission from all bodily substances, including blood in the saliva, to which other children might be exposed in the TMH classroom. Accordingly, we remand with directions that the trial court make findings as to the overall risk of transmission so that it can determine whether Eliana is otherwise qualified to attend classes in the TMH classroom.

If the risk of transmission supports a finding that Eliana is not "otherwise qualified" to attend classes with the other children in the TMH classroom, the court must consider whether reasonable accommodations would make her so. In evaluating possible accommodations, a trial court must consider the effect of each proposed accommodation on the handicapped child and the institution. . . . The court must be guided by the requirement that, to the maximum extent appropriate, these accommodations place the child in the least restrictive environment that would make the child otherwise qualified. Additionally, the court must consider the financial burden the accommodation would impose on the institution. . . .

We vacate the judgment of the district court and remand the case so that the district court may make the further required findings. The district court should receive such additional evidence as it deems necessary in light of such requirements. It should thereafter enter such judgment as is appropriate.

Vacated and remanded with instructions.

NOTE

1. The Eleventh Circuit Court of Appeals remanded *Martinez* to the Federal District Court, and the court ruled:

The Court has seriously considered the allegations now being raised that the risk to Eliana far outweighs any benefit to her from attending school with other children. . . . The decision must balance the risk to the child versus the benefit which flows from the attendance at school. Keeping this child out of school does not guarantee her safety and long life; death if it seeks and takes Eliana may come from various sources which are available to her without restriction: the park, the mall, or her home. Upon conscientious consideration of the issue from all sides, the Court cannot find that the risk is significant enough to counterbalance the benefit and rights to this child inherent in attending school with other children. . . .

[The court concluded:]

1. The appropriate educational placement for Eliana Martinez under the Education for All Handicapped Children would be the regular Trainable Mentally Handicapped classroom if she did not suffer from AIDS.
2. The possibility of transmission with respect to tears, saliva, and urine is remote and theoretical and does not rise to the "significant" risk level that is required to bar Eliana Martinez from the regular Trainable Mentally Handicapped classroom.
3. The evidence does not support a finding that the overall risk of transmission from all bodily substances, including blood in the saliva, rises to the "significant" risk level of requiring this child's exclusion from the classroom. . . .
4. The Court finds that Eliana Martinez is "otherwise qualified" to attend the Trainable Mentally Handicapped classroom at Manhattan Elementary School, which is the most appropriate educational setting for this child pursuant to the EHA.
5. Since the Court finds Eliana Martinez "otherwise qualified" to attend this classroom, it is unnecessary for the Court to consider the effect of any accommodation.
6. The Court readopts its previous conclusion of law stating that if there is a question of the advisability of Eliana being in the classroom on a certain day, the school nurse should be consulted for an evaluation of either Eliana, or another child, if the danger may be an infection from another child to Eliana. It is not necessary for Eliana, nor the rest of the TMH students, to be seen by the nurse or other health practioner on a daily basis to determine if Eliana should be in the integrated classroom that day.
7. The Court will require that the Hillsborough County School Board provide educational programs to the school parent population, and, student population as far as is practicable, that will be associated with Eliana Martinez in the classroom, with the aim of educating and informing them regarding the realities of AIDS, and, the proper procedures in order to deal with the situation and minimize the risk of transmission to others. In addition a copy of this Order is to be made available to the public at the Office of Manhattan Elementary School. Accordingly, it is Ordered that Defendant, The School Board of Hillsborough County, Florida, admit Plaintiff Eliana Martinez to the Trainable Mentally Handicapped classroom of Manhattan Elementary School within the parameters of this order.

Done and ordered.

Martinez v. School Board of Hillsborough County, Florida 711 F.Supp. 1066 (M.D. Fla. 1989)

◼ ENDNOTES

1. Public Law 101–46, 104 Stat. 1103.
2. Donald F. Moores, *Educating the Deaf: Psychology, Principles and Practices* (Boston: Houghton Mifflin, 1978).
3. Ibid.
4. Resolve for Erecting a Lunatic Hospital (1831), Resolves of the General Court of the Commonwealth of Massachusetts.
5. Jonathan Messerli, *Horace Mann* (New York: Alfred A. Knopf, 1972).
6. Samuel A. Kirk and James J. Gallagher, *Educating Exceptional Children*, 4th ed. (Boston: Houghton Mifflin, 1983).
7. Watson v. City of Cambridge, 157 Mass. 561, 32 N.E. 864 (1893).

8. State ex rel. Beattie v. Board of Education, 169 Wis. 231, 172 N.W. 153 (1919).

9. Ibid., p. 154.

10. Ralph B. Kimbrough and Michael Y. Nunnery, *Educational Administration* (New York: Macmillan Publishing Company, Inc., 1976).

11. Ibid.

12. Brown v. Board of Education, 347 U.S. 483, 74 S.Ct. 686 (1954).

13. Ibid.

14. Pennsylvania Association for Retarded Children v. Commonwealth, 334 F.Supp. 1257 (E.D.Pa.1971), 343 F.Supp. 279 (E.D.Pa.1972).

15. Ibid.

16. 348 F.Supp. 866 (D.D.C.1972).

17. Ibid.

18. Vocational Rehabilitation Act of 1973.

19. Ibid.

20. Ibid.

21. Ibid., §§ 84.33, 84.34.

22. Doe , State of Hawaii, v. Katherine D., 531 F.Supp. 517 (D.Hawaii 1982), *affirmed in part and reversed in part as to attorneys fees*, 727 F. 2d 809 (1984).

23. Doe v. Dolton Elementary School Dist. No. 148, 694 F.Supp. 440 (N.D. Ill. 1988).

24. Grove City College v. Ball, 465 U.S. 555, 104 S.Ct. 1211 (1984).

25. 20 U.S.C.A. § 1681(a).

26. Gallagher v. Pontiac School Dist., 807 F.2d 75 (6th Cir. 1986).

27. 480 U.S. 273, 107 S.Ct. 1123 (1987).

28. Public Law 100–259. See also Laura F. Rothstein, *Special Education Law* (New York: Longman, 1990), pp. 26–28.

29. The Education for All Handicapped Children Act, 20 U.S.C.A., § 1400(b).

30. Ibid., § 1401(16–91).

31. Ibid.

32. Public Law 95–561, 92 Stat. 2364 (1978); Public Law 98–199, 97 Stat. 1357 (1983); Public Law 99–372, 100 Stat. 796 (1986); and Public Law 99–457, 100 Stat. 1145 (1986).

33. Education of the Handicapped Act Amendments of 1983: Report of Mr. Hatch to Accompany S. 1341, Comm. on Labor and Human Resources, S. Rep. No. 191, 98th Cong., 1st Sess. 7 (1983).

34. Ibid.

35. Senate Report No. 315, 99th Cong., 2d Sess. 3, 5 (1986). See also House Report No. 860, 99th Cong., 2d Sess., *reprinted in* 1986 U.S. Code Cong. & Admin. News 2401.

36. 20 U.S.C.A. § 1422.

37. § 1415.

38. § 1401(18).

39. Board of Education of Hendrick Hudson Central School District Bd. of Educ. v. Rowley, 458 U.S. 176, 201, 102 S.Ct. 3034, 3048 (1982).

40. Ibid., at 206, 102 S.Ct. at 3051.

41. Ibid., White dissenting 212, 102 S.Ct. at 3054.

42. 875 F.2d 954 (1st Cir. 1989).

43. 629 F.2d 269 (3d Cir. 1980).

44. Ibid., at 272.

45. Ibid., at 277.

46. Ibid., at 280.

47. 708 F.2d 1028, 1035, (5th Cir. 1983).

48. Georgia Association of Retarded Citizens v. McDaniel, 511 F.Supp. 1263 (N.D. Ga. 1981), affirmed 716 F.2d 1565 (11th Cir. 1983).

49. Battle v. Commonwealth of Pennsylvania, *supra.*

50. Yaris v. Special School District of St. Louis, 558 F.Supp. 545 (E.D. Mo. 1983), affirmed 728 F.2d 1055 (8th Cir. 1984).

51. Crawford v. Pittman, *supra.*

52. Georgia Association of Retarded Citizens v. McDaniel, 511 F.Supp. 1263 (N.D. Ga. 1981), affirmed 716 F.2d 1565 (11th Cir. 1983).

53. Alamo Heights Ind. School Dist. v. State Bd. of Educ., 790 F.2d 1153, 1159 (5th Cir. 1986).

54. Ibid.

55. Ibid., at 1158.

56. 921 F.2d 1022 (10th Cir. 1990).

57. Polk v. Central Susquehanna Intermediate Unit 16, 853 F.2d 171 (3d Cir. 1988).

58. Board of Education Hendrick Hudson v. Rowley, *supra*, at 3049.

59. Johnson v. Independent School Dist. No. 4 of Bixby, 921 F.2d 1022 (10th Cir. 1990).

60. Cordrey v. Euckert, 917 F.2d 1460, 1464 (6th Cir. 1990).

61. Ibid., at 1471.

62. Ibid., at 1472.

63. Board of Educ. Hendrick Hudson v. Rowley, *supra.*

64. § 1415(c).

65. Speilberg v. Henrico County Public Schools, 853 F.2d 256 (4th Cir. 1988).

66. Burke County Bd. of Educ. v. Denton, 895 F.2d 973 (4th Cir. 1990).

67. Doe v. Defendant I, 898 F.2d 1186, 1190 (6th Cir. 1990).

68. § 1415(c).

69. § 1415(e)(3).

70. Honig v. Doe, 484 U.S. 305, 108 S.Ct. 592 (1988).

71. § 1415(e)(2).

72. Georgia Ass'n of Retarded Citizens v. McDaniel, 716 F.2d 1565 (11th Cir. 1983), *vacated on other grounds*, 468 U.S. 1213, 104 S.Ct. 3581 (1984): see on remand 740 F. 2d 902 (1984).

73. 20 U.S.C.A. § 1400. See also Honig v. Doe, *supra.*

74. 20 U.S.C.A. § 1412(5)(B); 34 C.F.R. § 300.551.

75. 45 C.F.R. §§ 300.551 and 300.552(d).

76. 34 C.F.R. § 300.551.

77. Rothstein, *op cit.*, p. 112.

78. 700 F.2d 1058 (6th Cir. 1983).

79. Ibid.

80. Ibid.

81. Lachman v. Illinois Board of Education, 852 F.2d 290 (7th Cir. 1988).

82. Grkman v. Scanlon, 528 F.Supp. 1032 (W.D.Pa. 1981), vacated and remanded 707 F.2d 1388 (3d Cir. 1982), rehearing 563 F.Supp. 793 (W.D.Pa. 1983); Silvio v.

Commonwealth, 64 Pa.Cmwlth. 192, 439 A.2d 893 (1982); Bales v. Clarke, 523 F.Supp. 1366 (E.D.Va. 1981).

83. Bales v. Clarke, 523 F.Supp. 1366, 1370 (E.D.Va. 1981).

84. Education for All Handicapped Children Act, 34 C.F.R. § 300.302.

85. 45 C.F.R. § 121(a) 302.

86. Devries v. Fairfax County School Board, 882 F.2d 876 (4th Cir. 1989).

87. 471 U.S. 359, 370, 105 S.Ct. 1996, 2003 (1985).

88. Leonard v. McKenzie, 869 F.2d 1558 (D.C.Cir. 1989).

89. Drew P. v. Clarke County School District, 877 F.2d 927 (11th Cir. 1989).

90. Ibid.

91. § 1401(17).

92. Irving Independent School District v. Tatro, 468 U.S. 883, 104 S.Ct. 3371 (1984).

93. Public Law 94–142.

94. Irving Independent School District v. Tatro, op. cit.

95. Ibid., at 894, 104 S.Ct. at 3378.

96. T. G. v. Board of Educ. of Piscataway, 576 F.Supp. 420 (D.N.J. 1983).

97. Alamo Heights Ind. School Dist. v. State Bd. of Educ., op. cit.

98. Metropolitan Government v. Tennessee Department of Educ., 771 S.W.2d 427, 429 (Tenn. App. 1989).

99. Corbett v. Regional Center for the East Bay, Inc., 676 F.Supp. 964 (N.D. Cal. 1988), *injunction modified*, 699 F.Supp. 230 (1988).

100. Stuart v. Nappi, 443 F.Supp. 1235 (D.Conn. 1978); Doe v. Koger, 480 F.Supp. 225 (N.D.Ind. 1979).

101. Stuart v. Nappi, op. cit.

102. S–1 v. Turlington, 635 F.2d 342 (5th Cir. 1981), cert. denied 454 U.S. 1030, 102 S.Ct. 566 (1981).

103. Ibid.

104. Doe v. Koger, 480 F.Supp. 225 (N.D.Ind. 1979).

105. S–1 v. Turlington, op cit. See also School Board of Prince William County, Va. v. Malone, 662 F.Supp. 978 (E.D.Va. 1984), affirmed 762 F.2d 1210 (4th Cir. 1985).

106. Jackson v. Franklin County School Board, 765 F.2d 535 (5th Cir. 1985); and Victoria L. v. District School Board of Lee County, Florida, 741 F.2d 369 (11th Cir. 1984).

107. 468 U.S. 992, 104 S.Ct. 3457 (1984).

108. Arons v. New Jersey State Board of Education, 842 F.2d 58 (3d Cir. 1988).

109. Eggers v. Bullitt County School District, 854 F.2d 892 (6th Cir. 1988).

110. Dellmuth v. Muth, 491 U.S. 223, 109 S.Ct. 2397 (1989). See also The Education of the Handicapped Act (EHA), 84 Stat. 175, as amended, 20 U.S.C.A. § 1400 et seq.

111. Atascadero State Hospital v. Scanlon, 473 U.S. 234, 105 S.Ct. 3142 (1985).

112. 42 U.S.C.A. § 2000–7(a)(1).

113. Ray v. School District of Desoto County, 666 F.Supp. 1524 (M.D.Fla. 1987).

114. Doe v. Dolton Elementary School District No. 148, 694 F.Supp. 440 (N.D.Ill. 1988).

115. Ray v. School District of Desoto County, 666 F.Supp. 1524 (M.D.Fla. 1987).

116. Ibid.

117. Doe v. Dolton Elementary School District No. 148, op. cit.

118. Arline, 480 U.S. at 288, 107 S.Ct. at 1131.

119. U.S. Public Health Service, *Surgeon General's Report on Acquired Immune Deficiency,* at 13 (1986).

120. 20 U.S.C.A. § 1401(a)(1) (italics added).

121. 34 C.F.R. § 300.5(b)(7) (italics added).

122. Doe v. Belleville Public School District No. 118, 672 F.Supp. 342, 344–345 (S.D.Ill. 1987).

CHAPTER 10

Desegregation

No one could have predicted that the pre-1850 education of a five-year-old child by the name of Sarah Roberts would have had such a profound effect on the historical development of the public schools. Sarah left home each day and walked through the streets of the city of Boston past five elementary schools for white children to reach the Smith Grammar School, which had been established in 1820 for blacks.

Not only was the school remote from the child's home, but an evaluation committee had reported that the school was in poor condition—"the school rooms are too small, the paint is much defaced" and the equipment needed repair. Sarah's father tried repeatedly to place her in the better nearby schools for whites, but each time his efforts had failed. After persistent rebuffs, Mr. Roberts sought the most able lawyer, civil rights enthusiast, and later United States Senator, Charles Sumner, to represent his child and challenge the unequal treatment. From the ensuing legal conflict, the now infamous doctrine of "separate-but-equal" was born.

Citing passages from the Massachusetts Constitution, which would later be likened to the Equal Protection Clause of the Fourteenth Amendment, Sumner maintained that compelling black children to attend separate schools was to effectively "brand a whole race with the stigma of inferiority and degradation."[1] Eloquently, Sumner pointed out that segregated schools could not be considered equivalent to white schools because of the stigma of caste that mandatory attendance attached thereto. Sumner effectively expounded the same constitutional position that

was to be the heart of the plaintiff's successful contention over one hundred years later in *Brown v. Board of Education,* that a separate school "exclusively devoted to one class must differ essentially, in its spirit and character, from that public school known to the law, where all classes meet together in equality."[2]

Justice Shaw of the Massachusetts Court was, however, unconvinced and in his historical opinion set forth the separate-but-equal doctrine that was to prevail for so long. In theory, he agreed with "the great principle" advanced by Sumner that all persons ought to stand equal before the law, but he went on to conclude contrarily that the standard of equality did not imply that all men and women were legally clothed with the same civil and political powers, but that all were merely entitled to equal consideration and protection for their maintenance and security. What exactly the protected rights were was dependent on the laws adapted to their "respective relations and conditions." As one of these conditions, race was seen to be a legitimate rationale for classification. Judge Shaw failed to show, however, that there was any reasonable relationship between racial classification and legitimate objectives of the school system; he merely asserted that school segregation was for the good of both races. With this decision, separate-but-equal was born into education, and it would not expire for over one hundred years. During the intervening years the Civil War would be fought, civil rights laws would be enacted by the United States Congress to little or no avail, and the United States Supreme Court itself would transplant the unfortunate standard from the

Massachusetts Constitution to the Constitution of the United States.

In 1868, the Fourteenth Amendment was ratified to assure the constitutionality of reconstruction statutes that had been enacted to proscribe racial discrimination. The third clause of the critical second sentence of the amendment stated: "Nor shall any State . . . deny to any person within its jurisdiction the equal protection of the laws." In spite of the strength of the wording, the amendment was to have little immediate effect, as was evidenced by the civil rights cases wherein the Supreme Court held that no application could be made to private enterprise discrimination such as occurred in inns, conveyances, restaurants, and places of entertainment.[3]

The move from private discrimination to state-sanctioned discrimination came about through interplay of an educationally irrelevant issue concerning interstate commerce, by which a Mississippi statute requiring segregated train cars was upheld because it pertained solely to transportation within the state.[4] The Equal Protection Clause was thereby circumvented and state-enforced classification of citizens by race was made possible. In the South, state action began transforming the private custom of discrimination into state law. Jim Crow laws began in Florida in 1887, and soon engulfed the South.[5] Justice Powell, commenting much later, said: "the Equal Protection Clause was virtually strangled in its infancy by post–Civil War judicial reactionism."[6]

The capstone of segregation, though, came in 1896 with *Plessy v. Ferguson*,[7] in which the separate-but-equal rationale of the Roberts Court was implanted as a national standard applying to the Fourteenth Amendment. In *Plessy*, the Supreme Court maintained that an 1890 Louisiana law entitled "An Act to Promote the Comfort of Passengers" providing that "all railway companies carrying passengers in their coaches in this State, shall provide equal but separate accommodations for the white and colored races, by providing two or more passenger coaches for each passenger

train, or by dividing the passenger coaches by a partition so as to secure separate accommodations" was not unconstitutional, because state legislatures have wide discretion in promoting public peace and good order, and such actions will be upheld so long as they are reasonable. In a now-infamous passage, Justice Brown said:

> In determining the question of reasonableness it (legislature) is at liberty to act with reference to the established usages, customs and traditions of the people, and with a view to the promotion of their comfort, and the preservation of the public peace and good order. Gauged by this standard, we cannot say that a law which authorizes or even requires the separation of the two races in public conveyances is unreasonable. . . . [8]

In essence, the Court made the Equal Protection Clause subject to custom and tradition in accordance with legislative interpretation, no matter how blatantly and objectionably the law affected a particular classification of people.

In a lonely dissent in *Plessy*, Justice Harlan attacked the majority opinion and enunciated the law that would eventually become the prevailing view over fifty years later. He maintained, "Our constitution is color-blind, and neither knows nor tolerates classes among its citizens. In respect to civil rights, all citizens are equal before the law."[9] He maintained that separation of the races was a "badge of servitude."

After *Plessy*, the precedent of separation of the races was quickly transferred to education and further extended. In Richmond County, Georgia, the school board, discovering that it needed more facilities at the grade school level to accommodate black children, discontinued the black high school and turned the building into a black elementary school.[10] The board advised the black high school students to seek their education in church-affiliated schools. Upon challenge, the United States Supreme Court held that in this matter the only interest of the federal judiciary was to see that all citizens share equitably in the tax burden, but that the matter of education and how it was conducted, supported by that taxation, was solely a state concern.

Further expansion of segregation in education was justified in 1908 in *Berea College v. Kentucky*,[11] wherein the Supreme Court upheld a state law that forbade any institution as a corporation to provide instruction to both races at the same time unless the classes were conducted at least twenty-five miles apart. The law, the "Day Law" as it was named after its author,[12] was enacted specifically to prohibit integration at Berea College, a small private college that had been founded in 1859 to provide nondiscriminatory education for needy students, both black and white. In upholding the law and sidestepping the direct issue of state-enforced racial discrimination in the private sector, the Court simply asserted that the college, as a corporation of Kentucky, was subject to state regulation and was not entitled to all the immunities to which individuals were entitled. Since the college was the plaintiff and not black students, the Court was free to say that "a state may withhold from its corporations privileges and powers of which it cannot constitutionally deprive individuals."[13]

The *Plessy, Cumming,* and *Berea College* cases had not only fully established that the state could constitutionally maintain a separate system of education for blacks and whites, but that the arm of the state could reach into private education and require that it be segregated as well. Beyond this, *Cumming* laid the groundwork for almost unlimited state discretion in defining what constituted separate-but-equal. The federal courts would not intervene. Separation of the races in education was subsequently expanded to include not only black and white, but also yellow, brown, and red. In *Gong Lum v. Rice*,[14] in 1927, the Supreme Court held that states could segregate a Mongolian child from the Caucasian schools and compel her to attend a school for black children. Segregation of the *Gong Lum* type was practiced in many states, both North and South.

■ EROSION OF SEPARATE-BUT-EQUAL

As long as state legislatures had plenary power to define the limits of separate-but-equal, the concept was accepted with little or no argument. By the 1930s, however, the National Association for the Advancement of Colored People (NAACP) initiated a movement that was to pursue racial abuse and seek judicial clarification of the limits of separate-but-equal as a legal basis for segregation. At first, the intention was to attack segregation where equal facilities were obviously inadequate or nonexistent. As a result of these efforts, in 1938 a landmark desegregation case, *Missouri ex rel. Gaines v. Canada,* was handed down by the Supreme Court.[15] By a vote of seven to one, the Supreme Court held a Missouri law prohibiting blacks from entering the University of Missouri Law School unconstitutional because there were no other public law schools in the state to which blacks could go as an alternative. The ruling was singularly important because it not only placed some outward boundaries on implementation of separate-but-equal but more significantly it represented a reassertion of judicial authority in construing the Equal Protection Clause as a limitation on previously unfettered state action in education.

With the World War II years intervening, little was accomplished during the next decade, but slowly a public attitude against separate-but-equal began to materialize that would set the stage for more direct judicial action. The foundation of separate-but-equal was shaken by the Supreme Court in 1950, in another case involving a law school, this time the University of Texas.[16] Law schools were good targets for desegregation attorneys because judges and lawyers could more readily see the disparate condition in the legal field. In this case, a black Houston mail carrier by the name of Sweatt sought admission to the University of Texas Law School. Since the state had no law school for blacks, under the precedent of *Gaines,* a lower Texas court ordered that the state set up a law school for blacks. The school that was established was woefully inadequate and Sweatt further challenged, reasserting his claim to be admitted to the University of Texas Law School. Here, the Supreme Court was presented with a rather different dilemma of comparing two schools and rendering a judgment as to their comparability. Thus, the high Court found itself in the uneasy role of a super-accreditation agency. In ordering Sweatt admitted to the all-white law school, Chief Justice Fred Vinson pointed out that the new law school "could never hope to be equal in reputation of the faculty, experience of the administration, position and influence of the alumni, standing in the community, tradition and prestige."[17]

Vinson virtually eliminated the use of separate law schools for blacks by further observing that

> the law school to which Texas is willing to admit [Sweatt] excludes from its student body members of the racial groups which number 85 percent of the population of the State and include most of the lawyers, witnesses, jurors, judges, and other officials with whom [he] will inevitably be dealing when he becomes a member of the Texas Bar. With such a substantial and significant segment of society excluded, we cannot conclude that the education offered [Sweatt] is substantially equal to that which he would receive if admitted to the University of Texas Law School.[18]

The obvious educational infirmity of the separate-but-equal doctrine emerged with litigation in this case. Limitations on curriculum, faculty, educational atmosphere, and professional development combined to draw into serious constitutional question the further maintenance of separate higher-education facilities for both blacks and whites. On the same day that *Sweatt* was handed down, the Supreme Court ruled that if a state chose not to establish separate and substantially equal facilities for blacks, it could not segregate them within the white school.[19] McLaurin, a black doctoral student in the College of Education at the University of Oklahoma, was allowed to

enroll in the white school but was compelled to sit and study in designated sections for blacks while in the classrooms, library, and dining hall. The Court held this treatment unconstitutional as well.

Even though these cases served to expound the frailties of separate-but-equal, they did little to help the black elementary and secondary school children who were denied equal opportunity with no relief in sight. With *Cumming* as the precedent, the black child attended school in ramshackle facilities, had poor instructors, and in most cases attended schools that were in session for only a minor portion of the year. This circumstance could not be corrected so long as the separate-but-equal doctrine stood.

■ BROWN AND THE DEMISE OF SEGREGATED SCHOOLS

Several cases began making their way through the lower courts, each case holding potential for challenging the separate-but-equal doctrine head-on. Eventually five cases from Kansas, South Carolina, Virginia, Delaware, and Washington, D.C., reached the Supreme Court,[20] and were first argued in December 1952.

Lower courts in each case, with the exception of the Delaware case, had denied relief to black children. In Delaware, a decision by the Delaware Court of Chancery holding for the plaintiffs, requiring that black children be admitted to schools previously attended only by white children, was affirmed by the Supreme Court of Delaware. The defendants in this case applied for *certiorari* to the United States Supreme Court, challenging the immediate admission of black children to the white schools. In *Brown v. Board of Education*, the plaintiffs were black children of elementary age residing in Topeka. They brought action to enjoin a state statute that permitted, but did not require, cities in Kansas of more than 15,000 population to maintain separate facilities for black and white students. Under that authority, the Topeka Board of Education chose to establish segregated elementary schools. The lower federal court held that segregation in public education had a detrimental effect on black children but denied plaintiffs relief because the facilities were substantially equal. In both the South Carolina and Virginia cases, the lower courts had found the black schools to be inferior and had ordered improvements for equalization, but had not required admission of the black children to the schools for white children during the transition period. In the Washington, D.C., case, black children directly challenged school segregation in the nation's capital, alleging that segregation deprived them of due process of law under the Fifth Amendment. It was necessary to couch this latter claim in the Fifth Amendment since the Fourteenth Amendment did not apply to Congress.

These cases combined presented a range of situations by which the Supreme Court could comprehensively view the segregation issue. The Kansas case involved permissive segregation legislation in a northern state for elementary children; in the Virginia case a compulsory segregation law was used to segregate high school students in an upper southern state; South Carolina represented the deep South, and Delaware a border state.[21] The District of Columbia case drew due process and congressional power into question. The differing circumstances and the wide geographical distribution gave the decision more importance and imbued it with a national flavor and aura.

The importance of the case was reflected in the Court's hesitancy to rush to judgment. Though the case was first argued on 9 December 1952, the Court reached no decision and on 8 June 1953, the Court issued an order setting the case for reargument that fall and submitted a series of questions for litigants to address. In the first question, the Court asked what evidence there was to indicate that Congress and the states contemplated that the Fourteenth Amendment, when ratified, was intended to abolish school segregation. Sec-

ond, the Court asked whether Congress had the power to abolish school segregation and what the limits of the Court's own powers were. Third, the Court sought opinions on the extent of its own powers to resolve the issue, should the answer to the first two questions be inconclusive. Fourth, the Court asked whether, in the event of a decision in favor of plaintiffs, desegregation should be immediate or gradual, and whether the plaintiff children's grievance was personal and present. The fifth question concerned the procedural form the final decree should take.[22]

Within the parameters of these issues, several alternatives were open to the Court. Ashmore listed those that appeared to be within the realm of possibility.[23]

1. That there was no need to rule on the constitutionality of segregation per se, since each case might be disposed of on other grounds. (The Supreme Court had repeatedly declared that it would not rule on questions of a constitutional nature if a case could be decided by any other means.)
2. That the separate-but-equal doctrine was still the law, and when the separate facilities were unequal the Court would allow a reasonable period for the facilities to be made equal in fact.
3. That the separate-but-equal doctrine was still the law, but when separate facilities were unequal the Court would require immediate admission of blacks to the white schools pending the achievement of actual equality of facilities.
4. That the separate-but-equal doctrine was still the law, but the Court might require nonsegregation in certain phases of public education that it deemed impossible of equality within the separate framework. (In other words, the Court might conceivably hold that a particular course of activity could not be provided equally under segregation, as it had at least implied in the higher education cases.)
5. That whether segregation in a given case was a denial of equal protection of the laws was a question of fact, to be decided as are other questions of fact in the lower trial court.

6. That segregation was unconstitutional; the Court recognized the need for orderly progress of transition to nonsegregation; but the Court would limit itself to minimum personal relief of the plaintiffs, leaving to Congress the job of legislating detailed rules for implementing desegregation in the schools generally. (This would be in keeping with the idea that the administration of local school systems involves a "political question.")

7. That separate-but-equal was a clear denial of equal protection of the laws and thus unconstitutional; but the Court would permit a gradual change-over to a nonsegregated system under the supervision of the District Courts, or under the direction of a master appointed by the Supreme Court itself.

8. That separate-but-equal was unconstitutional and must be ended immediately; black plaintiffs in the case before the Court must be admitted at once to the white schools.

Realistically, the major point of the case could only have been decided one way, that separate-but-equal was unconstitutional. When asked how the Court would decide, the Solicitor General of the United States responded that the court "properly could find only one answer."[24] The final judgment came in a unanimous decision written by Chief Justice Earl Warren. The Court ruled: "We conclude that in the field of public education the doctrine of separate but equal has no place. Separate educational facilities are inherently unequal."[25] For directness and finality, the decision was a model. In overturning separate-but-equal, Warren did not dwell on other judicial precedents, because the precise issue before the Court had not been presented before. The validity of separate-but-equal, since *Roberts*, had been assumed but had never been argued and validly established.

The case was not only a watershed in American education, but was one of the most important decisions ever rendered by the Supreme Court. For sheer impact on society, it undoubtedly had the most far-reaching impact. Pollak commented: "Except for waging and winning the Civil War and World Wars I and II, the decision in the *School Segregation Cases* was probably the most important Amer-

ican governmental act of any kind since the Emancipation Proclamation."[26]

Separate-but-Equal Facilities Are Inherently Unequal

Brown v. Board of Education of Topeka

Supreme Court of the United States, 1954.
347 U.S. 483, 74 S.Ct. 686.

Mr. Chief Justice WARREN delivered the opinion of the Court. These cases come to us from the States of Kansas, South Carolina, Virginia, and Delaware. They are premised on different facts and different local conditions, but a common legal question justifies their consideration together in this consolidated opinion.

In each of the cases, minors of the Negro race, through their legal representatives, seek the aid of the courts in obtaining admission to the public schools of their community on a nonsegregated basis. In each instance, they have been denied admission to schools attended by white children under laws requiring or permitting segregation according to race. This segregation was alleged to deprive the plaintiffs of the equal protection of the laws under the Fourteenth Amendment. In each of the cases other than the Delaware case, a three-judge federal district court denied relief to the plaintiffs on the so-called "separate but equal" doctrine announced by this Court in *Plessy v. Ferguson*, 163 U.S. 537, 16 S.Ct. 1138, 41 L.Ed. 256. Under that doctrine, equality of treatment is accorded when the races are provided substantially equal facilities, even though these facilities be separate. In the Delaware case, the Supreme Court of Delaware adhered to that doctrine, but ordered that the plaintiffs be admitted to the white schools because of their superiority to the Negro schools.

The plaintiffs contend that segregated public schools are not "equal" and cannot be made "equal," and that hence they are deprived of the equal protection of the laws. Because of the obvious importance of the question presented, the Court took jurisdiction. Argument was heard in the 1952 Term, and reargument was heard this Term on certain questions propounded by the Court.
. . .

In the first cases in this Court construing the Fourteenth Amendment, decided shortly after its adoption, the Court interpreted it as proscribing all state-imposed discriminations against the Negro race. The doctrine of "separate but equal" did not make its appearance in this Court until 1896 in the case of *Plessy v. Ferguson*, supra, involving not education but transportation. American courts have since labored with the doctrine for over half a century. In this Court, there have been six cases involving the "separate but equal" doctrine in the field of public education. In *Cumming v. Board of Education of Richmond County*, 175 U.S. 528, 20 S.Ct. 197, 44 L.Ed. 262, and *Gong Lum v. Rice*, 275 U.S. 78, 48 S.Ct. 91, 72 L.Ed. 172, the validity of the doctrine itself was not challenged. In more recent cases, all on the graduate school level, inequality was found in that specific benefits enjoyed by white students were denied to Negro students of the same educational qualifications.
. . . In none of these cases was it necessary to re-examine the doctrine to grant relief to the Negro plaintiff. And in *Sweatt v. Painter*, the Court expressly reserved decision on the question whether *Plessy v. Ferguson* should be held inapplicable to public education.

In the instant cases, that question is directly presented. Here, unlike *Sweatt v. Painter*, there are findings below that the Negro and white schools involved have been equalized, or are being equalized, with respect to buildings, curricula, qualifications and salaries of teachers, and other "tangible" factors. Our decision, therefore, cannot turn on merely a comparison of these tangible factors in the Negro and white schools involved in each of the cases. We must look instead to the effect of segregation itself on public education.

In approaching this problem, we cannot turn the clock back to 1868 when the Amendment was adopted, or even to 1896 when *Plessy v. Ferguson* was written. We must consider public education in the light of its full development and its present place in American life throughout the Nation. Only in this way can it be determined if segregation in public schools deprives these plaintiffs of the equal protection of the laws.

Today, education is perhaps the most important function of state and local governments. Compulsory school attendance laws and the great expenditures for education both demonstrate our recognition of the importance of education to our democratic society. It is required in the performance of our most basic public responsibilities, even service in the armed forces. It is the very foundation of good citizenship. Today it is a principal instrument in awakening the child to cultural values, in preparing him for later professional training, and in helping him to adjust normally to his environment. In these days, it is doubtful that any child may reasonably be expected to succeed in life if he is denied the opportunity of an education. Such an opportunity, where the state has undertaken to provide it, is a right which must be made available to all on equal terms.

We come then to the question presented: Does segregation of children in public schools solely on the basis of race, even though the physical facilities and other "tangible" factors may be equal, deprive the children of the minority group of equal educational opportunities? We believe that it does.

In *Sweatt v. Painter*, in finding that a segregated law school for Negroes could not provide them equal educational opportunities, this Court relied in large part on "those qualities which are incapable of objective measurement but which make for greatness in a law school." In *McLaurin v. Oklahoma State Regents*, the Court, in requiring that a Negro admitted to a white graduate school be treated like all other students, again resorted to intangible considerations: "his ability to study, to engage in discussions and exchange views with other students, and, in general, to learn his profession." Such considerations apply with added force to children in grade and high schools. To separate them from others of similar age and qualifications solely because of their race generates a feeling of inferiority as to their status in the community that may affect their hearts and minds in a way unlikely ever to be undone. The effect of this separation on their educational opportunities was well stated by a finding in the Kansas case by a court which nevertheless felt compelled to rule against the Negro plaintiffs:

> Segregation of white and colored children in public schools has a detrimental effect upon the colored children. The impact is greater when it has the sanction of the law; for the policy of separating the races is usually interpreted as denoting the inferiority of the Negro group. A sense of inferiority affects the motivation of a child to learn. Segregation with the sanction of law, therefore, has a tendency to [retard] the educational and mental development of Negro children and to deprive them of some of the benefits they would receive in a racial[ly] integrated school system.

Whatever may have been the extent of psychological knowledge at the time of *Plessy v. Ferguson,* this finding is amply supported by modern authority. Any language in *Plessy v. Ferguson* contrary to this finding is rejected.

We conclude that in the field of public education the doctrine of "separate but equal" has no place. Separate educational facilities are inherently unequal. Therefore, we hold that the plaintiffs and others similarly situated for whom the actions have been brought are, by reason of the segregation complained of, deprived of the equal protection of the laws guaranteed by the Fourteenth Amendment. This disposition makes unnecessary any discussion whether such segregation also violates the Due Process Clause of the Fourteenth Amendment.

Because these are class actions, because of the wide applicability of this decision, and because of the great variety of local conditions, the formulation of decrees in these cases presents problems of considerable complexity. On reargument, the consideration of appropriate relief was necessarily subordinated to the primary question—the constitutionality of segregation in public education. We have now announced that such segregation is a denial of the equal protection of the laws. In order that we may have the full assistance of the parties in formulating decrees, the cases will be restored to the docket, and the parties are requested to present further argument on Questions 4 and 5 previously propounded by the Court for the reargument this Term. The Attorney General of the United States is again invited to participate. The Attorney General of the states requiring or permitting segregation of public education will also be permitted to appear as *amici curiae* upon request to do so by September 15, 1954, and submission of briefs by October 1, 1954.

It is so ordered.

NOTES

1. On the same day as *Brown,* the Court also announced a decision stating that "racial segregation in the public schools of the District of Columbia is a denial of the due process of law guaranteed by the Fifth Amendment to the Constitution." The Fourteenth Amendment applies to the states, but not to the District of Columbia. It found racial segregation of the District schools a denial of due process under the Fifth Amendment. The Court stated: "Classifications based solely on race must be scrutinized with particular care, since they are contrary to our traditions and hence constitutionally suspect . . . ." *Bolling v. Sharpe,* 347 U.S. 497, 74 S.Ct. 693 (1954).

2. One commentator has written as follows about the second *Brown* decision:

> The admission of a few dozen children to a few dozen schools would have presented no very grave difficulties calling for a study of means of gradual adjustment. Seen in its totality, however, as involving some 5,000 school districts, nearly nine million white children and nearly three million colored, the situation exhibited great variety and complexity. To begin with, a vast number of statutes and regulations incorporating centrally or marginally the rule of segregation, would require change in order to conform to the new principle. Bickel, A., *The Least*

Dangerous Branch (Bobbs-Merrill, New York, 1962), p. 248.

_____

▒▒ INTERPRETING BROWN

Over a generation after *Brown*, judicial decisions are still required to settle social and legal issues emanating from the circumstances surrounding desegregation. Full realization of the complexities brought on by the decision were probably, to a degree, foreseen by the Supreme Court when it first rendered its decision in 1954. Because of this awareness the Court delayed granting specific relief and invited the United States Attorney General and Attorneys General of all the States to submit their views regarding the ultimate order of the Court.

After due consideration of courses of action for implementation, the Court, with Chief Justice Warren again delivering the opinion, said that consideration should be given to "the public interest," as well as the "personal interest of the plaintiffs." In viewing this dichotomy, the Court directed lower courts to fashion remedies that would permit desegregation "with all deliberate speed."[27] In retrospect, the wisdom of the decision in *Brown II* has been called into question. Today, some maintain that the implementation decision, *Brown II,* allowed too much flexibility; others claimed not enough. But from the Supreme Court's perspective, the wisest course was to allow the local federal district courts to settle the individual complaints on a case-by-case basis with due regard for equity for all concerned, and, during the periods of transition, the lower courts were to retain jurisdiction to see that desegregation was properly implemented. The Supreme Court sought to avoid unreasonable delays by requiring specifically that the lower courts "require that the defendants make a prompt and reasonable start toward full compliance with our May 17, 1954, ruling."[28]

Considerable conflict followed the *Brown* decisions. Perhaps one of the most dramatic episodes occurred in Little Rock, Arkansas, where at first the National Guard was used to prevent black children from entering school, and later federal troops and the National Guard were used to protect the entrance of black children into the formerly white public schools.[29] Ultimately, the Supreme Court was called on to render a judgment in the Little Rock case. The question of nullification and interposition, the Civil War question, was again raised by the governor and the legislature of Arkansas, who asserted that they had no duty to obey federal court orders directed to them to effectuate desegregation.[30] The Court's response was direct and unambiguous:

> In short, the constitutional rights of children not to be discriminated against in school admission on grounds of race or color declared by this Court in the *Brown* case can neither be nullified openly and directly by state legislators or state executive or judicial officers, nor nullified indirectly by them through evasive schemes for segregation whether attempted "ingeniously or ingenuously."[31]

During the years immediately after *Brown,* school districts experimented with various devices to avoid desegregation. Initially, some states sought to provide funding for private schools through tuition or voucher arrangements. The most blatant example of this transpired in Virginia where, in Prince Edward County, the public schools were closed and private schools were operated with state and county assistance. In holding this scheme to be unconstitutional, the Supreme Court said that "the record in the present case could not be clearer that Prince Edward's public schools were closed and private schools operated in their place . . . for one reason, and one reason only: to ensure . . . that white and colored children in Prince Edward County would not, under any circumstances, go to the same school."[32]

Brown definitely proscribed government action that compelled or encouraged segregation, but did it require government intervention to integrate or mix the races in the schools?

When the *Briggs* case, a companion to *Brown*, was remanded to a federal district court in South Carolina, the lower-court judge discussed desegregation versus integration and defined the situation thusly:

> [A]ll that is decided, is that a state may not deny to any person on account of race the right to attend any school that it maintains. . . . The Constitution, in other words, does not require integration. It merely forbids segregation.[33]

The difference between desegregation and integration was also emphasized later by northern courts, which held that

> there is no constitutional duty on the part of the board to bus Negro or white children out of their neighborhoods or to transfer classes for the sole purpose of alleviating racial imbalance. . . .[34]

Contrarily, in another case in the South, the United States Court of Appeals for the Fifth Circuit held that there was indeed an affirmative duty on the part of government to integrate the schools were *de jure* segregation had existed prior to *Brown*.[35] *This court distinguished de facto* segregation, caused by housing patterns, from *de jure* segregation that had governmentally promulgated and enforced discrimination in the South.

These cases taken together enunciated a rule of law that required affirmative action by school boards in the South, *de jure* states, but did not compel school boards in the North, *de facto* states, to act affirmatively to move children about to assure that black children attended school with white children.

This issue was not treated by the United States Supreme Court until 1968, when it held that "freedom of choice" was an acceptable plan for desegregation only if it did in fact erase the vestiges of the past dual system of education. The Court said: "The school officials have the continuing duty to take whatever action may be necessary to create a unitary, nonracial system."[36] The constitutionality of an "open door" or "freedom of choice" policy could be judged only in light of its utility in bringing about desegregation. Effectively, the courts dismissed the distinc-

tion between integration and desegregation. The standard required that school districts be unitary and not dual. Where *de jure* segregation existed before, the state had an obligation to affirmatively assert itself to remove barriers to desegregation.

After waiting for fifteen years for the lower courts to effectuate the desegregation mandate of *Brown II,* the Supreme Court acted in 1969 to require that all school districts operating in states that had legal segregation in 1954 immediately become unitary.[37] The standard "with all deliberate speed" was replaced with an "immediately" standard. Whether this was accomplished through rezoning, busing, or other devices was not of concern to the Court; it simply required that all districts become unitary without further delay.

State's Closing of Public Schools and Contributing to the Support of Private Segregated Schools Is Unconstitutional

— — · — — · — — · —

Griffin v. County School Board of Prince Edward County

— — · — — · — — · —

Supreme Court of the United States, 1964.
377 U.S. 218, 84 S.Ct. 1226.

Mr. Justice BLACK delivered the opinion of the Court. This litigation began in 1951 when a group of Negro school children living in Prince Edward County, Virginia, filed a complaint in the United States District Court for the Eastern District of Virginia alleging that they had been denied admission to public schools attended by white children and charging that Virginia laws requiring such school segregation denied complainants the equal protection of the laws in violation of the Fourteenth Amendment. On May 17, 1954, ten years ago, we held that the Virginia segregation laws did deny equal protection. *Brown v. Board of Education,* 347 U.S. 483, 74 S.Ct. 686, 98 L.Ed. 873 (1954). On May 31, 1955, after reargument on the nature of relief, we remanded this case, along with others heard with it, to the District Courts to enter such orders as "necessary and proper to admit [complainants] to public schools on a racially nondiscriminatory basis with all deliberate speed . . . ." *Brown v. Board of Education,* 349 U.S. 294, 301, 75 S.Ct. 753, 757, 99 L.Ed. 1083 (1955).

Efforts to desegregate Prince Edward County's schools met with resistance. In 1956, Section 141 of the Virginia Constitution was amended to authorize the General Assembly and local governing bodies to appropriate funds to assist students to go to public or to nonsectarian private schools. In addition to those owned by the State or by the locality. The General Assembly met in special session and enacted legislation to close any public schools where white and colored children were enrolled together, to cut off state funds to such schools, to pay tuition grants to children in nonsectarian private schools, and to extend state retirement benefits to teachers in newly created private schools. The legislation closing mixed schools and cutting off state funds was later invalidated by the Supreme Court of Appeals of Virginia, which held that these laws violated the Virginia Constitution. *Harrison v. Day,* 200 Va. 439, 106 S.E.2d 636 (1959). In April 1959, the General Assembly abandoned "massive resistance" to desegregation and turned instead to what was called a "freedom of choice" program. The Assembly repealed the rest of the 1956 legislation, as well as a tuition grant law of January 1959, and enacted a new tuition grant program. At the same time the Assembly repealed Virginia's compulsory attendance laws and instead made school attendance a matter of local option.

In June 1959, the United States Court of Appeals for the Fourth Circuit directed the Federal District Court (1) to enjoin discriminatory practices in Prince Edward County schools, (2) to require the County School Board to take "immediate steps" toward admitting students without regard to race to the white high school "in the school term beginning September 1959," and (3) to require the Board to make plans for admissions to ele-

mentary schools without regard to race. *Allen v. County School Board of Prince Edward County,* 266 F.2d 507, 511 (C.A.4th Cir.1959). Having as early as 1956 resolved that they would not operate public schools "wherein white and colored children are taught together," the Supervisors of Prince Edward County refused to levy any school taxes for the 1959–1960 school year, explaining that they were "confronted with a court decree which requires the admission of white and colored children to all the schools of the county without regard to race or color." As a result, the county's public schools did not reopen in the fall of 1959 and have remained closed ever since, although the public schools of every other county in Virginia have continued to operate under laws governing the State's public school system and to draw funds provided by the State for that purpose. A private group, the Prince Edward School Foundation, was formed to operate private schools for white children in Prince Edward County and, having built its own school plant, has been in operation ever since the closing of the public schools. An offer to set up private schools for colored children in the county was rejected, the Negroes of Prince Edward preferring to continue the legal battle for desegregated public schools, and colored children were without formal education from 1959 to 1963, when federal, state, and county authorities cooperated to have classes conducted for Negroes and whites in school buildings owned by the county. During the 1959–1960 school year the Foundation's schools for white children were supported entirely by private contributions, but in 1960 the General Assembly adopted a new tuition grant program making every child, regardless of race, eligible for tuition grants of $125, or $150 to attend a nonsectarian private school or a public school outside his locality, and also authorizing localities to provide their own grants. The Prince Edward Board of Supervisors then passed an ordinance providing tuition grants of $100, so that each child attending the Prince Edward School Foundation's schools received a total of $225 if in elementary school or $250 if in high school. In the 1960–1961 session, the major source of financial support for the Foundation was in the indirect form of these state and county tuition grants, paid to children attending Foundation schools. At the same time, the County Board of Supervisors passed an ordinance allowing property tax credits up to 25 percent for contributions to any "nonprofit, nonsectarian private school" in the county.

In 1961 petitioners here filed a supplemental complaint, adding new parties and seeking to enjoin the respondents from refusing to operate an efficient system of public free schools in Prince Edward County and to enjoin payment of public funds to help support private schools which excluded students on account of race. The District Court, finding that "the end result of every action taken by that body [Board of Supervisors] was designed to preserve separation of the races in the schools of Prince Edward County," enjoined the county from paying tuition grants or giving tax credits so long as public schools remained closed. . . . At this time the District Court did not pass on whether the public schools of the county could be closed but abstained pending determination by the Virginia courts of whether the constitution and laws of Virginia required the public schools to be kept open. Later, however, without waiting for the Virginia courts to decide the question the District Court held that "the public schools of Prince Edward County may not be closed to avoid the effect of the law of the land as interpreted by the Supreme Court, while the Commonwealth of Virginia permits other public schools to remain open at the expense of the taxpayers." . . . Soon thereafter, a declaratory judgment suit was brought by the County Board of Supervisors and the County School Board in a Virginia Circuit Court. Having done this, these parties asked the Federal District Court to abstain from further proceedings until the suit in the state courts had run its course, but the District Court declined; it repeated its order that Prince Edward's public schools might not be closed to avoid desegregation while the other public schools in Virginia remained open. The Court of Appeals reversed, Judge Bell dissenting, holding that the District Court should have abstained to await state court determination of the validity

of the tuition grants and the tax credits, as well as the validity of the closing of the public schools. *Griffin v. Board of Supervisors of Prince Edward County,* 322 F.2d 332 (C.A.4th Cir.1963). We granted certiorari, stating:

> In view of the long delay in the case since our decision in the *Brown* case and the importance of the questions presented, we grant certiorari and put the case down for argument March 30, 1964, on the merits, as we have done in other comparable situations without waiting for final action by the Court of Appeals. 375 U.S. 391.

For reasons to be stated, we agree with the District Court that, under the circumstances here, closing the Prince Edward County schools while public schools in all the other counties of Virginia were being maintained denied the petitioners and the class of Negro students they represent the equal protection of the laws guaranteed by the Fourteenth Amendment. . . . The case has been delayed since 1951 by resistance at the state and county level, by legislation, and by lawsuits. The original plaintiffs have doubtless all passed high school age. There has been entirely too much deliberation and not enough speed in enforcing the constitutional rights which we held in *Brown v. Board of Education,* supra, had been denied Prince Edward County Negro children. We accordingly reverse the Court of Appeals' judgment remanding the case to the District Court for abstention, and we proceed to the merits.

In *County School Board of Prince Edward County v. Griffin,* 204 Va. 650, 133 S.E.2d 565 (1963), the Supreme Court of Appeals of Virginia upheld as valid under state law the closing of the Prince Edward County public schools, the state and county tuition grants for children who attend private schools, and the county's tax concessions for those who make contributions to private schools. The same opinion also held that each county had "an option to operate or not to operate public schools," 204 Va., at 671, 133 S.E.2d, at 580. We accept this case as a definitive and authoritative holding of Virginia law, binding on us, but we cannot accept the Virginia court's further holding, based largely on the Court of Appeals' opinion in this case, 322 F.2d 332, that closing the county's public schools under the circumstances of the case did not deny the colored school children of Prince Edward County equal protection of the laws guaranteed by the Federal Constitution.

Since 1959, all Virginia counties have had the benefits of public schools but one: Prince Edward. However, there is no rule that counties, as counties, must be treated alike; the Equal Protection Clause relates to equal protection of the laws "between persons as such rather than between areas." *Salsburg v. Maryland,* 346 U.S. 545, 551, 74 S.Ct. 280, 283, 98 L.Ed. 281 (1954). Indeed, showing that different persons are treated differently is not enough, without more, to show a denial of equal protection. . . .

Virginia law, as here applied, unquestionably treats the school children of Prince Edward differently from the way it treats the school children of all other Virginia counties. Prince Edward children must go to a private school or none at all; all other Virginia children can go to public schools. Closing Prince Edward's schools bears more heavily on Negro children in Prince Edward County since white children there have accredited private schools which they can attend, while colored children until very recently have had no available private schools, and even the school they now attend is a temporary expedient. Apart from this expedient, the result is that Prince Edward County school children, if they go to school in their own county, must go to racially segregated schools which, although designated as private, are beneficiaries of county and state support.

A State, of course, has a wide discretion in deciding whether laws shall operate statewide or shall operate only in certain counties, the legislature "having in mind the needs and desires of each." *Salsburg v. Maryland,* supra, 346 U.S., at 552, 74 S.Ct., at 284. A State may wish to suggest, as Maryland did in *Salsburg,* that there are reasons why one county ought not to be treated like another. But the record in the present case could not be clearer that Prince Edward's public schools were closed and private schools operated in their place with state and county assistance, for one reason, and one reason only: to ensure, through measures taken by the county and the State, that white and colored children in Prince Edward County would not, under any circumstances, go to the same school. Whatever nonracial grounds might support a State's allowing a county to abandon public schools, the object must be a constitutional one, and grounds of race and opposition to desegregation do not qualify as constitutional. . . .

Accordingly, we agree with the District Court that closing the Prince Edward schools and meanwhile contributing to the support of the private segregated white schools that took their place denied petitioners the equal protection of the laws. . . .

The District Court held that "the public schools of Prince Edward County may not be closed to avoid the effect of the law of the land as interpreted by the Supreme Court, while the Commonwealth of Virginia permits other public schools to remain open at the expense of the taxpayers." . . . At the same time the court gave notice that it would later consider an order to accomplish this purpose if the public schools were not reopened by September 7, 1962. That day has long passed, and the schools are still closed. On remand, therefore, the court may find it necessary to consider further such an order. An order of this kind is within the court's power if required to assure these petitioners that their constitutional rights will no longer be denied them. The time for mere "deliberate speed" has run out, and that phrase can no longer justify denying these Prince Edward County school children their constitutional rights to an education equal to that afforded by the public schools in the other parts of Virginia.

The judgment of the Court of Appeals is reversed, the judgment of the District Court is affirmed, and the cause is remanded to the District Court with directions to enter a decree which will guarantee that these petitioners will get the kind of education that is given in the State's public schools. And, if it becomes necessary to add new parties to accomplish this end, the District Court is free to do so. It is so ordered.

Judgment of Court of Appeals reversed, judgment of the District Court affirmed and cause remanded with directions.

Mr. Justice CLARK and Mr. Justice HARLAN disagree with the holding that the federal courts are empowered to order the reopening of the public schools in Prince Edward County, but otherwise join in the Court's opinion.

State Must Institute Affirmative Action Where "Freedom of Choice" Fails to Create Unitary System

—·—·—·—·—·—

Green v. County School Board of New Kent County, Virginia

—·—·—·—·—·—

Supreme Court of the United States, 1968.
391 U.S. 430, 88 S.Ct. 1689.

Mr. Justice BRENNAN delivered the opinion of the Court. The question for decision is whether, under all the circumstances here, respondent School Board's adoption of a "freedom-of-choice" plan which allows a pupil to choose his own public school constitutes adequate compliance with the Board's responsibility "to achieve a system of determining admission to the public schools on a nonracial basis . . . ." *Brown v. Board of Education of Topeka, Kan.,* 349 U.S. 294, 300–301, 75 S.Ct. 753, 756, 99 L.Ed. 1083 *(Brown II).*

Petitioners brought this action in March 1965 seeking injunctive relief against respondent's continued maintenance of an alleged racially segregated school system. . . .

The pattern of separate "white" and "Negro" schools in the New Kent County school system established under compulsion of state laws is precisely the pattern of segregation to which *Brown I* and *Brown II* were particularly addressed, and which *Brown I* declared unconstitutionally denied Negro school children equal protection of the laws. Racial identification of the system's schools was complete,

extending not just to the composition of student bodies at the two schools but to every facet of school operations—faculty, staff, transportation, extracurricular activities and facilities. In short, the State, acting through the local school board and school officials, organized and operated a dual system, part "white" and part "Negro."

It was such dual systems that fourteen years ago *Brown I* held unconstitutional and a year later *Brown II* held must be abolished; school boards operating such school systems were *required* by *Brown II* "to effectuate a transition to a racially nondiscriminatory school system." 349 U.S., at 301, 75 S.Ct. at 756. It is of course true that for the time immediately after *Brown II* the concern was with making an initial break in a long-established pattern of excluding Negro children from schools attended by white children. The principal focus was on obtaining for those Negro children courageous enough to break with tradition a place in the "white" schools. See, e.g., *Cooper v. Aaron,* 358 U.S. 1, 78 S.Ct. 1401, 3 L.Ed.2d 5. Under *Brown II* that immediate goal was only the first step, however. The transition to a unitary, nonracial system of public education was and is the ultimate end to be brought about; it was because of the "complexities arising from the transition to a system of public education freed of racial discrimination" that we provided for "all deliberate speed" in the implementation of the principles of *Brown I.* 349 U.S., at 299–301, 75 S.Ct. at 755. Thus we recognized the task would necessarily involve solution of "varied local school problems." Id., at 299, 75 S.Ct. at 756. . . .

It is against this background that thirteen years after *Brown II* commanded the abolition of dual systems we must measure the effectiveness of respondent School Board's "freedom-of-choice" plan to achieve that end. The School Board contends that it has fully discharged its obligation by adopting a plan by which every student, regardless of race, may "freely" choose the school he will attend. The Board attempts to cast the issue in its broadest form by arguing that its "freedom-of-choice" plan may be faulted only by reading the Fourteenth Amendment as universally requiring "compulsory integration," a reading it insists the wording of the Amendment will not support. But that argument ignores the thrust of *Brown II.* In the light of the command of that case, what is involved here is the question whether the Board has achieved the "racially nondiscriminatory school system" *Brown II* held must be effectuated in order to remedy the established unconstitutional deficiencies of its segregated system. In the context of the state-imposed segregated pattern of long standing, the fact that in 1965 the Board opened the doors of the former "white" school to Negro children and of the "Negro" school to white children merely begins, not ends, our inquiry whether the Board has taken steps adequate to abolish its dual, segregated system. *Brown II* was a call for the dismantling of well-entrenched dual systems tempered by an awareness that complex and multifaceted problems would arise which would require time and flexibility for a successful resolution. School boards such as the respondent then operating state-compelled dual systems were nevertheless clearly charged with the affirmative duty to take whatever steps might be necessary to convert to a unitary system in which racial discrimination would be eliminated root and branch. . . . The constitutional rights of Negro school children articulated in *Brown I* permit no less than this; and it was to this end that *Brown II* commanded school boards to bend their efforts.

In determining whether respondent School Board met that command by adopting its "freedom-of-choice" plan, it is relevant that this first step did not come until some eleven years after *Brown I* was decided and ten years after *Brown II* directed the making of a "prompt and reasonable start." This deliberate perpetuation of the unconstitutional dual system can only have compounded the harm of such a system. Such delays are no longer tolerable, for "the governing constitutional principles no longer bear the imprint of newly enunciated doctrine." . . . The burden on a school board today is to come forward with a plan that promises realistically to work, and promises realistically to work *now*.

The obligation of the district courts, as it always has been, is to assess the effectiveness of a proposed plan in achieving desegregation. There is no universal answer to complex problems of desegregation; there is obviously no one plan that will do the job in every case. The matter must be assessed in light of the circumstances present and the options available in each instance. It is incumbent upon the school board to establish that its proposed plan promises meaningful and immediate progress toward disestablishing state-imposed segregation. It is incumbent upon the district court to weigh that claim in light of the facts at hand and in light of any alternatives which may be shown as feasible and more promising in their effectiveness. Where the court finds the board to be acting in good faith and the proposed plan to have real prospects for dismantling the state-imposed dual system "at the earliest practicable date," then the plan may be said to provide effective relief. Of course, the availability to the board of other more promising courses of action may indicate a lack of good faith; and at the least it places a heavy burden upon the board to explain its preference for an apparently less effective method. Moreover, whatever plan is adopted will require evaluation in practice, and the court should retain jurisdiction until it is clear that state-imposed segregation has been completely removed. . . .

We do not hold that "freedom of choice" can have no place in such a plan. We do not hold that a "freedom-of-choice" plan might of itself be unconstitutional, although that argument has been urged upon us. Rather, all we decide today is that in desegregating a dual system a plan utilizing "freedom of choice" is not an end in itself. . . .

The New Kent School Board's "freedom-of-choice" plan cannot be accepted as a sufficient step to "effectuate a transition" to a unitary system. In three years of operation not a single white child has chosen to attend Watkins school and although 115 Negro children enrolled in New Kent school in 1967 (up from 35 in 1965 and 111 in 1966) 85 percent of the Negro children in the system still attend the all-Negro Watkins school. In other words, the school system remains a dual system. Rather than further the dismantling of the dual system, the plan has operated simply to burden children and their parents with a responsibility which *Brown II* placed squarely on the School Board. The Board must be required to formulate a new plan and, in light of other courses which appear open to the Board, such as zoning, fashion steps which promise realistically to convert promptly to a system without a "white" school and a "Negro" school, but just schools.

The judgment of the Court of Appeals is vacated insofar as it affirmed the District Court and the case is remanded to the District Court for further proceedings consistent with this opinion. It is so ordered.

Dual School Systems Are to Be Terminated at Once and Unitary Systems Are to Begin Immediately

Alexander v. Holmes County Board of Educ.

Supreme Court of the United States, 1969.
396 U.S. 19, 90 S.Ct. 29, rehearing denied 396 U.S. 976, 90 S.Ct. 437 (1969).

PER CURIAM. This case comes to the Court on a petition for certiorari to the Court of Appeals for the Fifth Circuit. The petition was granted on October 9, 1969, and the case set down for early argument. The question presented is one of paramount importance, involving as it does the denial of fundamental rights to many thousands of school children, who are presently attending Mississippi schools under segregated conditions contrary to the applicable decisions of this Court. Against this background the Court of Appeals should have denied all motions for additional time because continued operation of segregated schools under a standard of allowing "all deliberate speed" for desegregation is no longer constitutionally permissible. Under explicit holdings of this Court the obligation of every school district is to terminate dual

school systems at once and to operate now and hereafter only unitary schools. . . . It is hereby adjudged, ordered, and decreed:

The Court of Appeals' order of August 28, 1969, is vacated, and the case is remanded to that court to issue its decree and order, effective immediately, declaring that each of the school districts here involved may no longer operate a dual school system based on race or color, and directing that they begin immediately to operate as unitary school systems within which no person is to be effectively excluded from any school because of race or color. . . .

The Court of Appeals shall retain jurisdiction to insure prompt and faithful compliance with its order, and may modify or amend the same as may be deemed necessary or desirable for the operation of a unitary school system.

■■■ DE FACTO SEGREGATION

De facto segregation is not unconstitutional, whether it occurs in the South or in the North. President Nixon summarized the law in this regard in 1969. He said: "There is a fundamental distinction between so-called 'de jure' and 'de facto' segregation: de jure segregation arises by law or by the deliberate act of school officials and is unconstitutional; de facto segregation results from residential housing patterns and does not violate the Constitution."

This legal position concerning *de facto* segregation has been reiterated several times by the courts in various decisions. A notable early example was the *Bell* decision, in which the United States Court of Appeals for the Seventh Circuit said: "there is no affirmative United States constitutional duty to change innocently arrived at school attendance districts by the mere fact that shifts in population either increase or decrease the percentage of either Negro or white pupils."[38] Similarly, the Court of Appeals for the Fifth Circuit held that boards of education have no constitutional obligation to relieve racial imbalance that they do not cause or create. These are both decisions from northern states; but fundamentally the law is the same, whether the segregation occurs in the North or in the South. If segregation is created by law or official act, then an affirmative duty is required to integrate the schools. The Supreme Court summarized the constitutional standard in a Denver, Colorado, case:

> [W]e have held that where plaintiffs prove that a current condition of segregated schooling exists within a school district where a dual system was compelled or authorized by statute at the time of our decision in *Brown* . . . the State automatically assumes an affirmative duty to "effectuate a transition to a racially nondiscriminatory school system."[39]

In this case, the Supreme Court emphasized that the differentiating factor between *de jure* segregation and so-called *de facto* segregation is *purpose* or *intent*.

If school authorities practice purposeful segregation, then a *de jure* condition exists, and the school district will be required to take affirmative measures to correct racial imbalance in the schools.

School Board Actions May Have Effect of Creating Unconstitutional De Jure Segregation

– – · – – · – – · – –

Keyes v. School District No. 1, Denver

– – · – – · – – · – –

Supreme Court of the United States, 1973.
413 U.S. 189, 93 S.Ct. 2686.

Mr. Justice BRENNAN delivered the opinion of the Court. This school desegregation case concerns the Denver, Colorado, school system. That system has never been operated under a constitutional or statutory provision that mandated or permitted racial segregation in public education. Rather, the gravamen of this action, brought in June 1969 in the District Court for the District of Colorado by parents of Denver schoolchildren, is that respondent School Board alone, by use of various techniques such as the manipulation of student attendance zones, schoolsite selection and a neighborhood school policy, created or maintained racially or ethnically (or both racially and ethnically) segregated schools throughout the school district, entitling petitioners to a decree directing desegregation of the entire school district. . . .

The District Court found that by the construction of a new, relatively small elementary school, Barrett, in the middle of the Negro community west of Park Hill, by the gerrymandering of student attendance zones, by the use of so-called "optional zones," and by the excessive use of mobile classroom units, among other things, the respondent School Board had engaged over almost a decade after 1960 in an unconstitutional policy of deliberate racial segregation with respect to the Park Hill schools. The court therefore ordered the Board to desegregate those schools through the implementation of the three rescinded resolutions. D.C., 303 F.Supp. 279 and 289 (1969).

Segregation in Denver schools is not limited, however, to the schools in the Park Hill area, and not satisfied with their success in obtaining relief for Park Hill, petitioners pressed their prayer that the District Court order desegregation of all segregated schools in the city of Denver, particularly the heavily segregated schools in the core city area. But that court concluded that its finding of a purposeful and systematic program of racial segregation affecting thousands of students in the Park Hill area did not, in itself, impose on the School Board an affirmative duty to eliminate segregation throughout the school district. Instead, the court fractionated the district and held that petitioners had to make a fresh showing of *de jure* segregation in each area of the city for which they sought relief. Moreover, the District Court held that its finding of intentional segregation in Park Hill was not in any sense material to the question of segregative intent in other areas of the city. . . .

Before turning to the primary question we decide today, a word must be said about the District Court's method of defining a "segregated" school. Denver is a tri-ethnic, as distinguished from a bi-racial, community. The overall racial and ethnic composition of the Denver public schools is 66 percent Anglo, 14 percent Negro, and 20 percent Hispano. . . . What is or is not a segregated school will necessarily depend on the facts of each particular case. In addition to the racial and ethnic composition of a school's student body, other factors, such as the racial and ethnic composition of faculty and staff and the community and administration attitudes toward the school, must be taken into consideration. The District Court has recognized these specific factors as elements of the definition of a "segregated" school and we may therefore infer that the court will consider them again on remand.

We conclude, however, that the District Court erred in separating Negroes and Hispanos for purposes of defining a "segregated" school. We have held that Hispanos constitute an identifiable class for purposes of the Fourteenth Amendment. *Hernandez v. Texas,* 347 U.S. 475, 74 S.Ct. 667, 98 L.Ed. 866 (1954). . . . Indeed the District Court recognized this in classifying predominantly Hispano schools as "segregated" schools in their own right. But there is also much evidence that in the Southwest Hispanos and Negroes have a great many things in common. The United States Commission on Civil Rights has recently published two Reports on Hispano education in the Southwest. Focusing on students in the States of Arizona, California, Colorado, New Mexico, and Texas, the Commission concluded that Hispanos suffer from the same educational inequities as Negroes and American Indians. In fact, the District Court itself recognized that "[o]ne of the things which the Hispano has in common with the Negro is economic and cultural deprivation and discrimination." 313 F.Supp., at 69. This is agreement that, though of different origins, Negroes and Hispanos in Denver suffer identical discrimination in treatment when compared with the treatment afforded Anglo students. In that circumstance, we think petitioners are entitled to have schools with a combined predominance of Negroes and Hispanos included in the category of "segregated" schools.

In our view, the only other question that requires our decision at this time is . . . whether the District Court and the Court of Appeals applied an incorrect legal standard in addressing petitioners' contention that respondent School Board engaged in an unconstitutional policy of deliberate segregation in the core city schools. Our conclusion is that those courts did not apply the correct standard in addressing that contention.

Petitioners apparently concede for the purposes of this case that in the case of a school system like Denver's, where no statutory dual system has ever existed, plaintiffs must prove not only that segregated schooling exists but also that it was brought about or maintained by intentional state action. Petitioners proved that for almost a decade after 1960 respondent School Board had engaged in an unconstitutional policy of deliberate racial segregation in the Park Hill schools. . . . This finding did not relate to an insubstantial or trivial fragment of the school system. On the contrary, respondent School Board was found guilty of following a deliberate segregation policy at schools attended, in 1969, by 37.69 percent of Denver's total Negro school population . . . . Respondent argues, however, that a finding of state-imposed segregation as to a substantial portion of the school system can be viewed in isolation from the rest of the district, and that even if state-imposed segregation does exist in a substantial part of the Denver school system, it does not follow that the District Court could predicate on that fact a finding that the entire school system is a dual system. We do not agree. We have never suggested that plaintiffs in school desegregation cases must bear the burden of proving the elements of *de jure* segregation as to each and every school or each and every student within the school system. Rather, we have held that where plaintiffs prove that a current condition of segregated schooling exists within a school district where a dual system was compelled or authorized by statute at the time of our decision in *Brown v. Board of Education,* 347 U.S. 483, 74 S.Ct. 686, 98 L.Ed. 873 (1954) *(Brown I),* the State automatically assumes an affirmative duty "to effectuate a transition to a racially nondiscriminatory school system," *Brown v. Board of Education,* 349 U.S. 294, 301, 75 S.Ct. 753, 756, 99 L.Ed. 1083 (1955) *(Brown II);* see also *Green v. County School Board,* 391 U.S. 430, 437–438, 88 S.Ct. 1689, 1693–1694, 20 L.Ed.2d 716 (1968); that is, to eliminate from the public schools within their school system all "vestiges of state-imposed segregation." *Swann v. Charlotte-Mecklenburg Board of Education,* 402 U.S. 1, 15, 91 S.Ct. 1267, 1275, 28 L.Ed.2d 554 (1971).

This is not a case, however, where a statutory dual system has ever existed. Nevertheless, where plaintiffs prove that the school authorities have carried out a systematic program of segregation affecting a substantial portion of the students, schools, teachers, and facilities within the school system, it is only common sense to conclude that there exists a predicate for a finding of the existence of a dual school system. Several considerations support this conclusion. First, it is obvious that a practice of concentrating Negroes in certain schools by structuring attendance zones or designating "feeder" schools on the basis of race has the reciprocal effect of keeping other nearby schools predominantly white. Similarly, the practice of building a school — such as the Barrett Elementary School in this case — to a certain size and in a certain location, "with conscious knowledge that it would be a segregated school," 303 F.Supp., at 285, has a substantial reciprocal effect on the racial composition of other nearby schools. So also, the use of mobile classrooms, the drafting of student transfer policies, the transportation of students, and the assignment of faculty and staff on racially identifiable bases, have the clear effect of earmarking schools according to their racial composition, and this, in turn, together with the elements of student assignment and school construction, may have a profound reciprocal effect on the racial composition of residential neighborhoods, within a metropolitan area, thereby causing further racial concentration within the schools. We recognized this in *Swann* . . . .

In short, common sense dictates the conclusion that racially inspired school board actions have an impact beyond the particular schools that are subjects of those actions. This is not to say, of course, that there can never be

a case in which the geographical structure of, or the natural boundaries within, a school district may have the effect of dividing the district into separate, identifiable and unrelated units. Such a determination is essentially a question of fact to be resolved by the trial court in the first instance, but such cases must be rare. In the absence of such a determination, proof of state-imposed segregation in a substantial portion of the district will suffice to support a finding by the trial court of the existence of a dual system. . . .

Although petitioners had already proved the existence of intentional school segregation in the Park Hill schools, this crucial finding was totally ignored when attention turned to the core city schools. Plainly, a finding of intentional segregation as to a portion of a school system is not devoid of probative value in assessing the school authorities' intent with respect to other parts of the same school system. On the contrary where, as here, the case involves one school board, a finding of intentional segregation on its part in one portion of a school system is highly relevant to the issue of the board's intent with respect to the other segregated schools in the system. This is merely an application of the well-settled evidentiary principle that "the prior doing of other similar acts, whether clearly a part of a scheme or not, is useful as reducing the possibility that the act in question was done with innocent intent." 2 J. Wigmore, Evidence 200 (3d ed. 1940). . . .

Applying these principles in the special context of school desegregation cases, we hold that a finding of intentionally segregative school board actions in a meaningful portion of a school system, as in this case, creates a presumption that other segregated schooling within the system is not adventitious. It establishes, in other words, a prima facie case of unlawful segregative design on the part of school authorities, and shifts to those authorities the burden of proving that other segregated schools within the system are not also the result of intentionally segregative actions. This is true even if it is determined that different areas of the school district should be viewed independently of each other because, even in that situation, there is high probability that where school authorities have effectuated an intentionally segregative policy in a meaningful portion of the school system, similar impermissible considerations have motivated their actions in other areas of the system. We emphasize that the differentiating factor between *de jure* segregation and so-called *de facto* segregation to which we referred in *Swann* is *purpose* or *intent* to segregate. Where school authorities have been found to have practiced purposeful segregation in part of a school system, they may be expected to oppose system-wide desegregation, as did the respondents in this case, on the ground that their purposefully segregative actions were isolated and individual events, thus leaving plaintiffs with the burden of proving otherwise. But at that point where an intentionally segregative policy is practiced in a meaningful or significant segment of a school system, as in this case, the school authorities cannot be heard to argue that plaintiffs have proved only "isolated and individual" unlawfully segregative actions. In that circumstance, it is both fair and reasonable to require that the school authorities bear the burden of showing that their actions as to other segregated schools within the system were not also motivated by segregative intent.   . . .

In discharging that burden, it is not enough, of course, that the school authorities rely upon some allegedly logical, racially neutral explanation for their actions. Their burden is to adduce proof sufficient to support a finding that segregative intent was not among the factors that motivated their actions. The courts below attributed much significance to the fact that many of the Board's actions in the core city area antedated our decision in *Brown.* We reject any suggestion that remoteness in time has any relevance to the issue of intent. If the actions of school authorities were to any degree motivated by segregative intent and the segregation resulting from those actions continues to exist, the fact of remoteness in time certainly does not make those actions any less "intentional."   . . .

The respondent School Board invoked at trial its "neighborhood school policy" as explaining racial and ethnic concentrations within the core city schools, arguing that since the core city area population had long been Negro and Hispano, the concentrations were necessarily the result of residential patterns and not of purposefully segregative policies. We have no occasion to consider in this case whether a "neighborhood school policy" of itself will justify racial or ethnic concentrations in the absence of a finding that school authorities have committed acts constituting *de jure* segregation. It is enough that we hold that the mere assertion of such a policy is not dispositive where, as in this case, the school authorities have been found to have practiced *de jure* segregation in a meaningful portion of the school system by techniques that indicate that the "neighborhood school" concept has not been maintained free of manipulation.
. . .

In summary, the District Court on remand, *first,* will afford respondent School Board the opportunity to prove its contention that the Park Hill area is a separate, identifiable, and unrelated section of the school district that should be treated as isolated from the rest of the district. If respondent School Board fails to prove that contention, the District Court, *second,* will determine whether respondent School Board's conduct over almost a decade after 1960 in carrying out a policy of deliberate racial segregation in the Park Hill schools constitutes the entire school system a dual school system. If the District Court determines that the Denver school system is a dual school system, respondent School Board has the affirmative duty to desegregate the entire system "root and branch." *Green v. County School Board,* 391 U.S., at 438, 88 S.Ct. at 1694. If the District Court determines, however, that the Denver school system is not a dual school system by reason of the Board's actions in Park Hill, the court, *third,* will afford respondent School Board the opportunity to rebut petitioners' prima facie case of intentional segregation in the core city schools raised by the finding of intentional segregation in the Park Hill schools. There, the Board's burden is to show that its policies and practices with respect to schoolsite location, school size, school renovations and additions, student-attendance zones, student assignment and transfer options, mobile classroom units, transportation of students, assignment of faculty and staff, etc., considered together and premised on the Board's so-called "neighborhood school" concept, either were not taken in effectuation of a policy to create or maintain segregation in the core city schools, or, if unsuccessful in that effort, were not factors in causing the existing condition of segregation in these schools. Considerations of "fairness" and "policy" demand no less in light of the Board's intentionally segregative actions. If respondent Board fails to rebut petitioners' prima facie case, the District Court must, as in the case of Park Hill, decree all-out desegregation of the core city schools.

The judgment of the Court of Appeals is modified to vacate instead of reverse the parts of the Final Decree that concern the core city schools, and the case is remanded to the District Court for further proceedings consistent with this opinion. . . .

It is so ordered.

NOTES

1. In taking the position that there is no affirmative duty to integrate where *de facto* segregation exists, one commentator had this to say:

> Revolutionary as was the decision in *Brown* in its rendition and subsequent application, the Court has not sought to overturn the established principle of constitutional law that "the unlawful administration by state officers of a state statute fair on its face, resulting in its unequal application to those who are entitled to be treated alike, is not a denial of equal protection unless there is shown to be present in it an element of intentional or purposeful discrimination." *Snowden v. Hughes,* 321 U.S. 1, 64 S.Ct. 397 (1944).

In one of its first cases, *Virginia v. Rives,* 100 U.S. (10 Otto) 313 (1879), construing the Equal Protection Clause of the Fourteenth Amendment, the Court held that a mere showing that blacks were not included in a particular jury was not enough; there must be a showing of actual discrimination be-

cause of race. Down through the years, this has been the law of the land:

> The purpose of the Equal Protection Clause of the Fourteenth Amendment is to secure every person within the State's jurisdiction against intentional and arbitrary discrimination, whether occasioned by express terms of a statute or by its improper execution through duly constituted agents. *Sunday Lake Iron Co. v. Township of Wakefield,* 247 U.S. 350, 38 S.Ct. 495 (1918). No different purpose was attributed to the amendment by the Court either in *Brown* or any case since decided. Charles J. Bloch, "Does the Fourteenth Amendment Forbid De Facto Segregation?" 16 *Western Reserve L.Rev.* 542 (1965). Permission to quote granted by Wm. S. Hein and Company, Inc., Buffalo, New York.

2. The Equal Protection Clause protects minorities from the "tyranny of the majority." Laws passed with racial motivation by the majority are invalid. In 1978, the school board of the Seattle School District No. 1 enacted a desegregation plan that made use of extensive mandatory busing. Subsequently, in November 1978, a statewide initiative (Initiative 350) was passed that prohibited school boards from requiring, with certain exceptions, any student to attend a school other than the one geographically nearest to his or her home. The U.S. Supreme Court held that Initiative 350 violated Equal Protection because it directly and invidiously curtailed "the operation of political processes ordinarily to be relied upon to protect minorities." The Court concluded that such an initiative was no more permissible than a referendum by all the people to deny members of a racial minority the right to vote. *Washington et al. v. Seattle School District No. 1, et al.,* 458 U.S. 457, 102 S.Ct. 3187 (1982).

3. The Court of Appeals for the Fifth Circuit said in *United States v. Jefferson County Board of Education,* 372 F.2d 836 (5th Cir. 1966), that

> [t]he Constitution is both color blind and color conscious. To avoid a conflict with the

equal protection clause, a classification that denies a benefit, causes harm, or imposes a burden must not be based on race. But the Constitution is color conscious to prevent discrimination being perpetuated and to undo the effects of past discrimination. The criterion is the relevancy of color to a legitimate governmental purpose.

QUOTAS AND BUSING

If the vestiges of past state-sanctioned segregation remain, then the courts may do whatever is reasonably necessary to desegregate the schools. What constitutes legitimate remedies to overcome past segregation to bring into effect a unitary school system has been the subject of controversy since the days of "freedom of choice." Beyond freedom of choice, though, the state is required to assert a positive policy of placement of either students or facilities to bring about integration.

The problem really has two aspects: the measurement of inequality and the physical process used by the courts to effectuate integration. In determining the degree of inequality, the lower courts have tended to rely on quotas as a primary yardstick. In this regard, the Supreme Court has held that racial percentages of each school do not have to reflect the racial composition of the school system as a whole.[40] A fixed mathematical racial balance is not required and according to the Court should not be the sole criterion to determine appropriate movement toward a unitary state. The Supreme Court is consistent in this position in higher education as well as in elementary and secondary. In the celebrated *Bakke* decision,[41] the Supreme Court rejected the University of California's quota system for admission to medical school that specified a percentage of the student body be set aside for selected classifications of persons. The Court said that

> it is evident that the Davis special admission program involves the use of an explicit racial

classification never before countenanced by this court. It tells applicants who are not Negro, Asian, or "Chicano" that they are totally excluded from a specific percentage of the seats in an entering class. . . . The fatal flaw in petitioner's preferential program is its disregard of individual rights as guaranteed by the Fourteenth Amendment.[42]

In both higher education and the public schools, the Court has allowed the use of quotas or percentage as one criterion or as a starting point, but has never required nor permitted it to be used as the sole determinant.

Several alternatives have been approved by the Supreme Court in overcoming *de jure* racial imbalances, and transportation is one such acceptable remedy. Significantly, in *Swann v. Charlotte-Mecklenburg*, the court observed, "Desegregation plans cannot be limited to walk-in schools."

Busing to Overcome Racial Segregation Is a Judicially Acceptable Alternative Where De Jure Segregation Has Existed

---

Swann v. Charlotte-Mecklenburg Board of Education

Supreme Court of the United States, 1971.
402 U.S. 1, 91 S.Ct. 1267.

Mr. Chief Justice BURGER delivered the opinion of the Court. . . . This case and those argued with it arose in States having a long history of maintaining two sets of schools in a single school system deliberately operated to carry out a governmental policy to separate pupils in schools solely on the basis of race. That was what *Brown v. Board of Education* was all about. . . .

The Charlotte-Mecklenburg school system, the forty-third largest in the Nation, encompasses the city of Charlotte and surrounding Mecklenburg County, North Carolina. The area is large—550 square miles—spanning roughly twenty-two miles east-west and thirty-six miles north-south. During the 1968–1969 school year the system served more than 84,000 pupils in 107 schools. Approximately 71 percent of the pupils were found to be white and 29 percent Negro. As of June 1969 there were approximately 24,000 Negro students in the system, of whom 21,000 attended schools within the city of Charlotte. Two-thirds of those 21,000—approximately 14,000 Negro students—attended twenty-one schools which were either totally Negro or more than 99 percent Negro. . . .

In April 1969 the District Court ordered the school board to come forward with a plan for both faculty and student desegregation. Proposed plans were accepted by the court in June and August 1969 on an interim basis only, and the board was ordered to file a third plan by November 1969. In November the board moved for an extension of time until February 1970, but when that was denied the board submitted a partially completed plan. In December 1969 the District Court held that the board's submission was unacceptable and appointed an expert in education administration, Dr. John Finger, to prepare a desegregation plan. Thereafter, in February 1970, the District Court was presented with two alternative pupil assignment plans—the finalized "board plan" and the "Finger plan."

As finally submitted, the school board plan closed seven schools and reassigned their pupils. It restructured school attendance zones to achieve greater racial balance but maintained existing grade structures and rejected techniques such as pairing and clustering as part of a desegregation effort. The plan created a single athletic league, eliminated the previously racial basis of the school bus system, provided racially mixed faculties and administrative staffs, and modified its free-transfer plan into an optional majority-to-minority transfer system.

The board plan proposed substantial assignment of Negroes to nine of the system's ten high schools, producing 17 percent to 36 percent Negro population in each. The projected Negro attendance at the tenth school, Independence, was 2 percent. The proposed attendance zones for the high schools were typically shaped like wedges of a pie, extending outward from the center of the city to the suburban and rural areas of the county in order to afford residents of the center city area access to outlying schools.

As for junior high schools, the board plan rezoned the twenty-one school areas so that in twenty the Negro attendance would range from 0 percent to 38 percent. The other school, located in the heart of the Negro residential area, was left with an enrollment of 90 percent Negro.

The board plan with respect to elementary schools relied entirely upon gerrymandering of geographic zones. More than half of the Negro elementary pupils were left in nine schools that were 86 percent to 100 percent Negro; approximately half of the white elementary pupils were assigned to schools 86 percent to 100 percent white.

The plan submitted by the court-appointed expert, Dr. Finger, adopted the school board zoning plan for senior high schools with one modification: it required that an additional 300 Negro students be transported from the Negro residential area of the city to the nearly all-white Independence High School.

The Finger plan for the junior high schools employed much of the rezoning plan of the board, combined with the creation of nine "satellite" zones. Under the satellite plan, inner-city Negro students were assigned by attendance zones to nine outlying predominately white junior high schools, thereby substantially desegregating every junior high school in the system.

The Finger plan departed from the board plan chiefly in its handling of the system's seventy-six elementary schools. Rather than relying solely upon geographic zoning, Dr. Finger proposed use of zoning, pairing, and grouping techniques, with the result that student bodies throughout the system would range from 9 percent to 38 percent Negro. . . .

On February 5, 1970, the District Court adopted the board plan, as modified by Dr. Finger, for the junior and senior high schools. The court rejected the board elementary school plan and adopted the Finger plan as presented. Implementation was partially stayed by the Court of Appeals for the Fourth Circuit on March 5, and this Court declined to disturb the Fourth Circuit's order, 397 U.S. 978, 90 S.Ct. 1099, 25 L.Ed.2d 389 (1970).

On appeal the Court of Appeals affirmed the District Court's order as to faculty desegregation and the secondary school plans, but vacated the order respecting elementary schools. . . .

Nearly seventeen years ago this Court held, in explicit terms, that state-imposed segregation by race in public schools denies equal protection of the laws. At no time has the Court deviated in the slightest degree from that holding or its constitutional underpinnings. None of the parties before us challenges the Court's decision of May 17, 1954, that

> in the field of public education the doctrine of "separate but equal" has no place. Separate educational facilities are inherently unequal. Therefore, we hold that the plaintiffs and others similarly situated . . . are, by reason of the segregation complained of, deprived of the equal protection of the laws guaranteed by the Fourteenth Amendment. . . .

. . . The central issue in this case is that of student assignment, and there are essentially four problem areas:

1. to what extent racial balance or racial quotas may be used as an implement in a remedial order to correct a previously segregated system;
2. whether every all-Negro and all-white school must be eliminated as an indispensable part of a remedial process of desegregation;
3. what the limits are, if any, on the rearrangement of school districts and attendance zones, as a remedial measure; and
4. what the limits are, if any, on the use of transportation facilities to correct state-enforced racial school segregation.

Racial Balances or Racial Quotas

The constant theme and thrust of every holding from *Brown I* to date is that state-enforced separation of races in public schools is discrimination that violates the Equal Protection Clause. The remedy commanded was to dismantle dual school systems. . . .

Our objective in dealing with the issues presented by these cases is to see that school authorities exclude no pupil of a racial minority from any school, directly or indirectly, on account of race; it does not and cannot embrace all the problems of racial prejudice, even when those problems contribute to disproportionate racial concentrations in some schools.

In this case it is urged that the District Court has imposed a racial balance requirement of 71 percent–29 percent on individual schools. The fact that no such objective was actually achieved—and would appear to be impossible—tends to blunt that claim, yet in the opinion and order of the District Court of December 1, 1969, we find that court directing

> that efforts should be made to reach a 71–29 ratio in the various schools so that there will be no basis for contending that one school is racially different from the others . . . [t]hat no school [should] be operated with an all-black or predominantly black student body, [and] [t]hat pupils of all grades [should] be assigned in such a way that as nearly as practicable the various schools at various grade levels have about the same proportion of black and white students.

The District Judge went on to acknowledge that variation "from that norm may be unavoidable." This contains intimations that the "norm" is a fixed mathematical racial balance reflecting the pupil constituency of the system. If we were to read the holding of the District Court to require, as a matter of substantive constitutional right, any particular degree of racial balance or mixing, that approach would be disapproved and we would be obliged to reverse. The constitutional command to desegregate schools does not mean that every school in every community must always reflect the racial composition of the school system as a whole.

As the voluminous record in this case shows, the predicate for the District Court's use of the 71 percent–29 percent ratio was twofold: first, its express finding, approved by the Court of Appeals and not challenged here, that a dual school system had been maintained by the school authorities at least until 1969; second, its finding, also approved by the Court of Appeals, that the school board had totally defaulted in its acknowledged duty to come forward with an acceptable plan of its own, notwithstanding the patient efforts of the District Judge who, on at least three occasions, urged the board to submit plans. . . .

We see therefore that the use made of mathematical ratios was no more than a starting point in the process of shaping a remedy, rather than an inflexible requirement. From that starting point the District Court proceeded to frame a decree that was within its discretionary powers, as an equitable remedy for the particular circumstances. As we said in *Green,* a school authority's remedial plan or a district court's remedial decree is to be judged by its effectiveness. Awareness of the racial composition of the whole school system is likely to be a useful starting point in shaping a remedy to correct past constitutional violations. In sum, the very limited use made of mathematical ratios was within the equitable remedial discretion of the District Court.

One-race Schools

The record in this case reveals the familiar phenomenon that in metropolitan areas minority groups are often found concentrated in one part of the city. In some circumstances certain schools may remain all or largely of

one race until new schools can be provided or neighborhood patterns change. Schools all or predominantly of one race in a district of mixed population will require close scrutiny to determine that school assignments are not part of state-enforced segregation.

In light of the above, it should be clear that the existence of some small number of one-race, or virtually one-race, schools within a district is not in and of itself the mark of a system that still practices segregation by law. The district judge or school authorities should make every effort to achieve the greatest possible degree of actual desegregation and will thus necessarily be concerned with the elimination of one-race schools. . . . Where the school authority's proposed plan for conversion from a dual to a unitary system contemplates the continued existence of some schools that are all or predominately of one race, they have the burden of showing that such school assignments are genuinely nondiscriminatory. The court should scrutinize such schools, and the burden upon the school authorities will be to satisfy the court that their racial composition is not the result of present or past discriminatory action on their part.

An optional majority-to-minority transfer provision has long been recognized as a useful part of every desegregation plan. Provision for optional transfer of those in the majority racial group of a particular school to other schools where they will be in the minority is an indispensable remedy for those students willing to transfer to other schools in order to lessen the impact on them of the state-imposed stigma of segregation. In order to be effective, such a transfer arrangement must grant the transferring student free transportation and space must be made available in the school to which he desires to move. . . .
The court orders in this and the companion *Davis* case now provide such an option.

Remedial Altering of Attendance Zones

The maps submitted in these cases graphically demonstrate that one of the principal tools employed by school planners and by courts to break up the dual school system has been a frank — and sometimes drastic — gerrymandering of school districts and attendance zones. An additional step was pairing, "clustering," or "grouping" of schools with attendance assignments made deliberately to accomplish the transfer of Negro students out of formerly segregated Negro schools and transfer of white students to formerly all-Negro schools. More often than not, these zones are neither compact nor contiguous; indeed they may be on opposite ends of the city. As an interim corrective measure, this cannot be said to be beyond the broad remedial powers of a court.

Absent a constitutional violation there would be no basis for judicially ordering assignment of students on a racial basis. All things being equal, with no history of discrimination, it might well be desirable to assign pupils to schools nearest their homes. But all things are not equal in a system that has been deliberately constructed and maintained to enforce racial segregation. The remedy for such segregation may be administratively awkward, inconvenient, and even bizarre in some situations and may impose burdens on some; but all awkwardness and inconvenience cannot be avoided in the interim period when remedial adjustments are being made to eliminate the dual school systems.
. . .

We hold that the pairing and grouping of noncontiguous school zones is a permissible tool and such action is to be considered in light of the objectives sought. . . . Maps do not tell the whole story since noncontiguous school zones may be more accessible to each other in terms of the critical travel time, because of traffic patterns and good highways, than schools geographically closer together. Conditions in different localities will vary so widely that no rigid rules can be laid down to govern all situations.

Transportation of Students

The scope of permissible transportation of students as an implement of a remedial decree has never been defined by this Court and by the very nature of the problem it cannot be

defined with precision. No rigid guidelines as to student transportation can be given for application to the infinite variety of problems presented in thousands of situations. Bus transportation has been an integral part of the public education system for years, and was perhaps the single most important factor in the transition from the one-room schoolhouse to the consolidated school. . . .

The importance of bus transportation as a normal and accepted tool of educational policy is readily discernible in this and the companion case *Davis.* The Charlotte school authorities did not purport to assign students on the basis of geographically drawn zones until 1965 and then they allowed almost unlimited transfer privileges. . . .

Thus the remedial techniques used in the District Court's order were within that court's power to provide equitable relief; implementation of the decree is well within the capacity of the school authority.

The decree provided that the buses used to implement the plan would operate on direct routes. Students would be picked up at schools near their homes and transported to the schools they were to attend. The trips for elementary school pupils average about seven miles and the District Court found that they would take "not over thirty-five minutes at the most." This system compares favorably with the transportation plan previously operated in Charlotte under which each day 23,600 students on all grade levels were transported an average of fifteen miles one way for an average trip requiring over an hour. In these circumstances, we find no basis for holding that the local school authorities may not be required to employ bus transportation as one tool of school desegregation. Desegregation plans cannot be limited to the walk-in school.

An objection to transportation of students may have validity when the time or distance of travel is so great as to either risk the health of the children or significantly impinge on the educational process. . . . It hardly needs stating that the limits on time of travel will vary with many factors, but probably with none more than the age of the students. The reconciliation of competing values in a desegregation case is, of course, a difficult task with many sensitive facets but fundamentally no more so than remedial measures courts of equity have traditionally employed.

The Court of Appeals, searching for a term to define the equitable remedial power of the district courts, used the term "reasonableness." In *Green*, this Court used the term "feasible" and by implication, "workable," "effective," and "realistic" in the mandate to develop "a plan that promises realistically to work, and . . . to work *now*." On the facts of this case, we are unable to conclude that the order of the District Court is not reasonable, feasible, and workable. However, in seeking to define the scope of remedial power or the limits on remedial power of courts in an area as sensitive as we deal with here, words are poor instruments to convey the sense of basic fairness inherent in equity. Substance, not semantics, must govern, and we have sought to suggest the nature of limitations without frustrating the appropriate scope of equity.

At some point, these school authorities and others like them should have achieved full compliance with this Court's decision in *Brown I*. The systems would then be "unitary" in the sense required by our decisions in *Green* and *Alexander*.

It does not follow that the communities served by such systems will remain demographically stable, for in a growing, mobile society, few will do so. Neither school authorities nor district courts are constitutionally required to make year-by-year adjustments of the racial composition of student bodies once the affirmative duty to desegregate has been accomplished and racial discrimination through official action is eliminated from the system. This does not mean that federal courts are without power to deal with future problems; but in the absence of a showing that either the school authorities or some other agency of the State has deliberately attempted to fix or alter demographic patterns to affect the racial composition of the schools, further intervention by a district court should not be necessary.

For the reasons herein set forth, the judgment of the Court of Appeals is affirmed as to those parts in which it affirmed the judgment of the District Court. The order of the District Court, dated August 7, 1970, is also affirmed.

It is so ordered.

UNITARINESS

As indicated earlier, the central purpose of the Equal Protection Clause is to prevent governmental discrimination against a minority.[43] Plaintiffs seeking redress bear an initial burden of showing that the school board has intentionally created and maintained a racially segregated "dual" school system.[44] If the court finds that plaintiff's proof is sufficient, then the school board has an affirmative duty to change the "dual" system to a "unitary" one.[45]

The term "unitary" has been defined as the status a school system achieves "when it no longer discriminates between school children on the basis of race" or the status of a school system when it affirmatively removes all vestiges of race discrimination of the formerly dual system.[46] Alexander v. Board of Education defined a unitary system as one "within which no person is to be effectively excluded from any school because of race or color."[47]

Though the definition is clear, the operational application of unitary is more difficult. Appellate courts have provided few guidelines as to when and at what point unitary status is achieved. In *Flax v. Potts*[48] the court maintained that schools in a unitary school district are not identifiable by race and students and faculty are assigned in a manner that eliminates the vestiges of past segregation.[49]

The federal courts, however, are at odds as to whether unitary status can be reached incrementally or whether it is necessary to remedy the totality of segregative deficiencies before unitary status can be declared. The U.S. Court of Appeals for the Fifth Circuit[50] has agreed with the First Circuit[51] "that a school system can achieve unitary status incrementally and that, when it does so, the court will abdicate its supervisory role as to the particular aspect of the desegregation plan when proclaimed unitary."[52] This rationale was applied in *Ross v. Houston Independent School District*[53] where the Fifth Circuit ruled that the Houston school district was in fact unitary even though it still did not have a homogeneous student population. Giving weight to this view was the Tenth Circuit's decision in *Keyes* in 1990, which held that a school district can be declared "unitary in certain aspects, even though other aspects remain nonunitary."[54] Thus, a school district may be adjudged unitary and the district court can relinquish control if only a portion of the enumerated factors are achieved at any one time.

On the other hand, the "totality of deficiencies" standard maintains that the school system must fulfill all factors of unitariness at the same time. The factors that serve as the measurements of unitariness were set forth by the U.S. Supreme Court in *Green*[55]: (1) student assignment, (2) faculty, (3) staff, (4) transportation, (5) extracurricular activities, and (6) facilities. In *Pitts*, the Eleventh Circuit noted that a possible seventh category of "quality of education" was implicit in the six explicit standards and should be considered in conjunction with each and was not intended as a separate requirement.[56]

In *Pitts*,[57] the Eleventh Circuit, following the totality of deficiencies test, said:

> If the school system fulfills all six factors *at the same time* for several years, the court should declare that the school system has achieved unitary status. If the school system fails to fulfill all six factors at the same time for several years, the district court should retain jurisdiction.[58]

Finally, the *Pitts* court, in a specific rejection of the incremental standard, said: "A school system achieves unitary status or it does not."[59]

The U.S. Supreme Court has not resolved this dilemma, but has in a 1991 decision[60] quoted the *Green* test, saying that the district courts, in determining whether desegregation has been achieved, should "look not only at student assignments, but 'to every facet of school operations faculty, staff, transportation, extracurricular activities and facilities.'"[61] It does not, however, indicate how these indicia are to be applied. The Supreme Court, though, does reveal that the test should not "condemn a school district . . . to judicial tutelage for the indefinite future."[62]

Where Desegregation Plan Had Established a Racially Neutral System, District Court Exceeded Its Authority in Requiring Annual Readjustment of Attendance Zones

—·—·—·—·—·—

Pasadena City Board of Education v. Spangler

—·—·—·—·—·—

Supreme Court of the United States, 1976.
427 U.S. 424, 96 S.Ct. 2697.

Mr. Justice REHNQUIST delivered the opinion of the Court. In 1968, several students in the public schools of Pasadena, Cal., joined by their parents, instituted an action in the United States District Court for the Central District of California seeking injunctive relief from allegedly unconstitutional segregation of the high schools of the Pasadena City Board of Education, which operates the Pasadena Unified School District (PUSD).   . . .

On January 23, 1970, the court entered a judgment in which it concluded that the defendants' educational policies and procedures were violative of the Fourteenth Amendment. The court ordered the defendants "enjoined from failing to prepare and adopt a plan to correct racial imbalance at all levels in the Pasadena Unified School District." The defendants were further ordered to submit to the District Court a plan for desegregating the Pasadena schools.   . . .

The defendant school officials voted to comply with the District Court's decree and not to appeal. They thereupon set out to devise and submit the plan demanded by the District Court. In February the defendants submitted their proposed plan, the "Pasadena Plan," and on March 10, 1970, the District Court approved the plan, finding it "to be in conformance with the Judgment entered herein January 23, 1970." App. 96. The "Pasadena Plan" was implemented the following September, and the Pasadena schools have been under its terms ever since.

In January 1974, petitioners, successors to the original defendants in this action, filed a motion with the District Court seeking relief from the court's 1970 order. Petitioners sought four changes: to have the judgment modified so as to eliminate the requirement that there be "no school in the District, elementary or junior high or senior high school, with a majority of any minority students"; to have the District Court's injunction dissolved; to have the District Court terminate its "retained jurisdiction" over the actions of the Board; or, as an alternative, to obtain approval of petitioners' proposed modifications of the "Pasadena Plan."

The District Court held hearings on these motions and, on March 1, 1974, denied them in their entirety.   . . .

Petitioners requested the District Court to dissolve its injunctive order requiring that there be no school in the PUSD with a majority of any minority students enrolled. The District Court refused this request, and ordered the injunction continued. The court apparently based this decision in large part upon its view that petitioners had failed properly to comply with its original order. This conclusion was in turn premised upon the fact that although the School Board had reorganized PUSD attendance patterns in conformity with the court-approved Pasadena Plan, literal compliance with the terms of the court's order had been obtained in only the initial year of the plan's operation. Following the 1970–1971 school year, black student enrollment at one Pasadena school exceeded 50% of that school's total enrollment. The next year, four Pasadena schools exceeded this 50% black enrollment

figure; and at the time of the hearing on petitioners' motion some five schools, in a system of 32 regular schools, were ostensibly in violation of the District Court's "no majority of any minority" requirement. It was apparently the view of the majority of the Court of Appeals' panel that this failure to maintain literal compliance with the 1970 injunction indicated that the District Court had not abused its discretion in refusing to grant so much of petitioner's motion for modification as pertained to this aspect of the order. We think this view was wrong.   . . .

When the District Court's order in this case, as interpreted and applied by that court, is measured against what this Court said in its intervening decision in *Swann v. Charlotte-Mecklenburg Board of Education*, 402 U.S. 1, 91 S.Ct. 1267, 28 L.Ed.2d 554 (1971), regarding the scope of the judicially created relief which might be available to remedy violations of the Fourteenth Amendment, we think the inconsistency between the two is clear. The District Court's interpretation of the order appears to contemplate the "substantive constitutional right [to a] particular degree of racial balance or mixing" which the Court in *Swann* expressly disapproved.   . . . It became apparent, at least by the time of the 1974 hearing, that the District Court viewed this portion of its order not merely as a "starting point in the process of shaping a remedy," which *Swann* indicated would be appropriate . . . but instead as an "inflexible requirement," to be applied anew each year to the school population within the attendance zone of each school.

The District Court apparently believed it had authority to impose this requirement even though subsequent changes in the racial mix in the Pasadena schools might be caused by factors for which the defendants could not be considered responsible. Whatever may have been the basis for such a belief in 1970, in *Swann* the Court cautioned that "it must be recognized that there are limits" beyond which a court may not go in seeking to dismantle a dual school system.   . . . These limits are in part tied to the necessity of establishing that school authorities have in some manner caused unconstitutional segregation, for "[a]bsent a constitutional violation there would be no basis for judicially ordering assignment of students on a racial basis." While the District Court found such a violation in 1970, and while this unappealed finding afforded a basis for its initial requirement that the defendants prepare a plan to remedy such racial segregation, its adoption of the Pasadena Plan in 1970 established a racially neutral system of student assignment in the PUSD. Having done that, we think that in enforcing its order so as to require annual readjustment of attendance zones so that there would not be a majority of any minority in any Pasadena public school, the District Court exceeded its authority.

In so concluding, we think it important to note what this case does not involve. The "no majority of any minority" requirement with respect to attendance zones did not call for defendants to submit "step at a time" plans by definition incomplete at inception. . . . Nor did it call for a plan embodying specific revisions of the attendance zones for particular schools, as well as provisions for later appraisal of whether such discrete individual modifications had achieved the "unitary system" required by *Brown v. Board of Education,* 349 U.S. 294, 300, 75 S.Ct. 753, 756, 99 L.Ed. 1083 (1955). The plan approved in this case applied in general terms to all Pasadena schools, and no one contests that its implementation did "achieve a system of determining admission to the public schools on a nonracial basis," *id.,* at 300–301, 75 S.Ct., at 756.

There was also no showing in this case that those post-1971 changes in the racial mix of some Pasadena schools which were focused upon by the lower courts were in any manner caused by segregative actions chargeable to the defendants. The District Court rejected petitioners' assertion that the movement was caused by so-called "white flight" traceable to the decree itself. It stated that the "trends evidenced in Pasadena closely approximate the state-wide trends in California schools, both segregated and desegregated." 375 F.Supp., at 1306. The fact that black student enrollment at 5 out of 32 of the regular Pasadena schools came to exceed 50% during

the 4-year period from 1970 to 1974 apparently resulted from people randomly moving into, out of, and around the PUSD area. This quite normal pattern of human migration resulted in some changes in the demographics of Pasadena's residential patterns, with resultant shifts in the racial makeup of some of the schools. But as these shifts were not attributed to any segregative actions on the part of the petitioners, we think this case comes squarely within the sort of situation foreseen in *Swann:*

"It does not follow that the communities served by [unitary] systems will remain demographically stable, for in a growing, mobile society, few will do so. Neither school authorities nor district courts are constitutionally required to make year-by-year adjustments of the racial composition of student bodies once the affirmative duty to desegregate has been accomplished and racial discrimination through official action is eliminated from the system." 402 U.S., at 31–32, 91 S.Ct at 1283 1284.

. . . In this case the District Court approved a plan designed to obtain racial neutrality in the attendance of students at Pasadena's public schools. No one disputes that the initial implementation of this plan accomplished *that* objective. That being the case, the District Court was not entitled to require the PUSD to rearrange its attendance zones each year so as to ensure that the racial mix desired by the court was maintained in perpetuity. For having once implemented a racially neutral attendance pattern in order to remedy the perceived constitutional violations on the part of the defendants, the District Court had fully performed its function of providing the appropriate remedy for previous racially discriminatory attendance patterns. . . .

Because the case is to be returned to the Court of Appeals, that court will have an opportunity to reconsider its decision in light of our observations regarding the appropriate scope of equitable relief in this case. . . . The record in this case reflects the situation in Pasadena as it was in 1974. . . . And while any determination of compliance or noncompliance must, of course, comport with our holding today, it must also depend on factual determinations which the Court of Appeals and the District Court are in a far better position than we are to make in the first instance. Accordingly the judgment of the Court of Appeals is vacated, and the case is remanded to that court for further proceedings not inconsistent with this opinion.

So ordered.

NOTES

1. *Remedial Measures.* In determining what remedial measures should be undertaken after a finding of *de jure* segregation, the court should look for guidance to three factors. "First, the court must consider the nature and scope of the constitutional violation; second, the remedial objective sought is to be the restoration of the victims to the position they would have occupied absent the constitutional violation; and, third, consideration must be given to the interests of allowing state and local authorities to manage their own affairs." *Milliken v. Bradley (Milliken II)*, 433 U.S. 267, 97 S.Ct. 2749 (1977).

2. *Affirmative Action.* A school board cannot satisfy its duty to eliminate past segregation by merely abandoning its prior discriminatory purpose. Neither can it take any action that would subvert the process of conversion to a unitary system. Once a violation is found, "[t]he Board has . . . an affirmative responsibility to see that pupil [and faculty] assignment policies and school construction and abandonment practices 'are not used and do not serve to perpetuate or re-establish the dual school system.'" *Dayton Bd. of Educ. v. Brinkman*, 443 U.S. 526, 538, 99 S.Ct. 2971, 2979, 61 L.Ed.2d 720 (1979) *(Dayton II)* (quoting *Columbus Bd. of Educ. v. Penick*, 443 U.S. 449, 460, 99 S.Ct. 2941, 2948, 61 L.Ed.2d 666 (1979).

3. *White Flight.* School officials cannot use "white flight" as an excuse justifying failure to dismantle a dual school system, or as a pretext to resist or evade a present duty to desegregate. *United States v. Scotland Neck Board of Education*, 407 U.S. 484, 92 S.Ct. 2214

(1972). On the other hand, once a school system has been declared unitary, white flight cannot be used by plaintiffs to establish discriminatory intent on the part of the school board. *Riddick by Riddick v. School Board of City of Norfolk*, 784 F.2d 521 (4th Cir. 1986); *Pasadena City Board of Education v. Spangler*, 427 U.S. 424, 96 S.Ct. 2697 (1976).

4. *Desegregation.* Once a school district has been declared unitary and resegregation occurs, plaintiffs bear the burden of proving that discriminatory intent of the school board caused resegregation. In *Riddick*, the U.S. Court of Appeals, Fourth Circuit, held that resegregation due to population mobility and white flight did not require the school board to adopt a policy of mandatory busing to avoid the presumption of discriminatory intent. *Riddick by Riddick v. School Board of City of Norfolk*, 784 F.2d 521 (4th Cir. 1986).

5. *Effects of Unitary Status.* Once a formerly *de jure* segregated school system is declared unitary, school boards are free to act without federal court supervision so long as they do not purposefully and intentionally discriminate. *U.S. v. Overton*, 834 F.2d 1171 (5th Cir. 1987).

6. *Recision of Plan.* "Recision of a voluntary desegregation plan itself may be found to be an act of segregation for a school board which has been found to have practiced de jure segregation and has not completed the transition from a dual to a unitary school system." *NAACP v. Lansing Bd. of Ed.*, 559 F.2d 1042 (6th Cir.), cert. den. 434 U.S. 997, 98 S.Ct. 635, 54 L.Ed.2d 491 (1977). See *Riddick by Riddick v. School Bd. of City of Norfolk*, 784 F.2d 521 (4th Cir. 1986).

7. *Modification of Plan.* "In a school system that has not become unitary the school board is not barred from ever changing a desegregation plan. In such a situation, however, the board must show that the proposed changes are consistent with its continuing affirmative duty to eliminate discrimination." *Clark v. Board of Educ. of Little Rock School Dist.*, 706 F.2d 265 (8th Cir. 1983). See *Riddick*, op. cit.

Federal Court's Regulatory Control Over Previously de Jure Segregated School District Is Limited to the Time Necessary to Remedy the Effects of Past Intentional Discrimination

—··—··—··—··—

Board of Education of Oklahoma City Public Schools, Ind. School Dist. No. 89 v. Dowell

—··—··—··—··—

Supreme Court of the United States, 1991.
_____U.S. _____, 111 S.Ct. 630.

CHIEF JUSTICE REHNQUIST delivered the opinion of the Court. . . .

This school desegregation litigation began almost 30 years ago. In 1961, respondents, black students and their parents, sued petitioners, the Board of Education of Oklahoma City (Board), to end de jure segregation in the public schools. In 1963, the District Court found that Oklahoma City had intentionally segregated both schools and housing in the past, and that Oklahoma City was operating a "dual" school system—one that was intentionally segregated by race. . . . In 1965, the District Court found that the School Board's attempt to desegregate by using neighborhood zoning failed to remedy past segregation because residential segregation resulted in one race schools. . . . Residential segregation had once been state imposed, and it lingered due to discrimination by some realtors and financial institutions. The District Court found that school segregation had caused some housing segregation. . . . In 1972, finding that previous efforts had not been successful at eliminating state imposed segregation, the District Court ordered the Board to adopt the "Finger Plan" . . . under which kindergarteners would be assigned to neighborhood schools unless their parents opted otherwise; children in grades 1–4 would attend formerly all white schools, and thus black children would be bused to those schools; children in grade five would

attend formerly all black schools, and thus white children would be bused to those schools; students in the upper grades would be bused to various areas in order to maintain integrated schools; and in integrated neighborhoods there would be standalone schools for all grades.

In 1977, after complying with the desegregation decree for five years, the Board made a "Motion to Close Case." The District Court held in its "Order Terminating Case":

> The Court has concluded that [the Finger Plan] worked and that substantial compliance with the constitutional requirements has been achieved. The School Board, under the oversight of the Court, has operated the Plan properly, and the Court does not foresee that the termination of its jurisdiction will result in the dismantlement of the Plan or any affirmative action by the defendant to undermine the unitary system so slowly and painfully accomplished over the 16 years during which the cause has been pending before this court.
> . . .
>
> . . . The School Board, as now constituted, has manifested the desire and intent to follow the law. The court believes that the present members and their successors on the Board will now and in the future continue to follow the constitutional desegregation requirements.
>
> Now sensitized to the constitutional implications of its conduct and with a new awareness of its responsibility to citizens of all races, the Board is entitled to pursue in good faith its legitimate policies without the continuing constitutional supervision of this Court. . . .
>
> . . . Jurisdiction in this case is terminated ipso facto subject only to final disposition of any case now pending on appeal." No. Civ-9452 (WD Okla., Jan. 18, 1977). . . .

This unpublished order was not appealed.

In 1984, the School Board faced demographic changes that led to greater burdens on young black children. As more and more neighborhoods became integrated, more standalone schools were established, and young black students had to be bused further from their inner-city homes to outlying white areas. In an effort to alleviate this burden and to increase parental involvement, the Board adopted the Student Reassignment Plan (SRP), which relied on neighborhood assignments for students in grades K–4 beginning in the 1985–1986 school year. Busing continued for students in grades 5–12. Any student could transfer from a school where he or she was in the majority to a school where he or she would be in the minority. Faculty and staff integration was retained, and an "equity officer" was appointed.

In 1985, respondents filed a "Motion to Reopen the Case," contending that the School District had not achieved "unitary" status and that the SRP was a return to segregation. Under the SRP, 11 of 64 elementary schools would be greater than 90% black, 22 would be greater than 90% white plus other minorities, and 31 would be racially mixed. The District Court refused to reopen the case, holding that its 1977 finding of unitariness was res judicata as to those who were then parties to the action, and that the district remained unitary. . . . The District Court found that the School Board, administration, faculty, support staff, and student body were integrated, and transportation, extracurricular activities and facilities within the district were equal and nondiscriminatory. Because unitariness had been achieved, the District Court concluded that court ordered desegregation must end.

The Court of Appeals for the Tenth Circuit reversed. . . . It held that, while the 1977 order finding the district unitary was binding on the parties, nothing in that order indicated that the 1972 injunction itself was terminated. The court reasoned that the finding that the system was unitary merely ended the District Court's active supervision of the case, and because the school district was still subject to the desegregation decree, respondents could challenge the SRP. The case was remanded to determine whether the decree should be lifted or modified.

On remand, the District Court found that demographic changes made the Finger Plan unworkable, that the Board had done nothing for 25 years to promote residential segregation, and that the school district had bused students for more than a decade in good faith compliance with the court's orders. . . .

The District Court found that present residential segregation was the result of private decisionmaking and economics, and that it was too attenuated to be a vestige of former school segregation. It also found that the district had maintained its unitary status, and that the neighborhood assignment plan was not designed with discriminatory intent. The court concluded that the previous injunctive decree should be vacated and the school district returned to local control. . . .

The Court of Appeals again reversed . . . holding that "an injunction takes on a life of its own and becomes an edict quite independent of the law it is meant to effectuate." . . . That court approached the case "not so much as one dealing with desegregation, but as one dealing with the proper application of the federal law on injunctive remedies." . . . Relying on *United States v. Swift & Co.*, 286 U.S. 106 (1932), it held that a desegregation decree remains in effect until a school district can show "grievous wrong evoked by new and unforseen conditions" . . . and "dramatic changes in conditions unforseen at the time of the decree that . . . impose extreme and unexpectedly oppressive hardships on the obligor." . . . The Court of Appeals held that, despite the unitary finding, the Board had the "affirmative duty . . . not to take any action that would impede the process of disestablishing the dual system and its effects." . . .

We granted the Board's petition for certiorari to resolve a conflict between the standard laid down by the Court of Appeals in this case and that laid down in *Spangler v. Pasadena City Board of Education*, 611 F. 2d 1239 (CA9 1979), and *Riddick v. School Bd. of City of Norfolk*, 784 F.2d 521 (CA4 1986). We now reverse the Court of Appeals. . . .

The lower courts have been inconsistent in their use of the term "unitary." Some have used it to identify a school district that has completely remedied all vestiges of past discrimination. . . . Under that interpretation of the word, a unitary school district is one that has met the mandate of *Brown v. Board of Education*, 349 U.S. 294 (1955), and *Green v. New Kent County School Board*, 391 U.S. 430 (1968). Other courts, however, have used "unitary" to describe any school district that has currently desegregated student assignments, whether or not that status is solely the result of a courtimposed desegregation plan. . . . In other words, such a school district could be called unitary and nevertheless still contain vestiges of past discrimination. That there is such confusion is evident in *Georgia State Conference of Branches of NAACP v. Georgia,* 775 F. 2d 1403 (CA11 1985), where the Court of Appeals drew a distinction between a "unitary school district" and a district that has achieved "unitary status." The court explained that a school district that has not operated segregated schools as proscribed by *Green v. New Kent County School Board,* and *Swann v. Charlotte-Mecklenburg Bd. of Education* . . . "for a period of several years" is unitary, but that a school district cannot be said to have achieved "unitary status" unless it "has eliminated the vestiges of its prior discrimination and has been adjudicated as such through the proper judicial procedures." . . .

We think it is a mistake to treat words such as "dual" and "unitary" as if they were actually found in the Constitution. The constitutional command of the Fourteenth Amendment is that "[n]o State shall . . . deny to any person . . . the equal protection of the laws." Courts have used the terms "dual" to denote a school system which has engaged in intentional segregation of students by race, and "unitary" to describe a school system which has been brought into compliance with the command of the Constitution. We are not sure how useful it is to define these terms more precisely, or to create subclasses within them. But there is no doubt that the differences in usage described above do exist. The District Court's 1977 order is unclear with respect to what it meant by unitary and the necessary result of that finding. We therefore decline to overturn the conclusion of the Court of Appeals that while the 1977 order of the District Court did bind the parties as to the unitary character of the district, it did not finally terminate the Oklahoma City school litigation. In *Pasadena City Bd. of Education v. Spangler,* 427 U.S. 424 (1976), we held that a school board is entitled to a

rather precise statement of its obligations under a desegregation decree. If such a decree is to be terminated or dissolved, respondents as well as the school board are entitled to a like statement from the court.

The Court of Appeals relied upon language from this Court's decision in *United States v. Swift and Co.,* supra, for the proposition that a desegregation decree could not be lifted or modified absent a showing of "grievous wrong evoked by new and unforeseen conditions." . . . It also held that "compliance alone cannot become the basis for modifying or dissolving an injunction," . . . relying on *United States v. W. T. Grant Co.,* 345 U.S. 629, 633 (1953). We hold that its reliance was mistaken.

In Swift, several large meat packing companies entered into a consent decree whereby they agreed to refrain forever from entering into the grocery business. The decree was by its terms effective in perpetuity. The defendant meat packers and their allies had over a period of a decade attempted, often with success in the lower courts, to frustrate operation of the decree. It was in this context that the language relied upon by the Court of Appeals in this case was used.

United States v. United Shoe Machinery Corp., 391 U.S. 244 (1968), explained that the language used in Swift must be read in the context of the continuing danger of unlawful restraints on trade which the Court had found still existed. . . . "Swift teaches . . . a decree may be changed upon an appropriate showing, and it holds that it may not be changed . . . if the purposes of the litigation as incorporated in the decree . . . have not been fully achieved." . . . In the present case, a finding by the District Court that the Oklahoma City School District was being operated in compliance with the commands of the Equal Protection Clause of the Fourteenth Amendment, and that it was unlikely that the school board would return to its former ways, would be a finding that the purposes of the desegregation litigation had been fully achieved. No additional showing of "grievous wrong evoked by new and unforeseen conditions" is required of the school board.

In *Milliken v. Bradley (Milliken II)*, 433 U.S. 267 (1977), we said: "[F]ederal court decrees must directly address and relate to the constitutional violation itself. Because of this inherent limitation upon federal judicial authority, federal court decrees exceed appropriate limits if they are aimed at eliminating a condition that does not violate the Constitution or does not flow from such a violation . . . ." . . .

From the very first, federal supervision of local school systems was intended as a temporary measure to remedy past discrimination. Brown considered the "complexities arising from the transition to a system of public education free of racial discrimination" in holding that the implementation of desegregation was to proceed "with all deliberate speed." . . . Green also spoke of the "transition to a unitary, nonracial system of public education." . . .

Considerations based on the allocation of powers within our federal system, we think, support our view that quoted language from Swift does not provide the proper standard to apply to injunctions entered in school desegregation cases. Such decrees, unlike the one in Swift, are not intended to operate in perpetuity. Local control over the education of children allows citizens to participate in decisionmaking, and allows innovation so that school programs can fit local needs. . . . The legal justification for displacement of local authority by an injunctive decree in a school desegregation case is a violation of the Constitution by the local authorities. Dissolving a desegregation decree after the local authorities have operated in compliance with it for a reasonable period of time properly recognizes that "necessary concern for the important values of local control of public school systems dictates that a federal court's regulatory control of such systems not extend beyond the time required to remedy the effects of past intentional discrimination." . . .

A district court need not accept at face value the profession of a school board which has intentionally discriminated that it will cease to do so in the future. But in deciding whether to modify or dissolve a desegregation decree, a school board's compliance with previous court orders is obviously relevant. In this case the original finding of de jure segregation was entered in 1961, the injunctive decree from which the Board seeks relief was entered in 1972, and the Board complied with the decree in good faith until 1985. Not only do the personnel of school boards change over time, but the same passage of time enables the District Court to observe the good faith of the school board in complying with the decree. The test espoused by the Court of Appeals would condemn a school district, once governed by a board which intentionally discriminated, to judicial tutelage for the indefinite future. Neither the principles governing the entry and dissolution of injunctive decrees, nor the commands of the Equal Protection Clause of the Fourteenth Amendment, require any such Draconian result.

Petitioners urge that we reinstate the decision of the District Court terminating the injunction, but we think that the preferable course is to remand the case to that court so that it may decide, in accordance with this opinion, whether the Board made a sufficient showing of constitutional compliance as of 1985, when the SRP was adopted, to allow the injunction to be dissolved. The District Court should address itself to whether the Board had complied in good faith with the desegregation decree since it was entered, and whether the vestiges of past discrimination had been eliminated to the extent practicable.

In considering whether the vestiges of de jure segregation had been eliminated as far as practicable, the District Court should look not only at student assignments, but "to every facet of school operations faculty, staff, transportation, extracurricular activities and facilities." *Green*, 391 U.S., at 435. See also *Swann*, 402 U.S., at 18 ("[E]xisting policy and practice with regard to faculty, staff, transportation, extracurricular activities, and facilities" are "among the most important indicia of a segregated system").

After the District Court decides whether the Board was entitled to have the decree terminated, it should proceed to decide respondent's challenge to the SRP. A school district which has been released from an injunction imposing a desegregation plan no longer requires court authorization for the promulgation of policies and rules regulating matters such as assignment of students and the like, but it of course remains subject to the mandate of the Equal Protection Clause of the Fourteenth Amendment. If the Board was entitled to have the decree terminated as of 1985, the District Court should then evaluate the Board's decision to implement the SRP under appropriate equal protection principles. . . .

The judgment of the Court of Appeals is reversed, and the case is remanded to the District Court for further proceedings consistent with this opinion.

It is so ordered.

NOTE

1. *Unitariness.* The U.S. Court of Appeals, Tenth Circuit, has elaborated on its own view of unitariness and how it is to be determined. *Brown v. Board of Education of Topeka (Brown III)*, 892 F.2d 851 (10th Cir. 1989).

GENERAL PRINCIPLES OF UNITARINESS

. . . .

BURDEN OF PROOF. "To determine whether a school district has become unitary, . . . a court must consider what the school district has done or not done to fulfill its affirmative duty to desegregate, the current effects of those actions or inactions, and the extent to which further desegregation is feasible. After a plaintiff establishes intentional segregation at some point in the past and a current condition of segregation, a defendant then bears the burden of proving that its past acts have eliminated all traces of the past intentional segregation to the maximum feasible extent." . . .

CURRENT CONDITION OF SEGREGATION. "The actual condition of the school district at the time of trial is perhaps the most crucial consideration in a unitariness determination. The plaintiff bears the burden of showing the existence of a current condition of segregation. . . . In our view, a plaintiff must prove the existence of racially identifiable schools, broadly defined, to satisfy the burden of showing a current condition of segregation. Racially identifiable schools may be identifiable by student assignment alone, in the case of highly one-race schools, or by a combination of factors where the school is not highly one-race in student assignment." . . .

"Although virtual one-race schools 're-quire close scrutiny,' they are not always unconstitutional. *Swann,* 402 U.S. at 26, 91 S.Ct. at 1281. Their existence in a system with a history of *de jure* segregation, however, establishes a presumption that they exist as the result of discrimination and shifts the burden of proof to the school system. *Id.* The presence of essentially one-race schools is thus sufficient to satisfy a plaintiff's initial burden of showing a current condition of segregation." . . .

"However, no particular degree of racial balance is required by the Constitution. A degree of imbalance is likely to be found in any heterogeneous school system. Therefore, the existence of some racial imbalance in schools will often not be conclusive in itself." . . .

THE PARTIES' BURDENS. "Once a plaintiff has proven the existence of a current condition of segregation, the school district bears the substantial burden of showing that that condition is not the result of its prior *de jure* segregation. Under the relevant Supreme Court decisions, mere absence of invidious intent on the part of the school district is not sufficient to satisfy its "heavy burden" of proof; the district's duty is to act affirmatively, not merely to act neutrally."

. . .

"The school district must show that no causal connection exists between past and present segregation, not merely that it did not intend to cause current segregation. The causal link between prior and current segregation is not snapped by the absence of discriminatory intent alone, or even by a firm commitment to desegregation, where it is not accompanied by action that in fact produces a unified school district."

. . . .

"What the school district has done to integrate is crucial in determining whether the causal link between the prior segregation and the current disparities has been severed. The district may carry its burden by showing that it has acted affirmatively to desegregate. Absent such proof, the court must presume that current segregation is the result of prior intentional state action. A showing that the school district has not promoted segregation and has allowed desegregation to take place where neutral forces worked to that end is insufficient."

. . . .

"The ultimate test of what the school district has done is its effectiveness, most significantly its effectiveness in eliminating the separation of white and minority children. While a district is not always required to choose the most desegregative alternative when it selects a particular option, the results of the sum of the choices made by the district must be to desegregate the system to the maximum possible extent." . . .

MAXIMUM PRACTICABLE DESEGREGATION. "What more can and should be done, if anything, is the final component in a determination of unitary status. Essentially, a defendant must demonstrate that it has done everything feasible. Courts must assess the school district's achievements with an eye to the possible and practical, but they must not let longstanding racism blur their ultimate focus on the ideal."

"Where the school district has complied with the desegregation plan to the best of its ability, and has done what can be done in spite of the obstacles in its way, it is reasonable to conclude that no further desegregation is feasible."

"In sum, when a school system was previously *de jure*, a plaintiff bears the burden of showing that there is a current condition of segregation. It may do so by proving the existence of racially identifiable schools. The school district must then show that such segregation has no causal connection with the prior *de jure* segregation, and that the district has in fact carried out the maximum desegregation practicable for that district."

_____

REMEDIAL AND COMPENSATORY REMEDIES

Initial remedies in the early days of desegregation usually centered on movement of black and white students, teachers, and staff in an effort to make the racial make-up of the schools more homogeneous. More recently, though, the courts are allowing additional options as a part of the desegregation plans to enrich the learning experiences of minority students.[63] Rather than (or in addition to) the busing of students, various courts have approved programs for early childhood intervention,[64] curriculum development,[65] reduction in pupil-teacher ratios,[66] counseling and career guidance,[67] remedial reading,[68] and staff development.[69] Milliken II[70] is perhaps the leading case extending relief for remediation of individual educational harms as a method of overcoming the vestiges of past discrimination. In *Milliken II*, the U.S. Supreme Court set out three principles that govern a lower court's options in providing such remedies. First, the remedy should be commensurate with the nature and scope of the constitutional violation.[71] Second, the court's decree should be remedial in nature, fashioned as nearly as possible "to restore the victims of discriminatory conduct to the position they would have occupied in the absence of such conduct."[72] Third, in formulating a decree, the courts "must take into account the interest of state and local authorities in managing their own affairs, consistent with the Constitution."[73]

In keeping with these guidelines, the Supreme Court recognized the need to justify the creation of new educational programs to halt the ongoing effects of discrimination and to facilitate the process of desegregation.[74] Moreover, *Milliken II* recognized that it may be necessary for a lower federal court to require remedies that will alleviate the individual learning effects and deficiencies caused by segregation. The Supreme Court justified programmatic remedies in observing that

[c]hildren who have been thus educationally and culturally set apart from the larger com-

munity will inevitably acquire habits of speech, conduct, and attitudes reflecting their cultural isolation. They are likely to acquire speech habits, for example, which vary from the environment in which they must ultimately function and compete, if they are to enter and be a part of that community. . . .

Pupil assignment alone does not automatically remedy the impact of previous, unlawful educational isolation; the consequences linger and can be dealt with only by independent measures.[75]

Such remedies may be extensive and very costly, as was the case in *Missouri v. Jenkins.* Here the U.S. Supreme Court upheld a lower court's mandate for increased revenues and the imposition of a tax increase by the school district in order to fund several remedial and compensatory programmatic initiatives, including an effective schools program, reduction in class size, summer school, full-day kindergarten, before- and after-school tutoring, early childhood education, magnet schools, and facilities improvements.[76] Even though the *Missouri* case caused anguished cries of "taxation without representation," the Supreme Court upheld the validity of both the educational programs and the funding scheme as a proper means to overcome the effects of state-created segregation.[77]

Special programs designed solely for remediation of educational deficiencies caused by past discrimination may be supplemented or replaced by other programs as well. Optional plans that make core city schools more attractive for whites may be employed as well. For example, the creation of magnet programs in predominantly black schools and voluntary "majority to minority" transfers have been allowed.[78] In such an instance, the U.S. Court of Appeals, Eleventh Circuit, upheld the abandonment of mandatory busing, racial pairing of schools, and mandatory reassignment in favor of magnet programs, voluntary transfers and revised attendance zones. In way of justification the court observed: "The measure of a desegregation plan is its ultimate effectiveness. The type of plan employed is of little consequence so long as it effectively achieves the constitutionally required result that public schools be conducted on a unitary basis."[79]

Federal Courts Can Require School Districts to Levy Taxes in Excess of State Statutory Limits in Order to Fund Desegregation Remedies

———————

Missouri v. Jenkins

———————

Supreme Court of the United States, 1990.
____U.S. ____, 110 S.Ct. 1651.

Justice WHITE delivered the opinion of the Court. The United States District Court for the Western District of Missouri imposed an increase in the property taxes levied by the Kansas City, Missouri, School District (KCMSD) to ensure funding for the desegregation of KCMSD's public schools. We granted certiorari to consider the State of Missouri's argument that the District Court lacked the power to raise local property taxes. For the reasons given below, we hold that the District Court abused its discretion in imposing the tax increase. We also hold, however, that the modifications of the District Court's order made by the Court of Appeals do satisfy equitable and constitutional principles governing the District Court's power. . . .

. . . After a lengthy trial, the District Court found that KCMSD and the State had operated a segregated school system within the KCMSD. . . .

The District Court thereafter issued an order detailing the remedies necessary to eliminate the vestiges of segregation and the financing necessary to implement those remedies. . . . The District Court originally estimated the total cost of the desegregation remedy to be almost $88,000,000 over three years, of which it expected the State to pay $67,592,072 and KCMSD to pay $20,140,472. The court concluded, however, that several provisions of Missouri law would prevent KCMSD from being able to pay its share of the obligation. The Missouri Constitution limits local property taxes to $1.25 per $100 of assessed valuation unless a majority of the voters in the district approve a higher levy, up to $3.25 per $100; the levy may be raised above $3.25 per $100 only if two-thirds of the voters agree. Mo. Const., Art. X, § 11(b), (c). The "Hancock Amendment" requires property tax rates to be rolled back when property is assessed at a higher valuation to ensure that taxes will not be increased solely as a result of reassessments. Mo. Const. Art. X, § 22(a); Mo.Rev.Stat. § 137.073.2 (1986). The Hancock Amendment thus prevents KCMSD from obtaining any revenue increase as a result of increases in the assessed valuation of real property. "Proposition C" allocates one cent of every dollar raised by the state sales tax to a school's trust fund and requires school districts to reduce property taxes by an amount equal to 50% of the previous year's sales tax receipts in the district. Mo.Rev.Stat. § 164.013.1 (Supp.1988). However, the trust fund is allocated according to a formula that does not compensate KCMSD for the amount lost in property tax revenues, and the effect of Proposition C is to divert nearly half of the sales taxes collected in KCMSD to other parts of the State.

The District Court believed that it had the power to order a tax increase to ensure adequate funding of the desegregation plan, but it hesitated to take this step. It chose instead to enjoin the effect of the Proposition C rollback to allow KCMSD to raise an additional $4,000,000 for the coming fiscal year. The court ordered KCMSD to submit to the voters a proposal for an increase in taxes sufficient to pay for its share of the desegregation remedy in following years. . . .

The Court of Appeals for the Eighth Circuit affirmed the District Court's findings of liability and remedial order in most respects. . . . The Court of Appeals agreed with the State, however, that the District Court had failed to explain adequately why it had imposed most of the cost of the desegregation plan on the State. *Id.* at 684, 685. The Eighth Circuit ordered the District Court to divide the cost equally between the State and KCMSD. *Id.,* at 685. We denied certiorari. *Kansas City, Missouri, School Dist. v. Missouri,* 484 U.S. 816, 108 S.Ct. 70, 98 L.Ed.2d 34 (1987).

Proceedings before the District Court continued during the appeal. In its original remedial order, the District Court had directed KCMSD to prepare a study addressing the usefulness of "magnet schools" to promote desegregation. . . . A year later, the District Court approved KCMSD's proposal to operate six magnet schools during the 1986–1987 school year. The court again faced the problem of funding, for KCMSD's efforts to persuade the voters to approve a tax increase had failed, as had its efforts to seek funds from the Kansas City Council and the state legislature. Again hesitating to impose a tax increase itself, the court continued its injunction against the Proposition C rollback to enable KCMSD to raise an additional $6,500,000. . . .

In November 1986, the District Court endorsed a marked expansion of the magnet school program. It adopted in substance a KCMSD proposal that every high school, every middle school, and half of the elementary schools in KCMSD become magnet schools by the 1991–1992 school year. It also approved the $142,736,025 budget proposed by KCMSD for implementation of the magnet school plan, as well as the expenditure of $52,858,301 for additional capital improvements. . . .

The District Court next considered, as the Court of Appeals had directed, how to shift the cost of desegregation to KCMSD. The District Court concluded that it would be "clearly inequitable" to require the population of KCMSD to pay half of the desegregation cost, and that "even with Court help it would be very difficult for the KCMSD to fund more than 25% of the costs of the entire remedial plan." The court reasoned that the State should pay for most of the desegregation cost under the principle that "'the person who starts the fire has more responsibility for the damages caused than the person who fails to put it out,'" and that apportionment of damages between the State and KCMSD according to fault was supported by the doctrine of comparative fault in tort, which had been adopted by the Missouri Supreme Court in *Gustafson v. Benda,* 661 S.W.2d 11 (1983). The District Court then held that the State and KCMSD were 75% and 25% at fault, respectively, and ordered them to share the cost of the desegregation remedy in that proportion.

To ensure complete funding of the remedy, the court also held the two tortfeasors jointly and severally liable for the cost of the plan. . . .

Three months later, the District Court adopted a plan requiring $187,450,334 in further capital improvements. 672 F.Supp. 400, 408 (WD Mo.1987). By then it was clear that KCMSD would lack the resources to pay for its 25% share of the desegregation cost. KCMSD requested that the District Court order the State to pay for any amount that KCMSD could not meet. The District Court declined to impose a greater share of the cost on the State, but it accepted that KCMSD had "exhausted all available means of raising additional revenue." Finding itself with "no choice but to exercise its broad equitable powers and enter a judgment that will enable the KCMSD to raise its share of the cost of the plan," and believing that the "United States Supreme Court has stated that a tax may be increased if 'necessary to raise funds adequate to . . . operate and maintain without racial discrimination a public school system,' " . . . the court ordered the KCMSD property tax levy raised from $2.05 to $4.00 per $100 of assessed valuation through the 1991–1992 fiscal year. . . . KCMSD was also directed to issue $150,000,000 in capital improvement bonds. A subsequent order directed that the revenues generated by the property tax increase be used to retire the capital improvement bonds. . . .

The State appealed, challenging the scope of the desegregation remedy, the allocation of the cost between the State and KCMSD, and the tax increase. A group of local taxpayers (Clark Group) and Jackson County, Missouri, also appealed from an order of the District Court denying their applications to intervene as of right. . . .

We turn to the tax increase imposed by the District Court. The State urges us to hold that the tax increase violated Article III, the Tenth Amendment, and principles of federal/state comity. We find it unnecessary to reach the difficult constitutional issues, for we agree with the State that the tax increase contravened the principles of comity that must govern the exercise of the District Court's equitable discretion in this area.

It is accepted by all the parties, as it was by the courts below, that the imposition of a tax increase by a federal court was an extraordinary event. In assuming for itself the fundamental and delicate power of taxation the District Court not only intruded on local authority but circumvented it altogether. . . .

The District Court believed that it had no alternative to imposing a tax increase. But there was an alternative, the very one outlined by the Court of Appeals: it could have authorized or required KCMSD to levy property taxes at a rate adequate to fund the desegregation remedy and could have enjoined the operation of state laws that would have prevented KCMSD from exercising this power. . . . The difference between the two approaches is far more than a matter of form. Authorizing and directing local government institutions to devise and implement remedies not only protects the function of those institutions but, to the extent possible, also places the responsibility for solutions to the problems of segregation upon those who have themselves created the problems. . . .

The District Court therefore abused its discretion in imposing the tax itself. The Court of Appeals should not have allowed the tax increase to stand and should have reversed the District Court in this respect. . . .

We stand on different ground when we review the modifications to the District Court's order made by the Court of Appeals. As explained, . . . the Court of Appeals held that the District Court in the future should authorize KCMSD to submit a levy to the state tax collection authorities adequate to fund its budget and should enjoin the operation of state laws that would limit or reduce the levy below that amount. . . .

It is true that in *Milliken v. Bradley*, 433 U.S., at 291, 97 S.Ct., at 2763, we stated that the enforcement of a money judgment against the State did not violate principles of federalism because "[t]he District Court . . . neither attempted to restructure local governmental entities nor . . . mandat[ed] a particular method or structure of state or local financing." But we did not there state that a District Court could never set aside state laws preventing local governments from raising funds sufficient to satisfy their constitutional obligations just because those funds could also be obtained from the States. To the contrary, 42 U.S.C. § 1983 (1982 ed.), on which respondents' complaint is based, is authority enough to require each tortfeasor to pay its share of the cost of the remedy if it can, and apportionment of the cost is part of the equitable power of the District Court.   . . .

We turn to the constitutional issues. The modifications ordered by the Court of Appeals cannot be assailed as invalid under the Tenth Amendment. "The Tenth Amendment's reservation of nondelegated powers to the States is not implicated by a federal-court judgment enforcing the express prohibitions of unlawful state conduct enacted by the Fourteenth Amendment."   . . .

Finally, the State argues that an order to increase taxes cannot be sustained under the judicial power of Article III. Whatever the merits of this argument when applied to the District Court's own order increasing taxes, a point we have not reached,   . . .   a court order directing a local government body to levy its own taxes is plainly a judicial act within the power of a federal court.   . . .

The State maintains, however,   . . .   the federal judicial power can go no further than to require local governments to levy taxes *as authorized under state law.* In other words, the State argues that federal courts cannot set aside state-imposed limitations on local taxing authority because to do so is to do more than to require the local government "to exercise the power *that is theirs.*" We disagree. . . .

It is therefore clear that a local government with taxing authority may be ordered to levy taxes in excess of the limit set by state statute where there is reason based in the Constitution for not observing the statutory limitation. . . . Here the KCMSD may be ordered to levy taxes despite the statutory limitations on its authority in order to compel the discharge of an obligation imposed on KCMSD by the Fourteenth Amendment. To hold otherwise would fail to take account of the obligations of local governments, under the Supremacy Clause, to fulfill the requirements that the Constitution imposes on them. However wide the discretion of local authorities in fashioning desegregation remedies may be, "if a state-imposed limitation on a school authority's discretion operates to inhibit or obstruct the operation of a unitary school system or impede the disestablishing of a dual school system, it must fall; state policy must give way when it operates to hinder vindication of federal constitutional guarantees." *North Carolina State Bd. of Education v. Swann,* 402 U.S. 43, 45, 91 S.Ct. 1284, 1286, 28 L.Ed.2d 586 (1971). Even though a particular remedy may not be required in every case to vindicate constitutional guarantees, where (as here) it has been found that a particular remedy is required, the State cannot hinder the process by preventing a local government from implementing that remedy.

Accordingly, the judgment of the Court of Appeals is affirmed insofar as it required the District Court to modify its funding order and reversed insofar as it allowed the tax increase imposed by the District Court to stand. The case is remanded for further proceedings consistent with this opinion.

It is so ordered.

Justice KENNEDY, with whom THE CHIEF JUSTICE, Justice O'CONNOR, and Justice SCALIA join, concurring in part and concurring in the judgment.

■ INTERDISTRICT DESEGREGATION

Since school districts in the South are generally quite large, geographically, most of the litigation has involved intradistrict desegregation. The courts found that much integration could be accomplished without going beyond the school district boundaries. Few instances are extant in which it has been necessary to question the boundaries of the basic school district unit in order to effectuate a unitary educational system. Some cases have, however, been initiated in the South when it appeared that the school district boundaries were actually being used to thwart effective desegregation. In one such instance, a town in Virginia exercised its discretion under Virginia municipal law and withdrew from the county, forming an independent municipality.[80] At the time of withdrawal of municipal functions, the newly independent city decided to continue to operate the school system as a part of the overall county school system. Later, however, it was decided to also separate the independent city's school system from the countywide school district. This decision came about shortly after a federal district court had required a new desegregation plan for the entire county, replacing the older freedom-of-choice plan. The new reorganization resulted in an increase in the proportion of blacks in the county schools and a decrease in the city schools, although both systems retained a majority of blacks. The United States Supreme Court enjoined the reorganization, saying that the Court must look to the effect of such action on the segregation of the schools. When the effect is to exacerbate the problem of racial imbalance, the Court will frown on changing school district boundaries. The Supreme Court listed three factors supporting the conclusion under which such reorganizations may be judged constitutionally impermissible: first, the likelihood of increased segregation as white parents shifted their children to the new school district from private schools and the county system was apparent; second, the fact that the independent city schools in the state had traditionally been predominately white suggested that the same pattern might ensue here; third, the timing of the city's decision was psychologically poor since it made it appear that the rationale for separating the school system was based on the lower court's prohibition of the use of a freedom-of-choice plan for the entire school system. Effectively, then, the Supreme Court said that where segregation is perpetuated as a result of *de jure* governmental action, the Court will not be deterred from intervening even though the remedy goes beyond school district boundaries.[81]

In another case rendered on the same day as the decision just discussed, the Supreme Court refused to permit severance of Scotland Neck schools from those of surrounding Halifax County, North Carolina.[82] The Court reasoned that the motivation of Scotland Neck's departure from the county school system was prompted solely for purposes of segregation and the effect of the action would weld the two systems into a segregated pattern, the new city district being predominately white and the county schools being basically black.

An entirely different situation was presented in the notable Richmond, Virginia, case.[83] Here, a federal district court required the merger of three large and separate school districts to bring about desegregation. Chesterfield and Henrico County school districts are the suburban school district surrounding Richmond and, as in most large urban areas, the city school district had become progressively segregated over the years as white families moved beyond the city limits. Effectively, the federal district judge's decision would have made one large administrative unit of the three systems, with a complex system of rezoning and busing among the school centers. On appeal, the United States Court of Appeals for the Fourth Circuit reversed the lower court decision, holding that there was no evidence to indicate that there was ever any state action taken to keep blacks confined to a particular school district. The court said:

> This court believes that the root causes of the concentration of blacks in inner cities of America are simply not known and that the district court could not realistically place on the counties the responsibility for the effect that inner city decay has had on the public schools of Richmond . . . . . The facts of this case do not show that state establishment and maintenance of school districts coterminous with the political subdivision of the city of Richmond and the counties of Chesterfield and Henrico have been intended to circumvent any federally protected right.[84]

In review of this decision by the United States Supreme Court, eight justices were unable to render a decision, deadlocking four to four. Justice Powell had removed himself from the case because he had formerly been a member of the Richmond school board. Thus, the decision by the Court of Appeals stood.

A similar but more complicated situation arose in Michigan, where the school district pattern around Detroit was found by a lower federal district court to be so constituted as to create school segregation in the central city of Detroit.[85] Both the federal district court and the federal Court of Appeals concluded that desegregation of the Detroit schools was impossible, unless the racial composition of the entire metropolitan area was taken into account. Dismantling of segregation, therefore, according to these federal courts, required interdistrict busing between the Detroit core city and several suburban school districts. On appeal, the United States Supreme Court in reversing the decision held that there was no evidence in the record to show that the original boundaries of the Detroit School District or any other school districts in Michigan were established for the purpose of segregation of the races.

Subsequent to the Supreme Court's decision in *Milliken,* the United States Court of Appeals for the Sixth Circuit upheld a federal district court decision that effectively merged the Louisville and Jefferson County, Kentucky, school districts.[86] The court did not depart from the *Milliken* rationale, but reached a different result because of the special circumstances that were attendant to the Louisville situation. The court found that there still remained vestiges of past *de jure* discrimination in the two large school districts, which was not true in *Milliken.* The Court of Appeals found the crucial difference between the Louisville and Detroit cases to lie in the fact that in the past, school district boundaries in Louisville had been ignored in order to segregate the schools. For example, it was shown that in pre-*Brown* days, black high school students in the Jefferson County school district were sent to Central High School, located in the Louisville school district. This was done because the Jefferson County system had no black high school. It was also shown that another city high school was actually located

geographically in the county, and students of both systems had attended school there. No such interplay was present or had ever transpired between the suburban school districts of Detroit and the central city. Further, school districts in Kentucky had been legally segregated in pre-*Brown* days and, as such, evinced a record of a segregated past that was not present in Michigan.

The Detroit and Louisville cases, although reaching different results, continued a consistent legal rationale enunciating a rule of law that states essentially that school district integration will be required, by busing or other means, either within or among school districts, where it can be shown that segregation is the result of governmental action that tends to create, maintain, or perpetuate segregation of the races. The rule applies to northern as well as to southern states. In the North, although schools were not segregated by statute before *Brown* in 1954, it is quite possible for subsequent government acts, whether patent or latent, to discriminate in such a way as to create patterns of racial imbalance in the schools. In such instances, the segregation will not be viewed as *de facto* by the courts but as *de jure* and, therefore, unconstitutional.

Interdistrict Integration May Be an Improper Remedy to Overcome Single-district Segregation

— — — — — — — —

Milliken v. Bradley

— — — — — — — —

Supreme Court of the United States, 1974.
418 U.S. 717, 94 S.Ct. 3112.

Mr. Chief Justice BURGER delivered the opinion of the Court. We granted certiorari in these consolidated cases to determine whether a federal court may impose a multidistrict, areawide remedy to a single-district *de jure* segregation problem absent any finding that the other included school districts have failed to operate unitary school systems within their districts, absent any claim or finding that the boundary lines of any affected school district were established with the purpose of fostering racial segregation in public schools, absent any finding that the included districts committed acts which effected segregation within the other districts, and absent a meaningful opportunity for the included neighboring school districts to present evidence or be heard on the propriety of a multidistrict remedy or on the question of constitutional violations by those neighboring districts. . . . In *Brown v. Board of Education*, 349 U.S. 294, 75 S.Ct. 753, 99 L.Ed. 1083 (1955) *(Brown II)*, the Court's first encounter with the problem of remedies in school desegregation cases, the Court noted:

> In fashioning and effectuating the decrees, the courts will be guided by equitable principles. Traditionally, equity has been characterized by a practical flexibility in shaping its remedies and by a facility for adjusting and reconciling public and private needs. Id., at 300, 75 S.Ct., at 756.

In further refining the remedial process, *Swann* held, the task is to correct, by a balancing of the individual and collective interests, "the condition that offends the Constitution." A federal remedial power may be exercised "only on the basis of a constitutional violation" and, "[a]s with any equity case, the nature of the violation determines the scope of the remedy." 402 U.S., at 16, 91 S.Ct., at 1276.

Proceeding from these basic principles, we first note that in the District Court the complainants sought a remedy aimed at the *condition* alleged to offend the Constitution—the segregation within the Detroit City School District. The court acted on this theory of the case and in its initial ruling on the "Desegregation Area" stated:

> The task before this court, therefore, is now, and . . . has always been, how to deseg-

regate the Detroit public schools. 345 F.Supp., at 921.

Thereafter, however, the District Court abruptly rejected the proposed Detroit-only plans on the ground that "while [they] would provide a racial mix more in keeping with the black-white proportions of the student population [they] would accentuate the racial identifiability of the [Detroit] district as a black school system, and would not accomplish desegregation." Pet. App., 56a. "[T]he racial composition of the student body is such," said the court, "that the plan's implementation would clearly make the entire Detroit public school system racially identifiable" (Id., at 54a), "leav[ing] many of its schools 75 to 90 percent black." Id., at 55a. Consequently, the court reasoned, it was imperative to "look beyond the limits of the Detroit school district for a solution to the problem of segregation in the Detroit public schools . . . " since "[s]chool district lines are simply matters of political convenience and may not be used to deny constitutional rights." Id., at 57a. Accordingly, the District Court proceeded to redefine the relevant area to include areas of predominantly white pupil population in order to ensure that "upon implementation, no school, grade or classroom [would be] substantially disproportionate to the overall pupil racial composition" of the entire metropolitan area.

. . .

Viewing the record as a whole, it seems clear that the District Court and the Court of Appeals shifted the primary focus from a Detroit remedy to the metropolitan area only because of their conclusion that total desegregation of Detroit would not produce the racial balance which they perceived as desirable. Both courts proceeded on an assumption that the Detroit schools could not be truly desegregated—in their view of what constituted desegregation—unless the racial composition of the student body of each school substantially reflected the racial composition of the population of the metropolitan area as a whole. The metropolitan area was then defined as Detroit plus fifty-three of the outlying school districts. . . .

In *Swann,* which arose in the context of a single independent school district, the Court held:

> If we were to read the holding of the District Court to require, as a matter of substantive constitutional right, any particular degree of racial balance or mixing, that approach would be disapproved and we would be obliged to reverse. 402 U.S., at 24, 91 S.Ct., at 1280.

The clear import of this language from *Swann* is that desegregation, in the sense of dismantling a dual school system, does not require any particular racial balance in each "school, grade or classroom." See *Spencer v. Kugler,* 404 U.S. 1027, 92 S.Ct. 707, 30 L.Ed.2d 723 (1972).

Here the District Court's approach to what constituted "actual desegregation" raises the fundamental question, not presented in *Swann,* as to the circumstances in which a federal court may order desegregation relief that embraces more than a single school district. The court's analytical starting point was its conclusion that school district lines are no more than arbitrary lines on a map drawn "for political convenience." Boundary lines may be bridged where there has been a constitutional violation calling for interdistrict relief but the notion that school district lines may be casually ignored or treated as a mere administrative convenience is contrary to the history of public education in our country. No single tradition in public education is more deeply rooted than local control over the operation of schools; local autonomy has long been thought essential both to the maintenance of community concern and support for public schools and to quality of the educational process. . . .

The Michigan educational structure involved in this case, in common with most States, provides for a large measure of local control, and a review of the scope and character of these local powers indicates the extent to which the interdistrict remedy approved by the two courts could disrupt and alter the structure of public education in Michigan. The metropolitan remedy would require, in effect, consolidation of fifty-four independent school districts historically administered as separate units into a vast new super school district. Entirely apart from the logistical and other serious problems attending large-scale transportation of students, the consolidation would give rise to an array of other problems in financing and operating this new school system. Some of the more obvious questions would be: What would be the status and authority of the present popularly elected school boards? Would the children of Detroit be within the jurisdiction and operating control of a school board elected by the parents and residents of other districts? What board or boards would levy taxes for school operations in these fifty-four districts constituting the consolidated metropolitan area? What provisions could be made for assuring substantial equality in tax levies among the fifty-four districts, if this were deemed requisite? What provisions would be made for financing? Would the validity of long-term bonds be jeopardized unless approved by all of the component districts as well as the State? What body would determine that portion of the curricula now left to the discretion of local school boards? Who would establish attendance zones, purchase school equipment, locate and construct new schools, and indeed attend to all the myriad day-to-day decisions that are necessary to school operations affecting potentially more than three-quarters of a million pupils?

It may be suggested that all of these vital operational problems are yet to be resolved by the District Court, and that this is the purpose of the Court of Appeals' proposed remand. But it is obvious from the scope of the interdistrict remedy itself that absent a complete restructuring of the laws of Michigan relating to school districts the District Court will become first, a *de facto* "legislative authority" to resolve these complex questions, and then the "school superintendent" for the entire area. This is a task which few, if any, judges are qualified to perform and one which would deprive the people of control of schools through their elected representatives.

Of course, no state law is above the Constitution. School district lines and the present laws with respect to local control, are not sacrosanct and if they conflict with the Fourteenth Amendment federal courts have a duty to prescribe appropriate remedies. . . . But our prior holdings have been confined to violations and remedies within a single school district. We therefore turn to address, for the first time, the validity of a remedy mandating cross-district or interdistrict consolidation to remedy a condition of segregation found to exist in only one district.

The controlling principle consistently expounded in our holdings is that the scope of the remedy is determined by the nature and extent of the constitutional violation. *Swann,* 402 U.S., at 16, 91 S.Ct., at 1276. Before the boundaries of separate and autonomous school districts may be set aside by consolidating the separate units for remedial purposes or by imposing a cross-district remedy, it must first be shown that there has been a constitutional violation within one district that produces a significant segregative effect in another district. Specifically, it must be shown that racially discriminatory acts of the state or local school districts, or of a single school district have been a substantial cause of interdistrict segregation. Thus an interdistrict remedy might be in order where the racially discriminatory acts of one or more school districts caused racial segregation in an adjacent district, or where district lines have been deliberately drawn on the basis of race. In such circumstances an interdistrict remedy would be appropriate to eliminate the interdistrict segregation directly caused by the constitutional violation. Conversely, without an interdistrict violation and interdistrict effect, there is no constitutional wrong calling for an interdistrict remedy.

The record before us, voluminous as it is, contains evidence of *de jure* segregated conditions only in the Detroit schools; indeed, that was the theory on which the litigation was initially based and on which the District Court

took evidence. With no showing of significant violation by the fifty-three outlying school districts and no evidence of any interdistrict violation or effect, the court went beyond the original theory of the case as framed by the pleadings and mandated a metropolitan area remedy. To approve the remedy ordered by the court would impose on the outlying districts, not shown to have committed any constitutional violation, a wholly impermissible remedy based on a standard not hinted at in *Brown I* and *II* or any holding of this Court.

In dissent, Mr. Justice WHITE and Mr. Justice MARSHALL undertake to demonstrate that agencies having statewide authority participated in maintaining the dual school system found to exist in Detroit. They are apparently of the view that once such participation is shown, the District Court should have a relatively free hand to reconstruct school districts outside of Detroit in fashioning relief. Our assumption, *arguendo,* that state agencies did participate in the maintenance of the Detroit system, should make it clear that it is not on this point that we part company. The difference between us arises instead from established doctrine laid down by our cases. *Brown, Green, Swann, Scotland Neck* and *Emporia,* each addressed the issue of constitutional wrong in terms of an established geographic and administrative school system populated by both Negro and white children. In such a context, terms such as "unitary" and "dual" systems and "racially identifiable schools," have meaning, and the necessary federal authority to remedy the constitutional wrong is firmly established. But the remedy is necessarily designed, as all remedies are, to restore the victims of discriminatory conduct to the position they would have occupied in the absence of such conduct. Disparate treatment of white and Negro students occurred within the Detroit school system, and not elsewhere, and on this record the remedy must be limited to that system. *Swann,* supra, 402 U.S., at 16, 91 S.Ct., at 1276.

The constitutional right of the Negro respondents residing in Detroit is to attend a unitary school system in that district. Unless petitioners drew the district lines in a discriminatory fashion, or arranged for white students residing in the Detroit district to attend schools in Oakland and Macomb Counties, they were under no constitutional duty to make provisions for Negro students to do so. The view of the dissenters, that the existence of a dual system in *Detroit* can be made the basis for a decree requiring cross-district transportation of pupils, cannot be supported on the grounds that it represents merely the devising of a suitably flexible remedy for the violation of rights already established by our prior decisions. It can be supported only by drastic expansion of the constitutional right itself, an expansion without any support in either constitutional principle or precedent.

. . . The Court of Appeals . . . held the State derivatively responsible for the Detroit Board's violations on the theory that actions of Detroit as a political subdivision of the State were attributable to the State. Accepting, *arguendo*, the correctness of this finding of state responsibility for the segregated conditions within the city of Detroit, it does not follow that an interdistrict remedy is constitutionally justified or required. With a single exception, discussed later, there has been no showing that either the State or any of the eighty-five outlying districts engaged in activity that had a cross-district effect. The boundaries of the Detroit School District, which are coterminous with the boundaries of the city of Detroit, were established over a century ago by neutral legislation when the city was incorporated; there is no evidence in the record, nor is there any suggestion by the respondents, that either the original boundaries of the Detroit School District, or any other school district in Michigan, were established for the purpose of creating, maintaining, or perpetuating segregation of races. There is no claim and there is no evidence hinting that petitioner outlying school districts and their predecessors, or the thirty-odd other school districts in the tricounty area — but outside the District Court's "desegregation area" — have ever maintained or operated anything but unitary school systems. Unitary school systems have been required for more than a century by the Michigan Constitution as implemented by state law. Where the schools of only one district have been affected,

there is no constitutional power in the courts to decree relief balancing the racial composition of that district's schools with those of the surrounding district. . . .

We conclude that the relief ordered by the District Court and affirmed by the Court of Appeals was based upon an erroneous standard and was unsupported by record evidence that acts of the outlying districts effected the discrimination found to exist in the schools of Detroit. Accordingly, the judgment of the Court of Appeals is reversed and the case is remanded for further proceedings consistent with this opinion leading to prompt formulation of a decree directed to eliminating the segregation found to exist in Detroit city schools, a remedy which has been delayed since 1970.

Reversed and remanded.

NOTE

1. In a suit seeking desegregation of the Indianapolis public schools, the litigation followed a course similar to that of *Milliken*. In its first opinion, the District Court held that the Indianapolis City public schools were *de jure* segregated; the Court of Appeals affirmed and the United States Supreme Court denied *certiorari*. United States v. Board of School Commissioners 332 F.Supp. 655 (S.D.Ind.1971), affirmed 474 F.2d 81 (7th Cir. 1973), *certiorari* denied 413 U.S. 920, 93 S.Ct. 3066 (1973). In subsequent proceedings to select a remedy, the District Court concluded that Indianapolis' only desegregation plans were inadequate and ordered the preparation of a metropolitan desegregation plan. 368 F.Supp. 1191 (S.D.Ind.1973). In 1969, after the filing of the suit, the Indiana legislature had enacted a law consolidating the governments of Indianapolis and surrounding Marion County, but specifically excluding the area school districts from consolidation. The Court of Appeals for the Seventh Circuit vacated those portions of the District Court's opinion ordering a metropolitan remedy, citing *Milliken* 503 F.2d 68 (7th Cir.1974).

■ ENDNOTES

1. Roberts v. City of Boston, 59 Mass. (5 Cush.) 198 (1850).

2. Ibid.

3. See Jethro K. Lieberman, *Milestones, 200 Years of American Law* (New York: Oxford University Press and St. Paul, MN: West Publishing Company, 1976), pp. 256–57; Richard Kluger, *Simple Justice* (New York: Vintage Books, 1977), pp. 77–78.

4. Louisville, New Orleans and Texas Railway Co. v. Mississippi, 133 U.S. 587, 10 S.Ct. 348 (1890).

5. Lieberman, *Milestones,* p. 260.

6. Regents of University of Cal. v. Bakke, 438 U.S. 265, 98 S.Ct. 2733 (1978).

7. 163 U.S. 537, 16 S.Ct. 1138 (1896).

8. Ibid.

9. Ibid.

10. Cumming v. Board of Education of Richmond County, 175 U.S. 528, 20 S.Ct. 197 (1899).

11. 211 U.S. 45, 29 S.Ct. 33 (1908).

12. See Kern Alexander and Erwin Solomon, *College and University Law* (Charlottesville, Va.: The Michie Company, 1972), p. 518.

13. Berea College v. Commonwealth of Kentucky, op. cit.

14. 275 U.S. 78, 48 S.Ct. 91 (1927).

15. 305 U.S. 337, 59 S.Ct. 232 (1938).

16. Sweatt v. Painter, 339 U.S. 629, 70 S.Ct. 848 (1950).

17. Ibid.

18. Ibid.

19. McLaurin v. Oklahoma State Regents for Higher Education, 339 U.S. 637, 70 S.Ct. 851 (1950).

20. Brown v. Board of Education, 98 F.Supp. 797 (D.Kan.1951): Judgement reversed 349 U.S. 294, 75 S.Ct.753 (1955); Briggs v. Elliott, 98 F.Supp. 529 (E.D.S.C.1951); Davis v. County School Board, 103 F.Supp. 337 (E.D.Va.1952); Belton v. Gebhart, 32 Del.Ch. 343, 87 A.2d 862 (1952); and Bolling v. Sharpe, cert. granted 344 U.S. 873, 73 S.Ct. 173 (1952).

21. Loren Miller, "The Petitioners," from Harold W. Horowitz and Kenneth L. Karst, *Law Lawyers and Social Change* (Indianapolis: Bobbs-Merrill, 1969), pp. 181–82.

22. Ibid.

23. Harry S. Ashmore, *The Negro and the Schools* (Chapel Hill: The University of North Carolina Press, 1954), pp. 42–43.

24. Lieberman, *Milestones,* p. 276.

25. Brown v. Board of Education, 347 U.S. 483, 74 S.Ct. 686 (1954).

26. Louis H. Pollak, *The Constitution and the Supreme Court, A Documentary History,* vol. II (The World Publishing Company, 1966), p. 266.

27. Brown v. Board of Education of Topeka, 349 U.S. 294, 75 S.Ct. 753 (1955).

28. Ibid.

29. Cooper v. Aaron, 358 U.S. 1, 78 S.Ct. 1401 (1958).

30. Ibid.

31. Ibid.

32. Griffin v. County School Board of Prince Edward County, 377 U.S. 218, 84 S.Ct. 1226 (1964).

33. Briggs v. Elliott, 132 F.Supp. 776 (E.D.S.C.1955).

34. Bell v. School City of Gary, 324 F.2d 209 (7th Cir.1963), cert. denied 377 U.S. 924, 84 S.Ct. 1223 (1964); Deal v. Cincinnati Board of Education, 369 F.2d 55 (6th Cir.1966), cert. denied 389 U.S. 847, 88 S.Ct. 39 (1967).

35. United States v. Jefferson County Board of Education, 372 F.2d 836 (5th Cir.1966).

36. Green v. County School Board of New Kent County, Virginia, 391 U.S. 430, 88 S.Ct. 1689 (1968).

37. Alexander v. Holmes County Board of Educ., 396 U.S. 19, 90 S.Ct. 29 (1969), rehearing denied 396 U.S. 976, 90 S.Ct. 437 (1969).

38. Bell v. School City of Gary, 324 F.2d 209 (7th Cir.1963).

39. Keyes v. School District No. 1, Denver, 413 U.S. 189, 93 S.Ct. 2686 (1973).

40. Swann v. Charlotte-Mecklenburg Bd. of Education, 402 U.S. 1, 91 S.Ct. 1267 (1971).

41. Regents of the University of Cal. v. Bakke, 438 U.S. 265, 98 S.Ct. 2733 (1978).

42. Ibid.

43. Washington v. Davis, 426 U.S. 229, 96 S.Ct. 2040 (1976).

44. Of course, in the original *de jure* cases the burden shifted to the state automatically, because the segregation was enforced by statute.

45. Green v. County School Board, op. cit.

46. Columbus Bd. of Education v. Penick, 443 U.S. 449, 99 S.Ct. 2941 (1979).

47. Alexander v. Holmes County Board of Education, op. cit.

48. 915 F.2d 155 (5th Cir. 1990).

49. Ibid., citing Monteith v. St. Landry Parish School Bd., 848 F.2d 625 (5th Cir. 1988).

50. United States v. Overton, 834 F.2d 1171 (5th Cir. 1987).

51. Morgan v. Nucci, 831 F.2d 313 (1st Cir. 1987).

52. *Flax,* op. cit., p. 158.

53. 699 F.2d 218 (5th Cir. 1983).

54. Keyes v. School District No. 1, 895 F.2d 895 at 666 (10th Cir. 1990).

55. Green v. County School Board, op. cit.

56. Pitts by Pitts v. Freeman, 887 F.2d 1438 (11th Cir. 1989).

57. Ibid.

58. Ibid.

59. Ibid.

60. Board of Education of Oklahoma City Public Schools, Independent School Dist. No. 89 v. Dowell, ____ U.S. ____, 111 S.Ct. 630 (1991).

61. Ibid.

62. Ibid.

63. See Tracy Ellen Sivitz, "Eliminating the Continuing Effects of the Violation: Compensatory Education as a Remedy for Unlawful School Segregation," *Yale Law Journal* 97 (1988): 1173–92.

64. See, e.g., Jenkins v. Missouri, 639 F.Supp. 19, 32 (W.D.Mo.1985), affirmed 807 F.2d 657 (8th Cir. 1986), cert. denied 484 U.S. 816, 108 S.Ct. 70 (1987); Judgement affirmed in part, reversed in part by Missouri v. Jenkins 110 S.Ct. 1651, U.S. (1990); Liddell v. Board of Education,

567 F.Supp. 1037, 1050 (E.D. Mo. 1983), affirmed 731 F.2d 1294 (8th Cir.1984), cert. denied 469 U.S. 816, 105 S.Ct. 82 (1984); Arthur v. Nyquist, 514 F.Supp. 1133, 1139 (W.D.N.Y. 1981), affirmed mem. 661 F.2d 907 (2d Cir.1981), cert. denied 454 U.S. 1085, 102 S.Ct. 643 (1981).

65. See, e.g., Berry v. School Dist., 515 F.Supp. 344, 373–74 (W.D. Mich. 1981), affirmed 698 F.2d 813 (6th Cir.1983), cert. denied 464 U.S. 892, 104 S.Ct. 235 (1983); United States v. Board of School Com'rs of Indianapolis, 506 F.Supp. 657, 672 (S.D.Ind. 1979), vacated in part on other grounds 637 F.2d 1101 (7th Cir. 1980), cert. denied 449 U.S. 838, 101 S.Ct. 114 (1980); Evans v. Buchanan, 447 F.Supp. 982, 1016 (D. Del. 1978), affirmed 582 F.2d 750 (3d Cir. 1978) (en banc), cert. denied, 446 U.S. 923, 100 S.Ct. 1862 (1980).

66. See, e.g., Jenkins v. Missouri, 639 F.Supp. at 28–30; Liddell v. Board of Education, 567 F.Supp. at 1050.

67. See, e.g., United States v. Board of Educ. of Chicago, 588 F.Supp. 132, 167 (N.D. Ill. 1984), vacated on other grounds 744 F.2d 1300 (7th Cir. 1984), cert. denied 471 U.S. 1116, 105 S.Ct. 2538 (1985); United States v. Board of School Com'rs of Indianapolis, 506 F.Supp. at 672–73; Reed v. Rhodes, 455 F.Supp. 569, 599 (N.D. Ohio 1978), affirmed 607 F.2d 714 (6th Cir. 1979), cert. denied 445 U.S. 935, 100 S.Ct. 1329 (1980).

68. See, e.g., United States v. Board of School Com'rs of Indianapolis, 506 F.Supp. at 673; Reed v. Rhodes, 455 F.Supp. at 598–99; Evans v. Buchanan, 447 F.Supp. at 1015–16.

69. See, e.g., United States v. Yonkers Bd. of Educ., 635 F.Supp. 1538, 1551, app. C at 1572 (S.D.N.Y. 1986), affirmed 837 F.2d 1181 (2d Cir. 1987), cert. denied 486 U.S. 1055, 108 S.Ct. 2821 (1988); Berry v. School Dist., 515 F.Supp. at 376-79; Kelley v. Metropolitan County Bd. of Educ., 511 F.Supp. 1363, 1371 (M.D. Tenn. 1981), reversed in part on other grounds 687 F.2d 814 (6th Cir. 1982), cert. denied 459 U.S. 1183, 103 S.Ct. 834 (1983). See Sivitz, op. cit., for elaboration on remedies.

70. *Milliken v. Bradley,* 433 U.S. 267, 97 S.Ct. 2749 (1977).

71. Ibid.

72. Ibid.

73. Ibid.

74. Sivitz, op. cit., at 1178.

75. Milliken v. Bradley, op. cit., at 287–88.

76. ____ U.S. ____, 110 S.Ct. 1651 (1990).

77. See Charles J. Russo and Lawrence F. Rossow, "Missouri v. Jenkins: The Desegregation Battle Continues," 62 *Ed.Law Rep.* 399 (Nov. 22, 1990).

78. Stell v. Savannah-Chatham County Board of Education, 888 F.2d 82 (11th Cir. 1989).

79. Ibid.

80. Wright v. Council of the City of Emporia, 107 U.S. 451, 92 S.Ct. 2196 (1972).

81. See also: Lee v. Macon County Bd. of Education, 448 F.2d 746 (1971); Stout v. Jefferson County Bd. of Education, 448 F.2d 403 (1971); Haney v. County Bd. of Education, 410 F.2d 920 (1969).

82. United States v. Scotland Neck City Board of Education, 407 U.S. 484, 92 S.Ct. 2214 (1972).

83. Bradley v. Richmond School Board, 456 F.2d 6 (4th Cir.1972); 416 U.S. 696, 94 S.Ct. 2006 (1974).

84. Id.

85. Milliken v. Bradley, 418 U.S. 717, 94 S.Ct. 3112 (1974).

86. Newburg Area Council, Inc., v. Gordon, 521 F.2d 578 (1975); Newburg Area Council, Inc. v. Board of Education, 510 F.2d 1358 (1974).

CHAPTER 11

Torts

The law grants to each individual certain personal rights with regard to conduct that others must respect. Some of these rights arise through the execution of a contract between individuals, for breach of which financial liability may result. The law also grants to each individual certain personal rights not of a contractual nature, such as freedom from personal injury and security of life, liberty, and property. The law imposes corresponding duties and responsibilities on each individual to respect the rights of others. If, by speech or other conduct, one fails to respect these rights, thereby damaging another, a tort has been committed and the offending party may be held liable.

A tort is a civil wrong independent of contract. It may be malicious and intentional, or it may be the result of negligence and disregard for the rights of others. An action in tort compensates private individuals for harm caused to them by the unreasonable conduct of others. Social norms have provided the basis for legal precedent in the determination of that which is considered unacceptable or unreasonable conduct.

A legally proper relationship between two persons can be breached by injury caused by an act or an omission to act on the part of either party. The word "tort" is derived from the Latin word *"tortus"* or *"twisted."*[1] In personal relationships, the term "twisted" is applied to activity that deviates from a normally acceptable pattern of behavior.

A tort is different from a crime and emanates from a separate and distinct body of law. A civil action for tort is initiated and maintained by the injured party for the purpose of obtaining compensation for the injury suffered, whereas in a criminal proceeding the action is brought by the state to protect the public from actions of a wrongdoer. In a criminal case the state prosecutes not to compensate the injured person, but rather to protect the public from further wrongful acts. Since criminal law does not, and was never intended to compensate an injured individual, social justice demanded the birth of the action in tort.

Grounds for actions in tort can be divided into three categories: (1) intentional interference, (2) strict liability, and (3) negligence. Each of these can, at times, be applied to cases in public schools where pupils are injured.

INTENTIONAL INTERFERENCE

An intentional tort may result from an intended act whether accompanied by enmity, antagonism, maliciousness, or by no more than a good-natured practical joke.[2] With this type of tort, it is not necessary for the wrongdoer to be hostile or desire to do harm to the injured party. Even when a person does not plan to injure another but proceeds intentionally to act in a way that invades the rights of another, he or she commits an intentional tort. For intent to exist, the activity of an individual must, with substantial certainty, be the result of his or her act. If one does not know with substantial certainty the result of an act and injury

459

results, then it is negligence instead of an intentional tort.

Assault

An intentional tort can be committed even if no physical "touching" takes place. To have assault there must be an "overt act or an attempt, or the unequivocal appearance of an attempt, to do some immediate physical injury to the person of another." The overt act must be a display of force or menace of violence of such a nature as to cause reasonable apprehension of immediate bodily harm.[3] It is assault when a person stands within striking distance of another and with sword drawn says, "I intend to run you through." Such words and acts may be sufficient to put the plaintiff in immediate apprehension of imminent harm and it is apparent that the offender has the present ability to effectuate the harm. Thus, an intentional tort can be consummated by an act that, while not involving physical contact, places a person in immediate fear that such action will transpire.

Battery

Technically, battery is an intentional tort that comes about through physical contact. Prosser points out that it is battery to injure a man in his sleep, even though he does not discover the injury until later, while it is an assault to shoot at him while he is awake, and frighten but miss him.[4] In both cases, a person's interests are invaded. If a wrongdoer swings a bottle, intending to strike the plaintiff, and the plaintiff sees the movement and is apprehensive for his own safety, there is assault; if the attack is consummated and the blow is actually landed, both assault and battery are present.

Teachers accused of assault and battery for administering corporal punishment are usually given considerable leeway as to the reasonableness of their action. In one case, the court explained the rule of law: "To be guilty of an assault and battery, the teacher must not only inflict on the child immoderate chastise-

ment, but he must do so with legal malice or wicked motives or he must inflict some permanent injury."[5]

Cases involving assault and battery by a teacher usually result from a teacher's attempt to discipline a child. The courts generally allow wide latitude for teachers in chastisement of pupils, presuming that the teacher is innocent, has acted reasonably, and has done his or her duty, until the contrary is proved.

The courts still uphold the ancient doctrine of *in loco parentis,* which holds that the teacher stands in place of the parent and in such capacity has the right to chastise a pupil. The teacher's prerogatives are, of course, limited to the jurisdiction of the school and are not unlimited. Within these boundaries, the teacher may require pupils to abide by all reasonable commands and may inflict reasonable corporal punishment to enforce compliance. One court stated the situation in this manner:

> In the school, as in the family, there exists on the part of the pupils the obligations of obedience to lawful commands, subordination, civil deportment, respect for the right of other pupils, and fidelity to duty. Those obligations are inherent in any proper school system, and constitute, so to speak, the common law of the school.[6]

Courts do, however, make it quite clear that a teacher may be guilty of assault and battery if chastisement is cruel, brutal,[7] excessive,[8] or if administered in anger or insolence.[9] In one interesting old case, the court said that a teacher was not justified in beating a scholar so severely as to wear out two whips, strike two blows to the head with fists, and kick the scholar in the face, all because he misspelled a word and refused to try again.[10]

Chastisement of a pupil may become assault and battery if the teacher does not administer the punishment reasonably.[11] Criteria used by courts to identify excessive punishment include:

1. proper and suitable weapon,
2. part of person to which it is applied,
3. manner and extent of chastisement,

4. nature and gravity of offense,
5. age of pupil,
6. temper and deportment of the teacher,[12] and
7. history of pupil's previous conduct.

Both assault and battery may be criminal wrongs as well as tort where statutes so require. Criminal statutes usually define assault as attempted battery, requiring present ability. However, the reasoning pertaining to individual statutes may or may not have application to tort law.

Interference with Peace of Mind

In keeping with the theory that every man who is injured should have recompense, modern courts have had a tendency to recognize as a separate tort interference with peace of mind, the infliction of mental or emotional anguish. In such cases, it is necessary and quite difficult to prove mental suffering. The courts have been unable to precisely delineate between actual tortious actions and what may be considered everyday rough language or immoderate personal behavior that hurts one's feelings yet is so severe as to create an action in tort. One cannot recover damages simply because of hurt feelings.[13]

Courts have held that where an act is malicious, as distinguished from being merely negligent, there may be recovery for mental anguish, even though no physical injury results.[14] However, cases involving actions for mental anguish and suffering are easier to prove before a jury if the emotional distress has produced some visible or identifiable physical harm.

Another intentional tort is false imprisonment, sometimes called false arrest. Relatively few cases have occurred in this area, but the general rule is that an unauthorized person cannot detain or physically restrain the movements of another. This type of tort is not applicable to the situation in which a teacher confines a child in his classroom, since a teacher is charged with overseeing pupil activities in the school setting and is authorized to confine a pupil, if necessary, in order to discipline him.

◾◾◾ STRICT LIABILITY

Generally, liability for tort has been imposed with regard to "fault" on the part of the defendant. Both intentional interference and negligence are based on the supposition that someone was injured at the fault of another party. However, cases have arisen in which a person has been injured through no actual, identifiable fault of anyone. Such cases have forced some courts to hand down damage awards based on strict liability of the defendant. In these instances, a person may be liable even though he or she is not strictly at fault for the other party's injury. This rule was adopted in order to place the damages on the person best able to bear the burden. In these cases, the defendant's acts are not so important as the injury and suffering of the injured person. Underlying this type of decision is the older social justice reasoning that requiring "he who breaks must pay" regardless of whether the injury is knowingly or negligently caused.[15]

While fault is not a prerequisite to liability in these cases, the courts do generally require the defendant to have caused some unusual hazard to exist. The defendant's activity must involve abnormal danger to others.

Today in the United States, strict liability is not imposed unless the activity or thing is classified as hazardous or even "ultrahazardous."[16] While strict liability cases reported by appellate courts involving activities in the public schools are scarce, the possibility of such actions nevertheless exists. For example, the hazards in schools caused by laboratory experiments, shop activity, or field trips present possibilities of actions involving strict liability. However, this area makes up a small element of the total tort liability picture in schools.

Trampoline Is Not Abnormally Dangerous for the Purpose of Imposing Strict Liability

————————————

Fallon v. Indiana Trail School

————————————

Appellate Court of Illinois, Second District, 1986.
148 Ill. App. 3d 931, 102 Ill. Dec. 479,
500 N.E.2d 101.

Justice STROUSE delivered the opinion of the court. . . . The plaintiff's amended complaint sought to recover damages for spinal injuries suffered as a result of a trampoline accident which occurred on February 23, 1975. At that time the plaintiff was a sixth-grade student at the school and the defendants, Roach and Roynan-Leo, were physical education teachers. The incident occurred when the plaintiff attempted a "front-drop" maneuver on the trampoline during her physical education class. In her attempt to perform the maneuver, the plaintiff sustained spinal injuries.

. . . Count I alleged that the school and school district were strictly liable for the consequences of exposing pupils to an "abnormally dangerous instrumentality," a trampoline, during the physical education program. Count II alleged that the school and school district were negligent in the selection and use of an "abnormally dangerous" apparatus, a trampoline. . . .

In count I, the plaintiff alleged that the trampoline was an abnormally dangerous instrumentality, and the school district should, therefore, be held accountable under strict tort liability for any injuries due to its use. In count II, the plaintiff charged the school and school district with negligence as a result of a violation of section 10.20.8 of the School Code (Ill.Rev.Stat.1985, ch. 122, par. 10-20.8) because the trampoline was an abnormally dangerous instrumentality. We must, therefore, decide whether the plaintiff has alleged sufficient facts to support the

contention that the trampoline is an abnormally dangerous instrumentality and trampoline usage is an abnormally dangerous activity.

Illinois recognizes strict liability under two theories: unreasonably dangerous defective products . . . and the theory which plaintiff alleges is applicable to this case, ultrahazardous activities . . . . Sections 519 and 520 of the Restatement (Second) of Torts (1981) (Restatement) have formulated a definition of ultrahazardous activities. Under section 519(1) of the Restatement, "[o]ne who carries on an abnormally dangerous activity is subject to liability for harm to the person, land or chattels of another resulting from the activity, although he has exercised the utmost care to prevent the harm." (Restatement (Second) of Torts sec. 519(1) (1981).) Section 520 of the Restatement considers: "[E]xistence of a high degree of risk of some harm . . . ; likelihood that the harm that results from it will be great; inability to eliminate the risk by the exercise of reasonable care; extent to which the activity is not a matter of common usage . . . ." Restatement (Second) of Torts sec. 520 (1981).

Illinois has long recognized strict liability for damages caused by engaging in an ultrahazardous activity, although it has never explicitly relied upon the Restatement factors in determining whether a given activity is abnormally dangerous. In *City of Joliet v. Harwood* (1877), 86 Ill. 110, the Illinois Supreme Court held that blasting dynamite in a residential area was intrinsically dangerous and gave rise to strict liability for the blaster. . . .

The plaintiff concedes that there is no Illinois authority discussing either whether (1) trampoline usage of this sort is an ultrahazardous activity, or (2) the trampoline is an abnormally dangerous instrumentality. Indeed, the trial court, in its written disposition dismissing counts I and II, noted that most of the discussion which related to this subject had to do with such obviously dangerous instrumentalities and activities as blasting, transport of explosives, maintenance of high electrical current, large animals, and maintenance of water reservoirs. In support of her argument, the plaintiff attached Exhibit A, "Trampoline-Related Quadriplegia: Review of the Literature and Reflections on the American Academy of Pediatrics' Position Statement," a review documenting cervical spine injuries resulting from trampoline-related accidents.

After reviewing Exhibit A, the trial court's disposition, as well as the plaintiff's amended complaint, we believe the trial court was correct in finding that trampoline usage, as alleged in the present case, does not fall within the parameter of an abnormally dangerous activity. We also agree that the trampoline, as a matter of law, is not an abnormally dangerous instrumentality.

Trampolines are widely used in the school systems as well as other centers of gymnastic activity. The injuries that may be caused result not from the trampoline itself but rather from the manner of its use. The terms "ultrahazardous," "abnormally dangerous," or "intrinsically dangerous," as traditionally used, refer to that type of danger which is inherent in the instrumentality itself at all times and do not mean danger which arises from mere casual or collateral negligence of others with respect to it under the particular circumstances. More concisely, it means dangerous in its normal or nondefective state. . . . We conclude that although its negligent use can be the basis for liability, neither the trampoline itself nor its ordinary use is abnormally dangerous or ultrahazardous. . . . Therefore, counts I and II were properly dismissed.

. . .

Accordingly, for the reasons set forth above, the decision of the trial court is affirmed.

Affirmed.

■■■ **NEGLIGENCE**

Negligence differs from an intentional tort in that negligent acts are neither expected nor intended, whereas an intentional tort can be both anticipated and intended. With negligence[17] a reasonable man in the position of the actor could have anticipated the harmful results. A teacher, for example, could not have reasonably foreseen that a hidden can in an incinerator would explode and injure a child when the teacher had sent the child to empty the classroom wastebaskets.[18]

An accident that could not have been prevented by reasonable care does not constitute negligence. Many times what first appears to be an accident can be traced to someone's negligence; however, instances of pure accident do occur in which someone is injured and no one is actually at fault. For example, when a child closed a music room door, cutting off the tip of another student's finger, the court found no negligence, merely an accident.[19]

Standard of Conduct

A negligent act in one situation may not be negligence under a different set of circumstances. No definite rules as to what constitutes negligence apply. The standard of conduct of the actor is the key. The conditions embracing a negligent act have been described in this fashion:

> It is fundamental that the standard of conduct which is the basis of the law of negligence is determined by balancing the risk, in the light of the social value of the interest threatened, and the probability and extent of the harm, against the value of the interest which the actor is seeking to protect, and the expedience of the course pursued.[20]

For the court to strike a balance between the threatened harm and the actor's conduct,[21] the court must establish a standard by which such activity can be measured. In attempting to set boundaries for negligent acts committed in different factual situations, the courts have developed the reasonableness theory. For negligence to be present, someone must sustain an injury resulting from an "unreasonable risk" taken by another person.

To determine unreasonableness the courts personify the test in terms of the "reasonable man."

The Reasonable Man

The reasonable man (more appropriately the reasonable person) has been described by different courts as a prudent man, a man of average prudence, a man of ordinary sense using ordinary care[22] and skill, and as a reasonably prudent man. He is an ideal, a model of conduct and a community standard. The model for the reasonable man, although a community ideal, varies in every case. His characteristics are (1) the physical attributes of the defendant himself, (2) normal intelligence, (3) normal perception and memory with a minimum level of information and experience common to the community, and (4) such superior skill and knowledge as the actor has or holds himself out to the public as having.[23] While this standard of behavior provides a framework for the whole theory of negligence, the exact formula varies with attributes of the persons involved and with the circumstances.

The reasonable man then has the same physical characteristics as the actor himself, and the acts in question are measured accordingly. Correspondingly, the man who is crippled is not held to the same standard as the man with no physical infirmities. The courts have also made allowances for the weaknesses or attributes connected with the sex[24] and age[25] of the individual.

The courts have not, however, been so lenient with individuals who have mental deficiencies. The courts have traditionally held that a person with less mental ability than an average person must adjust and conform to the rules of society. No allowance is given by the courts for subnormal mentality, but, if a person is actually insane, a more convincing argument can be made for allowing the particular incapacity.[26]

One such case illustrating this point of law occurred when a junior high pupil entered school and shot and killed the principal and wounded three other people, including a teacher and two students. The student was ruled criminally insane, but the wounded teacher and student filed a civil action in tort. The court found that although a person was criminally insane, civil liability in damages was an appropriate remedy. The court said that "American courts have unanimously chosen to impose liability on an insane person rather than leaving the loss on the innocent victim."[27]

ELEMENTS OF NEGLIGENCE

To have a valid cause of action for negligence, certain prerequisites must exist and are frequently divided into four categories: (1) a *duty* to protect others, (2) a failure to exercise an appropriate *standard of care,* (3) an existence of a casual connection between the act and injury, *proximate* or *legal cause,* and (4) an *injury,* damage or loss, must exist.

Duty

The routine of everyday life creates situations in which persons constantly create risks and incur obligations for the safety of others. In negligence cases, a person has a duty to abide by a standard of reasonable conduct in the face of apparent risks.[28]

The courts generally hold that no duty exists when the defendant could not have reasonably foreseen the danger of risk involved. A duty owed by one person to another may well intensify as the risk increases. In other words, the duty to protect another is proportional to the risk or hazard of a particular activity. In certain school functions where risks are greater to children, a teacher has an increased level of obligation or duty to the children. For example, whenever children perform a dangerous experiment, the teacher has a greater obligation for the children's safety than when he or she is merely supervising a study hall. One judge has explained the duty requirement in this way:

> Every person is negligent when, without intending any wrong, he does such an act or omits to take such a precaution that under the

circumstances he, as an ordinary prudent person, ought reasonably to foresee that he will thereby expose the interest of another to an unreasonable risk of harm. A person is required to take into account such of the surrounding circumstances as would be taken into account by a reasonably prudent person and possess such knowledge as is possessed by an ordinary reasonable person and to use such judgment and discretion as is exercised by persons of reasonable intelligence under the same or similar circumstance.[29]

A school district generally has no duty to protect children who leave school grounds without permission and then are injured. However, a California court ruled a school district is not liable for injuries by a truant under all circumstances, but a school district may be legally responsible if negligent supervision of the student while on school grounds was the proximate cause of the injuries which occurred off school premised.[30]

Generally, the law holds that a person is not liable for an omission to act when there is not some definite relationship between the parties; no general duty exists to aid a person in danger. For example, even though a moral duty may be present, no legal duty mandates that a mere bystander aid a drowning person. If, however, a person acts affirmatively to assist another in peril, he or she assumes a duty to the person and all his or her subsequent acts must be performed reasonably. Because of this requirement, passersby in many situations will not assist victims of auto wrecks or other mishaps. Some states, in order to encourage more humanitarian responses and to protect well-meaning rescuers, have enacted laws that protect the "good Samaritan" from liability.

While a teacher has no more duty than anyone else to be a "good Samaritan" to the general public, he or she does have an obligation or duty to help a student under his or her jurisdiction when injured at school. Because of the teacher-student relationship, a teacher may be liable for an omission to act as well as for an affirmative act. In such a case, though, the teacher is required to provide only such assistance as a person with the same training and experience in similar circumstances could reasonably provide.

Standard of Care

A legally recognized duty requires the actor to conform to a certain standard of conduct or care. As the risk involved in an act increases, the standard of care required of the actor likewise increases.[31] The standard of care of a woodshop teacher is, of course, greater than that of the school librarian because the risk of injury involved in handling power tools is much greater than the risk of being injured while reading a book. Similarly, chemistry classes require a high standard of care.[32]

The standard of care required by the courts is not uniform among all persons. Children and aged persons have generally been given substantially more leeway in their activities than is allowed a normal adult. While both children and aged persons are liable for their torts, they are not held to the same standard as others without impairments of age. Although it is difficult to pinpoint precise standards for determining the reasonableness of a child because of the great variations in age, maturity, and capacity, the courts have nevertheless established as a subjective test that which is "reasonable to expect of children of like age, intelligence, and experience."[33]

While most courts appear to follow the preceding criteria for determining negligence of children, some courts have applied criminal law standards that prescribe the following criteria:

a. Children between one and seven years cannot be liable for negligence. They theoretically have no capacity for negligence.[34]
b. Children between the ages of seven and fourteen have a *prima facie* case for incapacity, but it can be rebutted. In other words, children in this age group are presumed not to be capable of negligence until proved to the contrary.

Authorities generally agree that while arbitrary age limits for negligence have been established by some courts, it is not a generally acceptable rule of law. One court has said that the rule providing for a specific age limit:

. . . is arbitrary and open to the objection that one day's difference in age should not be the dividing line as to whether a child is capable of negligence or not. Under present-day circumstances, a child of six is permitted to assume many responsibilities. There is much opportunity for him to observe and thus become cognizant of the necessity for exercising some degree of care. Compulsory school attendance, the radio (television), the movies, and traffic conditions all tend to have this effect. Under the arbitrary cut-off rule, a child may be guilty of the most flagrant violation of duty and still be precluded from any presumption of negligence.

With regard to teachers or others in the teaching profession, the generally accepted standard of care would be that of a reasonably prudent teacher, not that of a reasonably prudent layperson. A New York court has put it this way:

> The standard of care required of an officer or employee of a public school is that which a person of ordinary prudence charged with his duties, would exercise under the same circumstances.[35]

A Vermont court has defined the "standard of care" owed to a pupil by a teacher in the following manner. A teacher's

> relationship to the pupils under his care and custody differs from that generally existing between a public employee and a member of the general public. In a limited sense the teacher stands in the parents' place in his relationship to a pupil . . . and has such a portion of the powers of the parent over the pupil as is necessary to carry out his employment. In such relationship, he owes his pupils the duty of supervision.[36]

While this is the prevailing view, some courts have held teachers to a lesser degree of care. These courts have said that a teacher can be charged only with reasonable care such as any person of ordinary prudence would exercise under comparable circumstances.

Proximate or Legal Cause

"Proximate cause" or "legal cause" is the connection between the act and the resultant injury. The question the court will ask is: "Was the injury a natural and probable consequence of the wrongful act, and ought it to have been foreseen in light of the attendant circumstances?"[37] The *Restatement of Torts* explains the necessity of adequate causal relation in this way:

> In order that a negligent actor shall be liable for another's harm, it is necessary not only that the actor's conduct be negligent toward the other, but also that the negligence of the actor be a legal cause of the other's harm.[38]

To establish proximate cause, there must first be a duty or obligation on the part of the actor to maintain a reasonable standard of conduct. In most negligence cases, however, the courts do not refer to proximate cause but rely solely on the duty or obligation of the defendant and the standard of conduct required to avoid liability. Proximate cause as a criterion of liability has been used most often where some doubt exists as to whether the injured person was within the zone of obvious danger.[39]

In these cases, the courts require that the negligence of the defendant must be the "substantial" cause of the harm to the plaintiff. In other words, the cause must be substantial enough to lead reasonable people to conclude it is indeed the cause of injury. If the negligence is not a substantial factor in producing the harm, then no liability follows.

The actor's negligent act must be in continuous and active force up to the actual harm, and the lapse of time must not be so great that contributing causes and intervening factors render the original negligent act to be an unsubstantial or insignificant force in the harm. Therefore, a teacher may be relieved of liability for negligent conduct if some intervening act is sufficient to break the causal connection between the act and a pupil's injury. For example, where a principal gave pupils permission to hold a race in a street and a "recklessly negligent" pupil ran into and injured a pedestrian, the court held that the causal relation was too remote to hold the principal liable.[40]

To break the chain of events causing injury, the intervening act must legally supersede the original negligent act. This rule is illustrated in a case in which a student was cleaning a power saw in shop class and another student turned on the switch, starting the machine in violation of safety rules. In this instance, the court held that the board's negligence in not having a guard over the belt drive was not the proximate or legal cause of the injury.[41]

A different result might have been reached, however, if the intervening act had been foreseeable and could have been prevented by reasonable care on the part of the defendant. For example, if a teacher sends a child on an errand across a busy street and a motorist, while driving carelessly, injures the child, both the teacher and the motorist may be liable. Here the intervening negligent act is not substantial enough to entirely overcome the original act. In an actual case demonstrating this point, a school bus driver was negligent when a student was struck by an automobile after alighting from the bus. The driver of the automobile was also negligent; however, the court held that the negligent bus driver had a continuing obligation that was not ended by the negligence of the driver of the automobile. The automobile driver's negligence did not constitute a sufficient break in the causal connection to be a defense for the bus driver and was not a superseding or intervening cause.[42]

Injury or Actual Loss

A plaintiff, of course, cannot recover unless actual injury is suffered and the plaintiff is able to show actual loss or damages resulting from the defendant's act. If the harm suffered is caused by more than one person, then damages may be apportioned among the tortfeasors. Sometimes both school district and teacher are joined together by a plaintiff student in a case wherein it is claimed that the injury was caused by acts of both parties.

---

*Breach of a Duty of Reasonable Care Imposes
Liability on a School Board*

—–—·—–—·—–—

Brown v. Tesack

—–—·—–—·—–—

Supreme Court of Louisiana, 1990.
566 So.2d 955.

Shortess, Justice, Pro Tem. On the afternoon of August 28, 1984, during summer recess, Leonard Kisack, age 13, and Gerald Preston (over 12) obtained four partially-used cans of flammable duplicating fluid from a red metal garbage dumpster located in the rear of the Henderson H. Dunn Elementary School (Dunn School). . . . Dunn School has a significant history of break-ins and vandalism. . . .

Some time prior to August 28, 1984, an employee of the Dunn School disposed of a number of cans containing varying amounts of duplicating fluid in the dumpster. Leonard and Gerald took four cans from the dumpster to a courtyard in the Desire Housing Project where they lived and began to play with the fluid by creating small fires. Plaintiff lived in the project but was not a party to these activities. Gerald returned to the dumpster for an additional can of fluid later that evening and began pouring fluid onto an already burning plastic milk carton. Plaintiff came around a corner and onto the scene, was struck in the chest by a "fireball," and was severely burned over an extensive portion of his face and body.

The trial court held that the Board had a duty to properly dispose of the duplicating fluid, citing its knowledge of the likelihood that children would play in and around the dumpster and that the Dunn School was commonly the target of vandals. Wilbert F. Dunn, principal at Dunn School, . . . testified that he took significant precautionary measures to keep the fluid secure, including: storing the unused cans in a room to which only he, the assistant principal, and the chief custodian possessed keys; . . . and collecting partially used cans and storing them securely during school holidays. Dunn candidly explained the purpose of these safeguards:

> We were aware of the fact that Dunn School had a history of break-ins and vandalism and we did not want duplicating fluid to be used in setting fires . . .

The duty to properly dispose of the duplicating fluid arose *because* the liquid is flammable and the risk of harm, *i.e.* physical injury resulting from its flammability, was specifically recognized by the Board. . . .

. . . The testimony is uncontroverted that a "fireball" was projected from the can of fluid. Moreover, the Board's policy manifests a self-imposed duty to properly *store* the substance. Clearly, these precautions were taken to ensure that the fluid did not fall into the hands of third parties—possibly children; the risk that it could were these precautions not taken, therefore, was not only foreseeable but *foreseen*. The operative risk of harm here, misuse of the fluid causing injury to persons or property from fire, was no less foreseeable. The record establishes that Board personnel were well aware that children played on the school grounds and rummaged in the dumpster. A duty was owed both to these children and to their potential victims. *See Brown,* 556 So.2d at 89. (Plotkin, J., dissenting) ("there is no difference between the recognizable risk of a minor's misuse of an inherently dangerous object and the likelihood that the minor will cause personal or property damages to others). We agree . . . "children who possess a flammable substance can be expected to light it, to attract other children to join in the play and to commit criminal acts or engage in other misadventures."

We conclude that plaintiff's injuries were reasonably foreseeable. Additionally, the fact that the conduct (disposal of a flammable substance) was squarely within the duty and that the injuries were exactly those that the duty was imposed to prevent, is suggestive that the conduct fell short of that required by, *i.e.* was a breach of, the duty. . . . The recognition by the Board that this duplicating fluid was a dangerous substance to be treated with special precautions, leads directly to the conclusion that it was not reasonable to dispose of several partially full cans in the Dunn School dumpster.

We must conclude that the evidence does show a breach of the duty to properly dispose of the duplicating fluid, irrespective of the length of time that the cans remained in the dumpster prior to the accident. Dunn testified the gates at the school remained open in the summer time as no attempt was made to stop children from playing on the grounds, and it would be futile to try. The dumpster was there and easily accessible to anyone on the grounds. Putting children and flammable mixtures together, unfortunately, more often than not, produces combustion. The risk of burn injuries resulting from children playing with the duplicating fluid was squarely within the scope of the duty to properly dispose of the fluid, and the Board must share responsibility for plaintiff's injuries.

. . . We note that the School Board was aware of the danger that children might obtain the flammable substance and create fires and that the risk was significant inasmuch as fires could have been started in or spread to the nearby housing project. There was no suggestion that the duplicating fluid was old or otherwise unusable, thus disposal of partially full cans would seem unnecessary; if disposal was necessary, some other method should have been used. The Board occupied a superior position to the children; the duty to properly dispose of the fluid was imposed to prevent a situation where the conduct of third parties, possibly children, could cause injury. . . .

The judgments of the trial court and court of appeal dismissing plaintiff's suit against the School Board are reversed.

*School Bus Driver's Negligence Is
Proximate Cause of Injury*

—··—··—··—··—

Blair v. Board of Education of Sherburne-Earlville Central School

—··—··—··—··—

Supreme Court, Appellate Division,
Third Department, 1982.
86 A.D.2d 933, 448 N.Y.S.2d 566.

MEMORANDUM BY THE COURT. . . .
Bobby Wayne Blair allegedly sustained permanent serious injuries to his right eye when he was struck in that eye by an object thrown by one of the other passengers on the bus, and plaintiffs assert that these injuries were caused by defendants' negligence in failing to properly supervise and control the activities on the bus. Following a jury trial, a verdict was returned in the amounts of $100,000 in favor of Bobby Wayne Blair and $10,000 in favor of Richard C. Blair, and the trial court set aside the $10,000 verdict as excessive and ordered a new trial unless Richard C. Blair stipulated to accept $2,602.73. . . .

Seeking a reversal of the judgment at Trial Term, defendants basically argue that plaintiffs failed to prove at trial the existence of any culpable negligence on the part of defendants. We find their arguments unpersuasive. In his testimony, defendant Brown conceded that his duties as a school bus driver included the maintenance of order on the bus by the prevention of, *inter alia,* tomfoolery and the throwing of things around the bus. Significantly, there is also testimony from several of the passengers on this bus that this kind of activity had been occurring for fifteen minutes prior to Bobby Wayne Blair's injury and that defendant Brown took no action to stop it. One witness even testified that she told the bus driver of the unruly activity prior to the injury, but that he paid no attention to her. Under these circumstances, defendants' arguments that the disruptive and dangerous

actions of some of the pupils were unanticipated and that defendant Brown could not have foreseen the danger to his passengers arising from such activity ring hollow, and the jury could reasonably conclude that defendants' negligent supervision of the activity on bus No. 72 was a proximate cause of Bobby Wayne Blair's injuries. . . .

Judgment affirmed, with costs.

NOTES

1. *Adequate Supervision.* A student was awarded damages for an injury occurring when the student slipped and cut his face on rocks or glass on the playground during a fight with another student. The court found that the playground had not been adequately supervised and that the school district had allowed a hazard to exist that could injure students. *Laneheart v. Orleans Parish School Bd.,* 524 So. 2d 138 (La. App. 4th Cir. 1988).

2. *Adequate Supervision on a Field Trip.* A student on a field trip was hit by an automobile while crossing a street and sued two teachers for negligence. The court noted that the teachers had admonished the students to be careful in crossing the street, that the student was thirteen years old, and the street was not unreasonably dangerous. The court concluded that the teachers had not acted unreasonably and had no duty to personally escort students across streets. *King v. Kartanson,* 720 S.W. 2d 65 (Tenn. App. 1986).

3. *Hazardous Conditions.* The school district has a duty to maintain hazard-free conditions for students. A Massachusetts court held that glass panels, which were not shatterproof, constituted a dangerous condition rendering the city of Boston liable when a student lacerated tendons and injured nerves in his hand when he put his hand through a glass panel. *Johnson v. City of Boston,* 22 Mass. App. Ct. 24, 490 N.E. 2d 1204 (1986).

4. Dangerous conditions near or about school may require that the school district exercise extra care in protecting students from injury. Where a student was injured

on a construction site near school, the court held that daily warnings to students about the dangerous conditions were insufficient and that the school was negligent because it did not post a teacher to guard the construction site. *Dist. of Columbia v. Royal*, 465 A. 2d 367 (D.C. App. 1983).

5. The presence of rocks on playground does not create an unreasonably hazardous condition. *Hampton v. Orleans Parish School Board*, 422 So. 2d 202 (La. App. 1982).

6. *Proximate Cause.* In *Holler v. Lowery*, a Maryland case, the court said:

> There is no mystery in the doctrine of proximate cause. It rests upon common sense rather than legal formula. Expressed in the simplest terms it means that negligence is not actionable unless it, without the intervention of any independent factor causes the harm complained of. It involves of course the idea of continuity, that the negligent act continuously extends through every event, fact, act and occurrence related to the tortious conduct of the defendant and is itself the logical and natural cause of the injury complained of. In the statement of the doctrine an intervening cause means not a concurrent and contributing cause, but a superseding cause, which is itself the natural and logical cause of the harm. 175 Md. 149, 161, 200 A. 353, 358 (1938).

7. *Foreseeability.* The test of foreseeability was well stated in *McLeod v. Grant County School Dist. No. 128*, 42 Wn.2d 316, 255 P.2d 360 (1953), a case that held the school district answerable in damages to a girl who was attacked in an unlighted room adjacent to the school gymnasium. There the court said:

> Whether foreseeability is being considered from the standpoint of negligence or proximate cause, the pertinent inquiry is not whether the actual harm was of a particular kind which was expectable. Rather, the question is whether the actual harm fell within a general field of danger which

should have been anticipated. 42 Wn.2d at 321, 255 P.2d at 363.

The court further stated:

> The harm which came to appellant was not caused by the direct act or omission of the school district, but by the intervening act of third persons. The fact that the danger stems from such an intervening act, however, does not of itself exonerate a defendant from negligence. If, under the assumed facts, such intervening force is reasonably foreseeable, a finding of negligence may be predicated thereon. 42 Wn.2d at 320, 255 P.2d at 362.

8. The Supreme Court of California has held that another student's misconduct was the immediate precipitating cause of injury does not compel a conclusion that negligent supervision by the teacher was not the proximate cause of a student's death. Neither the mere involvement of a third party nor the party's own wrongful conduct is sufficient in itself to absolve the defendants of liability, once a negligent failure to provide adequate supervision is shown. *Dailey v. Los Angeles Unified School Dist.*, 2 Cal.3d 741, 87 Cal.Rptr. 376, 470 P.2d 360 (1970).

9. *Duty.* A Florida court has spoken about the duty owed by the school to the student:

> To sustain a cause of action in negligence, a complaint must allege ultimate facts which establish a relationship between the parties giving rise to a legal duty on the part of the defendant to protect the plaintiff from the injury of which he complains. It must also show that the defendant negligently breached that duty, and that the plaintiff's injury was proximately caused .by the defendant's negligence.
> *Ankers v. District School Board of Pasco County*, 406 So.2d 72 (Fla.App.1981).

10. *Intervening Act.* The intervening act of a student throwing a bamboo high-jump cross bar, after school hours, and striking another student in the eye was the sole

proximate cause of injury. High jumping equipment is not an "inherently dangerous" instrumentality that imposes a duty on teacher or school to provide supervision during nonschool hours. *Bush v. Smith*, 154 Ind.App. 382, 289 N.E.2d 800 (1972).

Intervening negligence of third party does not break proximate cause relieving original tortfeasor of his negligence if intervening negligence is foreseeable. *Leahy v. School Board of Hernando Co.*, 450 So.2d 883 (Fla.App. 1984).

11. A school district's responsibility does not extend off school grounds so as to incur liability unless a failure of reasonable care on the part of the school is the proximate cause of injury. Where a student was injured in an auto crash after he had obtained keys to a car, left school, and took other students joyriding, the court ruled that the failure of the school to notify parents of the students' truancy was not the proximate cause of the injury. *Palella v. Ulmer*, 136 Misc. 2d 34, 518 N.Y.S. 2d 91 (1987).

◼◼◼ DEFENSES FOR NEGLIGENCE

In all cases involving negligence, the defendant may attempt to show that he or she is not negligent because the injury was a mere accident, that his or her act was not the proximate or legal cause of injury, or that some other act intervened and was responsible for the injury. However, aside from these essentials of a tort claim, other rejoinders against negligence can be classified as defenses. The most common of these are (1) contributory negligence, (2) comparative negligence, (3) assumption of risk, and (4) immunity.

Of these defenses, contributory negligence and assumption of risk are most often used in school law cases. Immunity is a defense found in both common and statutory law that derives from the state's sovereignty. Each of these concepts is briefly explained below.

Contributory Negligence

Contributory negligence involves some fault or breach of duty on the part of the injured person, or failure to exercise the required standard of care for his or her own safety. One court explained contributory negligence as conduct on the part of the injured party that caused or contributed to the injury and that would not have been done by a person exercising ordinary prudence under the circumstances.[43] The *Restatement of Torts* defines contributory negligence in much the same manner:

> [C]onduct on the part of the plaintiff which falls below the standard to which he should conform for his own protection, and which is legally contributing cause cooperating with the negligence of the defendant in bringing about the plaintiff's harm.[44]

As previously pointed out, a child is capable of negligence and his or her failure to conform to a required standard of conduct for a child of the same age, physical characteristics, sex, and training will result in the court assigning fault to his or her actions. Thus, if an injured child is negligent and his or her negligence contributes to the harm, then a defendant, who is also negligent, may be completely absolved from liability. If the student has superior knowledge that would be protective, the courts will take it into consideration in adjudging fault. In a case in which students knew that chemicals should not be held near a flame and the students intentionally set fire to the experiment and injury resulted, the court held the students were contributorily negligent because they should have known the consequences.[45]

However, since a child is not expected to act with the same standard of care as an adult, teachers have more difficulty in showing contributory negligence than if the plaintiff were an adult. A child is by nature careless and often negligent and, knowing this, a teacher should allow for an additional margin of safety. This is especially true with younger children. In fact, courts have said that where a child is concerned, the test to be employed is whether the child has committed a gross disregard of safety in the face of known, perceived, and understood dangers.[46]

In a case in which contributory negligence was found, a boy climbed on top of wire screening, fell through a hole, and was injured. The jury found the boy to be contributorily at fault because he did not exercise a reasonable degree of care for his own protection.[47]

Another court has held that a pupil who was injured when he mixed chemicals in a school laboratory was guilty of contributory negligence because he knew the chemicals were dangerous.[48]

If a plaintiff's negligence or fault contributes to the injury, the court will bar recovery of any damages at all. Some courts have held that complete barring of any damages because of contributory fault is perhaps a little drastic and have, therefore, endeavored to prorate damages based on the degree of fault. This results in what is known as comparative negligence.

Comparative Negligence

When contributory negligence on the part of the plaintiff is shown, the defendant is usually completely absolved from all liability. This, some courts and legislatures have felt, works a hardship on the negligent plaintiff, who suffers injury but can recover nothing from the negligent defendant. This concern for the injured party has led legislatures in some states to enact statutes to determine degree of negligence and to allow recovery based on the relative degree of fault. While the specific provisions of "comparative negligence" statutes vary from state to state, the concept works this way: If the plaintiff's fault is found to be about equal to the defendant's, the plaintiff will recover one-half the damages and must bear the remainder of the loss himself. If the plaintiff's negligence amounted to one-third the fault and the defendant's two-thirds, the plaintiff could recover two-thirds of the damages.

Assumption of Risk

Assumption of risk is another defense against negligence. Here the plaintiff acts in a manner that effectively relieves the defendant of his or her duty or obligation of conduct. The plaintiff by expressed or implied agreement recognizes the danger and assumes the risk. The defendant is thereby under no legal duty to protect the plaintiff. With knowledge of the danger, the plaintiff voluntarily enters into a relationship with the defendant, and by so doing agrees to take his or her chances.[49]

Plaintiff's knowledge and awareness of the danger is an important factor in this defense. For example, a boy playing basketball was injured when his arm went through a glass pane in a door immediately behind the basketball backboard. The court later said that the boy had not assumed the risk of such an injury. The boy did not know the glass in the door was not shatterproof.[50] However, another court held that a boy had assumed the risk when he suffered an injury by colliding with a doorjamb in a brick wall while playing as a voluntary member of a team in a school gymnasium. The boy had played in the gym previously and knew the location of the basket, the door, and the wall and, therefore, was aware of the danger involved in voluntarily playing in this particular gymnasium.[51] In a case in which a batter in a softball game struck a classmate with the bat who was sitting on the third base line, the court said the child who was struck either assumed the risk or was contributorily negligent.[52]

Courts have generally established that the participant in athletic events, whether intramural or interscholastic, assumes the risk of the normal hazards of the game. This rule also applies to spectators attending sports or amusement activities. Spectators assume all the obvious or normal risks of being hurt by flying balls,[53] fireworks,[54] or the struggles of combatants.[55]

Everyone has seen spectators knocked down along the sidelines of football games by players careening off the field. A high school girl was injured precisely in this fashion as she was standing by the sidelines and was run over by football players. The court found against the plaintiff in following prevailing precedent and said that a spectator at a sporting event assumes risks incident to the game. This is especially true when the spectator chooses to stay at an unsafe place despite the availability of protected seating.[56]

Essential to the doctrine of assumption of risk is that the plaintiff have knowledge of the risks; if she is ignorant of the conditions and dangers, she does not assume the risk. If reasonable precautions are not taken to determine the hazards involved, then she has not assumed the risk but may have been contributorily negligent instead. However, neither a participant nor a spectator assumes the risk for negligence or willful or wanton conduct of others. For example, a spectator at an athletic contest does not assume the risk of the stands falling at a football game, nor does she assume that by attending a baseball game, a player will intentionally throw a bat into the stands.

Immunity

Immunity from tort liability is generally conferred on: (1) national and state governments, unless abrogated by statute; (2) public officials performing quasi-judicial or discretionary functions; (3) charitable organizations, granted immunity in some states; (4) infants, under certain conditions; and (5) in some cases, insane persons.

Where public schools are concerned, the defense of immunity is usually employed to protect the public school district against liability.[57] This governmental or sovereign immunity is a historical and common-law precedent that protects a state agency against liability for its torts. Because of the importance of this concept and its frequent applicability in public school tort cases, governmental or sovereign immunity is treated separately in Chapter 13.

Intervening Causative Factor May Absolve School from Liability

— — — — — — — —

Albers v. Independent School District No. 302 of Lewis County

— — — — — — — —

Supreme Court of Idaho, 1971.
94 Idaho 342, 487 P.2d 936.

McFADDEN, Justice. This action was instituted by appellant Ray Albers, the father of Morris Albers, a minor, to recover damages from Independent School District No. 302 of Lewis County, respondent, for personal injuries suffered by his son Morris. A motion for summary judgment was made by the school district which the trial court granted. We affirm this judgment. . . .

The record discloses that on December 23, 1967, during the Christmas holiday, Morris Albers, with five other boys, drove to the high school gymnasium of the district with the intention of playing an informal basketball game. Upon arrival they found the entrance locked; however, the custodian was working on the premises and was persuaded, perhaps reluctantly, to open the door and let the youths use the basketball court. The custodian went about his cleaning duties after admitting the boys.

Morris undertook to clean the playing surface of the gymnasium, by sweeping the court with a wide dust mop or broom for five or ten minutes, while his friends changed clothes. The boys then engaged in warming up activities, shooting baskets, using two worn leather basketballs which they found lying about, the equipment room of the gymnasium being locked.

At the time Morris was wearing standard basketball shoes and slacks. He was a member of the high school basketball team, an accomplished high school athlete, and participated in several other team sports. At least one of the other five boys was a teammate of his on the basketball team.

After warming up the boys split into two teams and played a "half-court" basketball game. Morris' deposition reflects that "it was a real clean game" from the standpoint of fouls and close calls. Sometime into their play a shot came off the backboard and "headed out towards [the] out of bounds line on the east side of the gym." Morris and an opposing player ran for the loose ball. As Morris reached to pick it up the two boys collided, Morris hitting his head against his opponent's hip. Morris fell to the floor on his back in a semi-conscious state. Morris suffered a fracture in the cervical area of his spine necessitating surgical correction and prolonged hospitalization. . . .

Generally, schools owe a duty to supervise the activities of their students whether they be engaged in curricular activities or non-required but school sponsored extracurricular activities. . . . Further, a school must exercise ordinary care to keep its premises and facilities in reasonably safe condition for the use of minors who foreseeably will make use of the premises and facilities. . . .

On the claim that the school district breached its duty to supervise the boys' game, the record lacks any evidence as to how the presence of a coach or teacher would have prevented the collision of the boys chasing the rebounding basketball. . . . Physical contact in such a situation in an athletic contest is foreseeable and expected. The general rule is that participants in an athletic contest accept the normal physical contact of the particular sport. . . . Nothing in the record would justify an exception to the rule here.

Regarding the allegation that the school district was negligent in allowing the youths to play on a dirty playing surface, the deposition of Morris Albers and his statements quoted above show there was no breach of any such duty. He had personally cleaned the floor and stated he saw no water spots or anything of that nature on the floor. . . .

The summary judgment of the trial court is affirmed. Costs to respondent.

Reasonable Supervision Does Not Require Constant Unremitting Scrutiny

—·—·—·—·—·—

Fagan v. Summers

—·—·—·—·—·—

Supreme Court of Wyoming, 1972.
498 P.2d 1227.

McINTYRE, Chief Justice. This case involves a suit for damages brought on behalf of seven-year-old George Fagan against a teacher's aide, Mrs. Lloyd Summers, and Park County School District No. 1.

During a noon recess a fellow student threw a small rock which hit a larger rock on the ground and then bounced up and struck George Fagan, causing him to lose the sight in his left eye. . . .

The trial court granted summary judgment for both Mrs. Summers and the school district. . . .

Regarding defendant Summers, she has stated by affidavit that she walked past the plaintiff and five or six other boys twice prior to the accident, while they were sitting on the ground near the school building. The boys were laughing and talking and she saw nothing out of the ordinary. After Mrs. Summers strolled by this group of youngsters, she had walked approximately twenty-five feet (taking about thirty seconds) when she heard an outcry from plaintiff. The accident happened in that interval.

There is no evidence or indication that Mrs. Summers' explanation is not true. Also, it is claimed on behalf of defendants that Mrs. Summers was reliable, conscientious and capable in her work and a good playground supervisor. This does not appear to be challenged in any of the evidence.

There is no requirement for a teacher to have under constant and unremitting scrutiny all precise spots where every phase of play activities is being pursued; and there is no compulsion that general supervision be continuous and direct at all times and all places. . . .

In *Butler v. District of Columbia,* 135 U.S.App.D.C. 203, 417 F.2d 1150, 1152, the court considered it common knowledge, susceptible of judicial notice, that small boys may indulge in horseplay when a teacher's back is turned. . . .

A teacher cannot anticipate the varied and unexpected acts which occur daily in and about the school premises. Where the time between an act of a student and injury to a fellow student is so short that the teacher has no opportunity to prevent injury, it cannot be said that negligence of the teacher is a proximate cause of the injury. . . .

As far as the instant case is concerned, counsel for appellant was asked during oral argument what should have been done by Mrs. Summers which was not done. His answer was to the effect that she could really not have done more than she did do and she could probably be dismissed from the suit. We consider counsel's answer frank and honest. In view of it and in view of what we have said about the absence of proximate cause on the part of Mrs. Summers, we hold summary judgment for her was proper.

When counsel for appellant was asked during oral argument what the district should have done which was not done, his answer was that the district should have put the playground in better shape and should have provided more supervisors.

There is evidence that construction of a new school building was taking place. In connection with this construction, the blacktop of the playground had been torn up leaving clods of blacktop and a rough playground. It is also shown that this condition remained for approximately two years.

Although plaintiff alleged in his complaint that he had been hit with a piece of torn-up blacktop, counsel for appellant conceded in oral argument, as far as the record is concerned, plaintiff was hit with a rock. Counsel then advanced the theory that when the blacktop was torn up, it left rocks from beneath exposed.

There would be a possibility of this set of facts being proved if trial were had. Therefore, we will assume, for purposes of considering the propriety of summary judgment, that the playground was rough for a long period of time, with the blacktop torn up and rocks from beneath exposed. Although there appears to be no evidence as to where the rock which struck plaintiff came from, we will assume it was one which had been beneath the blacktop prior to ripping up of such blacktop.

We realize there are cases which hold a school district can be liable for injury resulting from a dangerous and defective condition of a playground. We have found no case, however, which holds rocks on the ground to be a dangerous and defective condition. Left on the ground, a rock will hurt no one.

Therefore, if we were to assume the school district was negligent for allowing rocks to be on the playground, we would have to hold the act of a third person who throws one of the rocks and injures the plaintiff an intervening cause of the accident. . . .

In the case before us, plaintiff was not injured by negligence, if any, from rocks being on the playground. The injury was clearly caused by the intervening act of a third person—the boy who picked up and threw the rock. Appellant cites no authority for the proposition that such a result was reasonably foreseeable.

It is apparent from all we have said that the proximate cause of George Fagan's injury was the act of his fellow student in throwing a rock. It was not the failure of the Park County School District No. 1 to maintain the playground in a safe condition.

Appellant has made no effort to show that supervision of the playground was inadequate or that the accident would have been prevented if more supervisors had been present. We need not discuss counsel's casual suggestion that there may have been negligence in this regard.

Summary judgment for Mrs. Summers and for the school district was justified and proper. Affirmed.

Momentary Absence from Classroom Does Not Constitute Negligence

–– · –– · –– · –– · ––

Simonetti v. School District of Philadelphia

–– · –– · –– · –– · ––

Superior Court of Pennsylvania, 1982.
308 Pa.Super. 555, 454 A.2d 1038.

WIEAND, Judge. Richard Simonetti, a fifth-grade student, returned to the classroom from recess and was struck in the left eye by a pencil which had been propelled from the hand of a classmate when he tripped. The teacher, an employee of the School District of Philadelphia, was outside the classroom, standing at the door, when Simonetti was injured. There she was engaged in monitoring the return of her students from recess and talking with another teacher. The student who dropped or threw the pencil and two other students had been required to remain in the classroom during recess as punishment for misbehavior at breakfast. They had been talking with the teacher during the recess period and were instructed to take their seats when the teacher stepped outside the classroom to supervise the return of the students from recess.

In an action against the School District, it was contended by Simonetti that the teacher had been negligent in failing to provide adequate classroom supervision. . . . The teacher, it may confidently be observed, could not have been at two places at the same time. With equal confidence, it can be said that it was not negligence for the teacher to give priority to an entire class of approximately thirty students returning from recess rather than to remain in the classroom to supervise three students who had been required to stay in the classroom during the recess period.

It is common knowledge that children may indulge in horseplay. They may throw a pencil, shoot a paper clip or snap a rubber band when a teacher is absent or turns his or her back. In the instant case, the teacher attempted to guard against any horseplay by instructing the three students who were in the classroom to return to their seats and remain there. While these students were capable of free spirits and were even being punished for unrelated misconduct at breakfast, there is no evidence that they were hellions who required constant custody.

To require the teacher to anticipate the events which occurred while she was outside the classroom door would be to hold that a teacher is required to anticipate the myriad of unexpected acts which occur daily in classrooms in every school in the land. This is not the law, and we perceive no good reason for imposing such an absolute standard on teachers and school districts.

The judgment is reversed and is now entered for the appellant.

Injured Student with Knowledge of Risk Involved Is Contributorily Negligent

–– · –– · –– · –– · ––

Hutchison v. Toews

–– · –– · –– · –– · ––

Court of Appeals of Oregon, Department 2, 1970.
4 Or.App. 19, 476 P.2d 811.

LANGTRY, Judge. Plaintiff appeals from a judgment of involuntary nonsuit, entered on motion of both defendants at the conclusion of the plaintiff's case.

Plaintiff and his friend, Phillip Brown, both fifteen years old, attempted to shoot a homemade pipe cannon which exploded, injuring plaintiff's hands. They had made the explosive charge by mixing potassium chlorate and powdered sugar.

Brown, as plaintiff's witness, testified that he and the plaintiff had "badgered" defendant Toews, the chemistry teacher at Phoenix High School, for potassium chlorate to use in fireworks experimentation. He said they had asked Mr. Toews for the material about a dozen times. The plaintiff said five or six times. Finally, Mr. Toews had given them some powdered potassium chlorate, which they put in a baby food jar. A day or two later, when Mr. Toews left the separate chemical storage room unattended while he stepped into the adjoining chemistry classroom, Brown took, without Mr. Toews' knowledge or permission, some crystalline potassium chlorate also stored there. Brown positively identified this crystalline potassium chlorate as the substance used in the explosion. He was the one who mixed the ingredients. The plaintiff equivocated, first indicating that the powdered substance was what was used, but on cross-examination he said, "It looked like crystal." Brown waited approximately two years after the accident before he revealed to anyone that he had taken the crystalline substance and that it had caused the explosion. The plaintiff did not reveal that he knew the crystalline substance had been taken until after Brown's disclosure of the true facts. The injury occurred in November 1965. Plaintiff commenced this action for damages against defendant Toews only in June 1966, and filed an amended complaint in August 1967. In these complaints, plaintiff alleged that defendant Toews "supplied" the potassium chlorate to him.   . . .

Prosser says:

> [T]he kind of contributory negligence which consists of voluntary exposure to a known danger, and so amounts to assumption of risk, is ordinarily a defense   . . . . Prosser, Torts 539, § 78 (3rd ed.1964).

We think the evidence construed in the light most favorable to plaintiff . . . justifies the judgment of the court. The boys had purchased from a mail order firm in Michigan a pamphlet which gave 100 formulas for explosives. Together, they built the cannon and conducted their experiments. They admitted that they had looked at the warnings in the pamphlet. They had shown the pamphlet to defendant Toews, and he had cautioned them, and told them they should have supervision. He had declined their invitation to supervise them because of another commitment. Among other things, the pamphlet warned:

> Some of the formulas listed in this booklet are very dangerous to make. Therefore, it is strongly suggested that the making of fireworks be left in the hands of the experienced.

. . . They had previously experimented with homemade gunpowder in the cannon and in doing so had used up all of their fuses. When they mixed and placed the charge of potassium chlorate and powdered sugar in the cannon, they put the head of a paper match into the fuse hole and tried to light the paper end of the match in order to have time to take over before the explosion. When Brown tried to light the paper match, wind impeded him. On Brown's request, plaintiff held his hands around the fuse hole to shield it from the wind. The charge exploded, and the closed pipe end "peeled like a banana." Plaintiff's hands were severely injured. The evidence is lengthy, but it is replete with statements from both of the boys that they knew the experiment conducted was dangerous. Plaintiff testified on cross-examination he knew "That you might get burned if you held onto it, or if you stood too close to it when it did shoot . . . that it might fly up or hit you in the face . . . ."

Plaintiff testified he knew that the pamphlet said the formula was very powerful.

. . .

There are many cases involving tort liability of suppliers of explosives to children. No purpose is served by a detailed discussion of them here. We note that they usually turn on whether the plaintiff had or should have had knowledge and understanding so that he could have avoided the explosion.   . . .

In the case at bar, the only reasonable conclusion from the evidence was that plaintiff had knowledge of the risk involved, and that he was contributorily negligent as a matter of law.

Affirmed.

Student's Intervening Culpable Act in Stealing Chemicals Constituted Superseding Force Absolving School from Liability

------·---·---·---

Brazell v. Board of Education of Niskayuna Public Schools

------·---·---·---

Supreme Court, Appellate Division, Third Department, 1990.
161 A.D. 2d 1086, 557 N.Y.S.2d 645.

HARVEY, Justice. . . . Plaintiff commenced this personal injury action to recover for damages caused when her teen-aged son Colin stole an oxidizing agent (sodium chlorate) from defendant's science lab during school hours on April 23, 1987. A fire somehow started later that night at plaintiff's home and burned Colin's leg and personal property belonging to plaintiff. As a result, plaintiff basically alleges that defendant negligently supervised and allowed the boy to have access to the dangerous chemical without adequate warnings or precautions. Defendant denied these allegations and raised contributory negligence as a defense. Defendant brought a motion for summary judgment claiming, among other things, that Colin's wrongful act in stealing the chemicals was the sole proximate cause of his injuries. Supreme Court denied defendant's motion and this appeal ensued.

There must be a reversal. In our view, Supreme Court incorrectly denied defendant's motion for summary judgment. . . . In his testimony, Colin relates that his science class on the day of the accident was conducted from approximately 1:45 P.M. to around 2:30 P.M. An assignment that day was to measure out five grams of sodium chlorate with his lab partner to put aside for an experiment for the next class. After taking the container and measuring the five grams, Colin admitted he took an unspecified extra amount of the chemical and secreted it in his pants pocket so that he could take it home to burn with matches. He claims that he was told by another student that the chemical would burn and sparkle like fire crackers if ignited. Significantly, Colin admits that his teacher specifically told the class to never remove chemicals from the classroom and also that his teacher had gone over the safety procedures in the classroom with him. Once Colin had taken the chemical, he carried it around in his pocket all day until approximately 10:00 P.M. when he was upstairs in his bedroom with two younger cousins. At that time, Colin claimed that the chemical spontaneously ignited in his pocket causing him injuries. Although Colin claimed that there were no matches in his room, this assertion is contradicted by the police report attached to defendant's papers stating that two matchbook pieces were found at the scene.

Based on this and other information, defendant established its entitlement to summary judgment as a matter of law. Plaintiff argues that there are still questions of fact as to how detailed the science teacher's warnings were and how adequate the safety precautions were. Plaintiff points out, based on the teacher's deposition, that the chemical was not kept in a locked desk. However, because the chemical was being used in class that day and Colin received it from the teacher himself for class use, this fact is hardly surprising and raises no inference of negligence. In any event, it is our opinion that even if the science teacher was negligent in any way by reason of being unable to watch some 28 students every minute of the time they were there, Colin's intervening culpable act in intentionally stealing the chemical constituted a superseding force absolving defendant from any liability . . . . It is clear from Colin's own testimony that his conduct, aside from being unforeseeable by others, went beyond mere contributory negligence and rose to such a level of culpability as to replace any negligence on the part of defendant as the legal cause of the accident . . . ..

. . . Here, Colin's classroom was supervised, the rules were clear and there is no evidence that anyone knew, other than the teenaged boys themselves, that chemicals were being taken. . . . The fact that it was possible to sneak chemicals out of the room without the teacher's knowledge does not make the outcome that occurred in this case a probable one . . . . "In short, a series of new and unexpected causes intervened and had to intervene" before the injuries to Colin, some seven to eight hours after the theft, could occur. Because we perceive no issues of fact requiring resolution at trial, we reverse and grant defendant's motion for summary judgment dismissing the complaint.

Order reversed, on the law, without costs, motion granted, summary judgment awarded to defendant and complaint dismissed.

State Statute May Require Plaintiff to Show That the School District Is Grossly Negligent Before Liability May Ensue; Gross Negligence Requires a Higher, More Difficult Standard of Proof

- - - - - - - - - -

Richardson v. Hambright

- - - - - - - - - -

Supreme Court of South Carolina, 1988.
296 S.C. 504, 374 S.E. 2d 296.

HARWELL, Justice. . . .

This case centers around a District "Driving/Riding" policy requiring parental permission for students choosing to ride to the area vocational center in private vehicles instead of riding the bus provided by the District. Appellant and two other students were passengers in a pick-up truck driven by a fourth student. None of the four students had the required parental permission to travel in a private vehicle. While en route to the vocational center, the pick-up truck crashed into a large commercial vehicle. The driver and two other passengers were killed and appellant was seriously injured.

The policy provided that students who had parental permission would be issued special identification cards to carry. The policy provided that frequent car checks would occur and that "any member of the school administration, faculty, staff or law enforcement personnel" could conduct a check. Random checks were to be made at the vocational center once or twice a week. "All-school" checks were to be conducted once or twice a month. . . . Both appellant and his mother admitted knowledge of the policy. Appellant rode the bus on the first four days of the week, but rode in the truck on the last day. No checks were made during this week. Appellant submits that failing to conduct checks during this week amounted to gross negligence on the part of the District. We disagree.

Appellant's action is brought pursuant to the recently enacted "South Carolina Tort Claims Act", which provides that a " . . . governmental entity is not liable for loss resulting from: . . . responsibility or duty including but not limited to supervision, protection, control, confinement, or custody of any student . . . except when the responsibility or duty is exercised in a grossly negligent manner . . . " S.C.Code Ann. § 15–78–60(a)(25) (Cum.Supp.1987). Gross negligence is the intentional, conscious failure to do something which it is incumbent upon one to do or the doing of a thing intentionally that one ought not to do. . . . It is a failure to exercise slight care. . . . The District's failure to conduct an ID check during the one week of school when this accident occurred simply does not constitute an intentional and conscious failure. The District took steps to make all students aware of the policy by reviewing it with them during the first week of school. Copies of the policy were sent home to parents. This policy included a statement on safety; it also outlined enforcement procedures. The facts show, at the very least, that the District exercised "slight care."

We agree with the trial court's ruling that the District was not grossly negligent and that summary judgment was appropriate as a matter of law. It is not necessary to reach the remaining issues advanced by appellant. The judgment of the trial court is hereby

Affirmed.

NOTES

1. *Proper Supervision.* If a rule can be developed from the teacher liability cases, it is this: a teacher's absence from the classroom, or failure to properly supervise students' activities, is not likely to give rise to a cause of action for injury to a student, unless under all the circumstances the possibility of injury is reasonably foreseeable. In *Carroll v. Fitzsimmons,* 153 Colo. 1, 3, 384 P.2d 81, 82 (1963), the Supreme Court of Colorado had before it the question whether an allegation "that the plaintiff was struck in the eye by a rock thrown by a fellow student" and "that the defendant teacher permitted the rock to be thrown" stated a cause of action. In affirming the dismissal of the complaint, the court quoted from *Nestor v. City of New York,* supra, 28 Misc.2d 70, 71, 211 N.Y.S.2d 975, 977 (1961):

> There is no requirement that the teacher have under constant and unremitting scrutiny the precise spots wherein every phase of play activity is being pursued; nor is there compulsion that the general supervision be continuous and direct.

2. Requiring students to run to the dressing room when time between classes is short does not create an unreasonable risk. *Driscol v. Delphi Community School Corp.,* 155 Ind.App. 56, 290 N.E.2d 769 (1972).

3. In preparation of a project for a science fair, a girl was burned when students attempted to light a defective burner that had gone out and alcohol exploded after the teacher had set the experiment up, checked that it worked correctly, and returned to his regular class. The court, in holding the teacher liable for negligence, said: "where one creates, deals in, handles or distributes an inherently dangerous object or substance . . . an extraordinary degree of care is required of those responsible . . . . The duty is particularly heavy where children are exposed to

a dangerous condition which they may not appreciate." The duty was to either positively warn the students not to try to light the burner or to personally supervise; the teacher did neither. *Station v. Travelers Insurance Co.,* 292 So.2d 289 (La.App.1974).

4. Trade school welding student was not contributorily negligent when injured by exploding freon cylinder. *Danos v. Foret,* 354 So.2d 667 (La.App. 1977).

5. A chemistry experiment in an introductory high school course, requiring students to use materials that could explode, should be conducted under strictest supervision and personal attention of the teacher. *Mastrangelo v. West Side Union High School District of Merced County,* 2 Cal.2d 540, 42 P.2d 634 (1935).

6. *Suicide.* The Arkansas Supreme Court has said that the school cannot "shelter a growing child from every possible danger." Where a third grade child hanged himself in a school bathroom by a length of nylon cord attached to a large plywood bathroom pass, the court said that the school had taken adequate safety measures and that it was "manifestly futile" to protect students from all possibilities of injury, self-inflicted or otherwise. *Gathright v. Lincoln Ins. Co.,* 286 Ark. 16, 688 S.W.2d 931 (1985).

7. A coach is not liable for injury to a player on an opposing team resulting from a rule violation of player on his own team. The court said: "A coach cannot be held responsible for the wrongful acts of his players unless he teaches them to do the wrongful act or instructs them to commit the act." *Nydegger v. Don Bosco Preparatory High School,* 202 N.J. Super. 535, 495 A.2d 485 (1985).

8. *Damages.* The Supreme Court of Florida has attempted to set out an objective standard for review for damage awards. In the case of *Bould v. Touchette,* 349 So.2d 1181 (Fla. 1977) the court stated:

> Where recovery is sought for a personal tort, or where punitive damages are al-

lowed, we cannot apply fixed rules to a given set of facts and say that a verdict is for more than would be allowable under a correct computation. In tort cases damages are to be measured by the jury's discretion. The court should never declare a verdict excessive merely because it is above the amount which the court itself considers the jury should have allowed. The verdict should not be disturbed unless it is so inordinately large as obviously to exceed the maximum limit of a reasonable range within which the jury may properly operate.

9. *Liability of Teacher Aide for Pupil Injury.* When teacher aides are assigned tasks involving supervision, they are placed in a position of potential liability for pupil injury. In such a situation, liability is likely to arise out of negligence on the part of the aide. Any persons assigned such responsibilities are ignorant at their own peril. If they are not qualified to supervise playgrounds, they should not attempt to perform the task.

In cases involving pupil injury, the courts have traditionally held the teacher to a higher "standard of care" than that owed to the general public. Likewise, a teacher aide, when placed in a supervisory capacity, owes the pupils a greater "standard of care" than is normally required in other personal relationships.

10. *Liability of Administrator or Supervisor for Negligent Acts of Teacher Aide.* Where the administrator or supervisor appoints a well-qualified person to perform certain functions about the school and injury results, the administrator is not liable for negligence. The general rule of law is that in the public school situation the master is not liable for the commissions or omissions of his servant. In a Rhode Island case illustrating this principle, the court held that a school principal, who had authority over a school janitor, was not liable for injuries to a school teacher when the principal failed to warn her of a slippery floor in the school building. *Gray v. Wood,* 75 R.I. 123, 64 A.2d 191 (1949).

Therefore, a teacher or a principal is not liable for the negligent acts of a properly appointed and qualified teacher aide. On the other hand, if a teacher or a principal assigns duties for which the teacher aide is not qualified and the purposes of which do not fall within the scope of the aide's employment, the teacher or the principal may be liable for negligent acts by the aide.

11. An Illinois court in relating tort liability to the *in loco parentis* standard found that teachers are not subject to any greater liability than parents for injury to their children. Parents are liable only for willful and wanton misconduct, but not for mere negligence. *Montague v. School Board of the Thornton Fractional Township North High School District 215,* 57 Ill.App.3d 828, 15 Ill.Dec. 373, 373 N.E.2d 719 (1978).

Releases Required to Be Signed by Students or Parents as a Condition of Engaging in School Activities, Which Exculpate School Districts from Liability for Negligence, Are Invalid as Violative of Public Policy

Wagenblast v. Odessa School District No. 105-157-166J

Supreme Court of Washington, En Banc., 1988.
110 Wn. 2d 845, 758 P. 2d 968.

ANDERSEN, Justice.

In these consolidated cases we consider an issue of first impression—the legality of public school districts requiring students and their parents to sign a release of all potential future claims as a condition to student participation in certain school-related activities.

The plaintiffs in these cases are public school children and their parents.

Odessa School District students Alexander and Charles Wagenblast and Ethan and Katie

Herdrick all desired to participate in some form of interscholastic athletics. As a condition to such participation, the Odessa School District requires its students and their parents or guardians to sign a standardized form which releases the school district from "liability resulting from any ordinary negligence that may arise in connection with the school district's interscholastic activities programs." The releases are required by a group of small Eastern Washington school districts, including Odessa, which "pooled" together to purchase liability insurance.

The Seattle School District also requires students and their parents to sign standardized release forms as a condition to participation in interscholastic sports and cheerleading. When Richard and Paul Vulliet turned out for the Ballard High School wrestling team, they and their parents were required to sign release forms which released the Seattle School District, its employees and agents "from any liability resulting from any negligence that may arise in connection with the School District's wrestling program."

. . .

One issue is determinative of these appeals.

Can school districts require public school students and their parents to sign written releases which release the districts from the consequences of all future school district negligence, before the students will be allowed to engage in certain recognized school related activities, here interscholastic athletics?

We hold that the exculpatory releases from any future school district negligence are invalid because they violate public policy.

. . .

Probably the best exposition of the test to be applied in determining whether exculpatory agreements violate public policy is that stated by the California Supreme Court. In writing for a unanimous court, the late Justice Tobriner outlined the factors.   . . .

Thus the attempted but invalid exemption involves a transaction which exhibits some or all of the following characteristics. It concerns a business of a type generally thought suitable for public regulation. The party seeking exculpa

tion is engaged in performing a service of great importance to the public, which is often a matter of practical necessity for some members of the public. The party holds himself out as willing to perform this service for any member of the public who seeks it, or at least for any member coming within certain established standards. As a result of the essential nature of the service, in the economic setting of the transaction, the party invoking exculpation possesses a decisive advantage of bargaining strength against any member of the public who seeks his services. In exercising a superior bargaining power the party confronts the public with a standardized adhesion contract of exculpation, and makes no provision whereby a purchaser may pay additional reasonable fees and obtain protection against negligence. Finally, as a result of the transaction, the person or property of the purchaser is placed under the control of the seller, subject to the risk of carelessness by the seller or his agents.

. . . We agree.

Obviously, the more of the foregoing six characteristics that appear in a given exculpatory agreement case, the more likely the agreement is to be declared invalid on public policy grounds. In the consolidated cases before us, *all* of the characteristics are present in *each* case. We separately, then, examine each of these six characteristics as applied to the cases before us.

The agreement concerns an endeavor of a type generally thought suitable for public regulation.

Regulation of governmental entities usually means self-regulation. Thus, the Legislature has by statute granted to each school board the authority to control, supervise, and regulate the conduct of interscholastic athletics. In some situations, a school board is permitted, in turn, to delegate this authority to the Washington Interscholastic Activities Association (WIAA) or to another voluntary nonprofit entity. In the cases before us, both school boards look to the WIAA for regulation of interscholastic sports.   . . .

Clearly then, interscholastic sports in Washington are extensively regulated, and are a fit subject for such regulation.

The party seeking exculpation is engaged in performing a service of great importance to the public, which is often a matter of practical necessity for some members of the public.

This court has held that public school students have no fundamental right to participate in interscholastic athletics. Nonetheless, the court also has observed that the justification advanced for interscholastic athletics is their educational and cultural value. . . . Given this emphasis on sports by the public and the school system, it would be unrealistic to expect students to view athletics as an activity entirely separate and apart from the remainder of their schooling. . . .

In sum, under any rational view of the subject, interscholastic sports in public schools are a matter of public importance in this jurisdiction.

Such party holds itself out as willing to perform this service for any member of the public who seeks it, or at least for any member coming within certain established standards.

Implicit in the nature of interscholastic sports is the notion that such programs are open to all students who meet certain skill and eligibility standards. . . .

Because of the essential nature of the service, in the economic setting of the transaction, the party invoking exculpation possesses a decisive advantage of bargaining strength against any member of the public who seeks the services.

Not only have interscholastic sports become of considerable importance to students and the general public alike, but in most instances there exists no alternative program of organized competition. . . . While outside alternatives exist for some activities, they possess little of the inherent allure of interscholastic competition. . . . In this regard, school districts have near-monopoly power. And, because such programs have become important to student participants, school districts possess a clear and disparate bargaining strength when they insist that students and their parents sign these releases.

In exercising a superior bargaining power, the party confronts the public with a standardized adhesion contract of exculpation, and makes no provision whereby a purchaser may pay additional reasonable fees and obtain protection against negligence.

Both school districts admit to an unwavering policy regarding these releases; no student athlete will be allowed to participate in any program without first signing the release form as written by the school district. In both of these cases, students and their parents unsuccessfully attempted to modify the forms by deleting the release language. In both cases, the school district rejected the attempted modifications. Student athletes and their parents or guardians have no alternative but to sign the standard release forms provided to them or have the student barred from the program.

The person or property of members of the public seeking such services must be placed under the control of the furnisher of the services, subject to the risk of carelessness on the part of the furnisher, its employees or agents.

A school district owes a duty to its students to employ ordinary care and to anticipate reasonably foreseeable dangers so as to take precautions for protecting the children in its custody from such dangers. This duty extends to students engaged in interscholastic sports. . . . The student is thus subject to the risk that the school district or its agent will breach this duty of care.

In sum, the attempted releases in the cases before us exhibit all six of the characteristics . . . . Because of this, and for the aforesaid reasons, we hold that the releases in these consolidated cases are invalid as against public policy. . . .

The remaining aspect of these appeals which merits discussion is the Legislature's role in deciding such matters of public policy. By act of the territorial Legislature of 1869, school districts were made liable for their acts of negligence. At the 1917 session of the State Legislature, a bill to absolutely immunize school districts from negligence passed the

Senate, but the bill which was ultimately enacted that year was a compromise; that compromise barred actions against school districts for noncontractual acts or omissions relating to any park, playground, field house, athletic apparatus or appliance or manual training equipment. This compromise statute, in turn, was repealed some years later — by the 1967 Legislature. Thus, since territorial days, the State Legislature has generally followed a policy of holding school districts accountable for their negligence. Our decision today is in general accordance with that policy.

Legislative policies may, of course, change with changing conditions. This opinion is not to be construed as precluding school districts from attempting to convince the Legislature that their problems in this area require a legislative response of one kind or another. The Legislature through its hearing processes is well suited to making such inquiries and has tools and resources adequate to the task.

The decision of the trial court in the Odessa School District case is affirmed and the decision of the trial court in the Seattle School District case is reversed.

NOTES

1. Exculpatory clauses purporting to contract away liability for intentional conduct, recklessness, or gross negligence are unenforceable. *Adams v. Roark*, 686 S.W. 2d 73 (Tenn. 1985).
2. A permission slip is not a valid exculpatory release.
3. A Mississippi court has held that minors cannot sign exculpatory releases and no one can sign for them. A court in that state has said: "Minors can waive nothing. In the law they are helpless, so much so that their representatives can waive nothing for them." *Khoury v. Saik*, 203 Miss. 155, 33 So. 2d 616 (1948).
4. The Supreme Court of Connecticut has held that a parental release of liability is ineffective because a parent cannot release the child's action. *Doyle v. Bowdoin College*, 403 A. 2d 1206 (Me. 1979).
5. A Tennessee court has said that: "The law is clear that a guardian cannot, on behalf of

an infant or incompetent, exculpate or indemnify against liability, those organizations which sponsor activities for children and the mentally disabled." *Childress v. Madison County*, 777 S.W. 2d 1 (Tenn. App. 1989).

_____

■ EDUCATIONAL MALPRACTICE

Several courts in recent years have issued opinions on cases that fall under a general classification of educational malpractice. Such cases are not a separate area of law, but instead represent an expansion of the traditional tort law concept as applied to the educational setting. Basically, educational malpractice is an attempt to apply tort law to educational outcomes in such a way as to redress a student for knowledge deficiencies allegedly created by some substandard treatment of the student during the educational process.

Evidence to support an allegation of intentional tort would seem to be very difficult to support unless one could show that an educator, for some malicious purpose, set out to prevent a child from obtaining an education. The possibility of maintaining an action for intentional tort was recognized by a Maryland court when it stated: "It is our view that where an individual engaged in the education process is shown to have willfully and maliciously injured a child entrusted to his educational care, such outrageous conduct greatly outweighs any public policy considerations which would otherwise preclude liability so as to authorize recovery."[58]

The more common application of tort to redress a student's educational deficiencies is found in negligence. Here it is maintained that educators failed to act reasonably in administering to a student's educational needs. Such actions, though, have met with little or no success as the courts have established an imposing array of precedents denying students damages. The courts have generally denied redress for three reasons: "the absence of a workable rule of care against which defendant's conduct may be measured, the inherent uncertainty in determining the cause and nature of any damages, and the extreme burden which would be imposed on the already strained resources of the public school system to say nothing of the judiciary."[59]

The first reason given is, of course, related directly to the negligence question. How can a court enunciate a standard of care without a clear determination of the actual duty owed to the student? Does the educator have a duty to fill the vessel of the student's mind with a given amount of knowledge, and if the vessel remains half-full, does the educator, student, parent, or society bear the blame?

The problem of delineating an actionable duty was recognized by a California court in *Peter W.*[60] when it explained:

> The "injury" claimed here is plaintiff's inability to read and write. Substantial professional authority attests that the achievement of literacy in the schools, or its failure, is influenced by a host of factors which affect the pupil subjectively, from outside the formal teaching process, and beyond the control of its ministers. They may be physical, neurological, emotional, cultural, environmental; they may be present but not perceived, recognized but not identified.

In such a situation, the court could not find that the student had suffered injury within the meaning of negligence law, nor could it identify a workable "rule of care" that could be applied. Neither could the court find a causal relationship between any perceived injury and the alleged negligent commission or omission by the defendant. A New York court had drawn a conclusion similar to that in *Peter W.* and further maintained that judicial interference in this area would constitute a "blatant interference" with the administration of the public school system.[61] In agreement with these courts, the court in *Hunter* said that "to allow petitioners asserted negligence claims to proceed would in effect position the courts of this state as overseers of both the day-to-day operation of our educational process as well as the formulation of its governing policies. This responsibility we are loath to impose on our courts."[62]

Other courts have likewise rejected plaintiffs' tort claims in negligence actions.[63]

Educational Malpractice Is Not a Cognizable Cause of Action in Tort Law

Donohue v. Copiague Union Free School District

Court of Appeals of New York, 1979.
47 N.Y.2d 440, 418 N.Y.S.2d 375, 391 N.E.2d 1352.

JASEN, Judge. This appeal poses the question whether a complaint seeking monetary damages for "educational malpractice" states a cause of action cognizable in the courts.

Appellant entered Copiague Senior High School in September, 1972, and graduated in June, 1976. The thrust of appellant's claim is that notwithstanding his receipt of a certificate of graduation he lacks even the rudimentary ability to comprehend written English on a level sufficient to enable him to complete applications for employment. His complaint attributes this deficiency to the failure of respondent to perform its duties and obligations to educate appellant. To be more specific, appellant alleges in his complaint that respondent through its employees "gave to [appellant] passing grades and/or minimal or failing grades in various subjects; failed to evaluate [appellant's] mental ability and capacity to comprehend the subjects being taught to him at said school; failed to take proper means and precautions that they reasonably should have taken under the circumstances; failed to interview, discuss, evaluate and/or psychologically test [appellant] in order to ascertain his ability to comprehend and understand such matter; failed to provide adequate school facilities, teachers, administrators, psychologists, and other personnel trained to take the necessary steps in testing and evaluation processes insofar as [appellant] is concerned in order to ascertain the learning capacity, intelligence and intellectual absorption on the part of [appellant]."

Based upon these acts of commission and omission, appellant frames two causes of action, the first of which sounds in "educational malpractice" and the second of which alleges the negligent breach of a constitutionally imposed duty to educate. To redress his injury, appellant seeks the sum of $5,000,000. Upon respondent's motion, Special Term dismissed appellant's complaint for failure to state a cause of action. The Appellate Division affirmed, with one Justice dissenting. There should be an affirmance.

The second cause of action need not detain us long. The State Constitution (art. XI, § 1) commands that "[t]he legislature shall provide for the maintenance and support of a system of free common schools, wherein all the children of this state may be educated." Even a terse reading of this provision reveals that the Constitution places the obligation of *maintaining and supporting* a system of public schools upon the *Legislature.* To be sure, this general directive was never intended to impose a duty flowing directly from a local school district to individual pupils to ensure that each pupil receives a minimum level of education, the breach of which duty would entitle a pupil to compensatory damages. . . .

Appellant's first cause of action bears closer scrutiny. It may very well be that even within the strictures of a traditional negligence or malpractice action, a complaint sounding in "educational malpractice" may be formally pleaded. Thus, the imagination need not be overly taxed to envision allegations of a legal duty of care flowing from educators, if viewed as professionals, to their students. If doctors, lawyers, architects, engineers and other professionals are charged with a duty owing to the public whom they serve, it could be said that nothing in the law precludes similar treatment of professional educators. Nor would creation of a standard with which to judge an educator's performance of that duty necessarily pose an insurmountable obstacle. . . . As for proximate causation, while this element might indeed be difficult, if not impossible to prove in view of the many collateral factors involved in the learning process, it perhaps assumes too much to conclude that it could never be established. This would leave only the element of injury and who can in good faith deny that a student who upon graduation from high school cannot comprehend simple English—a deficiency allegedly attributable to the negligence of his educators—has not in some fashion been "injured."

The fact that a complaint alleging "educational malpractice" might on the pleadings state a cause of action within traditional notions of tort law does not, however, require that it be sustained. The heart of the matter is whether, assuming that such a cause of action may be stated, the courts should, as a matter of public policy, entertain such claims. We believe they should not. . . .

To entertain a cause of action for "educational malpractice" would require the courts not merely to make judgments as to the validity of broad educational policies—a course we have unalteringly eschewed in the past—but, more importantly, to sit in review of the day-to-day implementation of these policies. Recognition in the courts of this cause of action would constitute blatant interference with the responsibility for the administration of the public school system lodged by Constitution and statute in school administrative agencies. . . . Of course, "[t]his is not to say that there may never be gross violations of defined public policy which the courts would be obliged to recognize and correct.". . . .

Finally, not to be overlooked in today's holding is the right of students presently enrolled in public schools, and their parents, to take advantage of the administrative processes provided by statute to enlist the aid of the Commissioner of Education in ensuring that such students receive a proper education. The Education Law (§ 310, subd. 7) permits any person aggrieved by an "official act or decision of any officer, school authorities, or meetings concerning any other matter under this chapter, or any other act pertaining to common schools" to seek review of such act or decision by the commissioner.

Accordingly, the order of the Appellate Division should be affirmed, with costs.

WACHTLER, Judge (concurring).

I agree that complaints of "educational malpractice" are for school administrative agencies, rather than the courts, to resolve.

There is, however, another even more fundamental objection to entertaining plaintiff's cause of action alleging educational malpractice. It is a basic principle that the law does not provide a remedy for every injury. . . . As the majority notes, the decision of whether a new cause of action should be recognized at law is largely a question of policy. Critical to such a determination is whether the cause of action sought to be pleaded would be reasonably manageable within our legal system. The practical problems raised by a cause of action sounding in educational malpractice are so formidable that I would conclude that such a legal theory should not be cognizable in our courts. These problems, clearly articulated at the Appellate Division, include the practical impossibility of proving that the alleged malpractice of the teacher proximately caused the learning deficiency of the plaintiff student.

Factors such as the student's attitude, motivation, temperament, past experience and home environment may all play an essential and immeasurable role in learning. Indeed as the majority observes proximate cause might "be difficult, if not impossible, to prove."

I would, therefore, affirm the order of the Appellate Division on the ground that educational malpractice, as here pleaded, is not a cognizable cause of action. . . .

Order affirmed.

NOTES

1. A case with a slightly different perspective, the Montana Supreme Court, in a narrow four-to-three decision, held the misplacement of a child in a special education class constituted a kind of "malpractice." This court said the school owed a "duty of reasonable care in testing and placing the child in an appropriate special education program." In a concurring opinion it was noted that the state's special education statutes created a "duty" that required "reasonable care." The court distinguished this situation from the *Peter W. and Donohue* cases. (See *Peter W.,* op. cit. and *Donohue,* op. cit.)

In reality, this case becomes a special education statutory case that is quite different from the cause of action described as a common-law tort for malpractice. It is a case of special education misplacement, not a case of tort based on negligence in provision of basic academic skills. *B.M. v. State,* 200 Mont. 58, 649 P.2d 425 (1982). See Michael A. Magone, "Educational Malpractice—Does The Cause of Action Exist?", *Montana Law Review* 49 (Winter 1988), p. 140.

2. A Pennsylvania court disagreed with the Montana court, saying that a misplacement of a handicapped student under special education law would support a common-law action for educational malpractice. *Agostine v. School District of Philadelphia,* 106 Pa. Cmwlth. 492, 527 A.2d 193 (1987). The same result was reached in *Savino v. Board of Education of School District No. 1,* Westbury N.Y., 123 A.D. 2d 314, 506 N.Y.S. 2d 210 (1986): See also same result in *Doe v. Board of Education in Montgomery County,* 295 Md. 67, 453 A. 2d 814 (1982). See also *D.S.W. v. Fairbanks North Star Borough School Dist.,* 628 P. 2d 554 (Alaska 1981).

3. A New York court held that a social services department could not be liable for negligence in plaintiffs' action for educational malpractice. The court said that public policy precluded an educational malpractice action against a public school or a child care agency. *Torres v. Little Flower Children's Services et al.,* 64 N.Y. 2d 119, 485 N.Y.S. 2d 15, 474 N.E. 2d 223 (1984).

▓▓ CIVIL RIGHTS OR CONSTITUTIONAL TORTS

An individual's constitutional rights may be protected through application of the Civil Rights Act of 1871, as codified in § 1983 of Title 42 U.S.C.A. § 1983. Under this statute, denial of an individual's constitutional or statutory rights can result in damages assessed by the court against the school board, individual school board member, administrator, or teacher; or against any governmental official or employee responsible for the denial. This act had been virtually dormant for almost a hundred years when it was revived in the early 1960s in the Supreme Court case of *Monroe v. Pape,*[64] at which time the Court applied the act to actions against public officials. The law itself states:

> Every person who, under color of any statute, ordinance, regulation, custom, or usage, of any State or Territory, subjects, or causes to be subjected, any citizen of the United States or other person within the jurisdiction thereof to the deprivation of any rights, privileges or immunities secured by the Constitution and laws, shall be liable to the party injured in an action at law, suit in equity, or other proper proceeding for redress.[65]

This law was enacted by the Congress on April 20, 1871, after a month of debate during which time it became clear that there was great sentiment toward providing legal redress against those southerners who repressed individual rights of southern blacks. The press at that time called the legislation the Southern-outrage Repression Bill.[66]

Persons

As written, the law provides for both injunctive and monetary relief to be awarded by the federal courts. Offenders against whom action may be instituted are statutory persons— "persons" as the law is written. The United States Supreme Court has had difficulty in deciding exactly who a "person" is, whether it is a public board or an individual official or employee. In *Monroe* the Court first held that Congress did not intend the word "person" to include municipalities or agencies of the government. Therefore, suits seeking relief under the act were filed only against school officials and not school districts as entities. The result was that from 1961 to 1978 school districts insured the school officials against damages that may have been incurred by lawsuit in

such cases, and the municipality was immune. On June 6, 1978, in *Monell v. Department of Social Services of City of New York,*[67] this all changed when the Supreme Court voted 7 to 2 to overrule *Monroe* insofar as it provided immunity for municipalities. The Court, in so ruling, did not upset the interpretation of the *respondeat superior* doctrine, that a public school district is not responsible for the wrongdoing of its employees, but it did say that the school district could be held liable under § 1983 if it adopts an unconstitutional policy or acquiesces in an unconstitutional custom. Justice Brennan stated:

> We conclude, therefore, that a local government may not be sued for an injury inflicted solely by its employees or agents. Instead, it is when execution of a government's policy or custom, whether made by its lawmakers or by those whose edicts or acts may fairly be said to represent official policy, inflicts the injury that the government as an entity is responsible under Section 1983.

Monell, therefore, taken in context with two other cases, *Wood v. Strickland,*[68] and *Carey v. Piphus,*[69] clearly permits courts to assess damages against either the governmental agency or an individual official of government if it or they suppress one's civil rights, whether it be a student, teacher, or some other party. *Wood* established the potential liability of school board members for denial of students' due process rights, *Carey* clarified the nature and extent of the damages that could be levied by the courts. In *Carey,* Justice Powell writing for the Court explained that there was a limitation to the damages that were possible under this kind of action. According to Powell, § 1983 was not intended to provide purely punitive relief whereby the court would punish the wrongdoer for ill deeds, but instead the act was designed to compensate the victim for detriment and damage caused by the denial. Compensatory damages of this nature are quite difficult to prove, and the Supreme Court places this burden squarely on the shoulders of the plaintiff. In the absence of such proof, the individual is entitled to collect only nominal damages.

School Board Liability

As noted above, the Supreme Court in *Monell* held that municipalities cannot be liable under § 1983 if the government itself does not cause the infliction of harm beyond the injury caused by one of the government's employees. According to the Supreme Court, governmental liability can only be imposed when the injury is caused by "the execution of a government's policy or custom, whether made by its lawmakers or by those whose edicts or acts may fairly be said to represent official policy."[70]

In *Pembaur v. Cincinnati,*[71] a 1986 case, the Supreme Court held that a school board cannot be held liable under § 1983 unless there is actual or constructive knowledge that an employee of the board has denied plaintiffs their constitutional rights.

The Fifth Circuit has further clarified by holding that a municipality must have an "underlying knowledge" of a custom or a policy that is violative of a citizen's constitutional rights.[72] The Fifth Circuit has explained:

> Actual knowledge must be shown by such means as discussions at council meetings or receipt of written information. Constructive knowledge may be attributed to the governing body on the ground that it would have known of the violations if it had properly exercised its responsibilities, as, for example, the violations were so persistent and widespread that they were the subject of prolonged public discussion and a high degree of publicity.[73]

Official Negligence

Even though the U.S. Supreme Court initially held that civil remedy under § 1983 could be afforded for negligence,[74] the Court later reversed itself, holding that lack of due care by a state official could not be the basis for relief under § 1983.[75] Mere negligence or an omission causing injury cannot be used as the basis to invoke the protections of the statute. Thus, the so-called constitutional tort founded under § 1983 has the important constraint of being inapplicable to cases of official negligence. The Supreme Court, however, has left open the question of liability if there is a callous or reckless disregard for plaintiffs' rights and injury ensues.

In applying this principle, the Eighth Circuit in *Rubek v. Barnhart*[76] found that parents seeking damages under § 1983 could not prevail in an action for constitutional "negligence" against teachers and administrators for violation of due process in administering corporal punishment to the plaintiff children. The court required plaintiffs to show that the defendants, in administering the corporal punishment, had demonstrated "a reckless disregard or deliberate indifference to plaintiff's constitutional rights."[77]

Thus, the prevailing view appears to be that a governmental entity will not be liable unless there is shown a "deliberate indifference" for a child's rights. For a school board to be liable, the plaintiff must bear the difficult burden of proving that constitutional rights had been taken away as a result of overt official school district policy or custom. Moreover, the plaintiff must show that the board had knowledge of the policy or custom that caused the deprivation. Moreover, the plaintiff must show that the injury was caused by the board's "callous indifference" to the plaintiff's constitutional rights.[78]

Individual Liability

Under certain circumstances, an employee or an official of a school district may be found to be individually liable even though a school board may not be. The individual employee or official cannot be liable unless the plaintiff shows that the action violated a clearly established law, and that the individual exhibited a "callous indifference" for the rights of the plaintiff.[79]

In *Davis,* the U.S. Supreme Court held:

> Officials are shielded from liability for civil damages insofar as their conduct does not violate the clearly-established statutory or constitutional rights of which a reasonable person would have known at the time of the incident involved.[80]

Therefore, employees and officials, in their individual capacities, are immune from liability under § 1983 unless they have exhibited a "callous indifference" to an individual's constitutional rights and have demonstrated "a lack of objective good faith."[81]

Horner has carefully summarized the law of liability as set forth in § 1983 for both school boards and individuals:

> Indeed courts generally look at two basic elements in determining whether Section 1983 should be imposed upon governmental entities and their employees. With respect to the liability of the entity, courts will impose liability only if a state official acts in a "callously indifferent" manner toward the rights of individuals pursuant to governmental policy or custom. In essence, a state official must not only perform an outrageous action, but such actions must also be common within that particular governmental entity. Individual liability revolves around the "callous indifference" standard. If an employee acts with "callous indifference" toward the rights of an individual, he or she may be subject to liability in his or her individual capacity.[82]

School Board Members May Be Liable, as Individuals, for Damages Under Section 1983 of the Civil Rights Act of 1871

— · — · — · — · — · — · —

Wood v. Strickland

— · — · — · — · — · — · —

Supreme Court of the United States, 1975.
420 U.S. 308, 95 S.Ct. 992.

Mr. Justice WHITE delivered the opinion of the Court. Respondents Peggy Strickland and Virginia Crain brought this lawsuit against petitioners, who were members of the school board at the time in question, two school administrators, and the Special School District of Mena, Ark., purporting to assert a cause of action under 42 U.S.C.A. § 1983, and claiming that their federal constitutional rights to due process were infringed under color of state law by their expulsion from the Mena Public

High School on the grounds of their violation of a school regulation prohibiting the use or possession of intoxicating beverages at school or school activities. The complaint as amended prayed for compensatory and punitive damages against all petitioners, injunctive relief allowing respondents to resume attendance, preventing petitioners from imposing any sanctions as a result of the expulsion, and restraining enforcement of the challenged regulation, declaratory relief as to the constitutional invalidity of the regulation, and expunction of any record of their expulsion. . . .

The violation of the school regulation prohibiting the use or possession of intoxicating beverages at school or school activities with which respondents were charged concerned their "spiking" of the punch served at a meeting of an extracurricular school organization attended by parents and students. At the time in question, respondents were sixteen years old and were in the tenth grade. The relevant facts begin with their discovery that the punch had not been prepared for the meeting as previously planned. The girls then agreed to "spike" it. Since the county in which the school is located is "dry," respondents and a third girl drove across the state border into Oklahoma and purchased two twelve-ounce bottles of "Right Time," a malt liquor. They then bought six ten-ounce bottles of a soft drink, and after having mixed the contents of the eight bottles in an empty milk carton, returned to school. Prior to the meeting, the girls experienced second thoughts about the wisdom of their prank, but by then they were caught up in the force of events and the intervention of other girls prevented them from disposing of the illicit punch. The punch was served at the meeting, without apparent effect. . . . The board voted to expel the girls from school for the remainder of the semester, a period of approximately three months.

The board subsequently agreed to hold another meeting on the matter, and one was held approximately two weeks after the first meeting. The girls, their parents, and their counsel attended this session. The board began with a reading of a written statement of facts as it had found them. The girls admitted mixing the malt liquor into the punch with the intent of "spiking" it, but asked the board to forgo its rule punishing such violations by such substantial suspensions. . . . The board voted not to change its policy and, as before, to expel the girls for the remainder of the semester.

The District Court instructed the jury that a decision for respondents had to be premised upon a finding that petitioners acted with malice in expelling them and defined "malice" as meaning "ill will against a person—a wrongful act done intentionally without just cause or excuse." In ruling for petitioners after the jury had been unable to agree, the District Court found "as a matter of law" that there was no evidence from which malice could be inferred.

The Court of Appeals, however, viewed both the instruction and the decision of the District Court as being erroneous. Specific intent to harm wrongfully, it held, was not a requirement for the recovery of damages. Instead, "[i]t need only be established that the defendants did not, in the light of all the circumstances, act in good faith. The test is an objective, rather than a subjective one."

Petitioners as members of the school board assert here, as they did below, an absolute immunity from liability under § 1983 and at the very least seek to reinstate the judgment of the District Court. If they are correct and the District Court's dismissal should be sustained, we need go no further in this case. Moreover, the immunity question involves the construction of a federal statute, and our practice is to deal with possibly dispositive statutory issues before reaching questions turning on the construction of the Constitution. . . . We essentially sustain the position of the Court of Appeals with respect to the immunity issue.

The nature of the immunity from awards of damages under § 1983 available to school administrators and school board members is not a question which the lower federal courts have answered with a single voice. There is general agreement on the existence of a "good faith" immunity, but the courts have either emphasized different factors as elements of

good faith or have not given specific content to the good-faith standard. . . .

Common-law tradition, recognized in our prior decisions, and strong public-policy reasons also lead to a construction of § 1983 extending a qualified good-faith immunity to school board members from liability for damages under that section. Although there have been differing emphases and formulations of the common-law immunity of public school officials in cases of student expulsion or suspension, state courts have generally recognized that such officers should be protected from tort liability under state law for all good-faith nonmalicious action taken to fulfill their official duties.

As the facts of this case reveal, school board members function at different times in the nature of legislators and adjudicators in the school disciplinary process. Each of these functions necessarily involves the exercise of discretion, the weighing of many factors, and the formulation of long-term policy. "Like legislators and judges, these officers are entitled to rely on traditional sources for the factual information on which they decide and act." . . . As with executive officers faced with instances of civil disorder, school officials, confronted with student behavior causing or threatening disruption, also have an "obvious need for prompt action, and decisions must be made in reliance on factual information supplied by others."

Liability for damages for every action which is found subsequently to have been violative of a student's constitutional rights and to have caused compensable injury would unfairly impose upon the school decision-maker the burden of mistakes made in good faith in the course of exercising his discretion within the scope of his official duties. School board members, among other duties, must judge whether there have been violations of school regulations and, if so, the appropriate sanctions for the violations. Denying any measure of immunity in these circumstances "would contribute not to principled and fearless decision-making but to intimidation". . . . The imposition of monetary costs for mistakes which were not unreasonable in the light of all the circumstances would undoubtedly deter even the most conscientious school decision-maker from exercising his judgment independently, forcefully, and in a manner best serving the long-term interest of the school and the students. The most capable candidates for school board positions might be deterred from seeking office if heavy burdens upon their private resources from monetary liability were a likely prospect during their tenure.

These considerations have undoubtedly played a prime role in the development by state courts of a qualified immunity protecting school officials from liability for damages in lawsuits claiming improper suspensions or expulsions. But at the same time, the judgment implicit in this common-law development is that absolute immunity would not be justified since it would not sufficiently increase the ability of school officials to exercise their discretion in a forthright manner to warrant the absence of a remedy for students subjected to intentional or otherwise inexcusable deprivations.

. . . We think there must be a degree of immunity if the work of the schools is to go forward; and, however worded, the immunity must be such that public school officials understand that action taken in the good-faith fulfillment of their responsibilities and within the bounds of reason under all the circumstances will not be punished and that they need not exercise their discretion with undue timidity. . . .

The disagreement between the Court of Appeals and the District Court over the immunity standard in this case has been put in terms of an "objective" versus a "subjective" test of good faith. As we see it, the appropriate standard necessarily contains elements of both. The official himself must be acting sincerely and with a belief that he is doing right, but an act violating a student's constitutional rights can be no more justified by ignorance or disregard of settled, indisputable law on the part of one entrusted with supervision of students' daily lives than by the presence of actual malice. To be entitled to a special exemption from the categorical remedial language of § 1983 in a case in which his action violated a student's constitutional

rights, a school board member, who has voluntarily undertaken the task of supervising the operation of the school and the activities of the students, must be held to a standard of conduct based not only on permissible intentions, but also on knowledge of the basic, unquestioned constitutional rights of his charges. Such a standard imposes neither an unfair burden upon a person assuming a responsible public office requiring a high degree of intelligence and judgment for the proper fulfillment of its duties, nor an unwarranted burden in light of the value which civil rights have in our legal system. Any lesser standard would deny much of the promise of § 1983. Therefore, in the specific context of school discipline, we hold that a school board member is not immune from liability for damages under § 1983 if he knew or reasonably should have known that the action he took within his sphere of official responsibility would violate the constitutional rights of the student affected, or if he took the action with the malicious intention to cause a deprivation of constitutional rights or other injury to the student. That is not to say that school board members are "charged with predicting the future course of constitutional law". . . . A compensatory award will be appropriate only if the school board member has acted with such an impermissible motivation or with such disregard of the student's clearly established constitutional rights that his action cannot reasonably be characterized as being in good faith.

The Court of Appeals based upon its review of the facts but without the benefit of the transcript of the testimony given at the four-day trial to the jury in the District Court, found that the board had made its decision to expel the girls on the basis of *no* evidence that the school regulation had been violated:

To justify the suspension, it was necessary for the Board to establish that the students possessed or used an "intoxicating" beverage at a school-sponsored activity. No evidence was presented at either meeting to establish the alcoholic content of the liquid brought to the campus. Moreover, the Board made no finding that the liquid was intoxicating. The only evidence as to the nature of the drink was that supplied by the girls, and it was clear that they did not know whether the beverage was intoxicating or not. 485 F.2d, at 190.

. . . In its statement of facts issued prior to the onset of this litigation, the school board expressed its construction of the regulation by finding that the girls had brought an "alcoholic beverage" onto school premises. The girls themselves admitted knowing at the time of the incident that they were doing something wrong which might be punished. In light of this evidence, the Court of Appeals was ill advised to supplant the interpretation of the regulation of those officers who adopted it and are entrusted with its enforcement. . . .

When the regulation is construed to prohibit the use and possession of beverages containing alcohol, there was no absence of evidence before the school board to prove the charge against respondents. The girls had admitted that they intended to "spike" the punch and that they had mixed malt liquor into the punch that was served. . . .

Given the fact that there *was* evidence supporting the charge against respondents, the contrary judgment of the Court of Appeals is improvident. It is not the role of the federal courts to set aside decisions of school administrators which the court may view as lacking a basis in wisdom or compassion. Public high school students do have substantive and procedural rights while at school. . . . But § 1983 does not extend the right to relitigate in federal court evidentiary questions arising in school disciplinary proceedings or the proper construction of school regulations. The system of public education that has evolved in this Nation relies necessarily upon the discretion and judgment of school administrators and school board members and § 1983 was not intended to be a vehicle for federal-court correction of errors in the exercise of that discretion which do not rise to the level of violations of specific constitutional guarantees. . . .

Respondents have argued here that there was a procedural due process violation which also supports the result reached by the Court of Appeals. . . . But because the District Court did not discuss it, and the Court of Appeals did not decide it, it would be preferable to have the Court of Appeals consider the issue in the first instance.

The judgment of the Court of Appeals is vacated and the case remanded for further proceedings consistent with this opinion.

So ordered.

School Officials May Be Liable under § 1983 for a Discriminatory Act

–– · –– · –– · ––

Ponton v. Newport News School Board

–– · –– · –– · ––

United States District Court,
Eastern District of Virginia 1986.
F.Supp. 1056.

MERHIGE, District Judge. Plaintiff, Pamela Brown Ponton, a teacher in the Newport News Public School System, has filed this action against the Newport News School Board and various employees of the Newport News Public School System. Plaintiff alleges that the defendants violated her rights by forcing her to take a leave of absence from her teaching position because she was single and pregnant. Plaintiff contends that this coerced leave constituted a violation of her constitutional rights to equal protection, privacy and due process and her statutory rights under 42 U.S.C. §§ 1981 and 1983, 20 U.S.C. § 1681 (Title IX of the Education Amendments of 1972) and 42 U.S.C. § 2000e et seq. (Title VII of the Civil Rights Act of 1964).

The matter has been tried before the Court and is accordingly ripe for disposition.

Plaintiff was hired by the Newport News School Board in January 1982 to teach vocational home economics at the Vocational Education Magnet School in Newport News, Virginia. Plaintiff was single at the time.

In May of 1983, plaintiff, then unmarried, learned that she was pregnant. Plaintiff notified her superior, Lettie Booker, of her condition, but did not at that time notify the Personnel Department.

On June 11, 1983, plaintiff signed a contract with the Newport News School Board providing for her continued employment at her school for the 1983–84 school year. Such employment was to commence on August 30, 1983.

In the early part of August, 1983, Booker inquired of plaintiff if she had gotten married. Plaintiff informed Booker that she had not. Booker advised plaintiff that plaintiff should discuss her situation with the Personnel Department.

Plaintiff contacted Crawford Smith in the Personnel Department, who informed plaintiff that the School System dealt with such situations by giving the pregnant teacher three options: (1) get married, (2) take a leave of absence, or (3) resign. Mr. Smith, who at the time had the responsibility to recruit and staff middle schools, referred the plaintiff to Hattie Webb, who was the Personnel Coordinator for the Newport News School District and was responsible for granting leaves.

Plaintiff told Booker of the three options that Smith had communicated to her and Booker again advised plaintiff that she should contact the Personnel Department to see if there was anything they could do to help. Plaintiff stated that she did not feel there was any need for her to go to Personnel, whereupon Booker replied that she would contact the Personnel Department herself.

On or about August 23, 1985, plaintiff received a phone call from defendant Hattie Webb. Webb told plaintiff that she had heard rumors that plaintiff was pregnant, and that if plaintiff failed to come in for an interview, plaintiff would no longer be teaching. A meeting between Webb and plaintiff was scheduled for August 25.

Webb told plaintiff at the August 25 meeting that plaintiff would not be allowed to teach while she was single and pregnant as such a situation would set a bad example for plaintiff's students. When plaintiff asked what would happen if she refused to accept Webb's decision, Webb replied that she would take the matter up with Wiley Waters, her superior, who in turn would go to the School Board.

Webb suggested that plaintiff take a parental leave of absence. . . .

On August 26, 1983, plaintiff submitted a written request for a parental leave of absence for the fall term of the 1983–84 school year. This request was subsequently approved by the Personnel Department and the School Board.

Plaintiff filed for unemployment benefits on August 24, 1983, claiming that she had been forced to take a leave of absence because she was single and pregnant. Plaintiff was found eligible for such benefits on September 7. The School District appealed this ruling and a hearing was held on November 2. On November 4, the Virginia Employment Commission issued an opinion ruling that plaintiff had been forced to take a leave of absence because she was single and pregnant.

Plaintiff gave birth to a male child on December 15, 1983. On December 31, 1983, plaintiff married the child's father.

In November of 1983 and April of 1984, plaintiff requested that she be reinstated in a teaching position; however, no suitable positions were available at either of those times. On October 9, 1985, the School Board offered plaintiff a position teaching living skills at the Magruder Middle School. Plaintiff accepted the offer and began working at Magruder on November 1, 1985; she is currently still teaching at Magruder.

Plaintiff had filed a complaint with the EEOC on September 12, 1983 alleging that she had been discriminated against on the basis of her sex. On February 4, 1985, plaintiff received a Notice of Right to Sue from the EEOC. Plaintiff filed the instant suit on May 2, 1985. . . .

Since it has been determined that plaintiff's constitutional and statutory rights have been violated, it must now be decided which of the defendants may be liable to plaintiff. As with the merits, the Court will discuss, first, plaintiff's constitutional claim and, second, plaintiff's statutory claim.

A. Constitutional

Plaintiff's recovery for the violation of her constitutional right to privacy is authorized by 42 U.S.C. § 1983. This section provides a cause of action against any person who, under color of state law, deprives any other person of the rights secured by the Constitution. The Court will discuss, first, the potential liability of the School Board under § 1983 and, second, the liability of the various individuals named as defendants to this suit.

Municipal bodies are considered "persons" within the meaning of § 1983 and may therefore be subject to liability in suits brought under that section. *Monell v. Department of Social Services,* 436 U.S. 658, 98 S.Ct. 2018, 56 L.Ed.2d 611 (1978). However, a municipality may only be held liable under § 1983 if the alleged deprivation was the result of a policy or custom of that body. A municipality is not liable for the unauthorized acts of its employees, for respondeat superior does not apply in actions brought under § 1983. Plaintiff may therefore only recover from the School Board for the violation of her constitutional rights if she can establish that her leave of absence was the product of a School Board policy or custom of excluding single, pregnant teachers from the classroom.

There are three ways in which a School Board policy or custom could be found. First, it could be shown that the School Board actually initiated the policy. Second, a policy or custom could be attributed to the Board if the policy was initiated by an employee who had the final authority to make the decision to force a teacher to take a leave of absence. . . . Finally, the action of an individual employee could be imputed to the Board if it were established that the Board was aware of the employee's action and implicitly ratified it. . . .

Plaintiff has not introduced any evidence showing that the School Board itself initiated a policy of excluding single, pregnant teachers from the classroom. The evidence introduced at trial does, however, support the conclusion that, at least among the administrators in the Personnel Department, it was understood that single, pregnant teachers would be excluded from the classroom. Crawford Smith, a Personnel Assistant in the Department, was the person who first informed plaintiff of this policy. Moreover, both Hattie Webb and Wiley Waters testified that they felt that single,

pregnant teachers should not be in the classroom. And finally, a previous single, pregnant teacher had been excluded from the classroom, presumably at the request of the Personnel Department.

This unofficial Personnel Department policy cannot, however, be imputed to the School Board, for none of the employees in the Personnel Department had the power to initiate School Board policy; they only had the authority to administer policies enacted by the Board. The acts of individual employees may be considered to represent the policy of the municipality in those areas in which the employee is "the final authority or ultimate repository of . . . power" for the municipality. . . . None of the Personnel Department employees had such power in this case, however, for it was the School Board that had the final authority over discharges and, it may be assumed, coerced leaves of absences.

Even though the Personnel Department did not have the power to initiate School Board policy, the Department's unwritten policy regarding unwed, pregnant teachers could be imputed to the School Board if it were shown that the Board was aware of this policy and implicitly ratified it. . . . None of the evidence presented at trial, however, indicates that, at the time plaintiff was forced to take the leave, the School Board approved, or was even aware, of the manner in which the Personnel Department dealt with single, pregnant teachers.

It does appear that a previous single teacher had been treated in a manner similar to that in which plaintiff was treated in the instant case. There was, however, no evidence that the School Board played any role in either that case or the instant one. It is true that ultimate approval of leaves of absence rests with the School Board; however, it does not appear that there was any reason for the Board to have suspected that plaintiff's request for a leave was anything but voluntary, for there was nothing in plaintiff's letter requesting leave that indicated that her request was involuntary. In sum, plaintiff has not introduced sufficient evidence to warrant a finding that, at the time she was forced to take a leave of absence, there was a School

Board policy or custom of excluding single, pregnant teachers from the classroom.

However, although the Board is not responsible for initially causing plaintiff to take the leave of absence, it does appear, as plaintiff argues, that the Board must have become aware at some point that plaintiff was claiming that she had been forced to take a leave because she was single and pregnant. The Board's failure to respond to plaintiff's claim could be interpreted as implicit approval of the Personnel Department's action. This approval could therefore form the basis for holding the Board liable to plaintiff for some of the damages which she suffered.

The Board approved plaintiff's request for a leave on September 21, 1983. Plaintiff had been ruled eligible for unemployment benefits on September 7. The School District, through defendant Webb, appealed this decision on September 19. The Employment Commission held a hearing on November 2; defendants Webb and Waters testified at this hearing, and the School District was represented by an attorney. The Commission issued an opinion on November 4 finding that plaintiff had been dismissed because she was single and pregnant. In addition, plaintiff filed a complaint with the EEOC on September 12, 1983, charging the School District with sex discrimination. The EEOC investigated plaintiff's complaint. During this investigation, the School District was required to provide certain information to the EEOC.

It would therefore appear that, between the Employment Commission and the EEOC proceedings, the Board must have been made aware at some point—possibly even before it approved plaintiff's request for a leave—that plaintiff was challenging the legality of her leave. The Board's failure to take any action to remedy plaintiff's situation might therefore be found to constitute an implicit ratification of the Personnel Department's actions. Since a municipality may be liable under § 1983, not only for those policies which it initiates, but also for those which it implicitly ratifies, the Board could be liable for those injuries which plaintiff suffered after the Board became aware that plaintiff was claiming that her rights had been violated.

The difficulty with the above theory of liability, however, is that it appears that all of plaintiff's injuries are attributable to her initial leave, for there does not seem to have been anything the Board could have done to mitigate plaintiff's injuries once her leave was granted by the Personnel Department. As has already been noted, teachers who take a semester leave are not guaranteed that they will be returned to their former jobs, while teachers who take a disability leave are provided such a guarantee. Although it is unclear to the Court why these two types of leave are treated differently, it would appear that teachers who take a semester leave are replaced by permanent replacements, while teachers who take a disability leave are replaced by teachers hired on a temporary basis. Therefore, the reason a teacher who takes a disability leave is not guaranteed her job back is simply that her former position is no longer available.

Accordingly, when plaintiff took her leave of absence, her former position was filled by a teacher who had been hired on a permanent basis. Therefore, even if the Board knew that plaintiff had been treated unfairly, there would have been nothing it could have done about the situation, for it would have been improper for the Board to have created a vacancy for plaintiff by firing a teacher who had been legitimately hired. Plaintiff conceded at trial that, after her semester leave expired, she was returned to the first available position for which she was certified and qualified. Accordingly, because plaintiff has not established that the School Board became aware of plaintiff's claim at a time when it was still possible for the Board to have remedied plaintiff's situation, the Board is not liable to plaintiff under § 1983.

In addition to the School Board, however, plaintiff has also named numerous individuals as defendants, most of them in both their official and individual capacities. There is no need to discuss the liability of any of the individual defendants in their official capacities, for a suit against an individual in his official capacity is in reality a suit against the governmental entity which he represents. . . . Since the Court has already discussed the School Board's potential liability, the only aspect of the individual defendants' liability that needs to be addressed is their liability in their personal capacities.

The only defendants who are liable to plaintiff in their individual capacities are defendants Webb and Waters. Plaintiff has introduced no evidence indicating any conduct on the part of Donald Bruno, the current School District Superintendent, Oliver Greenwood, the former Superintendent, or any of the current or former members of the School Board which would justify the imposition of personal liability on any of these defendants. Unlike the other individual defendants, however, Webb and Waters are liable to plaintiff in their individual capacities for the violation of plaintiff's constitutional rights, as they were both responsible for this violation. Both Webb and Waters testified that they felt it was improper for a single, pregnant teacher to be in the classroom. They also appear to have been the two highest ranking officials in the Personnel Department, and it may therefore reasonably be inferred that they were the initiators of the Personnel Department's informal policy regarding single, pregnant teachers. Most importantly, it was Webb who told plaintiff that plaintiff would not be allowed to teach. Waters was aware that plaintiff was pregnant and unmarried and that Webb was going to have a conference with plaintiff. It may therefore be inferred that Waters knew that Webb was going to force plaintiff to take a leave and that he implicitly approved of this action. Accordingly, the Court finds that, because Webb and Waters were responsible for violating plaintiff's constitutional rights by forcing her to take a leave of absence, they are both liable to plaintiff in their individual capacities under § 1983.

B. Statutory

Plaintiff's recovery under Title VII differs from her recovery under § 1983 for, under Title VII, she may recover, not only from Webb and Waters, but also from the School Board. Section 2000e(a), as amended, includes governments, governmental agencies and political subdivisions as persons for Title VII purposes. The School Board has stipulated that it is an "employer" as defined in § 2000e(b).

Further, . . . Webb and Waters are also "employers" under Title VII because they acted as the School Board's agents in their dealings with plaintiff.

Defendants Webb and Waters are liable to plaintiff under Title VII for the same reason they are liable to her under § 1983, namely, because they were the ones who forced plaintiff to take the leave of absence. Moreover, the School Board is also liable to plaintiff for, unlike § 1983 where respondeat superior does not apply, Title VII imposes strict liability on the employer for the discriminatory acts of its agents. . . . Therefore, since Webb and Waters were the School Board's agents at the time they committed the discriminatory act, plaintiff may recover from the School Board itself, whether or not the Board played any affirmative role in the violation of plaintiff's Title VII rights.

Plaintiff's constitutional right to privacy and her statutory rights under Title VII were violated when she was forced to take a leave of absence because she was single and pregnant. The School Board is only liable to plaintiff under Title VII. Defendants Webb and Waters, however, are personally liable to plaintiff under both § 1983 and Title VII.

The precise amount of damages to be awarded will be determined at a later hearing. Counsel are advised that the Court is tentatively of the view that plaintiff is entitled to only nominal damages under § 1983. Accordingly, it is suggested that counsel in their efforts to reach agreement as to the amount of damages and counsel fees to which plaintiff is entitled under Title VII concentrate on the statutory allowances.

An appropriate order shall issue.

NOTES

1. *Absolute Immunity.* The Supreme Court, in a series of cases, determined that absolute immunity was available as a defense for prosecutors in initiating and presenting the state's case, *Imbler v. Pachtman,* 424 U.S. 409, 96 S.Ct. 984 (1976), and for state legislators. *Tenney v. Brandhove,* 341 U.S. 367, 71 S.Ct. 783 (1951).

2. *Qualified or Conditional Immunity.* Prosecutors and legislators have absolute immunity; therefore it may appear that other state officials have absolute immunity, however, in *Scheuer v. Rhodes,* 416 U.S. 232, 94 S.Ct. 1683 (1974), the Supreme Court declared the governor of Ohio and other state officials have only qualified or conditional immunity. Qualified or conditional immunity from civil liability means individuals are not liable as long as they are acting clearly within the scope of their authority for the betterment of those they serve. If they venture outside the scope of their authority, and, in doing so, violate someone's rights, then they may be personally liable. Qualified immunity has been established by Supreme Court decision for superintendents of state hospitals, *O'Connor v. Donaldson,* 422 U.S. 563, 95 S.Ct. 2486 (1975); and for local school board members, *Wood v. Strickland,* 420 U.S. 308, 95 S.Ct. 992 (1975).

3. *Good Faith Immunity.* Although individuals may assert good faith as a defense in a constitutional tort action, a municipality has no immunity and may not assert a good faith defense, *Owen v. City of Independence,* 445 U.S. 622, 100 S.Ct. 1398 (1980).

4. *Punitive Damages.* Individuals are entitled to recover only nominal damages unless they can prove actual damages. The Supreme Court stated "that in the absence of proof of actual injury, the students are entitled to recover only nominal damages." *Carey v. Piphus,* 435 U.S. 247, 98 S.Ct. 1042 (1978). See also *Memphis Community School District v. Stachura,* 477 U.S. 299, 106 S.Ct. 2537 (1986).

A municipality is immune from punitive damages. The Supreme Court of the United States, in concluding that punitive damages should not be assessed against municipalities (or school districts), has said:

> Punitive damages by definition are not intended to compensate the injured party, but rather to punish the tortfeasor whose wrongful action was intentional or malicious, and to deter him and others from similar extreme conduct. . . . Regarding retribution, it remains true that an award of punitive damages against a municipality "punishes" only the taxpayers, who took no part in the commission of the tort. These damages are assessed over and above the amount necessary to compensate the injured party. Thus, there is no question here of equitably distributing the losses resulting from official misconduct. . . . Indeed, punitive damages imposed on a municipality are in effect a windfall to a fully compensated plaintiff, and are likely accompanied by an increase in taxes or a reduction of public services for the citizens footing the bill. Neither reason nor justice suggests that such retribution should be visited upon the shoulders of blameless or unknowing taxpayers.
>
> Under ordinary principles of retribution, it is the wrongdoer himself who is made to suffer for his unlawful conduct. If a government official acts knowingly and maliciously to deprive others of their civil rights, he may become the appropriate object of the community's vindictive sentiments. . . . A municipality, however, can have no malice independent of the malice of its officials. Damages awarded for *punitive* purposes, therefore, are not sensibly assessed against the governmental entity itself. *City of Newport v. Fact Concerts, Inc.,* 453 U.S. 247, 101 S.Ct. 2748 (1981).

■ ENDNOTES

1. William L. Prosser, *Law of Torts* (St. Paul, Minn.: West Publishing Co., 1971), p. 1.

2. Reynolds v. Pierson, 29 Ind.App. 273, 64 N.E. 484 (1902); State v. Monroe, 121 N.C. 677, 28 S.E. 547 (1897).

3. State v. Ingram, 237 N.C. 197, 74 S.E.2d 532 (1953).

4. Prosser, *Law of Torts,* p. 37.

5. Suits v. Glover, 260 Ala. 449, 71 So.2d 49 (1954).

6. State ex rel. Burpee v. Burton, 45 Wis. 150 (1878).

7. Gardner v. State, 4 Ind. 632 (1853).

8. Vanvactor v. State, 113 Ind. 276, 15 N.E. 341 (1888).

9. Cooper v. McJunkin, 4 Ind. 290 (1853).

10. Gardner v. State, op. cit.

11. Frank v. Orleans Parish School Bd., 195 So.2d 451 (La.App.1967).

12. Cooper v. McJunkin, 4 Ind. 290 (1853); Danenhoffer v. State, 69 Ind. 295 (1879).

13. Wallace v. Shoreham Hotel Corp., 49 A.2d 81 (D.C. Mun.App.1946).

14. Barnett v. Collection Service Co., 214 Iowa 1303, 242 N.W. 25 (1932).

15. Prosser, *Law of Torts*, p. 315.

16. *Restatement of Torts*, pp. 519–20.

17. See Kern Alexander and Erwin Solomon, *College and University Law* (Charlottesville, Va.: The Michie Co., 1972), pp. 590–602.

18. Prier v. Horace Mann Insurance Co., 351 So.2d 265 (La.App.1977).

19. Lewis v. St. Bernard Parish School Board, 350 So.2d 1256 (La.App.1977).

20. Terry, "Negligence," 29 *Harv.L.Rev.* 40 (1915); see also the *Restatement of Torts*, pp. 291–93.

21. Prosser, *Law of Torts*, p. 123.

22. Ibid., p. 124.

23. Lehmuth v. Long Beach Unified School District, 53 Cal.2d 544, 2 Cal.Rptr. 279, 348 P.2d 887 (1960).

24. Michigan Central Railroad Co., v. Hasseneyer, 48 Mich. 205, 12 N.W. 155 (1882).

25. Johnson v. St. Paul City Railway Co., 67 Minn. 260, 69 N.W. 900 (1897); Kitsap County Transportation Co. v. Harvey, 15 F.2d 166 (9th Cir.1927).

26. In criminal law the courts have applied the rule as established in M'Naghten's Case, 10 Ct. & F. 200, 8 E.R. 718 (1843), which holds the defense of insanity can be established only by showing that the accused was "laboring under such a defect of reason, from disease of the mind, as not to know the nature and quality of the act he was doing; or, if he did know it, that he did not know what he was doing was wrong."

27. Williams v. Kearbey, 13 Kan.App.2d 564, 775 P.2d 670, 672 (1989).

28. Morris v. Douglas County School District, No. 9, 241 Or. 23, 403 P.2d 775 (1965).

29. Osborne v. Montgomery, 203 Wis. 223, 234 N.W. 372 (1931).

30. Hoyem v. Manhattan Beach City School District 150 Col.Rptr. 1, 585 P.2d 851 (1978).

31. Cirillo v. Milwaukee, 34 Wis.2d 705, 150 N.W.2d 460 (1967).

32. Connett v. Freemont County School District No. 6, 581 P.2d 1097 (Wyo.1978).

33. Prosser, *Law of Torts*, p. 127.

34. *The Restatement of Torts* § 464 states that: "Age is only one of the elements to be considered, along with experience and judgment, the latter involving discretion and power of self control, being predominant."

35. Ohman v. Board of Education of City of New York, 300 N.Y. 306, 90 N.E.2d 474 (1949), reargument denied 301 N.Y. 662, 93 N.E.2d 927 (1950).

36. Eastman v. Williams, 124 Vt. 445, 207 A.2d 146 (1965).

37. Scott v. Greenville Pharmacy, 212 S.C. 485, 48 S.E.2d 324 (1948).

38. Restatement, Second, Torts, § 430.

39. Prosser, *Law of Torts*, p. 252. See Woodsmall v. Mt. Diablo Unified School District, 188 Cal.App.2d 262, 10 Cal.Rptr. 447 (1961); Munson v. Board of Education, 17 A.D.2d 687, 230 N.Y.S.2d 919 (1962), affirmed 13 N.Y.2d 854, 242 N.Y.S.2d 492, 192 N.E.2d 272 (1963).

40. McDonnell v. Brozo, 285 Mich. 38, 280 N.W. 100 (1938).

41. Meyer v. Board of Education, 9 N.J. 46, 86 A.2d 761 (1952).

42. Mikes v. Baumgartner, 277 Minn. 423, 152 N.W.2d 732 (1967).

43. Walsh v. West Coast Coal Mines, 31 Wash.2d 396, 197 P.2d 233 (1948).

44. Restatement, Second, Torts, § 463.

45. Rixmann v. Somerset Public Schools, 83 Wis.2d 571, 266 N.W.2d 326 (1978). See also Lemelle v. State, Through Board of Secondary and Elementary Education, 435 So.2d 1162 (La.App. 3 Cir.1983).

46. Cormier v. Sinegal, 180 So.2d 567 (La.App.1965).

47. Basmajian v. Board of Education, 211 App.Div. 347, 207 N.Y.S. 298 (1925).

48. Wilhelm v. Board of Education of City of New York, 16 A.D.2d 707, 227 N.Y.S.2d 791 (1962).

49. Prosser, *Law of Torts*, p. 303. See Passantino v. Board of Education of City of New York, 41 N.Y.2d 1022, 395 N.Y.S.2d 628, 363 N.E.2d 1373 (1977).

50. Stevens v. Central School District No. 1, 25 A.D.2d 871, 270 N.Y.S.2d 23 (1966).

51. Maltz v. Board of Education of New York City, 32 Misc.2d 492, 114 N.Y.S.2d 856 (1952).

52. Benedetto v. Travelers Insurance Co., 172 So.2d 354 (La.App.1965).

53. Brisson v. Minneapolis Baseball and Athletic Association, 185 Minn. 507, 240 N.W. 903 (1932).

54. Scanlon v. Wedger, 156 Mass. 462, 31 N.E. 642 (1891).

55. Dusckiewicz v. Carter, 115 Vt. 122, 52 A.2d 788 (1947).

56. Cadieux v. Board of Education of the City School Dist. for the City of Schenectady, 25 A.D.2d 579, 266 N.Y.S.2d 895 (1966).

57. Barr v. Bernhard, 562 S.W.2d 844 (Tex.1978).

58. Hunter v. Board of Education of Montgomery County, 292 Md. 481, 439 A.2d 582 (1982).

59. Ibid.

60. Peter W. v. San Francisco Unified School District, 60 Cal.App.3d 814, 131 Cal.Rptr. 854 (1976).

61. Donohue v. Copiague Union Free School District, 47 N.Y.2d 440, 418 N.Y.S.2d 375, 391 N.E.2d 1352 (1979).

62. Ibid., 439 A.2d at 585.

63. See D.S.W. v. Fairbanks North Star Borough School District, 628 P.2d 554 (Alaska 1981); Smith v. Alameda County Social Services Agency et. al., 90 Cal.App.3d 929, 153 Cal.Rptr. 712 (1979); Hoffman v. Board of Education of City of New York, 49 N.Y.2d 121, 424 N.Y.S.2d 376, 400 N.E.2d 317 (1979); Aubrey v. School District of Philadelphia, 63 Pa.Cmwlth. 330, 437 A.2d 1306 (1981).

64. Monroe v. Pape, 365 U.S. 167, 81 S.Ct. 473 (1961).

65. 42 U.S.C.A. § 1983 enacted 1871.

66. Ernest W. Williams, *Liability of Public Schools and Public School Officials for Damages Under 42 U.S.C. 1983*. JD thesis, Harvard Law School, 1975, p. 1.

67. 436 U.S. 658, 98 S.Ct. 2018 (1978).

68. 420 U.S. 308, 95 S.Ct. 992 (1975).

69. 435 U.S. 247, 98 S.Ct. 1042 (1978).

70. Monell v. Department of Social Services of City of New York, 436 U.S. 658, 98 S.Ct. 2018 (1978).

71. Pembaur v. City of Cincinnati, 475 U.S. 469, 106 S.Ct. 1292 (1986).

72. Bennett v. City of Slidell, 728 F.2d 762 (5th Cir. 1984).

73. Ibid.

74. Parrott v. Taylor, 451 U.S. 527, 101 S.Ct. 1908 (1981).

75. Daniels v. Williams, 474 U.S. 327, 106 S.Ct. 662 (1986).

76. 814 F.2d 1283 (8th Cir. 1987).

77. 814 F.2d at 1284. See also Garcia v. Miera, 817 F.2d 650 (10th Cir. 1987) and Taylor v. Ledbetter, 818 F.2d 791 (11th Cir. 1987).

78. Kibbe v. City of Springfield, 777 F.2d 801 (1st Cir. 1985), cert. granted 475 U.S. 1064, 106 S.Ct. 1374 (1986), cert. dismissed 480 U.S. 257, 107 S.Ct. 1114 (1987).

79. Mitchell v. Forsyth, 472 U.S. 511, 105 S.Ct. 2806 (1985).

80. Davis v. Scherer, 468 U.S. 183, 104 S.Ct. 3012 (1984).

81. Harlow v. Fitzgerald, 457 U.S. 800, 102 S.Ct. 2727 (1982).

82. Jeffrey J. Horner, "The Anatomy of a Constitutional Tort," *West's Education Law Reporter,* 47 Ed.Law Rep. 1 (1988), p. 13.

CHAPTER 12

Defamation and Student Records

Defamation is the imputation of immorality, dishonesty, or dishonorable conduct to another by spoken or written word. Defamation injures one's character or reputation by false aspersion or calumny. "Criticism" is distinct from "defamation" in that it is addressed to public matters and does not follow a person into private or personal affairs. A true critic never resorts to personal denigration or ridicule but confines his or her commentary to the merits of the particular issue under consideration.

■ DEFAMATION IN LEGAL HISTORY

Though defamation is considered to be a tort, it descends from a different historical lineage than the common tort of negligence. The Anglo-Saxon law of defamation has traces of historical development in Germanic and Roman law.[1] In early Anglo-Saxon law, insulting words raised by one person against another were sometimes punished by penalties as severe as excision of the tongue,[2] or as light as requiring the offender to hold his nose and call himself a liar.[3] The word "defamation" is a technical term derived from the Latin *diffamatus*, signifying a person of sufficiently notorious and evil reputation that the church was justified in accusing and placing him on trial. If the defendant was acquitted and his ill fame was determined to be unfounded, then his accusers could be tried for the calumny of committing a crime of false and hateful accusation.[4] In 1275, defamation became a criminal offense in the first of a long line of statutes that forbade insult of the king or his court.[5] This statute, known as *scandalum magnatum,* the slander of magnates, punished those who published false news producing discord between the king and his subjects. Because the nature of this offense was criminal and offenses were generally considered sedition, application did not extend beyond offenses against the crown.[6] Gradually, though, the common-law courts developed defamation as a civil wrong, reasoning that "libelling calumniation is an offense against the law of God."[7]

The law of defamation was greatly abused by the Star Chamber and upon the abolition of that court in 1641, the law lay dormant for some years. In the latter part of the seventeenth century, when the distinction between spoken and written defamation was established and became a permanent division in the law of defamation. The law of libel, written word, was developed as a supplement to the law of slander, spoken word. It was reasoned that spoken words imputing ill fame could be thoughtlessly conveyed in the heat of discussion and could, in many cases, be ignored; but libel, because it was written and, presumably, more carefully considered, suggested the presence of malice and was actionable for special damages.[8]

The elements of common-law defamation were well established by the eighteenth century, and the American courts generally followed the rationale and precedents of the early English courts. Today, the most important changes have occurred in state statute expanding or redefining certain elements of the law.

DEFAMATION IN PUBLIC SCHOOLS

Defamation is, therefore, constituted of the twin torts of libel and slander. On their faces, libel as written and slander as oral communication are easily distinguishable. However, other forms of communication such as acts or gestures, motion pictures, and radio or television complicate the dichotomy. Some courts simply maintain that defamation designed for visual perception is libel and that defamation designed for all other forms of communication is slander.[9] General acceptance by the courts is found in the following definitions: libel is a malicious publication, expressed in either printing or writing, or by signs and pictures, and slander is personal imputation effected by writings, pictures, or signs, both of which tend to injure a party's situation in society.[10]

Teachers and school administrators are particularly susceptible to actions in defamation because of the sensitivity of personal information that they come into contact with each day. Teachers, as a matter of routine, process and communicate information that relates to pupil performance, the misuse of which could potentially harm the student's reputation and stigmatize his or her future. The problem of the administrator is even more complex in communication of information concerning teacher performance to other administrators or to school board members. Public interest in education, though, makes it essential that proper pupil and teacher evaluations be made, and that public school officials and employees not be subjected to constant fear of personal liability.

Privilege

Because of this important public interest, the courts have generally recognized that statements regarding school matters are qualifiedly privileged if made by persons having a com-

mon duty or interest in the information and acting in good faith.[11] "In the absence of malice, a school official is not liable to a teacher for performing the duties of his office."[12] A teacher likewise has a qualified or conditional privilege when acting in good faith in school matters; but the qualified privilege is not unlimited, and no privilege attaches to a teacher's entry in a school register to the effect that a certain pupil "was ruined by tobacco and whiskey."[13] Absolute privileges are only afforded those individuals who perform vital governmental functions that the courts have defined as judicial proceedings, legislative proceedings, and certain executive proceedings. With the judiciary, absolute privilege extends only to the particular statements that are relevant or pertinent to the case at bar.[14] In the legislature, complete privilege extends to statements made in the course of debate, voting, or reports on work performed in committees.[15] Public officers holding executive positions also have absolute immunity for communications made in connection with the performance of their official duties.

While courts generally hold that school superintendents have a conditional or qualified privilege, some courts have maintained that public policy requires that superintendents be given an absolute privilege in evaluating teacher activities before a school board. Similarly, school board members have been held to have absolute privilege in imputing inefficiency and lack of qualification in evaluating a school superintendent's performance.[16]

The more common precedent to follow, though, is that officials, teachers, and others dealing in the public interest context have at least a qualified privilege. This conditional immunity can even extend to parents presenting a petition before a school board to the effect that a teacher was "incompetent."[17]

Good Faith

A qualified privilege protects the teacher or school official when statements are made in good faith and without malice. One court explained such privileges in this way:

If a communication comes within the class denominated absolute privileged or qualifiedly privileged, no recovery can be had. Privileged communications are divided and defined as follows: (1) that the communication was made by the defendant in good faith, without malice, not voluntarily but in answer to an inquiry, and in the reasonable protection of his own interest or performance of a duty to society; (2) that the defendant must honestly believe the communication to be true; (3) there must have been reasonable or probable grounds known to him for the suspicion; (4) that the communication, if made in answer to an inquiry, must not go further than to truly state the facts upon which the suspicion was founded, and to satisfy the inquirer that these were reasons for the suspicion.[18]

Under this definition, it is clear that the communication must be made in good faith, without malice, upon reasonable grounds, in answer to inquiry, and, importantly, it must be made with regard to assisting or protecting the interests of either of the parties involved or in performing a duty to society. The school official or employee's communication is qualifiedly privileged if it is prompted by a duty owed to either the public or a third party and is made in good faith and without malice.

Defamation Per Se and Per Quod

Words which in and of themselves, without extrinsic proof, injure one's reputation are defamatory *per se*. With defamation *per se*, the plaintiffs' cause of action is complete when he or she proves that the words have been articulated and conveyed. Plaintiff is not required to prove actual injury or out-of-pocket monetary loss, but rather must merely show that the words were of such kind as to impair one's reputation or standing in the community or to cause personal anguish, suffering, or humiliation. The plaintiff need not prove that he or she suffered special harm or direct loss.

A Maine court has helped define defamation *per se*.

We recognize that a good deal of confusion exists in the use of such terms as "libelous or slanderous per se" and "actionable per se." Courts and commentators often use these terms interchangeably, sometimes referring to technical common law pleading requirements that obviate the need to *allege* special damage and at other times referring to the nature of evidence at trial that obviate the need to *prove* special damages. . . . Specifically, the term slander per se refers to words that on their face without further proof or explanation injure the plaintiff in his business or occupation, i.e., are defamatory per se.[19]

Under American common law today, an action for defamation *per se* will lie without proof of special harm (damage) where (1) words impute (a) a criminal offense punishable by imprisonment, or (b) that plaintiff is guilty of a crime involving moral turpitude; (2) words impute to the plaintiff an existing venereal or other loathsome or communicable disease; (3) words impute to the plaintiff conduct, characteristics, or a condition incompatible with proper conduct of his or her lawful business, trade, or profession, or a public or private offense; and (4) words impute unchastity to a woman.

If the plaintiff is unable to bring his case under one of these categories, he or she must resort to proving special harm or actual damages by the communication[20] of defamation *per quod*.

Defamation *per quod* requires that the plaintiff prove actual damage. The plaintiff must show that publication of the defamation was the legal cause of special harm. The distinction between defamation *per se* and *per quod* may rest on whether a crime is imputed. For example, the law holds that it is defamation *per quod* and special damages must be proven if the words imputed to a teacher appear to harm the teacher's reputation, but do not relate to conduct of a crime, moral turpitude, unchastity, or damage the teacher in his or her profession. To say that a male teacher seduced a female student would, of course, be defamation *per se*. On the other hand, where a defendant had accused a headmaster of committing adultery with the school custodian's wife, the court found that the words had not been uttered in the context of the school nor in reference to the plaintiff as schoolmaster; the charge could be defamation *per quod,* requiring a showing of special and actual damage, a burden that the plaintiff could not sustain. Since a teacher's reputation among students and the community is so vital to performance of his or her professional responsibilities, it is easy to see how, in the majority of cases, false imputations against a teacher could fall into the category of defamation *per se.*[21]

Public Officials and Figures

Since *New York Times, Inc. v. Sullivan,*[22] a 1964 United States Supreme Court decision, the law of defamation as it pertains to freedom of speech and press has changed considerably. This case, and subsequent ones, hold the interest of the publisher to be of vital importance to a free and informed society. The position of the press is elevated above the normal law of defamation, and special rules apply as defined by *Sullivan.*

In *Sullivan,* a paid advertisement in the New York Times signed by a number of prominent individuals criticized the behavior of the Montgomery, Alabama, police in dealing with racial unrest. The police chief, Sullivan, claimed that the derogatory reference to police behavior amounted to defamation of him personally. The Alabama State Supreme Court held that the publication was libel *per se,* and that the *New York Times* was liable for half a million dollars without the plaintiff showing special damage or fault on the part of the *Times.*

The United States Supreme Court reversed the lower court, holding the guarantee of free speech under the First Amendment prohibits a *public official* from recovering damages for a defamatory falsehood relating to his *official* conduct, unless he or she proves the statement was made with "actual malice," and that the statement was made with knowledge that it was false or in reckless disregard of whether it was false or not. This protection extended to both the newspaper and to the private individuals who paid for the advertisement and signed it. Plaintiffs in the case were unable to show that the *New York Times* actually had

knowledge of the falsity of portions of the statement.

Before *Sullivan,* the common law of libel established three rules that, taken together, effectively required a publisher ensure the absolute accuracy of statements made in criticism of any person. These rules were first, the burden of proof was always placed on the publisher because defamatory statements were presumed to be false; second, false information was presumed to be published with malice regardless of whether it was merely a misstatement, mistake, or bad luck; and third, the aggrieved party did not need to prove actual harm to his or her reputation—damage to one's reputation was presumed by the simple fact of publication. These common-law rules of defamation applied to communications between private persons, and these common-law standards still prevail where the press is not involved.[23]

Sullivan, invoked "freedom of press" as a constitutional gloss on the common law and provided much more latitude for the press. Here, the Supreme Court weighed the individual's interest in reputation against the public's interest in free speech and concluded that special consideration must be given the press when it criticizes public officials. *Sullivan* made two major changes in the law; it created the category of public official, and it shifted the burden of proof to the plaintiff to prove that an untruth was conveyed with malice.[24]

Cases following *Sullivan* have dealt primarily with two major questions: (1) what is the definition of public official, and how broad is the term; and (2) what is the level of *privilege* of the press, and does it vary as the subject of the defamation becomes more remote from officialdom.[25]

In *Rosenblatt v. Baer,*[26] the Supreme Court further defined "public official," saying:

> It is clear, therefore, that the "public official" designation applies at the very least, to those among the hierarchy of government employees who have, or appear to have, substantial responsibility for or control over the conduct of governmental affairs.[27]

The definition of "public officials" in *Sullivan* was broadened in *Curtis Publishing Co. v. Butts*[28] to include "public figures."

The Supreme Court has characterized a "public figure" in the following manner: For the most part those who attain [the status of a public figure] have assumed roles of especial prominence in the affairs of society. Some occupy positions of such persuasive power and influence that they are deemed public figures for all purposes. More commonly, those classed as public figures have thrust themselves to the forefront of particular public controversies in order to influence the resolution of the issues involved. In either event, they invite attention and comment.[29]

Public officials must show malice and knowledge of or reckless disregard for the truth of the publication. The Constitution requires proof of knowledge or conscious indifference to falsity when imputations are made to either public officials or public figures.

Where a private individual is libeled by the press, liability of the press may be incurred by merely showing that the statement was untruthful. It is not necessary to show malice, nor is it required the plaintiff show the newspaper knew the publication was false. Whenever liability is imposed against the press for false publication, the damages must be limited to the actual injury sustained; general or punitive damages are not available.

Students and teachers are not usually considered to be public officials or public figures. Imputations against teachers by the student press are actionable if the teacher shows the student publisher was at fault by directing the defamation toward the teacher. Similarly, students cannot attack other students or school administrators personally without potential consequences. A former school board member running in a school board election is considered to be a public figure under the *Sullivan* precedent.

Malice

Malice in a legal sense characterizes all acts that are done with evil disposition and unlawful motive with intent to injure or cause harm to another. The law distinguishes at least two types of malice. The first is called "malice in law" or "implied malice," and is defamation *per se*. Here there is no excuse for the conveyance of hurtful information. Unsolicited, derogatory commentary, oral or written, may be of this form. Actual malice is the second form, and is dependent on the defendant's motive for making the statement. Actual malice requires proof that the defendant's motives and interest were wrongful, ill willed, and designed to harm the plaintiff's reputation.

A qualified privilege is an affirmative defense that must be pleaded and proved. Whether a privilege exists is a matter of law for the court to decide, not the jury. A qualified privilege can be overcome with a showing of malice. Punitive damages may not be available for malice in law or implied malice, but are generally assumed to be appropriate for actual malice.[30]

Parents have a qualified privilege to speak publicly before a school board regarding a teacher's instruction of his or her children. It is within the right of parents to oversee their children's education, to make statements pertaining to a teacher's competency, or inefficiency in the classroom. A qualified privilege raises a presumption of good faith and places the burden on the plaintiff of proving express malice. In this Florida case the court stated:

Where a person speaks upon a privileged occasion, but the speaker is motivated more by a desire to harm the person defamed than by a purpose to protect the personal or social interest giving rise to the privilege, then it can be said that there was express malice and the privilege is destroyed. Strong, angry, or intemperate words do not alone show express malice; rather, there must be a showing that the speaker used his privileged position "to gratify his malevolence." . . . If the occasion of the communication is privileged because of a proper interest to be protected, and the defamer is motivated by a desire to protect that interest, he does not forfeit the privilege merely because he also in fact feels hostility or ill will toward the plaintiff. The incidental gratification of personal feelings of indignation is not sufficient to defeat the privilege where the primary motivation is within the scope of the privilege.[31]

As we shall see later, it is actual malice that is required of public officials to overcome the privilege of the press as enunciated in *Sullivan v. New York Times*.[32] Thus, some courts refer to actual malice as "New York Times Malice."[33] The standard of proof required of a public official to establish New York Times malice may be greater because of the newspapers' "constitutional" privilege. In such cases, the plaintiff public official must show "by clear and convincing evidence" a reckless disregard for truth. On the other hand, the "common" law qualified privilege of a teacher or a parent may be overcome by a lesser standard of proof, the intent to injure the plaintiff by a "preponderance of the evidence."

Truth

Falsity is the basic ingredient in the tort of defamation. Conveyance of truth is not defamation. Yet in some states, courts have held that truth is a defense for libel only when published with good motives and justifiable ends. In *Farnsworth v. Tribune Co.*,[34] the court ruled that a person will not be allowed to resurrect a long-forgotten mistake of another and republish it. The prevailing view, though, is that truth of a defamatory statement affords a complete defense to defamation regardless of whether ill will or malice are present. "One who publishes a defamatory statement of fact is not subject to liability for defamation if the statement is true."[35]

Truth, as an absolute defense against defamation, emanated from the famous Peter Zenger case in 1735. Prior to Zenger, defamation of a public official was largely indefensible. One will recall that Zenger was indicted for printing an edition of *The New York Weekly Journal* that called the governor of New York a "rogue" and accused him of destroying the liberties of the citizenry. Zenger's lawyer argued that the charges were true and a jury agreed, acquitting Zenger. Although the Zenger affair was so imbued with politics that its importance was mitigated, the case nevertheless established that truth was a legitimate defense to libel; and that truth was a matter of fact to be decided by a jury, not a matter of law to be decided by a judge. After the Zenger case, it was popularly maintained that "Truth ought to govern the whole affair of libels."[36]

Under common-law tort, where the plaintiff is a private person, a defamatory statement is presumed to be false; and the defendant must prove that the statement was true. The burden of proof is on the defendant, but, as just noted, if the plaintiff is a "public official" or "public figure," the burden of proof shifts. The "public person" must present clear and convincing proof to the court that the defendant published false, defamatory information with knowledge of its falsity or with reckless disregard for the truth.

Thus, if a teacher has been the brunt of a defamatory statement, then the burden of proving truth is on the defendant because a teacher is generally a private person. If, for example, a parent or student published defamatory information about a teacher, the burden would be on the parent or student to prove the statement is true.

One could probably conceive of a situation in which a teacher could be a public figure if he or she had won fame for some reason, but this is generally not the case. So long as the teacher does not acquire the esteemed status of a public personage, then the burden of proving truth would be on the defendant if a publication harmed the teacher.

---

*Negative Recommendation Is Protected
by a Conditional Privilege*

– – – · – – – · – – – ·

Hett v. Ploetz

– – – · – – – · – – – ·

Supreme Court of Wisconsin, 1963.
20 Wis.2d 55, 121 N.W.2d 270.

GORDON, Justice. Hett brought this action to recover damages for injury to his professional reputation from an allegedly libelous publication by Ploetz. . . .

From 1956 to 1959 Hett had been employed as a speech therapist in the school system of the city of Cudahy, Wisconsin. His schedule required that he travel to six different schools and teach those pupils who were in need of his specialty. . . .

Based upon their analysis of Hett's qualifications, the principals of the six schools in which Hett taught reported to Ploetz that they did not recommend renewal of Hett's contract for the 1959–1960 school year.

While the principals did not recommend Hett's retention for that year, Ploetz decided that because he had been the superintendent for only six months it would be unfair to Hett to recommend his dismissal.

Ploetz informed Hett that his contract was not going to be renewed and told him that it would be in his best interest to resign so that a dismissal would not appear on his record. Hett resigned. . . .

On November 9, 1959, Hett applied for a position as a speech therapist at the Southern Wisconsin Colony and Training School, Union Grove, Wisconsin. In his application he stated that the reason he left the Cudahy school system was that there was a lack of advancement opportunities. He listed Ploetz as a reference and gave permission to the Southern Colony officials to communicate with Ploetz. . . .

The plaintiff contends that he was libeled by the defendant's response to an inquiry from a prospective employer of the plaintiff. Hett had not only given Ploetz's name as a reference but had also given express permission to the prospective employer to communicate with Ploetz.

We must resolve two questions. The first is whether any privilege insulates the defendant's letter; the second is whether an issue of malice exists for trial.

It is clear that Ploetz's allegedly defamatory letter was entitled to a conditional privilege. Ploetz was privileged to give a critical appraisal concerning his former employee so long as such appraisal was made for the valid purpose of enabling a prospective employer to evaluate the employee's qualifications. The privilege is said to be "conditional" because of

the requirements that the declaration be reasonably calculated to accomplish the privileged purpose and that it be made without malice. . . . Lord Blackburn has said:

> Where a person is so situated that it becomes right in the interests of society that he should tell to a third person facts, then, if he *bona fide* and without malice does tell them, it is a privileged communication.

The public school official who expresses an opinion as to the qualifications of a person who has submitted an application for employment as a school teacher should enjoy the benefits of a conditional privilege.

As previously noted, the employee had given Ploetz's name as a reference and had authorized that an inquiry be made of him. The letter contains certain factual matters as well as expressions of opinion. The factual portions are not contradicted by any pleading before this court. Thus, the following statement contained in the letter written by Ploetz stands unchallenged:

> Last year, our six Principals and Elementary Coordinator unanimously recommended that he be no longer retained in our system as a speech correctionist. He, therefore, was not offered a contract to return this year.

The expression of opinion of which Hett complains is contained in the following portion of the defendant's letter:

> We feel that Mr. Hett is not getting the results that we expected in this very important field. I, personally, feel that Mr. Hett does not belong in the teaching field. He has a rather odd personality, and it is rather difficult for him to gain the confidence of his fellow workers and the boys and girls with whom he works.

In our opinion, the record before us establishes that this expression of opinion is not founded in malice. The background of the relationship of Hett and Ploetz satisfactorily demonstrates that the latter's negative recommendation was grounded on the record and not upon malice. Ploetz was not an intermeddler; he had a proper interest in connection with the letter he wrote. . . .

The plaintiff has failed to recite any evidentiary facts which are sufficient to raise questions for trial. His allegations that the letter contains defamatory material are mere conclusions. No presumption of malice has arisen; no showing of express malice has been presented.

In Otten v. Schutt (1962), 15 Wis.2d 497, 503, 113 N.W.2d 152, 155, this court stated:

> The law relating to defamatory communications is based on public policy. The law will impute malice where a defamatory publication is made without sufficient cause or excuse, or where necessary to protect the interests of society and the security of character and reputation; but where the welfare of society is better promoted by a freedom of expression, malice will not be imputed. . . .

Public policy requires that malice not be imputed in cases such as this, for otherwise one who enjoys a conditional privilege might be reluctant to give a sincere, yet critical, response to a request for an appraisal of a prospective employee's qualifications.

. . . A thorough examination of the entire record compels our conclusion that the respondent is entitled to the benefit of a conditional privilege.

Judgment affirmed.

NOTES

1. If a statement is made by defendant in response to an inquiry by the plaintiff, then a conditional privilege may be elevated to the status of an absolute privilege. An "absolute privilege is confined to relatively few situations. It is accorded judicial proceedings, legislative proceedings, proceedings of executive officers charged with responsibility of importance, publications made *with consent of the plaintiff* and communications between husband and wife." Prosser, *Law of Torts,* 2nd ed., West Publishing Company; *Walker v. D'Alesandro,* 212 Md. 163, 129 A.2d 148 (1957).

The Supreme Court of Missouri invoked this rule when a superintendent responded to a question by a teacher in a hearing before the school board.

> When plaintiff asked the defendant at the board meeting why she was not going to be re-employed the following school year the superintendent should be at liberty to say to her, "Miss Williams, you have disobeyed school rules and regulations, you are insubordinate and are insufficient and inadequate with your students." In that situation he (superintendent) is absolutely protected in his explanation to plaintiff. *Williams v. School District of Springfield R–12,* 447 S.W.2d 256 (Mo.1969).

2. Statement made by a school board member at a school board meeting referring to the fact that marijuana cigarettes had been found in a student's car was privileged and the board member could not be found liable for defamation. The court reasoned that the board member held a conditional privilege that could not be overcome absent the showing of malice. The court said:

> Privileged communications are divided into two classes, namely, those which are absolutely privileged, and those which are qualifiedly or conditionally privileged. In cases where absolute privilege obtains there is no liability. Depending upon the circumstances of the case, there may or may not be liability with respect to qualifiedly or conditionally privileged communications. The distinction between the two classes is said to be that the protection of absolute privileged communications is not at all dependent upon their bona fides, while qualifiedly or conditionally privileged communications are merely freed from the legal imputation of malice, and become actionable only by virtue of the existence of express malice. *Morrison v. Mobile County Bd. of Educ.,* 495 So.2d 1086 (Ala. 1986).

3. A New York court held that a school social worker has an absolute privilege for the social worker's report to the child protection agency. The same court

ruled that a qualified privilege existed covering the information conveyed between the social worker and the school district committee to establish appropriate individualized educational programs for handicapped children. *Dunajewski v. Bellmore-Merrick Central High School District,* 138 A.D. 2d 557, 526 N.Y.S.2d 139 (2 Dept., 1988).

4. In the case of *DeBolt v. McBrien,* 96 Neb. 237, 147 N.W. 462 (1914), the court applied the absolute privilege rule to a state superintendent of public instruction's statement to the county supervisor accusing the plaintiff of playing poker and being under the influence of liquor.

5. The Oklahoma Appellate Court found that defamatory statements about the school librarian made by the president and dean of the medical school at a session of the board of regents were absolutely privileged. See *Hughes v. Bizzell,* 189 Okl. 472, 117 P.2d 763 (1941).

6. Parents and patrons of the school have a qualified privilege in disclosing information at a school board meeting. School patrons presented the school trustees with a letter charging that the teacher failed to keep proper order and discipline and allowed older boys to take improper privileges with her and girl students. The court held that if the defendants believed the school was conducted as stated, then it was their right to complain to the trustees since they were the only ones authorized to remedy it. According to the court, the central issue was whether the letter was presented with malicious intent. In reversing a judgment in favor of the teacher, the court remanded the case for jury determination of whether malice existed. According to the court, the jury should be instructed to find that malice was present if the publication by defendants was not made in good faith and had actually intended to injure the teacher, not merely to correct the school situation. *Malone v. Carrico,* 16 Ky.Law Rev. 155 (1894).

7. Residents and patrons of a school district were held to be protected by a qualified privilege when they presented a petition to the school board stating "we do not think she (plaintiff teacher) is a competent teacher and has but little control over the school." The court said that if the occasion, the motive, and the cause be proper, the publication or communication does not imply malice. To overcome a qualified privilege, malice must be proved by the person claiming to have been defamed, and the mere falsity of the alleged defamatory matter is not sufficient. *Hoover v. Jordan,* 27 Colo.App. 515, 150 P. 333 (1915); see also 40 A.L.R.3d 490.

8. A tenured teacher and assistant principal were responsible for investigating suspected drug involvement of students and counseling with students and their parents. Their communications to parents of high school student concerning the sale of drugs in plaintiffs' place of business were qualifiedly privileged. Comments were made in good faith, and on an occasion that properly served their duty, and under circumstances that were fairly warranted. The teacher and assistant principal were not liable to plaintiffs for defamation in the absence of express malice. The court defined *qualified privilege* in this way: "A communication, although it contains criminating matter, is privileged when made in good faith upon any subject in which the party communicating has an interest, or in reference to which he has a right or duty, if made to a person having a corresponding interest, right, or duty, and made upon an occasion to properly serve such right, interest, or duty, and in a manner and under circumstances fairly warranted by the occasion and the duty, right, or interest, and not so made as to unnecessarily or unduly injure another, or to show express malice." *Chapman v. Furlough,* 334 So.2d 293 (Fla. App. 1976).

In defining *good faith,* the court quoted an older Florida case, saying: "Good faith, a right, duty, or interest in a proper subject, a proper occasion, and a proper communication to those having a like right, duty, or interest, are all essential to constitute words spoken, that are actionable per se, a privileged communication, so as to make the proof by the Plaintiff of express malice essential to liability. In determining whether or not a communication is privileged, the nature of the subject, the right, duty, or interest of the parties in such subject, the time, place and circumstances of the occasion, and the manner, character, and extent of the communication, should all be considered. When all these facts and circumstances are conceded, a court may decide whether a communication is a privileged one, so as to require the Plaintiff to prove express malice . . ." *Abraham v. Baldwin,* 52 Fla. 151, 42 So. 591 (1906).

Qualified Privilege Protects Parents Who Convey Information About Teachers

— · — · — · — · —

Desselle v. Guillory

— · — · — · — · —

Court of Appeal of Louisiana, Third Circuit, 1981.407 So.2d 79.

SWIFT, Judge. . . . In July of 1979, Mrs. Jane Guillory was a counselor at a summer church camp for girls. She participated in a conversation with several of the girls who told her about incidents which they had heard or witnessed concerning certain teachers, including the plaintiffs, at Bordelonville High School. When Mrs. Guillory discussed with one of her church deacons the information, which included allegations that the teachers were fondling students, he advised her to inform the school principal.

The following month Mrs. Guillory took up the matter with Mr. Jimmy Bordelon, the principal of the high school, who assured her that he would observe the teachers' behavior.

On March 6, 1980, Mrs. Guillory visited with Mr. Bordelon to discuss a poor grade on a test given to her daughter by Maxwell Desselle. Mr. Desselle was called in to talk to Mrs. Guillory about it. They had a heated discussion concerning the test and the defendant also made a comment to the effect that she had something else on Desselle. After he returned to his classroom Mrs. Guillory told the principal that the teachers had continued to molest the children. She testified that prior to this visit Abigail Farbes had informed her that it was still going on. The principal told Mrs. Guillory he did not believe such rumors and had not observed any such behavior. Mrs. Guillory then informed the principal she would take her information to the superintendent.

That same afternoon Mrs. Guillory had a conversation with Mrs. Jeannette Huffmaster. When Mrs. Guillory informed her of what she had heard, Mrs. Huffmaster told her that she had seen Maxwell Desselle pat a girl on the buttocks in the presence of Mr. Bordelon.

On March 7, 1980, Mr. Bordelon met with the plaintiffs and informed them of what Mrs. Guillory had said. The four then went to the Guillory home to discuss the matter. At this meeting an argument ensued and at least one of the plaintiffs threatened to sue the Guillorys for defamation.

Later that night Mrs. Guillory called her attorney who advised her to obtain written statements from the girls who had given her the information about the teachers. Mrs. Guillory went to the homes of Abigail Farbes, Joan Hess, Tammy Lemoine, Beverly Martin and Terry Bringold to obtain such statements. She said she explained the situation and alleged incidents to their parents and got their permission before asking the girls to write "letters" as to what they saw or heard about the matter. Three of these persons and her daughter did so.

On March 10, 1980, Mrs. Guillory and Mrs. Huffmaster drew up a petition calling for an investigation by the Evangeline Parish School Board into wrongdoings at Bordelonville High School. The petition did not contain the names of the plaintiffs or of any specific facts concerning the alleged wrongdoings. These ladies then visited five or six homes in an attempt to obtain signatures on the petition. The school board directed a representative to make an investigation. Upon his failure to obtain any testimony of wrongdoing, the board concluded there was no basis for action against any teacher and closed the case. The recorded statements taken by the representative were destroyed and the interested parties were notified in writing of the board's decision. . . .

Beverly Martin testified she had told Mrs. Guillory that she had heard students say that some of the teachers played with the students. In particular, she had heard Kenneth Maillet would take girls in the bathroom after practice, but they wouldn't tell her what they did. She also told her that Garland Desselle was friendly with the girls and would allow them to sit in his lap and that he felt one girl during P.E. In addition she told Mrs. Guillory of an incident when Maxwell Desselle kissed her under the mistletoe. Abigail Farbes testified she had told Mrs. Guillory that Maxwell and Kenneth Maillet would flirt around with girls and that Beverly had told her that Maxwell Desselle once had grabbed Beverly and gave her a passionate kiss.

Joan Hess testified that before the Mardi Gras trip she had her majorette uniform on under her jeans and part of the uniform was showing. She stated Mr. Maillet tugged at the jeans and a button came undone from the jeans. Joan further testified she told Kaye Guillory, the defendant's daughter, that Kenneth Maillet tugged at her jeans pulling a button off.

Tammy Lemoine testified that in the written statement given Mrs. Guillory she said she heard that Kenneth Maillet and another girl "had something going on" and that Garland Desselle said "he was going to get some meat" from two girls "one of these days."

The testimony as to the content of the statements Mrs. Guillory made to the principal and the parents of high school students is in dispute. Mr. Bordelon, the principal, said Mrs. Guillory told him the teachers were fondling and molesting girls, although she never used the word "intercourse." Clara Laborde and Peggy Hess stated Mrs. Guillory had told them that one of the plaintiffs, Kenneth Maillet, had unzipped Mrs. Hess' daughter's pants before a Mardi Gras band trip and that the plaintiffs

were molesting the girls. She also said some teachers were starting this in the elementary grades and taking them to bed by the time they reached the high school grades.

Mrs. Guillory testified that she did not accuse the plaintiffs of anything, but merely told Mrs. Hess and Mrs. Laborde what she had heard from the girls and said she felt the plaintiffs might be having sexual relations with the students. Having heard things about these men, such as one girl having seen Kenneth Maillet with his pants down in the bathroom one night after basketball practice, she was trying to determine if they were true. She also stated at trial that she thought the parents had a right to know and she never intended to do any harm to the men allegedly involved.

The plaintiffs emphatically denied ever molesting or having intercourse with any high school students. Kenneth Maillet did not recall any incident where he unbuttoned a girl's jeans or did anything improper. Maxwell Desselle said he had harmlessly kissed Beverly Martin at a Christmas dinner. Mr. Bordelon and Maxwell Desselle denied the occurrence of Mr. Desselle patting a girl on the buttocks.

Concerning the statement Mr. Guillory made to James Armand, Mr. Armand stated Mr. Guillory told him certain teachers were molesting girls on a school trip and named the three plaintiffs. Mr. Guillory disputed this by saying he told him some of the girls had stated to his wife that some of the teachers were "messing around." He testified he did not intend any harm.

The issues presented by this appeal are: (1) whether or not the jury erred in rendering a verdict in favor of the defendants and (2) whether or not the jury erred in awarding the defendants attorney's fees under LSA–C.C. Article 2315.1.

In order to maintain an action in defamation, the plaintiff must establish the following elements: (1) defamatory words; (2) publication; (3) falsity; (4) malice, actual or implied; and (5) resulting injury.

The available defenses against an action in defamation are: (1) privilege and (2) truth.

The appellants argue that the evidence presented sufficiently proved the elements necessary for an action in defamation and the defendants failed to bear their burden of proving privilege or truth. Assuming the evidence was sufficient to prove the first three elements of defamation, we find that a qualified privilege existed between Mrs. Guillory and each person she discussed the rumors with.

A qualified privilege exists as to a communication, even if false, between parties sharing an interest or duty. However, to be a good defense such communication must be made in good faith and without malice.

In the present case Mrs. Guillory had discussions with the school principal and with several parents of girls attending Bordelonville High School concerning the alleged actions of certain teachers. The interests shared by each of these persons were to protect the welfare of their children at school and to provide good teachers in the public schools.

There was sufficient evidence for the jury to have found that Mrs. Guillory was in good faith and without malice in her communications to the principal and the parents. Several high school girls told her that certain teachers were playing with the female students. She had heard that one of the plaintiffs was taking girls into the bathroom after practice for an unmentioned purpose; that a teacher was allowing a girl to sit on his lap while he felt her body; that a teacher had unbuttoned the jeans of a girl; and that a teacher had kissed a student and he also had patted a girl on the buttocks. Hearing these things from the girls and a parent, it was not unreasonable for Mrs. Guillory to have believed that improprieties were occurring at the school. From these facts the jury could have concluded that Mrs. Guillory had reasonable grounds to believe her statements were true and were made in good faith and without malice. In such cases they were privileged. . . .

From our review of the record we are unable to say that the verdict of the jury favoring the defendants on the plaintiffs' demands is clearly wrong. . . .

We do not believe the filing of these suits was frivolous. Our decision is based on the defense of qualified privilege and the record contains no indication of any lack of sincerity on the part of plaintiffs as to their legal position. Therefore the jury award of $3,000 to the Guillorys for attorney's fees was in error and must be set aside. *Boyd v. Community Center Credit Corporation*, 359 So.2d 1048 (La. App. 4 Cir.1978).

For these reasons the judgment of the district court is reversed and set aside insofar as it awarded $3,000.00 at attorney's fees to the plaintiffs-in-reconvention. Otherwise, it is affirmed. The costs of this appeal are assessed one-half to plaintiffs and one-half to the defendants.

Affirmed in part and reversed in part.

Newspaper Article Accusing Coach of Being a Liar Is Not Entitled to Separate Constitutional Privilege for "Opinion"

— · — · — · — · —

Milkovich v. Lorain Journal Co.

— · — · — · — · —

Supreme Court of the United States, 1990.
____U.S. ____, 110 S.Ct. 2695.

Chief Justice REHNQUIST delivered the opinion of the Court. Respondent J. Theodore Diadiun authored an article in an Ohio newspaper implying that petitioner Michael Milkovich, a local high school wrestling coach, lied under oath in a judicial proceeding about an incident involving petitioner and his team which occurred at a wrestling match. Petitioner sued Diadiun and the newspaper for libel, and the Ohio Court of Appeals affirmed a lower court entry of summary judgment against petitioner. This judgment was based in part on the grounds that the article constituted an "opinion" protected from the reach of state defamation law by the First Amendment to the United States Constitution. We hold that the First Amendment does not prohibit the application of Ohio's libel laws to the alleged defamations contained in the article.

This case is before us for the third time in an odyssey of litigation spanning nearly 15 years. Petitioner Milkovich, now retired, was the wrestling coach at Maple Heights High School in Maple Heights, Ohio. In 1974, his team was involved in an altercation at a home wrestling match with a team from Mentor High School. Several people were injured. In response to the incident, the Ohio High School Athletic Association (OHSAA) held a hearing at which Milkovich and H. Don Scott, the Superintendent of Maple Heights Public Schools, testified. Following the hearing, OHSAA placed the Maple Heights team on probation for a year and declared the team ineligible for the 1975 state tournament. OHSAA also censored Milkovich for his actions during the altercation. Thereafter, several parents and wrestlers sued OHSAA in the Court of Common Pleas of Franklin County, Ohio, seeking a restraining order against OHSAA's ruling on the grounds that they had been denied due process in the OHSAA proceeding. Both Milkovich and Scott testified in that proceeding. The court overturned OHSAA's probation and ineligibility orders on due process grounds.

The day after the court rendered its decision, respondent Diadiun's column appeared in the News-Herald, a newspaper which circulates in Lake County, Ohio, and is owned by respondent Lorain Journal Co. The column bore the heading "Maple beat the law with the 'big lie,'" beneath which appeared Diadiun's photograph and the words "TD Says." The carryover page headline announced " . . . Diadiun says Maple told a lie." The column contained the following passages:

 . . . a lesson was learned (or relearned) yesterday by the student body of Maple Heights High School, and by anyone who attended the Maple–Mentor wrestling meet of last Feb. 8.

A lesson which, sadly, in view of the events of the past year, is well they learned early.

It is simply this: If you get in a jam, lie your way out.

If you're successful enough, and powerful enough, and can sound sincere enough, you stand an excellent chance of making the lie

stand up, regardless of what really happened.

The teachers responsible were mainly Maple wrestling coach, Mike Milkovich, and former superintendent of schools, H. Donald Scott. . . .

Anyone who attended the meet, whether he be from Maple Heights, Mentor, or impartial observer, knows in his heart that Milkovich and Scott lied at the hearing after each having given his solemn oath to tell the truth.

But they got away with it.

Is that the kind of lesson we want our young people learning from their high school administrators and coaches?

I think not. . . .

Petitioner commenced a defamation action against respondents in the Court of Common Pleas of Lake County, Ohio, alleging that the headline of Diadiun's article and the 9 passages quoted above "accused plaintiff of committing the crime of perjury, an indictable offense in the State of Ohio, and damaged plaintiff directly in his life-time occupation of coach and teacher, and constituted libel per se." . . .

 . . .

Subsequently, . . . the Ohio Court of Appeals in the instant proceedings affirmed a trial court's grant of summary judgment in favor of respondents, concluding that "it has been decided, as a matter of law, that the article in question was constitutionally protected opinion." . . . We granted certiorari . . . to consider the important questions raised by the Ohio courts' recognition of a constitutionally-required "opinion" exception to the application of its defamation laws. We now reverse.

Since the latter half of the 16th century, the common law has afforded a cause of action for damage to a person's reputation by the publication of false and defamatory statements. . . .

 . . . Defamation law developed not only as a means of allowing an individual to vindicate his good name, but also for the purpose of obtaining redress for harm caused by such statements. . . . As the common law developed in this country, apart from the issue of damages, one usually needed only allege an unprivileged publication of false and defamatory matter to state a cause of action for defamation. See, *e.g.,* Restatement of Torts § 558 (1938); *Gertz v. Robert Welch, Inc.,* 418 U.S., at 370, 94 S.Ct., at 3022 (WHITE, J., dissenting) ("Under typical state defamation law, the defamed private citizen had to prove only a false publication that would subject him to hatred, contempt, or ridicule"). The common law generally did not place any additional restrictions on the type of statement that could be actionable. Indeed, defamatory communications were deemed actionable regardless of whether they were deemed to be statements of fact or opinion. See, *e.g.,* Restatement of Torts, *supra,* §§ 565–567. As noted in the 1977 Restatement (Second) of Torts § 566, Comment *a:*

> Under the law of defamation, an expression of opinion could be defamatory if the expression was sufficiently derogatory of another as to cause harm to his reputation, so as to lower him in the estimation of the community or to deter third persons from associating or dealing with him. . . . The expression of opinion was also actionable in a suit for defamation, despite the normal requirement that the communication be false as well as defamatory. . . . This position was maintained even though the truth or falsity of an opinion—as distinguished from a statement of fact—is not a matter that can be objectively determined and truth is a complete defense to a suit for defamation.

However, due to concerns that unduly burdensome defamation laws could stifle valuable public debate, the privilege of "fair comment" was incorporated into the common law as an affirmative defense to an action for defamation. "The principle of 'fair comment' afford[ed] legal immunity for the honest expression of opinion on matters of legitimate public interest when based upon a true or privileged statement of fact." 1 F. Harper & F. James, Law of Torts § 5.28, p. 456 (1956) (footnote omitted). As this statement implies, comment was generally privileged when it concerned a matter of public concern, was upon true or privileged facts, represented the actual opinion of the speaker, and was not made solely for the purpose of causing harm.

See Restatement of Torts, *supra,* § 606. "According to the majority rule, the privilege of fair comment applied only to an expression of opinion and not to a false statement of fact, whether it was expressly stated or implied from an expression of opinion." Restatement (Second) of Torts, *supra,* § 566 Comment *a.* Thus under the common law, the privilege of "fair comment" was the device employed to strike the appropriate balance between the need for vigorous public discourse and the need to redress injury to citizens wrought by invidious or irresponsible speech.

In 1964, we decided in *New York Times Co. v. Sullivan,* 376 U.S. 254, 84 S.Ct. 710, 11 L.Ed.2d 686, that the First Amendment to the United States Constitution placed limits on the application of the state law of defamation. There the Court recognized the need for "a federal rule that prohibits a public official from recovering damages for a defamatory falsehood relating to his official conduct unless he proves that the statement was made with 'actual malice'—that is, with knowledge that it was false or with reckless disregard of whether it was false or not." . . . This rule was prompted by a concern that, with respect to the criticism of public officials in their conduct of governmental affairs, a state law " 'rule compelling the critic of official conduct to guarantee the truth of all his factual assertions' would deter protected speech." *Gertz v. Robert Welch, Inc.,* 418 U.S., at 334, 94 S.Ct., at 3004 (quoting *New York Times, supra,* 376 U.S., at 279, 84 S.Ct., at 725).

Three years later, in *Curtis Publishing Co. v. Butts,* 388 U.S. 130, 87 S.Ct. 1975, 18 L.Ed.2d 1094 (1967), a majority of the Court determined "that the *New York Times* test should apply to criticism of 'public figures' as well as 'public officials.' The Court extended the constitutional privilege announced in that case to protect defamatory criticism of non-public persons 'who are nevertheless intimately involved in the resolution of important public questions or, by reason of their fame, shape events in areas of concern to society at large.' " . . .

The next step in this constitutional evolution was the Court's consideration of a private individual's defamation actions involving statements of public concern. Although the issue was initially in doubt, . . . the Court ultimately concluded that the *New York Times* malice standard was inappropriate for a private person attempting to prove he was defamed on matters of public interest. . . . As we explained:

> Public officials and public figures usually enjoy significantly greater access to the channels of effective communication and hence have a more realistic opportunity to counteract false statements than private individuals normally enjoy. . . .
>
> [More important,] public officials and public figures have voluntarily exposed themselves to increased risk of injury from defamatory falsehood concerning them. No such assumption is justified with respect to a private individual. . . .

Nonetheless, the Court believed that certain significant constitutional protections were warranted in this area. First, we held that the States could not impose liability without requiring some showing of fault. . . . Second, we held that the States could not permit recovery of presumed or punitive damages on less than a showing of *New York Times* malice. . . .

Still later, in *Philadelphia Newspapers, Inc. v. Hepps,* . . . we held "that the common-law presumption that defamatory speech is false cannot stand when a plaintiff seeks damages against a media defendant for speech of public concern." . . . In other words, the Court fashioned "a constitutional requirement that the plaintiff bear the burden of showing falsity, as well as fault, before recovering damages." . . . Although recognizing that "requiring the plaintiff to show falsity will insulate from liability some speech that is false, but unprovably so," the Court believed that this result was justified on the grounds that "placement by state law of the burden of proving truth upon media defendants who publish speech of public concern deters such speech because of the fear that liability will unjustifiably result." . . .

Respondents would have us recognize, in addition to the established safeguards discussed above, still another First Amendment-based protection for defamatory statements which are categorized as "opinion" as opposed to "fact." For this proposition they rely principally on the following dictum from our opinion in *Gertz:*

> Under the First Amendment there is no such thing as a false idea. However pernicious an opinion may seem, we depend for its correction not on the conscience of judges and juries but on the competition of other ideas. But there is no constitutional value in false statements of fact. . . .

Read in context, though, the fair meaning of the passage is to equate the word "opinion" in the second sentence with the word "idea" in the first sentence. . . .

Thus we do not think this passage from *Gertz* was intended to create a wholesale defamation exemption for anything that might be labeled "opinion." . . . Not only would such an interpretation be contrary to the tenor and context of the passage, but it would also ignore the fact that expressions of "opinion" may often imply an assertion of objective fact.

If a speaker says, "In my opinion John Jones is a liar," he implies a knowledge of facts which lead to the conclusion that Jones told an untruth. Even if the speaker states the facts upon which he bases his opinion, if those facts are either incorrect or incomplete, or if his assessment of them is erroneous, the statement may still imply a false assertion of fact. Simply couching such statements in terms of opinion does not dispel these implications; and the statement, "In my opinion Jones is a liar," can cause as much damage to reputation as the statement, "Jones is a liar." As Judge Friendly aptly stated: "[It] would be destructive of the law of libel if a writer could escape liability for accusations of [defamatory conduct] simply by using, explicitly or implicitly, the words 'I think.'" . . .

We are not persuaded that, . . . an additional separate constitutional privilege for "opinion" is required to ensure the freedom of expression guaranteed by the First Amendment. The dispositive question in the present case then becomes whether or not a reasonable factfinder could conclude that the statements in the Diadiun column imply an assertion that petitioner Milkovich perjured himself in a judicial proceeding. We think this question must be answered in the affirmative. As the Ohio Supreme Court itself observed, "the clear impact in some nine sentences and a caption is that [Milkovich] 'lied at the hearing after . . . having given his solemn oath to tell the truth.' " . . . This is not the sort of loose, figurative or hyperbolic language which would negate the impression that the writer was seriously maintaining petitioner committed the crime of perjury. Nor does the general tenor of the article negate this impression.

We also think the connotation that petitioner committed perjury is sufficiently factual to be susceptible of being proved true or false. . . .

The numerous decisions discussed above establishing First Amendment protection for defendants in defamation actions surely demonstrate the Court's recognition of the Amendment's vital guarantee of free and uninhibited discussion of public issues. But there is also another side to the equation; we have regularly acknowledged the "important social values which underlie the law of defamation," and recognize that "[s]ociety has a pervasive and strong interest in preventing and redressing attacks upon reputation." . . . Justice Stewart put it with his customary clarity:

> The right of a man to the protection of his own reputation from unjustified invasion and wrongful hurt reflects no more than our basic concept of the essential dignity and worth of every human being—a concept at the root of any decent system of ordered liberty. . . .
>
> The destruction that defamatory falsehood can bring is, to be sure, often beyond the capacity of the law to redeem. Yet, imperfect though it is, an action for damages is the only hope for vindication or redress the law gives to a man whose reputation has been falsely dishonored. 86 S.Ct., at 679–680 (Stewart, J., concurring).

We believe our decision in the present case holds the balance true. The judgment of the Ohio Court of Appeals is reversed and the case remanded for further proceedings not inconsistent with this opinion.

Reversed.

NOTES

1. A father's statement regarding the competency of a teacher of his child is protected by a qualified privilege. For the teacher to bring a successful action against the parent, it must be shown that the information conveyed by the parent was not only false, but also exhibited malice. The fact that the father communicated his complaint within the established channels of the school was insufficient to show malice. Here the parent wrote a letter to the school principal accusing the teacher of treating his child "most unfairly" and displaying a "remarkable insensitivity and behavior that was most unprofessional" and "inconsistent with good teaching practice." The court held for the parent, saying that "a qualified privilege extends to all communications made *bona fide* upon any subject matter in which the party communicating has an interest, or in reference to which he has a duty, to a person having a corresponding interest or duty, and embraces cases where the duty is not a legal one but is of a moral or social character of imperfect obligation." *Swenson-Davis v. Martel*, 135 Mich. App. 632, 354 N.W. 2d 288 (Mich App. 1984); citing *Timmis v. Bennett*, 352 Mich. 355, 89 N.W. 2d 748 (1958).

2. In a New York case, a high school football coach sued a reporter for defamation for an article that indicated that the coach "showed himself to be a big loser," and that he cursed, belittled, and verbally abused the players. Testimony from game officials, cheerleaders, players, and parents verified that the charge against the coach was false. The coach, however, conceded that he was a "public figure," invoking the New York Times malice, (actual malice) as the standard of proof against the reporter. The court explained that public figure status

triggers three constitutionally based requirements that the plaintiff must meet in order to sustain a judgment against a newspaper:

a. Plaintiff is required to prove defamatory statements were published with actual malice.
b. Actual malice must be established by clear and convincing evidence.
c. Appellate review must include an independent review of the evidence germane to the actual malice determination to ensure that the determination rests upon clear and convincing evidence.

The court further observed that falsity and actual malice are distinct concepts. "It is one thing to publish a false statement and quite another to do so knowingly and recklessly." Here, the coach was unable to sustain the test of clear and convincing evidence of intentional and reckless disregard. *Mahoney v. Adirondack Publishing Co.,* 71 N.Y. 2d 31, 523 N.Y.S. 2d 480, 517 N.E. 2d 1365 (1987)

Evidence of Express Malice in Criticism of Teacher Insufficient to Overcome Parent's Conditional Privilege

- - - - - - - - - -

Nodar v. Galbreath

- - - - - - - - - -

Supreme Court of Florida, 1984.
462 So. 2d 803.

BOYD, Chief Justice. . . . The district court affirmed a judgment for compensatory and punitive damages for the tort of defamation. The district court's decision conflicts with past decisions of this Court. We have jurisdiction. . . . We hold that the statements found to be defamatory by the jury were conditionally privileged under Florida law and that the plaintiff failed to prove express malice. We therefore quash the district court decision and order reversal of the judgment.

The complaint alleged that defendant/petitioner Joseph J. Nodar committed a slander of the plaintiff/respondent Patricia Galbreath by making certain remarks, heard by others, impugning her professional ability. The plaintiff is a public high school teacher. Prior to and at the time of the communication charged as defamatory, the son of the defendant was a student in a class taught by the plaintiff. The class was a special tenth-grade English class for gifted students. The publication alleged as having been defamatory was made at a meeting of the governing board of the Broward County school district, specifically a portion of the school board meeting specially set aside for receiving the comments of members of the public. . . .

The record shows that the defendant was dissatisfied with the instruction his son was receiving in the class and believed that it was not in accord with the established curriculum for the tenth-grade gifted English class. The theory of the complaint was that the publication was a false and defamatory statement tending to impugn plaintiff's abilities in connection with her business or profession and thus was slander per se. A second count alleged that the statements were made with express malice and sought punitive damages. The jury found the remarks defamatory and maliciously made and returned verdicts for $5,000 compensatory damages and $5,000 punitive damages.

By motion to dismiss and by answer to the complaint the defense raised issues of qualified privilege, the lack of sufficient allegations of malice, the so-called "constitutional privilege" relating to public officials, public figures, and public concerns, and the lack of defamatory meaning in the communication. . . .

Petitioner correctly points out that the district court failed to recognize that the "actual malice" necessary to overcome the "constitutional privilege" of *New York Times Co. v. Sullivan* is different from the express malice necessary to avoid the common-law qualified privilege. The elements of "actual malice," and the standard of proof, differ from those of express malice. "Actual malice," which under federal constitutional law must be shown before a public official or public figure may recover for defamation relating to a matter of his official conduct or of public concern, consists of knowledge of falsity or reckless disregard of truth or falsity, and must be shown by clear and convincing evidence. Express malice under the common law of Florida, necessary to overcome the common-law qualified privilege, is present where the primary motive for the statement is shown to have been an intention to injure the plaintiff. . . . The plaintiff need only show this fact by a preponderance of the evidence, the ordinary standard of proof in civil cases. Thus the district court erred in concluding that the trial court's ruling on the "public official" question made no difference to the defendant's claim of privilege.

Petitioner argues that respondent is a public official and that the case is governed by the "actual malice" standard of *New York Times Co. v. Sullivan*. . . . It has been said of the *New York Times* rule: "What the *New York Times* rule ultimately protects is defamatory falsehood. No matter how gross the untruth, the *New York Times* rule deprives a defamed public official of any hope for legal redress without proof that the lie was a knowing one, or uttered in reckless disregard of the truth." *Rosenblatt v. Baer*, 383 U.S. 75, 92, 86 S.Ct. 669, 679, 15 L.Ed.2d 597 (1966). . . .

. . . [W]e cannot conclude that one who accepts a position as a teacher in a public high school thereby effects the same kind of surrender of the right to vindicate defamation as does one who seeks or accepts an elected or policymaking position with a public body or government institution. It should be remembered that the public official and public figure categories both serve the same purpose of preserving a free press. . . . Petitioner has not cited any binding authority for the proposition that the plaintiff here was a public official. It is enough to say that we decline to so characterize a public high school English teacher.

Because plaintiff was not a public official, *New York Times* does not apply. However, there are constitutional limits on defamation recovery even when the plaintiff is neither a public official nor a public figure. . . . We believe, . . . that the constitutionally protected right to discuss, comment upon, criticize, and debate, indeed, the freedom to speak on any and all matters is extended not only to the organized media but to all persons. If common-law remedies for defamation are to be constitutionally restricted in actions against media defendants, they should also be restricted in actions against private, non-media speakers and publishers.

Petitioner argues that his remarks were privileged as a matter of law. We find that there are several legal grounds for holding that the defendant's remarks were made upon a conditionally privileged occasion.

"One who publishes defamatory matter concerning another is not liable for the publication if (a) the matter is published upon an occasion that makes it conditionally privileged and (b) the privilege is not abused." Restatement (Second) of Torts § 593 (1976). The law of Florida embraces a broad range of the privileged occasions that have come to be recognized under the common law. *See* Rahdert & Snyder, *Rediscovering Florida's Common Law Defenses to Libel and Slander*, 11 Stetson L.Rev. 1 (1981). "A communication made in good faith on any subject matter by one having an interest therein, or in reference to which he has a duty, is privileged if made to a person having a corresponding interest or duty, even though it contains matter which would otherwise be actionable, and though the duty is not a legal one but only a moral or social obligation." 19 Fla.Jur.2d *Defamation and Privacy* § 58 (1980). . . .

This general rule of privilege finds expression in several established common-law legal grounds for holding that the defendant's statements to the school board were protected by a qualified privilege. The remarks of the defendant, addressed in person to a school board at a school board meeting concerning the curriculum and instruction in an English class at a public high school in which his son was enrolled and his son's difficulties with the class clearly came within the scope of the privilege based on mutuality of interest of speaker and listener. . . . The concern of a parent for the welfare of his child provides a privilege for the occasion of speaking to one having the power or duty to take action for the benefit of the child. Restatement (Second) of Torts, § 597 (1976).

Another ground for holding that the statement was conditionally privileged would be that the statement was made for the protection of the recipient's interest in receiving information on the performance of its employee. *See* Restatement (Second) of Torts § 595 (1976). In this connection, the value of the defendant's defamatory information to the school board in overseeing the operation of the public schools must be weighed against the extent of the harm likely to be done to the plaintiff's reputation as a result of the communication. . . . Under the American Law Institute's approach, the interest of the school board in the performance of a teacher, its employee, would give rise to a privilege in another to provide information concerning that performance even without a legal duty or a family relationship and even though the information is not requested but merely volunteered, if the publication is "within the generally accepted standards of decent conduct." . . .

Another recognized legal ground for holding that the defendant's statements were privileged is that they were the statements of a citizen to a political authority regarding matters of public concern, i.e., the school curriculum and the performance of a public employee. . . . All of these grounds of qualified privilege have existed in the law of Florida for many generations and have served to provide broad protection for freedom of speech and of the press long before the creation of the remedy fashioned in *New York Times v. Sullivan*.

. . . Here the circumstances and content of the statement were clear and undisputed. Therefore the defendant's statements to the school board were qualifiedly privileged as a matter of law and the trial judge erred in submitting the question of privilege to the jury. The trial court should have instructed the jury that the statements were made on a privileged occasion.

The legal conclusion that the defendant's remarks were privileged brings us to the question of express malice. If the statements were made without express malice — that is, if they were made for a proper purpose in light of the interests sought to be protected by legal recognition of the privilege — then there can be no recovery. The determination that a defendant's statements are qualifiedly privileged eliminates the presumption of malice attaching to defamatory statements by law. The privilege instead raises a presumption of good faith and places upon the plaintiff the burden of proving express malice — that is, malice in fact as defined by the common-law doctrine of qualified privilege.

> In cases of qualifiedly privileged publications the presumption which attends cases not so privileged of malice from the publication of libelous language does not prevail; the burden of proof is changed, and, in order for the plaintiff to recover, he is called upon affirmatively and expressly to show malice in the publisher. This malice may be inferred from the language itself, or may be proven by extrinsic circumstances. While the malice may be inferred from the communication, it is not inferable from the mere fact that the statements are untrue.

Coogler v. Rhodes, 38 Fla. at 249, 21 So. at 112.

As has already been stated, the jury found that the petitioner's statements were made with malice so that the privilege was lost and the defendant liable for defamation. Petitioner argues that under the evidence his statements were non-malicious expressions of opinion as a matter of law, that the trial court erred in improperly excluding evidence relevant to the issue of malice, and that the jury was improperly instructed on the issue of malice. Petitioner is correct in all three arguments. Because we find that the evidence of express malice was legally insufficient to overcome the qualified privilege, we need not address the trial errors which would otherwise entitle petitioner to a new trial.

The evidence was insufficient to show express malice and there should have been a directed verdict on this ground. There was some confusion below about the concept of express malice. . . . Where a person speaks upon a privileged occasion, but the speaker is motivated more by a desire to harm the person defamed than by a purpose to protect the personal or social interest giving rise to the privilege, then it can be said that there was express malice and the privilege is destroyed. Strong, angry, or intemperate words do not alone show express malice; rather, there must be a showing that the speaker used his privileged position "to gratify his malevolence." . . . If the occasion of the communication is privileged because of a proper interest to be protected, and the defamer is motivated by a desire to protect that interest, he does not forfeit the privilege merely because he also in fact feels hostility or ill will toward the plaintiff. . . . The incidental gratification of personal feelings of indignation is not sufficient to defeat the privilege where the primary motivation is within the scope of the privilege. . . .

The plaintiff's proof of malice consisted of the tone of the defamatory words themselves and the behavior of the defendant over a period of several months before he made his remarks at the school board meeting. Plaintiff's counsel at trial relied upon evidence of defendant's repeated complaints about his son's teacher and argued that they demonstrated "harassment" of the teacher and hostility towards her.

The words themselves, we believe, are not so extreme as to demonstrate express malice. Petitioner merely said that the teacher had harassed and verbally abused his son, that she was unqualified to teach the course, and that her performance as a teacher was victimizing his son. While we must accept the unchallenged conclusion of the jury that these words were defamatory, the words do not inherently demonstrate express malice. The accusation that the teacher gave the student a poor mark in retaliation for the father's complaints about her teaching, while clearly capable of stating defamatory meaning, does not show express malice. Examples of cases where the false and defamatory words themselves were so extreme as to intrinsically show express malice are *Loeb v. Geronemus*, 66 So.2d 241 (Fla.1953) (defendants said plaintiff was guilty of evil conduct, was of low moral character, was a disgrace, a troublemaker, was not respectable, had been compelled to leave Chicago) and *Brown v. Fawcett Publications, Inc.*, 196 So.2d 465 (Fla. 2d DCA 1967) (defendant said plaintiff was a murderer, rapist, and sodomite).

The fact that the defendant's remarks to the school board were preceded by many months of personal conversations, telephone calls, and letters to the teacher and her superiors does not demonstrate express malice. Indeed, it seems to us that this evidence tends to support rather than negate the claim of privilege, as it shows that defendant tried to seek redress of his grievances through private communications before he publicly revealed his complaints at the school board meeting. The series of personal visits, telephone calls, and letters, far from exhibiting a pattern of malicious harassment, demonstrates a degree of parental concern for the effectiveness of public schools which our state, through its courts of law, should attempt to encourage rather than discourage.

We therefore hold that the plaintiff's evidence was insufficient as a matter of law to carry the burden of proving express malice. . . .

For the foregoing reasons, we quash the decision of the district court of appeal and remand with directions that the judgment be reversed and a directed verdict be entered for the petitioner/defendant.

It is so ordered.

Teacher Is Not a Public Official and Is Not Required to Prove Actual Malice to Recover Compensatory Damages for Libel

---·---·---·---

Richmond Newspapers, Inc., et al. v. Lipscomb

---·---·---·---

Supreme Court of Virginia, 1987.
362 S.E. 2d 32.

WHITING, Justice. This action for defamation brought by a Richmond public school teacher, Vernelle M. Lipscomb (Lipscomb), against Richmond Newspapers, Inc. (the newspaper), a publisher, and its reporter, Charles E. Cox (Cox), arises out of the publication of a front-page article in the *Richmond Times Dispatch*. The trial judge sustained a jury's award of $45,000 in punitive damages against Cox, but required a remittitur of $900,000 of a $1,000,000 compensatory damage award against both defendants. We will affirm the reduced award of compensatory damages but reverse the award of punitive damages.

(1) Was Lipscomb, as a public school teacher, in that class of public officials which can only recover compensatory damages for defamation by establishing the constitutional malice described in *New York Times v. Sullivan*, 376 U.S. 254, 84 S.Ct. 710, 11 L.Ed.2d 686 (1964)?

(2) If not, was negligent publication by Cox and the newspaper subsumed in the jury's finding of a publication with reckless disregard for the truth; and, if so, was the evidence in this case sufficient to support a finding of negligent publication?

(3) Was the evidence in this case sufficiently clear and convincing to support the jury's finding of publication by Cox with a reckless disregard for the truth, which Lipscomb must establish to recover punitive damages?

Collateral issues must also be resolved as to the admissibility of an expert's opinion on the standard of care, the obligation of a trial court to segregate potentially defamatory evidence from non-defamatory evidence in its instructions to the jury, and the size of the jury's verdict.

The news article was in the Sunday newspaper a few weeks prior to the opening of school in the fall of 1981. The article identified Lipscomb by name and said that certain parents and their children:

> charge that a Thomas Jefferson High School teacher is disorganized, erratic, forgetful and unfair; that she returns graded papers weeks late and absents herself from the classroom for long periods; that she insists students stick to the rules, and flouts them herself. They say she demeans and humiliates students. The brighter they appear, the likelier they are to suffer at her hands, the parents protest.

One of Lipscomb's colleagues was quoted as saying that the teacher "might be out of her element in dealing with the students found in the honors course where most of the problems seem to have cropped up since the mid–1970's."

Dr. I. David Goldman, a physician and a teacher at the Medical College of Virginia and the father of one of Lipscomb's students, initiated the contact with Cox. Goldman allegedly told Cox that the school's principal "has had enough complaints about Ms. Lipscomb's performance over the years to know that there was trouble." . . .

The article quoted a student as saying, "She [Ms. Lipscomb] was patronizing, she was late for class, and she was missing from class a third of the time. When she was present she was so disorganized that few if any of [my] classmates understood what was expected of them. She didn't teach, I really learned nothing . . . her verbal excesses . . . caused . . . pain, I cried in class, I cried outside her class." Another student was quoted as saying she was a victim of the teacher's harassment tactics, "[i]f I asked her a question, she would come back with something like, 'That's a stupid question.'" Dr. Goldman's daughter allegedly told the reporter that, "[Ms. Lipscomb] seemed to hate what I represented, meaning middle-class, bright, articulate, assertive, questioning. . . . I questioned her grades, I questioned her before the others in the class. She really didn't like it [and] she was always chipping away at our self-confidence." . . .

Cox essentially confined his investigative activities to interviews with the complaining parents and students and to telephone conferences with Lipscomb's principal and two of Lipscomb's teaching colleagues. He obtained very little information from Lipscomb and the other school employees. The school board's attorney had advised Lipscomb and certain school administrative officials not to discuss the details of the Goldman complaints because of the law dealing with confidentiality of both student and individual teacher records and his fear of litigation over the Goldman issue with Lipscomb as a possible defendant.

We first consider whether the trial court correctly required Lipscomb to prove publication with a reckless disregard for the truth in her claim for compensatory damages. The answer to this question hinges upon whether the trial court properly classified Lipscomb as a "public official" under the *New York Times* malice rule.

New York Times prohibits "a public official from recovering damages for a defamatory falsehood relating to his official conduct unless he proves that the statement was made with 'actual malice' — that is, with knowledge that it was false or with reckless disregard of whether it was false or not." . . . "Actual malice" as described in *New York Times* might be confused with common law malice, which involves "motives of personal spite, or ill-will," . . . Therefore, we will refer to such actual malice as *"New York Times"* malice.

The Supreme Court said in *New York Times v. Sullivan* "[w]e have no occasion here to determine how far down into the lower ranks of government employees the 'public official' designation would extend for purposes of this rule." . . . [T]he Supreme Court pointed out that it "has not provided precise boundaries for the category of 'public official'; it cannot be thought to include all public employees, however." Nevertheless, that Court has left little doubt that other courts are to determine who is a "public official" in accordance with "the purposes of a national constitutional protection," *Rosenblatt v. Baer*, 383 U.S. 75, 84, 86 S.Ct. 669, 675, 15 L.Ed.2d 597 (1966), and not by reference to state law standards. . . .

Cases construing the "public official" standards of *New York Times* are legion, but we have found no federal cases concerning school teachers. The state defamation cases are split on the issue of whether public school teachers are "public officials" subject to the *New York Times* malice rule.

There has been no showing that Lipscomb, who was not an elected official, either influenced or even appeared to influence or control any public affairs or school policy. On the contrary, the evidence shows her to have limited her activities to teaching and acting as a temporary department head of a small number of other English teachers. We also note there was no criticism of Lipscomb as an acting department head — it is all leveled at her teaching activities.

. . . When Cox and the newspaper chose to assist Dr. Goldman in going beyond his normal remedy by publicizing his dispute, they became subject to the same duty of due care to ascertain the accuracy of their charges that every citizen must assume when issuing statements, the substance of which makes substantial danger to reputation apparent.

The same reasoning applies to the defendants' contention that because the school system did not respond to Dr. Goldman's satisfaction, the conflict escalated into a public issue of evaluation of teacher competence in general and accountability of the school administration to the parents and students in particular. . . .

We find that the public had no independent interest in Lipscomb's qualifications and performance "beyond its general interest in the qualifications and performance of all government employees," and, therefore, conclude that Lipscomb was not a "public official" under *New York Times* but a private person. Accordingly, we decide that the trial court erred in requiring Lipscomb to prove *New York Times* malice before she could recover compensatory damages.

Because the jury found the plaintiff established *New York Times* malice, we must next consider whether we properly may enter a judgment for Lipscomb for compensatory damages or whether the case should be remanded for a new trial on that issue. . . . Two factors influence this determination; first, is a finding of negligence subsumed in a jury's finding of a reckless disregard for the truth? Second, if so, is the evidence sufficient to support a finding that Cox's investigation was negligent? . . .

. . . All parties, including Cox and his editors, recognized a substantial danger of injury to Lipscomb's reputation, raising a duty to investigate the accuracy of the statements made to Cox.

A number of supervisors, a fellow teacher, and students, including some classmates of the complaining students, testified as to Lipscomb's good qualities as a teacher and contradicted virtually all the negative statements made by the persons Cox interviewed. The students who contradicted the negative testimony were all shown to have been readily available for interview in the Richmond area. While the school authorities would not furnish Cox with the names or addresses of other students in Lipscomb's classes, the jury could have inferred from the evidence that Cox could have obtained this information from the students he interviewed but negligently failed to do so. In fact, one student gave Cox the names of some of the other students, but Cox apparently did nothing with the information.

We find that the jury had ample evidence from which to conclude that a reasonably prudent news reporter writing this article could readily have contacted a number of other students to verify (or contradict) these accusations and should have done so. Moreover, because there is no issue as to Cox's agency, the newspaper company also is liable for his negligent performance under familiar principles of *respondeat superior*.

The jury awarded punitive damages against Cox. To sustain that award, Lipscomb, as a private person, is required to establish *New York Times* malice by clear and convincing proof. . . . To decide if that requirement has been met, we conduct an "independent examination of the whole record," . . . resolving disputed factual issues and inferences favorably to the plaintiff. Lipscomb maintains that Cox's reckless disregard for the truth is demonstrated by a consideration of the following six factors:

(1) Lipscomb says that the ill will Cox's sources bore Lipscomb was of such a character as to raise obvious doubts as to their veracity. . . .

Except for the bias suggested by their expressions of dissatisfaction with Lipscomb, there is nothing to impeach the credibility of the professor of medicine, the minister, the Richmond school teacher, and the state health department employee, who were the complaining parents, or of their four complaining children. We conclude that there was insufficient damaging evidence about the informants themselves to provide obvious reasons to doubt their veracity.

(2) Lipscomb claims Cox's testimony demonstrates a predetermination of the facts. The most persuasive testimony we can find to support this assertion is Cox's testimony that when Dr. Goldman first called him:

> He said that he had a story he wanted to talk to me about. And he told me in general about the thing. . . . He indicated enough to pique my interest about the thing. . . . [H]e had considerable documentation to present in this case, an extraordinary amount, obviously of documentation already built up in this case. There was a record there for the picking up. In other words . . . [h]e said that he thought it had a wide public interest. I thought so myself. I was impressed [by the long document Dr. Goldman had written the school board] and I made a lot of marks on this thing. . . . I'm cautious by nature and I considered this document and I considered Dr. Goldman rather carefully. I was interested in the story. I had been thinking about such a story for a long time. . . .

Lipscomb refers to three cases in support of her claim that Cox had "predetermined the facts" when he began writing the story and suppressed favorable evidence to achieve that end. A review of the facts in those cases illustrates the failure of Lipscomb's proof on this point. . . .

(3) Lipscomb argues that Cox not only resolved ambiguities in the story against her but actually omitted information that was favorable. Cox did fail to report that a substantial part of Lipscomb's extended absence from class was due to the death of her fiance, resulting in a leave of absence, which Lipscomb characterizes as a "brutal twisting of known facts." The omission of this favorable explanation for her absence may have been unfair, but we do not agree that it sufficiently evidenced either the "brutal twisting" claimed or a reckless disregard for the truth. . . .

Our review of the evidence convinces us that there is insufficient support for this claim.

(4) Lipscomb contends that the absence of deadline pressure "holds a libel defendant more accountable." While the cases cited by the plaintiff indicate that lack of a deadline is a factor to be considered, in each case there also was other evidence of conduct demonstrating a reckless disregard for truth. . . . Lipscomb cites no cases, however, where absence of deadline pressure, coupled with a biased source, was sufficient to establish *New York Times* malice.

. . . If the evidence available to Cox at the time of writing was legally insufficient to require a further investigation before publication, additional time to do such an investigation has no legal significance.

(5) Doubts of the newspaper staff members as to the accuracy of the story were said to be evidenced by their delay in publishing it until Cox returned from a vacation. Cox testified that upon his return his editors had fears and reservations because "[t]hey just wanted to be careful journalists. They wanted to be very, very sure of the sources on this . . . they wanted their hands held, to be reassured I had done all my work, as an employee, and I was able to tell them, I assume convincingly, that I had done my work, [they] wanted to be sure that what [I] had gotten was

accurate and the sources were reliable." This is hardly "sufficient evidence to permit the conclusion that [either of] the defendant[s] in fact entertained serious [doubt] as to the truth of his publication." . . .

(6) The evidence is insufficient to support Lipscomb's final charge that Cox threatened and intimidated her, the school board's attorney, and the principal, the only favorable sources cited by her. On the contrary, the evidence shows that Cox was trying to persuade them to give Lipscomb's side of the controversy. . . .

Lipscomb, when asked if Cox had said, "you really ought to respond to the charges or words to that effect" replied, "Words to that effect, but it was more or less like an intimidating thing, like 'you'd better talk to me.' He didn't say, 'You ought to talk to me.' It was more or less an intimidation thing . . . I just could detect something like a threat in his voice." Cox himself said, "I tried, I tried very hard to tell [Lipscomb] that these were serious charges. And it seemed to me that she ought to respond." . . .

We conclude that, even with the bias shown, no one of the six elements charged is legally sufficient to justify a jury's finding of a reckless disregard for the truth. We equally are convinced that a consideration of all these elements as a group demonstrates the same inadequacy. Although we are satisfied that the evidence was sufficient to create a factual issue of negligence, as stated above, we find it insufficient to establish *New York Times* malice by clear and convincing evidence. Accordingly, we will reverse the award of punitive damages against Cox. . . .

The defendants charge that the verdict for $1,000,000 in compensatory damages and $45,000 in punitive damages was the result of "passion, prejudice, or a misconception of the law" and that the verdict, therefore, should have been set aside in its entirety. . . .

. . . While we have found the evidence insufficient to show a reckless disregard for the truth by Cox, it is more than ample to justify a finding of negligence in his failure to interview other students and school officials before publishing manifestly damaging statements about Lipscomb. . . .

The defendants also complain that the size of the final awards—$100,000 in compensatory damages and $45,000 in punitive damages—was "so out of proportion to the damage sustained as to be excessive as a matter of law." We need not consider further the punitive damage award since we have set it aside.

. . . We believe an award of $1,000,000 clearly would have been excessive. However, the evidence does not demonstrate that the trial court abused its discretion in reducing the award to $100,000.

For the reasons assigned, we will affirm the judgment of $100,000 for compensatory damages against both defendants, will reverse the judgment of $45,000 for punitive damages against Cox, and will enter a final judgment of $100,000 against both defendants.

Affirmed in part, reversed in part, and final judgment.

■■■ STUDENT RECORDS

Teachers, guidance counselors, and principals are generally involved in the release of student information and records to other teachers, professional personnel within the school, prospective employers outside the school, or other educational institutions to which students may be applying for entrance. Considering these areas of pupil information flow and the potential harm that can result, common law suggests the following practices to be appropriate.

Practices Suggested by Common Law

First, information should not be conveyed to other teachers or administrators unless the motive and purpose are to assist and enhance the educational opportunities of the pupil. Transmittal should be made in the proper channels and to persons assigned the responsibility for the relevant educational function. Gossip or careless talk among teachers, which is not calculated to help the student, may be shown to be malicious and not protected by the cloak of qualified privilege. Second, pupil information should be transmitted to prospective employers only upon request. This protects the teacher from the presumption that the transmittal was made with intent to defame the student with malicious intent.[37] A qualified privilege has been upheld when a communicator responded to a questionnaire and only gave answers to specific questions.[38] It is a good practice not to release information over a telephone unless the identity of the caller is absolutely certain. Third, records should be released to colleges and other institutions only if there is statutory or regulatory requirement for the transmittals, or if the pupil requests the conveyance. Most states have laws or regulations that require the transfer of elementary and secondary school pupils' records when they change schools. This, of course, facilitates the transition for the pupil, as well as for the school, and provides needed data for placement and is, therefore, proper.

Beyond common-law protection of student privacy, both state and federal statutes may intervene to provide additional safeguards. The Family Education Rights and Privacy Act (FERPA) was passed in August 1974 as an amendment to the Omnibus Education Bill.[39] The act establishes standards to which school districts must adhere in handling student records. Failure to abide by the law can result in the withdrawal of federal education funds. Additionally, the Congress has included other privacy provisions in the 1978 General Education Provisions Act (GEPA);[40] and in the Education of All Handicapped Children Act of 1975.[41]

Family Education Rights and Privacy Act (FERPA)

Under FERPA, every school district is required to publish a pupil records policy that includes annual notification to parents and to students over 18 years of age.[42] These policies must adhere to certain requirements of the act, including

1. Records of individual students, containing "personally identifiable information," must

be kept confidential and cannot be released by the school without written consent of the parent,[43] or consent from the student if the student is over the age of 18.[44]

2. Parents and guardians of students under age 18, and those students over 18, have the right to inspect all school records concerning that student.[45]

3. The school district record-keeping system must be described in sufficient detail for parents to locate their child's records.[46]

4. School district staff members with access to student records must be identified by title.[47]

5. Each child's file must include a record of access, which must be signed by each staff member whenever they withdraw that student's file.[48]

6. Parents have a right to appeal anything in a student's file that is considered incorrect, and if the school is not willing to delete the challenged material, the parents may request a hearing and/or provide a written statement to be attached to the challenged material.[49]

7. The school policy must define what constitutes "directory information," and under what circumstances that information may be released without parental consent.[50] Treatment records "made or maintained by a physician, psychologist, or other recognized professional or paraprofessional acting in his or her professional capacity or assisting in a paraprofessional capacity" and used in the treatment of an eligible student, that is, a student over 18 years of age or any student in an institution of post-secondary education, are excluded from the definition of "education records" in FERPA[51] and are not automatically accessible to the student.

An exception to FERPA is recognized for disclosures that were required by state statutes before enactment of the act.[52] Further, "personal notes" that are defined as "not education records"[53] are exempted from parental access. Personal notes which are not accessible to other school staff members are exempted from student or parental access.

These personal notes are available to the substitutes of the original note-writers.[54]

FERPA Alone Does Not Provide for Redress in Damages, But May If Combined with § 1983

–––·–––·–––·–––

Fay v. South Colonie Central School District

–––·–––·–––·–––

United States Court of Appeals
Second Circuit, 1986.
802 F. 2d 21.

MESKILL, Circuit Judge. This is an appeal and cross-appeal from a judgment of the United States District Court for the Northern District of New York, Miner, J. The plaintiffs below were Robert E. Fay (Fay) and his children, Theresa M. Fay and Thomas R. Fay. The defendants were the South Colonie Central School District, its superintendent (hereinafter the district and its superintendent are collectively described as "the school district") and the New York Commissioner of Education. The district court partially granted the plaintiffs' summary judgment motion, holding the school district liable under 42 U.S.C. § 1983 (1982) for denying Robert Fay access to his children's education records, *see* 20 U.S.C. § 1232g(a)(1)(A) (1982), awarding nominal damages for the denial of access to the records and granting injunctive relief on a pendent state law claim for violation of his rights as a parent with joint legal custody of his children. The court dismissed all of the plaintiff's claims against Commissioner Ambach. It also dismissed Fay's claim under section 1983 that the school district violated Fay's due process right to control the upbringing of his children and his right to equal protection of the laws. . . .

This suit involves an attempt to have the federal courts resolve a dispute that could be more appropriately resolved either by the state courts or by mediation.

Under a separation agreement Fay and his ex-wife have joint legal custody of their two children. The children live with Fay during the summer and live with their mother during the school year. The separation agreement further provides that the ex-wife

must . . . consult with [Fay] concerning . . . schooling, relevant to which school [the children] should attend, whether public or private, matters concerning any special education courses which the children may pursue or desire to pursue and further, the [ex-]wife is to provide [Fay] with report cards of the children or photostatic copies thereof. . . .

. . . Fay alleges that his ex-wife has failed to comply fully with this provision.

Dissatisfied with the operation of this aspect of the separation agreement, Fay tried to get information regarding his children's activities and progress directly from the children's schools. In December 1980 Fay sent a letter to the superintendent of the school district demanding such information. Although Fay's original demand was inchoate, it later became clear that he sought information ranging from standardized test results and accident reports to notices about classroom parties and cafeteria menus. Instead of seeking to accommodate any of the demands, the superintendent responded that the school would "provide information to any person or organization whom the courts decide have a legal right to it." . . .

More letters were exchanged between Fay and the superintendent and in April 1981 the United States Department of Education advised the superintendent of Fay's rights under the Family Educational Rights and Privacy Act, 20 U.S.C. § 1232g (1982) (FERPA). Thereafter, the school district began mailing copies of the Fay children's education records to Fay. The school district continued to refuse to mail to Fay duplicates of all school-related notices mailed to his ex-wife or carried home by his children.

In May or June 1981 Fay initiated an appeal of this continuing refusal to the New York Commissioner of Education, Gordon Ambach. . . . The Commissioner dismissed Fay's appeal, . . .

The Commissioner did not confine his observations to procedural matters, however. He also stated that Fay's request to receive copies of all communications sent by the school to his ex-wife would place "an unreasonable burden" on the school district. . . .

Fay brought an Article 78 proceeding to annul Commissioner Ambach's ruling. . . . The New York Supreme Court dismissed the proceeding. . . . In January 1983 the Appellate Division of the New York Supreme Court dismissed Fay's appeal.

In August 1983 Fay brought this action for damages and injunctive relief on behalf of himself and his children. The complaint alleged that the school district, the superintendent (in his official capacity) and Commissioner Ambach violated Fay's statutory rights under FERPA, his constitutional right to control the upbringing of his children and his constitutional right to equal protection of the laws. . . .

Fay appeals from the dismissal of the claims against Commissioner Ambach, the dismissal of his claim for the violation of his right to control his children's upbringing and the award of nominal damages. . . .

. . . We note, however, that Fay will have an opportunity on remand of his FERPA claim to prove damages similar to those sought under his due process claim. We now turn to the FERPA claim.

E. The FERPA Claim

The school district argues that the district court erred in concluding that Fay could assert a cause of action under section 1983 for the school district's violation of FERPA between May 1980 and April 1981. This argument is without merit. Fay claims that the district court erred in awarding him only nominal damages for the FERPA violation. This claim has merit and we remand this portion of the complaint for further proceedings.

FERPA denies federal funds to a school "which has a policy of denying . . . the parents of students who are or have been in attendance at [the school] the right to inspect and review the education records of their children." 20 U.S.C. § 1232g(a)(1)(A) (1982). *See also id.* at § (a)(4)(A) & (B) (definition of education records). The statute requires that the "Secretary . . . take appropriate actions to enforce" its provisions. *Id.* at § 1232g(f).

FERPA itself does not give rise to a private cause of action. . . . Fay does not rely on a private cause of action under FERPA. Instead, he asserts the FERPA violation as the basis for a claim under section 1983. . . . The district court correctly determined that FERPA creates an interest that may be vindicated in a section 1983 action because Congress did not create so comprehensive a system of enforcing the statute as to demonstrate an intention to preclude a remedy under section 1983. . . . Although FERPA authorizes extensive enforcement procedures created by regulation, *see* 34 C.F.R. §§ 99.60–.67 (1985), these regulations do not demonstrate a congressional intent to preclude suits under section 1983 to remedy violations of FERPA. . . .

The school district "tacitly conceded liability" for violating FERPA for the eleven months between May 1980 and April 1981, . . . and it does not contest the entry of summary judgment on the issue of liability. Fay argues, however, that the district court erred in awarding him only nominal damages.

Where the amount of damages is not in dispute, a court may award damages on summary judgment. . . . In this case, however, the opposing arguments made in papers submitted in connection with Fay's motion to amend the judgment make it clear that there was no agreement among the parties as to what damages Fay suffered as a result of the violation of his right to inspect his children's education records.

A section 1983 violation is a species of tort liability in which the level of damages is determined by applying principles derived from tort law. . . . As a leading treatise notes, "even when plaintiff is successful . . . the grant is likely only to fore-

close the issue of liability and leave any unliquidated claim for damages" for resolution by the factfinder. . . . Fay is entitled to present evidence to support his claim for compensatory damages and in light of the factual dispute the district court erred in awarding damages for the FERPA violation on summary judgment. We remand the action to the district court for further proceedings to determine the amount, if any, of Fay's damages. . . .

. . . His FERPA claim is remanded for further proceedings to determine the amount of compensatory damages. The parties shall bear their own costs.

NOTES

1. Another New York court has held FERPA (20 U.S.C.A., § 1232g) implies that both parents have a right to inspect and review the education records of their children. The regulations implementing the act "allow inspection by either parent, without regard to custody, unless such access is barred by state law, court order or legally binding instrument." Thus, a natural father, living apart from the child under terms of a separation agreement, has a right to inspect his child's records despite the fact that the mother had signed a statement indicating that she did not wish or authorize the school district to transmit school records to the father. The court said:

   > It is beyond cavil that a non-custodial parent has not "abandoned" his child simply by reason of noncustody and, . . . while legal custody may be in one or both of the parents, the fact that it is placed in one does not necessarily terminate the role of the other as a psychological guardian and preceptor. Matter of Unido R., 109 Misc. 2d 1031, 441 N.Y.S.2d 325 (1981).

2. FERPA does not give a student the right to bring an action challenging a professor's grading process. Under the law, "Students' grades, as reflected in educational records, can only be inaccurate or misleading if they do not reflect what the grader intended or

if they are mathematically incorrect." The U.S. Court of Appeals, Fifth Circuit, has said that the provision in the act referring to "other rights of students" . . . , as amended, 20 U.S.C.A. § 1232g(a) (2), cannot be construed as Congressional intent to "afford students a federal right, enforced by federal regulations, to challenge their teachers' or educational institutions' grading process." Tarka v. Cunningham, 917 F.2d 890 (5th Cir. 1990).

3. In an Illinois case, a parent sought release of raw test data taken as oral responses from his child on the Rorschach inkblot test. The school withheld the data and maintained that the raw data did not constitute "test results" as governed by statute. The data taken from the students oral responses had been verbatim, but had not been physically entered and incorporated into the student's record. The court found that the raw data were, in fact, constructively a part of the student's "temporary" record and should have been classified as statutorily governed test results. The school was required to release the data to the parents. John K. v. Board of Educ. for School Dist. No. 65, 152 Ill. App. 3d 543, 105 Ill. Dec. 512, 504 N.E.2d 797 (1 Dist. 1987).

▰▰ ENDNOTES

1. Theodore F. T. Plucknett, *A Concise History of the Common Law* (Boston: Little, Brown and Company, 5th Ed., 1956).

2. III Edgar, 4 (C.946–C.961), cited in Plucknett, *A Concise History*, p. 983.

3. Borough Customs (Selden Society), i. 78; Plucknett, *A Concise History*, p. 483.

4. Plucknett, *A Concise History*, p. 484.

5. Ibid., p. 485.

6. Ibid., p. 486.

7. Ibid., p. 487.

8. King v. Lake, 1670; see Plucknett, *A Concise History*, p. 497.

9. 50 Am.Jur.2d 516.

10. Ibid.

11. *Restatement of Torts*, § 596; 12 A.L.R. 147; 50 A.L.R. 339.

12. Barton v. Rogers, 21 Idaho 609, 123 P. 478 (1912).

13. Dawkins v. Billingsley, 69 Okl. 259, 172 P. 69 (1918).

14. William L. Prosser, *Law of Torts* (St. Paul, Minn.: West Publishing Company, 1971), p. 609.

15. Coffin v. Coffin, 4 Mass. 1, 3 Am.Dec. 189 (1808).

16. Smith v. Helbraun, 21 A.D.2d 830, 251 N.Y.S.2d 533 (1964).

17. Ottinger v. Ferrell, 171 Ark. 1085, 287 S.W. 391 (1926).

18. Baskett v. Crossfield, 190 Ky. 751, 228 S.W. 673 (1921).

19. Ramirez v. Rogers, 540 A.2d 475 (Me. 1988).

20. Alexander and Alexander, *The Law of Schools, Students and Teachers in a Nutshell* (St. Paul, Minn.: West Publishing Co., 1984), p. 243.

21. Ibid., p. 244.

22. 376 U.S. 254, 84 S.Ct. 710 (1964).

23. Harry Kalven, Jr., *A Worthy Tradition Freedom of Speech in America* (New York: Harper and Row, 1988), pp. 60–61.

24. Ibid., pp. 70–71.

25. Ibid.

26. Rosenblatt v. Baer, 383 U.S. 75, 86 S.Ct. 669 (1966).

27. 383 U.S. at 85, 86 S.Ct. at 676.

28. 388 U.S. 130, 87 S.Ct. 1975 (1967).

29. Hutchinson v. Proxmire, 443 U.S. 111, 99 S.Ct. 2675 (1979) (quoting Gertz v. Robert Welch, Inc., 418 U.S. 323, 94 S.Ct. 2997 (1974); see also True v. Ladner, 513 A.2d 257 (Me. 1986).

30. Vinson v. Linn-Mar Community School Dist., 360 N.W.2d 108 (Iowa, 1984).

31. Nodar v. Galbreath, 462 So.2d 803 at 811 (Fla. 1984).

32. New York Times Inc. v. Sullivan, op. cit.

33. Richmond Newspapers, Inc. v. Lipscomb, 362 S.E.2d 32 (Va. 1987).

34. 43 Ill. 2d 286, 253 N.E.2d 408 (1969).

35. *Restatement 2d Torts*, §581A (1979).

36. Oscar and Lillian Handlin, *Liberty and Power 1600–1760*, Vol. 1 (New York: Harper and Row), p. 225.

37. Solow v. General Motors Truck Co. 64 F.2d 105 (2d Cir. 1944).

38. Hoff v. Pure Oil Co., 147 Minn. 195, 179 N.W. 891 (1920).

39. Education Amendment of 1974, Public Law 93–380, 20 U.S.C. § 1232g (sometimes referred to as the Buckley Amendment) See Appendix B.

40. 20 U.S.C.A. § 1232h (1978).

41. 20 U.S.C.A. § 1415 (b)(1)(A) (1975).

42. 20 U.S.C.A. § 1232 (g)(e) and 34 C.F.R. § 99.7(a).

43. 20 U.S.C.A. § 1232g(b) (1) and 34 C.F.R. § 99.30 (a)(3).

44. 20 U.S.C.A.§ 1232 (g)(d) and 34 C.F.R. § 99.5.

45. 20 U.S.C.A. § 1232 (a)(1)(A) and 34 C.F.R. § 99.10.

46. 37 C.F.R. § 99.6 (a)(2)(iv).

47. 34 C.F.R. § 99.6(a)(4).

48. 34 C.F.R. § 99.6(a)(5) and § 99.32.

49. 30 U.S.C.A. § 1232g(a)(2) and 34 C.F.R. § 99.6(a)(7).

50. 20 U.S.C.A. § 1232g(a)(5)(B) and 34 C.F.R. § 99.3 "Directory Information," § 99.6(a)(6) and § 99.37.

51. 34 C.F.R. § 99.3 "Education Records" (6)(1).

52. 34 C.F.R. § 99.31(a)(5).

53. 20 U.S.C.A. § 1232g(4)(B)(i) and 34 C.F.R. § 99.3 "Education Records."

54. See Mary H. B. Gelfman and Nadine Schwab, "School Health Services and Educational Records: Conflicts in the Law," 64 *Ed.Law Rep.* 319 (January 31, 1991).

CHAPTER 13

Governmental Immunity from Liability

All sovereign governments have the inherent prerogative to protect themselves from liability. This power has been exercised by differing means and in varying degrees, ranging from erecting virtually impervious shields to near total abrogation of immunity. While the common law defines the nature and extent of immunity generally, statutory law may change and modify it as legislatures see fit. The extent of the legal variations in this area is almost limitless, as evidenced by the precedents among the fifty states. Immunity is further complicated by the interaction of the states with the central government in our federal system. Because of the uncertainty of the prerogatives of government in the federal system, the Eleventh Amendment of the United States Constitution was enacted to define the limitations of federal power on states as well as the boundaries of liability between citizens and states.

This chapter discusses both the common-law and statutory precedents regarding aspects of governmental immunity. Considerable attention is given to the Eleventh Amendment as it affects the state and local education agencies.

◼◼◼ SOVEREIGN IMMUNITY

Governmental agencies have historically been immune from tort liability. As a general rule, common law asserts that government is inherently immune unless the legislature specifically abrogates the privilege. The immunity concept evolved to this country from England, where the king could, theoretically, do no wrong. Various legal scholars maintain the concept was a product of the dark ages, when custom established that the lord of the fief was also the lawmaker and judge. As such, the lord was singly responsible for all laws and justice, and since he made and implemented the laws, he could not be sued without his permission.[1] As the feudal system drew to a close and fiefdoms became consolidated into larger governmental units, immunity became enmeshed with the "divine right of kings," placing the king in a superior and preferred legal position.[2] Sovereign immunity became formalized in English law at least as early as the thirteenth century, at which time the king could not be sued in his own courts.[3] Sovereign immunity apparently reached its zenith in fifteenth-century England, where it stabilized as a prerogative of the monarch. Judicial recognition of this power was taken when an English court held in 1607 that the king was not liable for damages to private property caused by the government's digging for saltpeter that was to be used in the manufacture of gunpowder.[4] In spite of his judicial sanction affirming sovereign immunity, the great jurist Coke held in the same year that the king could not sit as a judge in his own case.[5] Effectively, this began a whittling away process of the sovereign immunity that was not to culminate until over 250 years later, when the House of Lords held that a public entity was liable for the damages caused by acts of its employees.[6] Later, this rationale was applied to schools in England when a court held that if negligence occurred resulting in student injury, either the teacher or the school could be liable.[7]

The sovereign immunity doctrine may have been transported across the Atlantic to the United States directly under the precedent of *Russell v. The Men Dwelling in the County of Devon*[8] as relied upon by a Massachusetts court in *Mower v. The Inhabitants of Leicester* in 1812.[9] It is unlikely, however, that the concept traversed the Atlantic through a single precedent, especially since the court in *Russell* attributed its holding of nonliability to (1) the lack of a public treasury, (2) general judicial apprehension that imposing liability would encourage a flow of such actions, (3) the belief that public inconvenience should be avoided, and (4) that no legislation existed imposing such liability. No direct judicial notice was taken of the doctrine of Crown Prerogative, or the "king can do no wrong" doctrine. It seems more likely that sovereign immunity came to be commonly accepted in this country through the use by early lawyers and judges of English legal books and materials such as Blackstone's Commentaries, which were used as standard references, and, of course, many of the notable jurists of early America received their legal training in the Inns of Court in London. Regardless of its origin, however, the United States Supreme Court and state courts adopted the principle that the sovereign could not be sued without its permission. The Supreme Court in 1869 commented that "It is a familiar doctrine of the common law, that the sovereign cannot be sued in his own courts without his consent"[10] and, in the same year in another case, the court stated that "Every government has an inherent right to protect itself against suits . . . .The principle is fundamental [and] applies to every sovereign power."[11] The federal government abrogated immunity to a statutorily prescribed extent in the *Federal Tort Claims Act of 1946.*

Beginning from the point of nearly universal adherence to the immunity doctrine, some state courts have moved away from the doctrine. Most significant is the *Molitor* case, which abolished immunity in Illinois and directly refuted the legal rationale that supported sovereign immunity.[12] In *Muskopf,* the California Supreme Court observed the trend away from immunity, saying:

> Only the vestigial remains of such governmental immunity have survived; its requiem has long been foreshadowed. For years the process of erosion of governmental immunity has gone on unabated. The Legislature has contributed mightily to that erosion. The courts, by distinction and extension, have removed much of the force of the rule. Thus, in holding that the doctrine of governmental immunity for torts for which its agents are liable has no place in our law we make no startling break with the past but merely take the final step that carries to its conclusion an established legislative and judicial trend.[13]

Since *Molitor,* sovereign immunity has been in a state of considerable change. Some state courts have abrogated immunity only to have it reinstated by the legislatures, while other courts have approached the issue in a piecemeal way by creating exceptions for proprietary functions, nuisances, or different standards for licenses and invitees. Several courts have dissected the school program, abolishing immunity for transportation injuries while maintaining it for the regular school program. Too, a trend exists for courts to sanction consensual waiver of liability by school boards through the acquisition of liability insurance.

Sovereign Immunity May Be Abrogated By the Courts

--- --- --- --- ---

Molitor v. Kaneland Community Unit District No. 302

--- --- --- --- ---

Supreme Court of Illinois, 1959.
18 Ill.2d 11, 163 N.E.2d 89.

KLINGBIEL, Justice. Plaintiff, Thomas Molitor, a minor, by Peter his father and next friend, brought this action against Kaneland

Community Unit School District for personal injuries sustained by plaintiff when the school bus in which he was riding left the road, allegedly as a result of the driver's negligence, hit a culvert, exploded and burned.   . . .

In his brief, plaintiff recognizes the rule, established by this court in 1898, that a school district is immune from tort liability, and frankly asks this court to abolish the rule *in toto* . . . .

Thus we are squarely faced with the highly important question—in the light of modern developments—should a school district be immune from liability for tortiously inflicted personal injury to a pupil thereof arising out of the operation of a school bus owned and operated by said district?   . . .

Historically we find that the doctrine of the sovereign immunity of the state, the theory that "the King can do no wrong," was first extended to a subdivision of the state in 1788 in *Russell v. Men of Devon*, 2 Term Rep. 671, 100 Eng.Rep. 359.   . . .

The immunity doctrine of *Russell v. Men of Devon* was adopted in Illinois with reference to towns and counties in 1870 in *Town of Waltham v. Kemper*, 55 Ill. 346. Then, in 1898, eight years after the English courts had refused to apply the *Russell* doctrine to schools, the Illinois court extended the immunity rule to school districts in the leading case of *Kinnare v. City of Chicago*, 171 Ill. 332, 49 N.E. 536, where it was held that the Chicago Board of Education was immune from liability for the death of a laborer resulting from a fall from the roof of a school building, allegedly due to the negligence of the Board in failing to provide scaffolding and safeguards. That opinion reasoned that since the State is not subject to suit nor liable for the torts or negligence of its agents, likewise a school district, as a governmental agency of the State, is also "exempted from the obligation to respond in damages, as master, for negligent acts of its servants to the same extent as is the State itself." Later decisions following the *Kinnare* doctrine have sought to advance additional explanations such as the protection of public funds and public property, and to prevent the diversion of tax moneys to the payment of damage claims.   . . .

Of all of the anomalies that have resulted from legislative and judicial efforts to alleviate the injustice of the results that have flowed from the doctrine of sovereign immunity, the one most immediately pertinent to this case is the following provision of the Illinois School Code: "Any school district, including any non-high school district, which provides transportation for pupils may insure against any loss or liability of such district, its agents or employees, resulting from or incident to the ownership maintenance or use of any school bus. Such insurance shall be carried only in companies duly licensed and authorized to write such coverage in this state. Every policy for such insurance coverage issued to a school district shall provide, or be endorsed to provide, that the company issuing such policy waives any right to refuse payment or to deny liability thereunder within the limits of said policy, by reason of the non-liability of the insured school district for the wrongful or negligent acts of its agents and employees, and, its immunity from suit as an agency of the state performing governmental functions." Ill.Rev.Stat.1957, c. 122, § 29–11a.

Thus, under this statute, a person injured by an insured school district bus may recover to the extent of such insurance, whereas, under the *Kinnare* doctrine, a person injured by an uninsured school district bus can recover nothing at all.

Defendant contends that the quoted provision of the School Code constitutes a legislative determination that the public policy of this State requires that school districts be immune from tort liability. We can read no such legislative intent into the statute. Rather, we interpret that section as expressing dissatisfaction with the court-created doctrine of governmental immunity and an attempt to cut down that immunity where insurance is involved. The difficulty with this legislative effort to curtail the judicial doctrine is that it allows each school district to determine for itself whether, and to what extent, it will be financially responsible for the wrongs inflicted by it.   . . .

It is a basic concept underlying the whole law of torts today that liability follows negligence, and that individuals and corporations are responsible for the negligence of their agents and employees acting in the course of their employment. The doctrine of governmental immunity runs directly counter to that basic concept. What reasons, then, are so impelling as to allow a school district, as a quasi-municipal corporation, to commit wrongdoing without any responsibility to its victims, while any individual or private corporation would be called to task in court for such tortious conduct?

The original basis of the immunity rule has been called a "survival of the medieval idea that the sovereign can do no wrong," or that "the King can do no wrong." (38 Am.Jur., Mun.Corps., sec. 573, p. 266.) In *Kinnare v. City of Chicago*, 171 Ill. 332, 49 N.E. 536, 537, the first Illinois case announcing the tort immunity of school districts, the court said: "The state acts in its sovereign capacity, and does not submit its action to the judgment of courts, and is not liable for the torts or negligence of its agents, and a corporation created by the state as a mere agency for the more efficient exercise of governmental functions is likewise exempted from the obligation to respond in damages, as master, for negligent acts of its servants to the same extent as is the state itself, unless such liability is expressly provided by the statute creating such agency." This was nothing more nor less than an extension of the theory of sovereign immunity. Professor Borchard has said that how immunity ever came to be applied in the United States of America is one of the mysteries of legal evolution. (Borchard, Governmental Liability in Tort, 34 Yale L.J. 1, 6.) And how it was then infiltrated into the law controlling the liability of local governmental units has been described as one of the amazing chapters of American common-law jurisprudence. . . .

We are of the opinion that school district immunity cannot be justified on this theory. As was stated by one court, "The whole doctrine of governmental immunity from liability for tort rests upon a rotten foundation. It is almost incredible that in this modern age of comparative sociological enlightenment, and in a republic, the medieval absolutism supposed to be implicit in the maxim, 'the King can do no wrong,' should exempt the various branches of the government from liability for their torts, and that the entire burden of damage resulting from the wrongful acts of the government should be imposed upon the single individual who suffers the injury, rather than distributed among the entire community constituting the government, where it could be borne without hardship upon any individual, and where it justly belongs." *Barker v. City of Santa Fe,* 47 N.M. 85, 136 P.2d 480, 482. Likewise, we agree with the Supreme Court of Florida that in preserving the sovereign immunity theory, courts have overlooked the fact that the Revolutionary War was fought to abolish that "divine right of kings" on which the theory is based.

The other chief reason advanced in support of the immunity rule in the more recent cases is the protection of public funds and public property. This corresponds to the "no fund" or "trust fund" theory upon which charitable immunity is based. . . . This reasoning seems to follow the line that it is better for the individual to suffer than for the public to be inconvenienced. From it proceeds defendant's argument that school districts would be bankrupted and education impeded if said districts were called upon to compensate children tortiously injured by the negligence of those districts' agents and employees.

We do not believe that in this present day and age, when public education constitutes one of the biggest businesses in the country, that school immunity can be justified on the protection-of-public-funds theory.

In the first place, analysis of the theory shows that it is based on the idea that payment of damage claims is a diversion of educational funds to an improper purpose. As many writers have pointed out, the fallacy in this argument is that it assumes the very point which is sought to be proved, i.e., that payment of damage claims is not a proper purpose. "Logically, the 'No-fund' or 'trust fund' theory is without merit because it is of value only after a determination of what is a proper school expenditure. To predicate immunity upon the theory of a trust fund is merely to argue in a circle, since it assumes an answer to the very question at issue, to wit, what is an educational purpose? Many disagree with the 'no-fund' doctrine to the extent of ruling that the payment of funds for judgments resulting from accidents or injuries in schools is an educational purpose. Nor can it be properly argued that as a result of the abandonment of the common-law rule the district would be completely bankrupt. California, Tennessee, New York, Washington and other states have not been compelled to shut down their schools." (Rosenfield, Governmental Immunity from Liability for Tort in School Accidents, 5 Legal Notes on Local Government, 376–377.) . . .

Neither are we impressed with defendant's plea that the abolition of immunity would create grave and unpredictable problems of school finance and administration. . . . While this factor may have had compulsion on some of the earlier courts, I seriously doubt that it has any great weight with the courts in recent years. In the first place, taxation is not the subject matter of judicial concern where justice to the individual citizen is involved. It is the business of other departments of government to provide the funds required to pay the damages assessed against them by the courts. . . . This argument is like so many of the horribles paraded in the early tort cases when courts were fashioning the boundaries of tort law. It has been thrown in simply because there was nothing better at hand. The public's willingness to stand up and pay the cost of its enterprises carried out through municipal corporations is no less than its insistence that individuals and groups pay the cost of their enterprises. "Tort liability is in fact a very small item in the budget of any well organized enterprise." (Green, Freedom of Litigation, 38 Ill.L.Rev. 355, 378.)

We are of the opinion that none of the reasons advanced in support of school district immunity have any true validity today. Further, we believe that abolition of such immunity may tend to decrease the frequency of school bus accidents by coupling the power to transport pupils with the responsibility of exercising care in the selection and supervision of the drivers. As Dean Harno said: "A municipal corporation today is an active and virile creature capable of inflicting much

harm. Its civil responsibility should be co-extensive. The municipal corporation looms up definitely and emphatically in our law, and what is more, it can and does commit wrongs. This being so, it must assume the responsibilities of the position it occupies in society." (Harno, Tort Immunity of Municipal Corporations, 4 Ill.L.Q. 28, 42.) School districts will be encouraged to exercise greater care in the matter of transporting pupils and also to carry adequate insurance covering that transportation, thus spreading the risk of accident, just as the other costs of education are spread over the entire district. . . .

We conclude that the rule of school district tort immunity is unjust, unsupported by any valid reason, and has no rightful place in modern day society.

Defendant strongly urges that if said immunity is to be abolished, it should be done by the legislature, not by this court. With this contention we must disagree. The doctrine of school district immunity was created by this court alone. Having found that doctrine to be unsound and unjust under present conditions, we consider that we have not only the power, but the duty, to abolish that immunity.

Where Legislature Has Statutorily Established Governmental Immunity, Court Will Refrain from Infringing on Legislative Policy-Making Authority

— - — - — - — - —

Richardson v. Rankin County School District

— - — - — - — - —

Supreme Court of Mississippi, 1989.
540 So.2d 5.

PRATHER, Justice, for the Court. This appeal revisits the doctrine of governmental immunity abandoned by this Court in *Pruett v. City of Rosedale*, 421 So.2d 1046 (Miss.1982) and seeks total and final abandonment of such doctrine again by this Court. Plaintiff Alma Jane Richardson suffered personal injury in an accident between her vehicle and a Rankin County School bus driven by Darlene Collier. . . .

Richardson filed her complaint alleging that on May 1, 1986, she was injured as a result of a collision involving her automobile and a school bus owned by the Rankin County School District and being operated by its employee, Darlene Collier. Richardson bases her theory of liability upon the statutory liability of the Rankin County School District, et al, as provided under Miss.Code Ann. § 37–41–37, et seq. (1986 Supp.) and upon the theory of negligence. . . .

On March 31, 1987, all of the defendants filed their answer setting forth their defenses, including the defense that the defendants are immune from liability under the theory of sovereign or governmental immunity and denying all material allegations of the complaint and denying that Richardson is entitled to recover any sums whatsoever. . . .

The question of whether or not the doctrine of governmental or sovereign immunity should be totally abolished has come before this Court on a number of occasions. Finally, in *Pruett v. City of Rosedale*, 421 So.2d 1046 (Miss.1982), this Court recognized that the doctrine of sovereign immunity was a creature of the judiciary, and it was time for the judiciary to abolish it. The Court recognized, however, that it was the legislature, not the judiciary, that had the duty and responsibility of controlling and policing sovereign immunity.

> [T]he control and policing of sovereign immunity is a legislative responsibility and not that of the judiciary. The sovereign immunity doctrine is a creature of the judiciary. We are of the opinion that it should not be so; but that as said above, the details of handling the question is legislative rather than judicial. As has been said by many of the State's highest courts, the judicial branch is leaving the matter to the legislative branch. It was judicially created and necessarily should be judicially abrogated. [*Pruett* at page 1047.]

Pruett made clear that the immunity that was being abolished was the immunity of the

sovereign, which means the state, the county, the municipality or any other local subdivision of the sovereign. This Court expressly noted that the abolition of sovereign immunity did not "apply to legislative, judicial and executive acts by individuals acting in their official capacity, or to similar capacities in local governments, either county or municipal." . . .

The legislature, in response to the *Pruett* decision, enacted what is now codified as Miss.Code Ann. § 11–46–1, et seq. (1988 Supp.) (1984 Immunity Act). The intent of the legislature is clear. Section 11–46–3, Miss.Code Ann. (1988 Supp.) states:

> The Legislature of the State of Mississippi finds and determines as a matter of public policy and does hereby declare that from and after July 1, 1989, the "state" and, from and after October 1, 1989, its "political subdivisions," as such terms are defined in Section 11–46–1, shall not be liable and shall be immune from suit at law or in equity on account of any wrongful or tortious act or omission, including libel, slander or defamation, by the state or its political subdivisions, or any such act or omission by any employee of the state or its political subdivisions, notwithstanding that any such act or omission constitutes or may be considered as the exercise or failure to exercise any duty, obligation or function of a governmental, proprietary, discretionary or ministerial nature and notwithstanding that such act or omission may or may not arise out of any activity, transaction or service for which any fee, charge, cost or other consideration was received or expected to be received in exchange therefor.

The Immunity Act grants general legislative immunity to the State and its political subdivisions, including local school districts. It also waives such immunity of the State and its political subdivisions from claims for money damages arising out of the torts of such governmental entities and the torts of their employees while acting within the course and scope of their employment. Such immunity is waived only to the extent of the maximum amount of liability as provided under the provisions of the above quoted statutes. Miss. Code Ann. § 11–46–15 (1988 Supp.) provides the limits of liability of a governmental entity or its employee. . . .

Thus, it is clear from the above statute that the Mississippi Legislature has, by appropriate legislation, given the state and its political subdivisions immunity from suit on account of any wrongful or tortious act or omission by any employee of the state or its political subdivisions, except as to the extent of liability permitted by statute.

There is no challenge to the constitutionality of the statute itself, only a request that this Court finally abolish governmental immunity. This request infringes upon the policy making authority of the legislature, and this Court refrains from infringing upon this legislative prerogative.

The trial court did not err in granting the Motion For Partial Summary Judgment below, and should, therefore, be affirmed.

Affirmed.

NOTE

1. "Within constitutional limitations, the legislature is empowered to control the liability to which the state and its agencies may be subjected for tort." *Bego v. Gordon,* 407 N.W. 2d 801, 808 (S.D. 1987).

The Doctrine of Sovereign Immunity May Protect Teacher from Liability for Pupil Injury

— · — · — · — · — · —

Lentz v. Morris

— · — · — · — · — · —

Supreme Court of Virginia, 1988.
236 Va. 78, 372 S.E.2d 608.

COMPTON, Justice. The sole question presented in this appeal is whether the doctrine of sovereign immunity protects a high school teacher supervising a physical education class from a negligence action for damages brought by a student injured while a member of the class. . . .

The plaintiff asserts that on November 9, 1984, the day of the injury, he was a student and defendant was a teacher of health and physical education at Kellam High School in Virginia Beach. He alleges that he was assigned to a physical education class conducted "under the supervision and in the presence of Defendant." He further asserts that, while participating with the class in activities on school grounds, he and other students were "playing tackle football without wearing any protective equipment," which activity defendant knew or should have known posed danger to the participants. Plaintiff also alleges that as the result of defendant's negligent supervision and control of the physical education activities, he was "tackled with great force and violence" which caused his injuries.

. . . [P]laintiff contends that the trial court erred in ruling that a school teacher is entitled to immunity "for his own acts of negligence." . . .

. . . [T]he plaintiff urges, "Insulation of this individual from responsibility for his own negligent acts does not achieve any of the purposes for which immunity is ordinarily extended to governmental employees." We do not agree.

Messina v. Burden [228 Va. 301, 321 S.E.2d 657 (1984)] was a watershed decision on the subject of sovereign immunity. In that case, we reviewed our prior decisions stemming from diverse factual settings and attempted to reconcile them. Reasserting the viability of the doctrine in the Commonwealth, we endeavored to explicate the circumstances under which "an employee of a governmental body is entitled to the protection of sovereign immunity," given the facts of the cases under consideration in *Messina.* . . .

Initially, we focused upon the purposes served by the doctrine. They include "protecting the public purse, providing for smooth operation of government, eliminating public inconvenience and danger that might spring from officials being fearful to act, assuring that citizens will be willing to take public jobs, and preventing citizens from improperly influencing the conduct of governmental affairs through the threat or use of vexatious litigation." . . . We then said that in order to fulfill those purposes, the reach of the doctrine could not be limited solely to the sovereign but must be extended to "some of the people who help run the government." . . . We noted that because the government acts only through individuals, it could be crippled in its operations if every government employee were subject to suit.

In *Messina,* against the background of the purposes of the doctrine, the general principles applicable to the concept, and the facts and circumstances of the cases at hand, we proceeded to engage in a necessary "line-drawing" exercise to determine which government employees were entitled to immunity. Thus, in one case, we held that a State supervisory employee who was charged with simple negligence while acting within the scope of his employment was immune, there being no charge of gross negligence or intentional misconduct. . . .

In the other *Messina* case, supra, we decided that an employee of a county, which shares the immunity of the State, was entitled to the benefits of sovereign immunity where his activities clearly involved the exercise of judgment and discretion. . . . In deciding that case, we outlined the test, . . . to be used to determine entitlement to immunity. The factors to be considered include: (1) the nature of the function the employee performs; (2) the extent of the governmental entity's interest and involvement in the function; (3) the degree of control and direction exercised by the governmental entity over the employee; and (4) whether the alleged wrongful act involved the exercise of judgment and discretion. . . .

. . .

We hold the trial court correctly ruled that the health and physical education teacher in this case was immune from suit. The facts expressly alleged, and the inferences flowing from those facts, state the following case. The defendant, an employee of an immune governmental entity, was charged with simple negligence in the supervision and control of the class to which he was assigned. The facts do not support a charge of either gross negligence or intentional misconduct. In addition, and contrary to the contention of the plaintiff on brief, implicit in the facts alleged is the conclusion that the defendant was acting within the scope of his employment at the time of the injury.

Therefore, factors included in the *Messina* test for entitlement to immunity are present in this case. The employee is performing a vitally important public function as a school teacher. The governmental entity employing the teacher, the local school board, has official interest and direct involvement in the function of student instruction and supervision, and it exercises control and direction over the employee through the school principal. . . . And, a teacher's supervision and control of a physical education class, including the decision of what equipment and attire is to be worn by the student participants, clearly involves, at least in part, the exercise of judgment and discretion by the teacher.

Consequently, the *Messina* test, given the purposes served by the doctrine, mandates immunity for this defendant. If school teachers performing functions equivalent to this defendant are to be haled into court for the conduct set forth by these facts, fewer individuals will aspire to be teachers, those who have embarked on a teaching career will be reluctant to act, and the orderly administration of the school systems will suffer, all to the detriment of our youth and the public at large.

For these reasons, the judgment of the trial court will be

Affirmed.

Whether Sovereign Immunity Is Waived May Depend on the Specific Terms of Liability Insurance Policy

— · — · — · — · — · —

Dugger v. Sprouse

— · — · — · — · — · —

Supreme Court of Georgia, 1988.
257 Ga. 778, 364 S.E.2d 275.

SMITH, Justice. Appellee Anthony Plavich is an employee of Murray County school system. A suit was filed by a student, appellant Darin

Dugger, for injuries he received when he was thrown from the back of a pickup truck while delivering wrestling mats from one county school to another. The appellee's motion for summary judgment, based upon the defense of sovereign immunity, was granted. We affirm.

If insurance coverage is obtained by a government entity, then the government entity (the county in this case) waives its sovereign immunity to the extent of such insurance coverage. . . . However, where the plain terms of the policy provide that there is no coverage for the particular claim, the policy does not create a waiver of sovereign immunity as to that claim. Here the trial court found that the policy did not provide coverage for the appellant's claim. Where there is no insurance coverage, there is no waiver of sovereign immunity.

Judgment affirmed.

All the Justices concur.

◼ PROPRIETARY FUNCTIONS

Some courts, being reluctant to totally abrogate immunity, have sought ways to avoid direct confrontation with the issue. To sidestep the overall problem, courts have settled tort actions in several states on the basis of the activity or function that was being performed by the school district when the injury occurred. In this regard, we should note that school districts operate in a dual capacity: performing functions that are strictly governmental the majority of the time they also, on some occasions, perform proprietary functions or functions that may be performed by a private corporation.

Proprietary functions have been defined as things not normally required by law or things not governmental in nature. If a function is within the scope of the public school operation, as expressed or implied by statute, then the function is governmental and not proprietary. Courts have generally held that school athletic contests are governmental functions.[14] While the courts have rather

consistently held that municipalities are liable for injuries arising out of functions for which admission is charged or some financial gain is realized, they have been reluctant to generally apply this standard to school districts.

Thus, if a spectator or participant is injured at an athletic contest, the courts do not usually impose liability on the school district, even when a fee is charged and the school has realized a profit. Of course, exceptions exist to all general rules, and in regard to this question, one court held that when a school district leased its football stadium to another for a fee, the lessor was held to have been engaged in a proprietary activity and was liable for injury to a spectator who was injured when a railing broke.

In following the rule that school districts are immune from liability for incidents arising during functions that charge fees, a Tennessee court said:

> The mere fact that an admission fee was charged by the high school does not make the transaction an enterprise for profit. . . . The duties of a County Board of Education are limited to the operation of the schools. This is a governmental function. Therefore, in legal contemplation, there is no such thing as such a Board acting in a proprietary capacity for private gain.[15]

A Kansas court[16] has said, *in dicta,* that if a school district can and does perform proprietary activities, then it must answer in damages when guilty in tort for injuries resulting from such functions. The Supreme Court of Oregon has laid down a test for distinguishing proprietary from governmental functions. "The underlying test is whether the act is for the common good of all without the element of special corporate benefit or pecuniary profit."[17]

The rule, therefore, may probably be summarized: as long as the purpose of the activity is educational and for the common good and the profit accrued is only incidental, the activity is governmental in nature.

This general rule is enunciated by a Michigan court in a 1984 decision:

We therefore conclude that a governmental function is an activity which is expressly or impliedly mandated or authorized by constitution, statute, or other law. When a governmental agency engages in mandated or authorized activities, it is immune from tort liability, unless the activity is *proprietary* in nature. (italics added).[18]

Not all courts agree with this rule, however. It is, of course, an entirely appropriate rejoinder to assert that because public schools have no legitimate function except as authorized by law that they cannot, in fact, legally perform proprietary functions. In this view, proprietary functions are *ultra vires* and, thereby, have no legal cognizance. This is precisely the position taken by an appellate court in Texas, which concludes simply that school districts cannot perform proprietary functions.[19] This court has stated:

> Since a school district is purely a governmental agency and exercises only such powers as are delegated to it by the state, it performs no proprietary functions that are separate from governmental functions.[20]

LICENSEE AND INVITEE

A school district owes a greater degree of care to an invitee than to a licensee. A licensee is one who steps beyond the limits of invitation, entering and using the premises by permission or by operation of law but without expressed or implied invitation.[21] A licensee does not commit trespass, because he or she has passive permission to enter. Passive permission is not an implied invitation. On the other hand, an invitee is a person who enters the premises upon the invitation of the owner. An invitation may be either *expressed*, when the owner invites another to come and use the premises; or the invitation may be *implied*, when the owner by his or her acts or conduct conveys the desire that the person enter the premises.

An owner of property normally does not owe a licensee particular duty, and is therefore not responsible for exercising any particular standard of care to protect the licensee. Some courts, however, have held that an owner may be liable for willful or wanton disregard for the safety of the licensee. In this regard, the owner should not knowingly let the licensee run upon "hidden peril or wilfully cause him harm."[22] The standard of care owed an invitee is much higher, and the duty owed by the owner is substantially greater.

Holder of a Free Pass to a Football Game Was an Invitee to Whom the School District Owed a Duty of Reasonable Care

Tanari v. School Directors of District No. 502

Supreme Court of Illinois, 1977.
69 Ill.2d 630, 14 Ill.Dec. 874, 373 N.E.2d 5.

UNDERWOOD, Justice. Plaintiff, Flora Tanari, brought an action . . . seeking damages for injuries she sustained when she allegedly was knocked to the ground by a group of children engaged in horseplay at a high school football game sponsored by defendant on its premises. The complaint alleged ordinary negligence on the part of defendant in failing to provide adequate supervision and control of children at the game. At the close of the evidence, the trial court granted the defendant's motion for a directed verdict on the ground that plaintiff was a licensee on defendant's premises; that defendant therefore only owed her the duty to refrain from wilful and wanton misconduct; and that breach of such duty had neither been alleged nor proved at trial. . . .

Plaintiff, age 64, was employed as a bus driver by an individual who had a contract with the defendant school district to transport students to and from school. She had been so employed for twenty-seven years and had attended all of the local high school football games for the last twenty-five years. On October 13, 1972, plaintiff attended the Hall Township High School homecoming football game with her daughter, son-in-law and grandchildren. The game was held on defendant's premises at a sports stadium under defendant's supervision and control. Plaintiff entered the stadium using a complimentary season pass issued by the defendant. As she was walking toward her seat, she noticed a crowd of boys and girls playing near the northwest end of the stadium, and the next thing she knew she had been knocked to the ground by a "big" boy who fell on top of her. The boy, who was never identified, got up, apologized and hurried away. . . .

The athletic director of Hall Township High School testified that he had hired off-duty policemen and teachers to keep order at all high school football games conducted by the defendant. . . . He responded in the affirmative when asked if he had seen boys and girls at almost every game "playing tag, or horseplaying and roughing it up" in the area in question. However, when he was later asked if there was "rowdiness and horseplaying by these kids in that area," he responded that he did not know whether it should be called rowdiness and horseplay, but the children were definitely there. He further testified that on previous occasions he had tried to "correct" the children but that, as soon as he left, they were back at it again. He knew from his personal observation that a policeman was in the area of the accident on the night in question.

The trial court allowed the defendant's motion for a directed verdict on the sole ground that plaintiff was a licensee on the defendant's premises and that there was no proof whatsoever that defendant had breached its duty to refrain from willful and wanton misconduct. . . . Considering the state of the record before us, we are unable to concur with the appellate court's conclusions regarding defendant's immunity . . . .

It is unnecessary to dwell at length on the common law distinctions between invitees and licensees which have evolved over the

years. It suffices to observe that the general definition of an invitee is a visitor who comes upon premises at the invitation of the owner in connection with the owner's business or related activity. . . . Licensees are persons who have not been invited to enter upon the owner's premises and who come there for their own purposes and not those of the owner. . . . However, their presence is condoned by the owner, which distinguishes them from trespassers. The trial court concluded in the case at bar that since the plaintiff had not purchased a ticket but rather had attended the football game using a complimentary season pass, there was an absence of "commercial benefit" to the defendant school district, and she must therefore be considered a licensee. For the reasons hereafter stated, we must disagree with that conclusion.

In determining whether or not a person is an invitee or a licensee in a given situation, appellate courts in this State have often looked at the surrounding circumstances to determine whether, as between the visitor and the owner, there was a "mutuality of interest in the subject to which the visitor's business relates" . . . "a mutually beneficial interest" . . . a "mutuality of interest" . . . a "mutuality of benefit or a benefit to the owner" . . . or whether the visitor had come to "transact business in which he and the owner have a mutual interest or to promote some real or fancied material, financial, or economic interest of the owner" . . . . Such inquiries into the purpose and nature of the visit were deemed relevant, particularly in cases involving implied invitations, to ascertain whether the visitor was upon the owner's premises within the scope and purpose of the invitation or for some other reason.

That type of analysis is not necessary here. In our opinion, the complimentary pass issued to plaintiff was tantamount to an express invitation to attend Hall Township High School football games, and there can be no question about the fact that at the time of her injury, plaintiff was acting within the scope of that invitation. Unlike a person who comes upon an owner's premises for his own purposes rather than those of the owner and whose presence is merely condoned by the owner, plaintiff in this case was expressly invited and encouraged to come to the defendant's football stadium to swell the crowd in support of its team. In this type of situation, it would be entirely illogical to conclude that a person attending the game using a complimentary pass provided by the school district should be owed a lesser duty of care than a person otherwise similarly situated who had purchased a ticket. In our view, both persons should be owed the same duty of reasonable care, and we so hold.

Upon application of a reasonable care standard to the case at bar, we cannot conclude that all of the evidence, when viewed in its aspect most favorable to the plaintiff, so overwhelmingly favors the defendant that no verdict for the plaintiff could ever stand. . . . The question of whether defendant failed to exercise reasonable care in supervising children attending the football game and whether such failure, if found to exist, was the proximate cause of plaintiff's injuries, should have been submitted to the jury. . . .

Reversed and remanded.

School District Not Immune Regardless of Whether It Was Performing a Governmental or Proprietary Function

—·—·—·—·—·—

Board of School Commissioners of Mobile County v. Caver

—·—·—·—·—·—

Supreme Court of Alabama, 1978.
355 So.2d 712.

BLOODWORTH, Justice. . . . Plaintiff, Caver, a student who was allegedly injured by a Mobile County School Board bus while she was standing in the school yard, brought suit for negligence, and the Board moved to dismiss her complaint because of sovereign immunity. . . .

Defendant, Board, contends that the issue of sovereign immunity was decided in its favor in *Sims v. Etowah County Board of Education,* 337 So.2d 1310 (Ala.1976), which held in a plurality decision, (based upon an interpretation of Tit. 52, § 99, Code of Alabama 1940) that a school board is immune from suit in tort.

Although at first blush, the Board's argument seems an appealing one, for *Sims* appears to foreclose further inquiry into this question, a close reading of *Sims* and an examination of Act No. 480, Acts of Alabama, Regular Session 1969, as well as § 270 of the Constitution of 1901, convinces us that the Mobile County School Board is amenable to suit in tort.

Mr. Justice Stakely, in *Morgan v. Board of School Commissioners of Mobile County,* 248 Ala. 22, 26 So.2d 108 (1946), gave the history of the Mobile County Board of School Commissioners. In that opinion, he pointed out that the Mobile County School Board has been exempted, in large part, from the general scheme of public school legislation ever since 1854 when the State of Alabama set up its first comprehensive school system.

That legislative policy, which is based upon the fact that Mobile County established its school system before the State did so, continues to this date, as evidenced by Section 270 of Article XIV of the Alabama Constitution. . . .

This limitation on legislative power is restrictive in its scope and purpose and is to be strictly construed. . . .

Act Number 480 (the latest amendatory act regulating the public schools in Mobile County) falls within neither one of these two exceptions. That act provides, *inter alia,* that, "The said Board shall be a body corporate; and may have a common seal; *may sue and be sued* . . . .." (Emphasis supplied.) Clearly, the authority to "sue and be sued" is not one of those educational areas in which the legislature may not act concerning the Mobile County School Board.

We stressed in *Sims v. Etowah County Board of Education,* supra, as well as in *Enterprise City Board of Education v. Miller,* 348 So.2d 782

(1977), that the sovereign immunity we held was due to be accorded those boards of education flowed directly from the statutes. In both cases, the pertinent statutes stated that the county and city boards of education, respectively, "may sue." There was no corresponding provision in those statutes that the respective boards could "be sued." For that reason, we said in each case, *inter alia,* that the respective boards of education were immune from suit in tort.

In the case at bar, by contrast, Act Number 480 clearly states that the Mobile County School Board "may sue and be sued." We hold, therefore, as we said in *Sims* and *Enterprise City Board,* that the statute must be given effect, and, therefore, the Mobile County School Board may be sued in tort.

Defendant Board argues, however, that the phrase "sue and be sued" is not an all-encompassing term, and that if the county school board may be sued, it may only be sued for acts performed in its corporate or proprietary capacity as opposed to acts performed in its governmental capacity. In other words, defendant Board would have us resort to determining whether the act is governmental or corporate. As we held in *Jackson v. City of Florence,* 294 Ala. 592, 320 So.2d 68 (1975). . . . however, these distinctions are tenuous, at best, and our continued reliance upon them, in the context of sovereign immunity cases, would serve no useful purpose.

For the foregoing reasons, we hold that the trial judge's order is due to be affirmed.

Affirmed.

School District Not Liable to Licensee Unless Conduct Causing Injury Is Willful and Wanton

– – · – – · – – · – – ·

Yates v. J.W. Campbell Electric Corporation

– – · – – · – – · – – ·

Court of Appeals of North Carolina, 1989.
95 N.C. App. 354, 382 S.E. 2d 860.

JOHNSON, Judge. Viewed in the light most favorable to plaintiffs, as we are required to do on motion by defendant for summary judgment, the evidence tends to show the following. On 2 January 1985, plaintiff Jewell Maxine Yates and her two children, plaintiff Lief Cymone Yates, then six months of age, and plaintiff Bianca Odessa Yates, then three years, were passengers in a 1982 Chevrolet van being operated by third-party defendant Tessie O. Yates. At approximately 5:45 p.m., it was dark and raining when Tessie Yates drove the van into a driveway to turn around in front of Northampton High School West from highway 186 which bounds the school on the south. Plaintiffs, who are residents of Washington, D.C. did not know that the driveway had no outlet and necessitated coming out in the same place they entered. There was a basketball game going on at the school when plaintiffs drove in. None of the plaintiffs, however, exited the van after it entered the driveway. Tessie Yates then backed the van straight out on to the westbound lane of highway 186. Plaintiffs' van was then hit on the passenger side by an oncoming automobile owned by defendant J.W. Campbell Electrical Corporation and driven by defendant Rex David Bass. Defendant Bass was traveling in the westbound lane of highway 186 when he collided with plaintiffs' van. Defendants Bass and Campbell Electrical Corporation are not involved in this appeal.

The issue before us is whether the trial court erred in granting summary judgment in favor of defendant Northampton County Board of Education (hereinafter the defendant). . . .

First, plaintiffs urge us to reverse the trial court's order because they contend that there is a genuine issue of material fact regarding their status while on the public property under defendant's control. They argue that their status was that of invitee rather than licensee, and that therefore defendant owed them the corresponding higher duty of care. We disagree.

Our Supreme Court has set forth the distinction between an invitee and a licensee as follows:

The distinction between an invitee and a licensee is determined by the nature of the business bringing a person to the premises. A licensee is one who enters on the premises with the possessor's permission, express or implied, *solely for his own purposes* rather than the possessor's benefit. An invitee is a person who goes upon the premises in response to an express or implied invitation by the landowner for the mutual benefit of the landowner and himself. . . .

Plaintiffs urge, however, that their status while on defendant's driveway was that of invitee because the high school is public property and at the time was open to the public for an athletic event. . . .

. . . Plaintiff Jewell Maxine Yates admitted in one set of interrogatories that no one in her van attended the athletic event taking place at Northampton High School West. She also made the following statements in a different set of interrogatories:

Where were you coming from at the time of the accident?

ANSWER: The District of Columbia.

Where were you going at the time of the accident?

ANSWER: To take my grandmother home.

Although plaintiffs allege in their unverified complaint that they attended the sporting event, they candidly admit in their brief that they "pulled into the Defendant's driveway to turn around." . . . [T]he Yates plaintiffs were there solely for their own benefit and not in response to any express or implied invitation of defendant's. . . .

It is well-settled in North Carolina that a landowner's duty of care to a licensee is to refrain from willful or wanton negligence, and from doing any affirmative acts which result in increased danger to the licensee while he is on the premises. . . . Plaintiffs, however, contend that even if the two minor plaintiffs were licensees, that the defendant owed them a higher degree of care because of their tender years. We recognize that a landowner owes a higher level of care to a young child who is unable to appreciate a potential danger even

though he is a licensee. . . . This higher level of care is not owed, however, when the child is accompanied by a parent or other custodial adult who has full knowledge of the potential hazard. . . . [D]efendant Tessie Yates, who was present and operating plaintiffs' van, should have realized the danger involved in backing out on to a highway at night. Plaintiffs, of course, assert that plaintiff Jewell Yates did not have full knowledge of the danger and therefore defendant owed a higher duty of care to the minor plaintiffs. We disagree, but find that the issue is moot, since the critical point is that there is no evidence that defendant was aware that the minor plaintiffs were on its property. Without such knowledge, defendant did not owe a higher measure of care to the young children. . . .

Last, allowing for the possibility that we would decide that plaintiffs lacked the status of invitee, as we have, plaintiffs urge us that summary judgment is inappropriate because defendant was willfully and wantonly negligent, and its negligence was active. We disagree.

. . .

" 'Wilful and wanton' negligence is conduct which shows either a deliberate intention to harm, or an utter indifference to, or conscious disregard for, the rights or safety of others. 'Carelessness and recklessness,' though more than ordinary negligence, is less than wilfulness or wantonness." . . .

Reviewing the record before us with these standards in mind, we find nothing to indicate that plaintiffs will be able to make out a *prima facie* case of willful or wanton negligence at trial. The principal of the high school testified that to his knowledge the driveway had never extended past the school and back to the street. Although he stated that he had previously discussed the possibility of installing a blinking light in front of the school to slow down logging trucks, this simply does not rise to the level of showing willful or wanton negligence.

Defendant's negligence, if any, in the design and maintenance of its driveway was at most ordinary and passive in nature. Plaintiffs have failed to forecast evidence that defendant was either willfully or wantonly negligent or that it acted to increase the danger while plaintiffs were on the premises. Therefore, the trial court's granting of summary judgment for the defendant Board of Education must be upheld.

Affirmed.

■■■ NUISANCE

Another device used by the courts to partially skirt the boundaries of immunity is the nuisance doctrine. A nuisance has been defined as "the existence or creation of a dangerous, unsafe, or offensive condition which is likely to cause injury, harm, or inconvenience to others." A more complete definition has been given by a Connecticut court:

> [T]o constitute a nuisance there must have arisen a condition, the natural tendency of which is to create danger or inflict injury upon person or property . . . there must be more than an act or failure to act on the part of the defendant . . . the danger created must have been a continuing one.[23]

A leading case in which a school district was held to have created a nuisance was one in which snow had fallen from the roof of a school building onto adjacent property, damaging the property. The owner was also injured when he fell on the ice. The court held that in this case there was both nuisance and trespass.

> The plaintiff had the right to the exclusive use and enjoyment of his property, and the defendant had no more right to erect a building in such a manner that the ice and snow would inevitably slide from the roof, and be precipitated upon the plaintiff's premises, than it would have to accumulate water upon its own premises, and then permit it to flow in a body upon his premises.[24]

In keeping with the legal definition, a dangerous condition must be created by the school district for nuisance to exist. In Kansas, an action was brought to recover damages for injury sustained by a nine-year-old pupil who slipped and fell on a wet lavatory floor. Pupils had made the floor wet and slippery by throwing wet paper towels and splashing water. The plaintiff claimed the district was maintaining a nuisance and was therefore liable. In response, the court held that the school did not create the nuisance since pupils could be expected to splash water and throw wet towels on the floor while using the lavatory, and that wash basins were a necessary part of the school building equipment.[25]

The adequacy of supervision on the part of school personnel was another matter. Adequacy of supervision is not a question to be dealt with in a nuisance action, since to constitute nuisance there must be a continuing hazard and there must be more than a mere failure to act on the part of the defendant.[26]

It seems safe to conclude that while the "nuisance" theory is a viable method of averting direct confrontation with the governmental immunity issue, the courts in other jurisdictions will not plunge headlong toward its use as piecemeal abrogation. This, of course, does not mean courts will never employ the device since it is an acceptable legal doctrine, but it does indicate a reluctance on the part of the courts to tamper with the doctrine of governmental immunity in this limited fashion.

Snow Pushed into Mounds on Playground Does Not Constitute Intentional Nuisance

— ·— ·— ·— ·—

Hendricks v. Southfield Public Schools

— ·— ·— ·— ·—

Court of Appeals of Michigan, 1989.
178 Mich. App. 672, 444 N.W. 2d 143.

PER CURIAM. . . . On appeal, plaintiffs argue that the public building exception to governmental immunity applies to their case because piles of snow located on a school playground constitute a dangerous condition of a public building. M.C.L. § 691.1406; M.S.A. § 3.996(106). We disagree. . . .

The public building exception to governmental immunity has been interpreted to include items permanently affixed to a public building. . . . Our Supreme Court has indicated that the public building exception will not be so expansively interpreted as to extend to all public places. . . .

We do not believe that the Legislature intended its immunity exception to include the temporary condition of snow piles. Accepting as true all of plaintiffs' factual allegations contained in their pleadings and the conclusions to be reasonably drawn therefrom, plaintiffs' claim was so clearly unenforceable as a matter of law that no factual development could justify plaintiffs' right to recovery. Hence the trial court did not err in granting summary disposition on the basis that the piles of snow did not fall within the public building exception to the defense of governmental immunity. . . .

We are also unpersuaded by plaintiffs' argument that the mounds of snow should be deemed an intentional nuisance by which the claim of governmental immunity could be overcome.

To establish a claim of intentional nuisance against a governmental agency, a plaintiff must show that there is a condition which is a nuisance and that the agency intended to create that condition. . . .

Because the injury of which plaintiffs complain resulted from the school's failure to remove the mound of snow from the playground after clearing the parking lot, we conclude that the trial court in this case did not err in granting summary disposition to defendant on the basis that plaintiffs' well-pled facts involve circumstances showing the school's failure to act in removing the piles of snow.

Further, an intentionally created nuisance requires proof that the party creating or continuing the nuisance knew or must have known that harm to a plaintiff was substantially certain to follow. . . . Here, it cannot be said that harm was substantially certain to follow from the presence of the amount of snow at issue.

Accepting as true all of plaintiffs' factual allegations contained in the pleadings and conclusions to be reasonably drawn therefrom, plaintiffs could not have proved an intentionally created nuisance. Accordingly, the trial court did not err in granting summary disposition on the basis that the piles of snow did not constitute an intentional nuisance. . . .

Affirmed.

■ ELEVENTH-AMENDMENT IMMUNITY

The Eleventh Amendment to the U.S. Constitution bars a private party from recovery of funds from a state treasury for a liability judgment against the state. The Eleventh Amendment provides that:

> [T]he judicial power of the United States shall not be construed to extend to any suit in law or equity, commenced or prosecuted against one of the United States by Citizens of another state, or by Citizens or Subjects of any Foreign State.

The Eleventh Amendment is an explicit limitation on the power of the judiciary and is a reinforcement of the sovereign legislative power of the states.[27]

Origins of Amendment

The Eleventh Amendment was enacted in 1795 in response to the issues presented in two early cases, one in 1791 and another in 1792. The former case permitted a group of Dutch bankers, as creditors to the state of Maryland, to sue the state for recovery of debts[28]; and the latter saw an action of two citizens of South Carolina against the state of Georgia.[29] The thought of the consequences of having foreign nationals and citizens of other states to invade the sovereignty of the various states "literally shocked the nation."[30] Sentiment to prevent such actions quickly gained momentum and five years later, during John Adams' presidency, the Eleventh Amendment was ratified.

The idea that states as sovereign entities should be immune was supported by both Madison and Hamilton. Madison said, "I do not conceive that any controversy can ever be decided, in these courts, between an American state and a foreign state, without consent of the parties."[31] Hamilton observed in the *Federalist*, No. 81, that "It is inherent in the nature of sovereignty not to be amenable to the suit of an individual *without its* (the state) *consent*." Such invasion on legislative prerogative, it was thought, would hinder the operation of states and unduly restrain the exercise of their sovereignty. The Supreme Court has held that the amendment, by implication, also bars suits against the state by any and all citizens, including the state's own citizenry.[32] The Supreme Court has thus stated the general rule of law as follows: "[A] suit by private parties seeking to impose a liability which must be paid from public funds in the state treasury is barred by the Eleventh Amendment."[33]

The Supreme Court has enunciated this rule on several occasions. A most notable statement emanates from a 1921 case, in which the Court explained:

> The entire judicial power granted by the United States Constitution does not embrace authority to entertain a suit by private parties against the state without the consent of the state, whether it is brought by citizens of another state or by subjects of a foreign state, in which case it is contrary to the fundamental rule that a state may not be sued without its consent.[34]

This rule, though, is not without limits. Where there is a conflict of constitutional interest and the state violates the Fourteenth-Amendment rights, then the Eleventh Amendment may be overridden and liability may be imposed on the state.

There are basically two ways that state immunity under the Eleventh Amendment can be abrogated; one is "if a State waives its immunity and consents to suit in Federal court."[35] Concerning the waiver, the Supreme Court held that "a State will be deemed to have waived its immunity only where stated by the most express language or by such

overwhelming implication from the text as leave no room for any other reasonable construction."[36] The second abrogation of Eleventh-Amendment immunity is by Congress through the Fourteenth Amendment. Section 5 of the Fourteenth Amendment states, "The Congress shall have power to enforce, by appropriate legislation, the provision of this article." Since the Fourteenth Amendment was enacted after the Eleventh Amendment, the Supreme Court has interpreted § 5 to mean that Congress meant to waive the Eleventh Amendment when exercising the rights of the Fourteenth Amendment. But this waiver must be "an unequivocal expression of congressional intent to overturn constitutionally guaranteed immunity of the several states."

In *Dellmuth v. Muth*[37] in 1989, the Supreme Court ruled that "The Education Handicapped Act does not abrogate the state's Eleventh Amendment immunity" because that intention by Congress was not "unmistakenly clear in the language of the statute." In the newly enacted Individuals with Disabilities Education Act, formerly EAHCA, Congress makes clear the intent to waive the Eleventh Amendment. Section 1403 of the act is titled "Abrogation of State sovereign immunity" and is as follows:

(a) A State shall not be immune under the eleventh amendment to the Constitution of the United States from suit in Federal court for a violation of this Act.

(b) In a suit against a State for a violation of this Act, remedies (including remedies both at law and in equity) are available for such a violation to the same extent as such remedies are available for such a violation in the suit against any public entity other than a State.

(c) The provisions of subsections (a) and (b) of this section shall take effect with respect to violations that occur in whole or part after the October 30, 1990.

Therefore, Congress left no doubt in waiving the Eleventh-Amendment immunity of the state with regard to the Individuals with Disabilities Education Act.

Prospective Relief

When relief is permitted, it is not retroactive, applying to prospective redress only. In *ex parte Young*, the court required the state to conform only its future conduct to the requirements of the Fourteenth Amendment.[38] However, if a state consents to be sued, by consenting the state agrees to forgo its Eleventh-Amendment immunity and pay damages. Consent by the states cannot be implied or merely constructive acquiescence; rather, it must be an express denial of its own immunity. The mere fact that a state participates in a federal program does not implicitly waive the state's immunity from suit.[39]

In *Edelman*, the Supreme Court forbade the payment of retroactive "equitable restitution" from state funds.[40] It should be noted, however, that Eleventh-Amendment immunity protection does not extend to suits against public officials as individuals.[41]

> [W]hen we are dealing with the sovereign exemption from judicial interference in the vital field of financial administration a clear declaration of the state's intention to submit its fiscal problems to other courts than those of its own creation must be found.[42]

It makes no difference whether the state had abrogated its common-law sovereign immunity[43]; the waiving of common-law immunity does not affect Eleventh-Amendment immunity.[44]

Application to Local Schools

Does Eleventh-Amendment immunity extend to local school districts? As observed earlier in this text, local school districts are actually state agencies; local school board members are legally state officials; and locally derived funds are, in fact, state funds. Because this is true, it would seem logical that Eleventh-Amendment immunity should extend to local school districts as agencies of the state. This conclusion has, though, run afoul of the practical problems that would ensue if all education treasuries, state and local, were declared immune from suits by citizens. The Supreme Court has therefore apparently concluded that the Eleventh Amendment requires a different test as to the state or local nature of school districts.

The Supreme Court held, in *Mt. Healthy*, that the Eleventh Amendment does not necessarily apply to "counties and similar corporations."[45] The Court has, though, concluded that the Eleventh Amendment bars suit against county officials if the consequences of a judgment effectively constitute a judgment against the state's treasury itself.[46]

The issue as to the local nature of school districts is, however, far from definitive. The Supreme Court set a precedent in *Mt. Healthy* that has caused considerable confusion and is not likely to be resolved soon. In *Mt. Healthy* the Court took the position that local school boards in Ohio are more like a "county or city" than they are like "an arm of the state." This conclusion is, of course, contrary to all previous state and federal precedents on the subject.

In maintaining that local school districts are not state agencies in Ohio, the Court perused the Ohio statutes and concluded that the "state" does not include "political subdivisions" and that local school districts fall within the category of "political subdivisions." The Court further noted that local school boards may levy taxes and issue bonds and are thereby local instead of state agencies. In so surmising, the Supreme Court ignored the Ohio Constitution, which clearly places the responsibility for provision of education in its entirety on the state legislature, not the locality.[47]

Regardless, the Supreme Court in *Mt. Healthy* held that a school board in Ohio is a local agency, distinct from a state agency, and is thereby not entitled to Eleventh-Amendment immunity. This demarcation of immunity between state and local agencies is consistent with the Supreme Court's rulings in *Monell*[48] and *Pugh*,[49] which did not distinguish public schools from other local governmental agencies.

These precedents have left the lower courts in a quandary in attempting to determine whether school districts are state or local. The lower courts are now split on the matter. For example, in applying the *Mt. Healthy* rationale to Louisiana, the U.S. Court of Appeals for the Fifth Circuit concluded that school parish boards in Louisiana are "local independent agents not shielded" by Eleventh-Amendment immunity.[50] On the other hand, the U.S. Court of Appeals for the Tenth Circuit has held that local school boards in New Mexico are arms of the state and, therefore, enjoy Eleventh-Amendment immunity.

Several conclusions can be drawn from this line of precedents. The foremost is that the Eleventh Amendment is a viable constitutional restraint on the judiciary, preserving immune status for state government unless Congress specifically and unequivocally abrogates it through the enforcement provision, § 5, of the Fourteenth Amendment. Where relief is granted, it cannot be in the form of retroactive monetary damages taken from the state treasury.

Whether the treasuries of local school boards are similarly immune is a matter of application of the Supreme Court's criteria to determine immunity status. The *Mt. Healthy* criteria are[51]

1. Whether state statutes and case law characterize the local school district as an arm of the state;
2. The source of funds to operate the schools;
3. The degree of autonomy enjoyed by the school district;
4. Whether the school district is concerned primarily with local, rather than statewide problems;
5. Whether the school district has authority to sue and be sued in its own name; and
6. Whether the school district has the right to hold and use property.[52]

These criteria will, of necessity, be applied by the courts in each case where Eleventh-Amendment immunity is raised as a defense by local school districts.

Local Parish School Board in Louisiana Does Not Enjoy Eleventh-Amendment Immunity, and the School Board Is Not Immune but Individual Members May Have Common-Law or Statutory Immunity

Minton v. St. Bernard Parish School Board

United States Court of Appeals, Fifth Circuit, 1986. 803 F.2d 129.

ALVIN B. RUBIN, Circuit Judge. A Mississippi resident in whose favor a final tort judgment has been rendered by a Louisiana court against a Louisiana parish school district has been unable to collect her damages because the parish school board refuses to appropriate the funds necessary to satisfy her claim.

. . .

In 1974, Connie Minton, a resident of Mississippi and a minor, was struck and injured by a school bus operated under the supervision of the St. Bernard Parish School Board. Shortly thereafter, she and the administrator of her estate, Isaac D. Minton, brought an action to recover for her injuries in a Louisiana state court, and obtained judgment in her favor. . . . That judgment is now final.

Since then Minton and her administrator have tried unsuccessfully to obtain from the Saint Bernard Parish School Board an appropriation of funds to satisfy the judgment.

. . .

. . . In their prayer for relief, the Mintons asked the district court for damages, including the unpaid portion of the judgment plus interest, attorney's fees, punitive damages, and any equitable relief the court deems appropriate.

The Saint Bernard Parish School Board relies first on the defense that the Mintons' suit constitutes a suit against the state that is prohibited by the eleventh amendment to the

United States Constitution. We must therefore determine whether the Saint Bernard Parish School Board is an arm of the state enjoying eleventh amendment immunity or whether it possesses an identity sufficiently distinct from that of the State of Louisiana to place it beyond that shield.

As Judge Garwood has recently stated in *Clark v. Tarrant County, Texas,* 798 F.2d 736 (1986); to draw that distinction "we 'must examine the particular entity in question and its powers and characteristics as created by state law . . . .'" The relevant factors include: (1) whether state statutes and case law characterize the agency as an arm of the state; (2) the source of funds for the entity; (3) the degree of local autonomy the entity enjoys; (4) whether the entity is concerned primarily with local, as opposed to statewide, problems; (5) whether the entity has authority to sue and be sued in its own name; and (6) whether the entity has the right to hold and use property.

These tests identify parish school boards as local independent agents not shielded by the state's eleventh amendment immunity. Although Louisiana courts have referred to school boards as "agencies" of the state, this characterization does not amount to an assertion that the boards are arms of the state within the meaning of the eleventh amendment. School boards generate funds for the operation of parish school districts through local ad valorem taxation, exercise a great deal of discretion in performing their functions and addressing their innately local concerns, have authority to sue or be sued in their own name, and can hold, use, or sell property as each local board determines necessary to fulfill its obligation to the public. In view of the inherently local nature of the interests of Louisiana school boards, the wide degree of local autonomy they are granted under state law, and the predominately local source of their funding, it cannot be said either that these entities are mere arms of the state or that monetary judgments against them would represent indirect impositions on the state treasury interfering with the state's fiscal autonomy. Louisiana school boards, therefore, are not entitled to eleventh amendment immunity to Section 1983 claims. . . .

. . . [T]he School Board asserts that the failure of its members to appropriate funds requested by the Mintons is a legislative action absolutely immune from federal court inquiry. . . . Qualified official immunity and absolute legislative immunity are doctrines that protect individuals acting within the bounds of their official duties, not the governing bodies on which they serve. Thus, even if the actions of the School Board members are legislative, rather than administrative, the School Board itself as a separate entity is not entitled to immunity for violation of the Mintons' constitutional rights.

Whether the Board members' legislative immunity requires the complaint to be dismissed insofar as it seeks relief from them is a more complicated question. In *Tenney v. Brandhove** the Supreme Court held that state legislators who are acting within the scope of their legislative duty are, like their federal counterparts, absolutely immune to civil suits for damages, "not for their private indulgence but for the public good."[†] This absolute immunity from suit under § 1983 was extended to regional legislators in *Lake Country Estates, Inc. v. Tahoe Regional Planning Agency*[‡] and to local legislators in *Hernandez v. City of Lafayette.*[§] Thus, when acting in their legislative capacity, local legislators are granted even greater protection than the qualified immunity generally granted school officials for actions taken in "good faith fulfillment of their responsibilities and within the bounds of reason . . . ." If the School Board members are entitled to absolute immunity from the charges made by the Mintons, they are entitled not only to avoid "the consequences of litigation's results but also . . . the burden of defending themselves."

As the Supreme Court noted in *Scheuer v. Rhodes,*[‖] official immunity "apparently rested, in its genesis, on two mutually dependent

---

[*]341 U.S. 367, 71 S.Ct. 783, 95 L.Ed. 1019 (1951).
[†]341 U.S. at 377, 71 S.Ct. at 788.
[‡]440 U.S. 391, 99 S.Ct. 1171, 59 L.Ed.2d 401 (1979).
[§]643 F.2d 1188 (5th Cir.1981), *cert. denied,* 455 U.S. 907, 102 S.Ct. 1251, 71 L.Ed.2d 444 (1982).
[‖]416 U.S. 232, 239–40, 94 S.Ct. 1683, 1688, 40 L.Ed.2d 90 (1974).

rationales: (1) the injustice, particularly in the absence of bad faith, of subjecting to liability an officer who is required, by the legal obligations of his position, to exercise discretion; (2) the danger that the threat of such liability would deter his willingness to execute his office with the decisiveness and the judgment required by the public good." Because, however, official immunity doctrines are premised upon the concern that the threat of personal liability may deter government officials from executing their offices with the decisiveness and good faith judgment required for the public good, the immunity does not protect officials when they are not threatened with personal liability. It does not, therefore, bar injunctive relief or suits in which officials are sued only in their official capacities and, therefore, cannot be held personally liable.

. . .

Local legislators who are acting within the scope of their legislative duty, enjoy absolute immunity from personal liability under civil liability suits. Legislative absolute immunity, however, is actually only an extension of the qualified immunity granted other government officials, its objective being the implementation of additional safeguards that fulfill the mandate of the Speech or Debate Clause* of the Constitution. Its protection, therefore, applies not only to legislators but to any other officials fulfilling legislative functions including the President when exercising his authority to approve bills, justices of a state supreme court exercising legislative functions, and a city mayor vetoing a city ordinance. But even for legislators, the absolute immunity doctrine does not provide blanket protection from burdensome litigation. Not "everything a Member of Congress may regularly do is . . . a legislative act within the protection of the Speech or Debate Clause." It follows that not everything an official with legislative duties does is protected by absolute immunity. When an official possessing legislative responsibilities engages in official activities insufficiently connected with the legislative process

to raise genuine concern that an inquiry into the motives underlying his actions will thwart his ability to perform his legislative duties vigorously, openly and forthrightly, he is not entitled to absolute immunity but only to the qualified immunity grounded in good faith that is bestowed upon other government officials. Although the School Board addressed this issue in cursory form in its brief, it would be inappropriate at this time for this court to attempt to resolve the issue. If absolute immunity is urged by the School Board members in the district court, that court must determine whether, under the statutory scheme in Louisiana, school board members' decisions whether to appropriate funds to pay a particular tort judgment involve the degree of discretion and public-policy-making traditionally associated with legislative functions or merely an administrative application of existing policies.

. . .

. . . We conclude only that the Mintons have stated a claim for denial of equal protection for which some form of relief may be granted and that such claim is not barred by the eleventh amendment, abstention doctrines, or with regard to at least the School Board by legislative immunity.

Local School Boards as Arms of the State Are Immune from Liability under the Eleventh Amendment

— — — — — — — — — — —

Martinez v. Board of Education of Taos Municipal School District

— — — — — — — — — — —

United States Court of Appeals,
Tenth Circuit, 1984.
748 F.2d 1393.

SETH, Circuit Judge. This is an action for damages against a local school board and against members in their individual and official capacities. Plaintiff asserts that he was

---

*U.S. Const. art. I, § 6.

terminated as Superintendent because of his "real or imagined" political activities in the school board election. . . .

This appeal by plaintiff is directed to the Eleventh Amendment issue and to jury instructions. . . .

On the Eleventh Amendment issue and the autonomy and who pays the judgment issue, the attorney for the plaintiff acknowledged in his brief and at argument that the judgment there sought would be paid by state funds and handled by the Risk Management Division of state government (§ 41–4–20(A) (2)). The Division uses the state public liability fund which receives appropriations from the legislature and insures some risks.

Plaintiff argues in substance that the source of funds used to pay judgments should not be used in an Eleventh Amendment analysis or should not be a substantial element. He urges that *Mt. Healthy City Board of Ed. v. Doyle,* 429 U.S. 274, 97 S.Ct. 568, 50 L.Ed.2d 471, and an examination of the Ohio statutes there considered permit this conclusion as does our *Unified School District No. 480 v. Epperson,* 583 F.2d 1118 (10th Cir.).

On the autonomy issue it is necessary to consider the relationship between the local school boards or districts and the state government. New Mexico from the outset has taken an extreme position on the responsibility of state government for the local school systems both as to administration and finances.

Thus the relation was established by the state constitution. Article XII, § 6, after creating a state department and state board of education and after stating that the state board "shall determine public school policy," provides that the state board:

> "shall have control, management, and direction of all public schools, pursuant to authority and powers provided by law."

It is difficult to conceive of broader powers in the state board than having "control, management and direction" of all public schools. This has to be well beyond the "some guidance" referred to in *Mt. Healthy City Board of Ed. v. Doyle,* 429 U.S. 274, 97 S.Ct. 568, 50 L.Ed.2d 471. . . . [T]he state board's powers are of

long standing. In the 1978 statutes, in subsections A to X of § 22–2–2, the duties of the state board are listed. Some are as follows:

> E. designate courses of instruction to be taught in all public schools in the state;
>
> . . . .
>
> G. determine the qualifications for . . . any person teaching. . . . ;
> H. suspend or revoke a certificate held by a . . . instructor or administrator according to law for incompetency, immorality or for any other good and just cause;
>
> . . . .
>
> J. prescribe courses of instruction, requirements for graduation and standards for all public schools . . . ;
> K. adopt regulations for the administration of all public schools. . . . ;
>
> . . . .
>
> O. accept and receive all grants of money from the federal government . . . and disburse the money. . . . ;
>
> . . . .
>
> V. provide for management . . . to operate any public school or school district which has failed to meet requirements of law, state board standards or state board regulations . . . ."

Some of these enumerated powers were in the Ohio statute considered in *Mt. Healthy,* but they were not in the context of the state board's "control, management and direction."

As indicated, the state board can operate districts which do not conform to the board's regulations and standards. The board or the state superintendent can suspend such a local board, and is required to do so. No prior hearing is required. This has been done on a number of recent occasions.

There exists with the above State Board of Education control a separate system of pervasive financial control over all school districts exercised by a different state agency. . . . The budget must be there certified to be valid. The statute provides that no expenditure can be made by a school district unless it is in accordance with the budget certified by the Department.

The Public School Finance Act also provides that the districts or boards cannot hold funds unless specifically permitted to do so by the state. If not so permitted, the County Treasurer holds and disburses the funds (§ 22–8–37).

The statutes provide each school budget *must* contain one of three methods to meet judgments obtained in civil rights actions. The three methods are: (1) establish reserves out of budgeted funds; (2) buy commercial insurance coverage; (3) participate in the New Mexico public liability fund.

Section 41–4–20 provides that the Department of Finance and Administration is prohibited from approving any school district budget which does not budget for the risk of civil rights judgments. This statutory provision is very significant on the particular issue here concerned.

The state control over budgets is complete because the budgeting is *of state funds* distributed to the schools. In the 1982–1983 school year 96% of the school district funds statewide were provided by the state. The small amount of "local funds" comes mostly from a share in motor vehicle fees collected by the state and distributed to the counties. In a companion case the record shows that state funds provided 98.8% of the last school budget in Mora County.

. . .

Bonding for capital improvements is a significant aspect of an effective educational system. The initial decision to provide for such improvements is with the local boards. There is, however, a greater or lesser degree of state control and the exercise of the right to approve or not with the state depending on the type of bonds proposed. This local authority is perhaps related to the fact that the boards are elected, but in any event, these two factors are the most important of a local nature. However, they are overwhelmed by the pervasive state authority over education in the state originating with the state constitution.

The authority of the districts to act must be examined in the overall control exercised by the state. Thus, for example, the districts can acquire and dispose of property, but the acquisition must be within the fiscal and bonding control. Improvements in most instances must be approved, and, if substantial, state approval of plans and specifications must

be obtained. The district may dispose of property, but this is subject to state approval (§ 13–6–2). . . .

Considering that the New Mexico State Board of Education has the "control," the "management" and "direction" of all public schools; that this authority has been implemented by the legislature in detail; that the fiscal-budgetary matters for the districts are fully controlled by the state; that the state taxing method for schools is a statewide system of state taxes; that the funds so generated for the schools are applied on a formula to equalize funding among the districts and basically on school attendance, we must hold that the local boards are indeed arms of the state system of education as provided in the state constitution. The local boards, of course, do perform significant functions as an arm of the state government and the members make a very important contribution to the educational system. . . .

. . . We conclude that the instructions given the jury were a proper statement of the law and presented the theories of the parties.

Affirmed.

NOTES

1. "The Eleventh Amendment is an explicit limitation of the judicial power of the United States." *Missouri v. Fiske*, 290 US. 18 25, 54 S. Ct. 18, 20 (1933). It deprives a federal court of power to decide certain claims against States that otherwise would be within the scope of Art. III's grant of jurisdiction. For example, if a lawsuit against state officials under 42 U.S.C.A. § 1983 alleges a constitutional claim, the federal court is barred from awarding damages against the state treasury even though the claim arises under the Constitution. See *Quern v. Jordan*, 440 U.S. 332, 99 S.Ct. 1139 (1979). Similarly, if a § 1983 action alleging a constitutional claim is brought directly against a state, the Eleventh Amendment bars a federal court from granting any relief on that claim. See *Alabama v. Pugh*, 438 U.S. 781, 98 S.Ct. 3057 (1978) (per curiam). The amendment thus is a specific constitutional bar against hearing even federal claims that otherwise would be within the jurisdiction of the federal courts. *Pennhurst State School & Hospital v. Halderman*, 465 U.S. 89, 104 S.Ct. 900 (1984).

2. The U.S. Court of Appeals, Tenth Circuit, followed *Martinez* in denying injunctive and declaratory relief to a former assistant school superintendent who sought damages against the school board, school board members, and the superintendent. *Maestas v. Board of Education of the Mora Independent School Dist.*, 749 F. 2d 591 (10th Cir. 1984).

3. The Eleventh Amendment does not bar suits for prospective injunctive relief from unconstitutional actions by state officials. Inferior governmental bodies such as local school districts do not share Eleventh-Amendment immunity simply because they receive state funds. *Fay v. South Colonie Central School District*, 802 F.2d 21 (2d Cir. 1986).

4. In *Will v. Michigan Department of State Police* 491 U.S. 58, 109 S.Ct. 2304 (1989), the U.S. Supreme Court determined that a "[s]uit against a state official in his or her official capacity is a suit not against the official, but rather against the official's office; as such, it is a suit no different from one against the state itself" and therefore barred by the Eleventh amendment. Recently in *Hafer v. Melo*, the U.S. Supreme Court, 1991 W.L. 221067 (1991) determined that the same state official may be liable when acting in his or her personal capacity. The court stated "The Eleventh Amendment does not bar [42 U.S.C.A.] Section 1983 personal-capacity suits against state officials in federal court."

———

▪ ENDNOTES

1. F. Pollock and F.W. Maitland, *The History of English Law Before the Time of Edward I* (Cambridge University Press, Boston: Little, Brown & Co., 1905).

2. Eugene T. Conners, "Governmental Immunity: Legal Basis and Implications for Public Education," Ph.D. dissertation, University of Florida, 1977.

3. Ibid.

4. *The Case of the King's Prerogative in Saltpetre*, 12 Co.Rep. 12 (1607).

5. *Prohibitions del Roy*, 12 Rep. 63 (1607).

6. Mersey Trustees v. Gibbs, L.R. 1 H.L. 93 (1866).

7. Crisp v. Thomas, 63 LINS 756 (1890).

8. 100 Eng.Rep. 359, 2 T.R. 667 (1788).

9. 9 Mass. 247 (1812).

10. The Siren, 74 U.S. (7 Wall.) 152 (1869).

11. Nichols v. United States, 74 U.S. (7 Wall.) 122 (1869).

12. Molitor v. Kaneland Community Unit District No. 302, 18 Ill.2d 11, 163 N.E.2d 89 (1959).

13. Muskopf v. Corning Hospital District, 55 Cal.2d 211, 11 Cal.Rptr. 89, 359 P.2d 457 (1961).

14. Sawaya v. Tucson High School District No. 1, 78 Ariz. 389, 281 P.2d 105 (1955).

15. Reed v. Rhea County, 189 Tenn. 247, 225 S.W.2d 49 (1949).

16. Koehn v. Board of Education of City of Newton, 193 Kan. 263, 392 P.2d 949 (1964).

17. Rankin v. School District No. 9, 143 Or. 449, 23 P.2d 132 (1933).

18. Ross v. Consumers Power Co., 420 Mich. 567, 363 N.W.2d 641 (1984).

19. Stout v. Grand Prairie Ind. School District, 733 S.W.2d 290 (Tex. App.-Dallas 1987).

20. Ibid., p. 296.

21. Boneau v. Swift & Co., 66 S.W.2d 172, 175 (Mo. App. 1934).

22. Beehler v. Daniels, 18 R.I. 563, 29 A. 6 (1984).

23. Bush v. City of Norwalk, 122 Conn. 426, 189 A. 608 (1937).

24. Ferris v. Board of Education of Detroit, 122 Mich. 315, 81 N.W. 98 (1899).

25. Jones v. Kansas City, 176 Kan. 406, 271 P.2d 803 (1954).

26. Rose v. Board of Education, 184 Kan. 486, 337 P.2d 652 (1959).

27. Missouri v. Fiske, 290 U.S. 18, 54 S.Ct. 18, 20 (1933).

28. Vanstophorst v. Maryland, 2 U.S. (2 Dall.) 401 (1791).

29. Chisholm v. Georgia, 2 U.S. (2 Dall.) 419 (1792).

30. Edelman v. Jordan, 415 U.S. 651, 94 S.Ct. 1347 (1974).

31. 3 Elliot's Debates, 553.

32. Hans v. Louisiana, 134 U.S. 1, 10 S.Ct. 504 (1890); Employees v. Department of Public Health and Welfare, 411 U.S. 279, 93 S.Ct. 1614 (1973).

33. Great Northern Life Insurance Co. v. Read, 322 U.S. 47, 64 S.Ct. 873 (1944).

34. In re New York, 256 U.S. 490, 497, 41 S.Ct. 588, 589 L.Ed. 1057 (1921).

35. Atascadero State Hospital v. Scanlon, 473 U.S. 234, 105 S.Ct. 3142 (1985).

36. Edelman, op. cit., p. 673, 94 S.Ct. at 1360.

37. 491 U.S. 223, 109 S.Ct. 2397 (1989).

38. 209 U.S. 123, 28 S.Ct. 441 (1908).

39. Edelman v. Jordan, 415 U.S. 651, 94 S.Ct. 1347 (1974). See also Atascadero State Hospital v. Scanlon, 473 U.S. 234, 105 S.Ct. 3142 (1985); Fitzpatrick v. Bitzer, 427 U.S. 445, 96 S.Ct. 2666 (1976); and Quern v. Jordan, 440 U.S. 332, 342, 99, 440 U.S. 332, 99 S.Ct. 1139 1140 (1979); S.Ct. 1139 1146 (1979).

40. Edelman, op. cit.

41. Ibid.

42. Ibid.

43. See Molitor, op. cit.

44. Edelman, op. cit., at 678, 94 S.Ct. at 1363.

45. Mt. Healthy City School Dist. Bd. of Educ. v. Doyle, 429 U.S. 274, 97 S.Ct. 568 (1977).

46. Edelman v. Jordan, op. cit.

47. Article VI, § 2 of the Ohio Constitution states, "The general assembly shall make such provision . . . , as, . . . will secure a thorough and efficient system of common schools throughout the state . . ."

48. Monell v. Department of Social Services of City of New York, 436 U.S. 658, 98 S.Ct. 2018 (1978).

49. Alabama v. Pugh, 438 U.S. 781, 98 S.Ct. 3057 (1978).

50. Minton v. St. Bernard Parish School Board, 803 F.2d 129 (5th Cir. 1986).

51. Mt. Healthy, op cit. See also Clark v. Tarrant County, Texas, 798 F.2d 736, 748 (5th Cir. 1986).

52. Minton, op. cit., p. 131.

CHAPTER 14

Certification, Contracts, and Tenure

The employment conditions of public school teachers are governed by state statutory and regulatory policy. Because public education is exclusively a state function, the state may set the criteria for eligibility, qualification, and certification of teachers. A state at its option may have no certificate requirements, or it can establish complex conditions precedent to employment with regard to experience, education, test scores, or any number of conditions that may be considered important to one's ability to teach. Too, the state may prescribe the contractual relationship between the teacher and the school board and, if it wishes, may create special contractual conditions pertaining to terms and conditions of employment. The actual contract between teacher and school board may be for any period of time, but is usually annual, or there may be a statutorily created long-term arrangement of indefinite length known as a tenure or continuing contract. The conditions for such contracts, though, are prescribed by law, and teachers must agree to the legal conditions if they are to have and retain public school employment.

Common-law precedents pertaining to contracts may be relied on by the courts when litigation arises regarding disputed statutory application or interpretation. Beyond specific statutory and regulatory provision and relevant common-law applications, the courts may, too, be called upon to determine the lawfulness of state restrictions or restraints on employment that may adversely affect teacher's constitutional rights.

Thus, the law pertaining to teacher employment in public schools derives from state statutory and regulatory prescription with a gloss of common-law precedents where there is a lack of clarity. Too, the employment relationship is greatly affected by state and federal constitutional prohibitions that prevent government from arbitrarily and unilaterally denying a teacher a basic and fundamental constitutional right or interest.

This chapter is concerned with the eligibility and certification of teachers, their limited and tenure contractual relationships with school boards, and the conditions under which those relationships can be terminated. This chapter also deals with constitutional interests of teachers to the extent that they are affected by the obligation-of-contracts provision of the U.S. Constitution. Teachers' due process interests, teacher rights, and freedoms under the U.S. Bill of Rights and Fourteenth Amendment, as well as the federal antidiscrimination statutory provisions, are discussed in subsequent chapters.

■■■ CERTIFICATION

All state legislatures have enacted laws relating to the certification of teachers, and when such laws are properly promulgated with no intent to discriminate, and are not arbitrary, they will be upheld by the courts. These laws run the gamut from great particularity to gross generality. Thus, it is necessary to consider the specific laws of each state individually to determine specific certification requirements.

The general rule is that if a teacher satisfies all the requirements set forth in the statutes and regulations relative to the issuance of a certificate, the certifying body may not arbitrarily refuse to issue the certificate. However, in most cases, the certificate-issuing body is vested with discretionary authority. Also, the issuing agency may, in many instances, prescribe higher standards for certification than are contained in laws enacted by a state legislature.

Background

Early schools in the United States were deficient for many reasons, but the most important reason was the lack of well-educated and trained professional teachers. Few teachers were well-versed in subject matter, and still fewer knew the techniques of teaching. Early schools were usually staffed by itinerant teachers, who were interviewed and hired by local school trustees, who themselves were ofttimes illiterate or only vaguely aware of the qualifications necessary to good teaching. Very little serious thought was given to the education and training of teachers in America until the mid-nineteenth century. The late beginnings of teacher education in this country tracked the general disinterest in public schools by parents who chose to send their children to private schools, where the teachers were equally poorly prepared, or ignored formal education entirely, placing their children directly in the work force at a very early age.

The Prussians had much earlier recognized the need for adequately trained teachers and had between 1750 and 1794 established dozens of seminaries for the special training of elementary school teachers. By 1808, the new French government under Napoleon had established the *Ecole Normale Superieure*, a higher-education normal school; between 1831 and 1833, France created thirty new normal schools for teacher training. It was not until 1839 that the first legislatively authorized normal school in America was established under the leadership of Horace Mann in Lexington, Massachusetts.[1] Cubberley has commented on the trials and tribulations of this first teacher training school.

> The opening of this first school was not particularly auspicious. Ignorance, bigotry, and economy were arrayed against the undertaking. Few knew what such a school was to be. Many teachers regarded its creation as derogatory to them. Many academies did not especially welcome its completion. Not a note of congratulations welcomed its new principal to his post.[2]

Slowly, other states began to create normal schools in the realization that teachers should be especially trained in both subject matter and teaching methods. Most knowledgeable persons agreed that the study of didactics by teachers was essential if the public school was to be efficient and effective. Providing for well-trained personnel, however, addressed only part of the problem. The local orientation and control of public schools had produced the prevailing practice of lay certification through examination with little or no statewide coordination for quality control or continuity. It was said that even with the development of teacher training programs, many localities continued to indulge in "schoolkeeping," a system in which young, unmarried and unqualified women taught while they were "anticipating marriage"; or in which "traveling Ichabod Cranes *kept* school rather than professional teachers *teaching*" school.[3]

It was at this time proposed that the solution to the quality problem lay in "establishing a well-organized state system of examinations" managed at the local level by professional educators, superintendents, and professional teachers.[4] It was reasoned that certification should be granted to teachers by professional educators, "for the same reason that only lawyers can legally examine law students applying for admission to the bar, that only physicians can legally examine medical students, and that only clergymen pass on the fitness of theological students to enter the ministry."[5] The nature of public schools as governmental agencies, however, prevented the implementation of such certification proposals. Eventually a quasi-professional system was adopted whereby teacher training colleges would train and recommend certification of teachers to a state education agency, which would in turn issue a teaching certificate. It was believed that this process was more effective than certification based upon lay examination or even statewide teacher tests for certification with little or no requisite education or training.

Partially because of the experiences of the past, the public today apparently believes that teachers should meet the rigors of certain prescribed academic attainment as evaluated by institutions of higher education as well as teacher tests in order to acquire a license to teach. This license itself is a certificate issued by the state, recognizing that a person is presumptively qualified to teach in the public schools. In this manner, the state extends some surety to the child and the taxpayer that the public schools are protected against "charlatans, ignoramuses, and humbugs"[6] masquerading as teachers.

Requirements

Most states require that an applicant for a teacher's certificate be of good moral character. To remain eligible for either continued certification or renewal of an existing certificate, the teacher must continue to evidence good moral character.

Besides good moral character, state law generally requires that applicants have successfully completed a predetermined number of college credits in the subject that the individual plans to teach (i.e., English). In 1980, only a few states required aspiring teachers to pass a test to become eligible for certification. By 1989–90, the number of states requiring state-prescribed standardized tests as a condition for entering the teaching profession numbered 39. All 50 states approve the content of teacher education programs conducted by colleges and universities.[7] States, too, generally require the individual to be of a specified age (usually eighteen or older) and a citizen of the United States. Some states require the pledging of loyalty to the state and/or federal constitution and, in recent

years, have required the completion of an examination, such as the National Teacher Examination.

Teacher certification does not guarantee employment. State legislatures have delegated the authority for employment of teachers to local school boards. Local boards have been given wide latitude and may place additional requirements or restrictions on employment as long as these rules do not contradict or reduce the effect of state requirements. Neither can such rules violate one's constitutional or statutory rights. Local boards cannot impose requirements that are arbitrary, capricious, or enacted in bad faith.

Some additional requirements that have been upheld include mandating greater academic credentials than those established by the state, or having employees take additional academic courses after employment.[8] School boards have been upheld in requiring teachers to establish residency within the boundaries of the school district,[9] restricting outside employment, adopting reasonable health and physical requirements (within federal and state provisions for the handicapped), assigning (within state statutes) teachers to teaching positions, and supervising extracurricular activities.

Statute Forbidding Certification to Persons Who Are Not Citizens and Have Manifested No Intent to Become Citizens Is Not Violative of Equal Protection

————·—·—·——

Ambach v. Norwick

————·—·—·——

Supreme Court of the United States, 1979.
441 U.S. 68, 99 S.Ct. 1589.

Mr. Justice POWELL delivered the opinion of the Court. This case presents the question whether a State, consistently with the Equal Protection Clause of the Fourteenth Amendment, may refuse to employ as elementary and secondary school teachers aliens who are eligible for United States citizenship but who refuse to seek naturalization.

New York Education Law § 3001(3) forbids certification as a public school teacher of any person who is not a citizen of the United States, unless that person has manifested an intention to apply for citizenship. The Commissioner of Education is authorized to create exemptions from this prohibition, and has done so with respect to aliens who are not yet eligible for citizenship. Unless a teacher obtains certification, he may not work in a public elementary or secondary school in New York.

Appellee Norwick was born in Scotland and is a subject of Great Britain. She has resided in this country since 1965 and is married to a United States citizen. Appellee Dachinger is a Finnish subject who came to this country in 1966 and also is married to a United States citizen. Both Norwick and Dachinger currently meet all of the educational requirements New York has set for certification as a public school teacher, but they consistently have refused to seek citizenship in spite of their eligibility to do so. Norwick applied in 1973 for a teaching certificate covering nursery school through sixth grade, and Dachinger sought a certificate covering the same grades in 1975. Both applications were denied because of appellees' failure to meet the requirements of § 3001(3). Norwick then filed this suit seeking to enjoin the enforcement of § 3001(3), and Dachinger obtained leave to intervene as a plaintiff.

. . .

Applying the rational basis standard, we held last term that New York could exclude aliens from the ranks of its police force. *Foley v. Connelie*, 435 U.S. 291, 98 S.Ct. 1067, 55 L.Ed.2d 287 (1978). Because the police function fulfilled "a most fundamental obligation of government to its constituency" and by necessity cloaked policemen with substantial discretionary powers, we viewed the police force as being one of those appropriately defined classes of positions for which a citizenship requirement could be imposed. Ac-

cordingly, the State was required to justify its classification only "by a showing of some rational relationship between the interest sought to be protected and the limiting classification."

The rule for governmental functions, which is an exception to the general standard applicable to classifications based on alienage, rests on important principles inherent in the Constitution. The distinction between citizens and aliens, though ordinarily irrelevant to private activity, is fundamental to the definition and government of a State. The Constitution itself refers to the distinction no less than eleven times, see *Sugarman v. Dougall* (Rehnquist, J., dissenting), indicating that the status of citizenship was meant to have significance in the structure of our government. The assumption of that status, whether by birth or naturalization, denotes an association with the polity which, in a democratic republic, exercises the powers of governance. The form of this association is important: an oath of allegiance or similar ceremony cannot substitute for the unequivocal legal bond citizenship represents. It is because of this special significance of citizenship that governmental entities, when exercising the functions of government, have wider latitude in limiting the participation of noncitizens.

In determining whether, for purposes of equal protection analysis, teaching in public schools constitutes a governmental function, we look to the role of public education and to the degree of responsibility and discretion teachers possess in fulfilling that role. Each of these considerations supports the conclusion that public school teachers may be regarded as performing a task "that go[es] to the heart of representative government."

Public education, like the police function, "fulfills a most fundamental obligation of government to its constituency." The importance of public schools in the preparation of individuals for participation as citizens, and in the preservation of the values on which our society rests, long has been recognized by our decisions:

Today, education is perhaps the most important function of state and local governments. Compulsory school attendance laws and the great expenditures for education both demonstrate our recognition of the importance of education to our democratic society. It is required in the performance of our most basic public responsibilities, even service in the armed forces. It is the very foundation of good citizenship. Today it is a principal instrument in awakening the child to cultural values, in preparing him for later professional training, and in helping him to adjust normally to his environment. *Brown v. Board of Education,* 347 U.S. 483, 493, 74 S.Ct. 686, 691, 98 L.Ed. 873 (1954).

. . . Other authorities have perceived public schools as an "assimilative force" by which diverse and conflicting elements in our society are brought together on a broad but common ground. . . . These perceptions of the public schools as inculcating fundamental values necessary to the maintenance of a democratic political system have been confirmed by the observations of social scientists. . . .

Within the public school system, teachers play a critical part in developing students' attitude toward government and understanding the role of citizens in our society. Alone among employees of the system, teachers are in direct, day-to-day contact with students both in the classrooms and in the other varied activities of a modern school. In shaping the students' experience to achieve educational goals, teachers by necessity have wide discretion over the way the course material is communicated to students. They are responsible for presenting and explaining the subject matter in a way that is both comprehensible and inspiring. No amount of standardization of teaching materials or lesson plans can eliminate the personal qualities a teacher brings to bear in achieving these goals. Further, a teacher serves as a role model for his students, exerting a subtle but important influence over their perceptions and values. Thus, through both the presentation of course materials and the example he sets, a teacher

has an opportunity to influence the attitudes of students toward government, the political process, and a citizen's social responsibilities. This influence is crucial to the continued good health of a democracy.

Furthermore, it is clear that all public school teachers, and not just those responsible for teaching the courses most directly related to government, history, and civic duties, should help fulfill the broader function of the public school system. Teachers, regardless of their specialty, may be called upon to teach other subjects, including those expressly dedicated to political and social subjects. More importantly, a State properly may regard all teachers as having an obligation to promote civic virtues and understanding in their classes, regardless of the subject taught. Certainly a State also may take account of a teacher's function as an example for students, which exists independently of particular classroom subjects. In light of the foregoing considerations, we think it clear that public school teachers come well within the "governmental function" principle recognized in *Sugarman* and *Foley.* Accordingly, the Constitution requires only that a citizenship requirement applicable to teaching in the public schools bears a rational relationship to a legitimate state interest. . . .

As the legitimacy of the State's interest in furthering the educational goals outlined above is undoubted, it remains only to consider whether § 3001(3) bears a rational relationship to this interest. The restriction is carefully framed to serve its purpose, as it bars from teaching only those aliens who have demonstrated their unwillingness to obtain United States citizenship. Appellees, and aliens similarly situated, in effect have chosen to classify themselves. They prefer to retain citizenship in a foreign country with the obligations it entails of primary duty and loyalty. They have rejected the open invitation extended to qualify for eligibility to teach by applying for citizenship in this country. The people of New York, acting through their elected representatives, have made a judgment that citizenship should be a qualification for teaching the young of the State in the public schools, and § 3001(3) furthers that judgment.

Reversed.

Employee Residency Requirements Are Constitutional

Wardwell v. Board of Education of the City School District of the City of Cincinnati et al.

United States Court of Appeals, Sixth Circuit, 1976. 529 F.2d 625.

WILLIAM E. MILLER, Circuit Judge. In December, 1972, plaintiff, Terry Wardwell, was hired to teach in the Cincinnati schools. As a condition of employment he agreed to move into the city school district pursuant to a rule announced by the school superintendent in November, 1972, that all newly employed teachers must establish residence within the district within thirty days after employment. In January, 1973, the Board adopted the following resolution, essentially ratifying the superintendent's rule:

> RESOLVED, That any employee hired by the Cincinnati Schools after November 13, 1972, must either reside within the Cincinnati School District, or agree, as a condition of employment, to establish residency within the district within ninety days of employment. Employees who live in the district must continue to reside therein as long as they are so employed. This policy does not affect in any way personnel hired before the above date.

Plaintiff Wardwell lived outside the district but within the State of Ohio. Despite the re-

quirement he failed to change his residence. He filed the present action in July, 1973, under 28 U.S.C. § 1343 and 42 U.S.C. § 1983, challenging the residency requirement on equal protection grounds and seeking injunctive relief and attorney's fees. No preliminary injunction was requested because enforcement of the rule had been stayed by a preliminary injunction issued by a state court. Since being hired, plaintiff Wardwell has taught at one time in a predominantly white school located within a ten-minute drive from his home and later at a predominantly black school about twenty minutes from his home outside the district.

The district court denied the request for an injunction and upheld the validity of the rule, relying heavily on the Fifth Circuit's reasoning in *Wright v. City of Jackson*, 506 F.2d 900 (5th Cir.1975).

Plaintiff argues that the Board's residency requirement infringes his constitutionally protected right to travel as defined in *Shapiro v. Thompson*, 394 U.S. 618, 89 S.Ct. 1322, 22, L.Ed.2d 600 (1969), and in *Dunn v. Blumstein*, 405 U.S. 330, 92 S.Ct. 995, 31 L.Ed.2d 274 (1972), extending the protection, as he contends, to both intrastate and interstate travel and embracing as a necessary corollary the right to remain in one place.

We find no support for plaintiff's theory that the right to intrastate travel has been afforded federal constitutional protection. An examination of *Shapiro*, supra, *Dunn*, supra, and the Supreme Court's more recent opinion in *Memorial Hospital v. Maricopa County*, 415 U.S. 250, 94 S.Ct. 1076, 39 L.Ed.2d 306 (1974), convinces us that the aspect of the right to travel with which the Court was concerned in those cases is not involved here. It is clear that the Court was dealing with the validity of durational residency requirements which penalized recent interstate travel. Such *durational* residency requirements or restrictions affecting the interstate aspect of travel will not pass constitutional muster "absent a compelling state interest."

In *Memorial Hospital*, supra . . . the Court at some length emphasized that *Shapiro* and the later cases were not to be construed as applying to bona fide *continuing,* as distinguished from *durational,* residency requirements when it said:

The right of interstate travel has repeatedly been recognized as a basic constitutional freedom. Whatever its ultimate scope, however, the right to travel was involved in only a limited sense in *Shapiro.* The Court was there concerned only with the right to migrate, "with intent to settle and abide" or, as the Court put it, "to migrate, resettle, find a new job, and start a new life." Even a bona fide residence requirement would burden the right to travel, if travel meant merely movement. But, in *Shapiro,* the Court explained that "[t]he residence requirement and the one-year waiting-period requirement are distinct and independent prerequisites" for assistance and only the latter was held to be unconstitutional. Later, in invalidating a durational residence requirement for voter registration on the basis of *Shapiro,* we cautioned that our decision was not intended to "cast doubt on the validity of appropriately defined and uniformly applied bona fide residence requirements."

Our conclusion that *Shapiro* and the other right-to-travel cases are not applicable to intrastate travel and *continuing* employee residency requirements is supported by *Detroit Police Officers Association v. City of Detroit,* 405 U.S. 950, 92 S.Ct. 1173, 31 L.Ed.2d 227 (1972), on which the district court in this case and the Fifth Circuit in *Wright,* supra, relied. The case involved a Detroit residency requirement for policemen. The Michigan Supreme Court, applying the "rational basis test," determined that the classification bore a reasonable relationship to the object of the legislation and was therefore valid. *Detroit Police Officers Association v. City of Detroit,* 385 Mich. 519, 190 N.W.2d 97 (1971). The Supreme Court in a brief order dismissed the appeal "for want of a substantial federal question." While we do not consider it necessary to base the result in the present case primarily on *Detroit Police Officers,* we recognize that the Supreme Court's dismissal of the appeal "for want of a

substantial federal question" is a decision on the merits of the case appealed. We conclude that the "compelling state interest" test is the applicable test in cases involving infringement of the right to interstate travel by *durational* residency requirements. On the other hand, where, as in the present case, a *continuing* employee residency requirement affecting at most the right of intrastate travel is involved, the "rational basis" test is the touchstone to determine its validity.

We find a number of rational bases for the residency requirement of the Cincinnati School Board. The Cincinnati school superintendent testified that promulgation of the rule was based on the following conclusions: (1) such a requirement aids in hiring teachers who are highly motivated and deeply committed to an urban educational system, (2) teachers who live in the district are more likely to vote for district taxes, less likely to engage in illegal strikes, and more likely to help obtain passage of school tax levies, (3) teachers living in the district are more likely to be involved in school and community activities bringing them in contact with parents and community leaders and are more likely to be committed to the future of the district and its schools, (4) teachers who live in the district are more likely to gain sympathy and understanding for the racial, social, economic, and urban problems of the children they teach and are thus less likely to be considered isolated from the communities in which they teach, (5) the requirement is in keeping with the goal of encouraging integration in society and in the schools. These conclusions appear to us clearly to establish rational bases for the residency requirement imposed by the Cincinnati Board.

Appellant insists that the basic purpose of the residency rule is to advance "quality integrated" education and to help in eliminating racial segregation in the community and school system. The rule is not rationally related to this objective, appellant claims, because school and community integration would only be promoted by requiring teachers to live in the attendance districts of the schools at which they teach. Integration is not encouraged, it is argued, by a regulation such as the present one which requires teachers to live somewhere in the district at large when the district itself contains many segregated areas. This argument overlooks the various other convincing and rational bases for adoption of the rule. Although it is possible that the rule will not materially contribute to racial integration, we consider that the numerous other legitimate objectives of the rule are wholly adequate to demonstrate that the residency classification fully comports with the rational basis test. Many other courts have recognized the importance of employees being highly committed to the area in which they work and motivated to find solutions for its problems. . . . Such commitment and motivation, it is not unreasonable to suppose, may best be fostered by requiring teachers to live and pay taxes in the place in which they are employed to work.

Other arguments against the validity of this residency requirement are advanced. First, it is said that the right to teach, which in Ohio is controlled by state law through the issuance of a teaching certificate, entitles a teacher to be considered for employment only on his merits as prescribed by statute. This right may not be withheld on constitutionally impermissible grounds. The state certification of teachers distinguishes teachers as a group from municipal employees performing other functions. We agree with appellee, however, that the possession of an Ohio certificate establishes only that a teacher has met certain minimum standards. It does not entitle him to a teaching position with any particular local school board. Local boards are free to impose additional qualifications and conditions of employment or to adopt higher standards.

Finally, appellant argues that the residency requirements is invalid because it requires newly hired teachers to move into and remain in the district and permits those already hired to remain or move outside the district. Appellee replies that distinguishing between new teachers and teachers with experience who may have tenure and who did

not know of the requirement when they accepted employment, is a reasonable distinction which the state is free to make. While we recognize that the limited applicability of the rule may be its most questionable feature, we do not believe that the residency requirement must fail because it does not apply to all teachers employed by the Cincinnati schools. The Supreme Court has pointed out that there is no constitutional requirement that regulations must cover every class to which they might be applied. It has further stated that "if the classification has some reasonable basis, it does not offend the constitution simply because the classification 'is not made with mathematical nicety or because in practice it results in some inequality.' "

Affirmed.

NOTES

1. Where a school board policy required that certified personnel reside within the district or within a 10-mile driving distance of the city limits of the school district and a teacher moved 17 miles outside the district, her contract was not renewed. The court found that the policy had a rational basis, such as the necessity of community involvement. *McClelland v. Paris Public Schools,* 294 Ark. 292, 742 S.W.2d 907 (1988). See also *Mogle v. Sevier County School District,* 540 F.2d 478 (10th 1976); *Simien v. City of San Antonio,* 809 F.2d 255 (5th Cir. 1987).

2. Some states have passed legislation prohibiting municipalities from establishing residency requirements. The California Constitution states, "A city or county . . . may not require that its employees be residents of such city, county, or district; except that such employees may be required to reside within a reasonable and specific distance of their place of employment or other designated location."

3. City employees employed prior to the effective date of a residency requirement may be exempt. *Providence Teachers Union*

Local No. 958 v. Napolitano, 554 A.2d 641 (R.I. 1989).

————

————

Certificate May Be Denied When State Board Has Evidence to Question Good Moral Character of Applicant

—·—·—·—·—·—

Application of Bay

—·—·—·—·—·—

Supreme Court of Oregon, 1963.
233 Or. 601, 378 P.2d 558.

PERRY, Justice. Dean Norman Bay petitioned the circuit court of Union County for judicial review of the decision of appellant State Board of Education denying him issuance of a five-year elementary teacher's certificate. From the decree of the circuit court reversing the Board's decision for lack of competent evidence, appeal is made to this court.

In December of 1953, petitioner was tried and convicted in the state of Washington for his acts of breaking, entering, and grand larceny of several stores, the American Legion Club, and the local high school, committed while employed as a night policeman. At the time these acts were perpetrated, petitioner was twenty-four years old. After serving eighteen months of a two-year sentence, he was paroled. He moved to La Grande, Oregon, where, in the fall of 1956 he enrolled at the Eastern Oregon College of Education. In 1958 the state of Washington restored to him his full civil rights.

In 1960 petitioner was granted a one-year elementary teacher's emergency certificate by the Superintendent of Public Instruction, and taught elementary school while completing his fourth year at the college. Following graduation he applied for a five-year elementary teacher's certificate, but his application was denied on June 14, 1961.

On September 13, 1961, a hearing was conducted before the Board, the primary purpose of which was to determine whether petitioner had furnished the evidence of good moral character which ORS 342.060(2) authorizes the superintendent to require of an applicant. Whereas numerous witnesses appeared at the hearing to testify of petitioner's good character and over-all reputation in the community, the sole evidence of bad character introduced was the record of the prior conviction. The Board concluded that petitioner had not met his burden of furnishing satisfactory evidence of good moral character and he thereupon petitioned the circuit court of Union County for review of the administrative order pursuant to ORS 183.480. The court held that evidence as to a prior conviction was irrelevant and immaterial in determining present character where not accompanied by other evidence which related the prior act to the present, and therefore adjudged there was no competent evidence to support the Board's findings. The Board was ordered to issue petitioner the certificate, from which order this appeal is taken. . . .

In order to properly discuss the issues presented it is first necessary to discuss the powers of the trial court in reviewing the Board's determination.

While the statute uses the language "as a suit in equity," it is quite clear that this language refers only to the fact that the review shall be made by the court, not a jury, and does not grant to a trial court the right on appeal to try the case de novo. That is, the reviewing court is not granted the power to weigh the evidence and substitute its judgment as to the preponderance thereof for that of the agency. The extent to which a reviewing court should review the action of an administrative agency has been expressed by this court as follows:

Generally, they go no further than to determine whether the agency (1) acted impartially; (2) performed faithfully the duties delineated in the legislative acts which conferred jurisdiction upon it; (3) stayed within its jurisdiction; (4) committed no error of law; (5) exercised discretion judiciously and not capriciously; and (6) arrived at no conclusion which was clearly wrong. *Richardson v. Neuner,* 183 Or. 558, 564, 194 P.2d 989, 991.

The learned trial court recognized these guideposts and reached the conclusion that the finding of the Board as to lack of good moral character could not be sustained by the record. This conclusion of the court is based upon a finding that there was no evidence of bad moral character at the time of application and therefore the Board's conclusion was clearly wrong.

Whether or not the Board arrived at a conclusion which was clearly wrong depends upon whether a review of the entire record discloses any facts from which the conclusion drawn by the Board could be reached by reasonable minds. . . .

The Board made the following findings of fact which are pertinent to this appeal:

1. That the applicant on December 9, 1953, was convicted of grand larceny of four counts in the Superior Court for Klickitat County, State of Washington and received a one- to fifteen-year sentence by the said Court. That thereafter this sentence was fixed at a term of two years by the State Board of Terms and Parole of the State of Washington, and the applicant served an eighteen-month term at the Monroe Reformatory in the State of Washington.

2. Thereafter upon his release he was placed on parole for approximately a year and moved to the City of LaGrande, Oregon, and in the fall of 1956 entered the Eastern Oregon College of Education and enrolled in a teacher education course.

3. That by act of the Governor of the State of Washington full civil rights were restored to him on July 3, 1958. . . .

8. The Board further finds the offenses committed by Mr. Bay consisted of breaking and entering various stores in Goldendale, Washington, and grand larceny, and included safe burglaries at the American Legion Club, and Goldendale High School. That at the time he committed the offenses for which he was imprisoned he had reached the age of twenty-four years; that

his offenses numbered not one but several; that he was a man of superior intelligence as evidenced by his scores on intelligence tests in his subsequent college record.

9. The Board further finds that at the time of the thefts he occupied a position of trust as a night policeman in the community and that while so engaged he committed the acts resulting in his conviction.

10. That a teacher in a public school is the key factor in teaching by precept and example the subjects of honesty, morality, courtesy, obedience to law, and other lessons of a steadying influence which tend to promote and develop an upright and desirable citizenry, as required by ORS 336.240 and related statutes.

11. That there has been no evidence submitted to the Board of any violations of law or deviations from normally considered moral conduct from the time of his release from the Monroe Reformatory to the present time.

The Board then made the following conclusions of law:

1. That the applicant has not furnished evidence of good moral character deemed satisfactory and necessary by the Board to establish the applicant's fitness to serve as a teacher.

In resolving the question of moral character there must be kept in mind the distinction between character and reputation. "Character is what a man or woman is morally, while reputation is what he or she is reputed to be." *Leverich v. Frank,* 6 Or. 212; *State v. Charlie Sing,* 114 Or. 267, 229 P. 921.

A person's "character" is usually thought to embrace all his qualities and deficiencies regarding traits of personality, behavior, integrity, temperament, consideration, sportsmanship, altruism, etc. which distinguish him as a human being from his fellow men. His disposition toward criminal acts is only one of the qualities which constitute his character.

Since the crux of the question before the Board was good moral character, the fact that he had been guilty of burglarizing properties while he held a position of trust was most pertinent. These actions of petitioner clearly evidenced a lack of the moral fiber to resist temptation. The trial court therefore erred in holding there was no evidence of lack of good moral character.

The petitioner offered numerous witnesses from which a conclusion might properly be reached that this lack of moral fiber no longer exists. However, this condition having been shown to have existed, it became a matter of judgment as to whether it had been overcome.

The power to decide such an issue was delegated by the legislature to the Board of Education, therefore, as previously pointed out, the courts are not permitted to substitute their judgment for that of the Board where there is substantial evidence to support the agency.

The judgment of the trial court is reversed with instructions to enter findings of fact and conclusions of law sustaining the action of the Board of Education.

NOTES

1. Under what circumstances and when would applicant Bay be eligible for a certificate?
2. One of the basic purposes of the certification laws is that a capable and competent instructor will be provided in every classroom. Consequently, a teacher's certificate is a prerequisite not only to employment and reemployment, but is necessary for schools to qualify for state aid. It is a common practice in several states to permit student teachers to assume complete control of a class in the absence of the regular teacher. This violates not only the spirit but also the letter of the law of many states because a student teacher is not a qualified teacher, but is seeking to become a qualified teacher. If a teacher teaches without a certificate, she is considered to be a volunteer and is entitled to no compensation for services rendered. See *Floyd County Board of Education v. Stone*, 307 S.W.2d 912 (Ky.1957).
3. A teacher who has no certificate when entering into an employment contract with a school board could not recover salary for services rendered, even though he had obtained the license prior to actually beginning work. *McCloskey v. School District*, 134

Mich. 235, 96 N.W. 18 (1903); *O'Conner v. Francis,* 42 App.Div. 375, 59 N.Y.S. 28 (1899); *Lee v. Mitchell,* 108 Ark. 1, 156 S.W. 450 (1913).

4. "Our contention and the legislative enactments support [teacher's] contention that the grant of a certificate from the State Board of Education inherently carries with it a presumption of competence, interest and training in the subjects designated." *Bauer v. Board of Education, Unified School District* No. 452, 244 Kan. 6, 765 P.2d 1129 (1988).

Teacher's Adultery Insufficient to Support Revocation of Certificate

Erb v. Iowa State Board of Public Instruction

Supreme Court of Iowa, 1974.
216 N.W.2d 339.

McCORMICK, Justice. In this appeal plaintiff Richard Arlan Erb challenges the revocation of his teaching certificate. The certificate was revoked by defendant Board of Educational Examiners after a hearing on July 16, 1971. Erb brought an action in certiorari alleging the board's action was illegal. After trial the writ of certiorari was annulled. Erb appealed. We reverse.

Under Code § 260.1, the State Board of Public Instruction constitutes the Board of Educational Examiners. Code § 260.2 empowers the examining board to issue teaching certificates "to applicants who are eighteen years of age or over, physically competent and morally fit to teach, and who have the [required] qualifications and training . . . ."

Erb, a native Iowan, military veteran, and holder of a master's degree in fine arts, received his Iowa teaching certificate in 1963. Since then he has taught art in the Nishna

Valley Community School which serves an area including the towns of Strahn, Emerson, Hastings, and Stanton. He resides in Emerson, is married and has two young sons. In addition to teaching he has coached wrestling, assisted with football, and acted as senior class sponsor.

The complaint against Erb was made by Robert M. Johnson, a farmer whose wife Margaret taught home economics in the Nishna Valley School. Johnson told the board his goal was removal of Erb from the school and not revocation of his teaching certificate. He read an extensive statement in which he detailed his observations relating to an adulterous liaison between Erb and Johnson's wife which began and ended in spring 1970.

Margaret planned to quit teaching and open a boutique in Red Oak. Her association with Erb began in early spring when he agreed to assist her with design of the store. They saw each other often. By May, Johnson became suspicious of Margaret's frequent late-night absences from home. He suspected Margaret and Erb were meeting secretly and engaging in illicit activity in the Johnson automobile. One night in May he hid in the trunk of the car. Margaret drove the car to school, worked there for some time, and later drove to a secluded area in the country where she met Erb. Margaret and Erb had sexual intercourse in the back seat of the car while Johnson remained hidden in the trunk. Johnson did not disclose his presence or his knowledge of the incident.

Instead he consulted a lawyer with a view toward divorcing Margaret. He told the board he was advised his interests in a divorce action would be better served if he had other witnesses to his wife's misconduct. After several days of fruitless effort to catch Margaret and Erb in a compromising situation, he and his "raiding party" eventually located them one night in June parked in a remote area. Johnson and the others surrounded the car and took photographs of Margaret and Erb who were partially disrobed in the back seat. Johnson told Margaret not to come home and that further communication would be through lawyers. He told Erb to disclose the affair to his wife.

Erb did so. He and Margaret terminated their affair. Erb offered to resign his teaching position, but the local school board unanimously decided not to accept his resignation. The board president testified Erb's teaching was highly rated by his principal and superintendent, he had been forgiven by his wife and the student body, and he had maintained the respect of the community. Erb was retained for the ensuing school year and continued to teach in the Nishna Valley School.

Witnesses before the board included Erb's past and present high school principals, his minister, a parent of children in the school, and a substitute teacher. All vouched for his character and fitness to teach. His superintendent gave essentially the same testimony in district court. . . . Trial court ruled in its pretrial order that under the admitted record Erb's teacher-student relationship had not been impaired by his conduct.

The [state] board voted five to four to revoke Erb's teaching certificate and, without making any findings of fact or conclusions of law, ordered it revoked. Revocation was stayed by trial court and then by this court pending outcome of the certiorari action and appeal. Trial court held Erb's admitted adulterous conduct was sufficient basis for revocation of his certificate and annulled the writ. . . . In this appeal Erb contends the board acted illegally . . . in revoking his teaching certificate without substantial evidence that he is not morally fit to teach.

. . .

Since the board made no findings there is no intelligible way to determine what interpretation the board gave to its statutory authorization to revoke the certificate of one not "morally fit to teach." But nothing prevents us from determining whether there is substantial evidence in the record which would have supported revocation if the proper standard had been applied. Erb contends there is not. We agree. We will first examine the standard and then the sufficiency of the evidence.

This court has not previously been called upon to decide what constitutes moral unfitness to teach. . . .

A teacher occupies a sensitive position. Since students are taught by example as well as lecture, the teacher's out-of-school conduct may affect his classroom fitness. . . .

The private conduct of a man, who is also a teacher, is a proper concern to those who employ him only to the extent it mars him as a teacher, who is also a man. Where his professional achievement is unaffected, where the school community is placed in no jeopardy, his private acts are his own business and may not be the basis of discipline.

The board contends the fact Erb admitted adultery is sufficient in itself to establish his unfitness to teach. This assumes such conduct automatically and invariably makes a person unfit to teach. We are unwilling to make that assumption. It would vest the board with unfettered power to revoke the certificate of any teacher whose personal, private conduct incurred its disapproval regardless of its likely or actual effect upon his teaching. . . . ("Where the courts have been presented with the question whether or not specific conduct of a teacher constitutes moral unfitness which would justify revocation, they have apparently required that the conduct must adversely affect the teacher-student relationship before revocation will be approved.")
. . .

Surely incidents of extramarital heterosexual conduct against a background of years of satisfactory teaching would not constitute "immoral conduct" sufficient to justify revocation of a life diploma without any showing of an adverse effect on fitness to teach.

We emphasize the board's power to revoke teaching certificates is neither punitive nor intended to permit exercise of personal moral judgment by members of the board. Punishment is left to the criminal law, and the personal moral views of board members cannot be relevant. A subjective standard is impermissible and contrary to obvious legislative intent. . . .

In *Morrison* the California court discussed factors relevant to application of the standard:

In determining whether the teacher's conduct thus indicates unfitness to teach the board may consider such matters as the likelihood that the conduct may have adversely affected students or fellow teachers, the degree of such adversity anticipated, the proximity or remoteness in time of the conduct, the type of teaching certificate held by the party involved, the extenuating or aggravating circumstances, if any, surrounding the conduct, the praiseworthiness or blameworthiness of the motives resulting in the conduct, the likelihood of the recurrence of the questioned conduct, and the extent to which disciplinary action may inflict an adverse impact or chilling effect upon the constitutional rights of the teacher involved or other teachers. 82 Cal.Rptr. at 186, 461 P.2d at 386.

These factors have relevance in deciding whether a teacher is morally fit to teach under Code § 260.2. Since the same standard is applicable in determining whether a certificate should be revoked under Code § 260.23, a certificate can be revoked only upon a showing before the board of a reasonable likelihood that the teacher's retention in the profession will adversely affect the school community.

There was no evidence of such adverse effect in the present case. No one even asserted such an effect. The complainant himself acknowledged his purpose was to remove Erb from the school rather than from teaching. The evidence showed Erb to be a teacher of exceptional merit. He is dedicated, hardworking and effective. There was no evidence to show his affair with Margaret Johnson had or is likely to have an adverse effect upon his relationship with the school administration, fellow teachers, the student body, or the community. Overwhelming and uncontroverted evidence of local regard and support for Erb is a remarkable testament to the ability of a community to understand, forgive and reconcile.

There was no evidence other than that Erb's misconduct was an isolated occurrence in an otherwise unblemished past and is not likely to recur. The conduct itself was not an open or public affront to community mores; it became public only because it was discovered with considerable effort and made public by others. Erb made no effort to justify it; instead he sought to show he regretted it, it did not reflect his true character, and it would not be repeated. . . .

The board acted illegally in revoking his certificate. Trial court erred in annulling the writ of certiorari.

Reversed.

■ TEACHER CONTRACTS

A teacher's contract must satisfy the same requirements applicable to contracts in general. A school district is a legal entity, a corporate body with the power to sue and be sued; purchase, receive, hold, and sell real and personal property; make contracts and be contracted with; and do all other things necessary to accomplish the purposes for which it is created.

The Standard Contract

Contracts of school districts must conform not only to the requirements of general contract law, but must satisfy other statutory and case law demands as well. A contract may be defined as an agreement between two or more competent persons for a legal consideration on a legal subject matter in the form required by law. This definition includes the five basic elements inherent in every valid contract, to wit: offer and acceptance, competent persons, consideration, legal subject matter, and proper form.

Offer and Acceptance

All contracts are agreements, but not all agreements are contracts. An agreement is an offer and an acceptance. Every valid contract contains an offer and acceptance. For example, a board of education offers a fifth-grade teaching position in a particular school to an individual. There is no agreement unless and until the individual accepts the offer.

Several significant factors concerning agreements should be kept in mind. An offer can be accepted only by the individual or individuals to whom it is made. Unless otherwise stated, an offer must be accepted within a reasonable time after it is made or it will be terminated automatically. Newspaper advertisements are usually considered to be invitations for offers and not offers. That is, the board of education is soliciting offers. Also, an offer cannot be accepted unless at the time the individual performed the act necessary to accept the offer, he or she knew of the existence of the offer. By way of illustration, let us assume that vandals broke into a school building, and that the board of education offered a reward for information leading to the arrest and conviction of the vandals. The information was provided to the police by a man who was unaware of the reward offer. A majority of the states hold that the man is not entitled to the reward, because he could not have accepted the offer since he was unaware of its existence—there was no meeting of the minds.

Competent Persons

Each valid contract must be entered into between two or more competent persons—persons who have the legal capacity to contract. As already indicated, a board of education is considered a competent person under the law with full capacity to enter into contracts. However, there are certain classes of people who have limited capacity to contract. These include minors, married women, insane persons, drunken persons, and corporations.

A minor has the right to disaffirm her contract until a reasonable time after reaching her majority (i.e., becoming an adult). If a board of education contracts with a minor, the minor has the prerogative of electing to avoid the contract within a reasonable time after she becomes an adult, and no penalties for a contractual breach will be imposed against the minor. A board of education would have no right or option to avoid its contract with the minor.

If an individual is so insane or drunk at the time he enters into a contract that he does not know what he is doing, he may have the contract set aside because there was no meeting of the minds, which is always essential in every valid contractual situation.

At the common law, married women did not possess the legal capacity to contract. This law was premised on the age-old concept that when a man and woman married, the two became one and the man was that one. This contractual limitation has been removed by statutes in all states, and women now possess the power to enter into contracts on the same basis as men.

Before entering into a contract with a corporation, a board of education should ascertain that the corporation has the power, by statute or under its articles of incorporation, to perform the services agreed upon.

Consideration

Valid contracts must be supported by consideration—something of value. Consideration is divided into three types. These are good, valuable, and a promise for an act.

Good consideration is love and affection. For example, a mother may convey property to a child for good consideration. This notion is seldom invoked by courts today.

Valuable consideration is cash or its equivalent. Most deeds will recite that the property is being conveyed for good and valuable consideration.

The third type of consideration is that found in a unilateral contract—a promise for an act. For example, a board of education promises a reward of $500 for information leading to the arrest and conviction of vandals who damaged school property. An individual, knowing of the offer, provides the information that leads to the arrest and conviction of the vandals; he is entitled to the reward. His consideration was the doing of the act requested.

Legal Subject Matter

All contracts, to be valid, must involve a legal subject matter. Most, if not all, states prohibit the holding of various types of assemblies, such as rooster fighting. If a board of education entered into a contract to lease school premises for the purposes of staging a rooster-fighting conclave, such a contract would involve an illegal subject matter and would be declared void.

Proper Form

Contracts, to be enforceable, must be in the form required by law. For example, all agreements, with respect to the sale or leasing of real estate, must be in writing to be enforceable. An oral agreement to sell real property, even if made in the town square before ten thousand people, is unenforceable in the courts. This is but one example of the requirement that contracts must be in the proper form to be enforceable. States require that teacher's contracts be in writing.

Beyond the technical statutory and common-law requirements that govern the contractual relationships between teachers and school boards, there are the even more pervasive requirements of the state and federal constitutions, which sanctify the contract and protect the individual against arbitrary use of contracts by the state. This aspect of the contract is discussed later.

A Contract between a School Trustee and a Teacher to Pay "Good Wages" Is Too Indefinite to Enforce

---

Fairplay School Township v. O'Neal

Supreme Court of Indiana, 1891.
127 Ind. 95, 26 N.E. 686.

ELLIOTT, J. The complaint of the appellee alleges that she was duly licensed to teach school, and that her license was in force on the 31st day of March, 1888; that she entered into a verbal contract with the school trustee on that day, wherein she undertook to teach school for the term to be held in the school year 1888; that the school trustee promised in said oral contract to pay her "good wages;" that she has been ready and willing to teach, but the trustee refused to permit her to do so. The question presented is whether there was such a contract as bound the school township, and made it liable for damages for a breach.

Our opinion is that there was no such contract. The trustee is an officer clothed with statutory power, and all who deal with him are bound to take notice of the nature and extent of his authority. . . . The authority of the trustee respecting schools is vested in him for a public purpose, in which all the citizens of the township have an interest, and upon many phases of which they have a right to be heard by petition or remonstrance. This is especially so with regard to the employment of teachers. It is necessary, for the information of the citizens, that contracts made with teachers should be certain and definite in their terms; otherwise the citizens cannot guard their interests, nor observe the conduct of their officer. It is necessary that the contract should be definite and certain, in order that when the time comes for the teacher to enter upon duty there may be no misunderstanding as to what his rights are. Any other rule would put in peril the school interests. Suppose, for illustration, that a contract providing for "good wages," "reasonable wages," "fair wages," or the like, is made, and when the time comes for opening the schools there arises a dispute as to what the compensation shall be. How shall it be determined, and in what mode can the teacher be compelled to go on with the duty he has agreed to perform? Until there is a definite contract, it can hardly be said that a teacher has been employed, and the public interest demands that there should be a definite agreement before the time arrives for the schools to open; otherwise the school corporation may be at the mercy of the teacher, or else there be no school. We think that a teacher cannot recover from the school corporation for the breach of an executory agreement, unless it is so full and definite as to be capable of specific enforcement. . . . There is much reason for scrutinizing with care contracts made so far in advance of the opening of the school year as was that here sued on, and sound policy requires that the terms should be so definitely fixed and made known that all interested may have full and reliable information. It is, we may say in passing, not altogether clear that the statute

does not require that all contracts shall be in writing and be recorded; but we do not deem it necessary to decide that question. Judgment reversed.

NOTES

1. Would the outcome of this case have been different if the contract had been written?
2. Teachers' general relationships with school boards are created by contract and governed by general principles of contract law. *Kirk v. Miller,* 83 Wn.2d 777, 522 P.2d 843 (1974).
3. Power to employ or discharge teachers is exclusively vested in the school board and cannot be delegated to any other body or official, such as a school superintendent. *Snider v. Kit Carson School District R–1,* in Cheyenne County, 166 Colo. 180, 442 P.2d 429 (1968).
4. In order to have a valid teacher employment contract, as in other discretionary matters, the school board must act as a board and not as individuals. *Landers v. Board of Education of Town of Hot Springs,* 45 N.M. 446, 116 P.2d 690 (1941).

Teacher Who Did Not Obtain Necessary Credit Hours During Specified Period Was Not Entitled Contract Renewal

─ ─ ─ ─ ─ ─ ─ ─ ─

Feldhusen v. Beach Public School District No. 3

─ ─ ─ ─ ─ ─ ─ ─ ─

Supreme Court of North Dakota, 1988.
423 N.W.2d 155.

VANDE WALLE, Justice. David Feldhusen appealed from a judgment dismissing his petition for a writ of mandamus. We affirm.

Feldhusen was employed by Beach Public School District No. 3 (Beach) as a teacher in the fall of 1981. His employment continued until his contract was nonrenewed in the spring of 1987.

Beach takes part in a voluntary "accreditation" program established by the State Deartment of Public Instruction. In order to be accredited a school district must establish and implement a policy for the professional growth of teachers. Beach implemented its policy through the following provision in its professional-negotiations agreement with the teachers in the school district:

Summer school & extension course attendance shall be as follows to advance on the salary schedule:
  −a. All plus hours must be graduate hours.
  −b. *Teachers with degrees must acquire 8 semester or 12 quarter hours every five years.*
  −c. Teachers may substitute 16 hours of certified in-service training for 1 quarter hour. See attached policy on in-service hours.
  −d. All credits must be earned from an accredited college or university.
  −e. *All teachers must provide written proof each year by the second Monday in September that they meet above accreditation standards as required by North Dakota Department of Public Instruction. No salary increase will be granted the year accreditation standards are not met and no teacher contract will be offered the following year unless accreditation standards are met.* [Emphasis added.]*
  . . .

Beach established this policy in 1981. The 1985–1986 school year was the fifth year of the cycle for Feldhusen. At the end of that school

---

* Schools are accredited and teachers are certified. See Section 15–21–04.1 and Chapter 15–36, N.D.C.C. Feldhausen was certified as a teacher. One of the standards required for accreditation of the school, a voluntary process, is that the school board establish and implement a policy of professional growth for each teacher and that it also locally establish the five-year period for each teacher who holds a life certificate. The language of the Beach policy requiring that teachers "meet . . . accreditation standards as required by North Dakota Department of Public Instruction" relates to the credits required of each teacher in order that the school meet the standards for accreditation.

year Feldhusen had completed only six of the requisite twelve quarter-hours.

In March of 1987 the Beach school board voted to contemplate nonrenewal of Feldhusen's teaching contract. A letter was sent to Feldhusen informing him of the contemplated nonrenewal for the reason of "teacher qualifications" based upon Feldhusen's failure to meet the accreditation standards. . . .

After the end of the 1986–1987 school year Feldhusen performed coursework which would have given him the number of credits or quarter-hours required by the Beach accreditation policy. This work was completed in June of 1987. In July of 1987 Beach hired another teacher to fill the position which Feldhusen had held. Subsequently Feldhusen petitioned for a writ of mandamus requiring Beach to give him a contract. After a hearing was held, the trial court issued a judgment dismissing the petition. It is from that judgment that Feldhusen appeals.

The question before us is whether the trial court erred in dismissing Feldhusen's petition for a writ of mandamus. . . .

Feldhusen . . . argues that he has a clear legal right to a contract from Beach because there was no statutory basis for the Beach school board's nonrenewal decision. We disagree. The nonrenewal of teacher contracts is governed by Section 15–47–38(5), N.D.C.C. A portion of that statute provides:

The reasons given by the board for not renewing a teacher's contract must be sufficient to justify the contemplated action of the board and may not be frivolous or arbitrary but must be related to the ability, competence, or qualifications of the teacher as a teacher, or the necessities of the district such as lack of funds calling for a reduction in the teaching staff.

Thus teachers' contracts can be nonrenewed for a lack of qualifications.

In this case Beach was voluntarily taking part in an accreditation program which required that it assure the professional growth of its teachers. In order to comply with the accreditation standards Beach, in tandem with its teachers, created a policy requiring its teachers to acquire a certain number of college credits in a five-year period. That policy became a part of the professional-negotiations agreement between the Beach school board and the teachers of Beach. It is readily apparent that one of the qualifications for a teacher in Beach was that the teacher abide by the contractual provision designed to retain Beach's accreditation. If a teacher failed to abide by the provision regarding the acquisition of college credits, the negotiated policy specified that no teacher contract would be offered the following year, thus justifying nonrenewal under Section 15–47–38(5). Therefore, we cannot conclude that the trial court abused its discretion in denying the petition for a writ of mandamus which was predicated upon a claim that nonrenewal could not be grounded in a teacher's failure to abide by the Beach policy as formulated in the professional-negotiations agreement.   .   .   .

The judgment is affirmed.

◼ THE TENURE CONTRACT

Tenure is a statutory right to hold office or employment and to receive the benefits and emoluments of the position. Tenure in its general sense is a mode of holding or occupying a position or a job.[10] After meeting designated academic and teaching requirements in a school district for a prescribed number of years, a teacher, if recommended for reemployment, may acquire tenure. The benefit of tenure is that it bestows on the teacher a right of continued employment in the school district, and dismissal cannot occur without a hearing and presentation of proof of sufficient cause to meet the statutory requirements for removal.

Many court cases have arisen concerning the transferring of a tenured teacher from a particular class or school to another educational setting. Generally, a tenured teacher, like a teacher on a limited contract, may be assigned to any class or school in the district if she is qualified to teach in that position. The courts frown, however, upon any attempt of a school board or administrator to use "undesirable reassignment" as a means of retribution against a teacher who has achieved continuing contract status. If a teacher has committed an act for which her contract may be terminated, the proper legal procedure should be followed to terminate the contract, rather than using subterfuges of questionable legality.

Grounds for Termination

Tenure laws specify the grounds for and the manner by which a teacher's employment may be terminated. These laws may apply in instances of dismissal during the period of an annual contract or to termination of teachers who have either continuing contracts or tenure. The most common grounds for dismissal are incompetency and insubordination.

Incompetency has been construed by the courts to mean any physical or mental condition that tends to incapacitate a teacher to perform effectively. This rather broad definition generally concerns a fitness to teach that contains a range of factors and has been used by many boards as a catchall for teacher dismissal. Insubordination, on the other hand, is of narrower meaning and imports a willful disregard for express or implied directions of the employer and repeated refusal to obey reasonable regulations.[11]

Other grounds for dismissal include immorality, misconduct, neglect of duty, and other good or just cause. Every teacher is charged with the responsibility of setting a good example. Not only must teachers be of good moral character, but their general reputation must attest to this fact. Teachers must be not only moral persons, but must conduct themselves in such a manner that others will know of their virtue. Although court opinions are not uniform on the subject, it may generally be concluded that misconduct is a broader term than immorality, and that different standards of proof are required for each.

Reassignment of Teacher from Secondary Grade to Elementary Grade Is Not an Impermissible Demotion

———·——·——·———

Appeal of Santee

———·——·——·———

Supreme Court of Pennsylvania, 1959.
397 Pa. 601, 156 A.2d 830.

PER CURIAM. The decree appealed from is affirmed on the following opinion of Judge Flannery for the court en banc.

Miss Clara N. Santee has been a professional employee of the School District of the City of Hazleton where, since 1925, she has held the status of a teacher.

For the school year 1956–1957 she was assigned to the D.A. Harman, Jr. High School teaching English and Mathematics in the ninth grade.

On August 22, 1957, she was assigned to teach a sixth-grade class in the Arthur Street School, which assignment she regarded as a demotion and accepted under protest. Her salary was not affected by the transfer and is not here involved.

Exercising her rights under the School Code she demanded restoration of her previous status and requested a hearing before the School Board. That was granted and her petition was denied. She appealed to the Superintendent of Public Instruction of the Commonwealth of Pennsylvania who, by decision dated June 11, 1958, dismissed her appeal. From that decision she appealed to this court, and on October 3, 1958, we affirmed the decision and order of the Superintendent of Public Instruction. . . .

The question is narrow. Does an assignment from the ninth to the sixth grade constitute a demotion in type of position as contemplated by the Code? We believe it does not.

The statute provides:

but there shall be no demotion of any professional employee either in salary or in type of

position without the consent of the employe, or, if such consent is not received, then such demotion shall be subject to the right to a hearing before the board of school directors and an appeal in the same manner as hereinbefore provided in the case of the dismissal of a professional employe.

. . . There was a salary distinction between "elementary and secondary schools" under the Act of May 18, 1911, P.L. 309, as amended and revised. . . . But this distinction was swept away in the amendment of July 5, 1947, P.L. 1266, which provided for minimum salaries based on certification and academic qualifications and not on assignment and this system has been retained under the amendments to the Code. . . .

Thus the Legislature has abolished the legal distinction between elementary and secondary schools and unless we can find in the law some differences between the two in importance, dignity, responsibility, authority and/or prestige—some distinguishing difference—the appellant cannot prevail.

The definition of professional employee, as mandated in the Code, must be kept in mind. It provides:

The term "professional employe" shall include teachers, supervisors, supervising principals, directors of vocational education, dental hygienists, visiting teachers, school secretaries the selection of whom is on the basis of merit as determined by eligibility lists, school nurses who are certified as teachers and any regular full-time employe of a school district who is duly certified as a teacher.

. . . We construe these to be the "type of position" referred to in Art. XI, Sec. 1151, which prohibits demotion of any professional employee either in salary or in type of position without the consent of the employee, as we have quoted above. Under this construction the appellant has not been demoted.

There is no less importance, dignity, responsibility, authority, prestige or compensation in the elementary grades than in secondary. Here the young student still pliant, still susceptible, still in the formative stage, receives his earlier impressions, his inspiration, his direction. Here personality traits are brought out and developed, tastes are instilled, habit patterns are established, character is formed. This is perhaps the most important period of life, the most crucial, the period which may determine a child's ultimate moral, ethical and intellectual stature. To be charged with the responsibility for children in this critical time of their lives is no demotion.

Decree affirmed at appellant's costs.

NOTES

1. Tenure laws are enacted to provide job security for experienced teachers and to ensure that they are not discharged for insufficient and inadequate reasons. A system of tenure has as its objective the maintenance of an able teaching force who have undergone a period of probation, with the concomitant result that because of such protections, more talented personnel will be attracted to the teaching profession. *State v. Redman,* 491 P.2d 157 (Alaska 1971), appeal after remand *Redman v. Department of Education,* 519 P.2d 760 (1974).

2. The broad purpose of teacher tenure is to protect worthy instructors from enforced yielding to political pressures and to guarantee employment regardless of the vicissitudes of politics. *School District No. 8, Pinal County v. Superior Court of Pinal County,* 102 Ariz. 478, 433 P.2d 28 (1967).

3. A continuing contract has as one of its central purposes the elimination of uncertainty in the employment plans of both teacher and school district. *Peters v. South Kitsap School District No. 402,* 8 Wn.App. 809, 509 P.2d 67 (1973).

4. Tenure laws are not grants of power to school districts, but rather constitute a limitation on the power of the school district to freely contract with teachers. *Carlson v. School District No. 6 of Maricopa County,* 12 Ariz.App. 179, 468 P.2d 944 (1970).

Incompetency and Immorality May Be Interpreted by the Courts to Broadly Mean a General Lack of Fitness

— · — · — · — · —

Horosko v. Mount Pleasant Township School District

— · — · — · — · —

Supreme Court of Pennsylvania, 1939.
335 Pa. 369, 6 A.2d 866.

LINN, Justice. This appeal is from an order of the Superior Court reversing an order of the Common Pleas which had affirmed the action of a school board in discharging a teacher. . . .

The difference of view between the two learned courts which have considered the case arises from a different construction of the following provision in section 1205(a), 24 P.S. § 1126(a): "(a) The only valid causes for termination of a contract in accordance with the provisions of this section shall be—Immorality, incompetency, intemperance, cruelty, willful and persistent negligence, mental derangement, persistent and willful violation of the school laws of this Commonwealth on the part of the professional employe. . . .

All the members of this court agree that the Superior Court's construction is much narrower than was apparently intended by the legislature; we also think the case calls for the application of the rule that findings of fact supported by competent evidence must be accepted on appeal. In the opinion of the Superior Court it is said—"It may be true, as counsel for appellee [the school board] argues, that appellant [teacher] now commands neither the respect nor the good will of the community, but these are not matters which the statute now recognizes as causes for dismissal." If the fact be that she "now commands neither the respect nor the good will of the community" and if the record shows that effect to be the result of her conduct within the clause quoted, it will be conclusive evidence of incompetency. It has always been the recognized duty of the teacher to conduct himself in such way as to command the respect and good will of the community, though one result of the choice of a teacher's vocation may be to deprive him of the same freedom of action enjoyed by persons in other vocations. Educators have always regarded the example set by the teacher as of great importance, particularly in the education of the children in the lower grades such as those attending the school in which this teacher had been employed; it was a country school with eighteen pupils classified into eight grades.

Difficulties between this teacher and the board had been existing some time and grew out of her conduct with respect to a restaurant maintained by a man whom she married in August 1936, during the course of the period involved. In this restaurant beer was sold and a pinball and a slot machine were maintained and dice were played. The restaurant was across the road and about one hundred and twenty five feet from the school. In the opinion filed by the learned trial judge, he said:

> The evidence in the case is that: (1) While Miss Horosko used and was known by the name of Evelyn Horosko she was in fact married to one William Connors and lived with him as his wife; (2) That the said Connors was the proprietor of a lunch room and beer garden in which Evelyn Horosko acted as waitress and, on occasion, as bartender, such services being performed after school hours and during the summer vacation; (3) That in this beer garden and in the presence of several of her pupils whom she was tutoring, she (a) took an occasional drink of beer; (b) served beer to customers; (c) shook dice with customers for drinks; (d) played, and showed customers how to play, a pinball machine on the premises. And further, that she was rated by A.H. Howell, County Superintendent of Schools, under the rating card provided by the Department of Education, as 43 percent competent, a rating of 50 percent being the "passing" or average rating.

Is such a course of conduct immoral or intemperate, and does it—in connection with her scholastic and efficiency rating—amount to incompetency? We hold it to be self evident that, under the intent and meaning of the act,

immorality is not essentially confined to a deviation from sex morality; it may be such a course of conduct as offends the morals of the community and is a bad example to the youth whose ideals a teacher is supposed to foster and to elevate. Nor need intemperance be confined strictly to overindulgence in alcoholic liquors— temperance implies moderation, and a person may be intemperate in conduct without being an alcoholic addict. And so as to incompetency; as we take it, this means under the Act incompetency as a teacher—but does this mean that competency is merely the ability to teach the "Three R's"?

He concluded that it would be "just" (the word used in clause (j) of section 1205) to affirm the action of the school board in dismissing the teacher.

The opinion of the Superior Court is based, as we understand it, on a narrower construction of the word "incompetency" than that adopted by the trial court. The Statutory Construction Act of 1937, P.L. 1019, in section 33, 46 P.S. § 533, provides:

> Words and phrases shall be construed according to rules of grammar and according to their common and approved usage; but technical words and phrases and such others as have acquired a peculiar and appropriate meaning or are defined in this act, shall be construed according to such peculiar and appropriate meaning or definition.
>
> General words shall be construed to take their meanings and be restricted by preceding particular words.

The provisions of clause (a), which include the words "incompetency" and "immorality," are therefore to be construed "according to their common and approved usage," having regard, of course, to the context in which the legislature used them.

Among the definitions of "immorality" is "conduct inconsistent with moral rectitude." A large body of public opinion regards gambling as immoral. Gambling with a pinball or a slot machine or with dice is prohibited by law. We are not prepared to say the learned judge erred in concluding that the teacher's shaking "dice with customers for drinks" and showing them how to play a pinball machine in the presence of school children supported the finding of incompetency in the circumstances shown.

The term "incompetency" has a "common and approved usage." The context does not limit the meaning of the word to lack of substantive knowledge of the subjects to be taught. Common and approved usage give a much wider meaning. For example, in 31 C.J., with reference to a number of supporting decisions, it is defined: "A relative term without technical meaning. It may be employed as meaning disqualification; inability; incapacity; lack of ability, legal qualifications, or fitness to discharge the required duty." In Black's Law Dictionary, 3rd edition, page 945, and in 1 Bouv.Law Dict., Rawle's Third Revision, p. 1528, it is defined as "Lack of ability or fitness to discharge the required duty." Cases construing the word to the same effect are found in 4 Words and Phrases, First Series, page 3510, and 2 Words and Phrases, Second Series, page 1013. Webster's New International Dictionary defines it as "want of physical, intellectual, or moral ability; insufficiency; inadequacy; specif., want of legal qualifications or fitness." Funk & Wagnalls Standard Dictionary defines it as "General lack of capacity of fitness, or lack of the special qualities required for a particular purpose."

In the circumstances, therefore, we must conclude that the order made in the Common Pleas was "just."

The order of the Superior Court is reversed and that of the Common Pleas is reinstated; each party to bear its own costs.

NOTES

1. *Incompetency.* As noted above, incompetency has been given broad interpretation by the courts. Incompetency is defined as "want of physical, intellectual, or moral ability; insufficiency; inadequacy; specific want of legal qualifications or fitnesses," (*Webster's New International Dictionary*) *Beilan v. Board of Education, School District of Philadelphia,* 357 U.S. 399, 78 S.Ct. 1317 (1958). It generally concerns a fitness to teach, which contains a broad range of factors. The courts have included in incom-

petency the lack of knowledge of subject matter, lack of discipline, unreasonable discipline, unprofessional conduct, and willful neglect of duty. Generally, when incompetency is involved, other charges are also presented. In one case, the dismissal notification listed fourteen specific charges and included inadequate maintenance of discipline during class, excessive and ineffective use of films, ineffective classroom teaching, and failure to cooperate with school administrators. Here, the school presented a preponderance of evidence that children were disruptive, daydreamed in class, and left the room without permission. Therefore the court upheld the dismissal. *Board of Directors of Sioux City v. Mroz,* 295 N.W.2d 447 (Iowa 1980).

The manner of offering evidence in incompetency cases is generally through testimony. Both the quantity and quality of evidence are important. The courts have liberally allowed opinions of principals, curricular supervisors, and other supervisory personnel to stand as expert testimony. Other testimony by students and parents may be important, but the actual observations, by supervisors, of what transpired in the classroom are very significant. One court said, "The court, in absence of proof of an abuse of discretion, cannot substitute its opinion for the decision of the school board and of the district court where both of these tribunals were presented with substantial evidence upon which to base their decisions." *Frank v. St. Landry Parish School Board,* 225 So.2d 62 (La.App. 1969).

A teacher who has been certified by the state is assumed to be competent, and it is the responsibility of the school board to prove incompetency. As long as school boards are not arbitrary or capricious, the courts generally do not interfere. The Fifth Circuit Court of Appeals stated that "[f]or sound policy reasons, courts are loathe to intrude upon the internal affairs of local school authorities in such matters as teacher competency." The dismissal of a tenured teacher, who had been teaching for 25 years, was upheld because the teacher used poor grammar and made spelling errors. The teacher also attempted to teach spelling before the children mastered the alphabet. *Blunt v. Marion County School Board,* 515 F.2d 951 (5th Cir. 1975).

Unauthorized or excessive punishment of pupils may constitute incompetency. A New York court upheld the dismissal of a tenured teacher when the board gave evidence that the teacher administered excessive punishment on three separate occasions. *Kinsella v. Board of Education,* 64 A.D.2d 738, 407 N.Y.S.2d 78 (1978).

Incompetency may be evidenced by poor classroom decorum. A school district dismissed a tenured teacher on grounds of incompetence because she was unable to maintain order in her classroom. The classroom was littered with sunflower seeds, paper, and "junk"; and the furniture and walls were covered with graffiti. The teacher also had not planned her lessons or given students proper directions. *Board of Education of the School District of Philadelphia v. Kushner,* 109 Pa. Cmwlth. 120, 530 A.2d 541 (Pa. 1987).

Teachers, though, cannot be dismissed for incompetency for nebulous and nondefinitive evaluations of competency. A tenured teacher, of 13 years service and had received satisfactory evaluations, requested and was granted a 1-year unpaid leave of absence. The board of trustees instituted a new policy that all teachers seeking positions or teachers seeking voluntary transfers participate in a structured interview. When the teacher came back from leave, she participated in the structured interviews and did poorly. The trustees dismissed her for incompetency. After 13 years of sufficient teaching, the structured interviews were not sufficient to meet the burden of dismissing a tenured teacher. *Trustees, Missoula County School District No. 1 v. Anderson,* 232 Mont. 501, 757 P.2d 1315 (1988).

Some states' statutes require that teachers be given an opportunity to improve or to remediate themselves. If a statute requires remediation, the school board must show that remediation was attempted or that the situation was irremediable. When a

teacher was charged with incompetency based on a number of items, such as lack of rapport with pupils; making irregular homework assignments; and grabbing children's hair, arms, and shoulders in a cruel manner; the teacher claimed the acts were remediable but the court disagreed and stated that "many causes, when standing alone, may be remediable, whereas those same causes in combination with others may well be irremediable. Here, we think it clear that the combination of a number of causes plus the continuous nature of the conduct were sufficient bases for a finding of irremediability." *Gilliland v. Board of Education of Pleasant View Consol. School Dist. No. 622,* 67 Ill.2d 143, 8 Ill.Dec. 84, 365 N.E.2d 322 (1977).

2. *Insubordination.* Courts have defined insubordination as "a willful disregard of express or implied directions of the employer and a refusal to obey reasonable orders." *School District No. 8, Pinal County v. Superior Court,* 102 Ariz. 478, 433 P.2d 28 (1967). Charges of insubordination are not supportable if

1. the alleged misconduct was not proved;
2. the existence of a pertinent school rule or a superior's order was not proved;
3. the pertinent rule or order was not violated;
4. the teacher tried, although unsuccessfully, to comply with the rule or order;
5. the teacher's motive for violating the rule or order was admirable;
6. no harm resulted from the violation;
7. the rule or order was unreasonable;
8. the rule or order was invalid as beyond the authority of its maker;
9. the enforcement of the rule or order revealed possible bias or discrimination against the teacher; or
10. the enforcement of the rule or order violated the First Amendment rights to free speech or academic freedom. (78 ALR3d 83, 87).

Insubordination is refusal or repeated refusal to follow directions. In a case where a teacher was charged with insubordination for inappropriate punishment of students and allowing card games to be played in study hall, the court ruled that there was no insubordination, though the conduct was highly questionable, because the teacher ceased the activities after being admonished by the principal. *Thompson v. Wake County Board of Education,* 31 N.C.App. 401, 230 S.E.2d 164 (1976), see 292 N.C. 406, 233 S.E.2d 538 (1977).

In another insubordination case, a teacher was told not to use J.D. Salinger's *Catcher in the Rye* in his classroom and had agreed not to use the novel. Afterward, he began to use the novel again and was requested to meet with the principal concerning the issue. The teacher walked out of the meeting after 5 minutes and was charged with two counts of insubordination: (1) breaking the previous agreement, and (2) walking out of the conference. The school board upheld the charges and dismissed the teacher. Upon appeal, the court determined the dismissal was too severe. Although the courts do not generally review administrative sanction, this decision was disproportionate to the offense and was not fair, since students were not harmed and there was no indication of lack of fitness to teach. *Harris v. Mechanicville Central School District,* 45 N.Y.2d 279, 408 N.Y.S.2d 384, 380 N.E.2d 213 (1978).

If teacher's insubordinate conduct engenders a detrimental environment in the school, then dismissal may be upheld. A tenured teacher informed the superintendent she planned to take a week off to take a trip to Jamaica with her husband. The superintendent denied the leave. When the teacher did not appear at school, the superintendent recommended she be dismissed for insubordination. After a hearing, the school committee dismissed the teacher, whereupon the teacher filed suit. The court stated, "[i]n wake of plaintiff's conduct come grave doubts among school administrators, recriminations and jealousy among teachers, and an attitude of laxity and self-indulgence, possibly affecting the entire school community. These are consequences which the law does not require school administrators to condone." *Fernald v. City of Ellsworth Superintending School Committee,* 342 A.2d 704 (Me. 1975).

A continued violation of school policy is usually sufficient grounds to establish insubordination. A coach's contract was nonrenewed for insubordination because the coach continued to let noncertified volunteers coach at games in violation of school board policy. *King v. Elkins Public Schools,* 22 Ark. App. 52, 733 S.W.2d 417 (1987).

———

Board's Inference That Teacher's Activities Constituted Social Misbehavior Was Arbitrary and Capricious

— ·— ·— ·— ·—

Fisher v. Snyder

— ·— ·— ·— ·—

United States Court of Appeals,
Eighth Circuit, 1973.
476 F.2d 375.

BRIGHT, Circuit Judge. Appellants, as members of the school board of a rural Nebraska county district, dismissed appellee, Frances Fisher, as a high school teacher at the close of the 1972 school year, giving as a reason her "unbecoming conduct" outside the classroom. Mrs. Fisher thereafter brought an action against the members of the board under 42 U.S.C.A. § 1983, alleging that constitutionally impermissible reasons underlay their dismissal action. The district court ordered her reinstatement, and the board members bring this appeal. We affirm the district court.

The relevant facts are not in dispute. Mrs. Fisher, a middle-aged divorcee, was employed at the high school in Tryon, Nebraska, from 1970 to 1972. Her married son, then twenty-six years old, lived and taught in the neighboring town of Stapleton, Nebraska. Mrs. Fisher lived alone in a one-bedroom apartment. On several occasions, young ladies, married couples, and young men, who were friends of her son, visited Tryon. Because hotel and motel accommodations were generally sparse and unavailable in Tryon, Mrs. Fisher followed the advice of the secretary of the school board and allowed these guests to stay overnight at her apartment. Cliff Rowan, age twenty-six, was a particularly frequent visitor. Rowan's parents lived in California. He, therefore, regularly visited Mrs. Fisher during his school vacations and at other times, and she referred to him as her second son. In the spring of 1972, Rowan spent about a week in Tryon visiting school classes as a means of fulfilling certain of his college requirements. Mrs. Fisher made arrangements with school administrators for this visitation and it was reported in the local newspaper.

Following Rowan's visit, the school board notified Mrs. Fisher that her contract would not be renewed at the end of the 1972 school year. At her request, pursuant to provisions of Nebraska law, the board afforded Mrs. Fisher a hearing relating to the notice of dismissal.
. . .

Nebraska by statute requires that notice and a hearing be given nontenured teachers who are to be terminated. Neb.Rev.Stat. § 79–1254. The appellees concede that the school board, in dismissing Fisher, complied with the statute, and its judgment, therefore, must be afforded judicial deference "so long as the board does not act unreasonably, arbitrarily, capriciously, or unlawfully." *Smith v. Board of Educ.*, 365 F.2d 770, 782 (8th Cir. 1966) . . . .

However, a high school teacher may successfully argue that his dismissal was arbitrary and capricious if he can prove

> that each of the stated reasons [underlying his dismissal] is trivial, or is unrelated to the educational process or to working relationships within the educational institution, or is wholly unsupported by a basis in fact. [*McEnteggart v. Cataldo*, 451 F.2d 1109, 1111 (1st Cir.1971), cert. denied, 408 U.S. 943, 92 S.Ct. 2878, 33 L.Ed.2d 767 (1972).]

Thus, while a school board may legitimately inquire into the character and integrity of its teachers . . . it must be certain that it does not arbitrarily or capriciously dismiss a teacher based on unsupported conclusions drawn from such inquiries.

In seeking to justify the dismissal in this case, the school board argues that the evidence developed at the board hearing supported its finding Mrs. Fisher guilty of conduct unbecoming a teacher. In the board's view, "the inferences from her social behavior are that there was a strong potential of sexual misconduct." The board does not actually accuse Mrs. Fisher of immoral conduct but "of social misbehavior that is not conducive to the maintenance of the integrity of the public school system." . . .

But here there is no proof of improper conduct. The only whit of evidence offered as support for the board's conclusion that Mrs. Fisher was guilty of unbecoming conduct was the fact that she had overnight guests. But the presence of these guests in her home provides no inkling beyond subtle implication and innuendo which would impugn Mrs. Fisher's morality. Idle speculation certainly does not provide a basis in fact for the board's conclusory inference that "there was strong potential of sexual misconduct" and that, therefore, Mrs. Fisher's activity was "social misbehavior that is not conducive to the maintenance of the integrity of the public school system." We agree with the district court that "At most, the evidence may be said to raise a question of Mrs. Fisher's good judgment in her personal affairs, when measured against an undefined standard which someone could suppose exists in a small town in Nebraska." . . .

The record, furthermore, contains considerable evidence tending to negate any inference of improper or immoral conduct by Mrs. Fisher. She did not attempt to conceal the presence of her house guests but instead openly inquired of the school board's secretary about motel accommodations in Tryon for these guests. She was advised to keep them in her home because other accommodations were so limited. She formally introduced one of her guests at school so that he might observe classes to satisfy college requirements. The local Avon lady, wife of the pastor of a church in Tryon, called at Mrs. Fisher's residence on a Saturday morning during the 1970–1971 school year. Although Mrs. Fisher was apparently awakened by the visit, she invited the pastor's wife into her apartment. A young man who had been an overnight guest was also present in the apartment, and the three drank coffee together.

Two citizens of Tryon called as witnesses for the school board were subpoenaed. Their testimony cast no aspersions upon Mrs. Fisher's character or her fitness as a teacher. No evidence of a community reaction against Mrs. Fisher has been presented . . . nor has she been shown incapable of maintaining discipline in her classes because of any inferences of impropriety drawn by her students or their parents.

This evidence, in the context of our review of the entire record, convinces us of the correctness of the district court's determination. The openness of the association, and the age differential between Mrs. Fisher and her guests, would seem to belie any inference of impropriety. The school board's inference of misconduct was arbitrary and capricious and therefore constituted an impermissible reason for terminating her employment, since the inference lacked any valid basis in fact.

Accordingly, we affirm the judgment of the district court.

Homosexuality of Teacher Is Immorality Justifying Dismissal

– – – · – – – · – – –

Gaylord v. Tacoma School District No. 10

– – – · – – – · – – –

Supreme Court of Washington, 1977.
88 Wa.2d 286, 559 P.2d 1340.

HOROWITZ, Associate Justice. Plaintiff-appellant, James Gaylord, appeals a judgment of the trial court upholding Gaylord's discharge from employment as a high school teacher by defendant school district. . . .

Defendant school district discharged Gaylord—who held a teacher's certificate—from his teaching position at the Wilson High School in Tacoma on the ground of "immorality" because he was a known homosexual.
. . .

We need consider only the assignments of error which raise two basic issues: (1) whether substantial evidence supports the trial court's conclusion plaintiff-appellant Gaylord was guilty of immorality; (2) whether substantial evidence supports the findings, that as a known homosexual, Gaylord's fitness as a teacher was impaired to the injury of the Wilson High School, justifying his discharge by the defendant school district's board of directors. The relevant findings of the trial court may be summarized as follows.

Gaylord knew of his homosexuality for twenty years prior to his trial, actively sought homosexual company for the past several years, and participated in homosexual acts. He knew his status as a homosexual, if known, would jeopardize his employment, damage his reputation and hurt his parents.

Gaylord's school superior first became aware of his sexual status on October 24, 1972, when a former Wilson High student told the school's vice-principal he thought Gaylord was a homosexual. The vice-principal confronted Gaylord at his home that same day with a written copy of the student's statement. Gaylord admitted he was a homosexual and attempted unsuccessfully to have the vice-principal drop the matter.

On November 21, 1972, Gaylord was notified the board of directors of the Tacoma School Board had found probable cause for his discharge due to his status as a publicly known homosexual. This status was contrary to school district policy No. 4119(5), which provides for discharge of school employees for "immorality." After hearing, the defendant board of directors discharged Gaylord effective December 21, 1972.

The court found an admission of homosexuality connotes illegal as well as immoral acts, because "sexual gratification with a member of one's own sex is implicit in the term 'homosexual.'" These acts were proscribed by RCW 9.79.120 (lewdness) and RCW 9.79.100 (sodomy).

After Gaylords' homosexual status became publicly known, it would and did impair his teaching efficiency. A teacher's efficiency is determined by his relationship with his students, their parents, the school administration and fellow teachers. If Gaylord had not been discharged after he became known as a homosexual, the result would be fear, confusion, suspicion, parental concern and pressure on the administration by students, parents and other teachers.

The court concluded "appellant was properly discharged by respondent upon a charge of immorality upon his admission and disclosure that he was a homosexual" and that relief sought should be denied.

Was Gaylord guilty of immorality?

Our concern here is with the meaning of immorality in the sense intended by school board policy No. 4119(5). School boards have broad management powers. RCW 28A.58. Under RCW 28A.58.100(1) the school board may discharge teachers for "sufficient cause." Policy No. 4119(5) adopted by the school board and in effect during the term of Gaylord's teaching contract with defendant school district permits the Tacoma School Board of Directors to treat "immorality" as sufficient cause for discharge.

"Immorality" as used in policy No. 4119(5) does not stand alone. RCW 28A.67.110 makes it the duty of all teachers to "endeavor to impress on the minds of their pupils the principles of morality, truth, justice, temperance, humanity, and patriotism . . . ." RCW 28A.70.140 requires that an applicant for a teacher's certificate be "a person of good moral character." RCW 28A.70.160 makes "immorality" a ground for revoking a teacher's certificate. Other grounds include the commission of "crimes against the laws of the state." The moral conduct of a teacher is relevant to a consideration of that person's fitness or ability to function adequately as a teacher of the students he is expected to teach—in this case high school students. . . .

"Immorality" as a ground of teacher discharge would be unconstitutionally vague if not coupled with resulting actual or prospective adverse performance as a teacher. . . . The basic statute permitting discharge for "sufficient cause" (RCW 28A.58.100(1)) has been construed to require the cause must adversely affect the teacher's performance before it can be invoked as a ground for discharge. . . .

The next question is whether the plaintiff's performance as a teacher was sufficiently impaired by his known homosexuality to be the basis for discharge. The court found that Gaylord, prior to his discharge on December 21, 1972, had been a teacher at the Wilson High School in the Tacoma School District No. 10 for over twelve years, and had received favorable evaluations of his teaching throughout this time. (Findings of fact Nos. 1 and 2.) The court further found that "while plaintiff's status as a homosexual [was] unknown to others in the school," his teaching efficiency was not affected nor did his status injure the school. When, however, it became publicly known that Gaylord was a homosexual "the knowledge thereof would and did impair his efficiency as a teacher with resulting injury to the school had he not been discharged." (Finding of fact No. 9.)

The court further found:

A teacher's efficiency is determined by his relationship with students, their parents, fellow teachers and school administrators. In all of these areas the continued employment of appellant after he became known as a homosexual would result, had he not been discharged, in confusion, suspicion, fear, expressed parental concern and pressure upon the administration from students, parents and fellow teachers, all of which would impair appellant's efficiency as a teacher and injure the school. (Finding of fact No. 10.)

Gaylord assigns error to findings of fact numbers 9 and 10, contending there is no substantial evidence to support either. We do not agree.

First, he argues his homosexuality became known at the school only after the school made it known and that he should not be responsible therefor so as to justify his discharge as a homosexual. The difficulty with this argument is twofold. First, by seeking out homosexual company he took the risk his homosexuality would be discovered. It was he who granted an interview to the boy who talked to him about his homosexual problems. The boy had been referred to Gaylord for that purpose by the homosexual friend to whom Gaylord had responded favorably in answering his advertisement in the paper of the Dorian Society. As a result of that interview the boy came away with the impression plaintiff was a homosexual and later told the assistant high school principal about the matter. The latter in turn conferred with plaintiff for the purpose of verifying the charge that had been made. It was the vice-principal's duty to report the information to his superiors because it involved the performance capabilities of Gaylord. The school cannot be charged with making plaintiff's condition known so as to defeat the school board's duty to protect the school and the students against the impairment of the learning process in all aspects involved.

Second, there is evidence that at least one student expressly objected to Gaylord teaching at the high school because of his homosexuality. Three fellow teachers testified against Gaylord remaining on the teaching staff, testifying it was objectionable to them both as teachers and parents. The vice-principal and the principal, as well as the retired superintendent of instruction, testified his presence on the faculty would create problems. There is conflicting evidence on the issue of impairment but the court had the power to accept the testimony it did on which to base complained of findings. . . . The testimony of the school teachers and administrative personnel constituted substantial evidence sufficient to support the findings as to the impairment of the teacher's efficiency.

It is important to remember that Gaylord's homosexual conduct must be considered in the context of his position of teaching high school students. Such students could treat the retention of the high school teacher by the school board as indicating adult approval of his homosexuality. It would be unreasonable to assume as a matter of law a teacher's ability to perform as a teacher required to teach principles of morality (RCW 28A.67.110) is not impaired and creates no danger of encouraging expression of approval and of imitation. Likewise to say that school directors must wait for prior specific overt expression of homosexual conduct before they act to prevent harm from one who chooses to remain "erotically attracted to a notable degree towards persons of his own sex and is psychologically, if not actually, disposed to engage in sexual activity prompted by this attraction" is to ask the school directors to take an unacceptable risk in discharging their fiduciary responsibility of managing the affairs of the school district.

We do not deal here with homosexuality which does not impair or cannot reasonably be said to impair his ability to perform the duties of an occupation in which the homosexual engages and which does not impair the effectiveness of the institution which employs him. However, even the federal civil service regulations on which Gaylord relies to show a change in attitude towards homosexuals provides:

> [W]hile a person may not be found unsuitable based on unsubstantiated conclusions concerning possible embarrassment to the Federal service, a person may be dismissed or found unsuitable for Federal employment where the evidence establishes that such person's sexual conduct affects job fitness. 2 CCH Employment Practice's Guide ;pg 5339 (1975).

It must be shown that "the conduct of the individual may reasonably be expected to interfere with the ability of the person's fitness in the job or against the ability to discharge its responsibility." These principles are similar to those applicable here. The challenged findings and conclusions are supported by substantial evidence.

Affirmed.

NOTES

1. *Immorality.* Immorality is specified by statute in a number of states as grounds for dismissal. Although the term "immorality" has been attacked as unconstitutionally vague, *Kilpatrick v. Wright,* 437 F.Supp. 397 (M.D.Ala. 1977), it generally has been upheld by the courts, especially when it relates to fitness to teach and where there is a rational nexus between the prohibited activity and the individual's position as a teacher. Immorality may include both heterosexual and homosexual activities, but

does not pertain to exclusively sexual activities.

> [W]e note that statutes from colonial days forward recognize the unique position of teachers as examples to our youth and charge them to "exert their best endeavors to impress on the minds of children and youth committed to their care and instruction" the values basic to our society . . . requiring school committees to have full and satisfactory evidence of a teacher's moral character. This special role of teachers on impressionable and not fully tutored minds distinguished them from other public officials. *Dupree v. School Committee of Boston*, 15 Mass.App.Ct. 535, 446 N.E.2d 1099 (1983).

Lying is considered to be immoral. Where a tenured teacher was denied permission to attend a conference, she left anyway, and upon her return submitted a request for excused absences because of illness. The board dismissed her based on immorality. The court upheld the board and said: "questions of morality are not limited to sexual conduct, but may include lying." *Bethel Park School District v. Krall*, 67 Pa.Cmwlth. 143, 445 A.2d 1377 (1982).

1. SEXUAL INVOLVEMENT WITH STUDENTS. Because of the exemplary nature of teaching, the courts have left little question about the seriousness of sexual involvement with students. In one instance, a tenured teacher, while on a field trip, tickled and touched female students on various parts of their bodies, including between the legs. He was observed lying on a motel bed with one of the female students, watching television. The teacher made sexual remarks and innuendos to the female students and the board subsequently dismissed him for immorality. Upon being charged with immorality, the teacher responded that the activities were but "good natured horse-play." The teacher, who had enjoyed a reputation as a good teacher with excellent rapport, contended there was no nexus between his classroom effectiveness and his conduct. The court determined his activities constituted unfitness to teach. *Weissman v. Board of Education of Jefferson County School District No. R–1*, 190 Colo. 414, 547 P.2d 1267 (1976).

In another similar case, a 41-year-old tenured art teacher was dismissed for immorality and unfitness to teach because he placed his hands on female students by giving them back rubs, which escalated to further sexual contact. Evidence was given that he had engaged in sexual intercourse at various places within the high school with at least two other students. The court upheld the dismissal. *Johnson v. Beaverhead City High School District*, 236 Mont. 532, 771 P.2d 137 (1989).

Dismissal for immoral conduct has also been upheld where a teacher placed his hand inside the jeans of a student in the area of her buttocks and on another occasion squeezed the breast of a female student. The court determined the conduct to be immoral and irremediable. *Fadler v. Illinois State Board of Education*, 153 Ill.App.3d 1024, 106 Ill. Dec. 840, 506 N.E.2d 640 (5 Dist. 1987).

2. SEXUAL INVOLVEMENT WITH NONSTUDENTS. The courts, when dealing with cases of sexual activity of teachers with nonstudents, attempt to determine if there has been an impact on the teacher's fitness to teach, and whether the activities were public or private. In a California case, a 48-year-old elementary teacher had her life certificate revoked by the State Board of Education for immorality. The plaintiff was arrested at a private club by an undercover police officer after he watched her commit three separate acts of oral copulation, a violation of the Penal Code. After plea bargaining, the charges were reduced to the misdemeanor of "outraging public decency." The teacher and her husband had also appeared on television, in disguise, discussing nonconventional sexual life-styles. Even though the teacher introduced into evidence her

classroom evaluations, which were satisfactory, and a contract from the local board offering to rehire her, the court held that the state board was correct in revoking her certificate. The evidence showed that the sex acts were witnessed by several strangers in a semipublic atmosphere and "[p]laintiff's performance certainly reflected a total lack of concern for privacy, decorum or preservation of her dignity and reputation." The court said a teacher "in the public school system is regarded by the public and pupils in the light of an exemplar, whose words and actions are likely to be followed by children coming under her care and protection." Obviously, participation in sex orgies fell short of this standard. *Pettit v. State Board of Education,* 10 Cal.3d 29, 109 Cal.Rptr. 665, 513 P.2d 889 (1973).

Dismissal of a homosexual for immorality by a board of education must demonstrate a rational nexus between the conduct of the teacher and fitness to teach. A showing of potential rather than actual harm to students will suffice. Factors such as adverse effect on students or fellow teachers, adversity anticipated within school system, surrounding circumstances, and possible chilling effects on discipline may be used to establish unfitness. *Morrison v. State Board of Education,* 1 Cal.3d 214, 82 Cal.Rptr. 175, 461 P.2d 375 (1969).

A sex change by a teacher may be held to affect fitness to teach. The dismissal of a teacher who underwent a change of sex has been held to constitute incapacity. The tenured teacher changed his external anatomy to that of a female and was subsequently dismissed by the board, which reasoned that the situation would cause emotional harm to students. The teacher's proficiency in the classroom was not in question. According to the court, a teacher's fitness to teach is not based entirely upon academic proficiency but depends on a broad range of factors. One of those factors, the court said, was the "teacher's impact and effect upon his or her students" and the impact in this case would be harmful to the children. *In re Grossman,* 127 N.J.Super. 13, 316 A.2d 39 (1974).

Being pregnant and unmarried does not constitute immorality. An unmarried pregnant teacher was dismissed for immorality. The school district argued that "unwed parenthood is per se proof of immorality and that a parent of an illegitimate child is unfit role model." But the school district could offer no support of either assertion. "Therefore, we hold that Avery's discharge was in violation of her rights under the equal protection clause of the Fourteenth Amendment." *Avery v. Homewood City Board of Education,* 674 F.2d 337 (5th Cir. 1982).

Consensual sexual conduct between a teacher and an adult of the opposite sex, committed off-campus, cannot without other extenuating circumstances constitute "good cause" for school board's rejection of superintendent's nomination of the teacher for reemployment. *Sherbourne v. School Board of Suwannee County,* 455 So.2d 1057 (Fla.App. 1984).

2. *Moral Turpitude.* Moral turpitude is "[a]n act of baseness, vileness, or depravity in the private and social duties which a man owes to his fellow men, or to society in general, contrary to the accepted and customary rule of right and duty between man and man." (*Black's Law Dictionary,* 1160.) Moral turpitude is difficult to clearly define because it is premised on the moral standards of the community.

Revocation of the teaching certificate of two teachers for growing 52 marijuana plants in the greenhouse has been upheld by a Florida court as violative of the moral standards of the community. The court concluded that since teachers are in a leadership capacity, and are obligated to maintain a high moral standard in the community, the possession of marijuana plants, and the ensuing publicity, seriously impaired their abilities to be effective teachers. *Adams v. State Professional Practices Council,* 406 So.2d 1170 (Fla.App. 1981), petition denied 412 So.2d 463 (Fla. 1982). In an earlier decision, a teacher was found not to be guilty of moral turpitude where he was found to be cultivating only one marijuana plant out of curiosity. *Board of Trustees v. Judge,* 50 Cal.App.3d 920, 123 Cal.Rptr. 830 (1975).

Conviction for mail fraud constitutes moral turpitude justifying revocation of teaching certificate. *Startzel v. Commonwealth of Pennsylvania,* Department of Education, 128 Pa. Cmwlth. 110, 562 A.2d 1005 (1989).

3. *Criminal Conviction.* Guilt of criminal conduct may constitute immorality. A teacher was arrested and charged with two counts of harassment by communication or address. The teacher was convicted of making approximately 35 telephone calls to a board member in the early morning hours. These calls were related to a protracted labor dispute between the board and the teacher's union. The school board brought charges of immorality against the teacher because of the criminal conviction. The court said "guilty verdict of criminal conduct will support a finding of immorality." *Covert v. Bensalem Township School District,* 104 Pa. Cmwlth. 441, 522 A.2d 129 (1987).

State statutes, in a number of states, provide that teachers may be dismissed for "a felony or crime of moral turpitude." A felony is "[a] crime of a graver or more atrocious nature than those designated as misdemeanors . . . [g]enerally an offense punishable by death or imprisonment in the penitentiary." (*Black's Law Dictionary,* Fourth Edition, West Publishing Company, 744.)

A teacher was charged with theft, assault and battery, and fleeing a police officer; and as a result was dismissed from his teaching position. The court upheld his dismissal and stated, "it cannot be said that a teacher's conduct outside the classroom bears no reasonable relation to his qualifications for employment." *Gary Teachers Union, Local 4, American Federation of Teachers v. School City of Gary,* 165 Ind.App. 314, 332 N.E.2d 256 (1975).

Dismissal for unfitness is not necessarily dependent on criminal conviction. A school board may dismiss a teacher for arrest for a felony, even though the trial does not result in conviction. In a case where a teacher was charged with a criminal act of engaging in oral copulation with another man and was acquitted of criminal charges, the school board dismissed the teacher for immorality and unfitness. The state code provided for school boards to dismiss teachers for sex offenses. The court held for the board and said that it was the responsibility of the board to determine the fitness of the employee even if he had been acquitted of criminal charges. The key is whether the act is a detrimental influence on the pupils of the school. *Board of Education v. Calderon,* 35 Cal.App.3d 490, 110 Cal.Rptr. 916 (1973), cert. denied and appeal dismissed 414 U.S. 807, 95 S.Ct. 19 (1974).

4. *Misdemeanor.* Included in the area of criminal convictions is the dismissal of a teacher for a misdemeanor. Misdemeanors are "[o]ffenses lower than felonies and generally those punishable by a fine, penalty, forfeiture, or imprisonment otherwise than in [a] penitentiary." (*Black's Law Dictionary,* 1150.)

In a case where a tenured teacher was arrested and charged with "disturbing the peace by being under the influence of intoxicants, attempting to fight, and display of a gun," his dismissal was upheld for good and just cause and the board's action was held not to be arbitrary, irrational, or unreasonable. *Williams v. School District No.*

40 of Gila County, 4 Ariz.App. 5, 417 P.2d 376 (1966).

5. *Drugs.* Teachers, in recent years, have been dismissed for possession and use of controlled substances. Since state statutes usually do not specify dismissal for drugs, teachers who have been involved with drugs have been dismissed under statutory provisions of fitness to teach, moral turpitude, immorality, misdemeanor, and felony convictions, plus other good and sufficient cause.

Such an example was found in Georgia, where a tenured teacher was arrested for possession of cocaine, glutethimide, and marijuana and pleaded guilty to violating that state's Controlled Substances Act. Since it was a first offense, the teacher was placed on probation. Because of the publicity, she was transferred to two other teaching positions during the remainder of the year. Finally, the board dismissed her for "immorality" and "other good and sufficient cause" based on her guilty plea. The court said "the proven fact of the teacher's possession of three dangerous drugs is evidence from which 'immorality' may be inferred, even in the absence of criminal purpose or intent." *Dominy v. Mays,* 150 Ga.App. 187, 257 S.E.2d 317 (1979). A similar result was reached in *Chicago Board of Education v. Payne,* 102 Ill.App.3d 741, 58 Ill.Dec. 368, 430 N.E.2d 310 (1981).

6. *Good Cause.* Both common law and statute usually provide for dismissal of tenured teachers for "cause" or "good cause." Where statutes specify the causes for dismissal, a teacher cannot be dismissed for causes beyond those specified. *People v. Maxwell,* 177 N.Y. 494, 69 N.E. 1092 (1904); *School City of Elwood v. State ex rel. Griffin,* 203 Ind. 626, 180 N.E. 471 (1932). If, however, no causes are specified and the statute merely provides for dismissal for cause, then what constitutes cause is subject to broader interpretation. See Newton Edwards, *The Courts and The Public Schools* (Chicago: The University of Chicago Press, 1955), p. 481.

Financial problems of a school district may constitute "just cause" for dismissal. In an Iowa case, just cause was given as to the reason for release of a tenured teacher with 17 years of experience. The reasons given for just cause were budgetary considerations, declining enrollments, and need to make more efficient use of staff. In 1975 the district had 757 pupils, 506 in 1985, and projected enrollments of 440 to 461 by 1989. The decline in enrollment had caused a loss of state revenues. Also, evidence was submitted to the court showing that the district was overstaffed. The court upheld the dismissal based on just cause. *Pocahontas Community School District v. Levene,* 409 N.W.2d 698 (Iowa App. 1987).

Where a tenured teacher applied for and received sabbatical leave to pursue graduate work and continued his absence even though he was not admitted to graduate school, the court found the teacher breached his professional responsibilities and constituted "good cause" for dismissal. "Good cause" must be determined on the facts of each case. *Stansberry v. Argenbright,* 227 Mont. 123, 738 P.2d 478 (Mont. 1987). Too, "good cause" has been established supporting dismissal where a tenured teacher (1) cohabitated with a female teacher, (2) used a human fetus in the classroom when discussing abortion, (3) talked about abortion, and (4) spoke to his classes about his personal living arrangements. *Yanzick v. School District No. 23, Lake County, Montana,* 196 Mont. 375, 641 P.2d 431 (Mont. 1982).

Violation of school policy may constitute cause. Dismissal of a tenured teacher was upheld for violating a school policy, which stated that "the board of education does not encourage corporal punishment." Over a 4-year period the teacher had kicked a student, struck another in the face, knocked a female to the floor, and committed other similar acts. *Tomczik v. State Tenure Commission,* 175 Mich. App. 495, 438 N.W.2d 642 (1989).

Refusal to accede to school rules prohibiting teaching of religious beliefs in the classroom may constitute cause for dismissal. After a tenured teacher was warned numerous times to stop religious activities such as writing "God is truth and truth is God" on the blackboard, the board dismissed him. The teacher did not deny the allegations, and said he would not stop because "he was a Christian and that part of his mission was a sense of evangelism." His actions and refusal constituted grounds for dismissal. *Rhodes v. Laurel Highlands School District,* 118 Pa.Cmwlth. 119, 544 A.2d 562 (1988).

Cause for dismissal may also be supported for violation of policy prohibiting corporal punishment. In a case where a teacher grabbed a child and kneed him in the back, causing him to cry, and shoved another child to the floor, the court found sufficient cause. *Ortbals v. Special School District,* 762 S.W.2d 437 (Mo.App. 1988).

"Reasonable and just cause" for dismissal has been upheld where a tenured teacher was discharged for inviting two females from his driver's education class to a party where they drank beer and smoked marijuana. *Barcheski v. Board of Education of Grand Rapids Public Schools,* 162 Mich.App. 388, 412 N.W.2d 296 (1987).

■ REDUCTION IN FORCE

Some school districts have been faced with declining student enrollments and, as a result, there has been a necessary, corresponding reduction in the number of professional employees. Reductions in force may be brought about through enrollment declines, financial exigencies, reorganization, or the elimination of programs. Therefore, even a tenured teacher may be removed from the work force if justification is substantiated.

Local school boards may, within their discretion, establish a reduction in force policy, absent contractual obligations created by statutory or collective bargaining agreements. Such policy should consider (1) the necessity

of reduction in force, (2) the positions eliminated, (3) the bad faith actions of school boards, and (4) seniority.[12]

Reduction in Force Must Be in Good Faith and for Constitutional Reasons

-- - -- - -- - --

Zoll v. Eastern Allamakee Community School District

-- - -- - -- - --

United States Court of Appeals,
Eighth Circuit, 1978.
588 F.2d 246.

Action was brought by former school teacher for reinstatement and back pay following nonrenewal of her contract. The United States District Court for the Northern District of Iowa . . . entered judgment in favor of teacher against superintendent and elementary principal, and superintendent and principal appealed and teacher cross-appealed. The Court of Appeals . . . held that: (1) there was sufficient evidence of illicit motive for nonrenewal of teacher's contract to support jury verdict of liability; (2) no reversible error was committed in charging jury on elements of teacher's case, but (3) district court failed to comply with requisite guidelines for attorney fee awards and decided back pay claims against school district without benefit of the Supreme Court's recent *Monell* decision, which foreclosed absolute immunity for local governing bodies.

Mrs. Zoll holds a Masters Degree in Elementary Administration and is certified by the State of Iowa as both a teacher and an administrator. Prior to the nonrenewal of her contract, she had been employed as a first-grade teacher in Allamakee County for twenty-nine years. The last fifteen years of her teaching career were with the Eastern Allamakee Community School District which was organized after she began teaching. She was promoted to elementary school principal in the Eastern Allamakee Community School District but resigned after two years to devote her full time to teaching.

In September 1973, Mr. Harold Pronga succeeded Mrs. Zoll as the elementary school principal. In June and July 1974, Mrs. Zoll wrote two letters to the editor of a local newspaper sharply criticizing Mr. Pronga, School Superintendent Duane Fuhrman, and school board members Lawrence Protsman, Hugh Conway, James Mettille and Roy Renk for a decline in administrative concern with academic excellence.

Mrs. Zoll complained that athletics were stressed over academics in the high school and that the quality of the elementary school was also in jeopardy. Her fears were based in part upon Mr. Pronga's refusal to authorize her requisition for work books and his suggestion that Mrs. Zoll teach her students to play "Fish" and "Concentration."

In August, 1974, on her second day at school following the summer vacation, Mrs. Zoll was summoned to Mr. Pronga's office to discuss the letters. Mr. Pronga had informed Superintendent Fuhrman of the planned meeting. At the outset of their discussion, Mr. Pronga read to Mrs. Zoll from his prepared notes: "I am very concerned and equally puzzled by your letters to the editor." Mr. Pronga accused Mrs. Zoll of misrepresenting facts and chastised her for failing to express her feelings through proper channels.

In December 1974, the school board followed the suggestion of the Iowa Department of Public Instruction in adopting a contingency plan for staff reduction in the event of a decline in enrollment. The plan included rules for determining the pool of teachers from which layoffs would be made. Selection from the pool would be by a 100-point system. A maximum of 40 points could be awarded for experience and training. The principal, superintendent and school board could award up to 20 points each, based on their subjective evaluations.

At the February 1975 school board meeting, the board was informed of a projected enrollment decline of first-grade students for the 1975–76 school year which would war-

rant a staff reduction. The board treated as a pool from which a lay-off would be made the three first-grade teachers: Mrs. Zoll, Mrs. Rebecca Okerlund and Mrs. Jane Meyer. The official decision of which teacher to terminate was postponed until the March board meeting. Mrs. Zoll was advised by a colleague of the school board president that the decision to terminate her was actually made at the closed executive session of the February board meeting.

Out of the potential 100 points, Mrs. Zoll received 57, Mrs. Okerlund 62½, and Mrs. Meyer 72. Mrs. Zoll was erroneously awarded 17 points for experience, although she was entitled to 20 points under the objective scale. Thus, she was actually awarded 54 points, although entitled to 57 points. Mrs. Zoll received the highest point totals on the objective evaluation of experience and training. Out of a possible 40 points, Mrs. Zoll received 40, Mrs. Okerlund 4½ and Mrs. Meyer 16. Mrs. Zoll received the lowest point totals on the subjective evaluations by Mr. Pronga, Mr. Fuhrman and the school board. Out of a possible 60 points, Mrs. Zoll received 17, Mrs. Okerlund 58, and Mrs. Meyer 56.

On April 8, 1975, the school board notified Mrs. Zoll that her contract would not be renewed for the 1975–76 school year. A public hearing was convened by the school board at Mrs. Zoll's request on June 9, 1975, pursuant to Iowa Code § 279.13 (1975). At the conclusion of the hearing, the board voted four to one not to renew her contract.

On December 15, 1975, Mrs. Zoll filed suit against Mr. Pronga, Mr. Fuhrman, and the four board members who voted not to renew her contract, alleging that they had refused to renew her teaching contract in retaliation for her exercise of First Amendment rights in violation of 42 U.S.C. § 1983 (1970). . . .

There is sufficient evidence of a retaliatory motive for the nonrenewal of Mrs. Zoll's contract to support the jury verdict. Mrs. Zoll's letters to the editor criticizing the school administration were published in the summer of 1974. On the second day of the 1974–75 school year, Mr. Pronga called Mrs. Zoll to his office to express his displeasure with the letters. Mr. Fuhrman had foreknowledge of the meeting. There was testimony that the decision to terminate Mrs. Zoll was made before the statistical evaluation. Mrs. Zoll's expert witness testified to inconsistencies between the points assigned Mrs. Zoll and the notes and testimony of Mr. Pronga and Mr. Fuhrman.

Under the staff reduction policy which the board had adopted in December 1974, teachers laid off pursuant to the policy were granted certain "recall rights" for a three-year period: "Any staff member laid off due to reduction of staff policy may be recalled if a vacancy exists within three years." Three vacancies arose during the year following Mrs. Zoll's termination. The vacancies were at the first grade, sixth grade and seventh-eighth grade levels. Mrs. Zoll applied for but was not offered any of these positions. Instead, two new teachers were hired and one teacher was transferred to fill the vacancies. The jury could reasonably have believed that the subjective rating of Mrs. Zoll by Mr. Pronga and Mr. Fuhrman was a pretext for discharging her for exercising her First Amendment rights. See *Mt. Healthy City Board of Education v. Doyle,* 429 U.S. 274, 97 S.Ct. 568, 50 L.Ed.2d 471 (1977). . . .

Accordingly, we affirm the entry of judgment of liability on the jury verdict, vacate the attorney's fee award and remand to the district court for reconsideration of the post-trial back pay issue and the attorney's fee award and for further proceedings consistent with this opinion.

Affirmed in part, vacated and remanded in part.

NOTE

1. A tenured teacher may have "bumping" rights in time of fiscal stress. A Montana court has held that a high school principal with tenure had the right to bump an untenured teacher in a subject matter area in which he was certified to teach. *Holmes v. Board of Trustees of School District Nos. 4, 47 and 2,* 243 Mont. 263, 792 P.2d 10 (1990).

■ CONSTITUTIONAL PROTECTION OF CONTRACTS

Both state[13] and federal[14] constitutions contain protections against unilateral alteration of contracts by the state to disadvantage individuals in their relationships with the government. Basically, these provisions ensure the citizen that the state will not modify or abolish a contract to which it is a party.

An inherent conflict, however, exists between the guaranteed sanctity of contracts and the police power of the state in subsequent legislatures to make and change laws in the interest of the common good. A legislature cannot be completely bound and restricted by agreements made by earlier legislatures. Thus, the constraints placed on legislatures by the contract provision of the state or federal constitutions must necessarily be hedged to allow for government to function freely. The U.S. Supreme Court has declared that

> it is settled that neither the "contract" clause nor the "due process" clause has the effect of overriding the power of the State to establish all regulations that are reasonably necessary to secure the health, safety, good order, comfort, or general welfare of the community; that this power can neither be abdicated nor bargained away, and is inalienable even by express grant; and all contract and property rights are held subject to its fair exercise.[15]

Whether the individual's right to a contract prevails over the state's interest in modifying the agreement is dependent on at least three conditions. First, an agreement between an individual and the state must be clearly a "contract" before it invokes the obligation of contract protection. It cannot be simply a privilege bestowed by the state or some other relationship defined as something other than a contract. Second, the rights under a contract are determined by the laws existing at the time that the contract was made.[16] Third, where, on balance, the interests of the state in modifying or abrogating the contract are sufficiently weighty and compelling, the interest of the individual must give way to the common and general interest of all the people.

The burden of proof is on the individual to show that a particular relationship with the state is in fact a contract. The Supreme Court of the United States in *Dodge v. Board of Education*[17] defined the conditions necessary for a statute to be regarded as a contract.

In determining whether a law tenders a contract to a citizen it is of first importance to examine the language of the statute. If it provides for the execution of a written contract on behalf of the state the case for an obligation binding upon the state is clear. . . . On the other hand, an act merely fixing salaries of officers creates no contract in their favor and the compensation named may be altered at will by the legislature. This is true also of an act fixing the term or tenure of a public officer or an employee of a state agency. The presumption is that such a law is not intended to create private contractual or vested rights but merely declares a policy to be pursued until the legislature shall ordain otherwise. He who asserts the creation of a contract with the state in such a case has the burden of overcoming the presumption.

The most important precedent rendered by the Supreme Court defining the extent of governmental prerogative with regard to contracts was the famous *Dartmouth College* case,[18] which gave form and substance to Art. I, § 10 of the Obligation of Contracts provision of the U.S. Constitution. That article states: "No State Shall . . . pass any law . . . impairing the Obligation of Contracts, . . . "

In *Dartmouth College*, the English crown had granted a charter to the college, which had been established in the colony of New Hampshire as a private institution.[19] The college was governed by a self-perpetuating board of twelve members. A conflict that had political ramifications developed between the college president and the board members. Reacting to this controversy, the legislature of New Hampshire, in 1816, enacted legislation that materially altered the charter, making the college a state institution. The college trustees brought an action and claimed, in part, that the act of the legislature was unconstitutional and impaired the obligation of their contract, the original charter. The opinion of the Court, delivered by Justice Marshall, stated:

The points for consideration are: 1. Is this contract protected by the Constitution of the United States? 2. Is it impaired by the acts under which the defendant holds?

1. On the first point, it has been argued, that the word "contract" in its broadest sense would comprehend the political relations between the government and its citizens, would extend to offices held within a state, for state purposes, and to many of those laws concerning civil institutions, which must change with circumstances, and be modified by ordinary legislation; which deeply concern the public, and which, to preserve good government, the public judgment must control . . . .

This (charter) is plainly a contract to which the donors, the trustees and the crown (to whose rights and obligation New Hampshire succeeds) were the original parties. It is a contract made on a valuable consideration. It is a contract for the security and disposition of property. It is a contract, on the faith of which, real and personal estate has been conveyed to the corporation. It is, then, a contract within the letter of the Constitution, and within its spirit also unless the fact that the property is invested by the donors in trustees, for the promotion of religion and education, for the benefit of persons who are perpetually changing, though the objects remain the same, shall create a particular exception, taking this case out of the prohibition contained in the Constitution. . . .

The opinion of the court, after mature deliberation, is, that this is a contract, the obligation of which cannot be impaired, without violating the Constitution of the United States. This opinion appears to us to be equally supported by reason, and by the former decisions of this court.

2. We next proceed to the inquiry, whether its obligation has been impaired by those acts of the legislature of New Hampshire, to which the special verdict refers?

From the review of this charter, which has been taken, it appears that the whole power of governing the college, of appointing and removing tutors, of fixing salaries, of directing the course of study to be pursued by the students, and of filling up vacancies created in their own body, was vested in the trustees. On the part of the crown it was expressly stipulated, that this corporation, thus constituted, should continue forever; and that the number of trustees should forever consist of twelve, and no more. By this contract the crown was bound, and could have made no violent alteration in its essential terms, without impairing its obligation.

By the Revolution the duties, as well as the powers, of government devolved on the people of New Hampshire. It is admitted, that among the latter was comprehended the transcendent power of parliament, as well as that of the executive department. It is too clear, to require the support of argument, that all contracts and rights respecting property, remained unchanged by the Revolution. The obligations, then, which were created by the charter to Dartmouth College, were the same in the new, that they had been in the old government. . . . But the Constitution of the United States has imposed this additional limitation, that the legislature of a state shall pass no act "impairing the obligation of contracts." . . . .

It results from this opinion, that the acts of the legislature of New Hampshire, which are stated in the special verdict found in this cause, are repugnant to the Constitution of the United States; and that the judgment on this special verdict ought to have been for the plaintiffs. The judgment of the state court must, therefore, be reversed.

Later, in an Indiana case, Art. I, § 10 of the Constitution of the United States was directly applied as a limitation on state legislative actions pertaining to public education. The Indiana legislature passed an act that repealed a 1927 law granting tenure to teachers and a teacher thereafter sought a *writ of mandamus* to compel her continued employment. She claimed the original act had granted her a continuing contract that could not be impaired nor breached by subsequent legislation. The original act provided:

It is further agreed by the contracting parties that all of the Teachers' Tenure Law, approved March 8, 1927, shall be in full force and effect in this contract.

The Supreme Court of Indiana ruled in favor of the defendant board of education, and the teacher appealed. The Supreme Court of the United States reversed the Indiana Court.[20]

Both of these decisions illustrate the constitutional requirements within which a state legislature must operate when dealing with contracts. Particular application may be noted where legislation such as tenure and retirement statutes may create a contract between the state and an individual.

There is a fine line between the constitutional rights of one individual and the rights of the people as exercised through the elected authority of the legislature to provide for the welfare of the state. This is demonstrated by the dissent of Justice Black in the *Anderson v. Brand* case, when he said that the Supreme Court should not interfere with the determination of educational policy by the Indiana legislature, because the legislature of a state cannot make and be held to a contract "with a few citizens, that would take from all the citizens, the continuing power to alter the educational policy for the best interests of Indiana school children . . . ."

Tenure Contracts between the State and Teacher Cannot Be Unilaterally Cancelled by the State

—‒—·—·—‒—‒—

State of Indiana Ex Rel. Anderson v. Brand

—‒—·—·—‒—‒—

Supreme Court of the United States, 1938.
303 U.S. 95, 58 S.Ct. 443.

Mr. Justice ROBERTS delivered the opinion of the Court. The petitioner sought a writ of mandate to compel the respondent to continue her in employment as a public school teacher. Her complaint alleged that as a duly licensed teacher she entered into a contract in September, 1924, to teach in the township schools and, pursuant to successive contracts, taught continuously to and including the school year 1932–1933; that her contracts for the school years 1931–1932 and 1932–1933 contained this clause: "It is further agreed by the contracting parties that all of the provisions of the Teachers' Tenure Law, approved March 8, 1927, shall be in full force and effect in this contract"; and that by force of that act she had a contract, indefinite in duration, which could be canceled by the respondent only in the manner and for the causes specified in the act. She charged that in July, 1933, the respondent notified her he proposed to cancel her contract for cause; that, after a hearing, he adhered to his decision and the county superintendent affirmed his action; that, despite what occurred in July, 1933, the petitioner was permitted to teach during the school year 1933–1934 and the respondent was presently threatening to terminate her employment at the end of that year. The complaint alleged the termination of her employment would be a breach of her contract with the school corporation. The respondent demurred on the grounds that (1) the complaint disclosed the matters pleaded had been submitted to the respondent and the county superintendent who were authorized to try the issues and had lawfully determined them in favor of the respondent; and (2) the Teachers' Tenure Law, Acts Ind.1927, c. 97, had been repealed in respect of teachers in township schools. The demurrer was sustained and the petitioner appealed to the state Supreme Court which affirmed the judgment. The court did not discuss the first ground of demurrer relating to the action taken in the school year 1932–1933, but rested its decision upon the second, that, by an act of 1933, Acts Ind.1933, c. 116, the Teachers' Tenure Law had been repealed as respects teachers in township schools; and held that the repeal did not deprive the petitioner of a vested property right and did not impair her contract within the meaning of the Constitution. . . .

As in most cases brought to this court under the contract clause of the Constitution, the question is as to the existence and nature of the contract and not as to the construction of the law which is supposed to impair it. The principal function of a legislative body is not to make contracts but to make laws which declare the policy of the state and are subject to repeal when a subsequent Legislature shall determine to alter that policy. Nevertheless, it is established that a legislative enactment may contain provisions which, when accepted as the basis of action by individuals, become contracts between them and the State or its subdivisions within the protection of article 1, § 10. If the people's representatives deem it in the public interest they may adopt a policy of contracting in respect of public business for a term longer than the life of the current session of the Legislature. This the petitioner claims has been done with respect to permanent teachers. . . .

The courts of Indiana have long recognized that the employment of school teachers was contractual and have afforded relief in actions upon teachers' contracts. An act adopted in 1899 required all contracts between teachers and school corporations to be in writing, signed by the parties to be charged, and to be made a matter of public record. A statute of 1921 enacted that every such contract should be in writing and should state the date of the beginning of the school term, the number of months therein, the amount of the salary for the term, and the number of payments to be made during the school year.

In 1927 the State adopted the Teachers' Tenure Act under which the present controversy arises. . . . By this act it was provided that a teacher who has served under contract for five or more successive years, and thereafter enters into a contract for further service with the school corporation, shall become a permanent teacher and the contract, upon the expiration of its stated term, shall be deemed to continue in effect for an indefinite period, shall be known as an indefinite contract, and shall remain in force unless succeeded by a new contract or canceled as provided in the act. The corporation may cancel the contract, after notice and hearing, for incompetency, insubordination, neglect of duty, immorality, justifiable decrease in the number of teaching positions, or other good or just cause, but not for political or personal reasons. The teacher may not cancel the contract during the school term nor for a period thirty days previous to the beginning of any term (unless by mutual agreement) and may cancel only upon five days' notice.

By an amendatory act of 1933 township school corporations were omitted from the provisions of the act of 1927. The court below construed this act as repealing the act of 1927 so far as township schools and teachers are concerned and as leaving the respondent free to terminate the petitioner's employment. But we are of the opinion that the petitioner had a valid contract with the respondent, the obligation of which would be impaired by the termination of her employment.

Where the claim is that the state's policy embodied in a statute is to bind its instrumentalities by contract, the cardinal inquiry is as to the terms of the statute supposed to create such a contract. The State long prior to the adoption of the act of 1927 required the execution of written contracts between teachers and school corporations, specified certain subjects with which such contracts must deal, and required that they be made a matter of public record. These were annual contracts, covering a single school term. The act of 1927 announced a new policy that a teacher who had served for five years under successive contracts, upon the execution of another was to become a permanent teacher and the last contract was to be indefinite as to duration and terminable by either party only upon compliance with the conditions set out in the statute. The policy which induced the legislation evidently was that the teacher should have protection against the exercise of the right, which would otherwise inhere in the employer, of terminating the employment at the end of any school term without assigned reasons and solely at the employer's pleasure. The state courts in earlier cases so declared.

The title of the act is couched in terms of contract. It speaks of the making and canceling of indefinite contracts. In the body the word "contract" appears ten times in section 1, defining the relationship; eleven times in section 2, relating to the termination of the employment by the employer; and four times in section 4, stating the conditions of termination by the teacher.

The tenor of the act indicates that the word "contract" was not used inadvertently or in other than its usual legal meaning. By section 6 it is expressly provided that the act is a supplement to that of March 7, 1921, supra, requiring teachers' employment contracts to be in writing. By section 1 it is provided that the written contract of a permanent teacher "shall be deemed to continue in effect for an indefinite period and shall be known as an indefinite contract." Such an indefinite contract is to remain in force unless succeeded by a new contract signed by both parties or canceled as provided in section 2. No more apt language could be employed to define a contractual relationship. By section 2 it is enacted that such indefinite contracts may be canceled by the school corporation only in the manner specified. The admissible grounds of cancellation, and the method by which the existence of such grounds shall be ascertained and made a matter of record, are carefully set out. Section 4 permits cancellation by the teacher only at certain times consistent with the convenient administration of the school system and imposes a sanction for violation of its requirements. Examination of the entire act convinces us that the teacher was by it assured of the possession of a binding and enforceable contract against school districts.   . . .

Our decisions recognize that every contract is made subject to the implied condition that its fulfillment may be frustrated by a proper exercise of the police power but we have repeatedly said that, in order to have this effect, the exercise of the power must be for an end which is in fact public and the means adopted must be reasonably adapted to that end, and the Supreme Court of Indiana has taken the same view in respect of legislation impairing the obligation of the contract of a state instrumentality. The causes of cancellation provided in the act of 1927 and the retention of the system of indefinite contracts in all municipalities except townships by the act of 1933 are persuasive that the repeal of the earlier act by the later was not an exercise of the police power for the attainment of ends to which its exercise may properly be directed.

As the court below has not passed upon one of the grounds of demurrer which appears to involve no federal question, and may present a defense still open to the respondent, we reverse the judgment and remand the cause for further proceedings not inconsistent with this opinion.

So ordered.

Constitutional Prohibition against Impairment of Contracts Is Not Violated by Additional Test Requirement for Retention of Teaching Certificate

_ _ _ . _ . _ . _ _ . _

State v. Project Principle, Inc.

_ _ _ . _ . _ . _ _ . _

Supreme Court of Texas, 1987.
724 S.W.2d 387.

CAMPBELL, Justice. This is a direct appeal from a temporary injunction prohibiting enforcement of Tex.Educ.Code § 13.047 (Vernon Supp.1987) on the ground that the statute is unconstitutional. Section 13.047 provides that public school educators, to retain their teaching certificates, must successfully complete an examination known as the Texas Examination for Current Administrators and Teachers, or TECAT. We hold the statute is constitutional and we reverse the judgment of the trial court and dissolve that court's injunction.   . . .

On July 3, 1984, the state legislature passed into law House Bill 72. The bill contained numerous educational reforms, including additional school funding, school finance reform, teacher salary increases, and teacher competency testing.   . . .

Section 13.047 provides for a testing program by the State Board of Education for continued certification of all educators who have not taken the test required by section 13.032(e) of the Code. However, the section 13.032(e) test was first administered on May 24, 1986; thus, all previously certified teachers, including all members of Project Principle, were required to take the TECAT.   . . .

The state argues that the trial court's injunction is in error because section 13.047 impairs no contract rights. Project Principle contends that teaching certificates are contracts with which the legislature may not interfere. We hold that a teaching certificate is not a contract within the meaning of article I, section 16. Rather, the certificate is a license, and like all licenses, is subject to such future restrictions as the state may reasonably impose.

The United States Supreme Court spoke to the impairment of contracts argument more than forty years ago in *Dodge v. Board of Education*, 302 U.S. 74, 79, 58 S.Ct. 98, 100, 82 L.Ed. 57 (1937). In *Dodge*, retired teachers challenged an act of the Illinois legislature which decreased the amounts of annuity payments to retired teachers of Chicago public schools. The teachers claimed that the Act impaired the obligation of contracts in contravention of article I, § 10 of the United States Constitution. The Supreme Court of Illinois held that in passing the statute providing for the annuities the state legislature evinced no intent to create a binding contract with teachers. The United States Supreme Court affirmed, stating "the presumption is that (a tenure) law is not intended to create private contractual or vested rights but merely declares a policy to be pursued until the legislature shall ordain otherwise."

As early as 1925 it was recognized in Texas that a teaching certificate is a license. In *Marrs v. Matthews*, 270 S.W. 586 (Tex.Civ.App.—Texarkana 1925, writ ref'd), a teacher claimed that the state superintendent could not cancel his "permanent teacher's certificate" because the language used in describing the offenses for which a certificate may be cancelled was void for vagueness. The teacher also claimed that the statute giving the superintendent the authority to cancel the certificate of any "unworthy" teacher was an attempt to confer judicial powers upon an executive department of the state government. In dissolving the trial court writ enjoining cancellation of the teaching certificate, the court stated that a teaching certificate "is merely a license granted by the state, and is revocable by the state." The court noted that the teacher had "voluntarily sought and secured a statutory privilege to be enjoyed subject to statutory conditions."

Because we hold a teaching certificate is not a contract, the constitutional prohibition against impairment of contracts is not violated when the legislature imposes new conditions for the retention of the certificate. Further, because the certificate is a license and confers no vested rights, the constitutional prohibition against retroactive laws is not violated. It is only when vested rights are impaired that a retroactive law is invalid. . . .

The state contends the trial court's injunction is in error because section 13.047 does not violate due process guarantees. Project Principle contends the statute violates federal and state guarantees of due process. . . . Project Principle argues that after the enactment of section 13.047, educators' certificates are subject to cancellation without a hearing or avenue for appeal upon failure to take the TECAT or to perform satisfactorily on the TECAT.

First, it must be noted that decertification is not automatic upon failure of the examination. Section 13.047 provides that "each teacher must be given more than one opportunity to perform satisfactorily" on the TECAT.

Second, provisions for appeal of "proceedings concerning the suspension, revocation, or cancellation of a (teaching) certificate" are contained in 19 Tex.Admin.Code § 157.1(b)(4) (1985). . . . This review provides procedural due process to any teacher who fails to perform satisfactorily on a competency examination. . . .

. . . Project Principle argues that the classification of teachers into a class composed of those who pass the test and a class composed of those who fail the test is subject to strict scrutiny under equal protection analysis. Strict scrutiny is applicable, Project Principle argues, because the classification impinges upon a fundamental right, the right to practice a profession.

. . . Likewise, we hold a person's interest in teaching is not a fundamental right.

The right to teach not being fundamental, a classification which impinges on that right is not subject to strict scrutiny. . . . Rather, the TECAT must be judged by a rational basis standard. We hold that competency testing bears a rational relation to the legitimate state objective of maintaining competent teachers in the public schools. . . .

We reverse the judgment of the trial court and dissolve that court's injunction.

■ SCOPE OF TEACHER'S DUTIES

Teachers are called upon to perform many duties outside the classroom. These may include supervision of athletic events and field excursions, selling of tickets at student activities, loading of school buses, and other related nonacademic duties too numerous to mention.

The court cases on this subject indicate that a teacher may be required to perform tasks incidental to regular classroom work. Teachers cannot be required to render such services as janitorial duties, traffic duty, school bus driving, and similar activities not coming within the implied duties of a teacher's contract. All such common-law legal principles can be altered, of course, by a collective bargaining contract.

Assignment of Teacher to Supervise Athletic Events of School Is Not Unreasonable and Is Within Scope of Teaching Duties

—·—·—·—·—·—

McGrath v. Burkhard

—·—·—·—·—·—

California District Court of Appeal,
Third District, 1955.
131 Cal.App.2d 367, 280 P.2d 864.

SCHOTTKY, Justice. Plaintiff, a teacher in the Sacramento Senior High School, commenced an action for declaratory relief against defendant Superintendent of Sacramento City Unified School District, the Board of Education of said district and the individual members of said board, and the principal of the Sacramento Senior High School. Plaintiff sought declaratory relief on the ground that the non-classroom assignments, as hereinafter detailed, did not fall within the scope of his duties as a teacher under the terms of his contract of employment, and that such duties were unprofessional in nature. Plaintiff asked the court to declare the rights and duties under the contract of employment; that the non-classroom work was not within the scope of employment; that plaintiff should not be assigned duties on a teaching day which required more than eight hours per day to perform competently; that if more than eight hours may be assigned the court should declare the number of hours per day plaintiff is obligated to perform under the contract; that no duties be assigned on days for which he is not paid, i.e., Saturdays, holidays and most non-teaching days. . . . Before discussing the contentions made by plaintiff and appellant we shall summarize the factual situation which is not in substantial dispute.

Appellant is a teacher in the Sacramento Senior High School. From 1942 to 1945 he was employed as a long term substitute teacher; from July, 1945, to July, 1948, he was employed as a probationary teacher and from July, 1948, to the date of this action he was employed as a permanent teacher. He achieved the status of tenure in 1948.

At all times appellant has been employed under a written contract, which incorporates the rules of the respondent Board of Education.

During his course of employment by respondents, appellant and other male teachers have been required to attend certain non-classroom activities and act in a supervisory capacity. The activities are school football and basketball games, which are under the auspices and control of the school authorities. These games may be held at places other than on the school grounds. Six of these athletic assignments are made to each male member of the faculty during each school year, three football games and three basketball games. At the beginning of the school year each male teacher selects the three football games at which he would prefer to supervise; at the end of such season he then selects the three basketball games at which he would prefer to

attend in a supervisory capacity. To the extent possible the requests of the teachers are complied with in the scheduling of these assignments, but at times a teacher receives an assignment on a date other than the one he had selected. The teachers are selected impartially and without discrimination. For many years past this administrative practice of assigning the male teachers to supervise at the school athletic contests in football and basketball has been carried out to protect the welfare of the students. The teachers have no authority to act as police officers, but policemen are present at the games to handle any situation in which their authority is needed. Appellant testified that the teacher's duties at these games consisted of maintaining order in the student section of the stands . . . controlling conduct of the students, preventing smoking in the gymnasium by students or adults and preventing spectators from entering the gymnasium with soft drinks, candy or other food. The female teachers of the school are given assignments to supervision of non-classroom activities, but of a different nature, as supervising in the cafeteria, variety shows and dances. . . .

Appellant first contends that he is under no contractual obligation in regard to the athletic assignments and that if so obligated, the required duties are unreasonable and not within the scope of teaching duties. He states that such obligation is nowhere set forth in the contract, the rules of the Board of Education, nor in the laws of the state of California. While it is true that this specific duty is not set forth, a study of the evidence and the provisions set forth in the Education Code and the Administrative Code reveals that the assignment complained of by appellant is and was within the contemplation of the parties when the contract of employment was entered into. Relevant portions of each are set out below:

Education Code, section 2204. The governing board of any school district shall: (a) Prescribe and enforce rules not inconsistent with law or with the rules prescribed by the State Board of Education, for its own government, and for the government of the schools under its jurisdiction.

Education Code, section 13201. The governing board of each school district shall fix and prescribe the duties to be performed by all persons in public school service in the school district.

These sections provide for the delegation of rule making authority, so that the correct body can prescribe exactly what the duties are. In connection with this, certain rules promulgated by the State Board of Education must be considered. The following excerpts are taken from the California Administrative Code, Title 5, Article 3, which is entitled "Duties of Principals and Teachers."

Section 16. Responsibility of Principal. The principal is responsible for the supervision and administration of his school.

Section 18. Playground supervision. Where playground supervision is not otherwise provided, the principal of each school shall provide for the supervision, by teachers, of the conduct and direction of the play of the pupils of the school or on the school grounds during recesses and other intermissions and before and after school. All athletic or social activities, wherever held, when conducted under the name or auspices of any public school, or any class or organization thereof, shall be under the direct supervision of the authorities of the district.

. . . These provisions relate to all teachers in the public school system. Of course, the State Board of Education has expressed other duties which are required of teachers, as shown in the above excerpts from the Administrative Code. The local governing board has power delegated to it to make the necessary rules and regulations which its district requires. Ed. Code, secs. 2204, 13201. And finally, the principal has the necessary power which is inherent in his office to properly administer and supervise his school.

Appellant's contract expressly set forth that it was subject to the laws of California, the rules of the State Board of Education and of the local governing board. The trial court found that the rule of the Sacramento City Unified School District with reference to the athletic assignments was a part of appellant's contract. The code provisions relating to the

duties of teachers do not set forth the particular duty which is the subject of this controversy. The rules promulgated by the State Board of Education do not set forth such specific duty. However, the rules in Article 3 of Title 5 of the Administrative Code do show that the principals and teachers are charged with certain duties . . . .

Appellant . . . asserts that the trial court should be reversed since the duties at the athletic contests were (1) in the nature of police work, (2) unprofessional, (3) foreign to the field of instruction, and (4) imposed unreasonable hours, and therefore were not within the scope of the teaching duties required by the contract. However, the record does not sustain appellant's contention in this regard. The teachers have no authority to act as police officers; in fact, they are expressly informed that their duties are supervisory only. At no time is a teacher to exert police powers. The teachers are to act in a supervisory capacity, much as they do at school assembly meetings, etc. They are acting to protect the welfare of the students. Appellant asserts that he has received no training for this type of work and that the evidence suggests, since women are not assigned this type of duty, that physical strength is a requisite and that the motivating reason for the assignments is to quell and put down disturbances, which is in the nature of police duty. The record refutes appellant's statement. From the deposition of Dr. Murphy, the principal at Sacramento Senior High School, it appears that he was asked questions directly on this point and he replied that the duties did not relate to physical strength or power . . . . Appellant states that the duties were degrading, humiliating and unprofessional. Certain instances are cited. Dr. Murphy admitted that the duty was disagreeable to some, but he felt that it was the same with some women with the cafeteria assignments, or with anyone when they have to perform a task which they do not like, and apparently this is especially so with some teachers when they are faced with these types of supervisory duties. All public school teachers have general duties as expressed by the Education Code, sections 13228, 13229 and 13230, supra, relating to the control of the conduct of pupils, endorsement of rules and the training of them to be good American citizens. Coupled with these are the rules of the State Board of Education in Article 3 of Title 5 of the Administrative Code, which relate to certain duties, and section 24 in particular, quoted supra, which requires principals and teachers to exercise careful supervision of moral conditions in the schools and not to tolerate participation by students in gambling, profanity, the use of intoxicating liquors, etc., on or off the schoolgrounds. Teachers are expected to perform these obligations. It is of great importance that the association of teacher and pupil should tend to inculcate in the latter principles of justice, fair-play, good sportsmanship, good citizenship and respect for rules and authority. Viewing the duties at the games in light of the above, it is apparent that they are not of an unprofessional nature. For as stated in the case of *Parrish v. Moss,* so strongly relied upon by appellant, "The day in which the concept was held that teaching duty was limited to classroom instruction has long since passed."

Appellant's final contention is that the duties here involved impose unreasonable hours. The record shows that six of these assignments are made in a school year from September to the following June. Generally, the hours are evening ones, from about six or seven o'clock to ten o'clock. Some assignments fall on Saturday evenings or on Thanksgiving Day. Appellant also claims that the Saturday or legal holiday on which an assignment occasionally occurs is a day of duty for which he is not paid. However, appellant is not paid on a basis of so much per hour worked. Teachers are engaged in a professional employment. Their salaries and hours of employment are fixed with due regard to their professional status and are not fixed upon the same basis as those of day laborers. The worth of a teacher is not measured in terms of a specific sum of money per hour. A teacher expects to and does perform a service. If that service from time to time requires additional hours of work, a teacher expects to and does perform it. If that service from time to time

requires additional hours of work, a teacher expects to and does put in the extra hours, without thought of measuring his or her compensation in terms of a given sum of money per hour. A teacher's duties and obligations to students and the community are not satisfied by closing the classroom door at the conclusion of a class. The direction and supervision of extracurricular activities are an important part of his duties. All of his duties are taken into consideration in his contract for employment at the annual salary. All of this is, of course, subject to the test of reasonableness. It does not appear that six of these athletic assignments in an entire school year are unreasonable, nor that the hours of such assignments are unreasonable, under the circumstances. What is reasonable must necessarily depend upon the facts of the situation and the teachers are protected in that regard by the appropriate administrative and judicial procedure. Supervising the students and being present to protect their welfare at school athletic and social activities, conducted under the name and auspices of the school, is within the scope of the contract and such assignments are proper so long as they are distributed impartially, they are reasonable in number and hours of duty and each teacher has his share of such duty.   . . .

We believe that respondent school authorities had the right under the law and the contract with appellant to assign appellant to attend and assist in supervising these athletic contests. We believe that the presence of teachers at such contests should be helpful not only to the students but should be of benefit to the teachers themselves. We believe that the school authorities had the right to determine that such duties should be performed by the teachers assigned thereto. As stated by the learned trial judge in his memorandum opinion, "Have the parents not the right to expect, and, indeed, to demand, that all such school activities be under the supervision of the school authorities? If not, then who is to be in control? The answers to these questions seem obvious."   . . .

The judgment is affirmed.

NOTES

1. In the case of *Parrish v. Moss,* 200 Misc. 375, 160 N.Y.S.2d 577 (1951), New York teachers contested the right of a school board to assign incidental duties. The court held that teachers could be assigned only those duties related to their respective subject fields. English teachers could be required to coach plays and assist debate teams; band leaders would have to go with the band on field excursions; and physical education instructors could be required to coach intramural and interschool athletic teams.

2. A school board may assign reasonable nonacademic duties to teachers. An Illinois court has stated: "it has been held that school authorities may assign teachers to supervise non-academic school activities outside of school hours. As long as such assignments are reasonably related to teaching duties and not unduly time-consuming or burdensome, school authorities may, in the exercise of their sound discretion, require teachers to perform them . . . . . A broad spectrum of implied incidental powers is to be inferred from the general power of boards of education to adopt all necessary rules for the management and government of the schools." *Littrell v. Board of Education, etc.,* 45 Ill.App.3d 690, 4 Ill.Dec. 355, 360 N.E.2d 102 (1977).

3. A school board has broad powers in assignment of teachers' duties. Incidental to the board's powers is the right to assign non-classroom duties. Teaching duties are not solely confined to the classroom, and additional responsibilities may be properly imposed so long as they are within the scope of the license held by the teacher. Extra duty requirements do not need to be specified in school board rules in order to be valid. Courts generally maintain that duties that are not onerous, demeaning, unusually time-consuming, or assigned in a discriminatory manner may be assigned even though the teacher considers them an inconvenience. *Thomas v. Board of Education*

   of Community Unit School District, 117 Ill.App.3d 374, 72 Ill. Dec. 845, 453 N.E.2d 150 (1983).

4. The Supreme Court of Iowa, citing *McGrath v. Burkhard,* supra, upheld the reassignment of a school principal to extra duties. An elementary school principal who administered two small elementary schools was given the assignment of coordinator of the outdoor educational program and attendance officer. The reason for the reassignment was that one of his small schools was closed because of declining enrollment. The court found the assignment to be within the school board's discretion. "The assignments objected to do not appear to have been onerous in nature or unreasonably time consuming and are not demeaning to the professional status . . . ." *Gere v. Council Bluffs Community School District,* 334 N.W.2d 307 (Iowa 1983).

5. Guidance counselors may also be assigned extra duties. In a case in which a counselor refused to supervise the school campus before school began each day and also refused to obey other directives from the assistant principal, the court upheld dismissal, observing that the major issue for dismissal was the failure to supervise the students, and when placed in concert with the other acts, "[t]here is sufficient evidence in the record to support his dismissal." *Jones v. Alabama State Tenure Commission,* 408 So.2d 145 (Ala. Cir. App. 1981).

6. A school board cannot justify reassignment of librarians and guidance counselors to substitute teaching positions if a genuine financial emergency does not exist. In examining the evidence, the court found that one guidance counselor had been assigned to a substitute teaching position for 5 of the past 6 years. This and other evidence indicated that the fiscal plight was not "truly extraordinary," and reassignment could not be justified on that basis. *Randolph County Board of Education v. Scalia,* 387 S.E. 2d 524 (W.V. 1989).

7. Supervisory responsibilities such as hall duty are within the scope of the normal

educational process. *Lockhart v. Board of Education of Arapahoe County School District No. 6*, 735 P.2d 913 (Colo.App. 1986).

8. A school district may require teachers to obtain training in cardiopulmonary resuscitation and life-saving. In an Iowa case, the teachers' association claimed that such a requirement was not within the scope of normal teaching duties, and that the district could not compel additional certification beyond the regular teacher certification. The court held for the school board, saying that "It is reasonable for the school district to require an employee to have minimal training to meet emergencies that may occur in the school setting. This requirement is nothing more." *Pleasant Valley Educ. Ass'n v. Pleasant Valley Community School Dist.*, 449 N.W.2d 894 (Iowa.App. 1989).

▉ ENDNOTES

1. Ellwood P. Cubberley, *Public Education in the United States* (Boston: Houghton Mifflin Company, 1934), p. 371.

2. Ibid., p. 381.

3. R. Freeman Butts and Lawrence A. Cremin, *A History of Education in American Culture* (New York: Henry Holt and Company, 1953), p. 399.

4. Ibid.

5. Ibid.

6. John Swett, "The Examination of Teachers," National Education Association, *Proceedings,* 1872, pp. 71–82, in *Butts* and *Cremin, History of Education,* p. 399.

7. Richard J. Coley and Margaret E. Goertz, *Educational Standards in the 50 States: 1990* (Princeton, New Jersey: Educational Testing Service, August, 1990), pp. 10–15.

8. Harrah Independent School District v. Martin, 440 U.S. 194, 99 S.Ct. 1062 (1979).

9. Wardwell v. Board of Education, 529 F.2d 625 (6th Cir. 1976). See McCarthy v. Philadelphia Civil Service Commission, 424 U.S. 645, 96 S.Ct. 1154 (1976).

10. *Black's Law Dictionary* (St. Paul, Minn.: West Publishing Company, 1968), p. 1639.

11. School District No. 8, Pinal County v. Superior Court of Pinal County, 102 Ariz. 478, 433 P.2d 28 (1967).

12. Phay, Robert, *Reduction in Force: Legal Issues and Recommended Policy* (Topeka: National Organization on Legal Problems of Education, 1980).

13. See Constitution of Virginia, Article I, § 11.

14. Constitution of the United States, Article I, § 10.

15. Atlantic Coast Line R. Co. v. City of Goldsboro, 232 U.S. 548, 558, 34 S.Ct. 364, 368 (1914). See also Manigault v. Springs, 199 U.S. 473, 26 S.Ct. 127, (1905); Stone v. Mississippi, 101 U.S. (11 Otto) 814 (1880).

16. Ogden v. Saunders, 25 U.S. (12 Wheat.) 213 (1827); Citizens Mut. Bldg. Ass'n v. Edwards, 167 Va. 399, 189 S.E. 453 (1937). For a definitive explanation, see A. E. Dick Howard, Commentaries on the Constitution of Virginia, vol. I (Charlottesville: University Press of Virginia, 1974), pp. 206–7.

17. Dodge v. Board of Education, 302 U.S. 74, 58 S.Ct. 98 (1936).

18. Trustees of the Dartmouth College v. Woodward, 17 U.S. (4 Wheat) 518 (1819).

19. Ibid.

20. State ex rel. Anderson v. Brand, 303 U.S. 95, 58 S.Ct. 443 (1938).

CHAPTER 15

Teacher Rights and Freedoms

The legal relationship between the teacher and the school board is dependent on essentially three sources of the law: (a) constitutional rights and freedoms of the teacher as a citizen, (b) statutory relationships that govern the conduct of the public schools, and (c) contractual conditions of employment that may be created and agreed to by both the teacher and the employer. These sources are not wholly independent of each other; in fact, they have substantial interdependence. As we have seen in earlier chapters, overlap may come from several perspectives. For example, the presence of a statutory tenure contract relationship creates a substantive due process interest as well as a constitutionally protected contract right on behalf of the teacher. Statutes, contracts, and agreements may generally create extenuating circumstances that vest the teacher with additional implicit rights beyond those emanating directly from the state or federal constitutions. As we also observed in other chapters, substantive due process interests evolve from the rights and expectations created by the state through statute, regulation, or implication, and do not emanate directly from the federal Constitution itself. The rights and freedoms referred to in the present chapter are different in that they are explicitly and directly derived from the federal Constitution.

These natural rights are of such importance to human existence that they are protected by explicit wording of the Constitution. These rights, according to Justice Black, are set out as a "remarkable collection of 'thou shalt nots' "[1] or prohibitions against governmental intrusion. The essence of constitutional preservation of these inviolate natural rights is found in the first five words of the First Amendment: "Congress shall make no law."

◼ THE BILL OF RIGHTS

The Bill of Rights consists of ten amendments to the Constitution, all are prohibitions against governmental intrusion into individual rights and freedoms. The body of the Constitution itself delegated specified powers to the central government and did not state what rights and freedoms were left to the people. This omission greatly concerned Jefferson, who criticized the new Constitution as promulgated in Philadelphia in 1787 because it contained no specific provisions guaranteeing individual rights and freedoms. Jefferson wrote to Madison from Paris (where he was ambassador) praising the new Constitution, but ended his letter with a denunciation of the convention for not including a bill of rights. He said: "Let me add that a bill of rights is what the people are entitled to against every government on earth, general or particular, and what no just government should refuse, or rest on inference."[2] Jefferson's concern was reflected by others as well, and the ratification of the Constitution by the states was made contingent on the passage of an attendant bill of rights. Madison wrote the proposed Bill of Rights and presented it to Congress on 25 September 1789, in order to "kill the opposition" to the new Constitution.[3] With the additional assurance protecting the individual from governmental overbearance, the requisite number of state legislatures ratified the Bill of Rights by 15 December 1791.

Among the specifications of "thou-shalt-nots" contained in the Bill of Rights, the most basic are religion, speech, press, assembly, and due process as well as freedom from warrantless searches and forced self-incrimination. It was not until much later, after the Civil War, that the Fourteenth Amendment's due process and equal protection provisions were added to form the formidable and complete array of specified individual rights that are enjoyed by Americans today.

Yet, it was not until well into the twentieth century that the original ten amendments were first applied to encroachments by state governments on individual rights and freedoms.[4] Until that time the protections were read literally by the courts to mean that only "Congress shall make no law."

In addition to the U.S. Bill of Rights, state constitutions have provided additional protections against encroachments of the state governments on rights of individuals. Most state constitutions have their own bills of rights, or provisions that are tantamount to such. Unfortunately, in many instances state courts historically have not been as dedicated to enforcement of individual rights as have the federal courts. More recently, though, state courts have shown new vigor and have greatly enhanced the importance of state constitutional provisions as restraints on unwarranted governmental action.

FIRST AMENDMENT: THE PRIMARY REPOSITORY

The First Amendment is the basic repository of the primary and essential rights and freedoms. At an earlier point in our nation's constitutional development, public employment was viewed as a privilege and not a right.[5] The basis for this logic, that public employees could not fully retain their political freedoms and hold public employment concurrently, was founded in Justice Holmes' often-quoted assertion, in an 1892 case, that "The petitioner may have a constitutional right to talk politics, but he has no constitutional right to be a policeman."[6]

Some earlier cases involving public school teachers followed this philosophy, holding that the contract provisions between the board and the teacher could prohibit the exercise of various rights and freedoms by teachers; and, if the teacher violated the provisions of the contract, even though they were repressive of the teacher's rights, dismissal could be upheld.[7] Under such rationale, some courts allowed dismissal of teachers for marriage,[8] absence from school for childbirth,[9] and for political discussion in the classroom.[10]

Although the courts were generally split and clearly uncertain as to the political rights and personal freedoms of teachers, the privilege-right dichotomy continued to exist. Where teachers did prevail, the courts based their conclusions on common-law reasonableness and not on constitutional rights or freedoms. The common-law standard maintained simply that school boards held an implicit common-law power, even in absence of statute, to dismiss teachers for valid reasons.[11] The validity of the reasons was many times spurious and bore little relationship to ability to teach. Where statutes did govern dismissals, the teachers' rights could be no less in jeopardy. Some statutes simply invested boards with the power to dismiss teachers at the pleasure of the board.[12] Thus, the teacher employment relationship with the school board was defined by common-law reasonableness, contract law, and statutory and regulatory provision of the state. It did not clearly reach to constitutional rights and freedoms until 1968.

The watershed case in application of constitutional standards to teacher employment came in 1968 in *Pickering v. Board of Education*,[13] The U.S. Supreme Court held that freedom of speech, while not absolute in all circumstances, is nevertheless sufficiently strong to require the state show a "compelling state interest" in order to overcome a teacher's right to speak out on issues of public importance. In so doing the Court equated the teachers' right of free speech with that of other members of the general public to criticize and comment on public policies and issues. Any lingering doubt about the legal dichotomy of privileges versus rights was extinguished by this case, and the dictum of Justice Holmes was repudiated.

After *Pickering,* in search of a new standard, the courts have developed a flexible rule that provides for balancing the public's interests against the private interest of the employee in each circumstance. This balancing, however, does not remove all state restraint on teacher activities; on the contrary, the courts have reflected a strong belief that because of their sensitive position in the classroom, teachers must be held accountable for certain activities both internal and external to the school.[14] The interest of the public is to a great extent dependent on the teachers' status, appearance, and stature in the community. The school board must preserve the integrity of the learning processes of the school. Yet, because a teacher enters the school setting with constitutional freedoms of speech and association, the school must have a compelling reason to overcome the teacher's interest. This means simply that the teacher's rights are not absolute and can be overcome if the public necessity is great enough. Valid rationale has been used by boards of education in dismissing teachers for activities ranging from in-school issues such as insubordination and incompetency to out-of-school activities that tend to reflect on the welfare of the school, such as sexual misconduct, and gambling.

The balancing of these interests with regard to freedom of speech was given new clarity by the U.S. Supreme Court in *Connick v. Myers.*[15]

Speech and the Connick Rule

Connick explains that First Amendment free speech is protected when the employee speaks out on "matters of public concern." These words from *Pickering*[16] mean the Court must weigh the employee's interest in speaking on matters of public concern against the state's interest in providing efficient public services. Speech or expression exercised by a public employee concerning matters of private or personal interest and not as a citizen upon matters of public concern is not protected by the First Amendment.

Connick and *Pickering* combined then form a free speech test that is a two-step process. First, the initial inquiry is whether the speech is a matter of public concern; in this regard *Connick* states:

> When employee expression cannot be fairly considered as relating to any matter of political, social, or other concern to the community, government officials should enjoy wide latitude in managing their offices, without intrusive oversight by the judiciary in the name of the First Amendment.[17]

Second, if the speech is found to be a matter of public concern, the court then must apply the *Pickering* balancing test. The interest of the public employee as a citizen in commenting on matters of public concern must be weighed against the interests of the state, as an employer to promote effective and efficient public service.[18]

In *Connick,* a public employee (Assistant District Attorney Myers), when informed that she would be transferred to prosecute cases in a different area of criminal law, opposed her transfer. In response, Myers passed out a questionnaire to other fellow assistant district attorneys, soliciting information about office morale and pressure to work in political campaigns. Myers was told the questionnaire constituted insubordination, and her employment was terminated. The Supreme Court upheld Myers' dismissal, finding that the matter was basically of a personal nature and not a matter of public concern of any particular weight or magnitude. Though a question posed did fall under the rubric of "public concern," Myers' First Amendment interest was outweighed by the disruptive nature of the other questions. The beliefs by the state that Myers' actions would disrupt the office, undermine authority, and destroy the close working relationships within the office were reasonably taken in view of the evidence. The fact that Myers issued the questionnaire immediately after the transfer dispute and suggested conflict involving confidence in the conduct of the office lent additional weight in balancing the scales on behalf of the state. In so holding, the Court rejected Myers' contention that the state must bear the burden of clearly demonstrating that the discharge was necessary because the speech "substantially interfered" with the operation of the office. The "substantial interference" standard originally placed on the state in *Tinker*, the armband case, was not applicable here because the extent of a public employee's interest in the exercise of speech was not of "public concern," whereas in *Tinker* a protest of the war in Vietnam was clearly a matter of great political significance.

The speech test of the public employee can be summarized as follows: (1) public speech is a fundamental constitutional right, and allegations regarding teacher dismissal for exercise of freedom of speech place the burden of proof on the state (or school board); (2) speech can be denied if the interests of the state outweigh the interests of the employee in the exercise of that right; (3) public speech involving matters of public concern imposes an extensive burden on the part of the state to justify denial, in which case the state must "clearly demonstrate" that denial was necessary in order to prevent "substantial interference"; (4) public speech involving private concerns involves a relatively low standard of proof by the state to justify dismissal, one that a school board can easily sustain by showing minimally, as was shown in *Connick*, that the exercise of speech can be reasonably believed to undermine authority, disrupt the decorum, or harm working relationships.

Of course, as discussed later in this text, if a teacher does not have tenure and is not dismissed during the term of contract, the school board does not need to give reasons for nonretention, unless the nontenured teacher establishes the denial of a fundamental right such as speech. In that event, the *Connick* test of public versus private concern is invoked.

Teachers Have a Constitutional Right to Speak Out Freely on Matters of Public Concern

––– – ––– – –––

Pickering v. Board of Education

––– – ––– – –––

Supreme Court of the United States, 1968.
391 U.S. 563, 88 S.Ct. 1731.

Mr. Justice MARSHALL delivered the opinion of the Court. Appellant Marvin L. Pickering, a teacher in Township High School District 205, Will County, Illinois, was dismissed from his position by the appellee Board of Education for sending a letter to a local newspaper in connection with a recently proposed tax increase that was critical of the way in which the Board and the district superintendent of schools had handled past proposals to raise new revenue for the schools. Appellant's dismissal resulted from a determination by the Board, after a full hearing, that the publication of the letter was "detrimental to the efficient operation and administration of the schools of the district" and hence, under the relevant Illinois statute, Ill.Rev.Stat., c. 122, § 10-22.4 (1963), that "interests of the schools require[d] [his dismissal]." . . .

The letter constituted, basically, an attack on the School Board's handling of the 1961 bond issue proposals and its subsequent allocation of financial resources between the schools' educational and athletic programs. It also charged the superintendent of schools with attempting to prevent teachers in the district from opposing or criticizing the proposed bond issue.

The Board dismissed Pickering for writing and publishing the letter. Pursuant to Illinois law, the Board was then required to hold a hearing on the dismissal. At the hearing the Board charged that numerous statements in the letter were false and that the publication of the statements unjustifiably impugned the "motives, honesty, integrity, truthfulness, responsibility and competence" of both the Board and the school administration. The

Board also charged that the false statements damaged the professional reputations of its members and of the school administrators, would be disruptive of faculty discipline, and would tend to foment "controversy, conflict and dissension" among teachers, administrators, the Board of Education, and the residents of the district. Testimony was introduced from a variety of witnesses on the truth or falsity of the particular statements in the letter with which the Board took issue. The Board found the statements to be false as charged. No evidence was introduced at any point in the proceedings as to the effect of the publication of the letter on the community as a whole or on the administration of the school system in particular, and no specific findings along these lines were made.

. . . It is not altogether clear whether the Illinois Supreme Court held that the First Amendment had no applicability to appellant's dismissal for writing the letter in question or whether it determined that the particular statements made in the letter were not entitled to First Amendment protection. In any event, it clearly rejected Pickering's claim that, on the facts of this case, he could not constitutionally be dismissed from his teaching position.

To the extent that the Illinois Supreme Court's opinion may be read to suggest that teachers may constitutionally be compelled to relinquish the First Amendment rights they would otherwise enjoy as citizens to comment on matters of public interest in connection with the operation of the public schools in which they work, it proceeds on a premise that has been unequivocally rejected in numerous prior decisions of this Court. . . . "[T]he theory that public employment which may be denied altogether may be subjected to any conditions, regardless of how unreasonable, has been uniformly rejected." *Keyishian v. Board of Regents,* supra, 385 U.S. at 605-606, 87 S.Ct. at 685. At the same time it cannot be gainsaid that the State has interests as an employer in regulating the speech of its employees that differ significantly from those it possesses in connection with regulation of the speech of the citizenry in general. The problem in any case is to arrive at a balance between the interests of the teacher, as a citizen, in commenting upon matters of public concern and the interest of the State, as an employer, in promoting the efficiency of the public services it performs through its employees.

The Board contends that "the teacher by virtue of his public employment has a duty of loyalty to support his superiors in attaining the generally accepted goals of education and that, if he must speak out publicly, he should do so factually and accurately, commensurate with his education and experience." Appellant, on the other hand, argues that the test applicable to defamatory statements directed against public officials by persons having no occupational relationship with them, namely, that statements to be legally actionable must be made "with knowledge that [they were] . . . false or with reckless disregard of whether [they were] . . . false or not" . . . should also be applied to public statements made by teachers. . . .

An examination of the statements in appellant's letter objected to by the Board reveals that they, like the letter as a whole, consist essentially of criticism of the Board's allocation of school funds between educational and athletic programs, and of both the Board's and the superintendent's methods of informing, or preventing the informing of, the district's taxpayers of the real reasons why additional tax revenues were being sought for the schools. The statements are in no way directed towards any person with whom appellant would normally be in contact in the course of his daily work as a teacher. Thus no question of maintaining either discipline by immediate superiors or harmony among coworkers is presented here. Appellant's employment relationships with the Board and, to a somewhat lesser extent, with the superintendent are not the kind of close working relationships for which it can persuasively be claimed that personal loyalty and confidence are necessary to their proper functioning. Accordingly, to the extent that the Board's position here can be taken to suggest that even comments on matters of public concern that are substantially correct . . . may furnish grounds for dismissal if they are sufficiently critical in tone, we unequivocally reject it.

We next consider the statements in appellant's letter which we agree to be false. The Board's original charges included allegations that the publication of the letter damaged the professional reputations of the Board and the superintendent and would foment controversy and conflict among the Board, teachers, administrators, and the residents of the district. However, no evidence to support these allegations was introduced at the hearing. So far as the record reveals, Pickering's letter was greeted by everyone but its main target, the Board, with massive apathy and total disbelief. . . .

In addition, the fact that particular illustrations of the Board's claimed undesirable emphasis on athletic programs are false would not normally have any necessary impact on the actual operation of the schools, beyond its tendency to anger the Board. For example, Pickering's letter was written after the defeat at the polls of the second proposed tax increase. It could, therefore, have had no effect on the ability of the school district to raise necessary revenue, since there was no showing that there was any proposal to increase taxes pending when the letter was written.

More importantly, the question whether a school system requires additional funds is a matter of legitimate public concern on which the judgment of the school administration, including the School Board, cannot, in a society that leaves such questions to popular vote, be taken as conclusive. On such a question free and open debate is vital to informed decision-making by the electorate. Teachers are, as a class, the members of a community most likely to have informed and definite opinions as to how funds allotted to the operation of the schools should be spent. Accordingly, it is essential that they be able to speak out freely on such questions without fear of retaliatory dismissal. . . .

What we do have before us is a case in which a teacher has made erroneous public statements upon issues then currently the subject of public attention, which are critical of his ultimate employer but which are neither shown nor can be presumed to have in any

way either impeded the teacher's proper performance of his daily duties in the classroom or to have interfered with the regular operation of the schools generally. In these circumstances we conclude that the interest of the school administration in limiting teachers' opportunities to contribute to public debate is not significantly greater than its interest in limiting a similar contribution by any member of the general public.

The public interest in having free and unhindered debate on matters of public importance—the core value of the Free Speech Clause of the First Amendment—is so great that it has been held that a State cannot authorize the recovery of damages by a public official for defamatory statements directed at him except when such statements are shown to have been made either with knowledge of their falsity or with reckless disregard for their truth or falsity. . . . It is therefore perfectly clear that, were appellant a member of the general public, the State's power to afford the appellee Board of Education or its members any legal right to sue him for writing the letter at issue here would be limited by the requirement that the letter be judged by the standard laid down in *New York Times*.

This Court has also indicated, in more general terms, that statements by public officials on matters of public concern must be accorded First Amendment protection despite the fact that the statements are directed at their nominal superiors. . . .

While criminal sanctions and damage awards have a somewhat different impact on the exercise of the right to freedom of speech from dismissal from employment, it is apparent that the threat of dismissal from public employment is nonetheless a potent means of inhibiting speech. We have already noted our disinclination to make an across-the-board equation of dismissal from public employment for remarks critical of superiors with awarding damages in a libel suit by a public official for similar criticism. However, in a case such as the present one, in which the fact of employment is only tangentially and insubstantially involved in the subject matter of the public communication made by a teacher, we conclude that it is necessary to regard the teacher as the member of the general public he seeks to be.

In sum, we hold that, in a case such as this, absent proof of false statements knowingly or recklessly made by him, a teacher's exercise of his right to speak on issues of public importance may not furnish the basis for his dismissal from public employment. Since no such showing has been made in this case regarding appellant's letter, his dismissal for writing it cannot be upheld and the judgment of the Illinois Supreme Court must, accordingly, be reversed and the case remanded for further proceedings not inconsistent with this opinion. It is so ordered.

Judgment reversed and case remanded with directions.

NOTES

1. Speech exercised by the secretary of a school district superintendent in opposing a bond issue was entitled to First-Amendment protection absent a showing that the speech interfered with the efficient functioning of the office of the superintendent or impeded the secretary's performance or the performance of those with whom she worked. The court found that there was no evidence that the secretary's speech had either effect. The court in explaining its reasoning elaborated on *Pickering* and *Connick,* saying:

> Under the *Pickering* test, an employee's First Amendment rights are protected " 'unless the employer shows that some restriction is necessary to prevent the disruption of official functions or to insure effective performance by the employee.' " The employer's burden to justify its restriction on speech increases in proportion to the value of that speech in the public debate. In focusing on the effective functioning of the employer's enterprise, a court should consider "whether the statement impairs discipline by superiors or harmony among co-workers, has a detrimental impact on close working

> relationships for which personal loyalty and confidence are necessary, or impedes the performance of the speaker's duties or interferes with the regular operation of the enterprise." *Ware v. Unified School District No. 492,* Butler County, State of Kansas, 881 F.2d 906 (10th Cir. 1989); and *Rankin v. McPherson,* 483 U.S. 378, 107 S.Ct. 2891, 2899, 97 L.Ed.2d 315 (1987).

2. In *Piver* the court interpreted *Pickering,* saying:

> *Pickering* teaches that a public employee's speech is not constitutionally protected, even if it addresses an issue of public concern, unless the employee's and the audience's interests in the speech at issue outweigh the harm caused by the speech to the defendant's interests in running the governmental office efficiently.

The court further observed that the interests of a teacher, in speaking out at a board meeting regarding the tenure of another teacher and the discussion of the issue with students in a class, were of public concern protected by the First Amendment. The school board's alleged interest in overcoming the threat of "turmoil" in school was not sufficient to counterbalance the teacher's rights. *Piver v. Pender County Board of Education,* 835 F.2d 1076 (4th Cir. 1987).

3. A teacher filing a grievance against the school principal involved topics of "public concern." *Wren v. Spurlock,* 798 F.2d 1313, 1317 (10th Cir. 1986), cert. denied, 479 U.S. 1085, 107 S.Ct. 1287 (1987).

4. A school principal's speech to the school board involving a proposed transfer of his wife, an English teacher, was a matter of "public concern." *Lewis v. Harrison School District No. 1,* 805 F.2d 310 (8th Cir. 1986), cert. denied, 482 U.S. 905, 107 S.Ct. 2481 (1987).

5. Teachers' letter of complaint to the Arkansas Department of Education concerning school's delay in implementing federally mandated programs for handicapped students constituted a matter of "public con-

cern." *Southside Public Schools v. Hill*, 827 F.2d 270 (8th Cir. 1987).

6. Matters involving a high school's use of collegiate registration, a procedure in which students were permitted to choose their own subjects and teachers, were not of "public concern" and were therefore not protected by the First Amendment. *Ferrara v. Mills*, 781 F.2d 1508 (11th Cir. 1986).

7. Free speech protection does not entitle a teacher to be excessively critical and derisive of duly constituted school authority and to personally denounce and abuse other teachers. *Amburgey v. Cassady*, 370 F.Supp. 571 (E.D.Ky.1974).

8. It is well settled that a teacher, as a citizen, can run for political office, but there is a difference between the right to run for public office and the right to continued public employment after being elected. Common law provides that a teacher or other public employee cannot hold positions simultaneously that are incompatible and, therefore, present a conflict of interest. Whether a teacher may hold political office and serve as a teacher is dependent upon statutes of the particular state. Some states have statutes that provide that the teacher cannot serve as a state legislator and teacher at the same time. But if a state does not have a statute prohibiting serving, then the courts generally have allowed them to serve. A board can reasonably request the teacher to take an unpaid leave of absence while serving in a public position.

9. Some states have passed legislation modeled after the Federal Hatch Act, which prohibits participation in partisan politics. The United States Supreme Court in *Broadrick v. Oklahoma*, 413 U.S. 601, 93 S.Ct. 2908 (1973), upheld an Oklahoma statute prohibiting public employees from participating in partisan politics. These statutes usually limit activities such as direct fundraising for candidates, becoming a candidate, starting a political party, or actively managing a campaign. See *United States Civil Service Commission v. National Association of Letter Carriers*, 413 U.S. 548, 93 S.Ct. 2880 (1973).

Evidence Must Show That Teacher's Exercise of Constitutional Right Was the Motivating Factor Not to Rehire Before Judicial Action Is Justified

Mt. Healthy City School District Board of Education v. Doyle

Supreme Court of the United States, 1977.
429 U.S. 274, 97 S.Ct. 568.

Mr. Justice REHNQUIST delivered the opinion of the Court. Respondent Doyle sued petitioner Mt. Healthy Board of Education in the United States District Court for the Southern District of Ohio. Doyle claimed that the Board's refusal to renew his contract in 1971 violated his rights under the First and Fourteenth Amendments to the United States Constitution. After a bench trial the District Court held that Doyle was entitled to reinstatement with back pay. The Court of Appeals for the Sixth Circuit affirmed the judgment. . . .

Doyle was first employed by the Board in 1966. He worked under one-year contracts for the first three years, and under a two-year contract from 1969 to 1971. In 1969 he was elected president of the Teachers' Association, in which position he worked to expand the subjects of direct negotiation between the Association and the Board of Education. During Doyle's one-year term as president of the Association, and during the succeeding year when he served on its executive committee, there was apparently some tension in relations between the Board and the Association.

Beginning early in 1970, Doyle was involved in several incidents not directly connected with his role in the Teachers' Association. In one instance, he engaged in an argument with another teacher which culminated in the other teacher's slapping him. Doyle subsequently refused to accept an apology and insisted upon some punishment for the other teacher. His persistence in the matter resulted in the suspension of both teachers for one day, which was followed by a walkout by a number of other teachers, which in turn resulted in the lifting of the suspensions.

On other occasions, Doyle got into an argument with employees of the school cafeteria over the amount of spaghetti which had been served him; referred to students, in connection with a disciplinary complaint, as "sons of bitches"; and made an obscene gesture to two girls in connection with their failure to obey commands made in his capacity as cafeteria supervisor. Chronologically the last in the series of incidents which respondent was involved in during his employment by the Board was a telephone call by him to a local radio station. It was the Board's consideration of this incident which the court below found to be a violation of the First and Fourteenth Amendments.

In February of 1971, the principal circulated to various teachers a memorandum relating to teacher dress and appearance, which was apparently prompted by the view of some in the administration that there was a relationship between teacher appearance and public support for bond issues. Doyle's response to the receipt of the memorandum—on a subject which he apparently understood was to be settled by joint teacher-administration action—was to convey the substance of the memorandum to a disc jockey at WSAI, a Cincinnati radio station, who promptly announced the adoption of the dress code as a news item. Doyle subsequently apologized to the principal, conceding that he should have made some prior communication of his criticism to the school administration.

Approximately one month later the superintendent made his customary annual recommendations to the Board as to the rehiring of nontenured teachers. He recommended that Doyle not be rehired. The same recommendation was made with respect to nine other teachers in the district, and in all instances, including Doyle's, the recommendation was adopted by the Board. Shortly after being notified of this decision, respondent requested a statement of reasons for the Board's actions. He received a statement citing "a notable lack

of tact in handling professional matters which leaves much doubt as to your sincerity in establishing good school relationships." That general statement was followed by references to the radio station incident and to the obscene gesture incident.

The District Court found that all of these incidents had in fact occurred. It concluded that respondent Doyle's telephone call to the radio station was "clearly protected by the First Amendment," and that because it had played a "substantial part" in the decision of the Board not to renew Doyle's employment, he was entitled to reinstatement with backpay. The District Court did not expressly state what test it was applying in determining that the incident in question involved conduct protected by the First Amendment, but simply held that the communication to the radio station was such conduct. The Court of Appeals affirmed in a brief *per curiam* opinion.

Doyle's claims under the First and Fourteenth Amendments are not defeated by the fact that he did not have tenure. Even though he could have been discharged for no reason whatever, and had no constitutional right to a hearing prior to the decision not to rehire him, *Board of Regents v. Roth*, 408 U.S. 564, 92 S.Ct. 2701, 33 L.Ed.2d 548 (1972), he may nonetheless establish a claim to reinstatement if the decision not to rehire him was made by reason of his exercise of constitutionally protected First Amendment freedoms. *Perry v. Sindermann*.

That question of whether speech of a government employee is constitutionally protected expression necessarily entails striking "a balance between the interests of the teacher, as a citizen, in commenting upon matters of public concern and the interest of the State as an employer, in promoting the efficiency of the public services it performs through its employees." *Pickering v. Board of Education*. There is no suggestion by the Board that Doyle violated any established policy, or that its reaction to his communication to the radio station was anything more than an ad hoc response to Doyle's action in making the memorandum public. We therefore accept the District Court's finding that the communication was protected by the First and Fourteenth Amendments. We are not, however, entirely in agreement with that court's manner of reasoning from this finding to the conclusion that Doyle is entitled to reinstatement with backpay.

The District Court made the following "conclusions" on this aspect of the case:

1. If a non-permissible reason, e.g., exercise of First Amendment rights, played a substantial part in the decision not to renew—even in the face of other permissible grounds—the decision may not stand (citations omitted).

2. A non-permissible reason did play a substantial part. That is clear from the letter of the Superintendent immediately following the Board's decision, which stated two reasons— the one, the conversation with the radio station clearly protected by the First Amendment. A court may not engage in any limitation of First Amendment rights based on "tact"—that is not to say that "tactfulness" is irrelevant to other issues in this case.

   At the same time, though, it stated that "in fact, as this Court sees it and finds, both the Board and the Superintendent were faced with a situation in which there did exist in fact reason . . . independent of any First Amendment rights or exercise thereof, to not extend tenure."

Since respondent Doyle had no tenure, and there was therefore not even a state law requirement of "cause" or "reason" before a decision could be made not to renew his employment, it is not clear what the District Court meant by this latter statement. Clearly the Board legally *could* have dismissed respondent had the radio station incident never come to its attention. One plausible meaning of the court's statement is that the Board and the Superintendent not only could, but in fact *would* have reached that decision had not the constitutionally protected incident of the telephone call to the radio station occurred. We are thus brought to the issue whether, even if that were the case, the fact that the protected conduct played a "substantial part" in the actual decision not to renew would necessarily amount to a constitutional violation justifying remedial action. We think that it would not.

A rule of causation which focuses solely on whether protected conduct played a part, "substantial" or otherwise, in a decision not to rehire, could place an employee in a better position as a result of the exercise of constitutionally protected conduct than he would have occupied had he done nothing. The difficulty with the rule enunciated by the District Court is that it would require reinstatement in cases where a dramatic and perhaps abrasive incident is inevitably on the minds of those responsible for the decision to rehire, and does indeed play a part in that decision—even if the same decision would have been reached had the incident not occurred. The constitutional principle at stake is sufficiently vindicated if such an employee is placed in no worse a position than if he had not engaged in the conduct. A borderline or marginal candidate should not have the employment question resolved against him because of constitutionally protected conduct. But that same candidate ought not to be able, by engaging in such conduct, to prevent his employer from assessing his performance record and reaching a decision not to rehire on the basis of that record, simply because the protected conduct makes the employer more certain of the correctness of its decision.

This is especially true where, as the District Court observed was the case here, the current decision to rehire will accord "tenure." The long term consequences of an award of tenure are of great moment both to the employee and to the employer. They are too significant for us to hold that the Board in this case would be precluded, because it considered constitutionally protected conduct in deciding not to rehire Doyle, from attempting to prove to a trier of fact that quite apart from such conduct Doyle's record was such that he would not have been rehired in any event.   . . .

Initially, in this case, the burden was properly placed upon respondent to show that his conduct was constitutionally protected, and that this conduct was a "substantial factor"—or to put it in other words, that it was a "motivating factor" in the Board's decision not to rehire him. Respondent having carried that burden, however, the District Court should have gone on to determine whether the Board had shown by a preponderance of the evidence that it would have reached the same decision as to respondent's reemployment even in the absence of the protected conduct.

We cannot tell from the District Court opinion and conclusions, nor from the opinion of the Court of Appeals affirming the judgment of the District Court, what conclusion those courts would have reached had they applied this test. The judgment of the Court of Appeals is therefore vacated, and the case remanded for further proceedings consistent with this opinion.

NOTES

1. The combined meaning of *Pickering, Mt. Healthy,* and *Connick* is interpreted by the Eighth Circuit Court of Appeals, in *Roberts v. Van Buren Public Schools,* 773 F.2d 949 (8th Cir. 1985).

> *Pickering v. Board of Education,* 391 U.S. 563, 88 S.Ct. 1731, 20 L.Ed.2d 811 (1968), held that "[p]ublic employee[s do] not relinquish First Amendment rights to comment on matters of public interest by virtue of government employment." *Connick v. Myers,* 461 U.S. 138, 140, 103 S.Ct. 1684, 1686, 75 L.Ed.2d 708 (1983). Consideration of such claims involves a three-step analysis. First, plaintiffs must demonstrate that their conduct was protected; second, plaintiffs must demonstrate that such protected conduct was a substantial or motivating factor in the adverse employment decision; and third, the employer may show that the employment action would have been taken even in the absence of the protected conduct. *Mt. Healthy City School District Board of Education v. Doyle,* 429 U.S. 274, 287, 97 S.Ct. 568, 576, 50 L.Ed.2d 471 (1977).
>
> Since *Connick,* identification of protected activity is a two-step process in itself. As a threshold matter, the speech must have addressed a "matter of public concern," then, the interest of the employee in so speaking must be balanced against "the interest of the State, as an employer, in promoting the efficiency of the public services it performs through its employees." *Pickering,* 391 U.S. at 568, 88 S.Ct. at 1735. This

"*Pickering* balance," as it has come to be known, looks to the following factors: (1) the need for harmony in the office or work place; (2) whether the government's responsibilities require a close working relationship to exist between the plaintiff and co-workers when the speech in question has caused or could cause the relationship to deteriorate; (3) the time, manner, and place of the speech; (4) the context in which the dispute arose; (5) the degree of public interest in the speech; and (6) whether the speech impeded the employee's ability to perform his or her duties.

2. Another explanation, combining *Pickering, Mt. Healthy,* and *Connick,* comes from the U.S. Court of Appeals, Fourth Circuit, in *Daniels v. Quinn,* 801 F.2d 687 (4th Cir. 1986), which explains the First Amendment free-speech rights of a public employee in terms of the three-part inquiry.

> The first step is to ask whether the speech was about a matter of legitimate public concern. This question is one of law, not of fact.
>
> If the speech was about a matter of public concern, the question becomes whether the employee would have been discharged "but for" the speech. The defendant-employer will not be liable if the discharge would have occurred for other reasons, such as the plaintiff's own incompetence. This classic motivational question is one of fact. The employee bears the burden of demonstrating that protected speech was a motivating factor in the discharge. The burden then shifts to the employer to show that it would have reached the same decision even in the absence of the protected conduct. *Mt. Healthy v. Doyle,* 429 U.S. at 287, 97 S.Ct. at 576.
>
> If protected speech was the "but for" cause of the discharge, courts must still inquire whether the degree of public interest in the employee's statement was nonetheless outweighed by the employer's responsibility to manage its internal affairs and provide "effective and efficient" service to the public. If so, then the employer will not be liable. This question is ultimately one of law. *Daniels v. Quinn,* 801 F.2d 687 (4th Cir. 1986).

3. A school board's transfer of a teacher to traveling teacher status was upheld as a consideration of public interest outweighing the teacher's individual interests. Memorandum by the teacher, commenting on grading policies, only one of which could be adjudged of public concern, were personal in scope and sarcastic in tone, and the relationship between the teacher and the school had deteriorated to be "filled with animosity." With regard to the *Mt. Healthy* test, the court found that the exercise of speech was not a "substantial and motivating factor in the adverse job action." *Hesse v. Board of Education of Township High School District* No. 211, Cook County, Illinois, 848 F.2d 748 (7th Cir. 1988).

4. The questionnaire distributed by Sheila Myers in *Connick v. Myers*, discussed in the text above, queried other employees.

> Please take the few minutes it will require to fill this out. You can freely express your opinion WITH ANONYMITY GUARANTEED.
>
> 1. How long have you been in the office?
> 2. Were you moved as a result of the recent transfers?
> 3. Were the transfers as they effected [sic] you discussed with you by any superior prior to the notice of them being posted?
> 4. Do you think as a matter of policy, they should have been?
> 5. From your experience, do you feel office procedure regarding transfers has been fair?
> 6. Do you believe there is a rumor mill active in the office?
> 7. If so, how do you think it effects [sic] overall working performance of A.D.A. personnel?
> 8. If so, how do you think it effects [sic] office morale?
> 9. Do you generally first learn of office changes and developments through rumor?
> 10. Do you have confidence in and would you rely on the word of:
>
> Bridget Bane
> Fred Harper
> Lindsay Larson
> Joe Meyer
> Dennis Waldron
>
> 11. Do you ever feel pressured to work in political campaigns on behalf of office supported candidates?
> 12. Do you feel a grievance committee would be a worthwhile addition to the office structure?
> 13. How would you rate office morale?
> 14. Please feel free to express any comments or feelings you have.
>
> *Thank you for your cooperation in this survey.*

The court in *Connick* determined the only question that was a matter of "public concern," and therefore constitutionally protected, was Question 11 referring to pressure on employees to work in political campaigns. Since one question was a matter of public concern the *Mt. Healthy* test was invoked.

Would Myers have been dismissed if the protected question were not considered? The employer must show that the employment action would have been taken even in the absence of the protected conduct.

> When a public employee speaks not as a citizen upon matters of public concern, but instead as an employee upon matters only of personal interest, absent the most unusual circumstances, a federal court is not the appropriate forum in which to review the wisdom of a personnel decision taken by a public agency allegedly in reaction to the employee's behavior. *Connick v. Myers,* 461 U.S. 138, 103 S.Ct. 1684, 75 L.Ed.2d 708 (1983).

5. The Superintendent in *Mt. Healthy* sent a statement to teacher Doyle citing a "Lack of tact in handling professional matters" and gave two specific incidents: (1) the radio station incident and (2) the obscene gesture. Since Doyle was untenured would it have been more prudent for the Superintendent not to mention the radio incident in his letter since it was protected speech?

Did mentioning the radio incident shift the burden of proof to the school board?

6. The burden of proof is on the teacher to show that he or she was not rehired because of constitutionally protected conduct. The teacher must also prove that this conduct was the "motivating factor" in the school board's decision not to rehire. From this point the burden shifts to the defendant school board, which must show by a preponderance of evidence that it would have reached the same decision regardless of whether the teacher had engaged in the constitutionally protected conduct. *McGee v. South Pemiscot School District R-V,* 712 F.2d 339 (8th Cir.1983).

Freedom of Speech Is Guaranteed to Teacher in Private Communication with Employer

— — — — — — — — —

Givhan v. Western Line Consolidated School District

— — — — — — — — —

Supreme Court of the United States, 1979.
439 U.S. 410, 99 S.Ct. 693.

Mr. Justice REHNQUIST delivered the opinion of the Court. Petitioner Bessie Givhan was dismissed from her employment as a junior high English teacher at the end of the 1970-1971 school year. At the time of petitioner's termination, respondent Western Line Consolidated School District was the subject of a desegregation order entered by the United States District Court for the Northern District of Mississippi. Petitioner filed a complaint . . . seeking reinstatement on the ground that nonrenewal of her contract . . . infringed her right of free speech secured by the First and Fourteenth Amendments of the United States Constitution. In an effort to show that its decision was justified, respondent school district introduced evidence of, among other things, a series of private en-

counters between petitioner and the school principal in which petitioner allegedly made "petty and unreasonable demands" in a manner variously described by the principal as "insulting," "hostile," "loud," and "arrogant." After a two-day bench trial, the District Court held that petitioner's termination had violated the First Amendment. Finding that petitioner had made "demands" on but two occasions and that those demands "were neither 'petty' nor 'unreasonable,' insomuch as all of the complaints in question involved employment policies and practices at [the] school which [petitioner] conceived to be racially discriminatory in purpose or effect," the District Court concluded that "the primary reason for the school district's failure to renew [petitioner's] contract was her criticism of the policies and practices of the school district, especially the school to which she was assigned to teach." . . .

The Court of Appeals for the Fifth Circuit reversed. Although it found the District Court's findings not clearly erroneous, the Court of Appeals concluded that because petitioner had privately expressed her complaints and opinions to the principal, her expression was not protected under the First Amendment. . . .

This Court's decisions in *Pickering, Perry,* and *Mt. Healthy* do not support the conclusion that a public employee forfeits his protection against governmental abridgment of freedom of speech if he decides to express his views privately rather than publicly. While those cases each arose in the context of a public employee's public expression, the rule to be derived from them is not dependent on that largely coincidental fact.

In *Pickering* a teacher was discharged for publicly criticizing, in a letter published in a local newspaper, the school board's handling of prior bond issue proposals and its subsequent allocation of financial resources between the schools' educational and athletic programs. Noting that the free speech rights of public employees are not absolute, the Court held that in determining whether a government employee's speech is constitutionally protected, "the interests of the [employee], as a citizen, in commenting upon matters of public concern" must be balanced against "the interest of the State, as an employer, in promoting the efficiency of the public services it performs through its employees." . . . The Court concluded that under the circumstances of that case "the interest of the school administration in limiting teachers' opportunities to contribute to public debate [was] not significantly greater than its interest in limiting a similar contribution by any member of the general public." Here the opinion of the Court of Appeals may be read to turn in part on its view that the working relationship between principal and teacher is significantly different from the relationship between the parties in *Pickering* . . . . But we do not feel confident that the Court of Appeals' decision would have been placed on that ground notwithstanding its view that the First Amendment does not require the same sort of *Pickering* balancing for the private expression of a public employee as it does for public expression.

Perry and *Mt. Healthy* arose out of similar disputes between teachers and their public employers. As we have noted, however, the fact that each of these cases involved public expression by the employee was not critical to the decision. Nor is the Court of Appeals' view supported by the "captive audience" rationale. Having opened his office door to petitioner, the principal was hardly in a position to argue that he was the "*unwilling* recipient" of her views.

The First Amendment forbids abridgment of the "freedom of speech." Neither the Amendment itself nor our decisions indicate that this freedom is lost to the public employee who arranges to communicate privately with his employer rather than to spread his views before the public. We decline to adopt such a view of the First Amendment.

While this case was pending on appeal to the Court of Appeals, *Mt. Healthy City Board of Education v. Doyle* was decided. In that case this Court rejected the view that a public employee must be reinstated whenever constitutionally protected conduct plays a "substantial" part in the employer's decision to terminate. Such a rule would require reinstatement of employees that the public em-

ployer would have dismissed even if the constitutionally protected conduct had not occurred and, consequently "could place an employee in a better position as a result of the exercise of constitutionally protected conduct than he would have occupied had he done nothing." Thus, the Court held that once the employee has shown that his constitutionally protected conduct played a "substantial" role in the employer's decision not to rehire him, the employer is entitled to show "by a preponderance of the evidence that it would have reached the same decision as to [the employee's] reemployment even in the absence of the protected conduct." Id., at 287, 97 S.Ct., at 576.

The Court of Appeals in the instant case rejected respondents' *Mt. Healthy* claim that the decision to terminate petitioner would have been made even if her encounters with the principal had never occurred:

> The [trial] court did not make an express finding as to whether the same decision would have been made, but on this record the [respondents] do not, and seriously cannot, argue that the same decision would have been made without regard to the "demands." Appellants seem to argue that the preponderance of the evidence shows that the same decision would have been justified, but that is not the same as proving that the same decision would have been made. . . . Therefore [respondents] failed to make a successful "same decision anyway" defense.

Since this case was tried before *Mt. Healthy* was decided, it is not surprising that respondents did not attempt to prove in the District Court that the decision not to rehire petitioner would have been made even absent consideration of her "demands." Thus, the case came to the Court of Appeals in very much the same posture as *Mt. Healthy* was presented in this Court. And while the District Court found that petitioner's "criticism" was the "primary" reason for the school district's failure to rehire her, it did not find that she would have been rehired *but for* her criticism. Respondents' *Mt. Healthy* claim called for a factual determination which could not, on this record, be resolved by the Court of Appeals.

Accordingly, the judgment of the Court of Appeals is vacated and the case remanded for further proceedings consistent with this opinion.

So ordered.

NOTES

1. "*Connick* did not hold that speech relating to employment grievances is always a personal matter, such a view would conflict with the Court's commitment to a case-by-case balancing" and would run counter to *Givhan. Piver v. Pender County Board of Education,* 835 F.2d 1076 (4th Cir. 1987).
2. "Criticism in private of a public employer's allegedly racially discriminatory policies can be of 'public concern.' " *Piver v. Pender County Board of Education,* supra.

Teacher Dress Policy Ruled Constitutional

East Hartford Education Association v. Board of Education

United States Court of Appeals,
Second Circuit, 1977.
562 F.2d 838.

MESKILL, Circuit Judge. Although this case may at first appear too trivial to command the attention of a busy court, it raises important issues concerning the proper scope of judicial oversight of local affairs. The appellant here, Richard Brimley, is a public school teacher reprimanded for failing to wear a necktie while teaching his English class. Joined by the teachers union, he sued the East Hartford Board of Education, claiming that the reprimand for violating the dress code deprived him of his rights of free speech and privacy. . . .

In the vast majority of communities, the control of public schools is vested in locally-elected bodies. This commitment to local political bodies requires significant public control over what is said and done in school. It is not the federal courts, but local democratic processes, that are primarily responsible for the many routine decisions that are made in public school systems. Accordingly, it is settled that "[c]ourts do not and cannot intervene in the resolution of conflicts which arise in the daily operation of school systems and which do not directly and sharply implicate basic constitutional values." *Epperson v. Arkansas,* 393 U.S. 97, 104, 89 S.Ct. 266, 270, 21 L.Ed.2d 228 (1968).

Federal courts must refrain, in most instances, from interfering with the decisions of school authorities. Even though decisions may appear foolish or unwise, a federal court may not overturn them unless the standards set forth in *Epperson* is met. . . .

Mr. Brimley claims that by refusing to wear a necktie he makes a statement on current affairs which assists him in his teaching. In his brief, he argues that the following benefits flow from his tielessness:

a. He wishes to present himself to his students as a person who is not tied to "establishment conformity."
b. He wishes to symbolically indicate to his students his association with the ideas of the generation to which those students belong, including the rejection of many of the customs and values, and of the social outlook, of the older generation.
c. He feels that dress of this type enables him to achieve closer rapport with his students, and thus enhances his ability to teach.

Appellant's claim, therefore, is that his refusal to wear a tie is "symbolic speech," and, as such, is protected against governmental interference by the First Amendment.

We are required here to balance the alleged interest in free expression against the goals of the school board in requiring its teachers to dress somewhat more formally than they might like. When this test is applied, the school board's position must prevail.

Obviously, a great range of conduct has the symbolic, "speech-like" aspect claimed by Mr. Brimley. To state that activity is "symbolic" is only the beginning, and not the end, of constitutional inquiry. . . . Even though intended as expression, symbolic speech remains conduct, subject to regulation by the state. As the Supreme Court has stated in discussing the difference between conduct and "speech in its pristine form":

> We emphatically reject the notion urged by appellant that the First and Fourteenth Amendments afford the same kind of freedom to those who would communicate ideas by conduct such as patrolling, marching, and picketing on streets and highways, as these amendments afford to those who communicate ideas by pure speech. . . . We reaffirm . . . that "it has never been deemed an abridgement of freedom of speech or press to make a course of conduct illegal merely because the conduct was in part initiated, evidenced, or carried out by means of language, either spoken, written, or printed.".

. . . As conduct becomes less and less like "pure speech" the showing of governmental interest required for its regulation is progressively lessened. In those cases where governmental regulation of expressive conduct has been struck down, the communicative intent of the actor was clear and "closely akin to 'pure speech.' " *Tinker v. Des Moines School District*, 393 U.S. 503, 505, 89 S.Ct. 733, 21 L.Ed.2d 731 (1969). Thus, the First Amendment has been held to protect wearing a black armband to protest the Vietnam War, *Tinker v. Des Moines School District*, supra, burning an American Flag to highlight a speech denouncing the government's failure to protect a civil rights leader, *Street v. New York*, 394 U.S. 576, 89 S.Ct. 1354, 22 L.Ed.2d 572 (1969), or quietly refusing to recite the Pledge of Allegiance, *Russo v. Central School District*, 469 F.2d 623 (2d Cir.1972), cert. denied, 411 U.S. 932, 93 S.Ct. 1899, 36 L.Ed.2d 391 (1973).

In contrast, the claims of symbolic speech made here are vague and unfocused. Through the simple refusal to wear a tie, Mr. Brimley claims that he communicates a comprehensive view of life and society. It may well be, in an age increasingly conscious of fashion, that a significant portion of the population seeks to make a statement of some kind through its clothes. However, Mr. Brimley's message is sufficiently vague to place it close to the "conduct" end of the "speech-conduct" continuum described above. While the regulation of the school board must still pass constitutional muster, the showing required to uphold it is significantly less than if Mr. Brimley had been punished, for example, for publicly speaking out on an issue concerning school administration.

At the outset, Mr. Brimley had other, more effective means of communicating his social views to his students. He could, for example, simply have told them his views on contemporary America; if he had done this in a temperate way, without interfering with his teaching duties, we would be confronted with a very different First Amendment case. The existence of alternative, effective means of communication, while not conclusive, is a factor to be considered in assessing the validity of a regulation of expressive conduct.

Balanced against appellant's claim of free expression is the school board's interest in promoting respect for authority and traditional values, as well as discipline in the classroom, by requiring teachers to dress in a professional manner. A dress code is a rational means of promoting these goals. As to the legitimacy of the goals themselves, there can be no doubt. In *James v. Board of Education*, Chief Judge Kaufman stated:

> The interest of the state in promoting the efficient operation of its schools extends beyond merely securing an orderly classroom. Although the pros and cons of progressive education are debated heatedly, a principal function of all elementary and secondary education is indoctrinative—whether it be to teach the ABCs or multiplication tables or to transmit the basic values of the community. 461 F.2d 566 (2d Cir.), cert. denied, 409 U.S. 1042, 93 S.Ct. 529 (1972).

This balancing test is primarily a matter for the school board. Were we local officials, and not appellate judges, we might find Mr. Brimley's arguments persuasive. However, our role is not to choose the better educational policy. We may intervene in the decisions of school authorities only when it has been shown that they have strayed outside the area committed to their discretion. If Mr. Brimley's argument were to prevail, this policy would be completely eroded. Because teaching is by definition an expressive activity, virtually every decision made by school authorities would raise First Amendment issues calling for federal court intervention. . . .

Mr. Brimley also claims that the "liberty" interest grounded in the due process clause of the Fourteenth Amendment protects his choice of attire. . . .

The Supreme Court dealt with a similar claim in *Kelley v. Johnson*, 425 U.S. 238, 96 S.Ct. 1440, 47 L.Ed.2d 708 (1976). That case involved a challenge to the hair-grooming regulations of a police department. The Court was careful to distinguish privacy claims made by government employees from those made by members of the public:

Respondent has sought the protection of the Fourteenth Amendment, not as a member of the citizenry at large, but on the contrary as an employee of the police force of Suffolk County, a subdivision of the State of New York. While the Court of Appeals made passing reference to this distinction, it was thereafter apparently ignored. We think, however, it is highly significant. In Pickering v. Board of Education, 391 U.S. 563, 568[, 88 S.Ct. 1731, 20 L.Ed.2d 811] (1968), after noting that state employment may not be conditioned on the relinquishment of First Amendment rights, the Court stated that "[a]t the same time it cannot be gainsaid that the State has interests as an employer in regulating the speech of its employees that differ significantly from those it possesses in connection with regulation of the speech of the citizenry in general." More recently, we have sustained comprehensive and substantial restrictions upon activities of both federal and state employees lying at the core of the First Amendment. If such state regulations may survive challenges based on the explicit language of the First Amendment, there is surely even more room for restrictive regulations of state employees where the claim implicates only the more general contours of

the substantive liberty interest protected by the Fourteenth Amendment.

The same distinction applies here. The regulation involved in this case affects Mr. Brimley in his capacity as a public school teacher. Of course, as he points out, the functions of policemen and teachers differ widely. Regulations well within constitutional bounds for one occupation might prove invalid for another. Nonetheless, we can see no reason why the same constitutional test should not apply, no matter how different the results of their constitutional challenges.

Kelley goes on to set forth the standard to be applied in such cases:

We think the answer here is so clear that the District Court was quite right in the first instance to have dismissed respondent's complaint. Neither this Court, the Court of Appeals, nor the District Court is in a position to weigh the policy arguments in favor of and against a rule regulating hairstyles as a part of regulations governing a uniformed civilian service. The constitutional issue to be decided by these courts is whether petitioner's determination that such regulations should be enacted is so irrational that it may be branded "arbitrary," and therefore a deprivation of respondent's "liberty" interest in freedom to choose his own hairstyle.

If Mr. Brimley has any protected interest in his neckwear, it does not weigh very heavily on the constitutional scales. As with most legislative choices, the board's dress code is presumptively constitutional. It is justified by the same concerns for respect, discipline and traditional values described in our discussion of the First Amendment claim. Accordingly, appellant has failed to carry the burden set out in *Kelley* of demonstrating that the dress code is "so irrational that it may be branded 'arbitrary,' " and the regulation must stand.

. . .

Each claim of substantive liberty must be judged in the light of that case's special circumstances. In view of the uniquely influential role of the public school teacher in the classroom, the board is justified in imposing this regulation. As public servants in a special position of trust, teachers may properly be subjected to many restrictions in their professional lives which would be invalid if generally applied. We join the sound views of the First and Seventh Circuits, and follow *Kelley* by holding that a school board may, if it wishes, impose reasonable regulations governing the appearance of the teachers it employs. . . . There being no material factual issue to be decided, the grant of summary judgment is affirmed.

NOTE

1. A Louisiana school board expanded its student dress code to prohibit employees from wearing beards. The Fifth Circuit Court of Appeals recognized the liberty interest of the individual in choosing how to wear one's hair, but ruled the school board had made a rational determination in establishing the rule as "a reasonable means of furthering the school board's undeniable interest in teaching hygiene, instilling discipline, asserting authority, and compelling uniformity." *Domico v. Rapides Parish School Board*, 675 F.2d 100 (5th Cir.1982).

Teacher's Letter to School Newspaper Responding to Allegations of Sexual Discrimination Addressed a Public Concern

— — — — — — —

Seemuller v. Fairfax County School Board

— — — — — — —

United States Court of Appeals,
Fourth Circuit, 1989.
878 F.2d 1578.

BUTZNER, Senior Circuit Judge. The sole issue in this appeal is whether a public school teacher's letter addressed a matter of public concern. Donald Seemuller, a physical educa-

tion teacher at Lake Braddock High School in Fairfax County, Virginia, appeals the district court's order directing a verdict in favor of the Fairfax County School Board and George Stepp, the principal of Lake Braddock, in this § 1983 action alleging violation of Seemuller's first amendment right to freedom of speech. Seemuller contends that the district court erred in ruling that his speech, a letter to the editor published in the school's newspaper, was not on a matter of public concern but was simply a personal response to criticism. Because we find that Seemuller's speech commented on a matter of public concern, we vacate the district court's order and remand for further proceedings.

In December 1986, Lake Braddock's school newspaper, *The Bear Facts*, published an anonymous letter to the editor written by students and captioned "Angered Girls Fight P.E. Discrimination." The letter complained about "a few male chauvinistic P.E. teachers" and gave several supporting examples. . . .

Seemuller responded to the complaint by submitting a letter to the newspaper. Before publication, the paper's faculty advisor and the principal read the letter. They did not object to its publication or ask Seemuller to withdraw it. The principal did not warn Seemuller that publication would lead to disciplinary action. He did not speak to Seemuller about the letter until after it was published.

The paper published the letter under the caption "P.E. Teacher Defends." The letter read as follows:

Dear Editor,
As a male physical education teacher at Lake Braddock, I was somewhat taken aback by the recent letter accusing some members of our staff of chauvinism. I cannot speak for every member of the staff, but as for myself, I like girls, and the many things they can accomplish. My two females at home are a sixteen year old whom I permit to chauffer my son to and from his many activities, and my wife who is an adequate cook and housekeeper. My wife also does light yard work enabling me to play golf, and pursue many other masculine activities.
Hopefully this letter will convince those girls in physical education at Lake Braddock

that we have the utmost respect for their feminine talents.

Sincerely,
Don Seemuller

In addition to being distributed to students at Lake Braddock, the school's newspaper is mailed to approximately 3,600 families in the school's community. The newspaper's policy is to publish letters to the editor from students, teachers, and parents.

Following publication of Seemuller's letter, the principal told Seemuller that he had received complaints from the community, faculty members, and the Lake Braddock Human Relations Committee. He also said that Seemuller might receive a "needs improvement" rating in "Professional Responsibility" in his final evaluation in April and suggested that Seemuller meet with the Human Relations Committee and write a letter of apology to the newspaper.

Seemuller met with the committee and submitted a letter of apology to the newspaper in May 1987 which appeared under the heading, "Seemuller Apologizes for Satirical Response." . . .

The paper appended the following statement to Seemuller's letter:

EDITOR'S NOTE

The editorial board respects Mr. Seemuller for discussing and confronting the sexual bias problem that some students see in the physical education department. However, this letter should have been unnecessary. Mr. Seemuller's original statement was facetious and not meant to be offensive. . . .

In his final evaluation in April 1987, as a result of the publication of his letter, Seemuller was rated as "Needs Improvement" in "Professional Responsibility." Seemuller alleges that because of this evaluation he did not receive his step increment in pay for the 1987-88 school year.

Seemuller filed a grievance in accordance with school board regulations and state law. The deputy superintendent of schools who was designated by the superintendent to consider Seemuller's grievance acknowledged that his letter "was published in the context of school and community concerns about the treatment of females in school programs." The deputy superintendent concluded that Seemuller was able to exercise his "freedom of speech because [his] letter was published." Without further explanation, the school board denied the grievance after reviewing the documents and recommendation of the superintendent. Seemuller then brought this action.

The Supreme Court has explained in a series of cases during the last two decades the principles governing our inquiry. The initial question in deciding a public employee's entitlement to the protection of the first amendment is whether his speech addresses a matter of public concern. . . . In the absence of unusual circumstances, a public employee's speech "upon matters only of personal interest" is not afforded constitutional protection. *Connick v. Myers*, 461 U.S. 138, 147, 103 S.Ct. 1684, 1690, 75 L.Ed.2d 708 (1983). In contrast, a government employee's speech is protected from disciplinary action by his employer if "the interests of the [employee], as a citizen, in commenting upon matters of public concern" outweigh "the interests of the State, as an employer, in promoting the efficiency of the public services it performs through its employees." *Pickering v. Board of Education*, 391 U.S. 563, 568, 88 S.Ct. 1731, 1734, 20 L.Ed.2d 811 (1968). In this case, because the district court found that Seemuller's letter did not comment on a matter of public concern, it did not reach the *Pickering* balancing test. Consequently, the only issue on appeal is whether Seemuller's letter may be "fairly characterized as constituting speech on a matter of public concern." *Connick*, 461 U.S. at 146, 103 S.Ct. at 1689.

Connick also explains that "[w]hether an employee's speech addresses a matter of public concern must be determined by the content, form, and context of a given statement, as revealed by the whole record." . . . In conducting this examination, an appellate court is obligated to make "an independent constitutional judgment on the facts of the case." . . .

Connick dealt with the complaint of an employee who was discharged after she circulated a questionnaire that primarily sought responses about employment conditions in the office where she worked. In ruling that the employee's questionnaire did not involve a matter of public concern, the Court said:

> When employee expression cannot be fairly considered as relating to any matter of political, social, or other concern to the community, government officials should enjoy wide latitude in managing their offices, without intrusive oversight by the judiciary in the name of the First Amendment. . . .
>
> We hold only that when a public employee speaks not as a citizen upon matters of public concern, but instead as an employee upon matters only of personal interest, absent the most unusual circumstances, a federal court is not the appropriate forum in which to review the wisdom of a personnel decision taken by a public agency allegedly in reaction to the employee's behavior. Our responsibility is to ensure that citizens are not deprived of fundamental rights by virtue of working for the government; this does not require a grant of immunity for employee grievances not afforded by the First Amendment to those who do not work for the State.

Connick, 461 U.S. at 146-47, 103 S.Ct. at 1689-90 (citation omitted). . . .

In applying the foregoing principles to the facts of this case, the starting point is the anonymous letters written by students about the physical education department. The paper's editor recognized its content by captioning it "Angered Girls Fight P.E. Discrimination." The letter protested that teachers practice discrimination based on sex. The letter addressed an issue that is no less a matter of public interest than a charge that a school system engages in discrimination based on race. . . .

Seemuller's letter, submitted for publication several weeks later, was a response to the anonymous letter. It starts out by stating that "I was somewhat taken aback by the recent letter accusing some members of our staff of chauvinism." The editor recognized Seemuller's letter as a defense of the department, for it was published with the caption: "P.E. Teacher Defends." Seemuller's

letter was intended to address and did address the complaint of discrimination based on sex—a matter of public concern. This is apparent from the letter itself and from Seemuller's testimony at trial: "I was poking fun or making light or telling them to lighten up a little bit, that maybe what they had heard wasn't what really was going on." Asked to describe the letter, he testified: "My letter is, it is a humorous attempt at satire to point out that misperceptions can occur."

In his letter of apology, Seemuller explicitly stated that in his first letter he addressed "male chauvinism in the physical education department" and that the "intent of the letter was satirical in nature." The editor understood that Seemuller's first letter was a "Satirical Response" to the anonymous letter protesting discrimination based on sex. The editor appended a note saying the letter of apology was unnecessary and expressing the hope that Seemuller's treatment will not "scare others from contributing." The editor was aware of the danger of chilling speech protected by the first amendment.

The deputy superintendent of schools who presided over the grievance hearing recognized that Seemuller's letter dealt with a matter of public concern. In her decision she found as a fact that Seemuller's "letter was published in the context of school and community concern about the treatment of females in school programs." The grievance decision acknowledges that Seemuller was exercising his freedom of speech.

The record discloses that even before the anonymous letter was published in December 1986 some girls had complained that they were treated as second class citizens in the school. The exchange of correspondence between the anonymous letter writer and Seemuller sparked much livelier discussion about discrimination based on sex. The day after Seemuller's letter was published the principal met with 32 girls regarding discrimination and assured them he would not tolerate it. Later the school human relations committee met, deplored discrimination based on sex, and urged the principal to take steps to prevent it. Some people, taking Seemuller's letter literally, were offended by it and criticized it as demeaning women. Nevertheless, the fact that some persons considered the letter to be inappropriate or controversial "is irrelevant to the question whether it deals with a matter of public concern." . . . "[T]he public expression of ideas may not be prohibited merely because the ideas are themselves offensive to some of their hearers." . . .

Seemuller's use of satire to comment on a matter of public concern did not deprive him of the protection afforded by the first amendment. From Greek and Roman antiquity until the present time, commentators on public affairs have colored their writing with satire — sometimes humorous, sometimes gentle, sometimes caustic. . . . A teacher's letter criticizing the board of education was spiced with satire, but he was not deprived of the first amendment's protection. . . . Writing in a different context, the Supreme Court has observed that the first amendment protects satirists. . . .

In sum, we conclude that a complaint published in a school newspaper that a public school discriminates on the basis of sex raises a question of public concern. Seemuller's published response to the complaint also commented on a matter of public concern.

The judgment of the district court is vacated, and the case is remanded for further proceedings consistent with this opinion. Seemuller shall recover his costs.

■ PRIVACY

The word "privacy" is not mentioned in the Constitution or the Bill of Rights; yet, the right of privacy is so basic and fundamental to individual freedom that it is assumed to emanate implicitly from several sources in the Bill of Rights.

Justice Douglas in *Griswold v. Connecticut*[19] stated that there is a broad right of privacy which may be inferred from several provisions of the Bill of Rights. Justice Stewart dissented in *Griswold* on the grounds that he "can find no" general rights of privacy in the Bill of Rights or any other section of the constitution. The court noted that previous courts had

never held that the Bill of Rights and/or other Amendments only protected those rights specifically mentioned by name. The court said that the various guarantees of the constitution "create zones of privacy."

> The right of association contained in the penumbra of the First Amendment is one. . . . The Third Amendment in its prohibition against the quartering of soldiers "in any house" in time of peace without the consent of the owner is another faced of that privacy. The Fourth Amendment explicitly affirms the "right of the people to be secure in their persons, houses, papers, and effects, against unreasonable searches and seizures." The Fifth Amendment in its Self-Incrimination Clause enables the citizen to create a zone of privacy which government may not force him to surrender to his detriment. The Ninth Amendment provides: "The enumeration in the Constitution, of certain rights, shall not be construed to deny or disparage others retained by the people.[20]

The Ninth Amendment, though rarely relied upon, is possibly the most inclusive of all, because it guarantees natural rights and freedoms to individuals that are not enumerated elsewhere in the Constitution. . . . This amendment was thought necessary by Madison, its author, because he feared that the enumeration of other rights in the first eight amendments would imply to later generations that this list was exhaustive, and no other rights were intended. The simple expedient that he used to combat this assumption was to include a "catchall" amendment to protect all other "great rights of mankind" against governmental intrusion.[21]

The right of privacy also finds basis in the substance of liberty of the Due Process Clause of the Fourteenth Amendment. This was the basis for the Supreme Court's decision in *Roe v. Wade*.[22] The connection between personal privacy and liberty is reinforced by the earlier precedents of *Pierce v. Society of Sisters*[23] and *Meyer v. Nebraska*.[24]

It is the confluence and implication of these specified constitutional rights and freedoms that create the penumbras of privacy that Justice Douglas spoke of in *Griswold*.

Because privacy is a fundamental right governmental restraint can be justified only by a showing of a "compelling state interest."[25]

The essence of the privacy right, because of its breadth, is relatively difficult to circumscribe. Killian, though, explains it best:

> Privacy as a concept appears to encompass at least two different but related aspects. First, it relates to the right or the ability of individuals to determine how much and what information about themselves is to be revealed to others. Second, it relates to the idea of autonomy, the freedom of individuals to perform or not perform certain acts or subject themselves to certain experiences.[26]

Teachers' Mental and Physical Examinations

Teachers have always served as role models for pupils, and school boards expect high moral standards consistent with this status. The courts have generally upheld school boards in regulating the personal conduct of teachers within reasonable limits. Litigation, though, may result when teachers allege school rules invade their privacy.

Most of the litigation concerning a teacher's right of privacy involves issues of morality or fitness to teach, and has included such issues as homosexual activities, heterosexual improprieties, and use of marijuana and other drugs. The courts attempt to determine a rational nexus between the conduct in question and the professional duties being performed. To sustain their case against a teacher, the school board must establish whether the outside activity has a detrimental impact on the teacher's effectiveness to teach. "No person can be denied government employment because of factors unconnected with the responsibilities of that employment."[27]

Teachers' use of the right of privacy has become more frequent in recent years, as schools have sought to test and examine teachers for various reasons. In one such case, a federal district judge rejected the privacy claim of a female teacher who refused to submit to a physical examination by a male physician employed by the school district. The court, in holding against the teacher, said that there was no right of privacy at stake, but rather a personal predilection against male physicians.[28]

In another recent case, a school principal's privacy claim was found to give way to the public interest where the school superintendent had reason to believe that the principal needed psychiatric attention.[29]

Drug Testing

In 1990 the Georgia General Assembly passed a number of bills aimed at fighting the drug problem. One of these acts required all state employment applicants to submit to urine testing to determine the presence of illegal drugs. In *Skinner v. Railway Labor Executives*,[30] the Supreme Court stated "[b]ecause it [is] clear that the collection and testing of urine intrudes upon expectations of privacy that society has long recognized as reasonable . . . these intrusions [are] searches under the Fourth Amendment." Recently, in *National Treasury Employees Union v. Von Raab*,[31] it was established that there are times when Fourth Amendment intrusion serves a special governmental need. When these special needs are present, then the privacy expectations of the individual must be balanced against the government's interest on whether it is impractical to require a search warrant or have a particularized individual suspicion. *Von Raab* concerned the testing of Custom Service employees who carried fire arms, enforced drug law, had access to classified information among other duties. The court found the need compelling that first line drug enforcement officials are drug free, and therefore be subject to drug testing. The facts of the Georgia case differ drastically since the state government justified the testing on a generalized governmental interest in maintaining a drug-free work place.

Therefore drug tests appear to be allowed if specific governmental reasons are articulated and the balancing analysis set forth in *Von Raab* is utilized. The court in the Georgia case ruled the act violated the Fourth and Fourteenth Amendments because the " . . . state's generalized interest in insuring [the] integrity of [the] work force was not sufficiently compelling to outweigh applicants' right to privacy . . . "[32]

*Requirement That Principal See a Psychiatrist Did
Not Violate His Right of Privacy*

- - - - - - - - - -

Daury v. Smith

- - - - - - - - - -

United States Court of Appeals,
First Circuit, 1988.
842 F.2d 9.

BOWNES, Circuit Judge. Plaintiff-appellant Jeffrey Daury appeals the grant of summary judgment in favor of defendants-appellees in his action for deprivation of constitutional rights under 42 U.S.C. § 1983. Daury, a "grade leader" in the Pittsfield, Massachusetts school system, alleged in three counts of his complaint that the defendants, by requiring him to consult a psychiatrist as a condition of continued employment, deprived him of his right to privacy as guaranteed by the ninth and fourteenth amendments and his right to liberty as guaranteed by the fourteenth amendment. Daury claimed that as a result of defendants' action he suffered emotional distress, mental anguish, and damage to his health and well-being. Daury further claims that the decision to require him to see a psychiatrist was made in retaliation for his "union activities and free speech" and constituted intentional infliction of emotional distress. . . .

Jeffrey Daury began work for the Pittsfield school system in 1970 as a school principal. Two general aspects of his tenure are relevant to this appeal. First, Daury's favorable work evaluations began to decline in 1979 because defendants received an above average number of complaints concerning Daury from parents. Daury admits that some complaints did issue, but denies the foundation for many of them. Second, from 1979 until some time in 1983, Daury was a member of the negotiating team for the Pittsfield Teacher's Association. Daury asserts that he was very vocal in this role, but concedes that nothing unusual—neither strikes nor picketing—occurred during any period of contract negotiations.

In May 1983, the school committee decided to close one of the schools in the district because of budgetary constraints. It, therefore, became necessary to demote one principal; the committee decided upon Daury, and he was demoted to his present position of grade leader. Daury initiated a grievance procedure, but subsequently abandoned it. The committee has averred that its decision was in strict accordance with the requirement under the collective bargaining agreement that it consider both seniority *and* performance in deciding upon the demotion of a school principal.

Defendants point to three incidents, as well as other matters, leading to their decision to require that Daury see a psychiatrist. The first incident took place in October 1982. During a meeting about school funds between Daury and Theodore Herberg, director of research for the Pittsfield schools, Daury brought up a personal matter. The conversation turned into a near physical altercation; Daury received a written reprimand from Superintendent Davis. Daury filed a grievance and an arbitrator upheld the reprimand.

The second incident occurred in November 1982. Daury discovered documents in his personnel file that he had not signed. This was contrary to the collective bargaining agreement, which required that any document placed in a teacher's personnel file must be first signed by the teacher. Later that same day, Daury encountered Davis and another school administrator in the school parking lot. An argument concerning the unsigned documents ensued, as a result of which Davis suspended Daury for three days without pay. Again Daury filed a grievance. The arbitrator reduced the suspension to one day, and ordered the documents removed from Daury's file.

The final incident which prompted the school committee to require that Daury see a psychiatrist took place on June 3, 1983. Daury was supervising students crossing the street when a boy (not, as it developed, a student at Daury's school) began to cross in an unsafe manner. Daury told the boy to stop, and the boy swore at him. Daury took hold of him. According to Daury, he held the boy's arm. Defendants were told that Daury grabbed the boy by the neck. A police officer intervened and the boy was released. The boy's parents initiated a criminal complaint against Daury for assault and battery. Two witnesses, including the police officer, testified at trial that Daury put a "stranglehold" on the boy. One of these witnesses, a woman who allegedly viewed the entire incident, had telephoned Davis reporting the incident soon after it happened. Daury was found not guilty and the presiding judge praised his behavior as responsible.

Prior to the criminal trial, Daury and his attorney met in Davis' office with a representative of the Massachusetts Teachers Association (MTA), Assistant Superintendent Bordeau, and Superintendent Davis. Both Bordeau and Davis assert that Daury stated at the meeting that he was under a great deal of pressure and that he thought he needed some tranquilizers. It was tentatively agreed that Daury would be put on a leave of absence with pay until the end of the school year—that is, until the end of June 1983.

The school committee formally approved the paid leave at a meeting held that same evening. In addition, the committee decided that Daury be required to see a psychiatrist before returning to work. . . .

On August 7, 1984, Daury filed suit against the defendants.

Daury alleges that the school committee's order that he see a psychiatrist violated his constitutional right to privacy. More specifically, he maintains that compelling him to submit to a psychiatric examination as a condition to his continued employment forced him to reveal information about his marriage, family history, and other personal relationships, and that this constituted an invasion of privacy regardless of the promise given by the school committee to keep the report confidential.

That a person has a constitutional right to privacy is now well established. . . . Such right includes "the individual interest in avoiding disclosure of personal matters . . . ." . . . The privacy right, however, must often give way to considerations of public interest. . . .

In *Lyons v. Sullivan,* 602 F.2d 7 (1st Cir.), *cert. denied,* 444 U.S. 876, 100 S.Ct. 159, 62 L.Ed.2d 104 (1979), we held that a matter of public concern overrode the right to privacy. Lyons, a public school teacher, filed an unusual complaint in a medical malpractice action, which led the school superintendent to question his mental stability. . . . We found that the superintendent had a reasonable basis for questioning Lyon's mental condition, and that there was no constitutional infirmity in the course of conduct pursued.

As *Lyons* implicitly recognizes, there is a legitimate public interest in providing a safe and healthy educational environment. A school committee, therefore, may justifiably compel a teacher or administrator to submit to a psychiatric examination as a condition of continued employment if the committee has reason to believe that the teacher or administrator may be jeopardizing the welfare of students under his or her supervision.

Viewing the evidence in the light most favorable to Daury, we find no violation of his constitutional rights in the school committee's requiring that Daury see a psychiatrist. The committee simply sought a professional opinion to insure that Daury would not, if he returned to work, jeopardize the school system's interest in providing a safe and healthy educational environment. . . . And Daury offered no specific evidence contradicting the committee's position that it had a reasonable basis for concern.

Daury argues that the June 3, 1983 incident could not have been a real basis for concern because he was eventually acquitted of the criminal charge filed against him. . . . Even if we assume, as Daury contends, that he grabbed the boy by the arm and not around the neck, the fact that the boy's parents filed a criminal complaint suggests that Daury's reaction to the boy's conduct was severe enough to question his ability to handle the supervision of children, some of whom may be disruptive at times.

In light of all of the information the school committee had—the June 3 incident, Daury's statement that he was under pressure and needed tranquilizers, the two incidents in which he precipitated physical confrontations, and the complaints by parents,—we think it was eminently reasonable for the school committee to require that Daury submit to a psychiatric examination. . . .

We think that on this record the school committee acted prudently in requiring that Daury see a psychiatrist. . . .

Plaintiff's complaint does not contain any count stating that defendants, in requiring him to submit to a psychiatric examination, did so in retaliation for plaintiff's union activities and exercise of his right to free speech. None of the counts use the words "retaliation," "union activities," "first amendment," or "free speech." The district court noted this omission but addressed the issue, apparently because plaintiff had argued it in a memorandum to the court. Plaintiff's brief to this court suggests that the allegation was included in Count II of his complaint. His brief states: "The complaint included claims pursuant to 42 U.S.C. 1983 for deprivation of the plaintiffs liberty interest by the defendants intentional infliction of emotional distress in retaliation for the plaintiff's union activities and free speech." . . .

We will not rewrite plaintiff's complaint to contain a count that was not included in it.
. . .

Affirmed.

FREEDOM OF RELIGION

All persons in this country have the right of religious freedom as guaranteed by the First Amendment. However, religion, as with other freedoms, is not without certain limits. For example, in *Palmer v. Board of Education of the City of Chicago,* a teacher refused to carry out certain aspects of the approved curriculum because of religious beliefs. The court acknowledged the teacher's right to freedom of belief, but also recognized a compelling state interest in the proper education of all its children. The court stated that education "cannot be left to individual teachers to teach the way they please." Teachers have "no

constitutional right to require others to submit to [their] views and to forego a portion of their education they would otherwise be entitled to enjoy."[33]

A teacher's religious freedom may extend into several aspects of the educational program. For example, if the tenets of a teacher's religion are violated by the Pledge of Allegiance to the American flag, the teacher cannot be compelled to recite the pledge, but, the teacher, in accordance with school board rules, must hold the pledge ceremony for student participation.[34] Religious freedom of teachers is sustained by the courts so long as the exercise of the freedom does not encroach on the rights of students or is not deleterious to the good conduct of the school.

Title VII

The right of religious freedom, where employment is concerned, has been expanded by the 1972 Amendments to the Civil Rights Act of 1964, Title VII. The original act prohibited an employer from discriminating against an employee because of race, color, or sex, but did not specify religion. The 1972 Amendments incorporated religion, stating:

> It shall be an unlawful employment practice for an employment agency to fail or refuse for employment, or otherwise to discriminate against, any individual because of his race, color, religion, sex, or national origin, or to classify or refer for employment any individual on the basis of his race, color, religion, sex, or national origin.

The act further states that "[t]he term religion includes all aspects of religious observances and practice, as well as belief, unless an employer demonstrates that he is unable to reasonably accommodate an employee's or prospective employee's religious observance or practice without undue hardship on the conduct of the employer's business.[35]

The burden of proof is on the teacher to initially show that the school board's decision was religiously motivated or involved the denial of the teacher's religious freedom. If the teacher is able to sustain this proof, then the burden of proof shifts to the school board to show that a good-faith effort was made to accommodate the teacher's religious beliefs. If this effort is unsuccessful, then the board must show that it could not address the teacher's religious concerns without undue hardship to the school district.

In a case where a teacher who was a member of the World Wide Church of God requested seven days off from school, without pay, to attend a religious festival, the board refused the request, and discharged the teacher when the teacher left school and attended anyway.[36] Before leaving, however, the teacher prepared lesson plans and consulted with the school counselor, who served as the substitute teacher. The court determined that the classes had run smoothly and the school district had suffered no undue hardship. The court concluded that the dismissal was unwarranted and violated the teacher's Title VII rights.

In a similar case, a Jewish teacher claimed that she needed more than two days leave to celebrate religious holidays.[37] She noted that Christian teachers had the benefit of more days that coincided with the regular school calendar. Effectively, the denial of religious holidays compelled the Jewish teacher to choose between employment and religious observances. The court, in holding for the teacher, said that Title VII was violated if "An employer . . . punishes an employee by placing the latter in a position in which he or she must ignore a tenet of faith in order to retain employment.[38]

One of the primary questions under the act is, what does an employer have to do to reasonably accommodate the religious beliefs of an employee? In *Trans World Airlines, Inc. v. Hardison*,[39] the Supreme Court addressed this issue. Title VII did not require TWA "to carve out special exemptions" to permit a special religious observance on Saturday instead of Sunday. TWA had claimed that special accommodation for an employee on other than regular Christian holidays forced it to incur extraordinary costs for scheduling and replacement personnel. "To require TWA to bear more than a *de minimis* cost, in order to

give the employee Saturdays off, is an undue hardship."

In *Ansonia Board of Education v. Philbrook* (Chapter 17) the employee and employer each proposed a reasonable accommodation. The court of appeals ruled the employer was required to accept the employee's proposal unless it caused any undue hardship on the employers business. The Supreme Court reversed the court of appeals and stated:

> An employer has met its obligation under § 701(j) when it demonstrates that it has offered a reasonable accommodation to the employee. The employer need not further show that each of the employee's alternative accommodations would result in undue hardship. The extent of undue hardship on the employer's business is at issue only where the employer claims that it is unable to offer any reasonable accommodation without such hardship.[40]

Neither Inhibit nor Promote Religion

The religious provisions of the First Amendment, of course, apply to teachers in their employment capacity. A school board action must meet all conditions of the tripartite test of *Lemon v. Kurtzman,* in order not to violate the establishment clause of the First Amendment. As discussed earlier in this textbook, these conditions specify that the action must (1) have a secular purpose, (2) neither inhibit nor promote religion, and (3) not cause excessive entanglement.[41]

Following the First Amendment rule, a New Jersey court held that a teacher-negotiated agreement that allowed for paid leaves of absences for religious believers, but made no allowance for nonbelievers, violated the First Amendment. The court cited an earlier Supreme Court case of *Torcaso v. Watkins,* which held that it was unconstitutional to "impose requirements which aid all religions as against non-believers."[42]

Religious Garb

Whether public school teachers can wear religious garb of any particular religious order or society has been litigated on several occasions. While there is no precise definition of what constitutes religious garments, some states have sought prohibition of any apparel that showed that the person belonged to a particular sect, denomination, or order.[43]

In 1894, the Supreme Court of Pennsylvania held that the wearing by nuns of garb and insignia of the Sisterhood of St. Joseph while teaching in the public schools did not constitute sectarian teaching.[44] The court reasoned that to deny wearing of such apparel would violate the teachers' religious liberty. Later, the legislature of Pennsylvania prohibited the wearing of garb by public school teachers while in performance of their duties. This statute was subsequently upheld by the Pennsylvania Supreme Court. This time the court maintained that the act was a reasonable exercise of state power in regulating the educational system to prevent sectarian control. The court found that the legislation "is directed against acts, not beliefs, and only against acts of the teacher while engaged in the performance of his or her duties as such teacher."[45]

Litigation over the years in other states has been split on the issue. A New York Court in 1906 held that "the influence of such apparel is distinctly sectarian."[46] Similarly, the Nebraska Supreme Court refused to mandate that the state superintendent distribute state school trust funds to a school because of the school's religious emblems, and the teachers wore distinctive garb, including the rosary, indicative of the Catholic sisterhood.[47]

On the other hand, the wearing of religious garb has been upheld by at least three state supreme courts. In a North Dakota case, the court held that there was no evidence that nuns imparted religious instruction even though they were dressed in religious garb of the Sisterhood of St. Benedict.[48]

Most recently, in a definitive analysis of the issue, the Supreme Court of Oregon held that a teacher's certification could be revoked for wearing religious garb.[49] In so holding, the court observed that the legislature had a legitimate objective in maintaining the neutrality of the public schools. While the denial of the wearing of religious garb could be interpreted by some as an impingement on

the teacher's personal religious freedom, it could just as logically be maintained the state's condoning of such garb favors that particular religion and, in fact, places the imprimatur of the state behind that particular religious sect. The Oregon court said "that the teacher's appearance in religious garb may leave a conscious or unconscious impression among young people and their parents that the school endorses the particular religious commitment of the person (teacher)."[50]

Any lack of consensus by the courts is due to their legitimate hesitancy to invade either the religious rights of teachers or students. The issue boils down to one of a weighing of interests in view of the particular facts of the case. As the Connecticut Supreme Court has said:

> The decisions in these cases, however, are, as is to be expected, based upon a wide diversity of facts. The only definite conclusion that may be drawn from them is that whether sectarian influence connected with a school is such as to affect its public character is ordinarily a question of fact for the trial court.[51]

Tenured Teachers Can Have Certificate Revoked for Violating State Statute Prohibiting the Wearing of Religious Garb in School

— - — · — · — — · —

Cooper v. Eugene School District No. 4J

— - — · — · — — · —

Supreme Court of Oregon, 1986.
301 Or. 358, 723 P.2d 298.

LINDE, Justice. When Janet Cooper, a special education teacher in the Eugene public schools, became a Sikh, she donned white clothes and a white turban and wore them while teaching her sixth and eighth grade classes. In a letter to the staff of the school where she taught, she wrote that she would wear the turban and often wear white clothing as part of her religious practice, and that she had explained this and other changes in her life to her students.* She continued to wear her white garb after being warned that she faced suspension if she violated a law against wearing religious dress at her work. The law provides, in ORS 342.650:

> No teacher in any public school shall wear any religious dress while engaged in the performance of duties as a teacher.

and, in ORS 342.655:

> Any teacher violating the provisions of ORS 342.650 shall be suspended from employment by the district school board. The board shall report its action to the Superintendent of Public Instruction who shall revoke the teacher's teaching certificate.

Persuant to these statutes, the school superintendent, acting for the school board, suspended Cooper from teaching and reported this action to the Superintendent of Public Instruction, who, after a hearing, revoked Cooper's teaching certificate. This order was challenged on constitutional grounds in the Court of Appeals, which set aside the revocation of the teaching certificate as an excessive sanction under the court's understanding of federal First Amendment doctrine. . . . On petitions by the school district and the Superintendent of Public Instruction, we allowed review. . . .

Cooper's case is not one of declining to comply with an otherwise valid law on grounds of personal religious belief. . . . ORS 342.650 is not neutral toward religion. On the contrary, the religious significance of the teacher's dress is the specific target of this law. The law singles out a teacher's religious dress because it is religious and to the extent that its religious significance is apparent when the wearer is engaged in teaching. The issue therefore is whether the law infringes the right guaranteed to "all men" by Article I, section 2, of the Oregon Constitution "to worship Almighty God according to the dic-

tates of their own consciences," or "control[s] the free exercise, and enjoyment of religious opinions, or interfere[s] with the rights of conscience" contrary to Article I, section 3. . . .

The guarantees of religious freedom in Article I provide:

> Section 2. All men shall be secure in the Natural right, to worship Almighty God according to the dictates of their own consciences.
> Section 3. No law shall in any case whatever control the free exercise, and enjoyment of religeous (sic) opinions or interfere with the rights of conscience.
> Section 4. No religious test shall be required as a qualification for any office of trust or profit.
> Section 5. No money shall be drawn from the Treasury for the benefit of any religeous (sic), or theological institution, nor shall any money be appropriated for the payment of any religeous (sic) services in either house of the Legislative Assembly.
> Section 6. No person shall be rendered incompetent as a witness, or juror in consequence of his opinions on matters of religeon (sic); nor be questioned in any Court of Justice touching his religeous (sic) belief to affect the weight of his testimony.
> Section 7. The mode of administering an oath, or affirmation shall be such as may be most consistent with, and binding upon the conscience of the person to whom such oath or affirmation may be administered.

This court in fact has interpreted the meaning of these guarantees independently, sometimes with results contrary to those reached by the United States Supreme Court. . . .

The religion clauses of Oregon's Bill of Rights, Article I, sections 2, 3, 4, 5, 6 and 7, are more than a code. They are specifications of a larger vision of freedom for a diversity of religious beliefs and modes of worship and freedom from state-supported official faiths or modes of worship. The cumulation of guarantees, more numerous and more concrete than the opening clause of the First Amendment, reinforces the significance of the separate guarantees. . . .

. . . If such a law is to be valid, it must be justified by a determination that religious dress necessarily contravenes the wearer's

---

* Cooper also had married and had changed her name to Karta Kaur Khalsa.

role or function at the time and place beyond any realistic means of accommodation.

The compatibility of religious dress with the role of public school teachers is an old issue under state laws and constitutions. Generally it involved teaching by nuns while wearing the habits of their orders. It is, of course, a different question whether a constitution itself is claimed to forbid the display of the teacher's religious commitment in the public school or whether a ban on religious dress adopted by law or properly delegated rule contravenes the teacher's religious freedom. . . .

The courts' tolerance of overt religious symbolism in public schools has differed over time and perhaps with the religious composition of different communities. Looking beyond the specific facts of the cases, however, the decisions generally have been that more than a teacher's religious dress is needed to show a forbidden sectarian influence in the classroom, but that a rule against such religious dress is permissible to avoid the appearance of sectarian influence, favoritism, or official approval in the public school. The policy choice must be made in the first instance by those with lawmaking or delegated authority to make rules for the schools. The courts' role is to see whether the rule stays within that authority and within the constitution and, if necessary, to give the rule a constitutional interpretation.

Here the policy choice was made by the legislature. There is no reason to believe that when the Legislative Assembly enacted ORS 342.650 in its present form in 1965, it had any aim other than to maintain the religious neutrality of the public schools, to avoid giving children or their parents the impression that the school, through its teacher, approves and shares the religious commitment of one group and perhaps finds that of others less worthy. . . .

Recognition that freedom of religion for all implies official sponsorship of none has grown with the growing diversity of the nation itself. Two hundred years ago religious toleration could mean toleration merely among Protestant denominations. *See, e.g.,* Massachusetts Declaration of Rights, Art III (1780). Even after

Catholics, Jews, other minority faiths, and nonbelievers were accorded the right to follow their own views, toleration did not imply that their views were as good as the community's dominant religion. For those to whom religion is a matter of truth or error rather than "opinion," as the constitution says, to tolerate error did not mean that those in a position to speak for the community should not officially proclaim what they firmly believe to be the truth. Those whose faiths thereby would be relegated to second-class status of course might see freedom of religion differently.

The main battleground has been the public schools, as the cases under the constitutional proscriptions of "sectarian influence" and later under the First Amendment show. Parents and lawmakers may and do assume that the hours, days, and years spent in school are the time and the place when a young person is most impressionable by the expressed and implicit orthodoxies of the adult community and most sensitive to being perceived as different from the majority of his or her peers; famous constitutional cases have involved this socializing rather than intellectual function of the schools. In excluding teachers whose dress is a constant and inescapable visual reminder of their religious commitment, laws like ORS 342.650 respect and contribute to the child's right to the free exercise and enjoyment of its religious opinions or heritage, untroubled by being out of step with those of the teacher.

The principle is most obvious when the teacher represents the community's dominant religion, but it cannot be limited to that situation. From the "Know-Nothing" nativism of the mid-19th century, through the battle over the "Blaine Amendment," to recent times, contention centered on the role of Catholicism in public schools, symbolized by the dress of priests and nuns, as distinct from mainstream Protestantism, represented by school prayers and the King James translation of the Bible. . . . It may be a far cry from these historic conflicts to perceive any threat of sectarian influence in the dress of a sect that, in this country, may seem an exotic curiosity. But we are examining the validity of the law against a charge that it denies teachers the freedom to adopt the dress of their respective religions. Neither their religious freedom nor that of their students can depend on calculations which faiths are more likely than others to snatch a young soul from a rival creed. The tides of immigration and of home-grown religions have changed before and are changing again, and what is exotic today may tomorrow gain many thousands of adherents and potential majority status in some communities.[*] . . .

We conclude that ORS 342.650 does not impose an impermissible requirement for teaching in the public schools if it is properly limited to actual incompatibility with the teaching function.

A court's obligation before invalidating a textually overbroad statute is to see whether it can be interpreted so as to save the legislative purpose as far as the constitution permits, leaving only marginal instances of potentially unconstitutional application to case-by-case decision. *State v. Moyle,* 299 Or. 691, 702, 705 P.2d 740 (1985). The Court of Appeals recognized the need to limit the potential reach of ORS 342.650. Compliance with the statute demands some sacrifice of religious self-expression by a teacher. The statute, of course, does not forbid the wearing of religious dress outright, but it does forbid doing so while teaching. The law could be described either as denying a teacher's right to practice her religion or as denying a person demonstratively committed to a religious vocation the opportunity to teach in the public schools. . . .

. . . The religious influence on children while in the public school that laws like ORS 342.650, in their concern with the employment of nuns wearing their special garb as public school teachers, legitimately seek to prevent is not the mere knowledge that a teacher is an adherent of a particular religion. Their concern is that the teacher's appearance in religious garb may leave a conscious or unconscious impression among young people and their parents that the school endorses the particular religious commitment of the person whom it has assigned the public role of teacher. This is what makes the otherwise privileged display of a teacher's religious commitment by her dress incompatible with the atmosphere of religious neutrality that ORS 342.650 aims to preserve, or so the school authorities may decide. The statute therefore would not be violated whenever a teacher makes an occasional appearance in religious dress, for instance on her way to or from a seasonal ceremony. . . . Only wearing religious dress as a regular or frequently repeated practice while teaching is grounds for disqualification.

We conclude that, when correctly interpreted and applied, ORS 342.650 survives challenge under Oregon's guarantees of religious freedom. As interpreted in this opinion, we believe it also does not violate the federal First Amendment.

The Court of Appeals thought that revocation of a teaching certificate was an excessive "sanction" discouraging even privileged exercise of First Amendment rights more than is necessary to achieve the law's purpose of maintaining religious freedom and neutrality in the public schools. We do not disagree with the court's general proposition that First Amendment decisions have required limitations on the exercise of First Amendment rights to be no more restrictive than necessary, although we note, as the district argues, that the decisions deal with the coverage of such limitations rather than with the consequence of violating a valid rule.

ORS 342.650 might indeed restrict a teacher's First Amendment rights to the "free

---

[*]From 1900 to 1980, Roman Catholics increased from 17 percent to 30 percent of the population while Protestants declined from 65 percent to about 41 percent. The approximate numbers of Buddhists in the United States increased from 30,000 to 80,000, Muslims from 10,000 to about 1,600,000, Hindus from 1,000 to about 400,000. World Christian Encyclopedia 711 (D.B. Barrett, ed. 1982). Among specifically American denominations that have evolved since Oregon became a state, Mormon church membership grew from a few thousand in 1840 to about 200,000 in 1900 and 1,500,000 in 1960. Christian Science churches and societies, which did not exist before 1879, numbered about 2,300 in 1960. Gaustad, Historical Atlas of Religion in America 87, 132 (1962).

exercise" of religion more than necessary if it were applied literally, but where ORS 342.650 can validly be applied, the revocation of a teaching certificate under ORS 342.655 is not a penalty. It is not a withdrawal of a privilege by reason of hostility to a religious or political belief, as when some states disqualified Communists from driving or practicing pharmacy or from living in public housing. . . . It is a disqualification from teaching in public schools based on one's doing so in a manner incompatible with that function. We doubt that the First Amendment draws a line between a law that disqualifies a public school teacher by compelling her discharge and another law that disqualifies her by revoking her certificate to teach in the public schools. ORS 342.655 does not forbid requalifying for a certificate.

Insofar as the decision of the Court of Appeals strikes down ORS 342.655 on that premise, it must be reversed. . . . Because ORS 342.650 and 342.655 can be interpreted to remain within constitutional limits and can be constitutionally administered, the Superintendent's order pursuant to ORS 342.655 is not unlawful for being based on an invalid statute. . . .

The decision of the Court of Appeals is reversed.

942, 107 S.Ct. 1597 (1987). The administrators in the Philadelphia school requested that a Muslim teacher not wear her religious garb to school. The teacher challenged the statute as a violation of Title VII of the Civil Rights Act of 1964. The court concluded that it would impose an undue hardship on the school board to accommodate the teacher and stated:

> Where the statute bans *all* religious attire and is being enforced by the Commonwealth in a non-discriminatory manner with respect to the Muslim teachers as well as Catholics, we conclude that it is irrelevant whether a portion of those who voted for the statute in 1895 were motivated by a desire to bar Catholic habit from the classroom. We therefore accept that the Commonwealth regards the wearing of religious attire by teachers while teaching as a significant threat to the maintenance of religious neutrality in the public school system, and accordingly conclude that it would impose an undue hardship to require the Commonwealth to accommodate Ms. Reardon and others similarly situated.

United States v. Board of Education of School District of Philadelphia, 911 F.2d 882 (3rd Cir. 1990)

NOTES

1. A teacher who was a member of the original African Hebrew Israelites of Ethiopia wore a headwrap to school and was dismissed and denied unemployment benefits. The court held for the teacher stating schools may have reasonable dress codes provided they do not infringe on constitutional rights. *Mississippi Employment Security Commission v. McGlothin*, 556 So.2d 324 (Miss. 1990).

2. Pennsylvania passed a religious garb statute, in 1895, which is nearly identical to the Oregon statute challenged in *Cooper v. Eugene School District No. 4J*, 301 Or. 358, 723 P.2d 298 (1986) appeal dismissed 489 U.S.

▮▮▮ PRIVILEGE AGAINST SELF-INCRIMINATION

The Fifth Amendment self-incrimination clause, which provides that a person shall not "be compelled in any criminal case to be a witness against himself," was absorbed into the due process clause of the Fourteenth Amendment,[52] and made applicable to the states in 1964. The right that no man is bound to accuse himself, *nemo tenetur seipsum prodere,* is extended by the Fifth Amendment to teachers as it is to all individuals. The right, itself, though, does not allow avoidance of questions regarding professional competency or fitness to teach. The self-incrimination clause was intended to protect a person against inquisitional extraction of incriminating evidence in criminal proceedings or in governmental hearings that may result in criminal prosecution. This right extends only to protecting one's self, not another person. If a teacher validly invokes the Fifth Amendment, there can be no presumption of guilt.

In *Slochower v. Board of Education*,[53] the Supreme Court held that the dismissal of a Brooklyn College professor for invoking the Fifth Amendment before a congressional committee was unconstitutional. This case cannot, however, be too broadly interpreted, for only a short time later the Supreme Court held in *Beilan v. Board of Education*[54] that a teacher could be dismissed for refusing to answer questions posed by the school superintendent about alleged past subversive activities. The Court found that the dismissal was not predicated on an impermissible inference of criminal guilt drawn from refusal to answer, but instead on a finding of insubordination emanating from the fact that the teacher refused to answer.[55] *Slochower* was distinguished from *Beilan* in that the refusal to answer in *Beilan* was directed toward questions posed by a superior in specific regard to fitness to teach, and incompetency was specifically cited as the reason for dismissal.

The rationale of *Beilan*, though, comes under a shadow, because the Court has ruled subsequently that disbarment of a lawyer for refusing to produce evidence in an ethical practices proceeding was unconstitutional.[56] Also, the dismissal of a policeman for invoking the Fifth Amendment privilege in refusing to answer questions regarding his fitness and concerning conduct that could open him to criminal prosecution was held to be unconstitutional.[57] Although these cases can be distinguished in that the former involved disbarment and denial of future employment and the latter related to criminal evidence, the strength of the *Beilan* decision is substantially diminished if the fitness of a teacher is viewed in the broader constitutional context of subsequent First Amendment and due process cases affecting teachers.

Failure of Teacher to Answer Questions Posed by Superintendent Concerning Loyalty May Be Incompetency

————·——·——·——

Beilan v. Board of Education School District of Philadelphia

————·——·——·——

Supreme Court of the United States, 1958.
357 U.S. 399, 78 S.Ct. 1317.

Mr. Justice BURTON delivered the opinion of the Court. The question before us is whether the Board of Public Education for the School District of Philadelphia, Pennsylvania, violated the Due Process Clause of the Fourteenth Amendment to the Constitution of the United States when the Board, purporting to act under the Pennsylvania Public School Code, discharged a public school teacher on the ground of "incompetency," evidenced by the teacher's refusal of his Superintendent's request to confirm or refute information as to the teacher's loyalty and his activities in certain allegedly subversive organizations. For the reasons hereafter stated, we hold that it did not.

On June 25, 1952, Herman A. Beilan, the petitioner, who had been a teacher for about twenty-two years in the Philadelphia Public School System, presented himself at his Superintendent's office in response to the latter's request. The Superintendent said he had information which reflected adversely on petitioner's loyalty and he wanted to determine its truth or falsity. In response to petitioner's suggestion that the Superintendent do the questioning, the latter said he would ask one question and petitioner could then determine whether he would answer it and others of that type. The Superintendent, accordingly, asked petitioner whether or not he had been the Press Director of the Professional Section of the Communist Political Association in 1944. Petitioner asked permission to consult counsel before answering and the Superintendent granted his request.

On October 14, 1952, in response to a similar request, petitioner again presented himself at the Superintendent's office. Petitioner stated that he had consulted counsel and that he declined to answer the question as to his activities in 1944. He announced he would also decline to answer any other "questions similar to it," "questions of this type," or "questions about political and religious beliefs . . . ." The Superintendent warned petitioner that this "was a very serious and a very important matter and that failure to answer the questions might lead to his dismissal." The Superintendent made it clear that he was investigating "a real question of fitness for [petitioner] to be a teacher or to continue in the teaching work." These interviews were given no publicity and were attended only by petitioner, his Superintendent and the Assistant Solicitor of the Board. . . . The only question before us is whether the federal Constitution prohibits petitioner's discharge for statutory "incompetency" based on his refusal to answer the Superintendent's questions.

By engaging in teaching in the public schools, petitioner did not give up his right to freedom of belief, speech or association. He did, however, undertake obligations of frankness, candor and cooperation in answering inquiries made of him by his employing Board examining his fitness to serve it as a public school teacher.

> A teacher works in a sensitive area in a schoolroom. There he shapes the attitude of young minds towards the society in which they live. In this, the state has a vital concern. It must preserve the integrity of the schools. That the school authorities have the right and the duty to screen the officials, teachers, and employees as to their fitness to maintain the integrity of the schools as a part of ordered society, cannot be doubted. *Adler v. Board of Education*, 342 U.S. 485, 493, 72 S.Ct. 380, 385.

As this Court stated in *Garner v. Board of Public Works*, 341 U.S. 716, 720, 71 S.Ct. 909, 912, "We think that a municipal employer is not disabled because it is an agency of the State from inquiring of its employees as to matters that may prove relevant to their fitness and suitability for the public service."

The question asked of petitioner by his Superintendent was relevant to the issue of petitioner's fitness and suitability to serve as a teacher. Petitioner is not in a position to challenge his dismissal merely because of the remoteness in time of the 1944 activities. It was apparent from the circumstances of the two interviews that the Superintendent had other questions to ask. Petitioner's refusal to answer was not based on the remoteness of his 1944 activities. He made it clear that he would not answer any question of the same type as the one asked. Petitioner blocked from the beginning any inquiry into his Communist activities, however relevant to his present loyalty. The Board based its dismissal upon petitioner's refusal to answer any inquiry about his relevant activities—not upon those activities themselves. It took care to charge petitioner with incompetency, and not with disloyalty. It found him insubordinate and lacking in frankness and candor—it made no finding as to his loyalty.

We find no requirement in the federal Constitution that a teacher's classroom conduct be the sole basis for determining his fitness. Fitness for teaching depends on a broad range of factors. The Pennsylvania tenure provision specifies several disqualifying grounds, including immorality, intemperance, cruelty, mental derangement and persistent and willful violation of the school laws, as well as "incompetency." However, the Pennsylvania statute, unlike those of many other States, contains no catchall phrase, such as "conduct unbecoming a teacher," to cover disqualifying conduct not included within the more specific provisions. Consequently, the Pennsylvania courts have given "incompetency" a broad interpretation. . . .

> The term "incompetency" has a "common and approved usage." The context does not limit the meaning of the word to lack of substantive knowledge of the subjects to be taught. Common and approved usage give a much wider meaning. For example, in 31 C.J.,

with reference to a number of supporting decisions, it is defined: "A relative term without technical meaning. It may be employed as meaning disqualification; inability; incapacity; lack of ability, legal qualifications, or fitness to discharge the required duty" . . . .

In the instant case, the Pennsylvania Supreme Court has held that "incompetency" includes petitioner's "deliberate and insubordinate refusal to answer the questions of his administrative superior in a vitally important matter pertaining to his fitness." 386 Pa. at page 91, 125 A.2d at page 331. This interpretation is not inconsistent with the federal Constitution.

Petitioner complains that he was denied due process because he was not sufficiently warned of the consequences of his refusal to answer his Superintendent. The record, however, shows that the Superintendent, in his second interview, specifically warned petitioner that his refusal to answer "was a very serious and a very important matter and that failure to answer the questions might lead to his dismissal." That was sufficient warning to petitioner that his refusal to answer might jeopardize his employment. Furthermore, at petitioner's request, his Superintendent gave him ample opportunity to consult counsel. There was no element of surprise.

Our recent decisions in *Slochower v. Board of Higher Education,* 350 U.S. 551, 76 S.Ct. 637, 100 L.Ed. 692, and *Konigsberg v. State Bar of California,* 353 U.S. 252, 77 S.Ct. 722, 1 L.Ed.2d 810, are distinguishable. In each we envisioned and distinguished the situation now before us. In the *Slochower* case, 350 U.S. at page 558, 76 S.Ct. at page 641, the Court said:

> It is one thing for the city authorities themselves to inquire into Slochower's fitness, but quite another for his discharge to be based entirely on events occurring before a federal committee whose inquiry was announced as not directed at "the property, affairs, or government of the city, or . . . official conduct of city employees." In this respect the present case differs materially from *Garner* [Garner v. Board of Public Works, 341 U.S. 716, 71 S.Ct. 909, 95 L.Ed. 1317], where the city was attempting to elicit information necessary to

determine the qualifications of its employees. Here, the Board had possessed the pertinent information for twelve years, and the questions which Professor Slochower refused to answer were admittedly asked for a purpose wholly unrelated to his college functions. On such a record the Board cannot claim that its action was part of a bona fide attempt to gain needed and relevant information.

. . . In the instant case, no inferences at all were drawn from petitioner's refusal to answer. The Pennsylvania Supreme Court merely equated refusal to answer the employing Board's relevant questions with statutory "incompetency."

Inasmuch as petitioner's dismissal did not violate the federal Constitution, the judgment of the Supreme Court of Pennsylvania is affirmed.

Plea of Constitutional Privilege Against Self-incrimination Bears No Presumption of Unfitness

— · — · — · — · —

Board of Public Education School District of Philadelphia v. Intille

— · — · — · — · —

Supreme Court of Pennsylvania, 1960.
401 Pa. 1, 163 A.2d 420.

CHARLES ALVIN JONES, Chief Justice. The three appellants (Angelina Intille, Thomas Deacon and Sadie T. Atkinson) were teachers in the public schools of Philadelphia until the Spring of 1954 when they were dismissed by the Board of Public Education of the School District on a charge of "incompetency," preferred by Dr. Louis P. Hoyer, Superintendent of the Philadelphia public schools. In each case, the dismissal was based *solely* on the teacher's refusal to answer certain questions propounded by a Subcommittee (also known as the Velde Committee) of the Un-American Activities Committee of the House of Representatives concerning the witness' alleged membership in and association with the Communist Party. In refusing to testify in such regard, each of the appellants expressly relied upon the privilege against self-incrimination guaranteed by the Fifth Amendment of the federal Constitution.

All of the proceedings below, which resulted in the final orders of dismissal, now before us, were conducted separately throughout but, since the basic legal questions raised (both federal and state), are the same in all three appeals, they will be disposed of in this one opinion.

The appellants contend that their dismissals as teachers (1) violated the due process clause of the Fourteenth Amendment and (2) abridged their privilege against self-incrimination under the Fifth Amendment in further violation of the Fourteenth Amendment and of Article VI of the federal Constitution.

There is also an additional question raised by the Board's contention that the appellants' plea of privilege against self-incrimination under the Fifth Amendment constituted incompetency within the intent of Pennsylvania's Public School Code of 1949.

As teachers under contract prescribed by the Public School Code of 1949, the appellants were entitled to tenure as professional employees and, by virtue of the same statutory authority, were subject to dismissal from their teaching positions *only* for cause upon notice, hearing and right of appeal. One of the specified causes for removal, as prescribed by the School Code, is incompetency, which is the charge upon which Superintendent Hoyer suspended these teachers and recommended their dismissal to the Board of Education. The Superintendent based his finding of incompetency solely upon the fact that the appellants had refused to answer questions asked them by the Congressional Committee in reliance on their pleas of privilege under the Fifth Amendment against self-incrimination.

. . .

It follows from what we have said that the appellants' dismissals by the Board of Education, because they refused to answer certain questions of the Congressional Committee on

a plea of the Fifth Amendment's protection against self-incrimination, deprived them of liberty and property without due process of law and, at the same time, worked abridgment by State action of the same constitutional privilege, all in violation of the Fourteenth Amendment. . . .

For a public school teacher to plead a constitutional privilege, in appropriate circumstances, does not prove the teacher's incompetency within the intended scope of that term as used in our Public School Code; the plea is not even relevant as evidence of incompetency. Just as remaining mute, upon a plea of the Fifth Amendment, carries no implication of guilt of the matter inquired about in the unanswered questions . . . so also does the plea not carry an implication of the pleader's *incompetency.* Nor is it of any materiality to a question of the pleader's competency whether or not the propriety of the plea against self-incrimination is conceded or rejected by the inquiring body so long as the plea is made in good faith and is not plainly frivolous. There is no prerequisite to the exercise of the privilege against self-incrimination that the pleader must first establish affirmatively his good faith and lack of frivolity in entering the plea. The appellants' pleas of the Fifth Amendment did not prove their incompetency within the meaning of the Public School Code and, since their refusal to answer the Committee's questions, in reliance on the Fifth Amendment privilege, was all that was proven against them, the Board failed to make out a case for their dismissal.

But, the Board presently advances the idea that a teacher who refuses to answer a Congressional Committee's questions, implying possible subversive affiliations on the part of the witness, is incompetent within the meaning of the tenure provisions of our Public School Code. Such a contention transgresses what was thought to have been decided in *Beilan,* where we were assured that no question of loyalty was in any way involved. If the refusal to answer a particular question is to be made a basis for the discharge of a professional employee, the question should, obviously, have for its purpose the eliciting of information concerning some matter material to the fitness of the employee to continue at work. This is so whether the question propounded be by a Congressional Committee or by the Board of Education itself. And, if the only material matter to which the question relates is possible disloyalty or subversion on the part of the employee, then any proceeding looking to his dismissal for refusal to answer questions relating to his possible disloyal or subversive activities or affiliations must be brought under the Pennsylvania Loyalty Act of December 22, 1951, P.L. 1726, 65 P.S. § 211 et seq. In a proceeding under that statute a teacher may be discharged if it is determined "by a fair preponderance of the evidence" that he is a disloyal or subversive person; and "If the appointing authority shall be comprised of three or more members, a vote of two-thirds of the members shall be necessary in order to discharge a person." See Section 7 of the Act (65 P.S. § 217). What the Board of Education has attempted to do in these cases is to avoid the requirement of the Pennsylvania Loyalty Act that disloyalty or subversion, as a ground for the discharge of a public school teacher, must be proven "by a fair preponderance of the evidence." The Board's action evidences a belief that it has found a way to dismiss, without any evidence at all, teachers whom it suspects of disloyalty or subversion. Anything in the *Beilan* case to the contrary is herewith overruled for the future. In searching out and eliminating disloyalty or subversion among teachers in public schools the procedures of the applicable statute enacted for that purpose must be faithfully pursued, and violence must no longer be done the meaning of the word "incompetency" in order to circumvent the procedures of the Loyalty Act.

The orders of the courts below, now here on appeal at Numbers 331, 332 and 352, are severally reversed, and the records remanded for further proceedings not inconsistent with this opinion.

▪ ENDNOTES

1. Reid v. Covert, 354 U.S. 1, 77 S.Ct. 1222, 1957.

2. Leonard W. Levy, *Constitutional Opinions, Aspects of the Bill of Rights (New York: Oxford University Press, 1986)*, p. 113.

3. Ibid., p. 105.

4. Gitlow v. New York, 268 U.S. 652, 45 S.Ct. 625 (1925); Fiske v. Kansas, 274 U.S. 380, 47 S.Ct. 655 (1927); Cantwell v. Connecticut, 310 U.S. 296, 60 S.Ct. 900 (1940); Near v. State of Minnesota, 283 U.S. 697, 51 S.Ct. 625 (1931); and DeJonge v. Oregon, 299 U.S. 353, 57 S.Ct. 255 (1937).

5. Justice Holmes' often-quoted statement in McAuliffe v. Mayor, Etc. of New Bedford, 155 Mass. 216, 29 N.E. 517 (1892) is thought to be the first reference to this idea: "The petitioner may have a constitutional right to talk politics, but he has no constitutional right to be a policeman."

6. Ibid.

7. Backie v. Cromwell Consolidated School District No. 13, 186 Minn. 38, 242 N.W. 389 (1932); Sheldon v. School Committee of Hopedale, 276 Mass. 230, 177 N.E. 94 (1931).

8. Guilford School Township v. Roberts, 28 Ind.App. 355, 62 N.E. 711 (1902); Ansorge v. City of Green Bay, 198 Wis. 320, 224 N.W. 119 (1929).

9. People v. Board of Education, 212 N.Y. 463, 106 N.E. 307 (1914); Auran v. Mentor School District No. 1, 233 N.W. 644 (N.D. 1930).

10. Goldsmith v. Board of Education, 66 Cal.App. 157, 225, 783 (1924).

11. Crawfordsville v. Hays, 42 Ind. 200 (____).

12. Gillan v. Board of Regents, 88 Wis. 7, 58 N.W. 1042, 24 A.L.R. 336 (1894).

13. 391 U.S. 563, 88 S.Ct. 1731 (1968).

14. See "Developments in the Law—Academic Freedom," Harvard Law Review 81 (1968): 1045–1159.

15. 461 U.S. 138, 103 S.Ct. 1684 (1983).

16. Pickering v. Board of Education, op. cit.

17. Connick v. Myers, 461 U.S. 138, 146, 103 S.Ct. 1684, 1690, 75 L.Ed.2d 708 (1983).

18. See Knapp v. Whitaker, 757 F.2d 827 (7th Cir. 1985).

19. 381 U.S. 479, 85 S.Ct. 1678 (1965).

20. 381 U.S. 479, 484, 85 S.Ct. 1678, 1681 (1965).

21. Leonard W. Levy, Original Intent and the Framers' Constitution (New York: Macmillan Publishing Company, 1988), p. 272.

22. 410 U.S. 113, 93 S.Ct. 705 (1973).

23. 268 U.S. 510, 45 S.Ct. 571 (1925).

24. 262 U.S. 390, 43 S.Ct. 625, (1923).

25. Roe v. Wade, op. cit.

26. Johnny H. Killian, (ed.), The Constitution of the United States of America, 1978 Supplement (Washington, D.C., U.S. Government Printing Office, 1979), p. 5191.

27. Morrison v. State Bd. of Educ., 1 Cal.3d 214, 82 Cal.Rptr. 175, 191, 461 P.2d 375, 391 (1969).

28. Garguil v. Tompkins, 525 F.Supp. 795 (N.D.N.Y. 1981). See also Hoffman v. Jannarone, 401 F.Supp. 1095 (D.N.J. 1975).

29. Daury v. Smith, 842 F.2d 9 (1st Cir. 1988).

30. 489 U.S. 602, 109 S.Ct. 1402, 1413 (1989).

31. 489 U.S. 656, 109 S.Ct. 1384 (1989).

32. Georgia Association of Educators v. Harris, 749 F.Supp. 1110 (N.D.G.A. 1990).

33. 603 F.2d 1271, 1274 (7th Cir. 1979), cert. denied 444 U.S. 1026, 100 S.Ct. 689 (1980).

34. Russo v. Central School District No. 1, 469 F.2d 623 (2d Cir. 1972), cert. denied 411 U.S. 932, 93 S.Ct. 1899 (1973).

35. The Civil Rights Act of 1964, Title VII, as amended 1972 (42 U.S.C.A. § 2000e et seq.).

36. Wangsness v. Watertown School District No. 14-4, 541 F.Supp. 332 (D.S.D. 1982).

37. Pinsker v. Joint School Dist. No. 28J, 554 F.Supp. 1049 (D.Colo. 1983).

38. Ibid.

39. 432 U.S. 63, 97 S.Ct. 2264 (1977).

40. Ansonia Board of Education 479 U.S. 60, 61, 107 S.Ct. 367, 368 (1986).

41. 403 U.S. 602, 91 S.Ct. 2105 (1971).

42. 367 U.S. 488, 81 S.Ct. 1680 (1961).

43. See Donald E. Boles, The Two Swords (Iowa State University Press, 1967), p. 222.

44. Hysong v. School District of Gallitzin Borough, 164 Pa. 629, 30 A. 482 (1894).

45. Commonwealth v. Herr, 229 Pa. 132, 78 A. 68 (1910).

46. O'Connor v. Hendrick, 184 N.Y. 421, 77 N.E. 612 (1906).

47. State ex rel. Public School Dist. No. 6 v. Taylor, 122 Neb. 454, 240 N.W. 573 (1932); see also Zellers v. Huff, 55 N.M. 501, 236 P.2d 949 (1951).

48. Gerhardt v. Heid, 66 N.D. 444, 267 N.W. 127 (1936); see also City of New Haven v. Town of Torrington, 132 Conn. 194, 43 A.2d 455 (1945) and Rawlings v. Butler, 290 S.W.2d 801 (Ky. 1956).

49. Cooper v. Eugene School District No. 4J, 301 Or. 358, 723 P.2d 298 (1986).

50. Ibid., at 313.

51. City of New Haven v. Town of Torrington, 132 Conn. 194, 43 A.2d 455 (1945).

52. Fourteenth Amendment, Constitution of the United States.

53. 350 U.S. 551, 76 S.Ct. 637 (1956).

54. 357 U.S. 399, 78 S.Ct. 1317 (1958).

55. "Developments in the Law—Academic Freedom," p. 1076.

56. Spevack v. Klein, 385 U.S. 511, 87 S.Ct. 625 (1967).

57. Garrity v. New Jersey, 385 U.S. 493, 87 S.Ct. 616 (1967).

CHAPTER 16

Due Process Rights of Teachers

No concept of fundamental law is more basic to individual rights and freedoms than due process. Both the Fifth and Fourteenth Amendments assure that no person shall be deprived of "life, liberty, or property, without due process of law." The due process clause was repeated in the post–Civil-War Fourteenth Amendment to make certain that the right extended to state governments.[1]

The purpose of due process is to extend justice and fairness to the individual in relationship to government. Due process provides a bulwark against the encroachment of the state on individual rights and interests. The importance of due process is to establish a fundamental balance between the rights of individuals and the exercise of the police power of the state.

Due process is founded in the Magna Carta, signed by King John at Runnymede in 1215. The most famous passage is clause 39, the grandfather of due process provisions of Anglo-American law, which states: "No free man shall be taken, imprisoned, disseised, outlawed, banished, or in any way destroyed, nor will we proceed against or prosecute him, except by the lawful judgment of his peers and by the law of the land." The "law of the land" of this passage has become known down through the centuries as due process of law.[2]

■ FOUR ASPECTS OF DUE PROCESS

Due process of law in the federal Constitution has four aspects, and each one has been called into play by the courts in litigation involving teachers: (1) substantive due process, (2) procedural due process, (3) the vagueness test, and (4) the irrationality and presumptions test.[3] Each aspect has special meaning in balancing the individual's interest against the state. Substantive due process is the essence of life, liberty, and property, both explicit and implicit; the nature and substance of the individual's interests. Procedural due process establishes the mechanics of ascertaining the truth about a particular situation. The vagueness rule protects the individual against arbitrary and capricious governmental action. The rationality or presumption test requires that there be legal logic to the state's action in taking or restricting individual rights or interests.

Substantive Due Process

Teachers have a substantive interest in their employment. A right to be employed in one's chosen occupation is protected by due process. The U.S. Supreme Court ruled in *Board of Regents v. Roth*[4] that to deny employment as a teacher may implicate both liberty and property interests under the Due Process Clause.

The substance of due process emanates from the words "life, liberty, and property," the implicit as well as the explicit meanings. These terms establish the boundaries beyond which government cannot go in expanding its reach into the personal affairs of the individual. Governmental incursion into the hallowed presence of an individual's "life, liberty, and property" is permitted only after justification is established by procedural due process. The state cannot deny a substantive right without a fair hearing.

In determining the substance of due process, the courts have held that the words "liberty" and "property" have extensive meaning beyond mere right to own and hold real property or the freedom from incarceration. The Court in *Roth* stated, "Liberty and property are broad and majestic terms. They are among the great constitutional concepts . . . purposely left to gather meaning from experience . . . They relate to the whole domain of social and economic fact, and the statesmen who founded this nation knew too well that only a stagnant society remains unchanged."[5]

The Supreme Court emphasized in *Roth*,[6] and its companion case *Perry v. Sindermann*,[7] three primary features of substantive due process. First, liberty and property interests are not created by the Constitution itself, but rather arise from an independent source such as employment contracts or state tenure laws. A due process interest is therefore different from an equal protection right, which emanates directly from the Constitution. Continued employment gains substantive due process status only if the state creates some formal condition vesting the employee with expectancy of reemployment. Second, if a liberty or property interest in employment is not created by the state, there exists no requirement of procedural due process should employment status be terminated. Third, if a teacher possesses a liberty or property interest in employment, then procedural due process is required.[8]

A substantive interest may be implicated if a teacher has tenure or is serving during the term of an annual or multi-year contract when the dismissal proceeding is instituted. Simple nonrenewal at the expiration of a specified contract term does not involve a substantive interest and, therefore, procedural due process is not necessary.[9] But if a teacher is not rehired at the end of a contract period, and the nonrenewal is based on reasons that affect substantive rights emanating from due process or other basic rights or freedoms, then initiation of procedural due process is required.

Liberty

The concepts of both "liberty" and "property" were given great breadth and scope as contemplated by the framers of the U.S. Constitution. Madison maintained that liberty is the counterbalance that holds an overbearing government in check. As adherents of Rousseau, most of the framers of the Constitution agreed that liberty is "the noblest faculty of man";[10] it is an essential gift of nature that every person is entitled to enjoy, and it cannot be unilaterally taken away by government except by proper processes of law.

The intent of the word "liberty," as it applies to a teacher's employment, can be simply stated as guaranteeing the right to live and work at whatever job he or she desires. A most complete definition of liberty is given by the Supreme Court of Virginia in a 1903 case:

> The word "liberty" as used in the Constitution of the United States and the several States, has frequently been construed, and means more than mere freedom from restraint. It means not merely the right to go where one chooses, but to do such acts as he may judge best for his interest, not inconsistent with the equal rights of others; that is, to follow such pursuits as may be best adapted to his facilities, and which will give him the highest enjoyment. The liberty mentioned is deemed to embrace the right of the citizen to be free in the enjoyment of all his faculties; to be free to use them in all lawful ways; to live and work where he will; to earn his livelihood by any lawful calling, and for that purpose to enter into all contracts which may be proper, necessary, and essential to his carrying out to a successful conclusion the purpose above mentioned. These are individual rights, formulated as such under the phrase "pursuit of happiness" in the Declaration of Independence, which begins with the fundamental proposition that all men are created equal; that they are endowed by their Creator with certain inalienable rights; that among these are life, liberty, and the pursuit of happiness.[11]

The U.S. Supreme Court applied liberty directly to the employment circumstance of a teacher in *Board of Regents v. Roth*[12] and quoted *Meyer v. Nebraska*,[13] saying: "Without doubt, it denotes not merely freedom from bodily restraint, but also the right of the individual to contract, to engage in any of the common occupations of life."

Any action by the state that stigmatizes a teacher to the degree that future employability is adversely affected is sufficient to implicate due process. As mentioned, a liberty interest is involved if a person is stigmatizes with terms such as "dishonesty and immorality." The courts have ruled that the stigmatizing terms must carry over into the employee's private life, mere criticism does not stigmatize.

An employee was charged with insubordination, incompetence, hostility toward authority and aggressive behavior. The court stated that

> [n]early any reason assigned for dismissal is likely to be to some extent a negative reflection on an individual's ability, temperament, or character. But not every dismissal assumes a constitutional magnitude. The concern is only with the type of stigma that seriously damages an individual's ability to take advantage of other employment opportunities. . . . These allegations certainly are not complimentary and suggest that [the teacher] may have problems in relating to some people, but they do not import serious character defects such as dishonesty or immorality . . . as contemplated by *Roth*.[14]

Property

According to the Supreme Court in *Roth*, property interests "may take many forms."[15] A person may have a property interest in employment. Such an interest, though, is not absolute and a person, in order to maintain a property interest in employment "must have more than an abstract need or desire for it." Rather, he or she must have a "legitimate claim of entitlement to it."[16] If a teacher has a continuing and unlimited employment status extending for an indefinite period of time or holds statutory tenure, then a property interest in the employment is presumed.

The fact that employment as a teacher comes within the scope of a "property" interest was encompassed in the original intent of the Bill of Rights. Madison discussed the question extensively, maintaining that not only does a man have "a right to his property," but he has "a property in his rights."[17] Madison further asserted that the right of property guaranteed the citizens "free use of their faculties and free choice of their occupations."[18] Madison saw individual rights of property as being so broad as to include "everything to which a man may attach a value and have a right."[19] Such broad interpretation extended far beyond the more simplistic and restricted sense of what constituted property and included the more comprehensive phraseology of "pursuit of happiness." In this broader sense, beyond land, merchandise, or money, Madison held that a man has property in his opinions and the free communication of them.

> He has a property of peculiar value in his religious opinions, and in the profession and practices dictated by them. He has property very dear to him in the safety and liberty of his person. He has an equal property in the free use of his faculties and free choice of the objects on which to employ them. In a word, as a man is said to have a right to his property, he may be equally said to have a property in his rights.[20]

Thus, property has pervasive substantive meaning, and the implications for teacher dismissal or nonrenewal are very broad indeed.

A substantive property interest in a teaching position may emanate from a teacher's possession of tenure, holding of a permanent or continuing contract, or having a legitimate claim or entitlement to continued employment created by state law or policy of the school board. Too, a continuing long-term, undefined relationship, which may lead a teacher to an objective expectancy of reemployment, may be sufficient to vest the teacher with a substantive property interest. While mere subjective expectancy does not suffice, it is possible for a school to create conditions of employment that suggest entitlement of a legitimate claim to a job, in which case the teacher cannot be terminated without procedural due process.[21]

In welfare cases, the Supreme Court has held that whether and to what extent procedural due process is afforded, the individual is influenced by (a) the extent to which he may be "condemned to suffer grievous loss" and (b) "whether the recipient's interest in avoiding that loss outweighs the governmental interest" that involves a determination of the private interest that has been affected by government action.[22]

The United States Court of Appeals, Fifth Circuit, found that a teacher's "expectancy of reemployment" could be of sufficient import to cause the court to invoke due process requirements.[23]

> [A] college can create an obligation as between itself and an instructor where none might otherwise exist under the legal standards for the interpretation of contract relationships regularly applied to transactions in the market place if it adopts regulations and standards of practice governing nontenured employees which create an expectation of reemployment.[24]

Whether there is an entitlement rests on a balancing of the public school's interest against the individual interest of the teachers.[25] The school's interest is the desirability of selecting and retaining an effective and competent teaching staff, while the teacher's interest is his or her future employability, professional reputation, and other career interests.[26]

In 1972, the Supreme Court of the United States helped to clarify the property interest issue when it held that nontenured teachers were afforded no "property" interest in the teaching position. This is true so long as dismissal does not permanently impair their future employment opportunities.[27]

On the other hand, in *Sindermann*,[28] the court said that although subjective "expectancy" of tenure is not protected by the due process clause, it is possible for a college [or school] to have a *de facto* tenure policy that entitles a teacher to a legitimate claim of job tenure that can be terminated only through a hearing process. Although upholding its denial of the validity of "expectancy of reemployment" in *Roth*, the Supreme Court in *Sindermann* found an unusual situation in which the college had created an implied tenure arrangement. In *Sindermann*, the fac-

ulty guide prepared by the college itself stated that "the College wishes the faculty member to feel that he has permanent tenure as long as his teaching services are satisfactory."[29] The Court concluded that such a provision may, with other conditions, constitute "an unwritten 'common law,'[30] in a particular university that certain employees shall have the equivalent of tenure."[31]

Procedural Due Process Is Not Required When Teacher Is Not Deprived of Constitutional Right

——————

Board of Regents of State Colleges v. Roth

——————

Supreme Court of the United States, 1972.
408 U.S. 564, 92 S.Ct. 2701.

Mr. Justice STEWART delivered the opinion of the Court. In 1968 the respondent, David Roth, was hired for his first teaching job as assistant professor of political science at Wisconsin State University-Oshkosh. He was hired for a fixed term of one academic year. The notice of his faculty appointment specified that his employment would begin on September 1, 1968, and would end on June 30, 1969. The respondent completed that term. But he was informed that he would not be rehired for the next academic year.

The respondent had no tenure rights to continued employment. Under Wisconsin statutory law a state university teacher can acquire tenure as a "permanent" employee only after four years of year-to-year employment. Having acquired tenure, a teacher is entitled to continued employment "during efficiency and good behavior." A relatively new teacher without tenure, however, is under Wisconsin law entitled to nothing beyond his one-year appointment. There are no statutory or administrative standards defining eligibility for reemployment. State law thus clearly leaves the decision whether to rehire a nontenured teacher for another year to the unfettered discretion of university officials.

The procedural protection afforded a Wisconsin State University teacher before he is separated from the University corresponds to his job security. As a matter of statutory law, a tenured teacher cannot be "discharged except for cause upon written charges" and pursuant to certain procedures. A nontenured teacher, similarly, is protected to some extent *during* his one-year term. Rules promulgated by the Board of Regents provide that a nontenured teacher "dismissed" before the end of the year may have some opportunity for review of the "dismissal." But the Rules provide no real protection for a nontenured teacher who simply is not reemployed for the next year. He must be informed by February 1 "concerning retention or nonretention for the ensuing year." But "no reason for nonretention need be given. No review or appeal is provided in such case."

In conformance with these Rules, the President of Wisconsin State University-Oshkosh informed the respondent before February 1, 1969, that he would not be rehired for the 1969–1970 academic year. He gave the respondent no reason for the decision and no opportunity to challenge it at any sort of hearing.

The respondent then brought this action in Federal District Court alleging that the decision not to rehire him for the next year infringed his Fourteenth Amendment rights. (He attacked the decision both in substance and procedure. First, he alleged that the true reason for the decision was to punish him for certain statements critical of the University administration, and that it therefore violated his right to freedom of speech. Second, he alleged that the failure of University officials to give him notice of any reason for nonretention and an opportunity for a hearing violated his right to procedural due process of law.)

The District Court granted summary judgment for the respondent on the procedural issue, ordering the University officials to provide him with reasons and a hearing. 310 F.Supp. 972. The Court of Appeals, with one judge dissenting, affirmed this partial sum-

mary judgment. 446 F.2d 806. We granted certiorari. 404 U.S. 909, 92 S.Ct. 227, 30 L.Ed.2d 181. The only question presented to us at this stage in the case is whether the respondent had a constitutional right to a statement of reasons and a hearing on the University's decision not to rehire him for another year. We hold that he did not.

The requirements of procedural due process apply only to the deprivation of interests encompassed by the Fourteenth Amendment's protection of liberty and property. When protected interests are implicated, the right to some kind of prior hearing is paramount. But the range of interests protected by procedural due process is not infinite.

The District Court decided that procedural due process guarantees apply in this case by assessing and balancing the weights of the particular interests involved. It concluded that the respondent's interest in reemployment at Wisconsin State University-Oshkosh outweighed the University's interest in denying him reemployment summarily. 310 F.Supp., at 977–979. Undeniably, the respondent's reemployment prospects were of major concern to him—concern that we surely cannot say was insignificant. And a weighing process has long been a part of any determination of the *form* of hearing required in particular situations by procedural due process. But, to determine whether due process requirements apply in the first place, we must look not to the "weight" but to the *nature* of the interest at stake. . . . We must look to see if the interest is within the Fourteenth Amendment's protection of liberty and property.

"Liberty" and "property" are broad and majestic terms. They are among the "[g]reat [constitutional] concepts . . . purposely left to gather meaning from experience. . . . [T]hey relate to the whole domain of social and economic fact, and the statesmen who founded this Nation knew too well that only a stagnant society remains unchanged." *National Mutual Ins. Co. v. Tidewater Transfer Co.,* 337 U.S. 582, 646, 69 S.Ct. 1173, 1195, 93 L.Ed. 1556 (Frankfurter, J., dissenting). For that reason, the Court has fully and finally rejected the wooden distinction between "rights" and "privileges" that once seemed to govern the applicability of procedural due process rights. The Court has also made clear that the property interests protected by procedural due process extend well beyond actual ownership of real estate, chattels, or money. By the same token, the Court has required due process protection for deprivations of liberty beyond the sort of formal constraints imposed by the criminal process.

Yet, while the Court has eschewed rigid or formalistic limitations on the protection of procedural due process, it has at the same time observed certain boundaries. For the words "liberty" and "property" in the Due Process Clause of the Fourteenth Amendment must be given some meaning.

> While this court has not attempted to define with exactness the liberty . . . guaranteed [by the Fourteenth Amendment], the term has received much consideration and some of the included things have been definitely stated. Without doubt, it denotes not merely freedom from bodily restraint but also the right of the individual to contract, to engage in any of the common occupations of life, to acquire useful knowledge, to marry, establish a home and bring up children, to worship God according to the dictates of his own conscience, and generally to enjoy those privileges long recognized . . . as essential to the orderly pursuit of happiness by free men. *Meyer v. Nebraska,* 262 U.S. 390, 399, 43 S.Ct. 625, 626, 67 L.Ed. 1042.

In a Constitution for a free people, there can be no doubt that the meaning of "liberty" must be broad indeed. See e.g., *Bolling v. Sharpe,* 347 U.S. 497, 499–500, 74 S.Ct. 693, 694, 98 L.Ed. 884; *Stanley v. Illinois,* 405 U.S. 645, 92 S.Ct. 1208, 31 L.Ed.2d 551.

There might be cases in which a State refused to reemploy a person under such circumstances that interests in liberty would be implicated. But this is not such a case.

The State, in declining to rehire the respondent, did not make any charge against him that might seriously damage his standing and associations in his community. It did not base the nonrenewal of his contract on a charge, for example, that he had been guilty of dishonesty, or immorality. Had it done so, this would be a different case. For "[w]here a person's good name, reputation, honor, or integrity is at stake because of what the government is doing to him, notice and an opportunity to be heard are essential." . . . In such a case, due process would accord an opportunity to refute the charge before University officials. In the present case, however, there is no suggestion whatever that the respondent's "good name, reputation, honor, or integrity" is at stake.

Similarly, there is no suggestion that the State, in declining to reemploy the respondent, imposed on him a stigma or other disability that foreclosed his freedom to take advantage of other employment opportunities. The State, for example, did not invoke any regulations to bar the respondent from all other public employment in state universities. Had it done so, this, again, would be a different case. For "[t]o be deprived not only of present government employment but of future opportunity for it certainly is no small injury . . . ."

To be sure, the respondent has alleged that the nonrenewal of his contract was based on his exercise of his right to freedom of speech. But this allegation is not now before us. The District Court stayed proceedings on this issue, and the respondent has yet to prove that the decision not to rehire him was in fact based on his free speech activities.

Hence, on the record before us, all that clearly appears is that the respondent was not rehired for one year at one university. It stretches the concept too far to suggest that a person is deprived of "liberty" when he simply is not rehired in one job but remains as free as before to seek another. . . .

The Fourteenth Amendment's procedural protection of property is a safeguard of the security of interests that a person has already acquired in specific benefits. These interests—property interests—may take many forms.

Thus, the Court has held that a person receiving welfare benefits under statutory and administrative standards defining eligibility for them has an interest in continued receipt of those benefits that is safeguarded by procedural due process. *Goldberg v. Kelly,* 397 U.S. 254, 90 S.Ct. 1011, 25 L.Ed.2d 287. . . . Similarly, in the area of public employment, the Court has held that a public college professor dismissed from an office held under tenure provisions, *Slochower v. Board of Education,* 350 U.S. 551, 76 S.Ct. 637, 100 L.Ed. 692, and college professors and staff members dismissed during the terms of their contracts, *Wieman v. Updegraff,* 344 U.S. 183, 73 S.Ct. 215, 97 L.Ed. 216, have interests in continued employment that are safeguarded by due process. Only last year, the Court held that this principle "proscribing summary dismissal from public employment without hearing or inquiry required by due process" also applied to a teacher recently hired without tenure or a formal contract, but nonetheless with a clearly implied promise of continued employment. *Connell v. Higginbotham,* 403 U.S. 207, 208, 91 S.Ct. 1772, 1773, 29 L.Ed.2d 418.

Certain attributes of "property" interests protected by procedural due process emerge from these decisions. To have a property interest in a benefit, a person clearly must have more than an abstract need or desire for it. He must have more than a unilateral expectation of it. He must, instead, have a legitimate claim of entitlement to it. It is a purpose of the ancient institution of property to protect those claims upon which people rely in their daily lives, reliance that must not be arbitrarily undermined. It is a purpose of the constitutional right to a hearing to provide an opportunity for a person to vindicate those claims.

Property interests, of course, are not created by the Constitution. Rather they are created and their dimensions are defined by existing rules or understandings that stem from an independent source such as state law — rules or understandings that secure certain benefits and that support claims of entitlement to those benefits. Thus, the welfare recipients in *Goldberg v. Kelly,* supra, had a claim of entitlement to welfare payments that was grounded in the statute defining eligibility for them. The recipients had not yet shown

that they were, in fact, within the statutory terms of eligibility. But we held that they had a right to a hearing at which they might attempt to do so.

Just as the welfare recipients' "property" interest in welfare payments was created and defined by statutory terms, so the respondent's "property" interest in employment at Wisconsin State University-Oshkosh was created and defined by the terms of his appointment. Those terms secured his interest in employment up to June 30, 1969. But the important fact in this case is that they specifically provided that the respondent's employment was to terminate on June 30. They did not provide for contract renewal absent "sufficient cause." Indeed, they made no provision for renewal whatsoever.

Thus, the terms of the respondent's appointment secured absolutely no interest in reemployment for the next year. They supported absolutely no possible claim of entitlement to reemployment. Nor, significantly, was there any state statute or University rule or policy that secured his interest in reemployment or that created any legitimate claim to it. In these circumstances, the respondent surely had an abstract concern in being rehired, but he did not have a *property* interest sufficient to require the University authorities to give him a hearing when they declined to renew his contract of employment.

Our analysis of the respondent's constitutional rights in this case in no way indicates a view that an opportunity for a hearing or a statement of reasons for nonretention would, or would not, be appropriate or wise in public colleges and universities. For it is a written Constitution that we apply. Our role is confined to interpretation of that Constitution.

We must conclude that the summary judgment for the respondent should not have been granted, since the respondent has not shown that he was deprived of liberty or property protected by the Fourteenth Amendment. The judgment of the Court of Appeals, accordingly, is reversed and the case is remanded for further proceedings consistent with this opinion. It is so ordered.

*Teacher with De Facto Tenure Is Entitled to a
Hearing Before Termination of Employment*

———·———·———·———

Perry v. Sindermann

———·———·———·———

Supreme Court of the United States, 1972.
408 U.S. 593, 92 S.Ct. 2694.

Mr. Justice STEWART delivered the opinion of
the Court. From 1959 to 1969 the respondent,
Robert Sindermann, was a teacher in the state
college system of the State of Texas. After
teaching for two years at the University of
Texas and for four years at San Antonio Junior
College, he became a professor of Government
and Social Science at Odessa Junior College in
1965. He was employed at the college for four
successive years, under a series of one-year
contracts. He was successful enough to be
appointed, for a time, the cochairman of his
department.

During the 1968–1969 academic year, however, controversy arose between the respondent and the college administration. The
respondent was elected president of the Texas
Junior College Teachers Association. In this
capacity, he left his teaching duties on several
occasions to testify before committees of the
Texas Legislature, and he became involved in
public disagreements with the policies of the
college's Board of Regents. In particular, he
aligned himself with a group advocating the
elevation of the college to four-year status—a
change opposed by the Regents. And, on one
occasion, a newspaper advertisement appeared over his name that was highly critical
of the Regents.

Finally, in May 1969, the respondent's
one-year employment contract terminated
and the Board of Regents voted not to offer
him a new contract for the next academic year.
The Regents issued a press release setting
forth allegations of the respondent's insubordination. But they provided him no official
statement of the reasons for the nonrenewal of
his contract. And they allowed him no oppor-

tunity for a hearing to challenge the basis of
the nonrenewal.

The respondent then brought this action in
Federal District Court. He alleged primarily
that the Regents' decision not to rehire him
was based on his public criticism of the policies
of the college administration and thus infringed his right to freedom of speech. He also
alleged that their failure to provide him an
opportunity for a hearing violated the Fourteenth Amendment's guarantee of procedural
due process. The petitioners—members of the
Board of Regents and the president of the
college—denied that their decision was made
in retaliation for the respondent's public
criticism and argued that they had no obligation to provide a hearing. On the basis of these
bare pleadings and three brief affidavits filed
by the respondent, the District Court granted
summary judgment for the petitioners. It
concluded that the respondent had "no cause
of action against the [petitioners] since his
contract of employment terminated May 31,
1969, and Odessa Junior College has not
adopted the tenure system."

The Court of Appeals reversed the judgment of the District Court. 430 F.2d 939. First,
it held that, despite the respondent's lack of
tenure, the nonrenewal of his contract would
violate the Fourteenth Amendment if it in
fact was based on his protected free speech.
Since the actual reason for the Regents'
decision was "in total dispute" in the pleadings, the court remanded the case for a full
hearing on this contested issue of fact. Second, the Court of Appeals held that, despite
the respondent's lack of tenure, the failure
to allow him an opportunity for a hearing
would violate the constitutional guarantee of
procedural due process if the respondent
could show that he had an "expectancy" of
reemployment. It, therefore, ordered that
this issue of fact also be aired upon remand.
We granted a writ of certiorari, 403 U.S. 917,
91 S.Ct. 2226, 29 L.Ed.2d 694, and we have
considered this case along with *Board of
Regents v. Roth,* 408 U.S. 564, 92 S.Ct. 2701,
33 L.Ed.2d 548.

The first question presented is whether the
respondent's lack of a contractual or tenure

right to reemployment, taken alone, defeats his claim that the nonrenewal of his contract violated the First and Fourteenth Amendments. We hold that it does not.

For at least a quarter-century, this Court has made clear that even though a person has no "right" to a valuable governmental benefit and even though the government may deny him the benefit for any number of reasons, there are some reasons upon which the government may not rely. It may not deny a benefit to a person on a basis that infringes his constitutionally protected interests — especially his interest in freedom of speech. For if the government could deny a benefit to a person because of his constitutionally protected speech or associations, his exercise of those freedoms would in effect be penalized and inhibited. This would allow the government to "produce a result which [it] could not command directly." *Speiser v. Randall*, 357 U.S. 513, 526, 78 S.Ct. 1332, 1342, 2 L.Ed.2d 1460. Such interference with constitutional rights is impermissible.   . . .

Thus, the respondent's lack of a contractual or tenure "right" to reemployment for the 1969–1970 academic year is immaterial to his free speech claim. Indeed, twice before, this Court has specifically held that the nonrenewal of a nontenured public school teacher's one-year contract may not be predicated on his exercise of First and Fourteenth Amendment rights.   . . .   We reaffirm those holdings here.

In this case, of course, the respondent has yet to show that the decision not to renew his contract was, in fact, made in retaliation for his exercise of the constitutional right of free speech. The District Court foreclosed any opportunity to make this showing when it granted summary judgment. Hence, we cannot now hold that the Board of Regents' action was invalid.

But we agree with the Court of Appeals that there is a genuine dispute as to "whether the college refused to renew the teaching contract on an impermissible basis — as a reprisal for the exercise of constitutionally protected rights." 430 F.2d, at 943. The respondent has alleged that his nonretention was based on his testimony before legislative committees and his other public statements critical of the Regents' policies. And he has alleged that this public criticism was within the First and Fourteenth Amendments' protection of freedom of speech. Plainly, these allegations present a bona fide constitutional claim. For this Court has held that a teacher's public criticism of his superiors on matters of public concern may be constitutionally protected and may, therefore, be an impermissible basis for termination of his employment. *Pickering v. Board of Education.*

For this reason we hold that the grant of summary judgment against the respondent, without full exploration of this issue, was improper.

The respondent's lack of formal contractual or tenure security in continued employment at Odessa Junior College, though irrelevant to his free speech claim, is highly relevant to his procedural due process claim. But it may not be entirely dispositive.

We have held today in *Board of Regents v. Roth*, 408 U.S. 564, 92 S.Ct. 2701, that the Constitution does not require opportunity for a hearing before the nonrenewal of a nontenured teacher's contract, unless he can show that the decision not to rehire him somehow deprived him of an interest in "liberty" or that he had a "property" interest in continued employment, despite the lack of tenure or a formal contract. In *Roth* the teacher had not made a showing on either point to justify summary judgment in his favor.

Similarly, the respondent here has yet to show that he has been deprived of an interest that could invoke procedural due process protection. As in *Roth*, the mere showing that he was not rehired in one particular job, without more, did not amount to a showing of a loss of liberty. Nor did it amount to a showing of a loss of property.

But the respondent's allegations — which we must construe most favorably to the respondent at this stage of the litigation — do raise a genuine issue as to his interest in continued employment at Odessa Junior College. He alleged that this interest, though not secured by a formal contractual tenure provision, was secured by a no less binding understanding fostered by the college administration. In particular, the respondent alleged that the college had a *de facto* tenure program, and that he had tenure under that program. He claimed that he and others legitimately relied upon an unusual provision that had been in the college's official Faculty Guide for many years:

> *Teacher Tenure:* Odessa College has no tenure system. The Administration of the College wishes the faculty member to feel that he has permanent tenure as long as his teaching services are satisfactory and as long as he displays a cooperative attitude toward his co-workers and his superiors, and as long as he is happy in his work.

Moreover, the respondent claimed legitimate reliance upon guidelines promulgated by the Coordinating Board of the Texas College and University System that provided that a person, like himself, who had been employed as a teacher in the state college and university system for seven years or more has some form of job tenure. Thus, the respondent offered to prove that a teacher with his long period of service at this particular State College had no less a "property" interest in continued employment than a formally tenured teacher at other colleges, and had no less a procedural due process right to a statement of reasons and a hearing before college officials upon their decision not to retain him.

We have made clear in *Roth* . . . that "property" interests subject to procedural due process protection are not limited by a few rigid, technical forms. Rather, "property" denotes a broad range of interests that are secured by "existing rules or understandings." . . . . A person's interest in a benefit is a "property" interest for due process purposes if there are such rules or mutually explicit understandings that support his claim of entitlement to the benefit and that he may invoke at a hearing.

A written contract with an explicit tenure provision clearly is evidence of a formal understanding that supports a teacher's claim of entitlement to continued employment un-

less sufficient "cause" is shown. Yet absence of such an explicit contractual provision may not always foreclose the possibility that a teacher has a "property" interest in reemployment. For example, the law of contracts in most, if not all, jurisdictions long has employed a process by which agreements, though not formalized in writing, may be "implied." 3 A. Corbin on Contracts §§ 561–572A. Explicit contractual provisions may be supplemented by other agreements implied from "the promisor's words and conduct in the light of the surrounding circumstances." Id., at § 562. And, "[t]he meaning of [the promisor's] words and acts is found by relating them to the usage of the past."

A teacher, like the respondent, who has held his position for a number of years, might be able to show from the circumstances of this service—and from other relevant facts—that he has a legitimate claim of entitlement to job tenure. Just as this Court has found there to be a "common law of a particular industry or of a particular plant" that may supplement a collective-bargaining agreement, *United Steelworkers v. Warrior & Gulf Nav. Co.*, 363 U.S. 574, 579 . . . so there may be an unwritten "common law" in a particular university that certain employees shall have the equivalent of tenure. This is particularly likely in a college or university, like Odessa Junior College, that has no explicit tenure system even for senior members of its faculty, but that nonetheless may have created such a system in practice. . . .

In this case, the respondent has alleged the existence of rules and understandings, promulgated and fostered by state officials, that may justify his legitimate claim of entitlement to continued employment absent "sufficient cause." We disagree with the Court of Appeals insofar as it held that a mere subjective "expectancy" is protected by procedural due process, but we agree that the respondent must be given an opportunity to prove the legitimacy of his claim of such entitlement in light of "the policies and practices of the institution." 430 F.2d, at 943. Proof of such a property interest would not, of course, entitle him to reinstatement. But such proof would obligate college officials to grant a hearing at his request, where he could be informed of the grounds for his nonretention and challenge their sufficiency.

Therefore, while we do not wholly agree with the opinion of the Court of Appeals, its judgment remanding this case to the District Court is affirmed.

Affirmed.

Mr. Justice POWELL took no part in the decision of this case.

NOTES

1. Nonreemployment without a hearing of a nontenured teacher because of general ineffectiveness as a teacher does not violate the First and Fourteenth Amendments. *Robinson v. Jefferson County Board of Education*, 485 F.2d 1381 (5th Cir.1973), rehearing denied 488 F.2d 1055 (5th Cir.1974).

2. When a nontenured teacher had taught for ten years in a state with no tenure law and was not rehired, the court held that no substantive due process rights existed on behalf of the teacher that would invoke a cause of action under the Civil Rights Act § 1983, even though the only rationale used by the school board for dismissal was that the students of the teacher scored below expected levels on achievement tests. *Scheelhaase v. Woodbury Central Community School District*, 488 F.2d 237 (8th Cir.1973).

3. A nontenured teacher's claim of entitlement to a position was, under the Illinois Tenure Act, insufficient to constitute a property interest within the Fourteenth Amendment. Appellant was unable to show that the tenure law limited in any way the authority of the school board to terminate employment prior to acquiring tenure status. *Miller v. School District Number 167*, Cook County, Illinois, 500 F.2d 711 (7th Cir.1974).

4. A probationary teacher had no expectancy of reemployment vesting him with a property interest. *McCullough v. Lohn*, 483 F.2d 34 (5th Cir.1973).

5. When a nontenured teacher was indicted for alleged sexual misconduct with stu-

dents, the court held that, should he be convicted, the school board was not obligated to provide him with a hearing; however, in the event that he was exonerated by the court, the school board must provide a hearing in order for him to clear his name. The court found, in referring to *Roth*, though, that when a teacher is indicted it is not the obligation of the school board to hold a hearing prior to his trial in order to determine his guilt or innocence. To do so, according to the court, would have placed the board in the untenable position of dispensing findings that "in one direction would have injured the interests of the state, and in another direction would have damaged those of the teacher." *Moore v. Knowles*, 482 F.2d 1069 (5th Cir.1973).

6. Notice of nonrenewal of a nontenured teacher that is not posted or published does not create a "stigma" upon the teacher's good name, reputation, honor, or integrity sufficient to deprive her of "liberty" under the Fourteenth Amendment. *Shirck v. Thomas*, 486 F.2d 691 (7th Cir.1973).

7. When nontenured elementary teachers distributed a poem to students imploring them to throw off the dull discipline of the moral environment of their home life and enter into a new world of love and freedom — freedom to use acid and grass, freedom to engage in sexual activities, and freedom to use vulgarities, the court denied the teachers recovery under the Civil Rights Act. In so doing, the court commented:

> We do not believe that however much the reach of the First Amendment has been extended and however eager today's courts have been to protect the many varieties of claims to civil rights, the appellee school board had to put up with the described conduct of appellants.

Brubaker v. Board of Education, School District 149, Cook County, Illinois, 502 F.2d 973 (7th Cir.1974).

8. A United States District Court in Minnesota listed five occasions when *Roth* and *Sindermann* dictated a hearing on nonrenewal:

    a. When the contract nonrenewal is related to the teacher's exercise of freedom of speech under the First Amendment.

    b. When the teacher is confronted with a charge that might seriously damage his or her standing and associations in the community.

    c. When the failure to reemploy the teacher imposes a stigma or other disability on him or her that forecloses future freedom to take advantage of other employment opportunities.

    d. When the teacher, by virtue of existing state policies, the contract terms, or similar understandings, has a reasonable expectancy of reemployment.

    e. When the adverse reports on which action is taken are prepared by the school's superiors or plaintiffs' compatriots and are fabricated, without any foundation or basis in fact whatsoever, or are maliciously designed so as to use the freedom of the probationary period for reasons of personal calumny, hatred, vindication, or dislike thus using the probationary period as a sword rather than a shield. *Ferris v. Special School District No. 1*, 367 F.Supp. 459 (D.Minn.1973).

9. When there was evidence that teachers' contracts had not been renewed in retaliation for their public comments regarding teacher's salaries and affiliation with a teacher's association, the court held that the nonrenewal of their contracts violated their First Amendment rights of freedom of speech and association. *Greminger v. Seaborne*, 584 F.2d 275 (8th Cir.1978).

10. An allegation by a teacher that nonrenewal of his contract was due to the failure to shave his beard was held by the court to be unfounded and wholly insubstantial. *Ball v. Board of Trustees of Kerrville Independent School District*, 584 F.2d 684 (5th Cir.1978). See also *Carmichael v. Chambers County Board of Education*, 581 F.2d 95 (5th Cir.1978); *Cain v. McQueen*, 580 F.2d 1001 (9th Cir.1978); *Graves v. Duganne*, 581 F.2d 222 (9th Cir.1978).

11. *Stigmatizing Reasons.* The Supreme Court established in *Perry v. Sindermann* and in *Roth v. Board of Regents* that a nontenured teacher has a liberty interest not to be stigmatized or to have anything be said that damages his or her good name or reputation. Although the Court established this as a standard, it did not define specifically what stigmatizing means. Case law has defined these liberty interests as presented below.

    a. Allegations of incompetence, inadequacy, and insubordination have not been found to be stigmatizing. "These allegations certainly are not complimentary and suggest that (the teacher) may have problems . . . but do not import serious character defects . . . as contemplated by *Roth*." *Gray v. Union County Intermediate Education District*, 520 F.2d 803 (9th Cir.1975).

    b. Charges of racism have been determined to be a deprivation of a liberty interest, reflecting on a professor's reputation and good name, and therefore required due process to be afforded to prove the charges. *Wellner v. Minnesota State Junior College Board*, 487 F.2d 153 (8th Cir.1973).

    c. A school board's charges of "apparent emotional instability" stigmatizes a teacher because it goes beyond job-related comments. *Bomhoff v. White*, 526 F.Supp. 488 (D.Ariz.1981).

Procedural Due Process

When action is taken against a teacher that may result in the loss of a substantive constitutional interest, the teacher is entitled to procedural due process. Courts require procedural due process when a teacher can show that his termination emanates from an exercise of one of his fundamental freedoms such as free speech, expression, and press, or substantive due process interests. The state must show a compelling interest in order to suspend a fundamental right. "Simply because teachers are on the public payroll does not make them second-class citizens in regard to their constitutional rights."[32] Courts will invalidate denial of reemployment when the denial rests on an unconstitutional restriction of a fundamental interest. In *Pred,* the court said the determination must rest on facts showing whether the denial of a continuing contract was "(a) a reprisal for these actions in expression of ideas, thoughts, or associations rather than permissable nondiscriminatory professional evaluations, and, if so, (b) whether under the circumstances in relation to the reasonable demands of a system of organized responsible learning these actions were protected."[33]

Most essential to due process is the requirement of "fair play."[34] Procedural due process embodies the legal and moral concept of natural justice, which has two main parts: (a) that no person should be condemned without a hearing, and (b) every judge must be free from bias.[35] The fairness of a full hearing sufficient to reveal the relevant facts to a tribunal is required by due process. Procedural due process requires that a person be given "notice and an opportunity to be heard before a final decision is made which would deprive him of life, liberty, or property."[36]

The necessity of procedural due process was well explained by the Virginia Supreme Court over a century ago:

> The authorities on this point are overwhelming, and the decision of all the tribunals of every country where an enlightened jurisprudence prevails, are all one way. It lies at the very foundation of justice, that every person who is to be affected by an adjudication should have the opportunity of being heard in defense, both in repelling the allegations of fact, and upon the matter of law.[37]

Hearing

As discussed earlier in this text in the chapter on student rights, the requirements of procedural due process have been extended from courts of law to administrative tribunals such as state and local school boards and munici-palities. The process due a student where loss of education is in balance requires two essentials. In *Dixon v. Alabama State Board of Education,*[38] the court said:

1. Notice should be given of the hearing "containing a statement of the specific charges and grounds", and
2. a hearing should be held providing the opportunity for both sides to present their stories in considerable detail.[39]

These basic elements of fair play apply to the teacher when his or her substantive interest in a teaching position is jeopardized. The courts require that the formality and intensity of the process due a teacher be dependent on the severity of the impending loss to be suffered.

Due process of law is not a concrete prescription; it is dependent on circumstances. The U.S. Supreme Court has said that due process requires "that the proceedings shall be fair, but fairness is relative, not an absolute concept . . . What is fair in one set of circumstances may be an act of tyranny in others."[40]

The requirement that all the facts be revealed to objective evaluation is the goal of due process. An English court commenting on due process as the essence of natural justice has concisely summarized the issue, saying that to "act in good faith and fairly listen to both sides . . . is a duty lying upon everyone who decides anything." It is a question of "being required to act fairly."

Impartiality

Fairness requires that the judge or hearing tribunal be free of bias. The old dictum "that justice should both be done and be manifestly seen to be done"[41] is essential in meeting the strictures of due process. Ultimately, the strength of due process rests not only on whether justice is done but also on whether the public perceives that justice has been served.

In this regard, the courts have generally held that an administrative agency such as a state or local school board constitutes an unbiased tribunal, even though its own rules may have been broken or it is a party to the action. The leading case on this point is *Hortonville*, in which the U.S. Supreme Court held that a school board, as an administrative agency, must of necessity possess quasi-judicial powers; and is presumed, by its nature, to be unbiased unless proven otherwise.[42]

School Board Is an Impartial and Unbiased Tribunal Even though It Is Both a Part to and Decision-maker in a Controversy with Teachers

---

Hortonville Joint School District No. 1 v. Hortonville Education Association et al.

Supreme Court of the United States, 1976.
426 U.S. 482, 96 S.Ct. 2308.

Mr. Chief Justice BURGER delivered the opinion of the Court. We granted certiorari in this case to determine whether School Board members, vested by state law with the power to employ and dismiss teachers, could, consistent with the Due Process Clause of the Fourteenth Amendment, dismiss teachers engaged in a strike prohibited by state law.

The petitioners are a Wisconsin school district, the seven members of its School Board, and three administrative employees of the district. Respondents are teachers suing on behalf of all teachers in the district and the Hortonville Education Association (HEA), the collective-bargaining agent for the district's teachers. . . .

The sole issue in this case is whether the Due Process Clause of the Fourteenth Amendment prohibits this School Board from making the decision to dismiss teachers admittedly engaged in a strike and persistently refusing to return to their duties. The Wisconsin Supreme Court held that state law prohibited the strike and that termination of the striking teachers' employment was within the Board's statutory authority. . . .

Respondents' argument rests in part on doctrines that have no application to this case. They seem to argue that the Board members had some personal or official stake in the decision whether the teachers should be dismissed, . . . and that the Board has manifested some personal bitterness toward the teachers, aroused by teacher criticism of the Board during the strike. . . . [T]he teachers did not show, and the Wisconsin courts did not find, that the Board members had the kind of personal or financial stake in the decision that might create a conflict of interest, and there is nothing in the record to support charges of personal animosity. The Wisconsin Supreme Court was careful "not to suggest . . . that the board members were anything but dedicated public servants, trying to provide the district with quality education . . . within its limited budget." That court's analysis would seem to be confirmed by the Board's repeated invitations for striking teachers to return to work, the final invitation being contained in the letter that notified them of their discharge.

The only other factor suggested to support the claim of bias is that the School Board was involved in the negotiations that preceded and precipitated the striking teachers' discharge. Participation in those negotiations was a statutory duty of the Board. The Wisconsin Supreme Court held that this involvement, without more, disqualified the Board from deciding whether the teachers should be dismissed:

> The board was the collective bargaining agent for the school district and thus was engaged in the collective bargaining process with the teachers' representative, the HEA. It is not difficult to imagine the frustration on the part of the board members when negotiations broke down, agreement could not be reached and the employees resorted to concerted activity. . . . They were . . . not uninvolved in the events which precipitated decisions they were required to make.

Mere familiarity with the facts of a case gained by an agency in the performance of its statutory role does not, however, disqualify a decisionmaker. . . . Nor is a decision-maker disqualified simply because he has taken a position, even in public, on a policy issue related to the dispute, in the absence of a showing that he is not "capable of judging a particular controversy fairly on the basis of its own circumstances." . . .

Respondents' claim and the Wisconsin Supreme Court's holding reduce to the argument that the Board was biased because it negotiated with the teachers on behalf of the school district without reaching agreement and learned about the reasons for the strike in the course of negotiating. From those premises the Wisconsin court concluded that the Board lost its statutory power to determine that the strike and persistent refusal to terminate it amounted to conduct serious enough to warrant discharge of the strikers. Wisconsin statutes vest in the Board the power to discharge its employees, a power of every employer, whether it has negotiated with the employees before discharge or not. The Fourteenth Amendment permits a court to strip the Board of the otherwise unremarkable power the Wisconsin Legislature has given it only if the Board's prior involvement in negotiating with the teachers means that it cannot act consistently with due process.

Due process, as this Court has repeatedly held, is a term that "negates any concept of inflexible procedures universally applicable to every imaginable situation." . . . Determining what process is due in a given setting requires the Court to take into account the individual's stake in the decision at issue as well as the State's interest in a particular procedure for making it. . . . Our assessment of the interests of the parties in this case leads to the conclusion that . . . the Board's prior role as negotiator does not disqualify it to decide that the public interest in maintaining uninterrupted classroom work required that teachers striking in violation of state law be discharged.

The teachers' interest in these proceedings is, of course, self-evident. They wished to avoid termination of their employment, obviously an important interest, but one that must be examined in light of several factors. Since the teachers admitted that they were engaged in a work stoppage, there was no possibility of an erroneous factual determination on this critical threshold issue. Moreover, what the teachers claim as a property right was the expectation that the jobs they had left to go and remain on strike in violation of law would remain open to them. . . .

State law vests the governmental, or policymaking, function exclusively in the School Board and the State has two interests in keeping it there. First, the Board is the body with overall responsibility for the governance of the school district; it must cope with the myriad day-to-day problems of a modern public school system including the severe consequences of a teachers' strike; by virtue of electing them the constituents have declared the Board members qualified to deal with these problems, and they are accountable to the voters for the manner in which they perform. Second, the state legislature has given to the Board the power to employ and dismiss teachers, as a part of the balance it has struck in the area of municipal labor relations; altering those statutory powers as a matter of federal due process clearly changes that balance. Permitting the Board to make the decision at issue here preserves its control over school district affairs, leaves the balance of power in labor relations where the state legislature struck it, and assures that the decision whether to dismiss the teachers will be made by the body responsible for that decision under state law.

Respondents have failed to demonstrate that the decision to terminate their employment was infected by the sort of bias that we have held to disqualify other decisionmakers as a matter of federal due process. A showing that the Board was "involved" in the events preceding this decision, in light of the important interest in leaving with the Board the power given by the state legislature, is not enough to overcome the presumption of honesty and integrity in policymakers with decisionmaking power. . . . Accordingly, we hold that the Due Process Clause of the Fourteenth Amendment did not guarantee respondents that the decision to terminate their employment would be made or reviewed by a body other than the School Board.

The judgment of the Wisconsin Supreme Court is reversed, and the case is remanded for further proceedings not inconsistent with this opinion.

Reversed and remanded.

Bias of One Board Member in Hearing Is Sufficient to Deprive Teacher of Due Process

———·——·——·———

Crump v. Board of Education of the Hickory Administrative School Unit

———·——·——·———

Supreme Court of North Carolina, 1990.
326 N.C. 603, 392 S.E. 2d 579.

MITCHELL, Justice. The issue before us is whether, at a teacher dismissal hearing, a single school board member's bias against the teacher taints the entire board's decision-making process, denying the teacher due process and entitling him to compensatory damages, regardless of whether the bias affected the correctness of the board's decision. We conclude that such bias makes the decision-making process inherently unfair and violates due process.

. . . On 7 June 1984, the defendant-appellants, the Hickory Board of Education and its individual members, dismissed the plaintiff-appellee, Eddie Ray Crump, from his teaching position at Hickory High School based on findings of immorality and insubordination. . . .

Bruce Crump (no relation to the plaintiff-appellee), another former teacher, testified that in the spring of 1984, prior to the Board's hearing, he witnessed Board member Lois Young tell Principal Williamson, "We're all together on this Crump thing." Bruce Crump also testified that no matters involving him were pending with the Board at the time he heard Young make the statement about the "Crump thing." Neither Young nor Williamson testified at trial.

The plaintiff-appellee Eddie Crump testified that he had a conversation with Board member Young after his dismissal. Crump testified that during their conversation, Young told him that prior to the Board's hearing Principal Williamson had promised the Board members that Crump would resign rather than endure a dismissal hearing and thus bring embarrassment upon his wife.

The jury found that the Board had failed to "provide [Crump] a fair hearing before an unbiased hearing body," and that Crump had suffered resulting actual damages of $78,000, but awarded no punitive damages. The trial court entered judgment accordingly. A divided panel of the Court of Appeals affirmed the trial court's judgment. . . .

The Court of Appeals concluded that in this separate civil action under § 1983, the trial court "correctly instructed the jury that the bias of *one* member of the Board was sufficient for the jury to find that Mr. Crump had been deprived of a fair hearing." *Crump v. Board of Education,* 93 N.C.App. 168, 185, 378 S.E.2d 32, 34 (1989) (emphasis added). For the reasons discussed below, we too find no error in the trial court's instructions and affirm the decision of the Court of Appeals. We begin our analysis with some foundational concepts concerning due process, bias, and school boards.

Whenever a government tribunal, be it a court of law or a school board, considers a case in which it may deprive a person of life, liberty or property, it is fundamental to the concept of due process that the deliberative body give that person's case fair and open-minded consideration. "A fair trial in a fair tribunal is a basic requirement of due process." . . . As a career teacher under N.C.G.S. § 115C–325, Crump had a cognizable property interest in his continued employment. *See, e.g., Board of Regents v. Roth,* 408 U.S. 564, 576–78, 92 S.Ct. 2701, 2708–09, 33 L.Ed.2d 548, 560–61 (1972). Further, Crump's constitutionally-protected liberty interest was implicated, since the

charge impair[ed] his reputation for honesty or morality. The procedural protections of due process apply if the accuracy of the charge is contested, there is some public disclosure of the charge, and it is made in connection with the termination of employment or the alteration of some right or status recognized by state law.

. . . With his fundamental rights so implicated, Crump was entitled to a hearing according with principles of due process. "[A] Board of Education conducting a [dismissal] hearing under G.S. 115–142 [now § 115C–325] must provide all essential elements of due process." . . .

We recognize that due process is a somewhat fluid concept, and that determining what process is "due" at a school board hearing is very different from evaluating the procedural protections required in a court of law. "Determining what process is due in a given setting requires the Court to take into account the individual's stake in the decision at issue as well as the State's interest in a particular procedure for making it." *Hortonville Dist. v. Hortonville Ed. Assn.*, 426 U.S. 482, 494, 96 S.Ct. 2308, 2315, 49 L.Ed.2d 1, 10 (1976) (citing cases).

An unbiased, impartial decision-maker is essential to due process. . . . As discussed below, this case turns on the question of what evidence will suffice to support a jury's determination, as here, that a decision-maker is biased, when the decision-maker is a group of persons.

While the word "bias" has many connotations in general usage, the word has few specific denotations in legal terminology. Bias has been defined as "a predisposition to decide a cause or an issue in a certain way, which does not leave the mind perfectly open to conviction," Black's Law Dictionary 147 (5th ed. 1979), or as "a sort of emotion constituting untrustworthy partiality," 10 C.J.S. *Bias* (1955 & supp. 1989) (footnote omitted). "Some sort of commitment is necessary for disqualification [due to bias], even though it is less than an irrevocable one." 3 Davis, *Administrative Law Treatise 2d* § 19:4 at 385 (1980). Bias can refer to preconceptions about facts, policy or law; a person, group or object; or a personal interest in the outcome of some determination. Crump's complaint commencing the civil action now before us on appeal alleged that one or more Board members came into his

hearing having already decided to vote against him, based on "factual" information obtained outside the hearing process. This type bias can be labeled a "prejudgment of adjudicative facts."

The trial court in this case gave the jury a lengthy explanation of the heavy burden a plaintiff must bear to succeed in proving that a school board acted towards him or her with bias. The trial court began by explaining the presumption of correctness afforded school board actions, then instructed the jury that:

> To prove impermissible bias of the hearing body the plaintiff must show or prove by its greater weight more than the fact that a board member or members had some knowledge of some fact or facts concerning a charge or charges against a teacher. Mere familiarity with a fact or facts or charge or charges does not automatically disqualify a board member as a decision maker. . . .
>
> I instruct you that a board member's obligation is to be able to put aside anything read or heard prior to a hearing and base a decision solely upon the sworn testimony and evidence during a hearing.
>
> To find impermissible bias you, the jury, must find by the greater weight of the evidence that the mind of a board member was predetermined and was fixed and not susceptible to change prior to the deliberating process of the hearing board, and that the decision was not based solely upon evidence during the hearing.

The quoted instructions given by the trial court concerning decision-maker bias were free of error. If a Board member had made a fixed decision, prior to the Board's hearing, to vote against Crump, that member was biased against him. One such Board member's participation in Crump's dismissal hearing would cause that hearing to deny Crump procedural due process, no matter what outcome the Board reached at the hearing.

Distinguishing a Board member's disqualifying *bias* against Crump from permissible pre-hearing *knowledge* about Crump's case is essential to our analysis. Members of a school board are expected to be knowledgable about school-related activities in their district. Board members will sometimes have discussed certain issues that later become the subject of board deliberations; such knowledge and discussions are inevitable aspects of their multifaceted roles as administrators, investigators and adjudicators. However, when performing their quasi-judicial function during a board hearing and any resulting deliberations, members must be able to set aside their prior knowledge and preconceptions concerning the matter at issue, and base their considerations solely upon the evidence adduced at the hearing. In an analogous case before the United States Court of Appeals for the Ninth Circuit, Judge (now Justice) Anthony Kennedy wrote:

> The key component of due process, when a decisionmaker is acquainted with the facts, is the assurance of a central fairness at the hearing. . . .
> . . . Members of a school board in smaller communities may well have some knowledge of the facts and individuals involved in incidents which they must evaluate. Their obligation is to act impartially and in a fair manner.

Vanelli v. Reynolds School Dist. No. 7, 667 F.2d 773, 779–80 (9th Cir.1982) (citations omitted).

In the present case, a Board member with pre-hearing knowledge regarding the allegations against Crump would neither necessarily nor presumptively be biased against him. "The mere exposure to evidence presented in nonadversary investigative procedures is insufficient in itself to impugn the fairness of the Board members at a later adversary hearing." . . . Indeed, because of their multifaceted roles as administrators, investigators and adjudicators, school boards are vested with a presumption that their actions are correct, and the burden is on a contestant to prove otherwise. . . .

If the Board in this case was biased, it was unable to provide Crump with the fair and open-minded consideration that due process demanded his case receive. . . . Here, there was substantial evidence that, at the Board's hearing, one or more Board members consciously concealed both prior knowledge of the allegations against Crump and a fixed

predisposition against him. Such evidence having been presented, the trial court properly submitted this case to the jury for its determination as to whether a Board member had in fact been biased against Crump.

The decision of our Court of Appeals is in accord with the view of the United States Court of Appeals for the Third Circuit, which has stated that "[l]itigants are entitled to an impartial tribunal whether it consists of one [person] or twenty and there is no way which we know of whereby the influence of one upon the others can be quantitatively measured." . . .

The Board argues that at worst the evidence only shows that one member of the body making the adjudication was not in a position to judge impartially. We deem this answer insufficient. Litigants are entitled to an impartial tribunal whether it consists of one [person] or twenty and there is no way which we know of whereby the influence of one upon the others can be quantitatively measured.

A critical component of any quasi-judicial hearing and decision-making by a deliberative body is the give and take which occurs when group members share their observations and opinions. There is a fundamental notion that each member will enter the hearing with an open mind, listen to and view the evidence, share his or her observations, analyses and opinions with the other board members, listen to the other members' comments, and *only then* finally commit to a vote. One biased member can skew the entire process by what he or she does, or does not do, during the hearing and deliberations. Since the Board's deliberations giving rise to this case were closed and unrecorded, there is no meaningful way to accurately review the process to determine the impact of any bias by one or more members during the hearing and deliberations. . . .

. . . Having established injury arising from the due process violation itself to a Catawba County jury's satisfaction, Crump was entitled to a verdict in his favor.

Bias is hard to prove. Given the level of pre-commitment by a board member that must be shown to make out a case of bias and a resulting denial of due process, we doubt that our decision in this case will open any floodgates of litigation or unduly prevent boards of education from dismissing bad teachers. Determining what procedure is required by principles of due process in a given situation requires that the cost of the procedure be evaluated in light of the potential harm flowing from that procedure. In this case, the cost of the procedure which we conclude due process required was whatever it would have taken for one or more Board members to candidly answer Crump's questions about their pre-hearing knowledge. The injury to Crump from being forced to participate in a hearing that the jury in this case determined was unfair, on the other hand, was valued by the Catawba County jury at $78,000. It should not cost that much to be candid; talk is cheap.

The Court of Appeals affirmed the judgment of the trial court awarding Crump $78,000 in compensatory damages. . . . This case is remanded to the Court of Appeals for its further remand to the Superior Court, Catawba County, with instructions that the judgment be modified and amended accordingly. Except as modified in this regard, the decision of the Court of Appeals affirming the judgment of the trial court is affirmed.

Modified and affirmed; remanded with instructions.

NOTE

1. The fact that a teacher had harassed board members prior to hearing did not establish bias on part of the board as to preclude employee from receiving due process in a dismissal proceeding. *Covert v. Bensalem Township School District*, 104 Pa. Cmwlth. 441, 522 A. 2d 129 (1987).

The Vagueness Test: Loyalty Oaths

The vagueness test has been commonly offended by state statutes that extract loyalty oaths as a condition of employment. Such statutes implicitly accuse a person of an offense, and the oath must be taken to gain absolution in the eyes of the state. If the oath is so vague as to be uncertain of meaning, then the oath taker stands accused of an indefinite offense or may be guilty of perjury if he or she did not understand the offense for which the forswearing was required.

During the red scare after World War I, several states enacted laws requiring special oaths as a condition of teaching in public schools. An increased fear of the spread of communism in the 1930s and a responding upsurge of radicalism led to the enactment of loyalty oaths in 21 states by 1936. Even today, legislatures, in fits of patriotism, periodically enact loyalty oaths. Traditionally, such oaths have been quite vague, making it most difficult to determine exactly to what one is swearing.[43]

In *Cramp v. Board of Public Instruction*,[44] the Supreme Court invalidated an oath requiring teachers to swear that they had never lent their "aid, support, advice, counsel, or influence to the Communist Party" because the oath was not sufficiently definitive and was lacking in "terms susceptible of objective measurement." Vagueness, as violative of due process, was also the bane of a 1955 Washington statute, which sought to define a "subversive person." The definition was disected and exposed to its infirmities by the U.S. Supreme Court in the case of *Baggett v. Bullitt*.[45] The Court observed that teachers are particularly vulnerable when required to swear that they have not aided, abetted, taught, or assisted in a subversive organization. The Baggett oath was stricken because the Court found that teaching, by its nature, could influence opinions and even indirectly support a subversive view without the teacher's knowledge or intent to overthrow or do violence to the nation. The Court ruled that statutory language of an oath that requires the "forswearing of an undefined variety of 'guiltless knowing behavior' is" violative of due process.[46]

Too, the uncertain meaning of oaths has the effect of offending the First and Fourteenth Amendments, because it hangs as a threat over the freedom of discussion in the classroom. In *Cramp*, the Court said that "[t]he vice of unconstitutional vagueness is further aggravated where . . . the statute in question operates to inhibit the exercise of individual freedoms affirmatively protected by the Constitution."[47] In the classroom, in particular, the vagueness of loyalty oaths forces the teacher to steer far wider of the unlawful zone "in the exercise of free speech than if the boundaries of the forbidden areas were clearly marked."[48]

Though loyalty oaths have been consistently invalidated by decisions of the U.S. Supreme Court, the Court has not said that a properly constituted oath is unconstitutional. Kalven has noted that "Loyalty oaths are not *per se* invalid, but the Court will not lift a finger on their behalf."[49]

For the court to uphold an oath and subject a false forswearer to criminal liability requires that the oath taker have (1) knowledge (scienter), (2) active membership in a subversive organization, and (3) specific intent to overthrow the government. Kalven observes that the combination of all these requirements is the "functional equivalent of participation in a literal conspiracy."[50]

Two cases indicate the permissible conditions under which oaths may be held valid: *Connell v. Higginbotham*,[51] a 1971 Florida case, and *Cole v. Richardson*,[52] a 1970 Massachusetts ruling. The *Connell* case illustrates the disenchantment that the court has with the negative test oath. Here, the Court invalidated a negative forswearing but let stand an affirmative oath of allegiance. In so ruling, the Court presumably concluded that an affirmative oath is permissible because it is merely an inoffensive ceremony. On the other hand, a negative test oath subjects the taker to criminal perjury sanctions and is intended as a device to either disqualify the taker from a public position or to convict him in a criminal proceeding.

In *Cole*, the Supreme Court upheld a Massachusetts oath with two clauses; the first clause, an affirmative swearing, said, "I do solemnly swear (or affirm) that I will uphold and defend the Constitution." This part was routine and valid, but the second clause involved the negative, stating that "I will oppose the overthrow of the government . . . by force, violence, or any other illegal or unconstitutional means." The plaintiff had maintained that the second clause tainted and invalidated the first clause. In a four-to-three decision, with Chief Justice Burger writing for the majority, the Court held that the whole oath itself was simply an amenity and that nothing objectionable was intended by the "oppose" clause. Justice Harlan in *Cole* when vacating the lower courts decision reflected a growing judicial weariness with the oath cases, saying:

> I am, however, content to acquiesce in the Court's action because of the manifest triviality of the impact of the oath under challenge . . . . . . [a]lmost any word or phrase may be rendered vague and ambiguous by dissection with a semantic scalpel. I do not, however, consider it a provident use of the time of this Court to coach what amounts to little more than verbal calisthenics. This kind of semantic inquiry, however interesting, should not occupy the time of federal courts unless fundamental rights turn on the outcome.[53]

In concluding that the oath in *Cole* was not unconstitutional, the Supreme Court held that:

1. The "oath provisions . . . are not inconsistent with the First Amendment."
2. The District Court properly held that the "uphold and defend" clause, a paraphrase of the constitutional oath, is permissible.
3. The "oppose the overthrow" clause was not designed to require specific action to be taken in some hypothetical or actual situation but was to assure that those in positions of public trust were willing to commit themselves to live by the constitutional processes of our government.
4. The oath is not void for vagueness. Perjury, the sole punishment, requires a knowing and willful falsehood, which removes the danger of punishment without fair notice; and there is no problem of punishment inflicted by mere prosecution, as there has

been no prosecution under the statute since its enactment nor has any been planned.

5. There is no constitutionally protected right to overthrow a government by force, violence, or illegal or unconstitutional means, and therefore there is no requirement that one who refuses to take Massachusetts' oath be granted a hearing for the determination of some other fact before being discharged.

Cole, then, represented a somewhat more tolerant view of oaths than was evidenced in earlier opinions. In the future the Supreme Court may give states slightly more latitude in the wording and requirements of oaths.

Kalven, in analyzing the intricacies of the oath cases, has drawn four generalizations about the rule of law.[54]

1. "It is safe to conclude that the Court will not openly hold that the oath format is itself unconstitutional; and this is true for negative oaths, as well as for oaths of affirmation." Parenthetically, though, one may conclude that negative oaths are more objectionable and will be subject to more intense judicial scrutiny.

2. "The oath, however, is a *disfavored device.* It will be construed with the eye of conscience, and, thus held to the most exacting standards of unambiguous drafting; and held also to the most explicit limitations to those of *scienter,* (knowing participation). Hence, while the oath format *per se* is not unconstitutional, it will be difficult in actuality to draft an oath that will pass muster."

3. "The legality of an oath will depend not simply on clarity of its wording, but, ultimately on the content of its disqualification."

. . .

4. "The Court will, to some extent, distinguish between oaths of affirmation and negative loyalty oaths. In theory, only the latter are objectionable; the former are routine, conventional amenities of daily life. *Baggett,* however, indicates that even oaths of affirmation, if they depart from traditional formulae, might be invalid. It is only this last conclusion that the Court's gratuitous performance in *Cole v. Richardson* can, as a matter of logic, be said to unsettle."

Vagueness of Oath Offends Due Process

— — · — · — · — — ·

Wieman v. Updegraff

— — · — · — · — — ·

Supreme Court of the United States, 1952.
344 U.S. 183, 73 S.Ct. 215.

MR. JUSTICE CLARK delivered the opinion of the Court. This is an appeal from a decision of the Supreme Court of Oklahoma upholding the validity of a loyalty oath prescribed by Oklahoma statute for all state officers and employees. . . . Appellants, employed by the State as members of the faculty and staff of Oklahoma Agricultural and Mechanical College, failed, within the thirty days permitted, to take the oath required by the Act. Appellee Updegraff, as a citizen and taxpayer, thereupon brought this suit in the District Court of Oklahoma County to enjoin the necessary state officials from paying further compensation to employees who had not subscribed to the   oath. . . . [The appellants] sought a mandatory injunction directing the state officers to pay their salaries regardless of their failure to take the oath. Their objections centered largely on the following clauses of the oath:

That I am not affiliated directly or indirectly . . . with any foreign political agency, party, organization or Government, or with any agency, party, organization, association, or group whatever which has been officially determined by the United States Attorney General or other authorized agency of the United States to be a communist front or subversive organization; . . . that I will take up arms in the defense of the United States in time of War, or National Emergency, if necessary; that within the five (5) years immediately preceding the taking of this oath (or affirmation) I have not been a member of . . . any agency, party, organization, association, or group whatever which has been officially determined by the United States Attorney General or other authorized public agency of the United States to be a communist front or subversive organization . . . .

. . . The purpose of the Act, we are told, "was to make loyalty a qualification to hold public office or be employed by the State." . . . During periods of international stress, the extent of legislation with such objectives accentuates our traditional concern about the relation of government to the individual in a free society. The perennial problem of defining that relationship becomes acute when disloyalty is screened by ideological patterns and techniques of disguise that make it difficult to identify. Democratic government is not powerless to meet this threat, but it must do so without infringing the freedoms that are the ultimate values of all democratic living. In the adoption of such means as it believes effective, the legislature is therefore confronted with the problem of balancing its interest in national security with the often conflicting constitutional rights of the individual. . . . We are thus brought to the question touched on in *Garner, Adler,* and *Gerende:* whether the Due Process Clause permits a state, in attempting to bar disloyal individuals from its employ, to exclude persons solely on the basis of organizational membership, regardless of their knowledge concerning the organizations to which they had belonged. For, under the statute before us, the fact of membership alone disqualifies. If the rule be expressed as a presumption of disloyalty, it is a conclusive one.

But membership may be innocent. A state servant may have joined a proscribed organization unaware of its activities and purposes. In recent years, many completely loyal persons have severed organizational ties after learning for the first time of the character of groups to which they had belonged. "They had joined, [but] did not know what it was, they were good, fine young men and women, loyal Americans, but they had been trapped into it—because one of the great weaknesses of all Americans, whether adult or youth, is to join something." At the time of affiliation, a group itself may be innocent, only later coming under the influence of those who would turn it toward illegitimate ends. Conversely, an organization formerly subversive and therefore designated as such may have subsequently freed itself from the influences which originally led to its listing.

There can be no dispute about the consequences visited upon a person excluded from public employment on disloyalty grounds. In the view of the community, the stain is a deep one; indeed, it has become a badge of infamy. Especially is this so in time of cold war and hot emotions when "each man begins to eye his neighbor as a possible enemy." Yet under the Oklahoma Act, the fact of association alone determines disloyalty and disqualification; it matters not whether association existed innocently or knowingly. To thus inhibit individual freedom of movement is to stifle the flow of democratic expression and controversy at one of its chief sources. We hold that the distinction observed between the case at bar and *Garner, Adler* and *Gerende* is decisive. Indiscriminate classification of innocent with knowing activity must fall as an assertion of arbitrary power. The oath offends due process . . . . We need not pause to consider whether an abstract right to public employment exists. It is sufficient to say that constitutional protection does extend to the public servant whose exclusion pursuant to a statute is patently arbitrary or discriminatory . . . .

Reversed.

MR. JUSTICE FRANKFURTER, whom MR. JUSTICE DOUGLAS joins, concurring. The times being what they are, it is appropriate to add a word by way of emphasis to the Court's opinion, which I join.

The case concerns the power of a State to exact from teachers in one of its colleges an oath that they are not, and for the five years immediately preceding the taking of the oath have not been, members of any organization listed by the Attorney General of the United States, prior to the passage of the statute, as "subversive" or "Communist-front." Since the affiliation which must thus be forsworn may

SIXTEEN: DUE PROCESS RIGHTS OF TEACHERS **663**

well have been for reasons or for purposes as innocent as membership in a club of one of the established political parties, to require such an oath, on pain of a teacher's loss of his position in case of refusal to take the oath, penalizes a teacher for exercising a right of association peculiarly characteristic of our people. See Arthur M. Schlesinger, Sr., Biography of a Nation of Joiners, 50 Am. Hist. Rev. 1 (1944), reprinted in Schlesinger, Paths To The Present, 23. Such joining is an exercise of the rights of free speech and free inquiry. By limiting the power of the States to interfere with freedom of speech and freedom of inquiry and freedom of association, the Fourteenth Amendment protects all persons, no matter what their calling. But, in view of the nature of the teacher's relation to the effective exercise of the rights which are safeguarded by the Bill of Rights and by the Fourteenth Amendment, inhibition of freedom of thought, and of action upon thought, in the case of teachers brings the safeguards of those amendments vividly into operation. Such unwarranted inhibition upon the free spirit of teachers affects not only those who, like the appellants, are immediately before the Court. It has an unmistakable tendency to chill that free play of the spirit which all teachers ought especially to cultivate and practice; it makes for caution and timidity in their associations by potential teachers.

The Constitution of the United States does not render the United States or the States impotent to guard their governments against destruction by enemies from within. It does not preclude measures of self-protection against anticipated overt acts of violence. Solid threats to our kind of government— manifestations of purposes that reject argument and the free ballot as the means for bringing about changes and promoting progress—may be met by preventive measures before such threats reach fruition. However, in considering the constitutionality of legislation like the statute before us it is necessary to keep steadfastly in mind what it is that is to be secured. Only thus will it be

evident why the Court has found that the Oklahoma law violates those fundamental principles of liberty "which lie at the base of all our civil and political institutions" and as such are imbedded in the due process of law which no State may offend. *Hebert v. Louisiana*, 272 U.S. 312, 316, 47 S.Ct. 103, 104, 71 L.Ed. 270.

That our democracy ultimately rests on public opinion is a platitude of speech but not a commonplace in action. Public opinion is the ultimate reliance of our society only if it be disciplined and responsible. It can be disciplined and responsible only if habits of open-mindedness and of critical inquiry are acquired in the formative years of our citizens. The process of education has naturally enough been the basis of hope for the perdurance of our democracy on the part of all our great leaders, from Thomas Jefferson onwards.

To regard teachers—in our entire educational system, from the primary grades to the university—as the priests of our democracy is therefore not to indulge in hyperbole. It is the special task of teachers to foster those habits of open-mindedness and critical inquiry which alone make for responsible citizens, who, in turn, make possible an enlightened and effective public opinion. Teachers must fulfill their function by precept and practice, by the very atmosphere which they generate; they must be exemplars of open-mindedness and free inquiry. They cannot carry out their noble task if the conditions for the practice of a responsible and critical mind are denied to them. They must have the freedom of responsible inquiry, by thought and action, into the meaning of social and economic ideas, into the checkered history of social and economic dogma. They must be free to sift evanescent doctrine, qualified by time and circumstance, from that restless, enduring process of extending the bounds of understanding and wisdom, to assure which the freedoms of thought, of speech, of inquiry, of worship are guaranteed by the Constitution of the United States against infraction by National or State government.

*Uncertainty of Meaning of Teacher Oath
Violates Due Process*

Keyishian v. Board of Regents of the University of the State of New York

Supreme Court of the United States, 1967.
385 U.S. 589, 87 S.Ct. 675.

MR. JUSTICE BRENNAN delivered the opinion of the Court. Appellants were members of the faculty of the privately owned and operated University of Buffalo, and became state employees when the University was merged in 1962 into the State University of New York, an institution of higher education owned and operated by the State of New York. As faculty members of the State University their continued employment was conditioned upon their compliance with a New York plan, formulated partly in statutes and partly in administrative regulations, which the State utilizes to prevent the appointment or retention of "subversive" persons in state employment.

Appellants Hochfield and Maud were Assistant Professors of English, appellant Keyishian an instructor in English, and appellant Garver, a lecturer in philosophy. Each of them refused to sign, as regulations then in effect required, a certificate that he was not a Communist, and that if he had ever been a Communist, he had communicated that fact to the President of the State University of New York. Each was notified that his failure to sign the certificate would require his dismissal. Keyishian's one-year-term contract was not renewed because of his failure to sign the certificate. . . .

The Feinberg Law charged the State Board of Regents with the duty of promulgating rules and regulations providing procedures for the disqualification or removal of persons in the public school system who violate the 1917 law or who are ineligible for appointment to or retention in the public school system under the 1939 law. The Board of Regents was further directed to make a list, after notice and hearing, of "subversive" organizations, defined as organizations which advocate the doctrine of overthrow of government by force, violence, or any unlawful means. Finally, the Board was directed to provide in its rules and regulations that membership in any listed organization should constitute prima facie evidence of disqualification for appointment to or retention in any office or position in the public schools of the State.

The Board of Regents thereupon promulgated rules and regulations containing procedures to be followed by appointing authorities to discover persons ineligible for appointment or retention under the 1939 law, or because of violation of the 1917 law. The Board also announced its intention to list "subversive" organizations after requisite notice and hearing, and provided that membership in a listed organization after the date of its listing should be regarded as constituting prima facie evidence of disqualification, and that membership prior to listing should be presumptive evidence that membership has continued, in the absence of a showing that such membership was terminated in good faith. Under the regulations, an appointing official is forbidden to make an appointment until after he has first inquired of an applicant's former employers and other persons to ascertain whether the applicant is disqualified or ineligible for appointment. In addition, an annual inquiry must be made to determine whether an appointed employee has ceased to be qualified for retention, and a report of findings must be filed. . . .

Section 3021 requires removal for "treasonable or seditious" utterances or acts. . . .

We cannot gainsay the potential effect of this obscure wording on "those with a conscientious and scrupulous regard for such undertakings." *Baggett v. Bullitt*, 377 U.S. 360, 374, 374, 84 S.Ct. 1316, 1323, 12 L.Ed.2d 377. Even were it certain that the definition referred to in § 105 was solely Penal Law § 160, the scope of § 105 still remains indefinite. The teacher cannot know the extent, if any, to which a "seditious" utterance must transcend mere statement about abstract doctrine, the extent to which it must be intended to and tend to indoctrinate or incite to action in furtherance of the defined doctrine. The crucial consideration is that no teacher can know just where the line is drawn between "seditious" and nonseditious utterances and acts.

Other provisions of § 105 also have the same defect of vagueness. Subdivision 1 (a) of § 105 bars employment of any person who "by word of mouth or writing wilfully and deliberately advocates, advises or teaches the doctrine" of forceful overthrow of government. This provision is plainly susceptible of sweeping and improper application. It may well prohibit the employment of one who merely advocates the doctrine in the abstract without any attempt to indoctrinate others, or incite others to action in furtherance of unlawful aims. . . . And in prohibiting "advising" the "doctrine" of unlawful overthrow does the statute prohibit mere "advising" of the existence of the doctrine, or advising another to support the doctrine? Since "advocacy" of the doctrine of forceful overthrow is separately prohibited, need the person "teaching" or "advising" this doctrine himself "advocate" it? Does the teacher who informs his class about the precepts of Marxism or the Declaration of Independence violate this prohibition?

Similar uncertainty arises as to the application of subdivision 1 (b) of § 105. That subsection requires the disqualification of an employee involved with the distribution of written material "containing or advocating, advising or teaching the doctrine" of forceful overthrow, and who himself "advocates, advises, teaches, or embraces the duty, necessity or propriety of adopting the doctrine contained therein." Here again, mere advocacy of abstract doctrine is apparently included. And does the prohibition of distribution of matter "containing" the doctrine bar histories of the evolution of Marxist doctrine or tracing the background of the French, American, or Russian revolutions? The additional requirement, that the person participating in distribution of the material be one who "advocates, advises, teaches, or embraces the duty, necessity or propriety of adopting the doctrine" of forceful overthrow, does not alleviate the uncertainty in the scope of the section, but exacerbates it. Like the language of § 105, subd. 1 (a), this language may reasonably be construed to cover mere expression of belief. For example, does the university librarian who recommends the reading of such materials thereby "advocate . . . the . . . propriety of adopting the doctrine contained therein"?

We do not have the benefit of a judicial gloss by the New York courts enlightening us as to the scope of this complicated plan. In light of the intricate administrative machinery for its enforcement, this is not surprising. The very intricacy of the plan and the uncertainty as to the scope of its proscriptions make it a highly efficient *in terrorem* mechanism. It would be a bold teacher who would not stay as far as possible from utterances or acts which might jeopardize his living by enmeshing him in this intricate machinery. The uncertainty as to the utterances and acts proscribed increases that caution in "those who believe the written law means what it says," *Baggett v. Bullitt, supra,* at 374, 84 S.Ct., at 1324. The result must be to stifle "that free play of the spirit which all teachers ought especially to cultivate and practice. . . ." That probability is enhanced by the provisions requiring an annual review of every teacher to determine whether any utterance or act of his, inside the classroom or out, came within the sanctions of the laws. . . .

There can be no doubt of the legitimacy of New York's interest in protecting its education system from subversion. But "even though the governmental purpose be legitimate and substantial, that purpose cannot be pursued by means that broadly stifle fundamental personal liberties when the end can be more narrowly achieved." *Shelton v. Tucker,* 364 U.S. 479, 488, 81 S.Ct. 247, 252, 5 L.Ed.2d 231. The principle is not inapplicable because the legislation is aimed at keeping subversives out of the teaching ranks. . . .

Our Nation is deeply committed to safeguarding academic freedom, which is of transcendent value to all of us and not merely to the teachers concerned. That freedom is therefore a special concern of the First Amendment, which does not tolerate laws that cast a pall of orthodoxy over the classroom. "The vigilant protection of constitutional freedoms is nowhere more vital than in the community of American schools." *Shelton v. Tucker, supra,* 364 U.S. at 487, 81 S.Ct. at 251. The classroom is peculiarly the "marketplace of ideas." The Nation's future depends upon leaders trained through wide exposure to that robust exchange of ideas which discovers truth "out of a multitude of tongues, [rather] than through any kind of authoritative selection." . . .

The regulatory maze created by New York is wholly lacking in "terms susceptible of objective measurement." *Cramp v. Board of Public Information, supra,* at 286, 82 S.Ct., at 280. It has the quality of "extraordinary ambiguity" found to be fatal to the oaths considered in *Cramp* and *Baggett v. Bullitt.* "[M]en of common intelligence must necessarily guess at its meaning and differ as to its application. . . . " *Baggett v. Bullitt, supra,* at 367, 84 S.Ct. at 1320. Vagueness of wording is aggravated by prolixity and profusion of statutes, regulations, and administrative machinery, and by manifold cross-references to interrelated enactments and rules.

We therefore hold that § 3021 of the Education Law and subdivisions 1 (a), 1 (b) and 3 of § 105 of the Civil Service Law as implemented by the machinery created pursuant to § 3022 of the Education Law are unconstitutional.

---

*Disclaimer Provisions of Loyalty Oath
Are Unconstitutional*

– – · – – · – – · – – · – –

Connell v. Higginbotham

– – · – – · – – · – – · – –

Supreme Court of the United States, 1971.
403 U.S. 207, 91 S.Ct. 1772.

PER CURIAM. This is an appeal from an action commenced in the United States District Court for the Middle District of Florida challenging the constitutionality of §§ 876.05–876.10 of Fla.Stat. (1965), and the various loyalty oaths

upon which appellant's employment as a school teacher was conditioned. The three-judge U.S. District Court declared three of the five clauses contained in the oaths to be unconstitutional, and enjoined the State from conditioning employment on the taking of an oath including the language declared unconstitutional. The appeal is from that portion of the District Court decision, 305 F.Supp. 445, which upheld the remaining two clauses in the oath: I do hereby solemnly swear or affirm (1) "that I will support the Constitution of the United States and of the State of Florida"; and (2) "that I do not believe in the overthrow of the Government of the United States or of the State of Florida by force or violence." [The clauses declared unconstitutional by the court below required the employee to swear: (a) "that I am not a member of the Communist Party"; (b) "that I have not and will not lend my aid, support, advice, counsel or influence to the Communist Party"; and (c) "that I am not a member of any organization or party which believes in or teaches, directly or indirectly, the overthrow of the Government of the United States or of Florida by force or violence."]

On January 16, 1969, appellant made application for a teaching position with the Orange County school system. She was interviewed by the principal of Callahan Elementary School, and on January 27, 1969, appellant was employed as a substitute classroom teacher in the fourth grade of that school. Appellant was dismissed from her teaching position on March 18, 1969, for refusing to sign the loyalty oath required of all Florida public employees, Fla.Stat. § 876.05.

The first section of the oath upheld by the District Court, requiring all applicants to pledge to support the Constitution of the United States and of the State of Florida, demands no more of Florida public employees than is required of all state and federal officers. U.S. Const., Art. VI, cl. 3. The validity of this section of the oath would appear settled. . . .

The second portion of the oath, approved by the District Court, falls within the ambit of decisions of this Court proscribing summary dismissal from public employment without hearing or inquiry required by due process. . . . That portion of the oath, therefore, cannot stand.

Affirmed in part, and reversed in part.

_____

Irrationality and Presumptions

The fourth test imposed by due process on the validity of state actions is the requirement of rationality. The Supreme Court requires that there be a rational connection between the fact proved and the ultimate end presumed.[55] The Court has said that "if the inference of the one from proof of the other is arbitrary because of lack of connection between the two in common experience,"[56] then due process is violated. Moreover, the individual cannot be effectively denied the opportunity to rebut an irrational presumption. Accordingly, the Court has found that irrebuttable presumptions deny due process.[57]

Resident Status

An unconstitutional presumption was found where a state presumed conclusively that a college student was nonresident, subject to nonresident tuition fees for the duration of his college education. The fact that the student had moved into the state and intended to remain a resident of the state and was a *bona fide* resident was insufficient to rebut the state's presumption of nonresident states.[58]

Pregnancy

Similarly, the Supreme Court has held, in *Cleveland Board of Education v. LaFleur*,[59] that due process is violated by school board rules that create a conclusive presumption that every pregnant teacher who reaches a particular point of pregnancy becomes physically incapable of continuing to teach. The Court's objection to irrebuttable presumptions is best explained by Corwin:

> Legislative fiat may not take the place of fact, however, in the determination of issues involving life, liberty, or property, and a statute creating a presumption which is entirely arbitrary and which operates to deny a fair opportunity to repel it or to present facts pertinent to one's defense is void.[60]

Even though *LaFleur* was later followed in another pregnancy case voiding a statute that made pregnant women ineligible for unemployment compensation for a period during pregnancy and after childbirth,[61] the Supreme Court, of late, has tended to avoid this aspect of due process. Instead, the Court, under the leadership of both Chief Justices Burger and Rehnquist, has maintained that the protections afforded under the rationality of due process are more logically extended under the Equal Protection Clause of the Fourteenth Amendment. This was the essence of the dissent enunciated in *Vlandis v. Kline*[62] and was reinforced by the majority in *Weinberger v. Salfi*. Here the Court imposed the traditional equal protection analysis of strict scrutiny to encompass due process challenges of statutory classification that create irrebuttable presumptions. Therefore, the Court does not appear to be prone to extend this part of due process to overlap the rights and guarantees already found in equal protection. In the future the Court will probably "limit the doctrine to those areas which involve fundamental rights or suspect classifications that would, in equal protection analysis, rise to strict, and perhaps intermediate scrutiny."[63] The technical effect is simply that plaintiffs in the future will avoid this aspect of due process in favor of equal protection whenever state statute or school board rules are thought to be irrational or unreasonable.

_____

Mandatory Leave Rules and Arbitrary Cutoff Dates for Pregnant Teachers Violate Due Process

_____

Cleveland Board of Education v. LaFleur

_____

Supreme Court of the United States, 1974.
414 U.S. 632, 94 S.Ct. 791.

Mr. Justice STEWART delivered the opinion of the Court. The respondents in No. 72–777 and the petitioner in No. 72–1129 are female public school teachers. During the 1970–1971 school year, each informed her local school board that she was pregnant; each was compelled by a mandatory maternity leave rule to quit her job without pay several months before the expected birth of her child. These cases call upon us to decide the constitutionality of the school boards' rules.

Jo Carol LaFleur and Ann Elizabeth Nelson, the respondents in No. 72–777, are junior high school teachers employed by the Board of Education of Cleveland, Ohio. Pursuant to a rule first adopted in 1952, the school board requires every pregnant school teacher to take maternity leave without pay, beginning five months before the expected birth of her child. Application for such leave must be made no later than two weeks prior to the date of departure. A teacher on maternity leave is not allowed to return to work until the beginning of the next regular school semester which follows the date when her child attains the age of three months. A doctor's certificate attesting to the health of the teacher is a prerequisite to return; an additional physical examination may be required. The teacher on maternity leave is not promised reemployment after the birth of the child; she is merely given priority in reassignment to a position for which she is qualified. Failure to comply with the mandatory maternity leave provisions is ground for dismissal. . . .

The petitioner in No. 72–1129, Susan Cohen, was employed by the School Board of Chesterfield County, Virginia. That school board's maternity leave regulation requires that a pregnant teacher leave work at least four months prior to the expected birth of her child. Notice in writing must be given to the school board at least six months prior to the expected birth date. A teacher on maternity leave is declared reeligible for employment when she submits written notice from a physician that she is physically fit for reemployment, and when she can give assurance that care of the child will cause only minimal interference with her job responsibilities. . . .

This Court has long recognized that freedom of personal choice in matters of marriage and family life is one of the liberties protected by the Due Process Clause of the Fourteenth Amendment. . . . There is a right "to be free from unwarranted governmental intrusion into matters so fundamentally affecting a person as the decision whether to bear or beget a child."

By acting to penalize the pregnant teacher for deciding to bear a child, overly restrictive maternity leave regulations can constitute a heavy burden on the exercise of these protected freedoms. Because public school maternity leave rules directly affect "one of the basic civil rights of man, " Skinner v. Oklahoma, supra, 316 U.S., at 541, 62 S.Ct., at 1113, the Due Process Clause of the Fourteenth Amendment requires that such rules must not needlessly, arbitrarily, or capriciously impinge upon this vital area of a teacher's constitutional liberty. The question before us in these cases is whether the interests advanced in support of the rules of the Cleveland and Chesterfield County School Boards can justify the particular procedures they have adopted.

The school boards in these cases have offered two essentially overlapping explanations for their mandatory maternity leave rules. First, they contend that the firm cutoff dates are necessary to maintain continuity of classroom instruction, since advance knowledge of when a pregnant teacher must leave facilitates the finding and hiring of a qualified substitute. Secondly, the school boards seek to justify their maternity rules by arguing that at least some teachers become physically incapable of adequately performing certain of their duties during the latter part of pregnancy. By keeping the pregnant teacher out of the classroom during these final months, the maternity leave rules are said to protect the health of the teacher and her unborn child, while at the same time assuring that students have a physically capable instructor in the classroom at all times.

It cannot be denied that continuity of instruction is a significant and legitimate educational goal. Regulations requiring pregnant teachers to provide early notice of their condition to school authorities undoubtedly facilitate administrative planning toward the important objective of continuity. But, as the Court of Appeals for the Second Circuit noted

in *Green v. Waterford Board of Education,* 473
F.2d 629, 635:

> Where a pregnant teacher provides the Board
> with a date certain for commencement of
> leave . . . that value [continuity] is
> preserved; an arbitrary leave date set at the end
> of the fifth month is no more calculated to
> facilitate a planned and orderly transition be-
> tween the teacher and a substitute than is a date
> fixed closer to confinement. Indeed, the latter
> . . . would afford the Board more, not less,
> time to procure a satisfactory long-term substi-
> tute. (Footnote omitted.)

Thus, while the advance-notice provisions
in the Cleveland and Chesterfield County
rules are wholly rational and may well be
necessary to serve the objective of continuity
of instruction, the absolute requirements of
termination at the end of the fourth or fifth
month of pregnancy are not. Were continuity
the only goal, cutoff dates much later during
pregnancy would serve as well as or better
than the challenged rules, providing that
ample advance notice requirements were retained. Indeed, continuity would seem just as
well attained if the teacher herself were
allowed to choose the date upon which to
commence her leave, at least so long as the
decision were required to be made and notice
given of it well in advance of the date selected.

In fact, since the fifth or sixth month
of pregnancy will obviously begin at different times in the school year for different
teachers, the present Cleveland and Chesterfield County rules may serve to hinder attainment of the very continuity objectives that
they are purportedly designed to promote.
For example, the beginning of the fifth month
of pregnancy for both Mrs. LaFleur and Mrs.
Nelson occurred during March of 1971. Both
were thus required to leave work with only a
few months left in the school year, even
though both were fully willing to serve
through the end of the term. Similarly, if
continuity were the only goal, it seems ironic
that the Chesterfield County rule forced Mrs.
Cohen to leave work in mid-December 1970
rather than at the end of the semester in
January as she requested.

We thus conclude that the arbitrary cutoff
dates embodied in the mandatory leave rules
before us have no rational relationship to the
valid state interest of preserving continuity of
instruction. As long as the teachers are required to give substantial advance notice of
their condition, the choice of firm dates later in
pregnancy would serve the boards' objectives
just as well, while imposing a far lesser burden
on the women's exercise of constitutionally
protected freedom.

The question remains as to whether the
cutoff dates at the beginning of the fifth and
sixth months can be justified on the other
ground advanced by the school boards—the
necessity of keeping physically unfit teachers
out of the classroom. There can be no doubt
that such an objective is perfectly legitimate,
both on educational and safety grounds. And,
despite the plethora of conflicting medical
testimony in these cases, we can assume,
arguendo, that at least some teachers become
physically disabled from effectively performing their duties during the latter stages of
pregnancy.

The mandatory termination provisions of
the Cleveland and Chesterfield County rules
surely operate to insulate the classroom from
the presence of potentially incapacitated pregnant teachers. But the question is whether the
rules sweep too broadly.   . . .

That question must be answered in the
affirmative, for the provisions amount to a
conclusive presumption that every pregnant
teacher who reaches the fifth or sixth month
of pregnancy is physically incapable of continuing. There is no individualized determination by the teacher's doctor—or the school
board's—as to any particular teacher's ability
to continue at her job. The rules contain an
irrebuttable presumption of physical incompetency, and that presumption applies even
when the medical evidence as to an individual woman's physical status might be
wholly to the contrary.

. . . While the medical experts in these
cases differed on many points, they unanimously agreed on one—the ability of any
particular pregnant woman to continue at
work past any fixed time in her pregnancy is
very much an individual matter. Even assum-

ing, *arguendo,* that there are some women who would be physically unable to work past the particular cutoff dates embodied in the challenged rules, it is evident that there are large numbers of teachers who are fully capable of continuing work for longer than the Cleveland and Chesterfield County regulations will allow. Thus, the conclusive presumption embodied in these rules . . . is neither "necessarily [nor] universally true," and is violative of the Due Process Clause.

. . . While the regulations no doubt represent a good-faith attempt to achieve a laudable goal, they cannot pass muster under the Due Process Clause of the Fourteenth Amendment, because they employ irrebuttable presumptions that unduly penalize a female teacher for deciding to bear a child.

In addition to the mandatory termination provisions, both the Cleveland and Chesterfield County rules contain limitations upon a teacher's eligibility to return to work after giving birth. Again, the school boards offer two justifications for the return rules — continuity of instruction and the desire to be certain that the teacher is physically competent when she returns to work. As is the case with the leave provisions, the question is not whether the school board's goals are legitimate, but rather whether the particular means chosen to achieve those objectives unduly infringe upon the teacher's constitutional liberty.

Under the Cleveland rule, the teacher is not eligible to return to work until the beginning of the next regular school semester following the time when her child attains the age of three months. A doctor's certificate attesting to the teacher's health is required before return; an additional physical examination may be required at the option of the school board.

The respondents in No. 72–777 do not seriously challenge either the medical requirements of the Cleveland rule or the policy of limiting eligibility to return to the next semester following birth. The provisions concerning a medical certificate or supplemental physical examination are narrowly drawn methods of protecting the school board's interest in teacher fitness; these requirements allow an individualized decision as to the teacher's condition, and thus avoid the pitfalls of the presumptions inherent in the leave rules. Similarly, the provision limiting eligibility to return to the semester following delivery is a precisely drawn means of serving the school board's interest in avoiding unnecessary changes in classroom personnel during any one school term.

The Cleveland rule, however, does not simply contain these reasonable medical and next-semester eligibility provisions. In addition, the school board requires the mother to wait until her child reaches the age of three months before the return rules begin to operate. The school board has offered no reasonable justification for this supplemental limitation, and we can perceive none. To the extent that the three-month provision reflects the school board's thinking that no mother is fit to return until that point in time, it suffers from the same constitutional deficiencies that plague the irrebuttable presumption in the termination rules. The presumption, moreover, is patently unnecessary, since the requirement of a physician's certificate or a medical examination fully protects the school's interests in this regard. And finally, the three-month provision simply has nothing to do with continuity of instruction, since the precise point at which the child will reach the relevant age will obviously occur at a different point throughout the school year for each teacher.

Thus, we conclude that the Cleveland return rule, insofar as it embodies the three-month age provision, is wholly arbitrary and irrational, and hence violates the Due Process Clause of the Fourteenth Amendment. The age limitation serves no legitimate state interest, and unnecessarily penalizes the female teacher for asserting her right to bear children.

We ·perceive no such constitutional infirmities in the Chesterfield County rule. In that school system, the teacher becomes eligible for reemployment upon submission of a medical certificate from her physician; return to work is guaranteed no later than the beginning of the next school year following the eligibility determination. The medical certificate is both a reasonable and narrow method of protecting the school board's interest in teacher fitness, while the possible deferring of return until the next school year serves the goal of preserving continuity of instruction. In short, the Chesterfield County rule manages to serve the legitimate state interests here without employing unnecessary presumptions that broadly burden the exercise of protected constitutional liberty.

For the reasons stated, we hold that the mandatory termination provisions of the Cleveland and Chesterfield County maternity regulations violate the Due Process Clause of the Fourteenth Amendment, because of their use of unwarranted conclusive presumptions that seriously burden the exercise of protected constitutional liberty. For similar reasons, we hold the three-month provision of the Cleveland return rule unconstitutional.

ENDNOTES

1. Due Process Clause, Fourteenth Amendment, Constitution of the United States.

2. A. E. Dick Howard, *Commentaries on the Constitution of Virginia,* Vol. I (Charlottesville: University Press of Virginia, 1974), p. 189.

3. Ibid., pp. 190–201.

4. Board of Regents of State Colleges v. Roth, 408 U.S. 564, 92 S.Ct. 2701 (1972).

5. Ibid.

6. Ibid.

7. Ibid.

8. See *1990 Deskbook Encyclopedia of American School Law* (Rosemount, Minnesota: Data Research, Inc. 1990), p. 298.

9. Board of Regents of State Colleges v. Roth, op. cit.

10. Jean-Jacques Rousseau, *The Social Contract and Discourses,* Translation and introduction by G. D. H. Cole (London: J. M. Dent & Sons Ltd., reprinted, 1988), p. 104.

11. Young v. Commonwealth, 101 Va. 853, 45 S.E. 327 (1903).

12. Board of Regents of State Colleges v. Roth, op. cit.

13. 262 U.S. 390, 43 S.Ct. 625 (1923).

14. Gray v. Union County Intermediate Education District, 520 F.2d 803 (9th Cir. 1975).

15. Board of Regents of State Colleges v. Roth, op. cit.

16. Ibid.

17. Leonard W. Levy, *Original Intent and the Framers' Constitution* (New York: MacMillan Publishing Company, 1988), pp. 276–77.

18. Ibid.

19. Ibid.

20. Ibid.

21. Board of Regents of State Colleges v. Roth, op. cit.

22. Goldberg v. Kelly, 397 U.S. 254, 90 S.Ct. 1011 (1970).

23. Ferguson v. Thomas, 430 F.2d 852 (1st Cir. 1970).

24. Ibid.

25. Board of Regents of State Colleges v. Roth, op. cit.

26. Ibid.

27. Ibid.

28. Perry v. Sindermann, 408 U.S. 593, 92 S.Ct. 2694 (1972).

29. Ibid.

30. Ibid.

31. Ibid.

32. Pred v. Board of Public Instruction of Dade County, 415 F.2d 851 (5th Cir. 1969).

33. Ibid.

34. Paul Jackson, *Natural Justice* (London: Sweet & Maxwell, 1973), p. 1.

35. Ibid.

36. 294 F.2d 150 (5th Cir. 1961), *cert. denied* 368 U.S. 930, 82 S.Ct. 368 (1961).

37. Underwood v. McVeigh, 61 Va. (23 Gratt.) 409, 418 (1973).

38. Dixon v. Alabama State Board of Education, op. cit.

39. Ibid.

40. Snyder v. Massachusetts, 291 U.S. 97, 116-117, 54 S.Ct. 330, 336-337 (1934).

41. Jackson, *Natural Justice,* p. 29.

42. Hortonville Joint School District No. 1 v. Hortonville Education Association, 426 U.S. 482, 96 S.Ct. 2308 (1976).

43. Ellen W. Schrecker, *No Ivory Tower, McCarthyism & the Universities* (New York: Oxford University Press, 1986), p. 68.

44. 368 U.S. 278, 82 S.Ct. 275 (1961).

45. 377 U.S. 360, 84 S.Ct. 1316 (1964).

46. Ibid.

47. Cramp v. Board of Public Instructor of Orange County, Fla. 368 U.S. 278, 287, 82 S.Ct. 275, 281 (1961).

48. Speiser v. Randall, 357 U.S. 513, 526, 78 S.Ct. 1332, 1342 (1958).

49. Harry Kalven, Jr., *A Worthy Tradition, Freedom of Speech in America,* (ed.) Jamie Kalven (New York: Harper & Row Publishers, 1988), p. 353.

50. Ibid., p. 359.

51. 403 U.S. 207, 91 S.Ct. 1772 (1971).

52. 405 U.S. 676, 92 S.Ct. 1332 (1972).

53. Cole v. Richardson, 397 U.S. 238, 240, 90 S.Ct. 1099, 1100.

54. Kalven, *A Worthy Tradition,* pp. 366–67.

55. Howard, *Commentaries on the Constitution,* p. 201.

56. Tot v. United States, 319 U.S. 463, 63 S.Ct. 1241 (1943).

57. Vlandis v. Kline, 412 U.S. 441, 93 S.Ct. 2230 (1973).

58. Ibid.

59. 414 U.S. 632, 94 S.Ct. 791 (1974).

60. Edward S. Corwin (ed.), *The Constitution of the United States of America* (Washington, D.C., U.S. Government Printing Office, 1952), p. 1212.

61. Turner v. Dept. of Employment Security, 423 U.S. 44, 96 S.Ct. 249 (1975).

62. Ibid., p. 459 and p. 463.

63. Johnny H. Killian (ed.), *The Constitution of the United States of America, 1978 Supplement* (Washington, D.C., U.S. Government Printing Office, 1979), p. S209.

CHAPTER 17

Discrimination in Employment

The social and political upheavals experienced in the United States after World War II brought about tremendous changes in employment practices. These movements have spawned both federal and state legislation that have attempted to overcome the effects of past discrimination against minorities and to ensure against reemergence of discrimination. Legislation, such as the Civil Rights Act of 1964, the Equal Pay Act, the Age Discrimination in Employment Act, the Pregnancy Discrimination Act, and the Rehabilitation Act, have all addressed issues of employment discrimination. This chapter discusses precedents bearing on race, sex, age, and handicap discrimination emanating from statutes, court decisions, and regulations that have influenced employment practices in public education.

The Equal Protection Clause is a general protection against invidious discrimination, whereas Title VII is a broad-based legislative prohibition specifically against discrimination due to race, color, religion, sex, or national origin. Other statutes, the Equal Pay Act and the Age Discrimination in Employment Act, prohibit practices that classify persons according to sex or age. (See Appendix B.) Discrimination against the handicapped is prohibited in the Rehabilitation Act of 1973 and in the Americans with Disabilities Act of 1990.

■ RACE DISCRIMINATION

Since *Brown v. Board of Education,* numerous employment practices have been litigated regarding discrimination in the public sector. Many cases have challenged hiring and testing practices, reduction of staff resulting in nonretention of minority employees, and reverse discrimination. Most of these cases have been brought under the Equal Protection Clause of the Fourteenth Amendment and Title VII of the Civil Rights Act of 1964.

Equal Protection

The standards under the Equal Protection Clause are not the same as under the various statutory provisions that have been designed by Congress to eradicate discrimination. The equal protection standard as developed in the school desegregation cases prohibits discrimination that can be ultimately traced to a racially motivated purpose.[1] As discussed in the chapter on desegregation, remedial action to overcome segregation is not required by the courts under the Equal Protection Clause unless it can be shown that segregation was caused by official actions, the *purpose* and *intent* of which were to discriminate.[2] To show merely that the *effect* of the employer's policy results in adverse impact on racial minorities is insufficient to prove a violation of the Equal Protection Clause.

If plaintiffs cannot show that segregation was a result of discriminatory purpose or intent, the state need only show that its actions were not irrational. On the other hand, if discriminatory intent is shown, the state must bear the burden of showing that it had a compelling reason to act as it did.

In contrast, Title VII imposes a more rigorous standard on the state. Under Title VII, Congress provides that where employment practices are concerned, discriminatory intent need not be proved; rather, the plaintiff need only show that the effect of the policy was to discriminate. Where such disparity is shown, it is insufficient for the employer to show merely a rational basis to justify the challenged practice.[3]

The Supreme Court has set out evidentiary guidelines that plaintiffs must sustain in supporting claims of a discriminatory intent under the Equal Protection Clause. Topically, these are (1) historical background, (2) specific sequence of events leading to the passage or implementation of the practice, (3) departure from accepted practices and normal procedures, (4) substantial departures, and (5) legislative and administrative history. In commenting further, the Supreme Court has said: "Determining whether invidious discriminatory purpose was a motivating factor demands a sensitive inquiry into such circumstances and direct evidence of intent as may be available."[4] The *impact* of the official action may be one aspect of the proof of *intent* to discriminate.[5]

Title VI

Title VI of the Civil Rights Act prohibits discrimination in federally assisted programs based on race, color, or national origin. (See Appendix B for exact wording of the statute.) With Title VI, Congress provided a statutory remedy against discrimination that could be administered by federal agencies in their regulatory capacity. The ultimate enforcement weapon given the federal agencies under this law is the denial of federal funds. It was under Title VI that *Adams v. Richardson*[6] originated, maintaining that the U.S. Department of Health, Education, and Welfare had been derelict in its enforcement responsibilities. In that case, a federal court assumed the responsibility for monitoring enforcement of federal regulations promulgated by the department pursuant to Title VI. The regulations require desegregation of faculty, administration, and other personnel positions in public schools and universities.

The Supreme Court has exhibited some uncertainty as to the application of Title VI. The problem lies in whether officials are required to redress *de jure* segregation only, or whether they have a corresponding statutory obligation to correct racial imbalance caused by *de facto* segregation as well. In the *Bakke* case Justice Powell, writing for a splintered majority, said that Title VI requirements were coterminous with those of the Equal Protection Clause, that neither required school officials to correct unintended racial imbalances.[7] On the other hand, four justices, while agreeing with Powell's general disposition of the case, disagreed with his interpretation of Title VI, maintaining that congressional intent was to prohibit discrimination, regardless of intent. Writing for these four judges, Justice Stevens said that "the meaning of the Title VI ban on exclusion is crystal clear: Race cannot be the basis of excluding anyone from participation in a federally funded program." He further maintained that it was not necessary to liken Title VI to the Equal Protection Clause, since Title VI's origins emanated from its own legislative intent and history. Having said this, however, the Court did not resolve the fundamental issue of whether Title VI requires affirmative administrative response for unintended segregation.

Some clarification of the intent questions under Title VI did come forth in 1983 in the case of *Guardians Association v. Civil Service Commission of New York.*[8] In this case, the Court held that a private person may be compensated for a state agency's violation of his or her Title VI rights, but only if the person is able to show intent to discriminate. In other words, as now written, intent must be shown to exist before Title VI is violated and federal funds can be withheld.

Title VII

When first enacted in 1964,[9] Title VII did not extend to discriminatory employment practices in educational institutions, but in 1972 the law was amended, eliminating this exemption.[10] As a result, it is Title VII that has been used most often to challenge discrimination in teacher and administrator employment.

An area of important concern in applying Title VII has been employee testing for purposes of hiring and promotion. The position of the United States Supreme Court on employee testing was enunciated in 1971 in *Griggs v. Duke Power Co.*[11] In this case, the Court found that Title VII of the Civil Rights Act prevented an employer from rejecting black job applicants on the basis of lack of completion of high school or on the results of a general intelligence test. Duke Power Company was unable to show that the general standards it had established were related to job performance. The Court said:

> The facts of this case demonstrate the inadequacy of broad and general testing devices as well as the infirmity of using diplomas or degrees as fixed measures of capability. Nothing in the Act precludes the use of testing or measuring procedures; obviously they are useful. What Congress has forbidden is giving these devices and mechanisms controlling force unless they are demonstrably a reasonable measure of job performance.[12]

After *Griggs,* several lower courts invalidated the use of the Graduate Record Examination and the National Teachers Examination as violative of due process and equal protection because the examinations were not job related. School districts, in these instances, were unable to shoulder the burden of showing job relatedness in the face of the high percentage of black teachers who were disqualified.[13]

According to *Griggs,* after the plaintiff successfully shows that the effect of a particular employment practice is to create a racial imbalance, the burden then shifts to the defendant to justify the practice by showing that the imbalance is related to job performance. The Supreme Court has attempted to further clarify the issues by creating a distinction between "disparate treatment" and "disparate impact" cases and has explained the two terms in this way:

> "Disparate treatment" . . . is the most easily understood type of discrimination. The employer simply treats some people less favorably than others because of their race, color, religion, sex, or national origin.; Proof of discriminatory motive is critical, although it can in some situations be inferred from the mere fact of differences in treatment . . . . Undoubtedly disparate treatment was the most obvious and Congress had it in mind when it enacted Title VII . . . . Claims of disparate treatment may be distinguished from claims that stress "disparate impact." The latter involves employment practices that are facially neutral in their treatment of different groups but in fact fall more heavily on one group than another and cannot be justified by business necessity . . . . Proof of discriminatory motive, we have held, is not required under a disparate impact theory.[14]

Disparate treatment cases generally occur when a single plaintiff challenges a particular practice that is detrimental to him or her personally. For example, a faculty member's claim that her promotion in a particular academic department was denied because of bias must be brought as a disparate treatment issue. The nature of the facts do not lend themselves to a showing of impact. On the other hand, disparate impact may be more easily shown in cases involving a number of persons who are affected by a particular employment practice, such as a requirement that all employees pass a test.

When a plaintiff shows evidence to substantiate a claim of disparate impact, the employer must then bear the burden of showing that the particular employment practice was justified as a "business necessity" or that it was "related to job performance." For example, a written examination indicating one's level of verbal skills has been held a valid device to select recruits for a police department.[15] Similarly, the use of the National Teachers Examination has been found to be a valid "job related" instrument to determine teacher qualifications for employment and pay.[16]

Thus the Supreme Court has enunciated two routes for plaintiffs to pursue discrimination under Title VII, disparate treatment and disparate impact. Under the former, the initial burden of proof is difficult to bear because the plaintiff must show a discriminatory motive. Under the latter, the initial burden of the plaintiff is less difficult to sustain, but this is offset because the courts have allowed substantial leeway to defendants in showing "business necessity" or "job relatedness." In either instance, taking into account trends and philosophy of the current Supreme Court, plaintiffs may have an increasingly difficult burden in supporting claims of discrimination in the future.

Employment Standards and Tests That Are Not Significantly Related to Job Performance Violate Title VII of the Civil Rights Act of 1964

— · — · — · — · — ·

Griggs v. Duke Power Co.

— · — · — · — · — ·

Supreme Court of the United States, 1971.
401 U.S. 424, 91 S.Ct. 849.

Mr. Chief Justice BURGER delivered the opinion of the Court. We granted the writ in this case to resolve the question whether an employer is prohibited by the Civil Rights Act of 1964, Title VII, from requiring a high school education or passing of a standardized general intelligence test as a condition of employment in or transfer to jobs when (a) neither standard is shown to be significantly related to successful job performance, (b) both requirements operate to disqualify Negroes at a substantially higher rate than white applicants, and (c) the jobs in question formerly had been filled only by white employees as part of a longstanding practice of giving preference to whites. . . .

The objective of Congress in the enactment of Title VII is plain from the language of the statute. It was to achieve equality of employment opportunities and remove barriers that have operated in the past to favor an identifiable group of white employees over other employees. Under the Act, practices, procedures, or tests neutral on their face, and even neutral in terms of intent, cannot be maintained if they operate to "freeze" the status quo of prior discriminatory employment practices.

The Court of Appeals' opinion, and the partial dissent, agreed that, on the record in the present case, "whites register far better on the Company's alternative requirements" than Negroes. . . . Because they are Negroes, petitioners have long received inferior education in segregated schools and this court expressly recognized these differences in *Gaston County v. United States,* 395 U.S. 285, 89 S.Ct. 1720 (1969). . . . Congress did not intend by Title VII, however, to guarantee a job to every person regardless of qualifications. In short, the Act does not command that any person be hired simply because he was formerly the subject of discrimination, or because he is a member of a minority group. Discriminatory preference for any group, minority or majority, is precisely and only what Congress has proscribed. What is required by Congress is the removal of artificial, arbitrary, and unnecessary barriers to employment when the barriers operate invidiously to discriminate on the basis of racial or other impermissible classification.

. . . The Act proscribes not only overt discrimination but also practices that are fair in form, but discriminatory in operation. The touchstone is business necessity. If an employment practice that operates to exclude Negroes cannot be shown to be related to job performance, the practice is prohibited.

On the record before us, neither the high school completion requirement nor the general intelligence test is shown to bear a demonstrable relationship to successful performance of the jobs for which it was used. Both were adopted, as the Court of Appeals noted, without meaningful study of their relationship to job-performance ability. . . .

The evidence, however, shows that employees who have not completed high school or taken the tests have continued to perform satisfactorily and make progress in departments for which the high school and test criteria are not used. The promotion record of present employees who would not be able to meet the new criteria thus suggests the possibility that the requirements may not be needed even for the limited purpose of preserving the avowed policy of advancement within the Company. . . .

The Court of Appeals held that the Company had adopted the diploma and test requirements without any "intention to discriminate against Negro employees." . . . But Congress directed the thrust of the Act to the *consequences* of employment practices, not simply the motivation. More than that, Congress has placed on the employer the burden of showing that any given requirement must have a manifest relationship to the employment in question.

The facts of this case demonstrate the inadequacy of broad and general testing devices as well as the infirmity of using diplomas or degrees as fixed measures of capability. . . .

Nothing in the Act precludes the use of testing or measuring procedures; obviously they are useful. What Congress has forbidden is giving these devices and mechanisms controlling force unless they are demonstrably a reasonable measure of job performance. Congress has not commanded that the less qualified be preferred over the better qualified simply because of minority origins. Far from disparaging job qualifications as such, Congress has made such qualifications the controlling factor, so that race, religion, nationality, and sex become irrelevant. What Congress has commanded is that any tests used must measure the person for the job and not the person in the abstract.

State Use of Test Scores for Both Certification Purposes and as a Salary Factor Does Not Violate Equal Protection Clause nor Title VII of Civil Rights Act

– · – · – · – · –

United States of America v. State of South Carolina

– · – · – · – · –

United States District Court, District of South Carolina, Columbia Div., 1977. 445 F.Supp. 1094, affirmed 434 U.S. 1026, 98 S.Ct. 756 (1978).

Before HAYNSWORTH and RUSSELL, Circuit Judges and SIMONS, District Judge. . . . The defendants are charged with violations of the Fourteenth Amendment to the Constitution of the United States and Title VII of the Civil Rights Act of 1964, as amended, 42 U.S.C. § 2000e, et seq., (1970), through the use of minimum score requirements on the National Teacher Examinations (hereinafter "NTE") to certify and determine the pay levels of teachers within the State. . . .

For over thirty years the State of South Carolina and its agencies have used scores on the NTE to make decisions with respect to the certification of teachers and the amount of state aid payable to local school districts. Local school boards within the State use scores on the NTE for selection and compensation of teachers. From 1969 to 1976, a minimum score of 975 was required by the State for its certification and state aid decisions. In June, 1976, after an exhaustive validation study by Educational Testing Service (ETS), and after a critical review and evaluation of this study by the Board of Education's Committee on Teacher Recruitment, Training and Compensation and the Department Staff, the State established new certification requirements involving different minimum scores in various areas of teaching specialization that range from 940 to 1198. . . .

Plaintiffs challenge each of the uses of the NTE. They contend that more blacks than whites historically have failed to achieve the required minimum score, and that this result creates a racial classification in violation of the constitutional and statutory provisions cited in their complaints. . . .

We first consider whether the use by the State and its Board of Education of a minimum score requirement on the NTE violates the equal protection clause of the Fourteenth Amendment. . . .

In disposing of the remaining constitutional claims, separate consideration must be given to the State's use of the test scores to certify teachers and to determine the amount of state aid for local school districts. Plaintiffs allege that the disparate racial impact of defendants' certification and compensation systems creates a racial classification in violation of the Fourteenth Amendment. In order to sustain that allegation, the Supreme Court's decision in *Washington v. Davis,* 426 U.S. 229, 96 S.Ct. 2040, 48 L.Ed. 2d 597 (1976), requires plaintiffs to prove that the State intended to create and use a racial classification. If plaintiffs fail to prove intent (or defendants adequately rebut that proof), then we must evaluate this classification under the rational relationship standard required by the Fourteenth Amendment as to all such classifications.

Because of its paramount importance under *Washington v. Davis,* we look first at whether the plaintiffs have proved that any of the challenged decisions of defendants were motivated by an intent to discriminate. The purpose or intent that we must assess is the purpose or intent that underlies the particular act or acts under review. . . .

CERTIFICATION. South Carolina requires persons who teach in the public schools to hold a certificate issued by the State Board of Education. S.C. Code § 21–354. From 1945 to the present the State has had four certification systems, each requiring prospective teachers to take the NTE. Candidates are able to take the NTE an unlimited number of times. (The tests are given by the State three or four times each year).

The record before us indicates that during this period, the racial composition of the South Carolina teacher force has closely paralleled the racial composition of the State's population. . . .

From 1945 through 1968, the State issued four grades of certificates: A, B, C and D. From 1945 through 1956, candidates were awarded certificates based on their relative standing with respect to test scores of all candidates in the State for the year. . . .

In 1957, a new system of absolute, rather than relative, requirements was instituted. Under this system, a score of 500 or more on the Common Examinations portion of the NTE was required for an *A* certificate; a score of 425 to 499 for a *B* certificate; a score of 375 to 424 for a *C* certificate; and a score of 332 to 374 for a *D* certificate. . . .

In 1969, the certification system was further revised by replacing the four-tiered system with two types of certificates: the professional certificate and the warrant. . . . Those who attained scores below 400 were not licensed. In the academic year 1969–70, the maximum score requirement of 400 on the Common Examinations eliminated approximately 41 percent of the graduates of predominantly black colleges and less than 1 percent of the graduates of predominantly white colleges. Similar results were obtained in succeeding years, despite the fact that a score of 400 is usually below the 11th percentile nationally, and almost 90 percent of the candidates who take these tests get a higher score.

In 1976, the certification system was again revised, the two-tiered system being replaced with a single certificate with separate minimum score requirements in each of the eighteen fields of teaching specialty replacing the single minimum score requirement. These combined scores on both Common Examinations and Area Examinations ranged from 940 in Agriculture to 1178 in Library and Media Specialties; . . . . There are no statistics in the record indicating the impact of the new score requirements because they will be applied first to the class of 1977; however, plaintiffs predict that, under these requirements the disparate impact may be even greater. . . .

With respect to the constitutional challenge to South Carolina's use of the NTE for certification purposes, we conclude that the plaintiffs have not demonstrated the required discriminatory intent with respect to any of the specific decisions setting certification standards based on NTE scores. This is especially true in connection with the State's 1976 change in requirements where there is no indication whatsoever that the State and its officers were motivated by anything more than a desire to use an accepted and racially neutral standardized test to evaluate the teacher applicants competing for relatively few jobs in South Carolina.

The NTE are developed and administered by ETS, an independent nonprofit organization of recognized professional reputation.

ETS recommends that minimum score requirements not be used as a sole determinant of certification decisions where other appropriate information or criteria are available.

In this case, the plaintiffs have come forth with no other reasonably appropriate criteria upon which certification may be properly based.

Neither have plaintiffs been able to establish any defect in the NTE indicating that the examinations themselves discriminate on the basis of race. The choices as to subject matter and question format are reasonable and well-documented on the record, and although other subject matters or other examination forms might be possible or even preferable, there is no proof of any inherent discrimination. The inference that plaintiffs would have us draw from the statistics which indicate that blacks as a group have lower average scores than whites is rebutted by the evidence with respect to the construction of the tests and their content validity. Since we find that the NTE create classifications only on permissible bases (presence or absence of knowledge or skill and ability in applying knowledge), and that they are not used pursuant to any intent to discriminate, their use in making certification decisions by the State is proper and legal.

PAY SCALES. Plaintiffs raise a separate constitutional challenge to South Carolina's use of the NTE as a partial determinant of the salaries paid to public school teachers. The use of the NTE for salary purposes is distinct from, and, in significant ways, unrelated to the use of the NTE for certification purposes. Accordingly, we must again examine plaintiffs' proof with respect to intent. . . .

We are unable to find a discriminatory intent from these facts, even though the historical background of a dual pay system and a delay in implementing a unitary system after the Fourth Circuit struck down a similar system in another state provide some support for such an inference. Such inference is adequately rebutted by the evidence with respect to what the Legislature actually did. The unitary pay system was based in part on the amount of educational training and years of teaching experience possessed by each teacher. Plaintiffs make no claim that the use of either of these factors was motivated by discriminatory intent, and it is evident that the monetary rewards available through these avenues alone, without regard to the grade of certificate, were significant. The link between the new unitary pay system and the new certification system is not without a reasoned basis. It was important to the State to use its limited resources to improve the quality of the teacher force and to put whatever monetary incentives were available in the salary schedule to that task. As before stated, we have found that no discriminatory intent has been established with respect to the decision in 1945 to adopt a certification system based in part on NTE scores; and, therefore, without independent proof, there is no associated discriminatory intent in linking the certification and salary systems. . . .

Plaintiffs urge that the Legislature was motivated by an intent to discriminate because the state aid schedule provided fewer benefits and incentives for two classifications of teachers in which there were relatively more blacks than whites; the classifications continued to be based, if only in part, on examination scores; and the developer of the tests was later opposed to their use for this purpose. In the absence of any competent or persuasive direct evidence of intent, plaintiffs would have us draw an inference from the facts that are available. But such an inference can stand only if there is no equally persuasive explanation consistent with a legitimate intent. Here the reordering of priorities with respect to the limited resources available for teacher salaries appears entirely consistent with an intent to obtain the maximum incentive for improvement that could be accomplished with a fixed number of dollars. We are unable to find an intent to discriminate.

In the absence of discriminatory intent, the classifications of teachers for both certification and pay purposes may be assessed under the "rational relationship" standard required by the Fourteenth Amendment of all classifications.

The Supreme Court has defined this standard in the following terms:

> Although no precise formula has been developed, the Court has held that the Fourteenth Amendment permits the States a wide scope of discretion in enacting laws which affect some groups of citizens differently than others. The constitutional safeguard is offended only if the classification rests on grounds wholly irrelevant to the achievement of the State's objective. State legislatures are presumed to have acted within their constitutional power despite the fact that, in practice, their laws result in some inequality. A statutory discrimination will not be set aside if any state of facts reasonably may be conceived to justify it. *McGowan v. Maryland*, 366 U.S. 420, 425–26, 81 S.Ct. 1101, 1105, 6 L.Ed.2d 393 (1961).

We conclude that the State's use of the NTE for both certification and pay purposes meets the "rational relationship" standard of *McGowan v. Maryland*, supra, and consequently does not violate the equal protection clause of the Fourteenth Amendment.
. . .

. . . [W]e find that the defendants have offered a legitimate and important governmental objective for their use of the NTE. The State has the right to adopt academic requirements and to use written achievement tests designed and validated to disclose the minimum amount of knowledge necessary to effective teaching. . . . The evidence in the record supports a finding that South Carolina officials were concerned with improving the quality of public school teaching, certifying only those applicants possessed of the minimum knowledge necessary to teach effectively, utilizing an objective measure of applicants coming from widely disparate teacher training programs, and providing appropriate financial incentives for teachers to improve their academic qualifications and thereby their ability to teach. We conclude that these are entirely legitimate and clearly important governmental objectives.

In considering whether defendants' use of the NTE bears a fair and substantial relationship to these governmental objectives, we conclude that it does.

The record supports the conclusion that the NTE are professionally and carefully prepared to measure the critical mass of knowledge in academic subject matter. The NTE do not measure teaching skills, but do measure the content of the academic preparation of prospective teachers. . . . the NTE program "is neutral on its face and rationally may be said to serve a purpose the Government is constitutionally empowered to pursue." . . . Plaintiffs have not contended nor proved that the NTE are racially biased or otherwise deficient when measured against the applicable professional and legal standards.

Furthermore, there is ample evidence in the record of the content validity of the NTE. The NTE have been demonstrated to provide a useful measure of the extent to which prospective teachers have mastered the content of their teacher training programs. In a similar challenge to a bar examination the Fourth Circuit has held that proof of such content validity is persuasive evidence that the equal protection clause has not been violated. *Richardson v. McFadden*, 540 F.2d 744 (4th Cir.1976). The Supreme Court has held that a substantial relationship between a test and a training program—such as is found here—is sufficient to withstand challenge on constitutional grounds. *Washington v. Davis*, 426 U.S. at 248–52, 96 S.Ct. 2040. State officials surely have the right to require graduation from approved teacher training programs as a prerequisite to being certified to teach in South Carolina. Plaintiffs have acknowledged the substantial relationship between the academic training program and the job of teaching by advocating that a requirement of graduation from an approved program *alone* is sufficient to protect the public interest.
. . .

We also conclude that defendants' use of the NTE for salary purposes bears the necessary relationship to South Carolina's objectives with respect to its public school teaching force. Although the NTE were not designed to evaluate experienced teachers, the State could reasonably conclude that the NTE provided a reliable and economical means for measuring one element of effective teaching — the degree of knowledge possessed by the teacher. . . .

We turn now to the question whether defendants' uses of the NTE violate Title VII, 42 U.S.C.A. § 2000e, et seq. . . .

The remaining claims under Title VII must be tested under statutory standards. In *Washington v. Davis,* 426 U.S. 229, 96 S.Ct. 2040, 48 L.Ed.2d 597 (1976), the Supreme Court summarized the order of proof:

> Under Title VII, Congress provided that when hiring and promotion practices disqualifying substantially disproportionate numbers of blacks are challenged, discriminatory purpose need not be proved, and that it is an insufficient response to demonstrate some rational basis for the challenged practices. It is necessary, in addition, that they be "validated" in terms of job performance in any one of several ways, perhaps by ascertaining the minimum skill, ability or potential necessary for the position at issue and determining whether the qualifying tests are appropriate for the selection of qualified applicants for the job in question. (Id. at 246, 96 S.Ct. at 2051).

Thus, it was held not sufficient for the governmental entity to prove that the classification resulting from the test scores had a rational basis, that is, that it differentiated between persons who did and did not have some minimum verbal and communication skill. It was necessary, in addition, for the governmental entity to demonstrate that the minimum verbal and communication skill, in turn, had some rational relationship to the legitimate employment objectives of the employer . . . that the employment practice must be a "business necessity." Id. at 431, 91 S.Ct. 849.

Plaintiffs have proved that the use of NTE scores by the State in its certification decisions disqualifies substantially disproportionate numbers of blacks. The burden of proof was thereby shifted to the defendants, and in an effort to meet this burden the State commissioned an extensive validity study by ETS. The design of this study is novel, but consistent with the basic requirements enunciated by the Supreme Court, and we accordingly hold such study sufficient to meet the burden placed on defendants under Title VII.

The study seeks to demonstrate content validity by measuring the degree to which the content of the tests matches the content of the teacher training programs in South Carolina. It also seeks to establish a minimum score requirement by estimating the amount of knowledge (measured by the ability to answer correctly test questions that have been content-validated) that a minimally qualified teacher candidate in South Carolina would have. . . .

We find that the results of the validity study are sufficiently trustworthy to sustain defendants' burden under Title VII. . . . Plaintiffs misconceive their burden once defendants have made a reasonable showing that the study was executed in a responsible, professional manner designed to produce trustworthy results. In order to rebut the presumption that trustworthy results were indeed produced, plaintiffs must not only show that the study was not executed as intended, but also that the results were adversely affected. . . .

There remains, however, the question whether the State has satisfied the "business necessity" requirement set out in *Griggs v. Duke Power Co.,* 401 U.S. 424, 91 S.Ct. 849, 28 L.Ed.2d 158 (1971). This "business necessity" doctrine appears neither in the explicit language nor the legislative history of Title VII. The Court in *Griggs* and subsequent Title VII cases did not establish judicial standards for determining whether a particular practice is a business necessity. The EEOC Guidelines are of little assistance because they were published before *Griggs* and have not been updated since that time.

We think that *Griggs* did not import into Title VII law the concept of "compelling interest" developed as a part of the "strict scrutiny" standard for assessing certain classifications under the Fourteenth Amendment. Under this concept, the Court would balance the disparate impact on blacks against the business purpose of the employer and uphold the business practice only if it were sufficiently "compelling" to overcome the disparate impact. It is our view that the Supreme Court intended an examination of the alternatives available with respect to the legitimate employment objective identified by the employer to determine whether there is available to the employer an alternative practice that would achieve his business purpose equally well but with a lesser disparate impact by race. In examining alternatives, the risk and cost to the employer are relevant.

Here, plaintiffs have suggested only one alternative to the use of the NTE for certification purposes. Plaintiffs contend that mere graduation from an approved program should be sufficient and would have a lesser disparate impact on blacks. We cannot find that this alternative will achieve the State's purpose in certifying minimally competent persons equally well as the use of a content-validated standardized test. The record amply demonstrates that there are variations in admissions requirements, academic standards and grading practices at the various teacher training institutions within the State. The approval that the State gives to the teacher training program is to general subject matter areas covered by the program, not to the actual course content of the program, and not to the means used within the program to measure whether individual students have actually mastered the course content to which they have been exposed. The standardized test scores do reflect individual achievement with respect to specific subject matter content, which is directly relevant to (although not sufficient in itself to assure) competence to teach, and thus the use of these scores for certification purposes survives the business necessity test under Title VII.

There remains, finally, the question whether the uses of the NTE for salary purposes are a violation of Title VII. . . .

We believe that a distinction for pay purposes between those who are qualified as well as between those who are not qualified

survives the business necessity test. There appears to be no alternative available to the State, within reasonable limits of risk and cost, for providing the incentive necessary to motivate thousands of persons to acquire, generally on their own time and at their own expense, the necessary additional academic training so that they will be minimally competent teachers. Having made the investment of four years in an undergraduate education, it seems reasonable to try to upgrade the talent of unqualified teachers where possible, rather than rejecting them altogether.

In accordance with the foregoing findings and conclusions, we conclude that plaintiff and plaintiff-intervenors have failed to establish their right to any of the relief sought in their respective complaints. It is, therefore,

Ordered that judgment be entered in favor of the defendants.

NOTES

1. Because of the difficulties of proving intent, most litigation has been concerned with disparate impact under Title VII. A disparate treatment plaintiff, in establishing a *prima facie* case, must show that four basic factors are true: "(i) that he belongs to a racial minority; (ii) that he applied and was qualified for a job for which the employer was seeking applicants; (iii) that, despite his qualifications, he was rejected; and (iv) that, after his rejection, the position remained open and the employer continued to seek applicants from persons of complainant's qualifications." *McDonnell-Douglas Corp. v. Green*, 411 U.S. 792, 93 S.Ct. 1817 (1973).

The *McDonnell-Douglas* standards for establishing a *prima facie* case are flexible. Facts will vary from case to case and specifications for *prima facie* proof will not necessarily be the same in every aspect. "A prima facie case under *McDonnell Douglas* raises an inference of discrimination only because we [the Courts] presume these acts, if otherwise unexplained, are more likely than not based on the consideration of impermissible factors." *Furnco Construc-*

tion Corp. v. Waters, 438 U.S. 567, 98 S.Ct. 2943 (1978).

Therefore, to dispel the adverse inference from a *prima facie* showing, all the employer needs to do is "articulate some legitimate, nondiscriminatory reason for the employee's rejection." *McDonnell-Douglas Corp. v. Green,* 411 U.S. 792, 93 S.Ct. 1817 (1973). After the employer has articulated some legitimate reason, the plaintiff must be afforded the opportunity to present evidence that this is no more than a pretext for discrimination.

2. In *Board of Trustees of Keene State College v. Sweeney,* 439 U.S. 24, 99 S.Ct. 295 (1978), the appeals court required the defendant university "to prove [the] absence of [a] discriminatory motive." The Supreme Court reaffirmed *Furnco* and distinguished between "articulate," "show," and "prove." "[W]e think that there is a significant distinction between merely 'articulating some legitimate, nondiscriminatory reason' and 'proving absence of discriminatory motive.'" The case was remanded to the lower court to allow the university to articulate a legitimate reason as established and defined by the Supreme Court.

3. Perhaps the best explanation of the evidentiary requirements of Title VII is set forth by Supreme Court Justice Sandra Day O'Conner in *Watson v. Fort Worth Bank and Trust,* 487 U.S. 977, 108 S.Ct. 2777 (1988). In *Watson,* Justice O'Conner clarifies the complexities of the Supreme Court precedents with regard to the proof requirements for both plaintiffs and defendants under *disparate treatment* and *disparate impact* analysis. In the *Watson* case, the Supreme Court vacated and remanded a U.S. Court of Appeals decision ruling "a Title VII challenge to a discretionary or subjective promotion system can only be analyzed under the disparate treatment model." In so overruling the lower court, the Supreme Court concluded that "disparate impact analysis is in principle no less applicable to subjective employment criteria than to objective or standardized tests," 487 U.S. at 978, 108 S.Ct. at 2779. The following material is quoted from Justice O'Conner's opinion in

Watson. (The side-heads are added for emphasis.)

DISPARATE TREATMENT. Several of our decisions have dealt with the evidentiary standards that apply when an individual alleges that an employer has treated that particular person less favorably than others because of the plaintiff's race, color, religion, sex, or national origin. In such "disparate treatment" cases, which involve "the most easily understood type of discrimination," . . . the plaintiff is required to prove that the defendant had a discriminatory intent or motive.

BURDEN OF PROOF. In order to facilitate the orderly consideration of relevant evidence, we have devised a series of shifting evidentiary burdens that are "intended progressively to sharpen the inquiry into the elusive factual question of intentional discrimination." . . . Under that scheme, a prima facie case is ordinarily established by proof that the employer, after having rejected the plaintiff's application for a job or promotion, continued to seek applicants with qualifications similar to the plaintiff's. . . . The burden of proving a prima facie is "not onerous," . . . and the employer in turn may rebut it simply by producing some evidence that it had legitimate, nondiscriminatory reasons for the decision. If the defendant carries this burden of production, the plaintiff must prove by a preponderance of all the evidence in the case that the legitimate reasons offered by the defendant were a pretext for discrimination.

PLAINTIFF BEARS ULTIMATE BURDEN. We have cautioned that these shifting burdens are meant only to aid courts and litigants in arranging the presentation of evidence: "The ultimate burden of persuading the trier of fact that the defendant intentionally discriminated against the plaintiff remains at all times with the plaintiff."

DISPARATE IMPACT. In *Griggs v. Duke Power Co.,* 401 U.S. 424, 91 S.Ct. 849, 28 L.Ed.2d 158 (1971), this Court held that a plaintiff need not necessarily prove intentional discrimination in order to establish that an employer has violated § 703. In certain cases, facially neutral employment practices that have significant adverse effects on protected *groups* have been held to violate the Act without proof that the employer adopted those practices with a discriminatory intent. The factual issues and the character of the evidence are inevitably somewhat different when the plaintiff is exempted from the need to prove intentional discrimination. . . . The evidence in these "disparate impact" cases usually focuses on statistical disparities, rather than specific incidents, and on competing explanations for those disparities.

FEATURES OF DISPARATE IMPACT. The distinguishing features of the factual issues that typically dominate in disparate impact cases do not imply that the ultimate legal issue is different than in cases where disparate treatment analysis is used. . . . Nor do we think it is appropriate to hold a defendant liable for unintentional discrimination on the basis of less evidence than is required to prove intentional discrimination. Rather, the necessary premise of the disparate impact approach is that some employment practices, adopted without a deliberately discriminatory motive, may in operation be functionally equivalent to intentional discrimination.

Perhaps the most obvious examples of such functional equivalence have been found where facially neutral job requirements necessarily operated to perpetuate the effects of intentional discrimination that occurred before Title VII was enacted. In *Griggs* itself, for example, the employer had a history of overt racial discrimination that predated the enactment of the Civil Rights Act of 1964. . . . Such conduct had apparently ceased thereafter, but the employer continued to follow employment policies that had "a markedly disproportionate" adverse effect on blacks. . . . The *Griggs* Court found that these policies, which involved the use of general aptitude tests and a high school diploma requirement, were not demonstrably related to the jobs for which they were used. . . .

FACIAL NEUTRALITY. Believing that diplomas and tests could become "masters of reality,"

which would perpetuate the effects of pre-Act discrimination, the Court concluded that such practices could not be defended simply on the basis of their facial neutrality or on the basis of the employer's lack of discriminatory intent.

This Court has repeatedly reaffirmed the principle that some facially neutral employment practices may violate Title VII even in the absence of a demonstrated discriminatory intent. We have not limited this principle to cases in which the challenged practice served to perpetuate the effects of pre-Act intentional discrimination.

SUBJECTIVE CRITERIA. Each of our subsequent decisions, however, like *Griggs* itself, involved standardized employment tests or criteria. . . . In contrast, we have consistently used conventional disparate-treatment theory, in which proof of intent to discriminate is required, to review hiring and promotion decisions that were based on the exercise of personal judgment or the application of inherently subjective criteria. . . .

Our decisions have not addressed the question whether disparate impact analysis may be applied to cases in which subjective criteria are used to make employment decisions. As noted above, the Court of Appeals are in conflict on the issue. In order to resolve this conflict, we must determine whether the reasons that support the use of disparate impact analysis apply to subjective employment practices, and whether such analysis can be applied in this new context under workable evidentiary standards. . . .

We are persuaded that our decisions in *Griggs* and succeeding cases could largely be nullified if disparate impact analysis were applied only to standardized selection practices.

SUBJECTIVE VERSUS OBJECTIVE CRITERIA. However one might distinguish "subjective" from "objective" criteria, it is apparent that selection systems that combine both types would generally have to be considered subjective in nature. Thus, for example, if the employer in *Griggs* had consistently preferred applicants who had a high school diploma and who passed the company's general aptitude test, its selection system could nonetheless have been considered "subjective" if it also included brief interviews with the candidates. So long as an employer refrained from making standardized criteria absolutely determinative, it would remain free to give such tests almost as much weight as it chose without risking a disparate impact challenge. If we announced a rule that allowed employers so easily to insulate themselves from liability under *Griggs,* disparate impact analysis might effectively be abolished.

We are also persuaded that disparate impact analysis is in principle no less applicable to subjective employment criteria than to objective or standardized tests. In either case, a facially neutral practice, adopted without discriminatory intent, may have effects that are indistinguishable from intentionally discriminatory practices. It is true, to be sure, that an employer's policy of leaving promotion decisions to the unchecked discretion of lower level supervisors should itself raise no inference of discriminatory conduct. Especially in relatively small businesses like respondent's, it may be customary and quite reasonable simply to delegate employment decisions to those employees who are most familiar with the jobs to be filled and with the candidates for those jobs. It does not follow, however, that the particular supervisors to whom this discretion is delegated always act without discriminatory intent. Furthermore, even if one assumed that any such discrimination can be adequately policed through disparate treatment analysis, the problem of subconscious stereotypes and prejudices would remain. . . . If an employer's undisciplined system of subjective decision-making has precisely the same effects as a system pervaded by impermissible intentional discrimination, it is difficult to see why Title VII's proscription against discriminatory actions should not apply. In both circumstances, the employer's practices may be said to "adversely affect [an individual's] status as an employee, because of such individual's race, color, religion, sex, or national origin." 42 U.S.C. §2000e-2 (a)(2). We conclude, accordingly, that subjective or discretionary employment prac-

tices may be analyzed under the disparate impact approach in appropriate cases. . . .

It is completely unrealistic to assume that unlawful discrimination is the sole cause of people failing to gravitate to jobs and employers in accord with the laws of chance. . . . It would be equally unrealistic to suppose that employers can eliminate, or discover and explain, the myriad of innocent causes that may lead to statistical imbalances in the composition of their work forces.

CONGRESSIONAL INTENT. Congress has specifically provided that employers are *not* required to avoid "disparate impact" as such:

> Nothing contained in [Title VII] shall be interpreted to require any employer . . . to grant preferential treatment to any individual or to any group because of the race, color, religion, sex, or national origin of such individual or group on account of an imbalance which may exist with respect to the total number or percentage of persons of any race, color, religion, sex, or national origin employed by any employer . . . in comparison with the total number or percentage of persons of such race, color, religion, sex, or national origin in any community, State, section, or other area, or in the available work force in any community, State, section, or other area. 42 U.S.C. § 2000e-2(j).

EMPLOYER RESPONSE. Preferential treatment and the use of quotas by public employers subject to Title VII can violate the Constitution; see, *e.g., Wygant v. Jackson Bd. of Education,* 476 U.S. 267, 106 S.Ct. 1842, 90 L.Ed.2d 260 (1986), and it has long been recognized that legal rules leaving any class of employers with "little choice" but to adopt such measures would be "far from the intent of Title VII." . . . [E]xtending disparate impact analysis to subjective employment practices has the potential to create a Hobson's choice for employers and thus to lead in practice to perverse results. If quotas and preferential treatment become the only cost-effective means of avoiding expensive litigation and potentially catastrophic liability, such measures will be widely adopted. The prudent employer will be careful to ensure that its programs are discussed in euphemistic terms, but will be equally careful to ensure that the quotas are met. Allowing the evolution of disparate impact analysis to lead to this result would be contrary to Congress' clearly expressed intent, and it should not be the effect of our decision today.

We do not believe that disparate impact theory need have any chilling effect on legitimate business practices. We recognize, however, that today's extension of that theory into the context of subjective selection practices could increase the risk that employers will be given incentives to adopt quotas or to engage in preferential treatment. Because Congress has so clearly and emphatically expressed its intent that Title VII not lead to this result, 42 U.S.C. § 2000e-2(j), we think it imperative to explain in some detail why the evidentiary standards that apply in these cases should serve as adequate safeguards against the danger that Congress recognized. Our previous decisions offer guidance, but today's extension of disparate impact analysis calls for a fresh and somewhat closer examination of the constraints that operate to keep that analysis within its proper bounds.

PLAINTIFF'S BURDEN. First, we note that the plaintiff's burden in establishing a prima facie case goes beyond the need to show that there are statistical disparities in the employer's work force. The plaintiff must begin by identifying the specific employment practice that is challenged. Although this has been relatively easy to do in challenges to standardized tests, it may sometimes be more difficult when subjective selection criteria are at issue. Especially in cases where an employer combines subjective criteria with the use of more rigid standardized rules or tests, the plaintiff is in our view responsible for isolating and identifying the specific employment practices that are allegedly responsible for any observed statistical disparities. . . .

CAUSATION. Once the employment practice at issue has been identified, causation must be provided; that is, the plaintiff must offer statistical evidence of a kind and degree sufficient to show that the practice in question has caused the exclusion of applicants for jobs or promotions because of their membership in a protected group. Our formulas, which have never been framed in terms of any rigid mathematical formula, have consistently stressed that statistical disparities must be sufficiently substantial that they raise such an inference of causation. . . .

STATISTICAL EVIDENCE. Nor are courts or defendants obliged to assume that plaintiffs' statistical evidence is reliable. . . . ("If the defendants in a Title VII suit believe there to be any reason to discredit plaintiffs' statistics that does not appear on their face, the opportunity to challenge them is available to the defendants just as in any other lawsuit. They may endeavor to impeach the reliability of the statistical evidence, they may offer rebutting evidence, or they may disparage in arguments or in briefs the probative weight which the plaintiffs' evidence should be accorded . . . ").

BUSINESS NECESSITY OR JOB RELATEDNESS. A second constraint on the application of disparate impact theory lies in the nature of the "business necessity" or "job relatedness" defense. Although we have said that an employer has "the burden of showing that any given requirement must have a manifest relationship to the employment in question," *Griggs*, 401 U.S., at 432, 91 S.Ct., at 854, such a formulation should not be interpreted as implying that the ultimate burden of proof can be shifted to the defendant. On the contrary, the ultimate burden of proving that discrimination against a protected group has been caused by a specific employment practice remains with the plaintiff at all times. Thus, when a plaintiff has made out a prima facie case of disparate impact, and when the defendant has met its burden of producing evidence that its employment practices are based on legitimate business reasons, the plaintiff must "show that other tests or selection devices, without a similarly undesirable racial effect, would also serve the employer's legitimate interest in efficient and trustworthy workmanship." . . . Factors such as the cost or other burdens of proposed alternative selection devices are relevant in determining whether they would be equally as effective as the challenged practice in serving the employer's legitimate business goals. The same factors would also be relevant in determining whether the challenged practice has operated as the functional equivalent of a pretext for discriminatory treatment.

EMPLOYER'S EVIDENCE. Our cases make it clear that employers are not required, even when defending standardized or objective tests, to introduce formal "validation studies" showing that particular criteria predict actual on-the-job performance. . . .

In the context of subjective or discretionary employment decisions, the employer will often find it easier than in the case of standardized tests to produce evidence of a "manifest relationship to the employment in question." It is self-evident that many jobs, for example those involving managerial responsibilities, require personal qualities that have never been considered amenable to standardized testing. In evaluating claims that discretionary employment practices are insufficiently related to legitimate business purposes, it must be borne in mind that "[c]ourts are generally less competent than employers to restructure business practices, and unless mandated to do so by Congress they should not attempt it." . . . ([The] criteria [used by a university to award tenure], however difficult to apply and however much disagreement they generate in particular cases, are job related. . . . It would be a most radical interpretation of Title VII for a court to enjoin use of an historically settled process and plainly relevant criteria largely because they lead to decisions which are difficult for a court to review"). In sum, the high standards of proof in disparate impact cases are sufficient in our view to avoid giving employers incentives to modify any normal and legitimate practices by introducing quotas or preferential treatment.

Percentage of Black Teachers in the School District Compared to Percentage of Blacks in the School Teacher Population in the Relevant Labor Market Is a Statistical Criterion of Discrimination

— — —— —— —·—

Hazelwood School District v. United States

— — —— —— —·—

Supreme Court of the United States, 1977.
433 U.S. 299, 97 S.Ct. 2736.

Mr. Justice STEWART delivered the opinion of the Court. The petitioner Hazelwood School District covers seventy-eight square miles in the northern part of St. Louis County, Mo. In 1973 the Attorney General brought this lawsuit against Hazelwood and various of its officials, alleging that they were engaged in a "pattern or practice" of employment discrimination in violation of Title VII of the Civil Rights Act of 1964, as amended, 42 U.S.C.A. § 2000e et seq. The complaint asked for an injunction requiring Hazelwood to cease its discriminatory practices, to take affirmative steps to obtain qualified Negro faculty members, and to offer employment and give backpay to victims of past illegal discrimination.

Hazelwood was formed from thirteen rural school districts between 1949 and 1951 by a process of annexation. By the 1967–1968 school year, 17,550 students were enrolled in the district, of whom only 59 were Negro; the number of Negro pupils increased to 576 of 25,166 in 1972–1973, a total of just over 2 percent.

From the beginning, Hazelwood followed relatively unstructured procedures in hiring its teachers. . . . Generally, those who had most recently submitted applications were most likely to be chosen for interviews.

Interviews were conducted by a department chairman, program coordinator, or the principal at the school where the teaching vacancy existed. Although those conducting the interviews did fill out forms rating the applicants in a number of respects, it is undisputed that each school principal possessed virtually unlimited discretion in hiring teachers for his school. The only general guidance given to the principals was to hire the "most competent" person available, and such intangibles as "personality, disposition, appearance, poise, voice, articulation, and ability to deal with people" counted heavily. The principal's choice was routinely honored by Hazelwood's superintendent and Board of Education.

. . . As a buyer's market began to develop for public school teachers, Hazelwood curtailed its recruiting efforts. For the 1971–1972 school year, 3,127 persons applied for only 234 teaching vacancies; for the 1972–1973 school year, there were 2,373 applications for 282 vacancies. A number of the applicants who were not hired were Negroes.

Hazelwood hired its first Negro teacher in 1969. The number of Negro faculty members gradually increased in successive years: six of 957 in the 1970 school year; 16 of 1,107 by the end of the 1972 school year; 22 of 1,231 in the 1973 school year. By comparison, according to 1970 census figures, of more than 19,000 teachers employed in that year in the St. Louis area, 15.4 percent were Negro. That percentage figure included the St. Louis City School District, which in recent years has followed a policy of attempting to maintain a 50 percent Negro teaching staff. Apart from that school district, 5.7 percent of the teachers in the county were Negro in 1970.

Drawing upon these historic facts the Government mounted its "pattern or practice" attack in the District Court upon four different fronts. It adduced evidence of (1) a history of alleged racially discriminatory practices, (2) statistical disparities in hiring, (3) the standardless and largely subjective hiring procedures, and (4) specific instances of alleged discrimination against fifty-five unsuccessful Negro applicants for teaching jobs. Hazelwood offered virtually no additional evidence in response, relying instead on evidence introduced by the Government, perceived deficiencies in the Government's case, and its own officially promulgated policy "to hire all teachers on the basis of training, preparation and recommendations, regardless of race, color or creed."

The District Court ruled that the Government had failed to establish a pattern or practice of discrimination. The court was unpersuaded by the alleged history of discrimination, noting that no dual school system had ever existed in Hazelwood. . . .

The Court of Appeals for the Eighth Circuit reversed. After suggesting that the District Court had assigned inadequate weight to evidence of discriminatory conduct on the part of Hazelwood before the effective date of Title VII, the Court of Appeals rejected the trial court's analysis of the statistical data as resting on an irrelevant comparison of Negro teachers to Negro pupils in Hazelwood. The proper comparison, in the appellate court's view, was one between Negro teachers in Hazelwood and Negro teachers in the relevant labor market area. Selecting St. Louis County and St. Louis City as the relevant area the Court of Appeals compared the 1970 census figures , showing that 15.4 percent of teachers in that area were Negro, to the racial composition of Hazelwood's teaching staff. In the 1972–1973 and 1973–1974 school years, only 1.4 percent and 1.8 percent, respectively, of Hazelwood's teachers were Negroes. This statistical disparity, particularly when viewed against the background of the teacher hiring procedures that Hazelwood had followed, was held to constitute a prima facie case of a pattern or practice of racial discrimination.

. . . Applying that standard, the appellate court found sixteen cases of individual discrimination, which "buttressed" the statistical proof. Because Hazelwood had not rebutted the Government's prima facie case of a pattern or practice of racial discrimination, the Court of Appeals directed judgment for the Government and prescribed the remedial order to be entered. . . .

This Court's recent consideration, in *International Brotherhood of Teamsters v. United States*, of the role of statistics in pattern or practice suits under Title VII provides substantial guidance in evaluating the arguments advanced by the petitioners. In that case we stated that it is the Government's burden to "establish by a preponderance of the evidence that racial discrimination was the[employer's] standard operating procedure – the regular rather than the unusual practice." We also noted that statistics can be an important source of proof in employment discrimination cases . . . .Where gross statistical disparities can be shown, they alone may in a proper case constitute prima facie proof of a pattern or practice of discrimination.

There can be no doubt, in light of the *Teamsters* case, that the District Court's comparison of Hazelwood's teacher work force to its student population fundamentally misconceived the role of statistics in employment discrimination cases. The Court of Appeals was correct in the view that a proper comparison was between the racial composition of Hazelwood's teaching staff and the racial composition of the qualified public school teacher population in the relevant labor market. The percentage of Negroes on Hazelwood's teaching staff in 1972–1973 was 1.4 percent and in 1973–1974 it was 1.8 percent. By contrast, the percentage of qualified Negro teachers in the area was, according to the 1970 census, at least 5.7 percent. Although these differences were on their face substantial, the Court of Appeals erred in substituting its judgment for that of the District Court and holding that the Government had conclusively proved its "pattern or practice" lawsuit.

The Court of Appeals totally disregarded the possibility that this prima facie statistical proof in the record might at the trial court level be rebutted by statistics dealing with Hazelwood's hiring after it became subject to Title VII. Racial discrimination by public employers was not made illegal under Title VII until March 24, 1972. A public employer who from that date forward made all its employment decisions in a wholly nondiscriminatory way would not violate Title VII even if it had formerly maintained an all-white work force by purposefully excluding Negroes. For this reason, the Court cautioned in the *Teamsters* opinion that once a prima facie case has been established by statistical work force disparities, the employer must be given

an opportunity to show "that the claimed discriminatory pattern is a product of pre-Act hiring rather than unlawful post-Act discrimination."

The record in this case showed that for the 1972–1973 school year, Hazelwood hired 282 new teachers, ten of whom (3.5%) were Negroes; for the following school year it hired 123 new teachers, five of whom (4.1%) were Negroes. Over the two-year period, Negroes constituted a total of fifteen of the 405 new teachers hired (3.7%). Although the Court of Appeals briefly mentioned these data in reciting the facts, it wholly ignored them in discussing whether the Government had shown a pattern or practice of discrimination. And it gave no consideration at all to the possibility that post-Act data as to the number of Negroes hired compared to the total number of Negro applicants might tell a totally different story.

What the hiring figures prove obviously depends upon the figures to which they are compared. The Court of Appeals accepted the Government's argument that the relevant comparison was to the labor market area of St. Louis County and St. Louis City, in which, according to the 1970 census, 15.4 percent of all teachers were Negro. The propriety of that comparison was vigorously disputed by the petitioners, who urged that because the City of St. Louis has made special attempts to maintain a 50 percent Negro teaching staff, inclusion of that school district in the relevant market area distorts the comparison. Were that argument accepted, the percentage of Negro teachers in the relevant labor market area (St. Louis County alone) as shown in the 1970 census would be 5.7 percent rather than 15.4 percent.

The difference between these figures may well be important; the disparity between 3.7 percent (the percentage of Negro teachers hired by Hazelwood in 1972–1973 and 1973–1974) and 5.7 percent may be sufficiently small to weaken the Government's other proof, while the disparity between 3.7 percent and 15.4 percent may be sufficiently large to reinforce it. In determining which of the two figures – or very possibly, what intermediate figure – provides the most accurate basis for comparison to the hiring figures at Hazelwood, it will be necessary to evaluate such considerations as (i) whether the racially based hiring policies of the St. Louis City School District were in effect as far back as 1970, the year in which the census figures were taken; (ii) to what extent those policies have changed the racial composition of that district's teaching staff from what it would otherwise have been; (iii) to what extent St. Louis' recruitment policies have diverted to the city teachers who might otherwise have applied to Hazelwood; (iv) to what extent Negro teachers employed by the city would prefer employment in other districts such as Hazelwood; and (v) what the experience in other school districts in St. Louis County indicates about the validity of excluding the City School District from the relevant labor market.

It is thus clear that a determination of the appropriate comparative figures in this case will depend upon further evaluation by the trial court. As this Court admonished in *Teamsters,* "statistics . . . come in infinite variety . . . . [T]heir usefulness depends on all of the surrounding facts and circumstances." Only the trial court is in a position to make the appropriate determination after further findings. And only after such a determination is made can a foundation be established for deciding whether or not Hazelwood engaged in a pattern or practice of racial discrimination in its employment practices in violation of the law.

We hold, therefore, that the Court of Appeals erred in disregarding the post-Act hiring statistics in the record, and that it should have remanded the case to the District Court for further findings as to the relevant labor market area and for an ultimate determination of whether Hazelwood engaged in a pattern or practice of employment discrimination after March 24, 1972. Accordingly, the judgment is vacated, and the case is remanded to the District Court for further proceedings consistent with this opinion.

It is so ordered.

NOTES

1. Section 703 of the Civil Rights Act of 1964, 42 U.S.C.A. § 2000e-2, provides:

   (a) It shall be an unlawful employment practice for an employer—

   1. to fail or refuse to hire or to discharge any individual, or otherwise to discriminate against any individual with respect to his compensation, terms, conditions, or privileges of employment, because of such individual's race, color, religion, sex, or national origin; or
   2. to limit, segregate, or classify his employees or applicants for employment in any way which would deprive or tend to deprive any individual of employment opportunities or otherwise adversely affect his status as an employee, because of such individual's race, color, religion, sex, or national origin. . . .

   (h) Notwithstanding any other provision of this subchapter, it shall not be an unlawful employment practice for an employer . . . to give and to act upon the results of any professionally developed ability test provided that such test, its administration or action upon the results is not designed, intended or used to discriminate because of race, color, religion, sex or national origin.

2. *BFOQ Defense.* If being of a particular sex, religion, or national origin is a necessary part of a job, then discrimination is justified. Title VII provides a statutory exemption for a *bona fide* occupational qualification (BFOQ), a trait necessary for the proper conduct of a job. The Montana Supreme Court has upheld a BFOQ requiring that a high school counselor be a woman. The school sought to maintain a staff of two counselors, one male and one female. Upon seeking to fill a vacancy for the position of the female counselor, a male applicant filed a complaint. Evidence presented by the school indicated that female students were uncomfortable discussing intimate personal matters with a

male counselor. The school had concluded that it needed a counselor of each sex. The court agreed that in this case gender was a BFOQ. *Stone v. Belgrade School District No. 44*, 217 Mont. 309, 703 P.2d 136 (1984).

Affirmative Action

Affirmative action in employment is a voluntary plan adopted by a school district in an effort to remediate past discrimination in that system. Such a plan is looked upon favorably by the courts so long as it is not too broadly fashioned as to either its remedy or justification. The Supreme Court has said that we must be mindful of "this Court's and Congress' consistent emphasis on 'the value of voluntary efforts to further the objectives of the law.' "[17] Yet, affirmative action in employment plans, if not justified, may result in unlawful reverse discrimination. The lawfulness of such plans has been tested under Title VII, Title VI, and the Equal Protection Clause.

Title VII "does not impose a duty to adopt a hiring procedure that maximizes hiring of minority employees,"[18] on the contrary, the act attempts to make employment practices neutral, prohibiting discrimination against any employee. Title VII states specifically that "Nothing contained in [Title VII] shall be interpreted to require any employer . . . to grant preferential treatment to any individual or any group because of the race, color, religion, sex or national origin of such individual or group. . . . "[19] Under Title VII, affirmative action is voluntary. In *McDonald*,[20] the Supreme Court stated: "Title VII, whose terms are not limited to discrimination against members of any particular race, prohibits racial discrimination in private employment against white persons upon the same standards as racial discrimination against nonwhites."[21]

An *affirmative action* employment plan adopted by a school district will not be unlawful *reverse discrimination* under Title VII

if (a) there exists a statistical disparity between the races or sexes in a particular job category, (b) if the institution was guilty of discrimination in the past, (c) the plan does not "unnecessarily trammel" the rights of nonminority employees, (d) the plan does not stigmatize nonminority employees, and (e) the plan is temporary in nature and is scheduled to terminate upon the achievement of a racially or sexually integrated work force.[22]

In 1979, in the case of *United Steelworkers, etc. v. Weber*,[23] employees of a steel company claimed reverse discrimination, citing Title VII. The United Steelworkers and Kaiser Aluminum had negotiated an agreement that included a provision for the elimination of racial imbalance at the Kaiser Aluminum plant. The agreement provided that craft-training positions would be reserved for minorities until the percentage of blacks in the craft work force equaled the percentage of blacks in the local labor market. In the first year of the agreement, thirteen individuals were selected for craft training, seven blacks and six whites. The most senior black of the group had less seniority than a number of white workers who were not selected. The white workers who were not selected filed suit. The Supreme Court ruled that the mutually agreed-upon contract did not violate Title VII because not all private, voluntary, race-conscious, affirmative action plans instituted by companies are prohibited.

In the case of the *Regents of the University of California v. Bakke*,[24] the University's medical school admissions program was challenged by a student applicant named Bakke. The school had established two admission programs. The first, the regular admission program, considered the applicant's grade point average, scores on the Medical College Admissions Test, and other requirements, such as recommendations. Under this plan applicants could be either minority or nonminority, and each year a few minorities were accepted into the medical school through this regular applicant process. The second admissions program was designated for blacks, Chicanos, Asians, and

American Indians. These candidates were screened on similar standards as those in the regular admissions process but were given special consideration because of their disadvantaged backgrounds. Minority candidates who did not qualify for the regular program were eligible for admission under the special admission program.

The plaintiff, Bakke, a white applicant, challenged the admission process, charging reverse discrimination based on the Equal Protection Clause of the Fourteenth Amendment and Title VI of the Civil Rights Act of 1964. Mr. Bakke stated that he was only allowed to apply for one of eighty-four positions, while a minority candidate could apply for one of the regular eighty-four slots and, if not successful in the regular process, could apply for one of the sixteen reserved positions.

The Supreme Court decided the case on Title VI grounds and did not address the Fourteenth Amendment issue of equal protection. The Court held that the use of "quotas" was not allowable and that the admission system was quota based. It also determined that race may be used as a factor in admission programs,[25] and it may even be "weighted" more heavily, but it cannot be the sole and decisive factor.

The Supreme Court has provided definitive guidance as to the boundaries between affirmative action and reverse discrimination under the Equal Protection Clause. In *Wygant* the Supreme Court invalidated a school board's "affirmative retention" policy, which discriminated against nonminority teachers.[26] Following *Wygant*, the U.S. Court of Appeals, Seventh Circuit, held that a "no minority layoff" clause in a collective bargaining agreement violated both Equal Protection and Title VII.[27] The court found that the plan, which laid off 48 white teachers with greater seniority than black teachers who were retained on the job, constituted an absolute racial preference and was not "narrowly tailored" to serve any remedial affirmative action purpose.

Affirmative action plans may, therefore, be found to be discriminatory if they are justified on the excessively broad grounds of rectifying social discrimination alone and/or are too broadly fashioned to serve the remedial pur-poses of removing the vestiges of past discrimination in the schools. In order to have a valid plan to remediate past discrimination, there must be convincing evidence of prior discrimination by the particular governmental unit and "[s]ocietal discrimination alone is insufficient to justify a racial classification."

Six different opinions were filed in *Wygant* by the Supreme Court justices, who in the end failed to agree on a standard of review for affirmative action programs in public employment. The Court did, though, reject race-based layoffs, the necessity for which was defended on the rationale that teachers were "role models" and, as such, minority teachers should be employed in the same percentages to all teachers as the minority student population is to all students. The Court was of the opinion that while hiring goals and promotion policies favorable to minorities are acceptable, the actual laying off of teachers from existing jobs is so intrusive and harmful to the individual nonminority teacher that Equal Protection is violated.

Affirmative Retention Policy Resulting in Layoffs of Nonminority Teachers with More Seniority Violates Equal Protection

–– – –– – –– – ––

Wygant v. Jackson Board of Education

–– – –– – –– – ––

Supreme Court of the United States, 1986.
476 U.S. 267, 106 S.Ct. 1842.

Justice POWELL announced the judgment of the Court and delivered an opinion in which THE CHIEF JUSTICE and Justice REHNQUIST joined, and which Justice O'CONNOR joined in parts I, II, III–A, III–B, and V.

This case presents the question whether a school board, consistent with the Equal Protection Clause, may extend preferential protection against layoffs to some of its employees because of their race or national origin.

In 1972 the Jackson Board of Education, because of racial tension in the community that extended to its schools, considered adding a layoff provision to the Collective Bargaining Agreement (CBA) between the Board and the Jackson Education Association (the Union) that would protect employees who were members of certain minority groups against layoffs. The Board and the Union eventually approved a new provision, Article XII of the CBA, covering layoffs. It stated:

> In the event that it becomes necessary to reduce the number of teachers through layoff from employment by the Board, teachers with the most seniority in the district shall be retained, except that at no time will there be a greater percentage of minority personnel laid off than the current percentage of minority personnel employed at the time of the layoff. In no event will the number given notice of possible layoff be greater than the number of positions to be eliminated. Each teacher so affected will be called back in reverse order for positions for which he is certificated maintaining the above minority balance.

When layoffs became necessary in 1974, it was evident that adherence to the CBA would result in the layoff of tenured nonminority teachers while minority teachers on probationary status were retained. Rather than complying with Article XII, the Board retained the tenured teachers and laid off probationary minority teachers, thus failing to maintain the percentage of minority personnel that existed at the time of the layoff. The Union, together with two minority teachers who had been laid off, brought suit in federal court, . . . *(Jackson Education Assn. v. Board of Education, (Jackson I)* (mem. op.)), claiming that the Board's failure to adhere to the layoff provision violated the Equal Protection Clause of the Fourteenth Amendment and Title VII of the Civil Rights Act of 1964. . . .

Petitioners' central claim is that they were laid off because of their race in violation of the Equal Protection Clause of the Fourteenth Amendment. Decisions by faculties and administrators of public schools based on race or ethnic origin are reviewable under the Four-

teenth Amendment. This Court has "consistently repudiated '[d]istinctions between citizens solely because of their ancestry' as being 'odious to a free people whose institutions are founded upon the doctrine of equality,'" . . . "Racial and ethnic distinctions of any sort are inherently suspect and thus call for the most exacting judicial examination." *Regents of University of California v. Bakke,* 438 U.S. 265, 291, 98 S.Ct. 2733, 2748, 57 L.Ed.2d 750 (1978) . . . .

The Court has recognized that the level of scrutiny does not change merely because the challenged classification operates against a group that historically has not been subject to governmental discrimination. . . . In this case, Article XII of the CBA operates against whites and in favor of certain minorities, and therefore constitutes a classification based on race. "Any preference based on racial or ethnic criteria must necessarily receive a most searching examination to make sure that it does not conflict with constitutional guarantees." *Fullilove v. Klutznick,* 448 U.S. 448, 491, 100 S.Ct. 2758, 2781, 65 L.Ed.2d 902 (1980) . . . . There are two prongs to this examination. First, any racial classification "must be justified by a compelling governmental interest." . . . Second, the means chosen by the State to effectuate its purpose must be "narrowly tailored to the achievement of that goal." . . . We must decide whether the layoff provision is supported by a compelling state purpose and whether the means chosen to accomplish that purpose are narrowly tailored.

The Court of Appeals, relying on the reasoning and language of the District Court's opinion, held that the Board's interest in providing minority role models for its minority students, as an attempt to alleviate the effects of societal discrimination, was sufficiently important to justify the racial classification embodied in the layoff provision. . . . The court discerned a need for more minority faculty role models by finding that the percentage of minority teachers was less than the percentage of minority students.

This Court never has held that societal discrimination alone is sufficient to justify a racial classification. Rather, the Court has insisted upon some showing of prior discrimination by the governmental unit involved before allowing limited use of racial classifications in order to remedy such discrimination. . . .

Unlike the analysis in *Hazelwood,* the role model theory employed by the District Court has no logical stopping point. The role model theory allows the Board to engage in discriminatory hiring and layoff practices long past the point required by any legitimate remedial purpose. Indeed, by tying the required percentage of minority teachers to the percentage of minority students, it requires just the sort of year-to-year calibration the Court stated was unnecessary in *Swann,* 402 U.S., at 31–32, 91 S.Ct., at 1283–1284 . . .

Moreover, because the role model theory does not necessarily bear a relationship to the harm caused by prior discriminatory hiring practices, it actually could be used to escape the obligation to remedy such practices by justifying the small percentage of black teachers by reference to the small percentage of black students. . . . Carried to its logical extreme, the idea that black students are better off with black teachers could lead to the very system the Court rejected in *Brown v. Board of Education,* 347 U.S. 483, 74 S.Ct. 686, 98 L.Ed. 873 (1954) *(Brown I).*

Societal discrimination, without more, is too amorphous a basis for imposing a racially classified remedy. The role model theory announced by the District Court and the resultant holding typify this indefiniteness. . . . No one doubts that there has been serious racial discrimination in this country. But as the basis for imposing discriminatory *legal* remedies that work against innocent people, societal discrimination is insufficient and over expansive. In the absence of particularized findings, a court could uphold remedies that are ageless in their reach into the past, and timeless in their ability to affect the future.

Respondents also now argue that their purpose in adopting the layoff provision was to remedy prior discrimination against minorities by the Jackson School District in hiring teachers. Public schools, like other public employers, operate under two interrelated constitutional duties. They are under a clear command from this Court, starting with *Brown v. Board of Education,* 349 U.S. 294, 75 S.Ct. 753, 99 L.Ed. 1083 (1955), to eliminate every vestige of racial segregation and discrimination in the schools. Pursuant to that goal, race-conscious remedial action may be necessary. . . . On the other hand, public employers, including public schools, also must act in accordance with a "core purpose of the Fourteenth Amendment" which is to "do away with all governmentally imposed distinctions based on race." . . . These related constitutional duties are not always harmonious; reconciling them requires public employers to act with extraordinary care. In particular, a public employer like the Board must ensure that, before it embarks on an affirmative action program, it has convincing evidence that remedial action is warranted. That is, it must have sufficient evidence to justify the conclusion that there has been prior discrimination.

Evidentiary support for the conclusion that remedial action is warranted becomes crucial when the remedial program is challenged in court by nonminority employees. . . . The ultimate burden remains with the employees to demonstrate the unconstitutionality of an affirmative action program. But unless such a determination is made, an appellate court reviewing a challenge to remedial action by nonminority employees cannot determine whether the race-based action is justified as a remedy for prior discrimination.

Despite the fact that Article XII has spawned years of litigation and three separate lawsuits, no such determination ever has been made. . . .

. . . Here, . . . the means chosen to achieve the Board's asserted purposes is that of laying off nonminority teachers with greater seniority in order to retain minority teachers with less seniority. We have previously expressed concern over the burden that a preferential layoffs scheme imposes on innocent parties. . . . In cases involving valid *hiring* goals, the burden to be borne by innocent individuals is diffused to a considerable extent among society generally. Though hiring goals may burden some innocent individuals, they simply do not impose the same kind of injury that layoffs impose. Denial of a future employment opportunity is not as intrusive as loss of an existing job.

Many of our cases involve union seniority plans with employees who are typically heavily dependent on wages for their day-to-day living. Even a temporary layoff may have adverse financial as well as psychological effects. A worker may invest many productive years in one job and one city with the expectation of earning the stability and security of seniority. "At that point, the rights and expectations surrounding seniority make up what is probably the most valuable capital asset that the worker 'owns,' worth even more than the current equity in his home." . . . Layoffs disrupt these settled expectations in a way that general hiring goals do not.

While hiring goals impose a diffuse burden, often foreclosing only one of several opportunities, layoffs impose the entire burden of achieving racial equality on particular individuals, often resulting in serious disruption of their lives. That burden is too intrusive. We therefore hold that, as a means of accomplishing purposes that otherwise may be legitimate, the Board's layoff plan is not sufficiently narrowly tailored. Other, less intrusive means of accomplishing similar purposes—such as the adoption of hiring goals—are available. For these reasons, the Board's selection of layoffs as the means to accomplish even a valid purpose cannot satisfy the demands of the Equal Protection Clause.

We accordingly reverse the judgment of the Court of Appeals for the Sixth Circuit.

It is so ordered.

NOTES

1. The court in *Wygant* distinguished *Hazelwood*, saying:

> [t]he Court in *Hazelwood* held that the proper comparison for determining the existence of actual discrimination by the school board was "between the racial composition of [the school's] teaching staff and the racial composition of the qualified public school teacher population in the relevant labor market" 433 U.S., at 308, 97 S.Ct. at 2742 (1977). In contrast, in *Wygant*, the lower court had justified the minority retention policy on a broader societal scale by basing the percentage of minority teachers on the percentage of minority students.

2. Following *Wygant*, the U.S. Court of Appeals, Seventh Circuit, held that the Equal Protection Clause was violated by a collective bargaining agreement provision that provided that no black teachers would be laid off until every white teacher was laid off. The rationale for the agreement was that in the event of economic downturns or shrinkages in student population, a reduction in teaching positions would result in a teaching force with greater percentages of black teachers. The court rejected the measure because it was not narrowly tailored to the goal of remedying previous discrimination, but created an absolute preference for black teachers. *Britton v. South Bend Community School Corporation*, 819 F.2d 766 (7th Cir. 1987).

■ SEX DISCRIMINATION

Sex-based discrimination in working conditions, compensation, prerequisites for employment, and work-related benefits came under criticism during the early 1960s, and Congress responded by passing legislation to prohibit such discrimination. In recent years lawsuits have been filed under the Equal Protection Clause of the Fourteenth Amendment, the Equal Pay Act of 1963, Title VII of the Civil Rights Act of 1964, and Title IX of the Education Amendment of 1972,[28] challenging discriminatory practices based on sex.

Title VII

Employment discrimination based on gender is prohibited by Title VII.[29] In part, the act provides that it shall be unlawful for an employer "to fail or refuse to hire or to discharge an individual or otherwise to discriminate against any individual, . . . because of such individual's race, color, religion, *sex* or national origin" (italics added). As with racial discrimination (discussed earlier), the plaintiff is required to show (1) that he or she is a member of a class protected by Title VII; (2) that he or she applied and was qualified for the position; (3) that despite such qualifications, plaintiff was rejected; and (4) that after plaintiff's rejection, the position remained open and the employer continued to seek similarly qualified applicants.[30] If plaintiff sustains this *prima facie* case of sex discrimination, then the burden falls on the defendant to show the employment decision was based on a legitimate nondiscriminatory reason.

The application of this test is as valid for school districts and universities as for the private sector.[31] If needs of the school district evolve, and become such that the qualifications for a position change, it may be possible for a school board to justify hiring a person of a particular sex.[32]

On the other hand, to pass over a female for promotion to administrative positions with equal or better qualifications than a male applicant violates Title VII.[33]

If a teacher establishes a *prima facie* case of discrimination, the school board must show that its rationale for the employment decision was based on nondiscriminatory reasons. Where a school board defended its decision not to promote a black female teacher on the subjective factors of her "lack of interpersonal and management skills" as well as "abrasive" personality, the court found that these reasons "articulated legitimate nondiscriminatory reasons" for the board's decision.[34]

If plaintiff establishes by direct evidence that an employer acted with discriminatory intent, the defense will fail unless the employer can show "that the same decision would have been reached absent illegal motive."[35] Where a female plaintiff presented direct evidence of discrimination, the board's defense in showing that "she would not have been promoted if she were a man" provided the defendants with a complete defense to plaintiff's charges.[36] In other words, the employment decision must be

gender neutral or that gender was irrelevant to the determination.[37]

The court must determine, based on proof, what the considerations were that led to the employer's decision. Was the decision based on considerations that were legitimate, illegitimate, or a mixture of the two? The Supreme Court in considering the dilemma of a mixture of the two has held that the language of Title VII which states, in part, *"because of* such individual's sex"[38] (italics added), means if the evidence is insufficient to discern the causal significance between legitimate and illegitimate considerations, then the court must conclude that the employment decision was made "because of" sex. According to the Court, plaintiffs should be spared the extremely difficult burden of precisely distinguishing causality as to the employer's motives. Therefore, if gender is not a discernible aspect of an array of reasons for a decision, the Court will assume that neutrality has not been maintained. In this way Title VII "forbids employers to make gender an indirect stumbling block to employment opportunity."[39] The Supreme Court has concluded with regard to the plaintiff's burden of proof that

> [i]t is difficult for us to imagine that, in the simple words "because of" Congress meant to obligate plaintiff to identify the precise causal role played by legitimate and illegitimate motivations in the employment decision she challenges. We conclude, instead, that Congress meant to obligate her to prove that the employer relied upon sex-based considerations in coming to its decision.[40]

Pregnancy

Employers are prohibited by the Pregnancy Discrimination Act of 1978 (PDA),[41] an amendment to Title VII, from discriminating on the basis of pregnancy. The courts have interpreted the act to require that employers treat pregnancy the same as any other disabling illness for purposes of health benefits and other related programs.[42] Leave provisions extended to employees for disabling illnesses must be extended to pregnancy, as well. The rules of proof in establishing discrimination apply to pregnancy allegations in the same manner as to other aspects of Title VII. The plaintiff must establish a *prima facie* case of disparate treatment and, if successful, the institution must articulate legitimate nondiscriminatory reasons for the employment decision against the woman.[43]

In an oft-litigated case that returned to the U.S. Court of Appeals, Fourth Circuit, three times, the circuit court held that the school district must show a "business necessity" to counter a *prima facie* case of pregnancy discrimination.[44] In this instance, the defendant school district's policy requiring pregnant teachers to report their pregnancies to school officials immediately upon discovery was challenged as a violation of Title VII. The plaintiff, as a result of such disclosure, was not given a contract renewal for the succeeding school year. The Fourth Circuit held that plaintiff had established a *prima facie* violation of federal law in the school's requirement that there was a burden of reporting pregnancies imposed solely on women teachers. The circuit court remanded the case back to the federal district court to decide if the school's interest in continuity of instruction was sufficient to establish a viable defense of "business necessity." Upon rehearing at the lower court level, the school district conceded this point and the plaintiff prevailed.[45]

Benefits

Insurance companies and others use actuarial tables in calculating payments and benefits for insurance and other types of benefit plans. The actuarial tables indicate, on average, that females live longer than males; therefore, females have been charged more at the initial pay-in stage or receive smaller monthly payments at the pay-out stage. These types of programs have been challenged as a form of sex discrimination under Title VII.

The Supreme Court held in the *Manhart* case in 1978 that a pension plan that required female employees to make larger contribu-

tions than males for equivalent benefits violated Title VII because the difference in treatment was based strictly on sex.[46]

The State of Arizona[47] developed a different approach with the differential at the pay-out as opposed to the pay-in stage. Employees were offered a deferred annuity plan and could select from three options: (1) a single lump-sum payment upon retirement, (2) payments at a specified amount for a fixed period of time, or (3) monthly annuity payments for the remainder of the employee's life. The first two options treated males and females equally and were not in dispute. But option three, the monthly annuity plan, was set up in accordance with sex-based mortality tables. If males and females retired at the same age, with the same contributions, males received a greater payment per month. Sex was thus the only factor used to classify the individuals. Citing *Manhart*, the Court ruled that the system violated Title VII.

■■■ SEXUAL HARASSMENT

Sexual harassment may range from verbal innuendo to an overt act, and the definition must be broad enough to encompass the diversity of behavior.[48] Employees are protected from sexual harassment in the workplace by Title VII of the Civil Rights Act of 1964. Court cases in the 1970s began recognizing sexual harassment as an aspect of sex discrimination, but it was not until 1980 that the Equal Employment Opportunity Commission (EEOC) promulgated regulations prohibiting sexual harassment. These regulations state:

> Harassment on the basis of sex is a violation of Sec. 703 of Title VII. Unwelcome sexual advances, requests for sexual favors, and other verbal or physical conduct of a sexual nature constitute harassment when (1) submission to such conduct is made explicitly or implicitly a term or condition of an individual's employment, (2) submission to or rejection of such conduct by an individual is used as a basis for em-

ployment decisions affecting such individual, (3) such conduct has the purpose or effect of unreasonably interfering with an individual's work performance or creating an intimidating, hostile, or offensive working environment.[49]

The EEOC guidelines suggest two types of sexual harassment, *quid pro quo* and *non quid pro quo*. The United States Supreme Court in *Meritor Savings Bank, FSB v. Vinson,*[50] the leading case on sexual harassment, provides definition:

[T]he guidelines provide that sexual conduct constitutes prohibited "sexual harassment," whether or not it is directly linked to the grant or denial of an economic *quid pro quo,* where "such conduct has the purpose or effect of unreasonably interfering with an individual's work performance or creating an intimidating, hostile, or offensive working environment [*non quid pro quo*]."[51]

In condemning sexual harassment and justifying its legal prohibition, the Eleventh Circuit Court of Appeals in *Henson v. Dundee*[52] has observed:

Sexual harassment which creates a hostile or offensive environment for members of one sex is every bit the arbitrary barrier to sexual equality at the workplace that racial harassment is to racial equality. Surely, a requirement that a man or woman run a gauntlet for the privilege of being allowed to work and make a living can be as demeaning and disconcerting as the harshest of racial epithets.

The EEOC guidelines further provide that an employer is held responsible

[f]or its acts and those of its agents and supervisory employees with respect to sexual harassment regardless of whether the specific acts complained of were authorized or even forbidden by the employer and regardless of whether the employer knew or should have known of their occurrence.[53]

Also, an employer is held responsible for acts of sexual harassment between fellow employees where the employer "knows or should have known of the conduct, unless it can show

that it took immediate and appropriate corrective actions."[54]

Principal's Sexual Relationship with Teacher Was Consensual and Did Not Constitute Sexual Harassment under Title VII or Equal Protection

— — — — — — — — —

Trautvetter v. Quick

— — — — — — — — —

United States Court of Appeals,
Seventh Circuit, 1990.
916 F.2d 1140.

KANNE, Circuit Judge. Plaintiff-appellant, Patsy L. Trautvetter, brought an action in the district court in which she alleged that the defendants had engaged in sexual discrimination in violation of Title VII of the Civil Rights Act of 1964, 78 Stat. 253, as amended 42 U.S.C. §§ 2000e *et seq.,* and 42 U.S.C. §§ 1983 and 1985(3). . . .

In the fall of 1975, Patsy Trautvetter began her first year of teaching in the Northeast School Corporation in Sullivan County, Indiana. In 1982, after six years of full-time teaching and one year of maternity leave, she was assigned to teach first grade at Hymera Elementary School. Beginning in the fall of 1985, Ms. Trautvetter returned to Hymera Elementary after a second maternity leave to teach second grade. She has since been teaching at Hymera Elementary continuously. Defendant, John Quick, began his term as the principal of Hymera Elementary in 1981 and, as such, was at all times relevant to these proceedings Trautvetter's immediate supervisor.

Beginning late in the 1985–86 school year and continuing into the 1986–87 school year, Quick made a number of romantic overtures towards Ms. Trautvetter. Initially, she put off these advances by either politely saying "no" or simply "laughing them off." Eventually, however, she began to respond to Quick's romantic suggestions. Indeed, the record reveals that Trautvetter became involved in a sexual relationship with Quick in which both parties participated actively. The "courtship" proceeded as follows.

Quick's first romantic overture towards Ms. Trautvetter occurred on the final day of the 1985–86 school year. A group of teachers, including Ms. Trautvetter and Mr. Quick, had gone out for the evening and eventually ended up at a local bar. Trautvetter left the bar early. After she had arrived home, however, she called the bar and asked that Quick be paged so she could explain to him, for the benefit of another teacher, a joke which had been played on the latter. During the course of that conversation, Quick asked Trautvetter whether her family was home. She responded that they were not. Quick thereafter asked her if she would like to "play house." She replied "no."

Later that fall, during a school dance which both Quick and Ms. Trautvetter were chaperoning, Quick came up beside Trautvetter and placed one of his hands next to one of hers such that the two were touching. Ms. Trautvetter testified that she moved her hand away without saying anything. At a second school dance that fall, Quick asked Ms. Trautvetter where her family was that evening. She replied that her children were at her grandparents and that her husband was at work. Quick asked if she would like to go out and "share a bottle of wine." Trautvetter simply ignored Quick's invitation. In like manner, Trautvetter ignored or laughed off other invitations which she received from Quick that fall to go out for drinks. At no point, however, did she indicate to Mr. Quick that she thought his conduct was inappropriate. . . .

Ms. Trautvetter recalled one instance in which Mr. Quick had called her that spring. His first words (beyond "hello") were "Who do you love? Who do you love?" Trautvetter responded, "Yes, I love you." She testified that she felt she had to say it. The record reveals, however, that this was not the only time that Trautvetter told Quick that she loved him. She testified that Quick, on numerous other occasions, would state, "I love you. Do you love me?" Her response on these occasions was, "Yes, I love you."

On March 13, 1987, Ms. Trautvetter telephoned Mr. Quick and asked him "what was going on." Quick responded that he had feelings for her and suggested that they get together and talk about it. She agreed to join him and the two subsequently arranged to meet in the parking lot of a local business establishment during spring break. Although the meeting lasted about an hour, Trautvetter testified that no physical contact occurred. Mr. Quick did, however, tell Trautvetter that since they were in a motel parking lot he could get a room and they could "settle this now." Trautvetter simply responded "no." Again, however, she did not tell Quick that she thought his conduct was inappropriate. . . .

In April of 1987, the two agreed to meet on at least two occasions at an abandoned school building in Colemont, Indiana; an out-of-the-way place about which Quick had told her. According to Trautvetter, she and Quick would drive around the surrounding countryside, kissing and petting along the way. On one of these occasions, Quick asked Trautvetter if he could fondle her breasts. She let him do so. Again, at no time either prior to or during this encounter did Ms. Trautvetter tell Quick that she thought his conduct was inappropriate.

At some point in April, Ms. Trautvetter gave Quick a tape of a love song. She testified that she did so because Quick had earlier given a tape of a song to her. The record reveals, however, that Ms. Trautvetter also called a radio station and requested that "their song" be played over the air. She called Mr. Quick and told him to listen for it. . . .

On May 8, 1987, Ms. Trautvetter and Mr. Quick drove in Ms. Trautvetter's car to a Regal 8 Motel where they had sexual intercourse. This rendezvous had been planned for a week. Trautvetter testified that she was nervous on this occasion. Trautvetter also testified that she felt no affection for Quick on this occasion, but engaged in intercourse with him only because she "felt she had to be there." The record reveals, however, that Trautvetter was not physically forced to show up at the motel, nor was she forced to engage in the sexual act. Moreover, the record reveals that shortly after that date, Trautvetter sent Quick a note which read, "I'll remember that night

[May 8th] and hope we will be friends forever." . . .

. . . A few days later, Quick telephoned Trautvetter and told her that his wife was out of town and asked if she could get a babysitter and come over to his house. She told him she could not do that. The following evening, Trautvetter told her husband what had been going on between herself and Quick. . . .

On June 4, 1987, Ms. Trautvetter and her husband (Calvin Trautvetter) went to visit Mr. Quick to discuss the problem. According to Ms. Trautvetter, Mr. Trautvetter informed Mr. Quick that he should stay away from his wife. He also advised Mr. Quick that he should inform his own wife of the situation. . . .

On June 9, 1987, the Trautvetters met with Richard Walters, the superintendent of the Northeast School Corporation. . . . Mr. Walters asked them to "keep it quiet." At this point, however, it is undisputed that Mr. Walters was not aware of Ms. Trautvetter's allegations of sexual harassment; she had not told him. Indeed, Ms. Trautvetter testified that she had not even told her husband of her allegations of sexual harassment at this juncture.

Early in the morning of June 8, 1987, Mr. Walters met with John Quick and his wife. At this meeting, Quick told Mr. Walters of his relationship with Ms. Trautvetter. . . .

On June 23, 1987, Ms. Trautvetter called Mr. Walters to express her concern about her job status for the upcoming school year. She also told Mr. Walters that there was more to her side of the story that she needed to tell him. She did not, however, reveal her side of the story to Mr. Walters on that date.

On June 26, 1987, Ms. Trautvetter met with Mr. Walters and George Baker, a representative of the Indiana State Teacher's Association. During this meeting, Mr. Walters was informed for the first time of Trautvetter's allegations that Quick had pressured her into entering into the sexual relationship. . . .

On July 14, 1987, Mr. Walters and the school corporation's legal counsel, Mr. Springer, met to begin the investigation into Ms. Trautvetter's allegations. . . . All of the persons interviewed (if they were aware of the relationship which existed between Trautvetter and Quick) indicated to Mr. Walters that they thought that relationship was consensual. Moreover, there was no indication from any of those persons that Quick had harassed Trautvetter sexually or otherwise. . . .

Mr. Walters subsequently concluded his investigation. He found that the relationship which existed between Ms. Trautvetter and Mr. Quick was consensual in nature and, as such, that it did not result from any sexual harassment on the part of Mr. Quick. . . . A letter was sent to both parties on July 22, 1987, informing them of that decision. That same letter advised both Ms. Trautvetter and Mr. Quick that a transfer would be considered by the board if either of them felt that their past relationship would interfere with their work relationship. Neither party made such a request for transfer. Although this letter did not constitute an official action of the board in that it had not been put to a "formal vote," it is undisputed that the board was presented with the letter and did not present any objections to its being mailed.

This appeal requires us to examine the often-blurred line which exists between human interaction in the workplace which is purely a private matter and human interaction in the workplace which gives rise to sexual harassment claims actionable under either Title VII or the equal protection clause of the fourteenth amendment. . . .

The district court's dismissal of Ms. Trautvetter's Title VII allegation was premised upon a determination that she had failed to raise a genuine issue of material fact as to whether Mr. Quick's sexual advances were "unwelcome" as they are required to be under the substantive law governing this type of Title VII sexual harassment claim. . . . We need not address this sensitive factual issue in that we conclude that Ms. Trautvetter's Title VII allegation has failed to allege any injury which can be redressed under Title VII's equitable remedy provisions. . . .

Ms. Trautvetter has not raised any claim for equitable relief. Moreover, we are not sure that she has such a claim for it is undisputed that Ms. Trautvetter was neither affirmatively nor constructively discharged from her position at Hymera Elementary in relation to or as a result of these allegations. Indeed, at the time of oral argument, Ms. Trautvetter was still teaching at Hymera Elementary, having rejected an offer from the Northeast School Corporation to be transferred to a separate school. Ms. Trautvetter has also failed to allege (or demonstrate) that Mr. Quick's sexual advances infringed in some manner upon her ability to obtain a promotion or other job-related benefit. Thus, we are left with no prayer upon which the equitable relief provided for under Title VII may be granted. Accordingly, we affirm the district court's dismissal of Ms. Trautvetter's Title VII claims.

. . . Ms. Trautvetter argues that the defendants' actions, in both their individual and official capacities, violated her constitutional rights. Her specific allegations refer to: (1) John Quick's sexual advances; and (2) the remaining defendants' alleged failure to take appropriate action which she argues served to condone and perpetuate Quick's acts of sexual harassment. . . .

The parameters of a cause of action alleging sexual harassment as a violation of the equal protection clause have not been precisely defined. We have noted, however, that such a claim generally follows the contours of a Title VII allegation of sexual harassment. . . . Under either cause of action, there must be a showing of sexual harassment or discrimination. There is, however, an important distinction for purposes of our review which exists between the two; intent to discriminate must be shown under equal protection while Title VII requires no such showing. Thus, a plaintiff wishing to sustain an equal protection claim of sexual harassment must show both "sexual harassment" and an "intent" to harass based upon that plaintiff's membership in a particular class of citizens—i.e., male or female. In light of this burden, our task in reviewing the district court's grant of summary judgment necessarily becomes one of determining whether Ms. Trautvetter's allegations have raised a genuine question of material fact as to either of these two requirements.

The "harassment" prong of this type of equal protection claim was discussed by this court in *Bohen v. City of East Chicago*, 799 F.2d 1180 (7th Cir.1986). Our analysis focused on the analogous burden which a plaintiff bears in showing actionable "sexual harassment" under Title VII. Citing *Meritor Savings Bank v. Vinson*, 477 U.S. 57, 67, 106 S.Ct. 2399, 2405, 91 L.Ed.2d 49 (1986), we stated, "the harassment 'must be sufficiently severe or pervasive "to alter the conditions of [the victim's] employment and create an abusive working environment." ' " . . .

In determining whether the alleged harassment rises to this level we must examine whether the alleged sexual advances were "unwelcome." . . . ("The gravamen of any sexual harassment claim is that the alleged sexual advances were 'unwelcome.' ")

Although this determination is one that is traditionally left to the trier of fact, . . . the district court concluded for Title VII purposes, based on an examination of the entire record, that Ms. Trautvetter had not raised any genuine issues of material fact as to whether Mr. Quick's sexual advances were "unwelcome." The district court stated, "[t]he fact that she [Ms. Trautvetter] sometimes said no to his [Mr. Quick's] suggestions or made excuses not to meet him does not imply that she did not welcome his advances, especially when she often did agree to meet him and participated actively in the relationship." Indeed, if the test focuses on the extent to which Ms. Trautvetter made it known that the sexual advances were "unwelcome," it might be difficult to disagree with the district court's conclusion that there was no genuine issue of material fact on this question. Beyond the fact that Ms. Trautvetter initially declined Mr. Quick's offers for drinks, etc., the record is void of any evidence showing that she declared those advances to be unwelcome. Much to the contrary, the course of conduct when reviewed in its entirety, appears to substantiate the district court's findings that Ms. Trautvetter grew to "welcome" Mr. Quick's advances and even participated in an active way so as to encourage them. The district court need not have addressed this issue of fact, however, and we will not address it further, in light of our conclusion that Ms. Trautvetter has failed to demonstrate that Mr. Quick's advances constitute the type of *intentional discrimination* based upon an individual's membership in a particular class which has traditionally been viewed as actionable under the equal protection clause of the fourteenth amendment.

Like any other equal protection claim, a claim of sexual harassment under the fourteenth amendment must show that the discrimination was intentional. As we previously noted in this precise context in *Huebschen v. Dep't of Health and Social Serv.*, 716 F.2d 1167 (7th Cir.1983):

> A person bringing an action under the Equal Protection Clause must show intentional discrimination against him because of his membership in a particular class, not merely that he was treated unfairly. . . . "[T]he decisionmaker [must have] selected or reaffirmed a particular course of action at least in part 'because of,' not merely 'in spite of,' its adverse effects *upon an identifiable group.*"

In light of this "intent" requirement, the issue which we are presented with in this context, . . . is whether Mr. Quick's sexual advances towards Ms. Trautvetter were "because of" her status as a woman or, in the alternative, whether those advances were inspired by characteristics, albeit some sexual, which were personal to Ms. Trautvetter. . . .

. . . Thus, while it is clear that an individual plaintiff may pursue a sexual discrimination claim under the fourteenth amendment based solely upon acts of discrimination directed towards her, it is also clear that such a claim must show an intent to discriminate *because of* her status as a

female and not because of characteristics of her gender which are personal to her. Without question, this line becomes indistinct when those factors which are personal to an individual include attributes of sexual attraction. In such a case, a careful analysis of the conduct which is alleged to be harassment is necessary to determine whether it is indeed "harassment" as that term is understood in the Title VII context—the first prong of our analysis. If this distinction—subtle as it is—is not maintained, any consensual workplace romance involving a state supervisor and employee which soured for one reason or another could give rise to equal protection claims if the employee simply alleges that his or her supervisor's conduct during the term of the romance constituted "sexual harassment." Such a scenario constitutes precisely the type of claim which the equal protection clause's "intent to discriminate" requirement was meant to discourage. . . .

. . . [W]e conclude that she has not raised a genuine issue of material fact as to whether Mr. Quick's sexual advances were *because of* her status as a woman. Certainly, the underlying fact is that Ms. Trautvetter is a woman. But, as we have noted, her status as a woman does not itself support an allegation of sexual harassment under the equal protection clause; she must demonstrate in a colorable manner that Mr. Quick's advances were because of her status as a woman as opposed to characteristics, albeit some no doubt sexual, which were personal to her. This she has failed to do. Indeed, there is nothing in the record to indicate that Mr. Quick's feelings were based on anything but a personal attraction to Ms. Trautvetter. Ms. Trautvetter's own testimony leads us to this conclusion:; in reference to the March 13, 1987 phone call, Ms. Trautvetter testified that Mr. Quick told her that he "had feelings for her" and he thought they should get together and talk about it.

Significantly, the same cannot be said for our decisions in which sexual harassment has been remedied under the equal protection clause of the fourteenth amendment. . . . Because there is nothing in this record to indicate that Mr. Quick's sexual advances were anything but personal in nature—that is, because there is no showing that Mr. Quick intended to "harass" Ms. Trautvetter simply because she was a woman—we conclude that Ms. Trautvetter has not raised a genuine issue of material fact as to Mr. Quick's intent and, accordingly, affirm the grant of summary judgment on that ground.

For all of the foregoing reasons, we affirm the decision of the district court.

NOTES

1. *Title IX.* Title IX of the Education Amendment of 1972 addresses sex discrimination and sexual harassment. The sexual harassment prohibition of Title IX is not as clear as in Title VII. Title IX specifies: "No person in the United States shall, on the basis of sex, be excluded from participation in, be denied the benefits of, or be subjected to discrimination under any education program or activity receiving federal financial assistance . . . ."

The Office of Civil Rights (OCR) of the United States Department of Education is the primary administrative agency charged with enforcing Title IX. But unlike the Equal Employment Opportunity Commission (EEOC), which enforces Title VII, the OCR has failed to promulgate regulations or official guidelines regarding sexual harassment. Despite the absence of guidelines, OCR maintains that sexual harassment is prohibited by Title IX. One of the problems with Title IX is that the scope and nature of relief available under the act is not clear. Whereas equitable relief in the form of back pay is available under Title VII, it is probably not available under Title IX. Withdrawal of federal funding from the institution may be the only remedy available under Title IX.

2. *Equal Protection.* The Seventh Circuit Court of Appeals in *Bohen v. City of East Chicago, Ind.* was the first federal court to recognize a sexual harassment claim under the Equal Protection Clause of the Fourteenth Amendment (as discussed earlier in *Trautvetter v. Quick*). This action opens another legal approach for public employees. To be successful, the plaintiff must show that the discrimination was intentional. This discrimination may be shown by a single event, but it is unlikely that one event will constitute denial of equal protection. In *Bohen*, the court said, "Forcing women and not men to work in an environment of sexual harassment is no different than forcing women to work in a dirtier or more hazardous environment than men simply because they were women." 799 F.2d 1180 (7th Cir. 1986). *Principal's Handbook: Current Issues in School Law,* (eds.) William E. Camp, Julie K. Underwood, and Mary Jane Connelly; "Sexual harassment in the Workplace," M. David Alexander and Mary F. Hughes, National Organization on Legal Problems of Education, Topeka, Kansas, 1989.

■ RELIGIOUS DISCRIMINATION

Employees' religious rights and freedoms (also see: Chapter 15) are protected by both the First Amendment of the U.S. Constitution and the Title VII of the Civil Rights Act of 1964, as amended in 1972.

The Civil Rights Act of 1964, Title VII, prohibits any employer from discriminating against an individual because of religion. The 1972 Amendment states: "The term religion includes all aspects of religious observance and practice, as well as belief, unless an employer demonstrates that he is unable to reasonably accommodate an employee's or prospective employee's religious observance or practice without undue hardship on the conduct of the employer's business." A primary question emerges as to what the employer must do to reasonably accommodate the religious beliefs of an employee.

In *Trans World Airlines, Inc. v. Hardison,*[55] the Supreme Court addressed this issue. Hardison, the plaintiff employee, challenged a company rule, claiming violation of Title VII, which prevented him from observance of Saturday as a religious holiday. The U.S. Supreme Court held for the defendant and said that Title VII did not require the company "to carve out special exemptions" to accommodate one's religious beliefs. To require the company, in this case Trans-World Airlines, "to bear more than a *de minimis* cost" in order to give Hardison Saturdays off is an undue hardship.

As with other aspects of Title VII, the burden of proof to show religious discrimination is borne by the plaintiff, who must show that the employer's decision was religiously related. If the plaintiff sustains this burden, then the employer must in turn show that the encroachment on the employee's religious beliefs could not be reasonably accommodated without undue hardship to the employer.

Employees' work schedules have also come in conflict with religious worship in other cases. In one such case a teacher was dismissed because of absence from the job, without permission, to attend a religious festival.[56] The teacher had arranged for a substitute teacher, instructed the substitute on lesson plans, and so on; and the classes had in fact run very smoothly. The court determined that to accommodate the teacher resulted in no undue hardship to the school and rendered judgment for the teacher.

In a similar case, the court held that it is a violation of one's freedom of religion to compel an employee to choose between employment and religion. The court said: " . . . [A]n employer who punishes an employee by placing the latter in a position in which he or she must ignore a tenet of faith in order to retain employment violates" Title VII.[57]

The free exercise of religion is also, and more broadly, protected by the First Amendment. As noted earlier in Chapter 5 of this text, the school district, as an arm of the state, cannot defend policies that do not meet the tripartite test of *Lemon v. Kurtzman*.[58] Thus, a provision in a negotiated bargaining agreement between a school district and a teachers' union may fail because it cannot be shown to have a secular purpose.[59]

School Board Has Met Its Obligation Under Title VII When It Has Offered Reasonable Accommodation of Teacher's Religion

— — — — — — — — —

Ansonia Board of Education v. Philbrook

— — — — — — — — —

Supreme Court of the United States, 1986.
479 U.S. 60, 107 S.Ct. 367.

Chief Justice REHNQUIST delivered the opinion of the Court. Petitioner Ansonia Board of Education has employed respondent Ronald Philbrook since 1962 to teach high school business and typing classes in Ansonia, Connecticut. In 1968, Philbrook was baptized into the Worldwide Church of God. The tenets of the church require members to refrain from secular employment during designated holy days, a practice that has caused respondent to miss approximately six school days each year. We are asked to determine whether the employer's efforts to adjust respondent's work schedule in light of his beliefs fulfills its obligation under § 701(j) of the Civil Rights Act of 1964, 42 U.S.C. § 2000e(j), to "reasonably accommodate to an employee's . . . religious observance or practice without undue hardship on the conduct of the employer's business."

Since the 1967–1968 school year, the school board's collective-bargaining agreements with the Ansonia Federation of Teachers have granted to each teacher 18 days of leave per year for illness, cumulative to 150 and later to 180 days. Accumulated leave may be used for purposes other than illness as specified in the agreement. A teacher may accordingly use five days' leave for a death in the immediate family, one day for attendance at a wedding, three days per year for attendance as an official delegate to a national veterans organization, and the like. . . . With the exception of the agreement covering the 1967–1968 school year, each contract has specifically provided three days' annual leave for observance of mandatory religious holidays, as defined in the contract. Unlike other categories for which leave is permitted, absences for religious holidays are not charged against the teacher's annual or accumulated leave.

The school board has also agreed that teachers may use up to three days of accumulated leave each school year for "necessary personal business." Recent contracts limited permissible personal leave to those uses not otherwise specified in the contract. This limitation dictated, for example, that an employee who wanted more than three leave days to attend the convention of a national veterans organization could not use personal leave to gain extra days for that purpose. Likewise, an employee already absent three days for mandatory religious observances could not later use personal leave for "[a]ny religious activity," . . . or "[a]ny religious observance." . . . Since the 1978–1979 school year, teachers have been allowed to take one of the three personal days without prior approval; use of the remaining two days requires advance approval by the school principal.

The limitations on the use of personal business leave spawned this litigation. Until the 1976–1977 year, Philbrook observed mandatory holy days by using the three days granted in the contract and then taking unauthorized leave. His pay was reduced accordingly. In 1976, however, respondent stopped taking unauthorized leave for religious reasons, and began scheduling required hospital visits on church holy days. He also worked on several holy days. Dissatisfied with this arrangement, Philbrook repeatedly asked the school board to adopt one of two alternatives. His preferred alternative would allow use of personal business leave for religious observance, effectively giving him three additional days of paid leave for that purpose. Short of this arrangement, respondent suggested that he pay the cost of a substitute and receive full pay for additional days off for religious observances. Petitioner has consistently rejected both proposals. . . .

We find no basis in either the statute or its legislative history for requiring an employer to choose any particular reasonable accommodation. By its very terms the statute directs that any reasonable accommodation by the employer is sufficient to meet its accommodation

obligation. The employer violates the statute unless it "demonstrates that [it] is unable to reasonably accommodate . . . an employee's . . . religious observance or practice without undue hardship on the conduct of the employer's business." Thus, where the employer has already reasonably accommodated the employee's religious needs, the statutory inquiry is at an end. The employer need not further show that each of the employee's alternative accommodations would result in undue hardship. . . .

. . . We accordingly hold that an employer has met its obligation under § 701(j) when it demonstrates that it has offered a reasonable accommodation to the employee.

The remaining issue in the case is whether the school board's leave policy constitutes a reasonable accommodation of Philbrook's religious beliefs. . . . We think that the school board policy in this case, requiring respondent to take unpaid leave for holy day observance that exceeded the amount allowed by the collective-bargaining agreement, would generally be a reasonable one. In enacting § 701(j), Congress was understandably motivated by a desire to assure the individual additional opportunity to observe religious practices, but it did not impose a duty on the employer to accommodate at all costs. . . . The provision of unpaid leave eliminates the conflict between employment requirements and religious practices by allowing the individual to observe fully religious holy days and requires him only to give up compensation for a day that he did not in fact work. Generally speaking, "[t]he direct effect of [unpaid leave] is merely a loss of income for the period the employee is not at work; such an exclusion has no direct effect upon either employment opportunities or job status." . . .

But unpaid leave is not a reasonable accommodation when paid leave is provided for all purposes *except* religious ones. A provision for paid leave "that is part and parcel of the employment relationship may not be doled out in a discriminatory fashion, even if the employer would be free . . . not to provide the benefit at all." . . . Such an arrangement would display a discrimination against religious practices that is the antithesis of reasonableness. Whether the policy here violates this teaching turns on factual inquiry into past and present administration of the personal business leave provisions of the collective-bargaining agreement. The school board contends that the necessary personal business category in the agreement, like other leave provisions, defines a limited purpose leave. Philbrook, on the other hand, asserts that the necessary personal leave category is not so limited, operating as an open-ended leave provision that may be used for a wide range of secular purposes in addition to those specifically provided for in the contract, but not for similar religious purposes. We do not think that the record is sufficiently clear on this point for us to make the necessary factual findings , and we therefore affirm the judgment of the Court of Appeals remanding the case to the District Court. The latter court on remand should make the necessary findings as to past and existing practice in the administration of the collective-bargaining agreement.

It is so ordered.

■■■ TITLE IX

Title IX of the Education Amendments of 1972 was enacted to protect the rights of individuals and to prohibit discrimination based on gender in educational programs or activities receiving federal funds. Title IX was closely patterned after Title VI of the Civil Rights Act of 1974. Title IX in its original form stated:

No person in the United States shall, on the basis of sex, be excluded from participation in, be denied the benefits of, or be subjected to discrimination under any educational program or activity receiving Federal financial assistance, ...

Because Title IX is patterned after Title VI, and covers students in educational institutions, some courts have ruled that Title IX did not cover employees. But the Supreme Court, in *North Haven Board of Education v. Bell*, stated, "[W]hile section 901(a) does not expressly include or exclude employees within its scope, its broad directive that 'no person' may be discriminated against on the basis of gender includes employees as well as students."[60]

Further controversy over the application of Title IX occurred as a result of the federal government's requirement that a private college, Grove City College, supply assurance of compliance.[61] The college refused, and the U.S. Department of Education cut off the students' federal financial assistance. The U.S. Supreme Court, in 1984, held that Title IX applied only to "programs" receiving federal assistance and not to the entire institution. Under a narrow interpretation of the statute, the Court held that the college was obliged to submit assurance of compliance for the office responsible for administration of student federal financial aid only, and not for the college as a whole.

This decision was the impetus for the Congress to amend Title IX with the Civil Rights Restoration Act of 1988,[62] correcting the loophole identified in the *Grove City* case. Effectively, *Grove City* not only narrowed the coverage of Title IX, but of Title VI of the Civil Rights Act of 1964, § 504 of the Rehabilitation Act of 1973, and the Age Discrimination in Employment Act of 1975 as well. The Civil Rights Restoration Act of 1988 restored institution-wide application of these laws. The 1988 law added no new language to the coverage or fund termination provisions of the four acts, but amended each of the affected statutes by adding a section defining the phrase "program or activity" and "program" to make it clear that discrimination is prohibited throughout the entire institutions or agencies if any part is the recipient of federal financial assistance.

The New Act provides that the entire institution or system is covered and not just the program receiving federal assistance. If federal aid is distributed to any part of a public school district, the entire school system is subject to compliance requirements. Private education corporations are also covered if they receive federal funding.

*Title IX of the Education Amendments of 1972
Protects Employees Against Gender Discrimination
in Educational Institutions*

_._._._._._._.

North Haven Board of Education v. Bell

_._._._._._._.

Supreme Court of the United States, 1982.
456 U.S. 512, 102 S.Ct. 1912.

Justice BLACKMUN delivered the opinion of the Court. At issue here is the validity of regulations promulgated by the Department of Education pursuant to Title IX of the Education Amendments of 1972, Pub.L. 92–318, 86 Stat. 373, 20 U.S.C. § 1681 et seq. These regulations prohibit federally funded education programs from discriminating on the basis of gender with respect to employment.

Title IX proscribes gender discrimination in education programs or activities receiving federal financial assistance. Patterned after Title VI of the Civil Rights Act of 1964, Pub.L. 88–352, 78 Stat. 252, 42 U.S.C. § 2000d et seq., Title IX, as amended, contains two core provisions. The first is a "program-specific" prohibition of gender discrimination:

> No person in the United States shall, on the basis of sex, be excluded from participation in, be denied the benefits of, or be subjected to discrimination under any education program or activity receiving Federal financial assistance . . . ." § 901(a).

Nine statutory exceptions to § 901(a)'s coverage follow. See §§ 901(a)(1)–(9).

The second core provision relates to enforcement. Section 902 authorizes each agency awarding federal financial assistance to any education program to promulgate regulations ensuring that aid recipients adhere to § 901(a)'s mandate. The ultimate sanction for noncompliance is termination of federal funds or denial of future grants.

In 1975, the Department of Health, Education, and Welfare (HEW) invoked its § 902 authority to issue regulations governing the operation of federally funded education programs. These regulations extend, for example, to policies involving admissions, textbooks, and athletics. Interpreting the term "person" in § 901(a) to encompass employees as well as students, HEW included among the regulations a series entitled "Subpart E," which deals with employment practices, ranging from job classifications to pregnancy leave. . . .

Petitioners are two Connecticut public school boards that brought separate suits challenging HEW's authority to issue the Subpart E regulations. Petitioners contend that Title IX was not meant to reach the employment practices of educational institutions.

The North Haven Board of Education (North Haven) receives federal funds for its education programs and activities and is therefore subject to Title IX's prohibition of gender discrimination. Since the 1975–1976 school year, North Haven has devoted between 46.8 percent and 66.9 percent of its federal assistance to the salaries of its employees; this practice is expected to continue.

In January 1978, Elaine Dove, a tenured teacher in the North Haven public school system, filed a complaint with HEW, alleging that North Haven had violated Title IX by refusing to rehire her after a one-year maternity leave. In response to this complaint, HEW began to investigate the school board's employment practices and sought from petitioner information concerning its policies on hiring, leaves of absence, seniority, and tenure. Asserting that HEW lacked authority to regulate employment practices under Title IX, North Haven refused to comply with the request. . . .

The Trumbull Board of Education (Trumbull) likewise receives financial support from the federal government and must therefore adhere to the requirements of Title IX and appropriate implementating regulations. In October 1977, HEW began investigating a complaint filed by respondent Linda Potz, a former guidance counselor in the Trumbull school district. Potz alleged that Trumbull had discriminated against her on the basis of gender with respect to job assignments, working conditions, and the failure to renew her contract. In September 1978, HEW notified Trumbull that it had violated Title IX and warned that corrective action, including respondent's reinstatement, must be taken.   .

Trumbull then filed suit in the United States District Court for the District of Connecticut, contending that HEW's Title IX employment regulations were invalid . . . .

Our starting point in determining the scope of Title IX is, of course, the statutory language. Section 901(a)'s broad directive that "no person" may be discriminated against on the basis of gender appears, on its face, to include employees as well as students. Under that provision, employees, like other "persons," may not be "excluded from participation in," "denied the benefits of," or "subjected to discrimination under" education programs receiving federal financial support.

Employees who directly participate in federal programs or who directly benefit from federal grants, loans, or contracts clearly fall within the first two protective categories described in § 901(a). In addition, a female employee who works in a federally funded education program is "subjected to discrimination under" that program if she is paid a lower salary for like work, given less opportunity for promotion, or forced to work under more adverse conditions than are her male colleagues.

There is no doubt that "if we are to give [Title IX] the scope that its origins dictate, we must accord it a sweep as broad as its language." Because § 901(a) neither expressly nor impliedly excludes employees from its reach, we should interpret the provision as

covering and protecting these "persons" unless other considerations counsel to the contrary. After all, Congress easily could have substituted "student" or "beneficiary" for the word "person" if it had wished to restrict the scope of § 901(a).

Petitioners, however, point to the nine exceptions to § 901(a)'s coverage set forth in §§ 901(a)(1)–(9). . . . The exceptions, the school boards argue, are directed only at students, and thus indicate that § 901(a) similarly applies only to students. But the exceptions are not concerned solely with students and student activities: two of them exempt an entire class of institutions— religious and military schools—and are not limited to student-related activities at such schools. See §§ 901(a)(3), (4). Moreover, petitioners' argument rests on an inference that is by no means compelled; in fact, the absence of a specific exclusion for employment among the list of exceptions tends to support the Court of Appeals' conclusion that Title IX's broad protection of "person[s]" does extend to employees of educational institutions.

Although the statutory language thus seems to favor inclusion of employees, nevertheless, because Title IX does not expressly include or exclude employees from its scope, we turn to the Act's legislative history for evidence as to whether Congress meant somehow to limit the expansive language of § 901. . . .

In our view, the legislative history thus corroborates our reading of the statutory language and verifies the Court of Appeals' conclusion that employment discrimination comes within the prohibition of Title IX. . . .

Whether termination of petitioners' federal funds is permissible under Title IX is a question that must be answered by the District Court in the first instance. Similarly, we do not undertake to define "program" in this opinion. Neither of the cases before us advanced beyond a motion for summary judgment, and the record therefore does not reflect whether petitioners' employment practices actually discriminated on the basis of gender or whether any such discrimination comes within the prohibition of Title IX. Neither school board opposed HEW's investigation into its employment practices on the grounds that the complaining employees' salaries were not funded by federal money, that the employees did not work in an education program that received federal assistance, or that the discrimination they allegedly suffered did not affect a federally funded program. Instead, petitioners disputed the Department's authority to regulate any employment practices whatsoever, and the District Court adopted that view, which we find to be error. Accordingly, we affirm the judgment of the Court of Appeals but remand the case for further proceedings consistent with this opinion.

It is so ordered.

◼◼◼ EQUAL PAY ACT

In 1963, the Fair Labor Standards Act of 1938 was amended to include what is commonly referred to as the Equal Pay Act. The Equal Pay Act was designed to eliminate discrimination regarding pay or wages based on sex, where equal work, equal skills, and equal effort are performed under the same working conditions.[63] The act specified that differential pay may be appropriate if the decision is based on (1) a seniority system, (2) a merit system, (3) a situation in which quantity and quality of production is a factor, and (4) situations in which pay differences are based on any factor other than sex.

The Equal Pay Act was incorporated into Title VII of the Civil Rights Act of 1964. Title VII and the Equal Pay Act have almost identical language except that Title VII covers not only sex, but also race, color, religion, and national origin. Title VII states that the employer may provide different compensation, "or different terms, conditions, or privileges of employment pursuant to a bona fide seniority

or merit system, or a system which measures earnings by quantity or quality of production or to employees who work in different locations, provided that such differences are not the result of an intention to discriminate because of race, color, religion, sex, or national origin."[64]

Not only are the reasons for differential pay the same under both the Equal Pay Act and Title VII, but the standard used to determine unequal pay for equal work is basically the same for both acts. This standard is stated: "To establish a claim of unequal pay for equal work a plaintiff has the burden of proof that the employer pays different wages to employees of opposite sexes for equal work on jobs the performance of which requires equal skill, effort, and responsibility, and which are performed under similar working conditions."[65] Congress did not intend pay to be exactly equal but intended to require substantial equality for commensurate skills, effort, responsibility, and working conditions. Each case must be reviewed on a case-by-case basis to see if the remedial remedies of Equal Pay or Title VII can be invoked. Once the employee has established that the pay is unequal for the same work, the burden shifts to the employer to show that the differential (pay scale) is justified under one of the act's four exceptions listed earlier.[66]

A school district that paid women coaches of girls' teams less than men's coaches of boys' teams was held to violate the Equal Pay Act.[67] The United States Seventh Circuit, Court of Appeals, concluded that the "employer cannot divide equal work into two job classifications that carry unequal pay, forbid women to compete for one of the classifications, and defend the resulting inequity in pay by reference to a factor other than the sex of the employees."[68]

The Equal Pay Act reaches into private schools through the coverage of the Fair Labor Standards Act.[69] A federal district court in Ohio held that the compelling interests of the Equal Pay Act substantially outweighed the minimal impact of religious beliefs in discriminating against women by giving men a head-of-household pay supplement.

*School District Did Not Violate Title VII Prohibition
Against Disparate Treatment in Not Hiring Female
for School Principalship*

—··—··—··—··—

Danzl v. North St. Paul — Maplewood — Oakdale Independent School District No. 622

—··—··—··—··—

United States Court of Appeals,
Eighth Circuit, 1983.
706 F.2d 813.

FAGG, Circuit Judge. Once again we are asked to determine whether the North St. Paul-Maplewood-Oakdale Independent School District discriminated on the basis of sex, in violation of Title VII of the Civil Rights Act of 1964, when it did not hire Agnes Danzl to fill a one-year high school principal position. The district court found that the school district's articulated nondiscriminatory reasons for not hiring Danzl were pretextual, and held that the school district intentionally discriminated against Danzl solely on the basis of her sex. Because we believe the district court's findings of pretext and intentional discrimination are clearly erroneous, we reverse.

In late July 1979, a vacancy arose for a high school principalship in the school district for the 1979–80 school year. Twelve individuals — ten male and two female — applied for the position. Director of Secondary Education Richard St. Germain selected four finalists — two male and two female — based upon his review of the papers submitted, phone conversations with the applicants and reference checks. Several male applicants with prior principal experience were eliminated by this investigatory process. Between August 15 and August 20, St. Germain interviewed the four finalists.

On August 21, a committee of male and female teachers from the high school interviewed the candidates. Following the interviews, the teachers discussed and rated the candidates, and then met with St. Germain. The teachers agreed that Agnes Danzl, a female, and Jack Edling, a male, were the two leading candidates, but favored Danzl slightly based on the interviews. St. Germain told the teachers committee that he favored Edling; he had contacted various persons regarding Edling, including both administrators and teachers, and the references were very positive. His two reference checks on Danzl, he said, were not as positive. St. Germain had contacted an administrator who knew both candidates and he stated that he would hire Edling over Danzl. Also, one of Danzl's supervisors had stated that he would hesitate to hire Danzl for a high school as large as Burnsville, where she was currently teaching. The teachers, concerned that only administrators had been contacted for Danzl, while both administrators and teachers had been contacted for Edling, asked for time to conduct their own investigation of Danzl. St. Germain was amenable to this procedure.

Three male and female committee members, independent of St. Germain and of one another, contacted three teachers at Burnsville. Each of the references were considered, on balance, unfavorable to Danzl and were similar in content. The references indicated that Danzl was inflexible, had certain staff relations problems, and was insensitive to student needs. After the teachers informed the other committee members of the reference checks, St. Germain polled each member of the committee by phone. Their unanimous choice for the interim principal position was Edling. St. Germain cross-checked the references from the teachers with a Burnsville administrator, who did not disagree, in general, with the unfavorable comments about Danzl. Edling was recommended to the school board which in turn appointed him to the principal position.

On May 28, 1980, Danzl filed a complaint in federal district court, alleging that the school district had declined to hire her as a high school principal for the 1979–80 school year because of her sex, in violation of Title VII of the Civil Rights Act of 1964, 42 U.S.C. § 2000e et seq. and 42 U.S.C. § 1983. The district court held that the defendants had discriminated against Danzl on the basis of her sex, in violation of Title VII, and ordered the school district to make available to Danzl for at least one school year either a secondary school principalship or a comparable position. . . . We held that the district court had erred in shifting to the school district the burden of proving that it had not hired Danzl because of nondiscriminatory reasons and remanded for further proceedings on whether the nondiscriminatory reasons articulated for not hiring Danzl were pretextual.

The district court held a remand hearing but heard no additional evidence on the pretext issue. Based on the original trial record, the district court concluded that the school district's reasons for not hiring Danzl were "nothing more than pretexts and that the real motive underlying Dr. Danzl not being hired was due to sex-based discrimination." The school district appeals, urging that the district court erred in its findings of pretext and intentional discrimination.

There is a three-step allocation of burdens and order of presentation of proof in a Title VII disparate treatment case. The initial burden is on the plaintiff to establish a prima facie case of discrimination. If the plaintiff succeeds, the burden then shifts to the defendant to rebut the inference of discrimination by producing evidence that the plaintiff was rejected, or someone else was preferred, for some legitimate nondiscriminatory reason. The defendant's evidence is sufficient if it raises a genuine issue of fact as to whether it discriminated against the plaintiff. In addition, the reasons given must be legally sufficient to justify a judgment for the defendant. Finally, should the defendant carry this burden of production, the plaintiff must demonstrate by a preponderance of the evidence that the proffered reasons were not the true reason for the challenged employment decision. The plaintiff may prove this either by means of affirmative evidence that a discriminatory reason played an impermissible role in the decision or by showing that the proferred nondiscriminatory reasons are unworthy of credence. At all times the ultimate burden of persuasion that the defendant committed intentional discrimination remains with the plaintiff. In discharging this burden, Danzl need not prove that her sex was the sole reason for the challenged employment decision, but need only prove that sex was a factor in the decision.

There is no dispute that plaintiff has established a prima facie case of disparate treatment. Similarly, there is no dispute that the school district has met its burden of articulating reasons for not hiring Danzl that are legitimate and nondiscriminatory: (1) the candidate who was hired, Jack Edling, was better qualified because he had experience as a high school principal; and (2) Agnes Danzl had received unfavorable reference checks. Thus, the sole issue before this court concerns the district court's finding that the school district's articulated reasons for not hiring Danzl were a pretext for intentional sexual discrimination. We may not set aside the district court's findings of fact unless they are clearly erroneous. A finding is clearly erroneous if it is not supported by substantial evidence, if it evolves from an erroneous conception of the applicable law, or if the reviewing court on the entire record is left with the definite and firm conviction that a mistake has been made. Moreover, it is now the law that we may reverse a finding of intentional discrimination only if the finding is clearly erroneous.

The first reason the school district proffered for not hiring Danzl was that Edling was better qualified, due to his experience as a high school principal. Rejecting this explanation, the district court first found that Danzl and Edling were equally qualified for the position. This finding is clearly erroneous. We have no doubt that both candidates were qualified for the position. Nevertheless, an employer could distinguish between Edling, who had seven years' experience as a principal and one year's experience as a school superintendent, and Danzl, who had only five years' experience as an associate principal. The district court implied that Danzl made up for any lack of experience with her superior educational qualifications. Danzl had a Ph.D. awarded by an unaccredited school for certain courses and papers, including a dissertation, conducted by correspondence. Edling had a master's degree. Unlike principal experience, an advanced degree was not listed as a qualification for the position. The district court cannot substitute its judgment for the employer's by saying that Danzl's advanced degree compensates for Edling's superior experience. . . .

The district court's alternative rationale for its finding of pretext was that several of the original twelve applicants had experience as a high school principal, but of the final four applicants only Edling possessed such experience. Hence, the district court concluded that if past experience as a secondary school principal was so important, then "Dr. St. Germain had already decided to hire Mr. Edling as of the date the finalists were chosen, and all subsequent selection activities were mere window dressing designed to obscure the true intent of the defendant to hire a male."

This finding is simply without support in the record. When St. Germain selected the four finalists, an extensive and real selection process remained, involving interviews, reference checks, and numerous meetings with administrators, teachers and school district members. It just does not follow that by considering experience as a factor, the school district had therefore preselected Edling among the four finalists. The school district has never contended that experience was an absolute requirement for the job; the vacancy notice stated only that it was a desirable qualification to be considered. Although the issue is not before us, the district court conceded that principal experience could have been a legitimate requirement for the job of interim principal under the disparate impact test of *Griggs v. Duke Power Co.*, 401 U.S. 424, 91 S.Ct. 849, 28 L.Ed.2d 158 (1971).

Because we find no evidence in the record to contradict the school district's first legitimate nondiscriminatory reason for not hiring Danzl, her lack of principal experience, we conclude that the district court's finding of pretext was clearly erroneous.

The school district's second articulated reason for not hiring Danzl was that it had received several negative references concerning Danzl. The references for Edling, in contrast, were very positive. The district court found this reason pretextual because the references "were not received by the defendants until after the decision to hire Mr. Edling had already been made." There is nothing in the record to support this finding. . . .

We have thoroughly searched the record in this case and have found nothing that supports the district court's finding of intentional discrimination. Both Danzl and Edling, as well as several others, were qualified candidates. Unremarkably, the school district hired the candidate with superior experience and superior references. Although this may not comport with the district court's view of how hiring practices should compensate for years of underrepresentation of women in educational administration, it does not violate Title VII. The employer is free to choose the best candidate for the position without regard to sex. Nothing more than that occurred in this case.

The judgment of the district court is reversed.

AGE DISCRIMINATION

In 1967, the federal government passed the Age Discrimination in Employment Act (ADEA),[70] which prohibits discrimination against individuals who are at least forty, but less than seventy years of age. This 1967 act was amended in 1986, striking out the language "but less than seventy years of age." The effect of the amendment is to remove the maximum age limitation applicable to employees who are protected under the act. The act applies equally to all governmental employees, with the exception of firefighters and law enforcement officers who, by virtue of the rigors of their job requirements, are considered separately.[71] Too, tenured faculty in higher education are exempted and can be compelled to retire at age seventy until 31 December 1993, when this exception expires. The act prohibits discrimination with respect to hiring, discharging, compensation, terms and conditions, privileges, retirement, and demotion. The act was not intended to increase the number of elderly in the work force, but only to prevent discrimination against them. The act is intended to supplement the protections provided under the Equal Protection Clause.

Two cases decided by the Supreme Court are important in understanding mandatory retirement statutes and age discriminations. In the first case, the Court upheld a Massachusetts statute requiring uniformed state police to retire at age fifty.[72] The Court held that government employment was not a fundamental constitutional right, nor age a suspect classification. Therefore, the Court required that the government show a rational interest to support its policy, but did not require it to bear the burden of showing a compelling interest in creating the policy. Because the purpose of the statute was to assure physical preparedness by having younger troopers patrolling the highways, the policy was not unconstitutional. The rationale that younger policemen are more physically capable and can provide better protection to all of society was held to be a proper and reasonable societal objective.

In another case, again using the rational interest test, the Supreme Court upheld a statute requiring Foreign Service employees to retire at age sixty. The Court said: "Congress . . . was legitimately intent on stimulating the highest performance in the Foreign Service by assuring that opportunities for promotion would be available despite [the] limits on [the] number of personnel in the Service, and plainly intended to create [a] relatively small, homogeneous and particularly able corps of foreign service officers . . . ."[73] This the Court found to be an acceptable objective.

Whether a *bona fide* occupational qualification (BFOQ) exemption is allowed under the ADEA depends on how narrowly the employer fashions the exemption. In *Western Air Lines, Inc. v. Criswell*,[74] the U.S. Supreme Court established a two-part test for evaluating an employer's exemption. First, the job qualifications must be reasonably necessary to the essence of the business; and second, the employer must be "compelled to rely on age as a proxy for a safety-related" job qualification by showing that there exists a factual basis for believing that all persons over a specified age are incapable of performing the duties in a safe and efficient manner, or that it is "impossible or highly impractical" to deal with older employees on an individual basis.

In applying this test to a school rule applying to only eight bus drivers, a lower federal court ruled that to broadbrush all persons of sixty-five and older as incapable was inappropriate when the entire group of drivers was such a small number that all could have been evaluated separately.[75]

Thus, the reasonableness of an exemption can be largely determined by the practicality of application and efficacy of implementation.

The courts have held that the party claiming age discrimination will be evaluated under the same factors as established for race discrimination. If the action is a private, nonclass action:

> the complainant has the burden of establishing a *prima facie* case, which he can satisfy by showing that (i) he belongs to a special minority; (ii) he applied and was qualified for a job the employer was trying to fill; (iii) though qualified, he was rejected; and (iv) therefore, the employer continued to seek applicants with complainant's qualifications.[76]

After establishing a *prima facie* case, the burden shifts to the employer, who must articulate legitimate, nondiscriminatory reasons for not employing the individual or individuals.

Equal Protection and Due Process Guarantees Were Not Violated When Teacher Was Forced to Retire at Age 70

— · — · — · — · — · —

Palmer v. Ticcione

— · — · — · — · — · —

United States Court of Appeals,
Second Circuit, 1978.
576 F.2d 459.

HAYS, Circuit Judge. Appellant, Lois Palmer, commenced this action under 42 U.S.C. § 1983 (1970) for age discrimination in violation of the equal protection and due process guarantees of the Fourteenth Amendment. The district court granted the defendants' motion to dismiss for want of a substantial federal question. For the reasons stated below, we affirm the dismissal of the complaint.

The facts are undisputed. Appellant has been a teacher since 1943. She has been employed by the defendent Copiague Union Free District #5 as a kindergarten teacher since the 1961–62 school year. She received tenure at the end of the 1963–64 school year. In February 1975, she reached the age of 70. On May 15, 1975, she met with defendant N. Paul Buscemi, the Copiague superintendent of schools. He informed her that she was to be retired at the end of the school year because she had reached the retirement age of 70. This decision was subsequently ratified by the Copiague school board, and the New York State Retirement System was directed to place Mrs. Palmer on retirement status as of August 25, 1975.

It is not disputed that appellant is willing and able to teach. Her performance as a teacher was rated satisfactory in each year of her employment. In the last evaluation, made just before she was retired in 1975, her principal recommended that she be rehired, "[s]ubject to review of compulsory retirement under New York State Education Law."

Appellant contends that retirement solely on the basis of her age violates her constitutional and state law rights. Essentially, she claims: that compulsory retirement at age 70 violates the equal protection clause; that it creates an irrebuttable presumption of incompetency based on age; that, as a tenured teacher, she is entitled to a hearing before termination; and that, in the alternative, the New York Education Law should be read to prohibit compulsory retirement or, if not, to require a hearing before termination.

Compulsory retirement systems have come under constitutional attack in several contexts. These equal protection and due process challenges have been rejected by this and other courts. The only exception is *Gault v. Garrison,* 569 F.2d 993 (7th Cir.1977). In that case, the Seventh Circuit ruled that a retired teacher is entitled to a trial on her age discrimination claim. Because *Gault* involves a factual situation very similar to that of the instant case—the major difference is that the retirement age in *Gault* was 65, not 70—and because we disagree with the *Gault* holding, we think it appropriate to focus on this issue once again.

The ruling in *Gault* is premised on the implications of the Supreme Court's most recent decision in this area. In *Massachusetts Board of Retirement v. Murgia,* 427 U.S. 307, 96 S.Ct. 2562, 49 L.Ed.2d 520 (1976), the Court upheld a state law requiring the mandatory retirement of uniformed police at age 50. First *Murgia* established that the proper standard for equal protection review in a case challenging a compulsory retirement statute is the rational basis test. Applying this standard, the Court found that forced retirement at age 50 did foster the purpose identified by the state; it assured the continued physical preparedness of the state's uniformed police. In *Murgia,* there had been a trial, and there was evidence in the record to support the conclusion that physical preparedness is rationally related to age.

As in the instant case, but unlike *Murgia,* *Gault* involved an appeal from an order dismissing the complaint. The *Gault* court assumed that the strongest justification for a retirement law for teachers is to remove those who are unfit. Working from that premise, it held that, absent an evidentiary showing, there was no reason to assume that there is any relationship between advancing age and fitness to teach. *Gault* distinguished *Murgia* as involving a question of whether physical fitness declines with age, and noted that there was evidence in the record to support the conclusion that it does. It contrasted this with the question whether teaching ability, which involves predominantly mental skills, similarly declines with age. Absent an evidentiary showing, the court saw no reason to assume that it does; in fact, it speculated that the knowledge and experience necessary for teaching increases with age. Accordingly, it remanded for further proceedings to determine whether compulsory retirement of teachers at age 65 is rationally based.

We decline to follow *Gault* for two reasons. First, while there is a valid distinction between the instant case and *Murgia*, we cannot distinguish the prior cases that have sustained compulsory retirement statutes for occupations that involve primarily mental skills. In *Johnson v. Lefkowitz*, we upheld the constitutionality of § 70 of the New York State Retirement and Social Security Law (McKinney's 1971), which requires tenured civil servants to retire at age 70. In *Johnson*, the plaintiff had been dismissed from his position as senior attorney in the Real Property Bureau of the state's law department. In *Rubino v. Ghezzi*, we upheld the constitutionality of the mandatory retirement of state judges at age 70. And, in *Weisbrod v. Lynn*, mandatory retirement of federal civil servants at age 70 was upheld as constitutional, even though the statute undoubtedly requires the retirement of some civil servants who are engaged in occupations that involve primarily mental skills. See also *Weiss v. Walsh*, (denial of state-endowed chair to college professor over 65 is not unconstitutional age discrimination).

Second, *Gault* too narrowly conceives the possible rational bases for a compulsory retirement statute. Unrelated to any notion of physical or mental fitness, a state might prescribe mandatory retirement for teachers in order to open up employment opportunities for young teachers—particularly in the last decade when supply has outpaced demand, or to open up more places for minori-

ties, or to bring young people with fresh ideas and techniques in contact with school children, or to assure predictability and ease in establishing and administering pension plans. A compulsory retirement system is rationally related to the fulfillment of any or all of these legitimate state objectives.

Thus it would seem clear that *Gault* notwithstanding, the New York State compulsory retirement system for teachers is immune from constitutional attack. However, appellant seeks to distinguish the instant case on two grounds. First, she argues that, since the statute must "rationally [further] the purpose *identified* by the State . . . ," *Murgia*, we may only look to the purpose of the compulsory retirement law as evidenced by the statutory scheme. Section 510(1)(b) of the New York Education Law (McKinney's 1969), which provides for compulsory retirement at the employer's discretion, is part of a statute governing retirement benefits. Thus, appellant contends that the only possible purpose of the statute is to further the efficient distribution of retirement benefits. She argues that compulsory retirement is not rationally related to this purpose because the statute provides for compulsory retirement at the discretion of the employer. This encourages unpredictability in the administration of the pension program. Also, she contends that, to the extent that able teachers are forced to retire at age 70, compulsory retirement defeats the purpose of the statute by adding unnecessarily to the retirement rolls. Second, appellant argues that because this case involves a statute that provides for discretionary rather than mandatory compulsory retirement, the precedents are inapposite.

Closer scrutiny of the statute provides the answer to the first argument. Section 510(1)(b) is permissive; it allows individual school boards to implement compulsory retirement policies. Thus, if an individual school board adopts a compulsory retirement policy, whether mandatory or discretionary, it may be to further any of the purposes suggested above, without regard to the narrow context of the empowering statute. Since such a board-adopted policy would be supportable as rationally based, we would be constrained to uphold it as a legitimate exercise of a statutorily authorized power.

With regard to the second argument, we fail to see its relevance. The record is inconclusive on whether Copiague has adopted a mandatory or discretionary retirement policy. There is nothing in the record to indicate that the appellant was discharged under anything other than an across-the-board, mandatory retirement policy. If so, then, as noted above, the board's action is clearly immune from constitutional attack. However, even if appellant was retired under a discretionary policy, the result would be the same. First, a discretionary retirement policy would still be rationally related to a legitimate state goal; it would further any of the purposes noted above, with the exception of those related to the maintenance of pension plans. Second, the *Johnson* case would still be on point. *Johnson* involved § 70 of the New York Retirement and Social Security Law (McKinney's 1971), a statute that is functionally equivalent to discretionary retirement. Subsection (c) provides that a civil servant may be retained beyond age 70 under certain conditions. If he or she is retained, however, he or she is subject to termination upon sixty days' notice. Johnson had been given two extensions and was then summarily retired. The court found no constitutional infirmity with that system. We find none in the instant case either.

We reach the same conclusion with regard to the due process attack on compulsory retirement as establishing an irrebuttable presumption. That claim is analytically very similar to the equal protection one. If the statutory classification is sustainable as rationally based, then it should not fall because it might also be labeled a presumption.   . . .

Appellant also claims that she was entitled to a due process hearing before being retired. However, we can see no purpose for a hearing if appellant was retired under an across-the-board, mandatory retirement system. And even if a discretionary system was employed, we would be constrained to follow *Johnson,* supra, and deny this claim. In *Johnson,* we held that a hearing is not required because the benefits of holding such a hearing are outweighed by the burdens imposed upon the state by requiring a hearing in every case. 566 F.2d at 869.

Today's decision is not intended as an endorsement of compulsory retirement for teachers or compulsory retirement in general. Rather, we are aware of the many older Americans who continue to be able and eager to work beyond age seventy. We are also aware of the debilitating effects that compulsory retirement has on many such individuals, with regard to their economic situation, their health, their outlook on life, and the continuing opportunities for fulfillment. However, in determining the desirability of compulsory retirement, these considerations must be weighed against the social goals that compulsory retirement furthers. This is precisely the type of clash of competing social goals that is best resolved by the legislative process. The federal courts should not second guess the wisdom or propriety of such legislative resolutions as long as they are rationally based.

Congress has recently considered this issue and, after extensive hearings, has amended the Age Discrimination in Employment Act of 1967. The amendments prohibit, with some exceptions, the compulsory retirement of people under seventy, and of federal employees at any age. The original Act requires the Secretary of Labor to make annual reports concerning the effects of the Act, taking into account demographic changes. The 1978 amendments impose on the Secretary the further duty of reporting, by 1981, on the effects of the amendments and the feasibility of extending their coverage. We note these developments because we are persuaded that they reinforce today's decision. There is no question but that the passage of the 1978 amendments to the Age Discrimination in Employment Act was the result of a process that was fair, deliberate, and well informed. Moreover, Congress has provided a mechanism for continually reassessing the effects and the wisdom of its actions on this issue. The superior ability of Congress to collect data and to resolve competing social goals, as well as the flexibility resulting from its ability to monitor the effects of its actions and to make adjustments accordingly, mark this issue as one which the Constitution has appropriately left to the legislative processes, both state and federal.

Affirmed.

NOTES

1. Discrimination based on age may place on plaintiffs a more difficult burden of proof that race or sex discrimination. The U.S. Court of Appeals, Eleventh Circuit, has observed that

> [a]ge discrimination is *qualitatively different from race or sex discrimination in employment*, because the basis of the discrimination is not a discreet and immutable characteristic of an employee which separates the members of the protected group indelibly from persons outside the protected group. Rather, age is a continuum along which the distinctions between employees are often subtle and relative ones. *Goldstein v. Manhattan Industries, Inc.*, 758 F.2d 1435 (11th Cir. 1985), cert. denied, 474 U.S. 1005, 106 S.Ct. 525 (1985).

2. Violation of the Age Discrimination in Employment Act can be demonstrated by plaintiff's showing of either disparate treatment or disparate impact. *Lowe v. Commack Union Free School District*, 886 F.2d 1364 (2d Cir. 1989).

3. The case supporting claim of disparate treatment can be established if plaintiff can show that age was a "significant contributing factor." Age Discrimination in Employment Act of 1967, §4(a)(1), 29 U.S.C.A. §623(a)(1). *Lowe v. Commack Union Free School District*, supra.

4. School districts' incentive retirement plan excluding teachers over sixty years of age, because they were near retirement anyway, was discriminatory as a willful violation of the Age Discrimination in Employment Act of 1967. Section 4(f)(2), as amended, 29 U.S.C.A. §623(f)(2); *Cipriano v. Board of Education of North Tonawanda, N.Y.*, 700 F.Supp. 1199 (W.D.N.Y. 1988).

▓▓▓ DISCRIMINATION AGAINST THE HANDICAPPED

Aware that over 43 million Americans have one or more physical or mental disabilities and are without general recourse for discrimination for these handicaps, the Congress in 1990 enacted the Americans with Disabilities Act of 1990 (ADA). In contrast to the Rehabilitation Act of 1973, § 504, which was conditioned on the receipt of federal funds, the new ADA covers all employees, in the public and private sector, who work for companies with fifteen or more employees.

The ADA is modeled after the Education for All Handicapped Act (EHA) in that it is both comprehensive and extensively prescriptive. The ADA covers virtually all aspects of society, including transportation, public accommodations, telecommunications, and other areas. For purposes of liability, the act specifically waives state immunity under the Eleventh Amendment. The act's coverage is categorically delimited to exclude coverage of illegal drug use and defines "disability" as excluding

> (1) transvestism, transsexualism, pedophilia, exhibitionism, voyeurism, gender identity disorders not resulting from physical impairment, or other sexual behavior disorders; (2) compulsive gambling, kleptomania, or pyromania; or (3) psychoactive substance use disorders resulting from current illegal use of drugs.[77]

Because of the recency of the legislation, litigation has not yet emerged as to various interpretations of the statute. One can be assured, however, that comprehensive legislation of this nature will produce a plethora of legal actions in the near future.

To the present, though, the focal point of employee litigation for handicapped persons has remained with the Vocational Rehabilitation Act of 1973, § 504. Section 504 is violated if a handicapped person is denied a position "solely by reason of his handicap."

> The standards for determining the merits of a case under Section 504 are contained in the

statute. First, the statute provides that the individual in question must be an "otherwise qualified handicapped individual"; second, the statute provides that a qualified handicapped individual may not be denied admission to any program or activity or denied the benefits of any program or activity . . . solely on the bases of handicap."[78]

If an individual is not otherwise qualified, he or she cannot be said to have been rejected solely because of handicap.

The leading case is *School Board of Nassau County v. Arline,*[79] where a teacher with tuberculosis had been hospitalized with resulting respiratory impairment and sought to return to the classroom. The Court held that tuberculosis was a physiological disorder covered by § 504. The questions then arose, was she "otherwise qualified" and could she be "reasonably accommodated." The Court remanded the case to the district court to determine, based on the development of facts, whether Arline was otherwise qualified. The Court provided guidance, saying that "[a]n otherwise qualified person is one who is able to meet all of a program's requirements in spite of his handicap."

In 1969 a blind English teacher who held a Professional Certificate from the Pennsylvania Department of Education was refused the opportunity to take the Philadelphia Teacher's Examination. The school district classified her as having a "chronic or acute physical defect" which included blindness. With persistence and legal assistance the teacher in 1974 was allowed to take the test which she passed. Because the school district refused to afford her seniority as of the time she properly should have been admitted to take the examination, she filed suit. The court held for the teacher, awarding her retroactive seniority.[80] Significantly, the Court held that a handicap could not be considered a suspect classification for equal protection purposes. Thus, the issue of handicap, as an equal protection issue, must be divided under the rational relationship test, not the more rigorous compelling interest standard. The fact that handicapped persons do not form a suspect class has important bearing on the necessity for sepa-

rate statutory protection as provided in § 504 and the new ADA.

In another equal protection case, bearing on the issue of suspect class, a blind teacher sued because school policy prevented him from obtaining an administrative position.[81] The policy required that an oral and written examination be completed by each prospective administrator. The plaintiff completed the written section of the test, with the aid of a reader, and performed very poorly. A committee also rated the plaintiff very low on the oral part of the examination. The court held that because physical handicaps were not to be treated as a suspect classification, the school district needed only to show a rational relationship between its policy and reasonably state its objective. Using this test, the court determined that the plaintiff did not possess the skills and qualifications to be an administrator. The school had a legitimate, rational purpose in seeking competent individuals, and the oral and written tests were reasonable devices to assure such competence.

Teacher Afflicted with Tuberculosis Was "Handicapped Individual" within the Meaning of Rehabilitation Act of 1973

— — — — — — — —

School Board of Nassau County, Florida v. Arline

— — — — — — — —

Supreme Court of the United States, 1987.
480 U.S. 273, 107 S.Ct. 1123.

Justice BRENNAN delivered the opinion of the Court. Section 504 of the Rehabilitation Act of 1973, 87 Stat. 394, as amended, 29 U.S.C. § 794 (Act), prohibits a federally funded state program from discriminating against a handicapped individual solely by reason of his or her handicap. This case presents the questions whether a person afflicted with tuberculosis, a contagious disease, may be considered a "handicapped individual" within the meaning of § 504 of the Act, and, if so, whether such an individual is "otherwise qualified" to teach elementary school.

From 1966 until 1979, respondent Gene Arline taught elementary school in Nassau County, Florida. She was discharged in 1979 after suffering a third relapse of tuberculosis within two years. After she was denied relief in state administrative proceedings, she brought suit in federal court, alleging that the School Board's decision to dismiss her because of her tuberculosis violated § 504 of the Act.

A trial was held in the District Court, at which the principal medical evidence was provided by Marianne McEuen, M.D., an assistant director of the Community Tuberculosis Control Service of the Florida Department of Health and Rehabilitative Services. According to the medical records reviewed by Dr. McEuen, Arline was hospitalized for tuberculosis in 1957. . . . For the next twenty years, Arline's disease was in remission. . . . Then, in 1977, a culture revealed that tuberculosis was again active in her system; cultures taken in March 1978 and in November 1978 were also positive. . . .

The superintendent of schools for Nassau County, Craig Marsh, then testified as to the School Board's response to Arline's medical reports. After both her second relapse, in the Spring of 1978, and her third relapse in November 1978, the School Board suspended Arline with pay for the remainder of the school year. . . . At the end of the 1978–1979 school year, the School Board held a hearing, after which it discharged Arline, "not because she had done anything wrong," but because of the "continued reoccurrence [sic] of tuberculosis." . . .

In her trial memorandum, Arline argued that it was "not disputed that the [School Board dismissed her] solely on the basis of her illness. Since the illness in this case qualifies the Plaintiff as a 'handicapped person' it is clear that she was dismissed solely as a result of her handicap in violation of Section 504." . . . The District Court held, however, that although there was "[n]o question that she suffers a handicap," Arline was nevertheless not "a handicapped person un-

der the terms of that statute." . . . The court found it "difficult . . . to conceive that Congress intended contagious diseases to be included within the definition of a handicapped person." The court then went on to state that, "even assuming" that a person with a contagious disease could be deemed a handicapped person, Arline was not "qualified" to teach elementary school. . . .

The Court of Appeals reversed, holding that "persons with contagious diseases are within the coverage of section 504," and that Arline's condition "falls . . . neatly within the statutory and regulatory framework" of the Act. . . .

The court remanded the case "for further findings as to whether the risks of infection precluded Mrs. Arline from being otherwise qualified" for her job and, if so, whether it was possible to make some reasonable accommodation for her in that teaching position" or in some other position. . . . We granted certiorari, . . . and now affirm.

In enacting and amending the Act, Congress enlisted all programs receiving federal funds in an effort "to share with handicapped Americans the opportunities for an education, transportation, housing, health care, and jobs that other Americans take for granted." 123 Cong.Rec. 13515 (1977) (statement of Sen. Humphrey). To that end, Congress not only increased federal support for vocational rehabilitation, but also addressed the broader problem of discrimination against the handicapped by including § 504, an antidiscrimination provision patterned after Title VI of the Civil Rights of 1964. Section 504 of the Rehabilitation Act reads in pertinent part:

> No otherwise qualified handicapped individual in the United States, as defined in section 706(7) of this title, shall, solely by reason of his handicap, be excluded from participation in, be denied the benefits of, or be subjected to discrimination under any program or activity receiving Federal financial assistance. . . . 29 U.S.C. § 794.

In 1974 Congress expanded the definition of "handicapped individual" for use in § 504 to read as follows:[3]

[A]ny person who (i) has a physical or mental impairment which substantially limits one or more of such person's major life activities, (ii) has a record of such an impairment, or (iii) is regarded as having such an impairment. 29 U.S.C. § 706(7)(B).

The amended definition reflected Congress' concern with protecting the handicapped against discrimination stemming not only from simple prejudice, but from "archaic attitudes and laws" and from "the fact that the American people are simply unfamiliar with and insensitive to the difficulties confront[ing] individuals with handicaps." . . . To combat the effects of erroneous but nevertheless prevalent perceptions about the handicapped, Congress expanded the definition of "handicapped individual" so as to preclude discrimination against "[a] person who has a record of, or is regarded as having, an impairment [but who] may at present have no actual incapacity at all." . . .

In determining whether a particular individual is handicapped as defined by the Act, the regulations promulgated by the Department of Health and Human Services are of significant assistance. As we have previously recognized, these regulations were drafted with the oversight and approval of Congress, . . . they provide "an important source of guidance on the meaning of § 504." . . . The regulations are particularly significant here because they define two critical terms used in the statutory definition of handicapped individual. "Physical impairment" is defined as follows:

[A]ny physiological disorder or condition, cosmetic disfigurement, or anatomical loss affecting one or more of the following body systems: neurological; musculoskeletal; special sense organs; respiratory, including speech organs; cardiovascular; reproductive, digestive, genito-urinary; hemic and lymphatic; skin; and endocrine. . . .

In addition, the regulations define "major life activities" as

functions such as caring for one's self, performing manual tasks, walking, seeing, hearing, speaking, breathing, learning, and working. . . .

Within this statutory and regulatory framework, then, we must consider whether Arline can be considered a handicapped individual. According to the testimony of Dr. McEuen, Arline suffered tuberculosis "in an acute form in such a degree that it affected her respiratory system," and was hospitalized for this condition. . . . Arline thus had a physical impairment as that term is defined by the regulations, since she had a "physiological disorder or condition . . . affecting [her] . . . respiratory [system]." . . . This impairment was serious enough to require hospitalization, a fact more than sufficient to establish that one or more of her major life activities were substantially limited by her impairment. Thus, Arline's hospitalization for tuberculosis in 1957 suffices to establish that she has a "record of . . . impairment" within the meaning of 29 U.S.C. § 706(7)(B)(ii), and is therefore a handicapped individual.

Petitioners concede that a contagious disease may constitute a handicapping condition to the extent that it leaves a person with "diminished physical or mental capabilities," . . . and concede that Arline's hospitalization for tuberculosis in 1957 demonstrates that she has a record of a physical impairment, ... Petitioners maintain, however, Arline's record of impairment is irrelevant in this case, since the School Board dismissed Arline not because of her diminished physical capabilities, but because of the threat that her relapses of tuberculosis posed to the health of others.

We do not agree with petitioners that, in defining a handicapped individual under § 504, the contagious effects of a disease can be meaningfully distinguished from the disease's physical effects on a claimant in a case such as this. Arline's contagiousness and her physical impairment each resulted from the same underlying condition, tuberculosis. It would be unfair to allow an employer to seize upon the distinction between the effects of a disease on others and the effects of a disease on a patient and use that distinction to justify discriminatory treatment. . . .

Allowing discrimination based on the contagious effects of a physical impairment would be inconsistent with the basic purpose of § 504, which is to ensure that handicapped individuals are not denied jobs or other benefits because of the prejudiced attitudes or the ignorance of others. By amending the definition of "handicapped individual" to include not only those who are actually physically impaired, but also those who are regarded as impaired and who, as a result, are substantially limited in a major life activity, Congress acknowledged that society's accumulated myths and fears about disability and disease are as handicapping as are the physical limitations that flow from actual impairment. Few aspects of a handicap give rise to the same level of public fear and misapprehension as contagiousness. Even those who suffer or have recovered from such noninfectious diseases as epilepsy or cancer have faced discrimination based on the irrational fear that they might be contagious. The Act is carefully structured to replace such reflexive reactions to actual or perceived handicaps with actions based on reasoned and medically sound judgments: the definition of "handicapped individual" is broad, but only those individuals who are both handicapped *and* otherwise qualified are eligible for relief. The fact that *some* persons who have contagious diseases may pose a serious health threat to others under certain circumstances does not justify excluding from the coverage of the Act *all* persons with actual or perceived contagious diseases. Such exclusion would mean that those accused of being contagious would never have the opportunity to have their condition evaluated in light of medical evidence and a determination made as to whether they were "otherwise qualified." Rather, they would be vulnerable to discrimination on the basis of mythology — precisely the type of injury Congress sought to prevent. We conclude that the fact that a person with a record of a physical impairment is also contagious does not suffice to remove that person from coverage under § 504.

The remaining question is whether Arline is otherwise qualified for the job of elementary school teacher. To answer this question in most cases, the District Court will need to conduct an individualized inquiry and make appropriate findings of fact. Such an inquiry is essential if § 504 is to achieve its goal of protecting handicapped individuals from deprivations based on prejudice, stereotypes, or unfounded fear, while giving appropriate weight to such legitimate concerns of grantees as avoiding exposing others to significant health and safety risks.[16] The basic factors to be considered in conducting this inquiry are well established.[17] In the context of the employment of a person handicapped with a contagious disease, we agree with *amicus* American Medical Association that this inquiry should include

> [findings of] facts, based on reasonable medical judgments given the state of medical knowledge, about (a) the nature of the risk (how the disease is transmitted), (b) the duration of the risk (how long is the carrier infectious), (c) the severity of the risk (what is the potential harm to third parties) and (d) the probabilities the disease will be transmitted and will cause varying degrees of harm. Brief for American Medical Association as *Amicus Curiae* 19.

In making these findings, courts normally should defer to the reasonable medical judgments of public health officials. The next step in the "otherwise-qualified" inquiry is for the court to evaluate, in light of these medical findings, whether the employer could reasonably accommodate the employee under the established standards for that inquiry. . . .

Because of the paucity of factual findings by the District Court, we, like the Court of Appeals, are unable at this stage of the proceedings to resolve whether Arline is "otherwise qualified" for her job. The District Court made no findings as to the duration and severity of Arline's condition, nor as to the probability that she would transmit the disease. Nor did the court determine whether Arline was contagious at the time she was discharged, or whether the School Board could have reasonably accommodated her. Accordingly, the resolution of whether Arline was otherwise qualified requires further findings of fact.

We hold that a person suffering from the contagious disease of tuberculosis can be a handicapped person within the meaning of the § 504 of the Rehabilitation Act of 1973, and that respondent Arline is such a person. We remand the case to the District Court to determine whether Arline is otherwise qualified for her position. The judgment of the Court of Appeals is
Affirmed.

NOTES

1. The Supreme Court in footnotes to *Arline* clarified the meanings of "otherwise qualified" and "reasonable accommodation," saying:

> *Otherwise Qualified.* "An otherwise qualified person is one who is able to meet all of a program's requirements in spite of his handicap." . . . In the employment context, an otherwise qualified person is one who can perform "the essential functions" of the job in question.
>
> *Reasonable Accommodation.* When a handicapped person is not able to perform the essential functions of the job, the court must also consider whether any "reasonable accommodation" by the employer would enable the handicapped person to perform those functions. Accommodation is not reasonable if it either imposes "undue financial and administrative burdens" on a grantee, or requires "a fundamental alteration in the nature of [the] program" . . . ("where reasonable accommodation does not overcome the effects of a person's handicap, or where reasonable accommodation causes undue hardship to the employer, failure to hire or promote the handicapped person will not be considered discrimination");
> . . .
> Employers have an affirmative obligation to make a reasonable accommodation for a handicapped employee. Although they are not required to find another job for an employee who is not qualified for the job he or she was doing, they cannot deny an employee alternative employment opportunities reasonably available under the employer's existing policies. . . .

2. The *Arline* court further commented on the undesirability of placing a teacher with infectious disease in the classroom. The Court said:

> A person who poses a significant risk of communicating an infectious disease to others in the workplace will not be otherwise qualified for his or her job if reasonable accommodation will not eliminate that risk. The Act would not require a school board to place a teacher with active, contagious tuberculosis in a classroom with elementary school children. Respondent conceded as much at oral argument.

3. The claim of a handicapping condition cannot be made as an afterthought as a defense for incompetence. In a case illustrating this point, a teacher whose primary certification was elementary education was reassigned to teach sixth grade reading, spelling, mathematics, and social studies after 17 years of exclusively teaching mathematics. The teacher was evaluated and given extensive recommendations for improvement. After failure to improve, the teacher was dismissed for incompetency. The teacher's documentation included numerous spelling, punctuation, and grammatical errors by the teacher, including the misspelling of the names of twenty-five of her students and even the misspelling of her own name. The teacher claimed that she was handicapped, and a clinical psychologist diagnosed her as having a learning disability that affected her spelling, punctuation, and grammar. The court upheld the dismissal. Her incompetency in being able to instruct her students, standing alone, was sufficient grounds for termination. *Beck v. James*, 793 S.W.2d 416 (Mo. App. 1990).

4. The question of whether a disease prevents an employee from actually performing the duties of the job is often at the heart of conflict between the school district and an employee. In one such case, when a school bus driver was diagnosed as having multiple sclerosis, the school district's physician found her to be medically unqualified to

drive a bus. The driver filed a complaint with the New York State Division of Human Rights, charging discrimination. An expert in neurology testified on behalf of the driver, saying she was capable of driving a bus. The court ruled "that the determination that the complainant was unlawfully discriminated against is supported by substantial evidence . . . ." The disease did not prevent her from doing her job in a reasonable manner. *Bayport-Blue Point School District v. State Division of Human Rights*, 131 A.D.2d A.D. 2d 849, 517 N.Y.S.2d 209 (2 Dept. 1987).

Teacher with AIDS Cannot Be Prevented from Returning to the Classroom Solely Because of Fear and Apprehension of Parents

— · — · — · — · —

Chalk v. United States District Court Central District of California

— · — · — · — · —

United States Court of Appeals, 1988.
840 F.2d 701.

POOLE, Circuit Judge. Petitioner Vincent L. Chalk is a certified teacher of hearing-impaired students in the Orange County Department of Education. In February of 1987, Chalk was diagnosed as having Acquired Immune Deficiency Syndrome (AIDS). Subsequently, the Department reassigned Chalk to an administrative position and barred him from teaching in the classroom. Chalk then filed this action in the district court, claiming that the Department's action violated § 504 of the Rehabilitation Act of 1973, 29 U.S.C.A. § 794 (West Supp.1987), as amended, which proscribes recipients of federal funds from discriminating against otherwise qualified handicapped persons.

Chalk's motion for a preliminary injunction ordering his reinstatement was denied by the district court, and Chalk brought this appeal. After hearing oral argument, we issued an order reversing the district court and directing it to issue the preliminary injunction. . . . In this opinion, we now set forth in full the reasons underlying our reversal. . . .

Chalk bases his claim on section 504 of the Rehabilitation Act of 1973, 29 U.S.C. § 794, as amended (the Act), which provides:

> No otherwise qualified individual with handicaps . . . shall, solely by reason of his handicap, be excluded from the participation in . . . or be subjected to discrimination under any program or activity receiving Federal financial assistance.

As the district court recognized, the Supreme Court recently held that section 504 is fully applicable to individuals who suffer from contagious diseases. *School Bd. of Nassau County v. Arline*, __ U.S. __, 107 S.Ct. 1123, 94 L.Ed.2d 307 (1987). . . .

In its opinion, the Court addressed the question which is of central importance to this case: under what circumstances may a person handicapped with a contagious disease be "otherwise qualified" within the meaning of section 504? Relying on its earlier opinion in *Southeastern Community College v. Davis*, 442 U.S. 397, 99 S.Ct. 2361, 60 L.Ed.2d 980 (1979), the Court said:

> An otherwise qualified person is one who is able to meet all of a program's requirements in spite of his handicap. In the employment context, an otherwise qualified person is one who can perform "the essential functions" of the job in question. When a handicapped person is not able to perform the essential functions of the job, the court must also consider whether any "reasonable accommodation" by the employer would enable the handicapped person to perform those functions. Accommodation is not reasonable if it either imposes "undue financial and administrative burdens" on a grantee, or requires a "fundamental alteration in the nature of [the] program."

Arline, 107 S.Ct. at 1131. . . .

In applying this standard to the facts before it, the Court recognized the difficult circumstances which confront a handicapped person, an employer, and the public in dealing with the possibility of contagion in the workplace. The problem is in reconciling the needs for protection of other persons, continuation of the work mission, and reasonable accommodation—if possible—of the afflicted individual. The Court effected this reconciliation by formulating a standard for determining when a contagious disease would prevent an individual from being "otherwise qualified":

> A person who poses a significant risk of communicating an infectious disease to others in the workplace will not be otherwise qualified for his or her job if reasonable accommodation will not eliminate that risk. The Act would not require a school board to place a teacher with active, contagious tuberculosis in a classroom with elementary school children. . . .

The application of this standard requires, in most cases, an individualized inquiry and appropriate findings of fact, so that "§ 504 [may] achieve its goal of protecting handicapped individuals from deprivations based on prejudice, stereotypes, or unfounded fear, while giving appropriate weight to such legitimate concerns of grantees as avoiding exposing others to significant health and safety risks." . . . Specifically, *Arline* requires a trial court to make findings regarding four factors: "(a) the nature of the risk (how the disease is transmitted), (b) the duration of the risk (how long is the carrier infectious), (c) the severity of the risk (what is the potential harm to third parties) and (d) the probabilities the disease will be transmitted and will cause varying degrees of harm." . . . Findings regarding these factors should be based "on reasonable medical judgments given the state of medical knowledge," and courts should give particular deference to the judgments of public health officials.

Chalk submitted in evidence to the district court, and that court accepted, more than 100 articles from prestigious medical journals and the declarations of five experts on AIDS, including two public health officials of Los Angeles County. Those submissions reveal an overwhelming evidentiary consensus of medical and scientific opinion regarding the nature and transmission of AIDS. . . .

Transmission of HIV is known to occur in three ways: (1) through intimate sexual contact with an infected person; (2) through invasive exposure to contaminated blood of certain other bodily fluids; or (3) through perinatal exposure (i.e., from mother to infant). Although HIV has been isolated in several body fluids, epidemiologic evidence has implicated only blood, semen, vaginal secretions, and possibly breast milk in transmission. Extensive and numerous studies have consistently found no apparent risk of HIV infection to individuals exposed through close, non-sexual contact with AIDS patients.

Based on the accumulated body of medical evidence, the Surgeon General of the United States has concluded:

> There is no known risk of non-sexual infection in most of the situations we encounter in our daily lives. We know that family members living with individuals who have the AIDS virus do not become infected except through sexual contact. There is no evidence of transmission (spread) of AIDS virus by everyday contact even though these family members shared food, towels, cups, razors, even toothbrushes, and kissed each other.

U.S. Public Health Service, *Surgeon General's Report on Acquired Immune Deficiency Syndrome* at 13 (1986) (hereinafter *Surgeon General's Report*). . . .

The district judge addressed each of the four *Arline* factors in his ruling. He found that the duration of the risk was long and the severity was "catastrophic," but that scientifically established methods of transmission were unlikely to occur and that the probability of harm was minimal. . . . He therefore concluded that Chalk "may very well win ultimately." Nonetheless, the district judge expressed skepticism about the current state of medical knowledge. He was troubled that there might be something yet unknown to science that might do harm. . . .

. . . Little in science can be proved with complete certainty, and section 504 does not require such a test. As authoritatively construed by the Supreme Court, section 504 allows the exclusion of an employee only if there is "a *significant* risk of communicating an infectious disease to others." . . . In addition, *Arline* admonishes courts that they "should defer to the reasonable medical judgments of public health officials." . . . The district judge ignored these admonitions. Instead, he rejected the overwhelming consensus of medical opinion and improperly relied on speculation for which there was no credible support in the record. . . .

Viewing Chalk's submissions in light of these cases, it is clear that he has amply demonstrated a strong probability of success on the merits. We hold that it was error to require that every theoretical possibility of harm be disproved. . . .

Nonetheless, we recognize that the parties and the district court will have to deal with the apprehensions of other members of the school community, as well as with the inexorable progress of Chalk's disease. Although the time frame is unpredictable, given the current state of medical knowledge, the course of petitioner's condition is reasonably certain. Chalk's immune system will deteriorate over time, leaving him increasingly susceptible to opportunistic infections. These infections do not cause AIDS, nor do they increase the risk of transmission of the AIDS virus, but some of them may themselves be communicable to others in a classroom setting. The district court is in the best position, guided by qualified medical opinion, to determine what reasonable procedures, such as periodic reports from petitioner's doctors, will best give assurance to the Department, the community and the court that no significant risk of harm will arise in the future from Chalk's continued presence in the classroom.

We conclude that petitioner met all of the requirements necessary to receive a preliminary injunction. We therefore reverse the district court's order and remand this action with direction to enter a preliminary injunction ordering defendants forthwith to restore petitioner to his former duties as a teacher of hearing-impaired children in the Orange County Department of Education. This panel will retain jurisdiction over any subsequent appeal.

Reversed and remanded

NOTE

1. The Supreme Court, in *Arline*, specifically delimited its decision to exclude consideration of AIDS as a physical impairment. In a footnote to the case, the Court said:

> The United States argues that it is possible for a person to be simply a carrier of a disease, that is, to be capable of spreading a disease without having a "physical impairment" or suffering from any other symptoms associated with the disease. The United States contends that this true in the case of some carriers of the Acquired Immune Deficiency Syndrome (AIDS) virus. From this premise the United States concludes that discrimination solely on the basis of contagiousness is never discrimination on the basis of a handicap. The argument is misplaced in this case, because the handicap here, tuberculosis, gave rise both to a physical impairment *and* to contagiousness. This case does not present, and we therefore do not reach, the questions whether a carrier of a contagious disease such as AIDS could be considered to have a physical impairment, or whether such a person could be considered, solely on the basis of contagiousness, a handicapped person as defined by the Act.

▮▮▮ ENDNOTES

1. Keyes v. School District No. 1, 413 U.S. 189, 93 S.Ct. 2686 (1973).

2. Swann v. Charlotte-Mecklenberg Board of Education, 402 U.S. 1, 91 S.Ct. 1267 (1971).

3. Washington v. Davis, 426 U.S. 229, 96 S.Ct. 2040 (1976).

4. Village of Arlington Heights v. Metropolitan Housing Development Corp., 429 U.S. 252, 97 S.Ct. 555 (1977).

5. Ibid.

6. 480 F.2d 1159 (D.C. Cir. 1973).

7. Regents of the University of California v. Bakkee, 438 U.S. 265, 98 S.Ct. 2733 (1978).

8. Guardians Association, etc., et al. v. Civil Service Commission of New York, 463 U.S. 582, 103 S.Ct. 3221 (1983).

9. 42 U.S.C.A. §2000e–1.

10. Equal Employment Opportunities Act of 1972, Public Law 92–261.

11. 401 U.S. 424, 91 S.Ct. 849 (1971).

12. Ibid.

13. Armstead v. Starkville Municipal Separate School District, 325 F.Supp. 560 (N.D. Miss. 1971), affirmed in part and reversed in part 461 F.2d 276 (5th Cir. 1972); Chance v. Board of Examiners, 458 F.2d 1167 (2d Cir. 1972); Baker v. Columbus Municipal Separate School District, 462 F.2d 1112 (5th Cir. 1972); United States v. Chesterfield County School District, 484 F.2d 70 (4th Cir. 1973); United States v. North Carolina, 400 F.Supp. 343 (E.D.N.C. 1975), vacated 425 F.Supp. 789 (E.D.N.C. 1977).

14. International Brotherhood of Teamsters v. United States, 431 U.S. 324, 97 S.Ct. 1843 (1977).

15. Washington v. Davis, 426 U.S. 229, 96 S.Ct. 2040 (1976).

16. United States v. South Carolina, 445 F.Supp. 1094 (D.S.C. 1977), affirmed 434 U.S. 1026, 98 S.Ct. 756 (1978).

17. Johnson v. Transportation Agency, Santa Clara County, Cal., 480 U.S. 616, 639–642, 107 S.Ct. 1442, 1456–1457 (1987), citing University of California v. Bakke, 438 U.S. 265, 98 S.Ct. 2733 (1978).

18. Furnco Construction Corp. v. Waters, 438 U.S. 567, 577, 98 S.Ct. 2943, 2950 (1978).

19. Title VII, 42 U.S.C.A. §2000e–2(j).

20. McDonald v. Sante Fe Trail Transportation Co., 427 U.S. 273, 96 S.Ct. 2574 (1976).

21. Ibid.

22. See United Steelworkers of America v. Weber, 443 U.S. 193, 99 S.Ct. 2721 (1979), and Johnson v. Transportation Agency, 480 U.S. 616, 107 S.Ct. 1442 (1987). See also Data Research, Inc., *Deskbook Encyclopedia of American School Law,* (Rosemount, Minn.: Data Research, Inc., 1991), pp. 251–52.

23. 443 U.S. 193, 99 S.Ct. 2721 (1979).

24. 438 U.S. 265, 98 S.Ct. 2733 (1978).

25. Ibid., at 315–318, 98 S.Ct. at 2761–62.

26. Wygant v. Jackson Board of Education, 476 U.S. 267, 106 S.Ct. 1842 (1986).

27. Britton v. South Bend Community School Corporation, 819 F.2d 766 (7th Cir. 1987), cert. denied 484 U.S. 925, 108 S.Ct. 288 (1987).

28. Kern Alexander and M. David Alexander, *The Law of Schools, Students, and Teachers* (St. Paul, MN: West Publishing Company, 1984).

29. 42 U.S.C.A. §§2000e to 20003–17.

30. McDonnell-Douglas Corp. v. Green, 411 U.S. 792, 802, 93 S.Ct. 1817, 1924 (1973).

31. Carlile v. South Routt School District RE–3J, 739 F.2d 1496, 1500 (10th Cir. 1984).

32. Ibid.

33. Spears v. Board of Education of Pike County, Kentucky, 843 F.2d 882 (6th Cir. 1988).

34. Patterson v. Masem, 774 F.2d 251 (8th Cir. 1985). See also Wardell v. School Board, 786 F.2d 1554 (11th Cir. 1986).

35. Conner v. Fort Gordon Bus Co., 761 F.2d 1495, 1489 (11th Cir. 1985). See also McCarthney v. Griffin-Spalding County Board of Education, 791 F.2d 1549 (11th Cir. 1986).

36. McCarthney v. Griffin-Spalding County Board of Education, op. cit.

37. Price Waterhouse v. Hopkins, 490 U.S. 228, 109 S.Ct. 1775 (1989).

38. 42 U.S.C.A. §§2000e–2(a)(1), (2).

39. Price Waterhouse v. Hopkins, supra, 490 U.S. at 241–242, 109 S.Ct. 1786.

40. Ibid.

41. Public Law 95–555, 42 U.S.C.A. §2000(e).

42. *Deskbook Encyclopedia of American School Law,* p. 241.

43. Sanderson v. St. Louis University, 586 F.Supp. 954 (E.D. Mo. 1984).

44. Mitchell v. Board of Trustees of Pickens County School District A, 599 F.2d 582 (4th Cir. 1979); *1980 West Law No. 251,* 1991.

45. Ibid.

46. City of Los Angeles, Department of Water and Power v. Manhart, 435 U.S. 702, 98 S.Ct. 1370 (1978).

47. Arizona Governing Committee v. Norris, 463 U.S. 1073, 103 S.Ct. 3492 (1983).

48. M. David Alexander and Mary F. Hughes, "Sexual Harassment in the Workplace." In *Principal's Handbook: Current Issues in School Law,* (eds.). William E. Camp, Julie K. Underwood, and Mary Jane Connelly. National Organization on Legal Problems of Education, (Topeka, Kan.: 1989).

49. 29 CFR § 1604.11(a)(1985).

50. 477 U.S. 57, 106 S.Ct. 2399 (1986).

51. Ibid., 477 U.S. at 65, 106 S.Ct. at 2404.

52. 682 F.2d 897, 902 (11th Cir. 1982).

53. 29 CFR § 1604.11(c).

54. Ibid.

55. 432 U.S. 63, 97 S.Ct. 2264 (1977).

56. Wangsness v. Watertown School District No. 14–4, 541 F.Supp. 332 (D.S.D. 1982).

57. Pinsker v. Joint District No. 28J, etc., 554 F.Supp. 1049 (D. Colo. 1983), judgment affirmed 735 F.2d 388 (10th Cir. 1984).

58. 403 U.S. 602, 91 S.Ct. 2105 (1971).

59. Hunterdon Central High School Board of Educ. v. Hunterdon Central High School Teachers' Ass'n, 174 N.J. Super. 468, 416 A.2d 980 (App. Div. 1980).

60. 456 U.S. 512, 512, 102 S.Ct. 1912 1914 (1982).

61. Grove City College v. Bell, 465 U.S. 555, 104 S.Ct. 1211 (1984).

62. Public Law 100–259.

63. 29 U.S.C.A. § 206(d)(1).

64. 42 U.S.C.A. § 2000e–2.

65. Odomes v. Nucare, Inc., 653 F.2d 246, 250 (6th Cir. 1981) See Corning Glass Works v. Brennan, 417 U.S. 188, 94 S.Ct. 2223 (1974).

66. Corning Glass Works v. Brennan, 417 U.S. 188, 94 S.Ct. 2223 (1974).

67. EEOC v. Madison Community Unit School District No. 12, 818 F.2d 577 (7th Cir. 1987).

68. Ibid.

69. Equal Employment Opportunity Commission v. Tree of Life Christian Schools, 751 F.Supp. 700 (S.D. Ohio 1990).

70. 29 U.S.C.A. § 621, as amended in 1986, Age Discrimination in Employment Act.

71. Public Law 99–592, 29 U.S.C.A. § 621–623.

72. Massachusetts Board of Retirement v. Murgia, 427 U.S. 307, 96 S.Ct. 2562 (1976).

73. Vance v. Bradley, 440 U.S. 93, ____, 99 S.Ct. 939 (1979).

74. 472 U.S. 400, 105 S.Ct. 2743 (1985).

75. Tullis v. Lear School, Inc., 874 F.2d 1489 (11th Cir. 1989).

76. McDonnell-Douglas Corp. v. Green, 411 U.S. 792, 801, 93 S.Ct. 1817, 1824 (1973).

77. 42 U.S.C.A. § 12114.

78. Pushkin v. Regents of University of Colorado, 658 F.3d 1372, 1384 (10th Cir. 1981).

79. 480 U.S. 273, 107 S.Ct. 1123 (1987).

80. Gurmankin v. Costanzo, 556 F.2d 184 (3d Cir. 1977). See also 626 F.2d 1115 (3d Cir. 1980).

81. Upshur v. Love, 474 F.Supp. 332 (N.D. Cal. 1979).

CHAPTER 18

Collective Bargaining

Labor law in public education encompasses collective bargaining, strikes, wages, hours, and working conditions. With such broad import for the operation of the schools, it is little wonder that the movement toward unionism has had such a profound effect on school administration. This has manifested itself at all levels, from statutory provisions down to the day-to-day contract administration by the school building principal. The result has been that the administrative role has, to a great extent, shifted from discretionary activities to duties that are ministerial in nature. Public school labor relations is the story of this legal transition.

Developments in public school labor relations closely track the precedents of the private sector of the 1930s. Differences do exist, however, between the public and private sectors that cannot be ignored, thus preventing direct transference of private sector legal precedents into public practice. Both common law and statutory law that govern public school labor relations are, effectively, a modification of the well-established private sector view of labor relations.

HISTORICAL DEVELOPMENT

"Labor Relations in the Public Sector," Charles M. Rehmus, Paper prepared for the 3rd World Congress, International Industrial Relations Association, London, England (September 3–7, 1973)

– – – – – – – – – – –

BACKGROUND OF PUBLIC EMPLOYEE LABOR RELATIONS. Workers in the industrial private sector in the United States were given the statutory right to organize and bargain collectively in the 1930s. By 1960, approximately 30 percent of all nonagricultural private sector employees were represented by unions. Yet by this same date, there was practically no unionization in the public sector other than in the traditionally organized postal service and in a few other isolated situations.

The reasons for the delay in union organization of employees in the public sector in the United States are complex. In part, they stem from certain philosophical ideas long prevalent in the nation. Traditional concepts of sovereignty asserted that government is and should be supreme, hence immune from contravening forces and pressures such as that of collective bargaining. Related to this concept was that of the illegality of delegation of sovereign power. This assertion was that public decision-making could be done only by elected or appointed public officials, whose unilateral and complete discretion was therefore unchallengeable.

More practical considerations also delayed the advent of public employee unionism in the United States. The private sector unions and their international federations were fully occupied in trying to increase the extent of organization in the private sector. They had neither the money nor energy to turn to the public sector until the 1960s. Equally or more importantly, public employees were not generally dissatisfied with their terms and conditions of employment and, therefore, except in isolated cases, did not press for collective bargaining rights. Though the wages and salaries of public employees in the United States had traditionally lagged slightly behind comparable private sector salaries, the greater fringe benefits and job security associated

729

with public employment were traditionally thought to be adequate compensation.

By the late 1950s and early 1960s, several of these practical considerations that had delayed public employee unionism had disappeared. Moreover, new factors came into play that are difficult to assess as to sequence or relative importance, but in total added to a new militancy. Change increasingly became endemic in American society as more and more groups, including public employees, found it commonplace to challenge the established order. Some public employees were made less secure by organizational and technological changes as government came under pressure to reduce tax increases and, therefore, turned to devices to increase efficiency and lower unit labor costs. Public employee wages and salaries began to lag further behind those in the unionized private sector as the post-war inflationary spiral continued. The private sector international unions saw the large and growing employment in the non-union public sector as a fertile alternative that might substitute for their failure after 1956 to increase membership steadily in the private sector. Finally, many observers of public employment, both in and out of government, began strongly and publicly to question the logic behind governmentally protected collective bargaining in the private sector and government's complete failure to grant similar privileges and protections in the public sector.

By the 1960s, these practical challenges to the traditional arguments of sovereignty and illegal delegation of powers came to be seen as overriding in a number of government jurisdictions. The City of New York, the school board of that same city, and the State of Wisconsin gave modified collective bargaining rights to their public employees. Most importantly, in 1962 President Kennedy by executive order gave federal employees a limited version of the rights that private employees had received thirty years before. These seminal breakthroughs in granting some form of bargaining right to public employees led increasingly to similar kinds of state legislation, particularly in the more industrialized states. . . . President Nixon in two subsequent executive orders expanded and clarified the bargaining rights of federal employees.

■■■ PRIVATE VERSUS PUBLIC SECTOR

Before 1932, labor relations in the United States was a product of common law. In our laissez faire economic system, the courts tended to favor industrial management since the damage done by work stoppages was both social and economic. In the period extending from about 1870 to 1930, business interests held hegemony in labor relations, and the courts backed it up by liberal use of the injunction to suppress strikes, picketing, and boycotts. Further, neither the courts nor the legislatures fashioned remedies for the employee to prevent employers from discriminating against union members. Consequently, by 1930, labor unions were quite weak and had relatively little influence on the American economic system.[1]

Aware of the onesidedness of the legal precedents and the suppressive nature of the injunction and its overuse by the courts, the Congress enacted the Norris-LaGuardia Act in 1932, which had as its primary purpose preventing federal courts from issuing injunctions against union activities occurring as a result of labor disputes. Several states followed suit and, within a few years, the scales were tipped in favor of unions making the use of the injunction almost impossible. Anti-injunction legislation was the seed that allowed labor to develop strength. Modern labor statutes have largely carried forth the anti-injunction theory, allowing injunctions only if union activities violate the law or place the national health and safety in peril.[2]

Following the anti-injunction statute of 1932, the first broad labor relations act was the National Labor Relations Act of 1935 (the Wagner Act). Its purpose was to encourage collective bargaining as a means of promoting industrial peace. The act established the National Labor Relations Board as a regulatory body to prosecute and remedy unfair labor practice. Additionally, the law created procedures for determining employee representation and placed a duty on both parties to bargain in good faith.

In 1947, the National Labor Relations Act was amended by the Labor Management Relations Act of 1947, more popularly known as the Taft-Hartley Act. With this law, more limitations were placed on union activities through more definitive regulation of unfair labor practices by the union. Later, in 1959, the Taft-Hartley Act itself was amended by the Labor Management Reporting and Disclosure Act. This act was necessitated by widespread union mismanagement and corruption. A Senate investigating committee had found that unions in many cases had misused funds, had been infiltrated by gangsters, and had failed to conduct union business in a democratic manner. Designed to curb these abuses, the 1959 act specifically delineated employee rights as protection against union abuse, prescribed union election procedures, and established criminal penalties for misappropriation of union funds.[3]

The experience of private sector labor relations laid the groundwork for present statutory and judicial regulation of union activity. State statutes governing public employee collective bargaining reflect this in many ways; for example, scope of bargaining, representation procedures, impasse redress, and so on all have earmarks of the private experience.

Private and public sectors are, however, substantially different, and the application of private labor relations to the public schools has proceeded slowly. Some contend, as did Franklin D. Roosevelt in 1937, that "The process of collective bargaining as usually understood cannot be transplanted into the public service."[4] This view maintains that decision-making in education is a sovereign prerogative that cannot be shared. Those who are elected and speak with the voice of the citizenry as a whole must exercise their discretion in such matters, and the decision process that reflects this public will cannot be impaired or delegated. Public employees reject this rationale, arguing that the sovereign, legislature, or public agency is merely another employer with the power to delegate labor-management issues to the decision-making process of the bargaining table.

Most commentators admit, however, that the theoretical differences between the private and public sectors are probably of less practical importance than the more pragmatic distinctions relating to the strike, the process of governmental decision-making, existing civil service systems, and the different economic forces and motivations that bear on government as opposed to industry.[5]

At the heart of collective bargaining is the right to strike. From the viewpoint of the employee, if employees cannot strike, effective negotiations may be a hollow exercise. Labor's position is simply that "One cannot negotiate without ability to reject the proffered terms. The only way in which employees can reject an employer's offer is to stop work. Consequently, collective bargaining can hardly exist without preserving the right to strike."[6] With few exceptions, though, the people through their state legislature have rejected the right of public school teachers to strike. Where collective bargaining is permitted by statute, legislation usually falls short of allowing strikes and, in most instances, provides express prohibition. No such restraint, of course, exists in the private sector.

Another essential difference is that in the public sector, especially where school teachers are concerned, statutory budget deadlines and taxing restrictions make the bargaining process dependent on direct legislative action. In states in which local school district taxing leeway is limited, much of the new money for education is derived each year from state tax revenues. In such a situation, the bargaining agreement for increased wages is usually subject to legislative appropriation regardless of the bargaining agreement.

A further very practical difference between the private and public sectors is that private employees have fewer inherent protections than public employees enjoy. In our system of government, as reviewed in other sections of this book, public school teachers have constitutional rights of equal protection and due process against arbitrary state action, a benefit not enjoyed by employees in the private sector. These constitutional protections coupled with statutory prohibitions of discrimination, state salary schedules, fringe benefits of teacher retirement systems, sick leave, vacation leave, and so forth are examples of a public response to public employee needs that would probably not be found in the private sector in the absence of collective bargaining.

Finally, the normal market pressures of the private sector do not exist in the public schools. Public schools cannot lock out employees, go out of business, or raise prices. Beyond this, when the legislature of a state becomes involved, laws can be enacted that quickly change the rules of the game, possibly entirely redefining the criteria or certification for the teacher work force or unilaterally altering the nature of the public service in its entirety.

These distinctions, though, are held by many union leaders to be more apparent than real, and it is certainly true that a substantial erosion of the differences between private and public bargaining has transpired. To a large extent, some of the traditional points of departure have become irrelevant, but throughout any discussion of this issue, one cannot help observing that essential differences remain. The employee in the public sector as a citizen, taxpayer, and human being has greater potential influence over his or her employment destiny than can be found in the private sector.

As Werne points out,

> The employee in the private sector, except for the very devious method of shareholder voting, has no control over his management, unless by union contract. In the public sector, the employee can remove his employer from office and in not a few cases has effected such removal. In short, the strict dichotomy between employer and employee in the private sector has no exact counterpart in the public sector.[7]

Thus, the law pertaining to labor relations in the public schools may, to a great extent, be characterized as an adaptation of the private sector experience to the differing circumstances of the public schools.

◼◼ THE RIGHT TO BARGAIN COLLECTIVELY

The right of public employees to engage in collective bargaining entails important legal aspects, such as the employees' right to organize, the authority of the school board to bargain, the right to strike, and the authority of the school board to submit to compulsory arbitration. Employees have a right to organize and join labor unions. A North Carolina law forbidding public employees from joining unions was held unconstitutional on its face as violative of the First and Fourteenth Amendments.[8] In *AFSCME v. Woodward*,[9] the court held that employees not only have a right to join labor unions, but may file suit for damages and injunctive relief under the Civil Rights Act of 1871 if this freedom is denied. In *Woodward* the court stated:

> The First Amendment protects the right of one citizen to associate with other citizens for any lawful purpose free from government interference. The guarantee of the "right of assembly" protects more than the "right to attend a meeting; it includes the right to express one's attitudes or philosophies by membership in a group or by affiliation with it or by other lawful means . . . ." *Griswold v. Connecticut*, 381 U.S. 479, 85 S.Ct. 1678, 14 L.Ed. 2d 510 (1965); *N.A.A.C.P. v. Alabama* ex. rel. Patterson, 357 U.S. 449, 78 S.Ct. 1163, 2 L.Ed. 2d 1488 (1958).[10]

In the absence of statute, authority to bargain may[11] be within the discretion of the local board,[12] but there is no constitutional duty to bargain collectively with an exclusive bargaining agent.

> The refusal of [the School Board] to bargain in good faith does not equal a constitutional violation of plaintiffs-appellees' positive rights of association, free speech, petition, equal protection, or due process. Nor does the fact that the agreement to collectively bargain may be enforceable against a state elevate a contractual right to a constitutional right.[13]

Statutes prohibiting public employees' right to strike do not violate the state or federal constitutional mandates of equal protection. This issue was settled in a New York case contesting the Taylor Law's prohibition against strikes. The New York Court of Appeals held:

> In view of the strong policy considerations which led to the enactment of the Taylor Law, it is our conclusion that the statutory prohibition against strikes by public employees is reasonably designed to effectuate a valid state policy in an area where it has authority to act.[14]

Similarly, the Supreme Court has ruled that public school teachers have no inherent right to strike,[15] and these judgments have been reinforced at the federal level where, following a strike by the United States postal workers in 1970, a three-judge panel held that government employees do not have a right to strike. The Court held that neither public nor private employees have an absolute right to strike without statutory authorization. The opinion stated:

> Given the fact that there is no constitutional right to strike, it is not irrational or arbitrary for the Government to condition employment on a promise to withhold labor collectively, and to prohibit strikes by those in public employment, whether because of the prerogative of the sovereign, some sense of higher obligation associated with public service, to assure the continuing functioning of the Government without interruption, to protect public health and safety or for other reasons.[16]

The public attitude against public employee strikes has become more moderate in recent years and even the courts, albeit usually in dissents, are tending to view the strike situation more liberally. In a dissent in an Indiana case involving teachers in the City of Anderson, Justice DeBruler summarized arguments in favor of public employee strikes.

1. State sovereignty is not necessarily infringed upon if collective bargaining and a limited right to strike are extended to public sector employees.
2. The difference between public and private sector employees is in many instances negligible.
3. The impact of a private sector strike might be more crippling than a strike by public employees.
4. Public employees are guaranteed the same irrevocable rights by the Constitution as employees working in the private sector.
5. Public employees must have some means to assert their rights, especially when such rights are not ensured through legislation.[17]

Compulsory interest arbitration has been used in the private sector as an alternative to the strike and may become more common in public education. Impasse resolution in this manner provides that either party may request arbitration of the dispute, and that the decision of the arbitrator is binding on both parties. Compulsory arbitration has been extended to firefighters in Wyoming, Rhode Island, Massachusetts, and New York. A statute in Oregon requires binding arbitration in the field of public education, and Minnesota law provides for the Director of Mediation to resolve impasses by sending the dispute to arbitration.[18]

Without authorization from statute, however, school boards cannot generally submit to binding arbitration. The Virginia Supreme Court has held that binding rights arbitration imposed by state board regulation constitutes an unlawful denial of local school board power and an unwarranted delegation of authority and as such violates the Virginia Constitution, which makes management of the teaching staff an essential function of the local school board.[19]

In Michigan, however, the courts have upheld a state statute that provided for compulsory arbitration. The city had maintained that the act violated the prerogative of city government as delineated in the Michigan Constitution. The court held that validity of the statute should be upheld "unless the contrary clearly appears."[20] Although this case was later reversed on other grounds, it clearly enunciated that a state statute imposing arbitration on local government will be presumed to be valid unless in direct conflict with the state constitution. In the absence of such statute, however, local agencies are not required to delegate their authority to an arbitrator.

Teachers May Organize and Bargain Collectively but Cannot Strike

–––·––·––·–––

Norwalk Teachers Association v. Board of Education of City of Norwalk

–––·––·––·–––

Supreme Court of Errors of Connecticut, 1951.
138 Conn. 269, 83 A.2d 482.

JENNINGS, Justice. This is a suit between the Norwalk Teachers' Association as plaintiff and the Norwalk board of education as defendant for a declaratory judgment. . . . The plaintiff is a voluntary association and an independent labor union to which all but two of the teaching personnel of approximately 300 in the Norwalk school system belong. In April, 1946, there was a dispute between the parties over salary rates. The board of estimate and taxation was also involved. After long negotiations, 230 members of the association rejected the individual contracts of employment tendered them and refused to return to their teaching duties. . . . The contracts, subject to conditions precedent therein set forth, recognize the plaintiff as the bargaining agent for all of its members, defined working conditions and set up a grievance procedure and salary schedule. Similar contracts were entered into for the succeeding school years, including 1950–1951. From September, 1946, to the present and particularly with reference to the contract for 1950–1951, much doubt and uncertainty have arisen concerning the rights and duties of the respective parties, the interpretation of the contract and the construction of the state statutes relating to schools, education and boards of education. "In addition," the complaint states, "there has been the possibility of strikes, work stoppage

or collective refusals to return to work by the teachers through their organization and the possibility of discharges or suspensions by the defendant by reason of difficult personnel relations, all of which tends to disharmony in the operation of the school system and to the ever present possibility that either, or both, the parties may be unwittingly violating statutes by reason of mistaken or erroneous interpretation thereof." The parties agreed that the contract for the school year 1949–1950 would govern their relations for the school year 1950–1951, that they would join in this action, and "that whatever contractual obligations exist will be forthwith modified so soon as they shall have received from the Court judgments and orders declaring their respective rights, privileges, duties and immunities." The specific points of dispute are stated in the questions reserved, printed in the footnote.* . . .

---

* The plaintiff claimed a declaratory judgment answering and adjudicating the following questions:
"(a) Is it permitted to the plaintiff under our laws to organize itself as a labor union for the purpose of demanding and receiving recognition and collective bargaining?
"(b) Is it permitted to the plaintiff organized as a labor union to demand recognition as such and collective bargaining?
"(c) Is it permissible under Connecticut law for the defendant to recognize the plaintiff for the purpose of collective bargaining?
"(d) Is collective bargaining to establish salaries and working conditions permissible between the plaintiff and the defendant?
"(e) May the plaintiff engage in concerted action such as strike, work stoppage, or collective refusal to enter upon duties?
"(f) Is arbitration a permissible method under Connecticut law to settle or adjust disputes between the plaintiff and the defendant?
"(g) Is mediation a permissible method under the Connecticut law to settle or adjust disputes between the plaintiff and the defendant?
"(h) If the answer to the previous questions is yes, are the State's established administrative facilities, such as the State Board of Mediation and Arbitration and the State Labor Relations Board, available, as they are available in industrial disputes, to the plaintiff and the defendant?
"(i) Does the continuing contract law, so-called, create a status of employment within which the plaintiff may claim employment subject to the right to bargain salaries and working conditions?
"(j) Has the plaintiff the right to establish rules, working conditions and grievance resolution by collective bargaining?"

Under our system, the government is established by and run for all of the people, not for the benefit of any person or group. The profit motive, inherent in the principle of free enterprise, is absent. It should be the aim of every employee of the government to do his or her part to make it function as efficiently and economically as possible. The drastic remedy of the organized strike to enforce the demands of unions of government employees is in direct contravention of this principle. It has been so regarded by the heads of the executive departments of the states and the nation. Most of the text writers refer to one or more of the following statements by three of our recent presidents. They are quoted, for example, in 1 Labor Law Journal 612 (May, 1950): "There is no right to strike against public safety by anybody anywhere at any time" (Calvin Coolidge on the Boston police strike). This same strike was characterized by President Wilson as "an intolerable crime against civilization." President Franklin D. Roosevelt said in a letter to the president of the National Federation of Federal Employees on August 16, 1937: "Particularly, I want to emphasize my conviction that militant tactics have no place in the functions of any organization of Government employees. . . . [A] strike of public employees manifests nothing less than an intent on their part to prevent or obstruct the operations of Government until their demands are satisfied. Such action, looking toward the paralysis of Government by those who have sworn to support it, is unthinkable and intolerable." As the author of the article cited says, "The above statement by President Roosevelt, who certainly was no enemy of labor unions, epitomizes the answer to the problem. It seems to be axiomatic."

. . .

Few cases involving the right of unions of government employees to strike to enforce their demands have reached courts of last resort. That right has usually been tested by an application for an injunction forbidding the strike. The right of the governmental body to this relief has been uniformly upheld. It has been put on various grounds: public policy; interference with governmental function; ille-gal discrimination against the right of any citizen to apply for government employment (where the union sought a closed shop).

. . .

The plaintiff, recognizing the unreasonableness of its claims in the case of such employees as the militia and the judiciary, seeks to place teachers in a class with employees employed by the municipality in its proprietary capacity. No authority is cited in support of this proposition. "A town board of education is an agency of the state in charge of education in the town . . . ." . . . In fulfilling its duties as such an agency, it is acting in a governmental, not a proprietary, capacity. . . .

In the American system, sovereignty is inherent in the people. They can delegate it to a government which they create and operate by law. They can give to that government the power and authority to perform certain duties and furnish certain services. The government so created and empowered must employ people to carry on its task. Those people are agents of the government. They exercise some part of the sovereignty entrusted to it. They occupy a status entirely different from those who carry on a private enterprise. They serve the public welfare and not a private purpose. To say that they can strike is the equivalent of saying that they can deny the authority of government and contravene the public welfare. The answer to question (e) is "No."

Questions (a) and (b) relate to the right of the plaintiff to organize itself as a labor union and to demand recognition and collective bargaining. The right to organize is sometimes accorded by statute or ordinance. See, for example, the Bridgeport ordinance adopted June 17, 1946 (Bridgeport Munic. Reg. [1947] p. 15), discussed in National Institute of Municipal Law Officers Report No. 129, p. 51. The right to organize has also been forbidden by statute or regulation. *Perez v. Board of Police Commissioners,* 78 Cal.App. 2d 638, 178 P.2d 537. In Connecticut the statutes are silent on the subject. Union organization in industry is now the rule rather than the exception. In the absence of prohibitory statute or regulation, no good reason appears why public employees should not organize as a labor union. *Springfield v. Clouse*, 356 Mo. 1239, 1246, 206 S.W.2d 539. It is the second part of the question (a) that causes difficulty. The question reads: "Is it permitted to the plaintiff under our laws to organize itself as a labor union for the purpose of demanding and receiving recognition and collective bargaining?" The question is phrased in a very preemptory form. The common method of enforcing recognition and collective bargaining is the strike. It appears that this method has already been used by the plaintiff and that the threat of its use again is one of the reasons for the present suit. As has been said, the strike is not a permissible method of enforcing the plaintiff's demands. The answer to questions (a) and (b) is a qualified "Yes." There is no objection to the organization of the plaintiff as a labor union, but if its organization is for the purpose of "demanding" recognition and collective bargaining the demands must be kept within legal bounds. What we have said does not mean that the plaintiff has the right to organize for all of the purposes for which employees in private enterprise may unite, as those are defined in § 7391 of the General Statutes. Nor does it mean that, having organized, it is necessarily protected against unfair labor practices as specified in § 7392 or that it shall be the exclusive bargaining agent for all employees of the unit, as provided in § 7393. It means nothing more than that the plaintiff may organize and bargain collectively for the pay and working conditions which it may be in the power of the board of education to grant.

Questions (c) and (d) in effect ask whether collective bargaining between the plaintiff and the defendant is permissible. The statutes and private acts give broad powers to the defendant with reference to educational matters and school management in Norwalk. If it chooses to negotiate with the plaintiff with regard to the employment, salaries, grievance procedure and working conditions of its members, thereis there is no stat-

ute, public or private, which forbids such negotiations. It is a matter of common knowledge that this is the method pursued in most school systems large enough to support a teachers' association in some form. It would seem to make no difference theoretically whether the negotiations are with a committee of the whole association or with individuals or small related groups, so long as any agreement made with the committee os is confined to members of the association. If the strike threat is absent and the defendant prefers to handle the matter through negotiation with the plaintiff, no reason exists why it should not do so. The claim of the defendant that this would be an illegal delegation of authority is without merit. The authority is and remains in the board. This statement is not to be construed as approval of the existing contracts attached to the complaint. Their validity is not in issue.

As in the case of questions (a) and (b), (c) and (d) are in too general a form to permit a categorical answer. The qualified "Yes" which we give to them should not be construed as authority to negotiate a contract which involves the surrender of the board's legal discretion, is contrary to law or is otherwise ultra vires. For example, an agreement by the board to hire only union members would clearly be an illegal discrimination. *Mugford v. Baltimore*, 185 Md. 266, 270, 44 A.2d 745; Rhyne, Labor Unions & Municipal Employee Law, pp. 34, 137, 157. Any salary schedule must be subject to the powers of the board of estimate and taxation. "The salaries of all persons appointed by the board of education . . . shall be as fixed by said board, but the aggregate amount of such salaries . . . shall not exceed the amount determined by the board of estimate and taxation . . . ." 21 Spec. Laws, p. 285, No. 315, § 3; *Board of Education of Stamford v. Board of Finance*, 127 Conn. 345, 349, 16 A.2d 601. One of the allegations of the complaint is that the solution of the parties' difficulties by the posing of specific issues is not satisfactory. Whether or not this is so, that course will be necessary if this discussion of general principles is an insufficient guide.

Question (f) reads, "Is arbitration a permissible method under Connecticut law to settle or adjust disputes between the plaintiff and the defendant?" The power of a town to enter into an agreement of arbitration was originally denied on the ground that it was an unlawful delegation of authority. *Griswold v. North Stonington,* 5 Conn. 367, 371. It was later held that not only the amount of damages but liability could be submitted to arbitration. *Hine v. Stephens,* 33 Conn. 497, 504; *Mallory v. Huntington,* 64 Conn. 88, 96, 29 A. 245. The principle applies to the parties to the case at bar. If it is borne in mind that arbitration is the result of mutual agreement, there is no reason to deny the power of the defendant to enter voluntarily into a contract to arbitrate a specific dispute. On a proposal for a submission, the defendant would have the opportunity of deciding whether it would arbitrate as to any question within its power. Its power to submit to arbitration would not extend to questions of policy but might extend to question of liability. Arbitration as a method of settling disputes is growing in importance and, in a proper case, "deserves the enthusiastic support of the courts." *International Brotherhood of Teamsters v. Shapiro,* 138 Conn. 57, 69, 82 A.2d 345. Agreements to submit all disputes to arbitration, commonly found in ordinary union contracts, are in a different category. If the defendant entered into a general agreement of that kind, it might find itself committed to surrender the broad discretion and responsibility reposed in it by law. For example, it could not commit to an arbitrator the decision of a proceeding to discharge a teacher for cause. So, the matter of certification of teachers is committed to the state board of education. General Statutes, §§ 1432, 1433, 1435. The best answer we can give to question (f) is, "Yes, arbitration may be a permissible method as to certain specific, arbitrable disputes."

From what has been said, it is obvious that, within the same limitations, mediation to settle or adjust disputes is not only permissible but desirable. The answer to question (g) is "Yes." The state board of mediation and arbitration and the state labor relations board, however, are set up to handle disputes in private industry and are not available to the plaintiff and defendant for reasons given in the opinion of the attorney general dated July 6, 1948. 25 Conn.Atty.Gen.Rep. 270. This was confirmed as to Norwalk teachers by an opinion dated June 12, 1950, not yet published. See also *United States v. United Mine Workers,* 330 U.S. 258, 269, 67 S.Ct. 677, 91 L.Ed. 884. The answer to question (h) is "No."

General Statutes, Sup.1949, § 160a, provides in part: "The contract of employment of a teacher shall be renewed for the following school year unless such teacher has been notified in writing prior to March first of that year that such contract will not be renewed." Question (i) asks whether this law creates "a status of employment within which the plaintiff may claim employment subject to the right to bargain salaries and working conditions?" The meaning of this is not clear and the briefs do not clarify it. It is the type of question that should be related to a specific state of facts. It cannot be answered in vacuo.

As to question (j), the plaintiff has no right to establish rules. As stated above, the right is and remains in the board.

Question (g) is answered, "Yes, but not under chapter 369 of the General Statutes as amended." Questions (e), (h) and (j) are answered "No." Question (i) is not answered. No purpose would be served by answering the other questions categorically. Questions (a) and (b) are answered, "Yes, with relation to the plaintiff's own members, provided its demands are kept within legal bounds." Questions (c) and (d) are answered, "Yes, with relation to the plaintiff's own members, provided that this answer shall not be construed as approval of any specific contract which has been or may be entered into between the parties." Question (f) is answered, "Yes, arbitration may be a permissible method as to certain specific, arbitrable disputes." In answering some of these questions we have gone beyond the requirements of the specific questions asked in order to render such assistance as we properly may in helping to solve the difficulties of the parties.

No costs will be taxed in this court to either party.

In this opinion the other judges concurred.

Public Employees Must Have Express Legislative Permission to Strike

-- -- · -- · -- · -- -- · --

Anderson Federation of Teachers, Local 519 v. School City of Anderson

-- -- · -- · -- · -- -- · --

Supreme Court of Indiana, 1969.
252 Ind. 558, 251 N.E.2d 15, rehearing denied 252
Ind. 558, 254 N.E.2d 329 (1970), cert. denied 399
U.S. 928, 90 S.Ct. 2243 (1970).

GIVEN, Judge. On May 6, 1968, the Superior Court of Madison County found the appellant, Anderson Federation of Teachers, Local 519, in contempt of court for the violation of a restraining order which had been issued without notice on the 2nd day of May, 1968, directing the appellant, teachers' union, and its members to refrain from picketing and striking against the appellee school corporation. It is from this judgment of contempt that this appeal is taken.

The appellant is an organization of public school teachers employed by the appellee.

The appellee is a municipal corporation organized under the statutes of this state for the purpose of operating the public schools within the boundaries of the School City of Anderson, Indiana.

In the spring of 1968 the appellant and the appellees entered into negotiations concerning salary schedules for the following year. These negotiations apparently were not satisfactory to the appellant for on May 1, 1968, the appellant instituted a strike against the school corporation and established picket lines at the various schools operated by appellee. Evidence discloses that school children were unloaded in the public streets because of the presence of the picket lines. It was this action of picketing by the appellant which precipitated the temporary restraining order issued on May 2, 1968, and it was the continuation of this activity without regard for the restraining order upon which the trial court based its judgment after a hearing on May 6, 1968, that the appellant was in contempt of court for violating the restraining order.

The trial court was in all things correct in its finding and judgment of contempt of court.

It is the contention of the appellant that Indiana's "Little Norris-LaGuardia Act," also known as the anti-injunction statute, the same being Burns' Ind.Stat.Ann. § 40–501 et seq., is applicable in this case. This act prohibits the issuance of restraining orders and injunctions in matters involving labor disputes between unions and private employers. We do not agree with the appellant that this act is applicable to disputes concerning public employees. The overwhelming weight of authority in the United States is that government employees may not engage in a strike for any purpose.

The Supreme Court of the United States clearly enunciated the proposition that public employees did not have a right to strike and that the injunctive processes might properly be used to prevent or halt such strikes in the case of *United States v. United Mine Workers (1947)*, 330 U.S. 258, 67 S.Ct. 677, 91 L.Ed. 884. This case has never been overruled or modified.   . . .

This same proposition has been followed generally in most of the other state jurisdictions where it has been repeatedly held that strikes by public employees are or should be prohibited and that injunctions should be granted to halt or prevent them.   . . .

We find only one case where an injunction to prevent a pending strike of public employees was denied. That case was *Board of Education of City of Minneapolis v. Public School Employees Union (1951)*, 233 Minn. 141, 45 N.W.2d 797, 29 A.L.R.2d 424. That case, however was overruled in 1966 by the Supreme Court of Minnesota in *Minneapolis Federation of Teachers Local 59, AFL-CIO v. Obermeyer,* supra. . . .

We thus see that both the federal and state jurisdictions and men both liberal and conservative in their political philosophies have uniformly recognized that to allow a strike by public employees is not merely a matter of choice of political philosophies, but is a thing which cannot and must not be permitted if the orderly function of our society is to be preserved. This is not a matter for debate in the political arena for it appears fundamental, as stated by Governor Dewey, public strikes would lead to anarchy, and, as stated by President Roosevelt, the public strike "is unthinkable and intolerable."

The Madison Superior Court, is, therefore, in all things affirmed.

Teachers' Sanctions Against Board Is Concerted Action Toward Illegal End

— — — · — — · — — · — —

Board of Education v. New Jersey Education Association

— — — · — — · — — · — —

Supreme Court of New Jersey, 1968.
53 N.J. 29, 247 A.2d 867.

WEINTRAUB, C.J. . . . In February 1967 a dispute arose between the secretary of the Board and defendant Haller, president of UBTA. Haller was a teacher in plaintiff's system but had not yet acquired tenure. On March 14, 1967 the Board met to consider teacher contracts for the following school year and decided not to offer one to Haller and two other nontenure teachers who were active in UBTA. Haller was so notified on March 29. UBTA held a special meeting of its membership on March 31 at which a lengthy resolution was adopted listing seventeen grievances. . . .

Meanwhile, on April 12 UBTA resolved that "sanctions be imposed" against the Board and requested NJEA to follow suit. On April 21 the NJEA resolved to "impose sanctions" on the Board, and gave wide circulation to its resolution. . . .

NJEA proclaimed through the local press that it would be "a violation of the professional code of ethics for any teacher to accept employment in Union Beach or for any administrator to offer employment in Union Beach as long as the sanctions which had been invoked were in effect."

[1] It has long been the rule in our State that public employees may not strike. . . .

Defendants deny there was a "strike." They seek to distinguish the usual concerted refusal to work from what transpired here. As to the teachers employed by the Board, defendants say they merely resigned as of a future date, and with respect to the interference with the Board's recruitment of replacements, defendants, as we understand them, say a refusal to accept employment is inherently different from a quit. But the subject is the public service, and the distinctions defendants advance are irrelevant to it, however arguable they may be in the context of private employment. Unlike the private employer, a public agency may not retire. The public demand for services which makes illegal a strike against government inveighs against any other concerted action designed to deny government the necessary manpower, whether by terminating existing employments in any mode or by obstructing access to the labor market. Government may not be brought to a halt. So our criminal statute, N.J.S. 2A:98–1, N.J.S.A., provides in simple but pervasive terms that any two or more persons who conspire "to commit any act" for the "obstruction of . . . the due administration of the laws" are guilty of a misdemeanor.

Hence, although the right of an individual to resign or to refuse public employment is undeniable, yet two or more may not agree to follow a common course to the end that an agency of government shall be unable to function. Here there was such collective action by agreement both as to the quitting and as to new employment. As to the mass resignations, an agreement to that end must be inferred from the very adoption by the members through their teachers union of the program of sanctions which, despite some verbal obscurity in this regard, quite plainly imports an understanding to withdraw services when the union officialdom "imposes sanctions" upon a school district. The use of "unethical" in condemning new employment because of working conditions must mean it is also "unethical" to continue an existing employment under the same conditions. The full understanding must be that upon the imposition of sanctions, all services will be withdrawn. We have no doubt that the agreement to strike was not articulated because of the established illegality of that course. In any event, if it should be thought the plan did not include the obligation to quit in connection with the imposition of sanctions, we think it clear that the teachers entered into an agreement to quit when they voted in favor of mass resignations and then executed thirty-six of them. Although the Board accepted the resignations and hence does not ask that work stoppage be ended, we are satisfied the stoppage was concerted action to an illegal end.

And with respect to blacklisting of the school district and the scheme of "sanctions" upon teachers who offer or take employment with a "sanctioned" school board, it can escape no one that the purpose is to back up a refusal of others to continue to work. At a minimum the object is to withhold additional services a school district may need to discharge its public duty, which, as we have said, is no less illegal. Such an illegal agreement may come into being at the time of the strike or may antedate it. If individuals enter into a union or association on terms that upon the occurrence of some stipulated event or signal they will impede government in its recruitment of services, that very arrangement constitutes an agreement the law denounces. An agreement not to seek, accept, or solicit employment in government whenever the upper echelon of the union makes a prescribed

pronouncement is, no less than an accomplished shutdown, a thrust at the vitality of government, and comes within the same policy which denounces a concerted strike or quit or slowdown or other obstruction of the performance of official duties.

. . . That the conventional terminology of a "strike" nowhere appears is of no moment. The substance of a situation and not its shape must control. A doctrine designed to protect the public interest is equal to any demand upon it. It does not yield to guise or ingenuity.

. . . The trial court expressly added that "There is no intention, however, of restraining defendants from exercising the right of free speech concerning what they think the conditions are in the Union Beach school system."

What reappears in defendants' argument is a protest that "sanctions" are no more than an expression of disapproval of conditions in the school district and of the conduct of the Board. It is difficult, even in the abstract, to take that view of the terms used. Far from importing a mere denunciation of men and their work, the "imposition of sanctions" imports the imposition of a penalty. . . .

The imposition of "sanctions" was the stipulated signal for unlawful activity. The right to utter even a pleasantry may be lost if it is the agreed call for lawlessness. It need hardly be said that freedom of speech does not included the right to use speech as an instrument to an unlawful end. . . .

The judgment is affirmed (for Board).

NOTE

1. Refusal to perform extracurricular duties constitutes a strike. "Extracurricular activities are a fundamental part of a child's education, making the supervision of such activities an integral part of a teacher's duty toward his or her students." *Board of Educ. of City of Asbury Park v. Asbury Park Educ. Ass'n*, 145 N.J. Super. 495, 368 A.2d 396 (1976).

Strike Creates a Clear and Present Danger to Health, Safety, or Welfare of the Public

Jersey Shore Area School District v. Jersey Shore Education Association

Supreme Court of Pennsylvania, 1988.
519 Pa. 398, 548 A.2d 1202.

STOUT, Justice. This appeal is brought by the members of the Jersey Shore Education Association, which represents the teachers of the Jersey Shore Area School District. In it we are asked to reconcile that provision of the Public Employees Relations Act (PERA), 43 Pa.Stat. Ann. §§ 1101.101–.2301 (Purdon Supp. Pamph.1988), which gives teachers the right to strike, with that provision of the Public School Code, 24 Pa.Stat.Ann. §§ 15–1501 to 16–1613 (Purdon 1962 & Supp.1988), which mandates that school districts provide 180 days of pupil instruction. Specifically, PERA provides:

> If a strike by public employes occurs after the collective bargaining processes set forth in Sections 801 and 802 of Article VIII of this act have been completely utilized and exhausted, it shall not be prohibited unless or until such a strike creates *a clear and present danger or threat* to the health, safety or welfare of the public.

43 Pa.Stat.Ann. § 1101.1003 (Purdon Supp. Pamph.1988) (emphasis added). On the other hand, the Public School Code provides: "All public kindergartens, elementary and secondary schools shall be kept open each school year for at least one hundred eighty (180) days of instruction for pupils." 24 Pa.Stat.Ann. § 15–1501 (Purdon 1962 & Supp.1988).

On September 10, 1984, after only four days of pupil instruction, the teachers struck against appellee, Jersey Shore Area School District. On October 8, 1984, the school district filed for an injunction in the Court of Common Pleas of Lycoming County, in an effort to force the teachers back to work. A hearing was held on October 10, 1984, following which the Chancellor issued an injunction ordering the teachers back to work on October 11. The Association filed for reconsideration and an additional hearing was held on October 23, 1984. The Chancellor refused to lift the injunction. The Association appealed to the Commonwealth Court, which affirmed *solely* on the basis of the Chancellor's finding that the school district's impending inability to schedule 180 days of instruction presented a clear and present danger to the public because of a threatened loss of state subsidies. . . . While we disagree with the Commonwealth Court that the threatened loss of state subsidies alone would support the issuance of an injunction, we nonetheless affirm on the record as a whole. . . .

At the first hearing the superintendent for the school district testified that he had prepared a revised school calendar. Allowing for six snow days and two nonmandatory holidays, the superintendent had concluded that October 15, 1984, would be the last date upon which the teachers could return to the classroom while still ensuring an educationally-sound schedule. In addition, the superintendent testified extensively as to the financial impact of the strike. He stated that the school district stood to lose $26,637.00 per day in state subsidies for each day it fell short of 180 days of instruction. At the time of the hearing the superintendent estimated that the strike had cost the school district $65,944.00 in unemployment compensation, additional salaries and other costs incidental to the strike.

With respect to the students, the superintendent stated that the strike placed the seniors at a competitive disadvantage in terms of SAT testing. Seniors also faced deadlines with respect to scholarship applications and were bereft of guidance counseling services. The longer the strike, the more deleterious its effect on the future of the seniors.

With respect to other grades, students would be at a competitive disadvantage in taking state-mandated tests to determine remedial needs. With only four days of instruction, some students could be placed in remedial courses which they would not otherwise have needed. Moreover, in the event the school district could not administer these tests due to the continuation of the strike, it would lose state funding for the remedial courses themselves.

The superintendent stated that interference with a regular pattern of study, as had occurred in this strike, results in a loss of learning capacity, which increases with the length of the interruption. In support of this hypothesis he cited test scores from a previous year showing a drop in student aptitudes following a strike.

Finally, the superintendent expressed his concern that the strike deprived eligible students of a free, hot lunch, possibly the only such meal they received, while working parents were experiencing difficulties with interim babysitting arrangements.

The school teachers presented the testimony of two experts. The first disputed the superintendent's interpretation of prior test scores insofar as their reflecting a decrease in pupil learning due to the previous strike. This expert opined that it was inappropriate to compare different student groups for such a purpose. The second expert testified that, as of the date of the hearing, the school district would actually have a net savings in salaries and benefits of $24,199.00 over the potentially lost subsidy.

Having heard this evidence, the Chancellor issued the injunction on the basis of his conclusion that all of the evidence had demonstrated the existence of a clear and present danger to the health and welfare of the community.

At the reconsideration hearing, little additional evidence was presented except that two officials of the Department of Education testified as to departmental policy with regard to withholding subsidies and as to their calculations with regard to the last possible date upon which the teachers would have to return to the classroom in order to ensure a 180–day calendar. Following this testimony, the Chancellor refused to lift the injunction. . . .

Since this is an issue of first impression for this Court, we shall begin our legal analysis with a brief review of the decisions of the Commonwealth Court that have addressed it. In *Armstrong School Dist. v. Armstrong Educ. Ass'n,* 5 Pa. Commw. 378, 291 A.2d 120 (1972), Commonwealth Court grappled with the definition of "clear and present danger or threat" in analogizing it to First Amendment, free speech and association cases. . . . The Court concluded:

> In this light, the determination of whether or not a strike presents a clear and present danger to the health, safety of welfare of the public must, therefore, require the court to find that the danger or threat is real or actual and that a strong likelihood exists that it will occur. Additionally, it seems to us that the "danger" or "threat" concerned must not be one which is normally incident to a strike by public employees. By enacting [PERA] which authorizes such strikes, the Legislature may be understood to have indicated its willingness to accept certain inconveniences, for such are inevitable, but it obviously intended to draw the line at those which pose a danger to the public health, safety or welfare.

. . . In reversing the issuance of an injunction, the Court stated that the disruption of routine administrative procedures and the cancellation of extracurricular activities were inconveniences inherent in a teacher's strike, inconveniences envisioned by the legislature which, if considered a "clear and present danger or threat," would virtually nullify the right to strike. . . . In *dicta* the Court also stated that if a strike lasted so long as to make the 180–day calendar an impossibility, and the cessation of subsidies a possibility, it properly could be enjoined.

In *Philadelphia Fed. of Teachers v. Ross,* 8 Pa.Commw. 204, 301 A.2d 405 (1973), the Court affirmed the issuance of an injunction where the board presented evidence of sharply increased gang activity that necessitated $133,000.00 per day in increased police protection, endemic student underachievement, possible loss of state subsidies, and the disqualification of seniors from entering college. . . .

. . . *See also Bethel Park School Dist. v. Bethel Park Fed. of Teachers*, 54 Pa.Commw. 49, 52, 420 A.2d 18, 19 (1980) (loss of state subsidies, instructional days, vocational job training, higher education and special education opportunities, counseling, social and health services, extracurricular programs and employees' work and wage opportunities constituted a clear and present danger to the community).

In *Bellefonte Area School Bd. v. The Bellefonte Area Educ. Ass'n*, 9 Pa. Commw. 210, 304 A.2d 922 (1973), the Court reversed the issuance of an injunction in concluding that the facts did not support a finding of "clear and present danger or threat." Since in that case sufficient make-up days remained to replace the thirteen strike days, therefore, the loss of state subsidies was not imminent. Moreover, the possible loss of participation in an educational quality assessment program was not deemed harmful enough to justify the injunction.

. . . .

This brief history reflects judicial difficulty, and at times divergence, in reconciling the right to strike with the requirement of 180 instructional days. While some cases have looked at a plethora of factors, including the loss of state subsidies, others have looked only at the loss of state subsidies in determining that it *per se* creates a clear and present danger or threat. We do not believe that the language of PERA necessitates judicial hand-wringing or hair-pulling. We hold that the loss of state educational subsidies for failure of a school district to schedule 180 days of instruction for pupils, alone, does not constitute a "clear and present danger or threat to the health, safety or welfare of the public." In this case the school district demonstrated beyond peradventure the existence of a "clear and present danger or threat to the health, safety or welfare of the public." Without focusing on any one of the myriad economic and other facts upon which the school board relied, without weighing the interests of seniors as weightier that those of kindergartners, we conclude that, in conjunction, these factors created a school district which, although perhaps able to "make up" a day or two of instruction, could not "make up" the actual, the impending and the ever-increasing harm which was being wrought upon its students. On this record, the health and welfare of the students, who cannot and must not be treated as a category separate from the public at large, was clearly endangered and threatened.

The order of the Commonwealth Court is affirmed.

NOTES

1. The Supreme Court of Michigan has held that teachers who strike may be discharged without a prior hearing. The court reasoned:

   > When public employees strike, the public employer must, like a private employer, be able to hire substitute employees so that the public business is not interrupted. In order to hire competent replacements, it may be necessary for the public employer to offer permanent employment and, thus, displace strikers. Where essential services have been suspended, the hiring of replacements often cannot await time-consuming adjudicatory processes.
   >
   > The predominant interest secured by pre-disciplinary hearings, . . . is protection against removal of the wrong person and, assuming ultimate employee vindication, protection against interim financial deprivation.
   >
   > The possibility of removal of a nonstriker is minimized when, as here, the school board gives each striking teacher personal notice of the opportunity to return to the classroom before disciplinary action is taken. While on strike, a teacher receives no compensation; striking teachers do not suffer additional interim financial deprivation when disciplined.

   Rockwell v. The Board of Education of School District of Crestwood, 393 Mich. 616, 227 N.W. 2d 736 appeal dismissed 96 S.Ct. 3184, 427 U.S. 901 (1976) (1975).

2. An injunction against a teacher work stoppage was upheld where the teachers refused to work unless the school board reinstated certain provisions in a previously expired contract. The board refused to extend the terms of the old contract, and

during the period when no contract was in existence, imposed interim operating regulations that eliminated protections of the old contract. The court said that the work stoppage was an illegal strike within the meaning of the state statute prohibiting such stoppages for the purpose of inducing a "change in the conditions" of employment. *Warren Education Association v. Adams,* 57 Mich.App. 496, 226 N.W. 2d 536 (1975).

3. Where an illegal teacher's strike caused the students to miss several school days, the school board was justified in shortening the school year and reducing teacher's salaries accordingly. *Ash v. Board of Education,* 699 F.2d 822 (6th Cir. 1983).

4. No civil action in tort can lie against teachers' union for striking when employee relations act provides other remedies. The court reasoned that "public policy considerations interdict the creation of a new cause of action, which would unsettle an already precarious labor-management balance in the public labor relations sector." *Lamphere Schools v. Lamphere Federation of Teachers,* 400 Mich. 104, 252 N.W.2d 818 (1977).

———

Binding Arbitration Is an Unlawful Delegation of Power Violating State Constitution

— · — · — · — · —

School Board of the City of Richmond v. Parham

— · — · — · — · —

Supreme Court of Virginia, 1978.
218 Va. 950, 243 S.E.2d 468.

CARRICO, Justice. This is an appeal from the final order of the trial court awarding Margaret W. Parham (hereinafter, Parham), a Richmond public schoolteacher, a writ of mandamus against the School Board of the City of Richmond (hereinafter, the School Board). The order compelled the School Board to

submit to arbitration a grievance Parham had brought pursuant to the "Procedure for Adjusting Grievances," adopted by the State Board of Education (hereinafter, the State Board). The same order awarded the State Board, an intervenor in the proceeding, a declaratory judgment upholding the constitutionality of a provision of the Procedure which requires binding arbitration of certain disputes between local school boards and their nonsupervisory employees. The sole question for decision is whether the provision for binding arbitration is constitutionally valid.

Adopted in 1973 and subsequently amended, the Procedure prescribes the method for settling employee grievances. . . .

In the present case, Parham unsuccessfully processed her grievance through the several administrative levels prescribed by the Procedure and ultimately presented the dispute to the School Board, where she received an adverse decision. When she called for arbitration, the School Board refused to arbitrate, stating that it questioned the constitutionality of the Procedure "insofar as it compels arbitration binding on school boards in Virginia." Parham then filed her petition for a writ of mandamus to compel the School Board to submit the matter to arbitration.

At the heart of the present controversy are the provisions of Article VIII of the Virginia Constitution, which article relates to education. In pertinent part, the article reads:

§ 2. *Standards of quality; State and local support of public schools.* — Standards of quality for the several school divisions shall be determined and prescribed from time to time by the Board of Education, subject to revision only by the General Assembly. . . .

§ 4. *Board of Education.* — The general supervision of the public school system shall be vested in a Board of Education . . . .

§ 5. *Powers and duties of the Board of Education.* — The powers and duties of the Board of Education shall be as follows. . . .

(e) Subject to the ultimate authority of the General Assembly, the Board shall have primary responsibility and authority for effectuating the educational policy set forth in this Article, and it shall have such other powers and duties as may be prescribed by law. . . .

§ 7. *School boards.* — The supervision of schools in each school division shall be vested in a school board . . . .

The School Board recognizes that § 4 of Article VIII places "general supervision" of the public school system in the hands of the State Board. The School Board notes, however, that, under § 7 of Article VIII, the "supervision" of schools is vested in local school boards and that, implementing this constitutional mandate, the General Assembly has conferred upon such local boards extensive authority to execute their supervisory duties. . . .

The School Board argues, however, that "management of a school board's teaching staff and other employees is . . . an essential function of supervision" and that neither the General Assembly nor the State Board can divest local school boards of this function and place it "in an authority other than the local boards." Yet, the School Board asserts, the effect of the binding arbitration provision of the Procedure is to permit "an outside agency, in the form of an arbitration panel . . . to divest the local board of its essential function by the substitution of [the panel's] judgment for that of the board." As a result of the panel's action, the School Board maintains, a local school board's policies, rules, and regulations relating to the work activity of employees could be altered or rendered meaningless. This, the School Board concludes, is constitutionally impermissible under § 7 of Article VIII. . . .

In analyzing the arguments of Parham and the State Board, it is interesting to note that neither of these parties specifically defends the binding arbitration provision of the Procedure; the arguments merely assert the validity of the Procedure in general. The closest approach to a defense of the provision is a statement that "the arbitration panel has no authority whatsoever to make or enforce any decisions as to how the local school is to be operated." This merely evades, rather than answers, the School Board's contention that the arbitration provision permits "an outside

agency, in the form of an arbitration panel . . . to divest the local board of its essential function [of managing its teaching staff] by the substitution of [the panel's] judgment for that of the board."

This contention of the School Board presents the real question in the case, viz., whether the binding arbitration provision of the Procedure produces an unlawful delegation of power. . . .

There can be no doubt that a delegation of power is involved in the binding arbitration provision. Indeed, the very section of the Procedure which provides that an arbitration panel shall have authority to make a final and binding decision also states that the local school board "hereby delegates such authority to the Panel."

Whether, however, the arbitration provision results in an *unlawful* delegation of authority is a more difficult question. . . .

Although not involving binding arbitration provisions, *Howard v. School Board of Alleghany County*, 203 Va. 55, 122 S.E.2d 891 (1961), is pertinent to resolution of the present case. There, a state statute required the sale of school property if such disposition was favored by a majority of voters in a referendum. Ruling the statute invalid, we said that it was an "essential function" of a local school board's power of supervision, granted by what is now § 7 of Article VIII of the Constitution, "to determine whether a particular property is needed for school purposes and the manner in which it shall be used." The effect of the disputed statute, we stated, was "to divest the board of the exercise of that function and lodge it in the electorate," thus stripping the board "of any or all authority to exercise its judgment in the matter." 203 Va. at 58, 122 S.E.2d at 894. This is but another way of saying that the statute produced an unlawful delegation of power.

We believe the binding arbitration provision involved in the present case has the same effect as the offending statute in *Howard*, viz., to remove from a local school board and transfer to others a function essential and indispensable to the exercise of the power of supervision vested by § 7 of Article VIII. . . .

Equally clear, the function of *applying* local policies, rules, and regulations, adopted for the management of a teaching staff, is a function essential and indispensable to exercise of the power of supervision vested by § 7 of Article VIII. This power of supervision would be an empty one, indeed, if a local school board, once having adopted a valid policy, rule, or regulation, found itself powerless to enforce what it had promulgated.

. . .

We conclude, therefore, that the binding arbitration provision of the Procedure produces an unlawful delegation of power, violative of § 7 of Article VIII of the Constitution.

. . .

Reversed and final judgment.

Binding Arbitration Is Not an Illegal Delegation of School Board Power

— · — · — · — · — · —

City of Biddeford v. Biddeford Teachers Association

— · — · — · — · — ·

Supreme Judicial Court of Maine, 1973.
304 A.2d 387.

WEATHERBEE, Justice. These two complaints necessitate our first examination of the provisions of the Municipal Employees Labor Relations Law, 26 M.R.S.A. Chap. 9–A, which was enacted by the Maine Legislature in 1969. The complaints direct our attention only to the application of the statute to teachers in the public schools.

In the fall of 1970 the Board of Education of the City of Biddeford and the representatives of the Biddeford Teachers Association entered into negotiations in an attempt to effect a contract for the professional services of teachers in the Biddeford public schools for the school year 1971–1972. When the Board and the Association were unable to reach an agreement, the fact-finding procedures provided in section 965(3) were called into play

but they proved unsuccessful. Finally, in August of 1971 the parties resorted to the arbitration process found in section 965(4).
. . .

The purpose of the Municipal Public Employees Labor Relations Law is stated by 26 M.R.S.A. § 961 as follows:

It is declared to be the public policy of this State and it is the purpose of this chapter to promote the improvement of the relationship between public employers and their employees by providing a uniform basis for recognizing the right of public employees to join labor organizations of their own choosing and to be represented by such organizations in collective bargaining for terms and conditions of employment.

. . . The Act makes it the obligation of the public employer and the bargaining agent to meet and bargain collectively and provides a four-step procedure consisting of negotiation, mediation (when jointly requested), fact finding and arbitration. The parties are first obligated to negotiate in good faith concerning "wages, hours, working conditions and contract grievance arbitration" — with the exception —

[T]hat public employers of teachers shall meet and consult but not negotiate with respect to educational policies . . . .

Secondly, if the parties are unable to agree after negotiation they may jointly agree upon mediation procedures. Thirdly, if mediation procedures are omitted or are unsuccessful, either one or both may request fact-finding and the parties are then obligated to present their contending positions to the fact-finding board which will, after hearing, submit its findings to the parties. If a thirty-day period of further effort to resolve the controversy is unsuccessful either party may make the findings public. Fifteen more days are then allowed to permit a further good faith effort to resolve the controversy. Fourth, and lastly, if, after another ten days they have not agreed as to an arbitration procedure, either party may request in writing that their differences shall be arbitrated in accordance with the procedure described in subsection 4.

In brief, this procedure requires each party to choose an arbitrator and the two so chosen shall name a "neutral" arbitrator. The three arbitrators shall then proceed to hear the matter. If the subject of the controversy has been salaries, pensions or insurance, the arbitrator shall *recommend* terms of settlement which are advisory only and may make findings of fact. As to other matters in dispute the arbitrators shall make determinations which are binding upon the parties and "the parties will enter into an agreement or take whatever other action that may be appropriate to carry out and effectuate such binding determinations." The determinations are subject to review in accordance with M.R.C.P., Rule 80B but, in the absence of fraud, the arbitrators' decisions upon questions of fact are final.

The Act obviously represents a fresh approach to municipal public employee labor relations problems and enters an area as yet unexplored here. In the field of education, particularly, it appears to clash with traditional concepts of school control and management. As a result, members of the Board here—as several school boards in other jurisdictions have done—protest that if the members entered into the proposed contract, as the arbitration award has ordered them to do—they would be surrendering their authority as public officers to persons who are in no way responsible to the electorate.   . . .

While the present actions present many issues concerning various areas of the arbitrators' award, we must first consider the constitutionality of the Act in so far as it requires local school boards, at the request of the teaching employees, to submit to binding arbitration disputes arising both out of the making of the labor contract and out of later employment under the contract. Can the superintending school committees constitutionally delegate this authority to arbitrators? In requiring them to do so, can the Legislature constitutionally take away the authority which local officials had traditionally exercised and repose it in persons who compose ad hoc boards of arbitration? If so, has there

been such a valid delegation of authority here?   . . .

It appears that most of the cases holding that agreements to submit public employee labor disputes to binding arbitration are invalid attempts to delegate official responsibility come from states that had no legislation authorizing such agreements. On the other hand, serious concern over the problem is apparent in all the decisions and several of those often spoken of as favorable to the position urged here by the Association limit their holdings to grievance arbitration of contracts which municipalities have already entered into. It may be that the Rhode Island statute is the only one imposing upon the municipalities binding arbitration in the areas of both interest and grievance, without specific constitutional authorization, which has been finally upheld. We consider that decisions involving arbitration in essential industries in the private sector such as hospitals and public utilities give us little assistance as to this problem.

With scant solid precedent to guide us, we return to our own situation. We find that our Constitution gave the Legislature full responsibility over the subject matter of public schools and education and empowered it to make all reasonable laws in reference to schools and education for the "benefit of the people of this state." Opinions of the Justices, 68 Me. 582 (1876). Except for the areas where the Legislature has from time to time seen fit to impose its own requirements and except for the authority later given to the Commissioner of Education, the responsibilities for operating the public schools have remained in the local school boards.

The Legislature has now decided to take from the school boards the ultimate authority they have exercised in certain areas of school management—that is, as to "hours, and working conditions" and contract grievance arbitration—and to give it to ad hoc boards of arbitration.

It is settled beyond question that the Legislature may properly conclude that the purposes of its legislation may best be carried out through agents and that it may delegate to the agents a portion of its power to facilitate the functioning of the legislative program.

There can be no doubt but that the Legislature, which is the source of all municipal authority, *Squires v. Inhabitants of City of Augusta,* 155 Me. 151, 153 A.2d 80 (1959), has also the power to take back from municipal officers portions of the authority it has earlier given them.

It is clear that the Legislature has recognized that the maintenance of a satisfactory quality of public education requires harmonious relations between school officials and the teaching staffs and that disagreements inevitably arise during the carrying out of their respective responsibilities. The abrasive effect of the existence of unresolved grievances is one of the threats to harmonious relations which the Legislature considers should be removed.

The lawmakers have recognized that policy-making decisions should remain in the local officials, responsible to the public, and that while the citizens may properly be subjected to moral suasion as to such matters as wages and pensions, the ultimate determination of such matters with such heavy impact upon — and so limited by — municipal appropriations should be made by local officials.

The Legislature has apparently concluded, on the other hand, that experience has taught that certain aspects of this dynamic and complicated municipal employer-employee relationship no longer need remain subject to arbitrary decision by the employer and that in the area of working conditions and hours and of contract grievances the interests of the employees must in fairness be examined by impartial persons. The Legislature appears to believe that this much can be done without serious disruption of the balancing of operating costs against municipal appropriations.

We realize that in providing that the contract-making process itself (as it affects working conditions and hours) is subject to binding arbitration, our Legislature has moved into an area forbidden by many courts. The Legislature must have concluded that the benefits which are sought by the statute can never be achieved if an impasse occurs at the very beginning of the relationship. This conclusion is not unreasonable.

True, the statute does not contemplate the delegation of authority to public administrative boards or agencies but instead gives it to ad hoc panels whose memberships are not to be controlled by governmental action. Here we are of the opinion that the Legislature, mindful of the denial to municipal employees of such economic weapons as strikes and work stoppages which are available to employees in private employment, has sought to avoid the disruptive feelings of resentment and bitterness which may result if the governmental employee may look only to the government for redress of his grievances.

Where the ultimate arbiter of the dispute is a representative of one side of the dispute, adverse decisions will be hard to accept and the tendency toward alienation will be strong.

We consider that there is a rational reason for the Legislature's decision that its purposes would be best effectuated if the parties are left to choose their own arbitrators in the limited non-policy areas which are subject to arbitration.

NOTES

1. A union's standing to file grievance as well as substantive issues may be subject to reasonable debate and therefore may be submitted to arbitrator for resolution. *Mora Federation of Teachers, Local 1802 v. Independent School Dist. No. 332,* 352 N.W.2d 489 (Minn.App.1984).

2. A collective bargaining agreement providing that preference in filling a vacancy would be given to the employee with the greatest seniority, when qualifications of applicants were otherwise equal, is binding on a public school board. *Mahoning County*

Board of Mental Retardation and Developmental Disabilities v. Mahoning County TMR Education Association, 22 Ohio St. 3d 80, 488 N.E. 2d 872 (1986).

■■ SCOPE OF BARGAINING

Collective bargaining in the public sector encompasses three general categories: "(1) mandatory subjects of bargaining, (2) permissive subjects of bargaining, and (3) unlawful subjects of bargaining."[21] In states where collective bargaining is required, school boards must bargain in good faith to the point of impasse.[22] In states where statutes do not require school boards to bargain, and the matter is one of discretion or the state is governed by a "meet and confer" statute, the employer is under no duty to bargain at all.[23]

Mandatory bargaining subjects are by and large determined by experience gained in the private sector under the Taft-Hartley Act, which requires bargaining over "wages, hours, and other terms and conditions of employment."[24] Whether a subject is mandatory is at times unclear and often becomes a matter of litigation. Wages and hours may include considerations of salary schedules, overtime, cost-of-living increases, fringe benefits, vacations, holidays, sick leave, retirement benefits, and so on. A Connecticut court has held that teacher loads—defined as number of classes, preparation periods per week, and class sizes—are mandatory subjects of bargaining.[25]

The Supreme Court of Connecticut has held that a statute that provides for teacher evaluations to be "established by the state board of education and such additional performance criteria as the local or regional board of education may, by mutual agreement, establish" implies sufficient flexibility to make teacher evaluations a permissive rather than a mandatory subject of bargaining. A school board may therefore refuse to negotiate with teachers regarding evaluations.[26]

The Supreme Court of Michigan has ruled that early retirement benefits are not wages or salaries; rather, they are working conditions within the meaning of the Michigan school code. A local school board therefore has the authority to include retirement benefits in the collective bargaining agreement.[27]

Other issues that are not clearly mandatory nor permissive, but are negotiable, include elimination of a teacher work period and the replacement of that period with an additional classroom period;[28] a change in the number of class hours per day;[29] length of workday, performance of nonteaching duties (such as cleaning venetian blinds and washing windows), workloads, and teacher hours;[30] moving expenses;[31] tuition-free schooling for children of staff members who reside outside school district;[32] tuition reimbursement for teachers attending approved graduate courses;[33] annual salary adjustments;[34] pay for unused sick leave;[35] a sick leave bank providing for teachers' sharing of sick leave;[36] and in-service education, association rights, and disciplinary actions against employees.[37]

The rights of management have been broadly interpreted in some jurisdictions so as to limit the scope of negotiable items. Management retains the general right to organize and maintain an efficient work force.[38] "The rule that seems to emerge from reported cases is that the unilateral action of the employer in creating new jobs or in merging jobs already in existence is appropriate . . . [if such action is not done] . . . in an arbitrary or capricious manner."[39] Nonnegotiable management rights have been interpreted to include the "right to make changes in job duties, to create new job classifications, to eliminate jobs, and to combine jobs," so long as the action is taken to improve efficiency of operation and is in good faith.[40]

Nonnegotiable items, in some jurisdictions, have been held to include academic and personal freedom, assignment and transfer, extracurricular compensation (with certain exceptions), recall and reduction of personnel, dismissal procedures, binding arbitration of grievances, procedure for contract nonrenewal, frequency of grade cards, sabbatical leave, number of contract days, supplemental contracts, class size, recall of teachers,[41] imposition of a no-smoking ban,[42] and assignment of special duties during emergency situations.[43]

Courts in other jurisdictions, where bargaining is undertaken voluntarily by school boards, have held that teachers have a right to engage in "meaningful negotiations, and not be foreclosed from considerations touching on school policy as to class size, time allocations, and other factors influencing the quality of the schools."[44] "Meaningful negotiation" includes the right to execute a written agreement incorporating the terms and conditions agreed upon by both parties and the right to press grievances.

The following case, *Kenai*, provides substantial guidance regarding the extent of management rights and the corresponding determination of what is negotiable in school board and teacher bargaining. As this case indicates, while prior private and public sector precedents are important, in the final analysis the scope of collective bargaining in public schools is dependent on state statutory requirements.

Scope of Negotiations Is Essentially a Question for Legislative Guidance

— · — · — · — · — · —

Kenai Peninsula Borough School District v. Kenai Peninsula Education Association

— · — · — · — · — · —

Supreme Court of State of Alaska, 1977.
572 P.2d 416.

CONNOR, Justice. These cases present important questions of labor law and constitutional law concerning the collective bargaining requirements for teachers in the public schools.
. . .

To facilitate the understanding of our more detailed legal discussion later in this opinion, we will summarize at the outset the contentions of the parties. The statutes at issue in this litigation are AS 14.20.550 and .610, which provide:

> Sec. 14.20.550. *Negotiation with certificated employees.* Each city, borough and regional school board shall negotiate with its certificated employees in good faith on matters pertaining to their employment and the fulfillment of their professional duties. (§ 1 ch 18 SLA 1970; am § 3 ch 71 SLA 1972; am § 21 ch 124 SLA 1975).
>
> Sec. 14.20.610. *Legal responsibilities of boards.* Nothing in §§ 550–600 of this chapter may be construed as an abrogation or delegation of the legal responsibilities, powers, and duties of the school board including its right to make final decisions on policies. (§ 21 ch 18 SLA 1970).

. . . The school boards contend that the submission of educational policies to a good faith collective bargaining requirement would remove the final decisions on such matters from the boards, contrary to the intent of the legislature expressed in AS 14.20.610. The boards contend that to require bargaining on questions of educational policy would also contravene the Alaska Constitution, art. VII, § 1, which makes education the exclusive domain of the legislature. See *Macauley v. Hildebrand*, 491 P.2d 120 (Alaska 1971). Delegation of part of the decision-making power on educational policy to labor unions is unconstitutional, they urge, because the union is a private organization, unaccountable to the public. The union can use the power for its own ends, and is under no duty to foster educational policies which are in the general public interest.

The unions argue that such delegation is perfectly proper, and that there is no delegation of decision-making power inherent in a labor negotiations requirement. They further argue that they represent professional employees, and that their participation in good faith collective bargaining labor negotiations is an attempt by the legislature to provide professional advice to school boards on the management of the schools. . . .

If we were to look to the law concerning bargaining between labor unions and private employers, we would conclude that the scope of negotiable issues is broad. The law relating to the private sector has always contained, and still does contain, uncertainties. But the general trend has been to require that employers bargain in good faith on a wide range of items with respect to wages, hours, and other conditions of employment, without regard to whether the employers consider the items bargained for to be within the prerogatives of management. . . .

When we turn to employment in the public sector, and particularly in education, the question of what is properly bargainable is thrown into more doubt. If teachers' unions are permitted to bargain on matters of educational policy, it is conceivable that through successive contracts the autonomy of the school boards could be severely eroded, and the effective control of educational policy shifted from the school boards to the teachers' unions. Such a result could threaten the ability of elective government officials and appointive officers subject to their authority, in this case the school boards and administrators, to perform their functions in the broad public interest. . . .

The school boards initially argue that to make matters of school operation and educational policy subject to collective bargaining amounts to an unconstitutional delegation of governmental power to the unions.

. . . [C]ourts in an earlier era often held laws unconstitutional on the ground that they delegated legislative power to private persons or groups. . . .

Furthermore, the statute merely requires the school board to negotiate with the union. It does not require the board to accept any particular proposal the union might offer. It does not require, and probably does not permit, the board to delegate to the union the sole power to make any decision. Therefore, cited cases invalidating outright grants of governmental power to private groups . . . are not apposite.

The cases in other states rejecting the argument that collective bargaining with teachers' unions is an unconstitutional delegation of power, all involve statutes which fairly narrowly constrict either the scope of bargainable issues, or the school boards' duty to accede to union proposals, or both. . . . In this opinion, we similarly construe the Alaska statute. A statute defining the scope of collective bargaining as broadly as the union would have us do, might well present a more troubling constitutional question. But we find no constitutional infirmity in AS 14.20.550 and .610. The delegation of power problem still bears upon our task of statutory interpretation, however, for in interpreting the relevant statutes we will not readily assume that the legislature intended to divest the school boards of their power to determine matters of educational policy and school system management. . . .

Put another way, a matter is more susceptible to bargaining the more it deals with the economic interests of employees and the less it concerns professional goals and methods. Bargaining over the latter topics presents particular problems because there is less likely to be any politically organized interest group other than the union concerned with these issues. The salaries of public employees have a direct financial effect on the taxpayers; on the other hand, a question such as teacher evaluation of administrators is unlikely to have any impact sufficiently direct to be discernible by laymen. Furthermore, it is such an abstract and abstruse subject that it is unlikely that any appreciable portion of the public will either understand it or care greatly about it. In such circumstances, the risk that effective power over the governmental decision will come to rest with the union is significantly greater. Moreover, it is more likely that there will be disagreements among union members on questions of this nature than on "bread and butter" issues; the risk that minority viewpoints within the union will not be meaningfully represented in the bargaining is a real one. . . .

We will now consider the Alaska situation in more detail. At the outset it appears to us that questions concerning salaries, the number of hours to be worked, and amount of leave time are all so closely connected with the economic well-being of the individual teacher that they must be held negotiable under our statutes. The troubling question is what other items are bargainable.

The various trial courts in these cases considered such items as (1) relief from non-professional chores, (2) elementary planning time, (3) para-professional tutors, (4) teacher specialist, (5) teacher's aides, (6) class size, (7) pupil-teacher ratio, (8) a teacher ombudsman, (9) teacher evaluation of administrators, (10) school calendar, (11) selection of instructional materials, (12) the use of secondary department heads, (13) secondary teacher preparation and planning time, and (14) teacher representation on school board advisory committees.

The testimony adduced in the trial courts does not provide us with much enlightenment as to why any of these items should fall on one side of the line or another. Realistically the two areas, i.e., (1) educational policy and (2) matters pertaining to employment and professional duties, merge into and blend with each other at many points. Logically and semantically it is nearly impossible to assign specific items to one category and not the other. . . . We are confronted, then, with a situation in which the legislature has not spoken with clarity and concerning which we possess no expertise. We can only conclude that salaries, fringe benefits, the number of hours worked, and the amount of leave time are negotiable . . . we conclude that the other specific items . . . are, under the existing statutory language, non-negotiable.

It would be helpful if the legislature, through future enactments, provided more specific guidance on a number of the items which the unions seek to negotiate. Lacking that guidance, however, we cannot confidently say that the legislature intended any of these items to be bargainable. We cannot, therefore, read the statutes expansively as to the scope of what is negotiable.

As to matters which affect educational policy and are, therefore, not negotiable, we believe that there is nevertheless implicit in our statutes the intention that the school boards meet and confer with the unions. It is desirable that the boards consider teacher proposals on such questions. This will encourage teachers to give the boards the benefit of their expertise, and to make their positions known for the board's use in establishing educational policy. . . .

Affirmed in part, reversed in part.

NOTES

1. Agreement by a school board to confine itself in hiring to those applicants within the system is beyond the scope of bargaining and is therefore unenforceable. *Board of Education of North Bergen Township v. North Bergen Federation of Teachers*, 141 N.J.Super. 97, 357 A.2d 302 (App. Div. 1976).

2. Early retirement benefits are not salaries; rather, they are "working conditions" within the meaning of the school code. Thus a board of education has the authority to provide for such benefits in its collective bargaining agreement with the teachers' association. In this case, the Attorney General had ruled that a school district could not agree in a collective bargaining agreement to provide supplemental retirement benefits beyond those established by statute for the public school retirement system. In disagreeing with the Attorney General, the court pointed out that the collective bargaining statute had authorized inclusion of early retirement benefits by providing for "working conditions . . . " and "other related benefits of an economic nature . . . ." The court said that the statutory "expression of 'other related benefits of an economic nature' refutes appel-

lant's claim that 'working conditions' is a narrowly defined term meaning only physical conditions of the workplace. Physical conditions of the workplace are not 'benefits of an economic nature,' and we, therefore, conclude that 'other working conditions' was intended to be more liberally interpreted than the noneconomic physical conditions of the workplace."

3. *Jurva v. Attorney General of State of Michigan,* 419 Mich. 209, 351 N.W. 2d 813 (1984).

◼ COLLECTIVE AND INDIVIDUAL RIGHTS

Public employee collective bargaining, while authorized and governed by statute, is, to a large degree, a creature of precedents arising from the common law of the courts and quasi-judicial tribunals. Too, the respective rights and powers in public collective bargaining are circumscribed by constitutional constraints at both the state and federal levels. Because statutes cannot prescribe each and every element and contingency created by the complexities of the bargaining process, judicial and administrative law judgments are required to maintain a smoothly functioning mechanism. The rights of the parties to the bargaining process are founded, more or less, in a utilitarian attitude of pragmatic understandings between management, union, and employee. Such understandings have produced what are considered to be established acceptable boundaries of bargaining rights.

Bargaining Rights

Rights of the bargaining process delineate the extent of management, union and employee powers, the acceptable retention of management power, the necessary reach of union prerogative, and the residual and pervasive power of the individual.

Management Rights

Management has the general right to manage school operations as empowered by statute, but is restricted by applicable law that divests certain of those rights in favor of the union or the employee. Even though the school board's rights are not expressly limited by statute, it is nevertheless bound by common law to bargain reasonably, in good faith and without arbitrariness or capriciousness, or with discriminatory intent and motive.[45]

Yet, because school board rights are primarily predicated on applicable state statutes, management rights vary widely from state to state. In the absence of statutorily defined management rights, it is assumed that public sector boards have certain inherent rights that are also found in the private sector as recognized by arbitration decisions.[46]

Union Rights

Union rights, as separate from employee rights, include the rights to represent employees, to bargain at the table, to enforce the contract, to grieve, to arbitrate, and, importantly, to union security.[47]

Employee Rights

Employees have rights to organize freely,[48] engage in meaningful negotiations, press grievances, and execute written agreements. The boundaries of employees' rights are not precisely coterminus with union rights and may be more extensive. Employees, as individuals, have the rights and freedoms as guaranteed by the state and federal constitutions.

◼ CONSTITUTIONAL RIGHTS OF INDIVIDUALS

Public school employees do not have a right to bargain collectively in all states; but, as individuals, have a right to join unions.[49] A state law forbidding public employees from joining unions violates the First and Fourteenth Amendments of the U.S. Constitution. Discrimination against public employees because of union activity may also violate the Civil Rights Act of 1871, as well as the First and Fourteenth Amendments.[50] As mentioned earlier in this chapter, the U.S. Court of Appeals has said:

> The guarantee of the 'right of assembly' protects more than the 'right to attend a meeting; it includes the right to express one's attitudes or philosophies by membership in a group or by affiliation with it or by other lawful means . . . .'

Bargaining agreements of public agencies have the potential of overreaching the legitimate scope of negotiations and encroaching on the constitutional rights of individuals.

The act of filing a grievance by a teacher does not elevate private speech[51] to the constitutionally protected level of public opinion, as defined by *Connick v. Myers*.[52] The filing of a grievance against a school board does not invoke a First-Amendment right to petition government for redress of grievances. A grievance is not a speech activity in the sense that it is of political or "public concern."[53]

The requirement of due process for a discharged employee is satisfied by the offer of arbitration by a school board. The U.S. Court of Appeals, Third Circuit, has held that to provide the employee with the alternative of arbitration fulfills notice and the opportunity for a hearing as envisaged under due process.[54] If a labor dispute results in an illegal strike and the board of education responds by reducing teacher pay for the days they missed while on strike, no substantive property interest is implicated.[55] Where teachers claimed that a pay reduction violated their employment contract, the court concluded that an amended school calendar with a corresponding reduction in teachers' salaries were not violative of due process, because the teachers had participated in an unlawful work stoppage.[56]

Where a school district dismissed a nontenured teacher, and gave as reasons generally poor performance and personality conflicts, the court found that evidence linked both deficiencies to the teacher's union activities.[57] The fact that the dismissal was caused by union activities violated the teacher's First-Amendment rights.[58]

At times the constitutional rights of the individual employee may come in conflict with bargaining rights of the union. Such conflict has occurred where unions have sought security of the agency shop.[59] The agency shop is a provision in the contract between the school board and the union that permits the union to charge a fee to all employees, regardless of whether they are union members. Such compulsory payment has been challenged by nonunion employees as a violation of First Amendment rights of free speech and association. In the leading case on the issue, the U.S. Supreme Court has held that employees can be charged dues or assessments only for union expenditures incurred in activities that are not politically or ideologically objectionable to the employee.[60] The Supreme Court reasoned that single representation promotes peaceful labor relations through strengthening exclusive union representation. It theorized that the stability gained by having one strong bargaining agent for employees enhances labor by reducing the potential of internal turmoil and assists management by having some assurance of continuity in labor's representation.[61] The Supreme Court's position has been that agency shop and union shop agreements are justified because of the government's interest in industrial peace.[62] Yet, the Supreme Court will not go so far as to require an employee to join a union or contribute to a union if the dues paid to the union will be used for political or ideological purposes that are objectionable to the employee. Here the constitutional rights of the individual—freedom of expression, association, belief, and conscience—supersede the interest of the government in advancing harmony with the labor unions.[63]

The Supreme Court has observed that a forced exaction of fees for union activities, if used to "subsidize the propagation of political or ideological views" to which the employee objects, violates the basic principles of freedom of belief defended by Madison in his *Memorial and Remonstrance:* "[T]he tyrannical character of forcing an individual to contribute even 'three pence' for the 'propagation of opinions which he disbelieves.'"[64]

Agency Shop Does Not Violate Nonunion Employees' Constitutional Rights unless Fees Are Used to Support Objectionable Political and Ideological Views

— — — · — · — · — — —

Abood v. Detroit Board of Education

— — — · — · — · — — —

Supreme Court of the United States, 1977.
431 U.S. 209, 97 S.Ct. 1782.

Mr. Justice STEWART delivered the opinion of the Court. The State of Michigan has enacted legislation authorizing a system for union representation of local governmental employees. A union and a local government employer are specifically permitted to agree to an "agency shop" arrangement, whereby every employee represented by a union—even though not a union member—must pay to the union, as a condition of employment, a service fee equal in amount to union dues. The issue before us is whether this arrangement violates the constitutional rights of government employees who object to public sector unions as such or to various union activities financed by the compulsory service fees. . . .

On November 7, 1969—more than two months before the agency-shop clause was to become effective—Christine Warczak and a number of other named teachers filed a class action in a state court, naming as defendants the Board, the Union, and several Union officials. Their complaint, as amended, alleged that they were unwilling or had refused to pay dues and that they opposed collective bargaining in the public sector. . . .

Consideration of the question whether an agency shop provision in a collective-bargaining agreement covering governmental employees is, as such, constitutionally valid must begin with two cases in this Court that on their face go far towards resolving the issue. The cases are *Railway Employes' Department v. Hanson* . . . and *International Association of Machinists v. Street,* 367 U.S. 740, 81 S.Ct. 1784, 6 L.Ed.2d 1141.

In the *Hanson* case a group of railroad employees brought an action in a Nebraska court to enjoin enforcement of a union-shop agreement. The challenged clause was authorized, and indeed shielded from any attempt by a State to prohibit it, by the Railway Labor Act, 45 U.S.C.A. § 152, Eleventh. . . .

The record in *Hanson* contained no evidence that union dues were used to force ideological conformity or otherwise to impair the free expression of employees, and the Court noted that "[i]f 'assessments' are in fact imposed for purposes not germane to collective bargaining, a different problem would be presented." Id., at 235, 76 S.Ct., at 720. (footnote omitted). But the Court squarely held that "the requirement for financial support of the collective-bargaining agency by all who receive the benefits of its work . . . does not violate . . . the First Amendment." Id., at 238, 76 S.Ct., at 721.

The Court faced a similar question several years later in the *Street* case, which also involved a challenge to the constitutionality of a union shop authorized by the Railway Labor Act. In *Street,* however, the record contained findings that the union treasury to which all employees were required to contribute had been used "to finance the campaigns of candidates for federal and state offices whom [the plaintiffs] opposed, and to promote the propagation of political and economic doctrines, concepts and ideologies with which [they] disagreed." 367 U.S., at 744, 81 S.Ct., at 1787.

The Court recognized that these findings presented constitutional "questions of the utmost gravity" not decided in *Hanson,* id., at 749, 81 S.Ct., at 1789, and therefore considered whether the Act could fairly be construed to avoid these constitutional issues. Id., at 749–750, 81 S.Ct., at 1789–90. The Court concluded that the Act could be so construed, since only expenditures related to the union's functions in negotiating and administering the collective bargaining agreement and adjusting grievances and disputes fell within "the reasons . . . accepted by Congress why authority to make union-shop agreements was justified," id., at 768, 81 S.Ct. at

1800. The Court rule, therefore, that the use of compulsory union dues for political purposes violated the Act itself. Nonetheless, it found that an injunction against enforcement of the union-shop agreement as such was impermissible under *Hanson*, and remanded the case to the Supreme Court of Georgia so that a more limited remedy could be devised.

. . . A union-shop arrangement has been thought to distribute fairly the cost of these activities among those who benefit, and it counteracts the incentive that employees might otherwise have to become "free riders"—to refuse to contribute to the union while obtaining benefits of union representation that necessarily accrue to all employees. . . .

To compel employees financially to support their collective bargaining representative has an impact upon their First Amendment interests. An employee may very well have ideological objections to a wide variety of activities undertaken by the union in its role as exclusive representative. His moral or religious views about the desirability of abortion may not square with the union's policy in negotiating a medical benefits plan. One individual might disagree with a union policy of negotiating limits on the right to strike, believing that to be the road to serfdom for the working class, while another might have economic or political objections to unionism itself. An employee might object to the union's wage policy because it violates guidelines designed to limit inflation, or might object to the union's seeking a clause in the collective-bargaining agreement proscribing racial discrimination. The examples could be multiplied. To be required to help finance the union as a collective-bargaining agent might well be thought, therefore, to interfere in some way with an employee's freedom to associate for the advancement of ideas, or to refrain from doing so, as he sees fit. But the judgment clearly made in *Hanson* and *Street* is that such interference as exists is constitutionally justified by the legislative assessment of the important contribution of the union shop to the system of labor relations established by Congress. "The furtherance of the common cause leaves some leeway for the leadership of the group. As long as they act to promote the cause which justified bringing the group together, the individual cannot withdraw his financial support merely because he disagrees with the group's strategy. If that were allowed, we would be reversing the *Hanson* case, *sub silentio*." . . .

The governmental interests advanced by the agency shop provision in the Michigan statute are much the same as those promoted by similar provisions in federal labor law. The confusion and conflict that could arise if rival teachers' unions, holding quite different views as to the proper class hours, class sizes, holidays, tenure provisions, and grievance procedures, each sought to obtain the employer's agreement are no different in kind from the evils that the exclusivity rule in the Railway Labor Act was designed to avoid. . . . The desirability of labor peace is no less important in the public sector, nor is the risk of "free riders" any smaller. . . .

While recognizing the apparent precedential weight of the *Hanson* and *Street* cases, the appellants advance two reasons why those decisions should not control decision of the present case. First, the appellants note that it is *government* employment that is involved here, thus directly implicating constitutional guarantees, in contrast to the private employment that was the subject of the *Hanson* and *Street* decisions. Second, the appellants say that in the public sector collective bargaining itself is inherently "political," and that to require them to give financial support to it is to require the "ideological conformity" that the Court expressly found absent in the *Hanson* case. 351 U.S., at 238, 76 S.Ct., at 721. We find neither argument persuasive. . . .

The distinctive nature of public-sector bargaining has led to widespread discussion about the extent to which the law governing labor relations in the private sector provides an appropriate model. To take but one example, there has been considerable debate about the desirability of prohibiting public employee unions from striking, a step that the State of Michigan itself has taken, Mich. Comp.Laws § 423.202. But although Michigan has not adopted the federal model of labor relations in every respect, it has determined that labor stability will be served by a system of exclusive representation and the permissive use of an agency shop in public employment. As already stated, there can be no principled basis for according that decision less weight in the constitutional balance than was given in *Hanson* to the congressional judgment reflected in the Railway Labor Act. The only remaining constitutional inquiry evoked by the appellants' argument, therefore, is whether a public employee has a weightier First Amendment interest than a private employee in not being compelled to contribute to the costs of exclusive union representation. We think he does not.

Public employees are not basically different from private employees; on the whole, they have the same sort of skills, the same needs, and seek the same advantages. "The uniqueness of public employment is *not in the employees* nor in the work performed; the uniqueness is in the special character of the employer." . . . The very real differences between exclusive agent collective bargaining in the public and private sectors are not such as to work any greater infringement upon the First Amendment interests of public employees. A public employee who believes that a union representing him is urging a course that is unwise as a matter of public policy is not barred from expressing his viewpoint. Besides voting in accordance with his convictions, every public employee is largely free to express his views, in public or private orally or in writing. With some exceptions not pertinent here, public employees are free to participate in the full range of political activities open to other citizens. Indeed, just this Term we have held that the First and Fourteenth Amendments protect the right of a public school teacher to oppose, at a public school board meeting, a position advanced by the teacher's union. . . . In so ruling we recognized that the principle of exclusivity cannot constitutionally be used to muzzle a public employee who, like any other citizen, might wish to express his view about governmental decisions concerning labor relations, id., 97 S.Ct. at 426.

There can be no quarrel with the truism that because public employee unions attempt to influence governmental policy-making, their activities—and the views of members who disagree with them—may be properly termed political. But that characterization does not raise the ideas and beliefs of public employees onto a higher plane than the ideas and beliefs of private employees. It is no doubt true that a central purpose of the First Amendment "was to protect the free discussion of governmental affairs." . . . But our cases have never suggested that expression about philosophical social, artistic, economic, literary, or ethical matters—to take a nonexhaustive list of labels—is not entitled to full First Amendment protection. Union members in both the public and private sector may find that a variety of union activities conflict with their beliefs. . . . Nothing in the First Amendment or our cases discussing its meaning makes the question whether the adjective "political" can properly be attached to those beliefs of the critical constitutional inquiry.

The differences between public and private sector collective bargaining simply do not translate into differences in First Amendment rights. Even those commentators most acutely aware of the distinctive nature of public-sector bargaining and most seriously concerned with its policy implications agree that "[t]he union security issue in the public sector . . . is fundamentally the same issue . . . as in the private sector. . . . No special dimension results from the fact that a union represents public rather than private employees." . . . We conclude that the Michigan Court of Appeals was correct in viewing this Court's decisions in *Hanson* and *Street* as controlling in the present case insofar as the service charges are applied to collective bargaining, contract administration, and grievance adjustment purposes.

. . . Our decisions establish with unmistakable clarity that the freedom of an individual to associate for the purpose of advancing beliefs and ideas is protected by the First and Fourteenth Amendments. . . . Equally clear is the proposition that a government may not require an individual to relinquish rights guaranteed him by the First Amendment as a condition of public employment. . . . The appellants argue that they fall within the protection of these cases because they have been prohibited not from actively associating, but rather from refusing to associate. They specifically argue that they may constitutionally prevent the Union's spending a part of their required service fees to contribute to political candidates and to express political views unrelated to its duties as exclusive bargaining representative. We have concluded that this argument is a meritorious one.

One of the principles underlying the Court's decision in *Buckley v. Valeo,* 424 U.S. 1, 96 S.Ct. 612, 46 L.Ed.2d 659, was that contributing to an organization for the purpose of spreading a political message is protected by the First Amendment. Because "[m]aking a contribution . . . enables like-minded persons to pool their resources in furtherance of common political goals," id., at 22, 96 S.Ct. at 636, the Court reasoned that limitations upon the freedom to contribute "implicate fundamental First Amendment interests," id., at 23, 96 S.Ct. at 636.

The fact that the appellants are compelled to make, rather than prohibited from making, contributions for political purposes works no less an infringement of their constitutional rights. For at the heart of the First Amendment is the notion that an individual should be free to believe as he will, and that in a free society one's beliefs should be shaped by his mind and his conscience rather than coerced by the State. . . . They are no less applicable to the case at bar, and they thus prohibit the appellees from requiring any of the appellants to contribute to the support of an ideological cause he may oppose as a condition of holding a job as a public school teacher.

We do not hold that a union cannot constitutionally spend funds for the expression of political views, on behalf of political candidates, or towards the advancement of other ideological causes not germane to its duties as collective bargaining representative. Rather, the Constitution requires only that such expenditures be financed from charges, dues, or assessments paid by employees who do not object to advancing those ideas and who are not coerced into doing so against

their will by the threat of loss of governmental employment.

There will, of course, be difficult problems in drawing lines between collective bargaining activities, for which contributions may be compelled, and ideological activities unrelated to collective bargaining, for which such compulsion is prohibited. . . . All that we decide is that the general allegations in the complaint, if proven, establish a cause of action under the First and Fourteenth Amendments. . . .

The judgment is vacated, and the case is remanded for further proceedings not inconsistent with this opinion.

It is so ordered.

NOTES

1. An agency shop fee or a "fair share fee" provided for in statute does not deny an individual teacher due process. In a case, decided by the Minnesota Supreme Court, the primary question was whether the fair share statute was constitutional since it did not provide for a hearing for individual nonunion teachers before imposition of the fair share fee. The court concluded that the governmental interest in securing the financial stability of the exclusive union representation was sufficiently strong to override the individual's interest in obtaining a prior determination of the fee's validity. *Robbinsdale Education Association v. Robbinsdale Federation of Teachers Local 872,* 307 Minn. 96, 239 N.W.2d 437 (1976), *vacated* and *remanded* 429 U.S. 880, 97 S.Ct. 225 (1976) *original decision reinstated* 316 N.W.2d 551 (1982).

2. An agency shop provision in a contract was held invalid in face of a statute that granted public employees the right to voluntarily join, form, and participate in organizations of their own choosing. The court found that the statute assured the "right not to join," and the forced payment of dues or their equivalent "is tantamount to coercion or, at the very least, toward participation" in the labor organization as expressly forbidden by statute. *Churchill v. S.A.D. No. 49 Teachers Association,* 380 A.2d 186 (Me.1977).

3. The United States Supreme Court has upheld a collective bargaining agreement between a board of education and a teacher union giving the union exclusive access to the interschool mail system and teacher mailboxes of the school system. Plaintiffs, a competing union, had claimed that the preferential access to the internal mail system violated the First Amendment and the Equal Protection Clause of the Fourteenth Amendment. With regard to the First Amendment, the Court pointed out that equivalent access to all parts of a school building is not guaranteed. "Nowhere [have we] suggested that students, teachers, or anyone else has an absolute constitutional right to use all parts of a school building or its immediate environs for. . . . unlimited expressive purposes." See *Grayned v. City of Rockford,* 408 U.S. 104, 92 S.Ct. 2294 (1972). According to the Court, persons do not have the right of access to all types of public property; access depends on the character of the property at issue. The Court delineated three types of public property: (1) streets and parks are types of public property that have "Immemorially been held in trust for public use for communication and assembly"; (2) facilities and meeting places where open forums have traditionally existed as on a university, *Widmar v. Vincent,* 454 U.S. 263, 102 S.Ct. 269 (1981); and (3) public property that has not traditionally been an open forum for public communication. Public school mail facilities fall into this third category. School officials may decide what type of selective access will be given to such facilities. The fact that school mail facilities had been opened to such groups as the Girl Scouts and Boys Clubs does not make them an open forum; instead, the Court said that such facilities remain a "limited" public forum that can be regulated by the school board. Thus, the incumbent union may be allowed access while another union is denied. *Perry Education Association v. Perry Local Educators' Association,* 460 U.S. 37, 103 S.Ct. 948 (1983).

Union Procedure Held Inadequate to Assure Fee Collection from Nonunion Employees Would Not Be Used for Impermissible Purposes

Chicago Teachers Union, Local No. 1, AFL-CIO v. Hudson

Supreme Court of the United States, 1986.
475 U.S. 292, 106 S.Ct. 1066.

Justice STEVENS delivered the opinion of the Court. In *Abood v. Detroit Board of Education,* 431 U.S. 209, 97 S.Ct. 1782, 52 L.Ed.2d 261 (1977), "we found no constitutional barrier to an agency shop agreement between a municipality and a teacher's union insofar as the agreement required every employee in the unit to pay a service fee to defray the costs of collective bargaining, contract administration, and grievance adjustment. The union, however, could not, consistently with the Constitution, collect from dissenting employees any sums for the support of ideological causes not germane to its duties as collective-bargaining agent." *Ellis v. Railway Clerks,* 466 U.S. 435, 447, 104 S.Ct. 1883, 1892, 80 L.Ed.2d 428 (1984). The *Ellis* case was primarily concerned with the need "to define the line between union expenditures that all employees must help defray and those that are not sufficiently related to collective bargaining to justify their being imposed on dissenters." In contrast, this case concerns the constitutionality of the procedure adopted by the Chicago Teachers Union, with the approval of the Chicago Board of Education, to draw that necessary line and to respond to nonmembers' objections to the manner in which it was drawn.

The Chicago Teachers Union has acted as the exclusive collective-bargaining representative of the Board's educational employees continuously since 1967. Approximately 95% of the 27,500 employees in the bargaining unit are members of the Union. Until December 1982, the Union members' dues financed the entire cost of the Union's collective bargaining and contract administration. Nonmembers received the benefits of the Union's representation without making any financial contribution to its cost.

In an attempt to solve this "free rider" problem, the Union made several proposals for a "fair share fee" clause in the labor contract. Because the Illinois School Code did not expressly authorize such a provision, the Board rejected these proposals until the Illinois General Assembly amended the School Code in 1981. In the following year, the Chicago Teachers Union and the Chicago Board of Education entered into an agreement requiring the Board to deduct "proportionate share payments" from the paychecks of nonmembers. The new contractual provision authorized the Union to specify the amount of the payment; it stipulated that the amount could not exceed the members' dues. The contractual provision also required the Union to indemnify the Board for all action taken to implement the new provision.

For the 1982–83 school year, the Union determined that the "proportionate share" assessed on nonmembers was 95% of union dues. At that time, the union dues were $17.35 per month for teachers and $12.15 per month for other covered employees; the corresponding deduction from the nonmembers' checks thus amounted to $16.48 and $11.54 for each of the 10 months that dues were payable.

Union officials computed the 95% fee on the basis of the Union's financial records for the fiscal year ending on June 30, 1982. They identified expenditures unrelated to collective bargaining and contract administration (which they estimated as $188,549.82). They divided this amount by the Union's income for the year ($4,103,701.58) to produce a percentage of 4.6%; the figure was then rounded off to 5% to provide a "cushion" to cover any inadvertent errors.

The Union also established a procedure for considering objections by nonmembers. Before the deduction was made, the nonmember could not raise any objection. After the deduction was made, a nonmember could object to the "proportionate share" figure by writing to the Union President within 30 days after the first payroll deduction. The objection then

would meet a three-stage procedure. First, the Union's Executive Committee would consider the objection and notify the objector within 30 days of its decision. Second, if the objector disagreed with that decision and appealed within another 30 days, the Union's Executive Board would consider the objection. Third, if the objector continued to protest after the Executive Board decision, the Union President would select an arbitrator from a list maintained by the Illinois Board of Education. The Union would pay for the arbitration, and, if there were multiple objections, they could be consolidated. If an objection was sustained at any stage of the procedure, the remedy would be an immediate reduction in the amount of future deductions for all nonmembers and a rebate for the objector.

In October 1982, the Union formally requested the Board to begin making deductions and advised it that a hearing procedure had been established for nonmembers' objections. The Board accepted the Union's 95% determination without questioning its method of calculation and without asking to review any of the records supporting it. The Board began to deduct the fee from the paychecks of nonmembers in December 1982. The Board did not provide the nonmembers with any explanation of the calculation, or of the Union's procedures. The Union did undertake certain informational efforts. It asked its member delegates at all schools to distribute flyers, display posters, inform nonmembers of the deductions, and invite nonmembers to join the Union with an amnesty for past fines. It also described the deduction and the protest procedures in the December issue of the Union newspaper, which was distributed to nonmembers.

Three nonmembers—Annie Lee Hudson, K. Celeste Campbell, and Walter Sherrill—sent identical letters of protest to the Union stating that they believed the Union was using part of their salary for purposes unrelated to collective bargaining and demanding that the deduction be reduced. A fourth nonmember—Beverly Underwood—objected to any deduction from her paycheck. The Union's response to each of the four briefly explained how the proportionate share fee had been calculated, described the objection procedure, enclosed a copy of the Union Implementation Plan, and concluded with the advice that "any objection you may file" would be processed in compliance with that procedure. None of the letters was referred to the Executive Committee. Only Hudson wrote a second letter; her request for detailed financial information was answered with an invitation to make an appointment for an "informational conference" at the Union's office, at which she could review the Union's financial records. The four nonmembers made no further effort to invoke the Union procedures; instead, they challenged the new procedure in court.

In March 1983, the four nonmembers, joined by three other nonmembers who had not sent any letters, filed suit in Federal District Court, naming as defendants, the Union, its officials, the Board, and the Board members. They objected to the Union procedure for three principal reasons: it violated their First Amendment rights to freedom of expression and association; it violated their Fourteenth Amendment due process rights; and it permitted the use of their proportionate shares for impermissible purposes. . . .

The question presented in this case is whether the procedure used by the Chicago Teachers Union and approved by the Chicago Board of Education adequately protects the basic distinction drawn in *Abood*. "[T]he objective must be to devise a way of preventing compulsory subsidization of ideological activity by employees who object thereto without restricting the Union's ability to require every employee to contribute to the cost of collective-bargaining activities." *Abood*, 431 U.S., at 237, 97 S.Ct., at 1800.

Procedural safeguards are necessary to achieve this objective for two reasons. First, although the government interest in labor peace is strong enough to support an "agency shop" notwithstanding its limited infringement on nonunion employees' constitutional rights, the fact that those rights are protected by the First Amendment requires that the procedure be carefully tailored to minimize the infringement. Second, the non-union employee—the individual whose First Amendment rights are being affected—must have a fair opportunity to identify the impact of the governmental action on his interests and to assert a meritorious First Amendment claim.

In *Ellis v. Railway Clerks*, 466 U.S. 435, 443, 104 S.Ct. 1883, 1889, 80 L.Ed.2d 428 (1984), we determined that, under the Railway Labor Act, a "pure rebate approach is inadequate." We explained that, under such an approach, in which the union refunds to the nonunion employee any money to which the union was not entitled, "the union obtains an involuntary loan for purposes to which the employee objects." We noted the possibility of "readily available alternatives, such as advance reduction of dues and/or interest-bearing escrow accounts," but, for purposes of that case, it was sufficient to strike down the rebate procedure.

In this case, we must determine whether the challenged Chicago Teachers Union procedure survives First Amendment scrutiny, either because the procedure upheld by the District Court was constitutionally sufficient, or because the subsequent adoption of an escrow arrangement cured any constitutional defect. We consider these questions in turn.

The procedure that was initially adopted by the Union and considered by the District Court contained three fundamental flaws. First, as in *Ellis*, a remedy which merely offers dissenters the possibility of a rebate does not avoid the risk that dissenters' funds may be used temporarily for an improper purpose. "[T]he Union should not be permitted to exact a service fee from nonmembers without first establishing a procedure which will avoid the risk that their funds will be used, even temporarily, to finance ideological activities unrelated to collective bargaining." *Abood*, 431 U.S., at 244, 97 S.Ct., at 1804 (concurring opinion). The amount at stake for each individual dissenter does not diminish this concern. For, whatever the amount, the quality of respondents' interest in not being compelled to subsidize the propagation of political or ideological views that they oppose is clear. In *Abood*, we emphasized this point by quoting the comments of Thomas Jefferson and

James Madison about the tyrannical character of forcing an individual to contribute even "three pence" for the "propagation of opinions which he disbelieves." A forced exaction followed by a rebate equal to the amount improperly expended is thus not a permissible response to the nonunion employees' objections.

Second, the "advance reduction of dues" was inadequate because it provided nonmembers with inadequate information about the basis for the proportionate share. In *Abood*, we reiterated that the nonunion employee has the burden of raising an objection, but that the union retains the burden of proof: " 'Since the unions possess the facts and records from which the proportion of political to total union expenditures can reasonably be calculated, basic considerations of fairness compel that they, not the individual employees, bear the burden of proving such proportion.'" *Abood*, 431 U.S., at 239–240, n. 40, 97 S.Ct., at 1801–1802, n. 40,. . . . Basic considerations of fairness, as well as concern for the First Amendment rights at stake, also dictate that the potential objectors be given sufficient information to gauge the propriety of the union's fee. Leaving the nonunion employees in the dark about the source of the figure for the agency fee—and requiring them to object in order to receive information—does not adequately protect the careful distinctions drawn in *Abood*.

In this case, the original information given to the nonunion employees was inadequate. Instead of identifying the expenditures for collective bargaining and contract administration that had been provided for the benefit of nonmembers as well as members—and for which nonmembers as well as members can fairly be charged a fee—the Union identified the amount that it admittedly had expended for purposes that did not benefit dissenting nonmembers. An acknowledgment that nonmembers would not be required to pay any part of 5% of the Union's total annual expenditures was not an adequate disclosure of the reasons why they were required to pay their share of 95%.

Finally, the original Union procedure was also defective because it did not provide for a reasonably prompt decision by an impartial decisionmaker. Although we have not so specified in the past, we now conclude that such a requirement is necessary. The nonunion employee, whose First Amendment rights are affected by the agency shop itself and who bears the burden of objecting, is entitled to have his objections addressed in an expeditious, fair, and objective manner.

The Union's procedure does not meet this requirement. As the Seventh Circuit observed, the "most conspicuous feature of the procedure is that from start to finish it is entirely controlled by the union, which is an interested party, since it is the recipient of the agency fees paid by the dissenting employees." 743 F.2d, at 1194–1195. The initial consideration of the agency fee is made by Union officials, and the first two steps of the review procedure (the Union Executive Committee and Executive Board) consist of Union officials. The third step—review by a Union-selected arbitrator— is also inadequate because the selection represents the Union's unrestricted choice from the state list.

Thus, the original Union procedure was inadequate because it failed to minimize the risk that nonunion employees' contributions might be used for impermissible purposes, because it failed to provide adequate justification for the advance reduction of dues, and because it failed to offer a reasonably prompt decision by an impartial decisionmaker. . . .

We hold today that the constitutional requirements for the Union's collection of agency fees include an adequate explanation of the basis for the fee, a reasonably prompt opportunity to challenge the amount of the fee before an impartial decisionmaker, and an escrow for the amounts reasonably in dispute while such challenges are pending.

The determination of the appropriate remedy in this case is a matter that should be addressed in the first instance by the District Court. The Court of Appeals correctly reversed the District Court's original judgment and remanded the case for further proceedings. That judgment of reversal is affirmed, and those further proceedings should be consistent with this opinion.

It is so ordered.

NOTE

1. When teachers voluntarily surrender their individual academic freedom in exchange for protection of collective action and a group contract, they cannot later avoid their contractual commitments by recalling their constitutional freedoms. Where teachers maintained that school board policy unduly restricted use of certain books, thus violating their First and Fourteenth Amendment rights, the court found that they had no redress since they had submitted themselves to an employer-employee contractual model that gave the school board the authority to control communication through the assignment of reading material. *Cary v. Board of Education of Adams-Arapahoe School District 28-J,* 427 F.Supp. 945 (D.Colo.1977).

Freedom of Nonunion Teacher to Speak at Open Meeting Cannot Be Curtailed

City of Madison v. Wisconsin Employment Relations Commission

Supreme Court of the United States, 1976.
429 U.S. 167, 97 S.Ct. 421.

Mr. Chief Justice BURGER delivered the opinion of the Court. The question presented on this appeal from the Supreme Court of Wisconsin is whether a State may constitutionally require that an elected Board of Education prohibit teachers, other than union representatives, to speak at open meetings, at which public participation is permitted, if such speech is addressed to the subject of pending collective-bargaining negotiations.

The Madison Board of Education and Madison Teachers, Inc. (MTI), a labor union, were parties to a collective-bargaining agreement during the calendar year of 1971. In January 1971 negotiations commenced for renewal of the agreement and MTI submitted a number of proposals. One among them called for the inclusion of a so-called "fair-share" clause, which would require all teachers, whether members of MTI or not, to pay union dues to defray the costs of collective bargaining. . . .

During the same month, two teachers, Holmquist and Reed, who were members of the bargaining unit, but not members of the union, mailed a letter to all teachers in the district expressing opposition to the "fair share" proposal. Two hundred teachers replied, most commenting favorably on Holmquist and Reed's position. Thereupon a petition was drafted calling for a one-year delay in the implementation of "fair share" while the proposal was more closely analyzed by an impartial committee. The petition was circulated to all teachers in the district on December 6, 1971. Holmquist and Reed intended to present the results of their petition effort to the school board and to MTI at the school board's public meeting that same evening.

. . . During a portion of the meeting devoted to expression of opinion by the public, the president of MTI took the floor and spoke on the subject of the ongoing negotiations. He concluded his remarks by presenting to the board a petition signed by 1,300–1,400 teachers calling for the expeditious resolution of the negotiations. Holmquist was next given the floor, after John Matthews, the business representative of MTI, unsuccessfully attempted to dissuade him from speaking. Matthews had also spoken to a member of the school board before the meeting and requested that the board refuse to permit Holmquist to speak. Holmquist stated that he represented "an informal committee of seventy-two teachers in forty-nine schools" and that he desired to inform the Board of Education, as he had already informed the union, of the results of an informal survey concerning the "fair share" clause. He then read the petition which had been circulated to the teachers in the district that morning and stated that in the thirty-one schools from which reports had been received 53 percent of the teachers had already signed the petition.

Holmquist stated that neither side had adequately addressed the issue of "fair share" and that teachers were confused about the meaning of the proposal. He concluded by saying: "Due to this confusion, we wish to take no stand on the proposal itself, but ask only that all alternatives be presented clearly to all teachers and more importantly to the general public to whom we are all responsible. We ask simply for communication, not confrontation." The sole response from the school board was a question by the president inquiring whether Holmquist intended to present the board with the petition. Holmquist answered that he would. Holmquist's presentation had lasted approximately two and one-half minutes.

Later that evening, the board met in executive session and voted a proposal acceding to all of the union's demands with the exception of "fair share." During a negotiating session the following morning, MTI accepted the proposal and a contract was signed on December 14, 1976.

In January 1972 MTI filed a complaint with the Wisconsin Employment Relations Commission (WERC) claiming that the board had committed a prohibited labor practice by permitting Holmquist to speak at the December 6 meeting. . . .

The Wisconsin court perceived "clear and present danger" based upon its conclusion that Holmquist's speech before the school board constituted "negotiation" with the board. Permitting such "negotiation," the court reasoned, would undermine the bargaining exclusivity guaranteed the majority union under Wis.Stat. § 111.70(3)(a)4. From that premise it concluded that teachers' First Amendment rights could be limited. Assuming, *arguendo,* that such a "danger" might in some circumstances justify some limitation of First Amendment rights, we are unable to read this record as presenting such danger as would justify curtailing speech.

The Wisconsin Supreme Court's conclusion that Holmquist's terse statement during the public meeting constituted negotiation with the board was based upon its adoption of the lower court's determination that, "[e]ven though Holmquist's statement superficially appears to be merely a 'position statement,' the court deems from the total circumstances that it constituted 'negotiating.' " This cryptic conclusion seems to ignore the ancient wisdom that calling a thing by a name does not make it so. Holmquist did not seek to bargain or offer to enter into any bargain with the board, nor does it appear that he was authorized by any other teachers to enter into any agreement on their behalf. Although his views were not consistent with those of MTI, communicating such views to the employer could not change the fact that MTI alone was authorized to negotiate and to enter into a contract with the board.

Moreover, the school board meeting at which Holmquist was permitted to speak was open to the public. He addressed the school board not merely as one of its employees but also as a concerned citizen, seeking to express his views on an important decision of his government. We have held that teachers may not be "compelled to relinquish the First Amendment rights they would otherwise enjoy as citizens to comment on matters of public interest in connection with the operation of the public school in which they work." . . . Where the State has opened a forum for direct citizen involvement, it is difficult to find justification for excluding teachers who make up the overwhelming proportion of school employees and are most vitally concerned with the proceedings. It is conceded that any citizen could have presented precisely the same points and provided the board with the same information as did Holmquist. . . .

The Employment Relations Commission's order was not limited to a determination that a prohibited labor practice had taken place in the past; it also restrains future conduct. By prohibiting the school board from "permitting employees to appear and speak at meetings of the Board of Education" the order constitutes an indirect, but effective, prohibition on persons such as Holmquist from communicating with their government. The order would have a substantial impact upon virtually all communication between teachers and the school board. The order prohibits speech by teachers "on matters subject to collective bargaining." As the dissenting opinion below noted, however, there is virtually no subject concerning the operation of the school system that could not also be characterized as a potential subject of collective bargaining. Teachers not only constitute the overwhelming bulk of employees of the school system, but they are the very core of that system; restraining teachers' expressions to the board on matters involving the operation of the schools would seriously impair the board's ability to govern the district. . . . The challenged portion of the order is designed to govern speech and conduct in the future, not to punish past conduct and as such it is the essence of prior restraint.

The judgment of the Wisconsin Supreme Court is reversed and the case is remanded to that court for further proceedings not inconsistent with this opinion.

Reversed and remanded.

ENDNOTES

1. *1975 Guidebook to Labor Relations* (Chicago: Commerce Clearing House, Inc., 1975), pp. 8–9.

2. Ibid.

3. Ibid., p. 11.

4. See Benjamin Werne, *Public Employment Labor Relations* (The Michie Company, 1974), p. 5.

5. Ibid., p. 6.

6. Speech by Jerry Wurf, International President of American Federation of State, County, and Municipal Employees, AFL–CIO, United States Conference of Mayors, Honolulu, Hawaii, 1967.

7. Werne, *Public Employment*, p. 11; see also *Collective Bargaining and Politics in Public Employment*, 19 *U.C.L.A.L. Rev.* 887 (1972).

8. Atkins v. City of Charlotte, 296 F.Supp. 1068 (W.D.N.C.1969).

9. 406 F.2d 137 (8th Cir.1969).

10. Ibid.

11. This rule can vary among jurisdictions. For example, the Virginia Supreme Court has held that school boards do not have either statutory or constitutional authority to enter into collective bargaining agreements. *Commonwealth v. County Board of Arlington County*, 217 Va. 558, 232 S.E.2d 30 (1977).

12. Chief of Police v. Town of Dracut, 357 Mass. 492, 258 N.E.2d 531 (1970).

13. 48 Am.Jur.2d, § 1027–1043.

14. City of New York v. DeLury, 23 N.Y.2d 175, 295 N.Y.S.2d 901, 243 N.E.2d 128 (1968); *Remittur Amended*, 296 N.Y.S.2d 958, 244 N.E.2d 472 (1968); *appeal dismissed*, 394 U.S. 455, 89 S.Ct. 1223 (1969).

15. Anderson Federation of Teachers v. School City of Anderson, 252 Ind. 558, 251 N.E.2d 15 (1969); *cert.* denied 399 U.S. 928, 905 S.Ct. 2243 (1970).

16. United Federation of Postal Clerks v. Blount, 325 F.Supp. 879 (D.D.C. 1971), affirmed 404 U.S. 802, 92 S.Ct. 80 (1971).

17. Anderson, op. cit.

18. Hugh D. Jascourt, "Can Compulsory Arbitration Work in Education Collective Bargaining: An Introduction," *Journal of Law and Education* 4, no. 4 (October 1975).

19. School Board of the City of Richmond v. Parham, 218 Va. 950, 243 S.E.2d 468 (1978).

20. Dearborn Fire Fighters Union Local No. 412 v. City of Dearborn, 42 Mich. App. 51, 201 N.W.2d 650 (1972).

21. Werne, *Public Employment*, p. 247.

22. Ibid.

23. Ibid.

24. Labor Management Relations Act, 9(a), 29 U.S.C.A. § 159 (a).

25. West Hartford Education Association v. Dayson DeCourcy, 162 Conn. 566, 295 A. 2d 526 (1972).

26. Wethersfield Board of Education v. Connecticut State Board of Labor Relations, 201 Conn. 685, 519 A.2d 41 (1986).

27. Jurva v. Attorney General, 419 Mich. 209, 351 N.W. 2d 813 (1984).

28. NEA v. Unified School District No. 259, 234 Kan. 512, 674 P.2d 478 (1983).

29. Dodge City NEA v. Unified School District No. 443, Kan.App. 2d 810, 635 P.2d 1263 (1981).

30. Byram Township Board of Education v. Byram Township Education Association, 152 N.J. Super. 12, 377 A.2d 745 (App. Div. 1977).

31. Kolcum v. Board of Education, 335 A.2d 618 (Del. Super. 1975).

32. Board of Education v. New Paltz United Teachers, 57 A.D. 2d 583, 393 N.Y.S. 2d 588 (2d Dept. 1977).

33. Barnett v. Durant Community School Dist., 249 N.W. 2d 626 (Iowa 1977).

34. Los Angeles City & County Employees Union v. Los Angeles City Board of Education, 12 Cal. 3d 851, 117 Cal. Rptr. 537, 528 P.2d 353 (1974).

35. Chee-Craw Teachers Ass'n v. Unified School District No. 247, 225 Kan. 561, 593 P.2d 406 (1979).

36. Allen v. Town of Sterling 367 Mass. 844, 329 N.E. 2d 756 (1975).

37. Tri-County Educators' Ass'n v. Tri-County Special Education Co-op No. 607, 225 Kan. 781, 594 P.2d 207 (1979).

38. Libby, McNeill, & Libby v. Longshoremen Local 142, 37 LA 466, 467 (1961): cited in Werne, *Public Employment*,

p. 153. Benjamin Werne, *The Law and Practice of Public Employment* (Charlottesville, Virginia: The Michie Company, 1974), p. 153.

39. Id.

40. Monsanto Chemical Co. v. Chemical Workers Local 12, 32 LA 260, 263 (1959): cited in Werne, *Public Employment,* p. 153.

41. Chee-Craw Teachers Ass'n v. Unified School District, op. cit.

42. Chambersburg Area School District v. Commonwealth, 60 Pa. Cmwlth. 29, 430 A.2d 740 (1981).

43. Byram Township Board of Education v. Byram Township Education Association, op. cit.

44. Werne, *Public Employment,* p. 124.

45. Ibid., p. 150.

46. Ibid., p. 152.

47. Ibid.

48. AFSCME v. Woodward, 406 F.2d 137 (8th Cir. 1969).

49. Atkins v. City of Charlotte, 296 F. Supp. 1068 (W.D.N.C. 1969).

50. AFSCME v. Woodward, op. cit.; see also Griswold v. Connecticut, 381 U.S. 479, 85 S.Ct. 1678 (1965); N.A.A.C.P. v. Alabama, 357 U.S. 449, 78 S.Ct. 1163 (1958); *reversed and remanded other grounds,* 360 U.S. 240, 79 S.Ct. 1001 (1959).

51. Day v. South Park Independent School Dist., 768 F.2d 696 (5th Cir. 1985).

52. 461 U.S. 138, 103 S.Ct. 1684 (1983).

53. Day v. South Park Independent School Dist., op cit.

54. Pederson v. South Williamsport Area School District, 677 F. 2d 312 (3d Cir. 1982).

55. Ash v. Board of Education, 699 F.2d 822 (6th Cir. 1983).

56. Ibid.

57. Hickman v. Valley Local School District, 619 F.2d 606 (6th Cir. 1980).

58. Ibid.

59. Bauch v. City of New York, 54 Misc. 2d 343, 282 N.Y.S. 2d 816 (1967); Board of School Directors of the City of Milwaukee v. Wisconsin Employment Relations Commission, 42 Wis. 2d 637, 168 N.W. 2d 92 (1969).

60. Abood v. Detroit Board of Education, 431 U.S. 209, 97 S.Ct. 1782 (1977).

61. Ellis v. Brotherhood of Railway Airline and S.S. Clerks, 466 U.S. 435, 104 S.Ct. 1883 (1984).

62. Ibid.

63. Elrod v. Burns, 427 U.S. 347, 96 S.Ct. 2673 (1976); Kusper v. Pontikes, 414 U.S. 51 94 S.Ct. 303 (1973); Abood v. Detroit Board of Education, 431 U.S. 209, 97 S.Ct. 1782 (1977).

64. Chicago Teachers Union, Local No. 1 v. Hudson, 475 U.S. 292, 106 S.Ct. 1066 (1986).

CHAPTER 19

Finance

State constitutional provisions empowering the legislature to provide for a system of public schools confer on the legislature the authority to tax and distribute funds for public schools. Where litigation does arise, it usually involves the methods used by the legislature to regulate and control revenues and expenditures in the exercise of this authority. A substantial amount of litigation is devoted to the legal requirements for taxation and taxpayers' remedies for payment of illegal taxes, as well as legal requirements for budgeting and accounting for school funds. Many cases question the legal authority of school districts to issue bonds, hold bond elections, and impose certain fees and charges on children and parents. Although the volume of cases is relatively small compared to other fiscal matters, the issue of constitutional rights of students and the resulting impact on state school finance has probably been the most widely publicized area of school finance litigation.

Litigation in state courts challenging the constitutionality of state school aid formulas under specific state constitutional provisions represents an evolutionary step in judicial expansion of constitutional protections. These cases have extended students' rights by placing new limitations on the police power of the state to regulate and control education. Courts once obliquely maintained that education was a privilege bestowed upon the individual by the good will of the state, and that it could be altered or even taken away at the state's discretion. This has changed and education is now being adjudged a fundamental right as guaranteed by the state constitution.

School finance cases, therefore, represent an important step in legal precedents, not only because they involve limitations on the police power of the state to regulate and control education but, also, because they restrict a legislature's power to devise and implement its own system of taxation. Each of these issues has traditionally formed separate precedents.

■■■ TAXATION FOR EDUCATION

The power of taxation is an inherent power of the state, limited only by the federal Constitution and the constitution of the state. A state cannot impose an arbitrary or discriminatory tax burden upon a segment of the population, but a state can impose a heavier tax on nonresidents than on residents. Reasonable classifications for tax purposes are permissible, but those that invidiously discriminate violate the Equal Protection Clause of the Fourteenth Amendment.

The courts have held that school districts have no inherent power to levy taxes. This power must be expressly conferred upon the school district by the legislature. In the levy and collection of taxes, school districts must adhere strictly to the language of the statutory authority; the courts are hesitant to extend powers of taxation by statutory implication. The power of a local school district to tax for education funds is not implied by statute to establish and operate a local school system. In the absence of contrary constitutional provisions, the legislature may choose to finance education entirely from a tax levied at the state level and redistributed to the school districts.

School districts must construe statutes strictly and expend the monies for the specific purposes as set out by the legislature. If a school tax levy is illegal because of failure to follow the prescribed procedure, the courts will make a determination depending on whether the statutory provision is mandatory or directory. If the provision is mandatory, the tax is invalid. However, the courts have established no clear guidelines for determining if a provision is mandatory or directory. In these situations, courts are generally faced with the perplexing problems that ensue from finding a tax levy invalid and thereby harming the educational program. Because of this, the courts are usually very liberal in this regard and are hesitant to call a tax invalid. If a procedural error is relatively minor and does not deprive the taxpayers of a substantial or fundamental right, the courts will allow the tax to stand.

The Development of the American State and Local Tax System

With permission of Jerome R. Hellerstein, Third Ed., West Publishing Company, St. Paul, Minn pp. 1-2 & pp. 70-72.

— — — — — — — — —

Colonial Taxation. The colonial governments in their early days subsisted on voluntary payments, subsidies and allowances abroad, quit-rents, and occasional fees and fines of early justice. When compulsory levies developed, the tax systems followed the pattern of the local economies. In the democratic New England communities almost everyone owned land; and the distribution of property was fairly equal. Consequently, in New England, in addition to the poll tax, the colonies levied a tax on the gross produce of land, either actual or computed, according to the extent and quality of the land held. Gradually, this levy grew into a real property tax, which was soon expanded into a general property tax. The town artisans and other townsmen who subsisted on the fruit of their labor,

instead of property, were not adequately taxed by the property levy. The "faculty tax" was added to reach these persons. The faculty tax was not an income tax, but instead a levy in a fixed amount, imposed rather arbitrarily, according to occupations and callings.

An entirely different development took place in the Southern colonies, dominated by an aristocratic landed gentry with large holdings. There, the land tax played an insignificant role. After slavery was introduced, it became difficult to retain even the poll tax, which became in a sense a property tax on slaves. Consequently, the Southern colonies turned to excise taxes, particularly on imports and exports, which bore heavily on poorer consumers.

The middle colonies, particularly the New Netherlands, reflected the dominance of the moneyed interests and trading classes, who brought with them a Dutch tradition. Here, there was neither the more or less equal distribution of wealth characteristic of New England, nor the preponderance of the landed interests typified by Virginia. Instead of a system of poll and property levies or of excises primarily on imports and exports, the fundamental characteristic of the tax structure was an excise system of taxation of trade, borrowed from Holland.

Each section, therefore, had a fiscal system more or less in harmony with its economic conditions. It was not until these conditions changed during the eighteenth century that the fiscal systems began somewhat to approach each other; and it was not until much later that we find throughout the country a general property tax based not on the produce, but on the market value of property.

The outstanding development in State and local taxation during the nineteenth century was the rise of the property tax. As stated by Professor Ely, during the period from 1796 to the Civil War "the distinguishing feature of the system of state and local taxation in America may be described in one sentence. It is the taxation of all property, movable or immovable, visible or invisible, or real or personal . . . at one uniform rate.

Nevertheless, the divergence of economic systems was reflected in the development of the State fiscal systems. In the Southern States, with imports and exports as a source of revenue cut off by the federal Constitution, land had to bear a large part of the tax burden. As increased revenues were needed, these States, dominated by landed proprietors at least until the Civil War, turned primarily to license and privilege taxes on peddlers, auctioneers, saloon keepers, traders in slaves and horses, keepers of ferries, toll bridges and turnpikes, and indeed virtually all occupations carried on outside the farms.

In the Northern States, where business interests were dominant, the license or privilege tax system did not take hold. To supplement property tax yields, banks, insurance companies, canals, railroads, and other businesses were taxed; and as corporations came to play a more important role in the economy, general corporate franchise taxes were enacted. These levies were the precursors of the present day corporate taxes on or measured by net income. The newer States adopted the current tax philosophy of the older States, making the property tax the cornerstone of their tax structures.   .   .   .

Early property taxation. Although property taxes were regarded as an extraordinary source of revenue in early history, they, nevertheless, have ancient origins. In Athens, the land tax was originally levied on gross produce, but it gradually developed into a property tax imposed not only on land and houses but also on slaves, cattle, furniture and money. Rome taxed many forms of personalty as well as realty. In Europe, the early property taxes were levied on land but were gradually extended to buildings and cattle, until they became general property taxes. As new types of movable and intangible property developed, evasion became prevalent and assessment difficult. The principle of the general property tax broke down and personal property taxes were gradually abandoned. By 1800, the base of European property taxes had largely dwindled down to land alone or land and buildings.

The development of the general property tax in the United States.   .   .   .   [T]he general property tax became formally established in this country for the States and localities during the nineteenth century.

At first the property tax was really a tax on land at a fixed sum per acre of different types of land—cleared and uncleared, cultivated and cleared, and so forth. It soon was expanded to include livestock, buildings, and personal property. Each item of taxable property was listed and taxed at a fixed sum for each cow, each barn, and so on. The increasing complexity of this taxable list led finally to (1) the general property tax—general taxation of all properties, instead of the growing lists of taxable specified properties; (2) appraisal of property—the tax rates were imposed as percentages of per millages of the property valuation, rather than as a fixed sum of money per unit of property; (3) the adoption of the principle of uniformity—whereas earlier laws provided for varying rates for different classes of property, the uniformity concept adopted by State constitutions required real and personal property to be taxed at a uniform proportion of value.

Authority to Levy Taxes Must Be Found in Express Legislative Provision

— · — · — · — · —

Marion & McPherson Railway Co. v. Alexander

— · — · — · — · —

Supreme Court of Kansas, 1901.
63 Kan. 72, 64 P. 978.

CUNNINGHAM, J. The plaintiff in error in this action seeks to enjoin the collection of all taxes levied for school purposes in school district No. 79, Marion county, Kan., in excess of 2 percent on the taxable property owned by it in said district. A graded school district, No. 79, had been organized, identical in boundaries and inhabitants with school district No. 79; such organization being authorized by article 7, c. 92, of the General Statutes of 1889.

That article generally provided for the organization of union or graded schools, its principal sections being as follows: Section 107 provides for the selection of a board of directors by the graded school district, and that such board shall consist of a director, clerk, and treasurer. Section 108 directs that such board of directors shall, in all matters relating to the graded schools, possess all the powers and discharge all the like duties of boards of directors in other districts. Section 109 provides that the union districts thus formed shall be entitled to an equitable share of the school funds, to be drawn from the treasurer of each district so uniting, in proportion to the number of children attending the said graded school for each district. Section 110: "The said union district may levy taxes for the purpose of purchasing a building or furnishing proper buildings, for the accommodation of the school or for the purpose of defraying necessary expenses and paying teachers, but shall be governed in all respects by the law herein provided for levying and collecting district taxes." Section 111 provides certain duties for the clerk of the union district in relation to reports, and that the district treasurer shall apportion the amount of school moneys due the union district, and pay the same over to the treasurer of the union district on order of the clerk and director thereof. Section 112, that the clerk of the union district shall make report to the county superintendent, and discharge all the duties of clerk in like manner as the clerk of the district. Section 113, that the treasurer of the district shall perform all the duties of treasurer as prescribed in the act in like manner as the district treasurer. Section 115, that any single district shall possess power to establish graded schools in like manner and subject to the same provisions as two or more districts united. Section 28 of the same chapter (being the section which gives the general power for levying district taxes) provides: "The inhabitants qualified to vote at a school meeting, lawfully assembled, shall have power: . . . . To vote a tax annually not exceeding 2 percent on the taxable property in the district, as the meeting shall deem sufficient for the various school purposes, and distribute the amount as the meeting shall

deem proper in the payment of teachers' wages, and to purchase or lease a site."

These are all the sections which afford light for the solution of the question involved. From these, it is contended by plaintiff in error that while the inhabitants of one or more school districts may form a union or graded district, and create the machinery to run the same and to maintain any and all schools therein, the total levy "for the various school purposes" cannot exceed 2 percent on the taxable property in any one district annually. It is contended by the defendants in error that the various sections quoted, conferring as they do upon the various members of the graded school district board all the powers of like officers of ordinary district boards, and erecting a separate entity for the purpose of managing a separate school, and conferring upon that entity the power to levy taxes as found in section 110, give the power to such graded school district to make within its bounds an additional levy not to exceed 2 percent; that is, that it may levy as much as the original school district may, and this in addition to what the original district levies, and not that the total of both levies must be the limit fixed in section 28. The court below took this view of the question. In this we do not agree. We think that by section 28 the entire levy may not exceed 2 percent; and we are strengthened in this conclusion by the language of section 109, which says that a union district shall be entitled to "an equitable share of the school funds," and also by that in section 111—"the district treasurer shall apportion the amount of school money due the union district and pay the same over to the union district." The law fixes the time for holding the annual meetings of the union or graded districts in June, while the annual meetings of school districts occur in July. All these provisions, taken together, indicate that it was the purpose of the legislature that, while the first meeting—that of the graded district—could suggest the levy desired for graded school purposes, the last one only possessed the power to vote the tax which for "the various school purposes" could not in any one year exceed 2 percent. Or, at least, there must be such harmony in the action of both bodies that the aggregate levy may not exceed the limit found in section 28. We may say that the question is not one entirely free from doubt, but can hardly believe that the legislature would have left it in that condition, had its purpose been to confer the right to so largely increase the burden of taxation. The authority to levy taxes is an extraordinary one. It is never left to implication, unless it is a necessary implication. Its warrant must be clearly found in the act of the legislature. Any other rule might lead to great wrong and oppression, and when there is a reasonable doubt as to its existence the right must be denied. Therefore to say that the right is in doubt is to deny its existence. . . .

The levies sought to be enjoined are those for the years 1894 and 1895, and our conclusion is that the judgment of the district court must be reversed, and it be directed to make the injunction perpetual, enjoining all of the defendants from collecting all of said school taxes in excess of 2 percent. All the justices concurring.

NOTES

1. "Neither municipalities nor school districts are sovereigns, and they have no original or fundamental power of legislation or taxation, but have only the right and power to enact those legislative and tax ordinances or resolutions which are authorized by act of the legislature." *Appeal of School District of City of Allentown,* 370 Pa. 161, 87 A.2d 480 (1952).

2. Taxes levied and collected for school purposes are state taxes whether they are collected by the school district or a municipality. In an Alabama case, the court said: "If the Constitution raises the fund and directs its use in furthering a state function, it continues to be such a state fund regardless of the sort of agency designated to administer it." *City Board of Education of Athens v. Williams,* 231 Ala. 137, 163 So. 802 (1935).

3. In relating legislative provisions for taxation to constitutional requirements, the courts have held that revenue statutes must be given a reasonable construction,

and no statute can circumvent positively stated constitutional provisions. *Mathews v. Board of Education of City of Chicago,* 342 Ill. 120, 174 N.E. 35 (1930).

4. "The authority to levy taxes is an extraordinary one. It is never left to implication, unless it is a necessary implication. Its warrant must be clearly found in the act of the legislature. Any other rule might lead to great wrong and oppression, and when there is a reasonable doubt as to its existence the right must be denied . . . ." *Marion and M. Ry. Co. v. Alexander,* County Treasurer, 63 Kan. 72, 64 P. 978 (1901).

5. "The power of the board of education of a non-high school district to levy taxes is statutory. The language granting the power is to be strictly construed and will not be extended beyond the plain import of the words used." *People ex rel. Smith, Co. Collector v. Wabash Railway Co. et al.,* 374 Ill. 165, 28 N.E.2d 119 (1940).

6. The intent of the legislature in enacting taxation statutes is often difficult to interpret. A Pennsylvania court in determining that a statute prescribing taxation for "amusements" included admissions to "fair grounds" had this to say about statutory interpretation:

> The language of a statute must be read in a sense which harmonizes with the subject matter and its general purpose and object. The general design and purpose of the law is to be kept in view . . . . *School Dist. of Cambria Township v. Cambria Co. Legion Recreation Association,* 201 Pa.Super. 163, 192 A.2d 149 (1963).

7. Courts will not interfere with the exercise of sound business judgment on the part of taxing authorities, but will intervene only to prevent a clear abuse by such officers of their discretionary powers. *People v. Baltimore & Ohio Southwestern Railway Co.,* 353 Ill. 492, 187 N.E. 463 (1933).

8. Where a wrongful tax is collected, the taxpayer may recover only on such remedies as are authorized by law, such as an appeal to set aside or cancel a tax deed and

a tax protest. *Wall v. M. & R. Sheep Co.*, 33 Cal. 2d 768, 205 P.2d 14 (1949).

9. A person who pays tax voluntarily and not under duress cannot recover the tax. *Harding v. Wiley*, 219 Ill.App. 1. A mere protest by a taxpayer is not sufficient to constitute payment under compulsion or duress.

10. A person may not question the legality of school funds unless he has a requisite interest in such funds. *Chalupnik v. Savall*, 219 Wis. 442, 263 N.W. 352 (1935).

11. Some states have statutory provisions for a taxpayer protest in a court or board of tax review. The findings of fact or judgment by the court or board will not be disturbed unless clearly arbitrary or against the weight of evidence.

12. Taxpayers may not sit idly by and allow illegal systems of taxation to be installed without protesting and then take advantage of the illegality of the system by collaterally attacking the system when they are sued. In such a case, the Court of Civil Appeals of Texas held that, although a scheme of taxation is illegal, the burden is on the taxpayers to show that they have suffered substantial financial loss as a result of the failure of the city and school district to assess property legally. *City of Houston v. McCarthy*, 371 S.W.2d 587 (Tex. Cir.App. 1963).

13. Tangible personal property that is located in a state other than that in which the owner is domiciled may be taxed at the place of its location. *Fennell v. Pauley*, 112 Iowa 94, 83 N.W. 799 (1900). The "domicile" of a person is the place where he has his principal, true, fixed, permanent home, and to which he has, whenever he is absent, the intention of returning, and it also means the habitation, fixed in any place, from which a person does not have any present intention of removing. *State v. Benny*, 20 N.J. 238, 119 A.2d 155 (1955).

14. Intangible personal property is generally taxable at the domicile of the owner. *Scripps v. Board of Review of Fulton Co.*, 183 Ill. 278, 55 N.E. 700 (1899). However, courts have upheld cases in which the state legislature provides that intangible personal property shall be taxed when located other than where the owner is domiciled. In arriving at this conclusion, a Minnesota court stated:

> For many purposes the domicile of the owner is deemed the situs of his personal property. This, however, is only a fiction, from motives of convenience, and is not of universal application, by yields to the actual situs of the property when justice requires that it should. It is not allowed to be controlling in matters of taxation. Thus, corporeal personal property is conceded to be taxable at the place where it is actually situated. A credit which cannot be regarded as situated in a place merely because the debtor resides there, must usually be considered as having its situs where it is owned, at the domicile of the creditor. The creditor, however, may give it a business situs elsewhere; as where he places it in the hands of an agent for collection or renewal, with a view to reloaning the money and keeping it invested as a permanent business . . . . The allegation to pay taxes on property for the support of the government arises from the fact that it is under the protection of the government. *In re Washington County v. Estate of Jefferson*, 35 Minn. 215, 28 N.W. 256 (1886).

▰▰▰ DISTRIBUTION OF STATE SCHOOL FUNDS

Where constitutionality of a statute is questioned, all reasonable doubt will be resolved in favor of the questioned authority and the act will be declared constitutional unless it can be clearly demonstrated that the legislature did not have the power or authority exercised or that its authority was exercised arbitrarily and capriciously, for instance, as to classification or delegation of authority, to the prejudice of the rights of some of the citizens. Particularly, is this true where the act in question is . . . of great public concern involving the performance of an absolute duty imposed on the legislature by the basic law of the state.[1]

This statement describes the traditional position of the courts toward the judicial regulation of such important legislative functions as taxation for public education. Nonintervention has been the watchword for decades when courts have been asked to examine the constitutionality of legislatively prescribed methods of taxation for financing of education.

The courts have steadfastly adhered to the philosophy that an act of the legislature will not be rendered invalid unless the act obviously violates certain prescribed constitutional standards. With regard to the constitutionality of state school finance programs, the courts have traditionally been asked to determine only whether such programs created unconstitutional classifications or violated equality and uniformity of taxation requirements. The Equal Protection Clause of the Fourteenth Amendment encompasses, but is not limited to, the same protections as the equality and uniformity of taxation provisions of most state constitutions.

Taxation and Equal Protection

The Equal Protection Clause was first described as a limitation on state revenue legislation by the Supreme Court of the United States in 1890. The "test" devised by the Supreme Court to determine constitutionality of state taxation has been restated by Justice Jackson:

> Equal protection does not require identity of treatment. It only requires that classification rest on real and not feigned differences, that the distinction have some relevance to the purpose for which the classification is made, and the different treatment be not so disparate, relative to the difference in classification, as to be wholly arbitrary.[2]

The Equal Protection Clause establishes a minimum standard of uniformity to which state tax legislation must conform in addition to, and beyond, similar limitations imposed by state constitutional requirements.[3]

Practically all state constitutions have the equivalent of an "equal protection" provision — that is, some constitutional restriction against "unreasonable classifications." While

the United States Supreme Court has the ultimate interpretative power regarding "reasonableness" under the federal Equal Protection Clause, state courts have the last word as to the meaning of reasonableness under their respective state constitutions.[4] The primary problem is, of course, the definition of reasonableness or unreasonableness of a classification.

Courts have been hesitant to invalidate legislative acts on the basis of unconstitutional classification because the source of taxation is often tightly interwoven with the government's plan for distribution of funds to local districts. The essence of an illegal constitutional classification is to arbitrarily classify local districts or persons with no regard for their actual conditions or needs. The United States Ninth Circuit Court of Appeals speaks of this as fitting tax programs to needs:

> Traditionally classification has been a device for fitting tax programs to local needs and usages in order to achieve an equitable distribution of the tax burden. It has, because of this, been pointed out that in taxation, even more than in other fields, legislatures possess the greatest freedom in classification. Since the members of a legislature necessarily enjoy a familiarity with local conditions which this court cannot have, the presumption of constitutionality can be overcome only by the most explicit demonstration that a classification is a hostile and oppressive discrimination against particular persons and classes. The burden is on the one attacking the legislative arrangement to negate every conceivable basis which might support it.[5]

Distribution Formulas and The Equal Protection Clause

Even though the Ninth Circuit denied that equality and uniformity of taxation requirements of both state and federal constitutions applied to the distribution of funds, it proceeded nevertheless to lay down "guiding principles" that govern the legislatures' distribution of tax funds. Quoting *Corpus Juris Secundum*, the court said:

> In the absence of constitutional regulation the method of apportioning and distributing a

school fund, accruing from taxes or other revenue, rests in the wise discretion of the state legislature, which method, in the absence of abuse of discretion or violation of some constitutional provision, cannot be interfered with by the courts . . . the fact that the fund is distributed unequally among the different districts or political subdivisions does not render it invalid.[6]

In other words, the needs of the various types of school districts and the resulting impact of methods of taxation is a matter that is to be determined by the legislature.

In 1965, however, the theory was advanced that education funding was a constitutionally protected right and must be provided to all on equal terms. Thus a state that gives fewer dollars for the child in a poorer school district may be held as denying equal protection rights.[7] It was argued that the state had no reasonable equal protection basis on which to justify making a child's education dependent on the wealth of the school district. The U.S. Supreme Court had laid the groundwork for this conclusion by previously holding that to classify persons on either the basis of poverty[8] or according to their location, homesite, or occupation was unreasonable.[9] Therefore, it was concluded, the quality of a child's education could not be contingent upon a state and local taxing and fund distribution system that is based on the property wealth of the local school district.

Litigation Under Federal Equal Protection

By 1968, several suits had been filed, each seeking to have state school finance programs rendered unconstitutional through the application of this logic.

Educators for some time had recognized that all children cannot be educated equally with equal resources. Some children with special learning deficiencies caused by cultural deprivation or mental or physical incapacities need extra funds, but, dollar differences due to wealth are unjustified.

In *McInnis v. Shapiro*,[10] the plaintiffs claimed that the Illinois finance system created large variations in expenditures per student from district to district, thereby providing some students with a good education and depriving others who have equal or greater educational need. The court concluded that equal educational expenditures are not required by the Fourteenth Amendment, and that variations created by taxation of property in the school districts do not discriminate.

> Unequal educational expenditures per student, based upon the variable property values and tax rates of local school districts, do not amount to an invidious discrimination. Moreover, the statutes which permit these unequal expenditures on a district to district basis are neither arbitrary nor unreasonable.[11]

The *McInnis* court declined to establish judicial standards for determining legislative allocations based on educational needs. Since *McInnis* was summarily affirmed by the U.S. Supreme Court,[12] this statement represented precedent and had substantial impact on legal thought at that time.

The position in *McInnis* was summed by saying that there were no "discoverable and manageable standards by which a court can determine when the Constitution is satisfied and when it is violated."[13]

McInnis was closely followed by a second case in Virginia, *Burruss v. Wilkerson*.[14] Specifically, plaintiffs claimed the state formula created and perpetuated substantial disparities in educational opportunities throughout the state of Virginia and failed to relate to any of the variety of educational needs present in the several counties and cities of Virginia. In following the hands-off course of *McInnis*, the federal district court in Virginia said:

> [T]he courts have neither the knowledge, nor the means, nor the power to tailor the public moneys to fit the varying needs of these students throughout the state. We can only see to it that the outlays on one group are not invidiously greater or less than that of another. No such arbitrariness is manifest here.[15]

Accordingly, *Burruss* denied relief to plaintiffs under both the "efficiency" provision of the Virginia Constitution and the Equal Protection Clause of the Fourteenth Amendment. The United States Supreme Court summarily affirmed this decision.

Only a short time elapsed between *McInnis* and the now-famous decision by the California Supreme Court in *Serrano v. Priest*.[16] In *Serrano*, the court handed down a well-reasoned decision that strongly documented the establishment of a new equal protection application to school finance.

In critically analyzing the California school finance system, the court pointed out that, although the basic state aid program in California tends to equalize among school districts, the total system, including state and local funds combined, created great disparities in school revenues; and the system as a whole generated school revenue proportional to the wealth of the individual school. After concluding that education was a "fundamental interest" and property wealth was a "suspect classification," the court applied the "strict scrutiny" standard and found the system of finance unconstitutional.

The Rodriguez Case

A significant decision by a federal three-judge court in Texas[17] followed *Serrano* and reached the same conclusion. There it was held that plaintiffs had been denied equal protection of the law by the Texas system of financing public schools. Plaintiffs contended that the educational finance system of the state makes education a function of the local property tax base. The court observed that the school finance system of Texas erroneously assumes that the value of property in the various districts will be sufficiently equal to maintain comparable expenditures among districts. This inequality is not corrected to any substantial degree by state funds, because when all state and local funds were combined to correct this unconstitutional inequality, there were still great disparities. *Rodriguez* required a standard of "fiscal neutrality," which in essence means that the quality of a child's education should not be a function of the district where the child resides, but determined by the wealth of the state as a whole. As was the case in *Serrano*, the court maintained

that fiscal neutrality did not require that all educational expenditures be equal for each child, but wealth neutral.

The rationale and precedents of the lower courts in *Serrano* and *Rodriguez*, that a child's education could not be contingent on the wealth of the local school district, were to no avail, however; for in 1973 the Supreme Court of the United States handed down a reversal of *Rodriguez*,[18] effectively terminating such state school finance litigation under the Equal Protection Clause. On rehearing *Serrano*, the California Supreme Court was forced to abandon the Fourteenth Amendment as the constitutional basis for overturning the state school aid formula and thereafter relied solely on an equal protection provision in the California Constitution.

Justice Powell, in upholding the constitutionality of the Texas method of financing its schools, maintained that education was not a "fundamental" constitutional right under the Equal Protection Clause, as had been presumed from reading *Brown*; and, thus, education could not be viewed in special favor by the court justifying strict judicial scrutiny. In so holding, the court reverted to the traditional judicial position of leaving such matters to the wisdom of the legislature. In this regard, Justice Powell concluded:

> Education, perhaps even more than welfare assistance, presents a myriad of "intractable economic, social and even philosophical problems." The very complexity of the problems of financing and managing a statewide public school system suggests that "there will be more than one constitutionally permissible method of solving them," and that, within the limits of rationality, "the legislature's efforts to tackle the problems" should be entitled to respect.[19]

Immediately after this decision, most if not all such litigation in the federal courts ceased. It was clear that any future actions, if they were to be successful in attacking methods of state school financing, would have to be pursued in reliance on state constitutional grounds rather than on the Fourteenth Amendment. Subsequent to and in accordance with the Supreme Court's decision in

Rodriguez, the Supreme Courts of Michigan[20] and Arizona[21] reversed precedent and upheld the constitutionality of their own state school finance programs. The Michigan Supreme Court had previously held that the Michigan school finance system violated the equal protection provision of the state constitution,[22] but on rehearing found no violation of either the state or federal equal protection clauses. Similarly, the Supreme Court of Arizona, in upholding that state's method of financing schools, followed *Rodriguez* in finding that education was not a fundamental right deserving of strict judicial scrutiny.

Litigation Under State Constitutions

Litigation in the realm of state school aid distribution has returned to state courts, and since *Rodriguez,* the actions now test state formulas in light of only state constitutional provisions. Bases for such litigation may be found in equal protection, uniformity, equality, thorough and efficient, or other provisions of state constitutions. *Rodriguez* continues, though, to have substantial influence in shaping state courts' views of their own constitutions. In a Louisiana case[23] the court held that the method of school financing in that state did not differ significantly from that of Texas (litigated in *Rodriguez*) and that, as such, it was not unconstitutionally discriminatory against the poor people in poor school districts. The Supreme Court of Idaho held, in a 3–2 decision, that the education finance law of that state did not violate the "uniform system" requirement of that state's constitution.[24] In so doing, the court refused to recognize education as a "fundamental interest" under the Idaho Constitution and, in the same vein, turned back the plaintiff's equal protection claim. Decisions in Illinois,[25] Kansas,[26] Montana,[27] Oregon,[28] New York,[29] and Georgia[30] have likewise denied relief to plaintiffs where challenges to the school finance law were predicated on state constitutional provisions. The Oregon Supreme Court observed that it could interpret the equal protection clause of the Oregon Constitution more broadly than that placed on the federal Constitution in *Rodriguez,* but it declined to do so. The court

refused to acknowledge that education was a fundamental right, and the fact that education was mentioned in the Oregon Constitution was not sufficient to establish its fundamentality. Further, the court found the word "uniform" in the constitution merely required the legislature to provide a minimum program of educational opportunity throughout the state. Complete uniformity, the court decided, would infringe on the state's reasonable objective to maintain local control of education.

In an important case that departed from the influence of *Rodriguez,* the New Jersey Supreme Court, in *Robinson v. Cahill,* relied on the state's "thorough and efficient" clause to invalidate the state school aid formula.[31] This court made it clear that the state had an obligation to correct the fiscal imbalances created by local school district organization and fiscal ability variations. It further found the "thorough and efficient" standard required equal educational opportunity, and that if local government fails to so provide, then the state must act either to compel local districts to meet the constitutional mandate or to meet the obligation itself. In broadly defining the "thorough and efficient" standard, the court said:

> The Constitution's guarantee must be understood to embrace that educational opportunity which is needed in the contemporary setting to equip a child for his role as a citizen and as a competitor in the labor market.[32]

Because of the variation in the education provisions of state constitutions and the diversity in state school finance formulas, one can expect little consistency in state court views on school finance equalization. While several courts have declined to intervene in school finance issues, others, as in *Robinson,* have held that methods of financing the schools are unconstitutional.

In Connecticut, the court held the equal protection provision of the state constitution was violated by the state educational finance formula, which allocated money to local school districts on a flat grant basis, not taking into consideration the fiscal ability of local school districts.[33] The court reasoned that, under the Connecticut Constitution, education was a fundamental right because it was explicitly recognized in Article VIII, § I, and the history and tradition of the state demonstrated a commitment to the education of children. In holding the system unconstitutional and mandating that the legislature redress the faults, the court observed absolute equality was not required, and cost differences due to variations in educational needs and economic conditions may be taken into account.

In 1983, the Supreme Court of Arkansas held that state's system of financing public schools was unconstitutional. The court noted that minimal educational programs are not enough to satisfy the equal opportunity demanded by equal protection. It said that "[B]are and minimal sufficiency does not translate into equal educational opportunity."[34]

By 1990, plaintiffs' challenges to state school finance programs had failed in fourteen cases[35] and had prevailed in twelve.[36] Franklin and Hickrod[37] observe the split in the views of the state courts is primarily due to whether the courts believe education is a fundamental right for equal protection purposes and apparently does not depend on the wording of the education clauses. Where the courts are influenced by *Rodriguez* in the interpretation of the Equal Protection Clause, the defendant state will most likely prevail. Where the state court goes beyond the *Rodriguez* equal protection interpretation and rules that state equal protection is broader and more encompassing than the federal version, then plaintiff poor school districts are most likely to prevail. This latter approach was followed in *Serrano* I,[38] wherein the California Supreme Court refused to restrict the meaning of the equal protection clause of the California Constitution to the more narrow definition imposed by *Rodriguez*.

Future Directions of Litigation

In states where plaintiffs have prevailed and state school finance programs have been held unconstitutional, the courts have put slightly different twists on their reasoning suggesting directions of future litigation. First, the *Serrano II*[39] type of rationale may be employed by the court, holding that education is a fundamental right and that malapportionment of school funds violates the state equal protection clause. Second, alternatively, the state school finance program may be held invalid under the *Robinson v. Cahill type* of reasoning, which relies solely on the education provision of state constitution without invoking equal protection.[40] Third, a state court may hold, as did the court in *Pauley v. Kelly*, the education provision of the state constitution is sufficient to establish fundamentality of education and that the two provisions (the education clause and the equal protection clause) work in concert to require strict judicial scrutiny of state school finance legislation.[41] In *Pauley*, the court viewed the state equal protection clause and the education provision as being "harmonious" and complementary to each other. Fourth, the state court may hold that the education provision alone — whether the wording is "equal," "uniform," "efficient," or "thorough and efficient" — by its inclusion in the state constitution establishes the fundamentality of education and thereby implicitly justifies more intensive judicial oversight of legislative discretion.[42]

Regardless of the rationale, though, a trend has developed for state courts to be less deferential to the state legislatures in matters pertaining to education. In particular, the school finance cases in Kentucky,[43] New Jersey,[44] and Texas[45] suggest a much more active role to be played by the state courts in interpreting the intent of education provisions of state constitutions.[46]

The Fundamentality Issue

Government could not function effectively if it were not permitted to classify persons for various reasons to alleviate problems, bestow benefits or, in some cases, to impose detriments. Government, however, cannot classify and create distinctions for illegitimate or discriminatory purposes. Some distinctions may be unimportant, while others may strike at the basic fabric of society and offend individuals and the common good of the state. Governmental discrimination is not in and of itself violative of equal protection unless the distinctions drawn affect "fundamental interests" and "suspect" classifications of people. Equal protection forbids only unreasonable discrimination or harmful and invidious discrimination.

One court explained the matter of equal protection in this way:

> There are a number of reasons why the Equal Protection Clause has not historically been thought to require that all legislation be applied equally to all citizens. First, government must be able to draw reasonable distinctions among its citizens in awarding benefits and imposing burdens. Second, there is the traditional deference of courts to the Legislature's expression of the will of the people. Third, any strictly egalitarian view of the Equal Protection Clause could not be justified historically in terms of the intention of those who drafted and ratified it. Fourth, "equality" is itself such an ephemeral concept that judicial review on an abstract "equality" standard is bound to be unmanageable.[47]

If disparate allocation of governmental benefits can be justified on a basis of reasonable classification or the interests involved are not fundamental, then statutes will be regarded as constitutional. On the other hand, if a statute divides persons into suspect classes, and if the benefits and detriments affect a fundamental interest, then the statute may be unconstitutional. On the other hand, if no fundamental interest is at stake, the effects of the disparity are by definition constitutionally inconsequential, then equal protection is not implicated.

In *Rodriguez,* cited above, the U.S. Supreme Court held that education is not a fundamental right, and disparate allocation of resources among school districts does not discriminate against any particular "suspect classification" of children. The court in *Rodriguez* basically ruled that a state legislature can heap benefits on some wealthy school districts and deprive others of fiscal resources and not offend the federal Equal Protection Clause.

Contrarily, the California Supreme Court has held that the equal protection clause of a state's constitution cannot be confined to the scope of federal equal protection, but can exceed it in breadth in application to state legislation.[49] In this regard, the *Serrano* court said:

> our state equal protection provisions, while substantially equivalent of the guarantees contained in the Fourteenth Amendment to the United States Constitution, are possessed of an independent vitality which, in a given case, may demand an analysis different from that which would obtain if only the federal standard were applicable.

Based on this "independent vitality," the California Supreme Court found that wealth differentials among school districts involves a suspect classification; and it further found the benefits and detriments bestowed on these suspect classes were highly significant because they affected a fundamental interest, education. Accordingly, the court elevated the judicial test from "rational relationship" to "strict scrutiny" and found the California state system of school finance to be constitutionally deficient.[50]

Even though the Supreme Court of Connecticut found an "independent vitality" in its own constitution, as well, the court found that sole reliance on equal protection was not necessary because that state's education provision (Article VIII, § 1) established education as a "fundamental right."[51]

The reasoning of the Connecticut court was basically similar to that of the West Virginia Supreme Court in *Pauley,* where the state equal protection clause and the education provision were adjudged to be complementary and harmonious, requiring a strict-scrutiny analysis of state school finance statutes.[52]

Several other state supreme courts, however, have not extended their own state equal protection clauses beyond the rationale of *Rodriguez.* For example, the Supreme Court of Georgia has found that education is not a fundamental right in that state, concluding, "[W]e hold that education, per se, is not a 'fundamental right' and that the Georgia public school system must stand if it satisfies the 'rational relationship' test."[53] Accordingly, this court found that the Georgia school finance system was not unconstitutional.

State Court precedent is divided as to whether education is a fundamental right for equal protection purposes.[54] More recently, though, the Supreme Courts of Kentucky[55] and Texas[56] have found it unnecessary to examine the "vitality" of their state equal protection clauses in order to declare that education is a fundamental interest. These state courts refused to be drawn into the technicalities of the federal judicial review tests of equal protection, in interpreting their own constitutions. Rather, they have concluded that the inherent importance of education to the republican form of government and the historical antecedents to the education provisions of their respective state constitutions provide ample evidence of the fundamentality of education. Both the Kentucky and Texas courts seemed to imply that education is fundamental because it could arguably be defended as a natural right[57] or as an aspect of natural justice, in the same context as liberty and property.[58] In this regard, the Kentucky court cited constitutional debates where it was strongly maintained that "public schools . . . are a part and parcel of our free institutions, woven into the very web and woof of popular government"[59] and the Texas court quoted favorably from its own constitutional convention record, which declared that "[education] must be classed among the abstract rights, based on apparent natural justice."[60]

The Supreme Court of Montana also found it unnecessary to deal with the equal protection issue because it had already found that education was a fundamental right, as evidenced by its inclusion in the education provision (Article X, § 1) of the Montana Constitution.[61]

There then appears to be a trend for the state courts to evaluate the constitutionality of state school finance programs in light of the state constitutions' education provisions rather than on the basis of the equal protection clauses. Their presumption is that where state constitutions specifically require state legislatures to provide for education, there is good reason to assume that the framers of the state constitutions viewed education as a fundamental right.

State School Finance System That Results in Revenue Disparities Based on Fiscal Ability of School Districts Does Not Violate the Equal Protection Clause of the Fourteenth Amendment

— · — · — · — · — ·—

San Antonio Independent School District v. Rodriguez

— · — · — · — · — ·—

Supreme Court of the United States, 1973.
411 U.S. 1, 93 S.Ct. 1278, rehearing denied 411
U.S. 959, 93 S.Ct. 1919 (1973).

Mr. Justice POWELL delivered the opinion of the Court. This suit attacking the Texas system of financing public education was initiated by Mexican-American parents whose children attend the elementary and secondary schools in the Edgewood Independent School District, an urban school district in San Antonio, Texas. They brought a class action on behalf of schoolchildren throughout the State who are members of minority groups or who are poor and reside in school districts having a low property tax base. Named as defendants were the State Board of Education, the Commissioner of Education, the State Attorney General, and the Bexar County (San Antonio) Board of Trustees. The complaint was filed in the summer of 1968 and a three-judge court was impaneled in January 1969. In December 1971 the panel rendered its judgment in a *per curiam* opinion holding the Texas school finance system unconstitutional under the Equal Protection Clause of the Fourteenth Amendment. The State appealed, and we noted probable jurisdiction to consider the far-reaching constitutional questions presented. . . . For the reasons stated in this opinion, we reverse the decision of the District Court. . . .

The school district in which appellees reside, the Edgewood Independent School

District, has been compared throughout this litigation with the Alamo Heights Independent School District. This comparison between the least and most affluent districts in the San Antonio area serves to illustrate the manner in which the dual system of finance operates and to indicate the extent to which substantial disparities exist despite the State's impressive progress in recent years. Edgewood is one of seven public school districts in the metropolitan area. Approximately 22,000 students are enrolled in its twenty-five elementary and secondary schools. The district is situated in the core-city sector of San Antonio in a residential neighborhood that has little commercial or industrial property. The residents are predominantly of Mexican-American descent: approximately 90 percent of the student population is Mexican-American and over 6 percent is Negro. The average assessed property value per pupil is $5,960 — the lowest in the metropolitan area — and the median family income ($4,686) is also the lowest. At an equalized tax rate of $1.05 per $100 of assessed property — the highest in the metropolitan area — the district contributed $26 to the education of each child for the 1967-1968 school year above its Local Fund Assignment for the Minimum Foundation Program. The Foundation Program contributed $222 per pupil for a state-local total of $248. Federal funds added another $108 for a total of $356 per pupil.

Alamo Heights is the most affluent school district in San Antonio. Its six schools, housing approximately 5,000 students, are situated in a residential community quite unlike the Edgewood District. The school population is predominantly "Anglo," having only 18 percent Mexican-Americans and less than 1 percent Negroes. The assessed property value per pupil exceeds $49,000, and the median family income is $8,001. In 1967-1968 the local tax rate of $.85 per $100 of valuation yielded $333 per pupil over and above its contribution to the Foundation Program. Coupled with the $225 provided from that Program, the district was able to supply $558 per student. Supplemented by a $36 per-pupil grant from federal sources, Alamo Heights spent $594 per pupil. . . .

Despite recent increases, substantial inter-district disparities in school expenditures found by the District Court to prevail in San Antonio and in varying degrees throughout the State still exist. And it was these disparities, largely attributable to differences in the amounts of money collected through local property taxation, that led the District Court to conclude that Texas' dual system of public school financing violated the Equal Protection Clause. The District Court held that the Texas system discriminates on the basis of wealth in the manner in which education is provided for its people. 337 F.Supp., at 282. Finding that wealth is a "suspect" classification and that education is a "fundamental" interest, the District Court held that the Texas system could be sustained only if the State could show that it was premised upon some compelling state interest. Id., at 282-284. On this issue the court concluded that "[n]ot only are defendants unable to demonstrate compelling state interests . . . they fail even to establish a reasonable basis for these classifications." Id., at 284.

Texas virtually concedes that its historically rooted dual system of financing education could not withstand the strict judicial scrutiny that this Court has found appropriate in reviewing legislative judgments that interfere with fundamental constitutional rights or that involve suspect classifications. If, as previous decisions have indicated, strict scrutiny means that the State's system is not entitled to the usual presumption of validity, that the State rather than the complainants must carry a "heavy burden of justification," that the State must demonstrate that its educational system has been structured with "precision," and is "tailored" narrowly to serve legitimate objectives and that it has selected the "less drastic means" for effectuating its objectives, the Texas financing system and its counterpart in virtually every other State will not pass muster. The State candidly admits that "[n]o one familiar with the Texas system would contend that it has yet achieved perfection." Apart from its concession that educational financing in Texas has "defects" and "imperfections," the State defends the system's rationality with vigor and disputes the District Court's finding that it lacks a "reasonable basis."

This, then, establishes the framework for our analysis. We must decide, first, whether the Texas system of financing public education operates to the disadvantage of some suspect class or impinges upon a fundamental right explicitly or implicitly protected by the Constitution, thereby requiring strict judicial scrutiny. If so, the judgment of the District Court should be affirmed. If not, the Texas scheme must still be examined to determine whether it rationally furthers some legitimate, articulated state purpose and therefore does not constitute an invidious discrimination in violation of the Equal Protection Clause of the Fourteenth Amendment.

The District Court's opinion does not reflect the novelty and complexity of the constitutional questions posed by appellees' challenge to Texas' system of school financing. In concluding that strict judicial scrutiny was required, that court relied on decisions dealing with the rights of indigents to equal treatment in the criminal trial and appellate processes, and on cases disapproving wealth restrictions on the right to vote. Those cases, the District Court concluded, established wealth as a suspect classification. Finding that the local property tax system discriminated on the basis of wealth, it regarded those precedents as controlling. It then reasoned, based on decisions of this Court affirming the undeniable importance of education, that there is a fundamental right to education and that, absent some compelling state justification, the Texas system could not stand.

We are unable to agree that this case, which in significant aspects is *sui generis,* may be so neatly fitted into the conventional mosaic of constitutional analysis under the Equal Protection Clause. Indeed, for the several reasons that follow, we find neither the suspect-classification nor the fundamental-interest analysis persuasive.

The wealth discrimination discovered by the District Court in this case, and by several other courts that have recently struck down school-financing laws in other States, is quite unlike any of the forms of wealth discrimination heretofore reviewed by this Court.
. . .

The case comes to us with no definitive description of the classifying facts or delineation of the disfavored class. Examination of the District Court's opinion and of appellees' complaint, briefs, and contentions at oral argument suggests, however, at least three ways in which the discrimination claimed here might be described. The Texas system of school financing might be regarded as discriminating (1) against "poor" persons whose incomes fall below some identifiable level of poverty or who might be characterized as functionally "indigent," or (2) against those who are relatively poorer than others, or (3) against all those who, irrespective of their personal incomes, happen to reside in relatively poorer school districts. Our task must be to ascertain whether, in fact, the Texas system has been shown to discriminate on any of these possible bases and, if so, whether the resulting classification may be regarded as suspect.

The precedents of this Court provide the proper starting point. The individuals, or groups of individuals, who constituted the class discriminated against in our prior cases shared two distinguishing characteristics: because of their impecunity they were completely unable to pay for some desired benefit, and as a consequence, they sustained an absolute deprivation of a meaningful opportunity to enjoy that benefit. . . .

Only appellees' first possible basis for describing the class disadvantaged by the Texas school-financing system — discrimination against a class of definably "poor" persons — might arguably meet the criteria established in . . . prior cases. Even a cursory examination, however, demonstrates that neither of the two distinguishing characteristics of wealth classifications can be found here. First, in support of their charge that the system discriminates against the "poor," appellees have made no effort to demonstrate that it operates to the peculiar disadvantage of any class fairly definable as indigent, or as composed of persons whose incomes are beneath any designated poverty level. Indeed, there is reason to believe that the poorest families are not necessarily clustered in the poorest property districts. A recent and exhaustive study of school districts in Connecticut concluded that "[i]t is clearly incorrect . . . to contend that the 'poor' live in 'poor' districts . . . . Thus, the major factual assumption of *Serrano*—that the educational financing system discriminates against the 'poor'—is simply false in Connecticut." Defining "poor" families as those below the Bureau of the Census "poverty level," the Connecticut study found, not surprisingly, that the poor were clustered around commercial and industrial areas—those same areas that provide the most attractive sources of property tax income for school districts. Whether a similar pattern would be discovered in Texas is not known, but there is no basis on the record in this case for assuming that the poorest people—defined by reference to any level of absolute impecunity—are concentrated in the poorest districts.

Second, neither appellees nor the District Court addressed the fact that, unlike each of the foregoing cases, lack of personal resources has not occasioned an absolute deprivation of the desired benefit. The argument here is not that the children in districts having relatively low assessable property values are receiving no public education; rather, it is that they are receiving a poorer quality education than that available to children in districts having more assessable wealth. Apart from the unsettled and disputed question whether the quality of education may be determined by the amount of money expended for it, a sufficient answer to appellees' argument is that, at least where wealth is involved, the Equal Protection Clause does not require absolute equality or precisely equal advantages. Nor indeed, in view of the infinite variables affecting the educational process, can any system assure equal quality of education except in the most relative sense. . . .

For these two reasons—the absence of any evidence that the financing system discriminates against any definable category of "poor" people or that it results in the absolute deprivation of education—the disadvantaged class is not susceptible of identification in traditional terms.

As suggested above, appellees and the District Court may have embraced a second or third approach, the second of which might be characterized as a theory of relative or comparative discrimination based on family income. Appellees sought to prove that a direct correlation exists between the wealth of families within each district and the expenditures therein for education. That is, along a continuum, the poorer the family the lower the dollar amount of education received by the family's children. . . . These questions need not be addressed in this case, however, since appellees' proof fails to support their allegations or the District Court's conclusions. . . .

This brings us, then, to the third way in which the classification scheme might be defined—*district* wealth discrimination. Since the only correlation indicated by the evidence is between district property wealth and expenditures, it may be argued that discrimination might be found without regard to the individual income characteristics of district residents. . . . Alternatively, as suggested in Mr. Justice MARSHALL's dissenting opinion, the class might be defined more restrictively to include children in districts with assessable property which falls below the statewide average, or median, or below some other artificially defined level.

However described, it is clear that appellees' suit asks this Court to extend its most exacting scrutiny to review a system that allegedly discriminates against a large, diverse, and amorphous class, unified only by the common factor of residence in districts that happen to have less taxable wealth than other districts. The system of alleged discrimination and the class it defines have none of the traditional indicia of suspectness: the class is not saddled with such disabilities, or subjected to such a history of purposeful unequal treatment, or relegated to such a position of political powerlessness as to command extraordinary protection from the majoritarian political process.

We thus conclude that the Texas system does not operate to the peculiar disadvantage of any suspect class. But in recognition of the fact that this Court has never heretofore held that wealth discrimination alone provides an adequate basis for invoking strict scrutiny, appellees have not relied solely on this contention. They also assert that the State's system impermissibly interferes with the exercise of a "fundamental" right and that accordingly the prior decisions of this Court require the application of the strict standard of judicial review. . . . It is this question— whether education is a fundamental right, in the sense that it is among the rights and liberties protected by the Constitution— which has so consumed the attention of courts and commentators in recent years. . . .

Nothing this Court holds today in any way detracts from our historic dedication to public education. We are in complete agreement with the conclusion of the three-judge panel below that "the grave significance of education both to the individual and to our society" cannot be doubted. But the importance of a service performed by the State does not determine whether it must be regarded as fundamental for purposes of examination under the Equal Protection Clause. . . . It is not the province of this Court to create substantive constitutional rights in the name of guaranteeing equal protection of the laws. Thus, the key to discovering whether education is "fundamental" is not to be found in comparisons of the relative societal significance of education as opposed to subsistence or housing. Nor is it to be found by weighing whether education is as important as the right to travel. Rather, the answer lies in assessing whether there is a right to education explicitly or implicitly guaranteed by the Constitution. . . .

Education, of course, is not among the rights afforded explicit protection under our federal Constitution. Nor do we find any basis for saying it is implicitly so protected. As we have said, the undisputed importance of education will not alone cause this Court to depart from the usual standard for reviewing a State's social and economic legislation. It is appellees' contention, however, that education is distinguishable from other services and benefits provided by the State because it bears a peculiarly close relationship to other rights and liberties accorded protection under the Constitution. Specifically, they insist that education is itself a fundamental personal right because it is essential to the effective exercise of First Amendment freedoms and to intelligent utilization of the right to vote. . . .

. . . We need not dispute any of these propositions. The Court has long afforded zealous protection against unjustifiable governmental interference with the individual's rights to speak and to vote. Yet we have never presumed to possess either the ability or the authority to guarantee to the citizenry the most *effective* speech or the most *informed* electoral choice. That these may be desirable goals of a system of freedom of expression and of a representative form of government is not to be doubted. These are indeed goals to be pursued by a people whose thoughts and beliefs are freed from governmental interference. But they are not values to be implemented by judicial intrusion into otherwise legitimate state activities.

Even if it were conceded that some identifiable quantum of education is a constitutionally protected prerequisite to the meaningful exercise of either right, we have no indication that the present levels of educational expenditures in Texas provide an education that falls short. Whatever merit appellees' argument might have if a State's financing system occasioned an absolute denial of educational opportunities to any of its children, that argument provides no basis for finding an interference with fundamental rights where only relative differences in spending levels are involved and where—as is true in the present case—no charge fairly could be made that the system fails to provide each child with an opportunity to acquire the basic minimal skills necessary for the enjoyment of the rights of speech and of full participation in the political process. . . .

We have carefully considered each of the arguments supportive of the District Court's finding that education is a fundamental right or liberty and have found those arguments unpersuasive. In one further respect we find this a particularly inappropriate case in which to subject state action to strict judicial scrutiny.

The present case, in another basic sense, is significantly different from any of the cases in which the Court has applied strict scrutiny to state or federal legislation touching upon constitutionally protected rights. Each of our prior cases involved legislation which "deprived," "infringed," or "interfered" with the free exercise of some such fundamental personal right or liberty. . . . A critical distinction between those cases and the one now before us lies in what Texas is endeavoring to do with respect to education. . . .

Every step leading to the establishment of the system Texas utilizes today—including the decisions permitting localities to tax and expend locally, and creating and continuously expanding the state aid—was implemented in an effort to *extend* public education and to improve its quality. Of course, every reform that benefits some more than others may be criticized for what it fails to accomplish. But we think it plain that, in substance, the thrust of the Texas system is affirmative and reformatory and, therefore, should be scrutinized under judicial principles sensitive to the nature of the State's efforts and to the rights reserved to the States under the Constitution.

It should be clear, for the reasons stated above and in accord with the prior decisions of this Court, that this is not a case in which the challenged state action must be subjected to the searching judicial scrutiny reserved for laws that create suspect classifications or impinge upon constitutionally protected rights.

We need not rest our decision, however, solely on the inappropriateness of the strict-scrutiny test. A century of Supreme Court adjudication under the Equal Protection Clause affirmatively supports the application of the traditional standard of review, which requires only that the State's system be shown to bear some rational relationship to legitimate state purposes. This case represents far more than a challenge to the manner in which Texas provides for the education of its children. We have here nothing less than a direct attack on the way in which Texas has chosen to raise and disburse state and local tax revenues. We are asked to condemn the State's judgment in conferring on political subdivisions the power to tax local property to supply revenues for local interests. In so doing, appellees would have the Court intrude in an area in which it has traditionally deferred to state legislatures. This Court has often admonished against such interferences with the State's fiscal policies under the Equal Protection Clause. . . .

Thus, we stand on familiar grounds when we continue to acknowledge that the Justices of this Court lack both the expertise and the familiarity with local problems so necessary to the making of wise decisions with respect to the raising and disposition of public revenues. Yet, we are urged to direct the States either to alter drastically the present system or to throw out the property tax altogether in favor of some other form of taxation. No scheme of taxation, whether the tax is imposed on property, income, or purchases of goods and services, has yet been devised which is free of all discriminatory impact. In such a complex arena in which no perfect alternatives exist, the Court does well not to impose too rigorous a standard of scrutiny lest all local fiscal schemes become subjects of criticism under the Equal Protection Clause.

In addition to matters of fiscal policy, this case also involves the most persistent and difficult questions of educational policy, another area in which this Court's lack of specialized knowledge and experience counsels against premature interference with the informed judgments made at the state and local levels. Education, perhaps even more than welfare assistance, presents a myriad of "intractable economic, social, and even philosophical problems." . . . The very complexity of the problems of financing and managing a statewide public school system suggests that "there will be more than one constitutionally permissible method of solving them," and that, within the limits of rationality, "the legislature's efforts to tackle the problems" should be entitled to respect. . . . On even the most basic questions in this area the scholars and educational experts are divided. Indeed, one of the major sources of controversy concerns the extent to which there is a demonstrable correlation between educational expenditures and the quality of education—and assumed correlation underlying virtually every legal conclusion drawn by the District Court in this case. Related to the questioned relationship between cost and quality is the equally unsettled controversy as to the proper goals of a system of public education. And the question regarding the most effective relationship between state boards of education and local school boards, in terms of their respective responsibilities and degrees of control, is now undergoing searching reexamination. The ultimate wisdom as to these and related problems of education is not likely to be divined for all time even by the scholars who now so earnestly debate the issues. In such circumstances, the judiciary is well advised to refrain from imposing on the States inflexible constitutional restraints that could circumscribe or handicap the continued research and experimentation so vital to finding even partial solutions to educational problems and to keeping abreast of ever-changing conditions.

It must be remembered, also, that every claim arising under the Equal Protection Clause has implications for the relationship between national and state power under our federal system. Questions of federalism are always inherent in the process of determining whether a State's laws are to be accorded the traditional presumption of constitutionality or are to be subjected instead to rigorous judicial scrutiny. While "[t]he maintenance of the principles of federalism is a foremost consideration in interpreting any of the pertinent constitutional provisions under which this Court examines state action," it would be difficult to imagine a case having a greater potential impact on our federal system than the one now before us, in which we are urged to abrogate systems of financing public education presently in existence in virtually every State.

The foregoing considerations buttress our conclusion that Texas' system of public school finance is an inappropriate candidate for strict judicial scrutiny. . . .

Apart from federal assistance, each Texas school receives its funds from the State and from its local school district. On a statewide average, a roughly comparable amount of funds is derived from each source. The State's contribution, under the Minimum Foundation

Program, was designed to provide an adequate minimum educational offering in every school in the State. . . .

By virtue of the obligation to fulfill its Local Fund Assignment, every district must impose an ad valorem tax on property located within its borders. The Fund Assignment was designed to remain sufficiently low to assure that each district would have some ability to provide a more enriched educational program. Every district supplements its Foundation grant in this manner. In some districts, the local property tax contribution is insubstantial, as in Edgewood where the supplement was only $26 per pupil in 1967. In other districts, the local share may far exceed even the total Foundation grant. In part, local differences are attributable to differences in the rates of taxation or in the degree to which the market value for any category of property varies from its assessed value. The greatest interdistrict disparities, however, are attributable to differences in the amount of assessable property available within any district. Those districts that have more property, or more valuable property, have a greater capability for supplementing state funds. . . .

The "foundation grant" theory upon which Texas legislators and educators based the Gilmer-Aikin bills, was a product of the pioneering work of two New York Educational reformers in the 1920s, George D. Strayer and Robert M. Haig. Their efforts were devoted to establishing a means of guaranteeing a minimum statewide educational program without sacrificing the vital element of local participation. The Strayer-Haig thesis represented an accommodation between these two competing forces. . . .

The Texas system of school finance is responsive to these two forces. While assuring a basic education for every child in the State, it permits and encourages a large measure of participation in and control of each district's schools at the local level. In an era that has witnessed a consistent trend toward centralization of the functions of government, local sharing of responsibility for public education has survived. . . .

The persistence of attachment to government at the lowest level where education is concerned reflects the depth of commitment of its supporters. In part, local control means, as Professor Coleman suggests, the freedom to devote more money to the education of one's children. Equally important, however, is the opportunity it offers for participation in the decision-making process that determines how those local tax dollars will be spent. Each locality is free to tailor local programs to local needs. . . . No area of social concern stands to profit more from a multiplicity of viewpoints and from a diversity of approaches than does public education.

. . . Appellees suggest that local control could be preserved and promoted under other financing systems that resulted in more equality in educational expenditures. While it is no doubt true that reliance on local property taxation for school revenues provides less freedom of choice with respect to expenditures for some districts than for others, the existence of "some inequality" in the manner in which the State's rationale is achieved is not alone a sufficient basis for striking down the entire system. . . . It may not be condemned simply because it imperfectly effectuates the State's goals. . . . Nor must the financing system fail because, as appellees suggest, other methods of satisfying the State's interest, which occasion "less drastic" disparities in expenditures, might be conceived. Only where state action impinges on the exercise of fundamental constitutional rights or liberties must it be found to have chosen the least restrictive alternative. . . . The people of Texas may be justified in believing that other systems of school financing, which place more of the financial responsibility in the hands of the State, will result in a comparable lessening of desired local autonomy. . . .

Appellees further urge that the Texas system is unconstitutionally arbitrary because it allows the availability of local taxable resources to turn on "happenstance." . . . But any scheme of local taxation—indeed the very existence of identifiable local governmental units—requires the establishment of jurisdictional boundaries that are inevitably arbitrary. It is equally inevitable that some

localities are going to be blessed with more taxable assets than others. . . .

Moreover, if local taxation for local expenditures were an unconstitutional method of providing for education then it might be an equally impermissible means of providing other necessary services customarily financed largely from local property taxes, including local police and fire protection, public health and hospitals, and public utility facilities of various kinds. We perceive no justification for such a severe denigration of local property taxation and control as would follow from appellees' contentions. It has simply never been within the constitutional prerogative of this Court to nullify statewide measures for financing public services merely because the burdens or benefits thereof fall unevenly depending upon the relative wealth of the political subdivisions in which citizens live.

In sum, to the extent that the Texas system of school financing results in unequal expenditures between children who happen to reside in different districts, we cannot say that such disparities are the product of a system that is so irrational as to be invidiously discriminatory. . . . In its essential characteristics, the Texas plan for financing public education reflects what many educators for a half century have thought was an enlightened approach to a problem for which there is no perfect solution. We are unwilling to assume for ourselves a level of wisdom superior to that of legislators, scholars, and educational authorities in fifty States, especially where the alternatives proposed are only recently conceived and nowhere yet tested. The constitutional standard under the Equal Protection Clause is whether the challenged state action rationally furthers a legitimate state purpose or interest. . . . We hold that the Texas plan abundantly satisfies this standard.

. . . The consideration and initiation of fundamental reforms with respect to state taxation and education are matters reserved for the legislative processes of the various States, and we do no violence to the values of federalism and separation of powers by staying our hand. We hardly need add that this Court's action today is not to be viewed as placing its judicial imprimatur on the status quo. The need is apparent for reform in tax systems which may well have relied too long and too heavily on the local property tax. And certainly innovative thinking as to public education, its methods, and its funding is necessary to assure both a higher level of quality and greater uniformity of opportunity. These matters merit the continued attention of the scholars who already have contributed much by their challenges. But the ultimate solutions must come from the lawmakers and from the democratic pressures of those who elect them.

Reversed.

NOTE

1. *The Three Level Standard.* Three years after the ruling in *Rodriguez,* the U.S. Supreme Court redefined the two level standard, rational relationship versus strict scrutiny, to include a third "intermediate" standard. The Court said:

> There are three standards generally accepted for determining constitutionality under the Equal Protection Provisions of both the U.S. and State Constitutions: (1) The rational relationship test; (2) The intermediate level of scrutiny; and (3) The strict judicial scrutiny standard. Under the rational relationship test a statutory classification is presumed valid and will comport with constitutional standards as long as it bears a *reasonable* relationship to a legitimate governmental purpose. The intermediate level of judicial scrutiny requires that a classification be *substantially* related to an *important* governmental objective. See, *Craig v. Boren,* 429 U.S. 190, 97 S.Ct. 451, 50 L.Ed.2d 397 (1976). Under the strict judicial scrutiny standard, which is employed when a classification involves socially stigmatic inequalities, such as those based on race . . . the governmental classification will fall unless the government demonstrates that the classification is *necessarily* related to a *compelling* governmental objective. See *San Antonio School District v. Rodriguez,* 411 U.S. 1, 93

S.Ct. 1278, 36 L.Ed.2d 16 (1973); *Graham v. Richardson,* 403 U.S. 365, 91 S.Ct. 1848, 29 L.Ed.2d 534 (1971); *Shapiro v. Thompson,* 394 U.S. 618, 89 S.Ct. 1322, 22 L.Ed.2d 600 (1969); *Mosgrove v. Town of Federal Heights,* 190 Colo. 1, 543 P.2d 715 (1975); *Bernzen v. Boulder,* 186 Colo. 81, 525 P.2d 416 (1974); *Jarmel v. Putnam,* 179 Colo. 215, 499 P.2d 603 (1972). Application of the strict scrutiny test means that the classification is not entitled to the usual presumption of validity and that the State bears the burden of proving that the classification system 'has been structured with "precision" and is "tailored" narrowly to serve legitimate objectives and that it has selected the less "drastic means" for effectuating its objectives.' *San Antonio School District v. Rodriguez, supra* [411 U.S.] at 16-17 [93 S.Ct. at 1287-88]. *Craig v. Boren, supra.*

Education Is Not a Fundamental Right in Georgia, and Disparities in School Funding Do Not Violate Either State Equal Protection or Education Adequacy Provision

McDaniel v. Thomas

Supreme Court of Georgia, 1981.
248 Ga. 632, 285 S.E. 2d 156.

SMITH, Justice. The basic question presented by this case is whether the current system of funding public education in Georgia conforms to the mandates of our state constitution.

Plaintiff-appellees are parents, children, and school officials who reside in school districts which, in relation to other school districts in the state, have a low property tax base. They brought a declaratory judgment action in the Superior Court of Polk County alleging that the existing system of financing public education 1) violates the equal protection provisions of our state constitution (Constitution of 1976, Art. I, Sec. II, Par. III (Code Ann. § 2-203); Art. I, Sec. II, Par. VII (Code Ann.

§ 2-207) and 2) deprives the children in their district of an "adequate education" in contravention of Art. VIII, Sec. I, Par. I (Code Ann. § 2-4901) and Art. VIII, Sec. VIII, Par. I (Code Ann. § 2-5601). The trial court agreed with plaintiffs' equal protection arguments and declared the existing school finance system unconstitutional. Defendants brought this appeal. The court, however, rejected plaintiffs' assertions regarding "adequate education," and they have filed a cross-appeal. . . .

Public education in Georgia is financed through federal, state and local funds. . . .

The great bulk of state support for local school systems, approximately 80 per cent, is allocated under the Adequate Program for Education in Georgia (APEG). See Code Ann. Chapter 32-6A. In fiscal year 1981, APEG was funded at a level of almost $800 million.

. . .

APEG is designed to meet basic educational needs. Because the basic needs of school districts vary, the amounts allocated to a particular school district within a particular APEG item also vary. Most allotments are based upon the number of pupils in the district in average daily attendance. . . .

APEG is not simply a grant from the state to local school districts. As a condition to participation in APEG, each local school district must contribute an amount obtained from ad valorem taxation. This amount is referred to as "required local effort" (RLE). Each school district's RLE is calculated on the basis of its proportionate share of the equalized adjusted school property tax digest multiplied by a total statewide local effort figure of 78.6 million. Because the RLE is determined on the basis of a school district's proportionate share of property wealth, the property tax rate imposed by each school district for RLE is virtually the same, approximately 2.15 mills. (A one mill rate imposes a tax of 1/10 cent on each dollar's worth of property.)

After a district's RLE is determined, it is deducted from the total amount to which the district is entitled under APEG. The remainder is provided by the state. With the total statewide RLE fixed at $78.6 million, APEG is currently funded 90% by state funds and 10% by RLE.

Theoretically, RLE is an equalizing component in the APEG system—the state provides less funds to school districts which, by virtue of local property values, are more capable of financing public education at the local level. . . .

In reality, however, RLE does little to equalize property rich and property poor districts. As indicated above, the total statewide RLE has been fixed at approximately $78.6 million. Meanwhile, educational costs have risen. Whereas, in the early 1970's, total RLE constituted almost 20 percent of APEG, it now amounts to only 10 percent. Total RLE is at such a low level, relative to total APEG expenditures, that it cannot have a significant equalizing effect as between property rich and property poor districts. Thus, to an extent, APEG has become a flat grant from the state to local districts wherein considerations relating to local wealth have no place.

If APEG were the only source of public school funding in this state, there would be no significant disparities between school districts insofar as revenues per student in ADA is concerned. However, APEG is not the only source of school revenues. In addition to the categorical aid referred to above, all 187 local school districts in Georgia supplement APEG with funds derived from local property tax assessments . . . It is this feature of the Georgia public school finance system which is largely responsible for the present action. . . .

The evidence in this case establishes beyond doubt that there is a direct relationship between a district's level of funding and the educational opportunities which a school district is able to provide its children. Due to differences in funding, instructional staffs in low wealth districts tend to have less formal training and experience than those in wealthy districts. Larger salary supplements and employee benefits provide wealthier districts with a substantial competitive edge. Further-

---

[T]he . . . wealthiest district, Heard County, was 7.9 times wealthier than the poorest system, Carroll County. In 1977–78, the highest spending district spent $1,682 per student in ADA, while the lowest spending district spent $777.

more, wealthy school districts are financially capable of hiring more teachers than poor districts and thus have a lower student-teacher ratio.

The curriculum in high wealth districts is also superior to that of low wealth districts. The evidence in record establishes that, in low wealth districts, opportunities are limited (or in some cases non-existent) in such areas as foreign language, higher mathematics and science, art, music, physical education, vocational education, special education and remedial education.

Disparities in funding also affect the availability of textbooks, library books, audio-visual equipment, supplies, counseling and testing services, and extra-curricular activities as well as the condition of school buildings and grounds.

The effect of major disparities between school districts is compounded when, as is sometimes the case, poor and wealthy school districts are in close proximity to one another. The superintendent of low wealth Whitfield County testified as follows: "We are compared with [neighboring] Dalton constantly and because of the tremendous difference in financial resources available we come out 'second-class.' This has a devastating impact on our children—educationally, psychologically and otherwise."

Based on the foregoing, the following conclusion of the trial court is unassailable: "[S]imilarly situated children receive very different amounts of educational resources as a result of disparities among school districts in taxable property wealth per pupil . . . The inequalities in the school finance system deny students in property poor districts equal educational opportunities." . . .

To clarify the issues, we shall deal with the cross-appeal first. Cross-appellants maintain that the trial court erred in finding that the existing systems of funding public education in Georgia does not violate Code Ann. §§ 2-4901 and 2-5601. They present two distinct arguments: 1) that the term "adequate education" as embodied in the constitution "incorporates equal educational opportunity as a basic concept;" and 2) that public education in some school districts is

so deficient in basic areas of study that it fails to meet the "adequacy" standard mandated by the state constitution. . . .

1. In addressing the merits of cross-appellants assertion the term "adequate education" "incorporates equal educational opportunity as a basic concept," it is necessary to have some understanding of the history of public education in Georgia prior to the ratification of the Constitution of 1945, wherein the "adequate education" language first appears. This history, it can be seen, is largely a chronicle of the quest for permanent and adequate financing for public education.

More important, for purposes of the instant case, is what this history reveals as to the circumstances existing when the education provision of the 1945 Constitution was formulated. It is clear that, between 1943 and 1945, significant inequalities between local school districts persisted. Moreover, these inequalities were the product of disparities in property values between school districts. Existing legislation helped minimize funding disparities arising from differences in local wealth, but by no means did it eliminate them.

The adoption of the term "adequate education" was not intended to fundamentally alter the existing obligation of the state with regard to education. Mr. Frank Gross, a member of the Constitutional Revision Commission, explained the purpose of the new language to the rest of the Commission: "We tried to make a broader definition of the general purpose of education and eliminated some of the language we thought was surplusage." Records of Constitutional Commission, Vol. I, p. 276. Although consolidation of local school districts as well as a statewide educational tax were discussed (Id., Vol. I, pp. 296, 302), the Commission decided that existing independent school districts should not be abolished. Mr. J. I. Allman expressed the following view: "[W]henever you abolish the average independent system in the larger community you lower the standard of the schools, because the county as a whole, together with what the State puts in the school system, cannot maintain all of the schools in the county on the level that the independent system now operates, and that is my reason for not having advocated its abolition. There is a philosophy on the other side." . . . The Constitutions of 1945 and 1976 preserve the independent school districts.

The framers of the 1945 Constitution envisioned a scheme under which the financing of county and independent school districts was largely based on ad valorem taxation within the district. They understood that disparities in wealth between districts existed and prohibited the formation of new independent school districts. They declined, however, to downgrade existing independent systems by mandating consolidation with county school systems. They acknowledged the "equalization fund" set up by the legislature, but did not give it constitutional status. Id., Vol. I, p. 323.

In 1962, Art. VIII, Sec. XIII, Par. II of the 1945 Constitution (former Code Ann. § 2-7503) was ratified by the voters of this state. It provides: "Freedom from compulsory association at all levels of public education shall be preserved inviolate. The General Assembly shall by taxation provide funds for an adequate education for the citizens of Georgia." The new provision, while expressly recognizing the obligation of the General Assembly "to provide funds for an adequate education" did not purport to impose an obligation on the legislature to *equalize* educational opportunities.

The Constitution of 1976 preserves the same basic financing structure as the 1945 Constitution (as amended). The requirement of local funding for education through ad valorem taxation is maintained.
. . .

The Georgia constitution thus contains very specific provisions relating to the obligation of localities to impose a tax for the maintenance of the public schools and general provisions imposing a duty on the state and General Assembly to provide its citizens an "adequate education." Nowhere in Article VIII of the Constitution is there any express statement as to the obligation of the state to equalize educational opportunities.

In view of the foregoing, we must conclude that the "adequate education" provisions of the constitution do not restrict local school districts from doing what they can to improve educational opportunities within the district, nor do they require the state to equalize educational opportunities between districts. . . .

2. Having determined that the term "adequate education" does not "incorporate equal educational opportunity as a basic concept," we must decide whether public education in some school districts is so deficient in basic areas of study that it fails to meet the "adequacy" standards of the state constitution.

The term "adequate education" is not defined in our constitution. Moreover, Georgia appears to be the only state in the union which employs such a phrase in its constitution to delineate the state's basic obligation with respect to education. . . . However, it is clear that even a "minimum" education must "provide each child with an opportunity to acquire the basic minimum skills necessary for the enjoyment of the rights of speech and of full participation in the political process." *San Antonio School District v. Rodriguez,* supra at 37 93 S.Ct. at 1299.

Beyond this minimum, then, lies an "adequate" education. However, this court has recently noted the inherent difficulty in establishing a "judicially manageable standard for determining whether or not pupils are being provided 'an adequate education.'" . . . We deal in an area where courts have "traditionally deferred to state legislatures." . . . Thus, while an "adequate" education must be designed to produce individuals who can function in society, it is primarily the legislative branch of government which must give content to the term "adequate." . . .

For the above reasons, the judgment on the cross-appeal is affirmed.

The issue presented in the main appeal is whether the trial court erred in holding that the current system of financing public education in Georgia violates the equal protection provisions of the state constitution. It is conceded that any challenge to the Georgia system under the equal protection clause of the U.S. Constitution is foreclosed by *San Antonio School District v. Rodriguez,* supra.

. . . The question now presented is whether the state equal protection provisions impose an *additional* obligation on the state to *equalize* educational opportunities.

What is disturbing about finding such an obligation under state equal protection is the fact that an entire article of the Georgia Constitution (Article VIII) is specifically devoted to education. . . .

In view of the extensive treatment afforded the subject of public education in our state constitution, we believe the absence of any provision imposing an affirmative duty on the General Assembly to equalize educational opportunities is of constitutional significance.
. . .

However, given the applicability of equal protection principles to the instant case, we must conclude that the existing Georgia public school finance system is not subject to appellees' attack.

Appellees have argued that education is a "fundamental right" for purposes of state equal protection and that the Georgia public school finance system is therefore subject to "strict scrutiny." They rely on the following statement in *San Antonio School District v. Rodriguez,* supra at 33-34, 93 S.Ct. at 1296-97: "[T]he key to discovering whether education is 'fundamental' is not to be found in comparisons of the relative societal significance of education as opposed to subsistence or housing. Nor is it to be found by weighing whether education is as important as the right to travel. Rather, the answer lies in assessing whether there is a right to education explicitly or implicitly guaranteed by the Constitution.
. . .

In our view, such an "answer" cannot govern state constitutional analysis. The "equal protection" clause of the Georgia Constitution itself provides: "*Protection to person and property is the paramount duty of government, and shall be impartial and complete.*" (Em-

phasis supplied.) Code Ann. § 2-203. The "explicit or implicit" guarantee model, it can be seen, is one without meaningful limitation insofar as our state constitution is concerned.

"This is not to say that public education is not vital. Of course it is. Rather we stress how difficult it would be to find an objective basis to say the equal protection clause selects education and demands inflexible statewide uniformity in expenditure. Surely no need is more basic than food and lodging . . . Essential also are police and fire protection, as to which the sums spent per resident vary with local decision. Nor are water and sundry public health services available [on an equalized basis]." *Robinson v. Cahill,* supra. at 495-496, 303 A. 2d 273.

"The prudent and correct path is to continue with an analysis of the equal protection argument along the traditional lines of the rational basis test." *Thompson v. Engelking,* supra at 803. . . . We reach this conclusion for several reasons.

First, "we stand on familiar ground when we continue to acknowledge that the Justices of this Court lack both the expertise and the familiarity with local problems so necessary to the making of wise decisions with respect to the raising and disposition of public revenues . . . No scheme of taxation . . . has yet been devised which is free of all discriminatory impact. In such a complex arena in which no perfect alternatives exist, the Court does well not to impose too rigorous a standard of scrutiny lest all local fiscal schemes become subjects of criticism under the Equal Protection Clause.

"In addition to matters of fiscal policy, this case also involves the most persistent and difficult questions of educational policy . . . Education, perhaps even more than welfare assistance, presents a myriad of 'intractable economic, social, and even philosophical problems.' . . . The very complexity of the problems of financing and managing a statewide public school system suggests that 'there will be more than one constitutionally permissible method of solving them,' and that, within the limits of rationality, 'the legislature's efforts to tackle the problems' should be entitled to respect

. . . [T]he judiciary is well advised to refrain from imposing on the States inflexible constitutional restraints that could circumscribe or handicap the continued research and experimentation so vital to finding even partial solutions to educational problems and to keeping abreast of ever-changing conditions." *San Antonio School District v. Rodriguez*, supra at 41-43, 93 S.Ct. at 1301-02.

Finally, we deem it important that the U.S. Supreme Court has found the Texas system of public school finance "an inappropriate candidate for strict judicial scrutiny" (Id. at 44 93 S.Ct. at 1302) and analyzed it under a "rational relationship" test. While the determination of the U.S. Supreme Court that education is not a "fundamental right" does not bind state courts to make the same determination, . . . the fact that education is not a "fundamental right" under the U.S. Constitution provides some guidance to the states. Consistency in constitutional adjudication, though not demanded, is preferred. . . . Consistent with the holding of the U.S. Supreme Court in *Rodriguez*, as well as the decisions of the highest courts in a number of sister states, we hold that education per se is not a "fundamental right" and that the Georgia public school finance system must stand if it satisfies the "rational relationship" test. . . . Thus, if the Georgia school financing system "has a rational and reasonable basis and meets the educational mandate of our constitution [it] should, unless otherwise [invidiously] discriminatory or capricious, be upheld." . . .

The trial court held that, even under a "rational relationship" test, the Georgia system of financing public education must fall. With this conclusion, we cannot agree. The primary purpose of the APEG system is to provide basic educational funding to children throughout the state, and with the exception of RLE which "discriminates" in favor of property poor school districts, it does so on an essentially equal basis. Beyond APEG, the Georgia public school finance system preserves the idea of local contribution, perhaps out of concern "that along with increased control of the purse strings at the state level will go increased control over local policies."

San Antonio School District v. Rodriguez, supra at 53, 93 S.Ct. at 1307. The fact that the state has not *funded* a large-scale equalization plan does not render the current public school finance system invidiously discriminatory. In terms of equalization the system is a poor one. However, the system does bear some rational relationship to legitimate state purposes and is therefore not violative of state equal protection. Accordingly, the judgment of the trial court on the main appeal must be reversed.

Our holding that the current system of financing public education in Georgia is not unconstitutional should not be construed as an endorsement by this court of the status quo. Constitutions are designed to afford *minimum* protections to society. Plaintiffs have shown that serious disparities in educational opportunities exist in Georgia and that legislation currently in effect will not eliminate them. It is clear that a great deal more can be done and needs to be done to equalize educational opportunities in this state. For the present, however, the solutions must come from our lawmakers.

Judgment reversed on main appeal; affirmed on cross appeal. All the Justices concur.

State Financing System That Causes Wide Disparities in Revenue Among Local School Districts Violates "Efficient" Provision of Education Clause of Texas Constitution

---

Edgewood Independent School District v. Kirby

Supreme Court of Texas, 1989.
777 S.W.2d 391.

MAUZY, Justice. At issue is the constitutionality of the Texas system for financing the education of public school children. Edgewood Independent School District, sixty-seven other school districts, and numerous individual school children and parents filed suit seeking a declaration that the Texas school financing system violates the Texas Constitution. . . .

The basic facts of this cause are not in dispute. The only question is whether those facts describe a public school financing system that meets the requirements of the Constitution. As summarized and excerpted, the facts are as follows.

There are approximately three million public school children in Texas. The legislature finances the education of these children through a combination of revenues supplied by the state itself and revenues supplied by local school districts which are governmental subdivisions of the state. Of total education costs, the state provides about forty-two percent, school districts provide about fifty percent, and the remainder comes from various other sources including federal funds. School districts derive revenues from local ad valorem property taxes, and the state raises funds from a variety of sources including the sales tax and various severance and excise taxes.

There are glaring disparities in the abilities of the various school districts to raise revenues from property taxes because taxable property wealth varies greatly from district to district. The wealthiest district has over $14,000,000 of property wealth per student, while the poorest has approximately $20,000; this disparity reflects a 700 to 1 ratio. The 300,000 students in the lowest-wealth schools have less than 3% of the state's property wealth to support their education while the 300,000 students in the highest-wealth schools have over 25% of the state's property wealth; thus the 300,000 students in the wealthiest districts have more than eight times the property value to support their education as the 300,000 students in the poorest districts. The average property wealth in the 100 wealthiest districts is more than twenty times greater than the average property wealth in the 100 poorest districts. Edgewood I.S.D. has $38,854 in property wealth per student; Alamo Heights I.S.D., in the same county, has $570,109 in property wealth per student.

The state has tried for many years to lessen the disparities through various efforts to supplement the poorer districts. Through the Foundation School Program, the state currently attempts to ensure that each district has sufficient funds to provide its students with at least a basic education. . . . Under this program, state aid is distributed to the various districts according to a complex formula such that property-poor districts receive more state aid than do property-rich districts. However, the Foundation School Program does not cover even the cost of meeting the state-mandated minimum requirements. Most importantly, there are no Foundation School Program allotments for school facilities or for debt service. The basic allotment and the transportation allotment understate actual costs, and the career ladder salary supplement for teachers is underfunded. For these reasons and more, almost all school districts spend additional local funds. Low-wealth districts use a significantly greater proportion of their local funds to pay the debt service on construction bonds while high-wealth districts are able to use their funds to pay for a wide array of enrichment programs.

Because of the disparities in district property wealth, spending per student varies widely, ranging from $2,112 to $19,333. Under the existing system, an average of $2,000 more per year is spent on each of the 150,000 students in the wealthiest districts than is spent on the 150,000 students in the poorest districts.

The lower expenditures in the property-poor districts are not the result of lack of tax effort. Generally, the property-rich districts can tax low and spend high while the property-poor districts must tax high merely to spend low. In 1985-86, local tax rates ranged from $.09 to $1.55 per $100 valuation. The 100 poorest districts had an average tax rate of 74.5 cents and spent an average of $2,978 per student. The 100 wealthiest districts had an average tax rate of 47 cents and spent an average of $7,233 per student. In Dallas County, Highland Park I.S.D. taxed at 35.16 cents and spent $4,836 per student while Wilmer-Hutchins I.S.D. taxed at $1.05 and spent $3,513 per student. In Harris County, Deer Park I.S.D. taxed at 64.37 cents and spent $4,846 per student while its neighbor North Forest I.S.D. taxed at $1.05 and yet spent only

$3,182 per student. A person owning an $80,000 home with no homestead exemption would pay $1,206 in taxes in the east Texas low-wealth district of Leveretts Chapel, but would pay only $59 in the west Texas high-wealth district of Iraan-Sheffield. Many districts have become tax havens. The existing funding system permits "budget balanced districts" which, at minimal tax rates, can still spend above the statewide average; if forced to tax at just average tax rates, these districts would generate additional revenues of more than $200,000,000 annually for public education.

Property-poor districts are trapped in a cycle of poverty from which there is no opportunity to free themselves. Because of their inadequate tax base, they must tax at significantly higher rates in order to meet minimum requirements for accreditation; yet their educational programs are typically inferior. The location of new industry and development is strongly influenced by tax rates and the quality of local schools. Thus, the property-poor districts with their high tax rates and inferior schools are unable to attract new industry or development and so have little opportunity to improve their tax base.

The amount of money spent on a student's education has a real and meaningful impact on the educational opportunity offered that student. High-wealth districts are able to provide for their students broader educational experiences including more extensive curricula, more up-to-date technological equipment, better libraries and library personnel, teacher aides, counseling services, lower student-teacher ratios, better facilities, parental involvement programs, and drop-out prevention programs. They are also better able to attract and retain experienced teachers and administrators.

The differences in the quality of educational programs offered are dramatic. For example, San Elizario I.S.D. offers no foreign language, no pre-kindergarten program, no chemistry, no physics, no calculus, and no college preparatory or honors program. It also offers virtually no extracurricular activities such as band, debate, or football. At the time of trial, one-third of Texas school districts did not even meet the state-mandated standards for maximum class size. The great majority of these are low-wealth districts. In many instances, wealthy and poor districts are found contiguous to one another within the same county.

Based on these facts, the trial court concluded that the school financing system violates the Texas Constitution's equal rights guarantee of article I, section 3, the due course of law guarantee of article I, section 19, and the "efficiency" mandate of article VII, section 1. The court of appeals reversed. We reverse the judgment of the court of appeals and, with modification, affirm the judgment of the trial court.

Article VII, section 1 of the Texas Constitution provides:

A general diffusion of knowledge being essential to the preservation of the liberties and rights of the people, it shall be the duty of the Legislature of the State to establish and make suitable provision for the support and maintenance of an efficient system of public free schools.

The court of appeals declined to address petitioners' challenge under this provision and concluded instead that its interpretation was a "political question." Said the court:

That provision does, of course, require that the school system be "efficient," but the provision provides no guidance as to how this or any other court may arrive at a determination of what is efficient or inefficient. Given the enormous complexity of a school system educating three million children, this Court concludes that which is, or is not, "efficient" is essentially a political question not suitable for judicial review.

761 S.W.2d at 867. We disagree. This is not an area in which the Constitution vests exclusive discretion in the legislature; rather the language of article VII, section 1 imposes on the legislature an affirmative duty to establish and provide for the public free schools. This duty is not committed unconditionally to the legislature's discretion, but instead is accompanied by standards. By express constitutional

mandate, the legislature must make "suitable" provision for an "efficient" system for the "essential" purpose of a "general diffusion of knowledge." While these are admittedly not precise terms, they do provide a standard by which this court must, when called upon to do so, measure the constitutionality of the legislature's actions. . . . We do not undertake this responsibility lightly and we begin with a presumption of constitutionality. . . . If the system is not "efficient" or not "suitable," the legislature has not discharged its constitutional duty and it is *our* duty to say so.

The Texas Constitution derives its force from the people of Texas. This is the fundamental law under which the people of this state have consented to be governed. In construing the language of article VII, section 1, we consider "the intent of the people who adopted it." . . .

The State argues that, as used in article VII, section 1, the word "efficient" was intended to suggest a simple and inexpensive system. Under the Reconstruction Constitution of 1869, the people had been subjected to a militaristic school system with the state exercising absolute authority over the training of children. . . . Thus, the State contends that delegates to the 1875 Constitutional Convention deliberately inserted into this provision the word "efficient" in order to prevent the establishment of another Reconstruction-style, highly centralized school system.

While there is some evidence that many delegates wanted an economical school system, there is no persuasive evidence that the delegates used the term "efficient" to achieve that end. . . . It must be recognized that the Constitution requires an "efficient," not an "economical," "inexpensive," or "cheap" system. The language of the Constitution must be presumed to have been carefully selected. . . . The framers used the term "economical" elsewhere and could have done so here had they so intended.

There is no reason to think that "efficient" meant anything different in 1875 from what it now means. "Efficient" conveys the meaning of effective or productive of results and connotes the use of resources so as to produce results with little waste; this meaning does not

appear to have changed over time. . . . One dictionary used by the framers defined efficient as follows:

> Causing effects; producing results; actively operative; not inactive, slack or incapable; characterized by energetic and useful activity. . . .

N. Webster, *An American Dictionary of the English Language* 430 (1864). In 1890, this court described "efficient" machinery as being "such as is capable of well producing the effect intended to be secured by the use of it for the purpose for which it was made." . . .

Considering "the general spirit of the times and the prevailing sentiments of the people," it is apparent from the historical record that those who drafted and ratified article VII, section 1 never contemplated the possibility that such gross inequalities could exist within an "efficient" system. . . . At the Constitutional Convention of 1875, delegates spoke at length on the importance of education for *all* the people of this state, rich and poor alike. The chair of the education committee, speaking on behalf of the majority of the committee, declared:

> [Education] must be classed among the abstract rights, based on apparent natural justice, which we individually concede to the State, for the general welfare, when we enter into a great compact as a commonwealth. I boldly assert that it is for the general welfare of all, rich and poor, male and female, that the means of a common school education should, if possible, be placed within the reach of every child in the State.

S. McKay, *Debates in the Texas Constitutional Convention of 1875* 198 (1930). Other delegates recognized the importance of a diffusion of knowledge among the masses not only for the preservation of democracy, but for the prevention of crime and for the growth of the economy. . . .

In addition to specific comments in the constitutional debates, the structure of school finance at the time indicates that such gross disparities were not contemplated. Apart from cities, there was no district structure for schools nor any authority to tax locally for school purposes under the Constitution of 1876. B. Walker and W. Kirby, *The Basics of Texas Public School Finance* 5, 86 (1986). The 1876 Constitution provided a structure whereby the burdens of school taxation fell equally and uniformly across the state, and each student in the state was entitled to exactly the same distribution of funds. *See* Tex. Const. art. VII, § 5 (1876). The state's school fund was initially apportioned strictly on a per capita basis. B. Walker and W. Kirby at 21. Also, a poll tax of one dollar per voter was levied across the state for school purposes. These per capita methods of taxation and of revenue distribution seem simplistic compared to today's system; however they do indicate that the people were contemplating that the tax burden would be shared uniformly and that the state's resources would be distributed on an even, equitable basis.

If our state's population had grown at the same rate in each district and if the taxable wealth in each district had also grown at the same rate, efficiency could probably have been maintained within the structure of the present system. That did not happen. Wealth, in its many forms, has not appeared with geographic symmetry. The economic development of the state has not been uniform. Some cities have grown dramatically, while their sister communities have remained static or have shrunk. Formulas that once fit have been knocked askew. Although local conditions vary, the constitutionally imposed state responsibility for an efficient education system is the same for all citizens regardless of where they live.

We conclude that, in mandating "efficiency," the constitutional framers and ratifiers did not intend a system with such vast disparities as now exist. Instead, they stated clearly that the purpose of an efficient system was to provide for a "*general* diffusion of knowledge." (Emphasis added.) The present system, by contrast, provides not for a diffusion that is general, but for one that is limited and unbalanced. The resultant inequalities are thus directly contrary to the constitutional vision of efficiency. . . .

By statutory directives, the legislature has attempted through the years to reduce disparities and improve the system. There have been good faith efforts on the part of many public officials, and some progress has been made. However, as the undisputed facts of this case make painfully clear, the reality is that the constitutional mandate has not been met.

The legislature's recent efforts have focused primarily on increasing the state's contributions. More money allocated under the present system would reduce some of the existing disparities between districts but would at best only postpone the reform that is necessary to make the system efficient. A band-aid will not suffice; the system itself must be changed.

We hold that the state's school financing system is neither financially efficient nor efficient in the sense of providing for a "general diffusion of knowledge" statewide, and therefore that it violates article VII, section 1 of the Texas Constitution. Efficiency does not require a per capita distribution, but it also does not allow concentrations of resources in property-rich school districts that are taxing low when property-poor districts that are taxing high cannot generate sufficient revenues to meet even minimum standards. There must be a direct and close correlation between a district's tax effort and the educational resources available to it; in other words, districts must have substantially equal access to similar revenues per pupil at similar levels of tax effort. Children who live in poor districts and children who live in rich districts must be afforded a substantially equal opportunity to have access to educational funds. Certainly, this much is required if the state is to educate its populace efficiently and provide for a general diffusion of knowledge statewide.

Under article VII, section 1, the obligation is the legislature's to provide for an efficient system. In setting appropriations, the legislature must establish priorities according to constitutional mandate; equalizing educational opportunity cannot be relegated to an "if funds are left over" basis. We recognize that there are and always will be strong public interests competing for available state funds. However, the legislature's responsibility to support public education is different because it is constitutionally imposed. Whether the legislature acts directly or enlists local government to help meet its obligation, the end product must still be what the constitution commands—i.e. an efficient system of public free schools throughout the state.   . . . This does not mean that the state may not recognize differences in area costs or in costs associated with providing an equalized educational opportunity to atypical students or disadvantaged students. Nor does it mean that local communities would be precluded from supplementing an efficient system established by the legislature; however any local enrichment must derive solely from local tax effort.

Some have argued that reform in school finance will eliminate local control, but this argument has no merit. An efficient system does not preclude the ability of communities to exercise local control over the education of their children. It requires only that the funds available for education be distributed equitably and evenly. An efficient system will actually allow for more local control, not less. It will provide property-poor districts with economic alternatives that are not now available to them. Only if alternatives are indeed available can a community exercise the control of making choices.

Our decision today is not without precedent. Courts in nine other states with similar school financing systems have ruled those systems to be unconstitutional for varying reasons.   . . .

Because we have decided that the school financing system violates the Texas Constitution's "efficiency" provision, we need not consider petitioners' other constitutional arguments. The Texas school financing system as set forth in the Texas Education Code, sections 16.001, *et seq.,* and as implemented in conjunction with local school districts containing unequal taxable property wealth, is unconstitutional under article VII, section 1 of the Texas Constitution.   . . .

Although we have ruled the school financing system to be unconstitutional, we do not now instruct the legislature as to the specifics of the legislation it should enact; nor do we

order it to raise taxes. The legislature has primary responsibility to decide how best to achieve an efficient system. We decide only the nature of the constitutional mandate and whether that mandate has been met. Because we hold that the mandate of efficiency has not been met, we reverse the judgment of the court of appeals. The legislature is duty-bound to provide for an efficient system of education, and only if the legislature fulfills that duty can we launch this great state into a strong economic future with educational opportunity for all.

Because of the enormity of the task now facing the legislature and because we want to avoid any sudden disruption in the educational processes, we modify the trial court's judgment so as to stay the effect of its injunction until May 1, 1990. However, let there be no misunderstanding. A remedy is long overdue. The legislature must take immediate action. We reverse the judgment of the court of appeals and affirm the trial court's judgment as modified.

NOTE

1. As observed in the text above, inequities in the distribution of funds for public schools have been challenged under (a) state equal protection clauses and/or (b) state education provisions. The state equal protection clauses are general constitutional provisions prohibiting government from invidiously discriminating against any particular class of persons by denial of fundamental rights. Equal protection is a prohibition, "a thou shalt not" that protects individuals against the state. On the other hand, the education provisions are affirmative mandates requiring that state legislatures provide for the education of the people. Plaintiffs have used both types of provisions in efforts to strike down state school finance programs that combine state and local revenues in a manner that greatly favors children in affluent school districts. The state courts have responded to these challenges in several basic ways. First, they have held that education is not a fundamental right, and disparity of resources is not irrational

and is not violative of equal protection. Second, they have held that education is a fundamental right, and that under a strict scrutiny analysis the state cannot succeed in showing that it has compelling interest in distributing funds in a disproportionate manner. Third, they have held that education is a fundamental right, and that the state's disparate allocation of school funds is defensible under strict scrutiny analysis. Fourth, they have found a declaration of fundamentality unnecessary and have held that the distribution of funds is not rational. Fifth, they have held that education is not fundamental for equal protection purposes and have found the funding method unconstitutional under the education provision of the state constitution. Sixth, they have held that education is fundamental, have found that widely unequal revenues per pupil violates the education provision of the state constitution, and have determined it unnecessary to rule on the application of equal protection.

The notes that follow summarize and consolidate these court decisions into three categories: (a) education is not fundamental, (b) education is fundamental, and (c) finding of fundamentality is not necessary to hold a state school finance program unconstitutional.

a. *Education Is Not a Fundamental Right.* Education is not a fundamental right under the Maryland Declaration of Rights, Maryland Constitution, Article XXIV. "The right to adequate education in Maryland is no more fundamental than the right to personal security, to fire protection, to welfare subsidies, to health care or like vital governmental services." The Maryland Supreme Court further held that Article VIII of the Maryland Constitution, which requires the General Assembly to establish and maintain a thorough and efficient system of free public schools throughout the state," is not alone sufficient to elevate education to fundamental status." *Hornbeck v. Somerset County Board of Education,* 295 Md. 597, 458 A. 2d 758, 786 (Md. 1983).

The Supreme Court of Colorado has said that the "heartfelt recognition and endorsement of the importance of education does not elevate public education to a fundamental interest warranting strict scrutiny." This court saw the property-poor school districts' plea for fiscal equity as ultimately an attack on local control. The Colorado court, in denying fundamental status to education, followed the reasoning of *Rodriguez* and held that the plaintiff children did not constitute a suspect class to justify the invoking of the strict-scrutiny test of equal protection. Moreover, it held that the wide disparity in revenues per pupil among Colorado school districts could be justified as rational because it furthered the objective of local control. *Lujan v. Colorado State Board of Education,* 649 P. 2d 1005 (Colo. 1982).

The fact that education is provided for in the state constitution does not make it a fundamental right for purposes of equal protection. The Oklahoma Supreme Court has held that provisions of the state constitution requiring establishment and maintenance of a public school system merely mandated establishment and maintenance of a system and did not guarantee equality of educational opportunity in the sense that expenditures should be equalized. *Fair School Finance Council of Oklahoma, Inc. v. State of Oklahoma,* 746 P. 2d 1135 (Okl. 1987).

The Georgia Supreme Court, as indicated in the text of the case above, has held that education is "vital" but not fundamental. This court adopted the *Rodriguez* position that education is more fundamental than food, lodging, police, fire protection, water, and health services, all of which are governed locally with wide differences in expenditures. The Georgia court, however, failed to reconcile the fact that education is the only one of these services set out and specified by the state constitution as a direct responsibility of the state legislature. *McDaniel v. Thomas,* 248 Ga. 632, 285 S.E. 2d 156 (1981).

The Court of Appeals of New York has also denied that education is a fundamental constitutional right. This court observed in the Levittown case that education is "unquestionably high on the list of priorities of governmental concern and responsibility . . . , enlisting most active attention of the citizenry and the legislature," but this "does not automatically entitle public education" to be classified as a fundamental right. *Board of Education, Levittown Union Free School District v. Nyquist,* 57 N.Y. 2d 27, 453 N.Y.S.2d 643, 439 N.E. 2d 359 (1982).

The Supreme Court of Idaho perceived a connection between fundamentality of education and the destruction of local control of education. This court said: "[W]e refuse to classify the right to education as a fundamental right which compels the State, for the purposes of financing, to wipe out local entities and finance on the basis of revenues raised by some sort of statewide system." *Thompson v. Engelking,* 96 Idaho 793, 537 P. 2d 635 (1975).

In Oregon, the court assumed that equity of funding and local control were incompatible. In choosing between the two, the court apparently felt local control was more important than equity. In this case, the court did not explicitly reject the fundamentality of education and the strict scrutiny standard, but created its own balancing test, whereby it weighed the detriment of unequal revenues against the "ostensible justification" of local control. *Olsen v. State,* 276 Or. 9, 554 P.2d 139 (1976).

Other cases finding that education is not a fundamental right, justifying the courts' strict scrutiny of school finance legislation, include: *Milliken v. Green,* 390 Mich. 389, 212 N.W.2d 711 (1973); *Danson v. Casey,* 484 Pa. 415, 58 Ohio St. 2d 368, 399 A.2d 360 (1979), and *Bensalem Township School District v. Commonwealth of Pennsylvania,* 105 Pa. Cmwlth. 388, 524 A.2d 1027 (1987); *Board of Education of the City School Dist. of Cincinnati v. Walter,* 390 N.E.2d 813 (1979), cert. denied, 444 U.S. 1015, 100 S.Ct. 665 (1980); *Britt v. North Carolina State Board of Education,* 357 S.E.2d 432 (1987); *School Board of the Parish of Livingston v. Louisiana State Board of Elementary and Secondary Education,* 830 F.2d 563 (5th Cir. 1987), cert. denied 487 U.S. 1223, 108 S.Ct. 2884 (1988); *Richland County v. Campbell,* 294 S.C. 346, 364 S.E.2d 470 (1988).

In *Shofstall v. Hollins,* 110 Ariz. 88, 515 P.2d 590 (1973), the Supreme Court of Arizona found that education was a fundamental right under the Arizona Constitution, but did not apply the strict-scrutiny standard in evaluating the state school finance program. Instead, the court required only that the program be "rational, reasonable and neither discriminatory nor capricious" to meet equal protection requirements. Taking this unique approach of mixing fundamentality with the "rational" standard, the court held for the defendants, finding that disparate revenues among school districts did not deny children in poor school districts of their fundamental right to an education.

b. *Education is a Fundamental Right.* The requirement of the State of Washington Constitution that the "legislature shall provide for a general and uniform system of public schools (Article IX, § 2) and that the legislature has a "paramount duty" to "make ample provision for education of all children" (Article IX, § 1) makes it clear that the children of Washington have a constitutionally "guaranteed education" in which the first priority is to provide "fully sufficient funds." Consequently, all children residing within Washington's borders "have a 'right' to be amply provided with an education." That "right" is constitutionally paramount and must be achieved through a "general and uniform system of public schools." Const. Art. IX, § 2. Further, the education that is provided must be "without distinction or preference on account of race, color, caste, or sex." West's RCWA Const. Art. 9, § 1. *Seattle School District No. 1 of King County v. State of Washington,* 90 Wn. 2d 476, 585 P.2d 71 (1978).

In *Pauley v. Kelly,* the Supreme Court of West Virginia held that the requirements of the state constitution mandating that the legislature provide for a "thorough and efficient system of free schools" makes education a "fundamental, constitutional right in West Virginia." (Article XII, § 1), 255 S.E.2d 859 (1979).

The Supreme Court of Kentucky held that education is a fundamental right for children in Kentucky and based its opinion on the "animus" of § 183 of the Kentucky Constitution, which requires that the General Assembly "provide an efficient system of common schools throughout the state." (The term "animus" is defined as the "intention, design, disposition or mind." *Black's Law Dictionary,* (St. Paul. West Publishing Company, 1968, p. 114). Thus, fundamentality of education derives from the intention and design of the framers of the affirmative constitutional mandate that the legislature provide for education. The Kentucky court having found that education is fundamental and that the system of financing the public schools was not "efficient," under § 183, concluded that an equal protection analysis was unnecessary. *Rose v. Council for Better Education, Inc.,* 790 S.W.2d 186 (Ky. 1989).

Other court decisions declaring that education is fundamental include *Knowles v. State Board of Education,* 219 Kan. 271, 547 P.2d 699 (1976); *Buse v. Smith,* 74 Wis. 2d 550, 247 N.W.2d 141 (1976), and *Kukor v. Grover,* 436 N.W.2d 568 (1989); *Serrano v. Priest,* 5 Cal. 3d 584, 96 Cal. Rptr. 601, 487 P.2d 1241 (1971) and *Serrano v. Priest,* 18 Cal. 3d 728, 135 Cal. Rptr. 345, 557 P.2d 929 (1976), cert. den., 432 U.S. 907, 97 S.Ct. 2951 (1977), and *Serrano v. Priest,* 200 Cal. App. 3d 897, 226 Cal Rptr. 584 (1986); *Horton v. Meskill,* 172 Conn. 615, 376 A.2d 359

(1977); *State ex rel. Board of Education for Grant County of Grant v. Manchin,* ___ W.Va. ___, 366 S.E. 2nd 743 (1988); *Washakie County School District No. One v. Herschler,* 606 P.2d 310 (Wyo. 1980), cert. denied sub nom.; *Hot Springs County School District Number One v. Washakie County School District Number 1,* 449 U.S. 824, 101 S.Ct. 86 (1980); *Edgewood Independent School District v. Kirby,* 777 S.W.2d 391 (Tex. 1989).

c. *Finding of Fundamentality is Unnecessary to Invalidate Funding Scheme.* On the other hand, the Supreme Court of Arkansas found it unnecessary to address the fundamentality question to justify strict scrutiny because from the evidence presented, the court was able to conclude that the system of school financing did not even meet the lesser test of rationality. In so holding, the court said that "we find no constitutional basis for the present system, as it has no rational bearing on the educational needs of the districts." *Dupree v. Alma School District No. 30 of Crawford County,* 279 Ark. 340, 651 S.W.2d 90 (1983).

Likewise, the Montana Supreme Court held it did not need to consider the fundamentality question under the equal protection provision of that state's constitution because the school funding scheme directly violated the education provision of the state constitution. Thus, recourse to the equal protection clause was obviated. *Helena Elementary School District No. 1 v. State,* 236 Mont. 44, 769 P.2d 684 (1989); opinion amended by 236 Mont. 44, 784 P.2d 412 (1990).

The New Jersey Supreme Court, in *Robinson v. Cahill,* set the initial precedent in holding a system of school financing unconstitutional without invoking fundamentality and the state's equal protection clause. The New Jersey Court foresaw unusual and unnecessary complications in attempting to address the educational equity issue in terms of equal protection. Instead, the court based its opinion of unconstitutionality of the New Jersey finance program on the "thorough and efficient" clause of the education provision of the New Jersey Constitution (Article VIII, § 4, Part 1).

The viability and conclusiveness of the New Jersey Court's 1973 decision relying on the "thorough and efficient" requirement of the education provision was recently reinforced by the same court in *Abbott v. Burke,* 119 N.J. 287, 575 A.2d 359 (1990), wherein the method of distributing funds among the school districts of New Jersey was again held to be unconstitutional.

and does not specify control or approval authority, the courts have held that the reviewing agency cannot reduce the budget.

A school district must expend moneys for the purpose for which they are collected. If a statute requires fund accounting for special tax money, the school board must establish and deposit the money in such a fund. In such a case, a taxpayer may not require an accounting for the school funds beyond seeing that they are used for the purpose for which they were levied and collected.

▄▄▄ BUDGETING AND ACCOUNTING FOR SCHOOL FUNDS

For the school district to effectively plan for educational activities and account for the expenditure of tax funds, provisions must be made for budgetary and accounting procedures. School boards are generally given wide latitude in the determination of how educational funds will be expended. The attitude of the courts has been that a school district, being charged with the responsibility for operating the schools, should have as much freedom as possible to determine how and where the funds will be spent.

This broad budgetary authority, of course, extends to teachers' salaries subject only to legislative or constitutional restraints against arbitrary, discriminatory, or unreasonable classifications.

The exception to this rule is where the legislature has prescribed that school boards be fiscally dependent on city government. In such cases, the board must submit its budget for review and approval by the city government. However, where a city council has the authority to fix the amount of the school budget, it may not direct the itemized expenditure of the gross amount authorized; the board may spend the money for any purpose permitted by law. In instances where the law requires only the submission of the budget

Funds Collected and Allocated for a Particular Public Purpose Cannot Be Lawfully Diverted to Another Purpose

---

San Benito Independent School District v. Farmers' State Bank

---

Court of Civil Appeals, Texas 1935.
78 S.W.2d 741.

SMITH, Justice. On May 16, 1932, Farmers' State Bank & Trust Company of San Benito was closed and its affairs were taken over by the state banking commissioner for administration, as provided by law. Up to that time San Benito Independent School District maintained four separate checking accounts in the bank, which was the district treasury, as follows:

First, an "interest and sinking fund account," from taxes assessed, collected, and deposited in said account for the purpose of paying interest and principal upon the district's bonded debt, in which account there was a balance, at the time the bank failed, of $12,942.68;

Second, a "local maintenance fund account," in which were deposited taxes assessed and collected for the specific purpose of local maintenance, exclusive of teachers' salaries, in which there was a balance of $318.25;

Third, an "interest and penalty refunding account," in which had been deposited interest and penalties unlawfully collected from the taxpayers, which under the law were required to be refunded to those paying them. In this account there was a balance, at the time the bank failed, of $124.16. The balances in the three foregoing accounts aggregated $13,385.09;

Fourth, a "state available warrant fund account," in which were deposited, as received, funds received from the state for the specific purpose of paying teachers' salaries. In this account, however, there was no balance on hand at the time the bank failed. Moreover, at that time the bank held unpaid district warrants drawn against that account in the aggregate amount of $3,409.18, which the bank carried, not as an overdraft, but as assets.

In this situation the district brought this action against the bank and banking commissioner to recover $13,385.09, being the amount of the balance of funds on deposit in the first three accounts mentioned, and prayed that the amount of the unpaid warrants held by the bank against the exhausted fourth, or "state available warrant fund account," be offset against the district's claim, leaving a balance of $9,975.91, for which net amount the district prayed judgment.

The bank and banking commissioner answered, setting up their claims of $3,409.18, represented by the unpaid district warrants held by them against the exhausted "state available warrant fund account," and, asserting that that claim against that fund could not lawfully be applied as an offset against the district's claim upon deposits in the other three specific fund accounts, prayed for direct judgment upon said warrants.

The trial court rendered judgment in favor of the district for the amount of its deposits in the bank, and in favor of the banking commissioner for the amount of the unpaid warrants held by him, but denied the district's prayer that the latter recovery be applied as an offset. The district has appealed.   . . .

It is too well settled to require citation, or any extended discussion, that a public fund collected and allocated for a particular public purpose cannot be lawfully diverted to the use of another particular public purpose. Under that wise rule, when applied here, when the taxpayer pays a certain tax for the specific purpose of liquidating a particular public bonded indebtedness of his school district, the funds derived therefrom cannot lawfully be used for the purpose of paying teachers' salaries, chargeable under the law to a different public fund; when lawful interest and penalties have been collected from the taxpayers and segregated into a particular fund, and is required by law to be refunded to the taxpayer, as is the case here, that fund may not lawfully be diverted to the payment of teachers' salaries chargeable to another specific fund, as is sought to be done by appellant; when a specific tax has been levied and assessed by a school district and paid by the taxpayers, for the particular purpose of "local maintenance" (exclusive of teachers' salaries), and the fund so collected has been segregated and allocated to that purpose, as was done here, the district may not divert that fund to another for the purpose of paying teachers' salaries, as is sought to be done by the district in this case.

So when the bank acquired the warrants against the district's "state available fund" account, which was exhausted, at least for the time being, it could not lawfully collect them by charging the amounts thereof to the accounts of the interest and sinking fund, or the local maintenance fund, or the interest and penalty refunding fund; it could only hold the warrants until the account against which they were drawn was replenished, and it was so holding them, as among its assets, when it ceased to do business.

The corporate school district, as are all municipal corporations, is but a trustee of guardian of the public funds coming into its possession under the law, and may disburse those funds only in the manner and for the purposes prescribed by law. As the funds in question were gathered in, the district, in obedience to law, allocated them to the several purposes for which they were paid in, and deposited them with the bank in appropriate separate accounts kept for each specific fund. When so segregated into separate accounts, the district had no power or authority to transfer any part of the funds from either account and apply it to the purposes of any other account, any more than a trustee of several persons or estates could divert the funds of one cestui que trust to the use of another. Nor could the bank, in this case, lawfully pay the warrants drawn on one particular account out of the funds of another particular account, any more than it could charge the draft of one individual depositor to the account of another. The rights, capacities and interests of the respective parties are thus fixed by settled principles of law, and there being no mutuality of rights, interests and capacities between the district as trustee of the "available state" fund and account, and the same entity as trustee of the other three specific funds and accounts, it could not appropriate the one to the uses of the others.

The inevitable conclusion is, then, that in balancing the accounts between the district and the bank, the claim of the latter against the "state available fund" of the former could not be applied as an offset against the obligations of the bank to the other three separate fund accounts. The bank could not enforce such offset in an action thereon, nor may the district enforce it in this action.

The judgment is affirmed.

NOTES

1. The extent of budget itemization necessary to meet statutory requirements has been described in an Arizona case. Arizona statute requiring budgetary information divided the school budget into major general categories and then subdivided these categories into subitems. The operating expense category was broken down into two broad sections administration and instruction. Each of these sections were divided into forty-one subitems. A controversy arose as to whether the forty-one subitems were merely explanatory of the major categories or were the expenditures of the board of education restricted to the amounts in the subitems making transfer of funds among subitems illegal. The statute governing this question stated:

   No expenditure shall be made for a purpose not particularly itemized and included in such budget, and no expenditure shall be made, and no debt, obligation or liability shall be incurred or created in any year for any purpose itemized in such budget in excess of the amount specified for such item.

   The court in interpreting this statute defined the word "purpose" in light of judicial principle that where the language of a statute may be subject to more than one interpretation, the court will adopt the one that is reasonable in view of the particular situation being litigated. The court said:

   Since the word "purpose" as used in (the statute) is susceptible of more than one interpretation, we are bound to declare as the intention of the legislature the alternative which is reasonable and convenient. It appears to us that to bind either the school district or the superintendent to a forty-one line operating expense budget, as advocated by the (treasurer), would be impractical, unduly restrictive, and lead to absurd results. *Isley v. School District No. 2 of Maricopa County*, 81 Ariz. 280, 305 P.2d 432 (1956).

2. An Oklahoma court upheld a state board of education directive requiring school districts to treat as a current expense certain items that taxpayers insisted should have been recorded as capital outlay expenditures. The state board of education had acted under a statute providing that the state board shall prescribe a list of appropriation accounts by which funds of school districts shall be budgeted. *St. Louis-San Francisco Railway Co. v. McCurtain County*, Okl., Excise Bd., 352 P.2d 896 (Okl. 1960).

3. Where a school tax levy raises revenues in excess of the requested budgetary amount, the school board is entitled to the surplus. In Montgomery County, Maryland, where the county levies the tax rate requested by the school district, the county tax collector on many occasions received more from the school tax levy than was requested by the school board. The surplus remained in the county treasury and amounted to over one million dollars. The school board brought

suit against Montgomery County to obtain the funds. The court held that when the levy was actually and unconditionally made by the county, the statutes were explicit in declaring that no part of the sum levied for the use of the public schools be used for any other purpose, and that the amount so levied each year be paid by the county treasurer to the school board. *Board of Education of Montgomery County v. Montgomery County,* 237 Md. 191, 205 A.2d 202 (1964).

4. In the case of a fiscally dependent school district, a Connecticut court has held that where a school budget is submitted to a municipal reviewing agency and the expenditures are for purposes described by statute to be within the board of education's authority to effectuate, the finance board has no power to refuse to include an appropriation for such expenditure in its budget. This statement is qualified by the fact that the reviewing agency may refuse appropriation if the financial condition of the town does not permit such expenditures. This is, of course, an extremely important limitation, since in Connecticut it is within the review board's authority to pronounce that the town is not in a financial position to support such expenditures for education and thereby cut the school budget. *Board of Ed. of Town of Stamford v. Board of Finance of Town of Stamford,* 127 Conn. 345, 16 A.2d 601 (1940).

5. In another case involving the authority of the town board of finance to control educational expenditures in Connecticut school districts, the court held that placement of certain funds to be used for school purposes in the general government budget contravened a statute permitting the board of education to transfer the unexpended or uncontracted-for portion of appropriations for school purposes to any other item, and this constituted an illegal restriction on the appropriation. *Board of Ed. of Town of Ellington v. Town of Ellington,* 151 Conn. 1, 193 A.2d 466 (1963).

6. A school district may not, in the absence of statute expressly permitting it, accumulate surpluses beyond that required to operate for the ensuing year. The theory is that a school district levying taxes sufficient to maintain a large surplus should reduce its tax levy. One court held that a tax levy that created a surplus of over 50 percent of the entire school district budget exceeded the amount reasonably contemplated for a contingency. The court went on to say:

> A tax levy is required to be a reasonable approximation of the amount required. It has not been the policy of the law to permit the creation of funds by taxation in large amounts for future use, except where statutory authorization exists as in the case of building funds, sinking funds, and the like. *Kissinger v. School District No. 49 of Clay County,* 163 Neb. 33, 77 N.W.2d 767 (1956).

Money or Property Derived Under the Auspices of the Public School Is Accountable in the Same Manner as Other Tax Funds

— · — · — — · — · —

Petition of Auditors of Hatfield Township School District

— · — · — — · — · —

Superior Court of Pennsylvania, 1947.
161 Pa. super. 388, 54 A.2d 833.

ARNOLD, Judge. This appeal is from an order of the court below directing the officers, directors and supervising principal of the Hatfield Joint Consolidated School District to comply with a duces tecum subpoena issued by the official auditors calling for the production of various books, vouchers and papers.

The Hatfield Joint Consolidated School District was formed by the school districts of the borough of Hatfield and the township of Hatfield. Its bank account is carried by its treasurer in the Hatfield National Bank under the name, "Hatfield Joint Consolidated School District," hereafter called the "official account." The warrants or vouchers thereon are executed by the proper officers of the district.

In the same bank is an account called "Hatfield Joint School Accounts," and the sole right to withdraw funds therefrom is possessed by Elmer B. Laudenslager, the supervising principal. This we will refer to as the "activities account." The appellants challenge the right of the statutory auditors to examine this account. . . .

Appellants have asked us to determine whether the activities account is subject to official audit even though no tax moneys were in it, and state: "This question is a matter of interest to every district in the Commonwealth. The decision in this case will affect every school district . . . [and] . . . will decide once and for all the status of such funds . . . even as the legislature established the status of the cafeteria funds. Section 8 of Act of 1931, P.L. 243, and Act of 1945, P.L. 688, 24 P.S. § 331." Indeed the evidence in this case disclosed four other nearby communities operating a similar system, and in fact the system is widespread. It is fraught with great danger. High school football and other athletics have achieved great popularity, and this means that almost any school district, depending in a degree upon the skill of the athletes, has athletic events the admission fees of which aggregate a large sum of money, probably in excess of $10,000. It would be a great blow to the public school system if by embezzlement or lack of care such funds should be lost. Not only has the school board a moral duty to perform but there is also a legislative imperative. The public school system of this commonwealth is entirely statutory. Within the constitutional limitations the legislature is supreme and there reposes in the courts no power to permit deviation from its commands; and neither the local school districts nor the State Department of Education may bypass the duties enjoined.

In the so-called activity accounts various situations obtain. Of course if pupils of a class give money to a supervising principal to purchase for them class jewelry or similar things the school district has no official duty (although it may have a moral duty), for the supervising principal acts as agent of the pupils. This is the smaller end of the problem. At the other pole, a school district, acting under the express provisions of § 405 of the Code, 24 P.S. § 339, has athletic events. These activities produce large sums of money from paid admissions. Under the instant system these sums of money are not disbursed through the treasurer, nor through a resolution of the board, but are solely at the command of one individual, who has no statutory standing or duty. It is possible that some school districts may neither *directly* nor *indirectly* furnish any money for the playing field or stadium; or for the coaching of the athletes, or for their uniforms or playing togs, or for the apparatus with which the sport is connected, or for the lighting of the field; although it is very doubtful whether such case exists. But it is certainly true that, if a school district operates and expends tax money for the acquisition, maintenance or lighting of the playing field, or for the payment of services of a coach, the admissions charged result from the use of public property and from the expenditure of tax moneys and are the property of the school district, must go into the official account of the treasurer thereof, and are subject to audit.

The moneys derived from the sale of admissions to witness the event in question come into being because of (1) the use and wear of the school building and grounds; (2) the use and wear of personal property owned by the district; (3) the payment to employees such as coaches for their services; (4) the payment by the district for light, heat and various maintenance charges, including janitor service. By reason of the use of these public funds the event takes place, and from it are reaped the admission fees paid to witness the performance. The pupils are not expected to and do not furnish any of the money. The admission fees could not belong to them, and indeed if taken they would be professionals instead of amateurs. The spectators are not to get their money back. No one has any investment except the school district. The money raised by admissions therefore belongs to the district, which by its property and funds made the admission fees possible.

Of lesser importance, but in the same category, are the admission fees charged for dramatic and musical enterprises held in the buildings of the district. These belong to the district for the same reasons and with the same results. For instance, the school districts usually and properly provide musical instruments, just as they provide equipment and uniforms for athletics. In the instant case admission fees were expended through the activities account for such instruments, but it was frankly admitted that when bought the instruments belonged to the district. So do the admission fees themselves.

We have not attempted to discuss each situation that may present itself, but where moneys or property are derived directly or indirectly through the use of school buildings, or from the expenditure of public funds of the district, the moneys thus derived are public property, must be handled exactly as tax moneys and be paid to the district treasurer.

. . .

Order affirmed.

◼◼ PUBLIC SCHOOL INDEBTEDNESS

The authority of school districts to issue bonds must be clearly and expressly conferred by statute. The failure of a school board to comply with the statutory conditions for school bond issuance will render the bonds illegal.

Bonds issued for a specific purpose must be used for that purpose and no other. It has been held that bonds approved by the voters for "erecting and constructing a new roof" for a school building were illegal when the statute provided for bonds to be issued for the purpose of "erecting and equipping, or purchasing and equipping" school houses.[62] In another case, a court held a statute authorizing a bond election for the "erection and enlargement" of school buildings could not be construed to include the issuance of bonds for the purpose of equipping school buildings.[63]

While earlier cases generally held statutory procedures for school bond elections were to be strictly followed and failure to do so would make the bonds illegal, more recent cases tend to allow some flexibility so long as irregularities do not affect the results of the election. It has been held that where the voters in a bond election authorize bonds for a greater amount than is consistent with the law, the voter authorization is not illegal, and the school board may issue bonds for the amount prescribed by law.

Generally the courts have held that a bondholder cannot recover on an illegal bond even if he is an innocent purchaser. This rule, however, has been modified in some states, where it has been held that where illegal bonds have been sold and the funds applied to the improvement of the district, the bondholder may recover under the *quantum meruit*. Also, the courts will permit the holder of an illegal bond to recover if the money is identifiable and has not been commingled with other funds of the district. The courts, in some cases, have allowed the holder to recover property purchased with illegal bond proceeds if no other money of the district was used in payment for the property.

Constitutions of most states make provision for debt limitations, the maximum percentage of which a local school district may not exceed. Courts have held that the percentage of indebtedness is to be computed using the amount of bonds that actually has been issued and not the amount that was projected at the time of a bond election. While a state legislature must conform to prescribed constitutional requirements regarding indebtedness, some state legislatures have sought to avoid stringent constitutional debt restrictions that severely limit educational facility construction. One such device resorted to by a few states is the "holding company" or the "local school building authority." This method of financing school construction effectively increases the debt capacity of a local school district and has been upheld by the courts.[64]

*Legislature Has Power to Direct Local Authorities
to Create Debt for Public School Building*

— · — · — · — · —

Revell v. Mayor, etc. of
City of Annapolis

— · — · — · — · —

Court of Appeals of Maryland, 1895.
81 Md. 1, 31 A. 695.

ROBINSON, C.J. The act of 1894, c. 620, provides for the erection of a public school building in the city of Annapolis, and, to pay for the same, it authorizes and directs the school commissioners of Anne Arundel county to borrow money, not exceeding the sum of $20,000, on bonds to be indorsed by the county commissioners; and for the same purpose it directs that the city of Annapolis shall issue bonds to the amount of $10,000, and that said bonds shall be issued without submitting the question of their issue to the voters of said city. The city of Annapolis has refused to issue the bonds as thus directed by the act, and the question is whether the legislature has the power to direct that the city authorities shall issue bonds to raise money to be applied to the erection of a public school building in said city. This power is denied, on the broad ground that it is not competent for the legislature to compel a municipal corporation to create a debt or levy a tax for a local purpose, in which the state has no concern, or to assume a debt not within the corporate powers of a municipal government. If the correctness of this general proposition be conceded for the purposes of this case, we do not see how it affects in any manner the validity of the act now in question. We cannot agree that the erection of buildings necessary for the public schools is a matter of merely local concern, in which the state has no interest. In this country the people are not only in theory, but in practice, the source of all governmental power, and the stability of free institutions mainly rests upon an enlightened public opinion. Fully recognizing this, the constitution declares that it shall be the duty of the legislature "to establish throughout the state a thorough and efficient system of free public schools, and to provide by taxation or otherwise" for their maintenance and support. . . . And the legislature has accordingly established a public school system, and has provided for its support by state and local taxation. It cannot be said, therefore, that the erection of buildings for public school purposes is a matter in which the state has no concern; nor can we agree that the creation of a debt for such purposes is not within the ordinary functions of municipal government. What is a municipal corporation? It is but a subordinate part of the state government, incorporated for public purposes, and clothed with special and limited powers of legislation in regard to its own local affairs. It has no inherent legislative power, and can exercise such powers only as have been expressly or by fair implication delegated to it by the legislature. The control of highways and bridges within the corporate limits; the power to provide for an efficient police force; to pass all necessary laws and ordinances for the preservation of the health, safety, and welfare of its people; and the power to provide for the support of its public schools by local taxation,—are all among the ordinary powers delegated to municipal corporations. And the public schools in Baltimore city are not only under the control and supervision of the city authorities, but are mainly supported by municipal taxation. It is no answer to say that the public schools in Annapolis are under the control of the school commissioners of Anne Arundel county, and that under its charter it has no power to create a debt or levy taxes for their support. The legislature may, at its pleasure, alter, amend, and enlarge its powers. It may authorize the city authorities to establish public schools within the corporate limits, and direct that bonds shall be issued to raise money for their support, payable at intervals during a series of years. There is no difference in principle between issuing bonds and the levying of a tax in one year sufficient to meet the necessary expenditure. . . .

If the legislature has the power to direct the city authorities to create a debt for a public school building, the exercise of this power in no manner depends upon their consent or upon the consent of the qualified voters of the city. We recognize the force of the argument that the question whether a municipal debt is to be created ought to be left to the discretion and judgment of the people who are to bear the burden. We recognize the fact that the exercise of this power by the legislature may be liable to abuse. But this abuse of a power is no argument against its exercise. The remedy, however, in such cases, is with the people to whom the members of the legislature are responsible for the discharge of the trust committed to them. It is a matter over which the courts have no control. If the debt to be created was for a private purpose, that would present quite a different question, for it is a fundamental principle, inherent in the nature of taxation itself, that all burdens and taxes shall be levied for public, and not for private, purposes. Be that as it may, it is well settled in this state that the legislature has the power to compel a municipal corporation to levy a tax or incur a debt for a public purpose, and one within the ordinary functions of a municipal government. . . .

In closing his argument, the counsel for the appellees suggested that the act was invalid because it was in conflict with the Fourteenth Amendment of the federal Constitution which forbids the taking of "property without due process of law." . . . It is a sufficient answer to this objection to say that the act in question, which requires the city authorities to issue bonds to raise money to pay the cost of a public school building, is a lawful exercise of legislature power, and, this being so, taxes levied to pay such bonds are not open to the objection of taking property without due process of law. Nor can we agree that the act is in conflict with section 33, art. 3, of the constitution, which declares that the general assembly shall pass no special law for any case for which provision has been made by an existing general law. The general law pro-

vides, it is true, that the school commissioners of Anne Arundel county shall have the control and supervision of the public schools in said county, with power to build, repair, and furnish schoolhouses. But it does not authorize the commissioners to borrow money upon bonds to be indorsed by the county commissioners for such purposes, nor does it provide for the apportionment of the cost of a public school building to be erected in the city of Annapolis between the county and the city. This could only be done by special act, and, this being so, the special act is not in conflict with the constitution, which forbids the passing of a special act for any purpose for which provision has been made by an existing general law. It follows from what we have said that the judgment sustaining the demurrer in this case must be overruled.

Issuance of Municipal Bonds without Statutory Authorization Is Ultra Vires

—————————

Hewitt v. Board of Education

—————————

Supreme Court of Illinois, 1880.
94 Ill. 528.

Mr. Chief Justice WALKER delivered the opinion of the Court. This was an action of assumpsit, brought by Hewitt in the circuit court of McLean county, against the "Board of Education of Normal School District," on a bond for $500, and two coupons of $25 each. The bond was dated the 1st of September, 1873, payable five years after its date, with ten percent interest, and it was payable to John Gregory or order. It was indorsed by him in blank, and he negotiated it to the Home Bank, of which appellant purchased, taking no further indorsement. . . .

The evidence tended to show that the bond was not issued to pay for a school house site, or to erect a building thereon. It also tended to prove that Gregory was, at the time the bond was issued to him, a member of the board, and that appellant was aware of the fact when he purchased the bond. As these were controverted facts, and were found by the circuit court against appellant, and as the Appellate Court has affirmed the judgment of the circuit court, we must take the affirmance as a finding of the facts as they were found by the circuit court, and we are precluded from reviewing these controverted facts, but are bound by the finding of the Appellate Court.

The fact, then, that the bond was not issued for an authorized purpose, undeniably rendered it void. Municipal corporations are not usually endowed with power to enter into traffic or general business, and are only created as auxiliaries to the government in carrying into effect some special governmental policy, or to aid in preserving the order and in promoting the well-being of the locality over which their authority extends. Where a corporation is created for business purposes, all persons may presume such bodies, when issuing their paper, are acting within the scope of their power. Not so with municipalities. Being created for governmental purposes, the borrowing of money, the purchase of property on time, and the giving of commercial paper, are not inherent, or even powers usually conferred; and unless endowed with such power in their charters, they have no authority to make and place on the market such paper, and persons dealing in it must see that the power exists. This has long been the rule of this court. . . . We might refer to other cases where it has been held that bonds issued without authority are void, even in the hands of purchasers before maturity and without actual notice.

A person taking bonds of a municipal corporation has access to the records of the body, and it is his duty to see that such instruments are issued in pursuance of authority, and when without power, they must be held void in whosesoever hands they are found. If, therefore, this bond was not issued to purchase a school house site, or for erecting a school building, as the Appellate Court seem to have found, the bond is void, as it was issued without power, and this, too, in the hands of a person taking without actual notice.

Again, this bond was issued without authority, and was void . . . .

The judgment of the Appellate Court is affirmed.

NOTES

1. The legislature may prescribe the conditions by which school bonds shall be issued. Failure to follow prescribed conditions will render the bonds illegal. *Dupont v. Mills*, 39 Del. 42, 196 A. 168 (1937).

2. A 1893 case, the Federal Circuit Court for the District of Nebraska held that a statute providing "any school district shall have power and authority to borrow money to pay for the sites of schoolhouses" does not confer authority on the school district to issue negotiable securities. Such securities issued by school districts are void even in the hands of an innocent purchaser. *Ashuelot Nat. Bank v. School District No. 7*, 56 Fed. 197 (C.C.A. Neb. 1893).

3. Statutes relating to school bond elections frequently state that the notice of election or resolution shall relate to a single purpose only. The notice or resolution must state specifically the issues in order that the voter can make a clear choice. Such a statutory provision in Ohio provides for the notice of a bond election for "one purpose," but defines one purpose quite broadly as being

> in the case of a school district, any number of school buildings; and in any case, all expenditures, including the acquisition of a site and purchase of equipment, for any one utility building, or other structure, or group of buildings or structures for the same general purpose . . . included in the same resolution.

Pursuant to this statute, an action was brought contesting a bond election for which the resolution had provided for (1) the acquisition of real estate, construction of fireproof school buildings, and the provision of furniture and furnishing therefore; and (2) improvement of nonfireproof school buildings and the provision of furniture and furnishings therefore. The court held that this resolution violated the statutory mandate for "one purpose" and stated:

> The purpose of the statute is to prevent the union in one act of diverse, incongruous and disconnected matters, having no relation to or connection with each other . . . ; to give electors a choice to secure what they desire without the necessity of accepting something which they do not want . . . ; and to prevent double propositions being placed before a voter having but a single expression to answer all propositions, thus making logrolling impossible . . . . In applying the rule, the courts invoke a test as to the existence of a natural relationship between the various structures or objects united in one proposition so that they form 'but one rounded whole.' . . . *State ex rel. Board of Education v. Thompson,* 167 Ohio St. 23, 145 N.E.2d 668 (1957).

4. One court has held that a statute authorizing the school district to issue bonds "for the purpose of raising funds to pay the cost of the equipping, enlarging, remodeling, repairing, and improving" the schoolhouse and "the purchase, repairing and installation of equipment thereof" did not authorize a rural high school district to issue bonds for the purpose of raising funds to pay the cost of removing a schoolhouse from one site to another. *Byer v. Rural High School District No. 4 of Brown County,* 169 Kan. 351, 219 P.2d 382 (1950).

5. Courts have held that school district indebtedness, subject to legal limitations, extends only to voluntary indebtedness. A judgment against a school district for a sum of money is not considered the creation of a debt within the meaning of constitutional debt limitations. Such debt is not subject to collateral attack by a taxpayers' suit to avoid taxation. *Edmundson v. Independent School District,* 98 Iowa 639, 67 N.W. 671 (1896).

6. It has generally been held that a school district whose boundaries overlap or are coterminous with a civil government has a separate computation in determining in-

debtedness. *Vallelly v. Board of Park Commissioners,* 16 N.D. 25, 111 N.W. 615, 171 A.L.R. 732 (1907).

7. In determining whether an indebtedness limit has been exceeded, the amount of indebtedness is determined at the time the bonds are issued and not at the time the bonds are voted. *Hebel v. School District R-1, Jefferson County,* 131 Colo. 105, 279 P.2d 673 (1955).

8. Refunding bonds do not increase the indebtedness of a school district. *Prohm v. Non-High School District* No. 216, 7 Ill. 2d 421, 130 N.E.2d 917 (1955).

9. The constitutions in Indiana and Kentucky limit the indebtedness of school districts and other political subdivisions to a mere 2 percent of the value of the taxable property in the district. These constitutional debt limitations are the lowest of any of the states in the nation. To bypass or avoid these uncommonly strict limitations, both states have enacted statutes that allow for the use of school building corporations in financing school construction. Such a procedure permits the formation of a holding company that is authorized to construct a school building and incur the indebtedness. The school building corporation contracts with the school district to lease the building to the district for a number of years, and when the rental payments have paid off the bonded indebtedness, the building becomes the property of the school district. This type of purchase on an installment arrangement does not increase the indebtedness of the school district. The Supreme Court of Indiana had this to say about the constitutionality of the procedure:

> The fact that the building company was willing to give the school building to the (school district) when the building company had been paid an amount equal to its investment . . . does not change the lease-contract into a contract to purchase. It is true that the (school district), through the device of a long term lease providing for annual rental payments, may become the owner of the school building which (under the constitutional limitation) it could not

have acquired . . . by issuing bonds. But it does not follow that either the arrangement or the result constitutes an evasion of the limitations of the (Constitution). The lease-contract is not in contravention of (the Constitution) unless it necessarily created a legally enforceable debt

obligation for an amount in excess of the amount permitted by (the Constitution). *Jefferson School Tp. v. Jefferson Tp. School Building Co.*, 212 Ind. 542, 10 N.E.2d 608 (1937); and *Kees v. Smith*, 235 Ind. 687, 137 N.E.2d 541 (1956).

ENDNOTES

1. This discussion is adapted from a chapter by Kern Alexander and K. Forbis Jordan in *Financing Education; Fiscal and Legal Alternatives,* edited by R. L. Johns, Kern Alexander, and K. Forbis Jordan (Charles Merrill Company), 1972. See also School District No. 25 of Woods County v. Hodge, 199 Okl. 81, 183 P.2d 575 (1947).

2. Bell's Gap Railroad Co. v. Pennsylvania, 134 U.S. 232, 10 S.Ct. 533 (1890).

3. Wade J. Newhouse, *Constitutional Uniformity and Equality in State Taxation* (Ann Arbor: Univ. of Michigan Law School, 1959), p. 602.

4. Ibid., p. 608.

5. Hess v. Mullaney, 213 F.2d 635 (9th Cir. 1954), cert. denied Hess v. Dewey, 348 U.S. 836, 75 S.Ct. 50 (1954).

6. 79 C.J.S. § 411.

7. "Is Denial of Equal Educational Opportunity Constitutional?" Administrator's Notebook, No. 6, XIII (Univ. of Chicago, Feb. 1965). See also Arthur E. Wise, *Rich Schools Poor Schools* (Chicago: The University of Chicago Press), 1968.

8. Griffin v. Illinois, 351 U.S. 12, 76 S.Ct. 585 (1956).

9. Baker v. Carr, 369 U.S. 186, 82 S.Ct. 691 (1962).

10. McInnis v. Shapiro, 293 F.Supp. 327 (N.D. Ill. 1968) affirmed sub nom. McInnis v. Ogilvie, 394 U.S. 322, 89 S.Ct. 1197 (1969).

11. McInnis v. Ogilvie, p. 336.

12. McInnis v. Ogilvie, 394 U.S. 322, 89 S.Ct. 1197 (1969)

13. McInnis v. Shapiro, op. cit.

14. 310 F.Supp. 572 (W.D. Va. 1969), affirmed 397 U.S. 44, 90 S.Ct. 812 (1970).

15. Ibid.

16. 5 Cal. 3d 584, 96 Cal. Rptr. 601, 487 P.2d 1241 (1971), appeal after remanded 18 Cal. 3d 728, 135 Cal. Rptr. 345, 557 P.2d 929 (1976), cert. denied 432 U.S. 907, 97 S.Ct. 2951 (1976).

17. San Antonio Independent School Dist. v. Rodriguez, 411 U.S. 1, 93 S.Ct. 1287 (1973).

18. Serrano v. Priest, 5 Cal. 3d 584, 96 Cal Rptr. 601, 487 P.2d 1241 (1971), appeal after remanded 18 Cal. 3d 728, 135 Cal. Rptr. 345, 557 P.2d 929 (1976) *cert. denied,* 432 U.S. 907, 97 S.Ct. 2951 (1977) and Serrano v. Priest, 200 Cal. App. 3d 897, 226 Cal. Rptr. 584 (1986).

19. San Antonio Independent School District v. Rodriguez, op. cit.

20. Milliken v. Green, 389 Mich. 1, 203 N.W.2d 457 (1972) vacated 390 Mich. 389, 212 N.W.2d 711 (1973).

21. Shofstall v. Hollins, 110 Ariz. 88, 515 p.2d 590 (1973).

22. Milliken v. Green, 389 Mich. 1 203 N.W.2d 457 (1972).

23. School Board of Parish of Livingston v. Louisiana State Board of Elementary & Secondary Education, 830 F.2d 563 (5th Cir. 1987).

24. Thompson v. Engelking, 96 Idaho 793, 537 P.2d 635 (1975).

25. Blase v. Illinois, 55 Ill. 2d 94, 302 N.E.2d 46 (1973).

26. Knowles v. State Board of Education, 219 Kan. 271, 547 P.2d 699 (1976).

27. Helena Elementary School District No. 1 v. State of Montana, 236 Mont. 44, 769 P.2d 684 (1989), opinion amended by Helena Elementary School District No. 1 v. State, 236 Mont. 44, 784 P.2d 412 (1990).

28. Olsen v. Oregon, 276 Or. 9, 554 p.2d 139 (1976).

29. Board of Education v. Nyquist, 94 Misc. 2d 466, 408 N.Y.S.2d 606 (1978), affirmed 83 A.D. 2d 217, 443 N.Y.S.2d 843 (1981) reversed 57 N.Y.2d 27, 453 N.Y.S.2d 643 439 N.E. 2d 359 (1982) appeal dismissed 459 U.S. 1139, 103 S.Ct. 775 (1983).

30. McDaniel v. Thomas, 248 Ga. 632, 285 S.E.2d 156 (1981).

31. 62 N.J. 473, 303 A.2d 273 (1973), 63 N.J. 196, 306 A.2d 65 (1973), 69 N.J. 449, 355 A.2d 129 (1976), opinion supplemented 70 N.J. 155, 358 A.2d 457 (1976) injunction dissolved 70 N.J. 464, 360 A.2d 400 (1976).

32. Robinson v. Cahill, op. cit., p. 295.

33. Horton v. Meskill, 172 Conn. 615, 376 A.2d 359 (1977), 187 Conn. 187, 445 A.2d 579 (1982), 195 Conn. 24, 486 A.2d 1099 (1985).

34. Dupree v. Alma School District No. 30, 279 Ark. 340, 651 S.W.2d 90 (1983).

35. Shofstall v. Hollins, 110 Ariz. 88, 515 P.2d 590 (1973); Milliken v. Green, 390 Mich. 389, 212 N.W. 2d 711 (1973); Thompson v. Engelking, 96 Idaho 793, 537 P.2d 635 (1975); Olsen v. State of Oregon, 276 Or. 9, 554 P.2d 139 (1976); Danson v. Casey, 484 Pa. 415, 399 A.2d 360 (1979) and Bensalem Township School District v. Commonwealth of Pennsylvania, 105 Pa. Cmwlth. 388, 524 A.2d 1027 (1987); Board of Education of City School Dist. of City of Cincinnati v. Walter, 58 Ohio St. 2d 368, 390 N.E. 2d 813 (1979), cert. denied 444 U.S. 1015, 100 S.Ct. 665 (1980); McDaniel v. Thomas, 248 Ga. 632, 285 S.E. 2d 156 (1981); Lujan v. Colorado State Board of Education, 649 P.2d 1005 (Colo. 1982); Board of Education, Levittown Union Free School District v. Nyquist, 94 Misc. 2d 466, 408 N.Y.S.2d 606 (1978) 408 N.Y.S. 2d (1978); *judgment modified* 443 N.Y.S. 2d 843 (1981); order modified, 453 N.Y.S. 2d 643 (1982); *appeal dismissed,* 459 U.S. 1138, 103 S.Ct. 775 (1983). Dumain v. Carey 133 A.D. 2d 206, 519 N.Y.S. 2d 17 (1987);

Hornbeck v. Somerset County Board of Education, 295 Md. 597, 458 A.2d 758 (1983); Fair School Finance Council of Oklahoma Inc. v. State of Oklahoma, 746 P.2d 1135 (Okl. 1987); Britt v. North Carolina State Board of Education, 86 N.C. App. 282, 357 S.E. 2d 432 (1987); School Board of the Parish of Livingston v. Louisiana State Board of Elementary and Secondary Education, 830 F. 2d 563 (5th Cir. 1987), cert. denied 487 U.S. 1223, 108 S.Ct. 2884 (1988); Richland County v. Campbell, 294 S.C. 346, 364 S.E. 2d 470 (1988).

36. Robinson v. Cahill, 62 N.J. 473, 303 A.2d 273 (1973), cert. denied 414 U.S. 976, 94 S.Ct. 292 (1973); Knowles v. State Board of Education, 219 Kan. 271, 547 P.2d 699 (1976); Buse v. Smith, 74 Wis. 2d 550, 247 N.W.2d 141 (1976) and Kukor v. Grover, 148 Wis. 2d 469, 436 N.W.2d 568 (1989); Serrano v. Priest, 5 Cal. 3d 584, 96 Cal. Rptr. 601, 487 P.2d 1241 (1971) and Serrano v. Priest, 557 P.2d 929 (1976), cert. denied 432 U.S. 907, 97 S.Ct. 2951 (1977) and Serrano v. Priest, 200 Cal. App. 3d 897, 226 Cal. Rptr. 584 (1986); Horton v. Meskill, 376 A.2d 359 (1977); Seattle School District No. 1 v. State of Washington, 90 Wn. 2d 476, 585 P.2d 71 (1978); Pauley v. Kelly, 162 W.Va. 672, 255 S.E. 2d 859 (1979) and State ex rel. Board of Education for Grant County v. Manchin, _____ W.Va. _____, 366 S.E. 2d 743 (1988); Washakie County School District No. One v. Herschler, 606 P.2d 310 (Wyo. 1980), cert. denied sub nom.; Hot Springs County School District Number 1 v. Washakie County School District Number 1, 449 U.S. 824, 101 S.Ct. 86 (1980); DuPree v. Alma School District No. 30, 279 Ark. 340, 651 S.W.2d 90 (1983); Helena Elementary School District No. 1 v. State of Montana, 236 Mont. 44, 769 P.2d 684 (1989) 236 Mont. 44, 784 P.2d 412 (1990); Rose et al. v. Council for Better Education, Inc., et al., 790 S.W. 2d 186 (Ky. 1989); Edgewood Independent School District v. Kirby, 777 S.W. 2d 391 (Tex. 1989).

37. David L. Franklin and G. Alan Hickrod, "School Finance Equity: The Courts Intervene," *Policy Briefs* (Normal, Illinois: North Central Regional Educational Laboratory), no. 6 & 7, 1990, pp. 1–2.

38. Serrano v. Priest, (1976), op. cit.

39. Serrano v. Priest, (1976), op. cit.

40. Robinson v. Cahill, op. cit.

41. 162 W.Va. 672, 255 S.E.2d 859 (1979); Pauley v. Bailey, _____ W.Va. _____, 324 S.E.2d 128 (1984).

42. See Kern Alexander, "The Common School Ideal and the Limits of Legislative Authority: The Kentucky Case, *Harvard Journal on Legislation* (Cambridge, Mass.: Harvard Law School) vol. 28, no. 2 (Summer 1991).

43. Rose v. Council for Better Education, Inc., 790 S.W.2d 186 (Ky. 1989).

44. Robinson v. Cahill, op. cit.

45. Edgewood Independent School District v. Kirby, 777 S.W.2d 391 (Tex. 1989). See also 804 S.W.2d 491 (Tex. 1991).

46. Alexander, "The Common School Ideal."

47. Milliken v. Green, 390 Mich. 389, 212 N.W. 2d 711 (1973).

48. San Antonio Independent School Dist. v. Rodriguez, op. cit.

49. Serrano v. Priest, op. cit.

50. Ibid.

51. Horton v. Meskill, op. cit.

52. Pauley v. Kelly, op. cit.

53. McDaniel v. Thomas, op. cit.

54. Franklin and Hickrod, "School Finance Equity."

55. Rose v. The Council for Better Education, Inc., op. cit.

56. Edgewood Independent School District v. Kirby, op. cit.

57. Kern Alexander, "The Common School Ideal," op. cit.

58. Edgewood Independent School District v. Kirby, op. cit.

59. Rose v. Council for Better Education, Inc., op. cit., 206.

60. Edgewood Independent School District v. Kirby, op. cit., citing S. McKay, Austin, Texas: *Debates in the Texas Constitutional Convention of 1875*, (1930), p. 198.

61. Helena Elementary School District No. 1 v. State of Montana, op. cit., 691.

62. School District No. Six in Chase County v. Robb, 150 Kan. 402, 93 P.2d 905 (1939).

63. Jewett v. School District No. 25 in Fremont County, 49 Wyo. 277, 54 P.2d 546 (1936).

64. Kees v. Smith, 235 Ind. 687, 137 N.E.2d 541 (1956); Waller v. Georgetown Board of Education, 209 Ky. 726, 273 S.W. 498 (1925).

CHAPTER 20

Property

School property is state property held in trust for public school purposes.[1] By vesting a local school district with the power to acquire and hold property, the legislature does not relinquish its control. School property remains the property of the state, and the power of the local district may be expanded or abolished at the will of the legislature. For example, it is conceivable that a state legislature may decide to vest the control of school property in another agency, other than a school district, at the local level. In such a case, the school district would, abiding by the statute, relinquish control over the property in favor of the other agency.

The same reasoning prevails when the legislature decides to reorganize many small school districts into larger, more comprehensive district units. The property now owned by the smaller district becomes, by statute, the property of the new, larger, consolidated district. The state legislature in this case has merely changed the trustee in which control of school property is vested.

Absent Legislation to the Contrary, a School District, as a State Agency, Is Not Subject to Local Municipal Zoning Ordinance

City of Bloomfield v. Davis County Community School District

Supreme Court of Iowa, 1963.
254 Iowa 900, 119 N.W.2d 909.

GARFIELD, Chief Justice. This is an action in equity by the City of Bloomfield to enjoin defendants, Davis County Community School District, and its contractor, Boatman, from installing in a restricted residence district in plaintiff city a bulk storage tank for gasoline and a pump to supply its school buses therewith. . . .

On September 19, 1933, the council of plaintiff city passed ordinance 84 designating and establishing a restricted residence district in the city. Section 2 of the ordinance provides: "That no buildings or other structures, except residences, school houses, churches, and other similar structures shall hereafter be erected, reconstructed, altered, repaired or occupied within said district without first securing from the city council permit therefor . . . ."

Section 3 of the ordinance provides: "Any building or structure erected, altered, repaired or used in violation of any of the provisions of this ordinance, is hereby declared to be a nuisance . . . ." . . .

The only contention of defendants we find it necessary to consider is that ordinance 84 should not be held applicable to them to prevent installation on this school-owned site of this gasoline facility for servicing its school buses because the school district is an arm of the state and proposes to use its property for a governmental purpose. . . .

The law seems quite well settled that a municipal zoning ordinance is not applicable to the state or any of its agencies in the use of its property for a governmental purpose unless the legislature has clearly manifested a contrary intent. . . .

C.J.S. Zoning, § 135 says, "Ordinarily, a governmental body is not subject to zoning restrictions in its use of property for governmental purposes."

The underlying logic of some of these authorities is, in substance, that the legislature could not have intended, in the absence of clear expression to the contrary, to give municipalities authority to thwart the state, or any of its agencies in performing a duty imposed upon it by statute.

There can be no doubt the school district is an arm or agency of the state and that the maintenance of public schools, including providing transportation to the pupils entitled to it as required by statute, is a governmental function. Certainly it is not a proprietary one. . . .

Code section 297.1, I.C.A. states, "The board of each school corporation may fix the site for each schoolhouse . . . ." Section 297.3 says, "Any school corporation . . . may take and hold an area equal to two blocks . . . for a schoolhouse site, and not exceeding thirty acres for school playground, stadium, or field house, *or other purposes for each such site.*" (Emphasis added.)

Section 285.10, which requires local school boards to provide transportation for each pupil legally entitled thereto, states, in subsection 2, that local school boards "Establish, maintain and operate bus routes for the transportation of pupils so as to provide for the economical and efficient operation thereof . . . ." Section 285.10 also provides, in subsection 5, that local boards "Exercise any and all powers and duties relating to transportation of pupils enjoined upon them by law."

Section 285.11 provides that in the operation of bus routes and contracting for transportation, "The boards shall take advantage of all tax exemptions on fuel, equipment, *and of such other economies as are available.*" (Emphasis added.)

We think furnishing economical transportation to pupils entitled to it is as much a school matter, over which the district has exclusive jurisdiction, as maintenance of the school buildings or location of the high school football field. (Plaintiff concedes a football stadium is generally held to come within the meaning of a schoolhouse. See also *Livingston*

v. Davis, 243 Iowa 21, 27, 50 N.W.2d 592, 596, 27 A.L.R.2d 1237.) . . .

No statute has come to our attention which indicates a clear legislative intent that the state or such of its agencies as defendant district, in the use of its property for a governmental purpose, must comply with a municipal zoning ordinance. Unless our decision is to be contrary to the uniform current of authority on the subject, we must hold defendant district, in the location of this tank and pump to supply fuel to its buses, is not subject to ordinance 84. . . .

We think this opinion does not conflict with our decision in *Cedar Rapids Community School Dist. v. City of Cedar Rapids,* supra, 252 Iowa 205, 106 N.W.2d 655, that the school district was subject to certain building ordinances of the city in renovating and constructing school buildings. No zoning ordinance or question as to the district's right to make use of its property in performing a duty enjoined on it by law—such as transportation of pupils—was there involved. The two cases are further to be distinguished on the ground that here the state appears to have taken over the field of legislation pertaining to transportation of pupils and therefore municipalities may not interfere in that field. See C.J.S. Zoning § 10.

Defendants are entitled to an injunction to restrain plaintiff from interfering with their installation of the gasoline tank and pump on the ground owned by the school district north of the high school football field. For decree accordingly the cause is—reversed and remanded.

All Justices concur.

School District Is Obliged to Adhere to Minimum Building Code Standards

––– –––– ––– –––

Edmonds School District No. 15 v. City of Mountlake Terrace

––– –––– ––– –––

Supreme Court of Washington, 1970.
77 Wn.2d 609, 465 P.2d 177.

HALE, Judge. A kind of sibling rivalry in governmental affairs brings the Edmonds School District and the City of Mountlake Terrace here on a declaratory judgment suit. The school district's claim of sovereign immunity from the city's building code is met by the city's equally vehement claim of sovereign authority to enforce the code. Failing to obtain in the superior court a declaratory judgment that it need not comply with the building code, the district now appeals from a judgment favoring its intergovernmental rival.

. . .

The school district brings this suit for a declaratory judgment asking that ordinance No. 391, the building code of the City of Mountlake Terrace, be held inapplicable to and not binding upon the school district in the construction of its high school addition. From a summary judgment denying this relief and dismissing the complaint with prejudice, the district appeals.

Each party claims superior rights over the other deriving from their common source of governmental power, the sovereign state. They present two main questions: Has the state designated which of the two agencies should exercise its sovereign authority with respect to building permits and minimum setback requirements? Is there an irreconcilable dichotomy between the delegation to the school district of the sovereign's constitutional duty to educate the children of the state and the city's exercise of the police power in adopting and enforcing a building code?

Are the two sets of delegated powers in conflict? The school district says that the city, in forcing compliance with its building code, is transgressing and trespassing upon its powers and duties as an agency of the sovereign state, to build, operate and maintain public high schools. The district's function of providing the land, materials and designs for school buildings cannot, it contends, be lawfully preempted nor frustrated in any way by a municipality any more than a city could enforce its standards upon the sovereign state against its will.

Education is one of the paramount duties of the state. The duty and power to educate the people are not only inherent qualities of

sovereignty but are expressly made an attribute of sovereignty in the State of Washington by the state constitution. Const. art. 9, §§ 1, 2. The state exercises its sovereign powers and fulfills its duties of providing education largely by means of a public school system under the direction and administration of the State Superintendent of Public Instruction, State Board of Education, school districts and county school boards.

School districts are, in law, municipal corporations with direct authority to establish, maintain and operate public schools and to erect and maintain buildings for that and allied purposes. RCW 28.58. In essence, a school district is a corporate arm of the state established as a means of carrying out the state's constitutional duties (RCW 28.57.135) and exercising the sovereign's powers in providing education. The state has thus made the local school district its corporate agency for the administration of a constitutionally required system of free public education. . . . The state now requires school districts to have the plans and specifications, including those features pertaining to heating, lighting, ventilating and safety, approved by the county superintendent of schools before entering into any school building construction contracts. RCW 28.58.301.

But in other spheres of governmental activity, the state has allocated some of its sovereign powers and responsibilities to cities, too. Under Const. art. 11, § 11, a city may make and enforce all police and sanitary regulations within its limits which do not conflict with general laws. By statute, cities are charged with the sovereign exercise of the police power to maintain peace and good government and to provide for the general welfare of their inhabitants through law not inconsistent with the constitution and statutes of the state. RCW 35.24.290(18). A city and other kinds of municipal corporations, too, are agencies of the state to accomplish these ends. *Columbia Irrigation Dist. v. Benton County,* 149 Wash. 234, 270 P. 813 (1928). Among these police powers, of course, is the capability of adopting and enforcing building codes. Just as the state has vested in the state superintendent, state board, and the school districts many of its attributes of sovereignty pertaining to education, it has done the same to incorporated cities with respect to the general police powers, among which are zoning and building regulations.

The City of Mountlake Terrace cannot, under existing statutes, supersede, set aside, invalidate or impair the educational processes of or limit the standards prescribed by the state for the operation of the public schools (*State ex rel. School Dist. No. 37 of Clark County v. Clark County,* 177 Wash. 314, 31 P.2d 897 (1934)), for that would be an infringement upon state sovereignty. But the state, in delegating to school districts power to build, maintain and operate public schools, has not prescribed minimum standards for street offsets, nor directed that building permits be waived in the construction of public school buildings or additions. It has left its subordinate municipalities free to regulate each other in those activities which traditionally are thought to lie within their particular competence and are more proximate to their respective functions. Fixing minimum offsets for streets, alleys, front, side and back yards would, unless the state has said otherwise, fit more relevantly into a city building code than into the general rules for the operation and maintenance of a high school. . . .

There is little doubt that the State of Washington . . . has the constitutional power to prescribe standards for and regulate school construction, and may, as an attribute of its sovereignty, deprive municipalities of any voice in these matters. But the state has not thus far exercised this power nor prohibited cities from exacting a building permit fee, nor relieved school districts within the corporate limits of a city from paying such fee or complying with the setback provisions of the municipal building code. Unless the state has, so to speak, preempted the field of building standards or specifically ousted the municipality of jurisdiction over school construction, we think the school district is obliged to comply with the minimum standards set forth in the city's building code.

Arguments of the district and amicus curiae convey a concern that, if the court holds a school district amenable to a municipal building code, the ruling will ultimately operate to permit cities—and counties—to interfere with or impinge upon the operation, management and control of the public schools. These fears, we think, are illusory. In the matter of education, a school district is deemed to be an arm of the state for the administration of the school system. . . . It follows that the school district exercises the paramount power of the state in providing education and carries out the will of the sovereign state as to all matters involved in the educational processes and in the conduct, operation and management of the schools. We find nothing in the constitution or existing law which would enable a city legislative body to trespass or impinge upon or interfere with the conduct and operation of the public schools. We do not apprehend that requiring the Edmonds School District to pay for a building permit and set back its new addition from the street or property lines in accordance with the city building code empowers the city to assume any responsibilities or control over the way the educational process is conducted. Such matters as curriculum, textbooks, teaching methods, grading, school hours and holidays, extracurricular school activities or those concerning the selection, tenure and compensation of school personnel—indeed, the thousand and one activities and facilities by which the school districts of the State of Washington afford an education to the children of the state, and adults, too—remain outside of the authority and control of the cities.

Affirmed.

NOTES

1. "A community unit school district, like any other school district established under enabling legislation, is entirely subject to the will of the legislature thereafter. With or without the consent of the inhabitants of a school district, over their protests, even without notice or hearing, the state may take the school facilities in the district, without giving compensation therefore, and vest them in other districts or agencies. The state may hold or manage the facilities directly or indirectly. The area of the district

may be contracted or expanded, it may be divided, united in whole or in part with another district, and the district may be abolished. The 'property of the school district' is a phrase which is misleading. The district owns no property, all school facilities, such as grounds, buildings, equipment, etc., being in fact and law the property of the state and subject to the legislative will." *People v. Deatherage*, 401 Ill. 25, 81 N.E.2d 581 (1948).

An Indiana court held: "Under the constitution and laws of this state, school property is held in trust for school purposes by the persons or corporations authorized for the time being by statute to control the same. It is in the power of the legislature, at any time, to change the trustee." *Carson v. State*, 27 Ind. 465 (1867).

2. The courts have consistently held that school property may be taken from one school district and vested in other agencies. In a school district organization case that has implications for the school district's control over property, an Illinois court held: "The state may, with or without the consent of the inhabitants or against their protest, and with or without notice or hearing, take their property [property of the district] without compensation and vest it in other agencies, or hold it itself, expand or contract the territorial area, divide it, unite our whole or part of it with another municipality, apportion the common property and the common burdens in accordance with the legislative will, and it may abolish the municipality [or school district] altogether." *People ex rel. Taylor v. Camargo Community Consol. School District No. 158*, 313 Ill. 321, 145 N.E. 154 (1924).

■ PURCHASE OF PROPERTY FOR SPECIAL PURPOSES

Taxpayers have, on many occasions, questioned a board of education's use of tax money for the purchase of property that does not fall strictly within the generally accepted defini-tions of a school or classroom instructional purpose. The purchase of property for such things as athletic fields, playgrounds, recreational centers, and camps have been litigated.

The weight of authority indicates that the courts tend to interpret the authority of a board of education in this area broadly and, especially in recent years, have expanded their interpretation of the purposes and objectives of public education. However, there are boundaries beyond which it may be questionable for a board of education to tread. For example, a "liberal-minded" Florida court held it permissible for a board of education to purchase property in another county for a camp and recreational grounds.[2] On the other hand, a more cautious Kentucky court has held that there was no authorization for a board of education to purchase a recreation center in another county.[3]

School Board Has the Implied Authority to Purchase Land Outside Geographical Boundaries of School District

In Re Board of Public Instruction of Alachua County

Supreme Court of Florida, 1948.
160 Fla. 490, 35 So.2d 579.

TERRELL, Justice. . . . The question for determination is whether or not the Board of Public Instruction of Alachua County is authorized to purchase and take title to lands outside the geographical limits of the county for the purpose of administering its public school program.

Appellants contend that this question should be answered in the negative. To support this contention they rely on certain provisions of Chapter 230, Florida Statutes 1941, F.S.A., particularly sections 230.22 and 230.23, defining the powers and duties of Boards of Public Instruction. . . . They contend that said statutes and decisions restrict the power of the Board of Public Instruction in the exercise of its school program to the county over which it exercises jurisdiction and that it is without authority to enter another county or to purchase lands beyond its borders for any purpose.

Prior to the enactment of Chapter 19,355, Acts of 1939, as amended by Chapter 23,726, Acts of 1947, F.S.A. § 227.01 et seq., hereafter referred to as the School Code, this contention might have been upheld, but as this Court pointed out in *Taylor et al. v. Board of Public Instruction of Lafayette County*, 157 Fla. 422, 26 So.2d 180, 181, the School Code "enlarged materially the scope of public school programs, public school plants, and public school activities." An adequate public school program is no longer limited to exploiting the three R's and acquiring such facilities as are necessary to do so. It contemplates the development of mental, manual and other skills that may not derive from academic training. It is predicated on the premise that a personality quotient is just as important as an intelligence quotient and that training the character and the emotions is just as important as training the mind if the product is to be a well balanced citizen.

. . . Section 230.23, among other things, authorizes the County Board of Public Instruction to assume such responsibilities as may be vested in it by law, or as may be required by the State Board of Education or as in the opinion of the County Board of Public Instruction are necessary to provide for the more efficient operation of the County school system in carrying out the purposes of the School Code. As to property ownership, the latter section provides that the County Board of Public Instruction shall retain possession of all property to which title is not held by the County Board and to attain possession of and accept and hold under proper title all property which may at any time be acquired by the County Board for educational purposes in the County.

. . . It is not at all clear that the legislature intended the words "in the county" to limit land purchase to lands in the county. It would be just as reasonable to conclude that the intent was to authorize the purchase of lands anywhere they might aid the county's school program.

The reason for purchasing the lands in question was to provide a camp and a recreational ground to aid the educational program of Alachua County. It was situated on a lake across the county line in Clay County but within easy reach of the schools of Alachua County. It is shown to be well adapted for that purpose and was being offered at a nominal price. Competitive sports are now a recognized part of the public school program. Eminent psychologists proclaim the doctrine that competitive sports contribute more to one's personality quotient and ability to work with people than any other school activity. Athletic coaches and physical directors tell us that the Olympic Games and other forms of physical competition have done more to put an end to class hatreds and promote international harmony than the United Nations Assembly, the reason being that they are conducted by a strict moral code that insures just treatment to all who participate in them.

This is a mere incident to the manner in which the public school program has been bounced out of its traditional groove and invaded by new experiments in education. An adequate school program is now as diversified as an experimental farm program and the very purpose of the School Code was to give sanction to such a program. The progenitors of the three R's would doubtless have "thrown a fit" if the School Board had talked about purchasing lands for a recreational center. The barn yard and the woodpile filled the need of a recreational center for them. It met the challenge of the time but its exponents, the three R's and the little red school house that symbolized it now repose in the museum of modern education. What we are concerned with is a system to cope with this machine age that we are in danger of becoming victims of if we do not become its masters.

We have learned that the public school program has a definite relation to the economy of our people, that the great majority of them must make their living with their hands and that those who do so must acquire different skills and trades from those who pursue the learned professions, various businesses and specialized activities. We have also learned that, while skill in the three R's was adequate for a rural democracy when the nearest neighbor was three miles away and it was sometimes three hundred yards from the front door to the front gate, it is entirely inadequate for an urban democracy where you speak to your neighbor through the window and sometimes live with a flock of them under the same roof. A democracy in which we cultivate our farms with machines, travel by automobile, send our mail by airplane and flip a gadget to warm the house, start breakfast and relieve much of the day's drudgery. Such is the social era that the public school program must prepare the citizen for and the School Code was designed to provide the wherewith for such a program. County lines may be treated as a fiction rather than a barrier to such a program.

It follows that the question confronting us impels an affirmative answer. To construe the School Code otherwise would render it impossible to bring about a public school program adequate for the needs contemplated by the legislature. So the fact that the lands in question were without the geographical limits of Alachua County is not material if they are essential to carry out its public school program.

Affirmed.

NOTES

1. In a ruling similar to the Alachua County case, the Kentucky Court of Appeals upheld a cooperative arrangement by which the Jefferson County Board of Education jointly with the Jefferson County Fiscal Court created a Jefferson County Board of Recreation. The activities of the recreation board were financed jointly by the cooperating agencies upon submission and approval of a budget by each agency. The primary legal question was, does a statute that provides that any school district may join with a city or county in "providing and conducting public playgrounds and recreational centers" extend sufficient authority for the school district to budget funds and purchase property for the establishment of playgrounds, parks, and recreation centers? The court said it did and reasoned: "We think the statute is plain in extending the authority; it is subject to no other construction. It is true that there is no explicit provision for the expenditure by the board of such sum or sums as may appear to it in the exercise of reasonable discretion to further the intended purpose. The force of the argument is that while the school district may join in 'providing and conducting' the enterprise, the county must bear all incident expenses. The power and authority granted by a statute is not always limited to that which is specifically conferred, but includes that which is necessarily implied as incident to the accomplishment of those things which are expressly authorized." *Dodge v. Jefferson County Board of Education*, 298 Ky. 1, 181 S.W.2d 406 (1944).

2. The authority of a school district to purchase or construct teachers' homes has been upheld by the courts. One court had this to say: "An adequate public school system program now contemplates the development of skills that flow from the head, the hand, the heart . . . . Expenditures for facilities that aid these purposes may be lawfully made from the public school funds." *Taylor v. Board of Public Instruction of Lafayette County, Fla.*, 157 Fla. 422, 26 So.2d 180 (1946). Evidently, the reasoning of this court was that homes for teachers would enhance the educational process to a sufficient degree to pay dividends through increased educational attainment of the pupils.

Conversely, it has been held that public school funds may not be used to provide a house for the school superintendent. *Fulk v. School Dist. No. 8 of Lancaster County*, 155 Neb. 630, 53 N.W.2d 56 (1952). However, this view seems to be in the minority.

■ SCHOOL BUILDINGS

Since much of the educational dollar goes for capital outlay, and by far the greatest portion of this money comes from local taxation, it is inevitable that people in the community will, from time to time, question the propriety of the expenditure of such money for certain capital construction purposes. In settling these disputes, the courts have found it necessary to define just what the legislature meant when it provided for local school boards to construct "school buildings" and "schoolhouses." Such an interpretation naturally reverts to a discussion of the parameters of educational purpose and the means by which to accomplish such purposes.

For example, in discussing educational purpose the courts have held both for and against the construction of football stadiums; however, the precedent seems to support the conclusion that stadiums do serve a school purpose and thereby constitute a schoolhouse within the meaning of statute. The rule seems to be that a schoolhouse is a place where instruction and training is given in any branch or branches of the educational endeavor, regardless of whether such exercises are mental or physical.

Term "Schoolhouse" Is Broad Enough to Imply
Authority to Build a Stadium

– · – · – · – · –

Alexander v. Phillips

– · – · – · – · –

Supreme Court of Arizona, 1927.
31 Ariz. 503, 254 P. 1056.

LOCKWOOD, J. Plaintiff brought this action for the purpose of restraining the issue of some $80,000 in bonds of the Phoenix union high school district of Maricopa County, Ariz. . . . The second question is the vital point in the case. In substance it is: May a high school district in Arizona issue bonds to build a "stadium"? The purpose for which school bonds may be issued is governed by the provisions of paragraph 2736, R.S.A.1913, Civil Code, as amended by chapter 24, Session Laws of 1925, which reads, so far as material to this feature of the case, as follows:

> 2736. The board of trustees of any school district may, whenever in their judgment it is advisable, and must, upon petition of fifteen per cent. of the school electors, as shown by the poll list at the last preceding annual school election, residing in the district, call an election for the following purposes: . . .
>
> (3) To decide whether the bonds of the district shall be issued and sold for the purpose of raising money for purchasing or leasing school lots, *for building schoolhouses,* and supplying same with furniture and apparatus, and improving grounds, or for the purpose of liquidating any indebtedness already incurred for such purposes. (Italics ours.)

The matter then for our determination is whether a stadium is a "schoolhouse" within the provision of paragraph 2736. The word "stadium" comes from the Greek, and was originally a measure of distance. From this, by easy transition, the term was applied first to a foot race of that distance, and then to the place where the race was run, usually an open area some 600 feet long, and flanked by terraced elevations providing seats for the spectators of the race. The modern definition follows the old one, but is somewhat broader in its scope and is technically given as:

> A similar modern structure with its enclosure used for athletic games . . . .Webster's New International Dictionary (1925 Ed.).

This is also the popular definition, and we may therefore assume that when the question was submitted to the electors of the district, it was understood by them that the proceeds of the bonds would be used to erect a structure where various forms of athletic games could be given by the students of the high school and spectators could be properly accommodated while watching them.

Is such a structure a "schoolhouse"? The terms "schoolhouse" and "school" are properly defined as follows:

Schoolhouse — a building which is appropriated for the use of a school or schools, or as a place in which to give instruction.

School — a place for instruction in any branch or branches of knowledge. Webster's New International Dictionary (1925 Ed.).

Was the stadium for which the bonds of the district were to be issued a "building which is appropriated for the use of a school or schools"? . . . No one would maintain that it was within the unfettered discretion of the pupils, the teachers, or any independent set of men or women to determine what should be taught in our public schools. Only the people, speaking through the proper authorities, can determine this question, and the law therefore provides in what branches of human knowledge instruction may be given. We therefore hold that the proper definition of a "schoolhouse" within the meaning of paragraph 2736, supra, is: Any building which is appropriated for a use prescribed or permitted by the law to public schools.

. . . The founders of our first public schools believed all that was necessary, or at least then advisable, was the most elementary mental training, and therefore for many years public school education was confined principally to the teaching of the "three R's." But as the world progressed, it was recognized more and more fully that man, using the language of the motto of one of our great philanthropic institutions, is composed of "body, mind, and spirit," and that the complete citizen must be trained in all three fields. . . . For this reason the new generation of educators has added to the mental education, which was all that was given by the public schools of the past, the proper training of the body, and a gymnasium is now accepted to be as properly a schoolhouse as is the chemical laboratory or the study hall. Not only is this true, but the public is realizing that, even on the mental side, the field is broadening, and, whereas fifty years ago such a thing as an auditorium with a stage was practically unheard of in connec-

tion with the public school, now even the rural school of three or four rooms is not considered to be properly equipped without such a structure, either separate or in combination with the ordinary lecture room.

We thus see that the branches of human knowledge taught in the public schools have been vastly expanded in the last few generations. Has this expansion been sufficient to bring within its scope a structure of the class in question? It is a well-known fact, of which this court properly takes judicial notice, that the large majority of the higher institutions of learning in the country are erecting stadiums differing from that proposed for the Phoenix union high school only in size, and it is commonly accepted that they are not only a proper but almost a necessary part of the modern college. This is true both of our privately endowed and our publicly maintained universities. That athletic games under proper supervision tend to the proper development of the body is a self-evident fact. It is not always realized, however, that they have a most powerful and beneficial effect upon the development of character and morale. To use the one game of football as an illustration, the boy who makes a successful football player must necessarily learn self-control under the most trying circumstances, courage, both physical and moral, in the face of strong opposition, sacrifice of individual ease for a community purpose, teamwork to the exclusion of individual glorification, and above all that "die in the last ditch" spirit which leads a man to do for a cause everything that is reasonably possible, and, when that is done, to achieve the impossible by sheer willpower. The same is true to a greater or lesser degree of practically every athletic sport which is exhibited in a stadium.

It seems to us that, to hold things of this kind are less fitted for the ultimate purpose of our public schools, to wit, the making of good citizens, physically, mentally, and morally, than the study of algebra and Latin, is an absurdity. Competitive athletic games therefore, from every standpoint, may properly be included in a public school curriculum. The question then is, Does the law of Arizona so include them?

The Eighth Legislature has specifically directed that all public school pupils not physically disabled must take, as part of the regular school work, a course in physical education, which is declared to include "athletic games and contests." So far as the instant case is concerned, this of course is merely illustrative of the present trend of thought along the lines of physical education. At the time the election referred to was held, paragraph 2733, R.S.A.1913, Civil Code, provided among other things, as follows:

> Under such conditions as are provided for by law, boards of trustees may employee such special teachers in drawing, music, domestic science, manual training, kindergarten, commercial work, agriculture and other special subjects as they shall deem advisable.

We think "other special subjects" reasonably includes physical education, and indeed, by virtue of this provision, not only practically all high schools in the state of Arizona, but many of the grammar schools, have for years employed physical and athletic directors, both men and women, and physical education for both boys and girls is a subject required in the courses of study adopted by a large majority of our high schools and approved by the state board of education in pursuance of paragraph 2778, R.S.A.1913; the Phoenix union high school being among this number.

If physical education be one of the special subjects permitted by law, it is a matter for the reasonable discretion of our school authorities as to how such subject should be taught and no parent who has ever had a child participate in any form of the athletic games and contests recognized and given by the various schools of this state, and who has noted the increased interest shown and effort put forth by the participants when such games and sports are open to the view of their schoolmates, friends, and parents, both in intra and inter mural competition, but will realize the educational value both of the games and of a suitable place for giving them.

For the foregoing reasons, we are of the opinion (1) that physical education is one of the branches of knowledge legally imparted in the Phoenix union high school; (2) that competitive athletic games and sports in both intra and inter mural games are legal and laudable methods of imparting such knowledge; and (3) that a structure whose chief purpose is to provide for the better giving of such competitive athletic games and sports as aforesaid is reasonably a schoolhouse within the true spirit and meaning of paragraph 2736, supra.

In view of the foregoing conclusions, it is not necessary to consider the other legal questions raised by plaintiff.

The judgment of the superior court of Maricopa county is affirmed.

NOTES

1. The Kentucky Court of Appeals has held that an auditorium-gymnasium is a "school building" within the meaning of statutes. *Rainer v. Board of Education of Prestonsburg Independent School Dist.* 273 S.W.2d 577 (Ky.1954). The court in this case distinguished its reasoning from an earlier case in which it held that a football stadium did not constitute a "school building." *Board of Education of Louisville v. Williams,* 256 S.W.2d 29 (Ky.1953). The court reasoned that in the *Rainer* case the use of the auditorium-gymnasium constituted a useful educational purpose where use of the stadium did not.

   In the 1953 *Louisville* case, the court disagreed with the ruling in the case of *Alexander v. Phillips,* the principal case presented above, and said: "The case of *Alexander v. Phillips,* apparently the leading case in point, differs in that the voters in that case specifically voted for construction of the stadium, where the Louisville voters only authorized an eight million dollar bond issue for 'school buildings.'" The Kentucky court further commented on the Arizona case, saying: "The court apparently reasoned that, since a school house was a place for instruction, and since some athletic instruction took place in a stadium, a stadium was therefore a school house. This dubious logic was supported by a eulogy on the spiritual values of interscholastic athletic contests, of which the court took judicial notice. We think *Alexander v. Phillips* is not persuasive as to the intent of the Kentucky legislature in authorizing special taxes and special bond issues for 'school buildings.' "

2. The Supreme Court of Oregon has ruled that a swimming pool falls within the statutory meaning of the term "school building." The court reasoned: "We believe that it was the legislative purpose to empower the issuance of bonds by school districts for the erection on school lands of any structure which the district was authorized to construct and which it deemed necessary or desirable in carrying out its educational program." In rejecting the criterion as to whether the pool was enclosed, the court further stated: "The statute reflects the intent to make the function of the structure rather than its architectural design the criterion in determining whether the bonds may be issued." *Petition of School Board of School Dist. No. U2-20 Jt., Multnomah County*, 232 Or. 593, 377 P.2d 4 (1962).

3. Courts in other jurisdictions have upheld the authority of the school district to construct buildings for a gymnasium, *Burlington ex rel. Board of School Commissioners v. Mayor of Burlington*, 98 Vt. 388, 127 A. 892 (1925); a building for dramatics and athletics, *Woodson v. School District No. 28*, 127 Kan. 651, 274 P. 728 (1929); a recreation field, *Wilkinsburg v. School District*, 298 Pa. 193, 148 A. 77 (1929); a building for gymnasium, home economics, and vocational training, *Young v. Linwood School District No. 17*, 193 Ark. 82, 97 S.W.2d 627 (1936).

4. In a case questioning a constitutional provision of taxes for "school purposes" included school buildings, the court held that:

> the unfettered term "school purpose" has an all-inclusive meaning including the erection of school buildings. In this case the court it seems used reverse implication in reasoning that: "If the General Assembly, [in redrafting the applicable constitutional amendment] had intended to limit the application of amendment to the usual and ordinary expenses of maintaining and operating schools

> or 'school district purposes excluding the erection of buildings,' it could have easily clarified the situation by the use of some such expression." *Rathjen v. Reorganized School Dist. R–11 of Shelby County*, 365 Mo. 518, 284 S.W.2d 516 (1955).

■■■ SCHOOL SITE SELECTION

A major responsibility of a school board is the location and selection of an appropriate property for the furtherance of the educational purposes of the school district. Many cases have arisen contesting the board's authority to select sites and the appropriateness of the selection. Usually such cases evolve from the efforts of a board to consolidate small schools into larger, more centralized schools that provide not only more efficient operation but also greater educational opportunities for the children.

The courts have uniformly held that it is within the discretion of a board of education to determine what school site will best meet the educational needs of the children, and the mere fact that others do not agree is not grounds for interfering with the board's decision.

Courts Will Not Intervene Unless Board's Decision Is Tainted with Fraud or Abuse of Discretion

–––·––·––·–––

Mullins v. Board of Education of Etowah County

–––·––·––·–––

Supreme Court of Alabama, 1947.
249 Ala. 44, 29 So.2d 339.

STAKELY, Justice. This is an appeal from a decree of the equity court sustaining the demurrer to the bill of complaint. . . . The purpose of the bill is to enjoin the respondents from constructing a proposed school building in a particular community in Etowah County or in the alternative to declare legal rights of the Board of Education and Superintendent of Education of Etowah County.

The allegations of the bill in substance show the following. The respondents have requested and received bids for the proposed construction of a school building to consist of eighteen rooms or more, to be located in the Southside Community in Etowah County, Alabama. The building is to "consist of grammar school and high school grades, a vocational school and an agricultural school."
. . .

The community now served by the John S. Jones Junior High School is more thickly populated and has more children of school age than the Southside Community. More students from the community served by the John S. Jones Junior High School would attend the proposed school than students of the Southside Community. The proposed plan would necessitate the transportation of a greater number of children for much greater distances and would remove the Junior High School grades from the John S. Jones Junior High School. . . .

The plan, if put into effect, will result in the construction in the Southside Community of a school building larger than needed by that community to care for the school children residing therein and a portion of the building so constructed would remain empty and unused. The respondents further propose to remove from neighboring communities, including the John S. Jones community, sufficient students to fill the proposed building, which will leave portions of the school facilities now being used in the John S. Jones community empty and unused. In either event the result will be a waste of funds and facilities held by respondents to the detriment of the taxpayers in the county and will prevent construction of much needed school buildings in other communities in Etowah County. The construction of a smaller and less expensive building for Southside High School will be adequate and sufficient to serve the needs of school children living in Southside Community.

It is further alleged that "the proposed action of the defendants . . . is a gross abuse of the discretion vested in them by the laws of the State of Alabama."

This court is committed to the view that the courts of this state will not ordinarily seek to control the exercise of the broad discretion given by the statutes to the county board of education since the powers vested in it are quasi-judicial as well as administrative. This principle prevails even though in the exercise of descretion there may have been error or bad judgment. The courts will act, however, if the acts of county boards of education are tainted with fraud or bad faith or gross abuse of discretion. . . .

It is conceded by appellants that there is nothing to show either fraud or bad faith in the present bill.

It is insisted, however, that the allegations of the bill present a case showing gross abuse of discretion. So far as we are aware this court has not attempted to define precisely "gross abuse of discretion," perhaps for the reason that it is best to allow the facts and c ..m- stances peculiar to each case to determine its presence or absence. In a general way, however, we say that it means such an arbitrary and unreasonable act or conclusion as to shock the sense of justice and indicate lack of fair and careful consideration. . . .

The broad powers conferred on the county board of education to which we have referred include the power to consolidate schools and to arrange for transportation of pupils to and from such consolidated school (§ 76, Title 52, Code of 1940), the power to determine the "kind, grade and location of schools" (§ 113, Title 52, Code of 1940) and the power to adopt "a building program adequate to the present and future needs of the schools in the county" (§ 116, Title 52, Code of 1940). Do the allegations of the bill remove the case from within the discretion of the board to an arbitrary, unreasonable and unjustifiable misuse of power? Do the allegations of the bill overcome the presumption which is in favor of the reasonableness and propriety of the action of the board? It does not appear so to us.

The proposed school is to replace a school destroyed by fire in a community now without a school. Construing the bill against the pleader, it does not appear with sufficient certainty how much money is to be used to consummate the plan or how much empty or waste space will be created in the new school or be left in the John S. Jones Junior High School. There is nothing to show the dimensions, area or topography of the proposed site. There is nothing to show to what extent the proposed site is or is not a suitable school center or in a central location from the standpoint of other communities, not just the community in which one school, the John S. Jones Junior High School, is located. There is nothing to show a bad location from the standpoint of roads or the condition thereof.

Beyond all this there is nothing to show that the plan is out of step with the future needs of the schools of the county so far as they may be reasonably foreseen. § 116, Title 52, Code of 1940, supra. In the absence of a contrary showing it must be assumed that the authorities gave careful and due consideration to the growing and expanding needs of education in the county. The statutes as well as the high purposes of education contemplate that a plan should be adopted that has vision and foresight. A sparsely settled community today may well be a populous community tomorrow. Matters which may create irritations today because of inconvenience, etc., may be relatively unimportant in comparison with a long range plan.

The allegations of the bill will not be aided by the general allegation that "the proposed action of the defendants is a gross abuse of discretion" because this is "merely to apply an epithet without defining the act." . . . The court acted correctly in sustaining the demurrer to the bill.

Affirmed.

NOTES

1. In a later Alabama case contesting the school board's selection of a school site for a high school, it was alleged that (1) the population of the proposed site area was not sufficient to support a high school, and (2) the geographical conditions were not suitable for a high school. The court cited the principle case above, *Mullins v. Board of Education of Etowah County*, 249 Ala. 44, 29 So.2d 339 (1947) and said that it would not interfere unless the board's action constituted "gross abuse of discretion," and in this case the selection of this particular school site did not demonstrate such gross abuse. The court further said that the complainants must show a "gross abuse of discretion," and the board's action must be "such an arbitrary and unreasonable act or conclusion as to shock the sense of justice and indicate lack of fair and careful consideration," and they had failed to do this. *Board of Ed. of Blount County v. Phillips*, 264 Ala. 603, 89 So.2d 96 (1956).

2. In an Indiana case, a taxpayer sought a *writ of mandamus* to compel the school trustee to build a school building at a specified site. The court denied the writ and held that *mandamus* does not lie to compel a school township trustee to provide for the construction of a school building—especially where it does not clearly appear that it is the trustee's duty to construct the building and that he has the means to do so. *Good v. Howard*, 174 Ind. 358, 92 N.E. 115 (1910). Of course, the authority of the old township trustee is of little relevance today, except that the axiom holds true that a taxpayer cannot substitute his or her discretion for that of a school board or a trustee and compel the construction of a school building.

3. When a board of education selected a site for a school building and a large group of taxpayers objected, signed a petition, and brought an action to prevent purchase of the site, the court found that the evidence concerning the adequacy of the site was conflicting and said: "We do not deem it necessary to go into a detailed analysis of the proof. It is not the court's duty to select a site; it is only to determine whether the board of education abused a sound discretion in performing that duty. The weight of proof is largely with the board of education; and, if we had any doubt upon the question, it must be resolved in favor of the board of education . . . . Not only does the good faith of the board of educa-

tion stand unimpeached; but, under the rule by which we will not set aside a finding of fact by the [board of education] where the proof is contradictory we will not disturb [its] judgment in the case." *Spaulding v. Campbell County Board of Education*, 239 Ky. 277, 39 S.W.2d 490 (1931).

■ EMINENT DOMAIN

Eminent domain is the power of the government to take private property for public use. Through the right of eminent domain the state can reassert, for reason of public exigency and for the public good, its dominion over any portion of the property of a state. Therefore, when statute so provides, a public board of education can condemn and take for public use property needed for public school purposes; but without legislative authorization, the right of eminent domain lies dormant and cannot be exercised.

Also, the power of eminent domain as exercised by local school boards must satisfy constitutional provisions of both the state and federal governments. Federal constitutional provisions that must be carefully observed are the Fifth Amendment, which prohibits depriving any person of life, liberty, or property without due process of law and from taking private property for public use without just compensation, and the Fourteenth Amendment, which prohibits any state from depriving any person of life, liberty, or property without due process of law and from denying any person within its jurisdiction the equal protection of the laws. Comparable clauses are included in state constitutions. Such constitutional provisions make it necessary that owners be justly compensated for their property. The question of what is just compensation has been the impetus for much litigation. Generally, however, the fair market value or the value of the property between a willing buyer and a willing seller is the measure of compensation to be awarded the owner.

In taking private property for public use, the public agency must show a necessity for the land, and therefore, cannot condemn more property than public necessity dictates.

It is a general rule that a school board cannot take land that is already being used by another public agency; however, it has been held, in some cases, that where two public agencies need land, the agency with the more necessary need will prevail.

Eminent Domain Can be Exercised to Condemn Property for "Public Use"

Oxford County Agricultural Society v. School District No. 17

Supreme Judicial Court of Maine, 1965.
161 Me. 334, 211 A.2d 893.

WEBBER, Justice. On appeal. The defendant School Administrative District No. 17, a quasi-municipal corporation charged with the responsibility of providing public school education, seeks to take property of the plaintiff Oxford County Agricultural Society by eminent domain. The District requires the property for the location of a new high school. It has general statutory authority to take by eminent domain for its lawful purposes but it has never been given specific legislative authority to take the property of this plaintiff.

The . . . issue is whether or not the Society's property is devoted to public uses to such an extent and in such a manner as to provide it with an exemption from condemnation. The plaintiff conducts an annual fair on the property in question which has all the usual attributes of an agricultural fair with which Maine people have long been familiar. . . . The plaintiff is a private voluntary corporation chartered by the Legislature. It is not a political subdivision of the state nor is it invested with any political or governmental function. It was not created to assist in the conduct of government nor was it created by the sovereign will of the Legislature without the consent of the persons who constitute it. These persons may decline or refuse to execute powers granted by legislative charter. They may at any time dissolve and abandon it and are under no legal obligation to conduct an annual fair or to carry on or continue any of the activities which are said to benefit the public. The principles governing exemption from condemnation were well stated in *Tuomey Hospital v. City of Sumter* (1964), 134 S.E.2d (S.C.) 744, 747:

> We recognize that it is difficult to give an accurate and comprehensive definition of the term "public use." The distinction between public and private use lies in the character of the use and must to a large extent depend upon the facts of each case. There are, however, certain essential characteristics which must be present if the use is to be deemed public and not private within the meaning of the law of eminent domain.   . . .
>
> The general rule, to which we adhere, was thus stated in the case of the *President and Fellows of Middlebury College v. Central Power Corporation of Vermont*, 101 Vt. 325, 143 A. 384, 388: "It is essential to a public use, as the term is used in proceedings involving the law of condemnation or eminent domain, that the public must, to some extent, be entitled to use or enjoy the property, not by favor, but as a matter of right.   . . . The test whether a use is public or not is whether a public trust is imposed upon the property; whether the public has a legal right to the use, which cannot be gainsaid or denied, or withdrawn at the pleasure of the owner."

We are satisfied that the statement set forth in 18 Am.Jur. 720, Sec. 94, accurately summarizes the requirements for exemption:

> To exempt property from condemnation under a general grant of the power of eminent domain, it is not enough that it has been voluntarily devoted by its owner to a public or semipublic use. If the use by the public is permissive and may be abandoned at any time, the property is not so held as to be exempt. The test of whether or not property has been devoted to public use is what the owner must do, not what he may choose to do. It is immaterial how the property was acquired; if its owner has devoted it to a public use which he is under a legal obligation to maintain, it comes within the protection of the rule exempting it from condemnation.

We conclude, as did the justice below, that the property of the Society is not immune from condemnation by the District.   . . .

Appeal denied.

"Proper School Purpose" Provision in Eminent Domain Statute Allows School District to Condemn Property for Parking Facilities and School Administration Building

——— · — · — · — · — ———

In Re School Dist. of Pittsburgh

——— · — · — · — · — ———

Supreme Court of Pennsylvania, 1968.
430 Pa. 566, 244 A.2d 42.

EAGEN, Justice.   . . . The precise issue presented here is whether the lower court correctly determined that the acquisition of land for parking facilities for employees and visitors to the School Administration Building is not a "proper school purpose" within the meaning of the Act of March 10, 1949.

· · ·

On June 21, 1966, the Board of Public Education of the School District of Pittsburgh [hereinafter Board] passed a resolution authorizing the filing of declarations of taking for the involved properties [primarily to provide parking facilities at the School Administration Building].   . . . The lower court sustained the preliminary objections solely because it concluded that the Board's condemnation power does not extend to the acquisition of land for parking facilities for administrative employees.

The Board's condemnation power flows from the Act of March 10, 1949, P.L. 30, Art. VII, 24 P.S. § 7–701 et seq. Section 703, 24 P.S. § 7–703 provides:

In order to comply with the provisions of this act, and subject to the conditions thereof, the board of school directors of each district is hereby vested with the necessary power and authority to acquire, in the name of the district, by purchase, lease, gift, devise, agreement, condemnation, or otherwise, any and all such real estate . . . as the board of school directors may deem necessary to furnish suitable sites for proper school purposes for said district . . . .

Section 721, 24 P.S. § 7–721 provides:

Whenever the board of school directors of any district cannot agree on the terms of its purchase with the owner or owners of any real estate that the board has selected for school purposes, such board of school directors, after having decided upon the amount and location thereof may enter upon, take possession of, and occupy such land as it may have selected for school purposes, whether vacant or occupied, and designate and mark the boundary lines thereof, and thereafter may use the same for school purposes according to the provisions of this act . . . .

In interpreting the statute we must, of course, bear in mind that provisions conferring the power of eminent domain must be strictly construed. Act of May 28, 1937, P.L. 1019, Art. IV, § 58, 46 P.S. § 558. Strict construction does not require, however, that a statute be construed as narrowly as possible, or that it be construed so literally and without common sense that its obvious intent is frustrated. . . .

A close examination of Section 703 of March 10, 1949, supra, indicates that the power and authority of the Board to acquire real estate is limited to acquisition "for proper school purposes" not only when the acquisition is by condemnation, but also when it is by "purchase, lease, gift, devise, agreement . . . or otherwise." Thus, if the Board cannot condemn real estate for the purpose of using it as a parking lot, it apparently cannot lease, purchase or otherwise acquire real estate for parking purposes. To deny the Board this power is serious not only because off street parking usually is desirable for buildings located in congested urban areas,

but also because this Court has held that a school board may be compelled to comply with a zoning ordinance requiring provision for off street parking in the erection of a new building. . . .

In approaching the question of whether or not the legislature intended to deny the Board this power, it is significant that the phrase "proper school purposes" in Section 703 of the Act of March 10, 1949, supra, replaced the phrase "school buildings and playgrounds" in Section 602 of the Act of May 18, 1911, P.L. 309. This substitution, fairly read, not only left the Board's power less precisely defined, but also broadened it somewhat. Thus the acquisition of a building to be used solely for administration undoubtedly is for a proper school purpose although an administration building may not be unquestionably within the term "schoolbuilding," which could be read to imply a school house where classes are held.

We think that the acquisition of land for off street parking for school district facilities, including an administration building, is for a "proper school purpose." With particular reference to an administration building, there are two obvious reasons why numerous automobiles are incident to its operation. First, superintendents and supervisors that have central offices in an administration building must have occasion when duty requires their presence in scattered parts of the school district. The availability and effectiveness of these professionals no doubt is greatly enhanced by their use of automobile transportation. Second, teachers, principals and other staff scattered throughout the school system must have occasion when they are required to attend meetings together in the central administration building. To do so without an excessive investment in time, they frequently will have to use automobile transportation. With reference to any school district facility, automobiles will be incident to its operation for other reasons. For instance, professionals, as well as secretarial, clerical and maintenance staff, may not accept employment unless they can commute to and from work by automobile. This might be common in areas where public transportation does not serve either the employee's home or the school district's facility.

Even where public transportation is available, we must recognize that today a great part of the public is unwilling to use it because they are almost addicted to the convenience and independence provided by the automobile. Since automobiles are a necessary incident to the operation of school district facilities, off street parking is a practical necessity. The streets simply are not adequate and sometimes are not available for parking. Consequently, the acquisition of land for off street parking, which is a practical necessity to the effective and efficient operation of a school system, is certainly a "proper school purpose." To interpret the statute any more narrowly would be to frustrate its obvious intent to delegate to the Board authority to discharge the legislature's constitutional obligation to provide for an efficient public school system.

. . .

Reversed.

NOTES

1. A Florida statute illustrates a typical right of eminent domain conferred upon a school district. "There is conferred upon the county board in each of the several counties in the state the authority and right to take private property for any public school purpose or use when, in the opinion of the county board, such property is needed in the operation of any or all of the public schools within the county, including property needed for any school purpose or use in any school district or districts within the county. The absolute fee simple title to all property so taken and acquired shall vest in the county board of such county unless the county board seeks to appropriate a particular right or estate in such property." West's F.S.A. § 235.05.

2. Where a school district takes property by condemnation, and the statutes do not require title to be taken in fee simple, the courts have held that a school district obtains only an easement or a qualified fee. The court in a Pennsylvania case held that under a condemnation proceeding, "whatever kind of right, estate, or easement, the school district acquired, terminated when it ceased to use it for the purpose for which the land was appropriated, and the title reverted to the original owner or those who hold under him." *Lazarus v. Morris,* 212 Pa. 128, 61 A. 815 (1905).

3. To condemn property, boards of education must show that the property will be used for a public school use. An Alabama court has held that an administrative building for the school superintendent and his or her staff constitutes a public use and falls within statutory provisions that provide for condemnation for "other public school purposes." *Smith v. City Board of Education of Birmingham,* 272 Ala. 227, 130 So.2d 29 (1961).

4. The prevailing view is that one public agency may condemn property belonging to another public agency if a "more necessary need" exists. In a case illustrating this view, the Supreme Court of North Dakota held that "the convenience to the public arising out of the use of certain property as a school site and grounds exceeded the convenience to the public arising from the use as a park." *Board of Education of Minot v. Park District of Minot,* N.D., 70 N.W.2d 899 (N.D. 1955). A Massachusetts court held that school property could be taken for use as a public road. The court weighed the need for the road against the harm incurred and ruled that the road was the "more necessary need." The court said in part: "there is much greater freedom of choice as to where a schoolhouse shall be put than where roads shall run . . . ." *Easthampton v. County Commissioners of Hampshire,* 154 Mass. 424, 28 N.E. 298 (1891).

5. In a case illustrating the use of fair market value as the measure of damages, a school board in Louisiana contested a court's valuation of a condemned tract of land. The jury had assessed a value of $1,200 for a school site of 5.9 acres. On appeal, the board showed that similar land in the neighborhood was selling between $5.00 to $25.00 per acre. Based on this evidence, the total award was reduced to $300.00. *Ouachita Parish School Board v. Clark,* 197 La. 131, 1 So.2d 54 (1941).

6. Under condemnation procedures, the usual redress open to a landowner is an action to recover compensation and damages for the loss of property. The award to the owner is usually based on the appraised fair market value of property. However, some courts have used other measures such as the "substitute facility approach" in condemnation of special-purpose property. For example, where a highway intersects a school campus, cutting growth potential or isolating a building, the courts may apply this alternative standard. *Commonwealth, Department of Highways v. City of Winchester,* 431 S.W.2d 707 (Ky.1968). The United States Supreme Court has said: "[W]e are not to make a fetish of market value 'since it may not be the best measure of value in some cases'. Where the highest and best use of the property is for municipal or governmental purposes, as to which no market value properly exists, some other method of arriving at just compensation must be adopted, and the cost of providing property in substitution for the property taken may reasonably be the basis of the award." *United States v. Cors,* 337 U.S. 325, 69 S.Ct. 1086 (1949).

▰▰▰ ADVERSE POSSESSION

Adverse possession is a means of acquiring property that is of occasional concern to school district authorities. All states have statutes that limit the times during which certain actions may be brought. These are called statutes of limitation and apply not only to matters concerning property but to other areas of law, such as actions for contracts under seal, actions for wrongful death, and actions for liability for torts. Statutes of limitation for recovery of property have particular significance because the running of the statutes has not only procedural but also proprietary significance. In other words, if the statute of limitation for recovery of possession of property is twenty years and the owner of the land does not initiate an action within this

time against someone in actual open possession of the property, the owner loses his title to the land, his right of action is dead, and the person in possession of the property acquires title. However, in order to gain title to property by adverse possession, the occupant must exercise dominion over the property in a manner that is actual, uninterrupted, open, notorious, hostile, and exclusive, with a claim of ownership such as will notify parties seeking information that the property is not held in subordination to any claim by others, but is held against all titles and claims.[4]

Party Seeking to Acquire Property by Adverse Possession Must Establish an Open, Notorious, and Hostile Claim

––·––·––·––

Lovejoy v. School District No. 46, Sedgwick County

––·––·––·––

Supreme Court of Colorado, 1954.
129 Colo. 306, 269 P.2d 1067.

HOLLAND, Justice. . . . The sole question here involved is whether or not the district, by being in possession and holding school on the premises for a long period of time more than the statutory period of eighteen years, was entitled to possession and to have title quieted in it by adverse possession.

The fact that the district had established a school on the land involved about the year 1886, and that there had been continuously conducted a school thereon until the year 1947, is not disputed. The proof offered by the School District lacks any showing of a clear, positive and unequivocal act on the part of the district during any of the time involved that would disclose its claim or right to the land by adverse possession. Mere occupancy alone seems to be relied upon until after the spring of 1947, when a question arose between Phyllis Lovejoy, the fee owner of the quarter section, and District No. 68 as to the ownership of the building. Since the building was a permanent fixture, she authorized her attorney, on April 30, 1951, to write the president of School District No. 68, requesting the Board to remove the school building. This incident was notice to the District that she claimed ownership of the land, and there appears no denial of her claim at that time. If the District then claimed ownership of the land, there then was an open opportunity for it to assert such claim of ownership; however, it consulted an attorney and then decided to claim ownership by adverse possession. By such action, a strong presumption follows that the School District, in effect, admitted that its claim was not open, hostile and notorious, as is necessary in reliance upon adverse possession.

Numerous witnesses, of the community, were called by plaintiff, some of whom had resided there for many years, and one in particular who attended the second term of school in 1887. None of the witnesses could recall any incident whereby it was known that the District claimed ownership to the land, but all were of the same positive impression that the District owned the building.   . . .

The very essence of adverse possession is that the possession must be hostile, not only against the true owner, but against the world as well. An adverse claim must be hostile at its inception, because, if the original entry is not openly hostile or adverse, it does not become so, and the statute does not begin to run as against a rightful owner until the adverse claimant disavows the idea of holding for, or in subservience to another, it actually sets up an exclusive right in himself by some clear, positive and unequivocal act. The character of the possession must become hostile in order that it may be deemed to be adverse. And this hostility must continue for the full statutory period. 1 Am.Jur., p. 871, § 137. The statute begins to run at the time the possession of the claimant becomes adverse to that of the owner, and this occurs when the claimant sets up title in himself, by some clear, positive and unequivocal act.

No one representing School District No. 68 ever asserted that the District owned the land until immediately before the commencement of this action. The District, without color of title to possession, had to be in possession under an open and notorious claim of ownership. Under the circumstances here, mere occupancy was not sufficient to put any of the true owners on notice that the District claimed the land, and the burden of proof, as to open, notorious and hostile claim, is upon the District when it claims title by adverse possession without color of title. Every reasonable presumption is made in favor of the true owner as against adverse possession. *Evans v. Welch*, 29 Colo. 355, 68 P. 776.

In support of the general trend of the testimony that is was never known that the District claimed the land, only the building, it is to be noted that the District first claimed that it had a full acre after that time a right of way ditch cut across the corner of the section, which left an area of more than two acres, and the school land up to the ditch as a playground, and the fences along the ditch were not shown to have been placed there by the School District. Had the District been making a claim to the ground, it follows that there would have been no uncertainty as to the extent and boundaries thereof. The school board knew almost two years before this suit was commenced that Phyllis Lovejoy claimed ownership of the land when she asked them to remove the building. If originally this was a case of permission to use the ground, it would be in subordination to the title and here the burden was upon the District to prove that such notice was given, which it failed to meet.

There is no reason to discuss the question of the judgment for damages, since our determination of the rights of the parties involved necessitates a reversal of the judgment, and that the complaint be dismissed.

The judgment is reversed and the cause remanded with direction to the trial court to dismiss the complaint.

NOTES

1. Adverse possession must be open, visible, continuous, and exclusive, with a claim of ownership, such as will notify parties seeking information upon the subject that the premises are not held in subordination to

any claim of others, but against all titles and claimants.

The placing of a permanent school building and other necessary appendages on the land of another, and conducting school . . . thereon is evidence of adverse and hostile possession under which title may be claimed after fifteen years. *Liles v. Smith*, 206 Okl. 458, 244 P.2d 582 (1952).

2. A court in Wyoming had this to say about adverse possession and its relationship to title by the true owner: "[T]he general rule in the United States is that possession will be presumed to be in subservience to the title of the true owner, and that the burden to prove adverse possession is upon the party who relies thereon. 2 C.J. 264. These rules, however, must be construed in the light of other rules, which have been adopted by our courts. Thus the intention to claim may be manifested either by words, or by acts . . . . Further, the term 'claim of right' has been treated as the equivalent of a hostile claim. (Citing authorities). The character of possession may give rise to a presumption, and it is generally held that the actual occupation, use, and improvement of the premises of the claimant as if he were in fact the owner thereof will, in the absence of explanatory circumstances showing the contrary, be sufficient to raise a presumption of his entry and holding as absolute owner, and, unless rebutted, will establish the fact of a claim of right. (Citing authorities). . . . Thus it is said in the last case cited:

> All reasonable presumptions are to be made in favor of the true owners, including the presumption that actual possession is subordinate to the right of the true owner, subject, however, to the limitation that actual, continuous, exclusive possession for the statutory period, unexplained, displaces a presumption in favor of the true owner and creates a presumption of fact that such possession, and the commencement of it, were characterized by all the requisites to title by adverse possession. (Emphasis added.)"

City of Rock Springs v. Sturm, 39 Wyo. 494, 273 P. 908 (1929).

▮ REVERSION OF SCHOOL PROPERTY

Conveyance of land may be made to school districts upon the same rules of future interests as a similar transaction between private persons. Under common law, the only way a fee-simple estate could be created was by the use of the words, "and his heirs" or "and their heirs." However, under modern statutes, these words of inheritance are not necessary to create a fee-simple estate. The name of the grantee only is sufficient to take a fee-simple estate unless a lesser estate is described.[5]

When a school district acquires property and the words used in the conveyance are "to X school district" or to "X school district and his heirs," and the grantor does not indicate a lesser estate, the school district obtains title in fee-simple absolute. A fee-simple absolute estate is the largest, exclusive, and most extensive interest that can be enjoyed in land. It is an estate when lands are given to a person or, in our case, a school district, and to his or her heirs absolutely without limit or end.[6]

However, many times grantors who convey property to school districts for school purposes desire that the land will sooner or later revert to them when it is no longer used for school purposes. In such cases, deeds making the conveyances of land must be unmistakably clear as to their intent; without sufficient clarity, the courts will not permit a reversion. A New Jersey court had this to say about the interpretation of such deeds: "Conditions, when they tend to destroy estates, are stricti juris and to be construed strictly . . . . Conditions subsequent, especially when relied upon to work a forfeiture, must be created by express terms or clear implication, and are strictly construed . . . ."[7]

The condition subsequent of which the court speaks is a determinable fee, the limitations of which are usually identified by the words "so long as," "until," "while," or "during." An example of such a condition is: A, fee-simple owner, conveys Blackacre to school district for so long as said property is used for school purposes. In this case the school district has a determinable fee simple and A has a possibility of reverter.

In a case in which land was conveyed to a school district "for school purposes only," it was contended that the property should revert to the grantor when it was no longer used for school purposes. The court held that the words "for school purposes only" were neither preceded nor followed by words on condition such as those listed above. The court said: "The words upon which the appellant relies as debasing the fee are merely superfluous and not expressive of any intention of the parties to the conveyance as to the effect to be given to it."[8] In this case, the clause merely duplicated a limitation that was already imposed on school property anyway.

The following case discusses the relationship between the grantor and the school district when subsequent conditions exist or are alleged to exist.

Reversionary Interest Does Not Come into Play as Long as Property Is Used for School Purposes

— · — · — · — · —

Williams v. McKenzie

— · — · — · — · —

Court of Appeals of Kentucky, 1924.
203 Ky. 376, 262 S.W. 598.

TURNER, C. On the 29th of August, 1895, appellee, W.H. McKenzie, and one Melvin Fyffe conveyed to the trustees of common school district No. 8 of Johnson county a tract of land of less than one acre, about one-half of which was from the property of appellee, and the other half from that of Fyffe. The conveyance was made "in consideration of their

respect for the system of common schools of Johnson county," and was absolute on its face except as hereinafter pointed out. The habendum clause is:

> To have and to hold the same, with all the appurtenances thereon, to the second party and their heirs and assigns forever, with covenants of general warranty.

However, after the description of the property there is appended the following:

> It is expressly understood that the aforesaid property is to belong to the aforesaid school district so long as it is used for common school purposes, but whenever the same is no longer so used it is to revert back to the parties of the first part, and the party of the second part is to have the right to remove the school building and fixtures on said premises.

As indicated in the face of the instrument, the property conveyed had been probably for some years before the conveyance used for school purposes; at any rate, a schoolhouse was erected on it, and it has been continuously used for school purposes at all times since that day, and is yet so used.

Thereafter by operation of law the title so held by the common school district became vested in the county board of education, and in November, 1920, the board of education, in consideration of $50 and the customary royalty, leased the same for oil and gas development to the appellant Junior Oil Company. Thereafter the latter under the lease drilled a well on that part of the school lot formerly belonging to appellee, McKenzie, and brought in thereon a producing oil well, whereupon, in December, 1921, McKenzie instituted this equitable action seeking to cancel the deed of August, 1895, and the lease so made by the board and to have it adjudged the title thereto was in him, and to enjoin the oil company from entering upon the same, or using or claiming the same, and asking for an accounting for the oil taken therefrom.

The original petition alleges, in substance, that the board of education had no right or authority to make the lease to the oil company for oil and gas development, and that the oil company had moved onto the property for the purpose of developing the same for such purposes, and asserting the right so to do, whereby a cloud was cast upon plaintiff's title. It is further alleged that the board of education had title to such lot only for the purpose of conducting thereon a common school for educational purposes, and that the conversion of same by it to commercial purposes was equivalent to an abandonment by it of the original purpose for which the grant was made, and by such acts it abandoned the property for the original purpose, whereby the title to same reverted to plaintiff.   .   .   .

It will be observed that by the deed of August, 1895, appellee parted with his whole interest in the property. He made no reservation or exception, nor was there a condition or restriction of any nature upon the present title conveyed. He only provided that the title so conveyed should revert to him in the uncertain event that the property should ever cease to be used for common school purposes. He provided only for a mere possible reverter to himself if the property should ever cease to be used for such purposes. The questions, therefore, which it seems necessary to determine, are:

1. What estate did the grantees take in the deed of 1895, and what are their rights in the property while the same is still being used for common school purposes?
2. What estate, if any, remains in the grantor under that deed while the same continues to be used for common school purposes, and has he such a right or interest during that time as authorizes him to maintain an action for waste?
3. Have school authorities owning property in use for school purposes the right or power to lease the same for mineral development purposes, the funds, if any, derived therefrom to be used for schools?

Questions 1 and 2 are in effect one and the same, for, if the grantees in the deed took such estate as entitles them to the unrestricted use of the property before the reversion provided for takes place, then it is clear there is no such right or estate left in the grantor as entitles him to maintain an action for waste.

The grantor clearly parted with his whole present interest, and after parting with it engrafts upon the estate conveyed a possible reversionary interest in himself if the property should ever cease to be used for common school purposes, which is manifestly a thing which may or may never happen. The thing which will operate as a reversion in the grantor is and can be only the action of the grantees themselves or their successors in title.

A qualified or determinable fee is defined in 10 R.C.L. 652, as follows:

> A qualified or determinable fee is an estate limited to a person and his heirs, with a qualification annexed to it by which it is provided that it must determine whenever that qualification is at an end. Because the estate may last forever it is a fee; and because it may end on the happening of the event it is called a determinable or qualified fee.

Such an estate is defined in 21 C.J. 922, in the following way:

> Although distinctions have been made or discussed by some authorities, the terms "base fee," "qualified fee" and "determinable fee" are generally used interchangeably to denote a fee which has a qualification subjoined thereto, and which must be determined whenever the qualification annexed to it is at an end. This estate is a fee, because by possibility it may endure forever in a man and his heirs; yet as that duration depends upon the concurrence of collateral circumstances which qualify and debase the purity of the donation it is therefore a qualified or base fee.

Manifestly the estate passing under the deed in question is embraced by these definitions. The grantor parted with all present interest in the property, and conveyed it to the grantees without limitation or restriction of title, with the lone qualification that, if it should ever cease to be used for common school purposes, the title should revert to him.

In conveying such a title, with no other limitation or restriction, the grantor not only divests himself of all present title, but places the unlimited and unrestricted use and occupation of the property in his grantee until such time, if ever, the event happens which will determine the estate conveyed. Such an estate, being one which may last forever, is from necessity such as carries with it the unlimited right to use and control the property at all times before the happening of the event which will end the estate.

As said by Mr. Washburn (4th Ed. vol. 1, p. 89) in discussing the incidents of a determinable fee:

> So long as the estate in fee remains the owner in possession has all the rights in respect to it which he would have if tenant in fee simple, unless it be so limited that there is properly a reversionary right in another — something more than a possibility of reverter belonging to a third person, when, perhaps, chancery might interpose to prevent waste of the premises.

This quotation from Mr. Washburn was approved by this court in the case of *Landers v. Landers*, 151 Ky. 206, 151 S.W. 386. Ann. Cas.1915A, 223, and the court in that case held there was no equitable waste where one only used the property in such way a prudent man would have used his own.

In 21 C.J. 923, in discussing the incidents of such an estate, it is said:

> Until its determination such an estate has all the incidents of a fee simple; and, while this estate continues, and until the qualification upon which it is limited is at an end, the grantee or proprietor had the same rights and privileges over his estate as if it was a fee simple. He has an absolute right to the exclusive possession, use, and enjoyment of the land, and has complete dominion over it all for purposes as though he held it in fee simple.

. . . the holder of a determinable fee before its determination has all the rights of a fee simple title holder, and that the holder of a mere possible estate in reversion has not sufficient right or interest in the property to authorize him to maintain an action for waste [citations].

The property in this case has been used for school purposes now for thirty years or more, and there is nothing in the pleadings or evidence to suggest any purpose upon the part of the school authorities to abandon its use for such purpose, and consequently there is nothing to indicate that the title conveyed to the school trustees will at any time in the near future be determined by the cessation of the use of the property for such purposes.

Appellee, however, relies upon a certain class of cases holding that, where property has been conveyed for school purposes and a reversionary clause is inserted, its use for other purposes works a forfeiture of the original grant, and the reversion takes place. But that class of cases has no application here whatsoever, for the very plain and sufficient reason that the property here is not being used for other than school purposes, or in any such way as to interfere with the efficient and orderly administration of the school. There is no allegation that the oil development has or will so interfere with the school; and, even if there was, appellee, who is not now a resident of the school district, is not in position to make that question.

But it is earnestly argued that, the county board of education being the creature of the statute for a specific purpose, its only duty and authority lies in the administration of educational affairs; that it is not authorized to go into the field of speculation and engage in hazardous industrial affairs, even though such activities might result profitably, and for that reason alone the oil lease given by the school board was invalid and properly cancelled. In the first place, the mere leasing of its property to others for development purposes is not engaging in a commercial venture, but is, properly speaking, only an effort to get from its property the real values therefrom, to the end that there may be a more efficient administration of school affairs.

In support of this argument reliance is had upon the case of *Herald v. Board of Education*, 65 W.Va. 765, 65 S.E. 102, 31 L.R.A. (N.S.) 588. In that case it was held by a majority of the Supreme Court of West Virginia that a school board under the statutes of that state had no power to lease a schoolhouse lot for oil and gas purposes, even though the school authorities had the absolute fee simple title thereto.

Under the provisions of section 4437, Ky.Stats., 1915 Ed., which was in effect at the time the deed was made from appellee to the school board, such school trustees were authorized to "take, hold and dispose of real and personal estate for the maintenance, use and benefit of the common school of their district."

. . .

Oil and gas are fugitive minerals; they are connected by underground streams or crevices by which they may be drained from one property onto another, and there brought to the surface. There can be no sound or practical reason given that will deprive school authorities who own property under which there are valuable minerals from entering into contracts for its development, and particularly would this seem to be true when the character of the mineral is such that adjoining landowners may profit at the expense of the school property by the failure of the school authorities to enter into such contracts. It is shown in this record that there are on adjoining lands other producing oil wells very near to the property lines of the school lot, and it is perfectly apparent that if the well on the school lot had not been drilled the oil on the school lot would soon have been drained from it by such wells, and the school authorities would have thereby been deprived of the chief wealth on the property to which they had title for the benefit of the school. There was, however, in the West Virginia case referred to, a strong dissenting opinion, in which we fully concur. That opinion, after discussing the West Virginia statute, said:

> I think the statute not only expressly but impliedly gives this board ample power to lease this property. This ought especially to be so where the product, as in this case, is oil and gas, fugitive in nature and which will be drained and carried away by operations on adjoining lands.

We are of the opinion, therefore, that under the statute in existence at the time the title was conveyed to the school authorities the board of education had the right to execute the lease in question, and, having the right to do so, it was its duty to do so to prevent the valuable mineral product on the school property from being appropriated by others.

The views which we have here expressed make it unnecessary to discuss the other questions presented.

The judgment is reversed, with directions to set aside the judgment entered, to dismiss the plaintiff's petition, and on the counterclaim and cross-petition to quiet the present title of the school board and to enjoin appellee from further claiming any present right or interest in the school lot.

Whole court sitting.

NOTES

1. *Fee Simple Absolute.* "The terms 'fee,' 'fee simple,' and 'fee simple absolute' are equivalent. *Boon v. Boon,* 348 Ill. 120, 180 N.E. 792, 794 (1932). "A fee simple absolute is an estate limited absolutely to a man and his heirs and assigns forever without limitation or condition." *Rathbun v. State,* 284 Mich. 521, 280 N.W. 35, 40 (1938). "The word 'fee,' used alone, is sufficient designation of this species of estate, and hence 'simple' is not a necessary part of the title, but it is added as a means of clearly distinguishing this estate from a fee-tail or from a variety of conditional estates." *Black's Law Dictionary, supra.* "Fee tail is a freehold estate in which there is a fixed line of inheritable succession limited to the issue of the body of the grantee or devisee, and in which regular or general succession of heirs is cut off." *Coleman v. Shoemaker,* 147 Kan. 689, 78 P.2d 905, 907 (1938). "Fee" derives from feudal times when it constituted "a freehold estate in lands, held of a superior lord, as a reward for services, and on condition of rendering some service in return for it. The true meaning of the word 'fee' is the same as that of 'feud' or 'fief' . . . ." See Black's

Law Dictionary (St. Paul, Minn., West Publishing Co., 1968), pp. 741–42.

2. Whether a board of education by conveyance obtains a fee simple title or some type of defeasible fee is explained by the Kentucky Court of Appeals.

When a limitation merely states the purpose for which the land is conveyed, such limitation usually does not indicate an intent to create an estate in fee simple which is to expire automatically upon the cessation of use for the purpose named. Additional facts, however, can cause such an intent to be found. Among the facts sufficient to have this result are clauses in other parts of the same instrument, the relation between the consideration paid for the conveyance and the market value of the land in question, and the situation under which the conveyance was obtained. *Scott County Board of Education v. Pepper,* 311 S.W. 2d 189 (Ky. 1958).

3. Property obtained by a school district with a fee-simple determinable provision in the deed providing that if the land is abandoned and "not used for school purposes" then property reverts was held sufficient to take the property from the school district when the property was no longer in use. *School District No. Six in Weld County v. Russell,* 156 Colo. 75, 396 P.2d 929 (1964).

———————

ENDNOTES

1. Carson v. State, 27 Ind. 465 (1867).

2. In re Board of Public Instruction of Alachua County, 160 Fla. 490, 35 So.2d 579 (1948).

3. Wilson v. Graves County Board of Education, 307 Ky. 203, 210 S.W.2d 350 (1948).

4. Liles v. Smith, 206 Okl. 458, 244 P.2d 582 (1952).

5. Smith, Chester H., *Survey of the Law of Real Property* (St. Paul, Minn.: West Pub. Co., 1956), p. 85.

6. *Black's Law Dictionary,* Revised Fourth Edition (St. Paul, Minn.: West Pub. Co., 1968), p. 742.

7. Board of Education of Borough of West Paterson v. Brophy, 90 N.J. Eq. 57, 106 A. 32 (1919).

8. T.W. Phillips Gas and Oil Co. v. Lingenfelter, 262 Pa. 500, 105 A. 888 (1919).

APPENDIX A

Selected Constitutional Provisions

◼◼◼ CONSTITUTION OF THE UNITED STATES

We the People of the United States, in Order to form a more perfect Union, establish Justice, insure domestic Tranquillity, provide for the common defence, promote the general Welfare, and secure the Blessings of Liberty to ourselves and our Posterity, do ordain and establish this Constitution for the United States of America.

Article. I.

Section. 1. All legislative Powers herein granted shall be vested in a Congress of the United States, which shall consist of a Senate and House of Representatives.

Section. 2. The House of Representatives shall be composed of Members chosen every second Year by the People of the several States, and the Electors in each State shall have the Qualifications requisite for Electors of the most numerous Branch of the State Legislature.

. . .

Section. 7. All Bills for raising Revenue shall originate in the House of Representatives; but the Senate may propose or concur with amendments as on other Bills.

Every Bill which shall have passed the House of Representatives and the Senate, shall, before it become a Law, be presented to the President of the United States; If he approve he shall sign it, but if not he shall return it, with his Objections to that House in which it shall have originated, who shall enter the Objections at large on their Journal, and proceed to reconsider it. If after such Reconsideration two thirds of that House shall agree to pass the Bill, it shall be sent, together with the Objections, to the other House, by which it shall likewise be reconsidered, and if approved by two thirds of that House, it shall become a Law. But in all such Cases the Votes of both Houses shall be determined by yeas and Nays, and the Names of the Persons voting for and against the Bill shall be entered on the Journal of each House respectively. If any Bill shall not be returned by the President within ten Days (Sunday excepted) after it shall have been presented to him, the Same shall be a Law, in like Manner as if he had signed it, unless the Congress by their Adjournment prevents its Return, in which Case it shall not be a Law.

. . .

Section. 8. The Congress shall have Power To lay and collect Taxes, Duties, Imposts and Excises, to pay the Debts and provide for the common Defence and general Welfare of the United States; but all Duties, Imposts and Excises shall be uniform throughout the United States;

To borrow Money on the credit of the United States;

To regulate Commerce with foreign Nations, and among the several States, and with the Indian Tribes;

. . .

To promote the Progress of Science and useful Arts, by securing for limited Times to Authors and Inventors the exclusive Right to their respective Writings and Discoveries;

. . .

Section. 9. The Privilege of the Writ of Habeas Corpus shall not be suspended, unless when in Cases of Rebellion or Invasion the public Safety may require it.

No Bill of Attainder or ex post facto Law shall be passed.

. . .

Section. 10. No State shall enter into any Treaty, Alliance, or Confederation; grant Letters of Marque and Reprisal; coin Money; emit Bills of Credit; make any Thing but gold and silver Coin a Tender in Payment of Debts; pass any Bill of Attainder, ex post facto Law, or Law impairing the Obligation of Contracts, or grant any Title of Nobility.

. . .

Article. II.

Section. 1. The executive Power shall be vested in a President of the United States of America. . . .

Section. 2. The President shall be Commander in Chief of the Army and Navy of the United States, and of the Militia of the several States, . . .

He shall have Power, by and with the Advice and Consent of the Senate, to make Treaties, provided two thirds of the Senators present concur; and he shall nominate, and by and with the Advice and Consent of the Senate, shall appoint Ambassadors, other public Ministers and Consuls, Judges of the supreme Court, and all other Officers of the United States, whose Appointments are not herein otherwise provided for, and which shall be established by Law: but the Congress may by Law vest the Appointment of such inferior Officers, as they think proper, in the President alone, in the Courts of Law, or in the Heads of Departments. . . .

Section. 4. The United States shall guarantee to every State in this Union a Republican Form of Government, and shall protect each of them against Invasion; and on Application of the Legislature, or of the Executive (when the Legislature cannot be convened) against domestic Violence.

Article. III.

Section. 1. The judicial Power of the United States, shall be vested in one supreme Court, and in such inferior Courts as the Congress may from time to time ordain and establish. The Judges, both of the supreme and inferior Courts, shall hold their Offices during good Behaviour, and shall, at stated Times, receive for their Services, a Compensation, which shall not be diminished during their Continuance in Office.

Section. 2. The judicial Power shall extend to all Cases, in Law and Equity, arising under this Constitution, the Laws of the United States, and Treaties made, or which shall be made, under their Authority;—to all Cases affecting Ambassadors, other public Ministers and Consuls;—to all Cases of admiralty and maritime Jurisdiction;—to Controversies to which the United States shall be a Party;—to Controversies between two or more States;—between a State and Citizens of another State;—between Citizens of different States;—between Citizens of the same State claiming Lands under Grants of different States, and between a State, or the Citizens thereof, and foreign States, Citizens or Subjects.

. . .

The Trial of all Crimes, except in Cases of Impeachment, shall be by Jury; and such Trial shall be held in the State where the said Crimes shall have been committed; but when not committed within any State, the Trial shall be at such Place or Places as the Congress may by Law have directed.

Article. IV.

Section. 1. Full Faith and Credit shall be given in each State to the public Acts, Records, and judicial Proceedings of every other State. And the Congress may by general Laws prescribe the Manner in which such Acts, Records and Proceedings shall be proved, and the Effect thereof.

Section. 2. The Citizens of each State shall be entitled to all Privileges and Immunities of Citizens in the several States.

. . .

Section. 3. New States may be admitted by the Congress into this Union; but no new State shall be formed or erected within the Jurisdiction of any other State; nor any State be formed by the Junction of two or more States, or Parts of States, without the Consent of the Legislatures of the States concerned as well as of the Congress.

. . .

Article. V.

The Congress, whenever two thirds of both Houses shall deem it necessary, shall propose Amendments to this Constitution, or, on the Application of the Legislatures of two thirds of the several States, shall call a Convention for proposing Amendments, which, in either Case, shall be valid to all Intents and Purposes, as Part of this Constitution, when ratified by the Legislatures of three fourths of the several States, or by Conventions in three fourths thereof, as the one or the other Mode of Ratification may be proposed by the Congress; Provided that no Amendment which may be made prior to the Year One thousand eight hundred and eight shall in any Manner affect the first and fourth Clauses in the Ninth Section of the first Article; and that no State, without its Consent, shall be deprived of it's equal Suffrage in the Senate.

. . .

This Constitution, and the Laws of the United States which shall be made in Pursuance thereof; and all Treaties made, or which shall be made, under the Authority of the United States, shall be the supreme Law of the Land; and the Judges in every State shall be found thereby, any Thing in the Constitution or Laws of any State to the Contrary notwithstanding.

The Senators and Representatives before mentioned, and the Members of the several State Legislatures, and all executive and judicial Officers, both of the United States and of the several States, shall be bound by Oath or Affirmation, to support this Constitution; but no religious Test shall ever be required as a Qualification to any Office or public Trust under the United States.

Article. VII.

The Ratification of the Conventions of nine States, shall be sufficient for the Establishment of this Constitution between the States so ratifying the Same.

■■■ AMENDMENTS TO THE CONSTITUTION OF THE UNITED STATES OF AMERICA

Articles in Addition to, and Amendment of, the Constitution of the United States of America, Proposed by Congress, and Ratified by the Several States, Pursuant to the Fifth Article of the Original Constitution

Amendment [I.] [1791]

Congress shall make no law respecting an establishment of religion, or prohibiting the free exercise thereof; or abridging the freedom of speech, or of the press; or the right of the people peaceably to assemble, and to petition the Government for a redress of grievances.

Amendment II. [1791]

A well regulated Militia, being necessary to the security of a free State, the right of the people to keep and bear Arms, shall not be infringed.

Amendment III. [1791]

No Soldier shall, in time of peace be quartered in any house, without the consent of the Owner, nor in time of war, but in a manner to be prescribed by law.

Amendment IV. [1791]

The right of the people to be secure in their persons, houses, papers, and effects, against unreasonable searches and seizures, shall not be violated, and no Warrants shall issue, but upon probable cause, supported by Oath or affirmation, and particularly describing the place to be searched, and the persons or things to be seized.

Amendment V. [1791]

No person shall be held to answer for a capital, or otherwise infamous crime, unless on a presentment or indictment of a Grand Jury, except in cases arising in the land or naval forces, or in the Militia, when in actual service in time of War or public danger; nor shall any person be subject for the same offence to be twice put in jeopardy of life or limb; nor shall be compelled in any criminal case to be a witness against himself, nor be deprived of life, liberty, or property, without due process of law; nor shall private property be taken for public use, without just compensation.

Amendment VI. [1791]

In all criminal prosecutions, the accused shall enjoy the right to a speedy and public trial, by an impartial jury of the State and district wherein the crime shall have been committed, which district shall have been previously ascertained by law, and to be informed of the nature and cause of the accusation; to be confronted with the witnesses against him; to have compulsory process for obtaining witnesses in his favor, and to have the Assistance of Counsel for his defence.

Amendment VII. [1791]

In Suits at common law, where the value in controversy shall exceed twenty dollars, the right of trial by jury shall be preserved, and no fact tried by a jury, shall be otherwise re-examined in any Court of the United States, than according to the rules of the common law.

Amendment VIII. [1791]

Excessive bail shall not be required, nor excessive fines imposed, nor cruel and unusual punishments inflicted.

Amendment IX. [1791]

The enumeration in the Constitution, of certain rights, shall not be construed to deny or disparage others retained by the people.

Amendment X. [1791]

The powers not delegated to the United States by the Constitution, nor prohibited by it to the States, are reserved to the States respectively, or to the people.

Amendment XI. [1798]

The Judicial power of the United States shall not be construed to extend to any suit in law or equity, commenced or prosecuted against one of the United States by Citizens of another State, or by Citizens or Subjects of any Foreign State.

Amendment XIII. [1865]

Section 1. Neither slavery nor involuntary servitude, except as a punishment for crime whereof the party shall have been duly convicted, shall exist within the United States, or any place subject to their jurisdiction.

Section 2. Congress shall have power to enforce this article by appropriate legislation.

Amendment XIV. [1868]

Section 1. All persons born or naturalized in the United States and subject to the jurisdiction thereof, are citizens of the United States and of the State wherein they reside. No State shall make or enforce any law which shall abridge the privileges or immunities of citizens of the United States; or shall any State deprive any person of life, liberty, or property, without due process of law; nor deny to any person within its jurisdiction the equal protection of the laws.

Section 5. The Congress shall have power to enforce, by appropriate legislation, the provisions of this article.

Amendment XV. [1870]

Section 1. The right of citizens of the United States to vote shall not be denied or abridged by the United States or by any State on account of race, color, or previous condition of servitude.

Section 2. The Congress shall have power to enforce this article by appropriate legislation.

.   .   .

Amendment XIX. [1920]

The right of citizens of the United States to vote shall not be denied or abridged by the United States or by any State on account of sex.

Congress shall have power to enforce this article by appropriate legislation.

.   .   .

Amendment XXVI [1971]

Section 1. The right of citizens of the United States, who are eighteen years of age or older, to vote shall not be denied or abridged by the United States or by any State on account of age.

Section 2. The Congress shall have power to enforce this article by appropriate legislation.

APPENDIX B

Selected Federal Statutes

▋▋ CIVIL RIGHTS ACTS OF 1866, 1870 42 U.S.C. § 1981

Section 1981 provides:

"All persons within the jurisdiction of the United States shall have the same right . . . to make and enforce contracts, to sue, be parties, give evidence, and to the full and equal benefit of all laws and proceedings for the security of persons and property as is enjoyed by white citizens, and shall be subject to like punishments, pains, penalties, taxes, licenses, and exactions of every kind, and to no other."

▋▋ THE CIVIL RIGHTS ACT OF 1871 42 U.S.C. § 1983

Section 1983 provides:

"Every person who, under color of any statute, ordinance, regulation, custom or usage, of any State or Territory, subjects, or causes to be subjected, any citizen of the United States or other person within the jurisdiction thereof to the deprivation of any rights, privileges or immunities secured by the Constitution and laws, shall be liable to the party injured in an action at law, suit in equity, or other proper proceeding for redress."

▋▋ THE CIVIL RIGHTS ACT OF 1871 42 U.S.C. §§ 1985 AND 1986

Section 1985(3) provides:

"If two or more persons in any State or Territory conspire or go in disguise on the highway or on the premises of another, for the purpose of depriving, either directly or indirectly, any person or class of persons of the equal protection of the laws, or of equal privileges and immunities under the laws: or for the purpose of preventing or hindering the constituted authorities of any State or Territory from giving or securing to all persons within such State or Territory the equal protection of the laws . . . : in any case of conspiracy set forth in this section, if one or more persons engaged therein do, or cause to be done, any act in furtherance of the object of such conspiracy, whereby another is injured in his person or property, or deprived of having and exercising any right or privilege of a citizen of the United States, the party so injured or deprived may have an action for the recovery of damages, occasioned by such injury or deprivation, against any one or more of the conspirators."

Section 1986 provides:

"Every person who, having knowledge that any of the wrongs conspired to be done, and mentioned in Section 1985 of this title, are about to be committed, and having the power to prevent or aid in preventing the commission of the same, neglects or refuses so to do, if such wrongful act be committed, shall be liable to the party injured, or his legal representatives, for all damages caused by such wrongful act, which such person by reasonable diligence could have prevented; and such damages may be recovered in an action on the case; and any number of persons guilty of such wrongful neglect or refusal may be joined as defendants in the action. . . . "

▋▋ CIVIL RIGHTS ACTS OF 1866, 1870 42 U.S.C. § 1988

As amended 1976, § 1988 provides:

Proceedings in vindication of civil rights. The jurisdiction in civil and criminal matters conferred on the district courts by the provisions of this chapter and Title 18, for the protection of all persons in the United States in their civil rights, and for their vindication, shall be exercised and enforced in conformity with the laws of the United States, so far as such laws are suitable to carry the same into effect; but in all cases where they are not adapted to the object, or are deficient in the provisions necessary to furnish suitable remedies and punish offenses against law, the common law, as modified and changed by the constitution and statutes of the State wherein the court having jurisdiction of such civil or criminal cause is held, so far as the same is not inconsistent with the Constitution and laws of the United States, shall be extended to and govern the said courts in the trial and disposition of the cause, and, if it is of a criminal nature, in the infliction of punishment on the party found guilty. In any action or proceeding to enforce a provision of sections 1981, 1982, 1983, 1985, and 1986 of this title, title IX of Public Law 92–318, or in any civil action or proceeding, by or on behalf of the United States of America, to enforce, or charging a violation of, a provision of the United States Internal Revenue Code, or title VI of the Civil Rights Act of 1964, the court, in its discretion, may allow the prevailing party, other than the United States, a reasonable attorney's fee as part of the costs.

As amended Pub.L. 94–559, § 2, Oct. 19, 1976, 90 Stat. 2641.

■■■ CIVIL RIGHTS ACT OF 1964 TITLE VI (SELECTED PARTS) 42 U.S.C.A. §§ 2000D – D–1

FEDERALLY ASSISTED PROGRAMS

§ 2000d. Prohibition against exclusion from participation in, denial of benefits of, and discrimination under Federally assisted programs on ground of race, color, or national origin

No person in the United States shall, on the ground of race, color, or national origin, be excluded from participation in, be denied the benefits of, or be subjected to discrimination under any program or activity receiving Federal financial assistance.

Pub.L. 88–352, Title VI, § 601, July 2, 1964, 78 Stat. 252.

§ 2000d–1. Federal authority and financial assistance to programs or activities by way of grant, loan, or contract other than contract of insurance or guaranty; rules and regulations; approval by President; compliance with requirements; reports to Congressional committees; effective date of administrative action

Each Federal department and agency which is empowered to extend Federal financial assistance to any program or activity, by way of grant, loan, or contract other than a contract of insurance or guaranty, is authorized and directed to effectuate the provisions of section 2000d of this title with respect to such program or activity by issuing rules, regulations, or orders of general applicability which shall be consistent with achievement of the objectives of the statute authorizing the financial assistance in connection with which the action is taken. No such rule, regulation, or order shall become effective unless and until approved by the President. Compliance with any requirement adopted pursuant to this section may be effected (1) by the termination of or refusal to grant or to continue assistance under such program or activity to any recipient as to whom there has been an express finding on the record, after opportunity for hearing, of a failure to comply with such requirement, but such termination or refusal shall be limited to the particular political entity, or part thereof, or other recipient as to whom such a finding has been made and, shall be limited in its effect to the particular program, or part thereof, in which such noncompliance has been so found, or (2) by any other means authorized by law: *Provided, however,* That no such action shall be taken until the department or agency concerned has advised the appropriate person or persons of the failure to comply with the requirement and has determined that compliance cannot be secured by voluntary means. In the case of any action terminating, or refusing to grant or continue, assistance because of failure to comply with a requirement imposed pursuant to this section, the head of the Federal department or agency shall file with the committees of the House and Senate having legislative jurisdiction over the program or activity involved a full written report of the circumstances and the grounds for such action. No such action shall become effective until thirty days have elapsed after the filing of such report.

Pub.L. 88–352, Title VI, § 602, July 2, 1964, 78 Stat. 252.

■■■■ CIVIL RIGHTS ACT OF 1964 TITLE VII (SELECTED PARTS) 42 U.S.C.A. § 2000E – E–2

EQUAL EMPLOYMENT OPPORTUNITIES

§ 2000e–2. Unlawful employment practices

Employer practices

(a) It shall be an unlawful employment practice for an employer—

(1) to fail or refuse to hire or to discharge any individual, or otherwise to discriminate against any individual with respect to his compensation, terms, conditions, or privileges of employment, because of such individual's race, color, religion, sex, or national origin; or

(2) to limit, segregate, or classify his employees or applicants for employment in any way which would deprive or tend to deprive any individual of employment opportunities or otherwise adversely affect his status as an employee, because of such individual's race, color, religion, sex, or national origin.

Employment agency practices

(b) It shall be an unlawful employment practice for an employment agency to fail or refuse to refer for employment, or otherwise to discriminate against, any individual because of his race, color, religion, sex, or national origin, or to classify or refer for employment any individual on the basis of his race, color, religion, sex, or national origin. . . .

Training programs

(d) It shall be an unlawful employment practice for any employer, labor organization, or joint labor-management committee controlling apprenticeship or other training or retraining, including on-the-job training programs to discriminate against any individual because of his race, color, religion, sex, or national origin in admission to, or employment in, any program established to provide apprenticeship or other training.

Business or enterprises with personnel qualified on basis of religion, sex, or national origin; educational institutions with personnel of particular religion

(e) Notwithstanding any other provision of this subchapter, (1) it shall not be an unlawful employment practice for an employer to hire and employ employees, for an employment agency to classify, or refer for employment any individual, for a labor organization to classify its membership or to classify or refer for employment any individual, or for an employer, labor organization, or joint labor-management committee controlling apprenticeship or other training or retraining programs to admit or employ any individual in any such program, on the basis of his religion, sex, or national origin in those certain instances where religion, sex, or national origin is a bona fide occupational qualification reasonably necessary to the normal operation of that particular business or enterprise, and (2) it shall not be an unlawful employment practice for a school, college, university, or other educational institution or institution of learning to hire and employ employees of a particular religion if such school, college, university, or other educational institution or institution of learning is, in whole or in substantial part, owned, supported, controlled, or managed by a particular religion or by a particular religious corporation, association, or society, or if the curriculum of such school, college, university, or other educational institution or institution of learning is directed toward the propagation of a particular religion. . . .

Seniority or merit system; quantity or quality of production; ability tests; compensation based on sex and authorized by minimum wage provisions

(h) Notwithstanding any other provision of this subchapter, it shall not be an unlawful employment practice for an employer to apply different standards of compensation, or different terms, conditions, or privileges of employment pursuant to a bona fide seniority or merit system, or a system which measures earnings by quantity or quality of production or to employees who work in different locations, provided that such differences are not the result of an intention to discriminate because of race, color, religion, sex, or national origin, nor shall it be an unlawful employment practice for an employer to give and to act upon the results of any professionally developed ability test provided that such test, its administration or action upon the results is not designed, intended, or used to discriminate because of race, color, religion, sex or national origin. It shall not be an unlawful employment practice under this subchapter for any employer to differentiate upon the basis of sex in determining the amount of the wages or compensation paid or to be paid to employees of such employer if such differentiation is authorized by the provisions of section 206(d) of Title 29. . . .

Preferential treatment not to be granted on account of existing number or percentage imbalance

(j) Nothing contained in this subchapter shall be interpreted to require any employer, employment agency, labor organization, or joint labor-management committee subject to this subchapter to grant preferential treatment to any individual or to any group because of the race, color, religion, sex, or national origin of such individual or group on account of an imbalance which may exist with respect to the total number or percentage of persons of any race, color, religion, sex, or national origin employed by any employer, referred or clas-

sified for employment by any employment agency or labor organization, admitted to membership or classified by any labor organization, or admitted to, or employed in, any apprenticeship or other training program, in comparison with the total number or percentage of persons of such race, color, religion, sex, or national origin in any community, State, section, or other area, or in the available work force in any community, State, section, or other area.

Pub.L. 88–352, Title VII, § 703, July 2, 1964, 78 Stat. 255; Pub.L. 92–261, § 8(a), (b), Mar. 24, 1972, 86 Stat. 109.

▇▇▇ DISCRIMINATION BASED ON SEX TITLE IX (SELECTED PARTS) 20 U.S.C.A. § 1681

§ 1681. Sex

Prohibition against discrimination; exceptions

(a) No person in the United States shall, on the basis of sex, be excluded from participation in, be denied the benefits of, or be subjected to discrimination under any education program or activity receiving Federal financial assistance, except that:

Classes of educational institutions subject to prohibition

(1) in regard to admissions to educational institutions, this section shall apply only to institutions of vocational education, professional education, and graduate higher education, and to public institutions of undergraduate higher education;

Educational institutions commencing planned change in admissions

(2) in regard to admissions to educational institutions, this section shall not apply (A) for one year from June 23, 1972, nor for six years after June 23, 1972, in the case of an educational institution which has begun the process of changing from being an institution which admits only students of one sex to being an

institution which admits students of both sexes, but only if it is carrying out a plan for such a change which is approved by the Commissioner of Education or (B) for seven years from the date an educational institution begins the process of changing from being an institution which admits only students of only one sex to being an institution which admits students of both sexes, but only if it is carrying out a plan for such a change which is approved by the Commissioner of Education, whichever is the later;

Educational institutions of religious organizations with contrary religious tenets

(3) this section shall not apply to an educational institution which is controlled by a religious organization if the application of this subsection would not be consistent with the religious tenets of such organization;

Educational institutions training individuals for military services or merchant marine

(4) this section shall not apply to an educational institution whose primary purpose is the training of individuals for the military services of the United States, or the merchant marine;

Public educational institutions with traditional and continuing admissions policy

(5) in regard to admissions this section shall not apply to any public institution of undergraduate higher education which is an institution that traditionally and continually from its establishment has had a policy of admitting only students of one sex;

Social fraternities or sororities; voluntary youth service organizations

(6) this section shall not apply to membership practices—

(A) of a social fraternity or social sorority which is exempt from taxation under section 501(a) of Title 26, the active membership of which consists primarily of students in attendance at an institution of higher education, or

(b) of the Young Men's Christian Association, Young Women's Christian Association, Girl Scouts, Boy Scouts, Camp Fire Girls, and voluntary youth service organizations which are so exempt, the membership of which has traditionally been limited to persons of one sex and principally to persons of less than nineteen years of age;

Boy or girl conferences

(7) this section shall not apply to—

(A) any program or activity of the American Legion undertaken in connection with the organization or operation of any Boys State conference, Boys Nation conference, Girls State conference, or Girls Nation conference; or

(B) any program or activity of any secondary school or educational institution specifically for—

(i) the promotion of any Boys State conference, Boys Nation conference, Girls State conference, or Girls Nation conference; or

(ii) the selection of students to attend any such conference;

Father-son or mother-daughter activities at educational institutions

(8) this section shall not preclude father-son or mother-daughter activities at an educational institution, but if such activities are provided for students of one sex, opportunities for reasonably comparable activities shall be provided for students of the other sex; and

Institution of higher education scholarship awards in "beauty" pageants

(9) this section shall not apply with respect to any scholarship or other financial assistance awarded by an institution of higher education to any individual because such individual has received such award in any pageant in which the attainment of such award is based upon a combination of factors related to the personal appearance, poise, and talent of such individual and in which

participation is limited to individuals of one sex only, so long as such pageant is in compliance with other non-discrimination provisions of Federal law.

Preferential or disparate treatment because of imbalance in participation or receipt of Federal benefits; statistical evidence of imbalance

(b) Nothing contained in subsection (a) of this section shall be interpreted to require any educational institution to grant preferential or disparate treatment to the members of one sex on account of an imbalance which may exist with respect to the total number or percentage of persons of that sex participating in or receiving the benefits of any federally supported program or activity, in comparison with the total number or percentage of persons of that sex in any community, State, section, or other area: *Provided,* That this subsection shall not be construed to prevent the consideration in any hearing or proceeding under this chapter of statistical evidence tending to show that such an imbalance exists with respect to the participation in, or receipt of the benefits of, any such program or activity by the members of one sex.

Educational institution defined

(c) For purposes of this chapter an educational institution means any public or private preschool, elementary, or secondary school, or any institution of vocational, professional, or higher education, except that in the case of an educational institution composed of more than one school, college, or department which are administratively separate units, such term means each such school, college, or department.

Pub.L. 92–318, Title IX, § 901, June 23, 1972, 86 Stat. 373; Pub.L. 93–568, § 3(a), Dec. 31, 1974, 88 Stat. 1862; Pub.L. 94–482, Title IV, § 412(a), Oct. 12, 1976, 90 Stat. 2234.

■ EQUAL PAY ACT (SELECTED PARTS) 29 U.S.C.A. § 206

§ 206. Minimum wage

Prohibition of sex discrimination

(d)(1) No employer having employees subject to any provisions of this section shall discriminate, within any establishment in which such employees are employed, between employees on the basis of sex by paying wages to employees in such establishment at a rate less than the rate at which he pays wages to employees of the opposite sex in such establishment for equal work on jobs the performance of which requires equal skill, effort, and responsibility, and which are performed under similar working conditions, except where such payment is made pursuant to (i) a seniority system; (ii) a merit system; (iii) a system which measures earnings by quantity or quality of production; or (iv) a differential based on any other factor other than sex: *Provided,* That an employer who is paying a wage rate differential in violation of this subsection shall not, in order to comply with the provisions of this subsection, reduce the wage rate of any employee.

(2) No labor organization, or its agents, representing employees of an employer having employees subject to any provisions of this section shall cause or attempt to cause such an employer to discriminate against an employee in violation of paragraph (1) of this subsection.

(3) For purposes of administration and enforcement, any amounts owing to any employee which have been withheld in violation of this subsection shall be deemed to be unpaid minimum wages or unpaid overtime compensation under this chapter.

(4) As used in this subsection, the term "labor organization" means any organization of any kind, or any agency or employee representation committee or plan, in which employees participate and which exists for the purpose, in whole or in part, of dealing with

employers concerning grievances, labor disputes, wages, rates of pay, hours of employment, or conditions of work.

June 25, 1938, c. 676, § 6, 52 Stat. 1062; June 26, 1940, c. 432, § 3(e), (f), 54 Stat. 616; Oct. 26, 1949, c. 736, § 6, 63 Stat. 912; Aug. 12, 1955, c. 867, § 3, 69 Stat. 711; Aug. 8, 1956, c. 1035, § 2, 70 Stat. 1118; May 5, 1961, Pub.L. 87–30, § 5, 75 Stat. 67; June 10, 1963, Pub.L. 88–38, § 3, 77 Stat. 56; Sept. 23, 1966, Pub.L. 89–601, Title III, §§ 301–305, 80 Stat. 838, 839, 841; Apr. 8, 1974, Pub.L. 93–259, §§ 2–4, 5(b), 7(b)(1), 88 Stat. 55, 56, 62; Nov. 1, 1977, Pub.L. 95–151, § 2(a)–(d)(2), 91 Stat. 1245, 1246.

■ FAMILY RIGHTS AND PRIVACY ACT (BUCKLEY AMENDMENT) (SELECTED PARTS) 20 U.S.C.A. § 1232G

§ 1232G. Family educational and privacy rights

Conditions for availability of funds to educational agencies or institutions; inspection and review of education records; specific information to be made available; procedure for access to education records; reasonableness of time for such access; hearings; written explanations by parents; definitions

(a)(1)(A) No funds shall be made available under any applicable program to any educational agency or institution which has a policy of denying, or which effectively prevents, the parents of students who are or have been in attendance at a school of such agency or at such institution, as the case may be, the right to inspect and review the education records of their children. If any material or document in the education record of a student includes information on more than one student, the parents of one of such students shall have the right to inspect and review only such part of such material or document as relates to such

student or to be informed of the specific information contained in such part of such material. Each educational agency or institution shall establish appropriate procedures for the granting of a request by parents for access to the education records of their children within a reasonable period of time, but in no case more than forty-five days after the request has been made. . . .

(2) No funds shall be made available under any applicable program to any educational agency or institution unless the parents of students who are or have been in attendance at a school of such agency or at such institution are provided an opportunity for a hearing by such agency or institution, in accordance with regulations of the Secretary, to challenge the content of such student's education records, in order to insure that the records are not inaccurate, misleading, or otherwise in violation of the privacy or other rights of students, and to provide an opportunity for the correction or deletion of any such inaccurate, misleading, or otherwise inappropriate data contained therein and to insert into such records a written explanation of the parents respecting the content of such records. . . .

Release of education records; parental consent requirement; exceptions; compliance with judicial orders and subpoenas; audit and evaluation of Federally-supported education programs; record-keeping

(b)(1) No funds shall be made available under any applicable program to any educational agency or institution which has a policy or practice of permitting the release of education records (or personally identifiable information contained therein other than directory information, as defined in paragraph (5) of subsection (a) of this section) of students without the written consent of their parents to any individual, agency, or organization, other than to the following—

(A) other school officials, including teachers within the educational institution or local educational agency who have been determined by such agency or institution to have legitimate educational interests;

(B) officials of other schools or school systems in which the student seeks or intends to enroll, upon condition that the student's parents be notified of the transfer, receive a copy of the record if desired, and have an opportunity for a hearing to challenge the content of the record;

(C) authorized representatives of (i) the Comptroller General of the United States, (ii) the Secretary, (iii) an administrative head of an education agency (as defined in section 1221e–3(c) of this title), or (iv) State educational authorities, under the conditions set forth in paragraph (3) of this subsection;

(D) in connection with a student's application for, or receipt of, financial aid;

(E) State and local officials or authorities to whom such information is specifically required to be reported or disclosed pursuant to State statute adopted prior to November 19, 1974;

(F) organizations conducting studies for, or on behalf of, educational agencies or institutions for the purpose of developing, validating, or administering predictive tests, administering student aid programs, and improving instruction, if such studies are conducted in such a manner as will not permit the personal identification of students and their parents by persons other than representatives of such organizations and such information will be destroyed when no longer needed for the purpose for which it is conducted;

(G) accrediting organizations in order to carry out their accrediting functions;

(H) parents of a dependent student of such parents, as defined in section 152 of Title 26; and

(I) subject to regulations of the Secretary, in connection with an emergency, appropriate persons if the knowledge of such information is necessary to protect the health or safety of the student or other persons.

Nothing in clause (E) of this paragraph shall prevent a State from further limiting the number or type of State or local officials who will continue to have access thereunder.

(2) No funds shall be made available under any applicable program to any educational agency or institution which has a policy or practice of releasing, or providing access to, any personally identifiable information in education records other than directory information, or as is permitted under paragraph (1) of this subsection unless—

(A) there is written consent from the student's parents specifying records to be released, the reasons for such release, and to whom, and with a copy of the records to be released to the student's parents and the student if desired by the parents, or

(B) such information is furnished in compliance with judicial order, or pursuant to any lawfully issued subpoena, upon condition that parents and the students are notified of all such orders or subpoenas in advance of the compliance therewith by the educational institution or agency.   . . .

(C) With respect to this subsection, personal information shall only be transferred to a third party on the condition that such party will not permit any other party to have access to such information without the written consent of the parents of the student.   . . .

Students' rather than parents' permission or consent

(d) For the purposes of this section, whenever a student has attained eighteen years of age, or is attending an institution of post-secondary education the permission or consent required of and the rights accorded to the parents of the student shall thereafter only be required of and accorded to the student.   . . .

Pub.L. 90–247, Title IV, § 438, as added Pub.L. 93–380, Title V, § 513(a), Aug. 21, 1974, 88 Stat. 571, and amended Pub.L. 93–568 § 2(a), Dec. 31, 1974, 88 Stat. 1858.

§ 1232h. Protection of pupil rights

Inspection by parents or guardians of instructional material

(a) All instructional material, including teacher's manuals, films, tapes, or other supplementary instructional material which will be used in connection with any research or experimentation program or project shall be available for inspection by the parents or guardians of the children engaged in such program or project. For the purpose of this section "research or experimentation program or project" means any program or project in any applicable program designed to explore or develop new or unproven teaching methods or techniques.

Psychiatric or psychological examinations, testing, or treatment

(b) No student shall be required, as part of any applicable program, to submit to psychiatric examination, testing, or treatment, or psychological examination, testing, or treatment, in which the primary purpose is to reveal information concerning:

(1) political affiliations;

(2) mental and psychological problems potentially embarrassing to the student or his family;

(3) sex behavior and attitudes;

(4) illegal, anti-social, self-incriminating, and demeaning behavior;

(5) critical appraisals of other individuals with whom respondents have close family relationships;

(6) legally recognized privileged and analogous relationships, such as those of lawyers, physicians, and ministers; or

(7) income (other than that required by law to determine eligibility for participation in a program or for receiving financial assistance under such program), without the prior consent of the student (if the student is an adult or emancipated minor), or in the case of unemancipated minor, without the prior written consent of the parent.

(Jan. 2, 1968, P.L. 90–247, Title IV, Part C, Subpart 2, § 439, as added Aug. 21, 1974, P.L. 93–380, Title V, § 514(a), 88 Stat. 574; Nov. 1, 1978, P.L. 95–561, Title XII, Part D, § 1250, 92 Stat. 2355.)

■ AMERICANS WITH DISABILITIES ACT OF 1990 (SELECTED PARTS), PUBLIC LAW 101–336, 42 U.S.C. §12101

TITLE I – EMPLOYMENT

§ 101. Definitions.

As used in this title:

(1) Commission. – The term "Commission" means the Equal Employment Opportunity Commission established by section 705 of the Civil Rights Act of 1964 (42 U.S.C. 2000e–4).

(2) Covered entity. – The term "covered entity" means an employer, employment agency, labor organization, or joint labor-management committee.

(3) Direct threat. – The term "direct threat" means a significant risk to the health or safety of others that cannot be eliminated by reasonable accommodation.

(4) Employee. – The term "employee" means an individual employed by an employer.

(5) Employer. –

(A) In general. – The term "employer" means a person engaged in an industry affecting commerce who has 15 or more employees for each working day in each of 20 or more calendar weeks in the current or preceding calendar year, and any agent of such person, except that, for two years following the effective date of this title, an employer means a person engaged in an industry affecting commerce who has 25 or more employees for each working day in each of 20 or more calendar weeks in the current or preceding year, and any agent of such person.

(B) Exceptions. – The term "employer" does not include –

(i) the United States, a corporation wholly owned by the government of the United States, or an Indian tribe; or

(ii) a bona fide private membership club (other than a labor organization) that is exempt from taxation under section 501(c) of the Internal Revenue Code of 1986.

(7) PERSON, ETC.—The terms "person", "labor organization", "employment agency", "commerce", and "industry affecting commerce", shall have the same meaning given such terms in section 701 of the Civil Rights Act of 1964 (42 U.S.C. 2000e).

(8) QUALIFIED INDIVIDUAL WITH A DISABILITY.—The term "qualified individual with a disability" means an individual with a disability who, with or without reasonable accommodation, can perform the essential functions of the employment position that such individual holds or desires. For the purposes of this title, consideration shall be given to the employer's judgment as to what functions of a job are essential, and if an employer has prepared a written description before advertising or interviewing applicants for the job, this description shall be considered evidence of the essential functions of the job.

(9) REASONABLE ACCOMMODATION.—The term "reasonable accommodation" may include—

(A) making existing facilities used by employees readily accessible to and usable by individuals with disabilities; and

(B) job restructuring, part-time or modified work schedules, reassignment to a vacant position, acquisition or modification of equipment or devices, appropriate adjustment or modifications of examinations, training materials or policies, the provision of qualified readers or interpreters, and other similar accommodations for individuals with disabilities.

(10) UNDUE HARDSHIP.—

(A) IN GENERAL.—The term "undue hardship" means an action requiring significant difficulty or expense, when considered in light of the factors set forth in subparagraph (B).

(B) FACTORS TO BE CONSIDERED.—In determining whether an accommodation would impose an undue hardship on a covered entity, factors to be considered include—

(i) the nature and cost of the accommodation needed under this Act;

(ii) the overall financial resources of the facility or facilities involved in the provision of the reasonable accommodation; the number of persons employed at such facility; the effect on expenses and resources, or the impact otherwise of such accommodation upon the operation of the facility;

(iii) the overall financial resources of the covered entity; the overall size of the business of a covered entity with respect to the number of its employees; the number, type, and location of its facilities; and

(iv) the type of operation or operations of the covered entity, including the composition, structure, and functions of the workforce of such entity; the geographic separateness, administrative, or fiscal relationship of the facility or failities in question to the covered entity.

■ EDUCATION OF INDIVIDUALS WITH DISABILITIES (SELECTED PARTS), 20 U.S.C. SECS. 1400–1485.

Purpose

It is the purpose of this chapter to assure that all children with disabilities have available to them, within the time periods specified in section 1412(2)(B) of this title, a free appropriate public education which emphasizes special education and related services designed to meet their unique needs, to assure that the rights of children with disabilities and their parents or guardians are protected, to assist States and localities to provide for the education of all children with disabilities, and to assess and assure the effectiveness of efforts to educate children with disabilities.

§ 1401. Definitions

(1) The term "children with disabilities" means children—

(A) with mental retardation, hearing impairments including deafness, speech or language impairments, visual impairments including blindness, serious emotional disturbance, orthopedic impairments, autism, traumatic brain injury, other health impairments, or specific learning disabilities; and

(B) who, by reason thereof need special education and related services.   .   .   .

.   .   .

(15) The term "children with specific learning disabilities" means those children who have a disorder in one or more of the basic psychological processes involved in understanding or in using language, spoken or written, which disorder may manifest itself in imperfect ability to listen, think, speak, read, write, spell, or do mathematical calculations. Such disorders include such conditions as perceptual disabilities, brain injury, minimal brain dysfunction, dyslexia, and developmental aphasia. Such term does not include children who have learning problems which are primarily the result of visual, hearing, or motor disabilities, of mental retardation, of emotional disturbance, or of environmental, cultural, or economic disadvantage.

(16) The term "special education" means specially designed instruction, at no cost to parents or guardians, to meet the unique needs of a child with a disability, including—

(A) instruction conducted in the classroom, in the home, in hospitals and institutions, and in other settings; and

(B) instruction in physical education.

(17) The term "related services" means transportation, and such developmental, corrective, and other supportive services (including speech pathology and audiology, psychological services, physical and occupational therapy, recreation, including therapeutic recreation and social work services, and medical and counseling services,[1] including rehabilitation counseling, except that such medical services shall be for diagnostic and evaluation purposes only) as may be required to assist a child with a disability to benefit from special education, and includes the early identification and assessment of disabling conditions in children.

(18) The term "free appropriate public education" means special education and related services that—

(A) have been provided at public expense, under public supervision and direction, and without charge,

(B) meet the standards of the State educational agency,

(C) include an appropriate preschool, elementary, or secondary school education in the State involved, and

(D) are provided in conformity with the individualized education program required under section 1414(a)(5) of this title.

(19) The term "transition services" means a coordinated set of activities for a student, designed within an outcome-oriented process, which promotes movement from school to post-school activities, including postsecondary education, vocational training, integrated employment (including supported employment), continuing and adult education, adult services, independent living, or community participation. The coordinated set of activities shall be based upon the individual student's needs, taking into account the student's preferences and interests, and shall include instruction, community experiences, the development of employment and other post-school adult living objectives, and, when appropriate, acquisition of daily living skills and functional vocational evaluation.

(20) The term "individualized education program" means a written statement for each child with a disability developed in any meeting by a representative of the local educational agency or an intermediate educational unit who shall be qualified to provide, or supervise the provision of, specially designed instruction to meet the unique needs of children with disabilities, the teacher, the parents or guardian of such child, and, whenever appropriate, such child, which statement shall include—

(A) a statement of the present levels of educational performance of such child,

(B) a statement of annual goals, including short-term instructional objectives,

(C) a statement of the specific educational services to be provided to such child, and the extent to which such child will be able to participate in regular educational programs,

(D) a statement of the needed transition services for students beginning no later than age 16 and annually thereafter (and, when determined appropriate for the individual, beginning at age 14 or younger), including, when appropriate, a statement of the interagency responsibilities[2] or linkages (or both) before the student leaves the school setting.

(E) the projected date for initiation and anticipated duration of such services, and

(F) appropriate objective criteria and evaluation procedures and schedules for determining, on at least an annual basis, whether instructional objectives are being achieved. In the case where a participating agency, other than the educational agency, fails to provide agreed upon services, the educational agency shall reconvene the IEP team to identify alternative strategies to meet the transition objectives.

■ AGE DISCRIMINATION ACT — 29 U.S.C. § 621 (§ 623)

(a) It shall be unlawful for an employer —

(1) to fail or refuse to hire or to discharge any individual or otherwise discriminate against any individual with respect to his compensation, terms, conditions, or privileges of employment, because of such individual's age. . . .

(c) It shall be unlawful for a labor organization —

(1) to exclude or to expel from its membership, or otherwise to discriminate against, any individual because of his age. . . .

(3) to cause or attempt to cause an employer to discriminate against an individual in violation of this section. . . .

(f) It shall not be unlawful for an employer, employment agency, or labor organization —

(1) to take any action otherwise prohibited under subsections (a), (b), (c), or (e) of this section where age is a bona fide occupational qualification reasonably necessary to the normal operation of the particular business, or where the differen-

tiation is based on reasonable factors other than age. . . .

(3) to discharge or otherwise discipline an individual for good cause. . . .

■ EQUAL EDUCATION OPPORTUNITIES ACT — 20 U.S.C. § 1703

§ 1703 provides:

No State shall deny equal educational opportunity to an individual on account of his or her race, color, sex, or national origin, by —

(a) the deliberate segregation by an educational agency of students on the basis of race, color, or national origin among or within schools. . . .

(c) the assignment by an educational agency of a student to a school, other than the one closest to his or her place of residence within the school district in which he or she resides, if the assignment results in a greater degree of segregation of students on the basis of race, color, sex, or national origin. . . .

(d) discrimination by an educational agency on the basis of race, color, or national origin in the employment, employment conditions, or assignment to schools of its faculty or staff, except to fulfill the purposes of subsection (f) below. . . .

(e) the transfer by an educational agency, whether voluntary or otherwise, of a student from one school to another if the purpose and effect of such transfer is to increase segregation of students on the basis of race, color, or national origin among the schools of such agency; or

(f) the failure by an educational agency to take appropriate action to overcome language barriers that impede equal participation by its students in its instructional programs.

■ REHABILITATION ACT OF 1973 — 29 U.S.C. § 794 (§ 504)

The Act provides in part:

"No otherwise qualified handicapped individual . . . shall, solely by reason of his handicap, be excluded from the participation in, be denied the benefits of, or be subjected to discrimination under any program or activity receiving Federal financial assistance."

APPENDIX C

GLOSSARY OF TERMS*

Ab initio: From the beginning.

Ad valorem: According to the value, e.g., a duty or tax.

Adverse possession: A method of acquisition of title by possession for a statutory period under certain conditions.

Allegation: A statement of fact made in a legal proceeding.

Annotation: A remark, note, or commentary on some passage of a book, intended to illustrate its meaning.

Appeal: An application by an appellant to a higher court to rectify the order of the court below.

Appellant: One who appeals from a judicial decision.

Appellate court: A higher court which hears a case from a lower court on appeal.

Appellee: The person against whom an appeal is taken; the respondent to an appeal.

Arbitrary: Means in an "arbitrary" manner, as fixed or done capriciously or at pleasure, without adequate determining principle; not founded in the nature of things; nonrational; not done or acting according to reason or judgment; depending on the will alone; absolutely in power; capriciously; tyrannical; despotic.

Assault: Threatening to strike or harm.

Assumpsit: An early form of action in English law, later used in America, under which plaintiff seeks to recover damages for non-performance of a parol or simple contract.

Battery: Beating and wounding, including every touching or laying hold, however trifling, of another's person or clothes in an angry, insolent, or hostile manner.

Bill: A formal declaration, complaint, or statement of particular things in writing. As a legal term, this word has many meanings and applications, the more important of which are enumerated in *Black's Law Dictionary.*

Bona fide: With good faith, honestly, openly.

Breach: A breaking; either the invasion of a right, or the violation of a duty.

Certiorari: (To be more fully informed) An original writ or action whereby a cause is removed from an inferior to a superior court for trial. The record of proceedings is then transmitted to the superior court. The term is most commonly used when requesting the U.S. Supreme Court to hear a case from a lower court.

Citation: A writ issued out of a court of competent jurisdiction, commanding a person therein named to appear on a day named and do something therein mentioned, or show cause why he should not.

Civil action: An action which has for its object the recovery of private or civil rights, or compensation for their infraction.

Class bill or suit: One in which one or more members of a class sue either for themselves or for themselves and other members of a class.

---

*These definitions were selected from *Black's Law Dictionary* by Henry Campbell Black, West Publishing Company, St. Paul, Minn.

Code: A compilation of statutes, scientifically analyzed into chapters, subheadings, and sections with a table of contents and an index. A collection or system of laws.

Collateral: By the side of; indirect. Not directly concerned with the issue.

Collateral attack: An attempt to avoid, defeat, or evade a judicial proceeding, or deny its force and effect, in some incidental proceeding not provided by law for the express purpose of attacking it.

Common law: Legal principles derived from usage and custom, or from court decisions affirming such usages and custom, or from the acts of Parliament in force at the time of the American Revolution, as distinguished from law created by enactment of American legislatures.

Concurring opinion: An opinion, separate from that which embodies the views and decision of the majority of the court, prepared and filed by a judge who agrees in the general result of the decision, and which either reinforces the majority opinion by the expression of the particular judge's own views or reasoning, or (more commonly) voices his disapproval of the grounds of the decision or the arguments on which it was based, though approving the final result.

Consideration in contracts: The inducement to a contract. The cause, motive, price, or impelling influence that induces a contracting party to enter into a contract.

Contract: A promissory agreement between two or more persons that creates, modifies, or destroys a legal relation.

Contributory negligence: Negligence of the plaintiff which, combined with the negligence of the defendant, was the proximate cause of the injury complained of.

Court of record: A court that keeps a permanent record of its proceedings. Frequently appellate courts are called courts of record since their proceedings are published.

Curia: A court.

Damages: A pecuniary compensation or indemnity, which may be recovered in the courts by any person who has suffered loss, detriment, or injury, whether to his person, property, or rights through the unlawful act or omission or negligence of another.

Declaratory relief: The opinion of a court on a question of law that, without ordering anything to be done, simply declares the rights of the parties.

Decree: The judgment of a court of equity or admiralty, answering for most purposes to the judgment of a court of common law.

De facto: (In fact) A *de facto* officer is in actual possession of an office without lawful title. A *de facto* corporation may be reorganized as legally effective even though defective in some particular.

Defamation: Scandalous words written or spoken concerning another, tending to the injury of his reputation, for which an action on the case for damages would lie.

Defendant: One required to make answer in a suit—the one against whom the suit is brought.

Defendant in error: The distinctive term appropriate to the party against whom a writ of error is sued out.

De jure: (By right) A *de jure* officer has just claim and rightful title to an office, though not necessarily in actual possession thereof; a legal or true corporation or officer as opposed to one that is *de facto*.

De minimus: A matter that is insignificant or not worthy of judicial attention.

Demurrer: A plea by one of the parties to an action, who, while admitting for the sake of argument all the material facts properly pleaded by the opposing party, contends the existence of the facts does not constitute grounds for action.

Devise: A testamentary disposition of land or realty; a gift of real property by the last will and testament of the donor.

Dictum: The expression by a judge of an opinion on a point of law not necessary to the decision on the case; not binding on other judges.

Directory: A provision in a statute, rule of procedure, or the like, which is a mere direction or instruction of no obligatory force, and involves no invalidating consequence for its disregard, as opposed to an imperative or mandatory provision, which must be followed.

Discretionary power: Involves the exercise of judgment in reaching a decision; deciding whether to do something.

Dissenting opinion: An opinion disagreeing with that of the majority, handed down by one or more members of the court.

Due process: Law in the regular course of administration through courts of justice, according to those rules and forms that have been established for the protection of private rights.

Ejusdem generis: Of the same kind or nature.

Eminent domain: The power to take private property for public use.

En banc: In the bench, all judges sitting.

Enjoin: To require, command, positively direct. To require a person, by writ of injunction from a court of equity, to perform, or to abstain or desist from, some act.

Equity: A system of law that affords a remedy where there is no complete or adequate remedy at law. A court of law assesses damages; a court of equity renders a decision in mandamus, injunction, or specific performance.

Error case: Appeal on questions of law or a reference to a "writ of error" requesting reversal for a mistaken or incorrect judgment.

Estop: To stop, bar, or impede; to prevent, to preclude.

Estoppel: A man's own act or acceptance stops or closes his mouth to allege or plead the truth.

Et al: And others.

Ex cathedra: To speak with authority.

Exculpatory: Excusing, clearing from alleged fault or guilt.

Ex officio: By virtue of his office.

Ex parte: By or for one party.

Ex post facto: (After the fact) Act passed after another act that retroactively changes the legal consequences of that act. Federal Constitution prohibits passage of *ex post facto* criminal law.

Ex rel: (ex relatione) At the instance of; on behalf of; on relation of information.

Executory: That which is yet to be performed or accomplished.

Fee simple: A fee simple absolute is an estate limited absolutely to a man and his heirs and assigns forever without limitation or condition.

Governmental function: One imposed or required of a municipal corporation for the protection of the general public; a function relating to the corporation's purpose for existing.

Hearsay evidence: Evidence not proceeding from the personal knowledge of the witness, but from the mere repetition of what he has heard others say.

In loco parentis: In place of the parent; charged with some of the parents' rights, duties, and responsibilities.

In re: In the affair; in the matter of; concerning. This is the usual method of entitling a judicial proceeding in which there are no adversary parties.

Injunction: A prohibitive writ issued by a court of equity forbidding the defendant to do some act he is threatening, or forbidding him to continue doing some act that is injurious to the plaintiff and cannot be adequately redressed by an action at law.

Ipso facto: By the very act itself, i.e., as the necessary consequence of the act.

Ipso jure: By the mere operation of the law.

Laches: Negligence, or unreasonable delay in pursuing a legal remedy, whereby a person forfeits his right.

Legacy: A disposition of personalty by will.

Liability: The word is a broad legal term and has been referred to as of the most comprehensive significance, including almost every character of hazard or responsibility, absolute, contingent, or likely.

Libel: Defamation by printed or written communication.

Liquidated: Fixed, ascertained, e.g., damages, the exact amount of which must be paid, or may be collected, upon a default or breach of contract.

Liquidated damages: The term is applicable when the amount of the damages has been ascertained by the judgment in the action, or when a specific sum of money has been expressly stipulated by the parties to a bond or other contract as the amount of damages to be recovered by either party for a breach of the agreement by the other.

Mala in se (Malum in se): Acts wrong in themselves, whether prohibited by human law or not.

Mala prohibita (Malum prohibitum): Acts prohibited by human laws, but not necessarily wrong of themselves.

Malfeasance: The commission of an unlawful act.

Malice: Hatred, ill will; a formed design of doing an unlawful act.

Mandamus: A writ of mandamus is a command from a court of law directed to an inferior court, officer, corporate body, or person regarding him or them to do some particular thing.

Ministerial: Belonging to a minister or subordinate who is bound to follow instructions; opposed to judicial or discretionary.

Misfeasance: A wrongful act, negligence, or the improper performance of some lawful act.

Municipal corporation: A body politic created by the incorporation of the inhabitants as an agency of the state to regulate and administer the local affairs thereof; a voluntary corporation; a city, village, or borough. The term is sometimes used in a broader sense and includes all types of local governmental bodies including school districts.

Negligence: Want of care.

Nolens volens: Whether willing or unwilling; consenting or not.

Nominal damages: A trifling sum awarded to a plaintiff when no substantial loss or injury has occurred.

Nuisance: Anything that unlawfully results in harm, inconvenience, or damage.

Original jurisdiction: The jurisdiction of a court to entertain a case in its inception, as contrasted with the appellate jurisdiction.

Parol: By word of mouth.

Per curiam: By the court, opinion written by the whole court as opposed to an opinion written by any one judge.

Per se: By itself, alone.

Petition: Written application or prayer to the court for the redress of a wrong or the grant of a privilege or license.

Plaintiff: Person who brings an action, the one who sues by filing a complaint.

Plenary: Full; conclusive.

Police power: Inherent or plenary legislative power to enact laws for the comfort, health, and prosperity of the state. The right to modify for the common good. In short, the right of the sovereign to govern.

Prayer: The request contained in a bill in equity that the court will grant the process, aid, or relief that the complainant desires.

Precedent: A decision considered as furnishing an example or authority for an identical or similar case afterward arising on a similar question of law.

Prima facie: At first view; on the first aspect. Prima facie evidence, presumptions, etc., are such as will prevail, if not rebutted or disproved.

Privies of parties: Persons connected with mutual interest in the same action.

Proprietary functions: Those functions exercised by a municipality for the improvement of the territory within the corporate limits, or the doing of such things as inure to the benefit, pecuniarily or otherwise, of the municipality. Things not normally required by law or things not governmental in nature. Operation of an athletic contest where a fee is charged may be an example in some states.

Punitive damages: An award to punish.

Quantum meruit: (As much as he has earned) Action brought by a party to a contract against the other, not founded on the contract itself, but on an implied promise to pay for so much as the party suing has done, or as much as reasonably deserved for work or labor.

Quasi: As if; almost.

Quasi-municipal corporation (or quasi corporation): A political or civil subdivision of the state, created by law, to assist the state in administering the state's affairs—an involuntary corporation. Example: a school district.

Quid pro quo: "Something for something"; a consideration.

Quo warranto: (By what authority) A writ, or proceeding, by which the government inquires into the right of a person, or corporation, to hold an office, or exercise a franchise, which was never lawfully held, or which has been forfeited by neglect or abuse.

Ratification: In a broad sense, the confirmation of a previous act done either by the party himself or by another; confirmation of a voidable act.

Remand a case: An action by an appellate court to send the case back to the court from which it came for further proceedings there.

Res judicata: A matter judicially decided.

Respondeat superior: The responsibility of a master for the acts of his servants.

Respondent: The one making an answer— the defendant.

Restrain: To prohibit from action; to enjoin.

Restraining order: An injunction.

Reversion: The residue of an estate left by operation of law in the grantor or his heirs, or in the heirs, or in the heirs of a testator, commencing in possession on the determination of a particular estate granted or devised.

Slander: Defamation by spoken word.

Specific performance: A requirement by a court of equity that both parties go through with a contract.

Star Chamber: A court in English law established to provide equitable relief for aggrieved parties who could find no relief at common law. Abuse of power by this court eventually led to its abolition.

Stare decisis: Adherence to precedent. When the court has made a declaration of legal principle it is the law until changed by a competent authority.

Statute: Law enacted by the legislative power of a country or state.

Subpoena duces tecum: A process by which a court commands a witness to produce some document or paper that is pertinent to the controversy being litigated.

Substantive law: The positive law of rights and duties.

Tenure: Right to perform duties and receive emoluments thereof.

Title to property: Title is the means whereby the owner of lands has the just possession of his property.

Tort: Legal injury or wrong committed upon the person or property of another independent of contract.

Trespass: The unauthorized entry upon, taking, or interfering with the property of another. Also, common law form of action brought to obtain damages for unlawful injury.

Ultra vires: An *ultra vires* contract is one beyond the powers of the corporation to make. In other words, it is one the corporation had no authority to make.

Void: Null; ineffectual; nugatory; having no legal force or binding effect; unable, in law, to support the purpose for which it was intended.

Voidable: That may be avoided, or declared void; not absolutely void, or void in itself.

INDEX

E